Lecture Notes in Computer Science   8690

Commenced Publication in 1973
Founding and Former Series Editors:
Gerhard Goos, Juris Hartmanis, and Jan van Leeuwen

David Fleet   Tomas Pajdla   Bernt Schiele
Tinne Tuytelaars (Eds.)

Computer Vision – ECCV 2014

13th European Conference
Zurich, Switzerland, September 6-12, 2014
Proceedings, Part II

 Springer

Volume Editors

David Fleet
University of Toronto, Department of Computer Science
6 King's College Road, Toronto, ON M5H 3S5, Canada
E-mail: fleet@cs.toronto.edu

Tomas Pajdla
Czech Technical University in Prague, Department of Cybernetics
Technicka 2, 166 27 Prague 6, Czech Republic
E-mail: pajdla@cmp.felk.cvut.cz

Bernt Schiele
Max-Planck-Institut für Informatik
Campus E1 4, 66123 Saarbrücken, Germany
E-mail: schiele@mpi-inf.mpg.de

Tinne Tuytelaars
KU Leuven, ESAT - PSI, iMinds
Kasteelpark Arenberg 10, Bus 2441, 3001 Leuven, Belgium
E-mail: tinne.tuytelaars@esat.kuleuven.be

Videos to this book can be accessed at
http://www.springerimages.com/videos/978-3-319-10604-5

ISSN 0302-9743   e-ISSN 1611-3349
ISBN 978-3-319-10604-5   e-ISBN 978-3-319-10605-2
DOI 10.1007/978-3-319-10605-2
Springer Cham Heidelberg New York Dordrecht London

Library of Congress Control Number: 2014946360

LNCS Sublibrary: SL 6 – Image Processing, Computer Vision, Pattern Recognition,
and Graphics

Typesetting: Camera-ready by author, data conversion by Scientific Publishing Services, Chennai, India

Printed on acid-free paper

Springer is part of Springer Science+Business Media (www.springer.com)

Foreword

The European Conference on Computer Vision is one of the top conferences in computer vision. It was first held in 1990 in Antibes (France) with subsequent conferences in Santa Margherita Ligure (Italy) in 1992, Stockholm (Sweden) in 1994, Cambridge (UK) in 1996, Freiburg (Germany) in 1998, Dublin (Ireland) in 2000, Copenhagen (Denmark) in 2002, Prague (Czech Republic) in 2004, Graz (Austria) in 2006, Marseille (France) in 2008, Heraklion (Greece) in 2010, and Florence (Italy) in 2012. Many people have worked hard to turn the 2014 edition into as great a success. We hope you will find this a mission accomplished.

The chairs decided to adhere to the classic single-track scheme. In terms of the time ordering, we decided to largely follow the Florence example (typically starting with poster sessions, followed by oral sessions), which offers a lot of flexibility to network and is more forgiving for the not-so-early-birds and hard-core gourmets.

A large conference like ECCV requires the help of many. They made sure there was a full program including the main conference, tutorials, workshops, exhibits, demos, proceedings, video streaming/archive, and Web descriptions. We want to cordially thank all those volunteers! Please have a look at the conference website to see their names (http://eccv2014.org/people/). We also thank our generous sponsors. Their support was vital for keeping prices low and enriching the program. And it is good to see such a level of industrial interest in what our community is doing!

We hope you will enjoy the proceedings ECCV 2014.

Also, willkommen in Zürich!

September 2014

Marc Pollefeys
Luc Van Gool
General Chairs

Preface

Welcome to the proceedings of the 2014 European Conference on Computer Vision (ECCV 2014) that was in Zurich, Switzerland. We are delighted to present this volume reflecting a strong and exciting program, the result of an extensive review process. In total, we received 1,444 paper submissions. Of these, 85 violated the ECCV submission guidelines and were rejected without review. Of the remainder, 363 were accepted (26,7%): 325 as posters (23,9%) and 38 as oral presentations (2,8%). This selection process was a combined effort of four program co-chairs (PCs), 53 area chairs (ACs), 803 Program Committee members and 247 additional reviewers.

As PCs we were primarily responsible for the design and execution of the review process. Beyond administrative rejections, we were not directly involved in acceptance decisions. Because the general co-chairs were permitted to submit papers, they played no role in the review process and were treated as any other author.

Acceptance decisions were made by the AC Committee. There were 53 ACs in total, selected by the PCs to provide sufficient technical expertise, geographical diversity (21 from Europe, 7 from Asia, and 25 from North America) and a mix of AC experience (7 had no previous AC experience, 18 had served as AC of a major international vision conference once since 2010, 8 had served twice, 13 had served three times, and 7 had served 4 times).

ACs were aided by 803 Program Committee members to whom papers were assigned for reviewing. There were 247 additional reviewers, each supervised by a Program Committee member. The Program Committee was based on suggestions from ACs, and committees from previous conferences. Google Scholar profiles were collected for all candidate Program Committee members and vetted by PCs. Having a large pool of Program Committee members for reviewing allowed us to match expertise while bounding reviewer loads. No more than nine papers were assigned to any one Program Committee member, with a maximum of six to graduate students.

The ECCV 2014 review process was double blind. Authors did not know the reviewers' identities, nor the ACs handling their paper(s). We did our utmost to ensure that ACs and reviewers did not know authors' identities, even though anonymity becomes difficult to maintain as more and more submissions appear concurrently on arXiv.org.

Particular attention was paid to minimizing potential conflicts of interest. Conflicts of interest between ACs, Program Committee members, and papers were based on authorship of ECCV 2014 submissions, on their home institutions, and on previous collaborations. To find institutional conflicts, all authors,

Program Committee members, and ACs were asked to list the Internet domains of their current institutions. To find collaborators, the DBLP (www.dblp.org) database was used to find any co-authored papers in the period 2010–2014.

We initially assigned approximately 100 papers to each AC, based on affinity scores from the Toronto Paper Matching System and authors' AC suggestions. ACs then bid on these, indicating their level of expertise. Based on these bids, and conflicts of interest, approximately 27 papers were assigned to each AC, for which they would act as the primary AC. The primary AC then suggested seven reviewers from the pool of Program Committee members (in rank order) for each paper, from which three were chosen per paper, taking load balancing and conflicts of interest into account.

Many papers were also assigned a secondary AC, either directly by the PCs, or as a consequence of the primary AC requesting the aid of an AC with complementary expertise. Secondary ACs could be assigned at any stage in the process, but in most cases this occurred about two weeks before the final AC meeting. Hence, in addition to their initial load of approximately 27 papers, each AC was asked to handle three to five more papers as a secondary AC; they were expected to read and write a short assessment of such papers. In addition, two of the 53 ACs were not directly assigned papers. Rather, they were available throughout the process to aid other ACs at any stage (e.g., with decisions, evaluating technical issues, additional reviews, etc.).

The initial reviewing period was three weeks long, after which reviewers provided reviews with preliminary recommendations. Three weeks is somewhat shorter than normal, but this did not seem to cause any unusual problems. With the generous help of several last-minute reviewers, each paper received three reviews.

Authors were then given the opportunity to rebut the reviews, primarily to identify any factual errors. Following this, reviewers and ACs discussed papers at length, after which reviewers finalized their reviews and gave a final recommendation to the ACs. Many ACs requested help from secondary ACs at this time.

Papers, for which rejection was clear and certain, based on the reviews and the AC's assessment, were identified by their primary ACs and vetted by a shadow AC prior to rejection. (These shadow ACs were assigned by the PCs.) All papers with any chance of acceptance were further discussed at the AC meeting. Those deemed "strong" by primary ACs (about 140 in total) were also assigned a secondary AC.

The AC meeting, with all but two of the primary ACs present, took place in Zurich. ACs were divided into 17 triplets for each morning, and a different set of triplets for each afternoon. Given the content of the three (or more) reviews along with reviewer recommendations, rebuttals, online discussions among reviewers and primary ACs, written input from and discussions with secondary ACs, the

AC triplets then worked together to resolve questions, calibrate assessments, and make acceptance decisions.

To select oral presentations, all strong papers, along with any others put forward by triplets (about 155 in total), were then discussed in four panels, each comprising four or five triplets. Each panel ranked these oral candidates, using four categories. Papers in the two top categories provided the final set of 38 oral presentations.

We want to thank everyone involved in making the ECCV 2014 Program possible. First and foremost, the success of ECCV 2014 depended on the quality of papers submitted by authors, and on the very hard work of the reviewers, the Program Committee members and the ACs. We are particularly grateful to Kyros Kutulakos for his enormous software support before and during the AC meeting, to Laurent Charlin for the use of the Toronto Paper Matching System, and Chaohui Wang for help optimizing the assignment of papers to ACs. We also owe a debt of gratitude for the great support of Zurich local organizers, especially Susanne Keller and her team.

September 2014

David Fleet
Tomas Pajdla
Bernt Schiele
Tinne Tuytelaars

Organization

General Chairs

Luc Van Gool   ETH Zurich, Switzerland
Marc Pollefeys   ETH Zurich, Switzerland

Program Chairs

Tinne Tuytelaars   KU Leuven, Belgium
Bernt Schiele   MPI Informatics, Saarbrücken, Germany
Tomas Pajdla   CTU Prague, Czech Republic
David Fleet   University of Toronto, Canada

Local Arrangements Chairs

Konrad Schindler   ETH Zurich, Switzerland
Vittorio Ferrari   University of Edinburgh, UK

Workshop Chairs

Lourdes Agapito   University College London, UK
Carsten Rother   TU Dresden, Germany
Michael Bronstein   University of Lugano, Switzerland

Tutorial Chairs

Bastian Leibe   RWTH Aachen, Germany
Paolo Favaro   University of Bern, Switzerland
Christoph Lampert   IST Austria

Poster Chair

Helmut Grabner   ETH Zurich, Switzerland

Publication Chairs

Mario Fritz   MPI Informatics, Saarbrücken, Germany
Michael Stark   MPI Informatics, Saarbrücken, Germany

Demo Chairs

Davide Scaramuzza   University of Zurich, Switzerland
Jan-Michael Frahm   University of North Carolina at Chapel Hill,
                             USA

Exhibition Chair

Tamar Tolcachier   University of Zurich, Switzerland

Industrial Liaison Chairs

Alexander Sorkine-Hornung   Disney Research Zurich, Switzerland
Fatih Porikli   ANU, Australia

Student Grant Chair

Seon Joo Kim   Yonsei University, Korea

Air Shelters Accommodation Chair

Maros Blaha   ETH Zurich, Switzerland

Website Chairs

Lorenz Meier   ETH Zurich, Switzerland
Bastien Jacquet   ETH Zurich, Switzerland

Internet Chair

Thorsten Steenbock   ETH Zurich, Switzerland

Student Volunteer Chairs

Andrea Cohen   ETH Zurich, Switzerland
Ralf Dragon   ETH Zurich, Switzerland
Laura Leal-Taixé   ETH Zurich, Switzerland

Finance Chair

Amael Delaunoy   ETH Zurich, Switzerland

Conference Coordinator

Susanne H. Keller   ETH Zurich, Switzerland

Area Chairs

Lourdes Agapito	University College London, UK
Sameer Agarwal	Google Research, USA
Shai Avidan	Tel Aviv University, Israel
Alex Berg	UNC Chapel Hill, USA
Yuri Boykov	University of Western Ontario, Canada
Thomas Brox	University of Freiburg, Germany
Jason Corso	SUNY at Buffalo, USA
Trevor Darrell	UC Berkeley, USA
Fernando de la Torre	Carnegie Mellon University, USA
Frank Dellaert	Georgia Tech, USA
Alexei Efros	UC Berkeley, USA
Vittorio Ferrari	University of Edinburgh, UK
Andrew Fitzgibbon	Microsoft Research, Cambridge, UK
JanMichael Frahm	UNC Chapel Hill, USA
Bill Freeman	Massachusetts Institute of Technology, USA
Peter Gehler	Max Planck Institute for Intelligent Systems, Germany
Kristen Graumann	University of Texas at Austin, USA
Wolfgang Heidrich	University of British Columbia, Canada
Herve Jegou	Inria Rennes, France
Fredrik Kahl	Lund University, Sweden
Kyros Kutulakos	University of Toronto, Canada
Christoph Lampert	IST Austria
Ivan Laptev	Inria Paris, France
Kyuong Mu Lee	Seoul National University, South Korea
Bastian Leibe	RWTH Aachen, Germany
Vincent Lepetit	TU Graz, Austria
Hongdong Li	Australian National University
David Lowe	University of British Columbia, Canada
Greg Mori	Simon Fraser University, Canada
Srinivas Narasimhan	Carnegie Mellon University, PA, USA
Nassir Navab	TU Munich, Germany
Ko Nishino	Drexel University, USA
Maja Pantic	Imperial College London, UK
Patrick Perez	Technicolor Research, Rennes, France
Pietro Perona	California Institute of Technology, USA
Ian Reid	University of Adelaide, Australia
Stefan Roth	TU Darmstadt, Germany
Carsten Rother	TU Dresden, Germany
Sudeep Sarkar	University of South Florida, USA
Silvio Savarese	Stanford University, USA
Christoph Schnoerr	Heidelberg University, Germany
Jamie Shotton	Microsoft Research, Cambridge, UK

Kaleem Siddiqi	McGill, Canada
Leonid Sigal	Disney Research, Pittsburgh, PA, USA
Noah Snavely	Cornell, USA
Raquel Urtasun	University of Toronto, Canada
Andrea Vedaldi	University of Oxford, UK
Jakob Verbeek	Inria Rhone-Alpes, France
Xiaogang Wang	Chinese University of Hong Kong, SAR China
Ming-Hsuan Yang	UC Merced, CA, USA
Lihi Zelnik-Manor	Technion, Israel
Song-Chun Zhu	UCLA, USA
Todd Zickler	Harvard, USA

Program Committee

Gaurav Aggarwal	Joao Barreto	Kristin Branson
Amit Agrawal	Jonathan Barron	Steven Branson
Haizhou Ai	Adrien Bartoli	Francois Bremond
Ijaz Akhter	Arslan Basharat	Michael Bronstein
Karteek Alahari	Dhruv Batra	Gabriel Brostow
Alexandre Alahi	Luis Baumela	Michael Brown
Andrea Albarelli	Maximilian Baust	Matthew Brown
Saad Ali	Jean-Charles Bazin	Marcus Brubaker
Jose M. Alvarez	Loris Bazzani	Andres Bruhn
Juan Andrade-Cetto	Chris Beall	Joan Bruna
Bjoern Andres	Vasileios Belagiannis	Aurelie Bugeau
Mykhaylo Andriluka	Csaba Beleznai	Darius Burschka
Elli Angelopoulou	Moshe Ben-ezra	Ricardo Cabral
Roland Angst	Ohad Ben-Shahar	Jian-Feng Cai
Relja Arandjelovic	Ismail Ben Ayed	Neill D.F. Campbell
Ognjen Arandjelovic	Rodrigo Benenson	Yong Cao
Helder Araujo	Ryad Benosman	Barbara Caputo
Pablo Arbelez	Tamara Berg	Joao Carreira
Vasileios Argyriou	Margrit Betke	Jan Cech
Antonis Argyros	Ross Beveridge	Jinxiang Chai
Kalle Astroem	Bir Bhanu	Ayan Chakrabarti
Vassilis Athitsos	Horst Bischof	Tat-Jen Cham
Yannis Avrithis	Arijit Biswas	Antoni Chan
Yusuf Aytar	Andrew Blake	Manmohan Chandraker
Xiang Bai	Aaron Bobick	Vijay Chandrasekhar
Luca Ballan	Piotr Bojanowski	Hong Chang
Yingze Bao	Ali Borji	Ming-Ching Chang
Richard Baraniuk	Terrance Boult	Rama Chellappa
Adrian Barbu	Lubomir Bourdev	Chao-Yeh Chen
Kobus Barnard	Patrick Bouthemy	David Chen
Connelly Barnes	Edmond Boyer	Hwann-Tzong Chen

Tsuhan Chen
Xilin Chen
Chao Chen
Longbin Chen
Minhua Chen
Anoop Cherian
Liang-Tien Chia
Tat-Jun Chin
Sunghyun Cho
Minsu Cho
Nam Ik Cho
Wongun Choi
Mario Christoudias
Wen-Sheng Chu
Yung-Yu Chuang
Ondrej Chum
James Clark
Brian Clipp
Isaac Cohen
John Collomosse
Bob Collins
Tim Cootes
David Crandall
Antonio Criminisi
Naresh Cuntoor
Qieyun Dai
Jifeng Dai
Kristin Dana
Kostas Daniilidis
Larry Davis
Andrew Davison
Goksel Dedeoglu
Koichiro Deguchi
Alberto Del Bimbo
Alessio Del Bue
Hervé Delingette
Andrew Delong
Stefanie Demirci
David Demirdjian
Jia Deng
Joachim Denzler
Konstantinos Derpanis
Thomas Deselaers
Frederic Devernay
Michel Dhome

Anthony Dick
Ajay Divakaran
Santosh Kumar Divvala
Minh Do
Carl Doersch
Piotr Dollar
Bin Dong
Weisheng Dong
Michael Donoser
Gianfranco Doretto
Matthijs Douze
Bruce Draper
Mark Drew
Bertram Drost
Lixin Duan
Jean-Luc Dugelay
Enrique Dunn
Pinar Duygulu
Jan-Olof Eklundh
James H. Elder
Ian Endres
Olof Enqvist
Markus Enzweiler
Aykut Erdem
Anders Eriksson
Ali Eslami
Irfan Essa
Francisco Estrada
Bin Fan
Quanfu Fan
Jialue Fan
Sean Fanello
Ali Farhadi
Giovanni Farinella
Ryan Farrell
Alireza Fathi
Paolo Favaro
Michael Felsberg
Pedro Felzenszwalb
Rob Fergus
Basura Fernando
Frank Ferrie
Sanja Fidler
Boris Flach
Francois Fleuret

David Fofi
Wolfgang Foerstner
David Forsyth
Katerina Fragkiadaki
Jean-Sebastien Franco
Friedrich Fraundorfer
Mario Fritz
Yun Fu
Pascal Fua
Hironobu Fujiyoshi
Yasutaka Furukawa
Ryo Furukawa
Andrea Fusiello
Fabio Galasso
Juergen Gall
Andrew Gallagher
David Gallup
Arvind Ganesh
Dashan Gao
Shenghua Gao
James Gee
Andreas Geiger
Yakup Genc
Bogdan Georgescu
Guido Gerig
David Geronimo
Theo Gevers
Bernard Ghanem
Andrew Gilbert
Ross Girshick
Martin Godec
Guy Godin
Roland Goecke
Michael Goesele
Alvina Goh
Bastian Goldluecke
Boqing Gong
Yunchao Gong
Raghuraman Gopalan
Albert Gordo
Lena Gorelick
Paulo Gotardo
Stephen Gould
Venu Madhav Govindu
Helmut Grabner

Roger Grosse
Matthias Grundmann
Chunhui Gu
Xianfeng Gu
Jinwei Gu
Sergio Guadarrama
Matthieu Guillaumin
Jean-Yves Guillemaut
Hatice Gunes
Ruiqi Guo
Guodong Guo
Abhinav Gupta
Abner Guzman Rivera
Gregory Hager
Ghassan Hamarneh
Bohyung Han
Tony Han
Jari Hannuksela
Tatsuya Harada
Mehrtash Harandi
Bharath Hariharan
Stefan Harmeling
Tal Hassner
Daniel Hauagge
Søren Hauberg
Michal Havlena
James Hays
Kaiming He
Xuming He
Martial Hebert
Felix Heide
Jared Heinly
Hagit Hel-Or
Lionel Heng
Philipp Hennig
Carlos Hernandez
Aaron Hertzmann
Adrian Hilton
David Hogg
Derek Hoiem
Byung-Woo Hong
Anthony Hoogs
Joachim Hornegger
Timothy Hospedales
Wenze Hu

Zhe Hu
Gang Hua
Xian-Sheng Hua
Dong Huang
Gary Huang
Heng Huang
Sung Ju Hwang
Wonjun Hwang
Ivo Ihrke
Nazli Ikizler-Cinbis
Slobodan Ilic
Horace Ip
Michal Irani
Hiroshi Ishikawa
Laurent Itti
Nathan Jacobs
Max Jaderberg
Omar Javed
C.V. Jawahar
Bruno Jedynak
Hueihan Jhuang
Qiang Ji
Hui Ji
Kui Jia
Yangqing Jia
Jiaya Jia
Hao Jiang
Zhuolin Jiang
Sam Johnson
Neel Joshi
Armand Joulin
Frederic Jurie
Ioannis Kakadiaris
Zdenek Kalal
Amit Kale
Joni-Kristian
    Kamarainen
George Kamberov
Kenichi Kanatani
Sing Bing Kang
Vadim Kantorov
Jörg Hendrik Kappes
Leonid Karlinsky
Zoltan Kato
Hiroshi Kawasaki

Verena Kaynig
Cem Keskin
Margret Keuper
Daniel Keysers
Sameh Khamis
Fahad Khan
Saad Khan
Aditya Khosla
Martin Kiefel
Gunhee Kim
Jaechul Kim
Seon Joo Kim
Tae-Kyun Kim
Byungsoo Kim
Benjamin Kimia
Kris Kitani
Hedvig Kjellstrom
Laurent Kneip
Reinhard Koch
Kevin Koeser
Ullrich Koethe
Effrosyni Kokiopoulou
Iasonas Kokkinos
Kalin Kolev
Vladimir Kolmogorov
Vladlen Koltun
Nikos Komodakis
Piotr Koniusz
Peter Kontschieder
Ender Konukoglu
Sanjeev Koppal
Hema Koppula
Andreas Koschan
Jana Kosecka
Adriana Kovashka
Adarsh Kowdle
Josip Krapac
Dilip Krishnan
Zuzana Kukelova
Brian Kulis
Neeraj Kumar
M. Pawan Kumar
Cheng-Hao Kuo
In So Kweon
Junghyun Kwon

Junseok Kwon
Simon Lacoste-Julien
Shang-Hong Lai
Jean-François Lalonde
Tian Lan
Michael Langer
Doug Lanman
Diane Larlus
Longin Jan Latecki
Svetlana Lazebnik
Laura Leal-Taixé
Erik Learned-Miller
Honglak Lee
Yong Jae Lee
Ido Leichter
Victor Lempitsky
Frank Lenzen
Marius Leordeanu
Thomas Leung
Maxime Lhuillier
Chunming Li
Fei-Fei Li
Fuxin Li
Rui Li
Li Jiu Li
Chia-Kai Liang
Shengcai Liao
Joerg Liebelt
Jongwoo Lim
Joseph Lim
Ruei-Sung Lin
Yen-Yu Lin
Zhouchen Lin
Liang Lin
Haibin Ling
James Little
Baiyang Liu
Ce Liu
Feng Liu
Guangcan Liu
Jingen Liu
Wei Liu
Zicheng Liu
Zongyi Liu
Tyng-Luh Liu

Xiaoming Liu
Xiaobai Liu
Ming-Yu Liu
Marcus Liwicki
Stephen Lombardi
Roberto Lopez-Sastre
Manolis Lourakis
Brian Lovell
Chen Change Loy
Jiangbo Lu
Jiwen Lu
Simon Lucey
Jiebo Luo
Ping Luo
Marcus Magnor
Vijay Mahadevan
Julien Mairal
Michael Maire
Subhransu Maji
Atsuto Maki
Yasushi Makihara
Roberto Manduchi
Luca Marchesotti
Aleix Martinez
Bogdan Matei
Diana Mateus
Stefan Mathe
Yasuyuki Matsushita
Iain Matthews
Kevin Matzen
Bruce Maxwell
Stephen Maybank
Walterio Mayol-Cuevas
David McAllester
Gerard Medioni
Christopher Mei
Paulo Mendonca
Thomas Mensink
Domingo Mery
Ajmal Mian
Branislav Micusik
Ondrej Miksik
Anton Milan
Majid Mirmehdi
Anurag Mittal

Hossein Mobahi
Pranab Mohanty
Pascal Monasse
Vlad Morariu
Philippos Mordohai
Francesc Moreno-Noguer
Luce Morin
Nigel Morris
Bryan Morse
Eric Mortensen
Yasuhiro Mukaigawa
Lopamudra Mukherjee
Vittorio Murino
David Murray
Sobhan Naderi Parizi
Hajime Nagahara
Laurent Najman
Karthik Nandakumar
Fabian Nater
Jan Neumann
Lukas Neumann
Ram Nevatia
Richard Newcombe
Minh Hoai Nguyen
Bingbing Ni
Feiping Nie
Juan Carlos Niebles
Marc Niethammer
Claudia Nieuwenhuis
Mark Nixon
Mohammad Norouzi
Sebastian Nowozin
Matthew O'Toole
Peter Ochs
Jean-Marc Odobez
Francesca Odone
Eyal Ofek
Sangmin Oh
Takahiro Okabe
Takayuki Okatani
Aude Oliva
Carl Olsson
Bjorn Ommer
Magnus Oskarsson
Wanli Ouyang

Geoffrey Oxholm
Mustafa Ozuysal
Nicolas Padoy
Caroline Pantofaru
Nicolas Papadakis
George Papandreou
Nikolaos
  Papanikolopoulos
Nikos Paragios
Devi Parikh
Dennis Park
Vishal Patel
Ioannis Patras
Vladimir Pavlovic
Kim Pedersen
Marco Pedersoli
Shmuel Peleg
Marcello Pelillo
Tingying Peng
A.G. Amitha Perera
Alessandro Perina
Federico Pernici
Florent Perronnin
Vladimir Petrovic
Tomas Pfister
Jonathon Phillips
Justus Piater
Massimo Piccardi
Hamed Pirsiavash
Leonid Pishchulin
Robert Pless
Thomas Pock
Jean Ponce
Gerard Pons-Moll
Ronald Poppe
Andrea Prati
Victor Prisacariu
Kari Pulli
Yu Qiao
Lei Qin
Novi Quadrianto
Rahul Raguram
Varun Ramakrishna
Srikumar Ramalingam
Narayanan Ramanathan

Konstantinos
  Rapantzikos
Michalis Raptis
Nalini Ratha
Avinash Ravichandran
Michael Reale
Dikpal Reddy
James Rehg
Jan Reininghaus
Xiaofeng Ren
Jerome Revaud
Morteza Rezanejad
Hayko Riemenschneider
Tammy Riklin Raviv
Antonio Robles-Kelly
Erik Rodner
Emanuele Rodola
Mikel Rodriguez
Marcus Rohrbach
Javier Romero
Charles Rosenberg
Bodo Rosenhahn
Arun Ross
Samuel Rota Bul
Peter Roth
Volker Roth
Anastasios Roussos
Sebastien Roy
Michael Rubinstein
Olga Russakovsky
Bryan Russell
Michael S. Ryoo
Mohammad Amin
  Sadeghi
Kate Saenko
Albert Ali Salah
Imran Saleemi
Mathieu Salzmann
Conrad Sanderson
Aswin
  Sankaranarayanan
Benjamin Sapp
Radim Sara
Scott Satkin
Imari Sato

Yoichi Sato
Bogdan Savchynskyy
Hanno Scharr
Daniel Scharstein
Yoav Y. Schechner
Walter Scheirer
Kevin Schelten
Frank Schmidt
Uwe Schmidt
Julia Schnabel
Alexander Schwing
Nicu Sebe
Shishir Shah
Mubarak Shah
Shiguang Shan
Qi Shan
Ling Shao
Abhishek Sharma
Viktoriia Sharmanska
Eli Shechtman
Yaser Sheikh
Alexander Shekhovtsov
Chunhua Shen
Li Shen
Yonggang Shi
Qinfeng Shi
Ilan Shimshoni
Takaaki Shiratori
Abhinav Shrivastava
Behjat Siddiquie
Nathan Silberman
Karen Simonyan
Richa Singh
Vikas Singh
Sudipta Sinha
Josef Sivic
Dirk Smeets
Arnold Smeulders
William Smith
Cees Snoek
Eric Sommerlade
Alexander
  Sorkine-Hornung
Alvaro Soto
Richard Souvenir

Anuj Srivastava
Ioannis Stamos
Michael Stark
Chris Stauffer
Bjorn Stenger
Charles Stewart
Rainer Stiefelhagen
Juergen Sturm
Yusuke Sugano
Josephine Sullivan
Deqing Sun
Min Sun
Hari Sundar
Ganesh Sundaramoorthi
Kalyan Sunkavalli
Sabine Süsstrunk
David Suter
Tomas Svoboda
Rahul Swaminathan
Tanveer
  Syeda-Mahmood
Rick Szeliski
Raphael Sznitman
Yuichi Taguchi
Yu-Wing Tai
Jun Takamatsu
Hugues Talbot
Ping Tan
Robby Tan
Kevin Tang
Huixuan Tang
Danhang Tang
Marshall Tappen
Jean-Philippe Tarel
Danny Tarlow
Gabriel Taubin
Camillo Taylor
Demetri Terzopoulos
Christian Theobalt
Yuandong Tian
Joseph Tighe
Radu Timofte
Massimo Tistarelli
George Toderici
Sinisa Todorovic

Giorgos Tolias
Federico Tombari
Tatiana Tommasi
Yan Tong
Akihiko Torii
Antonio Torralba
Lorenzo Torresani
Andrea Torsello
Tali Treibitz
Rudolph Triebel
Bill Triggs
Roberto Tron
Tomasz Trzcinski
Ivor Tsang
Yanghai Tsin
Zhuowen Tu
Tony Tung
Pavan Turaga
Engin Türetken
Oncel Tuzel
Georgios Tzimiropoulos
Norimichi Ukita
Martin Urschler
Arash Vahdat
Julien Valentin
Michel Valstar
Koen van de Sande
Joost van de Weijer
Anton van den Hengel
Jan van Gemert
Daniel Vaquero
Kiran Varanasi
Mayank Vatsa
Ashok Veeraraghavan
Olga Veksler
Alexander Vezhnevets
Rene Vidal
Sudheendra
  Vijayanarasimhan
Jordi Vitria
Christian Vogler
Carl Vondrick
Sven Wachsmuth
Stefan Walk
Chaohui Wang

Jingdong Wang
Jue Wang
Ruiping Wang
Kai Wang
Liang Wang
Xinggang Wang
Xin-Jing Wang
Yang Wang
Heng Wang
Yu-Chiang Frank Wang
Simon Warfield
Yichen Wei
Yair Weiss
Gordon Wetzstein
Oliver Whyte
Richard Wildes
Christopher Williams
Lior Wolf
Kwan-Yee Kenneth
  Wong
Oliver Woodford
John Wright
Changchang Wu
Xinxiao Wu
Ying Wu
Tianfu Wu
Yang Wu
Yingnian Wu
Jonas Wulff
Yu Xiang
Tao Xiang
Jianxiong Xiao
Dong Xu
Li Xu
Yong Xu
Kota Yamaguchi
Takayoshi Yamashita
Shuicheng Yan
Jie Yang
Qingxiong Yang
Ruigang Yang
Meng Yang
Yi Yang
Chih-Yuan Yang
Jimei Yang

Bangpeng Yao
Angela Yao
Dit-Yan Yeung
Alper Yilmaz
Lijun Yin
Xianghua Ying
Kuk-Jin Yoon
Shiqi Yu
Stella Yu
Jingyi Yu
Junsong Yuan
Lu Yuan
Alan Yuille
Ramin Zabih
Christopher Zach

Stefanos Zafeiriou
Hongbin Zha
Lei Zhang
Junping Zhang
Shaoting Zhang
Xiaoqin Zhang
Guofeng Zhang
Tianzhu Zhang
Ning Zhang
Lei Zhang
Li Zhang
Bin Zhao
Guoying Zhao
Ming Zhao
Yibiao Zhao

Weishi Zheng
Bo Zheng
Changyin Zhou
Huiyu Zhou
Kevin Zhou
Bolei Zhou
Feng Zhou
Jun Zhu
Xiangxin Zhu
Henning Zimmer
Karel Zimmermann
Andrew Zisserman
Larry Zitnick
Daniel Zoran

Additional Reviewers

Austin Abrams
Hanno Ackermann
Daniel Adler
Muhammed Zeshan
    Afzal
Pulkit Agrawal
Edilson de Aguiar
Unaiza Ahsan
Amit Aides
Zeynep Akata
Jon Almazan
David Altamar
Marina Alterman
Mohamed Rabie Amer
Manuel Amthor
Shawn Andrews
Oisin Mac Aodha
Federica Arrigoni
Yuval Bahat
Luis Barrios
John Bastian
Florian Becker
C. Fabian
    Benitez-Quiroz
Vinay Bettadapura
Brian G. Booth

Lukas Bossard
Katie Bouman
Hilton Bristow
Daniel Canelhas
Olivier Canevet
Spencer Cappallo
Ivan Huerta Casado
Daniel Castro
Ishani Chakraborty
Chenyi Chen
Sheng Chen
Xinlei Chen
Wei-Chen Chiu
Hang Chu
Yang Cong
Sam Corbett-Davies
Zhen Cui
Maria A. Davila
Oliver Demetz
Meltem Demirkus
Chaitanya Desai
Pengfei Dou
Ralf Dragon
Liang Du
David Eigen
Jakob Engel

Victor Escorcia
Sandro Esquivel
Nicola Fioraio
Michael Firman
Alex Fix
Oliver Fleischmann
Marco Fornoni
David Fouhey
Vojtech Franc
Jorge Martinez G.
Silvano Galliani
Pablo Garrido
Efstratios Gavves
Timnit Gebru
Georgios Giannoulis
Clement Godard
Ankur Gupta
Saurabh Gupta
Amirhossein Habibian
David Hafner
Tom S.F. Haines
Vladimir Haltakov
Christopher Ham
Xufeng Han
Stefan Heber
Yacov Hel-Or

David Held
Benjamin Hell
Jan Heller
Anton van den Hengel
Robert Henschel
Steven Hickson
Michael Hirsch
Jan Hosang
Shell Hu
Zhiwu Huang
Daniel Huber
Ahmad Humayun
Corneliu Ilisescu
Zahra Iman
Thanapong Intharah
Phillip Isola
Hamid Izadinia
Edward Johns
Justin Johnson
Andreas Jordt
Anne Jordt
Cijo Jose
Daniel Jung
Meina Kan
Ben Kandel
Vasiliy Karasev
Andrej Karpathy
Jan Kautz
Changil Kim
Hyeongwoo Kim
Rolf Koehler
Daniel Kohlsdorf
Svetlana Kordumova
Jonathan Krause
Till Kroeger
Malte Kuhlmann
Ilja Kuzborskij
Alina Kuznetsova
Sam Kwak
Peihua Li
Michael Lam
Maksim Lapin
Gil Levi
Aviad Levis
Yan Li

Wenbin Li
Yin Li
Zhenyang Li
Pengpeng Liang
Jinna Lie
Qiguang Liu
Tianliang Liu
Alexander Loktyushin
Steven Lovegrove
Feng Lu
Jake Lussier
Xutao Lv
Luca Magri
Behrooz Mahasseni
Aravindh Mahendran
Siddharth Mahendran
Francesco Malapelle
Mateusz Malinowski
Santiago Manen
Timo von Marcard
Ricardo Martin-Brualla
Iacopo Masi
Roberto Mecca
Tomer Michaeli
Hengameh Mirzaalian
Kylia Miskell
Ishan Misra
Javier Montoya
Roozbeh Mottaghi
Panagiotis Moutafis
Oliver Mueller
Daniel Munoz
Rajitha Navarathna
James Newling
Mohamed Omran
Vicente Ordonez
Sobhan Naderi Parizi
Omkar Parkhi
Novi Patricia
Kuan-Chuan Peng
Bojan Pepikj
Federico Perazzi
Loic Peter
Alioscia Petrelli
Sebastian Polsterl

Alison Pouch
Vittal Premanchandran
James Pritts
Luis Puig
Julian Quiroga
Vignesh Ramanathan
Rene Ranftl
Mohammad Rastegari
S. Hussain Raza
Michael Reale
Malcolm Reynolds
Alimoor Reza
Christian Richardt
Marko Ristin
Beatrice Rossi
Rasmus Rothe
Nasa Rouf
Anirban Roy
Fereshteh Sadeghi
Zahra Sadeghipoor
Faraz Saedaar
Tanner Schmidt
Anna Senina
Lee Seversky
Yachna Sharma
Chen Shen
Javen Shi
Tomas Simon
Gautam Singh
Brandon M. Smith
Shuran Song
Mohamed Souiai
Srinath Sridhar
Abhilash Srikantha
Michael Stoll
Aparna Taneja
Lisa Tang
Moria Tau
J. Rafael Tena
Roberto Toldo
Manolis Tsakiris
Dimitrios Tzionas
Vladyslav Usenko
Danny Veikherman
Fabio Viola

Minh Vo
Christoph Vogel
Sebastian Volz
Jacob Walker
Li Wan
Chen Wang
Jiang Wang
Oliver Wang
Peng Wang
Jan Dirk Wegner
Stephan Wenger
Scott Workman
Chenglei Wu

Yuhang Wu
Fan Yang
Mark Yatskar
Bulent Yener
Serena Yeung
Kwang M. Yi
Gokhan Yildirim
Ryo Yonetani
Stanislav Yotov
Chong You
Quanzeng You
Fisher Yu
Pei Yu

Kaan Yucer
Clausius Zelenka
Xing Zhang
Xinhua Zhang
Yinda Zhang
Jiejie Zhu
Shengqi Zhu
Yingying Zhu
Yuke Zhu
Andrew Ziegler

Table of Contents

Structure from Motion and Feature Matching

Coarse-to-Fine Auto-Encoder Networks (CFAN) for Real-Time Face Alignment

Jie Zhang[1,2], Shiguang Shan[1], Meina Kan[1], and Xilin Chen[1]

[1] Key Lab of Intelligent Information Processing of Chinese Academy of Sciences (CAS), Institute of Computing Technology, CAS, Beijing 100190, China
[2] University of Chinese Academy of Sciences, Beijing 100049, China
{jie.zhang,shiguang.shan,meina.kan,xilin.chen}@vipl.ict.ac.cn

Abstract. Accurate face alignment is a vital prerequisite step for most face perception tasks such as face recognition, facial expression analysis and non-realistic face re-rendering. It can be formulated as the nonlinear inference of the facial landmarks from the detected face region. Deep network seems a good choice to model the nonlinearity, but it is non-trivial to apply it directly. In this paper, instead of a straightforward application of deep network, we propose a Coarse-to-Fine Auto-encoder Networks (CFAN) approach, which cascades a few successive Stacked Auto-encoder Networks (SANs). Specifically, the first SAN predicts the landmarks quickly but accurately enough as a preliminary, by taking as input a low-resolution version of the detected face holistically. The following SANs then progressively refine the landmark by taking as input the local features extracted around the current landmarks (output of the previous SAN) with higher and higher resolution. Extensive experiments conducted on three challenging datasets demonstrate that our CFAN outperforms the state-of-the-art methods and performs in real-time(40+fps excluding face detection on a desktop).

Keywords: Face Alignment, Nonlinear, Deep Learning, Stacked Auto-encoder, Coarse-to-Fine, Real-time.

1 Introduction

Face alignment or facial landmark detection plays an important role in face recognition, facial expression recognition, face animation, *etc.* Therefore, it has received more and more attentions in recent years. However, it remains a challenging problem due to the complex variations in face appearance caused by pose, expression, illumination, partial occlusion, *etc.* Generally speaking, the existing approaches can be categorized into holistic feature based methods [7,21,14,34,19,6] and local feature based methods [8,10,15,23,9,25,35,32,31,2,28,11].

As a typical model, Active Appearance Models (AAM) [7,21] firstly use Principal Component Analysis (PCA) to model the shape and texture separately and then integrate them together with another PCA to get the generative appearance model. In the testing stage, the shape of a new face image is inferred by optimizing the model parameters to minimize the difference between the observed

D. Fleet et al. (Eds.): ECCV 2014, Part II, LNCS 8690, pp. 1–16, 2014.
© Springer International Publishing Switzerland 2014

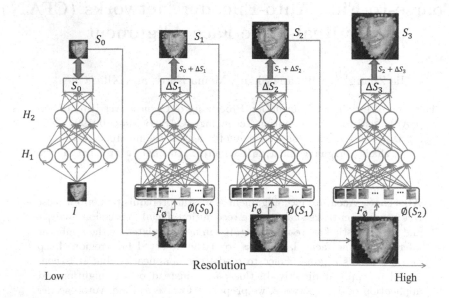

Fig. 1. Overview of our Coarse-to-Fine Auto-encoder Networks (CFAN) for real-time face alignment. H_1, H_2 are hidden layers. Through function F_Φ, the joint local features $\Phi(S_i)$ are extracted around facial landmarks of current shape S_i.

face image and the image generated by the appearance model. However, these methods generally fail in case of complex appearance variations in real-world applications, mainly because a single linear model can hardly cover all the non-linear variations in facial appearance. To address this problem, Zhao et al. [34] propose a locally linear AAM method to approximate the global nonlinear model and report good performance. However the initialization of this approach needs eyes locations. Moreover, it is difficult for AAM-like holistic methods to handle partial occlusion problems.

Instead of modeling appearance with the entire face, local feature based methods like ASMs [8,15,23], CLM [9] build appearance models with local image patches which are generally sampled around the current facial landmarks. In these methods, partial occlusion problem can be easily handled by including a shape constraint. But the shape constrains employed in these methods are relatively weak so that they are prone to local minimum due to ambiguous local regions [8,9]. Saragih et al. [25] propose a Regularized Landmark MeanShift fitting method to solve the optimization problem of CLM, which achieves higher performance for generic face alignment scenario. Recently, Asthana et al. propose a promising method named as discriminative response map fitting with constrained local models (DRMF) [2], which learns the dictionaries of probability response maps based on local features and adopts linear regression-based fitting method in the CLM framework. In another state-of-the-art work [31], a

 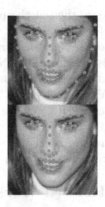

Fig. 2. Facial landmark detection under the partial occlusion scenario (from Helen datasets [18]): Results of DCNN [26] (top row) and our CFAN (bottom row)

Fig. 3. Denition of 68 (top) and 49 (bottom) facial landmarks

supervised descent method (SDM) is proposed to solve nonlinear least squares optimization problem and achieves significant success in facial landmark detection.

SDM [31] achieves promising performance by using the supervised descent strategy, but it is initialized by using the mean shape on the detected face region which makes it heavily rely on the face detection results. Moreover, in each stage of the cascades architecture of SDM, linear regression is exploited to model the mapping from shape-index feature [12] to face shape, which may be insufficient for the complex non-linear process from shape-index feature to face shape. In contrast, the DCNN [26] employs a deep CNN model with the global feature to predict the landmark locations as the initialization, which is more accurate than the mean shape. After the initialization, the successive network of DCNN refines each landmark separately without any shape constraints, which may fail in case of partial occlusions as shown in the first row of Fig. 2. Therefore it is necessary for the first stage to provide a strong shape prior for the following stages.

In this paper, we further push the frontier of the area by resorting to deep network and elaborately adapting it to disintegrate progressively the complex nonlinearity in face shape inference. We propose an architecture named Coarse-to-Fine Auto-encoder Networks (CFAN), as illustrated in Fig. 1, and show how it can further beat the state-of-the-art methods such as SDM and DRMF. As seen from Fig.1, instead of a single stacked auto-encoder network (SAN), our CFAN is comprised of several successive SANs, each figuring out part of the nonlinearity. Specifically, the first SAN predicts the face shape quickly by taking holistically a low-resolution version of the detected face as input; the following SANs then progressively refine the landmark locations by taking as input the joint local features extracted around the current landmarks (output of the previous SAN) in higher and higher resolution. By using such a progressive and resolution-variable strategy, the search space of each SAN, or in other words the difficulty of the task for each SAN, is well controlled and thus more tractable. Benefitted from the advantages of joint local features, our method is more robust to partial occlusions than DCNN [26] as shown in the last row of Fig. 2.

Extensive evaluation results on several public databases, *i.e.*, XM2VTS [22], LFPW [3] and HELEN [18], show that our method achieves impressively better accuracies, compared with the state-of-the-art methods, such as SDM and DRMF. Furthermore, our method (in Matlab codes) takes about 23 milliseconds per image to predict 68 facial points excluding the face detection time, on an desktop machine with Intel i7-3770 (3.4 GHz CPU).

2   Related Works

2.1   Local Models with Regression Fitting

Recently local model methods with Regression Fitting [28,11,33,31,2] make great progresses on facial point detection, especially SDM [31]. Local methods like ASMs [8,15,23] and CLMs [9,25] solve the optimization problems with Gauss-Newton method. Yet, instead of computing the Jacobian and Hessian matrices, SDM learns generic descent directions and re-scaling factors by using the linear regression. Specifically, given an image $x \in \mathbf{R}^d$, S denotes the shape vector containing the coordinates of the facial points. The objective of most regression fitting model can be formulated as optimizing a sequence of successive update ΔS for shape as follows:

$$f(S_0 + \Delta S) = ||\Phi(S_0 + \Delta S) - \Phi(S_g)||_2^2, \qquad (1)$$

where S_0 and S_g denote the initial shape and ground truth shape respectively and Φ is a nonlinear feature extraction function from a shape. The shape update ΔS can be obtained by employing Newton's method as follows:

$$\Delta S = -H^{-1}J_f = -2H^{-1}J_\phi^T(\Phi(S_0) - \Phi(S_g)), \qquad (2)$$

where J_f and H are the Jacobian and Hessian matrices.

SDM directly estimates the descent direction $R_1 = -2H^{-1}J_\phi^T$ by using a linear regression between the appearance information and the shape deviation to avoid the complex computations of Jacobian and inverse of Hessian matrices. Thus, in SDM, Eq. (2) is formulated as bellow:

$$\Delta S_1 = R_1\Phi_0 + b_1, \qquad (3)$$

where b_1 is a bias term corresponding to $\Phi(S_g)$. In a similar way, SDM can learn a sequence of generic descent directions R_k and bias term b_k after k iterations.

$$\Delta S_k = R_k\Phi_{k-1} + b_k. \qquad (4)$$

For most methods including SDM, the mean shape is used as the initialization, which may suffer from local minimum problem in case of bad initializations. To depress the effects from bad initializations, Cao et al. [6] use multiple initializations strategy and Burgos-Artizzu et al. [5] adopt smart restarts technique, but it still leaves a long way to go.

2.2 Deep Models

Recently, deep models like Deep Auto-encoders(DAEs), Convolutional Neural Networks(CNNs), Restricted Boltzmann Machines(RBMs) and their variants are widely used in the field of computer vision [4]. They have achieved great success in many challenging tasks such as image classification [17], scene parsing [13], human pose estimation [27], face alignment and facial feature tracking [26,30].

Sun et al. [26] propose a cascaded regression approach for facial points detection with three-stage deep convolutional network. At the first stage, the carefully designed convolutional neural networks provide accurate initial estimations of facial points when given the full face as input. Then the initial estimations are refined during next two stages. Impressive results are achieved on two public datasets, BioID [16] and LFPW [3]. However, in the layers after the first one, each landmark is refined separately, which makes it depend on and sensitive to the accuracy of the first layer more heavily. Another interesting work [30] constructs a face shape prior model by using RBMs and their variants for facial feature tracking under varying facial expressions and face poses. In [30], Wu et al. use deep belief networks(DBNs) to capture the face shape variations from facial expressions and handle pose variations with a 3-way RBM model. Luo et al. [20] also use DBNs for facial component detection and then train the facial component segmentators with deep auto-encoders.

Most of these deep models achieve promising results on facial landmarks detection and tracking, benefitted from its favorable ability for modeling the nonlinearity, which can work well for the nonlinear mapping from the a face image to the face shape. Some major concerns in these deep works are the time complexity and the local minima, due to the highly nonlinear optimization.

3 Coarse-to-Fine Auto-Encoder Networks

In this paper, we present a novel Coarse-to-Fine Auto-encoder Networks method (CFAN) for real-time facial landmark detection. Firstly, we will illustrate the overview of the proposed framework; secondly, we will describe the details about two components of CFAN, *i.e.*, global SAN and local SANs; and finally we will give a detailed discussion about the difference from some existing works.

3.1 Method Overview

As shown in Fig. 1, the proposed CFAN attempts to design the general cascade-regression framework in a coarse-to-fine architecture, with the regression in each stage modeled as a nonlinear deep network. Specifically, the CFAN framework consists of several successive Stacked Auto-encoder Networks (SANs). Each SAN attempts to characterize the nonlinear mappings from face image to face shape in different scales based on the shape predicted from the previous SAN.

The first SAN (referred as global SAN) endeavors to roughly approximate the facial landmark locations, and therefore a low-resolution image is exploited for a large search step. A large step can alleviate the suffering from local minima and meanwhile promise a fast model. Moreover, rather than local shape-indexed feature from mean shape, the global image feature is employed as input to avoid the inaccuracy of mean shape. As a result, the global SAN can approach the ground truth facial landmark locations more accurately and more quickly.

After getting an estimation S_0 of face shape from the first SAN, the successive SANs (referred as local SANs) make an effort to refine the shape by regressing the deviation ΔS between the current locations and the ground truth locations step by step. The nonlinear regression model SAN is still exploited to model the nonlinearity between the current feature and the ground truth shape. To characterize fine variations, the shape-indexed feature extracted from current shape at higher resolution is exploited to enforce smaller search step and smaller search region. Furthermore, the shape-indexed features of all facial points are concatenated together to enforce all facial points updated jointly so as to insure a reasonable solution, even under the partial occlusion scenario.

3.2 Global SAN

The first SAN of the proposed coarse-to-fine deep networks, *i.e.*, the global SAN, directly estimates the face shape based on global raw features at a low-resolution image. Given a face image $x \in \mathbf{R^d}$ of d pixels, $S_g(x) \in \mathbf{R^p}$ denotes the ground truth locations of p landmarks. The face landmark detection is to learn a mapping function $\mathbf{F}$ from the image to the face shape as follows:

$$\mathbf{F} : S \leftarrow x. \tag{5}$$

Generally, $\mathbf{F}$ is complex and nonlinear. To achieve this goal, k single hidden layer auto-encoders are stacked as a deep neural network to map the image to the corresponding shape. Specifically, the face alignment task is formulated as minimizing the following objective:

$$\mathbf{F^*} = \arg \min_{\mathbf{F}} ||S_g(x) - f_k(f_{k-1}(...f_1(x)))||_2^2, \tag{6}$$

$$f_i(a_{i-1}) = \sigma(W_i a_{i-1} + b_i) \triangleq a_i, i = 1, ..., k - 1, \tag{7}$$

$$f_k(a_{k-1}) = W_k a_{k-1} + b_k \triangleq S_0. \tag{8}$$

where $\mathbf{F} = \{f_1, f_2, ..., f_k\}$, f_i is the mapping function of ith layer in the deep network, σ is a sigmoid function and a_i is the feature representations of each layer. Nonlinear mapping in term of sigmoid function is employed by the first $k - 1$ layers to characterize the nonlinearity between the image feature and the face shape. However, the output range of sigmoid function is [0 1] which is inconsistent with the location range, therefore, linear regression is exploited in the last layer f_k to get an accurate shape estimation S_0.

To prevent over-fitting, a regularization term $\sum_{i=1}^{k}||W_i||_F^2$(a weight decay term) is added which tends to decrease the magnitude of the weights. The objective function is further re-formulated as bellow:

$$\mathbf{F}^* = \arg\min_{\mathbf{F}} ||S_g(x) - f_k(f_{k-1}(...f_1(x)))||_2^2 + \alpha \sum_{i=1}^{k} ||W_i||_F^2. \qquad (9)$$

The function $\mathbf{F}$ contains lots of parameters and it is easy to fall into local minimum during optimization. To achieve a better optimization, firstly, we adopt the unsupervised pre-train process to initialize the first $k - 1$ layers in a stacked strategy and random initialization for the kth layer; secondly, fine tune the whole network in a supervised way.

For the ith layer, it is pre-trained by optimizing the following objective function:

$$\{f_i^*, g_i^*\} = \arg\min_{f_i, g_i} ||a_{i-1} - g_i(f_i(a_{i-1}))||^2 + \alpha(||W_i||_F^2 + ||W_i^T||_F^2), \qquad (10)$$

where $f_i(x) = \sigma(W_i x + b_i)$, $g_i(x) = \sigma(W_i^T x + b_i')$, $i = 1, 2, ..., k - 1$.

Then the output of this single hidden layer network $a_i = f_i(a_{i-1})$ is used as the input of the next layer. For the first layer, the input is the raw image feature, i.e., $a_0 = x$.

After the initialization with Eq. (10), all layers of the whole network are fine-tuned according to Eq. (9). As a result, the first few layers of a stacked auto-encoder network tend to capture the low-level features such as texture patterns in an image, while the higher layers tend to capture higher-level features containing context information of texture patterns.

After the optimization, the prediction of the facial landmarks is achieved as S_0, which is a rough but robust and fast approximation of the ground truth.

3.3 Local SANs

The global SAN described above will give a rough shape estimation S_0 of input image x, which is already close to the ground truth locations but not close enough due to the highly complicated variations in expression, pose, identity, etc. To achieve finer locations, several successive SANs are employed to iteratively predict the deviation ΔS_j between current shape S_{j-1} and the ground truth S_g based on joint local shape-indexed features, referred as local SANs.

Shape-indexed features extracted around the landmark points have been proved to be efficient and effective for face alignment [12,6,31,5]. The local feature from each facial point can only capture the information from itself while ignore the relevance with the other points. Therefore, the facial points are modeled jointly in our local SAN, by concatenating all local shape-indexed feature together as the input.

Similarly as the global SAN, the successive local SAN is also designed as a stacked deep auto-network to deal with the nonlinearity of predicting the face shape, but with the local shape-indexed feature as input. With the estimated

Fig. 4. Local patches extracted around the landmark points with different resolutions. For the sake of concise display, we choose two eye centers and 17 facial points on the face contour to describe the multi-resolution strategy used in each local SAN.

shape S_0 from global SAN, the shape-indexed features, *i.e.*, SIFT, can be extracted around each facial point, denoted as $\phi(S_0)$. The objective of the first local SAN is to achieve a nonlinear regression $\mathbf{H}_1$ from the shape-indexed feature $\phi(S_0)$ to the deviation $\Delta S_1 = S_g - S_0$ as follows:

$$\mathbf{H}_1^* = \arg\min_{\mathbf{H}_1} ||\Delta S_1(x) - h_k^1(h_{k-1}^1(...h_1^1(\phi(S_0))))||_2^2 + \alpha \sum_{i=1}^{k} ||W_i^1||_F^2, \quad (11)$$

where $\mathbf{H}_1 = \{h_1^1, h_2^1, ..., h_k^1\}$, $\sum_{i=1}^{k} ||W_i^1||_F^2$ is the weight decay term. Similar to the global SAN, the whole deep network is firstly initialized by using the unsupervised pre-training, and then fine-tuned according to Eq. (11).

After getting the face shape update $(\Delta \hat{S}_1)$ by the first local SAN, an updated face shape can be obtained as $S_1 = S_0 + \Delta \hat{S}_1$. Then the successive local SAN extracts local features around the new shape, and optimizes a deep network to minimize the new deviation between the current location and the ground truth. The objective of the jth local SAN is shown as follows:

$$\mathbf{H}_j^* = \arg\min_{\mathbf{H}_j} ||\Delta S_j(x) - h_k^j(h_{k-1}^j(...h_1^j(\phi(S_{j-1}))))||_2^2 + \alpha \sum_{i=1}^{k} ||W_i^j||_F^2. \quad (12)$$

For each Local SAN, local features around the landmark points are extracted in a local patch of the same size but at different resolutions as shown in Fig. 4. Local patches of the same size at low-resolution face images contain more context information and thus lead to a larger searching region for the Local SAN. It is necessary for the anterior SANs to approximate with a large search step when the current location is relatively far from the ground truth. On the other hand, the local patches of the same size but at high resolution face images actually constrain the searching within a small region which means that the posterior SAN can refine the location with a tiny step leading to more accurate results.

3.4   Discussions

Differences with SDM   [31]. A sequence of generic descent directions are learned by several successive local SANs as well as SDM [31], but they differ in the following aspects: 1) SDM employs linear regression to model the mapping from shape-indexed features to a face shape, while our CFAN employs nonlinear regression, *i.e.*, deep auto networks, to model the mapping from shape-indexed feature to face shape, which can achieve lower regression error. 2) SDM employs the mean shape as the initialization of the shape-indexed feature, which may be trapped when the initialization is far away from the ground truth, especially under the linear model. On the contrary, our CFAN designs a deep auto network to directly predict a rough estimation of the face shape from the global image feature rather than shape-indexed feature, and this can obtain a more accurate initialization of the shape for the following local SANs.

Differences with DCNN [26]. Both DCNN and our CFAN follow the cascade framework and use a global nonlinear regression as the first stage to achieve a rough estimation of face shape. The differences lie on two aspects: 1) In DCNN, after the global estimation, each facial point is refined independently, which may distort the whole shape without the constraint between facial points. On the contrary, all facial points are refined jointly in our CFAN and this can ensure an effective shape, especially when several landmarks are occluded in which case the rest will provide supports for locating the obscured one. 2) The separate refinement of each point makes DCCN framework rely on and sensitive to the accuracy of the first level more heavily than ours.

4   Implementation Details

Data Augmentation. To train a robust global SAN model, we augment the training data by perturbing each training sample with random changes in translation, rotation and scaling. This can effectively prevent the deep models from over-fitting and achieve robustness to various changes in the wild data.

Parameter Setting. The global SAN has four layers with three hidden layers followed by a linear regression layer that is capable of learning non-linear mappings from a full face with 50×50 pixels to a face shape. Numbers of hidden units in each layer are respectively $1600, 900, 400$. For local SANs, SIFT features are extracted around each landmark. The resolution of face images in each layer becomes higher and higher gradually during the successive local SANs. Numbers of hidden units in each layer of local SAN are respectively $1296, 784, 400$. The weight decay parameter α controls the relative importance of the two terms, the average sum-of-squares error term and the weight decay term. Although α can be set different, the same value $\alpha = 0.001$ is used for both global SAN and local SANs for simplicity.

5   Experiments

In this section, we firstly illustrate the experimental settings for the evaluations including the datasets and methods to compare; and then investigate the alignment results of each stage in our method; finally, compare the proposed CFAN with the state-of-the-art methods.

5.1   Datasets and Methods for Comparison

To evaluate the effectiveness of the proposed CFAN algorithm, four public datasets are used for our experiments, *i.e.*, XM2VTS [22], LFPW [3], HELEN [18] and AFW [35]. The images in XM2VTS dataset are collected under laboratory conditions, while the images in LFPW, HELEN and AFW datasets are collected in the wild environment formulating a more challenging scenario than XM2VTS. Face detection results can be achieved from ibug websit [1], and the ground truth annotations of 68 facial points (as shown in Fig. 3) are provided by [24].

We evaluate a few state-of-the-art methods, *i.e.*, DRMF [2], SDM [31], Zhu et al. [35] and Yu et al. [32]. For Zhu et al.'s method, we use the model released by Asthana et al. [2], which performs better as illustrated in [2]. The 68 facial landmarks predicted by Zhu et al. [35] are shown in Fig 3. Both of the publicly available codes from [2] and [32] predict 66 facial points (as shown in Fig. 3 except two inner mouth corners), and the released code of SDM only estimates 49 landmarks (as shown in Fig. 3) located in the inner regions of the face. For fair comparisons with these methods, we implement the SDM algorithm to estimate 68 points using the same training set, among which the common 66 facial points are used for evaluation. The normalized root mean squared error (NRMSE) is employed to measure the error between the estimated facial landmark locations and the ground truth. The NRMSE is normalized by the distance between centers of eyes. The cumulative distribution function (CDF) of NRMSE is applied for performance evaluation.

5.2   Investigation of Each SAN in CFAN

As the proposed CFAN method consists of several successive SANs, we investigate how each SAN contributes to the performance improvement for facial landmark detection. The experiments are conducted on LFPW dataset in terms of average detection accuracy of 66 facial points, *i.e.*, CDF. The images from LFPW training set [3], HELEN [18] and AFW [35] are used for training and the images in LFPW test set [3] are used for evaluation.

The evaluation results are shown in Fig. 5. As seen, the CDF of global SAN is 0.65 when NRMSE is 0.1, which is much better than mean shape. However, the estimated shape is still far away from the ground truth since global SAN just gives a roughly accurate estimation of facial landmark locations. But benefited from this more accurate shape estimation rather than the mean shape as shape initialization for local SANs, accuracy of facial landmark detection is significantly improved by 25% in the first local SAN. In the second local SAN, the detection accuracy is improved up to about 5.7% when NRMSE is 0.1 and 44% when NRMSE is 0.05. In the third local SAN, no improvement when NRMSE is 0.1, and the improvement is up to 11% when NRMSE is 0.05. It demonstrates that the former SANs mainly handle the large variations due to pose and expression and the latter ones precisely refine the landmark locations in a smaller search region as the resolution becomes higher and higher.

Besides the performance, another important factor is the time complexity. We evaluate the run time of each SAN on LFPW as shown in Table 1. The method is run in matlab 2012 on a desktop (Intel i7-3770 3.4 GHz CPU). To avoid the influence of random factors, the method is repeated several times, and the average of running time is reported. As shown in the table, it takes only 0.25 millisecond per image for global SAN to give a rough estimation of the face shape. Each local SAN costs about 7 milliseconds and only 3 local SANs are enough. So, totally our CFAN takes less than 25 milliseconds per image for 68 facial points locating, which can easily meet the real-time requirement.

5.3   Comparison on XM2VTS Dataset

Firstly, we evaluate our CFAN and the existing methods under the controlled settings on XM2VTS dataset [22]. The XM2VTS dataset contains 2360 face images of 295 individuals collected over 4 sessions. In this experiment, our CFAN is trained by using the images from LFPW training set [3], HELEN [18] and AFW [35] and all methods are tested on XM2VTS. For DRMF method [2], the Viola-Jones face detector [29] is employed since all images in XM2VTS are almost frontal. For a fair comparison, only the common images with face detected by all methods are employed for the testing.

The cumulative error distribution curves of these methods are shown in Fig. 6. As seen, DRMF performs better than [35,32], followed by SDM which benefits from its supervised descent solution. Furthermore, our method performs the best on this dataset, even better than SDM, which attributes to the nonlinear model and coarse-to-fine strategy. The training set of our CFAN is composed of different datasets including large variations from pose, expression, illumination, partial occlusions *etc*, and while the major variation of XM2VTS is from the identity with similar pose, expression and illumination. This means that the distribution of training set of our CFAN is extremely different from the testing samples. Even trained from a different distribution, CFAN still works well, which demonstrate our method is robust to the out-of-database scenario.

Table 1. Run time of each stage in terms of millisecond (ms)

	Global SAN	Local SAN1	Local SAN2	Local SAN3	Total
Run Time (ms)	0.25	7.63	7.28	7.68	22.84

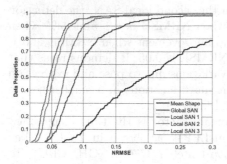

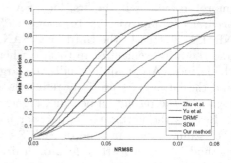

Fig. 5. The cumulative error distribution curves from LFPW of each SAN

Fig. 6. Comparison on XM2VTS

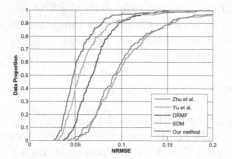

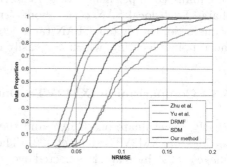

Fig. 7. Comparison on LFPW

Fig. 8. Comparison on Helen

Furthermore, we compare our CFAN with DCNN [26] on this dataset in terms of five landmarks for a fair comparison since only the model of five landmarks is released. We directly run the model provided by [26] on XM2VTS dataset. The comparison results are shown in Fig. 9(a). As seen, our CFAN outperforms DCNN in general.

5.4   Comparison on LFPW Dataset

Furthermore, we evaluate the methods on the Labeled Face Parts in the Wild (LFPW) dataset [3] which is collected from wild condition. LFPW dataset consists of 1132 training images and 300 test images with large variations in pose, expression, illumination, partial occlusion, *etc*, which makes the facial point detection quite challenging on this dataset. The original URLs of images are provided by [3], but some of them are not available any longer. So, the 811 training samples and 224 test samples provided by ibug websit mentioned above are directly used for training and testing. For our method, we directly use the landmark detector trained for XM2VTS experiments for the evaluation. For DRMF method, the tree-based face detector is used to achieve more accurate face detection.

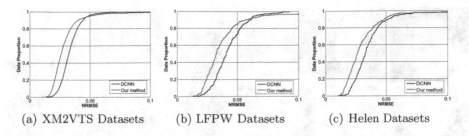

(a) XM2VTS Datasets   (b) LFPW Datasets   (c) Helen Datasets

Fig. 9. Comparison with DCNN [26]

The performance of all methods are shown in Fig. 7. As seen, SDM still performs the best among the existing methods, and our method achieves a better detection accuracy with an improvement up to about 15% than SDM when NRMSE is below 0.05. Similarly, we also compare our CFAN with DCNN [26] in terms of five landmarks. As seen from the Fig. 9(b), our CFAN performs much better than DCNN when NRMSE is below 0.06, but comparable or a little worse when NRMSE is 0.1. On average, our CFAN outperforms DCNN in terms of five landmarks, and a further significant improvement can be expected in terms of more points, *e.g.*, 68 points, especially considering those hard points around the contour.

5.5   Comparison on Helen Dataset

Similar to LFPW, the Helen dataset [18] is also collected under uncontrolled condition, *i.e.*, *Flicker*. Helen consists of 2330 high-resolution images with large variations in pose, lighting, expression, occlusion, and identity. For our CFAN, the images from the Helen training set, the LFPW training set [3], and AFW [35] are used for training the model. All methods are valuated on the 330 images from the Helen test set.

The comparison results are shown in Fig. 8. As seen, our CFAN still performs the best, which demonstrates the superiority to the existing methods again. As analyzed in Sec. 3.4, DCNN cannot well handle partial occlusion problem since each landmark is refined independently without any support from other points. Some failed examples are shown in Fig. 2. On the contrary, our method is more robust than DCNN under the partial occlusion scenario. Fig. 9(c) further shows that our CFAN performs better than DCNN on this dataset.

Fig. 10 shows the detection results of CFAN on some extremely challenging example faces from XM2VTS, LFPW and HELEN. It can be observed that our algorithm is robust to the variations from pose, expression, beard, sunglass and partial occlusion. However, as shown in the last column of Fig. 10, the performance of CFAN degrades on some images with simultaneous large out-of-plane rotations and exaggerated expressions, partially due to the lack of such samples in training set. Models specific to large pose or with latent pose estimation will be considered in the future.

Fig. 10. Example results from XM2VTS, LFPW and HELEN. The first five column samples contain diverse variations in pose, expression, beard, sunglass and occlusion respectively. Some failure cases are shown in the last column.

6   Conclusions and Future Works

Aiming at dealing with the nonlinearity in inferring face shapes from face images, we make use of a sequence of Stacked Auto-encoder Networks in a coarse-to-fine architecture, each of which figures out part of the nonlinearity. The first SAN takes directly a low-resolution version of the detected face as input, to globally estimate a roughly accurate shape. Then, the subsequent SANs take as input the shape-index local features at higher and higher resolution to refine the shape better and better. Such a coarse-to-fine strategy is proved well matching the capacity of SAN and the difficulty of the problem to solve, thus achieves better results than the state-of-the-art methods, such as SDM and DRMF, on three databases with extensive variations. Furthermore, our method can work rather efficiently, with 40+ fps even with Matlab codes on a common desktop with no parallel programming.

Our work further validates the effectiveness of regression-based methods for facial landmarks localization. By decomposing the nonlinearity of the image-to-shape mapping elaborately into a cascaded stages, facial landmarks can be accurately predicted progressively. In the future, we will try other types of deep networks with similar principle.

Acknowledgements. This work is partially supported by Natural Science Foundation of China under contracts Nos. 61390511, 61222211, 61173065, and 61272319.

References

1. 300 faces in-the-wild challenge, http://ibug.doc.ic.ac.uk/resources/300-W/
2. Asthana, A., Zafeiriou, S., Cheng, S., Pantic, M.: Robust discriminative response map fitting with constrained local models. In: IEEE Conference on Computer Vision and Pattern Recognition (CVPR), pp. 3444–3451 (2013)
3. Belhumeur, P.N., Jacobs, D.W., Kriegman, D.J., Kumar, N.: Localizing parts of faces using a consensus of exemplars. In: IEEE Conference on Computer Vision and Pattern Recognition (CVPR), pp. 545–552 (2011)
4. Bengio, Y.: Learning deep architectures for AI. Foundations and Trends® in Machine Learning 2(1), 1–127 (2009)
5. Burgos-Artizzu, X.P., Perona, P., Dollár, P.: Robust face landmark estimation under occlusion. In: IEEE International Conference on Computer Vision, ICCV (2013)
6. Cao, X., Wei, Y., Wen, F., Sun, J.: Face alignment by explicit shape regression. In: IEEE Conference on Computer Vision and Pattern Recognition, CVPR, pp. 2887–2894 (2012)
7. Cootes, T.F., Edwards, G.J., Taylor, C.J.: Active appearance models. IEEE Transactions on Pattern Analysis and Machine Intelligence (TPAMI) 23(6), 681–685 (2001)
8. Cootes, T.F., Taylor, C.J., Cooper, D.H., Graham, J.: Active shape models-their training and application. Computer Vision and Image Understanding (CVIU) 61(1), 38–59 (1995)
9. Cristinacce, D., Cootes, T.F.: Feature detection and tracking with constrained local models. In: British Machine Vision Conference (BMVC), vol. 17, pp. 929–938 (2006)
10. Cristinacce, D., Cootes, T.F.: Boosted regression active shape models. In: British Machine Vision Conference (BMVC), pp. 1–10 (2007)
11. Dantone, M., Gall, J., Fanelli, G., Van Gool, L.: Real-time facial feature detection using conditional regression forests. In: IEEE Conference on Computer Vision and Pattern Recognition (CVPR), pp. 2578–2585 (2012)
12. Dollár, P., Welinder, P., Perona, P.: Cascaded pose regression. In: IEEE Conference on Computer Vision and Pattern Recognition (CVPR), pp. 1078–1085 (2010)
13. Grangier, D., Bottou, L., Collobert, R.: Deep convolutional networks for scene parsing. In: International Conference on Machine Learning Workshops, vol. 3 (2009)
14. Gross, R., Matthews, I., Baker, S.: Generic vs. person specific active appearance models. Image and Vision Computing (IVC) 23(12), 1080–1093 (2005)
15. Gu, L., Kanade, T.: A generative shape regularization model for robust face alignment. In: Forsyth, D., Torr, P., Zisserman, A. (eds.) ECCV 2008, Part I. LNCS, vol. 5302, pp. 413–426. Springer, Heidelberg (2008)
16. Jesorsky, O., Kirchberg, K.J., Frischholz, R.W.: Robust face detection using the hausdorff distance. In: International Conference on Audio-and Video-based Biometric Person Authentication (AVBPA), pp. 90–95 (2001)
17. Krizhevsky, A., Sutskever, I., Hinton, G.: Imagenet classification with deep convolutional neural networks. In: Advances in Neural Information Processing Systems (NIPS), pp. 1106–1114 (2012)
18. Le, V., Brandt, J., Lin, Z., Bourdev, L., Huang, T.S.: Interactive facial feature localization. In: Fitzgibbon, A., Lazebnik, S., Perona, P., Sato, Y., Schmid, C. (eds.) ECCV 2012, Part III. LNCS, vol. 7574, pp. 679–692. Springer, Heidelberg (2012)

19. Liu, X.: Discriminative face alignment. IEEE Transactions on Pattern Analysis and Machine Intelligence (TPAMI) 31(11), 1941–1954 (2009)
20. Luo, P., Wang, X., Tang, X.: Hierarchical face parsing via deep learning. In: IEEE Conference on Computer Vision and Pattern Recognition (CVPR), pp. 2480–2487 (2012)
21. Matthews, I., Baker, S.: Active appearance models revisited. International Journal of Computer Vision (IJCV) 60(2), 135–164 (2004)
22. Messer, K., Matas, J., Kittler, J., Luettin, J., Maitre, G.: Xm2vtsdb: The extended m2vts database. In: International Conference on Audio and Video-based Biometric Person Authentication (AVBPA), vol. 964, pp. 965–966 (1999)
23. Milborrow, S., Nicolls, F.: Locating facial features with an extended active shape model. In: Forsyth, D., Torr, P., Zisserman, A. (eds.) ECCV 2008, Part IV. LNCS, vol. 5305, pp. 504–513. Springer, Heidelberg (2008)
24. Sagonas, C., Tzimiropoulos, G., Zafeiriou, S., Pantic, M.: A semi-automatic methodology for facial landmark annotation. In: IEEE Conference on Computer Vision and Pattern Recognition Workshops (CVPRW), pp. 896–903 (2013)
25. Saragih, J.M., Lucey, S., Cohn, J.F.: Face alignment through subspace constrained mean-shifts. In: IEEE International Conference on Computer Vision (ICCV), pp. 1034–1041 (2009)
26. Sun, Y., Wang, X., Tang, X.: Deep convolutional network cascade for facial point detection. In: IEEE Conference on Computer Vision and Pattern Recognition (CVPR), pp. 3476–3483 (2013)
27. Toshev, A., Szegedy, C.: Deeppose: Human pose estimation via deep neural networks. In: IEEE Conference on Computer Vision and Pattern Recognition, CVPR (2014)
28. Valstar, M., Martinez, B., Binefa, X., Pantic, M.: Facial point detection using boosted regression and graph models. In: IEEE Conference on Computer Vision and Pattern Recognition (CVPR), pp. 2729–2736 (2010)
29. Viola, P., Jones, M.: Rapid object detection using a boosted cascade of simple features. In: IEEE Conference on Computer Vision and Pattern Recognition (CVPR), vol. 1, p. I–511 (2001)
30. Wu, Y., Wang, Z., Ji, Q.: Facial feature tracking under varying facial expressions and face poses based on restricted boltzmann machines. In: IEEE Conference on Computer Vision and Pattern Recognition (CVPR), pp. 3452–3459 (2013)
31. Xiong, X., De la Torre, F.: Supervised descent method and its applications to face alignment. In: IEEE Conference on Computer Vision and Pattern Recognition, CVPR (2013)
32. Yu, X., Huang, J., Zhang, S., Yan, W., Metaxas, D.N.: Pose-free facial landmark fitting via optimized part mixtures and cascaded deformable shape model. In: IEEE International Conference on Computer Vision, ICCV (2013)
33. Zhao, X., Kim, T.K., Luo, W.: Unified face analysis by iterative multi-output random forests. In: IEEE Conference on Computer Vision and Pattern Recognition, CVPR (2014)
34. Zhao, X., Shan, S., Chai, X., Chen, X.: Locality-constrained active appearance model. In: Asian Conference on Computer Vision (ACCV), pp. 636–647 (2013)
35. Zhu, X., Ramanan, D.: Face detection, pose estimation, and landmark localization in the wild. In: IEEE Conference on Computer Vision and Pattern Recognition (CVPR), pp. 2879–2886 (2012)

From Manifold to Manifold: Geometry-Aware Dimensionality Reduction for SPD Matrices

Mehrtash T. Harandi, Mathieu Salzmann, and Richard Hartley

Australian National University, Canberra, ACT 0200, Australia
NICTA*, Locked Bag 8001, Canberra, ACT 2601, Australia

Abstract. Representing images and videos with Symmetric Positive Definite (SPD) matrices and considering the Riemannian geometry of the resulting space has proven beneficial for many recognition tasks. Unfortunately, computation on the Riemannian manifold of SPD matrices –especially of high-dimensional ones– comes at a high cost that limits the applicability of existing techniques. In this paper we introduce an approach that lets us handle high-dimensional SPD matrices by constructing a lower-dimensional, more discriminative SPD manifold. To this end, we model the mapping from the high-dimensional SPD manifold to the low-dimensional one with an orthonormal projection. In particular, we search for a projection that yields a low-dimensional manifold with maximum discriminative power encoded via an affinity-weighted similarity measure based on metrics on the manifold. Learning can then be expressed as an optimization problem on a Grassmann manifold. Our evaluation on several classification tasks shows that our approach leads to a significant accuracy gain over state-of-the-art methods.

Keywords: Riemannian geometry, SPD manifold, Grassmann manifold, dimensionality reduction, visual recognition.

1 Introduction

This paper introduces an approach to embedding the Riemannian structure of Symmetric Positive Definite (SPD) matrices into a lower-dimensional, more discriminative Riemannian manifold. SPD matrices are becoming increasingly pervasive in various domains. For instance, diffusion tensors naturally arise in medical imaging [16]. In computer vision, SPD matrices have been shown to provide powerful representations for images and videos via region covariances [20]. Such representations have been successfully employed to categorize textures [20,6], pedestrians [21], faces [15,6], actions and gestures [18].

SPD matrices can be thought of as an extension of positive numbers and form the interior of the positive semidefinite cone. It is possible to directly employ the Frobenius norm as a similarity measure between SPD matrices, hence analyzing

---

* NICTA is funded by the Australian Government as represented by the Department of Broadband, Communications and the Digital Economy, as well as by the Australian Research Council through the ICT Centre of Excellence program.

D. Fleet et al. (Eds.): ECCV 2014, Part II, LNCS 8690, pp. 17–32, 2014.
© Springer International Publishing Switzerland 2014

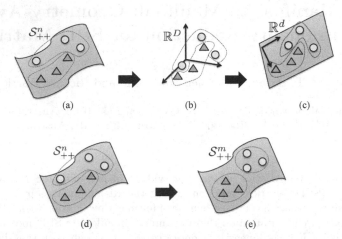

Fig. 1. Conceptual comparison of typical dimensionality reduction methods on the manifold [4,22] and our approach. **Top row (existing techniques):** The original manifold (a) is first flattened either via tangent space computation or by Hilbert space embedding. The flattened manifold (b) is then mapped to a lower-dimensional, optionally more discriminative space (c). The distortion incurred by the initial flattening may typically make this mapping more complicated. **Bottom row (our approach):** The original manifold (d) is directly transformed to a lower-dimensional, more discriminative manifold (e).

problems involving such matrices via Euclidean geometry. However, as several studies have shown, undesirable phenomena may occur when Euclidean geometry is utilized to manipulate SPD matrices [16,21,8]. One example of this is the *swelling effect* that occurs in diffusion tensor imaging (DTI), where a matrix represents the covariance of the local Brownian motion of water molecules [16]: When considering Euclidean geometry to interpolate between two diffusion tensors, the determinant of the intermediate matrices may become strictly larger than the determinants of both original matrices, which is a physically unacceptable behavior. In [16], a Riemannian structure for SPD matrices was introduced to overcome the drawbacks of the Euclidean representation. This Riemannian structure is induced by the Affine Invariant Riemmanian Metric (AIRM), and is referred to as the SPD or tensor manifold.

As shown in several studies [16,21,6,8], accounting for the geometry of SPD manifolds can have a highly beneficial impact. However, it also leads to challenges in developing effective and efficient inference methods. The main trends in analyzing SPD manifolds are to either locally flatten them via tangent space approximations [21,18], or embed them in higher-dimensional Euclidean spaces [6,2,8]. In both cases, the computational cost of the resulting methods increases dramatically with the dimension of the SPD matrices. As a consequence, very low-dimensional SPD matrices are typically employed (*e.g.*, region covariance descriptors obtained from a few low-dimensional features), with the exception of a few studies where medium-size matrices were used [15,6]. While the matrices obtained from low-dimensional features have proven sufficient for specific problems, they are bound to be less powerful and discriminative than the high-dimensional features typically used in computer vision.

To overcome this limitation, here, we introduce an approach that lets us handle high-dimensional SPD matrices. In particular, from a high-dimensional SPD manifold, we construct a lower-dimensional, more discriminative SPD manifold. While some manifold-based dimensionality reduction techniques have been proposed [4,22], as illustrated in Fig. 1, they typically yield a Euclidean representation of the data and rely on flattening the manifold, which incurs distortions. In contrast, our approach directly works on the original manifold and exploits its geometry to learn a representation that (i) still benefits from useful properties of SPD manifolds, and (ii) can be used in conjunction with existing manifold-based recognition techniques to make them more practical and effective.

More specifically, given training SPD matrices, we search for a projection from their high-dimensional SPD manifold to a low-dimensional one such that the resulting representation maximizes an affinity-weighted similarity between pairs of matrices. In particular, we exploit the class labels to define an affinity measure, and employ either the AIRM, or the Stein divergence [19] to encode the similarity between two SPD matrices. Due to the affine invariance property of the AIRM and of the Stein divergence, any full rank projection would yield an equivalent representation. This allows us, without loss of generality, to model the projection with an orthonormal matrix, and thus express learning as an unconstrained optimization problem on a Grassmann manifold, which can be effectively optimized using a conjugate gradient method on the manifold.

We demonstrate the benefits of our approach on several tasks where the data can be represented with high-dimensional SPD matrices. In particular, our method outperforms state-of-the-art techniques on three classification tasks: image-based material categorization and face recognition, and action recognition from 3D motion capture sequences. A Matlab implementation of our algorithm is available from the first author's webpage.

2   Related Work

We now discuss in more details the three techniques that also tackle dimensionality reduction of manifold-valued data.

Principal Geodesic Analysis (PGA) was introduced in [4] as a generalization of Principal Component Analysis (PCA) to Riemannian manifolds. PGA identifies the tangent space whose corresponding subspace maximizes the variability of the data on the manifold. PGA, however, is equivalent to flattening the Riemannian manifold by taking its tangent space at the Karcher, or Fréchet, mean of the data. As such, it does not fully exploit the structure of the manifold. Furthermore, PGA, as PCA, cannot exploit the availability of class labels, and may therefore be sub-optimal for classification.

In [22], the Covariance Discriminative Learning (CDL) algorithm was proposed to embed the SPD manifold into a Euclidean space. In contrast to PGA,

CDL utilizes class labels to learn a discriminative subspace using Partial Least Squares (PLS) or Linear Discriminant Analysis (LDA). However, CDL relies on mapping the SPD manifold to the space of symmetric matrices via the principal matrix logarithm. While this embedding has some nice properties (*e.g.*, diffeomorphism), it can also be thought of as embedding the SPD manifold into its tangent space at the identity matrix. Therefore, although supervised, CDL also exploits data potentially distorted by the use of a single tangent space, as PGA.

Finally, in [5], several Nonlinear Dimensionality Reduction techniques were extended to their Riemannian counterparts. This was achieved by introducing various Riemannian geometry concepts, such as Karcher mean, tangent spaces and geodesics, in Locally Linear Embedding (LLE), Hessian LLE and Laplacian Eigenmaps. The resulting algorithms were applied to several unsupervised clustering tasks. Although these methods can, in principle, be employed for supervised classification, they are limited to the transductive setting since they do not define any parametric mapping to the low-dimensional space.

In this paper, we learn a mapping from a high-dimensional SPD manifold to a lower-dimensional one without relying on tangent space approximations of the manifold. Our approach therefore accounts for the structure of the manifold and can simultaneously exploit class label information. The resulting mapping lets us effectively handle high-dimensional SPD matrices for classification purposes. Furthermore, by mapping to another SPD manifold, our approach can serve as a pre-processing step to other Riemannian-based approaches, such as the manifold sparse coding of [6], thus making them practical to work with more realistic, high-dimensional features. Note that, while our formulation is inspired from graph embedding methods in Euclidean spaces, *e.g.*, [24], here we work with data lying on more challenging non-linear manifolds.

To the best of our knowledge, this is the first work that shows how a high-dimensional SPD manifold can be transformed into another SPD manifold with lower intrinsic dimension. Note that a related idea, but with a very different approach, was introduced in [9] to decompose high-dimensional spheres into submanifolds of decreasing dimensionality.

3   Riemannian Geometry of SPD Manifolds

In this section, we discuss some notions of geometry of SPD manifolds. Throughout this paper we will use the following notation: $\mathcal{S}_{++}^n$ is the space of real $n \times n$ SPD matrices; $\mathbf{I}_n \in \mathbb{R}^{n \times n}$ is the identity matrix; $\mathrm{GL}(n)$ is the general linear group, *i.e.*, the group of real invertible $n \times n$ matrices.

Definition 1. *A real and symmetric matrix* $\mathbf{X} \in \mathbb{R}^{n \times n}$ *is said to be SPD if* $\mathbf{v}^T \mathbf{X} \mathbf{v}$ *is positive for any non-zero* $\mathbf{v} \in \mathbb{R}^n$.

The space of $n \times n$ SPD matrices is obviously not a vector space since multiplying an SPD matrix by a negative scalar results in a matrix which does not belong to $\mathcal{S}_{++}^n$. Instead, $\mathcal{S}_{++}^n$ forms the interior of a convex cone in the n^2-dimensional Euclidean space. The $\mathcal{S}_{++}^n$ space is mostly studied when endowed with a Riemannian metric and thus forms a Riemannian manifold [16]. A natural way to measure closeness on a manifold is by considering the geodesic distance between two points on the manifold. Such a distance is defined as the length of the shortest curve connecting the two points. The shortest curves are known as geodesics and are analogous to straight lines in $\mathbb{R}^n$. The Affine Invariant Riemannian Metric (AIRM) is probably the most popular Riemannian structure for analyzing SPD matrices [16]. Let P be a point on $\mathcal{S}_{++}^n$. The AIRM for two tangent vectors $v, w \in T_P \mathcal{S}_{++}^n$ is defined as

$$\langle v, w \rangle_P := \langle P^{-1/2} v P^{-1/2}, P^{-1/2} w P^{-1/2} \rangle = \mathrm{Tr}\left(P^{-1} v P^{-1} w \right) . \qquad (1)$$

Definition 2. *The geodesic distance* $\delta_g : \mathcal{S}_{++}^n \times \mathcal{S}_{++}^n \to [0, \infty)$ *induced by the AIRM is defined as*

$$\delta_g^2(X, Y) = \| \log(X^{-1/2} Y X^{-1/2}) \|_F^2 , \qquad (2)$$

where $\log(\cdot)$ *is the matrix principal logarithm.*

More recently, Sra introduced the Stein metric on SPD manifolds [19]:

Definition 3. *The Stein metric* $\delta_S : \mathcal{S}_{++}^n \times \mathcal{S}_{++}^n \to [0, \infty)$ *is a symmetric type of Bregman divergence and is defined as*

$$\delta_S^2(X, Y) = \ln \det \left(\frac{X + Y}{2} \right) - \frac{1}{2} \ln \det(XY) . \qquad (3)$$

The Stein metric shows several similarities to the geodesic induced by the AIRM while being less expensive to compute [3]. In addition to the properties studied by Sra [19], we provide the following important theorem which relates the length of curves under the two metrics.

Theorem 1. *The length of any given curve is the same under* δ_g *and* δ_s *up to a scale of* $2\sqrt{2}$.

Proof. Given in supplementary material. □

One of the motivations for projecting a higher-dimensional SPD manifold to a lower-dimensional one is to preserve the properties of δ_g^2 and δ_S^2 [16,19]. One important such property, especially in computer vision, is affine invariance [16].

Property 1 (Affine invariance). For any $M \in \mathrm{GL}(n)$,

$$\delta_g^2(X, Y) = \delta_g^2(M X M^T, M Y M^T),$$
$$\delta_S^2(X, Y) = \delta_S^2(M X M^T, M Y M^T).$$

This property postulates that the metric between two SPD matrices is unaffected by the action of the affine group. In the specific case where the SPD matrices are region covariance descriptors [20], this implies that the distance between two descriptors will remain unchanged after an affine transformation of the image features, such as a change of illumination when using RGB values. Note that, in addition to this specific implication, we will also exploit the affine invariance property for a different purpose when deriving our learning algorithm in the next section.

4   Geometry-Aware Dimensionality Reduction

We now describe our approach to learning an embedding of high-dimensional SPD matrices to a more discriminative, low-dimensional SPD manifold. More specifically, given a matrix $X \in \mathcal{S}_{++}^n$, we seek to learn the parameters $W \in \mathbb{R}^{n \times m}$, $m < n$, of a generic mapping $f : \mathcal{S}_{++}^n \times \mathbb{R}^{n \times m} \to \mathcal{S}_{++}^m$, which we define as

$$f(X, W) = W^T X W. \tag{4}$$

Clearly, if $\mathcal{S}_{++}^n \ni X \succ 0$ and W has full rank, $\mathcal{S}_{++}^m \ni W^T X W \succ 0$.

Given a set of SPD matrices $\mathcal{X} = \{X_1, \cdots, X_p\}$, where each matrix $X_i \in \mathcal{S}_{++}^n$, our goal is to find a transformation W such that the resulting low-dimensional SPD manifold preserves some interesting structure of the original data. Here, we encode this structure via an undirected graph defined by a real symmetric affinity matrix $A \in \mathbb{R}^{p \times p}$. The element A_{ij} of this matrix measures some notion of affinity between matrices X_i and X_j, and may be negative. We will discuss the affinity matrix in more details in Section 4.2.

Given A, we search for an embedding such that the affinity between pairs of SPD matrices is reflected by a measure of similarity on the low-dimensional SPD manifold. In this paper, we propose to make use of either the AIRM or the Stein metric to encode (dis)similarities between SPD matrices. For each pair (i, j) of training samples, this lets us write a cost function of the form

$$\mathcal{J}_{ij}(W; X_i, X_j) = A_{ij} \delta^2 \left(W^T X_i W, W^T X_j W \right), \tag{5}$$

where δ is either δ_g or δ_S. These pairwise costs can then be grouped together in a global empirical cost function

$$L(W) = \sum_{i,j} \mathcal{J}_{ij}(W; X_i, X_j), \tag{6}$$

which we seek to minimize w.r.t. W.

To avoid degeneracies and ensure that the resulting embedding forms a valid SPD manifold, i.e., $W^T X W \succ 0$, $\forall X \in \mathcal{S}_{++}^n$, we need W to have full rank. Here, we enforce this requirement by imposing orthonormality constraints on W, i.e., $W^T W = I_m$. Note that, with either the AIRM or the Stein divergence, this entails no loss of generality. Indeed, any full rank matrix $\tilde{W}$ can be expressed as MW, with W an orthonormal matrix and $M \in \mathrm{GL}(n)$. The affine invariance property of the AIRM and of the Stein metric therefore guarantees that

$$\mathcal{J}_{ij}(\tilde{W}; X_i, X_j) = \mathcal{J}_{ij}(MW; X_i, X_j) = \mathcal{J}_{ij}(W; X_i, X_j).$$

Finally, learning can be expressed as the minimization problem

$$W^* = \underset{W \in \mathbb{R}^{n \times m}}{\arg\min} \sum_{i,j} A_{ij} \delta^2 \left(W^T X_i W, W^T X_j W \right) \quad \text{s.t. } W^T W = I_m. \tag{7}$$

In the next section, we describe an effective way of solving (7) via optimization on a (different) Riemannian manifold.

4.1 Optimization on Grassmann Manifolds

Recent advances in optimization methods formulate problems with orthogonality constraints as optimization problems on Stiefel or Grassmann manifolds [1]. More specifically, the geometrically correct setting for the minimization problem $\min L(\boldsymbol{W})$ with the orthogonality constraint $\boldsymbol{W}^T\boldsymbol{W} = \mathbf{I}_m$ is, in general, on a Stiefel manifold. However, if the cost function $L(\boldsymbol{W})$ possesses the property that for any rotation matrix $\boldsymbol{R}$ (i.e., $\boldsymbol{R} \in \mathrm{SO}(m)$, $\boldsymbol{R}\boldsymbol{R}^T = \boldsymbol{R}^T\boldsymbol{R} = \mathbf{I}_m$), $L(\boldsymbol{W}) = L(\boldsymbol{W}\boldsymbol{R})$, then the problem is on a Grassmann manifold.

Since both the AIRM and the Stein metric are affine invariant, we have

$$\mathcal{J}(\boldsymbol{X}_i, \boldsymbol{X}_j, \boldsymbol{W}) = \mathcal{J}(\boldsymbol{X}_i, \boldsymbol{X}_j, \boldsymbol{W}\boldsymbol{R}),$$

and thus $L(\boldsymbol{W}) = L(\boldsymbol{W}\boldsymbol{R})$, which therefore identifies (7) as an (unconstrained) optimization problem on the Grassmann manifold $\mathcal{G}(m, n)$.

In particular, here, we utilize a nonlinear Conjugate Gradient (CG) method on Grassmann manifolds to minimize (7). A brief description of the steps of this algorithm is provided in supplementary material. For a more detailed treatment, we refer the reader to [1]. As for now, we just confine ourselves to saying that nonlinear CG on Grassmann manifolds requires the $n \times m$ Jacobian matrix of $L(\boldsymbol{W})$ w.r.t. $\boldsymbol{W}$. For the Stein metric, this Jacobian matrix can be obtained by noting that

$$D_{\boldsymbol{W}} \ln \det \left(\boldsymbol{W}^T\boldsymbol{X}\boldsymbol{W}\right) = 2\boldsymbol{X}\boldsymbol{W}\left(\boldsymbol{W}^T\boldsymbol{X}\boldsymbol{W}\right)^{-1}, \tag{8}$$

which lets us identify the Jacobian of the Stein divergence as

$$D_{\boldsymbol{W}}\delta_S^2(\boldsymbol{W}^T\boldsymbol{X}_i\boldsymbol{W}, \boldsymbol{W}^T\boldsymbol{X}_j\boldsymbol{W}) - (\boldsymbol{X}_i + \boldsymbol{X}_j)\boldsymbol{W}\left(\boldsymbol{W}^T\frac{\boldsymbol{X}_i + \boldsymbol{X}_j}{2}\boldsymbol{W}\right)^{-1}$$
$$- \boldsymbol{X}_i\boldsymbol{W}(\boldsymbol{W}^T\boldsymbol{X}_i\boldsymbol{W})^{-1} - \boldsymbol{X}_j\boldsymbol{W}(\boldsymbol{W}^T\boldsymbol{X}_j\boldsymbol{W})^{-1}.$$

For the AIRM, we can exploit the fact that $\mathrm{Tr}(\log(\boldsymbol{X})) = \ln\det(\boldsymbol{X}), \forall \boldsymbol{X} \in \mathcal{S}_{++}^n$. We can then derive the Jacobian by utilizing Eq. 8, which yields

$$D_{\boldsymbol{W}}\left(\delta_g^2\left(\boldsymbol{W}^T\boldsymbol{X}_i\boldsymbol{W}, \boldsymbol{W}^T\boldsymbol{X}_j\boldsymbol{W}\right)\right) = D_{\boldsymbol{W}}\left(\left\|\log\left((\boldsymbol{W}^T\boldsymbol{X}_j\boldsymbol{W})^{-1/2}\boldsymbol{W}^T\boldsymbol{X}_i\boldsymbol{W}(\boldsymbol{W}^T\boldsymbol{X}_j\boldsymbol{W})^{-1/2}\right)\right\|_F^2\right)$$
$$= 2D_{\boldsymbol{W}}\left\{\mathrm{Tr}\left(\log\left((\boldsymbol{W}^T\boldsymbol{X}_j\boldsymbol{W})^{-1/2}\boldsymbol{W}^T\boldsymbol{X}_i\boldsymbol{W}(\boldsymbol{W}^T\boldsymbol{X}_j\boldsymbol{W})^{-1/2}\right)\right)\right\}\cdot$$
$$\cdot\log\left((\boldsymbol{W}^T\boldsymbol{X}_j\boldsymbol{W})^{-1/2}\boldsymbol{W}^T\boldsymbol{X}_i\boldsymbol{W}(\boldsymbol{W}^T\boldsymbol{X}_j\boldsymbol{W})^{-1/2}\right)$$
$$= 2D_{\boldsymbol{W}}\left(\ln\det\left(\boldsymbol{W}^T\boldsymbol{X}_i\boldsymbol{W}(\boldsymbol{W}^T\boldsymbol{X}_j\boldsymbol{W})^{-1}\right)\right)\log\left((\boldsymbol{W}^T\boldsymbol{X}_j\boldsymbol{W})^{-1/2}\boldsymbol{W}^T\boldsymbol{X}_i\boldsymbol{W}(\boldsymbol{W}^T\boldsymbol{X}_j\boldsymbol{W})^{-1/2}\right)$$
$$= 4\left(\boldsymbol{X}_i\boldsymbol{W}(\boldsymbol{W}^T\boldsymbol{X}_i\boldsymbol{W})^{-1} - \boldsymbol{X}_j\boldsymbol{W}(\boldsymbol{W}^T\boldsymbol{X}_j\boldsymbol{W})^{-1}\right)\log\left((\boldsymbol{W}^T\boldsymbol{X}_j\boldsymbol{W})^{-1/2}\boldsymbol{W}^T\boldsymbol{X}_i\boldsymbol{W}(\boldsymbol{W}^T\boldsymbol{X}_j\boldsymbol{W})^{-1/2}\right).$$

The pseudo-code for our SPD manifold learning (SPD-ML) method is given in Algorithm 1, where $\nabla_{\boldsymbol{W}}L(\boldsymbol{W})$ denotes the gradient on the manifold obtained from the Jacobian $D_{\boldsymbol{W}}L(\boldsymbol{W})$, and $\tau(\boldsymbol{H}, \boldsymbol{W}_0, \boldsymbol{W}_1)$ denotes the parallel transport of tangent vector $\boldsymbol{H}$ from $\boldsymbol{W}_0$ to $\boldsymbol{W}_1$ (see supplementary material for details).

4.2 Designing the Affinity Matrix

Different criteria can be employed to build the affinity matrix $\boldsymbol{A}$. In this work, we focus on classification problems on $\mathcal{S}_{++}^n$ and therefore exploit class labels to

Algorithm 1. SPD Manifold Learning (SPD-ML)

Input:
A set of SPD matrices $\{X_i\}_{i=1}^p$, $X_i \in \mathcal{S}_{++}^n$
The corresponding labels $\{y_i\}_{i=1}^p$, $y_i \in \{1, 2, \cdots, C\}$
The dimensionality m of the induced manifold

Output:
The mapping $W \in \mathcal{G}(m, n)$

Generate A using (9), (10) and (11)
$W_{old} \leftarrow I_{n \times m}$ (*i.e.*, the truncated identity matrix)
$W \leftarrow W_{old}$
$H_{old} \leftarrow 0$
repeat
    $H \leftarrow -\nabla_W L(W) + \eta \tau(H_{old}, W_{old}, W)$
    Line search along the geodesic $\gamma(t)$ from $W = \gamma(0)$ in the direction H to find
    $W^* = \underset{W}{\operatorname{argmin}} \ L(W)$
    $H_{old} \leftarrow H$
    $W_{old} \leftarrow W$
    $W \leftarrow W^*$
until convergence

---

construct A. Note, however, that our framework is general and also applies to unsupervised or semi-supervised settings. For example, in an unsupervised scenario, A could be built from pairwise similarities (distances) on $\mathcal{S}_{++}^n$. Solving (7) could then be understood as finding a mapping where nearby data pairs on the original manifold $\mathcal{S}_{++}^n$ remain close in the induced manifold $\mathcal{S}_{++}^m$.

Let us assume that each point $X_i \in \mathcal{S}_{++}^n$ belongs to one of C possible classes and denote its class label by y_i. Our aim is to define an affinity matrix that encodes the notions of intra-class and inter-class distances, and thus, when solving (7), yields a mapping that minimizes the intra-class distances while simultaneously maximizing the inter-class distances (*i.e.*, a discriminative mapping).

More specifically, let $\{(X_i, y_i)\}_{i=1}^p$ be the set of p labeled training points, where $X_i \in \mathcal{S}_{++}^n$ and $y_i \in \{1, 2, \cdots, C\}$. The affinity of the training data on $\mathcal{S}_{++}^n$ can be modeled by building a within-class similarity graph G_w and a between-class similarity graph G_b. In particular, we define G_w and G_b as binary matrices constructed from nearest neighbor graphs. This yields

$$G_w(i, j) = \begin{cases} 1, & \text{if } X_i \in N_w(X_j) \text{ or } X_j \in N_w(X_i) \\ 0, & \text{otherwise} \end{cases} \tag{9}$$

$$G_b(i, j) = \begin{cases} 1, & \text{if } X_i \in N_b(X_j) \text{ or } X_j \in N_b(X_i) \\ 0, & \text{otherwise} \end{cases} \tag{10}$$

where $N_w(\boldsymbol{X}_i)$ is the set of ν_w nearest neighbors of $\boldsymbol{X}_i$ that share the same label as y_i, and $N_b(\boldsymbol{X}_i)$ contains the ν_b nearest neighbors of $\boldsymbol{X}_i$ having different labels. The affinity matrix $\boldsymbol{A}$ is then defined as

$$A = G_w - G_b \,, \tag{11}$$

which resembles the Maximum Margin Criterion (MMC) of [11]. In practice, we set ν_w to the minimum number of points in each class and, to balance the influence of $\boldsymbol{G}_w$ and $\boldsymbol{G}_b$, choose $\nu_b \leq \nu_w$, with the specific value found by cross-validation. We analyze the influence of ν_b in supplementary material.

4.3 Discussion in Relation to Region Covariance Descriptors

In our experiments, we exploited Region Covariance Matrices (RCMs) [20] as image descriptors. Here, we discuss some interesting properties of our algorithm when applied to these specific SPD matrices.

There are several reasons why RCMs are attractive to represent images and videos. First, RCMs provide a natural way to fuse various feature types. Second, they help reducing the impact of noisy samples in a region via their inherent averaging operation. Third, RCMs are independent of the size of the region, and can therefore easily be utilized to compare regions of different sizes. Finally, RCMs can be efficiently computed using integral images [21,18].

Let I be a $W \times H$ image, and $\mathbb{O} = \{\boldsymbol{o}_i\}_{i=1}^r$, $\boldsymbol{o}_i \in \mathbb{R}^n$ be a set of r observations extracted from I, e.g., $\boldsymbol{o}_i$ concatenates intensity values, gradients along the horizontal and vertical directions, filter responses,... for image pixel i. Let $\mu = \frac{1}{r}\sum_{i=1}^r \boldsymbol{o}_i$ be the mean value of the observations. Then image I can be represented by the $n \times n$ RCM

$$C_I = \frac{1}{r-1} \sum_{i=1}^r (\boldsymbol{o}_i - \mu)(\boldsymbol{o}_i - \mu)^T = \boldsymbol{O}\boldsymbol{J}\boldsymbol{J}^T\boldsymbol{O}^T \,, \tag{12}$$

where $\boldsymbol{J} = r^{-3/2}(r\mathbf{I}_r - \mathbf{1}_{r \times r})$. To have a valid RCM, $r \geq n$, otherwise $\boldsymbol{C}_I$ would have zero eigenvalues, which would make both δ_g^2 and δ_S^2 indefinite.

After learning the projection $\boldsymbol{W}$, the low-dimensional representation of image I is given by $\boldsymbol{W}^T\boldsymbol{O}\boldsymbol{J}\boldsymbol{J}^T\boldsymbol{O}^T\boldsymbol{W}$. This reveals two interesting properties of our learning scheme. 1) The resulting representation can also be thought of as an RCM with $\boldsymbol{W}^T\boldsymbol{O}$ as a set of low-dimensional observations. Hence, in our framework, we can create a valid $\mathcal{S}_{++}^m$ manifold with only m observations instead of at least n in the original input space. This is not the case for other algorithms, which require having matrices on $\mathcal{S}_{++}^n$ as input. In supplementary material, we study the influence of the number of observations on recognition accuracy. 2) Applying $\boldsymbol{W}$ directly the set of observations reduces the computation time of creating the final RCM on $\mathcal{S}_{++}^m$. This is due to the fact that the computational complexity of computing an RCM is quadratic in the dimensionality of the features.

5   Empirical Evaluation

In this section, we study the effectiveness of our SPD manifold learning approach. In particular, as mentioned earlier, we focus on classification and present results on two image datasets and one motion capture dataset. In all our experiments, the dimensionality of the low-dimensional SPD manifold was determined by cross-validation. Below, we first briefly describe the different classifiers used in these experiments, and then discuss our results.

Classification algorithms: The SPD-ML algorithm introduced in Section 4 allows us to obtain a low-dimensional, more discriminative SPD manifold from a high-dimensional one. Many different classifiers can then be used to categorize the data on this new manifold. In our experiments, we make use of two such classifiers. First, we employ a simple nearest neighbor classifier based on the manifold metric (either AIRM or Stein). This simple classifier clearly evidences the benefits of mapping the original Riemannian structure to a lower-dimensional one. Second, we make use of the Riemannian sparse coding algorithm of [6] (RSR). This algorithm exploits the notion of sparse coding to represent a query SPD matrix using a codebook of SPD matrices. In all our experiments, we formed the codebook purely from the training data, *i.e.*, no dictionary learning was employed. Note that RSR relies on a kernel derived from the Stein metric. We therefore only applied it to the Stein metric-based version of our algorithm. We refer to the different algorithms evaluated in our experiments as:

NN-Stein: Stein metric-based Nearest Neighbor classifier.
NN-AIRM: AIRM-based Nearest Neighbor classifier.
NN-Stein-ML: Stein metric-based Nearest Neighbor classifier on the low-dimensional SPD manifold obtained with our approach.
NN-AIRM-ML: AIRM-based Nearest Neighbor classifier on the low-dimensional SPD manifold obtained with our approach.
RSR: Riemannian Sparse Representation [6].
RSR-ML: Riemannian Sparse Representation on the low-dimensional SPD manifold obtained with our approach.

In addition to these methods, we also provide the results of the PLS-based Covariance Discriminant Learning (CDL) technique of [22], as well as of the state-of-the-art baselines of each specific dataset.

5.1   Material Categorization

For the task of material categorization, we used the UIUC dataset [12]. The UIUC material dataset contains 18 subcategories of materials taken in the wild from four general categories (see Fig. 2): *bark, fabric, construction materials*, and *outer coat of animals*. Each subcategory has 12 images taken at various scales. Following standard practice, half of the images from each subcategory was randomly chosen as training data, and the rest was used for testing. We report the average accuracy over 10 different random partitions.

Fig. 2. Samples from the UIUC material dataset

Small RCMs, such as those used for texture recognition in [6], are hopeless here due to the complexity of the task. Recently, SIFT features [13] have been shown to be robust and discriminative for material classification [12]. Therefore, we constructed RCMs of size 155×155 using 128 dimensional SIFT features (from grayscale images) and 27 dimensional color descriptors. To this end, we resized all the images to 400×400 and computed dense SIFT descriptors on a regular grid with 4 pixels spacing. The color descriptors were obtained by simply stacking colors from 3×3 patches centered at the grid points. Each grid point therefore yields one 155-dimensional observation o_i in Eq. 12. The parameters for this experiments were set to $\nu_w = 6$ (minimum number of samples in a class), and $\nu_b = 3$ obtained by 5-fold cross-validation.

Table 1 compares the performance of our different algorithms and of the state-of-the-art method on this dataset (SD) [12]. The results show that appropriate manifold-based methods (*i.e.*, RSR and CDL) with the original 155×155 RCMs already outperform SD, while NN on the same manifold yields worse performance. However, after applying our learning algorithm, NN not only outperforms SD significantly, but also outperforms both CDL and RSR. RSR on the learned SPD manifold (RSR-ML) further boosts the accuracy to 66.6%.

To further evidence the importance of geometry-aware dimensionality reduction, we replaced our low-dimensional RCMs with RCMs obtained by applying PCA directly on the 155 dimensional features. The AIRM-based NN classifier used on these RCMs gave 42.1% accuracy (best performance over different PCA dimensions). While this is better than the performance in the original feature space (*i.e.*, 35.6%), it is significantly lower than the accuracy of our NN-AIRM-ML approach (*i.e.*, 58.3%). Finally, note that performing NN-AIRM on the original data required 490s on a 3GHz machine with Matlab. After our dimensionality reduction scheme, this only took 9.7s.

5.2 Action Recognition from Motion Capture Data

As a second experiment, we tackled the problem of human action recognition from motion capture sequences using the HDM05 database [14]. This database contains the following 14 actions: 'clap above head', 'deposit floor', 'elbow to knee', 'grab high', 'hop both legs', 'jog', 'kick forward', 'lie down floor', 'rotate both arms backward', 'sit down chair', 'sneak', 'squat', 'stand up lie' and 'throw basketball' (see Fig. 3 for an example). The dataset provides the 3D locations of 31 joints over time acquired at the speed of 120 frames per second. We describe an action of a K joints skeleton observed over m frames by its joint covariance

Table 1. Mean recognition accuracies with standard deviations for the UIUC material dataset [12]

Method	Accuracy
SD [12]	$43.5\% \pm N/A$
CDL [22]	$52.3\% \pm 4.3$
NN-Stein	$35.8\% \pm 2.6$
NN-Stein-ML	$58.1\% \pm 2.8$
NN-AIRM	$35.6\% \pm 2.6$
NN-AIRM-ML	$58.3\% \pm 2.3$
RSR [6]	$52.8\% \pm 2.1$
RSR-ML	$\mathbf{66.6\% \pm 3.1}$

Table 2. Recognition accuracies for the HDM05-MOCAP dataset [14]

Method	Accuracy
CDL [22]	79.8%
NN-Stein	61.7%
NN-Stein-ML	68.6%
NN-AIRM	62.8%
NN-AIRM-ML	67.6%
RSR [6]	76.1%
RSR-ML	81.9%

Fig. 3. Kicking action from the HDM05 motion capture sequences database [14]

descriptor [7], which is an SPD matrix of size $3K \times 3K$. This matrix is computed as in Eq. 12 by taking o_i as the 93-dimensional vector concatenating the 3D coordinates of the 31 joints in frame i.

In our experiments, we used 2 subjects for training (*i.e.*, 'bd' and 'mm') and the remaining 3 subjects for testing (*i.e.*, 'bk', 'dg' and 'tr')[1]. This resulted in 118 training and 188 test sequences for this experiment. The parameters of our method were set to $\nu_w = 5$ (minimum number of samples in one class), and $\nu_b = 5$ by cross-validation.

We report the performance of the different methods on this dataset in Table 2. Again we can see that the accuracies of NN and RSR are significantly improved by our learning algorithm, and that our RSR-ML approach achieves the best accuracy of 81.9%. As on the UIUC dataset, we also evaluated the performance RCMs built by reducing the dimensionality of the features using PCA. This yielded an accuracy of 63.3% with an AIRM-based NN classifier (best performance over different PCA dimensions). Again, while this slightly outperforms the accuracy of NN-AIRM (*i.e.*, 62.8%), it remains clearly inferior to the performance of our NN-AIRM-ML algorithm (*i.e.*, 67.6%).

---

[1] Note that this differs from the setup in [7], where 3 subjects were used for training and 2 for testing. However, with the setup of [7] where an accuracy of 95.41% was reported, all our algorithms resulted in about 99% accuracy.

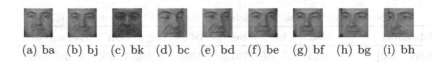

(a) ba   (b) bj   (c) bk   (d) bc   (e) bd   (f) be   (g) bf   (h) bg   (i) bh

Fig. 4. Samples from the FERET dataset [17]

5.3   Face Recognition

For face recognition, we used the 'b' subset of the FERET dataset [17], which contains 1800 images from 200 subjects. Following common practice [6], we used cropped images, downsampled to 64×64. Fig. 4 depicts samples from the dataset.

We performed six experiments on this dataset. In all these experiments, the training data was composed of frontal faces with expression and illumination variations (*i.e.*, images marked as 'ba', 'bj' and 'bk'). The six experiments correspond to using six different non-frontal viewing angles as test data (*i.e.*, images marked as 'bc','bd', 'be', 'bf', 'bg' and 'bh', respectively).

To represent a face image, we block diagonally concatenated three different 43×43 RCMs: one obtained from the entire image, one from the left half and one from the right half. This resulted in an RCM of size 129×129 for each image. Each 43×43 RCM was computed from the features

$$o_{x,y} = [\ I(x,y),\ x,\ y,\ |G_{0,0}(x,y)|,\qquad,\ |G_{4,7}(x,y)|\ ]\ ,$$

where $I(x,y)$ is the intensity value at position (x,y), $G_{u,v}(x,y)$ is the response of a 2D Gabor wavelet [10] centered at (x,y) with orientation u and scale v, and $|\cdot|$ denotes the magnitude of a complex value. Here, following [6], we generated 40 Gabor filters at 8 orientations and 5 scales.

In addition to our algorithms, we evaluated the state-of-the-art Sparse Representation based Classification (SRC) [23] and its Gabor-based extension (GSRC) [25]. For SRC, we reduced the dimensionality of the data using PCA and chose the dimensionality that gave the best performance. For GSRC, we followed the recommendations of the authors to set the downsampling factor in the Gabor filters, but found that better results could be obtained with a larger λ than the recommended one, and thus report these better results obtained with $\lambda = 0.1$. The parameters for our approach were set to $\nu_w = 3$ (minimum number of samples in one class), and $\nu_b = 1$ by cross-validation.

Table 3 reports the performance of the different methods. Note that both CDL and RSR outperform the Euclidean face recognition systems SRC and GSRC. Note also that even a simple Stein-based NN on 129×129 RCMs performs roughly on par with GSRC and better than SRC. More importantly, the representation learned with our SPD-ML algorithm yields significant accuracy gains when used with either NN or RSR for all different viewing angles, with more than 10% improvement for some poses.

Table 3. Recognition accuracies for the FERET face dataset [17]

Method	bc	bd	be	bf	bg	bh	average acc.
SRC [23]	9.5%	37.5%	77.0%	88.0%	48.5%	11.0%	45.3% ± 3.3
GSRC [25]	35.5%	77.0%	93.5%	97.0%	79.0%	38.0%	70.0% ± 2.7
CDL [22]	35.0%	87.5%	**99.5%**	**100.0%**	91.0%	34.5%	74.6% ± 3.1
NN-Stein	29.0%	75.5%	94.5%	98.0%	83.5%	34.5%	69.2% ± 3.0
NN-Stein-ML	40.5%	88.5%	97.0%	99.0%	91.5%	44.5%	76.8% ± 2.7
NN-AIRM	28.5%	72.5%	93.0%	97.5%	83.0%	35.0%	68.3% ± 3.0
NN-AIRM-ML	39.0%	84.0%	96.0%	99.0%	90.5%	45.5%	75.7% ± 2.6
RSR [6]	36.5%	79.5%	96.5%	97.5%	86.0%	41.5%	72.9% ± 2.7
RSR-ML	**49.0%**	**90.5%**	98.5%	100%	**93.5%**	**50.5%**	**80.3% ± 2.4**

6   Conclusions and Future Work

We have introduced a learning algorithm to map a high-dimensional SPD manifold into a lower-dimensional, more discriminative one. To this end, we have exploited a graph embedding formalism with an affinity matrix that encodes intra-class and inter-class distances, and where the similarity between two SPD matrices is defined via either the Stein divergence or the AIRM. Thanks to their invariance to affine transformations, these metrics have allowed us to model the mapping from the high-dimensional manifold to the low-dimensional one with an orthonormal projection. Learning could then be expressed as the solution to an optimization problem on a Grassmann manifold. Our experimental evaluation has demonstrated that the resulting low-dimensional SPD matrices lead to state-of-the art recognition accuracies on several challenging datasets.

In the future, we plan to extend our learning scheme to the unsupervised and semi-supervised scenarios. Finally, we believe that this work is a first step towards showing the importance of preserving the Riemannian structure of the data when performing dimensionality reduction, and thus going from one manifold to another manifold of the same type. We therefore intend to study how this framework can be applied to other types of Riemannian manifolds.

References

1. Absil, P.A., Mahony, R., Sepulchre, R.: Optimization Algorithms on Matrix Manifolds. Princeton University Press, Princeton (2008)
2. Caseiro, R., Henriques, J.F., Martins, P., Batista, J.: Semi-intrinsic mean shift on riemannian manifolds. In: Fitzgibbon, A., Lazebnik, S., Perona, P., Sato, Y., Schmid, C. (eds.) ECCV 2012, Part I. LNCS, vol. 7572, pp. 342–355. Springer, Heidelberg (2012)
3. Cherian, A., Sra, S., Banerjee, A., Papanikolopoulos, N.: Jensen-bregman logdet divergence with application to efficient similarity search for covariance matrices. IEEE Transactions on Pattern Analysis and Machine Intelligence 35(9), 2161–2174 (2013)

4. Fletcher, P.T., Lu, C., Pizer, S.M., Joshi, S.: Principal geodesic analysis for the study of nonlinear statistics of shape. IEEE Transactions on Medical Imaging 23(8), 995–1005 (2004)
5. Goh, A., Vidal, R.: Clustering and dimensionality reduction on riemannian manifolds. In: Proc. IEEE Conference on Computer Vision and Pattern Recognition (CVPR), pp. 1–7. IEEE (2008)
6. Harandi, M.T., Sanderson, C., Hartley, R., Lovell, B.C.: Sparse coding and dictionary learning for symmetric positive definite matrices: A kernel approach. In: Fitzgibbon, A., Lazebnik, S., Perona, P., Sato, Y., Schmid, C. (eds.) ECCV 2012, Part II. LNCS, vol. 7573, pp. 216–229. Springer, Heidelberg (2012)
7. Hussein, M.E., Torki, M., Gowayyed, M.A., El-Saban, M.: Human action recognition using a temporal hierarchy of covariance descriptors on 3d joint locations. In: Proc. Int. Joint Conference on Artificial Intelligence, IJCAI (2013)
8. Jayasumana, S., Hartley, R., Salzmann, M., Li, H., Harandi, M.: Kernel methods on the riemannian manifold of symmetric positive definite matrices. In: Proc. IEEE Conference on Computer Vision and Pattern Recognition (CVPR) (June 2013)
9. Jung, S., Dryden, I.L., Marron, J.: Analysis of principal nested spheres. Biometrika 99(3), 551–568 (2012)
10. Lee, T.S.: Image representation using 2d Gabor wavelets. IEEE Transactions on Pattern Analysis and Machine Intelligence 18(10), 959–971 (1996)
11. Li, H., Jiang, T., Zhang, K.: Efficient and robust feature extraction by maximum margin criterion. IEEE Transactions on Neural Networks 17(1), 157–165 (2006)
12. Liao, Z., Rock, J., Wang, Y., Forsyth, D.: Non-parametric filtering for geometric detail extraction and material representation. In: Proc. IEEE Conference on Computer Vision and Pattern Recognition (CVPR). IEEE (2013)
13. Lowe, D.G.: Distinctive image features from scale-invariant keypoints. IJCV 60(2), 91–110 (2004)
14. Müller, M., Röder, T., Clausen, M., Eberhardt, B., Krüger, B., Weber, A.: Documentation: Mocap database HDM05. Tech. Rep. CG-2007-2, Universität Bonn (2007)
15. Pang, Y., Yuan, Y., Li, X.: Gabor-based region covariance matrices for face recognition. IEEE Transactions on Circuits and Systems for Video Technology 18(7), 989–993 (2008)
16. Pennec, X., Fillard, P., Ayache, N.: A riemannian framework for tensor computing. Int. Journal of Computer Vision (IJCV) 66(1), 41–66 (2006)
17. Phillips, P.J., Moon, H., Rizvi, S.A., Rauss, P.J.: The feret evaluation methodology for face-recognition algorithms. IEEE Transactions on Pattern Analysis and Machine Intelligence 22(10), 1090–1104 (2000)
18. Sanin, A., Sanderson, C., Harandi, M., Lovell, B.: Spatio-temporal covariance descriptors for action and gesture recognition. In: IEEE Workshop on Applications of Computer Vision (WACV), pp. 103–110 (2013)
19. Sra, S.: A new metric on the manifold of kernel matrices with application to matrix geometric means. In: Proc. Advances in Neural Information Processing Systems (NIPS), pp. 144–152 (2012)
20. Tuzel, O., Porikli, F., Meer, P.: Region covariance: A fast descriptor for detection and classification. In: Leonardis, A., Bischof, H., Pinz, A. (eds.) ECCV 2006. LNCS, vol. 3952, pp. 589–600. Springer, Heidelberg (2006)
21. Tuzel, O., Porikli, F., Meer, P.: Pedestrian detection via classification on riemannian manifolds. IEEE Transactions on Pattern Analysis and Machine Intelligence 30(10), 1713–1727 (2008)

22. Wang, R., Guo, H., Davis, L.S., Dai, Q.: Covariance discriminative learning: A natural and efficient approach to image set classification. In: Proc. IEEE Conference on Computer Vision and Pattern Recognition (CVPR), pp. 2496–2503. IEEE (2012)
23. Wright, J., Yang, A.Y., Ganesh, A., Sastry, S.S., Ma, Y.: Robust face recognition via sparse representation. IEEE Transactions on Pattern Analysis and Machine Intelligence 31(2), 210–227 (2009)
24. Yan, S., Xu, D., Zhang, B., Zhang, H.J., Yang, Q., Lin, S.: Graph embedding and extensions: a general framework for dimensionality reduction. IEEE Transactions on Pattern Analysis and Machine Intelligence 29(1), 40–51 (2007)
25. Yang, M., Zhang, L.: Gabor feature based sparse representation for face recognition with Gabor occlusion dictionary. In: Daniilidis, K., Maragos, P., Paragios, N. (eds.) ECCV 2010, Part VI. LNCS, vol. 6316, pp. 448–461. Springer, Heidelberg (2010)

Pose Machines: Articulated Pose Estimation via Inference Machines

Varun Ramakrishna, Daniel Munoz, Martial Hebert,
James Andrew Bagnell, and Yaser Sheikh

The Robotics Institute, Carnegie Mellon University, USA

Abstract. State-of-the-art approaches for articulated human pose estimation are rooted in parts-based graphical models. These models are often restricted to tree-structured representations and simple parametric potentials in order to enable tractable inference. However, these simple dependencies fail to capture all the interactions between body parts. While models with more complex interactions can be defined, learning the parameters of these models remains challenging with intractable or approximate inference. In this paper, instead of performing inference on a learned graphical model, we build upon the *inference machine* framework and present a method for articulated human pose estimation. Our approach incorporates rich spatial interactions among multiple parts and information across parts of different scales. Additionally, the modular framework of our approach enables both ease of implementation without specialized optimization solvers, and efficient inference. We analyze our approach on two challenging datasets with large pose variation and outperform the state of the art on these benchmarks.

1 Introduction

There are two primary sources of complexity in estimating the articulated pose of a human from an image. The first arises from the large number of degrees of freedom (nearly 20) of the underlying articulated skeleton which leads to a high dimensional configuration space to search over. The second is due to the large variation in appearance of people in images. The appearance of each part can vary with configuration, imaging conditions, and from person to person.

To deal with this complexity, current approaches [1,2,3,4,5,6] adopt a graphical model to capture the correlations and dependencies between the locations of the parts. However, inference in graphical models is difficult and inexact in all but the most simple models, such as a tree-structured or star-structured model. These simplified models are unable to capture important dependencies between locations of each of the parts and lead to characteristic errors. One such error— double counting (see Figure 1)—occurs when the same region of the image is used to explain more than one part. This error occurs because of the symmetric appearance of body parts (e.g., the left and right arm usually have similar appearance) and that it is a valid configuration for parts to occlude each other. Modeling this appearance symmetry and self-occlusion with a graphical model

D. Fleet et al. (Eds.): ECCV 2014, Part II, LNCS 8690, pp. 33–47, 2014.
© Springer International Publishing Switzerland 2014

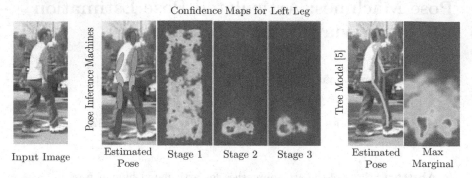

Fig. 1. **Reducing double counting errors.** By modelling richer interactions we prevent the double counting errors that occur in tree models. On the left we show the belief for the left foot of the person in each stage from our method. The belief quickly converges to a single sharp peak. On the right, we see that the tree-structured model [5] has a max-marginal for the left foot with multiple peaks and resulting in both legs being placed on the same area in the image.

requires additional edges and induces loops in the graph. Such non-tree structured graphical models typically require the use of approximate inference (e.g., loopy belief propagation), which makes parameter learning difficult [7].

A second limitation of graphical models is that defining the potential functions requires careful consideration when specifying the types of interactions. This choice is usually dominated by parametric forms such as simple quadratic models in order to enable tractable inference [1]. Finally, to further enable efficient inference in practice, many approaches are also restricted to use simple classifiers such as mixtures of linear models for part detection [5]. These are choices guided by tractabilty of inference rather than the complexity of the data. Such trade-offs result in a restrictive model that do not address the inherent complexity of the problem.

Our approach avoids this complexity vs. tractability trade-off by directly training the inference procedure. We present a method for articulated human pose estimation that builds off the hierarchical inference machine originally used for scene parsing [8,9]. Conceptually, the presented method, which we refer to as a *Pose Machine*, is a sequential prediction algorithm that emulates the mechanics of message passing to predict a confidence for each variable (part), iteratively improving its estimates in each stage. The inference machine architecture is particularly suited to tackle the main challenges in pose estimation. First, it incorporates richer interactions among multiple variables at a time, reducing errors such as double counting, as illustrated in Figure 1. Second, it learns an expressive spatial model directly from the data without the need for specifying the parametric form of the potential functions. Third, its modular architecture allows the use of high capacity predictors which are better suited to deal with the highly multi-modal appearance of each part. Inspired by recent work [10,11] that has demonstrated the importance of conditioning finer part detection on the detection of larger composite parts in order to improve localization, we incorporate these multi-scale cues in our framework by also modeling a hierarchy of parts.

Our contributions include a method that simultaneously addresses the two said primary challenges of articulated pose estimation using the architecture of an inference machine. Additionally, our approach is simple to implement, requiring no specialized optimization solvers at test time, and is efficient in practice. Our analysis on two challenging datasets demonstrates that our approach improves upon the state-of-the-art and offers an effective, alternative framework to address the articulated human pose estimation problem.

2   Related Work

There is a vast body of work on the estimation of articulated human pose from images and video. We focus on methods to estimate the 2D pose from a single image. The most popular approach to pose estimation from images has been the use of *pictorial structures*. Pictorial structure models [1,2,3,4,5,6], express the human body as a tree-structured graphical model with kinematic priors that couple connected limbs. These methods have been successful on images where all the limbs of the person are visible, but are prone to characteristic errors such as double-counting image evidence, which occur because of correlations between variables that are not modeled by a tree-structured model.

Pictorial structure models with non-tree interactions have been employed [12,13,14,15] to estimate pose in a single image. These models augment the tree-structure to capture occlusion relationships between parts not linked in the tree. Performing exact inference on these models is typically intractable and approximate methods at learning and test time need to be used. Recent methods have also explored using part hierarchies [16,17] and condition the detection of smaller parts that model regions around anatomical joints on the localization of larger composite parts or poselets [11,10,18,19] that model limbs in canonical configurations and tend to be easier to detect.

The above models usually involve some degree of careful modeling. For example, [3] models deformation priors by assuming a parametric form for the pairwise potentials, and [5] restricts the appearance of each part to belong to a mixture model. These trade-offs are usually required to enable tractable learning and inference. Even so, learning the parameters of these models usually involves fine-tuned solvers or approximate piecewise methods. Our method does not require a tailor-made solver, as its modular architecture allows us to leverage well-studied algorithms for the training of supervised classifiers.

In [20], the authors use a strong appearance model, by training rotation dependent part detectors with separate part detectors for the head and torso while using a simple tree-structured model. In [21] better part detectors are learned by using multiple stages of random forests. However this approach uses a tree-structured graphical model to enforce spatial consistency. Our approach generalizes the notion of using the output of a previous stage to improve part localization, learns a spatial model in a non-parametric data-driven fashion and does not require the design of part-specific classifiers.

Our method bears some similarity to deep learning methods [22] in a broad sense of also being a multi-layered modular network. However, in contrast to deep-learning methods which are trained in a global fashion (e.g., using back-propagation), each module is trained locally in a supervised manner.

Our method reduces part localization to a sequence of predictions. The use of sequential predictions—feeding the output of predictors from a previous stage to the next—has been revisited in the literature from time to time. Methods such as [23,24] applied sequential prediction to natural language processing tasks. While [25] explored the use of context from neighboring pixel classifiers for computer vision tasks. Our approach is based on the hierarchical inference machine architecture [8,9] that reduces structured prediction tasks to a sequence of simple machine learning subproblems. Inference machines have been previously studied in image and point cloud labeling applications [8,26]. In this work, our contribution is to extend and analyze the inference machine framework for the task of articulated pose estimation.

3   Pose Inference Machines

3.1   Background

We view the articulated pose estimation problem as a structured prediction problem. That is, we model the pixel location of each anatomical landmark (which we refer to as a part) in the image, $Y_p \in \mathcal{Z} \subset \mathbb{R}^2$, where $\mathcal{Z}$ is the set of all (u, v) locations in an image. Our goal is to predict the structured output $Y = (Y_1, \ldots, Y_P)$ for all P parts. An inference machine consists of a sequence of multi-class classifiers, $g_t(\cdot)$, that are trained to predict the location of each part. In each stage $t \in \{1 \ldots T\}$, the classifier predicts a confidence for assigning a location to each part $Y_p = z$, $\forall z \in \mathcal{Z}$, based on features of the image data $\mathbf{x}_z \in \mathbb{R}^d$ and contextual information from the preceeding classifier in the neighborhood around each Y_p. In each stage, the computed confidences provide an increasingly refined estimate for the variable. For each stage t of the sequence, the confidence for the assignment $Y_p = z$ is computed and denoted by

$$b_t(Y_p = z) = g_t^p \left(\mathbf{x}_z ; \bigoplus_{i=1}^{P} \psi(z, \mathbf{b}_{t-1}^i) \right), \tag{1}$$

where

$$\mathbf{b}_{t-1}^p = \{b_{t-1}(Y_p = z)\}_{z \in \mathcal{Z}}, \tag{2}$$

is the set of confidences from the previous classifier evaluated at every location z for the p'th part. The feature function $\psi : \mathcal{Z} \times \mathbb{R}^{|\mathcal{Z}|} \to \mathbb{R}^{d_c}$ computes contextual features from the classifiers' previous confidences, and $\bigoplus$ denotes an operator for vector concatenation.

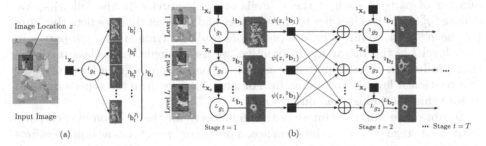

Fig. 2. (a) **Multi-class prediction.** A single multiclass predictor is trained for each level of the hierarchy to predict each image patch into one of $P_l + 1$ classes. By evaluating each patch in the image, we create a set of confidence maps $^l\mathbf{b}_t$. (b) **Two stages of a pose inference machine.** In each stage, a predictor is trained to predict the confidence of the output variables. The figure depicts the message passing in an inference machine at test time. In the first stage, the predictors produce an estimate for the confidence of each part location based on features computed on the image patch. Predictors in subsequent stages, refine these confidences using additional information from the outputs of the previous stage via the context feature function ψ.

Unlike traditional graphical models, such as pictorial structures, the inference machine framework does not need explicit modeling of the dependencies between variables via potential functions. Instead, the dependencies are arbitrarily combined using the classifier, which potentially enables complex interactions among the variables. Directly training the inference procedure via a sequence of simpler subproblems, allows us to use any supervised learning algorithm to solve each subproblem. We are able to leverage the state-of-the-art in supervised learning and use a sophisticated predictor capable of handling multi-modal variation. As detailed in the following section, our approach to articulated pose estimation takes the form of a *hierarchical* mean-field inference machine [8], where the contextual information that each variable uses comes from neighboring variables in *both* scale and space in the image.

3.2 Incorporating a Hierarchy

Recent work [11,10] has shown that part detections conditioned on the location of larger composite parts improves pose estimation performance; however, these composite parts are often constructed to form tree graph structures [16]. Inspired by these recent advances, we design a hierarchical inference machine that similarly encodes these interactions among parts at different scales in the image. We define a hierarchy of parts from smaller atomic parts to larger composite parts. Each of the L levels of the hierarchy have parts of a different type. At the coarsest level, the hierarchy is comprised of a single part that captures the whole body. The next level of the hierarchy is comprised of composite parts that model full limbs, while the finest level of the hierarchy is comprised of small parts that model a region around an anatomical landmark. We denote by $P_1, \ldots, P_L$, the number of parts in each of the L levels of the hierarchy. In the following, we denote ${}^l g_t^p(\cdot)$ as the classifier in the tth stage and l^{th} level that predicts the score for the pth part. While separate predictors could be trained for each part p in each level l of the hierarchy, in practice, we use a single multi-class predictor that produces a set of confidences for all the parts from a given feature vector at a particular level in the hierarchy. For simplicity, we drop the superscript and denote this multi-class classifier as ${}^l g_t(\cdot)$.

To obtain an initial estimate of the confidences for the location of each part, in the first stage ($t = 1$) of the sequence, a predictor ${}^l g_1(\cdot)$ takes as input features computed on a patch extracted at an image location z, and classifies the patch into one of P_l part classes or a background class (see Figure 2a), for the parts in the lth level of the hierarchy. We denote by $\mathbf{x}_z^l$, the feature vector of an image patch for the lth level of the hierarchy centered at location z in the image. A classifier for the lth level of the hierarchy in the first stage $t = 1$, therefore produces the following confidence values:

$$
{}^l g_1(\mathbf{x}_z^l) \rightarrow \left\{ {}^l b_1^p(Y_p = z) \right\}_{p \in 0 \ldots P_l}, \tag{3}
$$

where ${}^l b_1^p(Y_p = z)$ is the score predicted by the classifier ${}^l g_1$ for assigning the pth part in the lth level of the hierarchy in the first stage at image location z. Analogous to Equation 2, we represent all the confidences of part p of level l evaluated at every location $z = (u, v)^T$ in the image as ${}^l \mathbf{b}_t^p \in \mathbb{R}^{w \times h}$, where w and h are the width and height of the image, respectively. That is,

$$
{}^l \mathbf{b}_t^p[u, v] = {}^l b_t^p(Y_p = (u, v)^T). \tag{4}
$$

For convenience, we denote the collection of confidence maps for all the parts belonging to level l as ${}^l \mathbf{b}_t \in \mathbb{R}^{w \times h \times P_l}$ (see Figure 2a).

In subsequent stages, the confidence for each variable is computed similarly to Equation 1. In the order to leverage the context across scales/levels in the hierarchy, the prediction is defined as

$$
{}^l g_t \left(\mathbf{x}_z^l, \bigoplus_{l \in 1 \ldots L} \psi(z, {}^l \mathbf{b}_{t-1}) \right) \rightarrow \left\{ {}^l b_t^p(Y_p = z) \right\}_{p \in 0 \ldots P_l}. \tag{5}
$$

As shown in Figure 2b, in the second stage, the classifier ${}^l g_2$ takes as input the features $\mathbf{x}_z^l$ and features computed on the confidences via the feature function ψ for each of the parts in the previous stage. Note that the the predictions for a part use features computed on outputs of all parts *and* in all levels of the hierarchy ($\{ {}^l \mathbf{b}_{t-1} \}_{l \in 1 \ldots L}$). The inference machine architecture allows learning potentially complex interactions among the variables, by simply supplying features on the outputs of the previous stage (as opposed to specifying potential functions in a graphical model) and allowing the classifier to freely combine contextual information by picking the most predictive features. The use of outputs from all neighboring variables, resembles the message passing mechanics in variational mean field inference [9].

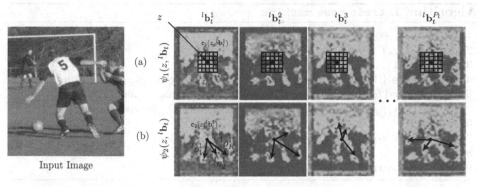

Input Image

Fig. 3. Context Feature Maps (a) Context patch features are computed from each score map for each location. The figure illustrates a 5×5 sized context patch (b) The context offset feature comprises of offsets to a sorted list of peaks in each score map.

3.3 Context Features

To capture the spatial correlations between the confidences of each part with respect to its neighbors, we describe two types of factors with associated "context" feature maps denoted by ψ_1 and ψ_2.

Context Patch Features. The feature map ψ_1 at a location z takes as input the confidence maps for the location of each part in a hierarchy level l and produces a feature that is a vectorized patch of a predefined width extracted at the location z in the confidence map ${}^l\mathbf{b}_t^p$ (see Figure 3a). We denote the set of patches extracted and vectorized at the location z, from the beliefs of the parts in the hierarchy level l, by $\mathbf{c}_1(z, {}^l\mathbf{b}_{t-1}^p)$. The feature map ψ_1 is therefore given by:

$$\psi_1(z, {}^l\mathbf{b}_{t-1}) = \bigoplus_{p \in 0 \ldots P_l} \mathbf{c}_1(z, {}^l\mathbf{b}_{t-1}^p). \tag{6}$$

In words, the context feature is a concatenation of scores at location z extracted from the confidence maps of all the parts in each level the hierarchy. The context patch encodes neighboring information around location z as would be passed as messages in a factor graph. Note that because we encode the context from all parts, this would be analogous to having a graphical model with a complete graph structure and would be intractable to optimize.

Context Offset Features. We compute a second type of feature, ψ_2, in order to encode long-range interactions among the parts that may be at non-uniform, relative offsets. First, we perform non-maxima suppresion to obtain a sorted list of K peaks from each of the P_l confidence maps ${}^l\mathbf{b}_{t-1}^p$ for all the parts in the l'th hierarchy level. Then, we compute the offset vector in polar coordinates from location z to each kth peak in the confidence map of the pth part and l^{th} level denoted as as ${}^l o_k^p \in \mathbb{R}^+ \times \mathbb{R}$ (see Figure 3b). The set of context offset features computed from one part's confidence map is defined as:

$$\mathbf{c}_2(z, {}^l\mathbf{b}_{t-1}^p) = \left[{}^l o_1^p; \ldots; {}^l o_K^p\right]. \tag{7}$$

Algorithm 1. train_pose_machine

1: Initialize: $\left\{{}^{l}\mathbf{b}_0 = \emptyset\right\}_{l \in 1, \ldots, L}$
2: **for** $t = 1 \ldots T$ **do**
3:     **for** $i = 1 \ldots N$ **do**
4:         Create $\{{}^{l}\mathbf{b}_{t-1}\}_{l=1}^{L}$ for each image i using predictor ${}^{l}g_{t-1}$ using Eqn. 5.
5:         Append features extracted from each training image i, and from corresponding $\{{}^{l}\mathbf{b}_{t-1}\}_{l=1}^{L}$ (Eqns. 6 & 8), to training dataset $\mathcal{D}_t$, for each image i.
6:     **end for**
7:     Train ${}^{l}g_t$ using $\mathcal{D}_t$.
8: **end for**
9: **Return:** Learned predictors $\{{}^{l}g_t\}$.

Then, the context offset feature map ψ_2 is formed by concatenating the context offset features $\mathbf{c}_2(z, {}^{l}\mathbf{b}_{t-1}^p)$ for each part in the the hierarchy:

$$\psi_2(z, {}^{l}\mathbf{b}_{t-1}) = \bigoplus_{p \in 1 \ldots P_l} \mathbf{c}_2(z, {}^{l}\mathbf{b}_{t-1}^p). \tag{8}$$

The context patch features (ψ_1) capture coarse information regarding the confidence of the neighboring parts while the offset features (ψ_2) capture precise relative location information. The final context feature ψ is computed by concatenating two: $\psi(\cdot) = [\psi_1(\cdot) \; ; \; \psi_2(\cdot)]$.

3.4   Training

Training the inference procedure involves directly training each of the predictors, $\{{}^{l}g_t\}$, in each level $l \in \{1, \ldots, L\}$, and for each stage $t \in \{1, \ldots, T\}$. We describe our training procedure in Algorithm 1. Training proceeds in a stage-wise manner. The first set of predictors $\{{}^{l}g_1\}$ are trained using a dataset $\mathcal{D}_0$ consisting of image features on patches extracted from the training set of images at the annotated landmarks. For deeper stages, the dataset $\mathcal{D}_t$ is created by extracting and concatenating the context features from the confidence maps $\{{}^{l}\mathbf{b}_{t-1}\}_{l=1}^{L}$ for each image, at the annotated locations.

3.5   Stacking

Training the predictors of such an inference procedure is prone to overfitting. Using the same training data to train the predictors in subsequent stages will cause them to rely on overly optimistic context from the previous stage, or overfit to idiosyncrasies of that particular dataset. Ideally we would like to train the subsequent stages with the output of the previous stages similar to that encountered at test time. In order to achieve this, we use the idea of stacked training [27,23].

Stacked training aims to prevent predictors trained on the output of the first stage from being trained on same training data. Stacking proceeds similarly to

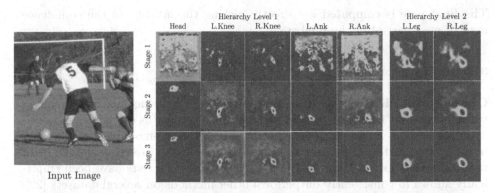

Fig. 4. The output of a three stage pose inference machine at each stage.
An inference machine iteratively produces more refined estimates of the confidence for
the location of each part. In the first stage, the estimate produced only from image
features is noisy and has multiple modes. Subsequent stages refine the confidence based
on predictions from neighboring factors to a sharp unimodal response at the correct
location and suppress false positive responses in the background. The confidences from
left to right are for the *head, left-knee, right-knee, left-ankle, right-ankle, left-leg, right-
leg.*

cross-validation by making M splits of the training data $\mathcal{D}$ into training and
held-out data $\{\mathcal{D}^m, \mathcal{D}/\mathcal{D}^m\}_{m=1...M}$. For each predictor we aim to train in the
first stage, we make M copies, each trained on one of the M splits of the training
data. To create the training data for the next stage, for each training sample, we
use the copy of the predictor that has not seen the sample (i.e., the sample is in
the held-out data for that predictor). Proceeding in this way creates a dataset
to train the next stage on the outputs of the previous stage, ensuring that the
outputs mimic test-time behavior. We repeat the stacking procedure for each
subsequent stage. The stacking procedure is only performed during training to
create a training dataset for subsequent stages. At test time, we use a predictor
in each stage that is trained using all of the data.

3.6 Inference

At test time, inference proceeds in a sequential fashion as show in Figure 2b.
Features are extracted from patches of different scales (corresponding to each
of the L levels of the hierarchy) at each location in the image and input to the
first stage classifiers $\{^l g_1\}_{l=1}^L$, resulting in the output confidence maps $\{^l \mathbf{b}_1\}_{l=1}^L$.
Messages are passed to the classifiers in the next stage, by computing context
features via the feature maps ψ_1, ψ_2 on the confidences $^l \mathbf{b}_1$ from the previous
stage. Updated confidences $\{^l \mathbf{b}_2\}_{l=1}^L$ are computed by the classifiers $^l g_2$ and this
procedure is repeated for each stage. The computed confidences are increasingly
refined estimates for the location of the part as shown in Figure 4. The location
of each part is then computed as,

$$\forall l, \forall p, \quad {}^l y_p^* = \underset{z}{\operatorname{argmax}} \; {}^l \mathbf{b}_T^p(z). \tag{9}$$

The final pose is computed by directly picking the maxima of the confidence map of each part after the final stage.

3.7 Implementation

Choice of Predictor. The modular nature of the inference machine architecture allows us to insert any supervised learning classifier as our choice of multiclass predictor g. As the data distribution is highly multi-modal, a high-capacity non-linear predictor is required. In this work, we use a boosted classifier [28] with random forests for the weak learners, because random forests have been empirically shown to consistently outperform other methods on several datasets [29]. We learn our boosted classifier by optimizing the non-smooth hinge loss [30]. We use 25 iterations of boosting, with a random forest classifier. Each random forest classifier consists of 10 trees, with a maximum depth of 15 and with a split performed only if a node contained greater than 10 training samples.

Training. To create positive samples for training, we extract patches around the annotated anatomical landmarks in each training sample. For the background class, we use patches sampled from a negative training corpus as in [5]. In addition, in subsequent stages, we sample negative patches from false positive regions in the positive images.

Image Features. We extract a set of image features from a patch at each location in the image. We use a standard set of simple features to provide a direct comparison and to control for the effect of features on performance. We use *Histogram of Gradients (HOG)* features, *Lab* color features, and gradient magnitude. The HOG features are defined based on the structure of the human poses labeled in the respective datasets, which we detail in the follow section. In the FLIC dataset [11], only an upper-body model is annotated and we use 6 orientations with a bin size 4. In the LEEDS dataset [6], a full body model is annotated and we use 6 orientations with a bin size of 8 in the finest level of the hierarchy. We increase the bin size by a factor of two for the coarser levels in the hierarchy. For the upper body model, we model each part in the finest level of the hierarchy with 9×9 HOG cells, while we use 5×5 HOG cells for the full body model. These parameter choices are guided by previous work using these datasets [11,5].

Context Features. For the context patch features, we use a context patch of size 21×21, with max-pooling in each 2×2 neighborhood resulting in a set of 121 numbers per confidence map. For the context offset features we use $K = 3$ peaks.

4   Evaluation

We evaluate and compare the performance of our approach on two standard pose estimation datasets to the current state-of-the-art methods.

Table 1. Quantitative performance on LEEDS Sports Pose dataset. Performance is measured by the PCP metric on the test set of the LEEDS sports dataset. Our algorithm outperforms all current methods.

Method	Torso	Upper Legs	Lower Legs	Upper Arms	Lower Arms	Head	Total
Ours	**93.1**	**83.6**	**76.8**	**68.1**	42.2	85.4	**72.0**
Pishchulin [20]	88.7	78.8	73.4	61.5	**44.9**	85.6	69.2
Pishchulin [10]	87.5	75.7	68.0	54.2	33.8	78.1	62.9
Yang&Ramanan [5]	84.1	69.5	65.6	52.5	35.9	77.1	60.8
Eichner&Ferrari [31]	86.2	74.3	69.3	56.5	37.4	80.1	64.3

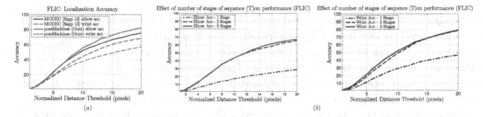

Fig. 5. (a) **Comparison to state-of-the-art on FLIC** Elbow and wrist localization accuracy on the FLIC dataset. We achieve higher accuracies for both joints compared to the state-of-the-art [11]. (b) **Effect of number of stages.** We plot the change in accuracy with the number of stages in the sequence. We observe that including a second stage which uses contextual information greatly increases the performance. We also observe a slight improvement with the incorporation of an additional third stage.

LEEDS Sports Pose Dataset. We evaluate our approach on the LEEDS sports dataset [6] which consists of 1,000 images for training and 1,000 images for testing. The images are of people in various sport poses. We use the observer-centric annotations as used in [10] for training and testing. We train a full body model comprised of a 2-level hierarchy. The second level of the hierarchy comprises of the 14 parts corresponding to each of the annotated joints. The first level comprises of 6 composite parts formed by grouping parts belonging to each of the limbs, a composite part for the head and shoulders and a composite part for the torso. Parameter choices were guided by a grid search using a development subset of the training dataset comprising of 200 images. We use the *Percentage Correct Parts* (PCP) metric to evaluate and compare our performance on the dataset. The results are listed in the Table 1. We outperform existing methods and achieve an average PCP score of 72.0. We show qualitative results of our algorithm on a few representative samples from the LEEDS dataset in Figure 7.

FLIC Upper Body Pose Dataset. We also evaluate our approach on the FLIC dataset [11] which consists of still frames from movies. The dataset consists of 4,000 images for training and 1,000 images for testing. We use a model trained

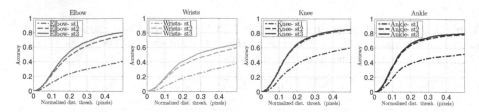

Fig. 6. Effect of number of stages on LSP. We plot the change in accuracy with the number of stages in the sequence for difficult landmarks on the LEEDS Sports dataset. The additional stages improve the performance especially of difficult parts like the elbows and wrists.

to recognize the pose of the upper body. We employ a two-level hierarchy, with the finest level of the hierarchy comprising of seven parts corresponding to the annotated anatomical landmark locations, the second level comprising of three composite parts corresponding to each of the arms and one for the head and shoulders. Parameter choices were guided by a grid search using a development subset of the training dataset comprising of 200 images. We use the accuracy metric specified in [11]. In Figure 5a we plot the accuracy of the wrist and elbow joints. Our approach shows a significant improvement over the state of the art [11]. We show qualitative results of our algorithm on samples from the FLIC dataset in Figure 8.

Fig. 7. Qualitative example results on the LEEDS sports dataset. Our algorithm is able to automatically learn a spatial model and correctly localize traditionally difficult parts such as the elbows and wrists.

Effect of the Number of Stages. We study the effect of increasing the number of stages T in the inference machine. Figure 5b plots the part localization accuracy as a function of the distance from the ground truth label on the FLIC dataset. We see that predicting part location only based on image features ($T=1$) results in poor performance. The addition of a second stage ($T=2$) that incorporates contextual information results in a dramatic increase in the accuracy. An additional third stage ($T=3$) adds a minor increase in performance on this dataset. Setting the number of stages is similar to how the number of iterations are set for message-passing algorithms such as belief propagation. For datasets of different sizes the number of stages can be set by evaluating the change in loss after each iteration.

We plot the change in accuracy with the number of stages in the sequence for difficult landmarks on the LEEDS Sports dataset (see Figure 6). We observe that including a second stage which uses contextual information greatly increases the performance. We also observe slight improvements for the knees and ankles, and a significant improvement for the wrists and elbows upon adding a third stage.

Fig. 8. Qualitative example results on the FLIC dataset. Our algorithm is able to automatically learn a spatial model and correctly localize traditionally difficult parts such as the elbows and wrists.

Fig. 9. Failure Modes. Typical failure modes include severe occlusion of parts and rare poses, for which too few training samples exist in the training set. The method is also prone to error when there are multiple people in close proximity.

5 Discussion

We have presented an inference machine for articulated human pose estimation. The inference machine architecture allows us to learn a rich spatial model and incorporate high-capacity supervised predictors, resulting in substantially improved pose estimation performance. One of the main challenges that remain is to correctly handle occluded poses, which is one of the failure modes of the algorithm (see Figure 9). A second failure mode is due to rare poses for which there are too few similar training instances. Tackling these challenges will need an understanding of the requirements from a human pose dataset for training an algorithm to work *in the wild*. The ability to handle complex variable dependencies leads to interesting directions for future work that include extending the method to monocular video by incorporating temporal cues, directly predicting poses in 3D, and adapting the method for different categories of articulated objects.

Acknowledgements. This material is based upon work supported by the National Science Foundation under Grants No. 1353120 and 1029679 and the NSF NRI Purposeful Prediction project.

References

1. Felzenszwalb, P.F., Huttenlocher, D.P.: Pictorial structures for object recognition. In: IJCV (2005)
2. Ramanan, D., Forsyth, D.A., Zisserman, A.: Strike a Pose: Tracking people by finding stylized poses. In: CVPR (2005)
3. Andriluka, M., Roth, S., Schiele, B.: Monocular 3D Pose Estimation and Tracking by Detection. In: CVPR (2010)
4. Andriluka, M., Roth, S., Schiele, B.: Pictorial Structures Revisited: People Detection and Articulated Pose Estimation. In: CVPR (2009)
5. Yang, Y., Ramanan, D.: Articulated pose estimation with flexible mixtures-of-parts. In: CVPR (2011)
6. Johnson, S., Everingham, M.: Clustered pose and nonlinear appearance models for human pose estimation. In: BMVC (2010)
7. Kulesza, A., Pereira, F.: Structured learning with approximate inference. In: NIPS (2007)

8. Munoz, D., Bagnell, J.A., Hebert, M.: Stacked hierarchical labeling. In: Daniilidis, K., Maragos, P., Paragios, N. (eds.) ECCV 2010, Part VI. LNCS, vol. 6316, pp. 57–70. Springer, Heidelberg (2010)
9. Ross, S., Munoz, D., Hebert, M., Bagnell, J.A.: Learning message-passing inference machines for structured prediction. In: CVPR (2011)
10. Pishchulin, L., Andriluka, M., Gehler, P., Schiele, B.: Poselet conditioned pictorial structures. In: CVPR (2013)
11. Sapp, B., Taskar, B.: MODEC: Multimodal Decomposable Models for Human Pose Estimation. In: CVPR (2013)
12. Wang, Y., Mori, G.: Multiple tree models for occlusion and spatial constraints in human pose estimation. In: Forsyth, D., Torr, P., Zisserman, A. (eds.) ECCV 2008, Part III. LNCS, vol. 5304, pp. 710–724. Springer, Heidelberg (2008)
13. Sigal, L., Black, M.J.: Measure locally, reason globally: Occlusion-sensitive articulated pose estimation. In: CVPR (2006)
14. Lan, X., Huttenlocher, D.P.: Beyond trees: Common-factor models for 2d human pose recovery. In: ICCV (2005)
15. Karlinsky, L., Ullman, S.: Using linking features in learning non-parametric part models. In: Fitzgibbon, A., Lazebnik, S., Perona, P., Sato, Y., Schmid, C. (eds.) ECCV 2012, Part III. LNCS, vol. 7574, pp. 326–339. Springer, Heidelberg (2012)
16. Tian, Y., Zitnick, C.L., Narasimhan, S.G.: Exploring the spatial hierarchy of mixture models for human pose estimation. In: Fitzgibbon, A., Lazebnik, S., Perona, P., Sato, Y., Schmid, C. (eds.) ECCV 2012, Part V. LNCS, vol. 7576, pp. 256–269. Springer, Heidelberg (2012)
17. Sun, M., Savarese, S.: Articulated part-based model for joint object detection and pose estimation. In: ICCV (2011)
18. Gkioxari, G., Arbeláez, P., Bourdev, L., Malik, J.: Articulated pose estimation using discriminative armlet classifiers. In: CVPR. IEEE (2013)
19. Wang, Y., Tran, D., Liao, Z.: Learning hierarchical poselets for human parsing. In: CVPR. IEEE (2011)
20. Pishchulin, L., Andriluka, M., Gehler, P., Schiele, B.: Strong appearance and expressive spatial models for human pose estimation. In: ICCV (2013)
21. Dantone, M., Gall, J., Leistner, C., Van Gool, L.: Human pose estimation using body parts dependent joint regressors. In: CVPR (2013)
22. Bengio, Y.: Learning deep architectures for AI. Foundations and trends in Machine Learning (2009)
23. Carvalho, V., Cohen, W.: Stacked sequential learning. In: IJCAI (2005)
24. Daumé III, H., Langford, J., Marcu, D.: Search-based structured prediction. Machine Learning (2009)
25. Bai, X., Tu, Z.: Auto-context and its application to high-level vision tasks and 3d brain image segmentation. In: PAMI (2009)
26. Xiong, X., Munoz, D., Bagnell, J.A., Hebert, M.: 3-d scene analysis via sequenced predictions over points and regions. In: ICRA (2011)
27. Wolpert, D.H.: Stacked Generalization. Neural Networks (1992)
28. Friedman, J.H.: Greedy function approximation: a gradient boosting machine. Annals of Statistics (2001)
29. Caruana, R., Niculescu-Mizil, A.: An empirical comparison of supervised learning algorithms. In: ICML (2006)
30. Grubb, A., Bagnell, J.A.: Generalized boosting algorithms for convex optimization. In: ICML (2011)
31. Eichner, M., Ferrari, V.: Appearance sharing for collective human pose estimation. In: Lee, K.M., Matsushita, Y., Rehg, J.M., Hu, Z. (eds.) ACCV 2012, Part I. LNCS, vol. 7724, pp. 138–151. Springer, Heidelberg (2013)

Piecewise-Planar StereoScan: Structure and Motion from Plane Primitives

Carolina Raposo, Michel Antunes, and Joao P. Barreto

Institute of Systems and Robotics
University of Coimbra, 3030 Coimbra, Portugal

Abstract. This article describes a pipeline that receives as input a sequence of images acquired by a calibrated stereo rig and outputs the camera motion and a Piecewise-Planar Reconstruction (PPR) of the scene. It firstly detects the 3D planes viewed by each stereo pair from semi-dense depth estimation. This is followed by estimating the pose between consecutive views using a new closed-form minimal algorithm that relies in point correspondences only when plane correspondences are insufficient to fully constrain the motion. Finally, the camera motion and the PPR are jointly refined, alternating between discrete optimization for generating plane hypotheses and continuous bundle adjustment. The approach differs from previous works in PPR by determining the poses from plane-primitives, by jointly estimating motion and piecewise-planar structure, and by operating sequentially, being suitable for applications of SLAM and visual odometry. Experiments are carried in challenging wide-baseline datasets where conventional point-based SfM usually fails.

Keywords: Structure and Motion, Piecewise-Planar Reconstruction.

1 Introduction

Although multi-view stereo has been an intensive field of research in the last few decades, current methods still have difficulty in handling situations of weak or repetitive texture, variable illumination, non-lambertian reflection, and high surface slant [11]. In this context, it makes sense to explore the fact that man-made environments are usually dominated by large plane surfaces to improve the accuracy and robustness of 3D reconstruction. This is the key idea behind the so-called Piecewise-Planar Reconstruction (PPR) methods that use the strong planarity assumption as a prior to overcome the above mentioned issues [11,9,22,2,26,10,18]. In addition, piecewise-planar 3D models are perceptually pleasing and geometrically simple, and thus their rendering, storage, and transmission is substantially less complex when compared to conventional point-cloud models [1,23]. The usefulness of plane primitives is not limited to multi-view stereo reconstruction as shown by recent works in SLAM for RGB-D cameras that estimate the motion from plane correspondences [24,21]. Taguchi et al. highlight that plane features are much less numerous than point features, favoring fast correspondence and scalability, and that the global character of

D. Fleet et al. (Eds.): ECCV 2014, Part II, LNCS 8690, pp. 48–63, 2014.

Fig. 1. Back-propagation of planes across stereo pairs: a closer view of the top horizontal plane allows its correct detection and propagation to previous stereo pairs. Note that the overlaid planes in the output images are identified by different colors.

plane-primitives helps avoiding local minima issues [24]. Also, man-made environments are often dominated by large size planes that enable correspondence across wide baseline images and, since plane-primitives are mostly in the static background, the motion estimation is specially resilient to dynamic foreground [21].

This article describes a pipeline for passive stereo that combines the benefits of PPR and plane-based odometry by recovering both structure and motion from plane-primitives. The algorithm receives as input an image sequence acquired by a calibrated stereo rig and outputs the camera motion and 3D planes in the scene. These planes are segmented in each stereo pair using a standard Markov-Random Field (MRF) labeling [11,22,4], and the final piecewise-planar model is obtained by simply concatenating the PPR results from consecutive frames.

The pipeline builds on the work of Antunes et al. [2] in PPR from semi-dense depth estimation using symmetry energy, which proved to outperform competing methods for the case of two calibrated views [4]. We start by running a simplified version of Antunes' algorithm in each input stereo pair and use these initial plane detections to compute the relative pose between consecutive frames. It is well known that the registration of two sets of 3D planes can be carried in closed-form from a minimum of 3 plane correspondences [13]. In our case, the estimation of the relative pose from plane-primitives raises two issues: establishing plane correspondences across stereo pairs, and determining the motion whenever the available planes do not fully constrain the problem [24]. The first issue is efficiently solved by matching triplets of planes using the angles between their normals. False correspondences are also pruned in [13,20,24] using this angular metric. Concerning the second issue it is shown that the undetermined situations can be overcome by either using 2 planes and 1 image point correspondence, or 1 plane and 3 image point correspondences [21] [1]. We derive closed-form minimal solutions for these cases and apply them in a hierarchical RANSAC that estimates the relative pose using point matches only when strictly necessary.

The next step is the joint refinement of camera motion and initial plane detections to obtain a coherent piecewise-planar model of the scene. In general, independent stereo detections of the same 3D plane are slightly different and must be merged into a single hypothesis before proceeding to bundle adjust-

---

[1] In this paper *image point correspondences* refer to inter-stereo point correspondences meaning point matches between the images of two different stereo pairs.

ment [11]. Moreover, and as shown in Fig. 1, it often happens that the same plane is wrongly reconstructed in a faraway view and correctly detected in a closer view, which means that the first plane hypothesis must be discarded and replaced by the second. We show that linking, fusing, and back-propagating plane hypotheses across stereo pairs can be conveniently formulated as a multi-model fitting problem that is efficiently solved using global energy minimization [15,17,6]. Thus, we propose to carry the joint refinement of motion and structure using a PEARL framework [15] that alternates between a discrete optimization step, whose objective is to re-assign plane hypotheses to stereo pairs, and a continuous bundle adjustment step that refines the reconstruction results using the symmetry-energies arising from the initial semi-dense depth estimations [2,4].

In summary, the contributions of these article are threefold: (i) a method for estimating the relative pose between two stereo cameras that preferentially uses plane-primitives. This method differs from the algorithm for RGB-D cameras [24] because it uses image correspondences instead of 3D points for handling the undetermined cases; (ii) a PEARL formulation for simultaneously refining camera motion and piecewise-planar model of the scene; and (iii) a complete stereo pipeline for PPR and motion estimation that is validated in challenging wide-baseline sequences for which conventional point-based SfM fails.

1.1   Related Work

Our work relates with previous methods for PPR [9,22,11,26,10,18] that operate in a batch manner by first applying point-based SfM to estimate the relative pose between monocular views [23], and then reconstructing the plane surfaces from all images in simultaneous. Unlike these methods, the algorithm herein described carries the 3D modeling in a sequential manner using a sliding window approach to concatenate the contributions of consecutive stereo pairs. This is an important difference that enables applications in visual odometry and SLAM. Since the article also proposes a method for estimating relative camera pose, it relates with prior works in visual odometry for stereo cameras [19,12,16,7,25]. We ran comparative experiments against the broadly used LIBVISO2 algorithm [12] that confirm the benefits of using plane-primitives, as opposed to image point matches, to recover the camera motion. In particular our method outperforms LIBVISO2 in the case of little overlap between stereo pairs.

2   Background

This section gives a brief review of background concepts that are useful for better understanding the proposed pipeline. It uses energy-based methods for solving two multi-model fitting problems, for which the theoretical basis is presented. Moreover, it builds on top of the PPR framework proposed in [2], whose main aspects are introduced in section 2.2.

2.1   Energy-Based Multi-Model Fitting

Several PPR methods start by obtaining a sparse 3D reconstruction of the scene, and solve a multi-model fitting problem for generating likely plane hypotheses. It has been recently stated in [15] that formulating the multi-model fitting as an optimal labeling problem with a global energy function is usually preferable than using RANSAC-based [11] or histogram-based [22] methods, mostly because they tend to ignore the overall classification of the input data.

The optimization problem that arises from the multi-model fitting can be cast as an Uncapacitated Facility Location (UFL) problem, whenever the relationships between data nodes is not taken into account. The objective is to assign a label to each data point by minimizing a global energy function, $E = D + L$, that consists of data, D, and label costs, L. UFL problems can be efficiently solved using a message passing inference algorithm [17].

Whenever the dependencies between the data points are taken into account, a smoothness term S must be added to the previous energy function. In this case, the multi-model fitting can be formulated as an optimization problem using the PEARL algorithm [15]. The objective is also to assign a label to each data point, but this time by minimizing an energy function in the form $E = D + S + L$, which is efficiently achieved using α-expansion [15].

2.2   Semi-dense Piecewise Planar Stereo Reconstruction

Our method starts by obtaining a semi-dense PPR of the scene for each stereo pair using the method proposed in [2]. This framework was chosen as our starting point since it reported superior results when compared to other PPR methods [22,11] in stereo reconstruction, both in terms of accuracy and computational time. The method starts by employing a sparse set of M virtual cut planes Φ_j intersecting the baseline in its midpoint for obtaining the energy E for each virtual plane using the SymStereo framework [3] (refer to Fig. 2(a)). This can be thought of as an image created by a virtual camera that is located between the cameras (cyclopean eye), where each epipolar plane Ψ_r projects onto one row and each virtual plane Φ_j projects onto one column of the cyclopean image. Each pixel of the cyclopean eye is originated from the back-projection ray $\mathbf{d}_{j,r}$. For a particular virtual cut plane, each pixel in E provides the matching likelihood of a certain pair of pixels in the stereo views. The energy E is used as input to a Hough transform for extracting a set of line segments, which are the intersections of the virtual planes with the scene planes, and then each set of two lines provides a plane hypothesis. This is illustrated in the third step of the scheme in Fig. 2(a).

PPR is a *chicken-and-egg* problem since the accuracy of the plane hypotheses is inevitably limited by the accuracy of the initial 3D reconstruction that significantly depends on taking into account the fact of the scene being dominated by planar surfaces. Methods for PPR such as [22,11] that treat stereo matching and plane detection in a sequential and independent manner are affected by this problem. In [2], the multi-model plane fitting is formulated in a simultaneous and integrated manner as an optimization problem using the PEARL algorithm,

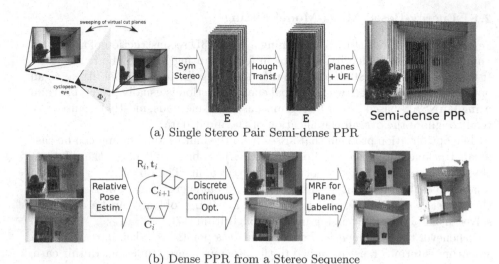

(a) Single Stereo Pair Semi-dense PPR

(b) Dense PPR from a Stereo Sequence

Fig. 2. Different steps of the proposed pipeline. (a) For each stereo pair, a semi-dense PPR is computed as described in section 3.1. The inlier set of planes for each view, along with the corresponding energies, is the input to the pipeline in (b), for which an overview is given in section 3.2. After the optimization step, colors identify planes. Note that a plane was randomly assigned to the black areas of the door due to its very weak texture, and the reconstructed points were removed.

overcoming this issue. Our pipeline follows this idea while fusing several stereo pairs. The objective in the formulation is to assign to each back-projection ray of the cyclopean eye a plane label of the initial plane set. They showed that the symmetry energy can be improved by repositioning the virtual cut plane according to the surface slant [4]. We use this idea in the continuous optimization step for improved performance. As a final step, a MRF formulation for labeling pixels is proposed. Our pipeline also contains this post processing step to obtain individual stereo reconstructions that are subsequently merged.

3   Overview of the Approach

We propose a structure and motion framework that is able to automatically recover the camera positions and orientations along with a piecewise planar reconstruction (PPR) of the scene from a stereo sequence. For each stereo pair, a semi-dense reconstruction is obtained using a simplified version of the algorithm described in section 2.2. The motion between consecutive frames is initialized in a RANSAC-like framework, where plane primitives are favoured over point correspondences. A sliding window approach is then used in an optimization step where the energy-based multi-model fitting algorithm PEARL [15] is applied.

3.1   Semi-dense PPR from a Single Stereo Pair

For each stereo pair, a semi-dense piecewise planar reconstruction of the 3D scene is obtained (Fig. 2(a)). This is done by using a modified version of the method proposed in [2] and briefly reviewed in section 2.2. The original work formulates the multi-model plane fitting as an optimization problem using the PEARL algorithm. However, this problem can be cast as a UFL problem whenever no smoothness term is considered. This provides a less accurate but sufficiently good semi-dense PPR of the scene, being much faster than the original method.

3.2   PPR from a Stereo Sequence

Our algorithm takes as input the semi-dense labeling computed individually for each stereo pair i and a set of plane hypotheses $\mathbf{\Pi}_k^i, k = 1, \ldots K$, and outputs the semi-dense labeling of a sequence of stereo pairs in conjunction with the relative pose between the consecutive pairs in the sequence, as illustrated in Fig. 2(b).

Although the explanation is given for a sequence of only two stereo pairs, it is extended to longer sequences in a straightforward manner. Our method consists of two main steps, which are an initialization of the relative pose $\mathsf{R}_i, \mathsf{t}_i$ between cameras C_i and C_{i+1}, and a subsequent bundle adjustment step that alternates between discrete and continuous optimization for refining pose and structure.

The relative pose estimation is carried out using the planes from stereo pairs i and $i + 1$ in a hierarchical scheme in the sense that it is obtained using the highest possible number of corresponding planes. A detailed explanation of this step is given in section 4. The energy-based multi-model fitting algorithm PEARL is applied in the optimization step. It consists of a discrete optimization step, where planes detected in cameras C_i and C_{i+1} are assigned to pixels of the cyclopean eye of those cameras, by minimizing an energy function with data, smoothness and label terms. Next, the chosen planes and the relative pose are jointly optimized in the continuous step. Further details are given in section 5.

For visualization purposes, a dense labeling for each stereo pair is generated in a MRF approach. By concatenating the individual reconstructions, it is possible to obtain a dense piecewise planar reconstruction for the complete sequence.

4   Relative Pose Estimation

Consider two consecutive stereo pairs C_i and C_{i+1} and two sets of plane detections. Let $\mathbf{\Pi}_k^{(i)}$ and $\mathbf{\Pi}_k^{(i+1)}$, with $k = 1 \ldots K$ be putative plane correspondences across the two pairs. Our objective is to use these plane correspondences to estimate the relative pose $(\mathsf{R}_i, \mathsf{t}_i)$ between the stereo cameras. In [13], it was first shown that two sets of 3D planes can be registered in a closed-form manner from a minimum of 3 correspondences as long as their normals span the entire 3D space. More recently, Taguchi et al. [24] used this registration algorithm as a starting point for their plane-based SLAM method for RGB-D cameras. They studied the singular configurations and showed how to use reconstructed

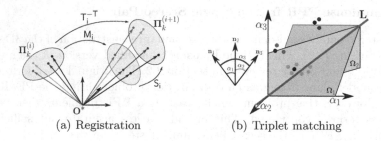

(a) Registration   (b) Triplet matching

Fig. 3. (a) The relative pose estimation can be cast as a point registration problem in the dual projective space $\mathcal{P}^{3*}$. (b) A descriptor is computed for the plane triplets and used in a nearest-neighbors approach for finding putative matches between the planes. Similarities between angles in the descriptor give rise to different hypotheses, depicted by the points near planes Ω_1 and Ω_2 and line L.

3D points to disambiguate motion whenever the information provided by planes was insufficient. We revisit this registration problem and show how to disambiguate the motion by directly using inter-stereo image point correspondences, in order to avoid having to reconstruct points from passive stereo.

4.1   Relative Pose from 3 Plane Correspondences

The registration problem between stereo pairs i and $i+1$ is the one of estimating R_i and $\mathbf{t}_i$ such that

$$\mathbf{\Pi}_k^{(i+1)} \sim \underbrace{\begin{bmatrix} R_i & \mathbf{0} \\ -\mathbf{t}_i^\mathsf{T} R_i & 1 \end{bmatrix}}_{T_i^{-\mathsf{T}}} \mathbf{\Pi}_k^{(i)} \sim \underbrace{\begin{bmatrix} I_3 & \mathbf{0} \\ -\mathbf{t}_i^\mathsf{T} & 1 \end{bmatrix}}_{S_i} \underbrace{\begin{bmatrix} R_i & \mathbf{0} \\ \mathbf{0} & 1 \end{bmatrix}}_{M_i} \mathbf{\Pi}_k^{(i)}, k = 1, 2, 3 \qquad (1)$$

verifies, where I_3 is the 3×3 identity matrix, and the 3D planes have the homogeneous representation $\mathbf{\Pi}_k^{(i)} \sim [\mathbf{n}_k^\mathsf{T} \ 1]^\mathsf{T}$ and $\mathbf{\Pi}_k^{(i+1)} \sim [\mathbf{m}_k^\mathsf{T} \ 1]^\mathsf{T}$. Knowing that points and planes are dual entities in 3D - a plane in the projective space $\mathcal{P}^3$ is represented as a point in the dual space $\mathcal{P}^{3*}$, and vice-versa - equation (1) can be seen as a projective transformation in $\mathcal{P}^{3*}$ that maps points $\mathbf{\Pi}_k^{(i)}$ into points $\mathbf{\Pi}_k^{(i+1)}$ through a rotation transformation M_i followed by a projective scaling S_i, as is illustrated in Fig. 3(a). R_i is firstly computed by applying the algorithm from [14] that provides a unique solution for aligning two sets of unitary vectors.

By replacing R_i in equation (1), it can be shown after some algebraic manipulation that $\mathbf{t}_i$ is computed by solving the following linear system of equations

$$\underbrace{\begin{bmatrix} \mathbf{m}_1^\mathsf{T}\mathbf{m}_1 & 0 & 0 \\ 0 & \mathbf{m}_2^\mathsf{T}\mathbf{m}_2 & 0 \\ 0 & 0 & \mathbf{m}_3^\mathsf{T}\mathbf{m}_3 \end{bmatrix} \begin{bmatrix} \mathbf{n}_1^\mathsf{T} \\ \mathbf{n}_2^\mathsf{T} \\ \mathbf{n}_3^\mathsf{T} \end{bmatrix}}_{N_i} R_i^\mathsf{T}\mathbf{t}_i = \begin{bmatrix} \mathbf{m}_1^\mathsf{T}\mathbf{m}_1 - \mathbf{m}_1^\mathsf{T}R_i\mathbf{n}_1 \\ \mathbf{m}_2^\mathsf{T}\mathbf{m}_2 - \mathbf{m}_2^\mathsf{T}R_i\mathbf{n}_2 \\ \mathbf{m}_3^\mathsf{T}\mathbf{m}_3 - \mathbf{m}_3^\mathsf{T}R_i\mathbf{n}_3 \end{bmatrix}. \qquad (2)$$

From this equation, it comes in a straightforward manner that if the three normals do not span the entire 3D space, then N_i is rank deficient and the problem of determining the translation becomes underdetermined.

4.2   Relative Pose Estimation in Case N_i Has Rank 2

The matrix of the normal vectors N_i can have rank 2 whenever there are only two corresponding planes available or the three planes have a configuration such that their normals are co-planar. An example of this situation happens when at least two planes are parallel. The rotation R_i is estimated using Horn's algorithm [14] since two corresponding planes suffice. However, there is a 2D space for translation, and thus there is one remaining DOF to be estimated. Given an image point correspondence $x^{(i)}, x^{(i+1)}$ between the reference views of the two stereo pairs C_i and C_{i+1}, the translation t_i can be fully determined by stacking the epipolar constraint $x^{(i+1)^T} E_i x^{(i)} = 0$, where $E_i = [t_i]_\times R_i$ is the essential matrix, to the two linear constraints in equation 2.

4.3   Relative Pose Estimation in Case N_i Has Rank 1

Whenever there is a single plane correspondence or the putative plane correspondences are all parallel, the registration leads to the computation of 2 DOF for the rotation. In this case N_i has rank 1, and thus 1 DOF for the translation can be estimated. We show for the first time that in this case the relative pose can be determined from a minimum of 3 additional image point correspondences $x_k^{(i)}, x_k^{(i+1)}$, $k = 1 \ldots 3$. Related to this problem is the work described in [8], where a minimal solution for the case of two known orientation angles is given. Our problem differs from it because we have an extra constraint for the translation.

Our reasoning is explained in the 3D space instead of the dual space. Both stereo cameras C_i and C_{i+1} are independently rotated so that the z axes of their reference views are aligned with the plane normal, through transformations P_i and P_{i+1}. This implies that the rotated cameras become related by an unknown rotation around the z axis, $R_u(\theta)$, and a translation $t_u = [t_x \quad t_y \quad t_z]^T$, where t_z can be computed as follows. In the rotated configuration, equation 1 becomes

$$\begin{bmatrix} 0 \\ 0 \\ z_2 \\ 1 \end{bmatrix} \sim \begin{bmatrix} R_u & \mathbf{0} \\ -[t_x \quad t_y \quad t_z]R_u & 1 \end{bmatrix} \begin{bmatrix} 0 \\ 0 \\ z_1 \\ 1 \end{bmatrix}. \tag{3}$$

Thus, t_z can be determined by $t_z = -\frac{z_1/z_2 - 1}{z_1}$. The remaining 3 DOF ($\theta$, t_x and t_y) can then be determined from 3 point correspondences using the epipolar constraint. The essential matrix E_i has a simplified form as in [8], allowing the epipolar constraint to be written as $A[t_x \quad t_y \quad 1]^T = \mathbf{0}$, where the 3×3-matrix A depends on θ, which can be computed using the hidden variable method. This originates up to 4 solutions for the motion in the rotated configuration, T_u. The real motion T_i can then be retrieved by simply computing $T_i = P_{i+1}^{-1} T_u P_i$.

4.4   Robust Algorithm for Computing the Relative Pose

Our relative pose estimation algorithm uses an hierarchical RANSAC scheme that works by considering the maximum number of planes present in the image pair, and only using point correspondences when strictly necessary. It first attempts to compute the pose from 3 plane correspondences, using subsequently less plane correspondences in case of failure, meaning that it tries to carry the registration with 2 planes and 1 point, and if this fails, with 1 plane and 3 points.

The method starts by building a descriptor (refer to Fig. 3(b))) for matching triplets of planes, which consists of the 3 angles between the plane normals sorted by increasing value, in both stereo pairs. Putative matches are established using a nearest neighbors approach. Remark that the descriptor implicitly establishes plane correspondences between elements in the triplet and that typically there is a relatively small number of triplets for each view. In case the angles in the descriptor are sufficiently different from each other, the descriptor establishes plane correspondences directly. However, if two of the angles are similar, two possible sets of element-wise correspondences are considered. This is the case in Fig. 3(b) where the point in the descriptor space is close to plane Ω_2 that defines $\alpha_1 = \alpha_2$ (and identical for plane Ω_1 that defines $\alpha_2 = \alpha_3$). Similarly, if all three angles are close, six possible hypotheses for matches must be considered. This is the case when the point is close to the line L that defines $\alpha_1 = \alpha_2 = \alpha_3$.

For each triple correspondence, a solution is computed using the procedure in subsection 4.1. The semi-dense PPR step generates a set of line cuts in each frame associated to each reconstructed scene plane. A patch containing the pixels around the projection of each line cut in the left image of camera C_i is selected and projected onto the left image of camera C_{i+1}, using the homography induced by the respective plane. Line cuts that have a photo-geometric error below a predefined threshold are considered for computing a score ϵ.

The pose estimation is performed in a RANSAC framework. If there are no matching triplets of planes or the number of inlier line cuts for the computed solutions originates a score too low, the algorithm attempts to use 2 plane correspondences. A descriptor consisting of the angle between the 2 plane normals is considered for both stereo pairs and matches are established using a nearest-neighbors approach. Since there is only one angle, each match gives rise to two hypotheses. A local feature detector (SURF [5]) is used for extracting point features and solutions are computed in a RANSAC framework from two planes and one point correspondences (subsection 4.2). The models' inliers are computed as in the previous stage. Similarly, if there are no acceptable corresponding pairs of planes, the motion is estimated using one plane and three point-correspondences, as described in subsection 4.3. Note that in theory the scoring metric might fail if the planes surfaces lack texture. An hybrid score metric that mixes planes and points raises other type of issues, such as normalization. The metric used in this work always provided acceptable results, and thus it was kept unaltered.

5 Discrete-Continuous Bundle Adjustment

This section describes the optimization step that is carried for jointly refining the motion and the piecewise planar structure. From the previous single stereo PPR and relative pose estimation steps come two sets of planes defined in the reference frames of cameras C_i and C_{i+1}, $\mathbf{\Pi}_k^{(i)}, k = 1 \ldots K_i$ and $\mathbf{\Pi}_k^{(i+1)}, k = 1 \ldots K_{i+1}$, respectively, and an initialization for the relative pose R_i, $\mathbf{t}_i$ between the cameras. The optimization is achieved using the PEARL algorithm that consists in three steps: (i) propose an initial set of plausible models (labels) from the data, (ii) expand the label set for estimating its spatial support (inlier classification), and (iii) re-estimate the inlier models by minimizing some error function.

The initial set of plane models $\mathcal{P}_0$ for PEARL is the union of the $(K_i + K_{i+1})$ planes detected in each stereo pair separately. Then, the objective is to expand the models and estimate their spatial support. Consider the cyclopean eye relative to camera i, whose back-projection rays are denoted by $\mathbf{d}_{j,r}^{(i)}$, where r indexes a particular epipolar plane (refer to section 2.2). The objective is to estimate the point on $\mathbf{d}_{j,r}^{(i)}$ that most likely belongs to a planar surface. As stated previously, this problem can be cast as a labeling problem, in which the nodes of the graph are the back-projection rays $\mathbf{d}_{j,r}^{(i)} \in \mathcal{D}$, and to which we want to assign a plane label $f_{\mathbf{d}_{j,r}^{(i)}}$. The set of possible labels is $\mathcal{F} = \{\mathcal{P}_0, f_\emptyset\}$, where $f_\emptyset$ is the discard label and is mostly used for identifying non-planar structures. This labeling problem is solved by minimizing an energy function E defined by

$$E(\mathbf{f}) = \underbrace{\sum_i \sum_{\mathbf{d}_{j,r}^{(i)} \in \mathcal{D}} D_{\mathbf{d}_{j,r}^{(i)}}(f_{\mathbf{d}_{j,r}^{(i)}})}_{\text{data term}} + \lambda_S \underbrace{\sum_i \sum_{\mathbf{d}_{j,r}^{(i)}, \mathbf{e}_{j,r}^{(i)} \in \mathcal{N}} V_{\mathbf{d}_{j,r}^{(i)}, \mathbf{e}_{j,r}^{(i)}}(f_{\mathbf{d}_{j,r}^{(i)}}, f_{\mathbf{e}_{j,r}^{(i)}})}_{\text{smoothness term}} + \underbrace{\lambda_L \cdot |\mathcal{F}_f|}_{\text{label term}},$$

(4)

where λ_S and λ_L are weighting constants, $\mathbf{f}$ is the labeling being analyzed, $\mathcal{N}$ is the neighborhood of $\mathbf{d}_{j,r}^{(i)}$ and V is the spacial smoothness term. The label term forces the algorithm to use as few plane surfaces as possible. The data term $D_{\mathbf{d}_{j,r}^{(i)}}$ for the back-projection ray $\mathbf{d}_{j,r}^{(i)}$ is defined as

$$D_{\mathbf{d}_{j,r}^{(i)}}(f) = \begin{cases} \min(1 - \mathrm{E}_j^{(i)}(r, x_f), \tau) & \text{if } f \in \mathcal{P}_0 \\ \tau & \text{if } f = f_\emptyset \end{cases}$$

where the coordinate x_f is the column defined by the hypothesis f, corresponding to the intersection of $\mathbf{d}_{j,r}^{(i)}$ with the plane indexed by f. Using the camera pose, we can transform the planes detected in the stereo rig $i + 1$ to the stereo rig i, and vice versa. This allows us to use all the structure information available simultaneously and reconstruct planes in a particular view even if they were detected by a different camera. The smoothness term V is used to describe the relationships between nodes. No penalization is assigned to neighboring nodes receiving the same plane label, while in the case of one node obtaining the discard label, a non-zero cost is added to the plane configuration $\mathbf{f}$. For each camera i, the smoothness term V is defined as in [2], which encourages label transitions near crease or occlusions edges . For further details refer to that work.

The output of this step is a set of planes shared by cameras C_i and C_{i+1}. Given the inliers of a particular plane label f, the corresponding energies $\mathbf{E}^{(i)}$ can be recomputed to enhance the likelihood measure with respect to a particular range of slant values [4]. These energies are used in the third step of PEARL.

Let $\mathbf{\Pi}_f$ be the plane associated to f to which has been assigned a non-empty set of inliers $\mathbf{D}(f) = \{\mathbf{d} \in \mathcal{D} | f_{\mathbf{d}} = f\}$. All the inlier planes $\{\mathbf{\Pi}_{f_k}\}$ and the relative pose R_i, $\mathbf{t}_i$ are refined simultaneously by minimizing the error function:

$$\{\mathsf{R}_i^*, \mathbf{t}_i^*, \{\mathbf{\Pi}_{f_k}^*\}\} = \min_{\mathsf{R}_i, \mathbf{t}_i, \{\mathbf{\Pi}_{f_k}\}} \sum_i \sum_k \sum_{\mathbf{d}_{j,r}^{(i)} \in \mathbf{D}(f)} \left(1 - \mathbf{E}_j^{(i)}(r, x_{\mathbf{\Pi}_{f_k}})\right) + \delta e_{ph}, \quad (5)$$

where $x_{\mathbf{\Pi}_{f_k}}$ is the column defined by the intersection of $\mathbf{d}_{j,r}^{(i)}$ with $\mathbf{\Pi}_{f_k}$, δ is a parameter that is zero whenever the optimization is carried out using 3 shared planes that span the 3D space and larger than zero otherwise, and e_{ph} is the photo-consistency error computed in a planar patch. The new set of plane labels $\mathcal{P}_1 = \left\{\mathbf{\Pi}_{f_k}^*\right\}$ is then used in a new expand step, and we iterate between discrete labeling and plane refinement until the α-expansion optimization does not decrease the energy of Equation 4.

A sliding window approach is applied where at most one relative pose is refined. The exchange of planes between cameras, described previously, has an important role in the 3D modeling process since it allows planar surfaces that are only properly detected in subsequent frames to be back-propagated and accurately reconstructed in previous images. Remark that plane information is only exchanged between different cameras inside the sliding window. In order to overcome this issue, a connected list is maintained containing the plane linking information across views and is updated whenever a new plane is back-propagated inside the considered window of cameras.

6   Experimental Results

In this section several experiments are shown in order to highlight the different advantages of the proposed method. The datasets were acquired using a stereo camera with a 24 cm baseline and a resolution of 1024×768 pixels. Experiments on short sequences of 3 to 6 images are presented, and the motion estimation is compared to the result obtained with the point-based method LIBVISO2 [12] (Fig. 4). LIBVISO2 only leads to plausible results in some of the experiments, in which cases the images of the 3D reconstructions include camera symbols in red and blue, if they were computed using our algorithm or LIBVISO2, respectively. For every experiment, the left images of all the stereo pairs that were used are shown with the overlaid MRF labeling, where each color identifies one plane.

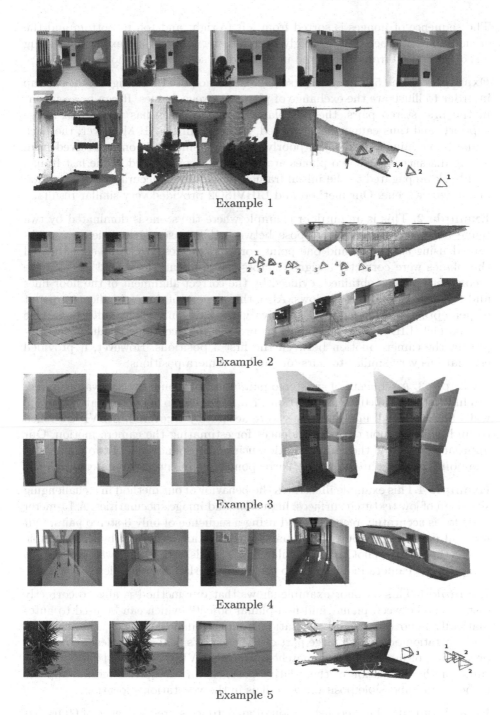

Example 1

Example 2

Example 3

Example 4

Example 5

Fig. 4. Structure and motion results, different colors identify different planes. Red/blue cameras represent the motion computed using our approach/LIBVISO2.

The sequence of images is sorted from left to right and top to bottom and the cameras are numbered accordingly. A 140-meter loop-closing experiment using a sequence of 60 frames acquired in an outdoor scene is also shown (Fig. 5).

Example 1. The 5-frame stereo sequence was acquired with significant overlap in order to illustrate the exchange of planes between frames. It can be seen that in the first stereo pairs, the top plane of the entrance has very small image support, and thus cannot be recovered, as shown in Fig. 1. Moreover, the back plane (containing the door) is poorly estimated since it is only observed from a long distance. These two planes are correctly reconstructed in the last frame, and back propagated to the initial frames, providing an accurate reconstruction of the whole scene. Our method and LIBVISO2 provided very similar results.

Example 2. This is an outdoor example where the scene is dominated by two plane directions. The relative pose between the consecutive cameras was obtained using two plane and one point correspondences. It can be seen that all the planes were correctly assigned across the different views, and an accurate reconstruction was obtained, evinced by the correct alignment of the floor lines and the detection of the windows. Also, this scene contains a significant amount of perceptual aliasing since consecutive views have only slight differences. Due to this fact, LIBVISO2 was unable to provide an acceptable result when computing the camera motion between the first 3 positions. However, it provided estimations very similar to ours for the last camera positions.

Example 3. A sequence of six stereo pairs with minimum overlap was acquired, originating a detailed reconstruction of a door. It can be seen that the white walls and the small interior planes were accurately recovered. LIBVISO2 failed to find sufficient point correspondences for estimating the camera motion. Our approach computed the camera motion using correspondences of two planes and one point, as there are no triplet correspondences in consecutive stereo pairs.

Example 4. This example illustrates the behavior of our method in a challenging situation of low textured surfaces, high slant and image specularities. A 14-meter corridor is accurately reconstructed using a sequence of only 3 stereo pairs. Our method does not rely on the Manhattan assumption, as shown by this example where the board is not perpendicular to the walls. LIBVISO2 was not able to compute the camera motion due to the small overlap between views.

Example 5. This outdoor example shows that our method is able to correctly distinguish between planar and non-planar objects, which can be used to automatically remove trees and vegetation from the final 3D model. The fact that the vegetation occupies a large part of the camera's field of view leads to a large percentage of incorrect point matches. Thus, LIBVISO2 provided very poor results for the estimation of the relative pose. As an example, camera 3 appears to be in an impossible position since it is in the vegetation's location.

Final Example. The reconstruction of an outdoor stereo sequence of 60 frames is shown in Fig. 5. The camera traveled 136.6 meters in loop, and the final loop closing error was 2.17% in translation and 2.67% in rotation. For validation and

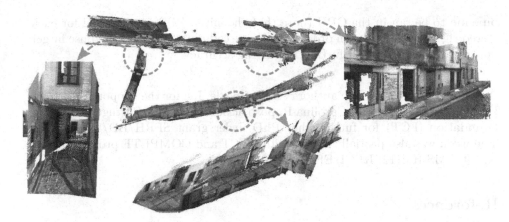

Fig. 5. Final example of a 137-meter loop closing experiment. Despite the challenging conditions, a good 3D reconstruction of the whole scene was obtained. A video is attached as supplementary material where some results can be seen in more detail.

computational time purposes, the selected size of the optimization window is two. The trajectory can be seen in the top view of the reconstructed scene, depicted by red camera symbols, showing that there is a large displacement between most of the positions, which translates into small overlap between consecutive stereo pairs. Moreover, the camera usually pointed forward, meaning that the algorithm dealt with strong surface slant. Under these circumstances, it was able to provide an accurate reconstruction of the scene. Images in different viewpoints are included to better illustrate the obtained results, where good alignment can be observed. Due to this acquisition conditions, LIBVISO2 was unable to find sufficient point matches to provide a plausible motion estimation.

7 Conclusions

We describe the first pipeline for sequential piecewise-planar reconstruction from images acquired by a moving stereo rig. The relative pose between consecutive frames is preferentially estimated using plane-primitives, and motion and structure are jointly refined within a PEARL framework [15] that alternates between discrete optimization to enforce coherent PPR across stereo frames, and continuous bundle adjustment to improve the accuracy of results. The experiments show that the use of plane-primitives to recover camera motion enables to handle sequences with little overlap that are very challenging for conventional SfM approaches. The approach proved to successfully handle situations of weak texture, high surface slant, repetitive structure, and non-lambertian reflection, being able to render detailed piecewise-planar models of the scene in cases of minimum visual coverage. We are using a straightforward MATLAB implementation for validation purposes. For getting an idea about the current runtime, our pipeline took around 2 hours for computing the motion and reconstructing the scene depicted in Fig. 5. As future work, we intend to develop a parallel version of the pipeline to be ran in the GPU (note that the initial PPR is computed for each stereo rig independently) in order to decrease computational time and use larger optimization windows for further improving accuracy.

Acknowledgments. The authors thank Google, Inc for the support through a Faculty Research Award. Carolina Raposo acknowledges the Portuguese Science Foundation (FCT) for funding her PhD under grant SFRH/BD/88446/2012. The work was also partially supported by FCT and COMPETE program under Grant AMS-HMI12: RECI/EEI-AUT/0181/2012.

References

1. P.F. Alcantarilla, C. Beall, F. Dellaert.: Large-scale dense 3D reconstruction from stereo imagery. In: 5th Workshop on Planning, Perception and Navigation for Intelligent Vehicles (PPNIV13) (2013)
2. Antunes, M., Barreto, J.P.: Semi-dense piecewise planar stereo reconstruction using symstereo and pearl. In: 3DimPVT (2012)
3. Antunes, M., Barreto, J.P., Zabulis, X.: Plane surface detection and reconstruction using induced stereo symmetry. In: BMVC (2011)
4. Antunes, M.: Phd thesis: Stereo reconstruction using induced symmetry and 3D scene priors (2014), http://www2.isr.uc.pt/~michel/files/final.pdf
5. Bay, H., Ess, A., Tuytelaars, T., Gool, L.V.: Speeded-up robust features (surf). Comput. Vis. Image Underst. 110(3), 346–359 (2008)
6. Delong, A., Osokin, A., Isack, H., Boykov, Y.: Fast approximate energy minimization with label costs. International Journal of Computer Vision 96(1), 1–27 (2012), http://dx.doi.org/10.1007/s11263-011-0437-z
7. Dunn, E., Clipp, B., Frahm, J.M.: A geometric solver for calibrated stereo egomotion. In: 2011 IEEE International Conference on Computer Vision (ICCV), pp. 1187–1194 (November 2011)
8. Fraundorfer, F., Tanskanen, P., Pollefeys, M.: A minimal case solution to the calibrated relative pose problem for the case of two known orientation angles. In: Daniilidis, K., Maragos, P., Paragios, N. (eds.) ECCV 2010, Part IV. LNCS, vol. 6314, pp. 269–282. Springer, Heidelberg (2010)
9. Furukawa, Y., Curless, B., Seitz, S., Szeliski, R.: Manhattan-world stereo. In: IEEE Conference on Computer Vision and Pattern Recognition, CVPR 2009, pp. 1422–1429 (June 2009)
10. Furukawa, Y., Curless, B., Seitz, S., Szeliski, R.: Reconstructing building interiors from images. In: 2009 IEEE 12th International Conference on Computer Vision, pp. 80–87 (September 2009)
11. Gallup, D., Frahm, J.M., Pollefeys, M.: Piecewise planar and non-planar stereo for urban scene reconstruction. In: 2010 IEEE Conference on Computer Vision and Pattern Recognition (CVPR), pp. 1418–1425 (June 2010)
12. Geiger, A., Ziegler, J., Stiller, C.: Stereoscan: Dense 3D reconstruction in real-time. In: Intelligent Vehicles Symposium (IV) (2011)
13. Grimson, W., Lozano-Pérez, T.: Model-based recognition and localization from sparse range or tactile data. International Journal of Robotics Research 3(3), 3–35 (1984), http://lis.csail.mit.edu/pubs/tlp/AIM-738.pdf

14. Horn, B.K.P.: Closed-form solution of absolute orientation using unit quaternions. J. Opt. Soc. Am. A 4(4), 629–642 (1987)
15. Isack, H., Boykov, Y.: Energy-based geometric multi-model fitting. IJCV (2012)
16. Kazik, T., Kneip, L., Nikolic, J., Pollefeys, M., Siegwart, R.: Real-time 6D stereo visual odometry with non-overlapping fields of view. In: 2012 IEEE Conference on Computer Vision and Pattern Recognition (CVPR), pp. 1529–1536 (June 2012)
17. Lazic, N., Frey, B.J., Aarabi, P.: Solving the uncapacitated facility location problem using message passing algorithms. Journal of Machine Learning Research (2010)
18. Micusik, B., Kosecka, J.: Piecewise planar city 3d modeling from street view panoramic sequences. In: 2009 IEEE Conference on Computer Vision and Pattern Recognition, CVPR 2009, pp. 2906–2912 (June 2009)
19. Nister, D., Naroditsky, O., Bergen, J.: Visual odometry. In: Proceedings of the 2004 IEEE Computer Society Conference on Computer Vision and Pattern Recognition, CVPR 2004, vol. 1, pp. I-652–I-659 (June 2004)
20. Pathak, K., Birk, A., Vaskevicius, N., Poppinga., J.: Fast registration based on noisy planes with unknown correspondences for 3D mapping. IEEE Transactions on Robotics 26(3), 424–441 (2010)
21. Raposo, C., Lourenco, M., Antunes, M., Barreto, J.P.: Plane-based odometry using an rgb-d camera, pp. 1–11 (September 2013)
22. Sinha, S., Steedly, D., Szeliski, R.: Piecewise planar stereo for image-based rendering. In: 2009 IEEE 12th International Conference on Computer Vision, pp. 1881–1888 (September)
23. Snavely, N., Seitz, S.M., Szeliski, R.: Modeling the world from internet photo collections. Int. J. Comput. Vision 80(2), 189–210 (2008), http://dx.doi.org/10.1007/s11263-007-0107-3
24. Taguchi, Y., Jian, Y.D., Ramalingam, S., Feng, C.: Slam using both points and planes for hand held 3d sensors. In: Proceedings of the 2012 IEEE International Symposium on Mixed and Augmented Reality, ISMAR 2012, pp. 321–322. IEEE Computer Society, Washington, DC (2012), http://dx.doi.org/10.1109/ISMAR.2012.6402594
25. Vasconcelos, F., Barreto, J., Nunes, U.: A minimal solution for the extrinsic calibration of a camera and a laser-rangefinder. IEEE Transactions on Pattern Analysis and Machine Intelligence PP(99), 1 (2012)
26. Werner, T., Zisserman, A.: New techniques for automated architectural reconstruction from photographs. In: Heyden, A., Sparr, G., Nielsen, M., Johansen, P. (eds.) ECCV 2002, Part II, LNCS, vol. 2351, pp. 541–555. Springer, Heidelberg (2002), http://dl.acm.org/citation.cfm?id=645316.649194

Nonrigid Surface Registration and Completion from RGBD Images*

Weipeng Xu[1,2], Mathieu Salzmann[2,3], Yongtian Wang[1], and Yue Liu[1]

[1] School of Optoelectronics, Beijing Institute of Technology (BIT), China
[2] NICTA, Canberra, Australia
[3] Australian National University (ANU), Australia

Abstract. Nonrigid surface registration is a challenging problem that suffers from many ambiguities. Existing methods typically assume the availability of full volumetric data, or require a global model of the surface of interest. In this paper, we introduce an approach to nonrigid registration that performs on relatively low-quality RGBD images and does not assume prior knowledge of the global surface shape. To this end, we model the surface as a collection of patches, and infer the patch deformations by performing inference in a graphical model. Our representation lets us fill in the holes in the input depth maps, thus essentially achieving surface completion. Our experimental evaluation demonstrates the effectiveness of our approach on several sequences, as well as its robustness to missing data and occlusions.

Keywords: Nonrigid registration, surface completion, RGBD images.

1 Introduction

Shape registration is a crucial process when handling sequences of 3D data. It allows us to progress from observing a set of unrelated point clouds to having a coherent 4D (space and time) shape representation, thus opening the way to a better understanding of the dynamic scene at hand. In the rigid scenario, many mature techniques are now available (e.g., [14,7]). Here, we focus on the challenging problem of nonrigid surface registration, which has many more degrees of freedom and typically suffers from many ambiguities.

In the nonrigid case, much of the existing literature has focused on registering volumetric data, where the point clouds represent (the surface of) a full 3D volume (e.g., [4,3,40,13,19,25,29]). Such volumetric data is typically acquired with multiple cameras placed around the scene of interest. Therefore, given sufficiently many cameras, it comes with relatively low noise and few holes in the point clouds. With the recent availability of low-cost RGBD sensors, 3D data can be acquired in much less constraining environments. However, this comes at the cost of (i) only having

---

* Electronic supplementary material -Supplementary material is available in the online version of this chapter at http://dx.doi.org/10.1007/978-3-319-10605-2_5. Videos can also be accessed at http://www.springerimages.com/videos/978-3-319-10604-5

D. Fleet et al. (Eds.): ECCV 2014, Part II, LNCS 8690, pp. 64–79, 2014.
© Springer International Publishing Switzerland 2014

(a) Input RGB image   (b) Side view of the input data   (c) Our registration result

Fig. 1. Nonrigid surface registration and completion: Given noisy RGBD images, such as the one depicted by (a) and (b), our approach computes a coherent shape across the images and lets us fill in the missing observations.

access to the 3D measurements of an inherently 2D surface instead of a 3D volume; and **(ii)** having to handle much noisier data with potentially many missing observations. While some techniques perform registration in this setting, with the exception of [10,11], they either acquire a model of the surface as a pre-processing step [15,16,6], or are designed for specific shapes, such as the human body [31].

In this paper, we introduce an approach to nonrigid surface registration from RGBD images that does not rely on a global surface model. To this end, we represent the observed surface as a collection of deformable patches. This makes our approach agnostic to the specific shape of the surface and thus applicable in more general scenarios. Furthermore, our patch-based representation gives us the means to fill in the gaps in the observations, and thus perform shape completion, as well as to account for newly visible surface parts in an online manner.

More specifically, we express nonrigid registration as an inference problem in a Conditional Markov Random Field (CRF) where each node represents a surface patch. The variables in our CRF are continuous and encode the deformations of the patches. This lets us formulate an energy function that comprises terms such as color constancy, coherence of the predicted 3D patches with the observed depth, surface smoothness and coherence across neighboring patches. The resulting energy is pairwise, which lets us employ a Fusion Moves strategy [18] to perform inference in our continuous CRF.

We evaluate our formulation on several sequences of deforming surfaces, such as the one depicted in Fig. 1. Our experiments evidence the benefits of our approach over model-free and model-based baselines in various scenarios including missing data and occlusions.

2   Related Work

In recent years, nonrigid registration has received a lot of attention. In particular, many methods have focused on the problem of registering, or matching, point clouds representing the surface of an entire 3D volume [4,3,40,13,19,25,29]. In this context, a patch-based representation of the surface was also employed in [4]. Note, however, that, in contrast to our deformable patches, the patches in [4] were assumed to move quasi-rigidly. More importantly, the above-mentioned techniques, as well as others designed for depth maps [20], ignore all appearance information of the object of interest. In [36,8,33], appearance was further included in the registration process. However, since the volumetric data was acquired with a multi-camera setup, the resulting techniques were able to exploit multiple views of the surface. In contrast, here, we make use of a low-cost RGBD sensor that only provides us with a single view of the surface, and whose 3D measurements are therefore not volumetric.

The measurements acquired with depth sensors are known to be noisy and to suffer from missing data. As a consequence, many techniques perform shape completion and denoising by fusing multiple depth images of the same scene [30,5]. This was further extended to incorporating appearance information in the fusion process [38,24]. While the previous methods rely on the availability of multiple depth maps of a rigid scene, depth super-resolution has also recently been investigated in the single image scenario. However, existing techniques require either having access to a large number of depth exemplars [21], or that the scene is redundant (i.e., has some repetitive patterns) [12].

Registering multiple depth maps to simultaneously perform denoising and build a model of a large scene has also been investigated [14,7]. While effective for rigid scenes, these techniques currently mostly treat nonrigid components as noise in the scene [17]. In [39], the nonrigid (articulated) case was explicitly handled. However, this was achieved by combining the information from multiple Kinects simultaneously acquiring images from different viewpoints.

Here, we aim to perform nonrigid registration from a single depth sensor. While some methods have been proposed to tackle this scenario, most of them rely on a global model of the observed shape. For instance, the technique of [31] is specifically designed for human pose estimation. While dealing with more general shapes, [6] relies on acquiring the global shape model from a separate RGBD sequence. In contrast, [15,16] build the shape model from the first frame of the sequence. However, this assumes that all parts of the surface are visible in this frame. To the best of our knowledge, [10,11] are the only RGBD-based methods that do not exploit knowledge of the shape at hand, and thus work in similar settings as our approach. Both methods, however, formulate the problem in terms of pixelwise flow, and thus are typically more sensitive to noise than model-based approaches.

Since RGBD sensors essentially provide us with 3D data corresponding to an inherently 2D surface (as opposed to full volumetric data), our work is also related to monocular nonrigid 3D reconstruction techniques [27]. These techniques can be categorized into template-based approaches [28,22,2] and nonrigid structure-from-motion methods [32,34,26,35,9]. Note that, in both classes, patch-based approaches were proposed [28,34,26]. As the name suggests, template-based methods make use of a reference model of the shape of interest. While nonrigid structure-from-motion techniques do not, they rely on tracking interest points across the sequence and are therefore sensitive to noise and occlusions. In contrast, since we exploit RGBD sensors that are now readily available in many scenarios, our approach can robustly track a surface throughout a sequence despite occlusions and missing data.

3   Nonrigid Surface Registration and Completion

We now present our approach to nonrigid surface registration. Ultimately, given a sequence of RGBD images depicting a deforming surface, our goal is to obtain a coherent surface representation across the entire sequence along with its deformations in each frame. We formulate this as nonrigid registration between pairs of neighboring frames, which lets us propagate information throughout the sequence. Note that, while we consider the video scenario, our registration approach could in principle be applied to any pair of images. In the remainder of this section, we first discuss our patch-based surface model and then describe our continuous CRF formulation of the nonrigid registration problem.

3.1   Nonrigid Patch-Based Surface Model

As mentioned earlier, we do not assume the availability of a global model of the surface of interest. This allows us to model surfaces of arbitrary shapes, and makes the design of deformation models easier. To this end, we represent the observed surface with a collection of overlapping, deformable patches.

Given an RGBD image of a nonrigid surface, we first compute a supervoxel segmentation of the observed data based on depth and color information [37]. Each supervoxel now corresponds to one patch in our representation. To parameterize the deformations of each patch, we make use of the linear deformation model of [28]. More specifically, each patch i is represented by a triangulated mesh with V vertices whose 3D coordinates are stored in the vector $\mathbf{m}_i \in \mathbb{R}^{3V}$. The deformation of this mesh can then be expressed as

$$\mathbf{m}_i = \mathbf{m}_i^0 + \Lambda \mathbf{c}_i \,, \tag{1}$$

where $\mathbf{m}_i^0$ is the rest shape of the mesh, Λ is the $3V \times Q$ matrix of deformation modes, and $\mathbf{c}_i \in \mathbb{R}^Q$ is the vector of mode coefficients determining the deformation. As in [28], the deformation modes were obtained by applying Principal Component Analysis (PCA) to a set of randomly generated deformations of $\mathbf{m}_i^0$.

In this formalism, our goal now is to fit 3D mesh patches to the observed supervoxels. To this end, we first perform a rigid registration by aligning the centroid and the normal vector of patch i to that of its corresponding supervoxel, which yields $\mathbf{m}_i^0$. From this first registration, we estimate the barycentric coordinates $\mathbf{b}_{i,j} \in \mathbb{R}^3$ with respect to $\mathbf{m}_i^0$ of each observed point $\mathbf{x}_{i,j}$ belonging to supervoxel i. These barycentric coordinates are obtained by casting a ray from $\mathbf{x}_{i,j}$ in the direction of the supervoxel normal and intersecting it with $\mathbf{m}_i^0$. They are thus given with respect to 3 mesh vertices. Fitting $\mathbf{m}_i$ to the supervoxel points $\mathbf{x}_i = [\mathbf{x}_{i,1}^T, \cdots, \mathbf{x}_{i,N_i}^T]^T$ can be expressed as the optimization problem

$$\min_{\mathbf{c}_i} \left\| \mathbf{B}_i \left(\mathbf{m}_i^0 + \Lambda \mathbf{c}_i \right) - \mathbf{x}_i \right\|^2 + w_r \left\| \Sigma^{-1/2} \mathbf{c}_i \right\|^2 \,, \tag{2}$$

where $\mathbf{B}_i$ is the $3N_i \times 3V$ matrix grouping the barycentric coordinates of all the points, w_r is a regularization weight[1], and Σ is the diagonal $Q \times Q$ matrix

---

[1] The weight w_r was set to 3 in all our experiments.

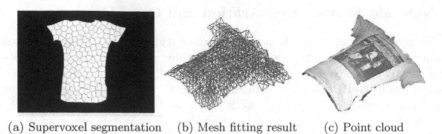

(a) Supervoxel segmentation   (b) Mesh fitting result   (c) Point cloud

Fig. 2. Mesh fitting: Given the supervoxel segmentation (a), we fit a mesh patch to each supervoxel. In (c), we visualize the surface points computed using barycentric coordinates with respect to the mesh vertices.

containing the eigenvalues obtained when applying PCA to the training meshes to create the deformation modes. These eigenvalues encode the importance of each mode on the deformation. Thus the second term in the objective function simply regularizes the deformation coefficients. Note that this optimization problem is a least-squares problem. Therefore, its solution can be obtained in closed-form. In Fig. 2, we illustrate the process of fitting patches to observed supervoxels.

3.2 Nonrigid Registration as Inference in a CRF

In this paper, we address nonrigid registration as an inference problem in a CRF with continuous variables. By making use of the model introduced in Section 3.1, we define each node in our CRF as one surface patch. We employ the mode coefficients c_i as random variable for node i, which can be thought of as a Q-dimensional continuous label.

Given two images I_0 and I_1 and their corresponding depth maps D_0 and D_1, the joint distribution over the deformation coefficients of the N surface patches registering frame 0 to frame 1 can be expressed as

$$P(\mathbf{c}|I_0, I_1, D_0, D_1) = \frac{1}{Z(\mathbf{c})} \exp\left(-\sum_{i=1}^{N} \phi_i(\mathbf{c}_i|I_0, I_1, D_0, D_1) - w_p \sum_{(i,i') \in \mathcal{E}} \phi_{ii'}(\mathbf{c}_i, \mathbf{c}_{i'})\right),$$

where $\phi_i(\cdot)$ is a unary potential function encoding the local evidence for a patch configuration, $\phi_{ii'}(\cdot, \cdot)$ is a pairwise potential function defined over the edges $\mathcal{E}$ of the CRF and accounting for the relation of two neighboring patches, w_p is a weight regulating the influence of both terms, and $Z(\cdot)$ is the partition function. Inference in the CRF is then performed by computing a MAP estimate of $\mathbf{c}$, which can be achieved by minimizing the corresponding energy

$$E(\mathbf{c}) = \sum_{i \in \mathcal{N}} \phi_i(\mathbf{c}_i|I_0, I_1, D_0, D_1) + w_p \sum_{(i,i') \in \mathcal{E}} \phi_{ii'}(\mathbf{c}_i, \mathbf{c}_{i'}). \tag{3}$$

In the remainder of this section, we describe our unary and pairwise potentials, as well as the inference strategy used to obtain a MAP estimate.

Unary Potential. Our unary potential comprises three terms, and can thus be expressed as

$$\phi_i(\mathbf{c}_i) = w_c \phi_i^c(\mathbf{c}_i) + w_d \phi_i^d(\mathbf{c}_i) + w_s \phi_i^s(\mathbf{c}_i) , \tag{4}$$

where we omitted the explicit dependencies on the images and depth maps for ease of notation. These three terms encode color constancy (ϕ_i^c), depth coherence (ϕ_i^d) and patch smoothness (ϕ_i^s), respectively.

The color constancy term ϕ_i^c measures the intensity disagreement between corresponding pixels in I_0 and I_1. To this end, let us define the function $\Pi(\cdot)$, which projects a 3D point to its 2D image coordinates. The projection of a 3D point $\mathbf{x} = [x, y, z]^T$ can thus be written as

$$\mathbf{u} = \Pi(\mathbf{x}) = \begin{pmatrix} \frac{x}{z} f_x + c_x \\ \frac{y}{z} f_y + c_y \end{pmatrix} , \tag{5}$$

where f_x and f_y are the focal lengths of the sensor, and c_x and c_y define the optical center. This lets us write our color constancy term as

$$\phi_i^c(\mathbf{c}_i) = \left\| I_1 \left(\Pi \left(\mathbf{B}_i(\mathbf{m}_i^0 + \Lambda \mathbf{c}_i) \right) \right) - I_0 \left(\Pi(\mathbf{B}_i \mathbf{m}_i^0) \right) \right\|_1 , \tag{6}$$

where $\mathbf{m}_i^0$ corresponds to the mesh configuration in frame 0 for patch i. Note that, to simplify notation, we assume that a vector input to the functions Π, I_0 and I_1 yields elementwise evaluations of the functions. Here, we utilize the ℓ_1 norm to increase the robustness of our method to outliers.

The depth coherence term ϕ_i^d penalizes depth disagreement between the deformed mesh patches and the target depth map D_1. By again making use of a robust ℓ_1 norm formulation, this term can be expressed as

$$\phi_i^d(\mathbf{c}_i) = \left\| D_1 \left(\Pi \left(\mathbf{B}_i(\mathbf{m}_i^0 + \Lambda \mathbf{c}_i) \right) \right) - \left(\mathbf{B}_i(\mathbf{m}_i^0 + \Lambda \mathbf{c}_i) \right)_z \right\|_1 , \tag{7}$$

where $(\cdot)_z$ extracts the z-components of the input vector.

Finally, the smoothness term ϕ_i^s penalizes large deviations of the deformation coefficients $\mathbf{c}_i$ from the training data. Similarly as in Section 3.1, this term can be expressed as

$$\phi_i^s(\mathbf{c}_i) = \left\| \Sigma^{-1/2} \mathbf{c}_i \right\|^2 , \tag{8}$$

and can be thought of as assuming a Q-dimensional zero-mean Gaussian prior on $\mathbf{c}_i$ with (diagonal) covariance Σ.

Pairwise Potential. Our unary potentials try to fit each individual mesh patch to the data observed in frame 1. Of course, this can be subject to ambiguities, since parts of the surface may be poorly-textured. This in turn would yield to inconsistencies between the different patches. To prevent these inconsistencies, we introduce a pairwise potential defined on adjacent mesh patches, i.e., patches that overlap when fitting the meshes to the supervoxels.

More specifically, let us denote by $\hat{\mathbf{x}}_{i,j}$ the 3D location of point j predicted by patch i. This prediction can be written as

$$\hat{\mathbf{x}}_{i,j} = \mathbf{B}_{i,j}(\mathbf{m}_i^0 + \Lambda \mathbf{c}_i) , \tag{9}$$

where $\mathbf{B}_{i,j}$ is the $3 \times 3V$ submatrix of $\mathbf{B}_i$ corresponding to point j. Similarly, if point j also belongs to patch i', we have the prediction

$$\hat{\mathbf{x}}_{i',j} = \mathbf{B}_{i',j}(\mathbf{m}_{i'}^0 + \Lambda \mathbf{c}_{i'}) \, . \tag{10}$$

To enforce coherence across adjacent patches, our pairwise potential therefore encourages these two predictions to agree. By summing over the $N_{i,i'}$ points in the overlap between patch i and patch i', this can be written as

$$\phi_{ii'}(\mathbf{c}_i, \mathbf{c}_{i'}) = \sum_{j=1}^{N_{i,i'}} \left\| \mathbf{B}_{i,j}(\mathbf{m}_i^0 + \Lambda \mathbf{c}_i) - \mathbf{B}_{i',j}(\mathbf{m}_{i'}^0 + \Lambda \mathbf{c}_{i'}) \right\|^2 \, . \tag{11}$$

Together, our unary and pairwise potentials define an energy that encourages the patches to fit the data and form a coherent surface. We now turn to the problem of minimizing this energy, i.e., performing inference in our CRF.

Inference. One of the challenges of performing inference in our graphical model is that its variables are continuous. While many inference methods have been proposed for the discrete case, the literature on continuous inference remains limited. Here, we perform inference using the Fusion Moves strategy introduced in [18]. Fusion Moves have proven effective to minimize nonlinear and non-convex objective functions in different contexts, such as optical flow estimation [18] and monocular nonrigid surface reconstruction [35]. In our framework, they are particularly better suited than gradient-based techniques to handle non-smooth robust error terms, such as ϕ_i^c and ϕ_i^d. Fusion Moves perform inference by iteratively merging a set of two proposals per node in the graph, which can be expressed as a binary labeling problem. While global convergence cannot be ensured, Fusion Moves guarantee that the energy decreases at each iteration.

As mentioned earlier, our deformation model was computed via PCA, and thus assumes a Gaussian distribution of the deformation coefficients. To generate proposals, we therefore make use of this assumption, and draw random samples for each patch according to

$$\mathbf{c}_i \sim \mathcal{N}(\mathbf{0}, \varepsilon \Sigma) \, , \tag{12}$$

where we exploit the covariance matrix of the coefficients Σ modulated by a constant scalar ε that encodes the degree of deformation expected between frame 0 and frame 1[2]. At each iteration, we draw one such sample per patch and make use of the current best solution as second proposal in the Fusion Moves. We iterate until the change of global energy is smaller than a predefined tolerance within ten iterations.

To tackle the video scenario, which we are most interested in, we use the method described in Section 3.1 to obtain the initial surface patches in the first frame of the video. We then track the deformations of these patches throughout the entire sequence by making use of the solution at time t as initialization

---

[2] We used $\varepsilon = 0.05$ in all our experiments.

for the Fusion Moves inference at time $t + 1$. As a consequence, we obtain a coherent surface model across the video sequence. In the presence of occlusions and missing data, the unobserved parts of the surface can then be inferred from the deformed mesh patches, thus effectively performing surface completion. Note that, while we do not model occlusions explicitly, our method has proven robust to moderate occlusions. For larger ones, a strategy such as the one used in [16] could easily be included in our framework. As will be evidenced by our experiments, our inference strategy makes our approach robust to error accumulation that can typically occur in a tracking scenario such as considered here.

3.3 Incorporating New Patches

One of the benefits of relying on patches instead of a global model is that we can easily incorporate new patches in an online manner, as previously-hidden parts of the surface become visible. To this end, we adopt the following strategy. After registering the previous frame to the current one, we search for parts in the point cloud that are not explained by the current patches. These parts correspond to newly visible surface areas. We then compute superpixels [1] in the input image corresponding to these areas only, and add a new patch for each sufficiently large superpixel (i.e., of similar size as the original patches). These patches are then registered to the RGBD image following the procedure of Section 3.1, and thus incorporated in our surface representation for the following frame.

4   Experimental Results

In this section, we study the effectiveness of our approach in different scenarios. In particular, we provide quantitative and qualitative results on two publicly available RGBD sequences[3] depicting dynamically deforming objects (a sheet of paper and a T-shirt) captured using a single Kinect. We also evaluate the robustness of our approach to missing data and occlusions, and illustrate its use to add patches online. In all our experiments, both the color images and the depth maps were acquired at the resolution of 640×480. We used square mesh patches with 5×5 vertices and retained $Q = 20$ deformation modes. The weights in Eqs. 3 and 4 were set to $w_p = 2500$, $w_c = 30$, $w_d = 25$, and $w_s = 10000$ for all sequences, which corresponds to making all the terms in the energy of similar magnitudes. The videos of our results are provided as supplementary material.

We compare our results with those obtained with two methods that, as ours, do not require a global model of the surface: (i) The Coherent Point Drift (CPD) algorithm of [23][4], which does not exploit RGB intensities; and (ii) RGBD-Flow [11][5], which extends state-of-the-art optical flow techniques to RGBD images. Furthermore, we also compare our results with a baseline obtained by replacing our local patches with the global NURBS representation of [16], in

---

[3] Publicly available at http://cvlab.epfl.ch/data/dsr

[4] Code available at https://sites.google.com/site/myronenko/research/cpd

[5] Code available at http://homes.cs.washington.edu/~eherbst/useful-code/

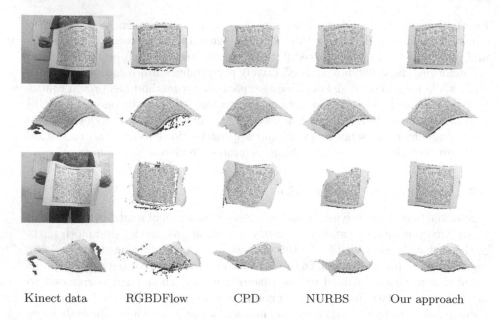

Kinect data   RGBDFlow   CPD   NURBS   Our approach

Fig. 3. Registration results for 2 frames of the paper sequence. We show the front view and side view of our results and of the baselines. Note that RGBDFlow introduces some noise in the results, while CPD and the NURBS model do not respect the texture of the surface. Our approach yields smooth and accurate surfaces.

conjunction with their regularizer and optimization technique (CMA-ES). For all baselines, we follow a similar strategy as with our approach to propagate information across the video sequence.

4.1 Comparison with the Baselines

In Figs. 3 and 4, we provide some examples of the registration results obtained with our approach and with the baselines on the paper and T-shirt sequences. To be able to better evaluate the registration quality, we warped the first RGBD image according to the registration results, and display the result of this warping procedure as colored point clouds seen from a different viewpoint.

From these examples, we can see that, while reasonably accurate in the middle of the surface, RGBDFlow yields very noisy point locations at the boundaries. In contrast, CPD and the NURBS model yield fairly smooth surfaces. However, the artifacts that can be observed on the warped texture of the surface suggest that registration is not very accurate. Our method simultaneously yields smooth results and accurate warped texture, thus indicating accurate registration.

The benefits of our approach are further evidenced by our quantitative results. In Fig. 5, we report depth errors for all methods, computed as the mean absolute depth difference between depth maps generated from the results of the different methods and the original Kinect depth maps. Note that the error of RGBDFlow

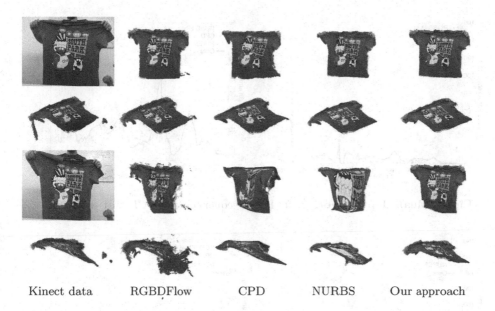

Kinect data   RGBDFlow   CPD   NURBS   Our approach

Fig. 4. Registration results for 2 frames of the T-shirt sequence. Note again that our approach yields smoother results than RGBDFlow and less distorted warped textures than CPD and the NURBS model, thus indicating more accurate registration.

increases over time, thus suggesting error accumulation. In contrast, CPD, the NURBS model and our approach yield lower errors and are more stable over time. Importantly, even when our accuracy drops for one frame (e.g., frame 45 in the T-shirt sequence), our Fusion Moves inference strategy, which performs more global optimization, is able to recover and get back to accurate registration in later frames. While it may seem that CPD, the NURBS model and our approach perform similarly, the front views of Figs. 3 and 4 suggest that our registration results are more accurate. To quantify this, we employed the following strategy: We manually selected 15 interest points spread over the surface every 20 frames of the paper and T-shirt sequences. The shapes predicted by our algorithm and the baselines give us estimates of the 3D locations of these points, which we can then compare against the manually selected locations. This gives us a better notion of registration error than the previous depth error, which does not take point correspondence into account and thus does not penalize points sliding on the surface. As evidenced by Fig. 6, our approach yields more accurate registration than the baselines.

On a laptop with a four-core CPU, 8GB memory and a Geforce 765M graphics card, the runtimes for the 4 methods are of the order of 1 min per frame for RGBDFlow, 10 min per frame for CPD, 10 min per frame for the NURBS model and 3 min per frame for our approach. Note that RGBDFlow benefits from a GPU implementation. In contrast, the current implementation of our approach only runs on the CPU.

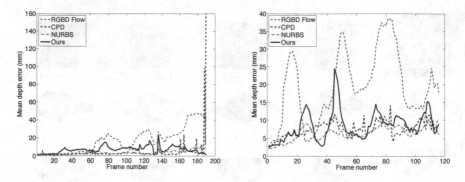

Fig. 5. Mean depth error: (Left) Paper sequence. (Right) T-shirt sequence.

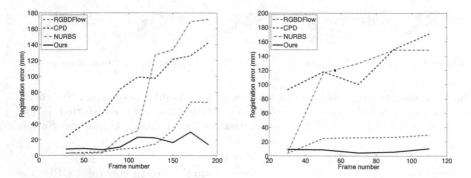

Fig. 6. Registration error: (Left) Paper sequence. (Right) T-shirt sequence.

4.2   Missing Data and Occlusions

In this section, we evaluate the robustness of our algorithm to missing data and partial occlusions. For the missing data case, we first made use of the paper sequence, and synthetically removed some amount of depth observations. To this end, and to model the fact that the noise in the depth sensor is often structured, we randomly removed square areas of 20×20 pixels from the depth maps of 10 consecutive frames in the sequence. We repeated this operation for different numbers of removed areas, corresponding to different percentages of missing data. Fig. 7 depicts the mean depth errors of the baselines and of our approach on the last of the 10 frames as a function of the percentage of missing points. Note that, while the errors of RGBDFlow and of the NURBS model tend to increase with the percentage of missing data, our errors remain stable. While the errors of CPD, and in some cases of the NURBS model, appear to be very low, they should again be considered jointly with the front view of the results (see Fig. 9) which suggests worse registration accuracy than for our approach.

To illustrate the fact that our approach is also robust to the missing data problem in a real scenario, we selected the images in the T-shirt sequence that

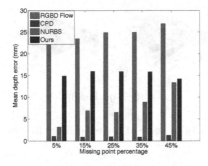 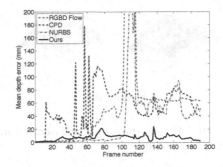

Fig. 7. Robustness to missing data: Mean depth error of the baselines and of our approach as a function of the percentage of missing points. The data was generated by randomly removing areas from some frames of the paper sequence

Fig. 8. Robustness to occlusion: Mean depth error of the baselines and of our approach as a function of the frame number. The data was generated by adding an occluder to the paper sequence

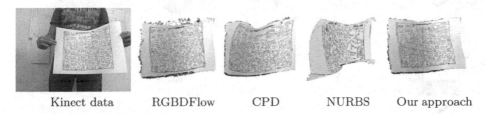

| Kinect data | RGBDFlow | CPD | NURBS | Our approach |

Fig. 9. Robustness to missing data: Front view of the registration results for the largest amount of missing data in Fig. 7

most suffer from this problem. These results are depicted in Figs. 1 and 10. Note that we can accurately fill in the holes in the original Kinect data.

To evaluate the robustness of our approach to partial occlusion, we employed the paper sequence and synthetically augmented it with an occluder passing in front of the surface, as shown in the first column of Fig. 11. Note that the resulting depth maps contained the depth of the occluder, thus truly mimicking occlusion. Fig. 11 compares our results on this occluded sequence with the results of the baselines. While the latter are strongly affected by the presence of the occluder, our approach performs essentially the same as without any occlusion. This is further evidenced by the quantitative errors provided in Fig. 8. Note that our results can also be used to fill in the gap in the observed data.

4.3 Incorporating New Patches

To illustrate the ability of our approach to incorporate new patches in an online manner, we employed the paper sequence, and augmented the data with a synthetic occluder that hides roughly half of the surface in the first frame. This

Missing data   Self-occlusion

Fig. 10. Missing data and self occlusion: Results on some of the most noisy frames of the T-shirt sequence

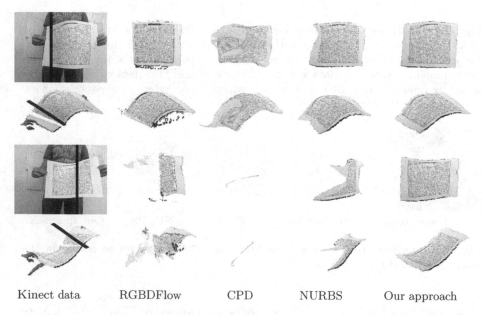

Kinect data   RGBDFlow   CPD   NURBS   Our approach

Fig. 11. Robustness to occlusions: While the baselines all suffer from the presence of an occluder in the sequence, our approach remains virtually unaffected

occluder was then progressively removed throughout the sequence. As shown in Fig. 12, our approach lets us augment the surface with new patches as parts of the object that were previously hidden become visible. Note that this would not be possible with a global model acquired in the first frame of the sequence.

4.4 Video Editing

Finally, we illustrate the use of our approach as a tool to achieve video editing. To this end, we re-textured the data in the first frame of the video and then made use of our registration results to transfer the new texture across the entire sequence. Fig. 13 depicts a few frames of the result of this process applied to the paper sequence. Note that, thanks to our registration accuracy, the resulting images look realistic, up to shading effects which are not modeled here.

Fig. 12. Incorporating Patches: Our approach lets us incorporate new patches as previously hidden parts of the surface become visible

Fig. 13. Video editing: Our registration results let us re-texture the surface in the paper sequence to create realistic RGBD images of a different object

5   Conclusion

We have introduced an approach to performing nonrigid surface registration and completion from a low-cost RGBD sensor. Thanks to our patch-based representation, our approach can be applied to surfaces of arbitrary shapes. Our experimental evaluation has demonstrated the effectiveness of our method in various scenarios. In the future, we plan to push our technique in the direction of augmented reality, as well as extend it to modeling more general 3D scenes.

Acknowledgement: This work was supported in part by National Program on Key Basic Research Project of China (973 Program) 2013CB328805, National High-tech R&D Program of China (863 Program) 2012AA013802 and National Natural Science Foundation of China (NSFC) 61370134. The authors would also acknowledge the financial support from China Scholarship Council. NICTA is funded by the Australian Government as represented by the

Department of Broadband, Communications and the Digital Economy, as well as by the Australian Research Council through the ICT Centre of Excellence program.

References

1. Achanta, R., Shaji, A., Smith, K., Lucchi, A., Fua, P., Susstrunk, S.: Slic superpixels compared to state-of-the-art superpixel methods. IEEE Transactions on Pattern Analysis and Machine Intelligence 34(11), 2274–2282 (2012)
2. Bartoli, A., Pizarro, D., Collins, T.: A robust analytical solution to isometric shape-from-template with focal length calibration. In: ICCV (2013)
3. Bronstein, A.M., Bronstein, M.M., Kimmel, R., Mahmoudi, M., Sapiro, G.: A Gromov-Hausdorff Framework with Diffusion Geometry for Topologically-Robust Non-Rigid Shape Matching. IJCV (2010)
4. Cagniart, C., Boyer, E., Ilic, S.: Free-form mesh tracking: a patch-based approach. In: CVPR (2010)
5. Cui, Y., Schuon, S., Chan, D., Thrun, S., Theobalt, C.: 3d shape scanning with a time-of-flight camera. In: CVPR (2010)
6. Dou, M., Fuchs, H., Frahm, J.M.: Scanning and tracking dynamic objects with commodity depth cameras. In: ISMAR (2013)
7. Endres, F., Hess, J., Engelhard, N., Sturm, J., Cremers, D., Burgard, W.: An evaluation of the rgb-d slam system. In: ICRA (2012)
8. Gall, J., Stoll, C., de Aguiar, E., Theobalt, C., Rosenhahn, B., Seidel, H.P.: Motion capture using joint skeleton tracking and surface estimation. In: CVPR (2009)
9. Garg, R., Roussos, A., Agapito, L.: Dense Variational Reconstruction of Non-Rigid Surfaces from Monocular Video. In: CVPR (2013)
10. Hadfield, S., Bowden, R.: Kinecting the dots: Particle based scene flow from depth sensors. In: ICCV (2011)
11. Herbst, E., Ren, X., Fox, D.: Rgb-d flow: Dense 3-d motion estimation using color and depth. In: ICRA (2013)
12. Hornacek, M., Rhemann, C., Gelautz, M., Rother, C.: Depth super resolution by rigid body self-similarity in 3d. In: CVPR (2013)
13. Huang, P., Budd, C., Hilton, A.: Global temporal registration of multiple non-rigid surface sequences. In: CVPR (2011)
14. Izadi, S., Kim, D., Hilliges, O., Molyneaux, D., Newcombe, R., Kohli, P., Shotton, J., Hodges, S., Freeman, D., Davison, A., Fitzgibbon, A.: Kinectfusion: Real-time 3d reconstruction and interaction using a moving depth camera. In: UIST (2011)
15. Jordt, A., Koch, R.: Fast tracking of deformable objects in depth and colour video. In: BMVC (2011)
16. Jordt, A., Koch, R.: Direct model-based tracking of 3d object deformations in depth and color video. IJCV (2013)
17. Keller, M., Lefloch, D., Lambers, M., Izadi, S., Weyrich, T., Kolb, A.: Real-time 3d reconstruction in dynamic scenes using point-based fusion. In: 3DV (2013)
18. Lempitsky, V., Rother, C., Roth, S., Blake, A.: Fusion moves for markov random field optimization. PAMI (2010)
19. Letouzey, A., Boyer, E.: Progressive shape models. In: CVPR (2012)
20. Li, H., Sumner, R.W., Pauly, M.: Global correspondence optimization for non-rigid registration of depth scans. In: SGP (2008)

21. Mac Aodha, O., Campbell, N.D.F., Nair, A., Brostow, G.J.: Patch based synthesis for single depth image super-resolution. In: Fitzgibbon, A., Lazebnik, S., Perona, P., Sato, Y., Schmid, C. (eds.) ECCV 2012, Part III. LNCS, vol. 7574, pp. 71–84. Springer, Heidelberg (2012)
22. Malti, A., Hartley, R., Bartoli, A., Kim, J.H.: Monocular template-based 3d reconstruction of extensible surfaces with local linear elasticity. In: CVPR (2013)
23. Myronenko, A., Song, X.: Point set registration: Coherent point drift. PAMI (2010)
24. Park, J., Kim, H., Tai, Y.W., Brown, M.S., Kweon, I.: High quality depth map upsampling for 3d-tof cameras. In: ICCV (2011)
25. Rouhani, M., Sappa, A.D.: Non-rigid shape registration: A single linear least squares framework. In: Fitzgibbon, A., Lazebnik, S., Perona, P., Sato, Y., Schmid, C. (eds.) ECCV 2012, Part VII. LNCS, vol. 7578, pp. 264–277. Springer, Heidelberg (2012)
26. Russell, C., Fayad, J., Agapito, L.: Energy Based Multiple Model Fitting for NRSFM. In: CVPR (2011)
27. Salzmann, M., Fua, P.: Deformable Surface 3D Reconstruction from Monocular Images. Morgan Kaufmann (2010)
28. Salzmann, M., Fua, P.: Linear Local Deformation Models for Monocular Reconstruction of Deformable Surfaces. PAMI (2011)
29. Santa, Z., Kato, Z.: Correspondence-less non-rigid registration of triangular surface meshes. In: CVPR (2013)
30. Schuon, S., Theobalt, C., Davis, J., Thrun, S.: Lidarboost: Depth superresolution for tof 3d shape scanning. In: CVPR (2009)
31. Taylor, J., Shotton, J., Sharp, T., Fitzgibbon, A.: The vitruvian manifold: Inferring dense correspondences for one-shot human pose estimation. In: CVPR (2012)
32. Torresani, L., Hertzmann, A., Bregler, C.: Nonrigid Structure-From-Motion: Estimating Shape and Motion with Hierarchical Priors. PAMI (2008)
33. Ulusoy, A.O., Biris, O., Mundy, J.L.: Dynamic probabilistic volumetric models. In: ICCV (2013)
34. Varol, A., Salzmann, M., Tola, E., Fua, P.: Template-Free Monocular Reconstruction of Deformable Surfaces. In: ICCV (2009)
35. Vicente, S., Agapito, L.: Soft inextensibility constraints for template-free non-rigid reconstruction. In: Fitzgibbon, A., Lazebnik, S., Perona, P., Sato, Y., Schmid, C. (eds.) ECCV 2012, Part III. LNCS, vol. 7574, pp. 426–440. Springer, Heidelberg (2012)
36. Vlasic, D., Baran, I., Matusik, W., Popovic, J.: Articulated mesh animation from multi-view silhouettes. In: SIGGRAPH (2008)
37. Weikersdorfer, D., Gossow, D., Beetz, M.: Depth-adaptive superpixels. In: ICPR (2012)
38. Yang, Q., Yang, R., Davis, J., Nister, D.: Spatial-depth super resolution for range images. In: CVPR (2007)
39. Ye, G., Liu, Y., Hasler, N., Ji, X., Dai, Q., Theobalt, C.: Performance capture of interacting characters with handheld kinects. In: Fitzgibbon, A., Lazebnik, S., Perona, P., Sato, Y., Schmid, C. (eds.) ECCV 2012, Part II. LNCS, vol. 7573, pp. 828–841. Springer, Heidelberg (2012)
40. Zeng, Y., Wang, C., Wang, Y., Gu, X., Samaras, D., Paragios, N.: Dense non-rigid surface registration using high-order graph matching. In: CVPR (2010)

Unsupervised Dense Object Discovery, Detection, Tracking and Reconstruction

Lu Ma and Gabe Sibley

Autonomous Robotics and Perception Group
The George Washington University
Washington DC, USA
{luma,gsibley}@gwu.edu

Abstract. In this paper, we present an unsupervised framework for discovering, detecting, tracking, and reconstructing dense objects from a video sequence. The system simultaneously localizes a moving camera, and discovers a set of shape and appearance models for multiple objects, including the scene background. Each object model is represented by both a 2D and 3D level-set. This representation is used to improve detection, 2D-tracking, 3D-registration and importantly subsequent updates to the level-set itself. This single framework performs dense simultaneous localization and mapping as well as unsupervised object discovery. At each iteration portions of the scene that fail to track, such as bulk outliers on moving rigid bodies, are used to either seed models for new objects or to update models of known objects. For the latter, once an object is successfully tracked in 2D with aid from a 2D level-set segmentation, the level-set is updated and then used to aid registration and evolution of a 3D level-set that captures shape information. For a known object either learned by our system or introduced from a third-party library, our framework can detect similar appearances and geometries in the scene. The system is tested using single and multiple object data sets. Results demonstrate an improved method for discovering and reconstructing 2D and 3D object models, which aid tracking even under significant occlusion or rapid motion.

Keywords: Structure From Motion, SLAM, 3D Tracking, 3D Reconstruction, Dense Reconstruction, Learning, Level-Set Evolution.

1 Introduction

Object detection, tracking and 3D reconstruction are fundamental early-vision tasks that are often addressed independently. Here, we present a unified and unsupervised framework that places dense-object tracking and reconstruction in feedback with one another, allowing us to discover, detect, track and reconstruct multiple objects simultaneously. Rigid bodies are automatically and recursively detected and tracked based on appearance, geometry and motion information. A 2D level-set evolution is used to update the object's 2D contour. This contour and appearance model is useful for detection, and for image based 3D object tracking

D. Fleet et al. (Eds.): ECCV 2014, Part II, LNCS 8690, pp. 80–95, 2014.

estimation when no 3D depth data is available. Pixels inside a 2D contour are used to register and update an object's 3D model – this in itself is an object-oriented dense simultaneous localization and mapping (SLAM) system where the object models are fused and improved over time. However, the proposed system is also able to discover new objects based on coherent portions of the scene that that fail to match with any known object. Rigid bodies with distinct motion are hence natural candidates for new object creation.

In recent years, sparse structure from motion has been used for model inference from video [5]. Dense techniques have also been demonstrated[18], as well as level-set based fusion techniques[8], though not for multi-object simultaneous dense tracking and reconstruction in real-time.

KinectFusion, is a wonderful example of dense data fusion using signed distance functions (SDF) [14,10]. Using a single RGB-D camera, this system creates high-quality 3D models from live scenes. Similar results are also possible using monocular cameras alone [15,20]. The system presented in this paper extends 3D level-set fusion to model both the scene and also distinct objects. Further, we find that combining 3D level-set shape models with 2D level-set appearance models leads to a novel method for unsupervised object discovery tightly coupled with tracking, detection and reconstruction.

Normally, dense fusion techniques use the whole scene, and do not isolate objects for tracking or reconstruction purposes. There are notable exceptions which track 3D objects within a full-SLAM framework but do not automatically discover novel objects [16,19]. There have also been recent advances in fast detection and tracking, such as the Pixel-wise Posterior tracker (PWP)[3,4], which is a probabilistic 2D multiple-object tracking and segmentation method based on level-sets. We extend PWP to extract objects from the scene for 3D reconstruction purposes, and also more accurately represent changing contours in 3D [7].

Shape and semantic priors have recently been used to improve dense static object tracking and reconstruction [9,2]. Recently, PWP has also been extended to handle real-time 3D object tracking [16]. This system can track a moving object in a video sequence robustly and precisely even under rapid motion. There are also recent SLAM frameworks that detect and track multiple objects in real-time [19]. However, both [16] and [19] require known a priori 3D object models. Perhaps the most similar work to ours is [17]. They present a framework that simultaneously tracks a single object while reconstructing a 3D model using RGB-D data. There are, however, key methodological differences. First, while [17] selects the foreground (target) manually, we do this automatically by segmenting unexplained portions of the image using motion outliers. Second, our system can track and reconstruct multiple objects simultaneously. Third, they initialize an object's 3D model with a shape primitive model and update the model at each frame while we initialize and update the object's 3D model with its own geometry data. Finally, the presented framework can detect many objects simultaneously that are similar to other given objects (either learned by the system online or provided by a third-party library) in the scene.

2   Overview

The system aims to track and reconstruct $n + 1$ objects (rigid bodies), $O = O_{\emptyset}, O_1, O_2, \cdots, O_n$, which are present in a given video sequence. For an object O_i, its corresponding camera pose in the reference frame (time $k - 1$) and live frame (time k) are T^i_{wr} and T^i_{wl}, respectively. For a camera c with known calibration intrinsic matrix K, the transformation between its pose and world frame is $T_{wc} \in SE(3)$. A 3D point can be described as $x_c = (x, y, z)^{\top}$ and dehomogenisation by $\pi(x_c) = (x/z, y/z)^{\top}$. A pixel $\mathbf{u} = (u, v)^{\top}$ in the image domain can be back-projected to a 3D point as $\chi = \frac{1}{d} \cdot K^{-1} \cdot (\mathbf{u}; 1)$ with depth value d.

Figure 1 shows the representation of the 2D and 3D model of an object. An object's 2D model refers to its shape (contour) and appearance (RGB histogram), where the 2D shape is implicitly represented by the zero level-set of the object's 2D SDF Φ (Section 4.1). A contour C segments the image domain Ω into foreground Ω_f and background Ω_b, with appearance models M_f and M_b respectively. Specifically, we use Ω_f^{Φ}, Ω_b^{Φ} to denote the foreground and background region segments by the zero level-set of Φ.

An object's 3D model refers to its 3D shape (geometry), which is implicitly represented by the zero level-set surface of its 3D SDF $\mathcal{S}$ (more specifically, we use truncated signed distance function, TSDF). We also use $\mathcal{S}_i$ to denote the 3D SDF of an object O_i, where $\mathcal{S}_{\emptyset}$ refers to the 3D SDF of the dominant object. $\mathcal{S}$ is stored as a n^3 volume cube, where n is the number of voxels in one dimension. The size of each voxel is $v_m = \frac{2r}{n}$, where r is the radius of the volume. The volume is initialized and updated by SDF Fusion (Section 4.2). By setting a camera in different poses, we can ray cast the implicit surface of $\mathcal{S}$ and generate virtual images (Section 4.2).

Ω_b

Ω_f

Ω

$\emptyset(\mathrm{x})=0$

Virtual image of
an object's 3D SDF $\boldsymbol{S}$

Fig. 1. Representation of an object's 2D and 3D model

Our system goes through the following stages (Figure 2):

Initialization. The system is initialized by creating a 3D model of the first frame (the scene). We call this initial 3D model the *dominant object*, $O_{\emptyset}$ (in our approach, the scene itself is considered an object). $\mathcal{S}_{\emptyset}$ is represented by a 512^3 resolution volume, where the radius of the volume is based on the scene size.

Discovery. The system tracks and reconstructs $O_{\emptyset}$, frame by frame, and discovers (Section 3) a contour set $C_D = C_{D1}, C_{D2}, \cdots, C_{Dp}$ of potential rigid bodies, by portions of the scene that fail to track with $O_{\emptyset}$.

Detection. Given object O_i with known 2D and 3D models, the system also detects (Section 3) objects similar to O_i in the scene and extracts contours $C_L = C_{L1}, C_{L2}, \cdots, C_{Lq}$. The final contour set is $C = C_D \cup C_L$.

Tracking. Given $C_j \in C$ with foreground domain Ω_f^j, if C_j fails to match with any known objects, the system will initialize a new object with C_j. If C_j matches a known object O_i, the 2D SDF $\Phi(x_i)$ of O_i is updated by Ω_f^j to $\Phi'(x_i)$ via LSE producing $\Omega_f^{\Phi'}$. Tracking is achieved by estimating the relative camera pose between Ω_f^{Φ} and $\Omega_f^{\Phi'}$.

Reconstruction. The 3D SDF of O_i is then updated by fusing every pixel from $\Omega_f^{\Phi'}$ (instead of Ω_f^j) into the S_i. This is done to reduce the noise sometimes associated with Ω_f^j.

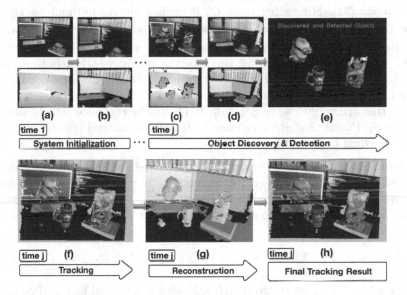

Fig. 2. System flow chart. Cyan represents missing depth data. (a) Initial RGB-D images. (b) Virtual images of $O_\emptyset$ (full scene) initialized by the first input frame. (c) Input RGB-D images at time j. (d) Virtual images of $S_\emptyset$ at time j. (e) Discovered and detected (learned) objects at time j, with ID on their top left side. (f) Objects 2D SDF are updated and tracked (shown as red/green/blue contour). (g) Reconstruction results of objects after updating their 3D SDF by 2D SDF from (f). (h) Final tracking results are implicitly represented by the virtual images of the 3D SDF of all objects (shown as red/green/blue transparent masks, arrows show the objects estimated velocities).

3 Discovery and Detection

Discovery. The system offers an unsupervised object discovery method by extracting potential objects from portions of the scene that fail to track with $O_\emptyset$. Once $O_\emptyset$ is tracked by estimating the relative pose $T_{rl}^\emptyset$ of its camera between the reference frame I_r and the live frame I_l via the ICP+RGB-D approach. (Section 4.1), we get $T^d_{wl} = T^\emptyset_{wr} \oplus T^\emptyset_{rl}$ where $\oplus$ indicate the composition of relative poses. Now, we can generate a virtual image I'_l of $\mathcal{S}_\emptyset$ from $T^\emptyset_{wl}$:

$$I'_l = \Upsilon(\mathcal{S}, T^\emptyset_{wl}) \tag{1}$$

here, $\Upsilon(\cdot)$ is a ray casting operator (Section 4.2). Equation (1) allows us to produce an outline image $I_o = I'_l - I_l$. By searching for disjoint contours in I_o that have a minimum number of pixels d_1 inside of the contour boundary, a contour set C_D of potential objects can be obtained:

$$C_D = \Gamma(I'_l - I_l) = \Gamma(\Upsilon(\mathcal{S}, T^\emptyset_{wl}) - I_l), C_D = C_{D1}, C_{D2}, \cdots, C_{Dp} \tag{2}$$

where $\Gamma(\cdot)$ is a contour detection operator that detects disjoint contours in image domain [21]. For each $C_{Dj} \in C$, it defines foreground and background regions Ω^j_f, Ω^j_b. Here, Ω^j_f is either used to initialize a new object, or used to update a known object. We then compute $I_c = \Omega^1_f + \Omega^2_f + \cdots + \Omega^n_f$ and $I_e = I_o - I_c$, where I_e consists of two kinds of pixels: (1), Pixels that should belong to I_c but were missed by a system error. (2), Pixels of $O_\emptyset$ which are occluded in the reference frame. By comparing the depth value of each pixel in I_e, pixels that are very close (e.g. 1 mm) to $O_\emptyset$ will be compiled into $I_\emptyset$ and used to update $\mathcal{S}_\emptyset$. Pixels that are very close to Ω^j_f will be merged into Ω^j_f and refine its corresponding contour C_{Dj}.

Detection. For an object O_i which is either predefined in an object database or learned by our system, the system automatically searches for other instances in the live image I_l. We start with an image $I'_l = h(I_l, O_i)$, where $h(\cdot)$ extracts pixels in I_l that agree with the appearance model of object O_i. We then extract contours from I'_l:

$$C_L = \Gamma(I'_l - I_l) = \Gamma(h(I_l, O_i) - I_l), C_L = C_{L1}, C_{L2}, \cdots, C_{Lq} \tag{3}$$

For each $C_{Lj} \in C_L$, we try to match Ω^{Lj}_f with the virtual image of $\mathcal{S}_i$ via the ICP+RGB-D approach. We then delete contours from C_L which correspondence Ω^{Lj}_f fail to match O_i.

Discovery and Detection Integration. Once our system finishes discovering and detecting contours in the live frame, the final contours set C based on equation (1) and (3) is:

$$C = C_D \cup C_L = \Gamma(\Upsilon(\mathcal{S}, T^\emptyset_{wl}) - I_l) \cup \Gamma(h(I_l, O_i) - I_l), C = C_1, C_2, \cdots, C_n \tag{4}$$

4   Tracking and Reconstruction

4.1   Tracking

Objects and Contours Matching. A key problem of our framework is, given a set of contours $C = C_1, C_2, \cdots, C_n$ in the live frame, where C_j derives a foreground region Ω_f^j, how to match Ω_f^j with a known object $O_i \in O$ in the reference frame? To address this question, we designed a simple score system to find a known object $O_i \in O$ that is best matched with Ω_f^j. The total score includes three different criteria: appearance (RGB Histogram), geometry (3D shape) and motion. The match score between O_i and Ω_f^j is represented by:

$$S(O_i, \Omega_f^j) = S_{Appearance_{i,j}} + S_{Motion_{i,j}} + S_{Geometry_{i,j}} \tag{5}$$

For the appearance score, $S_{Appearance_{i,j}} = r_a$ where r_a is the rate of pixels in Ω_f^j that agree with the appearance model of O_i. For the motion score, $S_{Motion_{i,j}} = p(P|P')$. Where $p(P|P') \sim \mathcal{N}(P', \Sigma)$ is the probability of P' appearing in P under Gaussian distribution with uncertainty Σ. Here, $P = (x, y, z)$ is the geometric center of Ω_f^j, $P' = (x', y', z')$ is the prediction of the geometric center of O_i in the live frame, which is estimated via a constant velocity motion model. For the geometry score, we match the depth image I_l of Ω_f^j and the virtual depth image I_r of $\mathcal{S}_i$ via the ICP+RGB-D approach (Section 4.1). Now, $S_{Geometry_{i,j}} = \frac{r_g}{rmse}$, where r_g is the percentage of pixels in I_r used in the ICP+RGB-D approach, $rmse$ is the error of the ICP+RGB-D approach.

The system computes score $S(O_i, \Omega_f^j)$ first by appearance, then motion, then geometry and will stop computing scores and set $S(O_i, \Omega_f^j)$ to 0 if any component is less than a threshold. Given a set of foreground regions $\Omega_f^k \in \Omega_f'$, we match O_i with $\Omega_f^k \in \Omega_f'$ if:

$$S(O_i, \Omega_f^k) > S(O_i, \Omega_f^l), \Omega_f^l \in \Omega_f', m, l \neq k \tag{6}$$

Notice that Ω_f^j may match several overlapping objects. However, each overlapping object can extract corresponding image regions from Ω_f^j via level-set evolution (LSE), which will be described in next Section.

Level Set Evolution. We use the level-set embedding function $\Phi(x_i)$, namely a 2D SDF, to implicitly represent an object's 2D contour (shape). Here $x_i = x_{i1}, x_{i2} \cdots, x_{in}$ is the set of pixel locations in the coordinate frame of O_i. We modify the Pixel-Wise Posteriors (PWP) segmentation method of [3] to use a new level-set evolution method described in [11] and propose $\mathcal{L}(\cdot)$:

$$\Phi(x_i)' = \mathcal{L}(\Phi(x_i), \Omega) \tag{7}$$

here, $\mathcal{L}(\cdot)$ is the level-set-evolution operation that evolves the object's 2D SDF $\Phi(x_i)$ to $\Phi(x_i)'$ in image domain Ω based on the 2D appearance and shape model of $\Phi(x_i)$. This operation can be achieved via:

$$\frac{\partial P(\Phi, p|\Omega)}{\partial \Phi} = \theta \cdot \Psi_p + \mu \cdot \Psi_d + \lambda \cdot \Psi_e + \alpha \cdot \Psi_a \tag{8}$$

The probability of updated $\Phi(x_i)$ appearing in location p (image warp parameters) depends on four terms. Ψ_p describes the probability of a pixel in the image domain belonging to the foreground or background under weight θ.

$$\Psi_p = \frac{(P_f - P_b)}{P_f H_\epsilon(\Phi) + P_b(1 - H_\epsilon(\Phi))} \tag{9}$$

where $H_\epsilon(\cdot)$ is a Heaviside step function, P_f, P_b are defined as:

$$P_f = \frac{P(y_i \mid M_f)}{\eta_f P(y_i \mid M_f) + \eta_b P(y_i \mid M_b)}, P_b = \frac{P(y_i \mid M_b)}{\eta_f P(y_i \mid M_f) + \eta_b P(y_i \mid M_b)} \tag{10}$$

here y_i is pixel value in input image, η_f and η_b is the area of foreground and background regions respectively:

$$\eta_f = \sum_{i=1}^N H_\epsilon(\Phi(x_i)), \eta_b = \sum_{i=1}^N (1 - H_\epsilon(\Phi(x_i)), \eta = \eta_f + \eta_b \tag{11}$$

Ψ_d is the distance regularization term that maintains the signed distance property of the level set function:

$$\Psi_d = div(d_p(|\nabla\Phi|\nabla\Phi)) \tag{12}$$

where $div(\cdot)$ is the divergence operator, $d_p(x) = \frac{p'(x)}{x}$.

Ψ_e is the edge term, which is minimized when the zero level set contour of $\Phi(x_i)$ reaches the object contour.

$$\Psi_e = \delta_\varepsilon(\Phi) div(g \frac{\nabla_\Phi}{|\nabla_\Phi|}) \tag{13}$$

here, $\delta_\epsilon(\cdot)$ is the derivative of the Heaviside step function. $g = \frac{1}{1+|\nabla G_\sigma \star I|^2}$ and ∇G_σ is a Gaussian kernel with standard deviation σ in image I.

Ψ_a is the area term, which speeds up the evolution of the level set. α is the weight of Ψ_a, where positive means shrink and negative means expand during the evolution of the level set function.

$$\Psi_a = g\delta_\epsilon(\Phi) \tag{14}$$

We seek $\frac{\partial log(P(\Phi,p|\Omega)}{\partial\Phi} = 0$ by using the gradient flow $\frac{\partial\Phi}{\partial t} = \frac{\partial log(P(\Phi,p|\Omega)}{\partial\Phi}$. In our implementation, we set weighting terms $\theta = 15$, $\mu = 0.015$, $\lambda = 5$, $\alpha = -4$, time step $t = 1$. level-set evolution (Equation 7) allows us update $\Phi(x_i)$ to $\Phi'(x_i)$ based on the appearance and shape of $\Phi(x_i)$, which provides a solution to obtain a more precise image domain $\Omega_f^{\Phi'}$ from noisy discovery or detection and overlapping objects for update the 3D SDF of an object (Section 4.2). Notice that LSE is not used for object's pose estimation. Instead, we use $\Phi'(x_i)$ to limit the pixels that are then used for shape and appearance based registration.

Pose Estimation. Once the 2D SDF of an object O_i is updated, object tracking is then achieved by estimating the relative camera pose T_{rl}^i between T_{wr}^i and T_{wl}^i, where $T_{wl}^i = T_{wr}^i \oplus T_{rl}^i$. Here, T_{rl}^i can be estimated by ICP based pose estimator [6] or RGB-D based (depth is only used for space warping) pose estimator [1]. However, both ICP and RGB-D approaches have drawbacks. The ICP approach highly depends on geometric information, and fails when tracking simple geometries (e.g. cups, dishes, etc). The RGB-D approach relies more heavily on intensity information, requires rich texture for good estimation. However, these shortcomings can be overcame by combining both approaches. We integrate the ICP approach with the RGB-D approach by using a weighting strategy [22]:

$$E = w_i \cdot E_{icp}(T_{rl}^i) + (1 - w_i) \cdot E_{rgbd}(T_{rl}^i) \tag{15}$$

here, $E_{icp}(T_{rl}^i)$ and $E_{rgbd}(T_{rl}^i)$ are the cost of ICP and RGB-D pose estimators, respectively. w_i is the weighting term, which is automatically set based on an object's color and geometric complexity during initialization. The pose is estimated by minimizing the $rmse$ of equation (15), which allows to have a ICP+RGB-D pose estimator $\mathcal{E}(\cdot)$:

$$T_{rl} = \mathcal{E}(I_r, I_l) \tag{16}$$

Where I_r and I_l are images in reference and live frame, T_{rl} is the relative pose we aim to estimate. This ICP+RGB-D pose estimator is also used to decide if two images match. Given images I_r and I_l for pose estimation, if the $rmse$ of ICP+RGB-D is higher than the threshold ε_1, or if the number of pixels used for estimation are fewer than the threshold ε_2, we assume that I_1 does not match with I_2. As I_r and I_l do not match in either color and geometric.

4.2 Reconstruction

SDF Fusion. Our system use SDF fusion [14] to initialize and update an object's 3D model. Given depth image I_D with world pose T_{wl}, SDF Fusion operation $\mathcal{F}(\cdot)$ fuses every valid point $\chi = (x, y, z)$ in I_D into the 3D SDF $\mathcal{S}$:

$$\mathcal{S}' = \mathcal{F}(\mathcal{S}, I_D, T_{wl}) \tag{17}$$

Given a contour $C_j \in C$, if C_j matches with a known object O_j, our framework uses the foreground domain Ω_f^{Φ} (derived by the updated 2D SDF Φ of O_j) to update $\mathcal{S}_j$. If C_j does not match with any known object, the system will initialize a new object O_k with C_j. The initialization of $\mathcal{S}_j$ depends on the 'type' of C_j. (1) If C_j belongs to object discovery result C_D, the system will initialize $\mathcal{S}_j$ with the foreground domain defined by C_j. (2) If C_j comes from object detection result C_L, which has a model similar to that of a known object O_k, the system will initialize $\mathcal{S}_j$ by using $\mathcal{S}_k$ directly.

Ray Casting. Having a 3D SDF $\mathcal{S}$, we can ray cast [14] the zero level set surface of $\mathcal{S}$ to generate virtual image I_v (can be grey or depth images. we also rendered the 3D model with Phong shading) by setting the camera at pose T_{wc}, where the Ray Casting operation $\Upsilon(\cdot)$ is:

$$I_v = \Upsilon(\mathcal{S}, T_{wc}) \tag{18}$$

Since each object O_i has its own 3D SDF $\mathcal{S}_i$, the virtual image I_v contains the object O_i in the scene and the value of other pixels in I_v will be set to void.

2D and 3D SDF Interaction. For an object O_i, once the system updates its 3D SDF $\mathcal{S}_i$ and its corresponding camera pose T_{wl}^i, its 2D SDF $\Phi(x_i)$ can be refined by:

$$\Phi(x_i) = \nu(\Phi(x_i), \Upsilon(\mathcal{S}_i, T_{wr}^i)) \tag{19}$$

$\nu(\cdot)$ sets the zero level-set of $\Phi(x_i) = 0$ to be the object contour of $\Upsilon(\mathcal{S}_i, T_{wr}^i)$.

4.3   Tracking and Reconstruction Interaction

The 2D tracking result of an object O_i is implicitly represented by the matching result (Section, 4.1), which may be noisy or incomplete due to noisy input data or occlusion of its correspondence match contour $C_j \in C$. By ray casting the up-to-date 3D SDF of O_i, the system can generate a more complete and precise 2D tracking result with respect to the object's pose and shape, which can offer complete knowledge of objects even in the presence of significant occlusions.

In short, the input for updating an object's 3D SDF comes from the results of 2D tracking, while an object's 3D reconstruction results are used to inform the final 2D tracking results. This interaction between tracking and reconstruction improves tracking and reconstruction results simultaneously.

5   System Integration

Given a contour set C (Equation (4)), where $C_j \in C$ defines an image domain Ω^j that matches a known Object O_i, where O_i with camera pose T_{wr}^i, 2D SDF $\Phi(x_i)$ and 3D SDF $\mathcal{S}_i$ in the reference frame, $\Phi(x_i)$ can thus be updated to:

$$\Phi^{'}(x_i) = \mathcal{L}(\Phi(x_i), \Omega^j) \tag{20}$$

$\mathcal{L}(\cdot)$ is a level-set-evolution operator (Section 4.1). The relative pose T_{rl}^i between $\Phi_f(x_i)$ and $\Phi_f^{'}(x_i)$ can be estimated via ICP+RGB-D pose estimator $\mathcal{E}(\cdot)$:

$$T_{rl}^i = \mathcal{E}(\Phi_f(x_i), \Phi_f^{'}(x_i)) \tag{21}$$

Now $\mathcal{S}_i$ can be updated by SDF Fusion $\mathcal{F}(\cdot)$:

$$\mathcal{S}_i' = \mathcal{F}(\mathcal{S}_i, \Phi_f^{'}(x_i), T_{wl}^i) = \mathcal{F}(\mathcal{S}_i, \Phi_f^{'}(x_i), T_{wr}^i \oplus \mathcal{E}(\Phi_f(x_i), \Phi_f^{'}(x_i))) \tag{22}$$

here, The unknown parameters are the 2D SDF $\Phi(x_i)$, 3D SDF $\mathcal{S}_i$ and camera pose T_{wr}^i. Equation (22) shows how the 2D and 3D model of an object is tracked and updated with respect to the change of the camera pose, which links object discovery, detection, tracking, and reconstruction together.

6   Results and Discussion

We test the system with single and multiple-object data sets. Each data set, lasting between 300 and 550 frames, is captured in 30 FPS via a hand-held moving RGB-D camera.

To evaluate our method, we first generate ground truth 3D models of all testing objects using synthetic RGB-D sequences. We then use the pose estimation approach described in Section 4.1 to track each ground truth object model in the testing video sequences. This allows us to generate a ground truth depth image D_g for each object in each frame. We then run our system in the same sequences and generate a virtual depth image D_l from each object's learned 3D SDF. The performance of the system is evaluated at pixel level by comparing each corresponding object's pixel p in D_g and D_l. We define a good match (true positive) if $abs(D_l(p) - D_g(p)) < d_\varepsilon$. We set $d_\varepsilon = 10mm$ in our experiments. We report per-frame precision and recall values for each learned object.

Figure 3 shows an examples of discovered objects and their corresponding matched object's 2D level-set after refine. It can be seen that LSE allows us to smooth noise from the raw detected contour (e.g. Fig. 3(c), 3(d)) and helps update the 2D SDF when objects overlap with each other (e.g. Fig. 3(r)). In totally, LSE is crucial as 1) it helps learn the unknown object based on its previous appearances and shape; 2) it helps track overlapping objects with significant occlusions; 3) without LSE, the reconstruction contour is often unusably noisy; 4) it allows object discovery and tracking when no depth is available. Once we update the 2D SDF, we are ready to track and reconstruct each object.

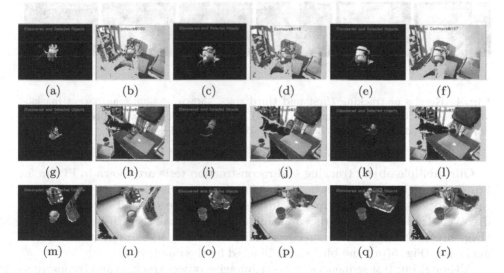

Fig. 3. Examples of raw discovered objects (odd columns, with ID on their top left side) and the zero level-sets refined by level-set-evolution (even columns), shown as red/green/blue outlines. Cyan represents missing depth data.

Figure 4 shows the tracking and reconstruction results for a cup and a yellow cartoon figure (Dave). As we move these objects, their shape and appearance is changed greatly to test the robustness of the system. The cup, which has a simple geometry, is used to test the ICP+RGB-D pose estimator. As motion is applied to the cup, it is slowly removed from the dominant object's 3D SDF $\mathcal{S}_\emptyset$ (Fig. 4(t)). This confirms that the system performs SLAM by simultaneously localization and mapping both the dominant object (desk and wall) and the singled out object (cup/Dave). It also shows that our system is able cope with limited input data, e.g. large portions of missing depth data (e.g. Fig. 4(f) 4(p)).

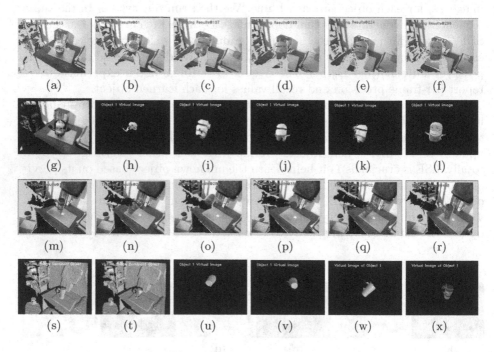

Fig. 4. Results of tracking (first and third rows, shown as blue transparent masks) and reconstruction (second and third rows) for single objects. Cyan represent missing depth data, red arrows show the objects estimated velocities.

Our multiple-object tracking and reconstruction tests are shown in Figure 5. For this experiment we focus on evaluating the performance of our system under rapid motions, overlapping and occlusions. Overall, we see that our system can discover, track and reconstruct multiple objects in a scene with high accuracy (Fig. 6(c)). Our system can recover the pose of an object even under severe occlusion (Fig. 5(m), the blue car is blocked by the donut bag).

Although our test sequences yield encouraging object tracking and reconstruction results, the precision and recall (Fig. 6) of our system changes with respect to an object's status. When our objects first appear (cup and Dave), the recall grows as the system continue to learn the objects' models.

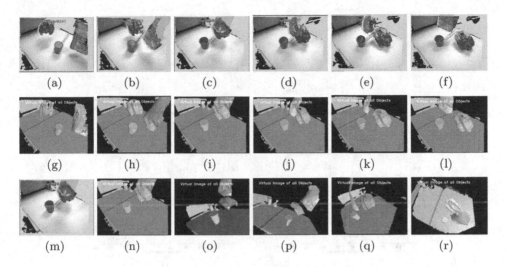

(a)   (b)   (c)   (d)   (e)   (f)

(g)   (h)   (i)   (j)   (k)   (l)

(m)   (n)   (o)   (p)   (q)   (r)

Fig. 5. Tracking (first row, shown as red/green/blue transparent masks) and reconstruction (second row) results of multiple objects. (m) Occluded car. (n)-(r) Multiple-view rendering of all objects during the occlusion shown in (m).

Objects without rapid motion − frame to frame translation in (x, y, z) less than 7 cm and rotation in $roll, pitch, yaw$ less than 12 degrees − can be tracked with high accuracy (precision over 90 % and recall over 80 %) for most frames with a true positive threshold of $d_\varepsilon = 10mm$ (cup/Dave/red can).

Drops in precision and recall that can be seen in Fig.(6) are due to rapid motions (e.g. the donut bag, frame to frame translation of more than 15cm in (x, y, z), and rotation of more than 15 degrees in $roll, pitch, yaw$) or occlusions (e.g. the blue car is 80 % occluded). In both cases, precision and recall recover to around 85% immediately after. When objects are highly occluded, (more than 90%, see blue car during frame 40 to 47 and frame 50 to 53 in Fig. 6(c) 6(d), corresponding tracking sequences in 5), both precision and recall are set to 0. While we don't yet have enough confidence to track occluded objects, our system proves adept at tracking objects that reappear after occlusion.

Over all, our system maintains good tracking and reconstruction performance (both precision and recall over 90%) when objects have less than 5cm frame to frame translations and 9 degrees frame to frame rotations. However, failure cases occur under significant motion blur, serious occlusions (more than 90% occluded), which predominantly hamper pose estimation.

Object Detection of Learned Objects. We demonstrate the learning and subsequent detection ability of the system with a coke can data set. Here, we grab a coke can in the left side of the scene (Fig. 7(a)). After the system has accrued enough 2D and 3D modeling information of the can (Fig. 7(b)), the system can detect other instances of the coke can, that will then be tracked and reconstructed (Fig 7(c)- 7(f)). This experiment shows that the system can discover new objects in the scene and learn similar objects without human intervention.

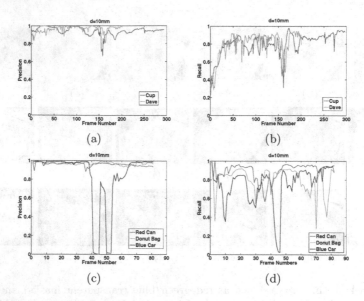

Fig. 6. Precision and Recall of system's performance under single (a), (b) and multiple-object (c),(d) data sets with true positive threshold of $d_\varepsilon = 10mm$. Frame number starts when motion is first applied to an object in test sequences.

System Run-Time. The system is implemented in C++. Both the reconstruction and the combined ICP and RGBD approach are GPU-based. We test our system with a single Nvidia TITAN GPU, Intel i7 CPU desktop, using 640×480 resolution of input images. Table 1 shows our system run-time in different stages.

Table 1. System Run-time of Different Stages, (*) Represent GPU-Based

	Discovery	Match Objects and Contours*	Single ICP+ RGB-D*	Single level-set evolution	Single Reconstruction*
Single Object	15 ms	24 ms	11 ms	31 ms	5 ms
Three Objects	15 ms	80 ms	11 ms	32 ms	5 ms

As table 1 shows, the most expensive stage comes when matching contours with objects. However, since computing the match score between each contour and a known object can be processed in parallel, we anticipate that running time can be significantly decreased. Discovery and the level-set-evolution are also amenable to GPU implementation where LSE is known to run in less than 6ms in [4]. Finally, tracking and reconstruction of each object can also be processed in parallel. With these enhancements and based on run-times reported in the literature [16,3], it is reasonable to conjecture that our system will run at 24Hz.

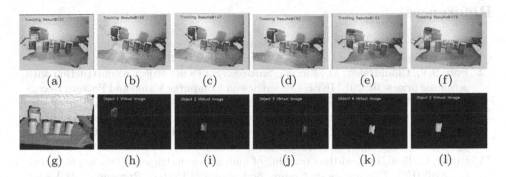

Fig. 7. Multiple instance detection. Above are shown tracking (first row, shown as different color transparent masks) and reconstruction (second row) results of detected (learned) objects (coke can) in the scene. After motion is applied to one coke can (a), all the other cans are detected.

7 Failure Cases and Future Work

Although the system is robust to many real-world operating conditions, it is not robust under significant motion blur, serious occlusions, etc., which predominantly hamper pose estimation. In future work, we aim to improve the resolution of the reconstructed models by [12,23] and enhanced the system with a single RGB camera techniques from [15,13]. We also see the potential applications in robot-object interaction and autonomous cars.

8 Conclusions

We present a novel unsupervised framework that is able to discover, detect, track and reconstruct multiple rigid bodies simultaneously. Instead of considering them independently, the presented system uses tracking results to refine reconstruction-models and reconstruction-models to aid detection and tracking. This allows objects tracking even under significant occlusion, missing data and rapid motion. Rigid bodies are automatically and recursively detected and tracked based on appearance, geometry and motion information. The system preforms dense SLAM on an object by object basis, and also discovers new objects it has not seen before. The system is tested using single and multiple object data sets. Results demonstrate an improved method for discovering and reconstructing 2D and 3D object models. To summarize, our primary contributions are: 1) a new framework, which unifies dense object discovery, detection, tracking and reconstruction; 2) an unsupervised approach to discover unknown objects; 3) a framework that not only learns objects but also detect similar objects based on learned models; and 4) present a new level-set evaluation method.

References

1. Baker, S., Matthews, I.: Lucas-kanade 20 years on: A unifying framework. International Journal of Computer Vision 56(3), 221–255 (2004)
2. Bao, S.Y., Chandraker, M., Lin, Y., Savarese, S.: Dense object reconstruction with semantic priors. In: 2013 IEEE Conference on Computer Vision and Pattern Recognition (CVPR), pp. 1264–1271. IEEE (2013)
3. Bibby, C., Reid, I.D.: Robust real-time visual tracking using pixel-wise posteriors. In: Forsyth, D., Torr, P., Zisserman, A. (eds.) ECCV 2008, Part II. LNCS, vol. 5303, pp. 831–844. Springer, Heidelberg (2008)
4. Bibby, C., Reid, I.: Real-time tracking of multiple occluding objects using level sets. In: 2010 IEEE Conference on Computer Vision and Pattern Recognition (CVPR), pp. 1307–1314. IEEE (2010)
5. Blais, G., Levine, M.D.: Registering multiview range data to create 3d computer objects. IEEE Transactions on Pattern Analysis and Machine Intelligence 17(8), 820–824 (1995)
6. Chen, Y., Medioni, G.: Object modelling by registration of multiple range images. Image and vision computing 10(3), 145–155 (1992)
7. Cremers, D., Rousson, M., Deriche, R.: A review of statistical approaches to level set segmentation: integrating color, texture, motion and shape. International Journal of Computer Vision 72(2), 195–215 (2007)
8. Curless, B., Levoy, M.: A volumetric method for building complex models from range images. In: Proceedings of the 23rd Annual Conference on Computer Graphics and Interactive Techniques, pp. 303–312. ACM (1996)
9. Dame, A., Prisacariu, V.A., Ren, C.Y., Reid, I.: Dense reconstruction using 3d object shape priors. In: 2013 IEEE Conference on Computer Vision and Pattern Recognition (CVPR), pp. 1288–1295. IEEE (2013)
10. Izadi, S., Kim, D., Hilliges, O., Molyneaux, D., Newcombe, R., Kohli, P., Shotton, J., Hodges, S., Freeman, D., Davison, A., et al.: Kinectfusion: real-time 3d reconstruction and interaction using a moving depth camera. In: Proceedings of the 24th Annual ACM Symposium on User Interface Software and Technology, pp. 559–568. ACM (2011)
11. Li, C., Xu, C., Gui, C., Fox, M.D.: Distance regularized level set evolution and its application to image segmentation. IEEE Transactions on Image Processin 19(12), 3243–3254 (2010)
12. Meilland, M., Comport, A.I.: Super-resolution 3d tracking and mapping. In: 2013 IEEE International Conference on Robotics and Automation (ICRA), pp. 5717–5723. IEEE (2013)
13. Newcombe, R.A., Davison, A.J.: Live dense reconstruction with a single moving camera. In: 2010 IEEE Conference on Computer Vision and Pattern Recognition (CVPR), pp. 1498–1505. IEEE (2010)
14. Newcombe, R.A., Davison, A.J., Izadi, S., Kohli, P., Hilliges, O., Shotton, J., Molyneaux, D., Hodges, S., Kim, D., Fitzgibbon, A.: Kinectfusion: Real-time dense surface mapping and tracking. In: 2011 10th IEEE International Symposium on Mixed and Augmented Reality (ISMAR), pp. 127–136. IEEE (2011)
15. Newcombe, R.A., Lovegrove, S.J., Davison, A.J.: Dtam: Dense tracking and mapping in real-time. In: 2011 IEEE International Conference on Computer Vision (ICCV), pp. 2320–2327. IEEE (2011)
16. Prisacariu, V.A., Reid, I.D.: Pwp3d: Real-time segmentation and tracking of 3d objects. International Journal of Computer Vision 98(3), 335–354 (2012)

17. Ren, C.Y., Prisacariu, V., Murray, D., Reid, I.: Star3d: Simultaneous tracking and reconstruction of 3d objects using rgb-d data
18. Rusu, R.B., Blodow, N., Marton, Z.C., Beetz, M.: Close-range scene segmentation and reconstruction of 3d point cloud maps for mobile manipulation in domestic environments. In: IEEE/RSJ International Conference on Intelligent Robots and Systems, IROS 2009. pp. 1–6. IEEE (2009)
19. Salas-Moreno, R.F., Newcombe, R.A., Strasdat, H., Kelly, P.H., Davison, A.J.: Slam++: Simultaneous localisation and mapping at the level of objects. In: 2013 IEEE Conference on Computer Vision and Pattern Recognition (CVPR), pp. 1352–1359. IEEE (2013)
20. Sibley, G., Keivan, N., Patron-Perez, A., Murphy, L., Lovegrove, S., Mamo, V.: Scalable perception and planning based control. In: International Symposium on Robotics Research (2013)
21. Teh, C.H., Chin, R.T.: On the detection of dominant points on digital curves. IEEE Transactions on Pattern Analysis and Machine Intelligence 11(8), 859–872 (1989)
22. Whelan, T., Johannsson, H., Kaess, M., Leonard, J.J., McDonald, J.: Robust tracking for real-time dense rgb-d mapping with kintinuous (2012)
23. Zhou, Q.Y., Miller, S., Koltun, V.: Elastic fragments for dense scene reconstruction. Environments 27(16), 7–35

Know Your Limits:
Accuracy of Long Range Stereoscopic Object Measurements in Practice

Peter Pinggera[1,2], David Pfeiffer[1], Uwe Franke[1], and Rudolf Mester[2,3]

[1] Environment Perception, Daimler R&D, Sindelfingen, Germany
[2] VSI Lab, Computer Science Dept., Goethe University Frankfurt, Germany
[3] Computer Vision Laboratory, Dept. EE, Linköping University, Sweden

Abstract. Modern applications of stereo vision, such as advanced driver assistance systems and autonomous vehicles, require highest precision when determining the location and velocity of potential obstacles. Sub-pixel disparity accuracy in selected image regions is therefore essential. Evaluation benchmarks for stereo correspondence algorithms, such as the popular Middlebury and KITTI frameworks, provide important reference values regarding dense matching performance, but do not sufficiently treat local sub-pixel matching accuracy. In this paper, we explore this important aspect in detail. We present a comprehensive statistical evaluation of selected state-of-the-art stereo matching approaches on an extensive dataset and establish reference values for the precision limits actually achievable in practice. For a carefully calibrated camera setup under real-world imaging conditions, a consistent error limit of $1/10$ pixel is determined. We present guidelines on algorithmic choices derived from theory which turn out to be relevant to achieving this limit in practice.

1   Introduction

Stereo vision has been an area of active research for several decades and applications have found their way into a wide variety of industrial and consumer products. Quite recently, stereo cameras have attracted renewed attention as the central sensor module in modern driver assistance systems, and even in first fully autonomous driving applications [7].

Part of the practicability and performance of modern stereo vision algorithms can arguably be attributed to the seminal Middlebury benchmark study [27], which first provided a comprehensive framework for evaluation and enabled algorithm analysis and comparison. Ten years later, the KITTI project [10] presented a new realistic and more challenging benchmark with stereo imagery of urban traffic scenes, triggering a new wave of improved stereo vision algorithms. These major benchmark studies focus on dense stereo correspondence and are naturally required to provide *both* dense *and* accurate ground truth data. Algorithm performance is mainly judged by the percentage of pixels whose disparity estimates fall within a given accuracy threshold. The threshold is commonly set to several pixels (KITTI), or half pixels at best (Middlebury).

D. Fleet et al. (Eds.): ECCV 2014, Part II, LNCS 8690, pp. 96–111, 2014.

 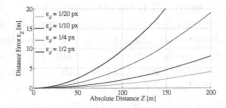

Fig. 1. Highway driving scene with relevant objects at distances of 80 and 140 m (left). Metric distance errors ϵ_Z increase non-linearly for given stereo disparity errors ϵ_d (right).

However, for safety-critical applications such as environment perception in autonomous driving, sub-pixel disparity accuracy is essential. Furthermore, not all parts of the considered images may require the same level of attention. Obstacles in the path of motion are most relevant to the driving task, and their location and velocity have to be determined with maximum precision. Fig. 1 illustrates such critical object locations and the significant impact of sub-pixel disparity errors on the respective distance estimates. Note that for a subsequent estimation of relative object *velocities*, these errors can have an even more serious influence. Unfortunately, this important aspect lies outside the scope of existing major stereo benchmarks, leaving open the question of the actually achievable disparity estimation accuracy where it matters most.

The present paper intends to fill this gap by providing an extensive statistical evaluation of object stereo matching algorithms and establishing a reference for the achievable sub-pixel accuracy limits in practice. We employ a large real-world dataset in an automotive scenario and consider various state-of-the-art stereo matching algorithms, including local differential matching and segmentation-based approaches as well as global optimization in both discrete and continuous settings. Moreover, we investigate possibilities for performance improvement rooted in signal- and estimation theory which are partly used in other areas of computer vision such as medical or super-resolution imaging. Finally, we provide practical guidelines on which algorithmic aspects are essential to achieving the accuracy limits and which are not, also taking into account the trade-off between precision and computational complexity.

2   Related Work

In major dense stereo correspondence benchmarks (Middlebury [27], KITTI [10]) the number of images is kept relatively small for practical reasons, and algorithm performance is derived from pixel-wise match evaluation, weighting each pixel equally. To determine the percentage of erroneous matches, the KITTI benchmark employs a minimum threshold of two pixels. Alternatively, the *average* disparity error on the dataset can be considered, where the top-ranking algorithms at the time of writing achieve a value of 0.9 pixels [33]. This value however provides no information on the matching accuracy for isolated salient objects.

Notably, all top-performing dense methods make use of generic smoothness constraints on the disparity solution, either by global optimization in discrete or continuous disparity space or by integrated image segmentation and parametric model refinement. Taking a closer look at sub-pixel matching precision, it becomes clear that techniques in a discrete setting entail inherent difficulties. Sub-pixel results are obtained by fractional sampling of the disparity space and/or a curve fit to the computed matching cost volume [30]. Depending on the used matching cost measure, these methods usually suffer from the so-called pixel-locking effect, i.e. an uneven sub-pixel disparity distribution. Various approaches have been proposed to alleviate this effect, including two-stage shifted matching [28], symmetric refinement [17], design of optimal cost interpolation functions [11] and disparity smoothing filters [9]. In contrast, methods set in a continuous framework [21] or based on segment model fitting [33] do not suffer from pixel-locking and have been shown to outperform discrete techniques in accuracy.

When shifting the focus from dense disparity maps to isolated objects, the properties of local area-based matching techniques have to be investigated. Within the context of image registration, Robinson and Milanfar [22] presented a comprehensive analysis of the fundamental accuracy limits under simple translatory motion. In low noise conditions, iterative differential matching methods [15] were shown to reach errors of below $1/100$ pixels. The corresponding Cramer-Rao Lower Bound (CRLB) for registration errors turns out to be a combination of noise and bias terms, with bias being caused by suboptimal methods for image derivative estimation and image interpolation as well as mathematical approximations. Similar results were reported in [29] for stereoscopic high-precision strain analysis applications. The optimal design of derivative filters and interpolation kernels was also identified as an essential issue in optical flow [26], super-resolution [3], and medical imaging [5,31] literature.

Perhaps most relevant to the present work is a recent study on local stereo block matching accuracy by Sabater et al. [24]. In contrast to the work mentioned above, realistic noise conditions were investigated and a theoretical formulation for the expected disparity error was derived. Results from a phase-correlation local matching algorithm were shown to agree with the presented theory, demonstrating an accuracy of down to $1/20$ pixel on pre-selected pixel locations. However, experiments were performed only on a set of three synthetic stereo pairs and the four classic Middlebury images. Finally, aiming at a more practical automotive setting, in [19] we proposed a joint differential matching and object segmentation approach, yielding errors of $1/10$ pixel on actual real-world data. However, our evaluation was also restricted to a very limited amount of sequences.

An important aspect, but outside the scope of the present object-based statistical evaluation, is the data-driven pre-selection of reliable matching points. For local differential methods, matching accuracy can be predicted based on the local image structure [6]. Point selection methods based on various confidence measures have been explored for local [25] as well as global methods [18].

3 Long Range Object Stereo: Algorithm Overview

All algorithms in the present evaluation assume a calibrated stereo camera setup and rectified image pairs. For each relevant object in the scene, a single representative disparity value is determined. This makes sense in the considered scenario, where it is sufficient to model the visible relevant objects as fronto-parallel planes. Note that at large distances, where accurate disparity estimation is actually most important, this model is also valid for more general scenarios.

For the purpose of this study, approximate image locations and sizes of objects are given in advance. Corresponding rectangular patches in the left stereo images are provided as input to the matching algorithms (cf. Fig. 1). Details on the generation of these object patches can be found in Sect. 4.1.

We first define a general stereo matching model by considering the discrete left and right image patch values $I_l(x,y)$ and $I_r(x,y)$ as noisy samples of the observed continuous image signal f at positions (x,y). In this simplified model, $\eta_l(x,y)$ and $\eta_r(x,y)$ represent additive Gaussian noise with variance σ^2, while the shift d denotes the object stereo disparity.

$$I_l(x,y) = f(x,y) + \eta_l(x,y) \tag{1}$$
$$I_r(x,y) = f(x+d,y) + \eta_r(x,y) \tag{2}$$

3.1 Local Differential Matching (LDM)

Iterative local differential matching methods, originally proposed by Lucas and Kanade [15], have proven to perform exceptionally well at high-accuracy displacement estimation [22,29,19]. The image difference $I_S(x,y) = I_r(x,y) - I_l(x,y)$ is approximated by linearization and Taylor expansion of f around $d = 0$, with f'_x denoting the signal derivative in direction x. Following (1), η now represents Gaussian noise with variance $\sigma_s{}^2 = 2\sigma^2$:

$$I_S(x,y) = f(x+d,y) - f(x,y) + \eta(x,y) \tag{3}$$
$$= d \cdot f'_x(x,y) + R_{res}(x,y,d) + \eta(x,y). \tag{4}$$

The disparity d is estimated as the least squares solution to $(d \cdot f'_x(x,y) - I_S(x,y))^2 \overset{!}{=} 0$, using all pixels of the input image patch. Applying this concept iteratively, the image patch I_r is successively warped by the current estimate of d, and additive parameter updates Δd are computed as described above. This effectively minimizes the influence of the residual R_{res} of the Taylor expansion, and the solution in fact converges to the Maximum Likelihood (ML) estimate. A good initial value for d is required and is commonly provided by a pyramidal implementation. In our sequences, we use a robust global stereo method (Sect. 3.4) for initialization or, if available, the estimation result from the previous frame. In most cases the algorithm converges in less than five iterations. To minimize errors due to global intensity offsets, image patches are mean-corrected before computation.

Table 1. Separable pre-smoothing (left) and derivative filter kernels (right). Complement symmetric and antisymmetric values respectively.

Scharr 3×3	$[\ldots, 0.5450, 0.2275]$	$[\ldots, 0, 0.5]$
Scharr 5×5	$[\ldots, 0.4260, 0.2493, 0.0377]$	$[\ldots, 0, 0.2767, 0.1117]$
Central Diff. 5×5	$[\ldots, 0.4026\ 0.2442, 0.0545]$	$\frac{1}{12}[1, -8, 0, 8, -1]$

Image Derivative Estimation. In practice, the signal derivatives f'_x in (4) are not known and have to be approximated from I_r using discrete derivative filters. However, inexact derivatives lead to matching bias [22,3], requiring the use of optimal filter kernels. Jähne [13] derived an optimized second order central differences kernel which requires a separate smoothing step for signal bandwidth limitation. Simoncelli and Scharr [5,26] on the other hand proposed the joint optimization of pairs of signal pre-smoothing and derivative filters. We investigate both methods, using 3×3 and 5×5 Scharr kernels as well as a 5×5 central difference kernel with a $5 \times 5/\sigma = 1$ Gaussian pre-smoother, cf. Table 1.

Inverse Compositional Algorithm (IC). In [2], Baker et al. presented the so-called inverse compositional algorithm, reversing the roles of the input images and introducing compositional parameter updates to the differential matching framework. This not only lowers the amount of required computations per iteration, but according to [29] also reduces matching bias. The estimated signal derivatives do not have to be warped in each iteration but are computed just once and only at integer pixel positions in I_l, which avoids errors from interpolating derivative kernel responses. In our evaluations, the IC variant is therefore used as the default LDM implementation.

Image Interpolation. Even when using the IC matching algorithm, the iterative nature of the approach still requires warping the image patch I_r in each iteration. Naturally, this step involves the evaluation of intensity values at sub-pixel positions and therefore makes a suitable image interpolation method necessary. In previous studies on image interpolation [31], approaches based on B-Spline representations clearly outperformed simpler methods such as cubic convolution [14] and bilinear interpolation. We investigate the impact of interpolation on disparity accuracy, with cubic B-Splines as the reference method [32].

Estimation-Theoretic Approach (LDM+). Looking at the derivation of the common LDM approach (cf. [15], Sect. 3.1), it can be seen that the algorithm actually computes the ML estimate for the model defined in (3), and not for the original measurement model from (1) and (2). In fact, only (2) depends on the parameter d, leading to the corresponding ML estimate

$$d_{ML} \leftarrow arg\,min_d(I_r(x,y) - f(x+d,y))^2, \tag{5}$$

which involves the unknown signal f. However, a recent theoretic study [16] argued that for the optimal solution of the correspondence problem *both* displacement *and* the unknown signal should be estimated at the same time. We follow this idea and implement a practical algorithm that performs a joint optimization (LDM+). The disparity is computed according to (5), while the signal f is re-estimated in each iteration as the mean of the respectively aligned input image patches. The signal derivatives are computed by applying derivative filters to the current estimate of f. Note that in this case the modifications used in the IC algorithm do not apply.

3.2   Joint Matching and Segmentation (SEG)

Common local matching techniques, such as the LDM algorithm, inherently make the assumption that all pixels in the input image patches conform to a single simple displacement model. Outliers corresponding to a different model can significantly distort estimation results. The approach presented in [19] handles this problem by jointly optimizing the patch shape and the corresponding parametric displacement model. A probabilistic multi-cue formulation integrating disparity, optical flow and pixel intensity is proposed to reliably segment the relevant object from its surroundings. At the same time the iterative approach refines disparity and optical flow parameters in an LDM manner.

We apply the method of [19] but do not make use of the optical flow cue for segmentation. As in the basic LDM algorithm, the results of our SEG algorithm thus depend only on the most recent image pair. After two segmentation iterations, the LDM+ approach as described above is applied for final disparity refinement.

Scene Flow Matching and Segmentation (SEG+). In order to investigate the impact of exploiting the full data from two consecutive stereo pairs, we again follow the approach of [19], but extend it by introducing an additional scene flow segmentation constraint and using all four images for disparity refinement.

In the original formulation, a Gaussian noise model is applied directly to the disparity d and optical flow vectors v, which allows for the formulation of probabilistic segmentation criteria by regarding the degraded versions $\tilde{d}$ and $\tilde{v}$ as conditionally independent random variables given $\ell, \mathcal{I}$. Here $\mathcal{I}$ denotes the stereo image data and ℓ the pixel labeling due to the segmentation result.

The scene flow constraint now couples the disparity displacements d between left and right stereo images at time t with the optical flow vectors v between consecutive left images, while the respective degradations due to noise are still considered to be conditionally independent. The constraint is expressed as

$$I_{l,t-1}(x + \tilde{v}_x, y + \tilde{v}_y,) = I_{r,t}(x - \tilde{d}, y). \tag{6}$$

Linearization and Taylor expansion as in (4) and [19] yields

$$I_{l,t-1}(x + \tilde{v}_x, y + \tilde{v}_y,) - I_{r,t}(x - \tilde{d}, y) \tag{7}$$
$$= df'_x(x,y) - v f'_v(x,y) + \eta(x,y), \tag{8}$$

where the noise term $\eta(x, y)$ with variance $f'^2_x \cdot \sigma^2_d + f'^2_v \cdot \sigma^2_v$ stems from the assumed degradation models of $\tilde{d}$ and $\tilde{v}$. Following [19], the additional random variable w representing the scene flow constraint can be derived from (8). The optimized patch shape is then computed by assigning optimal segment models for pixel intensity i, disparity d and optical flow v under the scene flow constraint w, thus maximizing the segmentation likelihood $p(\ell|\mathcal{I}, v, d, w, i)$.

Having obtained an optimized patch shape, for the final disparity refinement step we again resort to the LDM+ algorithm, but now aligning all four input images to estimate the unknown signal f.

3.3   Total Variation Stereo (TV)

As a representative for global stereo matching approaches in a continuous setting, we investigate a differential matching algorithm with variational optimization. Total Variation (TV) based algorithms, originally designed for optical flow estimation [35,34], have been shown to perform very well in stereo applications [21]. Specifically, we use a total variation Huber-L1 stereo implementation [20] adapted from [35]. The algorithm uses an iterative pyramidal approach to globally optimize an energy of the form

$$E = \int \int \lambda |I_r(x - d, y) - I_l(x, y)| + \sum_{k=1}^{2} |\nabla d_k|_\epsilon \, dy \, dx, \qquad (9)$$

where the regularization term $|\nabla d_k|_\epsilon$ penalizes the spatial variation of disparity values, using the robust Huber norm with threshold ϵ. For algorithm details we refer to [35]. We set $\epsilon = 0.01$, $\lambda = 25$ and use five image pyramid levels. For robustness with regard to changes in illumination, the structure-texture decomposition of [34] is applied.

Estimation-Theoretic Approach (TV+). Since the variational approach makes use of the same differential matching principle as the local LDM method on a pixel-wise basis, the estimation-theoretic considerations of the LDM+ algorithm can also be applied. We include a TV+ variant which performs the joint estimation of both displacement and unknown image signal at each iteration. To estimate the required image derivatives, a 3×3 Scharr kernel is used.

Object Measurement. While the resulting dense disparity map provided by the global algorithm is useful for many applications, an additional processing step is needed to arrive at representative disparity values for isolated objects. We compute the interquartile mean of the pixel disparities within the input image patch to obtain a robust object disparity estimate for evaluation.

3.4   Semi-Global Matching (SGM)

Finally, we evaluate the discrete Semi-Global Matching (SGM) algorithm of [12]. The method approximates a two-dimensional optimization with truly global constraints by first computing pixel-wise matching costs and then applying one-dimensional regularization along paths from eight directions at each pixel. The nature of the approach allows for efficient computation, and a fast implementation on specialized hardware has been presented in [8].

While all algorithms described above perform matching using image intensities directly, here we employ the census transform and corresponding Hamming distances as a matching cost. This provides a very robust algorithm suitable for challenging real-world scenarios [8]. Sub-pixel results are computed by a symmetric V-fit to three adjacent values in the regularized matching cost volume [11]. Again, we compute the interquartile mean to obtain object disparities.

Pixel Locking Compensation (SGM+PLC). As mentioned previously, matching methods in a discrete setting suffer from the so-called pixel-locking effect, i.e. a biased distribution of sub-pixel disparity values (cf. Fig. 7e). The severity of this effect depends on the used cost metric. While the census transform provides robust matching results, the associated pixel-locking effect is particularly prominent. For general stereo applications, different methods to alleviate the effect have been presented [28,11]. However, for the scenario at hand we propose a straightforward and efficient post-processing step, which largely neutralizes object-based pixel-locking errors. With ground truth data for the desired object disparities available, the systematic sub-pixel bias can be estimated from a set of raw measurements directly. To this end we project both expected and measured disparity values into the sub-pixel interval $[0, 1]$ and fit a low-order polynomial to the resulting two-dimensional point cloud. This curve is stored and directly provides the necessary offsets for an efficient online correction of the object disparities.

4 Evaluation

4.1 Dataset

A central aspect of the present evaluation is the use of an extensive dataset to allow for a meaningful statistical analysis. Furthermore, we exclusively use real-world data to be able to draw conclusions most relevant for practical applications.

The dataset consists of 70,000 grayscale image pairs recorded from a vehicle-mounted stereo camera system in highway scenarios at mostly sunny weather conditions. It includes approximately 250 unique vehicles representing relevant objects, which gives a total of more than 36,000 disparity measurements. The setup exhibits a baseline of 38 centimeters and a focal length of 1240 pixels, with spatial and radiometric resolutions of 1024×440 pixels and 12 bits, respectively.

We consider disparities between 9 and 3 pixels, corresponding to a distance range of approximately 50 to 160 meters. To also analyze matching accuracy as a function of absolute distance, we divide the overall range into intervals of two meters and evaluate each interval separately. The respective distribution of object observations in the dataset is visualized in Fig. 2.

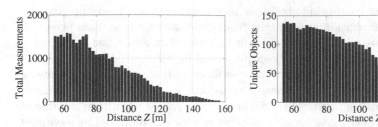

Fig. 2. Distribution of total measurements (left) and unique observed objects (right) in the dataset

Ground truth is provided by a long range radar sensor. Owing to its underlying measurement principle, radar is able to determine longitudinal distances of isolated moving objects with high precision. The used reference sensor yields a measurement uncertainty of $3\sigma \cong 0.5$ m over the full considered distance range.

Generation of Object Patches. To detect relevant objects in the images and provide them as input to the stereo algorithm evaluation, we apply a combined detection and tracking method. A texture-based pattern classifier using a multi-layer neural network with local receptive field features (NN/LRF) as described in [4] is used to first locate potential vehicles. These are then tracked over time, accumulating confidence in the process. For evaluation we consider objects which have been tracked for more than 15 frames. The objects are represented by a rectangular patch in the left stereo image, two examples can be seen in Fig. 1.

Note that, before passing the patches to the stereo algorithms, we optimize the patch fit around objects in order to minimize the amount of outlier pixels. We exploit a precomputed dense disparity result to estimate the mean disparity for each patch and decrease the patch size until the number of outliers falls below a given threshold. Subsequently, we shrink the patches by another 25%, except for the segmentation-based approaches, where we actually increase the size again by 25%. To determine the benefit of this adapted patch fit, we also apply the LDM+ algorithm to the *unmodified* patches, denoting this variant as **LDM-**.

4.2 Performance Measures

Disparity Error. The disparity error ϵ_d represents the deviation of the estimated stereo disparity from the ground truth radar value at each frame:

$$\epsilon_d = d - d_{radar}. \tag{10}$$

Temporal Disparity Error Variation. The disparity error ϵ_d as described above provides an *absolute* accuracy measure for all object observations, combining the measurements of multiple unique objects. However, it alone does not provide sufficient information on the *relative* accuracy for a single tracked object over time. This is essential if the velocities of single objects are to be determined. In this case, the relative accuracy between consecutive measurements of the object of interest is just as important as e.g. a possible constant disparity bias.

To describe the object-based relative measurement accuracy over time, we define $\nabla \epsilon_d$ as the disparity error variation using finite differences:

$$\nabla \epsilon_d = \epsilon_{d,t} - \epsilon_{d,t-1}. \tag{11}$$

We examine the distributions of ϵ_d and $\nabla \epsilon_d$ both over the complete dataset and as a function of absolute distance. In addition to robust estimates of the mean, we compute robust estimates of the standard deviation, using the location-invariant and statistically efficient scale estimator S_n of [23].

Runtime. Finally, as an important aspect for practical and possibly time critical applications, we also take the runtime requirements of the various algorithms into consideration. Timings are performed on a subset of the test data, with average unmodified object patch dimensions of approximately 30×30 pixels.

5   Results and Analysis

Table 2 gives an overview of the main quantitative results across the complete dataset. Fig. 3 shows the corresponding distributions of disparity error ϵ_d and error variation $\nabla \epsilon_d$. Examining the mean of the disparity error, it can be seen that the value consistently lies close to -0.1 pixel, varying by less than 1/30 pixel across all algorithms. Fig. 4 illustrates the consistency of this offset across the full distance range. These observations suggest a constant deviation in the stereo camera calibration, most likely caused by a minor squint angle offset.

While this fact illustrates the importance of accurate estimation *and* maintenance of calibration parameters in practice, the location-invariant scale estimates $S_n(\epsilon_d)$ and $S_n(\nabla \epsilon_d)$ provide more meaningful information regarding algorithmic matching accuracy. Note that the mean of $\nabla \epsilon_d$ is exactly zero for all algorithms, other values would in fact imply a temporal drift of the matching results.

Overall, we observe that after optimization of the selected algorithms, the differences in the results for $S_n(\epsilon_d)$ become very small. The best result of approximately 1/10 pixel is achieved by the TV approach, the combination of spatial regularization and mean object disparity estimation performing well across all object observations. However, TV performs worst with regard to temporal error variation, where it does not directly benefit from regularization. The local methods $S_n(\nabla \epsilon_d)$ do best in this category, yielding values as low as 1/20 pixel.

The order of the algorithms in terms of the specified performance measures is largely consistent over the distance range, as shown in Figs. 5 and 6. Given the properties of the used image data, the observed errors roughly agree with the results presented in [24] on synthetic data.

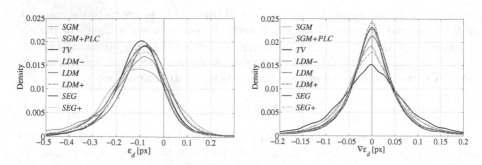

Fig. 3. Overall distributions of disparity error (left) and disparity error variation (right)

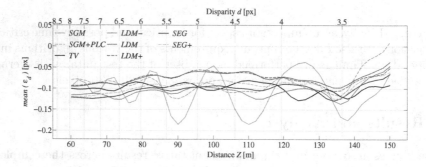

Fig. 4. Mean of disparity error over distance range

Estimation-Theoretic Approach. Now we examine the impact of the estimation-theoretic modifications used in LDM+ and TV+. As can be seen from Table 2 and Figs. 3 and 6, LDM+ yields the same results as LDM for $S_n(\epsilon_d)$, but performs slightly better in terms of error variation. TV and TV+ achieve virtually identical results, the global regularization effectively neutralizing the small differences in data terms.

Optimized Patch Fit. Optimizing the object patch fit has a relatively large impact on the disparity error, as LDM- performs notably worse than all other

Table 2. Overview of quantitative results. See text for details.

Method	SGM	SGM+PLC	TV	TV+	LDM-	LDM	LDM+	SEG	SEG+
$mean(\epsilon_d)$ [px]	-0.104	-0.090	-0.090	-0.097	-0.110	-0.080	-0.079	-0.109	-0.102
$S_n(\epsilon_d)$ [px]	0.139	0.117	**0.104**	**0.104**	0.135	0.113	0.112	0.114	0.111
$S_n(\nabla\epsilon_d)$ [px]	0.061	0.063	0.077	0.076	0.054	0.056	**0.049**	**0.049**	0.053
t_{avg} [ms]	25	25	65	65	∼**1**	∼**1**	∼**1**	40	80

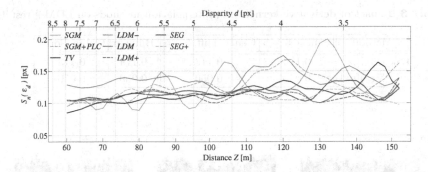

Fig. 5. Standard deviation estimate of disparity error over distance range

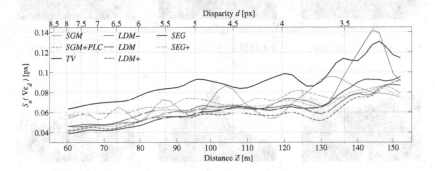

Fig. 6. Standard deviation estimate of disparity error variation over distance range

local algorithms at $S_n(\epsilon_d)$. The error variation scale $S_n(\nabla\epsilon_d)$ without optimized patch fit is also slightly higher than in the otherwise equivalent LDM+ implementation. The efficient adaptation of the rectangular patch fit leads to a similar level of accuracy as the more complex pixel-wise segmentation approaches SEG and SEG+.

Image Derivative Estimation and Interpolation. Interestingly, when comparing different derivative kernels and interpolation methods, we see only insignificant variations in the accuracy results of the differential matching algorithms. The LDM+ column of Table 2 represents our default variant, a 3×3 Scharr kernel and cubic B-Spline interpolation, whereas Table 3 displays the additional configurations. Only when looking at the actual sub-pixel disparity distributions of the different algorithms in Fig. 7, the differences between the interpolation methods become visible. Cubic B-Spline interpolation produces a nearly uniform distribution, while cubic convolution and bilinear interpolation result in a very slight bias towards half pixels. These small variations are in agreement with theoretical predictions presented in [29], but are not distinguishable by our practical disparity accuracy measures at this scale.

Table 3. Impact of derivative kernels and interpolation methods on LDM+ results

Method	Scharr 5 × 5	Centr. Diff. 5 × 5	Bilinear	Cubic Conv.
$S_n(\epsilon_d)$ [px]	0.119	0.118	0.114	0.113
$S_n(\nabla\epsilon_d)$[px]	0.054	0.050	0.050	0.050

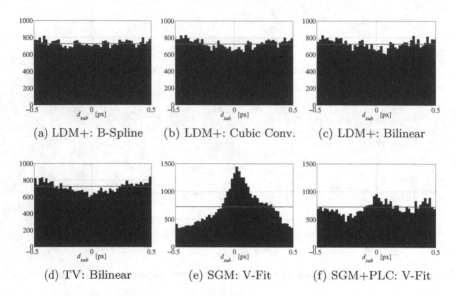

(a) LDM+: B-Spline   (b) LDM+: Cubic Conv.   (c) LDM+: Bilinear

(d) TV: Bilinear   (e) SGM: V-Fit   (f) SGM+PLC: V-Fit

Fig. 7. Sub-pixel disparity distributions resulting from different matching and interpolation methods. Plots show the interval $[-0.5, 0.5]$ centered on full pixel disparities

Pixel-Locking Compensation. In contrast, the systematic pixel-locking effect of the census-based SGM algorithm is clearly visible in both the disparity sub-pixel distribution (Fig. 7e) and in the error measures (Figs. 4, 5, 6). However, applying the proposed compensation method considerably reduces the effect, and SGM+PLC approaches the performance of the differential matching algorithms.

Scene Flow. Finally, our evaluation shows that utilizing the data of two consecutive stereo pairs for scene flow segmentation and disparity refinement as in SEG+ does not necessarily yield a measurable improvement. This might be due to the fact that, in order to align all images, two additional sets of two-dimensional displacements have to be estimated, introducing errors not present in the standard two-image computation. Also, applying a more sophisticated imaging model for estimating the unknown signal could further improve results.

Runtime. Table 2 illustrates average algorithm runtimes, where values for local methods represent the time taken per object, while global methods are timed per full image. Here, the time to compute object disparities from the dense disparity maps is negligible. Due to the different nature of the algorithms, the provided values are intended to serve as guidance values only. We execute the local methods on a modern four-core CPU while we make use of custom hardware implementations for the SGM (FPGA [8]) and TV (GPU [20]) algorithms.

For the considered patch sizes, the LDM versions vary only insignificantly in runtime and clearly outperform the other methods. The more complex local approaches SEG and SEG+ include an additional outer iteration loop for segmentation and require a significant amount of time for graph-cut based pixel labeling, even when using the speed-up methods of [1].

6   Conclusions

In this paper we depart from the common setting of major dense stereo benchmarks and examine the sub-pixel matching accuracy for isolated salient objects. This is motivated by modern safety-relevant applications of stereo vision, where highest sub-pixel accuracy is required in selected image areas. The presented analysis of various state-of-the-art matching approaches is based on an extensive real-world dataset, enabling meaningful statistical evaluation and providing valuable insights regarding the matching accuracy achievable in practice.

We note that the sole use of the mean absolute disparity error for evaluation proves to be problematic in practice, as even smallest deviations in the camera setup can distort results. We propose the use of robust statistical measures of scale, and additionally introduce an object-based temporal disparity error variation measure which is invariant to systematic disparity offsets. These observations also highlight the need for reliable online self-calibration algorithms.

Appropriate optimization of each selected stereo algorithm minimizes the observable differences in matching accuracy and yields consistent disparity error scale estimates of close to $1/10$ pixel. While global variational approaches achieve lowest values here, they perform worst in terms of temporal error variation.

Local differential matching methods perform very well in all performance measures, achieving a temporal error variation scale of $1/20$ pixel. Notably, the choice of derivative filter and interpolation method does not have a significant impact on the disparity accuracy here, while optimized patch shapes are essential. Furthermore, optimizations derived from estimation-theoretic considerations can slightly reduce the temporal error variation. Utilizing the full data of two consecutive stereo pairs does not necessarily yield the expected benefits, but shows potential for use with more sophisticated imaging and estimation models.

Pixel-locking effects of discrete matching methods such as SGM, which cause significant errors in sub-pixel disparity, can efficiently be alleviated by an object-based correction approach, moving discrete methods close to differential matching algorithms in terms of accuracy.

References

1. Alahari, K., Kohli, P., Torr, P.H.S.: Dynamic Hybrid Algorithms for MAP Inference in Discrete MRFs. TPAMI 32(10), 1846–1857 (2010)
2. Baker, S., Matthews, I.: Lucas-Kanade 20 Years On: A Unifying Framework: Part 1. IJCV 56(3), 221–255 (2004)
3. Elad, M., Teo, P., Hel-Or, Y.: On the Design of Filters for Gradient-Based Motion Estimation. Journal of Mathematical Imaging and Vision 23(3), 345–365 (2005)
4. Enzweiler, M., Hummel, M., Pfeiffer, D., Franke, U.: Efficient Stixel-Based Object Recognition. In: IV (2012)
5. Farid, H., Simoncelli, E.P.: Differentiation of Discrete Multidimensional Signals. TIP 13(4), 496–508 (2004)
6. Förstner, W.: Image Matching. In: Haralick, R.M., Shapiro, L.G. (eds.) Computer and Robot Vision, 2nd edn., ch. 16, pp. 289–372. Addison-Wesley (1993)
7. Franke, U., Pfeiffer, D., Rabe, C., Knoeppel, C., Enzweiler, M., Stein, F., Herrtwich, R.G.: Making Bertha See. In: ICCV Workshops (2013)
8. Gehrig, S.K., Eberli, F., Meyer, T.: A Real-Time Low-Power Stereo Vision Engine Using Semi-Global Matching. In: Fritz, M., Schiele, B., Piater, J.H. (eds.) ICVS 2009. LNCS, vol. 5815, pp. 134–143. Springer, Heidelberg (2009)
9. Gehrig, S.K., Franke, U.: Improving Stereo Sub-Pixel Accuracy for Long Range Stereo. In: ICCV 2007 Workshops (2007)
10. Geiger, A., Lenz, P., Urtasun, R.: Are We Ready for Autonomous Driving? The KITTI Vision Benchmark Suite. In: CVPR, pp. 3354–3361 (2012)
11. Haller, I., Nedevschi, S.: Design of Interpolation Functions for Subpixel-Accuracy Stereo-Vision Systems. TIP 21(2), 889–898 (2012)
12. Hirschmüller, H.: Stereo Processing by Semiglobal Matching and Mutual Information. TPAMI 30(2), 328–341 (2008)
13. Jähne, B.: Digital Image Processing - Concepts, Algorithms, and Scientific Applications, 3rd edn. Springer (1995)
14. Keys, R.G.: Cubic Convolution Interpolation for Digital Image Processing. ASSP 29(6), 1153–1160 (1981)
15. Lucas, B.D., Kanade, T.: An Iterative Image Registration Technique with an Application to Stereo Vision. In: Proc. Int. Joint Conf. on Artificial Intel. (1981)
16. Mester, R.: Motion Estimation Revisited: An Estimation-Theoretic Approach. In: SSIAI (2014)
17. Nehab, D., Rusinkiewiez, S., Davis, J.: Improved Sub-Pixel Stereo Correspondences Through Symmetric Refinement. In: ICCV, pp. 557–563 (2005)
18. Pfeiffer, D., Gehrig, S., Schneider, N.: Exploiting the Power of Stereo Confidences. In: CVPR, pp. 297–304 (2013)
19. Pinggera, P., Franke, U., Mester, R.: Highly Accurate Depth Estimation for Objects at Large Distances. In: Weickert, J., Hein, M., Schiele, B. (eds.) GCPR 2013. LNCS, vol. 8142, pp. 21–30. Springer, Heidelberg (2013)
20. Rabe, C.: Detection of Moving Objects by Spatio-Temporal Motion Analysis. Phd thesis, Christian-Albrechts-Universität zu Kiel (2011)
21. Ranftl, R., Gehrig, S., Pock, T., Bischof, H.: Pushing the Limits of Stereo Using Variational Stereo Estimation. In: IV (2012)
22. Robinson, D., Milanfar, P.: Fundamental Performance Limits in Image Registration. TIP 13(9), 1185–1199 (2004)
23. Rousseeuw, P.J., Croux, C.: Alternatives to the Median Absolute Deviation. Journal of the American Statistical Association 88(424) (1993)

24. Sabater, N., Morel, J.M., Almansa, A.: How Accurate Can Block Matches Be in Stereo Vision? SIAM Journal on Imaging Sciences 4(1), 472 (2011)
25. Sabater, N., Almansa, A., Morel, J.M.: Meaningful Matches in Stereovision. TPAMI 34(5), 930–942 (2012)
26. Scharr, H.: Optimal Filters for Extended Optical Flow. In: Jähne, B., Mester, R., Barth, E., Scharr, H. (eds.) IWCM 2004. LNCS, vol. 3417, pp. 14–29. Springer, Heidelberg (2007)
27. Scharstein, D., Szeliski, R.: A Taxonomy and Evaluation of Dense Two-Frame Stereo Correspondence Algorithms. IJCV 47(1-3), 7–42 (2002)
28. Shimizu, M., Okutomi, M.: Precise Sub-pixel Estimation on Area-Based Matching. In: ICCV, pp. 90–97 (2001)
29. Sutton, M.A., Orteu, J.J., Schreier, H.W.: Image Correlation for Shape, Motion and Deformation Measurements. Springer (2009)
30. Szeliski, R., Scharstein, D.: Sampling the Disparity Space Image. TPAMI 26(3), 419–425 (2004)
31. Thévenaz, P., Blu, T., Unser, M.: Interpolation Revisited. TMI 19(7) (2000)
32. Unser, M., Aldroubi, A., Eden, M.: B-Spline Signal Processing. TSP 41(2) (1993)
33. Vogel, C., Schindler, K., Roth, S.: Piecewise Rigid Scene Flow. In: ICCV (2013)
34. Wedel, A., Pock, T., Zach, C., Bischof, H., Cremers, D.: An Improved Algorithm for TV-L^1 Optical Flow. In: Cremers, D., Rosenhahn, B., Yuille, A.L., Schmidt, F.R. (eds.) Statistical and Geometrical Approaches to Visual Motion Analysis. LNCS, vol. 5604, pp. 23–45. Springer, Heidelberg (2009)
35. Werlberger, M., Trobin, W., Pock, T., Wedel, A., Cremers, D., Bischof, H.: Anisotropic Huber-L1 Optical Flow. In: BMVC, pp. 108.1–108.11 (2009)

As-Rigid-As-Possible Stereo
under Second Order Smoothness Priors

Chi Zhang[1], Zhiwei Li[2], Rui Cai[2], Hongyang Chao[1], and Yong Rui[2]

[1] Sun Yat-Sen University, China
[2] Microsoft Research Asia, China

Abstract. Imposing smoothness priors is a key idea of the top-ranked global stereo models. Recent progresses demonstrated the power of second order priors which are usually defined by either explicitly considering three-pixel neighborhoods, or implicitly using a so-called 3D-label for each pixel. In contrast to the traditional first-order priors which only prefer fronto-parallel surfaces, second-order priors encourage arbitrary collinear structures. However, we still can find defective regions in matching results even under such powerful priors, e.g., large textureless regions. One reason is that most of the stereo models are non-convex, where pixel-wise smoothness priors, i.e., *local constraints*, are too flexible to prevent the solution from trapping in bad local minimums. On the other hand, *long-range spatial constraints*, especially the segment-based priors, have advantages on this problem. However, segment-based priors are too rigid to handle curved surfaces. We present a mixture model to combine the benefits of these two kinds of priors, whose energy function consists of two terms 1) a Laplacian operator on the disparity map which imposes pixel-wise second-order smoothness; 2) a segment-wise matching cost as a function of quadratic surface, which encourages "as-rigid-as-possible" smoothness. To effectively solve the problem, we introduce an intermediate term to decouple the two subenergies, which enables an alternated optimization algorithm that is about an order of magnitude faster than PatchMatch [1]. Our approach is one of the top ranked models on the Middlebury benchmark at sub-pixel accuracy.

1 Introduction

Stereo correspondence is a core problem in computer vision. Following the terminology of [2], existing approaches are classified as local or global methods. For most of the top-ranked global methods, a clear clue is that they usually impose smoothness priors on disparity, e.g., first order priors [2][3][4], second-order priors [1][5] and segment-based priors [6][7][8][9]. Each kind of priors has special advantages as well as limitations. The goal of this paper is to develop a new global stereo model to combine advantages of second-order and segment-based priors.

1.1 Background

For a comprehensive discussion on dense two-frame stereo matching, we refer readers to the survey conducted by Scharstein and Szelisky [2]. In this paper, we

D. Fleet et al. (Eds.): ECCV 2014, Part II, LNCS 8690, pp. 112–126, 2014.

only discuss two categories of works related to smoothness priors, i.e., second-order and segment-based priors.

In contrast to the widely used first order prior defined on two-pixel neighborhoods p and q, $S(q, \{p\}) = \|D(p) - D(q)\|_1$, which increases monotonically as the neighborhood diverges from fronto-parallel, second-order priors defined on three-pixel neighborhoods, $S(q, \{p, r\}) = \|D(p) - 2D(q) + D(r)\|_1$, increases monotonically as the neighborhood diverges from collinearity. Using second-order priors in stereo matching has a long history since the early 1980s by Grimoson [10] and Terzopoulos [11]. It has been extended to piecewise second-order by Blake and Zisserman [12]. [13] argued that it is closer to the human visual system than first-order priors.

However, effectively applying second-order priors in stereo matching is not easy. Woodford et al. [14] imposed it by considering triple-cliques, which causes the energy function to be non-submodular and the corresponding pairwise graph representation is much more complex than that of the first-order priors. The QPBO-based fusion move algorithm was adopted to minimize the energy by considering many pre-computed disparity proposals [15], which makes the approach complicated and slow.

Assigning each pixel to a tangent plane specified by three parameters becomes a recent trend of sub-pixel accurate stereo models, which is sometimes termed as 3D-label stereo [16]. Olsson et al. have proved 3D-label is an implicit way to impose second-order priors on scalar disparities and leads to submodular pairwise potentials for planar proposals [16]. The PatchMatch work [1] demonstrated that it is an effective way to handle slanted planes thanks to its pixel-wise plane induced matching cost. Although PatchMatch is a "local" method, it has shown its ability to handle very challenge cases. [5][17][16] further developed PatchMatch into global models by adding explicit smoothness terms to regularize the local neighborhoods of 3D labels, i.e., equations of disparity planes. Despite of good results achieved, the necessity of parameterizing the scalar disparity by 3D label is sometimes arguable. Regularization on 3D labels significantly increases the computational cost.

Under an MRF-like energy minimization framework, smoothness priors are regularizers to prevent the solution from over-fitting to local minimums of matching cost volume [2]. However, both first and second-order priors are defined pixel-wise, that is, they are *local constraints*. Considering the fact that most of stereo models are non-convex, local constraints are usually too "weak" to prevent the solution from trapping in bad local minimums. On the contrary, *long-range spatial constraints*, especially the segment-based priors, have advantages on this problem by imposing the smoothness constraints in a rigid form [6][7][8][9]. A basic assumption is that disparity values vary smoothly in homogeneous regions, i.e., segments. And depth discontinuities are only expected to occur on region boundaries. A disparity plane is supposed to be sufficient to model disparity changes in a segment.

In segment-based methods, a disparity plane specified by three parameters $[c_1, c_2, c_3]^\top$, is usually individually fitted to each region. Given a disparity plane, the disparity of a pixel $[x, y]^\top$ is compute by $d = c_1 x + c_2 y + c_3$. These methods usually estimate many planes from a set of over-segmented regions according to some robust initial matches, and then determine the best matched plane for each region according to an aggregated matching cost defined inside the segment [6]. Robust initial matches are usually obtained by left-right consistency check.

Despite of the excellent accuracy and the relatively low computational cost, segment-based approaches are often challenged by curved surfaces. The rigidness is a double-edged sword. On one side it is very helpful to prevent over-fitting, while on the other side it leads to inaccurate results. Besides, a significant advantage of segment-based approaches is that they usually have much smaller number of parameters than pixel-wise 3D-label approaches.

In summary, both pixel-wise second-order priors and segment-based priors are very effective for stereo matching. Although both of them have limitations, their advantages are complementary for each other. If they can be considered in a single model, better results are very likely to be achieved. Our approach, to the best of our knowledge, is the first one to combine second-order and segment-based priors in a unified framework.

1.2   Contribution

In this paper we propose a novel segment-based global model, in which scalar disparities and parameterized disparity surfaces are jointly modeled. Our major contributions are three-folds:

First, we demonstrate that the second-order smoothness priors can be imposed on disparities by a well-defined Laplacian operator constructed on 4- or 8-pixel neighborhoods guided by color cues. Thus, it is able to preserve sharp discontinuities on edges as well as to encourage collinearity in smooth regions.

Second, unlike previous works where each segment is modeled by a disparity plane, we model a segment by a quadratic surface. Only with two additional parameters, we demonstrate that our approach is able to handle curved surfaces, as well as keeping the advantages of rigidness brought by segments.

Third, we propose an alternated optimization approach for the problem, which is about an order of magnitude faster than PatchMatch [1], making the proposed stereo model very practical.

The paper is organized as following. We present the general framework in Section 2, and a detailed implementation in Section 3. Experiments on benchmarks are given in Section 4. Finally, we conclude the paper in Section 5.

2   As-Rigid-As-Possible Stereo

Given a rectified stereo image pair $\{I_L, I_R\}$, the goal of stereo matching is to estimate the disparity map $\mathbf{u}$ for the reference view I_L. Most global stereo methods can be formulated in an energy minimization framework

$$E(\mathbf{u}) = E_S(\mathbf{u}) + E_D(\mathbf{u}) \tag{1}$$

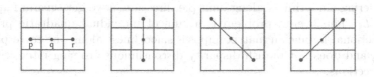

Fig. 1. Four types of Laplacian operators. From left to right are L_1, L_2, L_3 and L_4.

where E_D denotes the matching cost, and E_S denotes the smoothness constraints imposed on a local neighborhood of each pixel or segment. Different stereo models may use different terms or optimization algorithms. We present our proposal in the following sections.

2.1 Second-Order Smoothness Priors

Second-order smoothness priors are defined on three-pixel neighborhoods

$$S(q, \{p, r\}) = \|D(p) - 2D(q) + D(r)\|_1 \tag{2}$$

where p, q, r are the three pixels of a 3×1 patch, and $D(\cdot)$ is a disparity functional. We usually can define four types of 3×1 patches as shown in Fig. 1.

To avoid penalizing disparity discontinuities aligned with intensive edges, we add a weight for each 3×1 patch

$$w(q, \{p, r\}) = \exp\left(-\frac{\|c(p) - 2c(q) + c(r)\|_1}{\gamma}\right) \tag{3}$$

$$S(q, \{p, r\}) = \|w(q, \{p, r\})D(p) - 2w(q, \{p, r\})D(q) + w(q, \{p, r\})D(r)\|_1 \tag{4}$$

where $\|.\|_1$ is $L1$ normal of a vector, γ is a parameter controlling the significance of an edge, and $c(p)$ is the color vector of pixel p. To simplify notations, we will denote them by $w(q)$ and $S(q)$ at the rest of the paper. If the 3×1 patch crosses an edge between two regions, the corresponding weight $w(q)$ is likely to be zero, as well as $S(q)$. Therefore, this weighting scheme does not punish discontinuity of disparities on edges. Indeed $c(p) - 2c(q) + c(r)$ is the second derivative of the image. It is easy to verify that if the disparity function is linear, i.e., $D([x, y]^\top) = ax + by + c$, the smoothness term will be zero. Fox example, if $q = [x, y]^\top, p = [x - 1, y]^\top, r = [x + 1, y]^\top$, then

$$S(q) = \|w(q)(a(x-1)+by+c) - 2w(q)(ax+by+c) + w(q)(a(x+1)+by+c)\|_1 = 0 \tag{5}$$

Rewriting Eq. (4) in matrix form, the smoothness energy can be expressed as

$$E_S(\mathbf{u}) = \mathbf{u}^\top L^\top L \mathbf{u} \tag{6}$$

where $L = D - W$ is the Laplacian matrix [18], W is the weight matrix with $w_{qp} = w_{qr} = w(q, \{p, r\})$, and D is a diagonal matrix with $d_{qq} = \sum_i w_{qi}$.

By considering smoothness along multiple directions , we get several Laplacian matrices L_i. The overall problem is a sum of individual quadratic problem. Each directional Laplacian matrix imposes smoothness along one corresponding direction, and does not punish disparity discontinuous crossing intensity edges in any directions.

2.2 As-Rigid-As-Possible Smoothness and Data Cost

Segment-based smoothness prior is an implicit rigid regularization on disparities, which has been demonstrated to be very robust even in hard cases, e.g., autonomous driving stereo estimation [19]. Compared with pixel-wise smoothness priors, it has two major benefits 1) it is more robust to bad local minimum, and 2) the number of parameters is significantly reduced, which usually leads to faster models.

In order to exploit such advantages while avoiding over-rigidness, we reparameterize the disparity map $\mathbf{u}$ by a set of quadratic disparity surfaces that are fitted to each segment. In other word, we try to be "as-rigid-as-possible" (thus the name of the paper) by keeping using the segment-based scheme, while circumventing over-rigidness by fitting quadratic surfaces instead of planes. Specifically, given a segment list S of the input view, we define the segment-based data cost term, which has "built-in" as-rigid-as-possible smoothness, as

$$E_D(\mathbf{\Lambda}) = \sum_{\mathbf{s}} \sum_{p \in \mathbf{s}} \rho \left(\begin{bmatrix} p_x \\ p_y \end{bmatrix}, \begin{bmatrix} p_x - D_{\mathbf{s}}(p - \bar{p}_{\mathbf{s}}) \\ p_y \end{bmatrix} \right) \tag{7}$$

where $\mathbf{s}$ is a segment, p is a pixel in $\mathbf{s}$, $\bar{p}_{\mathbf{s}}$ is the barycenter of $\mathbf{s}$, and $D_{\mathbf{s}}([x, y]^\top) = dx^2 + ey^2 + ax + by + c$ is the disparity functional, $\mathbf{\Lambda}$ is a $|S| \times 5$ matrix representing the quadratic coefficients for all the $|S|$ segments, and $\rho(p, q)$ is the commonly used matching cost [1]

$$\rho(p, q) = (1 - \alpha) \min(\|I_1(p) - I_2(q)\|_1, \tau_{col}) + \alpha \min(\|\nabla I_1(p) - \nabla I_2(q)\|_1, \tau_{grad}) \tag{8}$$

where parameters τ_{col} and τ_{grad} truncate costs for robustness in occlusion regions. For clarity, we use $\rho(p, p - D_{\mathbf{s}}(p))$ to denote the ρ in the right hand side of (7) at the rest of the paper.

Actually, many different types of functionals can be adopted here to model a curved surface, e.g., the multiple-RBF proposed in [20]. Considering its simplicity, we choose the quadratic functional. If the two second-order parameters d and e are zero, the functional degenerates to a plane. Thus, it is a natural extension of the classical plane-fitting approaches [6]. In section 3.1 we will further show a straightforward way to initialize the functional.

However, the surfaces types that a quadratic functional can model are limited. To circumvent this problem, we propose to segment images to almost regular blocks by the super-pixel approach SLIC [21]. As shown in Fig. 2(a-b), the segmentation obtained by the SLIC is better than mean-shift [22] for our application. In each small regular grid, a quadratic functional could be a good approximation to the disparity surface.

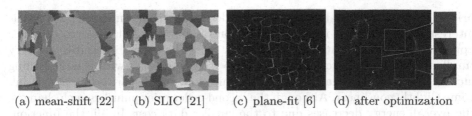

(a) mean-shift [22]   (b) SLIC [21]   (c) plane-fit [6]   (d) after optimization

Fig. 2. Some results of the Middlebury dataset Bowling2 [23]. (a-b) are segmentations. (c-d) shows the absolute residuals $\sum_i |L_i\mathbf{u}|$ with respect to disparity map $\mathbf{u}$ obtained by plane-fit[6] and our approach respectively. See text for more details.

2.3 Overall Energy

Combining the pixel-wise second-order smoothness (6) and the matching cost (7) with built-in "as-rigid-as-possible" smoothness , we obtain the energy

$$E_1(\mathbf{u}, \mathbf{\Lambda}) = \mathbf{u}^\top (\sum_i L_i^\top L_i)\mathbf{u} + \lambda \sum_{\mathbf{s}} \sum_{p\in\mathbf{s}} \rho(p, p - D_{\mathbf{s}}(p)) \tag{9}$$

where $\mathbf{u} = \mathbf{D}(\mathbf{\Lambda})$. However, this results in a tight dependence between the two energy terms, which is difficult to optimize. Inspired by the work [24][5], we introduce an intermediate term to decouple the tight dependence of the two subenergies. In summary, the overall energy is defined as

$$E_2(\mathbf{u}, \mathbf{\Lambda}) = \mathbf{u}^\top (\sum_i L_i^\top L_i)\mathbf{u} + \theta(\mathbf{u} - \mathbf{v})^\top G(\mathbf{u} - \mathbf{v}) + \lambda \sum_{\mathbf{s}} \sum_{p\in\mathbf{s}} \rho(p, p - D_{\mathbf{s}}(p)) \tag{10}$$

where $\mathbf{v} = \mathbf{D}(\mathbf{\Lambda})$ is the disparity map determined by the surface equations $\mathbf{\Lambda}$, G is an identity matrix[1], θ is a scalar determining the tightness of the couple between $\mathbf{u}$ and $\mathbf{v}$. When θ increases from 0 to a large value, the two disparity maps gradually converge to an agreement.

2.4 Interactions between the Two Priors

Without the segment-wise "as-rigid-as-possible" (ARAP) prior, the solution may easily get trapped in bad local minimums, such as those shown in Fig. 4, because the pixel-wise second-order prior itself is too flexible to handle this issue. Without the second-order prior term, the energy is almost the same as traditional segment-based approaches [6], which usually suffer from misalignments along segment boundaries. Fig. 2(c) shows the absolute residual $\sum_i |L_i\mathbf{u}|$ of a disparity map obtained by plane-fitting. We can easily find strong seams between regions while inside each region the residual is zero due to the collinearity. By combining the two priors, the over-flexible issue of the second-order prior is restricted by the ARAP prior. At the same time, the seams caused by the ARAP

---

[1] Each g_{ii} could be a confidence assigned to pixel i if we have that kind of information.

prior are smoothed out by the second-order prior, as shown in Fig. 2(d). It is interesting to note that in some regions on the bowling ball non-zero residuals appear, see the three patches of Fig. 2(d). Since the overall intensities are very small, we clip three patches and visualize their intensities with a large scaling factor. The reason is that after the optimization, the disparity functionals become slightly non-linear. Although the second-order prior punishes such changes, the overall energy decreases due to the smaller data cost. In all, the functionalities of the two priors are complementary to each other. As demonstrated in section 4, the two priors work together to generate accurate and seamless dense correspondences.

2.5 Optimization

The problem is solved by an alternative optimization approach. First, by fixing **u** we minimize the energy in (10) with respect to **Λ**

$$E_D(\mathbf{\Lambda}) = \theta(\mathbf{u} - \mathbf{D}(\mathbf{\Lambda}))^\top G(\mathbf{u} - \mathbf{D}(\mathbf{\Lambda})) + \lambda \sum_{\mathbf{s}} \sum_{p \in \mathbf{s}} \rho(p, p - D_\mathbf{s}(p)) \quad (11)$$

where $\mathbf{D}(\mathbf{\Lambda})$ denotes the functional vector. It is easy to verify that, given **u**, the optimizations for different segments are independent. Therefore, minimization can be conducted in parallel. Any derivative-free algorithms can be adopted to minimize it. We will present a specially designed approach in section 3.2. When θ is zero, optimizing (11) is similar as the plane-fitting approaches [6].

Second, by fixing $\mathbf{D}(\mathbf{\Lambda})$, that is **v**, we solve a quadratic programming problem with respect to **u**

$$E_S(\mathbf{u}) = \mathbf{u}^\top (\sum_i L_i^\top L_i)\mathbf{u} + \theta(\mathbf{u} - \mathbf{v})^\top G(\mathbf{u} - \mathbf{v}) \quad (12)$$

which has a closed-form solution by solving the linear equation

$$(\sum_i L_i^\top L_i + \theta G)\mathbf{u} = \theta G \mathbf{v} \quad (13)$$

Since $\sum_i L_i^\top L_i + \theta G$ is a sparse positive-semidefinite matrix, the equation can be efficiently solved by the Cholesky decomposition [25].

The alternated optimization is enclosed by an outer loop, which increases θ from zero to a large value. Thus, at the beginning, due to the loose couple, i.e., $\theta(\mathbf{u} - \mathbf{D}(\mathbf{\Lambda}))^\top G(\mathbf{u} - \mathbf{D}(\mathbf{\Lambda}))$ is small, both the two functionals **u** and **Λ** have freedom to change their values to decrease the total energy. While with the increase of θ, the couple of them becomes tighter. Finally, **u** and $\mathbf{D}(\mathbf{\Lambda})$ converge to an agreement. The whole algorithm is summarized in Algorithm 1.

3   Implementation

In this section, we present some further implementation notes to allow the readers to more easily replicate our method.

Algorithm 1. As-Rigid-As-Possible Stereo

---

compute Laplacian matrix L_i
set θ to zero
repeat
  repeat
    minimize Eq. (11) with respect to Λ by a derivative-free algorithm
    solve a quadratic programming Eq. (12) by sparse Cholesky decomposition
  until converged
  increase θ
until converged

3.1 Initialize

A good initialization will make the model converge fast. We adopt a similar plane-fitting approach as proposed in [6] to estimate a plane equation for each segment. Our approach consists of three steps:

1. A matching cost volume is computed based on Eq. (8).
2. Some robust matches are obtained by the WTA strategy followed by the left-right consistency check. The matches are not necessary to be accurate because the plane equations will further be optimized in the model.
3. A plane equation is estimated by RANSAC for each segment. Six matches are randomly sampled to estimate the three parameters of a plane equation, whose cost is then computed by querying pre-computed cost volume [6]. This process is repeated about 20 times[2], and the plane with lowest cost is kept as the result.

It is noted that, unlike in a traditional RANSAC algorithm where the number of inliers is used to evaluate the quality of an estimation, we use the matching cost as the quality measure. The objective of step 3 is coherent with the Eq. (9) where we try to minimize the matching cost too. For small segments or segments without initial matches, we just copy equations of the most similar (measured by mean colors) segment from the local neighborhood.

3.2 Optimize E_D

By the initialization step, we have obtained an approximately good equation for the three 1st-order parameters of each segment, then we randomly assign small values for the rest two 2nd-order parameters, d and e. As we have mentioned the analytical derivatives of Eq. (11) is difficult to compute, we adopt a derivative-free approach to optimize it. The Nelder-Mead simplex algorithm [26] is chosen because a good property of it is that we are able to customize the initialization

---

[2] Different from previous segment-based methods where the number is usually large to guarantee a good estimation, we only need a rough estimation because the surface will be optimized by consecutive steps.

of the $N+1$ vertices of the simplex, where $N = 5$ is the dimension of the variable being optimized. Starting from the space spanned by the initial simplex, better solutions are searched by effective rules of Nelder-Mead algorithm.

To minimize E_D with respect to a segment, we randomly pick six surface equations from its neighboring segments to initialize the Nelder-Mead simplex. This idea is motivated by the PatchMatch approach [1] where good estimations are propagated among adjacent pixels. The basic assumption is that adjacent segments are likely to share similar surface equations.

3.3   Optimize E_S

For large images, although a directional Lalpacian matrix L_i is very sparse, the $\sum_i L_i^\top L_i$ becomes a little dense. This fact causes the Cholesky decomposition slow. To address the problem, we suggest not to solve the linear equation exactly as in Eq. (13). Since Eq. (12) is a convex problem, we can use the gradient descent approach to find a better $\mathbf{u}^{(t+1)}$ from a start point instead of getting the best $\mathbf{u}$

$$\mathbf{u}^{(t+1)} = \mathbf{u}^{(t)} - \tau \nabla E_S \qquad (14)$$

where $\nabla E_S = 2(\sum_i L_i^\top L_i)\mathbf{u}^{(t)} + 2\theta G(\mathbf{u}^{(t)} - \mathbf{v})$ is the gradient of E_S, and τ is a step size.

3.4   Post-process

After optimization, we perform a left-right consistency check to label inconsistent pixels as unknown. The proposed model has a nature way to re-fill unknown pixels. In the G matrix of Eq. (12), we set the corresponding g_{ii} of unknown pixels to zero, then solve the quadratic programming again. Unknown pixels will then be filled by disparities of neighboring pixels with large weights in W. Therefore, disparities of occluded pixels are likely be filled by background instead of foreground, since the intensity edge between them leads to a small weights in W. No other post-processing is conducted.

4   Experiments

We tested our approach on the Middlebury stereo benchmark [2]. The experiments are conducted on a PC equipped with an i7-2600 3.40GHz CPU and 8GB memory. For the parameter setting, we choose $\{\alpha, \tau_{col}, \tau_{grad}\} = \{0.85, 20, 4\}$. The gradient feature is a 2-dimensional vector computed by the 3×3 Sobel operators in horizontal and vertical directions, preceded by a gaussian blur. The value of α is set relatively large to favor the gradient feature in order to deal with radiometric difference between left and right frames. On the other hand, the truncations τ_{col} and τ_{grad} are set to relatively small values to increase the robustness in occlusion. The weight λ which balances the smoothness and matching cost is set to 2. For the construction of the Laplacian matrix, we choose the

Table 1. Top ranked entries of the Middlebury stereo benchmark evaluated at 0.5 error threshold. Our method currently is ranked at the third place out of 143 competing algorithms. In each cell the number denotes bad pixel rate, and subscript denotes ranking.

	Avg.	Tsukuba			Venus			Teddy			Cones		
	Rank	nonocc	all	disc	nonocc	all	disc	nonocc	all	disc	nonocc	all	disc
1.GC+LSL	3.8	5.04_2	5.56_2	14.0_{10}	0.66_3	0.88_3	5.82_4	4.20_1	7.12_1	12.9_1	3.77_5	9.16_5	10.4_8
2.PM-Huber	6.0	7.12_9	7.80_{10}	13.7_8	1.00_9	1.40_{10}	7.80_{12}	5.53_4	9.36_2	15.9_5	2.70_1	7.90_1	7.77_1
3.Ours	6.1	7.17_{11}	7.67_8	16.0_{25}	0.64_2	0.87_2	6.17_5	5.52_3	10.7_4	15.6_4	3.00_3	8.55_3	8.35_3
$\vdots$		$\vdots$			$\vdots$			$\vdots$			$\vdots$		
7.PMBP	14.8	11.9_{44}	12.3_{40}	17.8_{48}	0.85_7	1.10_5	6.45_7	5.60_5	12.0_7	15.5_3	3.48_4	8.88_4	9.41_4
$\vdots$		$\vdots$			$\vdots$			$\vdots$			$\vdots$		
9.PatchMatch	22.2	15.0_{63}	15.4_{62}	20.3_{74}	1.00_{10}	1.34_9	7.75_{11}	5.66_6	11.8_6	16.5_6	3.80_6	10.2_7	10.2_6

same $\gamma = 20$ in Eq. (3) for all directions. To segment the input by SLIC [21], we use $\{k, m\} = \{500, 10\}$, where k is the number of desired superpixels, and m is a compactness parameter to regularize the shape of each superpixel. All these parameters are kept constant for the online evaluation.

4.1   Comparisons of Results

Our approach currently is ranked at the third place evaluated at the 0.5 error threshold. Table 1 details the error rates of top ranked methods. Disparity maps and bad pixel maps of our method are shown in Fig. 3. Fig. 4 compares results of our model and three PatchMatch-based models in a textureless region, the small region under the left arm of the teddy bear. It is clearly seen that Patch Match model mislabeled this region. Although the matching cost with slanted support window defined in PatchMatch is generally very powerful, it still suffers from the lack of regularization limitation in textureless regions, which is a common problem for local stereo methods. More interestingly, the two global extensions of PatchMatch (i.e., PM-Huber [5] and PMBP [17]) which have an explicit smoothness regularization of the 3D label still failed in this region. This may support our claim that pixel-wise smoothness constraints are somehow too flexible to prevent the solution from getting trapped in bad local minimums. In contrast, our method can correctly recover this area due to the "as-rigid-as-possible" constraints introduced by segment-based priors.

To demonstrate that our model can correctly handle curved surfaces, we show point clouds generated from our disparity maps, as well as their Phong shaded versions of the Bowling, Baby, and Cloth [23]. As observed in Fig. 5, our method successfully recovered the surface of the bowling ball, while PatchMatch introduced two pits on the left side of the ball. An interesting observation is that if we take a careful look at the left image, the two fault regions of PatchMatch

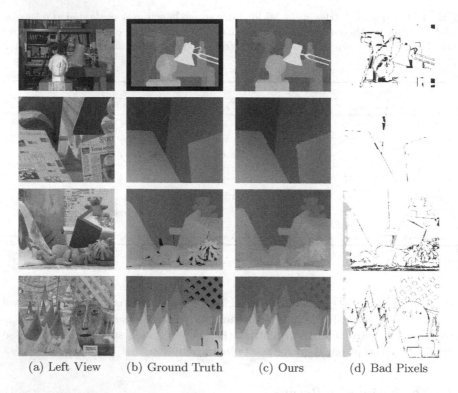

(a) Left View   (b) Ground Truth   (c) Ours   (d) Bad Pixels

Fig. 3. Our results on the four online testing images of Middlebury. The error maps shown in the last column are evaluated at 0.5 error threshold.

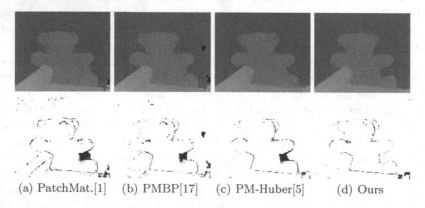

(a) PatchMat.[1]   (b) PMBP[17]   (c) PM-Huber[5]   (d) Ours

Fig. 4. Comparison of results in a textureless region. First row is the disparity maps. Second row is the bad pixel maps.

happen to be shadowed by the standing bottle, which probably results in ambiguous matching cost in these area. Local methods such as PatchMatch may probably fail in this situation. Fig. 6 shows more results. For the Baby case, the

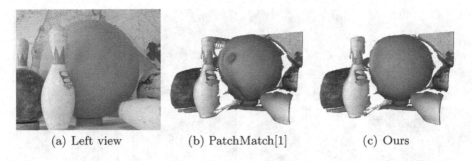

(a) Left view   (b) PatchMatch[1]   (c) Ours

Fig. 5. Comparison of the reconstructed point cloud between PatchMatch and our method

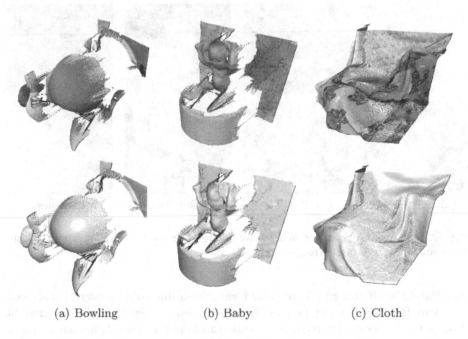

(a) Bowling   (b) Baby   (c) Cloth

Fig. 6. Point clouds and their Phong shaded versions obtained by our model

surface of the round table is correctly recovered, and the shape of the baby's body is well preserved too. The Cloth case is more challenging due to the surfaces with large curvature. However, our approach still works quite well under this hard condition.

In Fig. 7, we show more results of our method, compared with PatchMatch. We implemented the PatchMatch stereo algorithm following the parameters in the original paper [1]. Weighted median filtering is performed to pixels that fail to pass the left-right consistency check. For well textured scene such as the Rock case in the first row, both methods work well and the results are comparable. For weakly textured scene such as the Flowerpots case in the second

(a) Left View   (b) SLIC[21]   (c) PatchMatch[1]   (d) Ours

Fig. 7. More results. From the first to the last row are the Rocks, Flowerpots, Lampshade and Plastic datasets, respectively.

row, PatchMatch can still work considerably well due to its powerful matching cost. But the result is not perfect. It can be clearly seen that the upper-right most pot is not correctly recovered, while this is not a problem for our method. For scenes containing almost textureless regions, such as the Lampshade and Plastic case in the third and last row, disparities computed by PatchMatch are almost completely erroneous in those regions. In contrast, our method can naturally handle this problem. These results again support our basic idea that "as-rigid-as-possible" is effective for stereo matching.

4.2 Running Time

Speaking of running time, our current implementation takes on average 10 seconds for a Middlebury pair. It runs considerably faster than previous methods, e.g., PatchMatch [1] about 1 minute and PM-Huber [5] about 2 minutes. A key reason is that we handle segments, whose number (e.g., hundreds or thousands) is orderly smaller than image pixels. Let us give more details regarding to the implementation. First, the iteration number of the outer loop in Algorithm 1 is not necessarily to be large, since the disparity map usually converges in a few iterations. We increased θ from 0 to 1 by 10 uniform levels and performs two iterations of the inner loop for each level. Second, when solving for smoothness term in Eq. (12), it is not necessary to solve the large sparse linear system in Eq. (13) exactly. Since the energy in (12) is convex, we only need to perform a few steps of gradient descent instead. This results a huge acceleration. For an image of size 375×450, solving the sparse linear system requires approximately 4 seconds on our PC [25]. In contrast, we perform 10 steps of gradient descent, which only cost 0.1 seconds. Third, when solving for the segment-based matching cost term, we use the current best solutions of neighboring segments to initialize the simplex of current segment, which results in a faster convergence during Nelder-Mead search. We therefore keep the number of max iteration of Nelder-Mead low, i.e., 50 in out experiments. Finally since each segment can be optimized individually, we adopted OpenMP [27] for the parallelism.

5   Conclusion

We have presented a novel stereo model which simultaneously incorporates pixelwise second-order smoothness priors and the "as-rigid-as-possible" segment-based priors. The two priors work together to generate seamless, accurate and robust stereo correspondences. The model can be efficiently optimized by alternating between a quadratic programming and many parallel Nelder-Mead simplex search of surface equations. Experiments showed that our method can correctly handle curved surfaces, as well as large textureless regions. Compared to the powerful PatchMatch stereo algorithm, our method is about an order of magnitude faster and generally outperforms it.

References

1. Bleyer, M., Rhemann, C., Rother, C.: Patchmatch stereo - stereo matching with slanted support windows. In: BMVC, pp. 1–11 (2011)
2. Scharstein, D., Szeliski, R.: A taxonomy and evaluation of dense two-frame stereo correspondence algorithms. International Journal of Computer Vision 47(1-3), 7–42 (2002)
3. Zach, C., Pock, T., Bischof, H.: A duality based approach for realtime tv-l^1 optical flow. In: DAGM-Symposium, pp. 214–223 (2007)
4. Ranftl, R., Gehrig, S., Pock, T., Bischof, H.: Pushing the limits of stereo using variational stereo estimation. In: Intelligent Vehicles Symposium, pp. 401–407 (2012)
5. Heise, P., Klose, S., Jensen, B., Knoll, A.: Pm-huber: Patchmatch with huber regularization for stereo matching. In: ICCV, pp. 2360–2367 (2013)
6. Klaus, A., Sormann, M., Karner, K.F.: Segment-based stereo matching using belief propagation and a self-adapting dissimilarity measure. In: ICPR (3), pp. 15–18 (2006)
7. Hong, L., Chen, G.: Segment-based stereo matching using graph cuts. In: CVPR (1), pp. 74–81 (2004)

8. Tao, H., Sawhney, H.S., Kumar, R.: A global matching framework for stereo computation. In: ICCV, pp. 532–539 (2001)
9. Wang, Z.F., Zheng, Z.G.: A region based stereo matching algorithm using cooperative optimization. In: CVPR (2008)
10. Grimson, E.: From images to surfaces: a computational study of the human early visual system. MIT Press (1981)
11. Terzopoulos, D.: Multilevel computational processes for visual surface reconstruction. Computer Vision, Graphics, and Image Processing 24(1), 52–96 (1983)
12. Blake, A., Zisserman, A.: Visual Reconstruction. MIT Press (1987)
13. Ishikawa, H., Geiger, D.: Rethinking the prior model for stereo. In: Leonardis, A., Bischof, H., Pinz, A. (eds.) ECCV 2006. LNCS, vol. 3953, pp. 526–537. Springer, Heidelberg (2006)
14. Woodford, O.J., Torr, P.H.S., Reid, I.D., Fitzgibbon, A.W.: Global stereo reconstruction under second order smoothness priors. In: CVPR (2008)
15. Rother, C., Kolmogorov, V., Lempitsky, V.S., Szummer, M.: Optimizing binary mrfs via extended roof duality. In: CVPR (2007)
16. Olsson, C., Ulén, J., Boykov, Y.: In defense of 3d-label stereo. In: CVPR, pp. 1730–1737 (2013)
17. Besse, F., Rother, C., Fitzgibbon, A., Kautz, J.: Pmbp: Patchmatch belief propagation for correspondence field estimation. International Journal of Computer Vision, 1–12 (2012)
18. Forsyth, D.A., Ponce, J.: Computer Vision: A Modern Approach. Prentice Hall Professional Technical Reference (2002)
19. Yamaguchi, K., McAllester, D.A., Urtasun, R.: Robust monocular epipolar flow estimation. In: CVPR, pp. 1862–1869 (2013)
20. Zhou, X., Boulanger, P.: New eye contact correction using radial basis function for wide baseline videoconference system. In: Lin, W., Xu, D., Ho, A., Wu, J., He, Y., Cai, J., Kankanhalli, M., Sun, M.-T. (eds.) PCM 2012. LNCS, vol. 7674, pp. 68–79. Springer, Heidelberg (2012)
21. Achanta, R., Shaji, A., Smith, K., Lucchi, A., Fua, P., Süsstrunk, S.: Slic superpixels compared to state-of-the-art superpixel methods. IEEE Trans. Pattern Anal. Mach. Intell. 34(11), 2274–2282 (2012)
22. Comaniciu, D., Meer, P.: Mean shift: A robust approach toward feature space analysis. IEEE Trans. Pattern Anal. Mach. Intell. 24(5), 603–619 (2002)
23. Scharstein, D., Szeliski, R.: High-accuracy stereo depth maps using structured light. In: CVPR (1), pp. 195–202 (2003)
24. Steinbrücker, F., Pock, T., Cremers, D.: Large displacement optical flow computation withoutwarping. In: ICCV, pp. 1609–1614 (2009)
25. Chen, Y., Davis, T.A., Hager, W.W., Rajamanickam, S.: Algorithm 887: Cholmod, supernodal sparse cholesky factorization and update/downdate. ACM Trans. Math. Softw. 35(3) (2008)
26. Nelder, J., Mead, R.: A simplex method for function minimization (1965)
27. OpenMP Architecture Review Board: OpenMP application program interface version 3.0 (May 2008)

Real-Time Minimization of the Piecewise Smooth Mumford-Shah Functional

Evgeny Strekalovskiy and Daniel Cremers*

TU Munich, Germany

Abstract. We propose an algorithm for efficiently minimizing the piecewise smooth Mumford-Shah functional. The algorithm is based on an extension of a recent primal-dual algorithm from convex to non-convex optimization problems. The key idea is to rewrite the proximal operator in the primal-dual algorithm using Moreau's identity. The resulting algorithm computes piecewise smooth approximations of color images at 15-20 frames per second at VGA resolution using GPU acceleration. Compared to convex relaxation approaches [18], it is orders of magnitude faster and does not require a discretization of color values. In contrast to the popular Ambrosio-Tortorelli approach [2], it naturally combines piecewise smooth and piecewise constant approximations, it does not require an epsilon-approximation and it is not based on an alternation scheme. The achieved energies are in practice at most 5% off the optimal value for one-dimensional problems. Numerous experiments demonstrate that the proposed algorithm is well-suited to perform discontinuity-preserving smoothing and real-time video cartooning.

Keywords: Mumford-Shah functional, non-convex optimization, real-time, primal-dual.

1 Introduction

With over 4000 citations to date, the Mumford-Shah functional [15] is among the most influential publications in the field of image analysis. This and related publications by Blake and Zisserman [3] and others have sparked enormous research activity on discontinuity-preserving smoothing, piecewise-smooth approximations and minimal partition problems [14]. Yet, the computation of the *piecewise-smooth* approximation has rarely made it into practical image and video analysis methods because minimization of this non-convex functional is difficult and existing algorithmic solutions are far from real-time capability. The contribution of this paper is to propose what we believe to be the first real-time capable algorithm for computing piecewise smooth approximations of color images based on the Mumford-Shah functional.

---

* This work was supported by the ERC Starting Grant "ConvexVision".

D. Fleet et al. (Eds.): ECCV 2014, Part II, LNCS 8690, pp. 127–141, 2014.

Input image   Piecewise smooth approximation

Fig. 1. We propose a fast algorithm to approximately solve the piecewise smooth Mumford-Shah model. With 20 frames per second and above, it allows real-time image processing with applications such as denoising and cartooning.

1.1 The Mumford-Shah Problem

The Mumford-Shah functional [15] provides a prototypical form of all regularizers which aim at combining a smoothing of homogeneous regions with the enhancement of edges. Given a bounded open set $\Omega \subset \mathbb{R}^d$, $d \geq 1$, the vectorial Mumford-Shah problem is given by

$$\min_{u,K} \left\{ \int_\Omega |u - f|^2 \, dx + \alpha \int_{\Omega \setminus K} |\nabla u|^2 \, dx + \lambda \, |K| \right\}, \tag{1}$$

where $f : \Omega \to \mathbb{R}^k$ is a vector-valued input image with $k \geq 1$ channels. This model approximates f by a function $u : \Omega \to \mathbb{R}^k$ which is smooth everywhere in Ω except for a possible $(d-1)$-dimensional jump set K, at which u is discontinuous. The weight $\lambda > 0$ controls the length of the jump set K (less jumps for larger λ) and $\alpha > 0$ penalizes the smoothness of u outside of K. The limiting case $\alpha \to \infty$ imposes zero gradient outside K and is known as the *piecewise constant* Mumford-Shah model or the "cartoon" limit [15]. The norm of the gradient $|\nabla u|$ in (1) is the Euclidean norm $|\nabla u|^2 = \sum_i |\nabla u_i|^2$, and the norm in the term $|u - f|$ is also Euclidean.

Since the jump set K is defined as the union of the jump sets of the individual channels $u_i : \Omega \to \mathbb{R}$, we have a coupling among the channels assuring that jumps in different channels preferably coincide – see also [18].

1.2 Related Work

The Mumford-Shah problem has been intensively studied in the applied math community [14]. In practice its applicability is substantially limited because of its non-convexity. While it is often replaced by the convex total variation, this is a poor substitute because of its tendency to reduce the contrast at edges

Fig. 2. Comparison with the Ambrosio-Tortorelli model. The images show piecewise smooth approximation results for $\lambda = 0.1$, $\alpha = 100$ (top row) and $\lambda = 0.1$, $\alpha = 10000$ (bottom row). While the AT results vary with the parameter ε (and it is not clear how to choose it appropriately), our method has no additional parameters, is stable for every λ and α, and about 3–5 times faster.

and oversmooth flat regions (staircasing). As a consequence, researchers have developed different optimization strategies to tackle the non-convex Mumford-Shah problem.

Alternating Minimization Schemes. One kind of methods consists of non-convex approximations of the original Mumford-Shah functional, where one alternatingly minimizes for u and for K [2,20,11].

The Ambrosio-Tortorelli Approach. The non-convex phase-field model of Ambrosio and Tortorelli [2], for example, is given by:

$$\min_{u,s} \int_\Omega |u - f|^2 \, dx + \alpha \int_\Omega (1 - s)^2 |\nabla u|^2 \, dx + \lambda \int_\Omega \left(\varepsilon |\nabla s|^2 + \frac{1}{4\varepsilon} s^2 \right) dx \quad (2)$$

with a small parameter $\varepsilon > 0$. The key idea is to introduce the additional variable $s : \Omega \to \mathbb{R}$ as an edge set indicator, in the sense that points $x \in \Omega$ are part of the edge set K if $s(x) \approx 1$ and part of the smooth region if $s(x) \approx 0$.

It was shown in [2] that this approximation Γ-converges to the Mumford-Shah functional for $\varepsilon \to 0$, i.e. minimizers of (2) approach minimizers of (1). One finds u and s by alternating minimization, computing s for fixed u and vice versa. Each of these subproblems is elliptic and can be solved quickly, e.g. by the linearly converging primal-dual method [8]. Extensions of this approximation to color images have been proposed in [5].

One disadvantage of this model, beside its non-convexity, is its dependancy on an additional parameter ε. To obtain a good approximation of minimizers of (1),

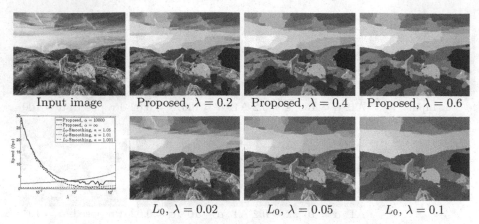

| Input image | Proposed, $\lambda = 0.2$ | Proposed, $\lambda = 0.4$ | Proposed, $\lambda = 0.6$ |
| L_0, $\lambda = 0.02$ | L_0, $\lambda = 0.05$ | L_0, $\lambda = 0.1$ |

Fig. 3. Real-time unsupervised segmentation. The proposed method (**top row**) directly includes the piecewise *constant* case $\alpha = \infty$, which allows to segment an image with an automatic selection of suitable color models in real-time. This is in contrast to L_0-Smoothing (**bottom row**, $\kappa = 1.05$), which leads to piecewise smooth solutions. Avoiding this by choosing small $\kappa > 1$ leads to significant run times.

ε will depend on α, λ and f. Generally, ε must be chosen small for increasing α, and for large α the dependancy becomes sensitive and a good choice is unclear. This makes the approach infeasible for the piecewise constant case $\alpha = \infty$.

The L_0-Smoothing Approach of Xu et al. For the piecewise constant case, Xu et al. [21] recently proposed a fast approximating method. Assuming the image domain has been discretized into a finite rectangular grid, again denoted by Ω, the piecewise constant Mumford-Shah limit corresponds to L_0 penalization of the gradient:

$$\min_u \sum_{x \in \Omega} |u(x) - f(x)|^2 + R_{MS_0}(\nabla u(x)) \tag{3}$$

where

$$R_{MS_0}(g) = \begin{cases} \lambda & \text{if } g \neq 0 \\ 0 & \text{else} \end{cases} \tag{4}$$

and the gradient $\nabla u = (\nabla u_i)_{1 \leq i \leq k}$ is discretized e.g. using forward differences. Intuitively, the regularizer R_{MS_0} summed up over all pixels counts how many times u changes its value. This way, it prefers regions of constancy instead of smooth variations. Xu et al. propose a quadratic decoupling strategy to solve (3), introducing new variables g which approximate the gradient:

$$\min_{u,g} \sum_{x \in \Omega} |u(x) - f(x)|^2 + \beta |\nabla u(x) - g(x)|^2 + R_{MS_0}(g(x)) \tag{5}$$

with a parameter $\beta > 0$ and the Euclidean norm for the coupling. This approximation is again solved via alternating minimization. After having computed the next u and g, the parameter β is increased to $\kappa\beta$ with a $\kappa > 1$ until a final $\beta_{\max}$

Fig. 4. Comparison with the convexification approach [18] for the MS model
(1). The images show denoising results for different parameters α and λ. While both
algorithms provide discontinuity-preserving smoothing, in the piecewise constant limit
(**bottom row**), the solutions of [18] appear too smooth or blurry. Moreover, since [18]
adds an additional dimension to the problem because of color quantization, it requires
much more memory (> 2 GB) and is about 50–500 times slower than our approach.

is reached. Starting value for β is chosen automatically as $\beta_0 = 2\lambda$. Multiplier
κ is set either to 2 (fast but smooth result) or 1.05 (slow and more piecewise
constant).

Because of the empirical nature of the coupling, it is not clear how the computed solutions u mathematically relate to the original model (3), or even to
(1). In fact, the computed solutions are actually not piecewise constant, but
vary smoothly over large areas.

Convex Relaxation Methods. In the recent past, several authors have
overcome the issue of non-convexity by suggesting convex relaxations for respective functionals [1,10]. Convex relaxations for the piecewise constant Mumford-Shah functional were proposed in [13,7,22]. Convex relaxations for the piecewise
smooth Mumford-Shah model were proposed for the scalar [16] and for the vectorial case [18]. The key idea is to rewrite the multi-label problem as a binary
labeling problem in a higher-dimensional space. Relaxation of the binary constraint leads to a convex problem which can be minimized optimally. Subsequent
binarization provides an approximate solution of the original problem.

Some of these approaches were clearly inspired by the Markov random field
(MRF) community, where the discrete variant of the Mumford-Shah regularizer
is typically referred to as a truncated quadratic penalizer [4,12,19].

Unfortunately, these methods to compute approximate minimizers are currently far from real-time capability because the added label space dimension
drastically increases memory and run time. For the Mumford-Shah model the

run time even grows quadratically in the number of considered color values. Thus, the problem of computing good approximate minimizers of the Mumford-Shah energy in real-time remains an important challenge.

1.3   Contribution

In this paper, we propose a novel algorithm to efficiently compute approximate minimizers of the full Mumford-Shah functional (1). It combines several important advantages:

- The Mumford-Shah energy is minimized directly, instead of alternatingly. Therefore there is a clear correspondence between the computed solutions and the original functional.

- In contrast to other methods like the Ambrosio-Tortorelli approximation or the L_0-Smoothing, our method naturally combines the piecewise smooth and the piecewise constant approximation. In the latter case, the solution is guaranteed to be piecewise constant, in contrast to the L_0-smoothing.

- The method runs in real-time. For VGA 640×480 images, the achieved frame rates are 15–20 Hz for piecewise smooth approximations, and still about 5–10 Hz for almost piecewise constant ones (α large).

- The algorithm is easy to implement It is based on a simple state-of-the-art primal-dual algorithm. In order to apply it to the non-convex MS regularizer, we reformulate one step of this algorithm in a slight but crucial way. All computations remain simple and elementary.

2   Proposed Finite-Difference Discretization

Similar to [21] we work with an already discretized image domain Ω. We propose to minimize the energy

$$\min_u E_{MS}(u) = \sum_{x \in \Omega} |u(x) - f(x)|^2 + R_{MS}(\nabla u(x)) \qquad (6)$$

with

$$R_{MS}(g) := \min \left(\alpha |g|^2, \lambda \right). \qquad (7)$$

Just as in the term $|\nabla u|$ in (1), the gradient norm in (7) is the Euclidean one, regarding the matrix $g = \nabla u = (\nabla u_i)_{1 \le i \le k} \in (\mathbb{R}^d)^k$ as an element of $\mathbb{R}^{dk}$. The gradient discretization can be done in several meaningful ways. In our implementation we used forward differences as they give visually good results at minimal implementation costs. Another possibility is to use a "staggered grid", where the gradient is computed in the middle point between four pixels [22].

The idea of (6) is to model the edge set explicitly in terms of the function u itself. Namely, the edge set K consists here of all points where the minimum value is λ in (7), i.e. where the gradient is large enough:

$$K_{MS} := \left\{ x \in \Omega \mid |\nabla u(x)| \ge \sqrt{\lambda/\alpha} \right\}. \qquad (8)$$

Indeed, for $x \in K_{MS}$ we have $R_{MS}(\nabla u(x)) = \lambda$, while for $x \notin K_{MS}$ we have $R_{MS}(\nabla u(x)) = \alpha |\nabla u(x)|^2$.

In the cartoon limit $\alpha \to \infty$ expression (7) becomes (4). Applying this regularizer in (6) yields *piecewise constant* approximations of the input image. This model is the same as (3) which is considered in [21]. Note that in contrast to convex relaxation methods [16,18] we do not need to discretize the range of $u : \Omega \to \mathbb{R}^k$ into a finite set in order to compute solutions, and therefore fully avoid the corresponding dramatic increase in memory consumption and computation time. The model (6) can be regarded as a natural discretization of the Mumford-Shah energy (1) for a discrete image domain, as will be explained next.

Connection to the Mumford-Shah Energy (1). For $2D$ scalar images, i.e. $k = 1$ and $d = 2$, in [9] Chambolle considered a variant E_{l^1} of the Mumford-Shah energy (1) where the usual Euclidean length $|K|$ of the edge set is replaced by the l^1-norm length $L_{l^1}(K)$. Intuitively, if K were approximated by small line pieces, everyone of which being either horizontal or vertical, $L_{l^1}(K)$ would be the usual length of this approximation. It was shown that, if the image domain is discretized into a finite rectangular grid of pixel width h, the discrete energies

$$E^h(u) = \sum_{x \in \Omega} h^2 |u(x) - f^h(x)|^2 + R_{MS}^h(\nabla u(x)) \qquad (9)$$

Γ-converge to E_{l^1} for $h \to 0$, with

$$R_{MS}^h(g) := \min\left(\alpha |g_1|^2, \tfrac{1}{h}\lambda\right) + \min\left(\alpha |g_2|^2, \tfrac{1}{h}\lambda\right) \qquad (10)$$

and $f^h(x) := \frac{1}{h^2} \int_{\text{Pixel } x} f^{\text{continuous}}(y) \, dy$. The gradient ∇ is discretized by forward differences. For instance, for the approximation of E_{l^1} by (9) we can choose $h = 1$, assuming the continuous domain has the size of the pixel grid.

Our proposed energy (6) is motivated by (9). Indeed, observe that penalizing $g_1 = \partial_x u$ and $g_2 = \partial_y u$ separately in (10) (no coupling) results in the l^1-norm length $L_{l^1}(K)$ for the edge set length. A natural conjecture is that, changing the coupling to the l^2-norm as in the proposed model (7), one would obtain the usual l^2-norm length $|K|$. Experiments suggest that this is indeed the case, since the obtained solutions do not show visible signs of grid dependance.

In addition to considering the l^2-coupling of the gradient in (7), we simultaneously extend the approach to the vectorial case $k \geq 1$, again by considering the l^2-norm of all possible derivatives of u in (7).

3   Minimization Algorithm

3.1   Algorithm for Convex Regularizers R

To give a motivation for our algorithm, we first consider the energy minimization problem (6) for *convex* regularizers R in place of R_{MS}. First we need a few definitions. For a function $R : \mathbb{R}^{d \times k} \to \mathbb{R}$ the Legendre-Fenchel *convex conjugate* [17] is defined as

$$R^*(p) := \sup_{g \in \mathbb{R}^{d \times k}} \langle p, g \rangle - R(g), \qquad (11)$$

where $\langle\cdot,\cdot\rangle$ is the standard scalar product on $\mathbb{R}^{d\times k}$. A well-known fact about the convex conjugate is that for convex and lower-semicontinuous R it holds $R = (R^*)^*$, i.e.

$$R(g) = \sup_{p\in\mathbb{R}^{d\times k}} \langle p, g\rangle - R^*(p). \tag{12}$$

For general R, expression (12) gives the *convex envelope* of R, which is the largest convex function pointwise below or equal to R. The *proximal operator* [8] of R is defined as

$$\operatorname{prox}_{\tau, R}(\tilde{g}) := \arg\min_{g\in\mathbb{R}^{d\times k}} \frac{|g - \tilde{g}|^2}{2\tau} + R(g) \tag{13}$$

for parameters $\tau > 0$ and arguments $\tilde{g} \in \mathbb{R}^{d\times k}$.

Primal-Dual Algorithm. Consider now the energy (6) with a *convex* (and lower-semicontinuous) regularizer R instead of R_{MS}. The first step is to use (12) as a means of variable decoupling. We get

$$E(u) = \sup_{p:\Omega\to\mathbb{R}^{d\times k}} \sum_{x\in\Omega} |u(x) - f(x)|^2 + \langle p(x), \nabla u(x)\rangle - R^*\big(p(x)\big). \tag{14}$$

Taking the minimum of (14) over u, we obtain a classical saddle-point problem. The state-of-the-art primal-dual algorithm [8] is developed especially for this kind of problems. Furthermore, we can use the accelerated Algorithm 2 of [8] since the data term $D(u) := \sum_{x\in\Omega} |u(x) - f(x)|^2$ in (14) is uniformly convex with constant $\gamma = 2$: for any u and u', $D(u) \geq D(u') + \langle 2f, u - u'\rangle + \frac{\gamma}{2}\|u - u'\|^2$. The update equations are as follows:

$$p^{n+1} = \operatorname{prox}_{\sigma_n, R^*}\left(p^n + \sigma_n \nabla \overline{u}^n\right), \tag{15}$$

$$u^{n+1} = \operatorname{prox}_{\tau_n, D}\left(u^n + \tau_n \operatorname{div} p^{n+1}\right), \tag{16}$$

$$\theta_n = \frac{1}{\sqrt{1+4\tau_n}}, \quad \tau_{n+1} = \theta_n\tau_n, \quad \sigma_{n+1} = \sigma_n/\theta_n, \tag{17}$$

$$\overline{u}^{n+1} = u^{n+1} + \theta_n(u^{n+1} - u^n). \tag{18}$$

The divergence $\operatorname{div} p = (\operatorname{div} p_i)_{1\leq i\leq k}$ for $p : \Omega \to \mathbb{R}^{d\times k} = (\mathbb{R}^d)^k$ is defined as the negative adjoint of the gradient [6]. The starting values u^0 and p^0 are arbitrary, with $\overline{u}^0 = u^0$ and time steps $\tau_0\sigma_0\|\nabla\|^2 < 1$. Since $\|\nabla\| < \sqrt{4d}$ [8], we can set $\tau_0 = \frac{1}{2d}$, $\sigma_0 = \frac{1}{2}$. As proved in [8], the iterates (u^n, p^n) converge to a solution of the saddle-point problem (14) with energy rate $\mathcal{O}(1/n^2)$.

The proximal operator for u in (16) can be easily computed explicitly:

$$\operatorname{prox}_{\tau, D}(\tilde{u}) = \frac{\tilde{u} + 2\tau f}{1 + 2\tau}. \tag{19}$$

Reformulation of (15) *by Moreau's Identity.* Note that the only place where the regularizer enters the algorithm is step (15), and this dependancy is in terms of the convex conjugate R^*. Plugging in an arbitrary, possibly non-convex regularizer R, through (12) this means that the algorithm would work as if the *convex*

Algorithm 1. Fast Mumford-Shah Minimization

Input: Image $f : \Omega \to \mathbb{R}^k$, parameters $0 < \alpha, \lambda \leq \infty$ and $\varepsilon > 0$ $(d = \dim \Omega)$
Initialize: $u^0 = f$, $\overline{u}^0 = u^0$, $p^0 = 0$, $\tau_0 = \frac{1}{2d}$, $\sigma_0 = \frac{1}{2}$

1 **for** $n \geq 0$ **until** $\|u^{n+1} - u^n\| < \varepsilon$ **do**

  // Dual ascent in p

2   $\tilde{p}(x) = p^n(x) + \sigma_n \nabla \overline{u}^n(x)$

3   $p^{n+1}(x) = \begin{cases} \frac{2\alpha}{\sigma_n + 2\alpha} \tilde{p}(x) & \text{if } |\tilde{p}(x)| \leq \sqrt{\frac{\lambda}{\alpha} \sigma_n(\sigma_n + 2\alpha)} \\ 0 & \text{else} \end{cases}$

  // Primal descent in u

4   $\tilde{u}(x) = u^n(x) + \tau_n \operatorname{div} p^{n+1}(x)$

5   $u^{n+1}(x) = \left(\tilde{u}(x) + 2\tau_n f(x)\right)/(1 + 2\tau_n)$

  // Extrapolation step

6   $\theta_n = \frac{1}{\sqrt{1+4\tau_n}}$, $\quad \tau_{n+1} = \theta_n \tau_n$, $\quad \sigma_{n+1} = \sigma_n/\theta_n$

7   $\overline{u}^{n+1} = u^{n+1} + \theta_n\left(u^{n+1} - u^n\right)$

8 **end**

---

envelope of R were given as the regularizer instead of R. For example, the convex envelope of R_{MS} is the zero function, so the algorithm for R_{MS} would behave as if there were no regularization at all.

To make the algorithm applicable also to non-convex R, the central idea is to reformulate step (15) by reducing the proximal operator of R^* to that of R. For this, we make use of Moreau's identity [17]:

$$\operatorname{prox}_{\sigma, R^*}(p) = p - \sigma \operatorname{prox}_{\frac{1}{\sigma}, R}(p/\sigma). \tag{20}$$

Applying this to (15), the algorithm only becomes written in a slightly different way. For convex R the sequence u^n is still the same and all convergence guarantees still hold.

3.2   Proposed Algorithm for the MS-Energy

The main advantage of reformulating the step (15) by (20) is that the algorithm now becomes applicable also to non-convex regularizers, because only R itself enters the right hand side of (20), and not R^*. We propose to apply the reformulated algorithm to the Mumford-Shah case with the *non-convex* regularizer R_{MS} in (7).

It remains to compute the right hand side of (20), and for this we need to compute the proximal operator

$$\operatorname{prox}_{\tau, R_{MS}}(\tilde{g}) = \arg\min_{g \in \mathbb{R}^{d \times k}} \frac{|g - \tilde{g}|^2}{2\tau} + \min\left(\alpha|g|^2, \lambda\right).$$

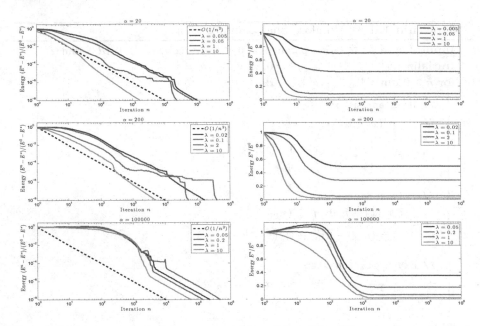

Fig. 5. Convergence of the proposed algorithm. For different values of α and λ the algorithm steadily decreases the energy (6) (**solid lines**) to a limit energy E^*, here approximated by $E^* = E(u^{10^6})$. Experimentally the convergence rate is roughly $\mathcal{O}(1/n^2)$ (**dashed lines**).

Although this energy is not convex, its simple structure allows us to find an *explicit formula* for the minimizer:

$$\text{prox}_{\tau, R_{MS}}(\tilde{g}) = \begin{cases} \frac{1}{1+2\tau\alpha}\, \tilde{g} & \text{if } |\tilde{g}| \leq \sqrt{\frac{\lambda}{\alpha}(1 + 2\tau\alpha)}, \\ \tilde{g} & \text{else.} \end{cases}$$

Inserting this into (20) results in

$$\text{prox}_{\sigma, R_{MS}^*}(\tilde{p}) = \begin{cases} \frac{2\alpha}{\sigma+2\alpha}\, \tilde{p} & \text{if } |\tilde{p}| \leq \sqrt{\frac{\lambda}{\alpha}\sigma(\sigma + 2\alpha)}, \\ 0 & \text{else.} \end{cases} \tag{21}$$

For the piecewise constant limit case $\alpha \to \infty$, the right hand side of (21) simplifies to

$$\text{prox}_{\sigma, R_{MS0}^*}(\tilde{p}) = \begin{cases} \tilde{p} & \text{if } |\tilde{p}| \leq \sqrt{2\lambda\sigma}, \\ 0 & \text{else.} \end{cases} \tag{22}$$

We obtain Algorithm 1 for the minimization of the proposed Mumford-Shah functional (6). The algorithm always converges experimentally, with roughly $O(1/n^2)$ energy rates, see Fig. 5. Although we do not have a proof of convergence yet, nonetheless we can prove the boundedness of u^n for the piecewise smooth case $\alpha < \infty$:

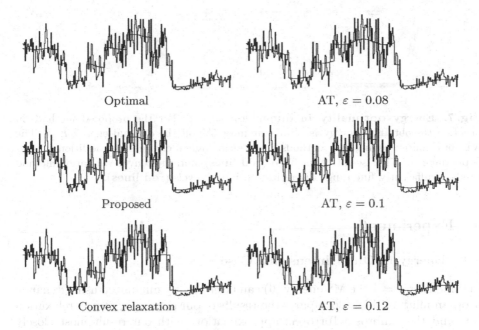

Fig. 6. **Denoising quality in dimension** $d = 1$ **with** $\alpha = 1000$ **and** $\lambda = 0.3$. Our approach yields a solution most closely resembling the optimal solution. We do not have any further parameters, while in contrast the AT method is highly sensitive w.r.t. ε.

Proposition 1. *The sequence* (u^n, p^n) *generated by Algorithm 1 is bounded and thus compact for* $\alpha < \infty$, *for instance it has a convergent subsequence.*

Proof. See supplementary material.

We terminate once the solution does not change significantly anymore. This will always be the case for any choice of the parameters, as stated in the following proposition:

Proposition 2. *Algorithm 1 always terminates, i.e.* $\|u_{n+1} - u_n\| \overset{n \to \infty}{\longrightarrow} 0$.

Proof. See supplementary material.

We set $\varepsilon = 5 \cdot 10^{-5}$. To reduce run time, we compute $\|u^{n+1} - u^n\|$ only once every 10 iterations, the norm here being defined as

$$\|\tilde{u}\| := \frac{1}{|\Omega|} \sum_{x \in \Omega} \sum_{1 \leq i \leq k} |\tilde{u}_i(x)|. \tag{23}$$

We use a parallel CUDA implementation on the NVIDIA GTX 680 GPU.

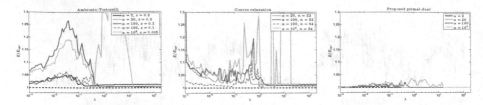

Fig. 7. Energy optimality in dimension $d = 1$**.** For the proposed method, in practice the obtained energy is always at most 5% off the optimal energy E_{opt}. The AT and convex relaxation methods both yield higher energies. In addition, the ε-dependancy of AT is sensitive for big α (**red lines**), and the convex relaxation method needs a sufficiently fine range discretization into n levels (**red lines**).

4   Experiments

4.1   Energy in One-Dimensional Case

In dimension $d = 1$ the MS energy (6) can be efficiently minimized using dynamic programming [9]. Fig. 6 compares the results of our approach, convex relaxation [18] and the Ambrosio-Tortorelli approximation, with our result most closely resembling the optimal solution (input is the lower row of the image in Fig. 3). In fact, in practice our obtained energy is always at most 5% off the optimal energy, see Fig. 7.

4.2   Comparison with Convex Relaxation

The method [18] computes *relaxed* solutions of (1) through convexification. Since it discretizes the color space, it requires huge amounts of memory (> 2 GB for VGA resolution and 32 levels for each channel) and is slow (30–300 seconds). In contrast, we only need about 15 MB and the run time is real-time. In general, our results are always visually similar with [18], see Fig. 4, which indicates the appropriateness of our method for solving the MS model. While the results of [18] are often too smooth and blurry, even for the piecewise constant case $\alpha = \infty$, our model yields results with visually well-defined sharp transitions.

4.3   Comparison with Ambrosio-Tortorelli

The AT approximation has an additional parameter ε. It is not clear how to choose a suitable ε given λ and α in order to obtain "true" minimizers of the MS model (1). The results depend on ε and this dependancy becomes more and more sensitive for larger α, see Fig. 2 and 6. In contrast, our method comes without any additional parameters, is stable in λ and α, and also turns out to be about 5–10 times faster. While the AT model requires alternating minimization and the two involved subproblems can be solved only approximately, we propose a direct well-defined algorithm which is also applicable for the case $\alpha = \infty$.

Input   [21], $\kappa = 1.01$ Proposed

Fig. 8. Grid artifacts of L_0-Smoothing [21]. The method [21] (**center**, $\lambda = 0.035$) measures edge lengths with the anisotropic l^1-norm. This leads to significant artifacts as result edges tend to align with coordinate axes. We use the l^2-norm (**right**, $\lambda = 0.82$, $\alpha = \infty$), yielding more natural results.

4.4 Comparison with L_0-Smoothing

The method [21] is devised for the piecewise constant case $\alpha = \infty$, but the solutions depend on a parameter $\kappa > 1$. To reduce smooth variations, it must be chosen near 1, which increases the run time significantly. In contrast, our method is directly applicable with $\alpha = \infty$ and the solutions are guaranteed to be piecewise constant, see Fig. 3. Because of the heuristic decoupling there is no clear relation between the parameter λ in (5) (through (4)) and the original parameter λ in (1). Since in (5) the g-subproblem is solved exactly, one can see that $R_0(g)$ then measure edges in the *anisotropic* l^1-norm. This leads to grid artifacts, see Fig. 8, in contrast to our primal-dual formulation.

4.5 Real-Time Unsupervised Image Segmentation

The proposed method naturally includes the piecewise constant limit $\alpha = \infty$, see Fig. 3. This allows one to segment an image with automatic selection of the most suitable color models in real-time. In contrast, results of the L_0-Smoothing always have smooth variations, which can only be avoided at considerable increase of run time. Also, [21] approximates (1) worse and worse when increasing the edge set penalization λ. This leads to artifacts such failing to get rid of small scale structures (grass) despite an overall smooth solution.

4.6 Real-Time Video Cartooning

The proposed method remains fast even when approaching the cartoon limit of the MS model (1), i.e. for large α, with more than 20 frames per second on three GPUs, and still about 5–10 frames per second on a single GPU. This allows us to apply the MS model to videos in real time, processing them frame by frame, see Fig. 9 and the supplementary material.

To reduce artificial solution variations from frame to frame, we employ temporal regularization at each pixel, yielding the energy

$$E_{MS}(u) + \gamma \sum_{x \in \Omega} |u(x) - u_{\text{prev}}(x)|^q \qquad (24)$$

Fig. 9. Video cartooning. The cartoon limit $\alpha \to \infty$ of our method allows to compute real-time cartoonings of video sequences (**top:** an input frame, **bottom:** cartooned frame), $\lambda = 1.5$, $\alpha = 500$, $\gamma = 0.4$ in (24). Average processing frame rate: 10.3 Hz.

with a small $\gamma > 0$, e.g. 0.4, and $q = 1.5$. This only affects the proximal operator (16), so that line 5 of the Algorithm 1 becomes slightly altered, see supplementary material. A practical side effect, in addition to regularization, is that this further accelerates the convergence of our algorithm.

The exponent $q = 1.5$ performs best in practice, having an effect between $q = 2$, where the results are blurry due to uniform averaging, and $q = 1$, where the previous frame influence is too strong, see supplementary material. Furthermore, to accommodate for low contrast edges, we use an adaptive variant of (7): $\min\left(\alpha|g|^2, \lambda w(x)\right)$ with $w(x) := \exp\left(-|\nabla f(x)|/s\right)$ and $s := \frac{1}{|\Omega|} \sum_{x \in \Omega} |\nabla f(x)|$.

5   Conclusion

We proposed an algorithm which allows to efficiently minimize the piecewise smooth and piecewise constant Mumford-Shah model. Using Moreau's identity to simplify respective proximal operators, we were able to generalize a recent primal-dual algorithm from convex to non-convex optimization. The resulting method computes piecewise smooth or piecewise constant approximations of color-images at 15-20 Hz at VGA resolution. Compared to existing convex relaxation methods, it does not require a discretization of color values and it is orders of magnitude faster. In contrast to the popular Ambrosio-Tortorelli approach, it does not require an epsilon-approximation and pursues a direct rather than an alternating minimization scheme. Numerous experiments demonstrate that the proposed algorithm is well-suited to perform discontinuity-preserving smoothing and real-time video cartooning.

References

1. Alberti, G., Bouchitté, G., Dal Maso, G.: The calibration method for the Mumford-Shah functional and free-discontinuity problems. Calc. Var. Partial Differential Equations 16(3), 299–333 (2003)
2. Ambrosio, L., Tortorelli, V.M.: Approximation of functionals depending on jumps by elliptic functionals via Γ–convergence. Comm. Pure Appl. Math. 43, 999–1036 (1990)
3. Blake, A., Zisserman, A.: Visual Reconstruction. MIT Press (1987)
4. Boykov, Y., Veksler, O., Zabih, R.: Fast approximate energy minimization via graph cuts. IEEE Trans. on Patt. Anal. and Mach. Intell. 23(11), 1222–1239 (2001)
5. Brook, A., Kimmel, R., Sochen, N.A.: Variational restoration and edge detection for color images. Journal of Mathematical Imaging and Vision 18(3), 247–268 (2003)
6. Chambolle, A.: An algorithm for total variation minimization and applications. J. Math. Im. Vis. 20(1-2), 89–97 (2004)
7. Chambolle, A., Cremers, D., Pock, T.: A convex approach to minimal partitions. SIAM Journal on Imaging Sciences 5(4), 1113–1158 (2012)
8. Chambolle, A., Pock, T.: A first-order primal-dual algorithm for convex problems with applications to imaging. J. Math. Imaging Vis. 40, 120–145 (2011)
9. Chambolle, A.: Image segmentation by variational methods: Mumford and Shah functional and the discrete approximations. SIAM J. Appl. Math. 55(3), 827–863 (1995)
10. Giaquinta, M., Modica, G., Souček, J.: Cartesian currents in the calculus of variations I, II., Ergebnisse der Mathematik und ihrer Grenzgebiete. 3, vol. 37-38, pp. 37–38. Springer, Berlin (1998)
11. Grady, L., Alvino, C.: The piecewise smooth Mumford-Shah functional on an arbitrary graph. IEEE Transactions on Image Processing 18(11) (2009)
12. Komodakis, N., Tziritas, G.: Approximate labeling via graph-cuts based on linear programming. IEEE Trans. on Patt. Anal. and Mach. Intell. 29(8), 1436–1453 (2007)
13. Lellmann, J., Schnörr, C.: Continuous multiclass labeling approaches and algorithms. SIAM J. Imaging Sciences 4(4), 1049–1096 (2011)
14. Morel, J.M., Solimini, S.: Variational Methods in Image Segmentation. Birkhäuser, Boston (1995)
15. Mumford, D., Shah, J.: Optimal approximations by piecewise smooth functions and associated variational problems. Comm. Pure Appl. Math. 42(5), 577–685 (1989)
16. Pock, T., Cremers, D., Bischof, H., Chambolle, A.: An algorithm for minimizing the piecewise smooth Mumford-Shah functional. In: ICCV (2009)
17. Rockafellar, R.T.: Convex Analysis. Princeton University Press (1996)
18. Strekalovskiy, E., Chambolle, A., Cremers, D.: A convex representation for the vectorial Mumford-Shah functional. In: CVPR (June 2012)
19. Veksler, O.: Graph cut based optimization for mrfs with truncated convex priors. In: CVPR (2007)
20. Vese, L., Chan, T.: A multiphase level set framework for image processing using the Mumford–Shah functional. Int. J. of Computer Vision 50(3), 271–293 (2002)
21. Xu, L., Lu, C., Xu, Y., Jia, J.: Image smoothing via l_0 gradient minimization. In: Proceedings of SIGGRAPH Asia, pp. 174:1–174:12. ACM (2011)
22. Zach, C., Hane, C., Pollefeys, M.: What is optimized in convex relaxations for multilabel problems: Connecting discrete and continuously inspired map inference. IEEE Transactions on Pattern Analysis and Machine Intelligence 36(1), 157–170 (2014)

A MAP-Estimation Framework
for Blind Deblurring
Using High-Level Edge Priors*

Yipin Zhou[1] and Nikos Komodakis[2]

[1] Brown University, USA
yipin_zhou@brown.edu
[2] Universite Paris-Est, Ecole des Ponts ParisTech, France
nikos.komodakis@enpc.fr

Abstract. In this paper we propose a general MAP-estimation framework for blind image deconvolution that allows the incorporation of powerful priors regarding predicting the edges of the latent image, which is known to be a crucial factor for the success of blind deblurring. This is achieved in a principled, robust and unified manner through the use of a global energy function that can take into account multiple constraints. Based on this framework, we show how to successfully make use of a particular prior of this type that is quite strong and also applicable to a wide variety of cases. It relates to the strong structural regularity that is exhibited by many scenes, and which affects the location and distribution of the corresponding image edges. We validate the excellent performance of our approach through an extensive set of experimental results and comparisons to the state-of-the-art.

1 Introduction

The problem of blind image deconvolution has regained lately a lot of research interest in the computer vision community [24,40,14,4,25,12,38,26,1,11,37,27,13,39,28,10,29,34,31,22,33,21,16]. By examining more closely the various state of the art algorithms that have been proposed recently, it becomes clear that there exist at least two elements that can play a crucial role for the success of blind image deconvolution: edge prediction and the use of proper priors.

The first element relates to the ability of one to correctly predict part of the true edges of the unknown deblurred image. The more of these edges can be detected during the deconvolution process, the better for the quality of the estimated results. Of course, the challenge is that this is often very difficult to achieve due to the inherent blurriness associated with the provided input image.

The second element is that the good performance of the recent blind deconvolution algorithms relies heavily on the successful use of various types of image

---

* Part of this work was done while the first author was an intern at Ecole des Ponts ParisTech.

D. Fleet et al. (Eds.): ECCV 2014, Part II, LNCS 8690, pp. 142–157, 2014.

priors, which naturally serve the purpose of reducing the severe ill-posedness
of the above problem. To mention just a few characteristic examples, there has
been recently made use of priors related to the distributions of image gradients
obeyed by natural images [7], color priors [15], normalized sparsity priors [20],
compactness priors over the so-called motion density function of the camera [9],
discrete MRF image priors [19], patch priors [32] as well as smoothness priors
that aim to reduce ringing artifacts [30].

Fig. 1. Scenes very often exhibit important structural regularities

In this paper we want to capitalize on the above two findings. In other words,
we wish to be able to utilize priors that are even more powerful, and which will
help us to estimate edges much more robustly during blind deconvolution. To do
that, in this paper we rely on an additional observation, which directly relates
to the fact that a large part of the images nowadays depict scenes that exhibit
strong geometric regularities with respect to the location and distribution of
the corresponding image edges. One of the many reasons that this happens,
for instance, is because a lot of these images display man-made objects or are
captured inside man-made environments (both indoor and outdoor). Actually,
one certain aspect of this phenomenon has been first noticed in an earlier work
by Coughlan and Yuille [6], where it has been experimentally shown to hold for
a large variety of scenes (not only urban but also rural ones).

The presence of such regularities suggests an opportunity for utilizing priors
that can significantly constrain (and thus hopefully improve) the estimation of
edges in this case. If we take a look at the images of Fig. 1, for instance,we
can immediately see that edge pixels do not appear isolated or in arbitrary
curves, but instead typically form line segments. Moreover, these segments are
not arbitrary either. Instead, many of them are collinear (*i.e.*, can be grouped
into lines) and, furthermore, many of the resulting lines converge into vanishing
points.

One of the goals of this work is exactly to allow successfully taking advantage of all such amount of scene-specific prior knowledge during the deblurring
process. More generally, our aim here is to propose a sound MAP-estimation
framework for blind deconvolution, based on which one would be able to incorporate in a principled, unified and robust manner multiple types of constraints
or priors, importantly including any available prior information regarding prediction of image edges.

In blind deconvolution, the idea of exploiting domain-specific properties had
been previously used for the deblurring of text images [3]. More generally, using

scene-specific prior knowledge for improving the performance of computer vision algorithms is an idea that has already been applied with great success in other contexts in the past. For instance, one characteristic example was in the context of camera orientation estimation [5], while two more recent examples are the works of Furukawa *et al.*[8] on multi-view stereo reconstruction, where significant improvements are shown through the use of a "Manhattan world" assumption, and Barinova *et al.*[35] on horizon estimation with also excellent results.

We conclude this section by briefly mentioning the main contributions of this work, which are as follows:

– It introduces the idea of utilizing *scene-specific* edge priors for tackling the blind image deblurring problem.
– It successfully makes use of one such prior (related to the strong regularities that exist in many of the existing images with respect to the location and distribution of their edges) for improving the performance of blind deconvolution. This prior is generic enough, goes beyond the Manhattan world assumption, and is applicable to a wide variety of cases.
– More generally, by building upon recent work [19] that shows the importance of utilizing sparse discrete MRF image priors in this context, it proposes a solid MAP-estimation framework that manages to formulate blind deconvolution as optimization over a *single unified* energy function that can take into account various types of constraints.
– Importantly, given the significance of correct edge prediction to blind deconvolution, such a framework enables one to incorporate available prior edge information (both low-level and high-level) into the deconvolution process in a principled, sound, and robust manner.

2   Our Blind Deconvolution Approach

In this section we describe the MAP-estimation framework that we propose for blind image deconvolution. As usual, we are considering a model where the blurry input image $\mathbf{I}$ is assumed to be the result of a convolution of a latent image $\mathbf{x}$ with a blur kernel $\mathbf{k}$ plus some additive noise $\mathbf{n}$, *i.e.*,

$$\mathbf{I} = \mathbf{x} \otimes \mathbf{k} + \mathbf{n}, \tag{1}$$

where the symbol $\otimes$ denotes the convolution operator.

In blind deconvolution, we need to recover both $\mathbf{x}$ and $\mathbf{k}$ using as only input the image $\mathbf{I}$. To that end, here we propose minimizing an energy function of the following form:

$$E(\mathbf{k}, \mathbf{x}, \mathbf{e}|\mathbf{I}) = E_{\text{data}}(\mathbf{k}, \mathbf{x}|\mathbf{I}) + E_{\text{kernel}}(\mathbf{k}) + E_{\text{img}}(\mathbf{x}|\mathbf{e}) + E_{\text{edge}}(\mathbf{e}|\mathbf{x}). \tag{2}$$

This energy consists of 4 main terms, corresponding to a data term $E_{\text{data}}(\mathbf{k}, \mathbf{x}|\mathbf{I})$, a prior-related term $E_{\text{kernel}}(\mathbf{k})$ concerning the kernel $\mathbf{k}$, a prior-related term $E_{\text{img}}(\mathbf{x}|\mathbf{e})$ for the image $\mathbf{x}$, and a prior-related term $E_{\text{edge}}(\mathbf{e}|\mathbf{x})$ concerning the image edges of the latent image $\mathbf{x}$ (where $\mathbf{e}$ is an appropriate set of variables used for specifying image edges).

The role of these terms is to properly constraint (in a soft manner) all the different elements involved in blind deconvolution with the goal of ensuring that, in the end, convergence towards the correct kernel will take place. The last two terms are of particular importance in this regard, since their role is to help together for correctly predicting some of the main structural elements of $\mathbf{x}$ that play a crucial role for obtaining high quality blur kernels. We next define each of the above terms, and also explain their role in more detail.

2.1 Data Term $E_{\text{data}}(\mathbf{k}, \mathbf{x}|\mathbf{I})$

This is a standard data term used in blind deconvolution, defined as

$$E_{\text{data}}(\mathbf{k}, \mathbf{x}|\mathbf{I}) = \|\mathbf{k} \otimes \mathbf{x} - \mathbf{I}\|^2. \tag{3}$$

It essentially corresponds to a negative log-likelihood term for the case where the noise $\mathbf{n}$ in equation (1) is assumed as white Gaussian.

2.2 Blur Kernel Prior Term $E_{\text{kernel}}(\mathbf{k})$

For the blur kernel $\mathbf{k}$ we select a Laplacian prior to impose on it. This leads to utilizing an l_1-norm penalty term as $E_{\text{kernel}}(\mathbf{k})$, *i.e.*,

$$E_{\text{kernel}}(\mathbf{k}) = \rho \cdot \|\mathbf{k}\|_1. \tag{4}$$

Such a term is known to be sparsity-inducing, leading to kernels with few non-zero entries, which is an assumption that holds true in most of the cases encountered in practice. This is especially true for kernels due to camera shake, which is the most common example. Of course, employing alternative priors for $\mathbf{k}$ (that might be more appropriate for other cases) is also possible within the proposed framework.

2.3 Image Prior Term $E_{\text{img}}(\mathbf{x}|\mathbf{e})$

For defining this term, we will draw upon recent work that shows the importance for blind deconvolution of imposing a discrete piecewise-constant MRF prior on image $\mathbf{x}$ (which inherently promotes sparsity). This, at first, means that the elements of image $\mathbf{x}$ are assumed to take values from a discrete label set, *i.e.*, $\mathbf{x} \in \mathcal{L}_n$, where $\mathcal{L}_n$ denotes the set of quantized images that contain a restricted number of at most n intensities or colors (n is supposed to be small).

Under this assumption, $E_{\text{img}}(\mathbf{x}|\mathbf{e})$ is then given by the following formula

$$E_{\text{img}}(\mathbf{x}|\mathbf{e}) = \sum_{(p,q)\in\mathcal{E}} w_{pq}(\mathbf{e})[x_p \neq x_q] + \lambda \sum_{(p,q)\in\mathcal{E}} (x_p - x_q)^2, \tag{5}$$

where $\mathcal{E}$ denotes the set of pairs of pixels that are considered to be neighbors in the MRF graph, and $[\cdot]$ equals 1 if the expression inside the brackets is true and zero otherwise.

The first term in eq. (5) above corresponds to a weighted discrete Potts model [2], which penalizes the assignment of different labels (*i.e.*, colors/intensities) to neighboring image pixels. By definition, such a model promotes L_0 sparsity and its role here is to impose a piecewise-constant structure on image $\mathbf{x}$. The idea of applying such a prior term to blind image deconvolution has been introduced recently in [19], where it was shown its importance for avoiding trivial blur kernel solutions (such as the no-blur one) and for obtaining very high quality blur kernels.

The associated weights w_{pq} play an important role in this regard, as they are used for determining the amount of penalty that should be assigned to an intensity (or color) discontinuity across pixels p, q of image $\mathbf{x}$. In this work, given that the variables $\mathbf{e}$ should already be predicting which of the pixels of the deblurred image $\mathbf{x}$ belong to image edges, we choose to define the weights w_{pq} in terms of these edge-related variables $\mathbf{e}$. More specifically, we use the following formula[1] for setting these weights:

$$w_{pq}(\mathbf{e}) = \begin{cases} w_{\text{edge}}, & \text{if } p \text{ or } q \text{ is edge pixel based on } \mathbf{e} \\ w_{\text{non-edge}}, & \text{otherwise,} \end{cases} \quad (6)$$

where w_{edge} and $w_{\text{non-edge}}$ are 2 parameters that satisfy $w_{\text{edge}} \ll w_{\text{non-edge}}$. The result of this is that label discontinuities in image $\mathbf{x}$ are penalized much less if there is evidence (according to variables $\mathbf{e}$) that there should actually exist an edge in the deblurred image. In doing so, the goal is to allow the edges of image $\mathbf{x}$ to be much better aligned with the true edges of the deconvolved image, which, as mentioned already, is important for high quality kernel estimation. In this manner we aim to be able to successfully transfer any edge-related prior knowledge (as encoded by variables $\mathbf{e}$) onto correctly estimating the structure of the image $\mathbf{x}$.

Last, concerning the term $\lambda \cdot \sum_{(p,q) \in \mathcal{E}} (x_p - x_q)^2$ also appearing in (5), its role here is to provide just a very small amount of extra regularization by penalizing large magnitude discontinuities (this can contribute a very slight image refinement in some cases). As a result, a small parameter λ, satisfying $\lambda \ll 1$ (*e.g.*, $\lambda = 10^{-3}$), should be used with it. We note that the role of this term is minor, and that the important term in (5) is the Potts term.

2.4   Edge Prior Term $E_{\text{edge}}(\mathbf{e}|\mathbf{x})$

This term serves the purpose of allowing us to encode any available prior knowledge with regard to the edges of the latent image $\mathbf{x}$. The rationale behind its introduction is to help in the correct prediction of these edges, which is an

---

[1] Other ways of expressing w_{pq} in terms of the variables $\mathbf{e}$ are also possible, but we found the above simple definition to be effective enough.

important factor for the success of blind deconvolution. Importantly, this permits us to incorporate in a principled manner various types of such priors into our framework (ranging rom low-level to higher-level ones), where the precise specification and meaning of the corresponding variables $\mathbf{e}$ is to be updated accordingly in each case, *i.e.*, depending on the specific choice that has been made. In the next section, we describe one particular prior of this type that will be used, which is applicable to a wide variety of cases and provides strong and very useful high-level constraints.

3   Geometric Parsing Prior for Blind Deconvolution

Our motivation for introducing the scene-specific prior described in this section comes from the well known observation that many of the images today depict scenes exhibiting strong structural regularities. Here we wish to be able to successfully take into account as many of these regularities as possible, imposing at the same time assumptions that are as general as possible. To that end, we are going to rely on a geometric image parsing prior similar to the one used in recent work [35]. Such a prior is generic enough and has already been shown to successfully apply to a wide variety of cases. Essentially, the main assumptions[2] that we make about the depicted scenes, in this case, are that many of the edge pixels appearing in image $\mathbf{x}$ are part of line segments, many of these line segments can possibly be grouped into lines, and many of the resulting lines can possibly be grouped into parallel line families. These parallel line families, therefore, converge (in the image plane) into a set of vanishing points (including the so-called zenith vanishing point as well as a set of horizontal vanishing points that lie close to the horizon line).

As a result, the set of variables $\mathbf{e} = \{\mathbf{s}, \mathbf{l}, \mathbf{h}, z\}$ used in this case consists of the set of 2d line segments $\mathbf{s} = \{s_i\}$, which represent the edge segments of image $\mathbf{x}$, the set of lines $\mathbf{l} = \{l_i\}$, the set of horizontal vanishing points $\mathbf{h} = \{h_i\}$, as well as the zenith vanishing point z. Deciding, therefore, if p is an edge pixel according to these variables (as needed by the formula used for setting the weights in (6)) simply requires checking if p belongs to one of the segments in $\mathbf{s}$, *i.e.*

$$p \text{ is edge pixel (according to } \mathbf{e}) \Leftrightarrow p \in \cup s_i \ . \tag{7}$$

The corresponding prior $E_{\text{edge}}(\mathbf{e}|\mathbf{x})$ is then defined as

$$E_{\text{edge}}(\mathbf{e}|\mathbf{x}) = \sum_i E_{\text{pixel}}(p_i|\mathbf{s}, \mathbf{x}) + \sum_i E_{\text{segment}}(s_i|\mathbf{l}) + \sum_i E_{\text{line}}(l_i|\mathbf{h}, z)$$
$$+ \sum_{i,j} E_{\text{horizon}}(h_i, h_j|z) + E_{\text{prior}}(\mathbf{s}, \mathbf{l}, \mathbf{h}). \tag{8}$$

The individual terms appearing in (8) are defined similarly to [35], and essentially encode all the assumptions that we mentioned above regarding the regularities of the depicted scenes. We next briefly describe each of these terms (and we refer to [35] for a detailed explanation):

---

[2] Note that these assumptions are more general than the so-called Manhattan world model.

– $E_{\text{pixel}}(p_i|\mathbf{s}, \mathbf{x})$: this term encodes how well an edge pixel p_i of image $\mathbf{x}$ is explained by one of the edge segments included in set $\mathbf{s}$

$$E_{\text{pixel}}(p|\mathbf{s}, \mathbf{x}) = E_p(\mathbf{s}) \cdot \sum_{q:(p,q)\in\mathcal{E}} [x_p \neq x_q],$$

where $E_p(\mathbf{s})$ is defined (for any pixel p) as

$$E_p(\mathbf{s}) = \min\Big(\theta_{\text{bg}}, \min_i \theta_{\text{dist}} \cdot d(p, s_i) + \theta_{\text{grad}} \cdot d_{\text{angle}}(p, s_i)\Big).$$

In the above, $d(p, s_i)$ denotes the minimum distance from p to segment s_i, and $d_{\text{angle}}(p, s_i)$ denotes the angular difference between the local edge direction at p and the direction of s_i. The role of the term $\sum_{q:(p,q)\in\mathcal{E}}[x_p \neq x_q]$ is to ensure that that only an *edge* pixel p of the discrete image $\mathbf{x}$ can contribute (proportional to $E_p(\mathbf{s})$) to the E_{pixel} term.

– $E_{\text{segment}}(s_i|\mathbf{l})$: this terms aims at measuring how well segment s_i is explained by one of the lines in $\mathbf{l}$. It is defined as

$$E_{\text{segment}}(s|\mathbf{l}) = \min\Big(\mu_{\text{bg}} \cdot \text{length}(s), \min_i \mu_{\text{dist}} \cdot d_{\text{area}}(s, l_i)\Big),$$

where $d_{\text{area}}(s, l_i)$ measures the distance between segment s and line l_i as the area of the figure between the line and the segment divided by the cosine of the corresponding angle between the line and the segment.

– $E_{\text{line}}(l|\mathbf{h}, z)$: this encodes if the line l passes close to one of the vanishing points $\mathbf{h} \cup z$ as follows

$$E_{\text{line}}(l|\mathbf{h}, z) = \min\Big(\eta_{\text{bg}}, \min_i(\eta_{\text{dist}} \cdot \phi(l, h_i), \eta_{\text{dist}} \cdot \phi(l, z))\Big),$$

where $\phi(l, h_i)$ measures the distance on the Gaussian sphere between the projection of l and the projection of a vanishing point h_i.

– $E_{\text{horizon}}(h_i, h_j|z)$: this term relates to measuring if the vanishing points in $\mathbf{h}$ lie close to a line in the image plane as they should. It is defined in the following manner

$$E_{\text{horizon}}(h_i, h_j|z) = \kappa_{\text{hor}} \cdot \tan\psi(h_i - h_j, L(z)),$$

where $L(z)$ is the line connecting the zenith and the principal point of the camera (assumed to lie at the center of image $\mathbf{x}$), and ψ is the absolute angle between $h_i - h_j$ and a perpendicular to $L(z)$.

– $E_{\text{prior}}(\mathbf{s}, \mathbf{l}, \mathbf{h})$: this term corresponds to an MDL-like prior that penalizes the number of lines segments $|\mathbf{s}|$ (taking also into account their length), the number of lines $|\mathbf{l}|$ and the number of vanishing points $|\mathbf{h}|$, aiming to favor explanations of the image edges of $\mathbf{x}$ involving as few elements as possible

$$E_{\text{prior}}(\mathbf{s}, \mathbf{l}, \mathbf{h}) = \lambda_{\text{line}}|\mathbf{l}| + \lambda_{\text{vp}}|\mathbf{h}| + \lambda_{\text{segm}} \sum_i \text{length}(s_i).$$

4   MAP-Estimation Inference

To perform blind image deconvolution, all we need is to optimize the energy function specified in the previous section. To that end, we follow a block coordinate descent approach by separately optimizing over $\mathbf{k}$, $\mathbf{x}$, and $\mathbf{e}$. We next describe the corresponding updates that result in such a process.

4.1   Optimizing over the Kernel k

If variables $\mathbf{x}$ and $\mathbf{e}$ are kept fixed, the updating of kernel $\mathbf{k}$ corresponds to solving the following minimization task

$$\min_{\mathbf{k}} \|\mathbf{x} \otimes \mathbf{k} - \mathbf{I}\|^2 + \rho\|\mathbf{k}\|_1 = \|\mathbf{M_x}\mathbf{k} - \mathbf{I}\|^2 + \rho\|\mathbf{k}\|_1, \tag{9}$$

where $\mathbf{M_x}$ denotes the matrix corresponding to a convolution by $\mathbf{x}$.

To efficiently compute a solution to the above problem, we resort to applying the Alternating Direction Method of Multipliers [36] in a manner similar to [19]. Essentially, this amounts to introducing a replicating variable together with a decoupling quadratic term for decomposing the problem into 2 subproblems and then applying alternating minimization between them.

4.2   Optimizing over the Latent Image

When $\mathbf{k}$ and $\mathbf{e} = \{\mathbf{s}, \mathbf{l}, \mathbf{h}, z\}$ are kept fixed, optimization of (2) over $\mathbf{x}$ reduces to the following problem

$$\min_{\mathbf{x} \in \mathcal{L}_n} E_{\text{data}}(\mathbf{k}, \mathbf{x}|\mathbf{I}) + E_{\text{img}}(\mathbf{x}|\mathbf{e}) + \sum_p E_{\text{pixel}}(p|\mathbf{s}, \mathbf{x}) =$$

$$\|\mathbf{k} \otimes \mathbf{x} - \mathbf{I}\|^2 + \lambda \cdot \sum_{(p,q)\in\mathcal{E}} (x_p - x_q)^2 +$$

$$\sum_{(p,q)\in\mathcal{E}} w_{pq}(\mathbf{e}) \cdot [x_p \neq x_q] + \sum_p \sum_{q:(p,q)\in\mathcal{E}} E_p(\mathbf{s}) \cdot [x_p \neq x_q].$$

To again decouple the above optimization task into easy-to-handle subproblems, we similarly introduce a replicating variable $\mathbf{x}'$ together with a quadratic penalty term $\beta\|\mathbf{x}' - \mathbf{x}\|^2 = \beta \sum_p (x'_p - x_p)^2$ (which penalizes deviations between $\mathbf{x}$ and $\mathbf{x}'$) [36], leading to the following objective function

$$\min_{\mathbf{x}' \in \mathcal{L}_n, \mathbf{x}} \|\mathbf{k} \otimes \mathbf{x} - \mathbf{I}\|^2 + \lambda \sum_{(p,q)\in\mathcal{E}} (x_p - x_q)^2 +$$

$$\sum_{(p,q)\in\mathcal{E}} \Big(w_{pq}(\mathbf{e}) + E_p(\mathbf{s}) + E_q(\mathbf{s})\Big)[x'_p \neq x'_q] + \beta\|\mathbf{x}' - \mathbf{x}\|^2 \tag{10}$$

Applying block coordinate descent to (10) with respect to $\mathbf{x}$ and $\mathbf{x}'$ leads to the 2 subproblems described next.

Optimizing over x. The subproblem with respect to $\mathbf{x}$ involves minimizing the following least squares objective

$$\min_{\mathbf{x}} \|\mathbf{k} \otimes \mathbf{x} - \mathbf{I}\|^2 + \lambda \sum_{(p,q)\in\mathcal{E}} (x_p - x_q)^2 + \beta\|\mathbf{x} - \mathbf{x}'\|^2, \qquad (11)$$

which amounts to solving the linear system shown below

$$\left(\mathbf{M_k}^T\mathbf{M_k} + \lambda(\mathbf{M_i}^T\mathbf{M_i} + \mathbf{M_j}^T\mathbf{M_j}) + \beta\right)\mathbf{x} = \mathbf{M_k}^T\mathbf{I} + \beta\mathbf{x}',$$

where $\mathbf{M_k}$, $\mathbf{M_i}$, $\mathbf{M_j}$ denote the convolution matrices for filters $\mathbf{k}$, $\mathbf{i} = [1, -1]$ and $\mathbf{j} = [1, -1]^T$.[3]

A solution is efficiently computed through the following frequency-domain operations

$$\mathbf{x} = \mathcal{F}^{-1}\left(\frac{\overline{\mathcal{F}(\mathbf{k})} \circ \mathcal{F}(\mathbf{I}) + \beta\mathcal{F}(\mathbf{x}')}{|\mathcal{F}(\mathbf{k})|^2 + \lambda(|\mathcal{F}(\mathbf{i})|^2 + |\mathcal{F}(\mathbf{j})|^2) + \beta}\right), \qquad (12)$$

where $\mathcal{F}^{-1}()$ and $\mathcal{F}()$ denote inverse and forward FFTs.

Optimizing over x'. The subproblem with respect to $\mathbf{x}'$ corresponds to minimizing the energy of a discrete MRF Potts model

$$\min_{\mathbf{x}'\in\mathcal{L}_n} \sum_p V_p(x_p') + \sum_{(p,q)\in\mathcal{E}} V_{pq}(x_p', x_q'),$$

that has unary potentials $V_p(x_p') = \beta \cdot (x_p' - x_p)^2$, and Potts pairwise potentials $V_{pq}(x_p', x_q') = \left(w_{pq}(\mathbf{e}) + E_p(\mathbf{s}) + E_q(\mathbf{s})\right)[x_p' \neq x_q']$. Several off-the-shelf state-of-the-art optimizers exist for this task (in our experiments we have used the FastPD algorithm due to its efficiency [18]).

4.3   Optimizing over the Edge-Related Variables e

With $\mathbf{k}$ and $\mathbf{x}$ being fixed, minimization of (2) over $\mathbf{e}$ reduces to

$$\min_{\mathbf{e}} E_{\text{edge}}(\mathbf{e}|\mathbf{x}) + \sum_{(p,q)\in\mathcal{E}} w_{pq}(\mathbf{e})[x_p \neq x_q]. \qquad (13)$$

Here the additional term $\sum_{p,q} w_{pq}(\mathbf{e})[x_p \neq x_q]$ encourages the edge segments determined by variables $\mathbf{s}$ to agree with the current edges of image $\mathbf{x}$.

The above energy function (13) is of the same form as $E_{\text{edge}}(\mathbf{e}|\mathbf{x})$, with the only difference being that the term $\sum_p E_{\text{pixel}}(p|\mathbf{s}, \mathbf{x}) = \sum_{(p,q)\in\mathcal{E}} \left(E_p(\mathbf{s}) + E_q(\mathbf{s})\right)[x_p \neq x_q]$ is now replaced by $\sum_{(p,q)\in\mathcal{E}} \left(E_p(\mathbf{s}) + E_q(\mathbf{s}) + w_{pq}(\mathbf{e})\right)[x_p \neq x_q]$. Given that the weights $w_{pq}(\mathbf{e})$ depend only on the variables $\mathbf{s}$ (see (6)), and not on $\{\mathbf{l}, \mathbf{h}, z\}$, the resulting objective function is of similar form to the energy function used in [35], and can therefore be optimized using the same method, which is highly efficient.

---

[3] W.l.o.g. here we assume 4-connectivity for the edges $\mathcal{E}$ of the MRF graph, which is what leads to the use of the filters $\mathbf{i}$ and $\mathbf{j}$ in this case.

4.4   Multi-resolution Inference

As is usually the case with blind deconvolution, optimization proceeds in a coarse-to-fine fashion. This is done in order to avoid bad local minima and to be able to deal with large kernels. We therefore use a multi-resolution image pyamid, and iterate the updates described in §4.1-§4.3 at each pyramid level. For efficiency and fast convergence, the variables $\mathbf{x}$ (§4.2), $\mathbf{x}'$ (§4.2), $\mathbf{e}$, $\mathbf{k}$ are maintained throughout the whole process, and are upsampled/upscaled when going from a coarser to a finer level in the pyramid. In practice, convergence at each level is very fast, with typically 3 iterations per level being enough on average.

Given the kernel $\mathbf{k}$, the final deconvolved image can be computed by applying (12) (using the final estimated image $\mathbf{x}'$ and a small β), or by using a more advanced non-blind deconvolution algorithm such as [38], [30].

5   Experimental Results

We next test our method on a wide variety of cases and also provide comparisons with the state of the art. We note that for all the experiments (paper and suppl. material), we used uniform parameter settings for our method. More specifically, we set $w_{non-edge} = 5 \cdot 10^2$, $w_{edge} = 0.05 \cdot w_{non-edge}$, $\lambda = 10^{-3}$, $n = 20$, while all parameters of energy E_{edge} were kept constant and set as in [35]. As already explained, λ should always be set to a small enough value (it is used only for adding a minor amount of regularization). Furthermore, it is enough that $w_{non-edge}$ is an order of magnitude larger than w_{edge}, while any reasonably small value of n (e.g., between 15 and 25) seems to suffice. In general, our method was quite robust (i.e., not very sensitive) with respect to how its parameters are set. As a result, we expect the above settings to work well for any other case.

We applied our framework to a wide variety of test examples, including blurred images of scenes with structural regularities, as well as general scenes, while using a variety of blurred kernels, and also comparing with the current state-of-the-art. For the scenes with structural regularities, we made use of images from the publicly available "Eurasian cities" and "York Urban" datasets. We first show results on kernel estimation, which is the most critical part in blind deconvolution. To that end, we experimented with a wide range of challenging kernels, including ones with large sizes that introduce very significant blur. Fig. 2 compares our method with several state-of-the-art blind deconvolution algorithms. Even visually, it is clear that our estimated kernels match the ground truth much more closely (both for small and large kernel sizes). Fig. 8(a) also shows the corresponding average SSD errors with respect to the correct blur kernels, verifying the much superior performance of our method.

We next show results concerning the estimated deblurred images. Fig. 9 again compares several state-of-the-art techniques (additional results are included in the supplemental material due to lack of space). Thanks to its more accurate blur kernel estimation, our method manages to recover much better images with

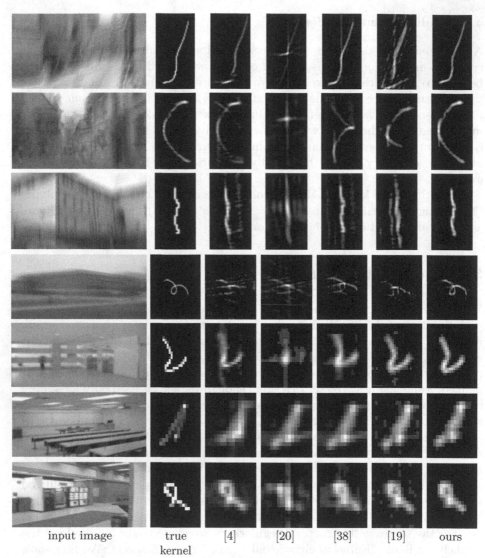

| input image | true kernel | [4] | [20] | [38] | [19] | ours |

Fig. 2. Ground truth and estimated blur kernels by different deconvolution algorithms

Fig. 3. More results by our method (input images [top], deblurred images [bottom])

more fine details as well as less ringing artifacts. We report in Fig. 8(a) the average PSNR and SSIM scores over all the test images (including the ones in the supplementary material). We also visualize in Fig. 8(b) some of the corresponding edge segments s (as estimated during the course of our method for two test cases from Fig. 9). Fig. 3 contains additional deblurring results by our method (with even more being included in the supplemental material for a variety of scenes, both indoor and outdoor).

Note that [19], which is a method that also utilizes a discrete MRF image prior, has been included in all of our comparisons above. This is for illustrating the important gains coming from the incorporation of the geometric parsing prior. Fig. 4 also shows an example of the sparse discrete images $x' \in \mathcal{L}_n$ that are estimated by [19] and our method. Notice, in our case, how much better x' can capture the true structure of the underlying latent image. To further illustrate the importance of the geometric parsing prior, we also show in Fig. 5 a comparison when this prior (*i.e.*, the term E_{edge}) is not used during blind deconvolution (in which case $w_{pq}(\mathbf{e})$ is set to a constant value).

 Blurry input image    True latent image    Our sparse discrete image x'  Sparse discrete image x' by [19]

Fig. 4. Sparse discrete images x' with our method and with method [19]

Blurry input images   Results with the geometric parsing prior   Results without the geometric parsing prior

Fig. 5. Results with and without the geometric parsing prior

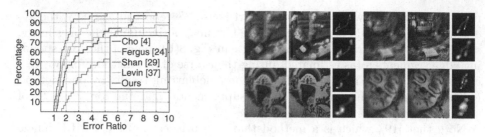

Fig. 6. Left: Error ratio evaluation for the benchmark dataset [24] (evaluation scores for other methods are taken from [23], [24]). **Right:** A few of our results for the dataset in [24] (for each one we show: input & deblurred images, true & estimated kernels).

Due to the fact that our edge-related prior is incorporated into our framework in a robust and principled manner, our method is perfectly capable of handling not just scenes with structural regularities but also general scenes. To demonstrate that, we also apply it to the benchmark datasets [24] and [17]. Figures 6, 7 contain quantitative evaluations that verify our method's state-of-the-art performance on these datasets. We also show in Fig. 6 a few indicative deblurring results from dataset [24] (a full set of results can be found in supp. material).

Cho	Xu	Shan	Fergus	Krishnan	Whyte(lsq)	Whyte(Kri)	Hirsch	Ours
28.98	29.41	25.89	22.73	25.72	27.84	28.07	27.77	**29.71**

Fig. 7. Average PSNR values of deblurred images for various methods on dataset [17]

	[4]	[26]	[7]	[28]	Ours
kernel SSD error	32.6	64.6	46.6	53.0	**17.9**
image PSNR	22.5	21.1	22.9	24.1	**26.78**
image SSIM	0.69	0.62	0.67	0.69	**0.80**

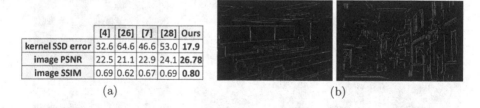

(a)   (b)

Fig. 8. In (a) the scores are computed using the best shifts for each of the estimated blur kernels and latent images. In (b) we show a visualization of the line segments s estimated during the course of our method for two of the test cases in Fig. 9.

6   Conclusions

We have proposed a sound MAP-estimation framework for blind image deconvolution, which uses a unified energy function that takes into account various types of constraints or priors, importantly including ones concerning the edges of the latent image. We have been able to successfully use this framework to take advantage of a very powerful prior of this type that relates to the strong structural

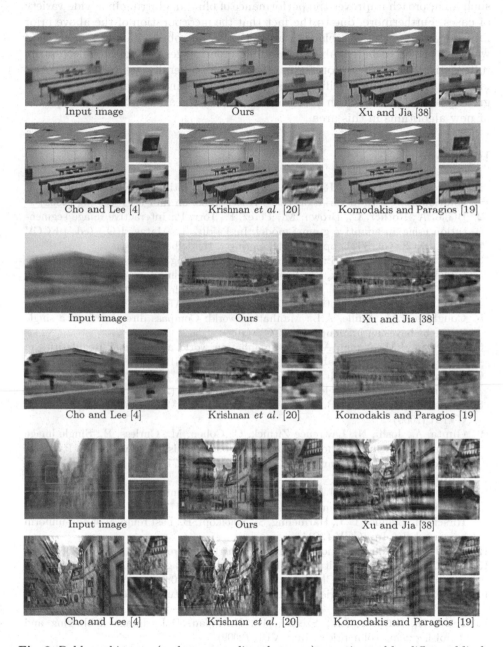

Fig. 9. Deblurred images (and corresponding close-ups) as estimated by different blind deconvolution methods. Additional results are included in the supplemental material.

regularities exhibited by many of the depicted scenes today. We have shown that such an approach improves the performance of blind deblurring in a wide variety of cases. Furthermore, due to the fact that the incorporation of the above prior into our framework takes place in a principled and robust manner, our method was also shown to be capable of handling even images that do not necessarily fully satisfy the above prior assumptions. More generally, we believe that our idea of utilizing scene-specific priors for improving blind deconvolution is one of great practical value, which can motivate further research and the development of new algorithms in this area.

References

1. Babacan, S.D., Molina, R., Katsaggelos, A.K.: Variational bayesian blind deconvolution using a total variation prior. IEEE Trans. on Image Processing (2009)
2. Blake, A., Rother, C., Brown, M., Perez, P., Torr, P.: Interactive image segmentation using an adaptive gmmrf model. In: Pajdla, T., Matas, J(G.) (eds.) ECCV 2004. LNCS, vol. 3021, pp. 428–441. Springer, Heidelberg (2004)
3. Cho, H., Wang, J., Lee, S.: Text image deblurring using text-specific properties. In: Fitzgibbon, A., Lazebnik, S., Perona, P., Sato, Y., Schmid, C. (eds.) ECCV 2012, Part V. LNCS, vol. 7576, pp. 524–537. Springer, Heidelberg (2012)
4. Cho, S., Lee, S.: Fast motion deblurring. In: SIGGRAPH ASIA (2009)
5. Coughlan, J.M., Yuille, A.L.: Manhattan world: Compass direction from a single image by bayesian inference. In: ICCV (1999)
6. Coughlan, J.M., Yuille, A.L.: The manhattan world assumption: Regularities in scene statistics which enable bayesian inference. In: NIPS (2000)
7. Fergus, R., Singh, B., Hertzmann, A., Roweis, S.T., Freeman, W.T.: Removing camera shake from a single photograph. SIGGRAPH (2006)
8. Furukawa, Y., Curless, B., Seitz, S.M., Szeliski, R.: Manhattan-world stereo. In: CVPR (2009)
9. Gupta, A., Joshi, N., Lawrence Zitnick, C., Cohen, M., Curless, B.: Single image deblurring using motion density functions. In: Daniilidis, K., Maragos, P., Paragios, N. (eds.) ECCV 2010, Part I. LNCS, vol. 6311, pp. 171–184. Springer, Heidelberg (2010)
10. Harmeling, S., Hirsch, M., Schölkopf, B.: Space-variant single-image blind deconvolution for removing camera shake. In: NIPS (2010)
11. Hirsch, M., Schuler, C.J., Harmeling, S., Schölkopf, B.: Fast removal of non-uniform camera shake. In: ICCV (2011)
12. Jia, J.: Single image motion deblurring using transparency. In: CVPR (2007)
13. Joshi, N., Kang, S.B., Zitnick, C.L., Szeliski, R.: Image deblurring using inertial measurement sensors. ACM Trans. Graph. 29, 30:1–30:9 (2010)
14. Joshi, N., Szeliski, R., Kriegman, D.J.: Psf estimation using sharp edge prediction. In: CVPR (2008)
15. Joshi, N., Zitnick, C.L., Szeliski, R., Kriegman, D.J.: Image deblurring and denoising using color priors. In: CVPR (2009)
16. Kim, T.H., Ahn, B., Lee, K.M.: Dynamic scene deblurring. In: ICCV (2013)
17. Köhler, R., Hirsch, M., Mohler, B., Schölkopf, B., Harmeling, S.: Recording and playback of camera shake: Benchmarking blind deconvolution with a real-world database. In: Fitzgibbon, A., Lazebnik, S., Perona, P., Sato, Y., Schmid, C. (eds.) ECCV 2012, Part VII. LNCS, vol. 7578, pp. 27–40. Springer, Heidelberg (2012)

18. Komodakis, N., Tziritas, G., Paragios, N.: Fast, approximately optimal solutions for single and dynamic MRFs. In: CVPR (2007)
19. Komodakis, N., Paragios, N.: MRF-based blind image deconvolution. In: Lee, K.M., Matsushita, Y., Rehg, J.M., Hu, Z. (eds.) ACCV 2012, Part III. LNCS, vol. 7726, pp. 361–374. Springer, Heidelberg (2013)
20. Krishnan, D., Tay, T., Fergus, R.: Blind deconvolution using a normalized sparsity measure. In: CVPR (2011)
21. Lee, H.S., Kwon, J., Lee, K.M.: Simultaneous localization, mapping and deblurring. In: ICCV (2011)
22. Lee, H.S., Lee, K.M.: Dense 3d reconstruction from severely blurred images using a single moving camera. In: CVPR (2013)
23. Levin, A., Weiss, Y., Durand, F., Freeman, W.T.: Efficient marginal likelihood optimization in blind deconvolution. In: CVPR (2011)
24. Levin, A., Weiss, Y., Durand, F., Freeman, W.: Understanding and evaluating blind deconvolution algorithms. In: CVPR (2009)
25. Levin, A.: Blind motion deblurring using image statistics. In: NIPS (2006)
26. Levin, A., Weiss, Y., Durand, F., Freeman, W.T.: Efficient marginal likelihood optimization in blind deconvolution. In: CVPR (2011)
27. Raskar, R., Agrawal, A., Tumblin, J.: Coded exposure photography: motion deblurring using fluttered shutter. In: SIGGRAPH, pp. 795–804 (2006)
28. Raskar, R., Agrawal, A., Tumblin, J.: Coded exposure photography: motion deblurring using fluttered shutter. In: SIGGRAPH, pp. 795–804 (2006)
29. Schmidt, U., Rother, C., Nowozin, S., Jancsary, J., Roth, S.: Discriminative non-blind deblurring. In: CVPR (2013)
30. Shan, Q., Jia, J., Agarwala, A.: High-quality motion deblurring from a single image. In: SIGGRAPH (2008)
31. Shan, Q., Xiong, W., Jia, J.: Rotational motion deblurring of a rigid object from a single image. In: ICCV (2007)
32. Sun, L., Cho, S., Wang, J., Hays, J.: Edge-based blur kernel estimation using patch priors. In: ICCP (2013)
33. Tai, Y.W., Du, H., Brown, M.S., Lin, S.: Correction of spatially varying image and video motion blur using a hybrid camera. PAMI (2010)
34. Tai, Y., Tan, P., Brown, M.: Richardson-lucy deblurring for scenes under a projective motion path. PAMI (2011)
35. Tretyak, E., Barinova, O., Kohli, P., Lempitsky, V.: Geometric image parsing in man-made environments. IJCV 97(3) (2012)
36. Wang, Y., Yang, J., Yin, W., Zhang, Y.: A new alternating minimization algorithm for total variation image reconstruction. SIAM Journal on Imaging Sciences (2008)
37. Whyte, O., Sivic, J., Zisserman, A., Ponce, J.: Non-uniform deblurring for shaken images. In: CVPR (2010)
38. Xu, L., Jia, J.: Two-phase kernel estimation for robust motion deblurring. In: Daniilidis, K., Maragos, P., Paragios, N. (eds.) ECCV 2010, Part I. LNCS, vol. 6311, pp. 157–170. Springer, Heidelberg (2010)
39. Yuan, L., Sun, J., Quan, L., Shum, H.Y.: Image deblurring with blurred/noisy image pairs. In: SIGGRAPH (2007)
40. Yuan, L., Sun, J., Quan, L., Shum, H.Y.: Progressive inter-scale and intra-scale non-blind image deconvolution. In: SIGGRAPH (2008)

Efficient Color Constancy
with Local Surface Reflectance Statistics

Shaobing Gao[1], Wangwang Han[1], Kaifu Yang[1], Chaoyi Li[1,2], and Yongjie Li[1]

[1] University of Electronic Science and Technology of China
[2] Shanghai Institutes for Biological Sciences, Chinese Academy of Sciences, China
{gao_shaobing,yang_kf}@163.com, cyli@sibs.ac.cn, liyj@uestc.edu.cn

Abstract. The aim of computational color constancy is to estimate the actual surface color in an acquired scene disregarding its illuminant. Many solutions try to first estimate the illuminant and then correct the image with the illuminant estimate. Based on the linear image formation model, we propose in this work a new strategy to estimate the illuminant. Inspired by the feedback modulation from horizontal cells to the cones in the retina, we first normalize each local patch with its local maximum to obtain the so-called locally normalized reflectance estimate (LNRE). Then, we experimentally found that the ratio of the global summation of true surface reflectance to the global summation of LNRE in a scene is approximately achromatic for both indoor and outdoor scenes. Based on this substantial observation, we estimate the illuminant by computing the ratio of the global summation of the intensities to the global summation of the locally normalized intensities of the color-biased image. The proposed model has only one free parameter and requires no explicit training with learning-based approach. Experimental results on four commonly used datasets show that our model can produce competitive or even better results compared to the state-of-the-art approaches with low computational cost.

Keywords: color constancy, illuminant estimation, reflectance, retina.

1 Introduction

To some extent, our visual system can constantly perceive the actual color of an object in a scene disregarding the large differences in illumination, which is called the ability of color constancy [17]. In contrast, the physical color of scenes captured with regular digital cameras or videos may be shifted by the varying external illuminant. Thus, for a robust color-based computer vision, removing the effect of light source color from the color-biased image is of very importance for many applications [1]. To solve this problem, one of the general ways is to estimate the scene illuminant and then utilize it to map the color-biased image to the so-called canonical image under white light source. According to the two steps mentioned above, many computational color constancy algorithms have been proposed (see [17,25,27] for recent overviews). For example, the classical

D. Fleet et al. (Eds.): ECCV 2014, Part II, LNCS 8690, pp. 158–173, 2014.

gamut mapping theory assumes that the distribution of RGB color values of an image captured under a canonical illuminant is a limited set, which is called canonical gamut [16]. So, for a color-biased image taken under an unknown illuminant will produce another gamut too, which is called observed gamut. The aim of gamut mapping is to compute the transformation that maps the observed gamut to the canonical gamut, and finally, the estimated illuminant could be derived from this transformation. Lately, the derivative structure of image was brought into the gamut mapping theory and achieved more robust color constancy performance than the standard gamut mapping algorithm [24].

Although the gamut mapping based methods have the elegant underlying theory to solve the problem of computational color constancy, the inherent drawbacks of these methods include their complication in implementation and the requirement of appropriate pre-processing [25]. Other typical approaches include learning-based methods [7,12,19], the bayesian color constancy [5,21], exemplar-based method [36], biologically-inspired methods [20,33], high level information-based methods [4,38], and physics-based methods [26,29,34].

Like most computer vision tasks, the problem of color constancy is ill-posed, and in general, most of the existing approaches mentioned above introduce specific assumptions based on, for example, the color distribution of per-pixel [16], filter-based structure of image [8,37], empirical prior distribution of light source color [5,13], etc, to estimate the illuminant. Based on the linear model $f(x) = \int_\omega S(\lambda)I(\lambda)C(x,\lambda)d\lambda$ [25], most existing methods put more emphasis on the relationship between the information of illuminant $I(\lambda)$ and the structure of image $f(x)$. In addition, though almost all the existing models employ various sort of a prior on distribution of reflectance in natural scenes, they generally suffer from certain assumption.

For example, the grey-world theory based models assume that the average surface reflectance (or the edge) of natural scenes is statistically achromatic [6,15,37]. This assumption is too strong to well match the statistic diversity of surface reflectance distribution in indoor and outdoor scenes of natural world [10]. As another typical model, white patch [28] assumes that there are points with perfect reflection in natural scenes and those points can be used to estimate the illuminant of environment. Similarly to the gray-world assumption, this hypothesis also can't satisfy the statistic diversity of surface reflectance. For example, it is not always easy to retrieve points with perfect reflection in scenes [25]. The bayesian color constancy usually assumes that the distribution of surface reflectance is independent identically distributed and is normally imitated using Gaussian models. Although the Gaussian distribution is simple for calculating, it does not always accord with the actual situations [21,30,35].

Different from the traditional models mentioned above that directly estimate the illuminant by probing into the relationship between the illuminant and the derivative structure of images (e.g., the edges), or the prior information of illuminant combining with pixel color distribution (e.g., the gamut), we introduce an efficient and simple method for color constancy based on the retinal mechanism and the suitable modeling of the distribution of surface reflectance. Inspired by the feedback modulation from horizontal cells to the cones in the retina [31], we first normalize each local patch of the image with its local maximum to obtain the so-called locally normalized reflectance estimate (LNRE). We then experimentally find that the global statistics of surface reflectances in an image could be well approached by the global statistics of LNRE. Based on this observation, we do not need to make any assumption about the distribution of the surface reflectances or the property of illuminant. Instead, the illuminant can be directly derived from the ratio between the global summation of per-pixels and the statistic summation of estimated surface reflectance in local regions according to the linear model of image formation [25]. We will also demonstrate that both the grey-world and white patch algorithms can be integrated into the proposed color constancy framework.

The rest of this paper is organized as follows. In section 2, the proposed model is described in details. Section 3 provides extensive performance evaluations of the proposed algorithm on four commonly used datasets. Finally, some discussion and concluding remarks are given in Section 4. The source codes of the work are available at http://www.neuro.uestc.edu.cn/vccl/home.html

2   Color Constancy with Local Surface Reflectance Estimation

Suppose that the scene is illuminated by a single light source, e.g., the outdoor daylight illuminant. Based on the common form of the linear imaging equation, The captured image values $f(x) = [f_R(x), f_G(x), f_B(x)]^T$ depend on the color of the light source $I(\lambda)$, the surface reflectance $C(x, \lambda)$ and the camera sensitivity function $S(\lambda) = [S_R(\lambda), S_G(\lambda), S_B(\lambda)]^T$, where x is the spatial coordinate and λ is the wavelength of the light (e.g., [25]):

$$f_c(x) = \int_\omega S_c(\lambda) I(\lambda) C(x, \lambda) d\lambda \tag{1}$$

where the integral is taken over the visible spectrum ω and $c \in \{R, G, B\}$ are sensor channels.

Among various color constancy algorithms, the color transform of image induced by the illuminant can be well approximated by a diagonal transform [11,14,25,27]. Thus, based on the diagonal transform assumption in color constancy, Eq (1) can be simplified as

$$f_c(x) = I_c C_c(x) \tag{2}$$

The aim of the color constancy method proposed in this work is to estimate the color of the light source I_c, $c \in \{R, G, B\}$. Given the color-biased image values of $f_c(x)$ and the illuminant estimate I_c, color constancy can be achieved by a transformation of $f_c(x)$ to the one appearing to be taken under a canonical (often white) light source. In general, I_c and $C_c(x)$ in Eq (2) are unknown and hence, given only the image values of $f_c(x)$, the estimation of I_c is an ill-posed inverse problem that cannot be solved without further assumptions [25].

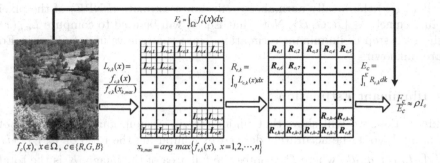

Fig. 1. The flowchart explaining the computational steps of the proposed algorithm

According to the linear multiplication relationship between the illuminant I_c and surface reflectance $C_c(x)$ in Eq (2), if we can first obtain the rough estimate of $C_c(x)$, the illuminant I_c could be simply derived by dividing $f_c(x)$ by the reflectance estimate $C_c(x)$ [25]. In this work, we are not to estimate the illuminant directly as did in most of the linear model based color constancy algorithms; in contrast, our philosophy is that we first estimate the reflectance $C_c(x)$ roughly based on certain appropriate assumption.

Fig. 1 shows the general flowchart of the proposed method, and the details will be described in the following sections.

2.1 Surface Reflectance Estimation in Local Region

The reflected lights entering into the eyes are first processed by the photoreceptors like cones (for color) and rods (for luminance). Then, at each spatial location, a horizontal cell (with large receptive field) pools a population of cones outputs within a relatively large region and then modulates the cones sensitivities via feedback [31]. In the following we simplify this retinal processing mechanism to modulate each local region by dividing by its local maximum.

We divide the full two dimensional (2D) area of the image $f_c(x)$ into K non-overlapped patches with equal size. Let

$$L_{c,k}(x) = \frac{f_{c,k}(x)}{f_{c,k}(x_{k,max})} \qquad (3)$$

where $x_{k,max}$ is the spatial coordinate of the maximum intensity pixel within the k-th local region:

$$x_{k,max} = arg\ max\{f_{c,k}(x), x = 1, 2, \cdots n\} \qquad (4)$$

Clearly, $L_{c,k}(x)$ is the intensity value of the pixel at x normalized by the local maximum of the intensity values within the k-th local region. Considering

$$L_{c,k}(x) = \frac{I_c C_{c,k}(x)}{I_c C_{c,k}(x_{k,max})} = \frac{C_{c,k}(x)}{C_{c,k}(x_{k,max})} \qquad (5)$$

we call $L_{c,k}(x)$ the locally normalized reflectance estimate (LNRE) of the pixel at x in channel $c \in \{R, G, B\}$. Note that Eq (3) will be used to compute $L_{c,k}(x)$ for the next step of illuminant estimation, since the true values of $C_c(x)$ in Eq (5) are unknown.

2.2   Illuminant Estimation

In this section, we will show that under certain assumption, the estimate of illuminant I_c could be accurately derived by computing the ratio of $\int_\Omega f_c(x)dx$ to $\int_1^K \int_\eta L_{c,k}(x)dxdk$, where Ω denotes the full area of the image, K is the total number of the local regions within the image. η represents the area of the k-th local region. Note that in our model, K is the only one free parameter, since for a given image with certain size, the value of η is determined by K. Let FR_c represent the ratio given by

$$FR_c = \frac{\int_\Omega f_c(x)dx}{\int_1^K \int_\eta L_{c,k}(x)dxdk} \qquad (6)$$

For a given color-biased image $f_c(x)$, we can easily obtain $FR_c, c \in \{R, G, B\}$. To exploit what information could be derived from FR_c, let us substitute Eq (2) into Eq (6), and we obtain:

$$FR_c = I_c \frac{\int_\Omega C_c(x)dx}{\int_1^K \int_\eta L_{c,k}(x)dxdk} = I_c \frac{T_c}{E_c} \qquad (7)$$

where

$$T_c = \int_\Omega C_c(x)dx \qquad (8)$$

$$E_c = \int_1^K \int_\eta L_{c,k}(x)dxdk \qquad (9)$$

where T_c represents the global summation of the true surface reflectance, and E_c denotes the global summation of locally normalized reflectance estimate (LNRE) computed with Eq (3).

To exploit the relationship of these two global summation measures, we used the Gehler-Shi dataset containing 568 linear images [32], the SFU indoor dataset including 321 linear images [2], the SFU HDR dataset containing 105 linear images [12,18], and the SFU grey ball dataset containing 11346 nonlinear images [9] for quantitative analysis. The known illuminant of each color-biased image provided in the datasets was used to correct the color-biased image to obtain the ground truth image, and the values of the ground truth image are equivalent to $C_c(x)$, which were then used to compute T_c.

The first column of Fig. 2 plots in three separate channels the 568 ratios of these two global summation measures, i.e., $\frac{T_c}{E_c}$ with $c \in \{R, G, B\}$, and each scatter point corresponds to one image in Gehler-Shi dataset. Similarly, the second column plots the 321 ratios for SFU indoor dataset, the third column

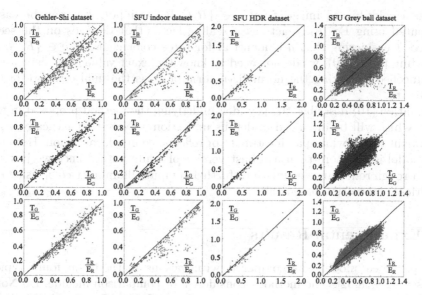

Fig. 2. Each point in the scatter plots represents the ratio of the statistic summation of real surface reflectance of an image (e.g. T_B) to the statistic summation of estimated surface reflectance in local regions of the image (e.g. E_B) in three separate color channels. These plots indicate that most of these scatter points in the three channels are closely aligned along the diagonal lines (the solid line).

plots the 105 ratios for SFU HDR dataset, and the fourth column plots the 11346 ratios for SFU grey ball dataset. Quite interestingly, from Fig. 2 we can clearly find that statistically, these scatter points are linearly correlated between any two channels of $\frac{T_c}{E_c}$, $c \in \{R, G, B\}$. More importantly, we can also obviously see that most of these scatter points in the three channels are closely aligned along the diagonal lines. These indicate that for most of the images, we have

$$\frac{T_R}{E_R} \approx \frac{T_G}{E_G} \approx \frac{T_B}{E_B} \approx \rho \qquad (10)$$

where ρ is a constant, which may be different for different images.

Equation (10) indicates that by choosing appropriate value of free parameter K involved in $E_c, c \in \{R, G, B\}$, we have great chance to get an accurate estimate of the direction of vector $[T_R, T_G, T_B]$ denoting the global statistics (i.e., summation) of true surface reflectance of a scene from the easily computed $[E_R, E_G, E_B]$ denoting the summation of surface reflectance estimate in local regions, with a scaling factor (i.e., ρ) between the magnitudes of the two vectors.

Substituting Eq (10) into (7), we now have:

$$FR_c \approx \rho I_c \qquad (11)$$

Based on this equation, we can estimate the color of the illuminant as

$$I_c \approx \frac{1}{\rho} FR_c \qquad (12)$$

Given a color-biased image $f_c(x), c \in \{R, G, B\}$ as input, FR_c can be easily computed using Eq (6). ρ acts as a scaling factor that depends on the scene viewed. Considering that ρ is identical for three color channels $c \in \{R, G, B\}$ according to Eq (10), we do not need to know the exact value of ρ, since ρ will be cancelled by taking the normalized form of I_c as the final estimate of the illuminant.

Equation (10) describes the key idea underlying the method proposed in this work, which will be discussed in details in Section 4. Note that basically, E_c is equivalent to the white-patch estimate of reflectance in a local region. However, our model is far more than a robust version of white patch, since we just use it as a rough reflectance estimate to further compute illuminant color using our empirical observation based rule.

3   Experimental Results

The proposed model was compared with various methods on foure typical datasets [2,9,18,32]. The methods considered for comparison include: Do Nothing (DN), inverse-intensity chromaticity space (IICS) [34], Grey World (GW) [6], White Patch (WP) [28], 1st-Grey Edge (GE1) and 2nd-Grey Edge (GE2) [37], Shades of Grey (SG) [15], general Grey World (GG), Bayesian (Bayes) [21], Regression (SVR) [19], automatic color constancy algorithm selection (AAS) [3], using natural image statistics (NIS) [23], spatial correlations (SC)[25], spatio-spectral statistics (SS (with reg.)) [8], pixel-based gamut mapping (GM(pixel)) [16], edge-based gamut mapping (GM(edge)) [24,25], Exemplar-based [36], Corrected-moment based (CM) [12]. Recently, the standard survey paper [25] reported the results for most of the methods mentioned above, here we directly use the result data from [22,25] for analysis and comparison except that results of SS and CM are from Ref [8] and [12], respectively.

The generally employed angular error is chosen as error metric [25].

$$\varepsilon = cos^{-1}\left((I_e \cdot I_g) / (\|I_e\| \cdot \|I_g\|) \right) \tag{13}$$

Where $I_e \cdot I_g$ is the dot product of the estimated illuminant I_e and the ground truth illuminant I_g, $\|\cdot\|$ is the Euclidean norm of a vector. Besides the commonly used measure of median angular error, we also reported the measure of mean, trimean, best-25%, and worst-25% for more comprehensive comparison.

3.1   Real-World Image Set

Gehler-Shi dataset [21,32] contains 568 high dynamic range linear images, including a variety of indoor and outdoor scenes, captured using a high-quality digital SLR camera in RAW format and therefore free of any color correction. In this study, the color-checker patch in each image used for computing ground truth illuminant was masked out in order to fully evaluate the performance of a specific model.

Table 1. Performance statistics of various methods on the Gehler-Shi dataset [32]

Methods		Median	Mean	Trimean	Best-25%	Worst-25%
Physics-based	DN	13.6°	13.7°	13.5°	10.4°	17.2°
	IICS	13.6°	13.6°	13.4°	9.5°	18.0°
(Static) low-level statistics -based	GW	6.3°	6.4°	6.3°	2.3°	10.6°
	WP	5.7°	7.5°	6.7°	1.5°	16.1°
	GE2	4.5°	5.3°	4.9°	1.9°	10.0°
	SG	4.0°	4.9°	4.4°	1.1°	10.2°
	GG	3.5°	4.7°	4.0°	1.0°	10.2°
Learning -based	SVR	6.7°	8.1°	7.4°	3.3°	14.9°
	SC	5.1°	5.9°	5.5°	2.4°	10.8°
	Bayes	3.5°	4.8°	4.1°	1.3°	10.5°
	AAS	3.3°	4.5°	3.7°	0.9°	10.1°
	NIS	3.1°	4.2°	3.5°	1.0°	9.2°
	SS(reg.)	3.0°	3.6°	3.2°	0.9°	7.4°
	GM(edge)	5.6°	6.7°	6.0°	2.0°	13.5°
	GM(pixel)	2.4°	4.2°	3.3°	0.5°	11.2°
	Exemplar	2.3°	2.9°	2.5°	0.8°	6.0°
	CM(19 Edge-Moments)	2.0°	2.8°	–	–	–
Proposed		2.6°	3.4°	2.9°	0.8°	7.2°

Table 2. Mean computation time taken to compute the illuminant for per image, which was averaged on 100 test images for one dataset with repeated 20 times using MATLAB codes. Here, we list the mean computation time of image from two typical datasets: one dataset with small image size of 360 ∗ 240 pixels [9] and one dataset with large image size of 2041 ∗ 1359 pixels [32]. Note that the time taken by GM(pixel) is only for the process of test, without including the process of training. Computer used here is Intel Core2, 2.53GHZ with 2.0G RAM.

Dataset	GM(pixel)	GE2	Proposed
SFU grey ball dataset [9]	1.44(s)	0.27(s)	0.22(s)
Gehler-Shi dataset [32]	9.21(s)	12.90(s)	1.36(s)

The results for various algorithms on this database are listed in Table 1. Fig. 3 shows examples of indoor and outdoor images corrected by different algorithms.

It can be seen from Table 1 that the performance of the proposed method almost arrives at (in terms of median angular error and best-25%) or beyond (in terms of other measures) the best performance of the state-of-the-art learning-based algorithms, e.g., the GM (pixel), GM (edge), SS(reg.), NIS, Exemplar, and CM. Note that the methods of GM (pixel), Exemplar, and CM perform better in terms of median angular error of 2.4°, 2.3°, and 2.0° respectively. In addition, Exemplar also performs better in terms of other measures.

However, compared to the complex implementation of the learning-based GM(pixel), Exemplar, and CM, our model is quite simpler, which endows our method with a remarkable advantage in saving computational cost. Table 2 shows

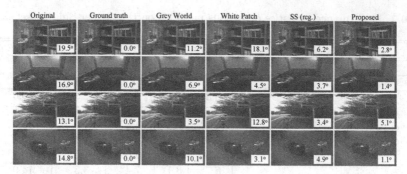

Fig. 3. Results of several algorithms on Gehler-Shi dataset, the angular error is given on the lower right corner of image

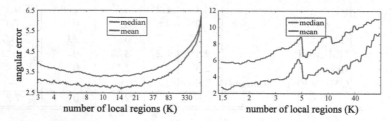

Fig. 4. The influence of parameter K of the proposed algorithm on the measure of median and mean angular error for two datasets. **Left**: real world Gehler-Shi dataset [32], **Right**: SFU indoor image dataset [2]. According to the two figures, for a real world image dataset, the suitable setting of parameter is $8 \leq K \leq 37$. For an indoor image dataset, the suitable setting of parameter is $1.5 \leq K \leq 4$. More discussion about parameter setting is given in the last section. Note the patch number $K = image\_size/patch\_size$, which may result in non-integer K. The curves were obtained with a step of $5 * 5$ pixels for patch size and the patches have no overlap.

that our model just takes about a seventh of the time needed by GM (pixel). Note that without the source codes of Exemplar and CM, we did not list the computation time of per image taken by them.

By visually comparing the performance of the proposed method with other algorithms on some examples shown in Fig. 3, we can find that for the indoor or outdoor scenes with various distributions of surface reflectance, it is difficult for a certain assumption (e.g., grey-world or white-patch) based model to perform well on all the scenes. For example, for the scene of grassland shown in the last row of Fig. 3, the distribution of surface reflectance is obviously not achromatic, which does not meet the grey-world assumption. In contrast, the proposed approach achieves the more robust performance with a suitable value for the only one parameter (i.e. K in Eq(6)) on the whole dataset.

Fig. 4 demonstrates the influence of the only one parameter K on the performance of the proposed method on two datasets: a real world Gehler-Shi dataset [32] and SFU indoor image dataset [2].

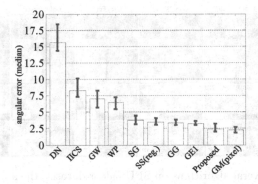

Fig. 5. Angular error (median) for different algorithms on SFU indoor dataset plotted with a 95% confidence interval

3.2 An Indoor Image Dataset in Laboratory

SFU lab dataset [2] contains 321 available images of 31 different objects captured with calibrated camera under 11 different lights in laboratory. Table 3 reports the results on this dataset for various algorithms (all methods are with optimal parameters). Similar to the results on the first dataset, we find that in terms of median angular error, our model performs better than both static- and learning-based algorithms on this dataset, but slightly worse than the method of GM(pixel) and CM. However, there is almost no significant difference between our model and GM(pixel) in terms of the measure of median angular error (Fig. 5). Note that though CM (9 Edge-moments) obtains the best performance, it required a special preprocessing on this dataset [12]. Fig. 6 presents some examples of images from SFU indoor dataset. As analyzed previously, no certain assumption can perform best on all of the scenes with various distribution of surface reflectance, even just in a simple indoor environment. However, the proposed approach still achieved competitive performance on those images comparing with the more complicated algorithm (Gamut (pixel)). We questioned

Table 3. Performance of various methods on the SFU indoor dataset

Methods	Median	Mean	Trimean	Best-25%	Worst-25%
DN	15.6°	17.3°	16.9°	3.6°	32.4°
IICS	8.2°	15.5°	12.0°	2.2°	40.0°
GW	7.0°	9.8°	8.1°	0.9°	23.3°
WP	6.5°	9.1°	7.6°	1.8°	20.9°
SG	3.7°	6.4°	5.0°	0.6°	16.4°
SS(with reg.)	3.5°	5.6°	4.8°	1.2°	12.8°
GG	3.3°	5.4°	4.1°	0.5°	13.7°
GE1	3.2°	5.6°	4.2°	1.0°	14.0°
GM(pixel)	2.3°	3.7°	2.7°	0.5°	9.3°
CM(9 Edge-Moments)	2.0°	2.6°	−	−	−
Proposed	2.4°	5.7°	4.1°	0.5°	15.0°

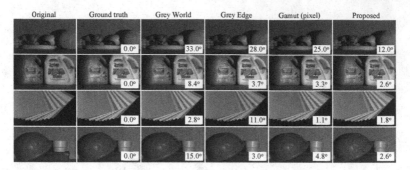

Fig. 6. Results of several algorithms on SFU indoor dataset, the angular error is given on the lower right corner of image

Table 4. Performance statistics of various methods on the SFU grey ball image dataset

Methods	Median	Mean	Worst-25%
GW	7.0°	7.9°	15.2°
DN	6.7°	8.3°	18.7°
GM(pixel)	5.8°	7.1°	14.7°
IICS	5.6°	6.6°	13.3°
WP	5.5°	6.8°	14.7°
GE2	4.9°	6.1°	13.2°
Proposed	5.1°	6.0°	11.9°

whether the high worst-25% of our model (15°) on this set was caused by black background of some images. To answer it, we tried to ignore the black background by using different levels of thresholding, and the performance varied as: median: $2.4° \rightarrow 2.3°$, mean: $5.7° \rightarrow 5.5°$, worst-25%: still 15.0°. This indicates that the high worst-25% might not be mainly caused by black background.

3.3 SFU Grey Ball Image Datasets

SFU grey-ball image dataset [9] contains 11346 nonlinear images. The images in this dataset have been processed with gamma-correction, automatic white balance, and other unknown post-processing in the camera (the image is more post-processed by camera, the more unknown factors affect the image and thus, the harder the illuminant estimation becomes [12]). So, the images in this datasets are no longer to meet the linear model of image formation described by Eq (1) [25]. Before this experiment, the grey sphere in the images, which were originally used to compute the ground truth, were masked in order to get a fair and full evaluation to the performance of a specific model.

Table 4 reports the measures on the entire dataset for several available static algorithms and gamut mapping algorithm (again all algorithms are with optimal parameters). From Table 4 we can see that among the multiple methods considered, the proposed algorithm produces the as best performance as that of GE2 on this dataset, in terms of all the three measures.

Table 5. Performance statistics for the SFU HDR image dataset. Here dash in table means that the result for that dataset was not reported by their authors.

Methods	Median	Mean	Worst-25%
DN	14.7°	15.1°	19.5°
GW	7.4°	8.0°	15.1°
MaxRGB (post-blur)	3.9°	6.3°	–
SG	3.9°	5.7°	12.9°
GE	3.8°	6.0°	13.8°
CM(9 Edge-Moments)	2.7°	3.5°	–
Proposed	2.9°	4.7°	10.8°

However, we also notice that none of the methods can provide a very low measure of median angular error (comparing with other three linear image datasets). One of the main possible reasons is that the unknown non-linear effects embedded in this dataset may seriously degrade the performances of most linear image formation based methods. For example, from Table 4 we observed that the median angular error of the grey world (GW) algorithm on this dataset is even higher than that of DN (i.e., do nothing on the original color biased images). For that reason, it could be expected that the linear image formation based methods would produce better performance when the camera dependent images are first transformed to the device independent raw images [25]. Note that on this dataset, the learning-based GM(pixel) also provides relatively poor performance.

3.4   SFU HDR Dataset

The SFU HDR dataset has been recently collected by [18] and includes 105 high dynamic range linear images with indoor and outdoor scenes. Also, a color checker were placed in the scenes for recording the overall light source color (again the color checker was masked during testing the illuminant estimation algorithms).

For comprehensive comparison, we also reported the results of GW, SG, and GE on this dataset by running the matlab codes downloaded from [22,37] with optimal parameters. The results of MaxRGB (post-blur) and Corrected-Moment (CM) are directly from paper [12]. Table 5 reports the performance statistics for various algorithms on this dataset.

On this dataset, our model also performed well comparing with other static-based models in terms of various measures. Although the performance of CM is slightly better than our method (in median angular error), CM needs to iteratively train a corrected matrix for every dataset with ground truth.

4   Discussion and Conclusion

We proposed in this work a new idea to estimate the illuminant of a scene, based on the experimental finding that the ratio of the global summation of the true surface reflectance to the global summation of locally estimated surface reflectance in a scene is almost achromatic. This so-called achromatic-ratio-mean observation inspired us to estimate the illuminant just by computing the ratio of the global summation of the observed intensities to the global summation of the locally normalized intensities of the color-biased image. There is only one free parameter in the proposed model, without the need for pre-learning. Extensive experimental tests on four commonly used datasets (three datasets with linear images and one with nonlinear images) indicated that the proposed model can produce quite competitive or even better results compared to the state-of-the-art approaches. In addition, our model shows significant advantage in terms of computational efficiency.

The main condition under which our model works well is the achromatic-ratio-mean observation described by Fig. 2 and Eq (10). Based on the derivation of equations, it is clear that we would obtain an accuracy of 100% if the ratio ρ defined by Eq (10) was always a constant, which is impossibly realized due to the complexity of scenes. Higher correlation between T_c and E_c makes ρ closer to be constant. Extensive empirical evidence on multiple datasets with large sizes and various scenes has already supported the visible correlation. For a given dataset, this requirement of high correlation could be matched as much as possible by choosing a suitable value for the only one free parameter K. In general, the distributions of the real reflectances in outdoor scenes are more complicated than the reflectance distributions in indoor scenes, since most of the indoor scenes are generally composed of only several simple color regions. Thus, based on the experimental results (Fig. 4), we suggest the bigger K values for outdoor images, because the estimated surface reflectance from a larger number of small local regions is able to better imitate the complex properties of surface reflectances in natural scenes. In contrast, for indoor images in laboratory, the model with smaller K values could work well.

Computationally, our model novelly combines the ideas of max-RGB (or White-Patch, WP) and Grey-World (GW), i.e., estimate each pixels reflectance in each local patch by normalizing the intensities with the local max (the idea of WP), then sum (or average) the estimated reflectances across the whole scene (the idea of GW). Then we estimate the light source color by computing the ratio of summation of observed intensities to the summation of estimated reflectances. Such idea underlying our model is quite different from others. For example, though the shade-of-grey (SG) also seems to balance the advantages of WP and GW, the difference is, SG averages intensities (different from the estimated reflectances in our model) that have been processed by emphasizing pixels with larger intensities (different from the WP based normalizing in each patch in our model). In addition, our achromatic-ratio-mean assumption is basically different from the GW theory assuming that the average reflectance in a scene under a neutral light source is achromatic. However, we can mathematically demonstrate that both the GW and WP assumptions are the extreme cases of Eq (10) (see Appendix).

Besides the achromatic-ratio-mean observation that was substantially validated across different datasets, a deeper insight explaining the good performance of our model is as follows. By applying the idea of WP in local patches, the influences of the pixels unexpected for WP (e.g. bright non-specularity or noise) could be limited within local regions, and meanwhile, the robustness of reflectance estimates could be enhanced by utilizing more normal bright patches.

Actually, a suitable value of parameter K may build a good balance between the gray world assumption [6] and the white patch assumption [28], which relaxes the strong limitation to the statistics distribution of surface reflectance in natural world assumed by these two theories, and hence, to better satisfy the diversity of the statistics distribution of surface reflectance in natural world.

5 Appendix

In the following, we mathematically derive how both grey world and white patch algorithms can be basically integrated into the proposed framework. When setting $K = 1$ in Eq (9), which is equivalent to set the whole input image as the only single local region, then Eq (9) is rewritten as

$$E_c = \int_1^K \int_\eta L_{c,k}(x)dxdk = \int_\Omega L_{c,k}(x)dx = \int_\Omega \frac{C_c(x)}{C_c(x_{max})}dx \qquad (14)$$

$c \in \{R, G, B\}$, where x_{max} is the spatial coordinate of the maximum of the intensity values within whole image. Thus, combining Eqs (8), (14), and (10) together, we have

$$C_R(x_{max}) \approx C_G(x_{max}) \approx C_B(x_{max}) \approx \rho \qquad (15)$$

This is just equivalent to the white patch algorithm (e.g. max-RGB) [28], which assumes the maximum reflectance in a scene is achromatic and then taking the maximum value of every channel of image as the estimated illuminant.

Similarly, when setting $K = N$ in Eq (9), where N is the pixel number of the full two dimensional area (Ω) of the image. This is equivalent to shrink each local region as small as one pixel, then Eq (9) is equal to

$$E_c = \int_1^K \int_\eta L_{c,k}(x)dxdk = \int_\Omega dk \qquad (16)$$

where $\int_\eta L_{c,k}(x)dx = 1$, since each local region contains only one pixel. Similarly, combining Eqs (8), (16), and (10) together, we get

$$\frac{\int_\Omega C_R(x)dx}{\int_\Omega dk} \approx \frac{\int_\Omega C_G(x)dx}{\int_\Omega dk} \approx \frac{\int_\Omega C_B(x)dx}{\int_\Omega dk} \approx \rho \qquad (17)$$

This is equivalent to the gray world algorithm [6], which hypothesizes that the average surface reflectance in a scene is achromatic and then computing the mean of every channel of image as the estimated illuminant.

Acknowledgments. We thank all anonymous reviewers for their thoughtful comments. This work was supported by the Major State Basic Research Program (#2013CB329401), the Natural Science Foundations of China (#61375115, #61075109, #91120013, #31300912), and the Doctoral Support Program of University of Electronic Science and Technology of China. The work was also supported by the 111 Project (#B12027) and PCSIRT (#IRT0910) of China.

References

1. Barnard, K., Martin, L., Coath, A., Funt, B.: A comparison of computational color constancy algorithms. ii. experiments with image data. IEEE Transactions on Image Processing 11(9), 985–996 (2002)
2. Barnard, K., Martin, L., Funt, B., Coath, A.: A data set for color research. Color Research & Application 27(3), 147–151 (2002)
3. Bianco, S., Ciocca, G., Cusano, C., Schettini, R.: Automatic color constancy algorithm selection and combination. Pattern Recognition 43(3), 695–705 (2010)
4. Bianco, S., Schettini, R.: Color constancy using faces. In: 2012 IEEE Conference on Computer Vision and Pattern Recognition (CVPR), pp. 65–72. IEEE (2012)
5. Brainard, D.H., Freeman, W.T.: Bayesian color constancy. JOSA A 14(7), 1393–1411 (1997)
6. Buchsbaum, G.: A spatial processor model for object colour perception. Journal of the Franklin Institute 310(1), 1–26 (1980)
7. Cardei, V.C., Funt, B., Barnard, K.: Estimating the scene illumination chromaticity by using a neural network. JOSA A 19(12), 2374–2386 (2002)
8. Chakrabarti, A., Hirakawa, K., Zickler, T.: Color constancy with spatio-spectral statistics. IEEE Transactions on Pattern Analysis and Machine Intelligence 34(8), 1509–1519 (2012)
9. Ciurea, F., Funt, B.: A large image database for color constancy research. In: Color and Imaging Conference, vol. 2003, pp. 160–164. Society for Imaging Science and Technology (2003)
10. Ebner, M.: Color constancy, vol, vol. 6. Wiley. com (2007)
11. Ebner, M.: Color constancy based on local space average color. Machine Vision and Applications 20(5), 283–301 (2009)
12. Finlayson, G.: Corrected-moment illuminant estimation. In: Proceedings of the IEEE International Conference on Computer Vision, pp. 1904–1911 (2013)
13. Finlayson, G.D.: Color in perspective. IEEE Transactions on Pattern Analysis and Machine Intelligence 18(10), 1034–1038 (1996)
14. Finlayson, G.D., Hordley, S.D.: Color constancy at a pixel. JOSA A 18(2), 253–264 (2001)
15. Finlayson, G.D., Trezzi, E.: Shades of gray and colour constancy. In: Color and Imaging Conference, vol. 2004, pp. 37–41. Society for Imaging Science and Technology (2004)
16. Forsyth, D.A.: A novel algorithm for color constancy. International Journal of Computer Vision 5(1), 5–35 (1990)
17. Foster, D.H.: Color constancy. Vision Research 51(7), 674–700 (2011)
18. Funt, B., Shi, L.: The rehabilitation of maxrgb. In: Color and Imaging Conference, vol. 2010, pp. 256–259. Society for Imaging Science and Technology (2010)

19. Funt, B., Xiong, W.: Estimating illumination chromaticity via support vector regression. In: Color and Imaging Conference, vol. 2004, pp. 47–52. Society for Imaging Science and Technology (2004)
20. Gao, S., Yang, K., Li, C., Li, Y.: A color constancy model with double-opponency mechanisms. In: Proceedings of IEEE International Conference on Computer Vision (ICCV), pp. 929–936 (2013)
21. Gehler, P.V., Rother, C., Blake, A., Minka, T., Sharp, T.: Bayesian color constancy revisited. In: IEEE Conference on Computer Vision and Pattern Recognition (CVPR), pp. 1–8 (2008)
22. Gijsenij, A.: Color constancy: research website on illuminant estimation, http://colorconstancy.com/ (accessed from)
23. Gijsenij, A., Gevers, T.: Color constancy using natural image statistics and scene semantics. IEEE Transactions on Pattern Analysis and Machine Intelligence 33(4), 687–698 (2011)
24. Gijsenij, A., Gevers, T., Van De Weijer, J.: Generalized gamut mapping using image derivative structures for color constancy. International Journal of Computer Vision 86(2-3), 127–139 (2010)
25. Gijsenij, A., Gevers, T., Van De Weijer, J.: Computational color constancy: Survey and experiments. IEEE Transactions on Image Processing 20(9), 2475–2489 (2011)
26. Gijsenij, A., Gevers, T., Van De Weijer, J.: Improving color constancy by photometric edge weighting. IEEE Transactions on Pattern Analysis and Machine Intelligence 34(5), 918–929 (2012)
27. Hordley, S.D.: Scene illuminant estimation: past, present, and future. Color Research & Application 31(4), 303–314 (2006)
28. Land, E.H., McCann, J.J., et al.: Lightness and retinex theory. Journal of the Optical society of America 61(1), 1–11 (1971)
29. Lee, H.C.: Method for computing the scene-illuminant chromaticity from specular highlights. JOSA A 3(10), 1694–1699 (1986)
30. Nascimento, S., Ferreira, F.P., Foster, D.H.: Statistics of spatial cone-excitation ratios in natural scenes. JOSA A 19(8), 1484–1490 (2002)
31. Schiller, P.H.: Parallel information processing channels created in the retina. Proceedings of the National Academy of Sciences 107(40), 17087–17094 (2010)
32. Shi, L., Funt, B.: Re-processed version of the gehler color constancy dataset of 568 images, http://www.cs.sfu.ca/~colour/data/ (accessed from)
33. Spitzer, H., Semo, S.: Color constancy: a biological model and its application for still and video images. Pattern Recognition 35(8), 1645–1659 (2002)
34. Tan, R.T., Nishino, K., Ikeuchi, K.: Color constancy through inverse-intensity chromaticity space. JOSA A 21(3), 321–334 (2004)
35. Tsin, Y., Collins, R.T., Ramesh, V., Kanade, T.: Bayesian color constancy for outdoor object recognition. In: Computer Vision and Pattern Recognition (CVPR), vol. 1, pp. I–1132 (2001)
36. Vaezi, J.H., Drew, M.: Exemplar-based colour constancy and multiple illumination. IEEE Transactions on Pattern Analysis and Machine Intelligence (2013)
37. Van De Weijer, J., Gevers, T., Gijsenij, A.: Edge-based color constancy. IEEE Transactions on Image Processing 16(9), 2207–2214 (2007)
38. Van De Weijer, J., Schmid, C., Verbeek, J.: Using high-level visual information for color constancy. In: International Conference on Computer Vision (ICCV), pp. 1–8 (2007)

A Contrast Enhancement Framework with JPEG Artifacts Suppression

Yu Li[1], Fangfang Guo[1], Robby T. Tan[2], and Michael S. Brown[1]

[1] National University of Singapore
[2] SIM University, Singapore

Abstract. Contrast enhancement is used for many algorithms in computer vision. It is applied either explicitly, such as histogram equalization and tone-curve manipulation, or implicitly via methods that deal with degradation from physical phenomena such as haze, fog or underwater imaging. While contrast enhancement boosts the image appearance, it can unintentionally boost unsightly image artifacts, especially artifacts from JPEG compression. Most JPEG implementations optimize the compression in a scene-dependent manner such that low-contrast images exhibit few perceivable artifacts even for relatively high-compression factors. After contrast enhancement, however, these artifacts become significantly visible. Although there are numerous approaches targeting JPEG artifact reduction, these are generic in nature and are applied either as pre- or post-processing steps. When applied as pre-processing, existing methods tend to over smooth the image. When applied as post-processing, these are often ineffective at removing the boosted artifacts. To resolve this problem, we propose a framework that suppresses compression artifacts as an integral part of the contrast enhancement procedure. We show that this approach can produce compelling results superior to those obtained by existing JPEG artifacts removal methods for several types of contrast enhancement problems.

Keywords: Contrast Enhancement, Dehazing, JPEG Artifacts Removal, Deblocking.

1 Introduction

A commonly applied procedure in low-level computer vision is contrast enhancement. This encompasses techniques that boost an image's global contrast through manipulations such as tone-curve adjustment, histogram equalization, and gradient-based enhancement. Such enhancement is beneficial for color segmentation, edge detection, image sharpening, image visualization, and many other tasks. In addition, spatially varying contrast enhancement is used to dramatically improve visibility in turbid media, such as haze, fog, rain, and underwater imaging.

Virtually all contrast enhancement algorithms operated on the assumption that the input image is uncompressed and free from significant noise. The reality, however, is that the vast majority of images available today on the internet

D. Fleet et al. (Eds.): ECCV 2014, Part II, LNCS 8690, pp. 174–188, 2014.
© Springer International Publishing Switzerland 2014

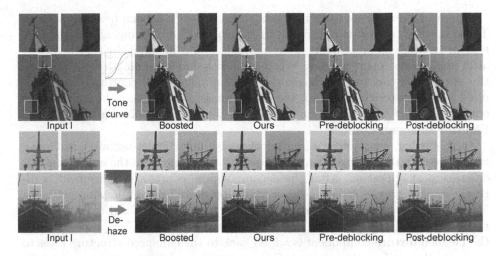

Fig. 1. This shows the noticeable compression artifacts after contrast enhancement. Top two rows are a tone-curve adjustment case ($Q40$) and the bottom two rows are a dehazing case ($Q70$). The zoomed-in regions are listed above to show the details. The characteristics of the blocking artifacts are distinctive in smooth regions (pointed out by the yellow arrows), while the ringing artifacts are along strong edges (pointed out by the red arrows). Comparison of our results with those of the deblocking method [10] applied before or after contrast enhancement results are shown. Note, our method produces more compelling results for reducing both blocking and ringing artifacts.

or from commodity imaging devices are compressed. Moreover, images coming from sources that would require contrast enhancement, e.g. surveillance cameras, often have notable amounts of image compression [13]. The most common compression scheme is by far JPEG and its extension to video, MPEG. The JPEG compression scheme breaks an input image into 8 × 8 pixel blocks and applies a discrete cosine transformation (DCT) to each block individually. To reduce storage space, the DCT coefficients are quantized at various levels – more quantization gives higher compression but lowers image quality (for more details see [25]). Lower-quality images exhibit what is termed collectively as "compression artifacts" that consist of the characteristic blocking artifacts resulting in discontinuities at the 8 × 8 borders, and oscillations or ringing artifacts next to strong edges.

Early JPEG compression methods use fixed quantization tables for different quality settings, however, most JPEG schemes now use what is referred to as *optimized JPEG* where quantization tables are customized based on the image's content [22]. This allows relatively high compression rates with little noticeable visual artifacts. However, when contrast boosting operations are applied, blocking and ringing artifacts become prominently visible as shown in Figure 1.[1]

---

[1] JPEG assigns a quality factor, QX, to indicate the subjective quality from 0 to 100 (from low quality to high quality).

There are several existing methods to reduce JPEG compression artifacts. These methods are often referred to as "deblocking" or "deringing". In the context of contrast enhancement, these methods would be applied either before or after the enhancement process. When applied before the enhancement process, the algorithms can smooth image details that have small contrast. When applied as a post-processing step, the effectiveness can be diminished due to the compression artifacts that were boosted by the contrast enhancement process. Figure 1 shows an example.

In this paper, we propose a framework based on structure-texture decomposition to remove the compression artifacts that are amplified in the image contrast enhancement operation. After the decomposition, contrast enhancement is directly applied to the structure layer, which is devoid of compression artifacts. Meanwhile, the texture layer, containing both image details and compress artifacts, is carefully processed to suppress only the artifacts. After proper scaling, the cleaned texture component is added back to the enhanced structure layer to generate the artifacts free output. Experimental results on various contrast enhancement task (*e.g.* Figure 1) demonstrate that our strategy can produce more compelling results (both qualitatively and quantitatively) than those of using general deblocking algorithms in either a pre- or post-processing manner. The details of our algorithm as well as comparisons with other methods are discussed in the following sections.

2   Related Work

We discuss relevant related work in the area of JPEG artifacts removal, contrast enhancement and multi-band image decomposition.

JPEG Artifacts Removal.   JPEG artifacts, particularly blocking artifacts, have long been recognized in the image processing community (*e.g.* [15,29]). Despite this, they remain unsolved and it is still an active area of research (*e.g.* [6,28]). Various methods have been used, which can be broadly categorized into three different approaches. The first approach treats the compression artifacts as non-Gaussian noise and attempts to remove them by adaptive local filtering which adjusts the filter kernel to remove block edges and preserve image edges (*e.g.* [10]). The second approach is a reconstruction based approach that incorporates knowledge on natural images and encodes it into an energy function as a prior. Commonly used priors include spatial smoothness [27], quantization constraints, total variation (*e.g.* [11]), and gradient constraints (*e.g.* Field of Experts [19]). The third approach for reducing compression artifacts relies on machine learning techniques to learn a mapping from compressed images to their uncompressed version [14,3]. While these approaches can reduce JPEG artifacts in images, their application as either a pre- or post-processing step can rarely outperform our method, which is designed explicitly for contrast enhancement.

Image Contrast Enhancement.   Contrast enhancement can be performed in many ways. The most direct way is to apply a function f to the original pixel intensity value, i.e. $I^e = f(I)$. This strategy is known as tone-curve adjustment. The function can be determined either manually or by selecting from pre-defined curves functions. Alternatively, the function can also be based on automatic histogram equalization, which obtains f by considering the input image's histogram. Aside from applying a certain function, local image gradients can also be used as a cost function that is optimized to boost contrast [17].

Recovering visibility in bad weather or underwater is, in fact, a specific contrast enhancement problem [20,12,5,1]. Optically, poor visibility in bad weather or underwater is due to the substantial presence of medium particles that have significant size and distribution [20]. Light from the atmosphere and light reflected from an object are absorbed and scattered by those particles, leading to contrast reduction and thus to the degraded images. Most current dehazing algorithms try to estimate either airlight or transmission map (see [20,9,12]). Regardless the algorithms, the outputs of visibility enhancement show clear increase of contrast.

Multi-band Image Decomposition. A common practice in solving computer vision and computational photography problems is to decompose images into different layers (or scales) and recombine them (*e.g.* multi-band image blending [4], optical flow estimation [26] *etc.*). The most related work to ours in this direction is tone-mapping methods (*e.g.* [7]), which attempt to reduce the contrast of a high dynamic range image to a limited range while preserving its details. This is usually achieved by reducing the contrast to the coarse layer and adding back the initial detail layer. Opposite to this tone-mapping methods' problem, however, we want to increase the contrast but not the noise/artifacts. As a result, we need to put more effort on processing the detail layer.

3   Proposed Method

Our basic pipeline is illustrated in Figure 2. It starts by decomposing the original input image into two layers: structure and texture layers. The input image can be considered as the superimposition of the two layers:

$$I = I_S + I_T, \tag{1}$$

where I_S is the structure layer corresponding to the main large objects in the image, and I_T is the texture layer corresponding to the fine details [2]. The contrast of the structure layer is then enhanced according to our task (e.g., tone-curve adjustment or dehazing). The texture layer is processed through a combination of image matting and deblocking to remove compression artifacts. Finally the two layers are recombined to produce the final output. In the following, the details of each step are discussed.

3.1   Structure-Texture Decomposition

To decompose the input image into a structure layer and texture (high-frequency) layer, any edge-aware smoothing operation (e.g. bilateral filter [21], weight least

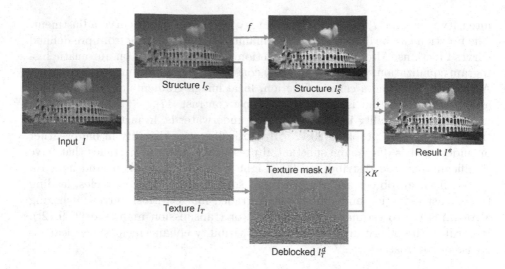

Fig. 2. The overview of our proposed method. The input image is decomposed into structure and texture components. The contrast of the structure component is then boosted directly; the texture component that contains the JPEG artifacts is processed to reduce compression artifact. The two components are recombined at the last step to render the final result. In the paper, we amplified the textural part by a factor of 10 and shift it by +0.5 for better visualization.

square filter [8]) can be applied. This procedure produces an image that retains strong structure and over-smooths out details. We take this image as the structure layer I_S, and obtain the texture layer by calculating the difference between the input image and its structure layer, $I_{T_i} = I_i - I_{S_i}$.

In our problem we applied the the total-variation (TV) image-reconstruction formulation based on Rudin-Osher-Fatemi method [18]. Based on the TV regularization, the structure layer I_S is obtained by minimizing the following objective function:

$$\min_{I_S} \sum_i (I_{S_i} - I_i)^2 + \lambda |\nabla I_{S_i}|, \qquad (2)$$

where i is the pixel index, λ is the regulation parameter and ∇ is the gradient operator. An efficient half-quadratic splitting scheme to solve Eqn.(2) is described in [23].

This structure-texture decomposition exploits the fact that most of the structure layer is related to larger gradient magnitudes, while the texture layer captures both fine image details and compression artifacts that exhibit smaller gradient magnitudes. The parameter λ is important for controlling this separation and needs to be adjusted according to the compression factor, i.e., more compression requires λ to be increased. We show the values of λ used for different compression levels in the experiments section. There are methods for deblocking using TV regularization (e.g. [11]). The main difference here is that they do not explicitly process the texture layer, while our method put significant effort on processing the texture

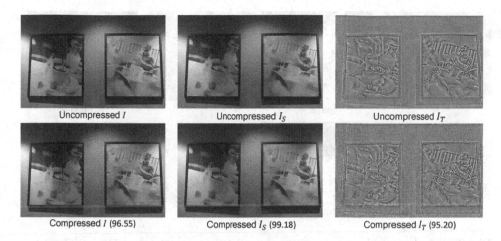

Fig. 3. This shows two examples of structure-texture decomposition in uncompressed and compressed image ($Q40$) pairs. The structure similarity index measurement (SSIM) [24] values (in ×100 scale in the paper) between each pair are shown in the brackets. Notice that most of the characteristic compression artifacts exist in the texture layer, while the structure layer of the compressed image resembles that of the uncompressed image.

layer as will be described later. As a result, TV-based deblocking methods tend to suffer from over-smoothing, while ours preserves more details.

Figure 3 shows two examples of the structure-texture decomposition results for the same images: one image is compressed and the other is not. As can be observed, unlike the texture layers that contain different information due to the artifacts, the structure layers are almost identical (both from the visual quality perspective and from the structure similarity index measurement, SSIM, perspective [24]). This shows the effectiveness of the TV regularization in producing a structure layer that significantly filter out any compression artifacts. As such, this image layer is considered to be artifacts free and suitable to be boosted using the desired enhancement operation directly, resulting in the enhanced version of the structure, I_S^e.

3.2   Reducing Artifacts in the Texture Layer

Since the texture layer contains both scene details and compression artifacts, it needs further refinement to be able to remove artifacts and to keep scene details. To do this, we create a mask M that separates regions, where the most scene details are presence, from the remaining regions. Having created the mask, for the regions inside the mask, we refine them further to remove potential ringing and blocking artifacts. For the remaining regions, which are those outside the mask, we remove the content altogether, since the content is most likely compression artifacts.

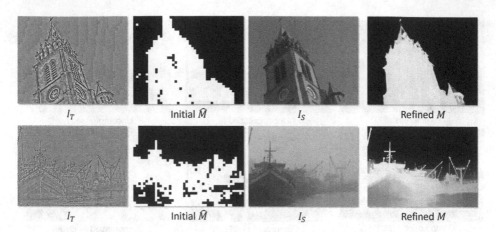

Fig. 4. This shows two examples of the scene detail map generation. The initial results obtained by checking DCT coefficients are rough estimations. A soft matting technique can help refine the map by applying it to the structure layer, and the result is well aligned with the objects in the images.

Scene Detail Extraction. To create the image mask, M, we apply the discrete cosine transform (DCT) to each 8×8 patches in the texture layer. We use the DCT high-frequency layer to serve as a likelihood of the scene details, i.e. stronger high-frequency DCT coefficients means more details. Denoting the 8×8 DCT of one block as matrix B, then the likelihood of this block to be part of the scene details can be expressed as:

$$t = \sum_{u,v} B_{u,v}^2 - B_{1,1}^2 - B_{1,2}^2 - B_{2,1}^2, \tag{3}$$

where u, v denotes the position in the DCT. We take the sum of squares of all DCT coefficients except $B_{1,1}, B_{1,2}$ and $B_{2,1}$, and apply a threshold to the likelihood to make a binary indication of each block. The threshold we use is empirically set to 0.1. This initial block-wise estimation of texture region, denoted as $\hat{M}$, is a coarse estimate, as shown in the second column of Figure 4.

This initial mask provides the regions of image details, but is too coarse for practical use. Thus, we apply a refinement step to better align the texture region with the structure layer. For this, we use a soft matting technique (inspired by [12]) by minimizing the following function on the scene detail map M:

$$\min_{\mathbf{m}} (\mathbf{m} - \hat{\mathbf{m}})^\top (\mathbf{m} - \hat{\mathbf{m}}) + \alpha \mathbf{m}^\top L_s \mathbf{m}, \tag{4}$$

where $\mathbf{m}$ and $\hat{\mathbf{m}}$ are the vector forms of matrix M and $\hat{M}$, respectively. L_s is Levin's [16] matting Laplacian matrix generated from I_S. The smallest eigenvectors of the matting Laplacian correspond to the partitioning of images [16]. The first term forces the agreement with the initial estimation $\hat{M}$, while the second term forces the output to be aligned with the structure layer I_S. We set the

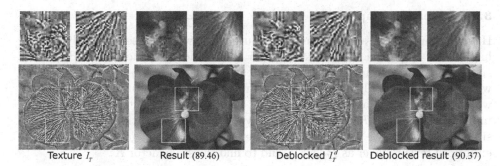

| Texture I_τ | Result (89.46) | Deblocked I_τ^d | Deblocked result (90.37) |

Fig. 5. This shows the effect of blocking artifacts reduction. The left side shows the textural layers and its corresponding final composition results without the blocking artifacts reduction step. The right side shows the same pair but with the effect of blocking artifacts reduction. As can be seen both in texture and final results that the block is less noticeable when we apply the block artifacts reduction. The similarity against ground truth using SSIM for with and without deblocking are also shown in the bracket.

regularization parameter α a large value (10^5 in our implementation), since it will provide clearer edges in the mask M. The last column of Figure 4 shows the texture region map after refinement using the structure I_S. Most of the values in the map are near 0 or 1 (close to binary), but some values are between the two.

The result is a mask M whose edges have been refined. Another benefit of aligning the mask to the structure layer is that small amounts of textures around edges, which are indicative to ringing artifacts, are removed.

Block Artifacts Reduction. Having created the mask indicating the regions of scene details, we now try to reduce the potential blocking artifacts in the regions. Denoting the texture image after blocking artifacts suppression as $I_{T_i}^d$, an objective function is defined as follows:

$$\min_{I_{T_i}^d} \sum_i (I_{T_i}^d - I_{T_i})^2 + \beta \sum_{i \in \eta} (\nabla I_{T_i}^d)^2, \tag{5}$$

where i is the pixel index, and η are the locations at the 8×8 block borders. The first term forces the output to be similar to the input, while the second term smooths the edges at the 8×8 block borders, since they are more likely to be block artifacts. The smoothness level is controlled by the weight term β. We empirically set it 0.5 to achieve a proper compromise between oversmoothness and noticeable artifacts. This is effective in reducing the blockings in the texture map and result in a higher quantitative score as can be seen in Figure 5.

182   Y. Li et al.

3.3 Layer Recomposition

Having removed the artifacts in the texture layer, we now need to apply an enhancement operation to the texture layer before adding it back to I_S^e. However, since most contrast functions f are not linear and thus $f(I_S+I_T) \neq f(I_S)+f(I_T)$, we cannot simply apply the same process and then sum them up. As a consequence, we have to approximate the enhancement function adjustment by finding a scale multiplication factor K, which should obey the following condition as much as possible: $f(I) = f(I_S) + KI_T$, where I is the original input image. By denoting the enhanced texture layer as I_T^e, we intend to find the scale factor K:

$$I_T^e = K \circ M \circ I_T^d, \tag{6}$$

where $\circ$ is the element-wise multiplication operator. $M \circ I_T^d$ combines the steps in the previous section that generates the masked texture layer with reduced artifacts.

Like in the case of enhancing contrast for the structure layer I_S, the scale factor depends on the applications. For the application of image tone-curve adjustment, the tone-curve function f is applied to the intensity values of the input image, I. Taylor series $f(t + \Delta t) \approx f(t) + f'(t)\Delta t$ allows us to write:

$$f(I_{S_i} + I_{T_i}) = f(I_{S_i}) + f'(I_{S_i})I_{T_i}. \tag{7}$$

Hence, from the last equation, we have the scale factor for the tone adjustment $K_i = f'(I_{S_i})$.

In the dehazing or underwater application, the enhancement should consider the optical model of scattering media, which according to [12], the output of the enhancement should follow the following equation:

$$I_i^e = \frac{I_i - A}{t_i} + A, \tag{8}$$

where the I_i is the input image, A is the atmospheric light, t_i is the transmission, and i is pixel index. Therefore, the scale factor, K_i, should be approximately equal to $\frac{1}{t_i}$, since A is a constant and I_i^e is in $\frac{I_i}{t_i} + k$ form. Following [12], t is obtained from dark channel prior and A is obtained from the patch with the brightest intensity in dark channel.

Having recovered both the structure and texture layers, the final result can be achieved by simply summing up the two layers: $I^e = I_S^e + I_T^e$.

4 Results

We evaluated our proposed framework by applying it to various contrast enhancement tasks: image tone-curve adjustment, dehazing and underwater visibility enhancement. Due to space limitation, only some of our results are shown here. More results are available in the supplemental material. Demo code and data are available at the author's webpage[2]. Experiments were performed on a

[2] http://www.comp.nus.edu.sg/~liyu1988/

| Low contrast (Q40) | Haze (Q80) | Underwater (Q30) |

Fig. 6. This figure shows the inputs in the section which require contrast boosting

Table 1. Average Runtime Comparison

Method	SA-DCT[10]	FoE[19]	NN[3]	Ours
Runtime(s)	20	287	25	15

PC with Intel I7 CPU (3.4GHz) with 8GB RAM. The test images were either self-taken or downloaded from the Internet. Three examples are shown in Figure 6. Note that, in these input images, there are often no noticeable artifacts. The artifacts become apparent after the contrast enhancement is applied.

The entire process for an image (approximately 500 × 600 in size) using our current un-optimized matlab implementation took about 15 seconds with the main bottleneck being the image matting which took more than 10 seconds. The only parameter that needs to be changed was the regulation term λ in the structure-texture decomposition in Eqn. (2). This parameter was set according to the compression level. Higher compression requires larger λ for the decomposition. $\lambda = 0.02, 0.03, 0.04, 0.05$ is used for $> Q70$, $Q50 - Q70$, $Q30 - Q50$ and $< Q30$, respectively.

Table 2. Quantitative Comparison

Method	simple boosted	FoE[19]	NN[3]	SA-DCT (Pre)[10]	SA-DCT (Post)[10]	Ours
Mean SSIM	90.79	91.14	91.88	92.03	91.79	**92.05**
Mean PSNR	29.17	29.69	29.94	**30.12**	29.42	29.76

We compared our approach with several state-of-the-art deblocking methods: a local filtering based method - shape adaptive DCT (SA-DCT) [10], a reconstruction based using Field of Experts (FoE) prior [19] as well as a learning based method using Neural Network (NN) [3]. These methods were all used as both a pre-processing and post-processing step for the contrast enhancement methods. We note that the comparison with NN is not fair since it is a more general algorithm targeting on any kinds of noise (i.e. not just JPEG artifacts). The average run-times of these algorithms are summarized in Table 1. Interestingly, even though we apply layer decomposition and matting as parts of our procedure, our method has the fastest performance among all.

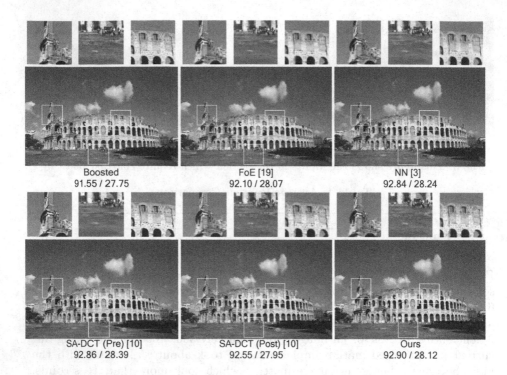

Fig. 7. This figure shows an example in image tone-curve adjustment using FoE [19], NN [3], SA-DCT [10] and our approach. Shown below the images are the comparison SSIM/PSNR(dB) with respect to the groundtruth.

For experiments involving tone-curve manipulation, we can also provide a quantitative comparison with the groundtruth. The groundtruth image is obtained by enhancing the uncompressed image using the same tone-curve. Quantitative results are reported using the perceptually-based quality measurement-structure similarity index (SSIM) [24] (in ×100 scale) as well as the peak signal-to-noise ratio (PSNR). Table 2 summarizes the average SSIM and average PSNR on all our 15 test cases and at different compression levels (from $Q20$ to $Q90$). Our approach achieves the highest SSIM but not the highest PSNR. As sometimes the case with PSNR, we believe it does not properly reflect the qualitative results. On visual inspection of the images, it is clear our approach is qualitatively better than the other methods.

Figure 7 shows a tone-curve adjustment comparison. As can be seen, FoE and NN successfully removed block artifacts which resulted in overall improvements in both PSNR and SSIM. However, they tended to smooth sharp edges and details in the image. SA-DCT lost its effectiveness in deblocking when used after the enhancement, but when used before the enhancement, SA-DCT did a good job and achieved the highest PSNR. However, upon close visual inspection, the

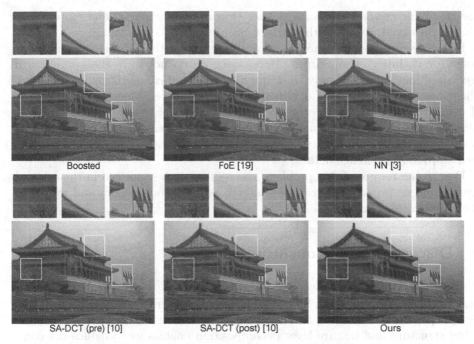

Fig. 8. This figure shows an example of dehazing using FoE [19], NN [3], SA-DCT [10] and our approach

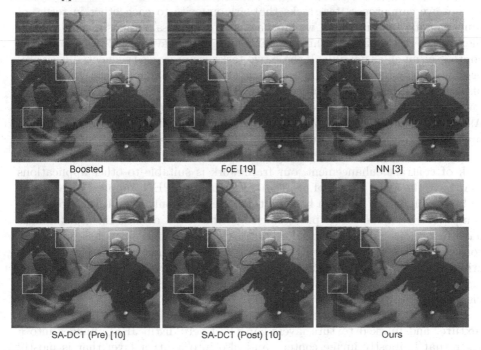

Fig. 9. This figure shows an example of underwater image enhancement using FoE [19], NN [3], SA-DCT [10] and our approach.

results of our method are much cleaner (less ringing artifacts) and more image details preserved, resulting the highest SSIM value.

Figures 8 and 9 show examples of applying our method to dehazing and underwater visibility enhancement. Here, since we do not have the groundtruth recovered image, we can only show qualitative visual comparisons. In these applications, the advantage of our method becomes more observable. The results of using FoE and NN are over smoothed, causing them to lose details. SA-DCT slightly outperformed FoE and NN in reducing the compression artifacts. Ours is better in terms of removing artifacts (particularly with much less ringings) as well as preserving image details.

Due to the nature of this problem, the results are best viewed in the original size. Thus, we provide larger images as well as more comparisons and results in the supplemental material.

5   Discussion and Conclusion

We have introduced a framework to suppress artifacts appearing in JPEG images that becomes prominently visible when applying contrast enhancement. While the proposed framework is admittedly engineering in nature, our strategy of using structure and texture layer decomposition enables us to reduce the compression artifacts in parallel with contrast enhancement, and to process them independently to each other. With this integrated framework, the key benefit is that we can process two tasks that are opposite to each other in terms of functionality. On one hand, we have a task to suppress noise as much as possible; on the other hand, within the same image, we have a task to enhance the content as much as possible. If these two tasks are processed sequentially, as pre- or post-processing, the results are not likely to be optimum. Since, the process of artifacts removal as pre-processing will remove the image content that have low contrast, and as post-processing will be affected by the enhanced artifacts. As shown in our experiments, we have demonstrated the effectiveness of the proposed framework using qualitative and quantitative measures.

While our approach targets suppressing JPEG compression artifacts for the task of contrast enhancement, our framework is suitable to other applications that have the same nature of problem. We consider JPEG compression artifacts to be an important problem because these are commonly troublesome for many computer vision and image processing algorithms that assume the input images have little noise. We also consider contrast enhancement, since it is one of the core operations in the low-level computer vision and image processing. Among other applications, it is crucially used to deal with turbid media, such as haze, fog, rain, and underwater, which has been addressed considerably in computer vision community recently.

Regarding our framework, the remaining question is whether our structure, texture, and masked texture layers can effectively distill JPEG images into a layer that is mostly image content and also into another layer that is mostly affected by compression artifacts. While our practical findings discussed in the paper have given us a positive answer (and we consider as a contribution that can be improved further), rigorous evaluation is still needed, and we will consider this in our future work.

Acknowledgement. This research was carried out at the SeSaMe Centre supported by the Singapore NRF under its IRC@SG Funding Initiative and administered by the IDMPO.

References

1. Ancuti, C., Ancuti, C.O., Haber, T., Bekaert, P.: Enhancing underwater images and videos by fusion. In: IEEE Conference on Computer Vision and Pattern Recognition (2012)
2. Aujol, J.F., Gilboa, G., Chan, T., Osher, S.: Structure-texture image decomposition–modeling, algorithms, and parameter selection. International Journal of Computer Vision 67(1), 111–136 (2006)
3. Burger, H.C., Schuler, C.J., Harmeling, S.: Image denoising: Can plain neural networks compete with bm3d? In: IEEE Conference on Computer Vision and Pattern Recognition (2012)
4. Burt, P.J., Adelson, E.H.: The laplacian pyramid as a compact image code. IEEE Transactions on Communications 31(4), 532–540 (1983)
5. Chiang, J.Y., Chen, Y.C.: Underwater image enhancement by wavelength compensation and dehazing. IEEE Transactions on Image Processing 21(4), 1756–1769 (2012)
6. Dong, W., Zhang, L., Shi, G.: Centralized sparse representation for image restoration. In: IEEE International Conference on Computer Vision (2011)
7. Durand, F., Dorsey, J.: Fast bilateral filtering for the display of high-dynamic-range images. ACM Transactions on Graphics (TOG) 21(3), 257–266 (2002)
8. Farbman, Z., Fattal, R., Lischinski, D., Szeliski, R.: Edge-preserving decompositions for multi-scale tone and detail manipulation. ACM Transactions on Graphics (TOG) 27(3), 67 (2008)
9. Fattal, R.: Single image dehazing. ACM Transactions on Graphics 27(3), 72 (2008)
10. Foi, A., Katkovnik, V., Egiazarian, K.: Pointwise shape-adaptive dct for high-quality denoising and deblocking of grayscale and color images. IEEE Transactions on Image Processing 16(5), 1395–1411 (2007)
11. Goto, T., Kato, Y., Hirano, S., Sakurai, M., Nguyen, T.Q.: Compression artifact reduction based on total variation regularization method for mpeg-2. IEEE Transactions on Consumer Electronics 57(1), 253–259 (2011)
12. He, K., Sun, J., Tang, X.: Single image haze removal using dark channel prior. IEEE Transactions on Pattern Analysis and Machine Intelligence 33(12), 2341–2353 (2011)
13. Jacobs, N., Burgin, W., Fridrich, N., Abrams, A., Miskell, K., Braswell, B.H., Richardson, A.D., Pless, R.: The global network of outdoor webcams: Properties and applications. In: ACM International Conference on Advances in Geographic Information Systems (2009)
14. Lee, K., Kim, D.S., Kim, T.: Regression-based prediction for blocking artifact reduction in jpeg-compressed images. IEEE Transactions on Image Processing 14(1), 36–48 (2005)

15. Lee, Y., Kim, H., Park, H.: Blocking effect reduction of jpeg images by signal adaptive filtering. IEEE Transactions on Image Processing 7(2), 229–234 (1998)
16. Levin, A., Lischinski, D., Weiss, Y.: A closed-form solution to natural image matting. IEEE Transactions on Pattern Analysis and Machine Intelligence 30(2), 228–242 (2008)
17. Majumder, A., Irani, S.: Perception-based contrast enhancement of images. ACM Transactions on Applied Perception 4(3), 17 (2007)
18. Rudin, L.I., Osher, S., Fatemi, E.: Nonlinear total variation based noise removal algorithms. Physica D: Nonlinear Phenomena 60(1), 259–268 (1992)
19. Sun, D., Cham, W.K.: Postprocessing of low bit-rate block dct coded images based on a fields of experts prior. IEEE Transactions on Image Processing 16(11), 2743–2751 (2007)
20. Tan, R.T.: Visibility in bad weather from a single image. In: IEEE Conference on Computer Vision and Pattern Recognition (2008)
21. Tomasi, C., Manduchi, R.: Bilateral filtering for gray and color images. In: IEEE International Conference on Computer Vision, pp. 839–846 (1998)
22. Wang, C.Y., Lee, S.M., Chang, L.W.: Designing jpeg quantization tables based on human visual system. Image Communication 16(5), 501–506 (2001)
23. Wang, Y., Yang, J., Yin, W., Zhang, Y.: A new alternating minimization algorithm for total variation image reconstruction. SIAM Journal on Imaging Sciences 1(3), 248–272 (2008)
24. Wang, Z., Bovik, A., Sheikh, H., Simoncelli, E.: Image quality assessment: From error visibility to structural similarity. IEEE Transactions on Image Processing 13(4), 600–612 (2004)
25. Watson, A.: Dct quantization matrices visually optimized for individual images. In: Proceedings of the International Society for Optics and Photonics, vol. 1913, pp. 202–216 (1993)
26. Wedel, A., Pock, T., Zach, C., Bischof, H., Cremers, D.: An improved algorithm for tv-l 1 optical flow. In: Cremers, D., Rosenhahn, B., Yuille, A.L., Schmidt, F.R. (eds.) Statistical and Geometrical Approaches to Visual Motion Analysis. LNCS, vol. 5604, pp. 23–45. Springer, Heidelberg (2009)
27. Yang, Y., Galatsanos, N.P., Katsaggelos, A.K.: Projection-based spatially adaptive reconstruction of block-transform compressed images. IEEE Transactions on Image Processing 4(7), 896–908 (1995)
28. Yim, C., Bovik, A.: Quality assessment of deblocked images. IEEE Transactions on Image Processing 20(1), 88–98 (2011)
29. Zakhor, A.: Iterative procedures for reduction of blocking effects in transform image coding. IEEE Transactions on Circuits and Systems for Video Technology 2(1), 91–95 (1992)

Radial Bright Channel Prior
for Single Image Vignetting Correction

Hojin Cho, Hyunjoon Lee, and Seungyong Lee

Pohang University of Science and Technology (POSTECH), Korea

Abstract. This paper presents a novel prior, *radial bright channel (RBC) prior*, for single image vignetting correction. The RBC prior is derived from a statistical property of vignetting-free images: for the pixels sharing the same radius in polar coordinates of an image, at least one pixel has a high intensity value at some color channel. Exploiting the prior, we can effectively estimate and correct the vignetting effect of a given image. We represent the vignetting effect as an 1D function of the distance from the optical center, and estimate the function using the RBC prior. As it works completely in 1D, our method provides high efficiency in terms of computation and storage costs. Experimental results demonstrate that our method runs an order of magnitude faster than previous work, while producing higher quality results of vignetting correction.

Keywords: radial bright channel prior, vignetting correction.

1 Introduction

In vignetting correction, image degradation is usually modeled as:

$$Z(r, \theta) = I(r, \theta) \cdot V(r), \tag{1}$$

where Z and I respectively represent the input and latent vignetting-free image in polar coordinates whose origin is the optical center of the image, and V represents the 1D vignetting function assuming the vignetting is rotationally symmetric. The goal of image vignetting correction is to estimate both V and I from a single input Z, which is an under-constrained problem.

Various approaches have been proposed for solving the vignetting correction problem, by utilizing a predefined template based photometric calibration [12,1,6,13] and multiple images of different intensity attenuation [10,3,5,9]. Although these methods can remove vignettes effectively, they require reference calibration images or multiple input images with known camera settings. On the other hand, single image based approaches attempt to restore vignetting-free images without any additional information [15,17]. Such methods can produce high quality results for various images in a fully automatic fashion, but they involve heavy computations and thus may not be directly applicable for consumer products. Since vignetting is an undesired artifact in many computer vision applications, an effective and efficient vignetting correction method is still highly demanded.

D. Fleet et al. (Eds.): ECCV 2014, Part II, LNCS 8690, pp. 189–202, 2014.

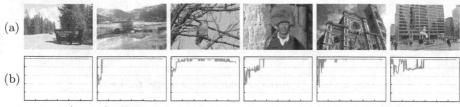

(x-axis): distance from optical center; (y-axis): intensity of RBC

Fig. 1. Radial bright channel (RBC). (a) vignetting-free images. (b) RBC values corresponding to (a), which form almost horizontal lines except near the optical centers.

In this paper, we propose a novel prior, *radial bright channel (RBC) prior*, for single image vignetting correction. Similar to the dark channel prior [4], the RBC prior is derived from a statistical property of vignetting-free natural images: for the pixels sharing the same radius in polar coordinates of an image, there frequently exists at least one pixel (called *radial bright pixel*) such that its intensity is close to the maximum intensity of the image, except near the optical center (Fig. 1a). By arranging radial bright pixels with respect to the distances from the optical center, we can extract a 1D curve called *radial bright channel*, which is an almost *horizontal* line (Figs. 1b and 2b). If an image is affected by vignetting, then the overall image intensities radially fall off away from the optical center, affecting the intensities of the RBC as well (Fig. 2d). Thus, the RBC of an image can provide a rough approximation of the vignetting effect.

Based the RBC prior, we develop an effective vignetting estimation algorithm. Instead of using the whole image pixels, our method only uses a 1D RBC to estimate the vignetting profile, assuming the vignetting is rotationally symmetric. Consequently, the proposed algorithm is computationally and memory efficient and runs an order of magnitude faster than previous methods [15,11,17]. To handle potential outliers in an image (e.g., objects near the optical center and over-exposed pixels), our vignetting estimation algorithm involves an iterative refinement process that evaluates and rejects the outliers. Experimental results demonstrate that our method outperforms previous single image vignetting correction algorithms in terms of result quality and speed.

Our contributions are summarized as follows:

- Novel image prior, called *radial bright channel prior*, that can be used for accurately characterizing the vignetting effects.
- Fast and robust single image based vignetting estimation algorithm which runs in the 1D spatial domain using the radial bright channel prior.

2   Related Work

There are a variety of vignetting correction techniques in the literature. An intuitive approach to estimate the vignetting is to calibrate the camera using a reference image taken under a uniform illumination [12,1,6,13]. This calibration-based approach can provide a plausible vignetting profile for known camera settings when the camera is available. However, the estimated vignettes would not correspond to images captured with different camera settings or lenses. This approach is barely suitable for arbitrary images downloaded from the internet.

Another related approach is to use multiple images taken with the same camera. In these methods, vignetting profiles are calibrated by utilizing overlapping views [10,7,3], different camera settings for exposure time and aperture [5], or a large number of images [9]. By considering the correspondence among multiple images with different intensity attenuations, ill-posedness of the vignetting problem can be reduced. However, this approach cannot be generally applied in practice as the corresponding multiple images are not often available.

Recently single image based vignetting correction has attracted more attention due to its flexibility [16,11,17]. An early approach in this category is based on image segmentation for classifying homogeneous regions with respect to color or texture, and estimates vignetting from intensity attenuation within each region [16]. This algorithm highly depends on image segmentation which is usually not robust for natural images, and is vulnerable to artifacts such as vignetting inconsistency between decomposed regions. A more sophisticated method utilizes the radial gradient symmetry of natural images [17]. This algorithm works well on a variety of natural images, but their asymmetry measure involves Kullback-Leibler divergence between positive and negative gradient distributions, which may not be robustly computed due to image noise and numerical instability. Similarly, inspired by [18,14] (the former version of [17]), statistical regularities of image derivatives have been exploited for vignetting correction [11], but there could be some ambiguity in the relationship between vignetting effects and image derivative distributions. Although several solutions exist for single image vignetting correction, they involve heavy computations due to nonlinear optimization with complicated priors for vignetting-free images.

3 Radial Bright Channel Prior

For a given image I, its radial bright channel (RBC) I^{RB} is formally defined as:

$$I^{RB}(r) = \max_{\theta} \left\{ \max_{C} I^{C}(r, \theta) \right\}, \tag{2}$$

where r is the radial distance from the optical center, $\theta \in [0, 2\pi)$, $C \in \{R, G, B\}$, and I^{C} is a color channel of I. For notational simplicity, we will omit the ranges of C and θ unless necessary. Fig. 2a illustrates how to compute $I^{RB}(r)$ for an image. The RBC prior can be summarized as: for almost all r, $I^{RB}(r)$ is close to the maximum channel value c_0 of an image, where $c_0 = \max_{r,\theta,C} I^{C}(r, \theta)$. That is, when we plot $I^{RB}(r)$ with respect to r, the curve is an almost horizontal line with the value of c_0 (Fig. 2b).

The RBC prior is based on the statistical property we can observe from natural images. In an ordinary image, we can easily observe high intensities, mainly due

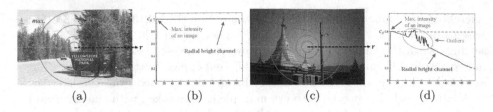

(a)   (b)   (c)   (d)

Fig. 2. RBC Computation. (a, c) computation of $I^{\mathrm{RB}}(r)$ in the 2D spatial domain. (b, d) resulting RBCs.

to two factors: 1) bright objects/surfaces; 2) colorful objects/surfaces that cause high values at some color channels. For many images, large portions of image regions (e.g., sky, sea, and ground for an outdoor scene, and wall and window for indoor) are usually well lit by the sunlight or other kinds of illuminations, as shown in Fig. 1a. These well-lit regions would contain almost uniformly high intensity values in some color channels. If we draw relatively large circles centered at the image center as illustrated in Fig. 2a, then some parts of the circles should intersect those well-lit regions and the maximum intensities for the circles will come from the intersected parts. Thus the intensity uniformity of well-lit regions will bring us the RBC prior.

To validate our observation, we downloaded various kinds of images from flickr.com and manually picked out vignetting-free images with proper brightness since vignetting is not well perceived in dark images. Among them, 3,000 images were randomly selected and uniformly scaled so that the distance from the image center to the farthest boundary pixel becomes 500 pixels. Then, to investigate how similar I^{RB} is to the maximum channel value of an image, we computed $I^{residual} = c_0 - I^{\mathrm{RB}}$ for image pixels (see Fig. 2b). We did not use all values of $I^{residual}$ because many natural images contain objects (e.g., human) near the image center. In our experiment, we rejected the first 30% of the distance range $[0, 500]$ as outliers, considering that generally vignetting does not strongly affect the pixels near the image center. In addition, we ignored the pixels with intensity values above 240, since they could have been over-exposed.

Fig. 3a shows the normalized histogram of $I^{residual}$ obtained from the 3,000 images. The total number of pixel samples used for the histogram is about one million. We observe that about 88% of the pixels in the RBCs have values equal to c_0. Considering the error tolerance, we find 94.5% and 99.5% of the residual values are below five and 15, respectively. Fig. 3b shows another meaningful statistics that most of the images have almost zero mean residual values. With these observations, our RBC prior can be considered strong enough to be applied for a large portion of natural images. The RBCs estimated for various natural images are shown in Fig. 1b.

For an image with vignetting, on the other hand, the overall image brightness is attenuated radially from the optical center and the RBC deviates from the maximum channel value of the image. Interestingly, however, the RBC extracted from such an image well captures the overall distribution of the vignetting effects,

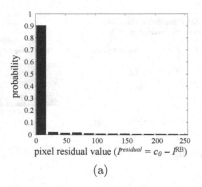 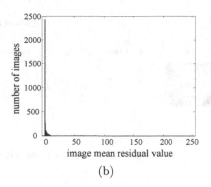

(a)   (b)

Fig. 3. RBC statistics. (a) normalized histogram of the residual values from about one million sample pixels in 3,000 images. The width of each bin is 16 intensity levels. (b) histogram of the mean residual values of the 3,000 images.

as shown in Fig. 2d. This property motivates our vignetting correction method, and the detailed algorithm will be described in Sec. 4.

Implementation Details. Similar to most vignetting correction methods, we assume the optical center of an input image is located at the image center. To robustly compute RBCs, we quantize the distance r between a pixel and the image center to discrete values. For each discrete value r, color channel values of the pixels belonging to r are stored into a histogram of 256 bins. Considering outliers (e.g., noise and saturation) in an image, we check each bin in the histogram and reject it if the bin size is smaller than a predefined empirical threshold T. Then the maximum channel value for r is chosen from the remaining bins. In the experiments, we set $T = 0.01 \times W$ for all images, where W is the maximum of image width and height.

4   Vignetting Correction Using RBC Prior

Fig. 4 shows the overall process of our vignetting correction algorithm using the RBC prior. From a given input image Z whose color channel values are ranged between 0 and 1, we first compute the RBC Z^{RB}. The vignetting function is then estimated using our iterative optimization technique, and finally the vignette-free image I is recovered with the estimated vignetting function.

4.1   Simple Estimation of the Vignetting Function

As described in Sec. 3, the RBC of an image exhibits the overall profile of vignetting effects. To utilize the RBC for vignetting correction, we first derive from Eq. (1) a relationship between the RBC and the vignetting profile. Note that in this paper, we assume that vignetting is rotationally symmetric and its effects are the same over all color channels.

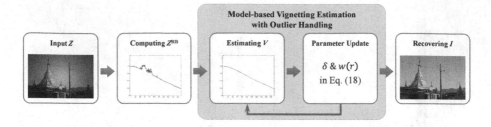

Fig. 4. Overview of our vignetting correction process

Taking two max operations over θ and color channels $\mathcal{C}$ in the image model of Eq. (1), we obtain

$$Z^{\mathrm{RB}}(r) = \max_\theta \left\{ \max_{\mathcal{C}} Z^{\mathcal{C}}(r, \theta) \right\} = \left[\max_\theta \left\{ \max_{\mathcal{C}} I^{\mathcal{C}}(r, \theta) \right\} \right] \cdot V(r), \qquad (3)$$

as V is independent of θ and $\mathcal{C}$. Using Eq. (2), we have

$$Z^{\mathrm{RB}}(r) = I^{\mathrm{RB}}(r) \cdot V(r). \qquad (4)$$

The statistics in Sec. 3 implies that I^{RB} is near constant with respect to r if we neglect outliers. Consequently, we can estimate the vignetting function V by substituting I^{RB} with a constant c_0 and minimizing the following term:

$$\underset{V, c_0}{\arg\min} \sum_{r=1}^{n} \left\| c_0 V(r) - Z^{\mathrm{RB}}(r) \right\|^2, \qquad (5)$$

where V becomes equivalent to Z^{RB} if $c_0 = 1$. However, this naive estimation of V would be vulnerable to outliers in Z, such as objects near the image center, saturated pixels, image noise, and dark backgrounds (Fig. 5b). We propose a model based solution to robustly handle outliers in vignetting estimation.

4.2 Model-Based Vignetting Estimation with Outlier Handling

From Eq. (4), we formulate the joint probability of I^{RB} and V with respect to Z^{RB} as

$$p\left(I^{\mathrm{RB}}, V | Z^{\mathrm{RB}}\right) \propto p\left(Z^{\mathrm{RB}} | I^{\mathrm{RB}}, V\right) p\left(I^{\mathrm{RB}}, V\right). \qquad (6)$$

To estimate V effectively and robustly in Eq. (6), we use a parametric representation for V by adopting the extended Kang-Weiss model [15]. In the Kang-Weiss model, a vignetting function is modeled with three factors: off-axis illumination

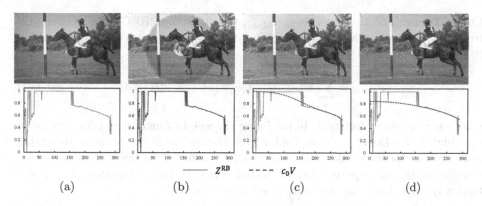

(a)   (b)   (c)   (d)

Fig. 5. Comparison of vignetting function estimation results. (a) input image. (b) naive estimation. (c) initial model-based estimation. (d) final model-based estimation with outlier handling. In (c), outliers in Z^{RB} near the image center are not properly filtered out, making the central region of the image darker than around the boundary. Such artifact is removed in (d) with our iterative refinement process.

factor A, geometric factor G, and tilt factor T. Among them, tilt factor is often ignored in practice and the vignetting function V is modelled as follows:

$$V(r) - A(r) \cdot G(r), \tag{7}$$

$$A(r) = \frac{1}{\{1 + (r/f)^2\}^2}, \tag{8}$$

$$G(r) = 1 - \sum_{i=1}^{p} \alpha_i \left(\frac{r}{n}\right)^p, \tag{9}$$

where f is the focal length of the camera and $\{\alpha_i\}$ are the coefficients of G.

By substituting I^{RB} with c_0 and plugging Eq. (7) into Eq. (6), we have

$$p\left(c_0, V | Z^{RB}\right) \propto p\left(Z^{RB} | c_0, f, \{\alpha_i\}\right) p\left(c_0, f, \{\alpha_i\}\right) \tag{10}$$

$$= p\left(Z^{RB} | c_0, f, \{\alpha_i\}\right) p(c_0) p(f) \prod_{i=1}^{p} p(\alpha_i),$$

with the assumption that all the model parameters are independent of each other. To estimate the parameters $\{c_0, f, \{\alpha_i\}\}$, we convert Eq. (10) into an energy function by taking negative log, and minimize the energy with some additional constraints:

$$\underset{c_0, f, \{\alpha_i\}}{\arg\min} \ \lambda_d E_{data} + \lambda_{c_0} E_{c_0} + \lambda_f E_f + \lambda_\alpha \sum_{i=1}^{p} E_{\alpha_i}, \tag{11}$$

$$\text{subject to} \ \forall_r V(r) \geq V(r+1) \ \text{and} \ 0 \leq c_0 \leq 1.$$

Data Term. For the data term E_{data}, we utilize our RBC prior. Differently from Eq. (5), we use a truncated L_1 distance which is known to be more robust to outliers so that:

$$E_{data} = \sum_{r=1}^{n} w(r) \cdot \min \left(\left| c_0 V(r) - Z^{\text{RB}}(r) \right|, \delta \right), \tag{12}$$

where w is a weight function. In modeling the weight function, it is important to give higher weights to the samples far from the optical center because vignetting appears more severely as r increases and Z^{RB} values near the optical center are unreliable. In our experiments, we tested several types of functions and found that a quadric function of r works well in most cases:

$$w(r) = \frac{r^2}{\sum_{r=1}^{n} r^2}. \tag{13}$$

In addition, we set the first 30% of w as zero to reject outliers near the optical center, as we did for computing the statistics in Sec. 3. w is updated during our optimization process to adaptively handle outliers in Z^{RB}, such as over-exposed pixels and pixels outside the image boundary.

Prior Terms. For computing E_{c_0}, we assume that c_0 is similar to the maximum value of Z^{RB} excluding outliers, and define

$$E_{c_0} = \left(\max(c_0 V | w) - \max(Z^{\text{RB}} | w) \right)^2, \tag{14}$$

where $\max(c_0 V | w)$ is the maximum among the values of $c_0 V(r)$ for which $w(r) \neq 0$, and $\max(Z^{\text{RB}} | w)$ is similarly defined.

To compute E_f, we use a well-known prior for the focal length [8] in which f is similar to the image size:

$$E_f = \left\{ (W - f) / W \right\}^2, \tag{15}$$

where W is the maximum of the image width and height.

For E_{α_i}, we enforce all the values of α_i to remain small since the vignetting function V should be smooth across the image. We thus formulate E_{α_i} as:

$$E_\alpha = \alpha_i^2. \tag{16}$$

Constraints. The first constraint in Eq. (11) makes V monotonically decreasing, which is a natural property of a vignetting function. Instead of assigning hard constraints, we transform it as soft constraints via an energy term as follows:

$$C_{dec} \equiv \lambda_{dec} \sum_{r=1}^{n-1} \max \left(V(r+1) - V(r), 0 \right)^2, \tag{17}$$

where C_{dec} is the non-increasing constraint. The boundary constraint for c_0 prohibits V from being bigger than 1, and is enforced as a hard constraint.

Algorithm 1. Model-based Vignetting Estimation with Outlier Handling

---

Input: radial bright channel Z^{RB} of an input image
Output: vignetting function V
    $c_0 \leftarrow 1,\, f \leftarrow W,\, \{\alpha_i\} \leftarrow 0$ ▷ Initialization
    for $iter = 1 : n_{iter}$ **do**
        $c_0, f, \{\alpha_i\} \leftarrow$ Estimate the parameters using Eq. (11)
        $V \leftarrow$ Reconstruct V using Eqs. (7)-(9)
        $w \leftarrow$ Update w with δ using Eq. (18)   ▷ Update for outlier handling
        $\delta \leftarrow \delta/2$
    end for

Iterative Optimization. The energy function in Eq. (11) can be solved with a non-linear constrained optimization method; in this paper, we used the Matlab implementation of trust-region-reflective algorithm [2]. The initial optimization result, however, might be inaccurate due to outliers in Z^{RB} and bad initial parameters, as shown in Fig. 5c. We thus use iterative refinement for more robust estimation of V.

We first optimize Eq. (11) and compute V, setting $\delta = 1$ in Eq. (12). Then, we update $w(r)$ by masking out outlier values of Z^{RB} using the following equation:

$$w(r) - \begin{cases} w(r), & \text{if } \left| c_0 V(r) - Z^{\text{RB}}(r) \right| < \delta \\ 0, & \text{otherwise.} \end{cases} \tag{18}$$

and halve δ to reject more outliers in the next iteration. The updated parameters δ and $w(r)$, as well as estimated model parameters $\{c_0, f, \{\alpha_i\}\}$, are passed to the next iteration to re-optimize Eq. (11). We iterate this process for 3∼4 times to obtain the final result. Fig. 5d shows an estimated 1D vignetting function.

In Eq. (11), we have several parameters for assigning relative weights between terms although our method is not sensitive to them. In this paper, we fix the parameters as $\lambda_d = \lambda_{dec} = 10^2, \lambda_{c_0} = \lambda_f = 10^{-4}$, and $\lambda_\alpha = 10^{-3}$ for all examples. For initial values of the model parameters, we set $c_0 = 1$, $f = W$, and $\{\alpha_i\} = 0$, where the number of elements in $\{\alpha_i\}$ is 8. Algorithm 1 summarizes our vignetting function estimation algorithm.

It is worth mentioning that the previous single image based methods [15,17] utilize the whole pixels of an image to estimate the vignetting function. In contrast, our estimation algorithm optimizes the vignetting function in the 1D spatial domain with the RBC prior. This strategy greatly reduces the complexity of the estimation algorithm, enabling fast and robust estimation of the vignetting function, despite the complicated energy terms and constraints for the objective function in Eq. (11).

4.3 Restoring the Vignetting-Free Image

Given an estimated V, we recover the vignetting-free image I by dividing $Z(r, \theta)$ with $V(r)$ for all $\theta \in [0, 2\pi)$. Restoring the final image increases the overall

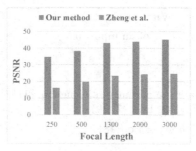

Fig. 6. Comparison with the state-of-the-art single image based method [17] of the mean PSNR values for 100 synthetic examples

brightness of an image, and some pixels of Z containing outliers (e.g., over-exposure and noise) can produce large values. We obtain the final result I as

$$I(r, \theta) = \min \left\{ \frac{Z(r, \theta)}{V(r)}, 1 \right\}. \qquad (19)$$

5   Results

In this section, we validate the effectiveness of our algorithm with various experimental results on synthetic and real images. We implemented our method using Matlab. Our testing environment is a PC running MS Windows 7 64bit version with Intel Core i7 CPU and 12GB RAM.

5.1   Synthetic Examples

To evaluate the performance of our vignetting estimation method, we built a dataset of synthetic images with vignetting effects. We first manually picked up 100 vignetting-free real images which contain indoor/outdoor scenes and complex scene objects (e.g., buildings, humans, animals, trees, grass, cars, sky, sea, etc), and resized each image to have the maximum of image width and height to be 600 pixels. Then we applied five different vignetting functions to each image. The vignetting functions were generated using the extended Kang-Weiss model (Eqs. (7)-(9)), with the five different focal lengths $f \in \{250, 500, 1300, 2000, 3000\}$ while neglecting the geometric factor. Setting the optical center as the image center, total 500 images were generated using Eq. (1). Finally, we compared our method with the state-of-the-art single image vignetting correction method proposed by Zheng et al. [17] using the dataset. The results of Zheng et al. were produced by the authors' implementation.

Fig. 6a shows PSNR values computed between ground truth images and results of each method. Since the effect of vignetting becomes weaker as the focal length increases, results of both methods tend to have higher PSNR values for larger focal lengths. The overall average PSNR value of our results is 40.97, while

(a) real input image   (b) our result

Fig. 7. Real example and its corresponding RBCs

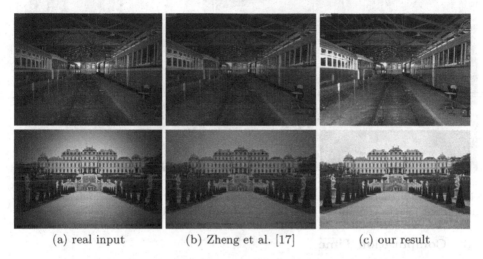

(a) real input   (b) Zheng et al. [17]   (c) our result

Fig. 8. Comparison with the state-of-the-art method on real photographs

that of Zheng et al. [17] is 21.57. Regardless of the focal length, our method can recover the original vignetting-free image more accurately.

We also estimated the running time of each method with the dataset. The average image size of our synthetic dataset is about 600 by 450 pixels. On average, our method took 1.43 seconds to process one image (i.e., estimating the vignetting function and recovering the corrected image), while Zheng et al.'s algorithm took 21.19 seconds.

5.2   Real Examples

Fig. 7 shows our result on a real example with the corresponding RBCs. As shown in Fig. 7a, the RBC of the input image with vignetting approximately represents the intensity attenuation. Although the image contains complex scene objects such as people and leaf textures, our algorithm recovers a visually pleasing result, making its RBC be a straight line away from the image center.

Fig. 8 shows a comparison with the state-of-the-art single image based method of Zheng et al. [17]. Although Zheng et al.'s approach could remove vignetting from images to a certain degree, vignetting were not fully corrected. In contrast, our method produced better results in terms of visual quality, despite severe vignetting effects in the input. More vignetting correction results on real photographs are included in Fig. 9 and the supplementary material.

Fig. 9. More vignetting correction results on real photographs. First and third rows show input images containing vignetting, and second and last rows show our results.

5.3   Computation Time

Table 1 summarizes the timing statistics of our method with various image sizes. Even with our unoptimized Matlab implementation, the total running time of our algorithm is about 8.8 seconds for an image of 4000×3000 pixels. This is an order of magnitude faster than the state-of-the-art single image vignetting correction method [17], implying the practical usefulness of our method.

Table 1. Timing data with various image sizes

Image size (in pixels)	800×600	$1,600 \times 1,200$	$3,200 \times 2,400$	$4,000 \times 3,000$
Computing Z^{RB}	0.27s	0.96s	3.61s	5.52s
Vignetting estimation	1.67s	2.39s	3.27s	2.65s
Final image restoration	0.04s	0.12s	0.45s	0.66s
Total	1.98s	3.47s	7.33s	8.83s

6   Discussion and Future Work

Our RBC prior provides a reliable measure for estimating the vignetting effects of an image. The proposed vignetting estimation algorithm is performed with 1D RBC data instead of 2D image pixels, enabling a high speed of the vignetting correction process. Despite its simplicity, experiments on both synthetic and real images demonstrate that our method can effectively restore high quality vignetting-free images. The RBC prior is a general image prior which successfully characterizes a statistical property of natural images. We expect it can be adopted for other computer vision and image processing applications than vignetting correction.

Extreme Cases and Limitations. Our RBC prior can capture the vignetting effects even when the illumination is non-uniform, by radially examining image regions and finding radial bright pixels. Still, in extreme cases such as radially non-uniform illumination and combination of non-uniform illumination and different object colors, our vignetting estimation using Eq. (11) may fall into a local minima as the RBC values become unstable. For an image with overall dark colors or low intensities, the RBC prior may not clearly hold. In this case, however, the vignetting itself is not clearly observable as well.

Although our method works well with various types of natural images for vignetting correction, our method may fail on images that do not follow our assumptions. Such cases include arbitrary outliers (e.g., night view and haze), chromatic aberration, or radially asymmetric vignetting effects caused by non-uniform illumination (Fig. 10). In our experiments, we assumed that the optical center corresponds to the image center. This assumption holds in many cases, but it might be broken with cropped images and images taken using special types of lenses. Our method would not produce optimal results for such images.

Future Work. A natural direction for future research will be overcoming the limitations of our method. Utilizing other image priors in conjunction with our RBC prior would enable more accurate and robust estimation of vignetting functions. Exploration of other applications of our RBC prior, such as white balancing, will be definitely interesting future work.

(a) color shading   (b) severe cropping

Fig. 10. Limitation examples. For each pair of image, the left is an input and the right is our result. In (a), color shading is emphasized after the vignetting has been removed. In (b), the image has been severely cropped and the optical center is located at the bottom of the image, causing incorrect estimation of the vignetting function.

Acknowledgments. We would like to thank the anonymous reviewers for their constructive comments. We also thank the following flickr users of creative commons license for the photos used in this paper: sagriffin305, Orin Zebest, Dominik Bartsch, Sherry's Rose Cottage, Beth Rankin, Maciek Lempicki, and Andrew Higgins. This work was supported in part by Basic Science Research Program of NRF (2012R1A1A2042837, 2013R1A1A2011692) and Samsung Electronics.

References

1. Asada, N., Amano, A., Baba, M.: Photometric calibration of zoom lens systems. In: Proc. International Conference on Pattern Recognition, vol. 1, pp. 186–190 (1996)
2. Coleman, T., Li, Y.: An interior trust region approach for nonlinear minimization subject to bounds. SIAM Journal on Optimization 6(2), 418–445 (1996)
3. Goldman, D.B.: Vignette and exposure calibration and compensation. IEEE Trans. Pattern Analysis and Machine Intelligence 32(12), 2276–2288 (2010)
4. He, K., Sun, J., Tang, X.: Single image haze removal using dark channel prior. IEEE Trans. Pattern Analysis and Machine Intelligence 33(12), 2341–2353 (2011)
5. Juang, R., Majumder, A.: Photometric self-calibration of a projector-camera system. In: Proc. CVPR, pp. 1–8 (2007)
6. Kang, S.B., Weiss, R.: Can we calibrate a camera using an image of a flat, textureless Lambertian surface? In: Vernon, D. (ed.) ECCV 2000. LNCS, vol. 1843, pp. 640–653. Springer, Heidelberg (2000)
7. Kim, S.J., Pollefeys, M.: Robust radiometric calibration and vignetting correction. IEEE Trans. Pattern Analysis and Machine Intelligence 30(4), 562–576 (2008)
8. Kŏseckà, J., Zhang, W.: Video compass. In: Heyden, A., Sparr, G., Nielsen, M., Johansen, P. (eds.) ECCV 2002, Part IV. LNCS, vol. 2353, pp. 476–490. Springer, Heidelberg (2002)
9. Kuthirummal, S., Agarwala, A., Goldman, D.B., Nayar, S.K.: Priors for large photo collections and what they reveal about cameras. In: Forsyth, D., Torr, P., Zisserman, A. (eds.) ECCV 2008, Part IV. LNCS, vol. 5305, pp. 74–87. Springer, Heidelberg (2008)
10. Litvinov, A., Schechner, Y.: Addressing radiometric nonidealities: A unified framework. In: Proc. CVPR, pp. 52–59 (2005)
11. Lyu, S.: Single image vignetting correction with natural image statistics in derivative domains. In: Proc. ICIP (2010)
12. Sawchuk, A.: Real-time correction of intensity nonlinearities in imaging systems. IEEE Trans. on Computers C-26(1), 34–39 (1977)
13. Yu, W.: Practical anti-vignetting methods for digital cameras. IEEE Trans. on Consumer Electronics 50(4), 975–983 (2004)
14. Zheng, Y., Kambhamettu, C., Lin, S.: Single-image optical center estimation from vignetting and tangential gradient symmetry. In: Proc. CVPR, pp. 2058–2065 (2009)
15. Zheng, Y., Lin, S., Kambhamettu, C., Yu, J., Kang, S.B.: Single-image vignetting correction. IEEE Trans. Pattern Analysis and Machine Intelligence 31(12), 2243–2256 (2009)
16. Zheng, Y., Lin, S., Kang, S.B.: Single-image vignetting correction. In: Proc. CVPR, pp. 461–468 (2006)
17. Zheng, Y., Lin, S., Kang, S.B., Xiao, R., Gee, J.C., Kambhamettu, C.: Single-image vignetting correction from gradient distribution symmetries. IEEE Trans. Pattern Analysis and Machine Intelligence 35(6), 1480–1494 (2013)
18. Zheng, Y., Yu, J., Kang, S.B., Lin, S., Kambhamettu, C.: Single-image vignetting correction using radial gradient symmetry. In: Proc. CVPR, pp. 1–8 (2008)

Tubular Structure Filtering by Ranking Orientation Responses of Path Operators*

Odyssée Merveille[1,2], Hugues Talbot[1], Laurent Najman[1], and Nicolas Passat[2]

[1] Université Paris-Est, LIGM, UPEMLV-ESIEE-CNRS, France
[2] Université de Reims Champagne-Ardenne, CReSTIC, France

Abstract. Thin objects in 3D volumes, for instance vascular networks in medical imaging or various kinds of fibres in materials science, have been of interest for some time to computer vision. Particularly, tubular objects are everywhere elongated in one principal direction – which varies spatially – and are thin in the other two perpendicular directions. Filters for detecting such structures use for instance an analysis of the three principal directions of the Hessian, which is a local feature. In this article, we present a low-level tubular structure detection filter. This filter relies on paths, which are semi-global features that avoid any blurring effect induced by scale-space convolution. More precisely, our filter is based on recently developed morphological path operators. These require sampling only in a few principal directions, are robust to noise and do not assume feature regularity. We show that by ranking the directional response of this operator, we are further able to efficiently distinguish between blob, thin planar and tubular structures. We validate this approach on several applications, both from a qualitative and a quantitative point of view, demonstrating noise robustness and an efficient response on tubular structures.

Keywords: mathematical morphology, non-linear filtering, path operators, thin structures, 3D imaging.

1 Introduction

Thin structures can be hard to detect in images. The difficulties stem from spatial sparsity, small size leading to partial volume effects, similarity with textured noise, potential tortuosity, the complexity of their topology when organised as networks and other problems. These difficulties are magnified in 3D applications (*e.g.*, in materials or angiographic imaging), due to structural issues (thin structures are no longer of codimension 1 in 3D) or computational burden.

Some solutions exist for filtering thin objects in 3D images, *i.e.*, for enhancing their signal and/or removing noise and artifacts that limit their detection. Most are based on scale-space and the differential properties of images, mainly via linear approaches (Sec. 2.1). This has led to the development of filters characterizing thin structures by

---

* This research was funded by *Agence Nationale de la Recherche* (Grant Agreement ANR-12-MONU-0010).

considering local information at various scales. Non-linear strategies have also been investigated, particularly in mathematical morphology (Sec. 2.2). To cope with the sparsity or thin structures, both linear and non-linear approaches either use a steerable approach or an orientation sampling procedure. Whereas directional sampling approaches are computationally feasible in 2D, in 3D they are often prohibitively expensive.

Recently, path operators have opened a promising way to take into account the strong anisotropy and non-local properties of thin structures. They are tailored to cope with the challenges of detecting thin, anisotropic, non-necessarily locally regular, and noisy structures. They are available in 3D, but by themselves they do not allow to distinguish between the various classes of thin objects.

In this article, we propose a 3D tubular structure filtering method based on path operators (Sec. 3). We describe this filter, formalised in the mathematical morphology framework (Sec. 4). In order to assess the behaviour of this filter, we compare it versus a gold-standard Hessian-based filter and a more traditional morphological approach. This comparative study is carried out both on synthetic and real data (Sec. 5). We finally summarise our contributions, and discuss further improvements (Sec. 6).

2   Related Works

The methods devoted to filtering thin structures can be divided – among many other classifications – into two categories, namely those relying on differential (mostly linear) operators (Sec. 2.1), and those relying on non-linear (often mathematical morphology) operators (Sec. 2.2).

2.1   Differential Filters

Thin structures filtering and detection based on second-order derivative properties of the image were first proposed in [29,21]. In these, the eigenvectors of multiscale Hessian matrices and their associated eigenvalues can be analysed to characterise isotropic (blobs), planar and tubular structures as well as their scale and orientation.

This strategy has led to the proposal of several "vesselness" measures, that combine differential information into heuristic formulations. The vesselness proposed by Frangi et al. in [13] is often considered as the current gold-standard. Many methods/variants have been proposed since then. Some of them also used the eigenvectors obtained from the Hessian matrix [18,8], for intance for guidance of a diffusion framework [23]. In [2] the second derivatives were associated to first derivatives and a Canny filter, while in [40], a strain energy function used a stress tensor computed from the Hessian tensor.

To achieve multiscale detection, derivative operators are typically combined with a differentiable convolution kernel. In order to avoid the induced blurring effects, these computations may be replaced by a gradient vector flow [1]. The use of a bi-Gaussian kernel was also proposed to better take into account the bimodal nature of tubular structures versus background [41]. This issue was also dealt with by considering optimally oriented flux [19].

Steerable filters [14] are anisotropic filters that can be expressed in term of a linear combination of basis filters. As such they are often used to detect oriented features such as tube-like structures. In [17], the convolution between a bar profile and the second derivative is used in a non-linear combination to introduce a multiscale approach. A framework for 3D steerable filters was first proposed in [9], using a nth Gaussian derivative basis filter. Then, it was proposed in [15] to use 3D steerable filters based on the 2nd and 4th Gaussian derivatives to detect dendritic profiles and used them as input for a classification approach.

Discrete gradients are also used in tube-like detection. In [27], tube-like orientation is first estimated using a set of discrete orientations called "sticks". Then instead of a classical low pass filter, an anisotropic non-linear filter, the L-filter, is used to enhance tube-like features. The Maximum Curvature [11,5] of tube-like structure is also computed by the 2nd derivative operator along the thirteen discrete lines of a $3 \times 3 \times 3$ kernel.

2.2 Non-linear Filters

Non-linear approaches include those based on mathematical morphology [26]. A common notion is the structuring element (SE), a geometric pattern from which basic operators (erosions, dilations, openings, closings, *etc.*) can be defined. Efficient operators using line segments in 2D were proposed in [31,32] and extended to 3D in [10]. Grey-level hit-or-miss transforms were explored as a way for detecting 3D vessels in angiographic data in [25]. Spatially-variant mathematical morphology also led to the development of approaches for anisotropic SE-based linear structure filtering, with reconnection purposes [42,36,12]. In these works, both linear and non-linear techniques were used in synergy.

A second notion is that of connectivity, generally handled on graphs. The key notion of connectivity is no longer the local notion of SE, but a more global notion of connected component. The resulting region-based approaches have been involved in the design of hierarchical filtering techniques, for instance via the notion of component tree [39], and their asymmetrical variants [34].

The SE- and connectivity-based approaches present dual intrinsic strengths and weaknesses. The SE-based approaches naturally handle anisotropy – which is highly desirable for linear structure filtering – but they still lead to mostly local filters. This also a weakness of differential operators. In comparison, the connectivity-based approaches lead to more global descriptors; but the underlying notion of adjacency remains too generic to efficiently model the anisotropy of linear structures.

To answer this problem, geodesic paths [6] have been introduced as a solution to consider long-range, non-local interactions while still coping with the constraints of thin objects, in particular noise. A thin object detector was proposed in [28] using geodesic voting, similar to path density. Polygonal path images [3] extended this idea allowing for better regularization and fewer artifacts. However these solutions are currently very costly in 3D.

The notion of morphological path operator, introduced in [4,16], constitutes a way to merge the strengths of these approaches, in the context of thin structure filtering. We present these operators in Sec. 4, however we now present our main strategy.

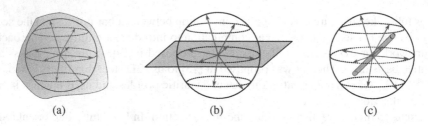

(a)   (b)   (c)

Fig. 1. When sampling orientations from a point, in an isotropic structure a.k.a. a blob (a), oriented operators all respond nearly identically (green arrows). In a plane (b), some proportion respond positively. In a tube (c), only a few orientations respond.

3 General Strategy

Our strategy for filtering tubular structures derives from the simple observation of Fig. 1. Let $\mathcal{F}_{\lambda,\phi}$ be the response of an oriented filter on image I depending on an orientation sampling of the unit sphere by longitude λ and latitude ϕ. Without loss of generality, we assume a bright feature on a dark background. For any orientation-dependent filter, be it linear or non-linear, sampling based or steerable, we will have that in any blob features of larger dimension than the considered scale, the response will be positive and similar in all directions. Conversely, assuming a horizontal planar feature, a positive response will only be observed in the directions where $\phi \equiv 0$. Finally, if the local feature is tubular, then there is only a narrow range of directions λ and ϕ where a positive response will be observed.

Therefore, if we consider a discretization $\{(\lambda_1, \phi_1), (\lambda_2, \phi_2), \ldots, (\lambda_n, \phi_n)\}$ of all possible orientations on the unit sphere, we could distinguish blobs, planes and tubes by counting the number of orientations where a positive response is observed. However this would not provide us with a filtering method. Instead, we can *rank* the responses pixelwise from highest to lowest, *i.e.*, at a particular position (x, y, z), we would have for $i, j, m \in [1, \ldots, n]$:

$$\mathcal{F}_{\lambda_i,\phi_i}[I](x,y,z) \geq \mathcal{F}_{\lambda_j,\phi_j}[I](x,y,z) \geq \ldots \geq \mathcal{F}_{\lambda_m,\phi_m}[I](x,y,z) \qquad (1)$$

This pixelwise ranking allows us to construct n response images $\mathcal{F}_1, \ldots, \mathcal{F}_n$ such that, for all points of I,

$$\mathcal{F}_1[I] \geq \mathcal{F}_2[I] \geq \ldots \geq \mathcal{F}_n[I] \qquad (2)$$

Here, $\mathcal{F}_1[I]$ is the image of maximum response and $\mathcal{F}_n[I]$ is the minimum response. In 2D, the oriented difference residual ODR = $\mathcal{F}_1[I] - \mathcal{F}_n[I]$ has been used before to distinguish between isotropic and oriented areas in image [32]. In 3D, this residual performs the same function, *i.e.*, it would provide a high response for Fig. 1(b) or (c) but not (a), and a fortiori the response would also be low in dark areas of the volume. Now, if we assume there is some level m such that in bright planar features, the response $\mathcal{F}_m$ is always high and always low in bright tubular features, then the tubular difference residual TDR = $\mathcal{F}_1[I] - \mathcal{F}_m[I]$ offers a high response only in tubular structures.

In many ways, this approach is similar to the Hessian analysis used in various vesselness measures. Principal feature directions are obtained by eigen-analysis instead of sampling directions, and response is replaced by rapid variation, modeled by curvature, *i.e.*, second derivatives of the intensities. Blobs are objects that have little variation along the three eigenvectors, planes have high variation in one direction, and tubes in two. However performing Hessian analysis imposes to consider a smoothed, isotropic, local neighborhood, at various scales. To improve on this, a non-local, anisotropic operator may be preferable. For efficiency, it is also crucial to consider operators that do not require sampling orientations with a high density. Amongst the possible tools satisfying these requirements, those based on paths are the most promising. However, most of them are currently too costly to be used in 3D image analysis. In the following, we introduce path operators which seems to be the most effective choice to date.

4   Ranking Orientation Responses of Path Operators

4.1   Path Operators

Morphological path operators lie at the convergence of mathematical morphology and graph-based path optimization. They include in particular the local minimal path approach [38], the polygonal path image [3] (both available only in the 2D case so far), and the path openings/closings, that we describe hereafter, and which constitutes the basis of our proposed filter. Without loss of generality we consider here the path opening for filtering bright objects on a dark background. Path closing would simply do the converse. Path openings were introduced in [4,16]. As stated, they derive from SE-based approaches, as they consider as structuring elements families of curvilinear paths. However, they also derive from connectivity-based approaches, since these paths are intrinsically linked to the topological structure mapped onto the image support.

Adjacency The support X of an image can be equipped with adjacency links, *i.e.*, a binary relation $\rightarrow$ that is irreflexive and possibly non-symmetric. Practically, the existence of a link $a \rightarrow b$ between two points a and b of X means that one can go locally from a to b in X. In other words, the couple $(X, \rightarrow)$ constitutes a (directed) graph. A path $\mathbf{a}$ of length L is then constituted of L points of X successively adjacent. More generally, we denote as $\Pi_L(X)$ the set of all the paths of length L on X, with respect to an adjacency relation. We note $\sigma(\mathbf{a})$ the set of points successively constituting the path $\mathbf{a}$. More formally, we have $\sigma(\mathbf{a}) = \{a_1, a_2, \ldots, a_L\}$ such that $a_i \rightarrow a_{i+1}$ for $i = 1$ to $L - 1$. The choice of the adjacency then controls the orientation, anisotropy degree and potential tortuosity of the induced paths.

Binary path opening The binary path opening $\alpha_L(X)$ of length L of a set X – viewed as a binary image – is defined as the union of all the paths of length L in X, *i.e.*

$$\alpha_L(X) = \bigcup \{\sigma(\mathbf{a}) \mid \mathbf{a} \in \Pi_L(X)\} \tag{3}$$

In other words, it preserves in $\alpha_L(X)$ all the points of X which belong to at least one path of length L. As a combination of openings, it is an (algebraic) opening.

Grey-level path opening Extension of path openings to the case of grey-level images is straightforward. Specifically the path opening of a grey-level image I, defined on X and taking its values in a finite set $\Lambda \subseteq \mathbb{Z}$ corresponds to stacking the results of the binary path openings at each grey-level value $\lambda \in \Lambda$, carried out on the subgraphs associated to the threshold sets $X_\lambda(I) = \{x \in X \mid I(x) \geq \lambda\}$. More formally, the grey-level path opening $A_L(I)$ is the grey-level image defined on X as

$$A_L(I)(x) = \max\{\lambda \in \Lambda \mid x \in \alpha_L(X_\lambda(I))\} \tag{4}$$

Path opening computation and robust path opening The adjacency considered for defining a given path opening operator is generally periodic and spatially invariant over the space X. This regularity allowed the development of efficient algorithms [33], and in any dimensions [22]. Since long paths can be sensitive to noise, an improved algorithm was also proposed, for coping with paths that include up to a maximum ratio of noisy nodes [33]. A simpler, more efficient approach, based on a local tolerance to noise led to the definition of Robust Path Openings (RPO) [7].

4.2   RPO-Based Filtering

If the considered adjacency is the standard 6- or 26-adjency, the grey-level path opening simply reduces to a standard, isotropic connected opening [26]. Path opening however authorizes the use of anisotropic adjacencies. These can model orientation in the considered space X. In the 3D discrete space $\mathbb{Z}^3$, 3, 7 or 13 principal orientations can naturally be defined. These rely on the grid's principal orientations, and its principal and the secondary diagonals, respectively. Adjacency configurations with 7 orientations are sufficient to accurately quantify the orientation space in a path-based paradigm. In this multi-directional framework it is then possible to develop an oriented version of path-based filtering for thin structure filtering.

4.3   Orientation Space Sampling

As stated above, we consider the 7 main orientations of the discrete space $\mathbb{Z}^3$, composed by the three principal orientations corresponding to the 3 vectors of the orthogonal basis $\{(0,0,1),(0,1,0),(1,0,0)\}$, denoted $\{\mathbf{e}_1, \mathbf{e}_2, \mathbf{e}_3\}$, plus the 4 vectors composing the principal diagonals $\{(1,1,1),(1,1,-1),(1,-1,1),(1,-1,-1)\}$, denoted $\{\mathbf{d}_1, \mathbf{d}_2, \mathbf{d}_3, \mathbf{d}_4\}$. We note $\mathcal{D}$ the set of these 7 vectors. In order to cover the whole space around these 7 axes, we consider a 3D discrete cone around each of them. In $\mathbb{R}^3$, such cover is obtained by associating to $\mathbf{e}_\star$ (resp. $\mathbf{d}_\star$) the cone $C_{\mathbf{e}_\star}$ (resp. $C_{\mathbf{d}_\star}$) bounded by 4 (resp. 3) edges composed by the vectors $\{\mathbf{d}_1, \mathbf{d}_2, \mathbf{d}_3, \mathbf{d}_4\}$ (resp. $\{\mathbf{e}_1, \mathbf{e}_2, \mathbf{e}_3\}$) that includes $\mathbf{e}_\star$ (resp. $\mathbf{d}_\star$). We note C_e the set of cones generated by $\mathbf{e}_\star$ and C_d the set of cones generated by $\mathbf{d}_\star$. Then C is the set of the 7 cones. These cones – which are unambiguously modelled in $\mathbb{Z}^3$ due to their discrete boundaries – are illustrated in Fig. 2.

The space $\mathbb{R}^3$ is fully covered by these 7 cones of C. More precisely, each point lies into exactly 2 cones over the 7, except points that lie into cone boundaries, that lie in at most 4 cones. Side effects of this property are discussed at the end of the section.

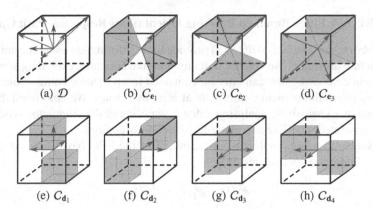

(a) $\mathcal{D}$ (b) $C_{\mathbf{e}_1}$ (c) $C_{\mathbf{e}_2}$ (d) $C_{\mathbf{e}_3}$

(e) $C_{\mathbf{d}_1}$ (f) $C_{\mathbf{d}_2}$ (g) $C_{\mathbf{d}_3}$ (h) $C_{\mathbf{d}_4}$

Fig. 2. (a) The 7 vectors of $\mathcal{D}$. (b–h) The 7 cones (in blue) of C. These cones form a cover of $\mathbb{R}^3$ (see text).

4.4 Cone-Oriented Robust Path Opening

For each cone $C_{\mathbf{c}}$ of C, it is possible to carry out a path opening, based on the graph induced by $C_{\mathbf{c}}$ on the support X of the image. This elementary opening operation is parametered by $C_{\mathbf{c}}$ and the length L of the paths that are preserved in the filtered image (see Eqs. (3–4)). These are the only two parameters that govern the behaviour of the path-opening. This small set of parameters have a physical meaning, since they refer to the orientation and size of the structures that the opening preserves. Consequently, they are easy to tune, based on application context.

In [7], noise-robust path opening consists of locally authorizing disconnections of up to K successive noise pixels. K is usually set to 1, which gives good results in practice. In the sequel, for a given cone $C_{\mathbf{c}}$, we note $R_{\mathbf{c}}^L(I)$ such robust path opening of the image I, for the path length L, and local noise tolerance $K = 1$.

4.5 Pointwise Rank Filtering

For an image I, we can compute the 7 RPO-filtered images $R_{\mathbf{c}}^L(I)$. These images then provide orientation information at every point $x \in I$. As seen in Sec. 3 the distribution of the values of these 7 images can provide an accurate characterisation of the image anisotropy at x. For instance, if all the values $R_{\mathbf{c}}^L(I)(x)$ are similar, the image intensity is necessarily homogeneous around x, characterising an isotropic structure. Contrariwise, if these values are high in some number of directions, and low in the others, the structure around x is anisotropic, thus characterising a thin structure.

Based on these remarks, we can build the 7 rank-filtered images $\phi_i^L(I)$, obtained by pointwise rank filters of the $R_{\mathbf{c}}^L(I)$. More formally, for $i \in [1, 7]$, we set

$$\phi_i^L(I)(x) = \mathrm{RF}_i\left\{R_{\mathbf{c}}^L(I)(x) \mid \mathbf{c} \in C\right\} \tag{5}$$

where RF_i is the rank-filter of order i, i.e., that yields the ith highest value within a set. In particular, $\phi_1^L(I)$, $\phi_4^L(I)$ and $\phi_7^L(I)$, are respectively the pointwise max, median and min filtered images obtained from the $R_{\mathbf{c}}^L(I)$ RPOs.

4.6 RORPO: A Filter Based on Ranking Orientations Responses Path Operator

As stated above, the 7 values of $R_c^L(I)(x)$ provide some information about the anisotropy of the structure around x. We can see that any line-like structure, excluding some limit cases we will deal with later, can only be contained in up to three cones at once. Conversely, any plane-like structure intersects at least five cones. We confirmed this geometric result by exhaustively analysing a dense sampling of the orientation space using randomly generated tube-like and plane-like discrete structures.

These validated results motivate our definition of the RPO-based filtering $\phi^L(I)$ as the tubular difference operator residual

$$\phi^L(I) = \phi_1^L(I) - \phi_4^L(I) \tag{6}$$

Less formally, the RPO-based filtering $\phi^L(I)$ is computed as the difference between the max and the median values of the pointwise rank-filters of the RPO images. We term our novel filter RORPO: Ranking Orientations Responses Path Operator.

4.7 Suppressing Artifacts Generated by Limit Cases

As stated above, tubular structures should be detected in at most three RPO orientations, but some limit cases occur. Indeed, the definition of orientations as discrete closed cones implies an overlap between neighboring RPO orientations. When one of these overlapping zones concerns more than two orientations, a tubular structure lying into this overlapping zone may be detected in more than three orientations and so is not considered tubular anymore. Experimental evidence suggests that tubes concerned by these limit orientations represent less than 4% of all tubes and can be classified into 2 patterns: 4-orientation tubes and 5-orientation tubes. 4-orientation tubes are detected in 2 of the 3 orientations defined by C_e plus 2 of the 4 orientations defined by C_d. 5-orientation tubes are detected in 1 of the 3 orientations defined by C_e plus the 4 orientations defined by C_d.

In order to keep 4 and 5-orientation tubes in the final result, we need to detect these special cases using extra processing. As 4 and 5-orientation tubes are defined as lying into overlapping of a finite set of RPO orientations, they can easily be isolated using intersection of orientations (see Eqs. (14) and (16)). We define the following cone sets, that correspond to relevant special cases:

$$O_1 = \{C_{e_1}, C_{e_2}, C_{d_2}, C_{d_3}\} \tag{7}$$

$$O_2 = \{C_{e_1}, C_{e_2}, C_{d_1}, C_{d_4}\} \tag{8}$$

$$O_3 = \{C_{e_2}, C_{e_3}, C_{d_1}, C_{d_2}\} \tag{9}$$

$$O_4 = \{C_{e_2}, C_{e_3}, C_{d_3}, C_{d_4}\} \tag{10}$$

$$O_5 = \{C_{e_1}, C_{e_3}, C_{d_2}, C_{d_4}\} \tag{11}$$

$$O_6 = \{C_{e_1}, C_{e_3}, C_{d_1}, C_{d_3}\} \tag{12}$$

We then detect the missing tubular structure by the following algorithm:

$$\Gamma_5 = \min_{c \in C_d}(R_c^L(I)(x)) \tag{13}$$

$$LC_5 = \Gamma_5 - \min(\Gamma_5, \gamma(\Phi_6^L, \Phi_4^L)) \tag{14}$$

$$\Gamma_4 = \max_{i \in \{1,...,6\}} \min_{c \in O_i}(R_c^L(I)(x)) \tag{15}$$

$$LC_4 = \Gamma_4 - \min(\Gamma_4, \gamma(\Phi_5^L, \Phi_4^L)). \tag{16}$$

where $\gamma(I, M)$ is the morphological reconstruction operator of image I under mask M (see [37]). Finally, we have

$$\text{RORPO}(I) = \max\{\phi^L(I), LC_4, LC_5\} \tag{17}$$

Thus, handling the limit cases simply consists of isolating the 4-orientation and 5-orientation tubes and to compose them to the result of RORPO. We note that this requires negligible additional computation as only simple operators are involved.

5 Experiments and Results

We now experimentally evaluate the RORPO filter. These evaluations are quantitatively carried out on synthetic data with ground truth, allowing to compute standard quality scores. The RORPO filter is then applied on challenging 3D images in the context of angiography.

5.1 Compared Methods and Quality Scores

In order to assess the efficiency of the RORPO filter, we consider two other methods, namely Frangi's vesselness, which is the gold-standard within the family of differential filters, and a classical morphological filter based on path-openings and a top-hat.

Frangi's vesselness [13]. As evoked in Sec. 2.1, Frangi's vesselness is a multiscale tubularity measure that relies on the eigenvalues, λ_1, λ_2 and λ_3, of the Hessian matrix. The values are then involved in the definition of a function $\mathcal{V}_0$ that quantifies the degree of vesselness of any given point x of an image, with respect to the local intensity profile in its neighbourhood:

$$\mathcal{V}_0(x) = \begin{cases} 0 & \text{if } \lambda_2 > 0 \text{ or } \lambda_3 > 0 \\ (1 - \exp(-\frac{\mathcal{R}_{\mathcal{A}}^2}{2\alpha^2}))\exp(-\frac{\mathcal{R}_{\mathcal{B}}^2}{2\beta^2})(1 - \exp(-\frac{\mathcal{S}^2}{2c^2})) & \text{otherwise} \end{cases} \tag{18}$$

$$\text{with} \quad \mathcal{R}_{\mathcal{A}} = \frac{|\lambda_2|}{|\lambda_3|} \quad \mathcal{R}_{\mathcal{B}} = \frac{|\lambda_1|}{\sqrt{|\lambda_2 \lambda_3|}} \quad \mathcal{S} = \sqrt{\lambda_1 + \lambda_2 + \lambda_3} \quad (|\lambda_1| \leq |\lambda_2| \leq |\lambda_3|) \tag{19}$$

The parameters α, β and c are set as originally proposed in [13]. A thorough optimization using an iteratively restarted Nelder-Meade simplex algorithm of the scale parameters (minimum, maximum, and number) was performed, in order to fairly compare this measure to the proposed RORPO filter.

A standard non-linear tubular structure filtering. We also compare the RORPO filter with another standard filter obtained by composing the Robust Path Opening (RPO) with a top-hat operator. This filter is applied for several values of lengths and noise tolerance, that are the same involved in the RORPO filter, thus leading to a multiscale approach.

Quality scores. In order to compare the results obtained by these three methods on synthetic data (Sec. 5.2), we considered ROC curves and two similarity criteria: Matthews Correlation Coefficient (MCC) and Dice Coefficient, defined as

$$MCC = \frac{TP \times TN - FP \times FN}{\sqrt{(TP + FP)(TP + FN)(TN + FP)(TN + FN)}} \tag{20}$$

$$Dice = \frac{2TP}{TP + FN + TN + FP} \tag{21}$$

where TP, TN, FP, FN are true/false positives/negatives, respectively.

As we deal with sparse features, the set of pixels belonging to the ground truth object (TP_{GT}) is always much smaller than the set of pixels belonging to its background (TN_{GT}). The considered ROC curves consider the true positive rate (TPR) as a function of the false positive rate (FPR), where both the TPR and the FPR are defined with respect to the ground truth object, *i.e.*, $TPR = \frac{TP}{TP_{GT}}$ and $FPR = \frac{FP}{TP_{GT}}$. Consequently, the FPR could well exceed 100%, but such values are uninteresting.

5.2 Synthetic Images

In these first experiments, we use a synthetic image containing both tubular, planar and blob structures (see Fig. 3(a,b)). A tubular structure is represented by a 3D simple helix with decreasing intensity, diameter and thickness. As a consequence, tube-like structures are represented in many orientations and with varying dimensions and degrees of tortuosity. Blobs were added using an additive Gaussian random field. The ground truth is a binary representation of the helix (see Fig. 3(c)).

The results of the three filters on this image are shown in Fig. 4. Qualitatively, we observe that RORPO is the only filter that fully removes the plane structure. The result of the vesselness is also much "noisier" than the other two. Indeed, these two morphological filters have the property that they always reduce the grey-level of the input image. This suppressive behaviour leads to cleaner images as seen on Fig. 4(a,c). In contrast, the vesselness does not share such a mathematical property. The visual analysis, that emphasises the good performance of RORPO filter is confirmed by the CCM and Dice measures.

Then, ROC curves have been computed from these filtered images by successive thresholding. To account for the 1-dimensional nature of the structures of interest, a skeletonization of the thresholded result was performed. The results, illustrated in Fig. 5(a), confirm that the RPO-top-hat is hindered by its inability to remove the planar structures. In this specific case, our RORPO filter outperforms Frangi's vesselness,

The last experiment quantifies the robustness of the RORPO filter with respect to noise. Various amounts of white Gaussian noise were added to the synthetic image,

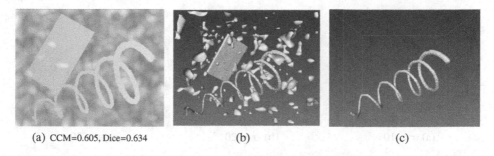

(a) CCM=0.605, Dice=0.634   (b)   (c)

Fig. 3. Synthetic image: (a) maximum intensity projection and (b) isosurface. (c) Ground truth. Optimal CCM and Dice scores obtained by thresholding are indicated for (a).

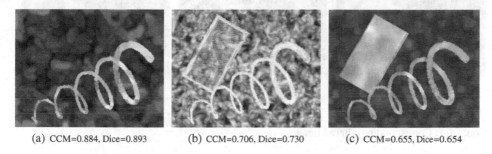

(a) CCM=0.884, Dice=0.893   (b) CCM=0.706, Dice=0.730   (c) CCM=0.655, Dice=0.654

Fig. 4. Filtered synthetic image: maximum intensity projection. (a) RORPO. (b) Frangi's vesselness. (c) and RPO-top-hat. Optimal CCM and Dice scores obtained by thresholding are indicated for (a–c).

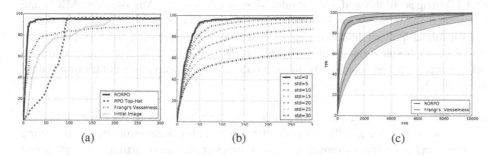

(a)   (b)   (c)

Fig. 5. ROC curves on synthetic data (a,b) and on real data (c). (a) Comparison of the three filters, plus the native image. (b) Noise robustness of the RORPO filter. (c) Comparison between RORPO and Frangi's vesselness on the Rotterdam repository. For both filtering, the central curve is the mean ROC curve and the other two are the mean plus or minus one standard deviation curves.

and ROC curves were computed in each case. The results are shown in Fig. 5(b), and partially illustrated in Fig. 6. In order to better take into account the quantitative effects of the noise, no skeletonization was performed in this evaluation. The most noticeable observation is the high robustness of the RORPO filter for low level noise. In particular, up to a standard deviation of 5 almost no difference can be observed.

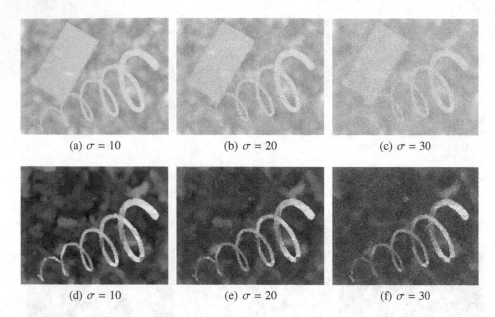

(a) $\sigma = 10$ (b) $\sigma = 20$ (c) $\sigma = 30$

(d) $\sigma = 10$ (e) $\sigma = 20$ (f) $\sigma = 30$

Fig. 6. (a–c) Synthetic image for various amounts of Gaussian noise: maximum intensity projection. (d–f) Corresponding filtered images.

5.3   Real Images

Finally we assessed the behaviour of the RORPO filter versus Frangi's vesselness, on real 3D images. To this end, we consider Magnetic Resonance Angiography (MRA) and Computed Tomography Angiography (CTA) images, that are among the most challenging for tubular pattern detection, due to the presence of acquisition noise, physiological artifacts, neighbouring anatomical structures, *etc.* The actual difficulties induced by vessel enhancement and detection from such data have motivated many contributions until now [20,35].

Brain MRA images. We first consider Time-of-Flight MRAs of the cerebral arterial tree, containing topologically and geometrically complex linear structures with varying diameter and intensity. Moreover, they are corrupted by various artifacts, and present a low SNR, since sequences capture the signal of moving structures, instead of stationary tissues [24]. The images considered here were acquired on a whole-body scanner (Siemens Magnetom Verio 3.0 T, gradient slope = 200 T/m/s, flow encoding sequence, TR = 42.7 ms, TE = 6.57 ms, resolution = $0.4 \times 0.4 \times 0.8$ mm^3). A 3D view of such MRA image is given in Fig. 7(a). The two filtering results are shown in Fig. 7(b–c).

Visually, Frangi's vesselness seems richer, and RORPO more accurate. This is a consequence of Frangi's enhancing behaviour, which in this case leads to false positives. Conversely RORPO suppressive behaviour may lead to potential false negatives. As well, the size of the vessels is overestimated by the vesselness (due to the Gaussian kernel convolution), while RORPO preserves the geometry of the vessels.

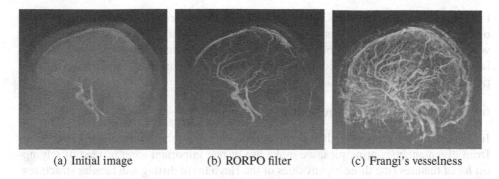

(a) Initial image   (b) RORPO filter   (c) Frangi's vesselness

Fig. 7. Brain arteries. (a) Time-of-flight magnetic resonance angiography, viewed in volume rendering (from low intensities, in red, to high intensities, in yellow). (b) RORPO filter: 8 lengths from $L = 30$px to 130px; computation time: 32mn. (c) Frangi's vesselness: 4 scales from 1 to 3; computation time: 13mn.

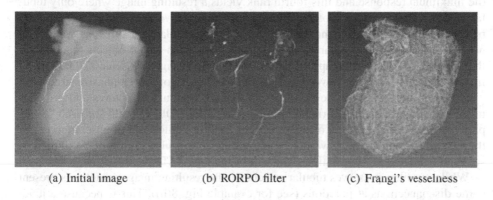

(a) Initial image   (b) RORPO filter   (c) Frangi's vesselness

Fig. 8. Coronary arteries. (a) Computed tomography angiography, viewed in volume rendering (from low intensities, in red, to high intensities, in yellow); the coronary medial axes are outlined in white. (b) RORPO filter: 4 scales from $L = 20$px to 50px; computation time: 50mn. (c) Frangi's vesselness: 4 scales from 0.4 to 1.8; computation time: 6mn.

Heart CTA images. We then consider CTAs of the coronary arteries of the heart from the Rotterdam repository [30]. These vascular structures are much simpler than cerebral MRAs. Coronary arteries are composed of only a few branches organised as a tree structure with homogeneous contrast due to contrast agent injection. Similar remarks can be derived as with the above MRA data. We observe that the RORPO filter leads to a noisier result than before, since it detects some parts of the origin of the aorta. The results obtained from Frangi's vesselness are also less satisfactory than for MRAs, essentially due to the presence of dense irregular tissues of the heart generating many false positives.

Coronary centerline ground truth is available in the Rotterdam database. ROC curves were computed on the 17 images of the training set of the Rotterdam repository. Two ground-truth images did not overlap a large part of the coronary tree for two patients so we chose to remove these images from the comparison study. We show in Fig. 5(c) results of the 15 ROC curves comparing RORPO and Frangi's Vesselness filtering. For each filtering method, the mean ROC curve was computed after normalizing each curve to 100% of true positive (TPR). Results on the 15 patients are almost identical. RORPO filter always gives better results for lower values of false positive than Frangi's Vesselness. The latter, in some cases, better recovers coronaries but only for unusably large values of false positive.

6   Discussion and Conclusion

In this article, we propose a filter aimed at removing non-tubular structures. Leveraging from eigen-analysis principles, we make use of one important idea: instead of relying on *local* features (the three eigenvalues of the Hessian) to distinguish tubular structures from planes or blobs, we use *semi-global* features: paths. As information are no longer local, we are now able to analyze the responses corresponding to the seven cones partitioning the 3D space. By ordering these responses from highest to lowest, we observe that tubular structures are absent from the fourth rank down. The difference between the maximum response and this fourth rank yields a resulting image where only tubular structures are present. Both qualitative and quantitative analysis demonstrate the promising capacities of our novel RORPO filter for tubular structures, as well as its noise robustness. In particular, it discriminates tubes from planar objects much better than previous top-hat-based approaches. Compared to Frangi's vesselness, the RORPO image contains noticeably fewer false positives and does not overemphasize structures.

However, the vesselness response is not limited to tubular structures and provides more information, such as orientation and scale. The RORPO scale we used in this paper is related to the length of the structures and not to the scale of observation as in the Gaussian scale-space. It would be interesting to complete the RORPO filter with scale and orientation information. This will be the topic of further research.

While our filter preserves tubular structures, the resulting image sometimes present some disconnections at junctions (see for example Fig. 8(b)). This is because a junction is not tubular but more like a blob. A future research direction is to cope with this problem, for example with a finer study of the direction behaviour at such connection points. The RORPO filter should be useful as a low level input in any pipeline for network extraction (such as coronary arteries segmentation), as a complement to other features, including vesselness measures. In future work, we aim to build such a complete segmentation algorithm, in the case of the cerebral vascular network.

A C++ implementation (with a test image and some usage explanations), as well as videos showing both Frangi's Vesselness and RORPO filtering on both the Heart and Brain images, are available at http://path-openings.github.io/RORPO/.

References

1. Bauer, C., Bischof, H.: A novel approach for detection of tubular objects and its application to medical image analysis. In: Rigoll, G. (ed.) DAGM 2008. LNCS, vol. 5096, pp. 163–172. Springer, Heidelberg (2008)
2. Bennink, H.E., van Assen, H.C., Streekstra, G.J., ter Wee, R., Spaan, J.A.E., ter Haar Romeny, B.M.: A novel 3D multi-scale lineness filter for vessel detection. In: Ayache, N., Ourselin, S., Maeder, A. (eds.) MICCAI 2007, Part II. LNCS, vol. 4792, pp. 436–443. Springer, Heidelberg (2007)

3. Bismuth, V., Vaillant, R., Talbot, H., Najman, L.: Curvilinear structure enhancement with the polygonal path image–application to guide-wire segmentation in X-ray fluoroscopy. In: Ayache, N., Delingette, H., Golland, P., Mori, K. (eds.) MICCAI 2012, Part II. LNCS, vol. 7511, pp. 9–16. Springer, Heidelberg (2012)
4. Buckley, M., Talbot, H.: Flexible linear openings and closings. In: ISMM. Computer Imaging and Vision, vol. 18, pp. 109–118. Kluwer (2000)
5. Chapman, B.E., Parker, D.L.: 3D multi-scale vessel enhancement filtering based on curvature measurements: Application to time-of-flight MRA. Med. Image Anal. 9, 191–208 (2005)
6. Cohen, L., Deschamps, T.: Segmentation of 3D tubular objects with adaptive front propagation and minimal tree extraction for 3D medical imaging. Comput. Meth. Biomech. Biomed. Eng. 10, 289–305 (2007)
7. Cokelaer, F., Talbot, H., Chanussot, J.: Efficient robust d-dimensional path operators. J. Sel. Top. Signal 6, 830–839 (2012)
8. Danielsson, P.E., Lin, Q., Ye, Q.Z.: Efficient detection of second-degree variations in 2D and 3D images. J. Vis. Commun. Image R 12, 255–305 (2001)
9. Derpanis, K.G., Gryn, J.M.: Three-dimensional nth derivative of Gaussian separable steerable filters. In: ICIP, vol. 3, pp. 553–556 (2005)
10. Dokládal, P., Jeulin, D.: 3-D extraction of fibres from microtomographic images of fibre-reinforced composite materials. In: Wilkinson, M.H.F., Roerdink, J.B.T.M. (eds.) ISMM 2009. LNCS, vol. 5720, pp. 126–136. Springer, Heidelberg (2009)
11. Du, Y.P., Parker, D.L., Davis, W.L.: Vessel enhancement filtering in three-dimensional MR angiography. JMRI-J Magn. Reson. Im. 5, 353–359 (1995)
12. Dufour, A., Tankyevych, O., Naegel, B., Talbot, H., Ronse, C., Baruthio, J., Dokládal, P., Passat, N.: Filtering and segmentation of 3D angiographic data: Advances based on mathematical morphology. Med. Image. Anal. 17, 147–164 (2013)
13. Frangi, A.F., Niessen, W.J., Vincken, K.L., Viergever, M.A.: Multiscale vessel enhancement filtering. In: Wells, W.M., Colchester, A.C.F., Delp, S.L. (eds.) MICCAI 1998. LNCS, vol. 1496, pp. 130–137. Springer, Heidelberg (1998)
14. Freeman, W.T., Adelson, E.H.: The design and use of steerable filters. IEEE T. Pattern Anal. 13, 891–906 (1991)
15. González, G., Aguet, F., Fleuret, F., Unser, M., Fua, P.: Steerable features for statistical 3D dendrite detection. In: Yang, G.-Z., Hawkes, D., Rueckert, D., Noble, A., Taylor, C. (eds.) MICCAI 2009, Part II. LNCS, vol. 5762, pp. 625–632. Springer, Heidelberg (2009)
16. Heijmans, H.J.A.M., Buckley, M., Talbot, H.: Path openings and closings. J. Math. Imaging Vis. 22, 107–119 (2005)
17. Koller, T., Gerig, G., Székely, G., Dettwiler, D.: Multiscale detection of curvilinear structures in 2D and 3D image data. In: ICCV, pp. 864–869 (1995)
18. Krissian, K., Malandain, G., Ayache, N., Vaillant, R., Trousset, Y.: Model-based detection of tubular structures in 3D images. Comput. Vis. Image Und. 80, 130–171 (2000)
19. Law, M.W.K., Chung, A.C.S.: Three dimensional curvilinear structure detection using optimally oriented flux. In: Forsyth, D., Torr, P., Zisserman, A. (eds.) ECCV 2008, Part IV. LNCS, vol. 5305, pp. 368–382. Springer, Heidelberg (2008)
20. Lesage, D., Angelini, E.D., Bloch, I., Funka-Lea, G.: A review of 3D vessel lumen segmentation techniques: Models, features and extraction schemes. Med. Image Anal. 13, 819–845 (2009)
21. Lorenz, C., Carlsen, I.C., Buzug, T.M., Fassnacht, C., Weese, J.: Multi-scale line segmentation with automatic estimation of width, contrast and tangential direction in 2D and 3D medical images. In: Troccaz, J., Mösges, R., Grimson, W.E.L. (eds.) CVRMed-MRCAS 1997, CVRMed 1997, and MRCAS 1997. LNCS, vol. 1205, pp. 233–242. Springer, Heidelberg (1997)
22. Luengo Hendriks, C.L.: Constrained and dimensionality-independent path openings. IEEE T. Image Process. 19, 1587–1595 (2010)

23. Manniesing, R., Viergever, M.A., Niessen, W.J.: Vessel enhancing diffusion: A scale space representation of vessel structures. Med. Image Anal. 10, 815–825 (2006)
24. Miyazaki, M., Lee, V.S.: Nonenhanced MR angiography. Radiology 248, 20–43 (2008)
25. Naegel, B., Passat, N., Ronse, C.: Grey-level hit-or-miss transforms—Part II: Application to angiographic image processing. Pattern Recogn. 40, 648–658 (2007)
26. Najman, L., Talbot, H. (eds.): Mathematical morphology: From theory to applications. ISTE/John Wiley & Sons (2010)
27. Orkisz, M., Hernández-Hoyos, M., Douek, P., Magnin, I.: Advances of blood vessel morphology analysis in 3D Magnetic Resonance Images. Machine Graph. Vis. 9, 463–472 (2000)
28. Rouchdy, Y., Cohen, L.D.: Image segmentation by geodesic voting. Application to the extraction of tree structures from confocal microscope images. In: ICPR, pp. 1–5 (2008)
29. Sato, Y., Nakajima, S., Atsumi, H., Koller, T., Gerig, G., Yoshida, S., Kikinis, R.: 3D multi-scale line filter for segmentation and visualization of curvilinear structures in medical images. In: Troccaz, J., Mösges, R., Grimson, W.E.L. (eds.) CVRMed-MRCAS 1997, CVRMed 1997, and MRCAS 1997. LNCS, vol. 1205, pp. 213–222. Springer, Heidelberg (1997)
30. Schaap, M., Metz, C.T., van Walsum, T., van der Giessen, A.G., Weustink, A.C., Mollet, N.R.A., Bauer, C., Bogunović, H., Castro, C., Deng, X., Dikici, E., O'Donnell, T., Frenay, M., Friman, O., Hernández Hoyos, M., Kitslaar, P.H., Krissian, K., Kühnel, C., Luengo-Oroz, M.A., Orkisz, M., Smedby, Ö., Styner, M., Szymczak, A., Tek, H., Wang, C., Warfield, S.K., Zambal, S., Zhang, Y., Krestin, G.P., Niessen, W.J.: Standardized evaluation methodology and reference database for evaluating coronary artery centerline extraction algorithms. Med. Image Anal. 13, 701–714 (2009)
31. Soille, P., Breen, E., Jones, R.: Recursive implementation of erosions and dilations along discrete lines at arbitrary angles. IEEE T. Pattern Anal. 18, 562–567 (1996)
32. Soille, P., Talbot, H.: Directional morphological filtering. IEEE T. Pattern Anal. 23, 1313–1329 (2001)
33. Talbot, H., Appleton, B.: Efficient complete and incomplete path openings and closings. Image Vision Comput. 25, 416–425 (2007)
34. Tankyevych, O., Talbot, H., Passat, N.: Semi-connections and hierarchies. In: Hendriks, C.L.L., Borgefors, G., Strand, R. (eds.) ISMM 2013. LNCS, vol. 7883, pp. 159–170. Springer, Heidelberg (2013)
35. Tankyevych, O., Talbot, H., Passat, N., Musacchio, M., Lagneau, M.: Angiographic image analysis. In: Medical Image Processing: Techniques and Applications, ch. 6, pp. 115–144. Springer (2011)
36. Tankyevych, O., Talbot, H., Dokládal, P.: Curvilinear morpho-Hessian filter. In: ISBI, pp. 1011–1014 (2008)
37. Vincent, L.: Morphological grayscale reconstruction in image analysis: Applications and efficient algorithms. IEEE T. Image Process. 2, 176–201 (1993)
38. Vincent, L.: Minimal path algorithms for the robust detection of linear features in gray images. In: ISMM. Computer Imaging and Vision, vol. 12, pp. 331–338. Kluwer (1998)
39. Wilkinson, M.H.F., Westenberg, M.A.: Shape preserving filament enhancement filtering. In: Niessen, W.J., Viergever, M.A. (eds.) MICCAI 2001. LNCS, vol. 2208, pp. 770–777. Springer, Heidelberg (2001)
40. Xiao, C., Staring, M., Shamonin, D.P., Reiber, J.H.C., Stolk, J., Stoel, B.C.: A strain energy filter for 3D vessel enhancement with application to pulmonary CT images. Med. Image Anal. 15, 112–124 (2011)
41. Xiao, C., Staring, M., Wang, Y., Shamonin, D.P., Stoel, B.C.: Multiscale bi-Gaussian filter for adjacent curvilinear structures detection with application to vasculature images. IEEE T. Image Process. 22, 174–188 (2013)
42. Zana, F., Klein, J.C.: Segmentation of vessel-like patterns using mathematical morphology and curvature evaluation. IEEE T. Image Process. 10, 1010–1019 (2001)

Optimization-Based Artifact Correction for Electron Microscopy Image Stacks*

Samaneh Azadi, Jeremy Maitin-Shepard, and Pieter Abbeel

EECS Department, University of California at Berkeley, USA

Abstract. Investigations of biological ultrastructure, such as comprehensive mapping of connections within a nervous system, increasingly rely on large, high-resolution electron microscopy (EM) image volumes. However, discontinuities between the registered section images from which these volumes are assembled, due to variations in imaging conditions and section thickness, among other artifacts, impede truly 3-D analysis of these volumes. We propose an optimization procedure, called EMISAC (EM Image Stack Artifact Correction), to correct these discontinuities. EMISAC optimizes the parameters of spatially varying linear transformations of the data in order to minimize the squared norm of the gradient along the section axis, subject to detail-preserving regularization.

Assessment on a mouse cortex dataset demonstrates the effectiveness of our approach. Relative to the original data, EMISAC produces a large improvement both in NIQE score, a measure of statistical similarity between orthogonal cross-sections and the original image sections, as well as in accuracy of neurite segmentation, a critical task for this type of data. Compared to a recent independently developed gradient-domain algorithm, EMISAC achieves significantly better NIQE image quality scores, and equivalent segmentation accuracy; future segmentation algorithms may be able to take advantage of the higher image quality.

In addition, on several time-lapse videos, EMISAC significantly reduces lighting artifacts, resulting in greatly improved video quality.

A software release is available at `http://rll.berkeley.edu/2014_ECCV_EMISAC`.

Keywords: Denoising, Volume Electron Microscopy, Connectomics, Optimization, Segmentation.

1 Introduction

Recent technological developments in automated volume electron microscopy (EM) enable the acquisition of multi-terravoxel volumes at near isotropic resolution in the range of 3–30 nm [12,14,24,31,26]. These high-resolution image volumes are critical to fields such as connectomics, which aims to comprehensively map neuronal circuits by densely reconstructing neuron morphology and identifying synaptic connections between neurons [16,15,6].

---

* This material is based upon work supported by the National Science Foundation under Grant No. 1118055.

D. Fleet et al. (Eds.): ECCV 2014, Part II, LNCS 8690, pp. 219–235, 2014.

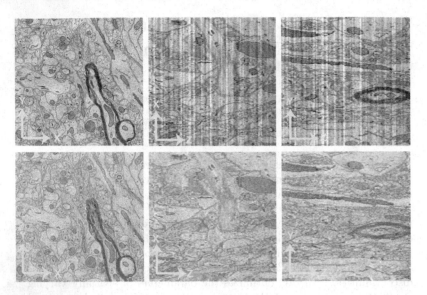

Fig. 1. Representative cross-sectional views of a $6 \times 6 \times 30$ nm ATUM-based SEM [31] image volume of mouse cortex. *First row:* The original, registered dataset clearly showing discontinuities along the Z (section) axis. *Second row:* Corrected data using our EMISAC algorithm.

All methods for volume electron microscopy, aside from tomography, which is only suitable for samples less than 1 micron in thickness, assemble the volume by spatially aligning a stack of two-dimensional images. Consequently, there can be substantial artifacts in the image volume, most notably serious discontinuities along the section axis. These are the result of variations in section thickness, sample deformations, and variations in imaging conditions. These artifacts are particularly a problem with ATUM-based SEM (Automated Tape Collecting Ultramicrotome-based Scanning Electron Microscopy) [31], a method that currently achieves the highest throughput and also has the advantage of preserving tissue sections, in contrast to the one-shot destructive imaging process of Serial Block Electron Microscopy (SBEM) [12] and Focused Ion Beam Scanning Electron Microscopy (FIBSEM) [24].

Figure 1 shows the artifacts typical in ATUM-based SEM volumes. In other imaging domains, improved imaging techniques and mathematical corrections have been devised for reducing artifacts in MRI and echo-planar images [13,2,1,11], and in 2-D electron microscopy images [21], but there has been less focus on three-dimensional EM volumes. [23]

When present, these artifacts prevent automated and manual analysis of volumes except as a series of 2-D images along the original sectioning axis, preventing in particular the extraction of truly 3-D image features. Given that structures, such as neurites in cortex, may have arbitrary 3-D orientations relative to the original sectioning axis, this limitation is a serious impediment. On SBEM and FIBSEM volumes without these artifacts, the ability to view cross sections along arbitrary axes has aided humans tasked with manually tracing neurites and detecting synapses [16,15], and automated algorithms for reconstructing neurite morphology (via segmentation) have depended on 3-D features. [18,33,17,19,4,3].

To eliminate these artifacts and enable truly 3-D analysis of such image volumes, we propose a coarse-to-fine optimization-based procedure EMISAC (EM Image Stack Artifact Correction). We note that a single per-section brightness and contrast adjustment (i.e. linear transform of intensity values) is inadequate on typical datasets for correcting discontinuities except very locally. EMISAC optimizes the parameters of spatially varying linear transformations of the data in order to minimize the squared norm of the gradient along the section axis, subject to detail-preserving regularization, as described in Section 2.

We applied EMISAC to a publicly available ATUM-based SEM volume of mouse cortex as well as to a serial section Transmission Electron Microscopy (ssTEM) volume of Drosophila larva ventral nerve cord. Figure 1 shows several cross-sectional views of the output of our algorithm. Qualitatively, EMISAC appears to completely eliminate all discontinuity artifacts while preserving all of the original detail.[1] (We did not attempt to address the problem of lower Z resolution than X-Y resolution.) Quantitatively, an evaluation based on the NIQE blind image quality metric [28] confirms the qualitative results. More importantly, we evaluated the effect of EMISAC as a preprocessing step on the accuracy of automated segmentation of neurites, a key challenge for this type of data; consistent with the NIQE scores, EMISAC dramatically improved segmentation accuracy.

After developing our approach independently, we became aware of a recent method [23] for addressing the same problem. Like our approach, this alternative method involves a quadratic optimization to minimize the squared norm of the gradient along the section axis, but uses a different parameterization and a different form of regularization and post-processing to preserve the intra-slice detail. We included this alternate method in our evaluations, and found EMISAC matches or outperforms it. In addition, we evaluated several other generic correction methods on the raw datasets including histogram equalization, contrast-limited adaptive histogram equalization [38], and local normalization, and found that EMISAC significantly outperforms all of them.

Furthermore, while designed primarily for electron microscopy image stacks, EMISAC is also applicable to lighting correction in time-lapse photography. Raw time-lapse image sequences typically have serious inter-frame lighting discontinuities. Although a few tools such as LRTimelapse[2] are designed to edit time-lapse sequences and correct these artifacts, our method does not require manual editing and can make local corrections to lighting as well. We evaluated EMISAC on several time-lapse videos exhibiting lighting problems; compared to the original videos, EMISAC produced a large qualitative improvement, and eliminated essentially all lighting discontinuities

---

[1] Our qualitative assessment was based on only a random subset of the cross-sections; we did not scrutinize every single cross-sectional view. Our quantitative assessment is more comprehensive.

[2] http://lrtimelapse.com

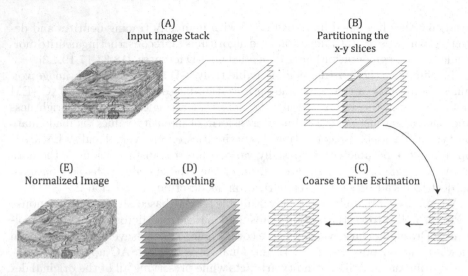

Fig. 2. Schematic of our approach. (A) An aligned EM image stack of 2-D slices. (B) The volume is optionally partitioned into a grid, which can be distributed across multiple processors; only limited communication is required between neighboring processors. (C) A coarse-to-fine procedure, in which both the data as well as the parameters are initially downsampled, speeds up the optimization of the objective in Eq. (3). From right to left: downsampled x-y slices and downsampled parameters (larger block size); downsampled parameters only; full parameters (small block size). (D) The parameters are spatially smoothed within each x-y slice to remove the blocking effect. Four blocks are shown for illustration purposes, but in practice there are many more blocks. (E) Corrected output image.

2   Artifact Correction Algorithm

In order to maximize the applicability of our approach, and avoid introducing a model bias[3] that could harm the accuracy of later stages of processing, we designed our approach to make as few and as simple assumptions as possible:

1. the true (undistorted) image volume is mostly continuous along the section axis;
2. the distortions in the volume can be expressed as *local* linear transformations of the intensity values, where the parameters of the linear transforms vary smoothly within each section (but are not smooth between sections).

The detailed formulation of our method is explained in the following sections. A summary of our approach is illustrated in Fig. 2.

---

[3] A denoising method based on a learned sparse-coding dictionary, for instance, could potentially introduce patterns that were not present in the original data.

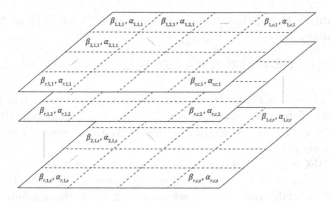

Fig. 3. EM image stack as a set of smaller blocks. The total number of blocks in the x-direction, y-direction, and z-direction are given by r, c, and s, respectively, resulting in a total of $r \cdot c \cdot s$ blocks. We have unique β and α parameters for each block.

2.1   Problem Formulation

As shown in Fig. 3, we partition each slice of the 3-D EM volume into small fixed-size two-dimensional blocks. Voxel intensity values are corrected by a linear transformation given by:

$$I'_{x,y,z} = \beta_{\lfloor x/w_x \rfloor, \lfloor y/w_y \rfloor, z} \cdot I_{x,y,z} + \alpha_{\lfloor x/w_x \rfloor, \lfloor y/w_y \rfloor, z} \tag{1}$$

where $I(x,y,z)$ refers to the scalar intensity value at position (x,y,z) of the volume, and (w_x, w_y) is the block size. The smaller the block size, the larger the number of parameters. Note that β and α correspond to correction of contrast and brightness, respectively. This block-based scheme effectively captures the local similarities within each slice and reduces the computational complexity.

We express our assumption of continuity in I' along z as a penalty on the squared norm of the gradient with respect to z. Likewise, the smoothness assumption on the the affine transforms is expressed as a penalty on the squared norms of the gradients of α and β with respect to the in-slice block positions. Thus, we formulate the optimization problem as follows:

$$\min_{\beta,\alpha} \sum_x \sum_y \sum_z (I'_{x,y,z+1} - I'_{x,y,z})^2$$

$$+ \gamma \sum_i \sum_j \sum_z \left[(\beta_{i+1,j,z} - \beta_{i,j,z})^2 + (\beta_{i,j+1,z} - \beta_{i,j,z})^2 \right. \tag{2}$$

$$\left. + (\alpha_{i+1,j,z} - \alpha_{i,j,z})^2 + (\alpha_{i,j+1,z} - \alpha_{i,j,z})^2 \right]$$

$$\text{s.t.} \quad \beta_{i,j,z} \geq 1, \quad \forall i,j,z.$$

The β parameters must be bounded to avoid the trivial null solution.

We reformulate the optimization problem given in Eq. (2) as the convex quadratic problem

$$\min_X \|D_z X\|_2^2 + \gamma(\|D_x X\|_2^2 + \|D_y X\|_2^2) \qquad \text{s.t.} \quad \beta \geq 1, \qquad (3)$$

where $X=[\beta, \alpha]$, $D_z = G_z A$, $D_x = G_x$, $D_y = G_y$, A is a matrix that maps the parameters X to a vector expressing I', and G_a is a matrix that maps a vectorized volume to a vector containing the finite-differences approximation of its gradient along axis a.

We use L-BFGS-B [37] to solve the optimization problem in Eq. (3). The optimization is stopped when the fractional decrease in objective between consecutive iterations falls below $\epsilon \cdot f$, where $\epsilon = 2^{-52}$ is the machine precision. To speed up the optimization process, we employ a coarse to fine estimation procedure detailed below.

2.2 Coarse-to-Fine Procedure

Rather than solving Eq. (3) with the final desired block size directly, we solve a sequence of optimization problems of the form shown in Eq. (3) with increasing image resolution in the x-y plane and/or decreasing block size. Each optimization after the first is initialized with the (appropriately upsampled) parameters that solved the previous optimization. In practice, we used (a single succession of) the following three steps:

1. The image resolution is reduced by a factor of 2 in x and y (using 2×2 averaging), as are the number of blocks.
2. The full image resolution is used, but the number of blocks remains reduced by a factor 2 in x and y.
3. The number of blocks is increased by a factor of 2 in x and y to its final size.

As the optimization is convex, the final solution obtained is unaffected by this procedure, but typically the running time is greatly reduced.

2.3 Removing the Blocking Effects

Ideally, the coarse-to-fine procedure is continued all the way down to a block size of $(1, 1)$. However, to reduce running time, it may be desirable to stop the procedure at a non-trivial block size. To avoid introducing artifacts from the blocking, after performing the final optimization, we upsample the α and β parameters to a block size of 1 using linear interpolation (rather than nearest neighbor interpolation).

2.4 Parallelization

For large image volumes, we can partition the volume into a grid along the x and y axes, which can be distributed across multiple processors or machines.

For simplicity, the grid cell boundaries should be aligned to block boundaries. Only the parameter gradients for blocks on the border of each grid cell must be communicated, at each iteration of the optimization, to the processors responsible for neighboring grid cells, which is in general a very small amount of data relative to the size of the image volume. As a simplifying approximation, we could even ignore the regularization term between neighboring grid cells and thereby require no communication between machines. In practice this may not significantly affect the result provided that the grid cells are large enough. In our experiments, we observed no loss of accuracy (in NIQE score) from using no communication between blocks, except for the final upsampling step.

3   Evaluation on Electron Microscopy Data

We tested EMISAC on a publicly available ATUM-based SEM volume of mouse cortex released by Kasthuri *et al.* [20] For a $1024 \times 1024 \times 100$ voxel portion of this dataset, a dense segmentation of neurites traced by a human expert is also publicly available as part of the SNEMI3D neurite segmentation challenge [5], which enabled us to evaluate the effect of EMISAC on segmentation accuracy. The dataset was acquired at a resolution of $3 \times 3 \times 30$ nm, but as the human-traced segmentation is provided only at the downsampled resolution of $6 \times 6 \times 30$ nm, we used the same downsampled resolution for all of our experiments. In addition, we tested EMISAC on another publicly available dataset, Cardona *et al.* 2010, collecting using a different imaging technique, ssTEM rather than ATUM-SEM, and of Drosophila larva ventral nerve cord rather than mouse cortex, with a resolution of $4 \times 4 \times 50$ nm [7,8].

We compared EMISAC against the original aligned but uncorrected image volume. We are aware of only one other method designed to address this same problem (of which we only became aware after independently developing our own algorithm), which we refer to as Kazhdan2013 [23]. As the authors of that method made publicly available their output [22] on the same mouse cortex volume on which we tested EMISAC, we were able to include the Kazhdan2013 algorithm in our evaluations without having to reimplement it. We also compared EMISAC against histogram equalization, contrast-limited adaptive histogram equalization (CLAHE) [38], and local normalization [30].

For EMISAC, we set the affine transform regularization parameter $\gamma = 0.4 \frac{w_x w_y}{d_x d_y}$ for all electron microscopy datasets, where d_x and d_y are the image downsampling factors in x and y respectively (relative to the $6 \times 6 \times 30$ and $4 \times 4 \times 30$ nm resolution data). The coefficient was selected to minimize NIQE score, which does not depend on any labeled data. Furthermore, results were fairly insensitive to several orders of magnitude change in γ.

3.1   Image Quality Evaluation

Although any corrected version of the data is only useful in so far as it aids an image analysis task of interest, such as neurite segmentation, it is convenient to be able to directly quantify the image quality independent of any particular later analysis step. A visual assessment by humans would be inherently subjective (and also inconvenient), and it is impossible to obtain a "ground truth" version of the data without any imaging artifacts, against which the corrected version might be compared. Furthermore, we have no way of knowing the true distortion model. We therefore rely on the "completely blind" Natural Image Quality Evaluator (NIQE) [28], which requires neither a model of expected distortions nor human assessments of distorted images as training data, but merely a set of high quality images from which to estimate a model of natural image statistics. On natural image benchmarks, this method is comparable to the best methods that *do* rely on human assessments as training data.

We trained a NIQE model on a random set of x-y sections from the dataset that were not part of any of the volumes on which we tested our approach. Thus, the NIQE score of a y-z or x-z cross section represents the statistical similarity of the orthogonal cross sections to the original image sections, a very reasonable metric given that the ultimate goal is to be able to analyze the 3-D volume without regard to a preferred orientation.

3.2 Segmentation Accuracy Evaluation

As one of the primary goals of our work on the artifact correction is the improvement of automated segmentation results for neural circuit reconstruction, we directly evaluated the impact of EMISAC on 3-D segmentation accuracy. The training of our machine-learning-based segmentation algorithm, as well as the evaluation of segmentation accuracy, were based on the SNEMI3D human expert-traced segmentation, which we treat as "ground truth."

Although the focus of this work is not on segmentation algorithms, for completeness we describe the three-step segmentation procedure that we used:

1. We use an unsupervised procedure to transform each position in the image volume into a 1-of-k binary feature vector, with $k = 624 \cdot 16$. We cluster $16 \times 16 \times 4$ patches of the image volume using k-means based on L_1 distance; the binary feature vector for each position is obtained by vector quantizing the image patch centered at that location. We take advantage of the assumed rotational covariance of the data (namely transposition and reflection in the x-y plane, and reflection along the z axis), which reduces the effective number of parameters by a factor of 16.

2. To predict the presence of a cell boundary between two adjacent voxels along the x, y, or z axes, we train a logistic regression classifier for each of the 3 axes. The feature vector for classification is obtained by concatenating all of the 1-of-k binary feature vectors within a $16 \times 16 \times 16$ window around the boundary (producing a very high-dimensional feature vector). We extracted boundary information for training examples directly from the human-provided ground-truth segmentation, and ensured that equal total weight was given to positive and negative training examples. We optimized the classification model using L-BFGS, using a quadratic approximation to dropout [35] (with $p = 0.5$) for

regularization. As for the unsupervised feature learning, we take advantage of the assumed rotational covariance to reduce the number of parameters to be learned by a factor of 16.

3. To produce a segmentation, we employ Gala [29], a state-of-the-art electron microscopy image segmentation algorithm, based on agglomeration of supervoxels, for which we use the cell boundary predictions as input.

We use half of the ground truth segmentation to train the boundary classifier, half of the remaining portion to train Gala, and the remainder for evaluation. The same training/testing procedures were used for the original data, the EMISAC output, and the Kazhdan2013 output. The results are averaged over 4 splits.

We evaluate the segmentation accuracy relative to the human-labeled ground-truth using Variation of Information (VI) [27], which has been used by recent prior work for evaluating EM segmentations. [29,3] The variation of information between two segmentations, S and U, is defined as the sum of two conditional entropy terms, $H(U|S)$ and $H(S|U)$, where each segmentation assigns to each voxel position a segment identifier, and the entropy terms are with respect to the distribution over joint segment assignments $(S(x), U(x))$ obtained by sampling positions x within the volume uniformly at random. Thus, $H(S|U)$ can be seen as a measure of false splits in S with respect to U, and $H(U|S)$ can be seen as a measure of false merges in S with respect to U. A lower score corresponds to greater accuracy.

4   Electron Microscopy Results

To guide later experiments, we initially evaluated the effect of varying the block size on running time and image quality (measured by NIQE score); the results are shown in Fig. 4. The running times reported for this and later experiments are based on our Python implementation running on an 8-core Intel Xeon X5570 2.93 GHz system, which consumed about 15 GB memory for each $1024 \times 1024 \times 100$ volume. Based on the observed trade-off between image quality and running time, we used a final block size of $(16, 16)$ for later experiments. We found that the NIQE score typically converged before reaching the threshold of $f = 10^{10}$.

4.1   Comparison of NIQE Scores

Using these parameters, we evaluated the improvement in NIQE score relative to the original data of EMISAC, Kazhdan2013, histogram equalization, contrast-limited adaptive histogram equalization [38], and local normalization. Figure 5 shows the distribution of NIQE scores for the SNEMI3D volume. Table 1 shows the improvement in NIQE score on both datasets. Under Welch's t-test, EMISAC attains a large and highly statistically significant improvement in both x-z ($p < 0.0001$) and y-z ($p < 0.0001$) NIQE score relative to Kazhdan2013 on the ATUM-SEM volume, without any considerable loss in x-y NIQE score. The preservation of detail is confirmed by the very high structural similarity (SS) [36] between the original and corrected x-y cross-sections. See Fig. 6 for a visual comparison.

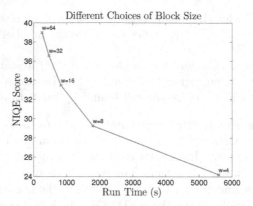

Fig. 4. Plot of average NIQE score versus EMISAC running time on the $1024 \times 1024 \times 100$ voxel SNEMI3D portion of the mouse cortex volume. The NIQE scores for all x-y, x-z, and y-z cross sections within the volume are averaged. w stands for the block size of (w, w). A lower NIQE score corresponds to higher image quality. The optimization was run in all cases with a stopping threshold of $f = 10^{10}$. These NIQE scores are consistent with the higher rate of visually apparent artifacts present when larger block sizes are used, which provides some confirmation of the validity of the NIQE score.

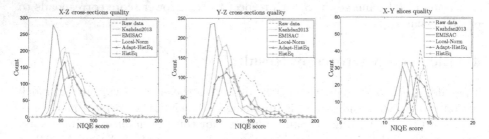

Fig. 5. Histogram of NIQE scores for the SNEMI3D volume. EMISAC uses a block size of $(16, 16)$ and stopping criteria of $f = 10^{10}$. Lower scores are better.

4.2   Comparison of Segmentation Accuracy

For the original data and each correction method, we evaluate the segmentation accuracy on each of the 4 boundary training/agglomeration training/test splits of the SNEMI3D volume. The Gala segmentation algorithm has a threshold parameter that trades off between false merges and false splits, as shown in Fig. 7; the optimal trade-off depends on the particular application, but in order to summarize results, we simply compute the minimum VI score (which gives equal weight to false splits and merges) over all thresholds.[4] For each correction method on each split, we compute the percent decrease in *minimum* VI score relative

---

[4] In actual use, we would have to pick the threshold based on cross-validation, as there would be no way to determine the true VI score for each threshold. However, this added complexity is irrelevant to our evaluation of artifact correction methods.

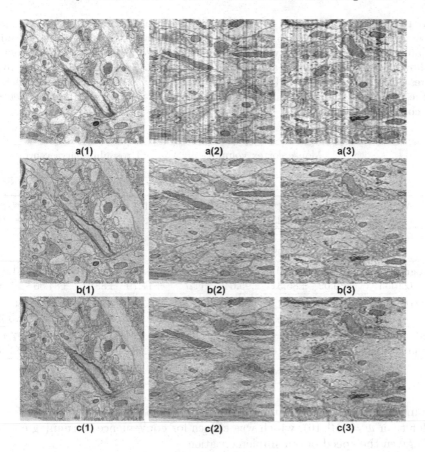

Fig. 6. Visual comparison of (a) the original data, and the corrected versions using (b) Kazhdan2013 and (c) our method EMISAC. From left to right we have the (1) x-y cross section, (2) x-z cross section, and (3) y-z cross-section. The two correction algorithms produce visually very similar results.

to the original data. To compare methods, we compute the mean and standard deviations of these decrease percentages. The results are shown in Table 2.

The nearly exact match in x-y NIQE scores between the original data and Kazhdan2013, as shown in Fig. 5 and Table 1, can be explained by the fact that Kazhdan2013 essentially copies the high-frequency content of the original x-y slices in its final step, and NIQE scores depend only on local (high-frequency) information.

While the NIQE scores were relatively insensitive to the stopping threshold f, we observed that the segmentation accuracy was highly sensitive, and therefore computed results for $f \in \{10^{10}, 10^9, 10^7, 10^6\}$, corresponding to increasing segmentation accuracy. Both Kazhdan2013 and EMISAC (for $f \leq 10^9$) achieve a similarly large improvement in accuracy over the original data. The difference between the two methods is not statistically significant ($p = 0.87$).

Table 1. NIQE score reduction (improvement) percentage, averaged over all x-y, x-z, and y-z cross-sections in the two EM datasets. The average structural similarity index (SS) [36] (as a percentage) between the original and corrected x-y cross-sections is also shown. Higher percentages are better. *First column:* Six $1024 \times 1024 \times 100$ voxel volumes of the mouse cortex ATUM-SEM volume [20] (five randomly sampled volumes plus the SNEMI3D volume). *Second column:* $512 \times 512 \times 30$ *Drosophila* larva ventral nerve cord ssTEM volume [8].

	Mouse cortex volume				Drosophila larva ventral nerve cord volume			
	x-y	x-z	y-z	SS	x-y	x-z	y-z	SS
EMISAC	6.59	**41.21**	**39.56**	96.4	-1.15	**11.04**	**11.82**	97.4
	±6.86	±19.25	±19.82	±2.20	±2.83	±25.05	±23.27	±1.06
Kazhdan2013	-1.85	35.24	35.06	98.3	-	-	-	-
	±0.82	±20.28	±20.02	±1.69				
Histogram	-4.53	-35.80	-42.31	69.5	-21.16	-68.54	-67.92	81.0
Equalization	±6.02	±86.31	±95.04	±6.47	±17.79	±88.76	±84.56	±3.64
CLAHE	-7.59	-39.77	-40.46	70.3	-14.02	-127	-133	80.1
	±6.19	±95.09	±96.56	±3.73	±9.43	±150	±154	±3.76
Local	2.51	13.04	13.79	93.3	3.05	-6.38	-8.51	97.4
Normalization	±4.91	±27.14	±27.20	±3.52	±1.93	±26.72	±28.85	±1.58

Figure 4 suggests that better results may be possible by using a block size smaller than $w = (16, 16)$, which was chosen for convenience in running experiments given the speed of our implementation.

We report running times of our Python implementation for comparison purposes, but by no means expect them to be comparable to those of a highly-optimized CPU or GPU implementation. Furthermore, L-BFGS-B is by no means the most effective algorithm for optimizing Eq. (3). The focus of our work was in evaluating correction models, rather than implementation speed.

Convolutional neural networks have shown good performance for neurite boundary detection [32,17,10], and may well perform better than the boundary classification method we used for our segmentation evaluation. Our choice was motivated by the fact that the state-of-the-art 3-D convolutional neural network approach for this problem is currently far from a settled matter, and we believe our method to be similar in performance; furthermore, it would have been highly impractical to spend the several weeks to months[5] of GPU time required to the train the network for each variant and data split that we tested.

---

[5] State-of-the-art 2-D networks often require several weeks of GPU training [10,25]; a comparable 3-D network can be expected to take at least as long, and possibly several times longer due to the larger number of parameters.

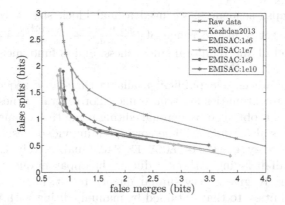

Fig. 7. Plot of the $H(S|U)$ (false split) vs. $H(U|S)$ (false merge) trade-off for segmentations based on the original image volume, Kazhdan2013, and EMISAC with several values of the stopping criteria f. Lower scores are better. Results are shown just for a single split, but results on other splits are similar. Note that the variation of information is simply $H(S|U) + H(U|S)$.

Table 2. Effect of artifact correction on segmentation accuracy ($n = 4$)

	Kazhdan2013	EMISAC			
		1e10	1e9	1e7	1e6
VI improvement(%)	29.19	19.83	26.43	27.23	27.97
	±13.12	±11.24	±10.03	±2.79	±1.88
Run Time (s)	-	828	1847	3963	4874

5 Lighting Correction of Time-Lapse Photography

Raw time-lapse photography sequences typically exhibit substantial flickering due to variations in lighting and exposure between frames [9]. Due to scene geometry, these variations are often local, such that a global brightness and contrast adjustment per frame is insufficient. We can directly apply EMISAC to the problem of correcting such lighting issues by treating time as the z-axis (taking the place of the section axis for the EM data); a separate set of α and β parameters are used for the red, green, and blue channels.

Quantitative evaluation of these time-lapse sequences cannot be done in the same way as for electron microscopy stacks, since the data distribution is obviously not invariant to transpositions between time and the x or y axis, as would be implied by comparing x-z and y-z cross-sections to the original x-y frames. In fact, we are unaware of any established method for quantitatively measuring lighting discontinuity in time-lapse sequences; while EMISAC's own objective function does measure this in some sense, it cannot reasonably be used for comparison to other methods nor can it be aggregated across datasets. Therefore, we are limited to qualitative assessment.

For all time-lapse sequences, we used a final block size of ($w_x = 4, w_y = 4$) and manually set γ in the range of $[\frac{39 \times 10^2 w_x w_y}{d_x d_y}, \frac{39 \times 10^4 w_x w_y}{d_x d_y}]$; γ trades off preservation of detail and temporal smoothness, and is fundamentally a matter of user preference.

For evaluation, we used 8 publicly available time-lapse sequences that exhibited lighting discontinuities between frames. For several of these sequences, a demonstration result obtained by manual editing using the commercial LRTime-Lapse software was also available. The corresponding video files can be found at http://rll.berkeley.edu/2014_ECCV_EMISAC. Qualitatively, EMISAC essentially eliminates all flickering without reducing the apparent quality of individual frames. It appears to give a very similar quality result, in terms of correcting lighting discontinuities, to that obtained by manual editing with the specialized LRTimeLapse software.

6   Discussion

Imaging artifacts, most notably discontinuities along the section (z) axis, have so far limited the use of image volumes acquired by ATUM-based SEM, one of the most promising high-throughput volume electron microscopy techniques, to essentially 2.5-D analysis [34,10]. Our limited assumptions about the data and distortion process lead naturally to a simple but highly effective optimization-based procedure: our method EMISAC appears to eliminate all visible discontinuities, without any loss of intra-section detail. On the key task of neurite segmentation, EMISAC substantially improves accuracy relative to the original data by about 28%, matching the improvement achieved by the recent independently-developed alternative method Kazhdan2013 [23]. In terms of NIQE score [28], our method significantly outperforms Kazhdan2013. Furthermore, the significant qualitative improvement in the video results demonstrates the applicability of EMISAC to time-lapse photography.

One explanation for the superior NIQE scores attained by EMISAC compared to Kazhdan2013 may be that EMISAC supports both local brightness as well as local contrast correction. Kazhdan2013 solves two sequential optimization problems, both of which apply an additive correction term to the original data, and penalize deviations in intra-slice gradients of the correction term. This implicitly allows smooth changes in brightness, as the gradient of the correction term is only affected by the gradient of the brightness factor. Even constant changes in contrast, however, are penalized heavily, as they have a *multiplicative* effect on the gradient of the correction term. While the lower NIQE scores of EMISAC relative to Kazhdan2013 did not correspond to better segmentation accuracy in our experiments, the segmentation performance may have been limited by the quality of the feature representation, and a future segmentation algorithm may indeed show improvement.

References

1. Alexander, A.L., Tsuruda, J.S., Parker, D.L.: Elimination of eddy current artifacts in diffusion-weighted echo-planar images: the use of bipolar gradients. Magnetic Resonance in Medicine 38(6), 1016–1021 (1997)
2. Andersson, J.L., Skare, S., Ashburner, J.: How to correct susceptibility distortions in spin-echo echo-planar images: application to diffusion tensor imaging. Neuroimage 20(2), 870–888 (2003)
3. Andres, B., Kroeger, T., Briggman, K.L., Denk, W., Korogod, N., Knott, G., Koethe, U., Hamprecht, F.A.: Globally optimal closed-surface segmentation for connectomics. In: Fitzgibbon, A., Lazebnik, S., Perona, P., Sato, Y., Schmid, C. (eds.) ECCV 2012, Part III. LNCS, vol. 7574, pp. 778–791. Springer, Heidelberg (2012)
4. Andres, B., Köthe, U., Helmstaedter, M., Denk, W., Hamprecht, F.A.: Segmentation of SBFSEM volume data of neural tissue by hierarchical classification. In: Rigoll, G. (ed.) DAGM 2008. LNCS, vol. 5096, pp. 142–152. Springer, Heidelberg (2008)
5. Berger, D.R., Schalek, R., Kasthuri, N., Tapia, J.C., Hayworth, K., Seung, H.S., Lichtman, J.W.: SNEMI3D challenge, http://brainiac2.mit.edu/SNEMI3D/home (training volume)
6. Briggman, K.L., Bock, D.D.: Volume electron microscopy for neuronal circuit reconstruction. Current Opinion in Neurobiology 22(1), 154–161 (2012)
7. Cardona, A., Saalfeld, S., Preibisch, S., Schmid, B., Cheng, A., Pulokas, J., Tomancak, P., Hartenstein, V.: An integrated micro-and macroarchitectural analysis of the Drosophila brain by computer-assisted serial section electron microscopy. PLoS Biology 8(10), e1000502 (2010)
8. Cardona, A., Saalfeld, S., Preibisch, S., Schmid, B., Cheng, A., Pulokas, J., Tomancak, P., Hartenstein, V.: Segmented serial section Transmission Electron Microscopy (ssTEM) data set of the Drosophila first instar larva ventral nerve cord (VNC) (2010), http://www.ini.uzh.ch/~acardona/data.html
9. Chylinski, R.: Time-Lapse Photography: A Complete Guide to Shooting, Processing and Rendering Time-Lapse Movies. Cedar Wings Creative (2012), http://books.google.com/books?id=7fDaLPhJB5IC
10. Ciresan, D.C., Giusti, A., Gambardella, L.M., Schmidhuber, J.: Deep neural networks segment neuronal membranes in electron microscopy images. In: NIPS, pp. 2852–2860 (2012)
11. Craddock, R.C., Jbabdi, S., Yan, C.G., Vogelstein, J.T., Castellanos, F.X., Di Martino, A., Kelly, C., Heberlein, K., Colcombe, S., Milham, M.P.: Imaging human connectomes at the macroscale. Nature Methods 10(6), 524–539 (2013)
12. Denk, W., Horstmann, H.: Serial block-face scanning electron microscopy to reconstruct three-dimensional tissue nanostructure. PLoS Biology 2(11), e329 (2004)
13. Haselgrove, J.C., Moore, J.R.: Correction for distortion of echo-planar images used to calculate the apparent diffusion coefficient. Magnetic Resonance in Medicine 36(6), 960–964 (1996)
14. Hayworth, K., Kasthuri, N., Schalek, R., Lichtman, J.: Automating the collection of ultrathin serial sections for large volume tem reconstructions. Microscopy and Microanalysis 12(S02), 86–87 (2006)
15. Helmstaedter, M.: Cellular-resolution connectomics: challenges of dense neural circuit reconstruction. Nature Methods 10(6), 501–507 (2013)

16. Helmstaedter, M., Briggman, K.L., Denk, W.: High-accuracy neurite reconstruction for high-throughput neuroanatomy. Nature Neuroscience 14(8), 1081–1088 (2011)
17. Jain, V., Bollmann, B., Richardson, M., Berger, D.R., Helmstaedter, M.N., Briggman, K.L., Denk, W., Bowden, J.B., Mendenhall, J.M., Abraham, W.C., et al.: Boundary learning by optimization with topological constraints. In: 2010 IEEE Conference on Computer Vision and Pattern Recognition (CVPR), pp. 2488–2495. IEEE (2010)
18. Jain, V., Murray, J.F., Roth, F., Turaga, S., Zhigulin, V., Briggman, K.L., Helmstaedter, M.N., Denk, W., Seung, H.S.: Supervised learning of image restoration with convolutional networks. In: IEEE International Conference on Computer Vision, pp. 1–8 (2007)
19. Jain, V., Turaga, S.C., Briggman, K.L., Helmstaedter, M.N., Denk, W., Seung, H.S.: Learning to agglomerate superpixel hierarchies. Advances in Neural Information Processing Systems 2(5) (2011)
20. Kasthuri, N., Lichtman, J.W.: Mouse S1 cortex Automatic Tape-Collecting Ultra Microtome (ATUM)-based Scanning Electron Microscopy (SEM) volume (2011), http://www.openconnectomeproject.org
21. Kaynig, V., Fischer, B., Müller, E., Buhmann, J.M.: Fully automatic stitching and distortion correction of transmission electron microscope images. Journal of Structural Biology 171(2), 163–173 (2010)
22. Kazhdan, M., Burns, R., Kasthuri, B., Lichtman, J., Vogelstein, J., Vogelstein, J.: Color corrected mouse S1 cortex Automatic Tape-Collecting Ultra Microtome (ATUM)-based Scanning Electron Microscopy (SEM) volume (2013), http://www.openconnectomeproject.org
23. Kazhdan, M., Burns, R., Kasthuri, B., Lichtman, J., Vogelstein, J., Vogelstein, J.: Gradient-domain processing for large em image stacks. arXiv preprint arXiv:1310.0041 (2013)
24. Knott, G., Marchman, H., Wall, D., Lich, B.: Serial section scanning electron microscopy of adult brain tissue using focused ion beam milling. The Journal of Neuroscience 28(12), 2959–2964 (2008)
25. Krizhevsky, A., Sutskever, I., Hinton, G.E.: Imagenet classification with deep convolutional neural networks. In: Advances in Neural Information Processing Systems, pp. 1106–1114 (2012)
26. Kuwajima, M., Mendenhall, J.M., Harris, K.M.: Large-volume reconstruction of brain tissue from high-resolution serial section images acquired by sem-based scanning transmission electron microscopy. In: Nanoimaging, pp. 253–273. Springer (2013)
27. Meilă, M.: Comparing clusterings–an information based distance. Journal of Multivariate Analysis 98(5), 873–895 (2007)
28. Mittal, A., Soundararajan, R., Bovik, A.C.: Making a completely blind image quality analyzer. IEEE Signal Processing Letters 20(3), 209–212 (2013)
29. Nunez-Iglesias, J., Kennedy, R., Parag, T., Shi, J., Chklovskii, D.B.: Machine learning of hierarchical clustering to segment 2d and 3d images. PloS One 8(8), e71715 (2013)
30. Sage, D.: Local normalization filter to reduce the effect of non-uniform illumination (March 2011), http://bigwww.epfl.ch/sage/soft/localnormalization/
31. Schalek, R., Wilson, A., Lichtman, J., Josh, M., Kasthuri, N., Berger, D., Seung, S., Anger, P., Hayworth, K., Aderhold, D.: Atum-based sem for high-speed large-volume biological reconstructions. Microscopy and Microanalysis 18(S2), 572–573 (2012)

32. Turaga, S., Briggman, K., Helmstaedter, M., Denk, W., Seung, S.: Maximin affinity learning of image segmentation. In: Bengio, Y., Schuurmans, D., Lafferty, J., Williams, C.K.I., Culotta, A. (eds.) Advances in Neural Information Processing Systems, vol. 22, pp. 1865–1873. MIT Press, Cambridge (2009)
33. Turaga, S.C., Murray, J.F., Jain, V., Roth, F., Helmstaedter, M., Briggman, K., Denk, W., Seung, H.S.: Convolutional networks can learn to generate affinity graphs for image segmentation. Neural Comput. 22(2), 511–538 (2010)
34. Vazquez-Reina, A., Gelbart, M., Huang, D., Lichtman, J., Miller, E., Pfister, H.: Segmentation fusion for connectomics. In: 2011 IEEE International Conference on Computer Vision (ICCV), pp. 177–184. IEEE (2011)
35. Wager, S., Wang, S., Liang, P.: Dropout training as adaptive regularization. In: Advances in Neural Information Processing Systems, pp. 351–359 (2013)
36. Wang, Z., Bovik, A.C., Sheikh, H.R., Simoncelli, E.P.: Image quality assessment: from error visibility to structural similarity. IEEE Transactions on Image Processing 13(4), 600–612 (2004)
37. Zhu, C., Byrd, R.H., Lu, P., Nocedal, J.: Algorithm 778: L-bfgs-b: Fortran subroutines for large-scale bound-constrained optimization. ACM Transactions on Mathematical Software (TOMS) 23(4), 550–560 (1997)
38. Zuiderveld, K.: Contrast limited adaptive histogram equalization. Graphic Gems, pp. 474–485 (1994)

Metric-Based Pairwise and Multiple Image Registration

Qian Xie[1], Sebastian Kurtek[2], Eric Klassen[1], Gary E. Christensen[3],
and Anuj Srivastava[1]

[1] Florida State University, Tallahassee, Florida, United States
qxie@stat.fsu.edu, klassen@math.fsu.edu, anuj@fsu.edu
[2] Ohio State University, Columbus, Ohio, United States
kurtek.1@stat.osu.edu
[3] University of Iowa, Iowa City, Iowa, United States
gary-christensen@uiowa.edu

Abstract. Registering pairs or groups of images is a widely-studied problem that has seen a variety of solutions in recent years. Most of these solutions are variational, using objective functions that should satisfy several basic and desired properties. In this paper, we pursue two additional properties – (1) invariance of objective function under identical warping of input images and (2) the objective function induces a proper metric on the set of equivalence classes of images – and motivate their importance. Then, a registration framework that satisfies these properties, using the L^2-norm between a novel representation of images, is introduced. Additionally, for multiple images, the induced metric enables us to compute a mean image, or a template, and perform joint registration. We demonstrate this framework using examples from a variety of image types and compare performances with some recent methods.

Keywords: metric-based registration, elastic image deformation, post-registration analysis, mean image, multiple registration.

1 Introduction

The problem of image registration is one of the most widely studied problems in medical image analysis. Given a set of observed images, the goal is to register points across the domains of these images. This problem has many names: registration, matching, correspondence, reparameterization, domain warping, deformation, etc., but the basic problem is essentially the same – which pixel/voxel on an image matches which pixel/voxel on the other image. The registration problem can be subdivided into categories in several ways. One way is to consider how many images are being registered: the *pairwise registration* where two images are matched and the *groupwise* or *multiple registration* where more than two images are being matched. Another possible division is based on modality - *unimodal registration* which is performed within a single modality and *multimodal registration* which is performed for images across multiple imaging modalities. In this

D. Fleet et al. (Eds.): ECCV 2014, Part II, LNCS 8690, pp. 236–250, 2014.

paper we will restrict to unimodal image registration since we are also interested in comparing and statistically analyzing registered images, beyond the problem of registration.

Although the registration problem has been studied for almost two decades, there continue to be some fundamental limitations in the popular solutions that make them suboptimal, difficult to evaluate and limited in scope. To explain these limitations let $\mathcal{F}$ be a certain set of $\mathbb{R}^n$-valued functions on a domain D, made precise later. A pairwise registration between any two images f_1, $f_2 \in \mathcal{F}$ is defined as finding a mapping γ, typically a diffeomorphism from D to itself, such that pixels $f_1(s)$ and $f_2(\gamma(s))$ are optimally matched to each other for all $s \in D$. To develop an algorithm for registration one needs: (1) an objective function for formalizing the notion of optimality, and (2) a numerical procedure for finding the optimal γ. Although the numerical techniques for optimization, i.e. item (2), have become quite mature over the last ten years, the commonly-used objective functions themselves have several fundamental shortcomings. It is the choice of objective function that is under the focus in this paper. The registration problems are commonly posed as variational problems, with the most common form of an objective function being

$$\mathcal{L}\left(f_1, f_2 \circ \gamma\right) \equiv \int_D \|f_1(s) - f_2(\gamma(s))\|^2 \, ds + \lambda R(\gamma), \ \gamma \in \Gamma, \qquad (1)$$

where $\|\cdot\|$ is the Euclidean norm, R is a regularization penalty on γ, typically involving its first and/or second derivatives, λ is a positive constant and Γ denotes the space of relevant deformations. Several variations of this functional are also used. We highlight shortcomings of these methods using a broader discussion about desired properties of an objective function in the next section.

1.1   Desired Properties in an Objective Function

We start with the question: What should be the properties of an objective function for registering images? The answer to this question is difficult since we may desire different results in different contexts. In fact, one can argue that we may never have a "perfect" objective function that matches an expert's intuition and solution. Still, there is a fundamental set of properties that is desirable, even essential, in for registration; some of these have been discussed previously in [3,17]. Some of them have been achieved in the previous papers while others have not. We list these properties next, starting with some notation. Note that some of them are overlapping, in the sense that they, individually or jointly with others, imply some others. Let $\mathcal{L}(f_1, (f_2, \gamma))$ denote the objective function for matching f_1 and f_2 by optimizing over γ (here γ is assumed to be applied to f_2 resulting in $(f_2, \gamma) \in \mathcal{F}$). The bracket (f, γ) denotes the group action where $\gamma \in \Gamma$ acts on $f \in \mathcal{F}$ defined by $(f, \gamma)(s) \equiv (f \circ \gamma)(s)$, $\forall s \in D$. Then, the *desired properties* of $\mathcal{L}$ are:

1. **Symmetry.** For any $f_1, f_2 \in \mathcal{F}$, we want

$$\mathcal{L}(f_1, f_2) = \mathcal{L}(f_2, f_1) \, .$$

2. **Positive Definiteness.** For any $f_1, f_2 \in \mathcal{F}$ we want $\mathcal{L}(f_1, f_2) \geq 0$ and

$$\mathcal{L}(f_1, f_2) = 0 \Leftrightarrow f_1 = f_2 \quad a.\ e.\ .$$

3. **Lack of Bias.** If f_1, f_2 are constant functions then for any $\gamma \in \Gamma$,

$$\mathcal{L}(f_1, f_2) = \mathcal{L}(f_1, (f_2, \gamma)) \ .$$

4. **Invariance to Identical Warping.** For any $f_1, f_2 \in \mathcal{F}$ and $\gamma \in \Gamma$, we have

$$\mathcal{L}(f_1, f_2) = \mathcal{L}\left((f_1, \gamma), (f_2, \gamma)\right) \ .$$

5. **Triangle Inequality.** For any $f_1,\ f_2,\ f_3 \in \mathcal{F}$,

$$\mathcal{L}(f_1, f_3) \leq \mathcal{L}(f_1, f_2) + \mathcal{L}(f_2, f_3) \ .$$

6. (An additional property of Γ.) **Γ is a group with composition.** For any γ, γ' and $\gamma" \in \Gamma$,
   i) $\gamma \circ \gamma' \in \Gamma$
   ii) $(\gamma \circ \gamma') \circ \gamma" = \gamma \circ (\gamma' \circ \gamma")$
   iii) there exists an $\gamma_{\text{id}} \in \Gamma$ such that $\gamma_{\text{id}} \circ \gamma = \gamma \circ \gamma_{\text{id}} = \gamma$
   iv) there exits a $h \in \Gamma$ such that $\gamma \circ h = h \circ \gamma = \gamma_{\text{id}}$.

Despite seemingly different appearances, the properties 1 to 4 are the same or closely related to those introduced previously in [17]. Specifically, properties 1, 4 and 6 together imply what was termed *"Symmetry"*, and property 4 and 6 imply *"Invariance under* SDiff$^+$ but are actually stronger. Property 5 is introduced to the list so that properties 1, 2 and 5 altogether imply that $\mathcal{L}$ is a proper *metric* on $\mathcal{F}$.

Property 4: **Invariance to Identical Warping** is listed as a standalone property not only because it is fundamental but also one of the most important. Why? Consider the two images f_1 and f_2 shown in the left panel of Fig. 1. Even though the two images are different, their corresponding pixels are nicely aligned. The middle panel shows an example of a warping function γ to be applied to both images and the right panel shows the warped images $f_1 \circ \gamma$ and $f_2 \circ \gamma$. It is easy to see that the correspondence between pixels across two images remains unchanged. Thus, since $\mathcal{L}$ is a measure of registration or correspondence between images, we need $\mathcal{L}(f_1, f_2) = \mathcal{L}\left((f_1, \gamma), (f_2, \gamma)\right)$. However, if we take the commonly used L^2-norm as an objective function (the first term in Eqn. 1), then function values are not the same, as shown below the images. In summary, an identical warping of any two images keeps their registration unchanged and, hence, in order to properly measure the level of registration, an objective function must have this property of invariance to identical warping. We seek a framework that achieves all of the properties listed above.

To specify the proposed framework, define an equivalence relation between images as follows: let $f \sim g$ iff there is a $\gamma \in \Gamma$ such that $g = (f, \gamma)$, and let

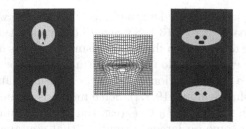

Fig. 1. Illustration of invariance to identical warping. The values of objective functions are not the same: $\|f_1 - f_2\|_{L^2} = 0.1085$ and $\|f_1 \circ \gamma - f_2 \circ \gamma\|_{L^2} = 0.1305$.

$[f] = \{g \mid g \sim f\}$ denote the orbit of an image f. Our goal is to establish a metric on the set of equivalence classes or orbits, the so-called quotient space of $\mathcal{F}$ under the action of Γ. However, since Γ is an open set, the resulting orbits are also open sets and it is difficult to establish a proper metric between these orbits. Thus, instead, we define the quotient space $\mathcal{F}/\Gamma$ as the set of *closures* of all equivalence classes, i.e. $\mathcal{F}/\Gamma = \{\text{closure}([f]) \mid f \in \mathcal{F}\}$. If $\mathcal{L}$ is a proper metric on $\mathcal{F}$ and, additionally, if properties 4 and 6 also hold, then it can be shown that the quantity $\inf_{\gamma \in \Gamma} \mathcal{L}(f_1, (f_2, \gamma))$ defines a proper metric on $\mathcal{F}/\Gamma$. The distance between any two equivalence classes $[f_1]$ and $[f_2]$ is well defined:

$$d([f_1], [f_2]) = \inf_{\gamma \in \Gamma} \mathcal{L}(f_1, (f_2, \gamma)) = \inf_{\gamma' \in \Gamma} \mathcal{L}(f_2, (f_1, \gamma')) . \tag{2}$$

This metric on the quotient space therefore provides us with a tool to measure the difference between registered images. Note that in case $\mathcal{L}$ is a proper metric, then property 4 implies the action of Γ on $\mathcal{F}$ is by isometries. It can be shown that if $d([f_1], [f_2]) = 0$, then $f_1 \in [f_2]$ and vice-versa.

This setup allows us to study another important property – "**inverse consistency**" – introduced in [3]. It states that for all $f_1, f_2 \in \mathcal{F}$, if

$$\tilde{\gamma} \in \operatorname*{argmin}_{\gamma \in \Gamma} \mathcal{L}(f_1, (f_2, \gamma)) \text{ then } \tilde{\gamma}^{-1} \in \operatorname*{argmin}_{\gamma \in \Gamma} \mathcal{L}(f_2, (f_1, \gamma)).$$

It is natural to have this property since it implies that the optimal registration between two images remains the same even if they are treated in the reverse order. Note that a combination of 1, 4 and 6, along with the definition in Eqn. 2, implies inverse consistency.

The requirement for Γ to be a group is important to derive other properties. While most papers use the full diffeomorphism group for Γ, some papers work with a subset of deformations, e.g. spline-based deformations, and that can be problematic as discussed later.

1.2   Past and Current Literature

While the objective function given in Eqn. 1 is one used most often, several variations have also been applied. For instance, sometimes the first term is replaced by mutual information [23,4], minimum description length [5,21], etc., or the second term is replaced by the length of a geodesic in the warping space (as in the LDDMM approach [6,20,1,13]). Some methods conceptualize the average image under the large deformation diffeomorphisms setting as an unbiased atlas ([8,12]). However, these methods do not use a formal metric for registration. Another idea is to impose regularization differently, e.g. using Gaussian smoothing of images (diffeomorphic demons [19,22]). Some methods optimize the objective function over a proper subgroup $\Gamma_0 \subset \Gamma$ (e.g. the set of volume-preserving diffeos [17]), some on Γ, some on larger a group Γ_b that contains Γ (e.g. the one including non-diffeomorphic mappings also) and some on even larger deformation spaces that are not groups (e.g. thin plate splines [2,16,7]). Rather than going through individual methods and their properties in details, we summarize their satisfaction of desired properties in Table 1. It is interesting to note that not a single past method satisfies property 4 without drastically restricting the deformation group Γ. The inverse consistency is, similarly, seldom satisfied.

Table 1. Properties of Objective Functions for Registration

Properties	1. Sym.	2. P.D.	3. Lack Bias	4. Inv.	5. Tri. Ineq.	6. Group
L^2	✓	✓	✓	✗	✓	✗
$L^2 + R(\gamma)$	✓	✓	✗	✗	✓	✗
CC [18]	✓	-	✗	✓	-	✓[1]
MI [23]	✓	-	✓	✗	-	✗
Demons [22]	✓	✓	✗	✗	✓	✗
LDDMM [1]	✓	✓	✗	✗	✓	✓
GL_2 [17]	✓	✓	✓	✓	✓	✓[2]
$GL_2 + R(\gamma)$	✓	✓	✗	✗	✓	✓

[1] is invariant to the general linear group.
[2] is invariant to the special group of volume and orientation preserving diffeomorphisms.
- indicates where the property is not proper to be evaluated under the context.

If we have a proper metric on the quotient space $\mathcal{F}/\Gamma$, it leads to additional tools for post-registration analysis. Here one analyzes registered images and applies statistical techniques such as PCA for dimension reduction and modeling. The question is: What should be the metric for these modeling procedures? Currently one performs registration using a certain objective function and then chooses a separate metric to perform post-registration analysis. Ideally, one would like an approach that can *align, compare, average, and model* multiple images in a **unified** framework that leads to efficient algorithms and consistent estimators. The objective function presented in this paper not only satisfies the invariance and the inverse consistency properties but also provides a metric on the quotient space for unified image comparison and analysis. Therefore, we have called our framework a metric-based method for registration, comparison and analysis of images. This idea was prompted by recent work on shape analysis of surfaces [10]. Although we utilize the same idea, the details are different because the representation and the Riemannian metric are not the same.

The rest of this paper is organized as follows. In Section 2, we introduce a new mathematical representation of images and a metric for image registration that satisfies all the desired properties. In Section 2.3, we develop the idea of mean images or templates under the chosen metric, and use these means to perform multiple image registration. Section 3 presents results on synthetic and real data. Finally, in Section 4, we present some concluding remarks.

2   Metric-Based Image Registration

In this section we lay out the framework for joint image registration and comparison under a new objective function which is a proper metric. This method applies to mathematical objects whose range space has dimension at least as high as that of their domain, as $f : D \to \mathbb{R}^n$, where $n \geq m = \dim(D)$. In case of 2D (3D) images, this means that pixels have at least two (three) coordinates which is the case for colored images, or multimodal images (with different imaging modalities as the pixel coordinates). The scalar (gray scaled) images can be transformed as described later to satisfy this condition.

2.1   Image Representation and Pairwise Registration

Let the image space be $\mathcal{F} = \{f : D \to \mathbb{R}^n \mid f \in C^\infty(D)\}$ and $\Gamma = \mathrm{Diff}^+(D)$ is a subgroup of Diff^+ (the orientation-preserving diffeomorphism group) that preserves the boundary of D. Hereafter we will use $\|f\|$ for the L^2-norm of any f and $|A|$ to denote the determinant of a square matrix A unless stated otherwise.

Definition 1. *The right action of Γ on $\mathcal{F}$ is defined by the mapping $\mathcal{F} \times \Gamma \to \mathcal{F}$ given by $(f, \gamma) = f \circ \gamma$.*

It is easy to see that this action is not by isometries under the L^2-metric. That is, for any two $f_1, f_2 \in \mathcal{F}$, and a general $\gamma \in \Gamma$, we have $\|f_1 - f_2\| \neq \|f_1 \circ \gamma - f_2 \circ \gamma\|$. Thus, the important property 4, invariance to simultaneous warping, is not satisfied and, consequently, one cannot work with the L^2-norm in the image space directly. Instead, we will use a mathematical representation of images defined by a mapping called the q-map, that has been prompted by recent work in shape analysis of surfaces [10]. Here, we adopt it for analyzing images as follows.

Let $(x^1, \ldots, x^m) : D \to \mathbb{R}^m$ be coordinates on (a chart of) D and $\mathbf{J}f(s)$ be the Jacobian matrix of f at s with the (j, i)-th element as $\partial f^j / \partial x^i(s)$. Define the "generalized area multiplication factor" of f at s for arbitrary $n \geq m$ as $a(s) = |\mathbf{J}f(s)|_V$ where $|\mathbf{J}f(s)|_V = \|\frac{\partial f}{\partial x^1} \wedge \frac{\partial f}{\partial x^2} \wedge \cdots \wedge \frac{\partial f}{\partial x^m}\|$. Here $\wedge$ denotes the wedge product. The two special cases are: if $m = n = 2$, then $a(s) = |\mathbf{J}f(s)|$; if $m = 2$ and $n = 3$, then $a(s) = \|\frac{\partial f}{\partial x^1}(s) \times \frac{\partial f}{\partial x^2}(s)\|$.

Definition 2. *For an $f \in \mathcal{F}$, define a mapping $Q : \mathcal{F} \to L^2$ such that for any $s \in D$, $Q(f)(s) = \sqrt{a(s)} f(s)$.*

For any $f \in \mathcal{F}$, we will refer to $q = Q(f)$ as its q-**map**; note that $q : D \to \mathbb{R}^m$. Also, we remark that this is a general version of q-map for arbitrary $\mathbb{R}^n$ that extends the work of [10]. Assuming the original set of images to be smooth, the set of all q-maps is a subset of the L^2-space. Intuitively, the q-map leaves uniform regions as zeros while preserving edge information in such a way that it is compatible with change of variables, i.e., stronger edges get higher values. The corresponding action of Γ on L^2 is given as follows.

Lemma 1. *The right action of Γ on the L^2-space, corresponding to the one given in Definition 1, is given by the mapping $L^2 \times \Gamma \to L^2$ as $(q, \gamma) = \sqrt{|\mathbf{J}\gamma|}(q \circ \gamma)$, where $\mathbf{J}\gamma(s)$ denotes the Jacobian matrix of γ at s.*

Note that the mapping Q is equivariant, i.e. it can be shown that for an image f and γ, $Q((f, \gamma)) = (Q(f), \gamma)$, where the action on the left side is given by Definition 1 and the action on the right is given by Definition 1.

This leads to the most important property of this mathematical representation as the following.

Proposition 1. *The reparametrization group Γ acts on the L^2-space by isometries under the L^2-norm, i.e. $\forall q_1, q_2 \in L^2, \forall \gamma \in \Gamma, \|(q_1, \gamma) - (q_2, \gamma)\| = \|q_1 - q_2\|.$*

Proof.

$$\|(q_1, \gamma) - (q_2, \gamma)\|^2 = \int_D |q_1(\gamma(s)) - q_2(\gamma(s))|^2 \, |\mathbf{J}\gamma(s)| \, ds = \|q_1 - q_2\|^2 . \quad (3)$$

Setting $q_2 \equiv 0$, $\forall q_1 \in L^2$ and $\gamma \in \Gamma$, we have $\|q_1\| = \|(q_1, \gamma)\|$. Thus, warping of images is actually a unitary operator under this representation.

Definition 3. *Define an objective function between any two images f_1 and f_2, represented by their q-maps q_1 and q_2, as $\mathcal{L}(f_1, (f_2, \gamma)) \equiv \|Q(f_1) - Q((f_2, \gamma))\| = \|q_1 - (q_2, \gamma)\|.$*

The registration is then achieved by minimizing the **objective function**:

$$\gamma^* = \operatorname*{arginf}_{\gamma \in \Gamma} \mathcal{L}(f_1, (f_2, \gamma)) = \operatorname*{arginf}_{\gamma \in \Gamma} \|q_1 - (q_2, \gamma)\| , \quad (4)$$

Upon closer inspection, Proposition 1 is exactly the same as property 4 – invariance to identical warping – in Section 1. In view of this, the L^2-norm between q-maps of images becomes a proper measure of registration between images since it remains the same if the registration is unchanged. This leads to a quantity that will serve as both the registration objective function and an extrinsic distance between registered images as defined in Eqn. 2. We will refer to the method as MBIR, i.e., the metric-based image registration method.

The objective function $\mathcal{L}$ given in Definition 3 satisfies **all** the properties listed earlier as those desired for registration. Specifically, it satisfies **invariance to simultaneous warping** (property 4). In case our transformation model Γ is a group then this framework satisfies the **inverse consistency** as stated in

Section 1. Additionally, the optimal registration is not affected by scaling and translations of image pixels: let $g_1 = c_1 f_1 + d_1$ and $g_2 = c_2 f_2 + d_2$ with $c_1, c_2 \geq 0$ and $d_1, d_2 \in \mathbb{R}^n$, if $\gamma^* = \arg\inf_\gamma \mathcal{L}(f_1, (f_2, \gamma))$ then $\gamma^* = \arg\inf_\gamma \mathcal{L}(g_1, (g_2, \gamma))$ as well. We point out that there are some unresolved mathematical issues concerning the existence of a unique global solution for γ^*, especially its existence inside Γ rather than being on its boundary. We leave this for a future discussion and focus on a numerical approach that estimates γ^*.

The proposed objective function in Eqn. 4 has only one term (similarity term) and the regularity term appears to be missing. However, the similarity term also has a built-in regularity, since it includes the determinant of the Jacobian, $|J_\gamma|$, in (q, γ). Additional regularity can also be introduced to the framework as is done in the LDDMM framework.

2.2   Gradient Method for Optimization Over Γ

The optimization problem over Γ stated in Eqn. 4 forms the crux of our registration framework and we will use a **gradient descent** method to solve it. Since Γ is a group, we use the gradient to solve for the incremental warping γ, on top of the previous cumulative warping γ_o, as follows. (In this way the required gradient is an element of $T_{\gamma_{\mathrm{id}}}(\Gamma)$, the tangent space of Γ at identity γ_{id}, and one needs to understand only that space.) We define a cost function with respect to γ as the functional

$$E(\gamma) = \|q_1 - \phi_{\tilde{q}_2}(\gamma)\|^2 , \tag{5}$$

where $\phi_q : \Gamma \mapsto [q]$ is defined to be $\phi_q(\gamma) = (q, \gamma)$ and $\tilde{q}_2 = (q_2, \gamma_o)$ with γ_o being the current deformation. Given a set of orthonormal basis elements, say $\mathbf{B}$, of $T_{\gamma_{\mathrm{id}}}(\Gamma)$, the gradient at γ_{id} takes the form $\nabla E(\gamma_{\mathrm{id}}) = \sum_{b \in \mathbf{B}} (\nabla_b E(\gamma_{\mathrm{id}})) b$, where $\nabla_b E(\gamma_{\mathrm{id}})$ is the directional derivative of E at γ_{id}. Let $\phi_{q,*}$ be the differential of ϕ_q at γ_{id} in the direction of b. Then $\nabla_b E(\gamma_{\mathrm{id}}) = \langle q_1 - \phi_{\tilde{q}_2}(\gamma_{\mathrm{id}}), \phi_{q,*}(b) \rangle$. Brackets denote the L^2 inner products. There exists an explicit form of $\phi_{q,*}$ such that for $b \in T_{\gamma_{\mathrm{id}}}(\Gamma)$ and $j = 1, 2, \dots, n$, the coordinate functions of $\phi_{q,*}(b)$ are given by:

$$\phi_{q,*}^j(b) = \frac{1}{2}(\nabla \cdot b)q^j + (\nabla q^j)b , \tag{6}$$

where $\nabla \cdot$ denotes the divergence operator. The form is the same as that is derived for parameterized surfaces in [10]. The basis elements are constructed using ideas of Fourier basis functions (See [24] for details).

2.3   Distance in the Quotient Space

Recall that in the LDDMM framework the regularity part of the objective function comes from a proper distance on Γ, computed as geodesic length under a Riemannian metric. If we study two images within an equivalence class using LDDMM (as A shown in Fig. 2), then the first term will go to zero and only the regularity term will remain. Thus, within equivalence classes, LDDMM provides a proper distance for comparing images. However, when two images are not

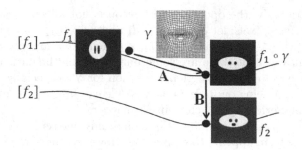

Fig. 2. Illustration of quotient space and orbits

equivalent, the variation left after registration is nonzero and needs a metric for
analysis. In other words, one needs a metric between equivalence classes (shown
in Fig. 2 as B), or a metric on the orbit space. Our framework naturally induces
a metric of that type. In case the variation in Γ is also of importance, we can
combine our metric (B) with a metric on A for analysis.

As stated in Eqn. 2, the minimal value of the objective function $\mathcal{L}$ introduced
in Definition 3 induces a distance in the quotient space $\mathcal{F}/\Gamma$. To explain further,
we define $\overline{[q]}$ to be the set of all warpings of a q-map. Since all elements of $\overline{[q]}$ can
be obtained using warpings (including the boundary of the orbit) of the same
image, we deem them equivalent from the perspective of registration. Let L^2/Γ
be the (quotient) set of all such equivalence classes of q-maps. Define

$$d([f_1], [f_2]) = d([q_1], [q_2]) \equiv \inf_{\gamma \in \Gamma} \mathcal{L}(f_1, (f_2, \gamma)) = \inf_{\gamma \in \Gamma} \|q_1 - (q_2, \gamma)\| , \quad (7)$$

It can be shown that the quantity $d([q_1], [q_2])$ (or $d([f_1], [f_2])$) forms a proper
distance on the quotient space L^2/Γ. At the same time since $g \in [f]$ indicates
$Q(g) \in [Q(f)]$, this quantity is a proper measure to quantify the level of registration.

Mean Image and Groupwise Registration
An important problem in image analysis, especially medical image analysis, is
to compute a "typical" or an "average" of several images from the same class
and use it as a template. Then, the individual images can be registered to the
sample mean in a pairwise manner, resulting in a group registration. By registering member images to the group mean, one can analyze their variations from
the typical template image. Suppose there is a set of N images, $\{f_i\}_{i=1}^N$. Their
Karcher mean is defined as the image that minimizes the sum of squares of the
distances to the given images, i.e. $[\mu] = \mathrm{argmin}_{f \in \mathcal{F}} \sum_{i=1}^n d^2([f_i], [f])$. The algorithm to find the Karcher mean is a standard one, and helps us find a mean
image f_μ deformable to the underlying image, such that $f_\mu \in [\mu]$. With this
mean, we can register groups of images to the mean image rather than to an
arbitrarily chosen template, as is often done in current methods.

3   Experiments

In this section we present various image registration results in order to validate our method. We provide examples of pairwise registration on both synthetic images and brain MRIs. In order to improve the registration of images with larger deformations, we also show results in landmark-aided registration for a better solution. We demonstrate the utility of our method to compute mean images as templates for registering multiple image. The problem of image classification is also considered using the proposed metric and the results are compared to those from other methods.

Recall that in case of grayscale images, with $n = 1$, our method does not apply directly since $n < dim(D)$. Instead, we make use of image gradients $\nabla f = (f_u, f_v)$ for $(u, v) \in [0, 1]^2$ and register objects in the form of $g = (f, f_u, f_v) \in \mathbb{R}^3$. In other words, the vector-valued image $g : D \to \mathbb{R}^3$ forms the input data for registration. Such image gradients are a type of edge measure and are often used in their own right as robust spatial features for image registration.

3.1   Pairwise Image Registration

We first present some results on synthetic images to demonstrate the use of the registration framework suggested in Eqn. 4. Fig. 3 shows images f_1 and f_2 that are registered twice, first by taking f_1 as the template image and estimating γ_{21} that optimally deforms f_2 using Eqn. 4. Then, the roles are reversed and f_2 is used as the template to obtain γ_{12}. We show the two converged objective functions, $\|(q_1, \gamma_{12}) - q_2\|$ and $\|q_1 - (q_2, \gamma_{21})\|$, associated with the optimal γ_{12} and γ_{21} to verify symmetry. The cumulative diffeomorphisms $\gamma_{21} \circ \gamma_{12}$ and $\gamma_{12} \circ \gamma_{21}$ are also used to demonstrate the inverse consistency of the proposed metric. As mentioned above, the theory shows that γ_{12} and γ_{21} are expected to be inverses of each other. We show the original images f_1 and f_2 with the matching warped images $f_2 \circ \gamma_{21}$ and $f_1 \circ \gamma_{12}$ respectively. The diffeomorphisms γ_{12} and γ_{21} used to register the images are also presented. By composing them in different orders we expect the resulting diffeomorphisms to be the identity map. In order to better visualize that the composed diffeomorphisms are close to identity, we apply them to checkerboard images and observe that the composed diffeomorphisms $\gamma_{21} \circ \gamma_{12}$ and $\gamma_{12} \circ \gamma_{21}$ are close to the identity map.

In Fig. 4, we present registration results using 2D brain MR images. In order to illustrate our method, in each of the two experiments, we show (1) the original images overlapped f_1/f_2 and (2) overlapped images after registration ($f_1/f_2 \circ \gamma_{21}$ and $f_2/f_1 \circ \gamma_{12}$). The overlapped images show image pairs in a common canvas such that red and green denote positive and negative image differences respectively.

Landmark-Aided Registration. Our framework can be extended to incorporate landmark information during registration and all of the nice mathematical properties of the objective function are preserved. Assume that there are a fixed

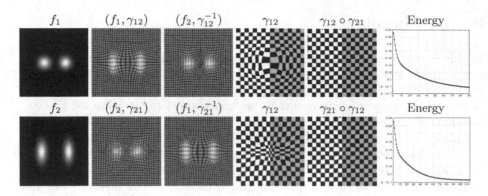

Fig. 3. Registering Synthetic Smooth Grayscale Images. $\gamma_{12} = \mathrm{argmin}_{\gamma \in \Gamma} \mathcal{L}(f_2, (f_1, \gamma))$ and $\gamma_{21} = \mathrm{argmin}_{\gamma \in \Gamma} \mathcal{L}(f_1, (f_2, \gamma))$. $\|q_1 - q_2\| = 0.2312$, $\|q_1 - (q_2, \gamma_{21})\| = 0.0728$ and $\|(q_1, \gamma_{12}) - q_2\| = 0.0859$.

number, say K, of distinct landmark points, $\mathcal{P} = \{p_1, p_2, \ldots, p_K\}$, in the image domain D. They are typically chosen according to the application but fixed within the analysis. The landmark-guided registration is achieved by defining a subgroup of Γ, denoted by $\Gamma_{\mathcal{P}}$, as:

$$\Gamma_{\mathcal{P}} = \{\gamma \in \Gamma \mid \gamma(p_i) = p_i, \quad i = 1, 2, \ldots, K\}. \tag{8}$$

Given two images f_1, f_2 with landmark information $\mathcal{P}$, the images can be registered in two steps in an iterative way:

1) Register the landmark points $\mathcal{P}$ and apply an initial deformation to f_1 to form $f_1^{\mathcal{P}}$ such that the landmarks are at the same locations in $f_1^{\mathcal{P}}$ and f_2.
2) Register $f_1^{\mathcal{P}}$ to f_2 using Eqn. 4 restricting to the subgroup $\Gamma_{\mathcal{P}}$.

Similar technique of forming landmark-constrained basis on $\mathbb{S}^2$ has been used on closed surfaces as described in [11]. In the second step, searching over $\Gamma_{\mathcal{P}}$ ensures correspondences of landmarks established in step 1 are preserved. The registration is refined without moving the landmarks. This search is based on a basis $\mathbf{B}^{\mathcal{P}}$ in $T_{\gamma_{id}}(\Gamma_{\mathcal{P}})$ constructed such that its elements, the vector fields on D, vanish at the landmark locations $\{p_i\}$.

We remark that $\Gamma_{\mathcal{P}}$ forms a subgroup of Γ and, as a result, the desired properties discussed earlier are still satisfied. This approach may be termed *landmark-guided* registration where the landmarks are treated as hard constraints.

We show results on MRIs with landmarks in Fig. 5. In the first example, presented in the first row of Fig. 5, the optimally deformed f_1 is displayed at the end as (f_1, γ). The deformation in the skull is so large that our original method fails to reach a global minimizer of the objective function. By adopting the landmark-aided registration, we at first get a deformed image $f_1^{\mathcal{P}}$, with nicely matched landmarks and the skull deformed correspondingly. Then, $f_1^{\mathcal{P}}$ is further deformed to register the intensity details without moving the landmarks. The final result $(f_1^{\mathcal{P}}, \gamma)$ matches f_2 with no artifacts around the skull. Another

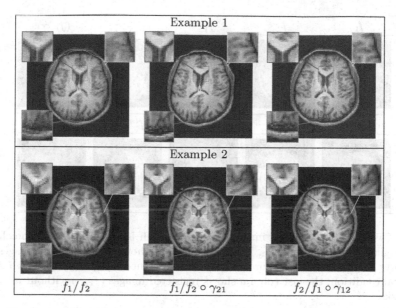

Fig. 4. Two examples of brain MR image registration. First columns show overlapped original images f_1 and f_2; second columns show overlapped images f_1 and deformed f_2; third columns show f_2 and deformed f_1.

example is shown in the bottom two rows of Fig. 5. Generally, the registration with landmarks outperforms the identity map as the initial condition of our procedure, especially when the deformations are large.

3.2 Registering Multiple Images

We use part of the MNIST database of handwritten digits to illustrate our method to compute the mean image and multiple image registration. In Fig. 6 we present the mean image of each digit computed without and with registration, respectively. We also show an example using brain MRIs in Fig. 7. Four brain images without alignment are shown on the top row with the corresponding mean image. This mean without registration appears blurred due to misalignment. On the bottom row, the images are aligned to the Karcher mean as described in Section 2.3. We can see that with multiple registration the mean image imporves the bluriness issue.

3.3 Image Classification

The framework introduced in this paper establishes a proper distance on the quotient space of q-maps of images. These distances can be used for pattern analysis of images such as clustering or classification. To illustrate this idea, we use a subset of the MNIST database of images of handwritten digits from 0 to 9. It contains ten images of handwritings for each digit. In addition to the

f_1	f_2	f_1^{lm}	(f_1^{lm}, γ)	(f_1, γ)

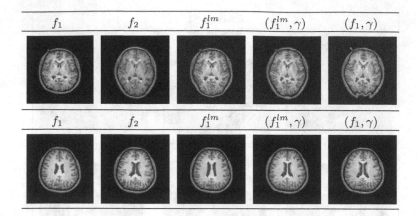

f_1	f_2	f_1^{lm}	(f_1^{lm}, γ)	(f_1, γ)

Fig. 5. Two examples of brain image registration with landmarks. First two columns show original images f_1 and f_2. The third column shows the deformed images f_1^{lm} using only landmarks; forth column shows final deformed images (f_1^{lm}, γ) with $f_1^{\mathcal{P}}$ as the initial condition; the last column shows registered images (f_1, γ) without involving landmarks.

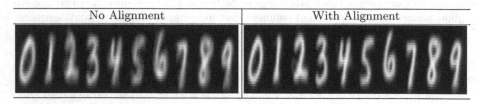

Fig. 6. First row contains the mean image without registration for digit groups (0-9); second row contains corresponding mean images with registration

baseline L^2-distance, or sum of squared distances (SSD) (without any warping), we compare our method to three other methods - diffeomorphic demons [22], FAIR [15] and NiftyReg [14].

For computing distance matrices between all pairs of images, the digits are registered in a pairwise manner using each of the three methods and then the SSD is computed for the registered images as a measure of distance. In the case of our method the distance defined in Eqn. 7 is used. Using the leave-one-out nearest-neighbor (LOO-NN) classifier, the rates of correct classification are listed in Table 2. Provided as a baseline, the L^2-distance without any registration provides a rate of classification of 76% with our method performing the best with 94%.

Table 2. Classification of MNIST Digits

Method	MBIR	Demons	FAIR	NiftyReg
%	94	86	85	83

No Alignment   Mean

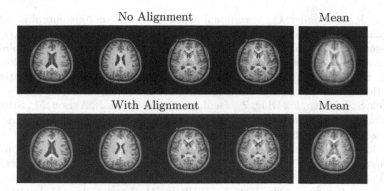

With Alignment   Mean

Fig. 7. Mean images of brain MRIs. Upper row: unregistered images and the cross-sectional mean; bottom row: mean with registration and images registered to it.

4   Conclusion

We have proposed a novel framework to register, compare and analyze images in a unified manner. This framework results in an objective function for registration that is both inverse consistent and invariant to random warpings of images. Furthermore, this function forms a proper metric on the quotient space of images, modulo the deformation group, and can be used to define and compute sample means of given images. This last item is based on computing an extrinsic distance between images in the representation space $\mathbb{L}^2$. With this framework, our method gives better results for pairwise registration and comparison, and multiple image registration and analysis. Furthermore, it allows the use of pre-determined (registered) landmark on images to help improve registration performance.

Acknowledgement. This research was supported in part by the NSF grants DMS 1208959, IIS 1217515, and CCF 1319658. We also thank the producers of datasets used here for making them available to public.

References

1. Beg, M., Miller, M., Trouvé, A., Younes, L.: Computing large deformation metric mappings via geodesic flows of diffeomorphisms. International Journal of Computer Vision 61, 139–157 (2005)
2. Bookstein, F.L.: Principal warps: Thin-plate splines and the decomposition of deformations. IEEE Transactions on Pattern Analysis and Machine Intelligence 11(6), 567–585 (1989)
3. Christensen, G., Johnson, H.: Consistent image registration. IEEE Transactions on Medical Imaging 20(7), 568–582 (2001)
4. Collignon, A., Vandermeulen, D., Marchal, G., Suetens, P.: Multimodality image registration by maximization of mutual information. IEEE Transactions on Medical Imaging 16(2), 187–198 (1997)
5. Davies, R., Twining, C., Cootes, T., Waterton, J., Taylor, C.: A minimum description length approach to statistical shape modeling. IEEE Transactions on Medical Imaging 21(5), 525–537 (2002)

6. Dupuis, P., Grenander, U.: Variational problems on flows of diffeomorphisms for image matching. Journal Quarterly of Applied Mathematics LVI (3), 587–600 (1998)
7. Eriksson, A., Astrom, K.: Bijective image registration using thin-plate splines. In: International Conference on Pattern Recognition, vol. 3, pp. 798–801 (2006)
8. Joshi, S., Davis, B., Jomier, B.M., Gerig, G.: Unbiased diffeomorphic atlas construction for computational anatomy. Neuroimage 23, 151–160 (2004)
9. Kurtek, S., Klassen, E., Ding, Z., Jacobson, S., Jacobson, J., Avison, M., Srivastava, A.: Parameterization-invariant shape comparisons of anatomical surfaces. IEEE Transactions on Medical Imaging 30, 849–858 (2011)
10. Kurtek, S., Klassen, E., Ding, Z., Srivastava, A.: A novel Riemannian framework for shape analysis of 3D objects. In: 2010 IEEE Conference on Computer Vision and Pattern Recognition, pp. 1625–1632 (2010)
11. Kurtek, S., Srivastava, A., Klassen, E., Laga, H.: Landmark-guided elastic shape analysis of spherically-parameterized surfaces. In: Computer Graphics Forum (Proceedings of Eurographics 2013, vol. 32(2), pp. 429–438 (2013)
12. Lorenzen, P., Davis, B., Joshi, S.: Unbiased atlas formation via large deformations metric mapping. In: Duncan, J.S., Gerig, G. (eds.) MICCAI 2005. LNCS, vol. 3750, pp. 411–418. Springer, Heidelberg (2005)
13. Miller, M., Trouve, A., Younes, L.: On the metrics and Euler-Lagrange equations of computational anatomy. Annual Review of Biomedical Engineering 4, 375–405 (2002)
14. Modat, M., Cardoso, M., Daga, P., Cash, D., Fox, N., Ourselin, S.: Inverse-consistent symmetric free form deformation. In: Dawant, B.M., Christensen, G.E., Fitzpatrick, J.M., Rueckert, D. (eds.) WBIR 2012. LNCS, vol. 7359, pp. 79–88. Springer, Heidelberg (2012)
15. Modersitzki, J.: FAIR: Flexible Algorithms for Image Registration. Society for Industrial and Applied Mathematics (2009)
16. Szeliski, R., Coughlan, J.: Spline-based image registration. International Journal of Computer Vision 22(3), 199–218 (1997)
17. Tagare, H., Groisser, D., Skrinjar, O.: Symmetric non-rigid registration: A geometric theory and some numerical techniques. Journal of Mathematical Imaging and Vision 34(1), 61–88 (2009)
18. Taquet, M., Macq, B., Warfield, S.: A generalized correlation coefficient: application to DTI and multi-fiber DTI. In: Mathematical Methods in Biomedical Image Analysis (2012)
19. Thirion, J.: Image matching as a diffusion process: an analogy with Maxwell's demons. Medical Image Analysis 2(3), 243–260 (1998)
20. Trouve, A.: Diffeomorphisms groups and pattern matching in image analysis. International Journal of Computer Vision 28(3), 213–221 (1998)
21. Twining, C., Marsland, S., Taylor, C.: Groupwise non-rigid registration: The minimum description length approach. In: Proceedings of the British Machine Vision Converence (BMVC), vol. 1, pp. 417–426 (2004)
22. Vercauteren, T., Pennec, X., Perchant, A., Ayache, N.: Diffeomorphic demons: Efficient non-parametric image registration. NeuroImage 45(suppl. 1), S61–S72 (2009)
23. Viola, P., Wells III, W.: Alignment by maximization of mutual information. In: Fifth International Conference on Computer Vision, pp. 16–23 (June 1995)
24. Xie, Q., Kurtek, S., Christensen, G., Ding, Z., Klassen, E., Srivastava, A.: A novel framework for metric-based image registration. In: Dawant, B.M., Christensen, G.E., Fitzpatrick, J.M., Rueckert, D. (eds.) WBIR 2012. LNCS, vol. 7359, pp. 276–285. Springer, Heidelberg (2012)

Canonical Correlation Analysis on Riemannian Manifolds and Its Applications

Hyunwoo J. Kim[1], Nagesh Adluru[1], Barbara B. Bendlin[1],
Sterling C. Johnson[1], Baba C. Vemuri[2], and Vikas Singh[1]

[1] University of Wisconsin–Madison, USA
[2] University of Florida, USA
http://pages.cs.wisc.edu/~hwkim/projects/riem-cca

Abstract. Canonical correlation analysis (CCA) is a widely used statistical technique to capture correlations between two sets of multi-variate random variables and has found a multitude of applications in computer vision, medical imaging and machine learning. The classical formulation assumes that the data live in a pair of *vector spaces* which makes its use in certain important scientific domains problematic. For instance, the set of symmetric positive definite matrices (SPD), rotations and probability distributions, all belong to certain curved Riemannian manifolds where vector-space operations are in general not applicable. Analyzing the space of such data via the classical versions of inference models is rather sub-optimal. But perhaps more importantly, since the algorithms do not respect the underlying geometry of the data space, it is hard to provide statistical guarantees (if any) on the results. Using the space of SPD matrices as a concrete example, this paper gives a principled generalization of the well known CCA to the Riemannian setting. Our CCA algorithm operates on the product Riemannian manifold representing SPD matrix-valued fields to identify meaningful statistical relationships on the product Riemannian manifold. As a proof of principle, we present results on an Alzheimer's disease (AD) study where the analysis task involves identifying correlations across diffusion tensor images (DTI) and Cauchy deformation tensor fields derived from T1-weighted magnetic resonance (MR) images.

1 Introduction

Canonical correlation analysis (CCA) is a powerful statistical technique to extract linear components that capture correlations between two multi-variate random variables [15]. CCA provides an answer to the following question: suppose we are given data of the form, $(\boldsymbol{x}_i \in \mathcal{X}, \boldsymbol{y}_i \in \mathcal{Y})_{i=1}^{N} \subset \mathcal{X} \times \mathcal{Y}$ where $\boldsymbol{x}_i \in \mathbf{R}^m$ and $\boldsymbol{y}_i \in \mathbf{R}^n$, find a model that explains *both* of these observations. More precisely, CCA provides an answer to this question by identifying a pair of directions where the projections (namely, u and v) of the random variables, $\boldsymbol{x}$ and $\boldsymbol{y}$ yield maximum correlation $\rho_{u,v} = \mathrm{COV}(u,v)/\sigma_u \sigma_v$. Here, $\mathrm{COV}(u,v)$ denotes the covariance function and σ. gives the standard deviation. During the last decade, the CCA formulation has been broadly applied to various unsupervised learning

D. Fleet et al. (Eds.): ECCV 2014, Part II, LNCS 8690, pp. 251–267, 2014.

problems in computer vision and machine learning including image retrieval [11], face/gait recognition [38], super-resolution [19] and action classification [24].

Beyond the applications described above, a number of works have recently investigated the use of CCA in analyzing neuroimaging data [3], which is a main focus of this paper. Here, for each participant in a clinical study, we acquire different types of images such as Magnetic Resonance (MRI), Computed Tomography (CT) and functional MRI. It is expected that each imaging modality captures a unique aspect of the underlying disease pathology. Therefore, given a group of N subjects and their corresponding brain images, we may want to identify strong relationships (e.g., anatomical/functional correlations) across different image types. When performed across different diseases, such an analysis will reveal insights into what is similar and what is different across diseases even when their symptomatic presentation may be similar. Alternatively, CCA may serve a feature extraction role. That is, the brain regions found to be strongly correlated can be used directly in downstream statistical analysis. In a study of a large number of subjects, rather than performing a hypothesis test on *all* brain voxels independently for each imaging modality, restricting the number of tests only to the set of 'relevant' voxels (found via CCA) is known to improve statistical power (since the False Discovery Rate correction will be less severe).

The classical version of CCA described above concurrently seeks two linear subspaces (straight lines) in *vector spaces* $\mathbf{R}^m$ and $\mathbf{R}^n$ for the two multi-variate random variables $\boldsymbol{x}$ and $\boldsymbol{y}$. The projection on to the straight line (linear subspace) is obtained by an inner product. This formulation is broadly applicable but encounters problems for manifold-valued data that are becoming increasingly important in present day research. For example, diffusion tensor magnetic resonance images (DTI) allow one to infer the diffusion tensor characterizing the anisotropy of water diffusion at each voxel in an image volume. This tensorial feature can be visualized as an ellipsoid and represented by a 3×3 symmetric positive definite (SPD) matrix at each voxel in the acquired image volume. Neither the individual SPD matrices nor the field of these SPD matrices lie in a vector space but instead are elements of a negatively curved Riemannian manifold where standard vector space operations are not valid. Hence, classical CCA is not applicable in this setting. For T1-weighted Magnetic resonance images (MRIs), we are frequently interested in analyzing not just the 3D intensity image on its own, but rather a quantity that captures the deformation field between each image and a *population template*. A registration between the image and the template yields the deformation field required to align the image pairs and the determinant of the Jacobian J of this deformation at each voxel is a commonly used feature that captures local volume changes [6,17]. Quantities such as the Cauchy deformation tensor defined as $\sqrt{J^T J}$ have been reported in literature for use in morphometric analysis [18]. The input to the statistical analysis is a 3D image of voxels, where each voxel corresponds to a matrix $\sqrt{J^T J} \succ 0$ (the Cauchy deformation tensor). Another example of manifold-valued fields is derived from high angular resolution diffusion images (HARDI) and can be used to compute the ensemble average propagators (EAPs) at each voxel of the given

HARDI data. The EAP is a probability density function that is related to the diffusion sensitized MR signal via the Fourier transform [5]. Since an EAP is a probability density function, by using a square root parameterization of this density function, it is possible to identify it with a point on the unit Hilbert Sphere. Once again, to perform any statistical analysis of these data derived features, we cannot apply standard vector-space operations since the unit Hilbert sphere is a positively curved manifold. When analyzing real brain imaging data, it is entirely possible that no meaningful correlations exist in the data. The key difficulty is that we do not know whether the experiment (i.e., inference) failed because there is in fact no statistically meaningful signal in the dataset or if the algorithms being used are sub-optimal.

Related Work. There are two somewhat distinct bodies of work that are related to and motivate this work. The first one relates to the extensive study of the classical CCA and its non-linear variants. These include various interesting results based on kernelization [1,4,12], neural networks [25,16], and deep architectures [2]. Most, if not all of these strategies extend CCA to arbitrary nonlinear spaces. However, this flexibility brings with it the associated issues of model selection (and thereby, regularization), controlling the complexity of the neural network structure, choosing an appropriate activation function and so on. It is an interesting question though not completely clear to us what type of a regularizer should be used if one were to explicitly impose a Riemannian structure on the objectives described in the works above. As opposed to regularization, the second line of work incorporates the specific geometry of the data directly within the estimation problem. Various statistical constructs have been generalized to Riemannian manifolds: these include regression [39,31], classification [36], kernel methods [21], margin-based and boosting classifiers [26], interpolation, convolution, filtering [10] and dictionary learning [14,27]. Among the most closely related are ideas related to projective dimensionality reduction methods. For instance, the generalization of Principal Components analysis (PCA) via the so-called Principal Geodesic Analysis (PGA) [9], Geodesic PCA [20], Exact PGA [33], Horizontal Dimension Reduction [32] with frame bundles, and an extension of PGA to the product space of Riemannian manifolds, namely, tensor fields [36]. It is important to note that except the non-parametric method of [34], most of these strategies focus on one rather than two sets of random variables (as is the case in CCA). Even in this setting, the first results on successful generalization of parametric regression models to Riemannian manifolds is relatively recent: geodesic regression [8,29] and polynomial regression [13] (note that the adaptive CCA formulation in [37] seems related to our work but is not designed for manifold-valued data).

   This paper provides a parametric model between two different tensor fields on a Riemannian manifold, which is a significant step beyond these recent works. The CCA formulation we present requires the optimization of functions over either a single product manifold or a pair of product manifolds (of different dimensions) concurrently. The latter problem involving product manifolds of different dimensions will not be addressed in this paper. Note that in general, on manifolds the projection operation does not have a nice closed form solution. So, we need to perform projections via an optimization scheme on the two manifolds and find the best pair of geodesic subspaces. We provide a precise solution to this problem. To our knowledge, this is the first extension of CCA to Riemannian manifolds. Our approach has two advantages relative to other non-linear extensions of CCA. The first advantage is that no model selection is required. Also our method incorporates the known geometry of data space. Our **key contributions** are: a) A principled generalization of CCA for Riemannian manifolds; b) First, a numerical optimization scheme for identifying the subspaces and later, single path algorithms with approximate projections (both these ideas may be applicable beyond the CCA formulation). c) Providing experimental evidence how the Riemannian CCA formulation expands the operating range of statistical analysis of neuroimaging data.

2   Canonical Correlation in Euclidean Space

First, we will briefly review the classical CCA in Euclidean space to motivate the rest of our presentation. Recall that Pearson's product-moment correlation coefficient is a quantity to measure the relationship of two random variables, $x \in \mathbf{R}$ and $y \in \mathbf{R}$. For one dimensional random variables,

$$\rho_{x,y} = \frac{\text{COV}(x,y)}{\sigma_x \sigma_y} = \frac{\mathbb{E}[(x - \mu_x)(y - \mu_y)]}{\sigma_x \sigma_y} = \frac{\sum_{i=1}^{N}(x_i - \mu_x)(y_i - \mu_y)}{\sqrt{\sum_{i=1}^{N}(x_i - \mu_x)^2}\sqrt{\sum_{i=1}^{N}(y_i - \mu_y)^2}} \quad (1)$$

For high dimensional data, $\boldsymbol{x} \in \mathbb{R}^m$ and $\boldsymbol{y} \in \mathbb{R}^n$, we cannot however perform a direct calculation as above. So, we need to project each set of variables on to a special axis in each space $\mathcal{X}$ and $\mathcal{Y}$. CCA generalizes the concept of correlation to random vectors (potentially of different dimensions). It is convenient to think of CCA as a measure of correlation between two multivariate data based on the *best* projection which maximizes their mutual correlation.

Canonical Correlation for $\boldsymbol{x} \in \mathbb{R}^m$ and $\boldsymbol{y} \in \mathbb{R}^n$ is given by

$$\max_{\boldsymbol{w}_x, \boldsymbol{w}_y} \text{corr}(\pi_{\boldsymbol{w}_x}(\boldsymbol{x}), \pi_{\boldsymbol{w}_y}(\boldsymbol{y})) = \max_{\boldsymbol{w}_x, \boldsymbol{w}_y} \frac{\sum_{i=1}^{N} \boldsymbol{w}_x^T(\boldsymbol{x}_i - \boldsymbol{\mu}_x)\boldsymbol{w}_y^T(\boldsymbol{y}_i - \boldsymbol{\mu}_y)}{\sqrt{\sum_{i=1}^{N}(\boldsymbol{w}_x^T(\boldsymbol{x}_i - \boldsymbol{\mu}_x))^2}\sqrt{\sum_{i=1}^{N}\left(\boldsymbol{w}_y^T(\boldsymbol{y}_i - \boldsymbol{\mu}_y)\right)^2}} \quad (2)$$

where $\pi_{\boldsymbol{w}_x}(\boldsymbol{x}) := \arg\min_{t \in \mathbb{R}} \text{d}(t\boldsymbol{w}_x, \boldsymbol{x})^2$. We will call $\pi_{\boldsymbol{w}_x}(\boldsymbol{x})$ the *projection coefficient* for $\boldsymbol{x}$ (similarly for $\boldsymbol{y}$). Define $S_{\boldsymbol{w}_x}$ as the subspace which is the span of $\boldsymbol{w}_x$. The projection of $\boldsymbol{x}$ on to $S_{\boldsymbol{w}_x}$ is given by $\Pi_{S_{\boldsymbol{w}_x}}(\boldsymbol{x})$. We can then verify that the relationship between the projection and the projection coefficient is,

$$\Pi_{S_{\boldsymbol{w}_x}}(\boldsymbol{x}) := \arg\min_{\boldsymbol{x}' \in S_{\boldsymbol{w}_x}} \text{d}(\boldsymbol{x}, \boldsymbol{x}')^2 = \frac{\boldsymbol{w}_x^T \boldsymbol{x}}{\|\boldsymbol{w}_x\|}\frac{\boldsymbol{w}_x}{\|\boldsymbol{w}_x\|} = \frac{\boldsymbol{w}_x^T \boldsymbol{x}}{\|\boldsymbol{w}_x\|^2}\boldsymbol{w}_x = \pi_{\boldsymbol{w}_x}(\boldsymbol{x})\boldsymbol{w}_x \quad (3)$$

In the Euclidean space, $\Pi_{S_{\boldsymbol{w}_x}}(\boldsymbol{x})$ has a closed form solution. In fact, it is obtained by an inner product, $\boldsymbol{w}_x^T\boldsymbol{x}$. Hence, by replacing the projection coefficient $\pi_{\boldsymbol{w}_x}(\boldsymbol{x})$ with $\boldsymbol{w}_x^T\boldsymbol{x}/\|\boldsymbol{w}_x\|^2$ and after a simple calculation, one obtains the form in (2). Without loss of generality, assume that x, y are centered. Then the optimization problem can be written as,

$$\max_{w_x, w_y} w_x^T X^T Y w_y \text{ subject to } w_x^T X^T X w_x = w_y^T Y^T Y w_y = 1 \qquad (4)$$

where $x, w_x \in \mathbb{R}^m$, $y, w_y \in \mathbb{R}^n$, $X = [x_1 \dots x_N]^T$ and $Y = [y_1 \dots y_N]^T$. The only difference here is that we remove the denominator. Instead, we have two equality constraints (note that correlation is scale-invariant).

3   Mathematical Preliminaries

We now briefly summarize certain basic concepts [7] which we will use later.

Riemannian Manifolds. A *differentiable manifold* [7] of dimension n is a set $\mathcal{M}$ and a family of *injective* mappings $\varphi_i : U_i \subset \mathbb{R}^n \to \mathcal{M}$ of open sets U_i of $\mathbb{R}^n$ into $\mathcal{M}$ such that: **(1)** $\cup_i \varphi_i(U_i) = \mathcal{M}$; **(2)** for any pair i, j with $\varphi_i(U_i) \cap \varphi_j(U_j) = W \neq \phi$, the sets $\varphi_i^{-1}(W)$ and $\varphi_j^{-1}(W)$ are open sets in $\mathbb{R}^n$ and the mappings $\varphi_j^{-1} \circ \varphi_i$ are differentiable, where $\circ$ denotes function composition. In other words, a differentiable manifold $\mathcal{M}$ is a topological space that is locally similar to an Euclidean space and has a globally defined differential structure. The tangent space at a point p on the manifold, $T_p\mathcal{M}$, is a vector space that consists of the tangent vectors of *all* possible curves passing through p.

A Riemannian manifold is equipped with a smoothly varying inner product. The family of inner products on all tangent spaces is known as the *Riemannian metric* of the manifold. The *geodesic distance* between two points on $\mathcal{M}$ is the length of the shortest *geodesic* curve connecting the two points, analogous to straight lines in $\mathbb{R}^n$. The geodesic curve from x_i to x_j can be parameterized by a tangent vector in the tangent space at y_i with an exponential map $\text{Exp}(y_i, \cdot) : T_{y_i}\mathcal{M} \to \mathcal{M}$. The inverse of the exponential map is the logarithm map, $\text{Log}(y_i, \cdot) : \mathcal{M} \to T_{y_i}\mathcal{M}$. Separate from these notations, matrix exponential (and logarithm) are given as $\exp(\cdot)$ (and $\log(\cdot)$).

Intrinsic Mean. Let $d(\cdot, \cdot)$ define the geodesic distance between two points. The intrinsic (or Karcher) mean of a set of points $\{x_i\}$ with non-negative weights $\{w_i\}$ is the minimizer of,

$$\bar{y} = \arg \min_{y \in \mathcal{M}} \sum_{i=1}^{N} w_i d(y, y_i)^2, \qquad (5)$$

which may be an arithmetic, geometric or harmonic mean depending on $d(\cdot, \cdot)$.

On manifolds, the Karcher mean with distance $d(y_i, y_j) = \|\text{Log}_{y_i} y_j\|$ is, $\sum_{i=1}^{N} \text{Log}_{\bar{y}} y_i = 0$. This identity implies that $\bar{y}$ is a local minimum which has a zero norm gradient [22], i.e., the sum of all tangent vectors corresponding to geodesic curves from mean $\bar{y}$ to all points y_i is zero in the tangent space $T_{\bar{y}}\mathcal{M}$. On manifolds, the existence and uniqueness of the Karcher mean is not guaranteed, unless we assume, for uniqueness, that the data is in a small neighborhood.

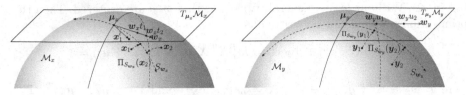

Fig. 1. CCA on Riemannian manifolds. CCA searches geodesic submanifolds (subspaces), S_{w_x} and S_{w_y} at the Karcher mean of data on each manifold. Correlation between projected points $\{\Pi_{S_{w_x}}(\boldsymbol{x}_i)\}_{i=1}^N$ and $\{\Pi_{S_{w_y}}(\boldsymbol{y}_i)\}_{i=1}^N$ is equivalent to the correlation between *projection coefficients* $\{t_i\}_{i=1}^N$ and $\{u_i\}_{i=1}^N$. Although $\boldsymbol{x}$ and $\boldsymbol{y}$ belong to the same manifold we show them in different plots for ease of explanation.

Geodesically Convex. A subset C of $\mathcal{M}$ is said to be a *geodesically convex set* if there is a minimizing geodesic curve in C between *any* two points in C. This assumption is commonly used [8] and essential to ensure that the Riemannian operations such as the exponential and logarithm maps are well-defined.

4   A Model for CCA on Riemannian Manifolds

We now present a step by step derivation of our Riemannian CCA model. Classical CCA finds the mean of each data modality. Then, it maximizes correlation between projected data on each subspace at the mean. Similarly, CCA on manifolds must first compute the intrinsic mean (i.e., Karcher mean) of each data set. It must then identify a 'generalized' version of a subspace at each Karcher mean to maximize the correlation of projected data. The generalized form of a subspace on Riemannian manifolds has been studied in the literature [33,26,20,9]. The so-called *geodesic submanifold* [9,36,23] which has been used for geodesic regression serves our purpose well and is defined as $S = \mathrm{Exp}(\boldsymbol{\mu}, \mathrm{span}(\{\boldsymbol{v}_i\}) \cap U)$, where $U \subset T_{\boldsymbol{\mu}}\mathcal{M}$, and $\boldsymbol{v}_i \in T_{\boldsymbol{\mu}}\mathcal{M}$ [9]. When S has only one tangent vector $\boldsymbol{v}$, then the geodesic submanifold is simply a geodesic curve, see Figure 1.

We can now proceed to formulate the precise form of projection on to a geodesic submanifold. Recall that when given a point, its projection on a set is the closest point in the set. So, the projection on to a geodesic submanifold (S) must be a function satisfying this behavior. This is given by,

$$\Pi_S(\boldsymbol{x}) = \arg \min_{\boldsymbol{x}' \in S} \mathrm{d}(\boldsymbol{x}, \boldsymbol{x}')^2 \tag{6}$$

In Euclidean space, the projection on a convex set (e.g., subspace) is unique. It is also unique on some manifolds under special conditions, e.g., quaternion sphere [30]. However, the uniqueness of the projection on geodesic submanifolds in general conditions cannot be ensured. Like other methods, we assume that given the specific manifold and the data, the projection is well-posed.

Finally, the correlation of points (*after* projection) can be measured by the distance from the mean to the projected points. To be specific, the projection on a geodesic submanifold corresponding to $\boldsymbol{w}_x$ in classical CCA is given by

$$\Pi_{S_{\boldsymbol{w}_x}}(\boldsymbol{x}) := \arg\min_{\boldsymbol{x}' \in S_{\boldsymbol{w}_x}} \|\mathrm{Log}(\boldsymbol{x}, \boldsymbol{x}')\|_{\boldsymbol{x}}^2 \qquad (7)$$

$S_{\boldsymbol{w}_x} := \mathrm{Exp}(\boldsymbol{\mu}_x, \mathrm{span}\{\boldsymbol{w}_x\} \cap U)$ where $\boldsymbol{w}_x$ is a basis tangent vector and $U \subset T_{\boldsymbol{\mu}_x}\mathcal{M}_x$ is a small neighborhood of $\boldsymbol{\mu}_x$. The expression for *projection coefficients* can now be given as

$$t_i = \pi_{\boldsymbol{w}_x}(\boldsymbol{x}_i) := \arg\min_{t_i' \in (-\epsilon, \epsilon)} \|\mathrm{Log}(\mathrm{Exp}(\boldsymbol{\mu}_x, t_i' \boldsymbol{w}_x), \boldsymbol{x}_i)\|_{\boldsymbol{\mu}_x}^2 \qquad (8)$$

where $\boldsymbol{x}_i, \boldsymbol{\mu}_x \in \mathcal{M}_x$, $\boldsymbol{w}_x \in T_{\boldsymbol{\mu}_x}\mathcal{M}_x, t_i \in \mathbf{R}$. The term, $u_i = \pi_{\boldsymbol{w}_y}(\boldsymbol{y})$ is defined analogously. t_i is a real value to obtain the point $\Pi_{S_{\boldsymbol{w}_x}}(\boldsymbol{x}) = \mathrm{Exp}(\boldsymbol{\mu}_x, t_i \boldsymbol{w}_x)$. As mentioned above, $\boldsymbol{x}$ and $\boldsymbol{y}$ belong to the same manifold. Note that we are dealing with a single manifold, however, we use two different notations $\mathcal{M}_x$, and $\mathcal{M}_y$ to show that they are differently distributed for ease of discussion.

Notice that we have $\mathrm{d}(\boldsymbol{\mu}_x, \Pi_{S_{\boldsymbol{w}_x}}(\boldsymbol{x}_i)) = \|\mathrm{Log}(\boldsymbol{\mu}_x, \mathrm{Exp}(\boldsymbol{\mu}_x, \boldsymbol{w}_x t_i))\|_{\boldsymbol{\mu}_x} = t_i \|\boldsymbol{w}_x\|_{\boldsymbol{\mu}_x}$. By inspection, this shows that the projection coefficient is proportional to the length of the geodesic curve from the base point $\boldsymbol{\mu}_x$ to the projection of $\boldsymbol{x}$, $\Pi_{S_{\boldsymbol{w}_x}}(\boldsymbol{x})$. Correlation is scale invariant, as expected. Therefore, the correlation between projected points $\{\Pi_{S_{\boldsymbol{w}_x}}(\boldsymbol{x}_i)\}_{i=1}^N$ and $\{\Pi_{S_{\boldsymbol{w}_y}}(\boldsymbol{y}_i)\}_{i=1}^N$ reduces to the correlation between the quantities that serve as projection coefficients here, $\{t_i\}_{i=1}^N$ and $\{u_i\}_{i=1}^N$.

Putting these pieces together, we obtain our generalized formulation for CCA,

$$\rho_{\boldsymbol{x}, \boldsymbol{y}} = \mathrm{corr}(\pi_{\boldsymbol{w}_x}(\boldsymbol{x}), \pi_{\boldsymbol{w}_y}(\boldsymbol{y})) = \max_{\boldsymbol{w}_x, \boldsymbol{w}_y, t, u} \frac{\sum_{i=1}^N (t_i - \bar{t})(u_i - \bar{u})}{\sqrt{\sum_{i=1}^N (t_i - \bar{t})^2}\sqrt{\sum_{i=1}^N (u_i - \bar{u})^2}} \qquad (9)$$

where $t_i = \pi_{\boldsymbol{w}_x}(\boldsymbol{x}_i)$, $\boldsymbol{t} := \{t_i\}$, $u_i = \pi_{\boldsymbol{w}_y}(\boldsymbol{y}_i)$, $\boldsymbol{u} := \{u_i\}$, $\bar{t} = \frac{1}{N}\sum_{i=1}^N t_i$ and $\bar{u} = \frac{1}{N}\sum_{i=1}^N u_i$. Expanding out components in (9) further, it takes the form,

$$\rho_{\boldsymbol{x}, \boldsymbol{y}} = \max_{\boldsymbol{w}_x, \boldsymbol{w}_y, t, u} \frac{\sum_{i=1}^N (t_i - \bar{t})(u_i - \bar{u})}{\sqrt{\sum_{i=1}^N (t_i - \bar{t})^2}\sqrt{\sum_{i=1}^N (u_i - \bar{u})^2}}$$

$$s.t. \quad t_i = \arg\min_{t_i \in (-\epsilon, \epsilon)} \|\mathrm{Log}(\mathrm{Exp}(\boldsymbol{\mu}_x, t_i \boldsymbol{w}_x), \boldsymbol{x}_i)\|^2, \forall i \in \{1, \ldots, N\} \qquad (10)$$

$$u_i = \arg\min_{u_i \in (-\epsilon, \epsilon)} \|\mathrm{Log}(\mathrm{Exp}(\boldsymbol{\mu}_y, u_i \boldsymbol{w}_y), \boldsymbol{y}_i)\|^2, \forall i \in \{1, \ldots, N\}$$

Directly, we see that (10) is a multilevel optimization and solutions from nested sub-optimization problems may be needed to solve the higher level problem. It turns out that deriving the first order optimality conditions suggests a cleaner approach.

Define $f(\boldsymbol{t}, \boldsymbol{u}) := \frac{\sum_{i=1}^N (t_i - \bar{t})(u_i - \bar{u})}{\sqrt{\sum_{i=1}^N (t_i - \bar{t})^2}\sqrt{\sum_{i=1}^N (u_i - \bar{u})^2}}$, $g(t_i, \boldsymbol{w}_x) := \|\mathrm{Log}(\mathrm{Exp}(\boldsymbol{\mu}_x, t_i \boldsymbol{w}_x), \boldsymbol{x}_i)\|^2$, and $g(u_i, \boldsymbol{w}_y) := \|\mathrm{Log}(\mathrm{Exp}(\boldsymbol{\mu}_y, u_i \boldsymbol{w}_y), \boldsymbol{y}_i)\|^2$. Then, we may replace the equality constraints in (10) with optimality conditions rather than another optimization problem for each i. Using this idea, we have

$$\rho(\boldsymbol{w}_x, \boldsymbol{w}_y) = \max_{\boldsymbol{w}_x, \boldsymbol{w}_y, \boldsymbol{t}, \boldsymbol{u}} f(\boldsymbol{t}, \boldsymbol{u})$$

$$s.t. \ \nabla_{t_i} g(t_i, \boldsymbol{w}_x) = 0, \nabla_{u_i} g(u_i, \boldsymbol{w}_y) = 0, \forall i \in \{1, \ldots, N\} \tag{11}$$

5   Optimization Schemes

We present two different algorithms to solve the problem of computing CCA on Riemannian manifolds. The first algorithm is based on a numerical optimization for (11). We only summarize the main model here and provide all technical details in the extended version for space reasons. Subsequently, we present the second approach which is based on an approximation for a more efficient algorithm.

5.1   An Augmented Lagrangian Method

The augmented Lagrangian technique is a well known variation of the penalty method for constrained optimization problems. Given a constrained optimization problem $\max f(\boldsymbol{x})$ s.t. $c_i(\boldsymbol{x}) = 0, \forall i$, the augmented Lagrangian method solves a sequence of the following models while increasing ν_k.

$$\max f(\boldsymbol{x}) + \sum_i \lambda_i c_i(\boldsymbol{x}) - \nu^k \sum_i c_i(\boldsymbol{x})^2 \tag{12}$$

The augmented Lagrangian formulation for our CCA formulation is given by

$$\max_{\boldsymbol{w}_x, \boldsymbol{w}_y, \boldsymbol{t}, \boldsymbol{u}} \mathcal{L}_A(\boldsymbol{w}_x, \boldsymbol{w}_y, \boldsymbol{t}, \boldsymbol{u}, \boldsymbol{\lambda}^k; \nu^k) = \max_{\boldsymbol{w}_x, \boldsymbol{w}_y, \boldsymbol{t}, \boldsymbol{u}} f(\boldsymbol{t}, \boldsymbol{u}) + \sum_i^N \lambda_{t_i}^k \nabla_{t_i} g(t_i, \boldsymbol{w}_x) +$$

$$\sum_i^N \lambda_{u_i}^k \nabla_{u_i} g(u_i, \boldsymbol{w}_y) - \frac{\nu^k}{2} \left(\sum_{i=1}^N \nabla_{t_i} g(t_i, \boldsymbol{w}_x)^2 + \nabla_{u_i} g(u_i, \boldsymbol{w}_y)^2 \right) \tag{13}$$

The pseudocode for our algorithm is summarized in Algorithm 1.

Remarks. Note that for Algorithm 1, we need the second derivative of g, in particular, for $\frac{d^2}{dwdt}g$, $\frac{d^2}{dt^2}g$. The literature does not provide a great deal of guidance on second derivatives of functions involving $\mathrm{Log}(\cdot)$ and $\mathrm{Exp}(\cdot)$ maps on general Riemannian manifolds. However, depending on the manifold, it can be obtained analytically or numerically (see extended version of the paper).

Approximate strategies. It is clear that the core difficulty in deriving the algorithm above was the lack of a closed form solution to projections on to geodesic submanifolds. If however, an approximate form of the projection can lead to significant gains in computational efficiency with little sacrifice in accuracy, it is worthy of consideration. The simplest approximation is to use a Log-Euclidean model. But it is well known that the Log-Euclidean is reasonable for data that are tightly clustered on the manifold and not otherwise. Further, the Log-Euclidean metric lacks the important property of affine invariance. We can obtain a more

---

Algorithm 1. Riemannian CCA based on the Augmented Lagarangian method

1: $x_1, \ldots, x_N \in \mathcal{M}_x$, $y_1, \ldots, y_N \in \mathcal{M}_y$
2: Given $\nu^0 > 0, \tau^0 > 0$, starting points (w_x^0, w_y^0, t^0, u^0) and $\boldsymbol{\lambda}^0$
3: **for** $k = 0, 1, 2 \ldots$ **do**
4:    Start at (w_x^k, w_y^k, t^k, u^k)
5:    Find an approximate minimizer (w_x^k, w_y^k, t^k, u^k) of $\mathcal{L}_A(\cdot, \boldsymbol{\lambda}^k; \nu^k)$, and terminate when $\|\nabla \mathcal{L}_A(w_x^k, w_y^k, t^k, u^k, \boldsymbol{\lambda}^k; \nu^k)\| \leq \tau^k$
6:    **if** a convergence test for (11) is satisfied **then**
7:       Stop with approximate feasible solution
8:    **end if**
9:    $\lambda_{t_i}^{k+1} = \lambda_{t_i}^k - \nu^k \nabla_{t_i} g(t_i, w_x), \forall i$
10:   $\lambda_{u_i}^{k+1} = \lambda_{u_i}^k - \nu^k \nabla_{u_i} g(u_i, w_y), \forall i$
11:   Choose new penalty parameter $\nu^{k+1} \geq \nu^k$
12:   Set starting point for the next iteration
13:   Select tolerance τ^{k+1}
14: **end for**

Algorithm 2. CCA with approximate projection

1: Input $X_1, \ldots, X_N \in \mathcal{M}_y$, $Y_1, \ldots, Y_N \in \mathcal{M}_y$
2: Compute intrinsic mean $\boldsymbol{\mu}_x, \boldsymbol{\mu}_y$ of $\{X_i\}, \{Y_i\}$
3: Compute $X_i^l = \text{Log}(\boldsymbol{\mu}_x, X_i)$, $Y_i^l = \text{Log}(\boldsymbol{\mu}_y, Y_i)$
4: Transform (using group action) $\{X_i^l\}, \{Y_i^l\}$ to the $T_I \mathcal{M}_x, T_I \mathcal{M}_y$
5: Perform CCA between $T_I \mathcal{M}_x, T_I \mathcal{M}_y$ and get axes $W_a \in T_I \mathcal{M}_x$, $W_b \in T_I \mathcal{M}_y$
6: Transform (using group action) W_a, W_b to $T_{\mu_x} \mathcal{M}_x, T_{\mu_y} \mathcal{M}_y$

---

accurate projection using the submanifold expression given in [36]. The form of projection is,

$$\Pi_S(x) \approx \text{Exp}(\mu, \sum_{i=1}^d v_i \langle v_i, \text{Log}(\mu, x) \rangle_\mu) \qquad (14)$$

where $\{v_i\}$ are *orthonormal basis* at $T_\mu \mathcal{M}$. The CCA algorithm with this approximation for the projection is summarized as Algorithm 2.

Finally, we provide a brief remark on one remaining issue. This relates to the question why we use group action rather than other transformations such as parallel transport. Observe that Algorithm 2 sends the data from the tangent space at the Karcher mean of the samples to the tangent space at Identity I. The purpose of the transformation is to put all samples at the Identity of the SPD manifold, to obtain a more accurate projection, which can be understood using (14). The projection and inner product depend on the anchor point μ. If μ is Identity, then there is no discrepancy between the Euclidean and the Riemannian inner products. Of course, one may use a parallel transport. However, group action may be substantially more efficient than parallel transport since the former does not require computing a geodesic curve (which is needed for parallel transport). Interestingly, it turns out that on SPD manifolds with a GL-invariant metric, parallel transport from an arbitrary point p to Identity I is *equivalent* to the transform using a group action. So, one can parallel transport tangent vectors from p to I using the group action more efficiently. The proof of Theorem 1 is available in the extended version.

Theorem 1. *On SPD manifold, let $\Gamma_{p \to I}(w)$ denote the parallel transport of $w \in T_p\mathcal{M}$ along the geodesic from $p \in \mathcal{M}$ to $I \in \mathcal{M}$. The parallel transport is equivalent to group action by $p^{-1/2}wp^{-T/2}$, where the inner product $\langle u, v \rangle_p = tr(p^{-1/2}up^{-1}vp^{-1/2})$.*

5.2   Extensions to the Product Riemannian Manifold

In the types of imaging datasets of interest in this paper, we seek to perform an analysis on an entire population of images (of multiple types). For such data, each image must be treated as a single entity, which necessitates extending the formulation above to a Riemannian product space.

Let us define a Riemannian metric on the product space $\mathcal{M} = \mathcal{M}_1 \times \ldots \times \mathcal{M}_m$. A natural choice is the following idea from [36].

$$\langle \boldsymbol{X}_1, \boldsymbol{X}_2 \rangle_{\boldsymbol{P}} = \sum_{j=1}^{m} \langle X_1^j, X_2^j \rangle_{P^j} \tag{15}$$

where $\boldsymbol{X}_1 = \left(X_1^1, \ldots, X_1^m\right) \in \mathcal{M}$, and $\boldsymbol{X}_2 = \left(X_2^1, \ldots, X_2^m\right) \in \mathcal{M}$ and $\boldsymbol{P} = \left(P^1, \ldots, P^m\right) \in \mathcal{M}$. Once we have the exponential and logarithm maps, CCA on a Riemannian product space can be directly performed by Algorithm 2. The exponential map $\mathrm{Exp}(\boldsymbol{P}, \boldsymbol{V})$ and logarithm map $\mathrm{Log}(\boldsymbol{P}, \boldsymbol{X})$ are given by

$$(\mathrm{Exp}(P^1, V^1), \ldots, \mathrm{Exp}(P^m, V^m)) \text{ and } (\mathrm{Log}(P^1, X^1), \ldots, \mathrm{Log}(P^m, X^m)) \tag{16}$$

respectively, where $\boldsymbol{V} = (V^1, \ldots, V^m) \in T_{\boldsymbol{P}}\mathcal{M}$. The length of tangent vector is $\|\boldsymbol{V}\| = \sqrt{\|V^1\|_{P^1}^2 + \cdots + \|V^m\|_{P^m}^2}$, where $V^i \in T_{P^i}\mathcal{M}_i$. The geodesic distance between two points $\mathrm{d}(\boldsymbol{X}_1, \boldsymbol{X}_2)$ on Riemannian product space is also measured by the length of tangent vector from one point to the other. So we have

$$\mathrm{d}(\boldsymbol{\mu}_x, \boldsymbol{X}) = \sqrt{\mathrm{d}(\mu_x^1, X^1)^2 + \cdots + \mathrm{d}(\mu_x^m, X^m)^2} \tag{17}$$

From our previous discussion of the relationship between *projection coefficients* and distance from the mean to points (after *projection*) in Section 4, we have $t_i = \mathrm{d}(\boldsymbol{\mu}_x, \Pi_{S_{\boldsymbol{W}_x}}(\boldsymbol{X}_i))/\|\boldsymbol{W}_x\|_{\boldsymbol{\mu}_x}$ and $t_i^j = \mathrm{d}(\mu_x^j, \Pi_{S_{W_x^j}}(X_i^j))/\|W_x^j\|_{\mu_x^j}$. By substitution, the *projection coefficients* on Riemannian product space are given by

$$t_i = \mathrm{d}(\boldsymbol{\mu}_x, \Pi_{S_{\boldsymbol{W}_x}}(\boldsymbol{X}_i))/\|\boldsymbol{W}_x\|_{\boldsymbol{\mu}_x} = \sqrt{\sum_{j}^{m} \left(t_i^j \|W_x^j\|_{\mu_x^j} \right)^2 / \sum_{j=1}^{m} \|W_x^j\|_{\mu_x^j}^2} \tag{18}$$

We can now mechanically substitute these "product space" versions of the terms in (18) to derive a CCA on Riemannian product space. The full model is provided in the extended version.

6   Experiments

6.1   CCA on SPD Manifolds

Diffusion tensors are symmetric positive definite matrices at each voxel in DTI. Let SPD(n) be a manifold for symmetric positive definite matrices of size $n \times n$. This forms a quotient space $GL(n)/O(n)$, where $GL(n)$ denotes the general linear group and $O(n)$ is the orthogonal group. The inner product of two tangent vectors $u, v \in T_p\mathcal{M}$ is given by $\langle u, v \rangle_p = \mathrm{tr}(p^{-1/2}up^{-1}vp^{-1/2})$. Here, $T_p\mathcal{M}$ is a tangent space at p (which is a vector space) is the space of symmetric matrices of dimension $(n+1)n/2$. The geodesic distance is $d(p,q)^2 = \mathrm{tr}(\log^2(p^{-1/2}qp^{-1/2}))$.

Here, the exponential map and logarithm map are defined as,

$$\mathrm{Exp}(p,v) = p^{1/2}\exp(p^{-1/2}vp^{-1/2})p^{1/2}, \quad \mathrm{Log}(p,q) = p^{1/2}\log(p^{-1/2}qp^{-1/2})p^{1/2} \quad (19)$$

and the first derivative of g in equation (11) on SPD(n) is given by

$$
\begin{aligned}
\frac{d}{dt_i}g(t_i, \boldsymbol{w}_x) &= \frac{d}{dt_i}\|\mathrm{Log}(\mathrm{Exp}(\mu_x, t_iW_x), X_i)\|^2 = \frac{d}{dt_i}\mathrm{tr}[\log^2(X_i^{-1}S(t_i))] \\
&= 2\mathrm{tr}[\log(X_i^{-1}S(t_i))S(t_i)^{-1}\dot{S}(t_i)], \text{ according to Prop. 2.1 in [28]}
\end{aligned}
\quad (20)
$$

where $S(t_i) = \mathrm{Exp}(\mu_x, t_iW_x) = \mu_x^{1/2}\exp^{t_iA}\mu_x^{1/2}$, and $\dot{S}(t_i) = \mu_x^{1/2}A\exp^{t_iA}\mu_x^{1/2}$ and $A = \mu_x^{-1/2}W_x\mu_x^{-1/2}$. The derivative of equality constraints, namely $\frac{d^2}{dWdt}g$, $\frac{d^2}{dt^2}g$ are calculated by numerical derivatives. Embedding the tangent vectors in the $n(n+1)/2$ dimensional space with orthonormal basis in the tangent space enables one to compute numerical differentiation. Details are provided in the extended paper.

6.2   Synthetic Experiments

In this section we provide experimental results using a synthetic dataset to evaluate the performance of Riemannian CCA. The samples are generated to be spread far apart on the manifold $\mathcal{M}(\equiv \mathrm{SPD}(3))$ so that the curvature of the manifold plays a key role in the maximization of the correlation function. In order to sample data from different regions of the manifold, we generate data around two well separated means $\mu_{x_1}, \mu_{x_2} \in \mathcal{X}$, $\mu_{y_1}, \mu_{y_2} \in \mathcal{Y}$ by perturbing the data randomly (see the extended version) in the corresponding tangent spaces. Fig. 2 shows the CCA results obtained by Riemannian and Euclidean methods. We can clearly see the improvements from the manifold approach by inspecting the correlation coefficients $\rho_{x,y}$ on the respective titles.

6.3   CCA for Multi-modal Risk Analysis

Motivation: We collected multi-modal magnetic resonance imaging (MRI) data to investigate the effects of risk for Alzheimer's disease (AD) on the white and gray matter in the brain. One of the central goals in analyzing this rich dataset

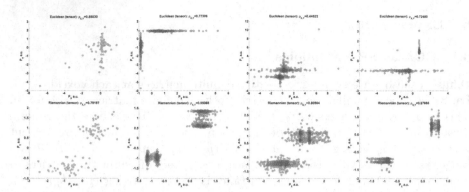

Fig. 2. Synthetic experiments showing the benefits of Riemannian CCA. The top row shows the projected data using the Euclidean CCA and the bottom using Riemannian CCA. P_X and P_Y denote the projected axes. Each column represents a synthetic experiment with a specific set of $\{\mu_{x_j}, \epsilon_{x_j}; \mu_{y_j}, \epsilon_{y_j}\}$. The first column presents results with 100 samples while the three columns on the right show with 1000 samples. The improvements in the correlation coefficients $\rho_{x,y}$ can be clearly seen from the corresponding titles.

is to find statistically significant AD risk $\leftrightarrow$ brain relationships. We can adopt many different ways of modeling these relationships but a potentially useful way is to analyze multi modality imaging data simultaneously, using CCA.

Risk for AD is characterized by their familial history (FH) status as well as APOE genotype risk factor. In the current experiments, we include a subset of 343 subjects and first investigate the effects of age and gender in a multimodal fashion since these variables are also important factors in healthy aging.

Brain structure is characterized by diffusion weighted images (DWI) for white matter and T1-weighted (T1W) image data for the gray matter. DWI data provides us information about the microstructure of the white matter. We use diffusion tensor ($\mathcal{D} \in \mathrm{SPD}(3)$) model to represent the diffusivity in the microstructure. T1W data can be used to obtain volumetric properties of the gray-matter. The volumetric information is obtained from Jacobian matrices (J) of the diffeomorphic mapping to a population specific template. These Jacobian matrices can be used to obtain the Cauchy deformation tensors which also belong to SPD(3).

Hippocampus and cingulum bundle (shown in Fig. 3) are two important regions in the brain. They are *a priori* believed to be significant in AD$\leftrightarrow$brain structure relationships, primarily due to the role of hippocampus in memory function and the projections of cingulum onto the hippocampus. However, detecting *risk*-brain relationships *before* the memory/cognitive function is impaired is difficult due to several factors (such as noise in the data, small sample and effect sizes, type I error due to multiple comparisons.). One approach to improve the statistical power in such a setting would be to perform tests on average properties in regions of interest (ROI) in the brain. This procedure reduces both noise and the number of comparisons/tests. However, taking averages will also dampen the signal of interest which is already weak in such pre-clinical studies.

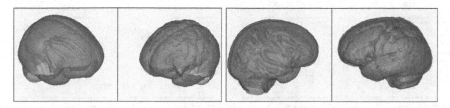

Fig. 3. Shown on the left are the bilateral cingulum bundles (green) inside a brain surface obtained from a population DTI template. Similarly on the right are the bilateral hippocampi. The gray and white matter ROIs are also shown on the right.

CCA can take the multi-modal information from the imaging data and project the voxels into a space where the signal of interest is likely to be stronger.

Experimental Design: The key multimodal linear relations we examine are

$$Y_{\text{DTI}} = \beta_0 + \beta_1 \text{Gender} + \beta_2 X_{\text{T1W}} + \beta_3 X_{\text{T1W}} \cdot \text{Gender} + \varepsilon,$$
$$Y_{\text{DTI}} = \beta_0' + \beta_1' \text{AgeGroup} + \beta_2' X_{\text{T1W}} + \beta_3' X_{\text{T1W}} \cdot \text{AgeGroup} + \varepsilon,$$

where the AgeGroup is defined as a categorical variable with 0 (middle aged) if the age of the subject ≤ 65 and 1 (old) otherwise. The sample under investigation is between 43 and 75 years of age. The statistical tests ask if we can reject the Null hypotheses $\beta_3 = 0$ and $\beta_3' = 0$ using our data at $\alpha = 0.05$. We report the results from the following four sets of analyses: **(i)** Classical ROI-average analysis: This is a standard type of setting where the brain measurements in an ROI are averaged. Here $Y_{\text{DTI}} = \overline{\text{MD}}$ i.e., the average mean diffusivity in the cingulum bundle. $X_{\text{T1W}} = \overline{\log |J|}$ i.e., the average volumetric change (relative to the population template) in the hippocampus. **(ii)** Euclidean CCA using scalar measures (MD and $\log |J|$) in the ROIs: Here, the voxel data is projected using the classical CCA approach [35] i.e., $Y_{\text{DTI}} = \mathbf{w}_{\text{MD}}^T \text{MD}$ and $X_{\text{T1W}} = \mathbf{w}_{\log |J|}^T \log |J|$. **(iii)** Euclidean CCA using $\mathcal{D}$ and $\mathcal{J}$ in the ROIs: This setting is an improvement to the setting above in that the projections are performed using the full tensor data [35]. Here $Y_{\text{DTI}} = \mathbf{w}_{\mathcal{D}}^T \mathcal{D}$ and $X_{\text{T1W}} = \mathbf{w}_{\mathcal{J}}^T \mathcal{J}$. **(iv)** Riemannian CCA using $\mathcal{D}$ and $\mathcal{J}$ in the ROIs: Here $Y_{\text{DTI}} = \langle \mathbf{w}_{\mathcal{D}}, \mathcal{D} \rangle_{\mu_{\mathcal{D}}}$ and $X_{\text{T1W}} = \langle \mathbf{w}_{\mathcal{J}}, \mathcal{J} \rangle_{\mu_{\mathcal{J}}}$.

The findings are shown in Fig. 4. We can see that the performance of CCA using the full tensor information improves the statistical significance for both Euclidean and Riemannian approaches. The weight vectors in the different settings for both Euclidean and Riemannian CCA are shown in Fig. 5 top row. We would like to note that there are several different approaches of using the data from CCA and we performed experiments with full gray matter and white matter regions in the brain whose results are included in the extended version. We show the representative weight vectors (in Fig. 5 bottom row) obtained using the full brain analyses. Interestingly, the weight vectors are spatially cohesive even without enforcing any spatial constraints. What is even more remarkable is that the regions picked between the DTI and T1W modalities are complimentary in a biological sense. Specifically, when performing our CCA on the ROIs, although the cingulum bundle extends into the superior mid-brain regions the weights are

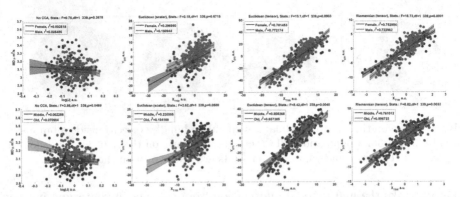

Fig. 4. Experimental evidence showing the improvements in statistical significance of finding the multi-modal risk-brain interaction effects. Top row shows the gender, volume and diffusivity interactions. Second row shows the interaction effects of the middle/old age groups.

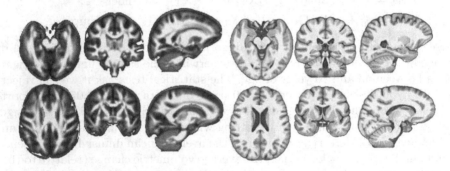

Fig. 5. Weight vectors (in red-yellow color) obtained from our Riemannian CCA approach. The weights are in arbitrary units. The top row is from applying Riemannian CCA on data from the cingulum and hippocampus ROIs (Fig. 3) while the bottom row is obtained using data from the entire white and gray matter regions of the brain. On the left (three columns) block we show the results in orthogonal view for DTI and on the right for T1W. The corresponding underlays are the population averages of the fractional anisotropy and T1W contrast images respectively.

non-zero in its hippocampal projections. In the case of entire white and gray matter regions, the volumetric difference (from the population template) in the inferior part of the corpus callosum seem to be highly cross-correlated to the diffusivity in the corpus callosum. Our CCA finds these projections without any a priori constraints in the optimization suggesting that performing CCA on the intrinsic nature of the data can reveal biologically meaningful patterns. Due to space constraints, we refer the interested reader to the extended version of the paper for additional details.

7 Conclusion

The classical CCA assumes that data live in a pair of vector spaces. However, many modern scientific disciplines require the analysis of data which belong to *curved* spaces where classical CCA is no longer applicable. Motivated by the properties of imaging data from neuroimaging studies, we generalize CCA to Riemannian manifolds. We employ differential geometry tools to extend operations in CCA to the manifold setting. Such a formulation results in a multi-level optimization problem. We derive solutions using the first order condition of projection and an augmented Lagrangian method. In addition, we also develop an efficient single path algorithm with approximate projections. Finally, we propose a generalization to the product space of SPD(n), namely, tensor fields allowing us to treat a full brain image as a point on the product manifold. On the experimental side, we presented neuroimaging findings using our proposed CCA on DTI and T1W imaging modalities on an Alzheimer's disease (AD) dataset focused on risk factors for this disease. Here, the proposed methods perform well and yield scientifically meaningful results. In closing, we note that our core optimization methods can be readily applied when maximizing correlation between data from two *different* types of Riemannian manifolds — this may open the doors to various other types of analysis not explicitly investigated in this paper.

Acknowledgments. This work was supported in part by NIH grants AG040396 (VS), AG037639 (BBB), AG021155 (SCJ), AG027161 (SCJ), NS066340 (BCV) and NSF CAREER award 1252725 (VS). Partial support was also provided by UW ADRC, UW ICTR, and Waisman Core grant P30 HD003352-45. The contents do not represent views of the Dept. of Veterans Affairs or the United States Government.

References

1. Akaho, S.: A kernel method for canonical correlation analysis. In: International Meeting on Psychometric Society (2001)
2. Andrew, G., Arora, R., Bilmes, J., Livescu, K.: Deep canonical correlation analysis. In: ICML (2013)
3. Avants, B.B., Cook, P.A., Ungar, L., Gee, J.C., Grossman, M.: Dementia induces correlated reductions in white matter integrity and cortical thickness: a multivariate neuroimaging study with SCCA. Neuroimage 50(3), 1004–1016 (2010)
4. Bach, F.R., Jordan, M.I.: Kernel independent component analysis. The Journal of Machine Learning Research 3, 1–48 (2003)
5. Callaghan, P.T.: Principles of nuclear magnetic resonance microscopy. Oxford University Press (1991)
6. Chung, M., Worsley, K., Paus, T., Cherif, C., Collins, D., Giedd, J., Rapoport, J., Evans, A.: A unified statistical approach to deformation-based morphometry. NeuroImage 14(3), 595–606 (2001)
7. Do Carmo, M.P.: Riemannian geometry (1992)
8. Fletcher, P.T.: Geodesic regression and the theory of least squares on riemannian manifolds. International Journal of Computer Vision 105(2), 171–185 (2013)

9. Fletcher, P.T., Lu, C., Pizer, S.M., Joshi, S.: Principal geodesic analysis for the study of nonlinear statistics of shape. Medical Imaging 23(8), 995–1005 (2004)
10. Goh, A., Lenglet, C., Thompson, P.M., Vidal, R.: A nonparametric Riemannian framework for processing high angular resolution diffusion images (HARDI), pp. 2496–2503 (2009)
11. Hardoon, D.R., Szedmak, S., Shawe-Taylor, J.: CCA: An overview with application to learning methods. Neural Computation 16(12), 2639–2664 (2004)
12. Hardoon, D.R., et al.: Unsupervised analysis of fMRI data using kernel canonical correlation. NeuroImage 37(4), 1250–1259 (2007)
13. Hinkle, J., Fletcher, P.T., Joshi, S.: Intrinsic polynomials for regression on Riemannian manifolds. Journal of Mathematical Imaging and Vision, 1–21 (2014)
14. Ho, J., Xie, Y., Vemuri, B.: On a nonlinear generalization of sparse coding and dictionary learning. In: ICML, pp. 1480–1488 (2013)
15. Hotelling, H.: Relations between two sets of variates. Biometrika 28(3/4), 321–377 (1936)
16. Hsieh, W.W.: Nonlinear canonical correlation analysis by neural networks. Neural Networks 13(10), 1095–1105 (2000)
17. Hua, X., Gutman, B., et al.: Accurate measurement of brain changes in longitudinal MRI scans using tensor-based morphometry. Neuroimage 57(1), 5–14 (2011)
18. Hua, X., Leow, A.D., Parikshak, N., Lee, S., Chiang, M.C., Toga, A.W., Jack Jr., C.R., Weiner, M.W., Thompson, P.M.: Tensor-based morphometry as a neuroimaging biomarker for Alzheimer's disease: an MRI study of 676 AD, MCI, and normal subjects. Neuroimage 43(3), 458–469 (2008)
19. Huang, H., He, H., Fan, X., Zhang, J.: Super-resolution of human face image using canonical correlation analysis. Pattern Recognition 43(7), 2532–2543 (2010)
20. Huckemann, S., Hotz, T., Munk, A.: Intrinsic shape analysis: Geodesic PCA for Riemannian manifolds modulo isometric Lie group actions. Statistica Sinica 20, 1–100 (2010)
21. Jayasumana, S., Hartley, R., Salzmann, M., Li, H., Harandi, M.: Kernel methods on the Riemannian manifold of symmetric positive definite matrices. In: CVPR, pp. 73–80 (2013)
22. Karcher, H.: Riemannian center of mass and mollifier smoothing. Communications on Pure and Applied Mathematics 30(5), 509–541 (1977)
23. Kim, H.J., Adluru, N., Collins, M.D., Chung, M.K., Bendlin, B.B., Johnson, S.C., Davidson, R.J., Singh, V.: Multivariate general linear models (MGLM) on Riemannian manifolds with applications to statistical analysis of diffusion weighted images. In: CVPR (2014)
24. Kim, T.K., Cipolla, R.: CCA of video volume tensors for action categorization and detection. PAMI 31(8), 1415–1428 (2009)
25. Lai, P.L., Fyfe, C.: A neural implementation of canonical correlation analysis. Neural Networks 12(10), 1391–1397 (1999)
26. Lebanon, G., et al.: Riemannian geometry and statistical machine learning. Ph.D. thesis, Carnegie Mellon University, Language Technologies Institute, School of Computer Science (2005)
27. Li, P., Wang, Q., Zuo, W., Zhang, L.: Log-Euclidean kernels for sparse representation and dictionary learning. In: ICCV, pp. 1601–1608 (2013)
28. Moakher, M.: A differential geometric approach to the geometric mean of symmetric positive-definite matrices. SIAM Journal on Matrix Analysis and Applications 26(3), 735–747 (2005)
29. Niethammer, M., Huang, Y., Vialard, F.X.: Geodesic regression for image time-series. In: MICCAI, pp. 655–662 (2011)

CCA on Riemannian Manifolds 267

30. Said, S., Courty, N., Le Bihan, N., Sangwine, S.J., et al.: Exact principal geodesic analysis for data on SO(3). In: Proceedings of the 15th European Signal Processing Conference, pp. 1700–1705 (2007)
31. Shi, X., Styner, M., Lieberman, J., Ibrahim, J.G., Lin, W., Zhu, H.: Intrinsic regression models for manifold-valued data. In: Yang, G.-Z., Hawkes, D., Rueckert, D., Noble, A., Taylor, C. (eds.) MICCAI 2009, Part II. LNCS, vol. 5762, pp. 192–199. Springer, Heidelberg (2009)
32. Sommer, S.: Horizontal dimensionality reduction and iterated frame bundle development. In: Nielsen, F., Barbaresco, F. (eds.) GSI 2013. LNCS, vol. 8085, pp. 76–83. Springer, Heidelberg (2013)
33. Sommer, S., Lauze, F., Nielsen, M.: Optimization over geodesics for exact principal geodesic analysis. Advances in Computational Mathematics, 1–31
34. Steinke, F., Hein, M., Schölkopf, B.: Nonparametric regression between general Riemannian manifolds. SIAM Journal on Imaging Sciences 3(3), 527–563 (2010)
35. Witten, D.M., Tibshirani, R., Hastie, T.: A penalized matrix decomposition, with applications to sparse principal components and canonical correlation analysis. Biostatistics 10(3), 515–534 (2009)
36. Xie, Y., Vemuri, B.C., Ho, J.: Statistical analysis of tensor fields. In: Jiang, T., Navab, N., Pluim, J.P.W., Viergever, M.A. (eds.) MICCAI 2010, Part I. LNCS, vol. 6361, pp. 682–689. Springer, Heidelberg (2010)
37. Yger, F., Berar, M., Gasso, G., Rakotomamonjy, A.: Adaptive canonical correlation analysis based on matrix manifolds. In: ICML (2012)
38. Yu, S., Tan, T., Huang, K., Jia, K., Wu, X.: A study on gait-based gender classification. IEEE Transactions on Image Processing 18(8), 1905–1910 (2009)
39. Zhu, H., Chen, Y., Ibrahim, J.G., Li, Y., Hall, C., Lin, W.: Intrinsic regression models for positive-definite matrices with applications to diffusion tensor imaging. Journal of the American Statistical Association 104(487) (2009)

Scalable 6-DOF Localization on Mobile Devices

Sven Middelberg[1], Torsten Sattler[2], Ole Untzelmann[1], and Leif Kobbelt[1]

[1] Computer Graphics Group, RWTH Aachen University, Aachen, Germany
[2] Department of Computer Science, ETH Zürich, Zürich, Switzerland

Abstract. Recent improvements in image-based localization have produced powerful methods that scale up to the massive 3D models emerging from modern Structure-from-Motion techniques. However, these approaches are too resource intensive to run in real-time, let alone to be implemented on mobile devices. In this paper, we propose to combine the scalability of such a global localization system running on a server with the speed and precision of a local pose tracker on a mobile device. Our approach is both scalable and drift-free by design and eliminates the need for loop closure. We propose two strategies to combine the information provided by local tracking and global localization. We evaluate our system on a large-scale dataset of the historic inner city of Aachen where it achieves interactive framerates at a localization error of less than 50cm while using less than 5MB of memory on the mobile device.

1 Introduction

Determining both position and orientation of a camera relative to a 3D model of a scene, also referred to as the image-based localization problem [26], is an important step in many applications, such as location recognition [21,26], navigation [10,16,30,22,24], and Augmented Reality (AR) [17,8,18,25].

We distinguish between two fundamental approaches to solve the image-based localization problem. *Local* methods operate in unknown environments, using simultaneous localization and mapping (SLAM) techniques to concurrently construct a 3D model and estimate the camera pose relative to it [8,9,11,17]. Due to the limited computational capabilities of mobile devices like smartphones and tablet PCs, local approaches for mobile localization, *e.g.*, PTAM [8,17], are usually confined to small workspaces. In contrast, *global* localization approaches assume that a 3D model of the scene is already available. Recent progress in Structure-from-Motion (SfM), allowing the rapid reconstruction of large scenes consisting of millions of 3D points [1], has lead to a focus on global image-based localization methods that are able to scale to such large datasets [21,26]. These approaches achieve impressive localization performance, but rely on powerful and memory intensive local descriptors such as SIFT [23] to establish 2D-3D matches between image features and scene points. As a result, they require computation and memory capacities that significantly exceed what current mobile devices can offer. Especially localization scenarios for micro aerial vehicles [30,24] place

D. Fleet et al. (Eds.): ECCV 2014, Part II, LNCS 8690, pp. 268–283, 2014.

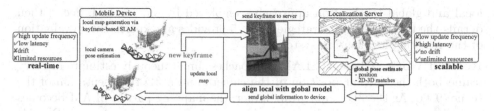

Fig. 1. We use a small local map, constructed on the mobile device, to perform real-time pose estimation. The keyframes used for the reconstruction are also send to a localization server to align the local map to the server reconstruction.

very hard restrictions on the available hardware due to weight and power constraints. Nevertheless, the flexibility of mobile devices creates a strong need for large-scale mobile localization, *e.g.*, for city-scale augmented reality. Recently, Lim *et al.* [22] and Ventura and Höllerer [29] proposed approaches for real-time, large-scale mobile pose tracking. However, both approaches require to keep a 3D model of the environment on the device, which can already consume more than 100MB for a scene of size 8m × 5m [22], limiting their applicability for mobile devices with their hard memory restrictions.

In this paper, we propose a truly scalable approach that is both real-time capable and memory efficient and thus ideally suited for mobile devices. The key idea, illustrated in Fig. 1, is to combine the information provided by local pose estimation running on the device and a global localization method running on an external server. Our system tracks the camera relative to a local map, built and maintained on the device using keyframe-based SLAM [17], in real-time. The localization server then provides global position estimates for the keyframes, allowing us to align the local map with the global one. Since the device only needs a small map of the relevant part of the scene, the run-time of the resulting algorithm is *independent of the size of the global model*. Since the global pose estimates are drift-free, there is no need to explicitly handle loop-closures.

2 Overall Approach

While very intuitive, our combination of local and global localization introduces some interesting challenges, as it requires to align two different coordinate systems. For this, we need to take into account that the accuracy of global pose estimates is unknown and incorporate means to detect and handle inaccurate global poses. In addition, the local mapping and tracking method has to be robust enough to handle a delay of up to multiple seconds before the global pose estimates are available, which is caused by the latency of querying the localization server. As the main contribution of our paper, we therefore propose two distinct alignment strategies, compare them experimentally in terms of localization accuracy and demonstrate that both strategies result in an image-based localization system that runs in real-time on mobile devices.

The paper is structured as follows. The remainder of this section reviews related work. Sec. 2 gives an overview of our approach, while Sec. 3 explains the local and global localization approaches employed by our method. Sec. 4 then details the two alignment strategies. Sec. 5 provides an experimental evaluation of the resulting localization systems.

Related Work. Classical SLAM approaches simultaneously estimate in every frame both the current position of the camera and a 3D representation of the scene [9,11]. As the 3D maps grows larger, the mapping part of SLAM becomes more expensive. To handle larger maps, *parallel tracking and mapping* (PTAM) approaches decouple the tracking and mapping part into two separate threads to prevent that mapping slows down tracking [17]. The mapping thread uses SfM techniques such as bundle adjustment [28] to generate a high quality map from certain *keyframes*. Advanced PTAM approaches are able to handle multiple 3D maps [8] or to run on mobile phones [18]. In contrast to SLAM and PTAM, which construct sparse maps from features found in images, *dense tracking and mapping* (DTAM) builds a dense 3D model by estimating depth maps [25]. This allows to track every pixel using the photometric error, which is much more stable under rapid movement than feature-based tracking. However, a powerful GPU is required to construct the map in real-time.

The localization approach of Arth *et al.* [5] uses SURF-like features [6] to determine the pose of a camera relative to a small 3D model. The model is kept out-of-core and is manually divided into multiple segments that fit into the memory of a mobile phone. Lim *et al.* propose to avoid complex, scale-invariant features [22]. Starting from an SfM point cloud, they extract more efficient descriptors for every 3D point across multiple scales to simulate scale-invariance. Once a pose is estimated from 2D-3D matches, they try to track the matching points over time using binary BRIEF descriptors [7]. Direct 2D-3D matching is only triggered if the number of currently tracked points is less than a threshold. The matching is distributed over several frames to keep processing times low. Ventura and Höllerer [29] propose to query an image-based localization server to estimate the camera pose of the first image, allowing subsequent real-time pose tracking relative to the server-side 3D model, which is also kept locally on the mobile device. To efficiently match features in the following images to this model, the pose of the previous image is used to cull 3D points behind the camera and outside the image. Image features are then matched to the remaining points via a patch-based approach similar to that of Klein and Murray [18].

In order to obtain an image-based localization method that is able to run in real-time on mobile devices with restricted computational and memory capabilities and that scales to very large datasets, *e.g.*, to a city-scale, we exploit the distinct advantages of local and global pose estimation approaches. Currently, global localization approaches do not achieve the interactive response times required for continuous camera pose tracking and are computationally too complex to run on mobile devices [21,26]. Thus, we employ a keyframe-based PTAM technique [17] to construct a local map of the environment on the mobile device itself and use it to track the camera pose in real-time [17,8]. While the keyframes are used to reconstruct the scene locally, we also send the corresponding images to a localization server, which computes and returns global localization results, *e.g.*, the position of the keyframe with respect to the server's 3D model. This global information is utilized to align the local map to the global server-side reconstruction. Hence, having properly aligned the local map to the global reconstruction, local tracking produces globally registered camera poses. Since the camera pose is tracked solely with respect to the globally aligned local map, the processing time and memory footprint on the mobile device only depend on its size, which, in turn, scales with the number of keyframes. The number of keyframes, however, increases with the length of the sequence. Thus, we keep only the currently relevant parts of the scene in the local map, by limiting the number of keyframes.

The crucial aspect of our approach is the alignment of the local map to the global reconstruction. If done right, this alignment implicitly avoids that our local model is affected by drift since the global localization is drift free. However, a simple affine transformation between the two coordinate frames is clearly not enough as avoiding drift requires us to non-affinely adapt the local map. To avoid drift, we need to carefully integrate the global information directly into the construction and refinement of the local map. There are two major aspects that need to be considered when performing such an integration. The first is that both the poses estimated locally on the device itself and the global information are not perfect but have certain, unrelated errors, which have to be handled accordingly to obtain a stable alignment, which preserves the consistency of the local map. The second challenge lies in the latency induced by sending an image to the server over 3G, 4G, or WiFi. The latter problem is overcome by decoupling pose tracking with respect to the local map from mapping and global alignment using two separate threads as in PTAM [17]. This way, local pose tracking can be continued, while the mapping thread handles the global alignment.

As a main contribution of this paper, we propose two strategies for incorporating global pose information into the local-to-global alignment process. The first strategy adapts the local map in a way that it aligns the keyframe positions estimated locally on the device with the corresponding global positions provided by the server, similar to the approach for fusion of SfM and GPS proposed by Lhuillier [20]. While this is a quite intuitive strategy, it is susceptible to inaccuracies in the global pose estimates. We therefore propose a second strategy that directly relies on the global 2D-3D matches used by the server to estimate the global poses instead of the keyframe positions themselves. We will discuss these two strategies in more detail in Sec. 4 before we compare them experimentally in Sec. 5. In the following, we offer a brief description of the local and global pose estimation methods currently employed by our method.

3 Local and Global Pose Estimation

Our localization approach consists of two separate modules handling the local and global camera pose estimation, respectively. The local pose estimation part, performed on the mobile device itself, has to run in real-time. Thus, we employ the inexpensive BRISK detector and its binary descriptor [19]. We consider only one scale-space octave and use a 256 bit, scale- but non-rotation-invariant version of the descriptor. The task of the global localization process, running on an external server, is to provide the information required to align the local map to the globally, geo-registered server reconstruction.

3.1   Local Pose Tracking Using SLAM

Following a PTAM approach [17], we use separate CPU threads for camera pose estimation and local map construction and alignment, since the latter does not need to run in real-time. We use some of the optimizations proposed by Lim *et al.* [22], such as simpler descriptors for tracking, to accelerate localization.[1]

Initializing the Local Model. Given two images, taken from viewpoints different enough to guarantee a certain baseline and similar enough to share enough feature matches, we initialize the local 3D model of the scene using SfM techniques [17]. Since IMUs belong to the standard equipment of modern smartphones and tablets, we exploit knowledge about the gravity direction by using a 3-point-relative-pose solver [13] to estimate the essential matrix inside a RANSAC loop [12]. We assume that the camera of the device is calibrated, but the internal calibration required by the solver could also be provided from the localization server. The initial local map is then obtained using triangulation followed by bundle adjustment [28].

Local Camera Pose Estimation. Following Lim *et al.*, we try to avoid BRISK descriptor matching between image features and scene points. Instead, we prefer to track already matched 3D points using simple 8×8 intensity patches as local descriptors. We extract the intensity patches only for BRISK keypoints in a 24×24 window surrounding the positions of the 3D points projected into the previous frame. The camera pose is then estimated using a 3-point-absolute-pose solver inside a RANSAC loop [12]. We consider a pose as valid if it has at least 10 inliers. To account for changes in viewpoint and scene structure that may occur during long sequences, we adapt the BRISK detection threshold dynamically following a simple strategy. With each new keyframe, we set the detection threshold to the maximal value, with which at least a number of η keypoints are found in the image. However, we enforce a lower limit of 30 for the detection threshold, to prevent the detection of features due to image noise. The value η is a framework parameter, which will be evaluated in Sec. 5.

Local Map Update. Once we have determined the pose of the current frame, we check whether it fulfills the keyframe properties and should thus be used to extend the local map. As in PTAM [17], the current frame becomes a keyframe if it could be successfully localized and it has a certain minimal distance to all previous keyframes. Additionally, to account for fast camera motion and viewpoint changes, we select a frame as a keyframe if the number of pose inliers is low and the majority of inliers is located in either the lower, upper, left or right half of the image. We then triangulate new map points from 2D-2D matches to the previous keyframes and apply bundle adjustment [28]. In order to limit the

---

[1] An iOS demo is available at http://www.graphics.rwth-aachen.de/localization.

computational load of maintaining the local map and its size in memory, we limit the number of keyframes to κ, which is an additional framework parameter. If more than κ keyframes are present, we delete the one that has the largest distance to the new keyframe. All associations between the deleted keyframe and points in the local map are removed. Finally, 3D points that are not observed by at least two of the remaining keyframes are deleted entirely.

3.2   Server-Based Global Localization

Besides using the keyframes to extend and refine the local map, we also send each of them to the localization server to obtain localization information relative to a large, global model, which covers the entire scene. We assume that the global model was reconstructed using SfM and we associate each 3D point with the RootSIFT descriptors [3,23] found in the images used for feature matching. Once we receive a keyframe, we employ the publicly available implementation by Sattler *et al.* [26] to establish 2D-3D matches between SIFT features found in the received image and the 3D points in the scene. Since we assume a calibrated camera, we also send its focal length to the server and apply a 3-point-absolute-pose solver to estimate the camera pose inside a RANSAC loop [12]. The resulting pose is accepted as correct if it has at least 12 inliers [26] and we subsequently refine the pose iteratively. Besides reporting the estimated position to the mobile device, we also send the 2D feature and 3D point positions of the inlier matches used to estimate the poses. Since [26] stops matching after finding 100 matches, the overhead of additionally transmitting the inlier data is negligible.

4   Aligning the Local Map Globally

The two crucial aspects of our localization approach are the alignment of the local map to a global, well-defined coordinate frame, as well as the prevention of drift. The latter cannot be accomplished by loop-closure methods, since only a constant number of keyframes is kept. Instead, the key idea of our framework is to manage both issues by exploiting the global, drift-free information provided by the localization server. The most simple approach to obtain such an alignment is to compute the affine transformation that best aligns the local and global keyframe positions. However, such a transformation does not correct inherent inaccuracies of the local map and thus cannot prevent drift. Instead, we need to incorporate the global localization information directly into the construction of the local map to enable a non-affine alignment. In the following, we first introduce our notation. We then detail our two alignment strategies outlined in Sec. 2. Both strategies are based on the idea of using global information in the bundle adjustment to "anchor" the local map. To prevent drift, we incorporate these constraints not only into the initial bundle adjustment after the map has been initialized, but also into the bundle adjustments that go along with the keyframe updates. The first method thereby uses the global keyframe positions while the second exploits the global 2D-3D matches between the images and the server reconstruction that were originally used to estimate the global poses. One might argue that it would also be reasonable to use 3D-3D correspondences between the local and global map points in the alignment. However, the local points are reconstructed from BRISK features [19] and the global points from SIFT features [23]. Thus, we do not expect a significant overlap between both point sets. Since we aim to achieve an as loose coupling as possible between the local tracker and the global localization approach to maintain a high degree of modularity, we consider the requirement that both map points are reconstructed from the same features too restrictive. For this reason, we do not explore the use of 3D-3D correspondences, although it might help in the alignment.

Let $\mathbf{P}_j^L$ and $\mathbf{P}_j^G$ denote the position of the j-th 3D point in the local and global map, respectively. Consequently, let $\mathbf{p}_j^i$ be the observed image position of the j-th point in the i-th keyframe. The local and global poses of a keyframe are defined by rotation matrices R_i^L, R_i^G and positions $\mathbf{t}_i^L$, $\mathbf{t}_i^G$ in the local and global coordinate system, respectively. Furthermore, let K_i denote the intrinsic matrix of the i-th keyframe. Since we assume a calibrated setting, K_i is known. Bundle adjustment adapts the camera parameters R_i^L, $\mathbf{t}_i^L$ and points $\mathbf{P}_j^L$ in order to minimize the sum of squared reprojection errors

$$\chi_1 = \sum_i \sum_j \delta_{i,j} \cdot d(\mathbf{p}_j^i, \mathrm{K}_i \mathrm{R}_i^L (\mathbf{P}_j^L - \mathbf{t}_i^L))^2 \ . \tag{1}$$

Here, $\delta_{i,j} \in \{0,1\}$ indicates whether the j-th point is visible in the i-th keyframe and $d(\mathbf{x}, \mathbf{y})$ is the 2D Euclidean distance between the 2D positions $\mathbf{x}$ and $\mathbf{y}$. The term $\mathrm{K}_i \mathrm{R}_i^L (\mathbf{P}_j^L - \mathbf{t}_i^L)$ is the projection of the j-th point onto the i-th keyframe.

Alignment Using the Global Keyframe Positions. Assuming that the global keyframe positions $\mathbf{t}_i^G$ returned by the server are sufficiently accurate, our first strategy to align the local and global 3D models tries to enforce that the local keyframe positions $\mathbf{t}_i^L$ closely match the estimates provided by the server. Therefore, we want to minimize the sum of squared Euclidean distances

$$\chi_2 = \sum_i \left|\left| \mathbf{t}_i^G - \mathbf{t}_i^L \right|\right|^2 \tag{2}$$

between the local and global keyframe positions. In order to be robust to errors in the global localization, we add a keyframe constraint $\left|\left| \mathbf{t}_i^G - \mathbf{t}_i^L \right|\right|^2$ to χ_2 only if the Euclidean distance between $\mathbf{t}_i^L$ and $\mathbf{t}_i^G$ is less than 2 meters. When refining the local map, we thus need to minimize both the sum of reprojection errors and the distances between the keyframe positions, resulting in the energy functional

$$e^1 = \chi_1 + \chi_2 \ . \tag{3}$$

Notice that the first term χ_1 minimizes a geometric error while the second term χ_2 minimizes an algebraic error. To combine both error types, we follow the idea of [20] and normalize our objective function using the initial values χ_1^0, χ_2^0 obtained by evaluating the terms using the original, unoptimized camera poses, to normalize both error terms. Thus the objective function becomes

$$e_\alpha^1 = (1 - \alpha) \cdot \chi_1/\chi_1^0 + \alpha \cdot \chi_2/\chi_2^0 \ , \tag{4}$$

where the parameter $\alpha \in [0,1]$ is used to weight the energy functionals χ_1 and χ_2 differently. A high value for α enforces a stronger alignment of the local and global keyframe positions while potentially lowering the quality of the local map. On the other hand, a low value for α preserves the consistency of the local map but may result in a poor alignment. Thus, the choice for α strongly influences the quality of global pose estimation and is evaluated experimentally in Sec. 5.

The minimization of e_α^1 has to be carried out iteratively by a non-linear least squares solver, which requires an adequate initialization. For this purpose, we compute an affine transformation $T_1(\mathbf{t}_i^L) = \mathbf{sRt}_i^L + \mathbf{t}$, with a scaling factor $\mathbf{s}$, a rotation $\mathbf{R}$ and a translation $\mathbf{t}$, that minimizes $\sum_i \left\| \mathbf{t}_i^G - T_1\left(\mathbf{t}_i^L\right) \right\|^2$. Since this transformation adapts the local map only affinely, this gives us a sufficient initial alignment while it preserves the consistency of the local map. Following the approach by Horn [15], we need at least three pairs $\left(\mathbf{t}_i^L, \mathbf{t}_i^G\right)$ to estimate T_1. However, if the server reconstruction is aligned with gravity, we can again utilize the gravity vectors provided by the device IMU to reduce the degrees of freedom of T_1 from 7 to 5, which enables us to compute T_1 from only two pairs $\left(\mathbf{t}_i^L, \mathbf{t}_i^G\right)$. Having computed T_1, we replace every local point $\mathbf{P}_j^L$ by $T_1(\mathbf{P}_j^L)$ and every camera pose $(\mathbf{R}_i^L, \mathbf{t}_i^L)$ by $T_1(\mathbf{R}_i^L, \mathbf{t}_i^L) = (T_1(\mathbf{R}_i^L), T_1(\mathbf{t}_i^L))$, where $T_1(\mathbf{R}_i^L) = \mathbf{R}_i^L \mathbf{R}^\mathsf{T}$. Note that this initial alignment has to be performed only once, when the local map is not yet aligned to the global coordinate frame. For later map updates, we assume that the local map is already adequately aligned to be used as initialization for the minimization of e_α^1 directly.

Alignment Using the Global 2D-3D Matches. The strategy described above implicitly assumes that the positions computed by the localization server are accurate enough to improve the quality of the local map. However, this assumption might be too strict. For example, the server localization approach might find 2D-3D matches only in a small region of the keyframe. This results in an unstable configuration for pose estimation and thus a larger error in the global position, which negatively impacts the alignment. However, a central observation is that even if the pose is inaccurate, most of the inlier 2D-3D matches from which it was estimated are still correct. Instead of relying on the accuracy of the global poses, our second strategy thus directly incorporates these global inlier matches into the bundle adjustment using the sum of squared global reprojection errors

$$\chi_3 = \sum_i \sum_k \delta_{i,k} \cdot d(\mathbf{p}_k^i, K_i \mathbf{R}_i^L (\mathbf{P}_k^G - \mathbf{t}_i^L))^2 \ , \tag{5}$$

resulting in the unweighted and weighted objective functions

$$e^2 = \chi_1 + \chi_3 \ , \tag{6}$$

$$e_\beta^2 = (1 - \beta) \cdot \chi_1 / n_L + \beta \cdot \chi_3 / n_G \ , \tag{7}$$

where n_L is the number of local matches and n_G is the number of global matches. In contrast to the first strategy, our second approach does not rely on accurate global pose estimation and integrates much more naturally into the map refinement process as only a single type of error is minimized. Again, a framework parameter $\beta \in [0,1]$ is used to weight χ_1 and χ_3 differently. Although both χ_1 and χ_3 represent the same type of error, a normalization is required since there are usually many more local than global matches. However, compared to the first strategy, the second strategy enables a fairer weighting of both χ_1 and χ_3 using the number of local and global matches. Notice that we do not refine the global 3D point positions $\mathbf{P}_k^G$. Since the global SfM point cloud was reconstructed offline using state-of-the-art SfM techniques, we can assume that they are highly accurate and thus do not need to be refined. Incorporating the globally matching points thus prevents drift in the local map without adding additional degrees of freedom to the optimization process.

Unlike χ_2, the sum of squared global reprojection errors χ_3 is highly susceptible to errors in the poses $\{\mathbf{R}_i^L, \mathbf{t}_i^L\}$. Without proper initialization, we observed convergence to bad local minima of e_β^2. Thus, we have to take further precautions to ensure a good initialization for the initial and all further map alignments as newly inserted keyframes may have poor local pose estimates. Thus, for the first alignment, the initialization with $\mathbf{T}_1$ is followed by a second affine mapping

$$\mathbf{T}_2 = \arg\min_{\mathbf{T}} \sum_i \sum_k \delta_{i,k} \cdot d(\mathbf{p}_k^i, \mathbf{K}_i \mathbf{T}(\mathbf{R}_i^L)(\mathbf{P}_k^G - \mathbf{T}(\mathbf{t}_i^L)))^2 , \qquad (8)$$

which is computed with a non-linear least squares solver. Since $\mathbf{T}_2$ does not affect the local reprojection errors, but minimizes the global reprojection errors it results in a better initialization for the minimization of e_β^2.

For subsequent alignments, we have to make sure that the pose estimate of a newly inserted keyframe is not only optimal with respect to the local, but also with respect to the global matches. Thus, in contrast to the first strategy, the local pose of a new keyframe is computed in a RANSAC-PnP solver [12] from both the local and the global matches. We expect a significantly higher number of local than global matches, since the global localization approach by Sattler *et al.* [26] returns at most 100 global matches as mentioned in Section 3.2. Thus, since we jointly process both types of matches in a RANSAC loop, this additionally allows to detect and remove outliers in the global matches, making the strategy robust to erroneous global localizations.

5   Experimental Evaluation

We experimentally evaluated our framework and the proposed alignment strategies on a second generation iPad Mini, which provides a dual-core 1.3 GHz Apple A7 CPU and 1GB of memory. In our implementation, we make intensive use of the Grand Central Dispatch multithreading API and the ARM Neon SIMD instruction set, *e.g.*, for detection, description, and matching of BRISK features. For bundle adjustment and other non-affine refinements, we use the Google Ceres optimization library [2]. The server reconstruction covers the historic inner city of Aachen (about 40k m^2), was computed from 3k images and consists of 1.5M 3D points and 7.28M SIFT descriptors [27]. In the following, we present evaluation results for 3 different sequences, which were captured with

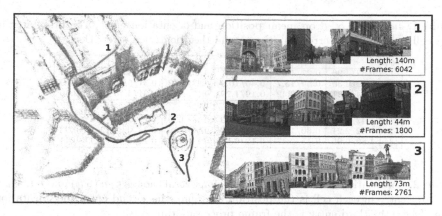

Fig. 2. Server reconstruction and ground truths of the evaluated sequences (*left*). Sample images from the sequences (*right*).

a Canon EOS 5D Mark II camera at a resolution of 1920×1080 and processed on the iPad at a resolution of 1024×576. The field of view has been adjusted to resemble that of mobile devices. We obtained ground truth pose estimates for each sequence by SfM, where we incrementally added the sequence images to the server reconstruction. For the initialization of the local map, we selected the first keyframe manually and set the second keyframe to the first sequence frame, which allowed us to evaluate the entire sequence. The gravity vectors were extracted from the ground truths. The low quality of current mobile device cameras accompanied by, *e.g.*, strong rolling shutter distortions prevented us from capturing trackable evaluation sequences with the iPad camera itself. However, with increasing quality of built-in cameras and ongoing research with the aim to overcome these issues [4,14], we expect our approach to be applicable to actual mobile device cameras in the near future. The server reconstruction and the evaluation sequences are depicted in Fig. 2.

5.1 Comparison of the Proposed Alignment Strategies

We compare the mean position and orientation error of both proposed alignment strategies e_α^1 and e_β^2 for Seq. 1, 2 and 3 and several choices for the weighting parameters α and β. Additionally, we also evaluated the pose accuracy for the respective unweighted alignments. To compute the position and orientation errors we compared each pose estimate against ground truth.

Table 1 reports the results. The orientation error for the objective functions e^1 and e_α^1 is always large, since this strategy does not incorporate any global orientation information. With respect to position error, the first strategy delivers the best results for $\alpha \geq 0.4$. Due to a significantly higher number of local than global matches, the unweighted functional of the second strategy e^2 performs poorly compared to the weighted versions. The best localization results are obtained for $\beta \geq 0.3$. As predicted, these results show that the second strategy outperforms

Table 1. Impact of α, β on mean position and orientation error. The first entry in each cell is the position error [m], the second the orientation error [Deg].

Seq.	e^1	$e^1_{0.1}$	$e^1_{0.2}$	$e^1_{0.3}$	$e^1_{0.4}$	$e^1_{0.5}$
1	0.52/4.96	0.27/4.03	0.78/12.7	0.40/6.55	0.30/4.33	0.27/4.10
2	0.52/2.39	0.54/13.7	0.40/10.9	0.43/9.42	0.31/5.83	0.34/7.99
3	0.24/1.81	0.20/2.42	0.19/1.79	0.17/2.41	0.21/4.40	0.17/2.50

Seq.	e^2	$e^2_{0.1}$	$e^2_{0.2}$	$e^2_{0.3}$	$e^2_{0.4}$	$e^2_{0.5}$
1	1.42/0.54	0.15/0.38	0.16/0.40	0.18/0.39	0.17/0.40	0.17/0.39
2	7.12/2.21	0.80/1.23	0.67/1.07	0.30/0.78	0.33/0.94	0.29/0.93
3	1.89/0.95	0.15/0.47	0.12/0.42	0.12/0.42	0.12/0.42	0.11/0.41

Table 2. Localization accuracy and timings for several choices of η (*left*) and κ (*right*). The first entry in each cell is the position error [m], the second entry the orientation error [Deg.], the third entry is the frame processing time [ms].

η	Seq. 1	Seq. 2	Seq. 3	κ	Seq. 1	Seq. 2	Seq. 3
500	0.19/0.38/42	0.24/0.76/39	0.11/0.40/41	5	0.21/0.41/48	0.31/0.85/47	0.13/0.44/45
1000	0.16/0.37/46	0.30/0.89/47	0.10/0.39/48	10	0.18/0.37/49	0.27/0.79/51	0.13/0.43/50
1500	0.17/0.39/53	0.29/0.93/61	0.11/0.41/53	15	0.17/0.39/53	0.29/0.93/61	0.11/0.41/53
2000	0.17/0.42/65	0.28/0.77/63	0.13/0.44/62	20	0.16/0.40/59	0.28/0.76/59	0.13/0.43/56

the first. Thus, if not explicitly stated otherwise, the following experiments were performed with alignment strategy $e^2_{0.5}$. One could argue that the first strategy could be improved by incorporating global keyframe orientations. While this is correct, we highly doubt that this would achieve the accuracy of the second strategy, since it would still rely on a single global pose estimate per keyframe. Furthermore, while the incorporation of the global matches results in an intuitive and simple objective function, the incorporation of orientations would require complex functions involving errors in the tangent space of SE(3).

Our framework depends on two additional parameters: the desired number of image features η and the maximum number of keyframes κ. Table 2 details the impact of different choices for η and κ. While these parameters do not affect the pose accuracy significantly, we observed that the smoothness of the pose estimates decreases with low values for η and κ. We decided for values of $\eta = 1500$ and $\kappa = 15$, which is a compromise in smoothness and processing time.

5.2   Accuracy, Efficiency and Scalability of Pose Estimation

Table 3 details localization results for the alignment strategies $e^1_{0.5}$ and $e^2_{0.5}$. Both strategies deliver accurate positions with mean errors between 0.11 and 0.34 m. However, only strategy $e^2_{0.5}$ is able to accurately estimate camera orientations. Furthermore, the standard deviations of the position and orientation errors are smaller for strategy $e^2_{0.5}$, which results in smoother trajectories. The mean size of the map is below 4MB for each sequence and for both strategies, which shows that our approach is suitable for large-scale mobile localization.

Fig. 4 depicts per frame statistics for Seq. 1 and strategy $e^2_{0.5}$. The threshold adaption is working properly as we constantly detect about 1500 features. The pose inaccuracies between frame 4000 and 4500 are caused by a rapid viewpoint

Table 3. Mean position and rotation error, processing time and map size for the alignment strategies $e^1_{0.5}$ and $e^2_{0.5}$

Seq.	$e^1_{0.5}$				$e^2_{0.5}$			
	P.Err.[m]	R.Err.[Deg.]	Time[ms]	Map[MB]	P.Err.[m]	R.Err.[Deg.]	Time[ms]	Map[MB]
1	0.27 ± 0.24	4.10 ± 4.48	53.8	3.99	0.17 ± 0.11	0.39 ± 0.23	52.8	3.20
2	0.34 ± 0.18	7.99 ± 6.27	56.4	2.79	0.29 ± 0.16	0.93 ± 0.68	60.1	3.41
3	0.17 ± 0.11	2.50 ± 2.73	54.0	3.17	0.11 ± 0.10	0.41 ± 0.33	52.6	3.98

Fig. 3. Part of Seq. 1 with a one-off alignment from the first two keyframes (*yellow*), strategies $e^1_{0.5}$ (*blue*), $e^2_{0.5}$ (*green*) and ground truth (*red*). Strategies $e^1_{0.5}$ and $e^2_{0.5}$ are well aligned to ground truth, while the one-off alignment is affected by drift. Strategy $e^2_{0.5}$ produces a smoother trajectory than $e^1_{0.5}$.

change. The peaks in the timing plot are caused by BRISK descriptor extraction and direct 2D-3D matching, which is triggered only if feature tracking fails. Besides feature detection, these tasks are most time consuming, as depicted in Fig. 5, which gives mean timings for the main components of pose estimation. As proposed by Lim *et al.* [22], descriptor extraction and direct matching could be distributed among multiple consecutive frames to achieve smoother timings, leaving feature detection as the main bottleneck. The total number of direct matching frames for Seq. 1 was 1304. The bottom curve in Fig. 4 demonstrates that the map size is nearly constant as soon as κ keyframes are in the map. Fig. 3 compares the trajectories for Seq. 1 and strategies $e^1_{0.5}$ and $e^2_{0.5}$, as well as a third trajectory that was aligned only once, from the first two keyframes, with ground truth. A single, initial alignment is not sufficient for robust large-scale pose estimation. However, by careful incorporation of additional global information with every new keyframe, the proposed strategies are able to prevent drift. Furthermore, strategy $e^2_{0.5}$ results in a much smoother trajectory than $e^1_{0.5}$.

Comparison to State-of-the-Art. We additionally evaluated our framework on the FLIGHT1 sequence of the state-of-the-art approach by Lim *et al.* [22]. Fig. 6 shows that the alignment strategy $e^2_{0.5}$ produces a qualitatively similar trajectory as the ground truth. Since we do not know the actual scale of the ground truth, we cannot compare the position error to the results of Lim *et al.*. The mean orientation error was 0.28 degree, compared to 1.7 degree with the approach of Lim *et al.*. Lim *et al.* state that the map is an 8m × 5m room that

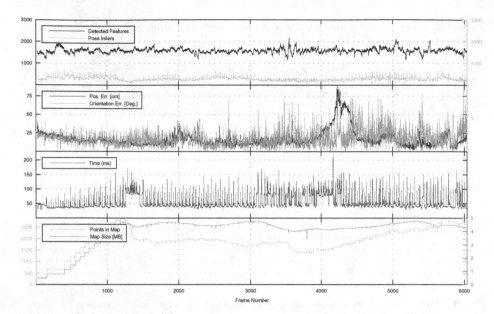

Fig. 4. Evaluation of Seq. 1. From top to bottom: detected features and inliers; position and orientation error; frame processing time; map points and size.

consumes 124MB of memory on the device. The mean memory footprint with our approach is only 1.03MB. The mean pose estimation time was 24.3ms.

The pose estimation approach by Ventura and Höllerer [29] relies on a single global pose estimate and is not capable to track the relative motion during the latency period. Thus, it is prone to both, high server latency and failed global localization. On the other hand, our approach is robust to these problems, since it is able to track the camera pose locally until sufficient global information is available for the alignment. Afterwards, if the server fails to localize a keyframe or the server response is pending, the global constraints belonging to this keyframe, but not the local reprojection errors, are omitted in the alignment.

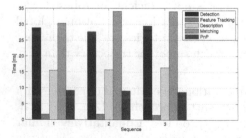

Fig. 5. Mean processing times of the main components of pose estimation

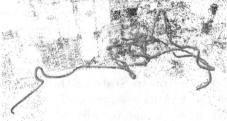

Fig. 6. FLIGHT1 sequence [22]: The $e_{0.5}^2$-trajectory (*green*) is qualitatively similar to the ground truth (*red*)

Table 4. Impact of false positive localizations on mean position and rotation error for Sequence 1 and strategies $e_0.5^1$ and $e_0.5^2$

False Positives	$e_{0.5}^1$		$e_{0.5}^2$	
	P.Err.[m]	R.Err.[Deg.]	P.Err.[m]	R.Err.[Deg.]
0%	0.27 ± 0.24	4.10 ± 4.48	0.17 ± 0.11	0.39 ± 0.23
10%	0.31 ± 0.35	6.63 ± 9.22	0.18 ± 0.15	0.40 ± 0.23
20%	0.32 ± 0.39	6.43 ± 9.39	0.18 ± 0.15	0.40 ± 0.23
30%	0.38 ± 0.51	7.48 ± 11.7	0.19 ± 0.15	0.40 ± 0.23
40%	0.44 ± 0.67	6.80 ± 8.20	0.19 ± 0.16	0.39 ± 0.23

Robustness to False Positive Global Localizations. As discussed in Section 4, both proposed alignment approaches take precautions to be robust to errors in the global localization. Li *et al.* [21] report false positive rates of less than 5.3%. Thus, to evaluate the robustness of the proposed strategies, we artificially set the number of false positive localizations to up to 40%. For every global localization, we randomly decided if it is a false positive localization. If so, we randomly selected a global keyframe pose and geometrically consistent global 2D-3D matches. Table 4 reports the impact on mean position and rotation errors for Sequence 1 and strategies $e_{0.5}^1$ and $e_{0.5}^2$. While the number of false positive global localizations has a notable impact on the localization accuracy and standard deviation for strategy $e_{0.5}^1$, it has almost no effect for strategy $e_{0.5}^2$.

6 Conclusion and Future Work

In this paper, we presented a truly scalable image-based localization approach that runs in real-time on a mobile device. The idea of our approach is to combine real-time pose tracking relative to a small 3D map constructed on the device itself with global pose information provided by a remote localization server. We proposed two strategies to align the local to the global model and to prevent drift in the camera pose. In the future, we would like to additionally utilize the localization server to overcome the major challenges of SLAM-based pose tracking, which are map initialization and recovery from tracking loss. While the proposed alignment approaches are intuitive and satisfying with regard to localization performance, we want to explore how additional global information, *e.g.*, 3D-3D correspondences between local and global map points or known scene geometry, can help to even further improve the alignment.

Acknowledgments. We gratefully acknowledge support by PREServ (EFRE 300268402). We also thank Sudipta N. Sinha for kindly providing the FLIGHT1 dataset and Tobias Weyand and Bastian Leibe for their valuable support.

References

1. Agarwal, S., Snavely, N., Simon, I., Seitz, S., Szeliski, R.: Building Rome in a Day. In: ICCV (2009)
2. Agarwal, S., Mierle, K.: Ceres Solver: Tutorial & Reference. Google Inc.
3. Arandjelović, R., Zisserman, A.: Three Things Everyone Should Know to Improve Object Retrieval. In: CVPR (2012)
4. Arth, C., Klopschitz, M., Reitmayr, G., Schmalstieg, D.: Real-Time Self-Localization from Panoramic Images on Mobile Devices. In: ISMAR (2011)
5. Arth, C., Wagner, D., Klopschitz, M., Irschara, A., Schmalstieg, D.: Wide Area Localization on Mobile Phones. In: ISMAR (2009)
6. Bay, H., Tuytelaars, T., Van Gool, L.: SURF: Speeded-Up Robust Features. In: Leonardis, A., Bischof, H., Pinz, A. (eds.) ECCV 2006, Part I. LNCS, vol. 3951, pp. 404–417. Springer, Heidelberg (2006)
7. Calonder, M., Lepetit, V., Strecha, C., Fua, P.: BRIEF: Binary Robust Independent Elementary Features. In: Daniilidis, K., Maragos, P., Paragios, N. (eds.) ECCV 2010, Part IV. LNCS, vol. 6314, pp. 778–792. Springer, Heidelberg (2010)
8. Castle, R.O., Klein, G., Murray, D.W.: Video-Rate Localization in Multiple Maps for Wearable Augmented Reality. In: ISWC (2008)
9. Davison, A.J., Reid, I.D., Molton, N., Stasse, O.: MonoSLAM: Real-Time Single Camera SLAM. PAMI 29(6), 1052–1067 (2007)
10. Dong, Z., Zhang, G., Jia, J., Bao, H.: Keyframe-Based Real-Time Camera Tracking. In: ICCV (2009)
11. Eade, E., Drummond, T.: Scalable Monocular SLAM. In: CVPR (2006)
12. Fischler, M., Bolles, R.: Random Sample Consensus: A Paradigm for Model Fitting with Applications to Image Analysis and Automated Cartography. Comm. ACM 24(6), 381–395 (1981)
13. Fraundorfer, F., Tanskanen, P., Pollefeys, M.: A Minimal Case Solution to the Calibrated Relative Pose Problem for the Case of Two Known Orientation Angles. In: Daniilidis, K., Maragos, P., Paragios, N. (eds.) ECCV 2010, Part IV. LNCS, vol. 6314, pp. 269–282. Springer, Heidelberg (2010)
14. Hedborg, J., Forssén, P.E., Felsberg, M., Ringaby, E.: Rolling Shutter Bundle Adjustment. In: CVPR (2012)
15. Horn, B.K.P.: Closed-Form Solution of Absolute Orientation Using Unit Quaternions. JOSA A 4(4), 629–642 (1987)
16. Irschara, A., Zach, C., Frahm, J.M., Bischof, H.: From Structure-from-Motion Point Clouds to Fast Location Recognition. In: CVPR (2009)
17. Klein, G., Murray, D.: Parallel Tracking and Mapping for Small AR Workspaces. In: ISMAR (2007)
18. Klein, G., Murray, D.: Parallel Tracking and Mapping on a Camera Phone. In: ISMAR (2009)
19. Leutenegger, S., Chli, M., Siegwart, R.: BRISK: Binary Robust Invariant Scalable Keypoints. In: ICCV (2011)
20. Lhuillier, M.: Fusion of GPS and Structure-from-Motion Using Constrained Bundle Adjustments. In: CVPR (2011)
21. Li, Y., Snavely, N., Huttenlocher, D., Fua, P.: Worldwide Pose Estimation Using 3D Point Clouds. In: Fitzgibbon, A., Lazebnik, S., Perona, P., Sato, Y., Schmid, C. (eds.) ECCV 2012, Part I. LNCS, vol. 7572, pp. 15–29. Springer, Heidelberg (2012)

22. Lim, H., Sinha, S.N., Cohen, M.F., Uyttendaele, M.: Real-Time Image-Based 6-DOF Localization in Large-Scale Environments. In: CVPR (2012)
23. Lowe, D.: Distinctive Image Features from Scale-Invariant Keypoints. IJCV 60(2), 91–110 (2004)
24. Meier, L., Tanskanen, P., Heng, L., Lee, G.H., Fraundorfer, F., Pollefeys, M.: PIX-HAWK: A Micro Aerial Vehicle Design for Autonomous Flight Using Onboard Computer Vision. Autonomous Robots 33(1-2), 21–39 (2012)
25. Newcombe, R.A., Lovegrove, S., Davison, A.J.: DTAM: Dense Tracking and Mapping in Real-Time. In: ICCV (2011)
26. Sattler, T., Leibe, B., Kobbelt, L.: Improving Image-Based Localization by Active Correspondence Search. In: Fitzgibbon, A., Lazebnik, S., Perona, P., Sato, Y., Schmid, C. (eds.) ECCV 2012, Part I. LNCS, vol. 7572, pp. 752–765. Springer, Heidelberg (2012)
27. Sattler, T., Weyand, T., Leibe, B., Kobbelt, L.: Image Retrieval for Image-Based Localization Revisited. In: BMVC (2012)
28. Triggs, B., McLauchlan, P., Hartley, R., Fitzgibbon, A.: Bundle Adjustment – A Modern Synthesis. In: Triggs, B., Zisserman, A., Szeliski, R. (eds.) Vision Algorithms: Theory and Practice. LNCS, vol. 1883, pp. 298–372. Springer, Heidelberg (2000)
29. Ventura, J., Höllerer, T.: Wide-Area Scene Mapping for Mobile Visual Tracking. In: ISMAR (2012)
30. Wendel, A., Irschara, A., Bischof, H.: Natural Landmark-based Monocular Localization for MAVs. In: ICRA (2011)

On Mean Pose and Variability
of 3D Deformable Models

Benjamin Allain[1], Jean-Sébastien Franco[1], Edmond Boyer[1], and Tony Tung[2]

[1] LJK, INRIA Grenoble Rhône-Alpes, France
[2] Graduate School of Informatics, Kyoto University, Japan
{firstname.lastname}@inria.fr, tung@vision.kuee.kyoto-u.ac.jp

Abstract. We present a novel methodology for the analysis of complex object shapes in motion observed by multiple video cameras. In particular, we propose to learn local surface rigidity probabilities (i.e., deformations), and to estimate a mean pose over a temporal sequence. Local deformations can be used for rigidity-based dynamic surface segmentation, while a mean pose can be used as a sequence keyframe or a cluster prototype and has therefore numerous applications, such as motion synthesis or sequential alignment for compression or morphing. We take advantage of recent advances in surface tracking techniques to formulate a generative model of 3D temporal sequences using a probabilistic framework, which conditions shape fitting over all frames to a simple set of intrinsic surface rigidity properties. Surface tracking and rigidity variable estimation can then be formulated as an Expectation-Maximization inference problem and solved by alternatively minimizing two nested fixed point iterations. We show that this framework provides a new fundamental building block for various applications of shape analysis, and achieves comparable tracking performance to state of the art surface tracking techniques on real datasets, even compared to approaches using strong kinematic priors such as rigid skeletons.

Keywords: Shape dynamics, Motion analysis, Shape spaces.

1   Introduction

Recent years have seen the emergence of many solutions for the capture of dynamic scenes, where a scene observed by several calibrated cameras is fully reconstructed from acquired videos using multiview stereo algorithms [24,12,1,20]. These techniques have many applications for media content production, interactive systems [2] and scene analysis [28] since they allow to recover both geometric and photometric information of objects' surface, and also their shape and evolution over time. Since these temporal evolutions were initially reconstructed as a sequence of topologically inconsistent 3D models, significant research work has been done for full 4D modeling and analysis of geometrically time-consistent 3D sequences.

In particular, several techniques propose to deform and match a template to either image data, or to intermediate 3D representations of the surface [25,17,9,26].

D. Fleet et al. (Eds.): ECCV 2014, Part II, LNCS 8690, pp. 284–297, 2014.

These methods allow the recovery of both shape and motion information. However they usually do not consider the intrinsic dynamic properties of a surface. These are either assumed, for instance through a kinematic structure (rigging) or through the surface tension parameters, or are simply ignored. Hence, there is a large interest in better understanding rigidity and motion properties of shapes, with the prospect of improving dynamic models, extracting more useful information, and better automation. In this work, we take the estimation a step further and investigate how to infer dynamics or statistical properties of shapes given temporal sequences.

Recovering this information is yet a largely open research topic with only few exploratory representations proposed for dynamics characteristics of surfaces, e.g. [11,29]. We propose a novel inference framework for the analysis of complex object shapes in motion that learns local surface rigidity probabilities (i.e., deformations), and estimates a mean pose over a temporal sequence. Based on recent advances in surface tracking techniques, we formulate a generative model of 3D temporal sequences using a probabilistic framework, which conditions shape fitting over all frames to a simple set of intrinsic surface rigidity properties. Surface tracking and rigidity variables can then be obtained iteratively using Expectation-Maximization inference by alternatively minimizing two nested fixed point iterations. Thus, our main contribution is a framework that allows the simultaneous tracking and inference of dynamic properties of object surfaces given temporal observations. We show how these properties contribute to a better understanding of surface motion and how they can be used for the dynamic analysis of 3D surface shapes through mean pose estimation and rigidity-based segmentation, while achieving competitive surface tracking.

The remainder of the paper is organized as follows. The next section discusses related work. Details on the mean pose inference model are given in Sect. 3. Section 4 presents various applications and experimental results. Section 5 concludes with a discussion on our contributions.

2   Related Work

The analysis of deformable surfaces captured by multi-video systems has gained lot of interest during the last decade due to the rapid progression of computer and image sensing technologies. We focus here on works that relate to dynamic properties of shapes.

Kinematic structures. Many popular tracking methods propose to rigidly constrain a model using an articulated structure, for instance a skeleton or a cage, which must be scaled and rigged to a 3D template, and optimally positioned through a sequence of models representing the observed subjects [4,30,17,19]. The template is usually deformed using a skinning technique, according to the optimized structure across the sequence [5]. Such kinematic structures provide intrinsic information on the associated shapes through their parameter evolutions (e.g. their averages can define a mean pose). These approaches require a priori knowledge on the observed shapes, such as the topology and the rigid parts, and cannot be applied to arbitrary object shapes. Moreover global template deformation across time is subject to loss of local details such as cloth wrinkles and folds.

Locally rigid structures. The literature also contains several methods that relax the constraint on the shape structure using looser rigidity priors. A body of works consider deformations that preserve local intrinsic surface properties, e.g. isometric deformations [21,8,22,23]. Such properties relate to local rigidities, for instance in [31,32] local surface distortions are constrained, however they are usually known priors. While efficient to register or match surfaces, intrinsic surface properties are not necessarily sufficient to track complex shapes such as human bodies. In that case, several approaches introduce local deformation models to drive surface evolutions. For instance, in [9], the observed surface is treated as a piece-wise body with locally rigid motions. We consider a similar model to represent surface deformations which is used to learn local rigidities as well as mean poses along with the tracking. Interestingly, recent approaches also in this category were proposed to characterize local surface deformations. In [11], the authors propose a probabilistic framework for rigid tracking and segmentation of dynamic surfaces where the rigid kinematic structure is learned along time sequences. Our framework does not assume such structure but learns instead local rigidities and mean poses. In [29], the authors model complex local deformation dynamics using linear dynamical systems by observing local curvature variations, using a shape index, and perform rigidity-based surface patch classification. The latter approach assumes surface alignment is given, in contrast to our proposed generative model that simultaneously performs surface tracking and local rigidity estimation.

Shape Spaces. Following the work of Kendall [18], a number of works consider shape spaces that characterize the configurations of a given set of points, the vertices of a mesh for instance. This has been used in medical imaging to estimate mean shapes through Procrustes analysis, e.g. [16]. In this case, the shape of the object is the geometrical information that remains when the pose (i.e., similarities) is filtered out. Thus Procrustes distances can be used to measure shape similarities and to estimate shape averages with Fréchet means. We follow here a different strategy where a shape space represents the poses of a single shape and where we estimate a mean pose instead of a mean shape. This relates to other works in this category that also consider shapes spaces to model shape poses with mesh representations. They can either be learned, e.g. [3,15] or defined a priori, e.g. [27] and are used to constrain mesh deformations when creating realistic animations [3,27] or estimating shape and poses from images[15]. While sharing similarities in the deformation model we consider, our objective is not only to recover meaningful shape poses but also to measure pose similarities and intrinsic shape properties. Unlike [3,15], we do not need a pose or shape database and the associated hypothesis of its representativeness. Moreover, our methodology specifically addresses robust temporal window integration.

3   Mean Pose Inference Model

We assume given a temporal sequence of 3D reconstructions, incoherent meshes or point clouds, obtained using a multi-view reconstruction approach, e.g. [12,1,20]. We also assume that a template mesh model of the scene is available, e.g. a particular instance within the reconstructed sequence under consideration. The problem of local surface rigidity and mean pose analysis is then tackled through the simultaneous tracking and intrinsic parameter estimation of the template model. We embed intrinsic motion parameters (e.g. rigidities) in the model, which control the motion behavior of the object surface. This implies that the estimation algorithm is necessarily performed over a sub-sequence of frames, as opposed to most existing surface tracking methods which in effect implement tracking through iterated single-frame pose estimation. We first describe in details the geometric model (§3.1) illustrated with Fig. 1, and its associated average deformation parameterization for the observed surface (§3.2). Second, we describe how this surface generates noisy measurements with an appropriate Bayesian generative model (§3.3). We then show how to perform estimation over the sequence through Expectation-Maximization (§3.4).

Fig. 1. Example of patch template used

3.1   Shape Space Parameterization

To express non-rigid deformability of shapes, while de-correlating the resolution of deformation parameters from mesh resolution, we opt for a patch-based parameterization of the surface similar to [9]. The reference mesh is partitioned in an overlapping set of patches, pre-computed by geodesic clustering of vertices. Each patch P_k is associated to a rigid transformation $\mathbf{T}_k^t \in SE(3)$ at every time t. Each position $\mathbf{x}_{k,v}$ of a mesh vertex v as predicted by the transform of P_k can then be computed from its template position $\mathbf{x}_v^0$ as follows:

$$\mathbf{x}_{k,v} = \mathbf{T}_k(\mathbf{x}_v^0). \tag{1}$$

We thus define a *pose* of the shape space as the set of patch transforms $\mathbf{T} = \{\mathbf{T}_k\}_{k \in \mathcal{K}}$ that express a given mesh deformation. Note here that a pose in the shape space does not necessarily correspond to a proper geometric realization of the reference mesh and, in practice, patch deformations are merged on the template to preserve the mesh consistency.

3.2 Mean Pose

To retrieve the mean pose of a given sequence, we provide a definition suitable for the analysis of complex temporal mesh sequences. Following Fréchet's definition of a mean [13], we introduce the *mean pose* $\bar{\mathbf{T}}$ of a given set of poses $\{\mathbf{T}^t\}_{t \in \mathcal{T}}$ over the time sequence $\mathcal{T}$ as the pose minimizing the sum of squared distances to all poses in the set:

$$\bar{\mathbf{T}} = \arg\min_{\mathbf{T}} \sum_{t \in \mathcal{T}} d^2(\mathbf{T}, \mathbf{T}^t), \tag{2}$$

where $d()$ is a distance that measures the similarity of two poses. This distance should evaluate the non-rigidity of the transformation between two poses of a shape and hence should be independent of any global pose. Such a distance is not easily defined in the non-Euclidean shape space spanned by the rigid motion parameters of the patches. However using the Euclidean embedding provided by the mesh representation, we can define a proper metric based on the vertex positions. Inspired by the deformation energy proposed by Botsch *et al.* [7] our distance is expressed as an internal deformation energy between two poses. Let $\mathbf{T}^i$ and $\mathbf{T}^j$ be two poses of the model, the distance can be written as a sum of per patch pair squared distances:

$$d^2(\mathbf{T}^i, \mathbf{T}^j) = \sum_{(P_k, P_l) \in \mathcal{N}} d_{kl}^2(\mathbf{T}^i, \mathbf{T}^j), \tag{3}$$

$$\text{with } d_{kl}^2(\mathbf{T}^i, \mathbf{T}^j) = \sum_{v \in P_k \cup P_l} \|\mathbf{T}_{k-l}^i(\mathbf{x}_v^0) - \mathbf{T}_{k-l}^j(\mathbf{x}_v^0)\|^2, \tag{4}$$

where $\mathbf{T}_{k-l}^i = \mathbf{T}_l^{i^{-1}} \circ \mathbf{T}_k^i$ is the relative transformation between patches P_k and P_l for pose i, and $\mathcal{N}$ is the set of neighboring patch pairs on the surface. The distance sums, for every pair of patches of the deformable model, its rigid deviation from pose i to j. This deviation is given by the sum over each vertex v belonging to the patch pair, of the discrepancy of relative positions of the vertex as displaced by P_k and P_l. It can be verified that d^2 defines a distance as it inherits this property from the L^2 norm used between vertices.

3.3 Generative Model

The expression (2) is useful to characterize the mean over a set of poses *already known*. Our goal however is to estimate this mean in the context where such poses are indirectly observed through a set of noisy and sparse 3D point clouds of the surface. Thus we cast the problem as the joint estimation of mean pose and fitting of the model to each set of observations. For our purposes, we assume the set of poses $\{\mathbf{T}^t\}_{t\in\mathcal{T}}$ are defined for a set $\mathcal{T}$ corresponding to observations in a temporal sequence. The observed point clouds are noted $\mathbf{Y} = \{\mathbf{Y}^t\}_{t\in\mathcal{T}}$, where $\mathbf{Y}^t = \{\mathbf{y}_o^t\}_{o\in\mathcal{O}_t}$ is the set of point coordinates $\mathbf{y}_o^t$ for an observation o among the set of observations $\mathcal{O}_t$ at time t. Note that this set $\mathcal{O}_t$ is different than $\mathcal{V}$ in general as it is obtained from a 3D reconstruction or depth camera, without any direct correspondence to the deformable shape surface model earlier defined.

To express the noisy predictions of observations, we follow the principle of EM-ICP [14] by introducing a set of assignment variables k_o^t indicating, for each observation o, which patch this observation is assigned to. We are also interested in retrieving information about the variations of the rigid deformation with respect to the mean shape. To keep this information in its simplest form, we express in the generative model that each pair of patches $(k, l) \in \mathcal{N}$ is assigned a *binary rigidity variable* $c_{kl} \in \{0, 1\}$, which will condition the patch pair to accordingly be rigid or flexible. This variable is an intrinsic parameter attached to the original deformable model and is thus time-independent. We note the full set of rigidity variables $C = \{c_{kl}\}_{(k,l)\in\mathcal{N}}$. This in turn will allow during inference the estimation of a rigid coupling probability for each patch pair (k, l). We express the generative model through the following joint probability distribution:

$$p(\bar{\mathbf{T}}, \mathbf{T}, \mathbf{Y}, C, K, \sigma) = p(\bar{\mathbf{T}}) \prod_{t\in\mathcal{T}} \left(p(\mathbf{T}^t \mid \bar{\mathbf{T}}, C) \prod_{o\in\mathcal{O}_t} p(\mathbf{y}_o^t \mid k_o^t, \mathbf{T}^t, \sigma^t) \right), \quad (5)$$

with $\sigma = \{\sigma^t\}_{t\subset\mathcal{T}}$ the set of noise parameters of the observation prediction model, and $K = \{k_o^t\}$ the set of all patch selection variables.

Observation Prediction Model. Each observation's point measurement is predicted from the closest vertex v within patch $P_{k=k_o^t}$. Because the prediction is noisy, this prediction is perturbed by Gaussian noise of variance σ^{t2}:

$$p(\mathbf{y}_o^t \mid k_o^t \ \mathbf{T}^t \sigma^t) = \mathcal{N}(\mathbf{y}_o^t \mid \mathbf{T}_{k_o^t}^t(\mathbf{x}_v^0), \sigma^t). \quad (6)$$

Pose Constraining Model. We constrain the fitted poses to be close to the mean pose, using the distance defined earlier (3). We embed the influence of rigidity variables in this term, by computing two versions of the distance, biased by rigidity variables C:

$$p(\mathbf{T}^t \mid \bar{\mathbf{T}}, C) \propto \exp\left(- \sum_{(k,l)\in\mathcal{N}} d_{kl}^2(\bar{\mathbf{T}}, \mathbf{T}^t, c_{kl}) \right), \quad (7)$$

$$\text{where } d_{kl}^2(\bar{\mathbf{T}}, \mathbf{T}^t, c_{kl}) = \sum_{v\in P_k\cup P_l} \beta_{kl}(v, c_{kl}) \left\| \mathbf{T}_{k-l}^i(\mathbf{x}_v^0) - \mathbf{T}_{k-l}^j(\mathbf{x}_v^0) \right\|^2, \quad (8)$$

with $\beta_{kl}(v, c_{kl})$ a uniform function over all vertices of the patch pair if $c_{kl} = 1$, which encourages common rigid behavior of the two patches, and a non-uniform function encouraging more elasticity when $c_{kl} = 0$:

$$\beta_{kl}(v, 0) \propto \exp(-\frac{b_{kl}(v)}{\eta \bar{D}}), \tag{9}$$

where $b_{kl}(v)$ is the distance between the vertex v and the border between P_k and P_l on the template, $\bar{D}$ is the average patch diameter and η is a global coefficient controlling the flexibility. The $\beta_{kl}(\cdot, 0)$ has larger values on the border between the patches, which allows more flexibility while enforcing continuity between the patches. The coefficients $\beta_{kl}(v, 0)$ are normalized such that $\sum_{P_k \cup P_l} \beta_{kl}(v, 0) = \sum_{P_k \cup P_l} \beta_{kl}(v, 1)$ in order to make both modes as competitive.

Mean Model Prior. In the absence of any prior, the mean pose is unconstrained and could theoretically have completely loose patches unrelated to each other. To avoid this and give the mean pose a plausible deformation, we consider the following a prior which expresses that the intrinsic mean pose should not significantly deviate from the original reference pose (represented by the identity transform **Id**):

$$p(\bar{\mathbf{T}}) \propto \exp(-d^2(\bar{\mathbf{T}}, \mathbf{Id})) \propto \exp\left(\sum_{(P_k, P_l) \in \mathcal{N}} \sum_{v \in P_k \cup P_l} \|\bar{\mathbf{T}}_k(\mathbf{x}_v^0) - \bar{\mathbf{T}}_l(\mathbf{x}_v^0)\|^2 \right), \tag{10}$$

3.4   Expectation-Maximization Inference

We apply Expectation-Maximization [10] to compute Maximum A Posteriori (MAP) estimates of the tracking and average shape parameters given noisy 3D measurements, using the joint probability described in (5) as described in [6]. The assignment variables K and rigidity coupling variables C are treated as latent variables, which we group by the name $Z = \{K, C\}$. For the purpose of clarity let us also rename all parameters to estimate as $\Theta = \{\bar{\mathbf{T}}, \mathbf{T}, \sigma\}$. Expectation-Maximization consists in iteratively maximizing the following auxiliary function Q given the knowledge of the previous parameter estimate Θ^m:

$$\Theta^{m+1} = \arg\max_{\Theta} Q(\Theta|\Theta^m) = \arg\max_{\Theta} \sum_Z p(Z|\mathbf{Y}, \Theta^m) \ln p(\mathbf{Y}, Z|\Theta). \tag{11}$$

The **E-Step** consists in computing the posterior distribution $p(Z|\mathbf{Y}, \Theta^m)$ of latent variables given observations and the previous estimate. It can be noted given the form of (5) that all latent variables are individually independent under this posterior according to the D-separation criterion [6], thus following the factorization of the joint probability distribution:

$$p(\mathbf{Y}, Z|\Theta^m) = \prod_{t \in \mathcal{T}} \left(\prod_{(k,l) \in \mathcal{N}} p(c_{kl}|\Theta^m) \prod_{o \in \mathcal{O}_t} p(k_o^t|\mathbf{Y}, \Theta^m) \right), \tag{12}$$

$$\text{where } p(c_{kl}|\Theta^m) = a \cdot \exp \left(- \sum_{v \in P_k \cup P_l} -d_{kl}^2(\mathbf{T}^{t,m}, \bar{\mathbf{T}}^m, c_{kl}) \right) \tag{13}$$

$$\text{and } p(k_o^t|\mathbf{Y}, \Theta^m) = b \cdot \mathcal{N}(\mathbf{y}_o^t \mid \mathbf{T}_{k_o^t}^{t,m}(v), \sigma^{t,m}), \tag{14}$$

where a, b are normalization constants ensuring the respective distributions sum to 1, and v is the closest vertex on patch k. Equations (13) and (14) are the E-step updates that need to be computed at every iteration for every latent variable. (13) corresponds to a reevaluation of probabilities of rigid coupling between patches, based on the previous m-th estimates of temporal and mean poses. (14) corresponds to the probability assignment table of time t's observation o to each patch in the model. This corresponds to the soft matching term commonly found in EM-ICP methods [14].

The **M-Step** maximizes expression (11), which can be shown to factorize similarly to (5) and (12), in a sum of three maximizable independent groups of terms, leading to the following updates:

$$\mathbf{T}^{t,m+1} = \arg\min_{\mathbf{T}^t} \sum_{(k,l) \in \mathcal{N}} \sum_{c_{kl}} p(c_{kl}|\Theta^m) \, d_{kl}^2(\bar{\mathbf{T}}^m, \mathbf{T}^t, c_{kl}) \tag{15}$$

$$+ \sum_{o \in \mathcal{O}_t} \sum_{k_o^t} p(k_o^t|\mathbf{Y}, \Theta^m) \|\mathbf{y}_o^t - \mathbf{T}_{k_o^t}^t(\mathbf{x}_v^t)\|^2,$$

$$\sigma^{t,m+1^2} = \frac{1}{3} \frac{\sum_{o \in \mathcal{O}_t} \sum_{k_o^t} p(k_o^t|\mathbf{Y}, \Theta^m) \, \|\mathbf{y}_o^t - \mathbf{T}_{k_o^t}^{t,m+1}(\mathbf{x}_v^t)\|^2}{\sum_{o \in \mathcal{O}_t} \sum_{k_o^t} p(k_o^t|\mathbf{Y}, \Theta^m)}, \tag{16}$$

$$\bar{\mathbf{T}}^{m+1} = \arg\min_{\bar{\mathbf{T}}} \ d^2(\bar{\mathbf{T}}, \mathbf{Id}) + \sum_{t \in \mathcal{T}} \sum_{(k,l) \in \mathcal{N}} \sum_{c_{kl}} p(c_{kl}|\Theta^m) d_{kl}^2(\bar{\mathbf{T}}, \mathbf{T}^{t,m+1}, c_{kl}). \tag{17}$$

Expression (15) corresponds to simultaneous updates of all patch transformations for a given time t, weighed by E-step probabilities. (16) updates the per-time frame noise parameter with an E-step weighed contribution of each observation. (17) computes the mean pose, accounting for all poses in the time sequence. Note that, for ease of resolution, we decouple the estimation of $\mathbf{T}^{t,m+1}$ and $\bar{\mathbf{T}}^{m+1}$, which is why (17) uses the result $\mathbf{T}^{t,m+1}$. We solve both systems with Gauss-Newton iterations, using a parametrization of the rigid transforms as a rotation matrix and translation.

4   Experiments

We evaluate the proposed generative model using 3D sequences reconstructed from real human performances captured by multiple view videos. We propose two datasets, GOALKEEPER and DANCER, which provide two different actions and clothing situations with high resolution inputs. These were processed by extracting visual hull reconstructions, and two neutral topology frames were selected to provide the template model after smoothing and simplifying the obtained mesh down to $5k$ vertices. Additionally, we also validate using two public datasets made available by the community. The FREE [25] dataset consists of a photocoherent mesh sequence of a dancer with approximately $135k$ vertices per frame, exhibiting particularly fast and difficult dancing motion. The MARKER dataset [19] provides another type of challenging situation with a two-person sequence of reconstructions, with martial art motions. It also provides markers on one of the persons which we will use for quantitative evaluation. For both these public sequences, we use the templates provided downsampled to $5k$ vertices.

In all visualizations, we render mesh poses by computing vertex position $\mathbf{x}_v^t$ at time t as a linear blend of positions $\mathbf{x}_k^t$ of expression (1), weighed by a set of Gaussian weights $\alpha_k(v)$ materializing the region of influence of patch P_k on the mesh. These are maximal at the center of mass of P_k and their sum over all non-zero patch influences are normalized to 1 for a given vertex v:

$$\mathbf{x}_v^t = \sum_k \alpha_k(v)\, \mathbf{x}_k^t \; . \tag{18}$$

We visualize the rigidity coupling probabilities over the surface with heat-colored probabilities, by diffusing this probability over vertices of influence of patch pairs to obtain a smooth rendering. We provide a supplemental video[1] with the processed results for these datasets.

4.1   Tracking Evaluation

We first evaluate the tracking performance of the algorithm. Full sequences may be processed but because of the motion of subjects in the sequence, all poses of the sequence cannot be initialized with a single static pose, as this would surely be susceptible to local minima. We thus process the four datasets using a sliding window strategy for $\mathcal{T}$, where processing starts with a single pose, then additional poses are introduced in the time window after the previous window converges. We provide tracking results with sliding window size 20 which corresponds to approximately one second of video. We show the resulting poses estimated by our algorithm on the four datasets in Fig. 4, Fig. 5a and Fig. 5b. Runtime is approximately 15 seconds per time step on a recent workstation and can be further improved.

We also provide a comparison with state of the art methods Liu *et al.* [19] and with a purely patch-based strategy [9], on the MARKER dataset. We reproduce

---

[1] http://hal.inria.fr/hal-01016981

[9] results by neutralizing mean updates and rigid coupling updates from our method, which corresponds to removing these terms from the energy and closely mimics [9]. Note that [19] is a kinematic tracking strategy, where both subjects are rigged to a kinematic skeleton providing a strong, fixed and dataset specific rigidity prior. On the other hand, [9] only use patch rigidity and inter-patch elasticity priors, that are weaker than [19] and our method. The MARKER dataset provides sparse marker positions, at which we estimate geometric positional error with respect to the surface. To this purpose we match the closest vertex on the template model provided, and follow it with the different methods, computing geometric errors in position with respect to the corresponding marker's position in these frames. The average errors are shown in Table 1. We also provide a temporal error graph for our method and [9] in Fig. 2.

Table 1. Mean error and standard deviation over the sequence of the MARKER dataset

method	mean error (mm)	standard deviation (mm)
no coupling, no mean pose [9]	55.11	48.02
our method	43.22	29.58
Liu *et al.* [19]	29.61	25.50

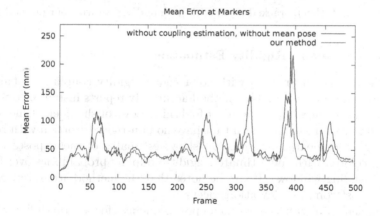

Fig. 2. Mean error for temporal evolution over MARKER dataset

Table 1 shows our method achieves comparable tracking performance to state of the art surface tracking techniques. The slightly higher error with respect to [19] is not unexpected given that they use a stronger kinematic skeleton prior. Regarding [9], the graph and table show a small advantage in error for our method along the sequence, as well as a smaller variance of the error, showing the better constraining provided by our framework. The graph also shows significantly higher error values with [9] than with our method around frames 60, 250, 325, 390 and 460. These error peaks are imputable to difficult segments of the input sequence where [9] loses track of limbs (see Fig. 3a and Fig. 3b) while our method does not. The high error values around frame 390 are due to ambiguous input meshes where the head of the second character (not seen in Fig. 3b) is out of the field of view. Around this frame, our method still outperforms [9] which misaligns an arm (see Fig. 3b). These results substantiate stronger robustness for our method over [9].

Regarding limitations, the model may fall into local minima when the noise level of inputs is too high similarly to all patch-based methods but this was not a strong limitation on the datasets. As the model favours rigidity and isometric surface deformations, the surface sometimes overfolds in non-rigid sections (as sometimes seen in video), which we will address in future work.

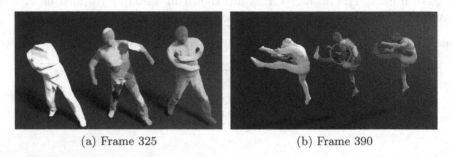

(a) Frame 325   (b) Frame 390

Fig. 3. Input mesh (left), tracked mesh with [9] (middle) and with our method (right)

4.2 Mean Pose and Rigidity Estimation

Fig. 5a shows tracking results with color coded rigidity coupling probabilities with sliding window size 20. The method accurately reports instantaneous rigidity deviation, such as when the subject folds his elbows or shoulders. Blue regions correspond to regions of the mesh that have no non-rigid distortion with respect to the estimated mean pose. Fig. 5b shows estimates of mean poses for full sequences, colored with the estimated rigidity coupling probabilities over full sequence (no sliding window). It can be noted that the method accurately reports where the most common deviations occur.

The supplemental video shows mean pose sequences for several sliding window sizes. We observe a temporal smoothing of the initial deformation: fast deformation is filtered out. This effect is stronger with wide windows. We interpret this phenomenon as follows: when the temporal window slides along the sequence, it produces a mean pose sequence analogous to the convolution of the estimated pose sequence with a gate function, with the same size as the window size. This process can be seen as a low-pass filtering of the sequence poses.

We also observe that the mean pose is not affected by global rigid motion of the shape (noticeable with the DANCER dataset). This is an expected consequence of using a pose distance that is invariant under global rigid transforms in (2).

Fig. 4. Tracking excerpts from the DANCER dataset. Colors code patches.

(a) Tracking Excerpts.   (b) Mean poses computed on
                                          full sequences.

Fig. 5. Tracking excerpts from GOALKEEPER, MARKER and FREE datasets. Best viewed in color. Please watch supplemental video for more visualizations.

5   Conclusions

We present a novel methodology for the analysis of complex object shapes in motion observed by multiple cameras. In particular, we propose a generative model of 3D temporal sequences using a probabilistic framework that simultaneously learns local surface rigidity probabilities and estimates a mean pose over temporal sequence. Hence, rigidity-based surface segmentation can be achieved using local deformation properties, while motion synthesis or surface alignment for compression or morphing applications can be achieved using a mean pose as a sequence keyframe or a cluster prototype.

Our model can also perform surface tracking with state of the art performance, and does not require a priori rigid (kinematic) structure, nor prior model learning from a database. Surface tracking and rigidity variable probabilities are obtained by solving an Expectation-Maximization inference problem which alternatively minimizes two nested fixed point iterations.

To our knowledge, this is the first model that achieves simultaneous estimation of mean pose, local rigidity, and surface tracking. Experimental results on real datasets show the numerous potential applications of the proposed framework for complex shape analysis of 3D sequences.

Acknowledgements. This work was funded by the Seventh Framework Programme EU project RE@CT (grant agreement no. 288369). It was also supported in part by the INRIA-JSPS Bilateral Program AYAME 146121400001 and the JSPS WAKATE B 26730089.

References

1. de Aguiar, E., Stoll, C., Theobalt, C., Ahmed, N., Seidel, H.P., Thrun, S.: Performance capture from sparse multi-view video. ACM Transactions on Graphics 27(3) (2008)
2. Allard, J., Ménier, C., Raffin, B., Boyer, E., Faure, F.: Grimage: Markerless 3d interactions. SIGGRAPH - Emerging Technologies (2007)
3. Anguelov, D., Srinivasan, P., Koller, D., Thrun, S., Rodgers, J., Davis, J.: Scape: Shape completion and animation of people. ACM Transactions on Graphics 24(3) (2005)
4. Ballan, L., Cortelazzo, G.M.: Marker-less motion capture of skinned models in a four camera set-up using optical flow and silhouettes. In: 3DPVT (2008)
5. Baran, I., Popović, J.: Automatic rigging and animation of 3D characters. ACM Transactions on Graphics 26(3), 72:1–72:8 (2007)
6. Bishop, C.M.: Pattern Recognition and Machine Learning (Information Science and Statistics). Springer-Verlag New York, Inc., Secaucus (2006)
7. Botsch, M., Pauly, M., Wicke, M., Gross, M.: Adaptive space deformations based on rigid cells. Comput. Graph. Forum 26(3), 339–347 (2007)
8. Bronstein, A.M., Bronstein, M.M., Kimmel, R.: Efficient computation of isometry-invariant distances between surfaces. SIAM Journal on Scientific Computing 28 (2006)

9. Cagniart, C., Boyer, E., Ilic, S.: Probabilistic deformable surface tracking from multiple videos. In: Daniilidis, K., Maragos, P., Paragios, N. (eds.) ECCV 2010, Part IV. LNCS, vol. 6314, pp. 326–339. Springer, Heidelberg (2010)
10. Dempster, A.P., Laird, N.M., Rubin, D.B.: Maximum likelihood from incomplete data via the em algorithm. Journal of the Royal Statistical Society, Series B (1977)
11. Franco, J., Boyer, E.: Learning temporally consistent rigidities. In: CVPR (2011)
12. Franco, J., Menier, C., Boyer, E., Raffin, B.: A distributed approach for real-time 3d modeling. In: CVPR Workshop (2004)
13. Fréchet, M.: Les éléments aléatoires de nature quelconque dans un espace distancié. Annales de l'institut Henri Poincaré 10, 215–310 (1948)
14. Granger, S., Pennec, X.: Multi-scale EM-ICP: A fast and robust approach for surface registration. In: Heyden, A., Sparr, G., Nielsen, M., Johansen, P. (eds.) ECCV 2002, Part IV. LNCS, vol. 2353, pp. 418–432. Springer, Heidelberg (2002)
15. Hasler, N., Ackermann, H., Rosenhahn, B., Thormählen, T., Seidel, H.P.: Multilinear pose and body shape estimation of dressed subjects from image sets. In: CVPR (2010)
16. Hufnagel, H., Pennec, X., Ehrhardt, J., Ayache, N., Handel, H.: Generation of a Statistical Shape Model with Probabilistic Point Correspondences and EM-ICP. IJCAR 2(5) (2008)
17. Gall, J., Stoll, C., de Aguiar, E., Theobalt, C., Rosenhahn, B., Seidel, H.P.: Motion capture using joint skeleton tracking and surface estimation. In: CVPR (2009)
18. Kendall, D.: Shape manifolds, procrustean metrics, and complex projective spaces. Bulletin of the London Mathematical Society 16(2), 81–121 (1984)
19. Liu, Y., Gall, J., Stoll, C., Dai, Q., Seidel, H.P., Theobalt, C.: Markerless motion capture of multiple characters using multi-view image segmentation. PAMI (2013)
20. Matsuyama, T., Nobuhara, S., Takai, T., Tung, T.: 3d video and its applications. Springer (2012)
21. Mémoli, F., Sapiro, G.: Comparing Point Clouds. SGP (2004)
22. Ovsjanikov, M., Mérigot, Q., Mémoli, F., Guibas, L.J.: One point isometric matching with the heat kernel. Comput. Graph. Forum 29(5) (2010)
23. Sahillioglu, Y., Yemez, Y.: 3D Shape correspondence by isometry-driven greedy optimization. In: CVPR (2010)
24. Starck, J., Hilton, A.: Model-based multiple view reconstruction of people. In: ICCV (2003)
25. Starck, J., Hilton, A.: Spherical matching for temporal correspondence of non-rigid surfaces. In: ICCV (2005)
26. Straka, M., Hauswiesner, S., Ruether, M., Bischof, H.: Simultaneous shape and pose adaption of articulated models using linear optimization (2012)
27. Sumner, R.W., Popović, J.: Deformation Transfer for Triangle Meshes. ACM Transactions on Graphics 23(3) (2004)
28. Tung, T., Matsuyama, T.: Topology dictionary for 3d video understanding. PAMI 34(8), 1645–1647 (2012)
29. Tung, T., Matsuyama, T.: Intrinsic characterization of dynamic surfaces. In: CVPR (2013)
30. Vlasic, D., Baran, I., Matusik, W., Popovic, J.: Articulated mesh animation from multi-view silhouettes. ACM Transactions on Graphics 27(3) (2008)
31. Windheuser, T., Schlickewei, U., Schmidt, F., Cremers, D.: Geometrically consistent elastic matching of 3d shapes: A linear programming solution. In: ICCV (2011)
32. Zeng, Y., Wang, C., Gu, X., Samaras, D., Paragios, N.: A Generic Deformation Model for Dense Non-Rigid Surface Registration: a Higher-Order MRF-based Approach. In: ICCV (2013)

Hybrid Stochastic / Deterministic Optimization for Tracking Sports Players and Pedestrians*

Robert T. Collins[1] and Peter Carr[2]

[1] The Pennsylvania State University, USA
[2] Disney Research Pittsburgh, USA

Abstract. Although 'tracking-by-detection' is a popular approach when reliable object detectors are available, missed detections remain a difficult hurdle to overcome. We present a hybrid stochastic/deterministic optimization scheme that uses RJMCMC to perform stochastic search over the space of detection configurations, interleaved with deterministic computation of the optimal multi-frame data association for each proposed detection hypothesis. Since object trajectories do not need to be estimated directly by the sampler, our approach is more efficient than traditional MCMCDA techniques. Moreover, our holistic formulation is able to generate longer, more reliable trajectories than baseline tracking-by-detection approaches in challenging multi-target scenarios.

1   Introduction

Multi-target tracking of pedestrians and sports players is difficult due to the presence of many similar-looking objects interacting in close proximity. For this reason there has been recent interest in sliding temporal window methods that recover tracking solutions by considering a batch of frames at a time. The motivation is that people who are occluded or otherwise difficult to disambiguate in a few frames will be easier to find in others, and that propagating temporal consistency constraints both backwards and forwards in time leads to better solutions than purely causal processing.

It is also advantageous to solve for detections and data association jointly, rather than computing detections first and then linking them into trajectories. Despite the obvious benefits, this holistic approach has received considerably less attention because the complexity of the search space of data association increases exponentially with the number of candidate detections in each frame, and therefore committing to a small set of high-quality discrete detections makes the later association problem more manageable. However, not being able to reconsider detection decisions puts a large burden on the data association algorithm to handle deficiencies such as missed detections and false positives.

---

* Electronic supplementary material -Supplementary material is available in the online version of this chapter at http://dx.doi.org/10.1007/978-3-319-10605-2_20. Videos can also be accessed at http://www.springerimages.com/videos/978-3-319-10604-5.

D. Fleet et al. (Eds.): ECCV 2014, Part II, LNCS 8690, pp. 298–313, 2014.
© Springer International Publishing Switzerland 2014

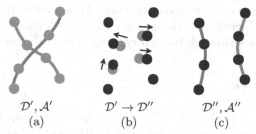

$\mathcal{D}', \mathcal{A}'$ $\mathcal{D}' \to \mathcal{D}''$ $\mathcal{D}'', \mathcal{A}''$
(a)   (b)   (c)

Fig. 1. Stochastic Detection/Deterministic Tracking. (a) An initial set of detections $\mathcal{D}'$ has a corresponding optimal data association solution $\mathcal{A}'$, shown here as red and blue trajectories. However, due to detection noise, we may have mistakenly swapped the identities of the two targets. (b) If we stochastically perturb the set of detections to generate a new hypothesis $\mathcal{D}''$, it may lead (c) to a better data association solution $\mathcal{A}''$. Conceptually, we are decomposing the joint optimization of $(\mathcal{D}, \mathcal{A})$ into a stochastic proposal of multi-frame detections $\mathcal{D}$ and a deterministic solution for $\mathcal{A}|\mathcal{D}$ (similar to 'line search') given each such proposal.

In this paper we present a Bayesian approach for simultaneous optimization over the space of detections and data associations (Figure 1). We develop a hybrid optimization algorithm that uses Reversible Jump Markov Chain Monte Carlo (RJMCMC) sampling over the space of detections to "drive" the estimation process, while leveraging recent results on deterministic polynomial-time algorithms for computing the globally optimal data association for a set of hypothesized multi-frame detections. Experimental results show that the method performs well, even on sports sequences where players perform rapid maneuvers in close proximity to each other.

Contributions

1) Our main contribution is a hybrid MCMC algorithm that uses deterministic solutions for blocks of variables to accelerate its stochastic mode-seeking behavior. Incorporating deterministic solutions within MCMC is nearly universally avoided [18] because it breaks detailed balance and threatens the integrity of the sampler. However, we note that using MCMC to guide discovery of the joint mode of a posterior distribution does not require faithful generation of samples representative of the whole distribution, and show that factoring a joint distribution into detection and association variables leads to a natural framework where MCMC sampling over detections is interleaved with a deterministic solution for the optimal set of associations. We show that our method yields a correct sampler with respect to a max-marginal distribution over detections, and that seeking the mode of this max-marginal allows efficient search for the joint mode of the original posterior with respect to both detections and associations.

2) Unlike the majority of tracking-by-detection methods for multi-frame, multi-target tracking, our approach iteratively revises (including adding and removing) detections over the sequence of frames. This leads to better results than fixing a set of detections once and for all prior to performing data association. Furthermore, interleaving data association with the search for detections has a

regularizing effect that encourages consistency of the number of detections across frames and of their locations with respect to a smooth path, without having to enforce those qualities through trajectory/motion smoothness priors.

2   Related Work

Tracking-by-detection [16,28,5,9,23,2,27] is a popular technique for multi-object tracking. A sequence of frames is preprocessed with an object detector to generate a finite set of object locations in space/time, and data association is then used to link detections across discrete time intervals, which effectively estimates a sampled trajectory for each object (to which a smoothed approximation can be estimated [2]). When the association objective function is limited to addition or multiplication of pairwise costs, the global optimum can be computed in polynomial time [5,23]. Most methods can easily handle false detections, but missed detections are more difficult since links must be hypothesized to span multi-frame gaps.

Breitenstein *et al.* [8] use detector confidence maps to hypothesize new locations when detections are missing. Our approach is similar to [8] in that we also hypothesize detections, however we hypothesize **all detections** for the entire multi-frame sequence, and not just detections which may have been missed by an object detector. Other approaches similar to ours, in that they attempt to simultaneously estimate both detections and trajectories, include: [19], where combined detection and trajectory estimation becomes an NP-hard quadratic boolean optimization problem, solved heuristically; the non-convex continuous energy minimization approach of [21], which contains transdimensional jump moves similar to RJMCMC, although applied in a deterministic way that can only decrease the energy; and [26], who propose a coupled detection and tracking approach where a sparsity-constrained detection solution is interleaved with min-cost flow data association in a Lagrangian optimization loop.

Markov Chain Monte Carlo (MCMC) sampling methods offer a general approach for exploring large problem spaces under expressive objective functions, and have been applied to problems of multi-target detection [29,13] and data association [20,7]. Previous MCMC Data Association (MCMCDA) approaches [14,22,4,20,7,17] have explicitly estimated the associations between detections. However, not only is the space of unknowns to be explored much larger when assignment links are included in the MCMC search, one has to design specialized moves that propose coordinated changes to multiple assignment variables to satisfy the one-to-one matching constraints necessary to maintain a feasible solution. A key difference of our work is that we do not explicitly estimate the data association variables using stochastic search. Instead, we address data association as a closed form solution contingent on the current hypothesized set of detections. As a result, we only need to consider relatively simple and well-understood sampler moves related to detections (e.g. birth, death and diffusion).

3   Approach

In multi-target tracking, the variables to be solved for are the number and location of objects (detections) in each frame of the sequence, and the inter-frame correspondences (associations) of those detections over time to form a set of trajectories.

3.1   Bayesian Formulation

We adopt a Bayesian approach where detections $\mathcal{D}$ and associations $\mathcal{A}$ are random variables, likelihood functions measure how well a hypothetical set of detections and associations explain the observed image sequence $\mathcal{Z}$, and priors encourage properties expected in "good" solutions. The goal is to maximize the joint posterior distribution over $\mathcal{D}$ and $\mathcal{A}$ given observations $\mathcal{Z}$:

$$A^*, D^* = \operatorname*{argmax}_{\mathcal{A}, \mathcal{D}} P(\mathcal{A}, \mathcal{D} | \mathcal{Z}) \tag{1}$$

$$= \operatorname*{argmax}_{\mathcal{A}, \mathcal{D}} P(\mathcal{A} | \mathcal{D}, \mathcal{Z}) P(\mathcal{D} | \mathcal{Z}) \tag{2}$$

where the second line follows by the definition of conditional probability.

Without loss of generality, we split the argmax and rewrite Eq. (2) as :

$$D^* = \operatorname*{argmax}_{\mathcal{D}} \left[\left(\max_{\mathcal{A}} P(\mathcal{A} | \mathcal{D}, \mathcal{Z}) \right) P(\mathcal{D} | \mathcal{Z}) \right] \tag{3}$$

$$A^* = \operatorname*{argmax}_{\mathcal{A}} P(\mathcal{A} | D^*, \mathcal{Z}) \ . \tag{4}$$

In practice the argmax A^* is found while computing the max over $\mathcal{A}$ in the inner parentheses of Eq. (3). This is equivalent to the joint maximization in Eq. (1) because both $P(\mathcal{A} | \mathcal{D}, \mathcal{Z})$ and $P(\mathcal{D} | \mathcal{Z})$ are non-negative by construction. Intuitively, this factors the joint estimation problem into detections, $P(\mathcal{D} | \mathcal{Z})$, and data associations, $P(\mathcal{A} | \mathcal{D}, \mathcal{Z})$. See Figure 2.

Previous tracking-by-detection approaches compute the following approximate solution to Eqs. (3–4):

$$D^* = \operatorname*{argmax}_{\mathcal{D}} P(\mathcal{D} | \mathcal{Z}) \tag{5}$$

$$A^* = \operatorname*{argmax}_{\mathcal{A}} P(\mathcal{A} | D^*, \mathcal{Z}) \ . \tag{6}$$

This is suboptimal even if the correct marginal $P(\mathcal{D} | \mathcal{Z}) = \int_{\mathcal{A}} P(\mathcal{A}, \mathcal{D} | \mathcal{Z})$ is used, because the mode of a marginal distribution does not necessarily correspond to the projection of the mode of the joint distribution. Furthermore, generating a fixed set of detections prior to determining associations makes it difficult if not impossible to recover when detections are missed due to occlusion or low detector confidence. It is better to allow association-based information such as

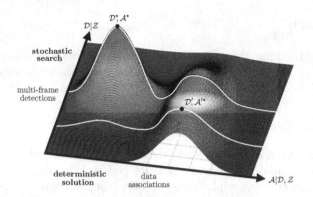

Fig. 2. Hybrid Stochastic/Deterministic Optimization. The goal is to determine the optimal set of detections $\mathcal{D}^*$ and associations $\mathcal{A}^*$ for observations $\mathcal{Z}$. We factor the joint optimization into stochastic search over detections $\mathcal{D}|\mathcal{Z}$ interleaved with deterministic solutions for associations $\mathcal{A}|\mathcal{D}, \mathcal{Z}$. Each hypothesized set of detections $\mathcal{D}'$ results in a reduced 'line search' for the corresponding best set of associations $\mathcal{A}'$ (which has a deterministic solution for energy functions of pairwise potentials).

high-confidence partial trajectories to guide estimation of hard-to-see detections during ambiguous portions of the sequence.

On the other hand, Eqs. (3–4) suggests that an algorithm for estimating the joint mode can be organized as a search over multi-frame configurations of detections while using a subroutine to solve the global data association problem for each hypothesized set of detections. That is the strategy taken in this paper: we present a hybrid optimization approach that uses RJMCMC to perform stochastic search over the space of detection configurations, interleaved with deterministic computation of the optimal multi-frame assignment for each proposed detection hypothesis.

The clearest way to think about our approach is to consider deterministic computation of assignments to be a closed-form function $A(\mathcal{D})$, and that we are performing stochastic optimization over a distribution $\Psi(\mathcal{D}) \propto A(\mathcal{D})P(\mathcal{D}|\mathcal{Z})$ that is a function only of detections.[1] It is not hard to recognize that $\Psi(\mathcal{D})$ is the **max-marginal** of $P(\mathcal{A}, \mathcal{D}|\mathcal{Z})$ computed by max'ing over $\mathcal{A}$ for each value of $\mathcal{D}$. One insight is that sampling from the max-marginal $\Psi(\mathcal{D})$ is sufficient to guide the search for (A^*, D^*), since $\Psi(\mathcal{D})$ has the same mode D^* as $P(\mathcal{A}, \mathcal{D}|\mathcal{Z})$, and, once D^* is found, it can be plugged into $A(\mathcal{D})$ to find A^*.

Unfortunately, $\Psi(\mathcal{D})$ is hard to sample from directly due to the implicit coupling between associations and detections. However, an MCMC sampler may propose samples from a simpler proposal distribution and rely on computation of the acceptance ratio to make sure accepted samples are distributed according to the desired target distribution. In this work we design an MCMC sampler that uses simple local updates to current detection configuration D_c to propose a new configuration D', for which the optimal data association $A' = A(D')$ is computed

---

[1] Note we overload $A(D)$ to refer to both the argmax as well as the value at the max.

deterministically, followed by using $\Psi(D')$ and $\Psi(D_c)$ to compute the likelihoods in the acceptance ratio that ensure $\Psi(\mathcal{D})$ is the correct target distribution of the sampler. The components of the sampler are presented below.

3.2 Observation Data

Our method uses a subsampled temporal window of N frames $I = \{I_1, I_2, \ldots, I_N\}$. Input RGB images are converted to YCbCr so that luminance information can be treated differently from chrominance. In addition to the raw pixel data, a set of binary foreground masks $F = \{F_1, F_2, \ldots, F_N\}$ is generated by background subtraction and thresholding in YCbCr color space, followed by denoising using morphological opening and dilation operators, and optional suppression of foreground data outside of a given region of interest.

To facilitate reasoning about locations of people in the ground plane, each foreground mask F_k is mapped to a monocular *occupancy proposal map* M_k such that $M_k(x, y)$ indicates the probability of ground location (x, y) being occupied. This is performed by a process similar to [10] where F_k is backprojected using camera calibration information onto 3D volume elements of the scene, followed by marginalizing over the height dimension. Together, the N triplets of color images, binary foreground masks and occupancy maps comprise the observation data $\mathcal{Z} = \{Z_1, Z_2, \ldots, Z_N\}$, with $Z_k = (I_k, F_k, M_k)$. See Figure 3 top row.

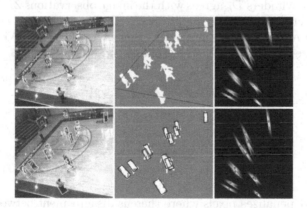

Fig. 3. Top row, left to right: color image I_k; foreground mask F_k (also showing region of interest); ground plane proposal map M_k. Bottom row: single frame detection results overlaid on each form of observation data.

3.3 Detections

A posterior distribution $P(\mathcal{D}|\mathcal{Z})$ over multi-frame detections is derived by Bayes rule and assumption of independence over frames

$$P(\mathcal{D}|\mathcal{Z}) \propto P(\mathcal{D})P(\mathcal{Z}|\mathcal{D}) = \prod_{k=1}^{N} P(D_k) \prod_{k=1}^{N} P(Z_k|D_k) . \tag{7}$$

Although independence is assumed, we note that later combination with the conditional posterior over associations, $P(\mathcal{A}|\mathcal{D}, \mathcal{Z})$, will have a regularizing effect on the set of detections found across frames.

Each person is modeled as a 3D cylinder C with ground plane location (x, y), height h and radius r. Holding r constant, the unknowns for each detected cylinder $d_i \in C$ are (x_i, y_i, h_i). A configuration in frame k is an unordered set of 0 or more cylinders $D_k \in \{\emptyset \cup C \cup C^2 \cup C^3 \cup \ldots\}$. To define a prior distribution over configurations, we restrict location (x, y) to range over a bounded subset W of $\mathbb{R}^2$ and to be distributed with respect to the homogeneous unit intensity Poisson process on W. Cylinder height h is uniformly distributed over a discrete set of heights, independent of location. Prior distribution $P(D_k)$ is therefore a so-called *marked point process* that couples a stochastic point process over the ground plane region of interest W with an additional distribution over a space of attributes at each point (*i.e.* height).

We assume that camera calibration information is known such that 3D locations in the scene can be projected into the 2D image plane, and define the detection likelihood function as a marked Gibbs point process

$$P(Z_k|D_k) \propto \exp\{-U(D_k, Z_k)\} \tag{8}$$

where energy function $U(\cdot)$ measures how well the projection of a hypothesized configuration of cylinders D_k agrees with the image observations Z_k. We compute this energy function using a *count image* S_k where each pixel $p \in S_k$ contains a count of how many cylinders project to that image location. With respect to this count image, the energy function contains two terms

$$U = \alpha_1 G_1(S_k, Z_k) + \alpha_2 G_2(S_k) \tag{9}$$

$$G_1 = \sum_{p \in S_k} \delta\left[\min(1, S(p)) \neq F(p)\right] \tag{10}$$

$$G_2 = \sum_{p \in S_k} (S(p) - 1). \tag{11}$$

Energy term G_1 penalizes pixels where there is disagreement between the count image and foreground mask over whether the image location is occupied. Energy term G_2 penalizes pixels where multiple people overlap, thereby encouraging solutions to have the smallest number of people that explain the data.

If association links are not needed or only one image is observed, we can search for the MAP estimate over detections with an RJMCMC sampler (see Section 3.5) having $P(\mathcal{D}|\mathcal{Z})$ as its target distribution. Due to the assumption of independence across frames, this is equivalent to estimating detections D_k independently for each frame k. Figure 3 (bottom row) shows such a single-frame detection result. It has been seen in previous work [29,13] that these single-frame solutions can be quite good at determining the number and location of multiple people whose projections partially occlude each other in the image.

3.4   Associations

The representation of association variables $\mathcal{A}$ is inspired by work on globally optimal data association based on network flow [5,23]. Consider the multi-frame detections in a configuration D to be nodes in a multi-stage trellis graph where each stage corresponds to one frame. Define an edge between each pair of detections in adjacent frames of the graph, *i.e.* such that $d_i \in D_k$ and $d_j \in D_{k+1}$ for $k = 1, \ldots, N - 1$. Paired with each edge is a binary *association link* variable f_{ij}. A value $f_{ij} = 1$ means d_i is to be linked with d_j to form one segment of a trajectory, whereas $f_{ij} = 0$ means the association link is turned off. With respect to detection d_k all edges f_{*k} are considered to be *incoming* edges, and all variables f_{k*} are called *outgoing* edges. Each detection d_k also has an incoming and outgoing dummy link ϕ allowing it to be the first or last node of a trajectory, or to be marked as a false positive.

Each edge has an associated cost

$$
c_{ij} = \begin{cases} \|d_i - d_j\|^2/\sigma^2 + \mathrm{EMD}(h_i, h_j) \; ; \|d_i - d_j\| \leq \rho \\ \beta \qquad\qquad\qquad\qquad\qquad\quad ; i = \phi \text{ or } j = \phi \\ \infty \qquad\qquad\qquad\qquad\qquad\quad ; \text{otherwise} \end{cases}
$$

combining distance information with color similarity measured by Earth Mover's Distance on color histograms h_i and h_j extracted from the image projection of each detection. Link variables with infinite cost can never be turned on and their edges can be excluded from the graph. Parameter ρ is a distance gating threshold, set to the maximum distance a person can travel from one sample frame to the next, σ^2 determines how much small displacements should be favored over larger ones, and β is a penalty for missed detections, which should be set at least as large as the largest gated detection cost would be, *e.g.* $\beta > \rho^2/\sigma^2$.

The likelihood over association variables is defined in Gibbs form as

$$
P(A|D, Z) \propto \exp\{-V(A, D, Z)\} \tag{12}
$$

where $V(\cdot)$ is a linear function of the association variables $\mathcal{A} = \{f_{ij}\}$:

$$
V = \alpha_3 G_3(A, D, Z) \tag{13}
$$

$$
G_3 = \sum_{f_{ij} \in \mathcal{A}} c_{ij} f_{ij}. \tag{14}
$$

Our goal is to choose binary values for variables f_{ij} that minimize the sum of costs in G_3 subject to constraints that exactly one incoming link and one outgoing link to and from each detection is set to 1, and all others to 0. If we connect all incoming dummy links to a distinguished *source* node, and outgoing dummy links to a *sink* node, this minimization can be addressed within a mincost network flow framework (e.g. [28]). However, the constraint that exactly one incoming and outgoing link are turned on makes the problem more natural to view as a multi-dimensional assignment problem [11], which can be be solved efficiently using an algorithm due to Shaffique[25].

Algorithm 1. HYBRID RJMCMC for maximizing $P(\mathcal{A}, \mathcal{D}|\mathcal{Z})$

Input: Z, ITERMAX
Output: A^*, D^*

Initialize D_c and A_c. Let $A^*, D^* = A_c, D_c$.
for $t = 1$ to ITERMAX
    choose a stochastic move and propose D'
    compute $A' = A(D')$ to maximize $P(\mathcal{A}|D', Z)$
    compute acceptance ratio $\alpha((D_c, A_c) \to (D', A'))$
    sample $u \sim U(0, 1)$
    if $\log(u) < \log(\alpha((D_c, A_c) \to (D', A')))$
        $D_c, A_c = D', A'$
    if $P(A_c, D_c|Z) > P(A^*, D^*|Z)$
        $A^*, D^* = A_c, D_c$
end

3.5 Optimization

We optimize over association and detection variables in $P(\mathcal{A}, \mathcal{D}|\mathcal{Z})$ by using a hybrid RJMCMC algorithm that samples over multi-frame detection configurations $\mathcal{D}$, interleaved with deterministic computation of multi-frame data association variables $\mathcal{A}$ with respect to each proposed set of detections (see Algorithm 1). Given a current state (D_c, A_c), the algorithm proposes a new state (D', A') by randomly perturbing the detection configuration $D_c \to D'$ and then deterministically computing the set of associations A' that maximize $P(A, D'|Z)$. This new state (D', A') is then accepted or rejected according to the Metropolis-Hastings-Green (MHG) ratio $\alpha((D_c, A_c) \to (D', A'))$ [15]. More details follow.

The stochastic moves used for proposing a transition $D_c \to D'$ are:

Birth: Choose a frame uniformly at random. Add a new detection to the unordered configuration with location (x_i, y_i) chosen by sampling from the proposal map for that frame and height h_i chosen from a discrete set of height options.

Death: Choose a frame uniformly at random. If there are no detections currently in that frame, no transition occurs. Otherwise, choose a detection uniformly at random and remove it from the configuration for that frame.

Diffusion: Choose a frame uniformly at random. If there are no detections currently in that frame, no transition occurs. Otherwise, choose a detection uniformly at random and perturb its (x_i, y_i) location to $(x_i + dx, y_i + dy)$ with $dx \sim U(-\Delta x, +\Delta x)$ and $dy \sim U(-\Delta y, +\Delta y)$. If the new location is outside the region of interest, no transition occurs. Also choose a new height h_i uniformly at random from the discrete set of height options.

Once a detection configuration D' is proposed, we seek an optimal multi-frame assignment A' to maximize $P(\mathcal{A}|D', Z)$. This is computed by a deterministic function $A' = A(D')$, leveraging the fact that the globally optimal solution to the multidimensional assignment problem of Section 3.4 can be found in strong polynomial time [25]. We prefer the multidimensional assignment framework rather than classical network flow because we want to explicitly penalize false positive detections, not ignore them (in MDA every detection must be explained; in network flow, false positives do not contribute to the cost of the solution if no flow is routed through them). It is important to have these penalties as feedback to encourage the exploration of detection configurations having fewer false positives and missed detections.

All stochastic proposal moves are local updates of detections only, and have a dimension matching Jacobian of 1, so the MHG acceptance ratio [15] reduces to the Metropolis-Hastings ratio:

$$\alpha((D_c, A_c) \to (D', A')) = \min\left(1, \frac{P(D', A'|Z)}{P(D_c, A_c|Z)} \frac{Q(D_c \to D')}{Q(D' \to D_c)}\right). \quad (15)$$

In this equation, $Q(a \to b)$ is the probability of proposing detection configuration b from the current configuration a, which is very easy to compute in all cases due to the highly localized effects of birth, death and diffusion moves.

3.6   Justification of Correctness

It is widely known that including deterministic moves in an MCMC sampler is dangerous because the chain may become non-ergodic and violate the detailed balance conditions that ensure a correct sampler [18]. Indeed, if our goal was to generate samples (D_c, A_c) representative of the joint distribution $P(A, D|Z)$ to make statistical inferences, such as computing expected values, our algorithm above would not be a correct sampler. This is because there are regions of joint A, D space that have nonzero probability under $P(A, D|Z)$ yet have zero probability of being transitioned to, since the deterministic solution $A = A(D)$ does not maintain any diversity of associations for a given detection configuration. Referring back to Fig. 2, note how only a single "point" along each line of constant D is ever generated by the sampler.

However, we are using MCMC not for statistical inferencing on $P(A, D|Z)$ but to guide search for its global mode. Recall that our sampler can be interpreted as searching for D^* from the max-marginal distribution $\Psi(D)$, and computing $A^* = A(D^*)$ deterministically from that. We therefore should be able to find the global mode A^*, D^* if our algorithm is a correct sampler over $\Psi(D)$. To prove this correctness, first note that $A(D)$ is strictly positive for any argument D, since assigning every detection as a false positive is always an option, and yields a positive value. As a distribution in Gibbs form, $P(D|Z)$ is also strictly positive for any configuration with countable number of detections. Therefore, any proposed configuration of detections D has a non-zero probability of being accepted. It suffices then to show that RJMCMC with the moves described earlier yields a sampler having stationary distribution $\Psi(D)$. The proof follows Appendix B of van Lieshout [11]. Specifically, the chain is positive recurrent and irreducible with respect to the null configuration of 0 detections in any frame, since any configuration can be transformed with positive probability to the null configuration by a finite series of death moves, and conversely any configuration can be recovered with positive probability by a finite series of birth moves.

Furthermore, there is a positive probability of staying in the null configuration for one or more time steps (for example, if a death move is proposed), and therefore the chain is also aperiodic. These properties are sufficient to ensure that target distribution $\Psi(\mathcal{D})$ is the unique stationary distribution of the chain.

4   Evaluation

In this section we present a proof of concept that the stochastic/deterministic sampler presented above works in practice. We evaluate our method on one in-house sequence and two publicly available video sequences. All were captured from stationary, calibrated cameras, allowing us to estimate object locations and trajectories in a metric ground-plane coordinate system.

Test Sequences: 1) The **Doohan** sequence is a short 20 second clip from an NCAA college basketball game recorded at 25fps and an image resolution of 1920×1456. All 10 players plus 2 referees are visible in the playing area through the whole sequence. Tracking of players is challenging due to their rapid and erratic motion, close proximity, and similar appearance. Ground truth locations were estimated by hand in a floor-plane coordinate system. 2) **APIDIS** sequence is a one minute video from the public APIDIS dataset[2]. It shares the same player tracking challenges as Doohan, but in addition players leave and reenter the field of view and extreme lighting causes saturated regions, long shadows, and poor color quality. The APIDIS dataset has been popular for testing multi-view volumetric tracking approaches [1,3,24]; however, we are interested in evaluating single-view tracking and only use camera 6, which views the right half of the court. Ground truth locations in the floor plane that were annotated every 1 second are distributed with the full APIDIS dataset. 3) The **Oxford Town-Centre** sequence [4] shows pedestrians walking along a busy street, recorded at 25fps with a resolution of 1920×1080[3]. The pedestrian paths are mostly smooth with constant velocity, however there are partial occlusions by signs and benches, and additional objects such as bicycles and strollers appear. This dataset only has meaningful annotations for head locations in the image plane. However, by assuming a constant height of 1.8 meters we approximate the corresponding ground location for each person. This leads to a bias in the "ground truth" for people who are not that tall; particularly noticeable for children in strollers.

Evaluation Metrics: We evaluate both detection and tracking results using the popular CLEAR MOT metrics [6]. MOTP is a measure of geometric accuracy of detections, and is measured for these sequences as distance in the ground plane. MOTA evaluates data association accuracy by penalizing ID swaps, false positives and missed detections along a trajectory. Also reported are precision, recall and average track length. In the online supplemental material we report all intermediate numbers used to compute these measures (e.g. TP, FN, FP, ID swaps),

[2] http://www.apidis.org/Dataset/
[3] http://www.robots.ox.ac.uk/ActiveVision/Publications/benfold_reid_cvpr2011/

and present additional evaluations with respect to 2D bounding box overlap rather than ground plane distance, evaluation of the effects of color appearance on algorithm performance, and measurement of performance improvement as the number of iterations of the MCMC algorithm increases.

Baseline Algorithms: For comparison, we developed four single-view baseline algorithms for multi-target detection and tracking, generated as the cross-product of two kinds of detectors and two kinds of data association. For detectors, **SF** is a single-frame version of our MCMC detection algorithm (Section 3.3), run on each frame independently, while **POM** is the probabilistic occupancy map detector of [12] run in single-frame mode using the same foreground mask used by our detector. For data association, **Oneshot** applies the deterministic multi-dimensional assignment algorithm [25] that we use solve for associations given a set of detections (Section 3.5), while **DC** applies the discrete-continuous linking and smoothing algorithm of [2] to a given set of detections. All four baseline algorithms (SF-Oneshot, SF-DC, POM-Oneshot, POM-DC) are non iterative, performing a single round of detection followed by a single round of data association, unlike our full algorithm, **HybridFull**, which iteratively performs a stochastic search through the space of multi-frame detection configurations while deterministically solving for the best data association for each configuration.

Results

Table 1 presents the quantitative evaluation results for each tested algorithm on each of the three sequences. Generally, our proposed stochastic/deterministic algorithm achieves the best performance across all measures and all sequences.

The discrete-continuous optimization algorithm [2] incorporates a trajectory smoothing stage, which appears to hinder performance when the temporal sampling is sparse. Additionally, this algorithm does not use appearance information, making it much more difficult to deduce the correct tracking when two objects are in close proximity. However, a clear trend among the algorithms is the longer track length produced by our method. The method of [2] tends to fragment long single-object trajectories into reliable, but short, tracks.

Our 'OneShot' algorithm is essentially the method of [25], but without the ability to infer associations across multi-frame gaps (*i.e.* it is not allowed to compensate for missed detections). In all sequences, HybridFull outperforms SF-OneShot indicating that the MCMC sampler was able to find a better set of detections than the initial solution. This reinforces the point that prematurely fixing the set of detections imposes a burden (e.g. gaps and false detections) that efficient polynomial time data association algorithms cannot overcome.

Figure 4 illustrates the regularizing effect that simultaneous estimation of data association has on estimated detections. Although there are no prior terms encouraging the number of detections in adjacent frames to be similar, the likelihood function $P(\mathcal{A}|\mathcal{D}, \mathcal{Z})$ for assignment variables contains penalty terms for unassigned detections, indirectly penalizing configurations having different numbers of detections in each frame. As a result, gaps are filled in and short trajectory fragments are linked together into longer, full trajectories.

Table 1. Quantitative evaluation on the Doohan (top), APIDIS (middle), and Oxford Towncentre (bottom) datasets. The match threshold for CLEAR MOT measures is 1 meter, applied in the ground plane. Lower values are better for MOTP; higher values are better for all other scores. Avglen is computed as (average detected path length / average ground truth path length) * 100.

Doohan sequence					
Algorithm	MOTP(m)	MOTA(-)	Prec(%)	Recall(%)	AvgLen(%)
SF-OneShot	0.27	86.38	96.14	96.14	33.40
SF-DC	**0.23**	64.63	**97.01**	85.77	8.40
HybridFull(ours)	0.26	**90.24**	96.74	**96.54**	**88.20**
APIDIS sequence					
Algorithm	MOTP(m)	MOTA(-)	Prec(%)	Recall(%)	AvgLen(%)
SF-OneShot	0.37	45.40	81.38	77.87	23.96
SF-DC	0.43	41.09	78.64	66.67	35.14
POM-OneShot	0.39	17.53	66.01	77.01	11.82
POM-DC	0.49	30.75	71.79	65.80	33.23
HybridFull(ours)	**0.34**	**62.64**	**85.50**	**81.32**	**60.70**
TownCentre sequence					
Algorithm	MOTP(m)	MOTA(-)	Prec(%)	Recall(%)	AvgLen(%)
SF-OneShot	0.46	29.88	65.06	72.59	32.90
SF-DC	0.59	-17.79	44.67	58.72	53.09
POM-OneShot	**0.40**	19.35	60.57	70.39	20.20
POM-DC	0.61	-5.51	49.19	59.38	59.61
HybridFull(ours)	0.45	**41.32**	**70.45**	**73.84**	**69.06**

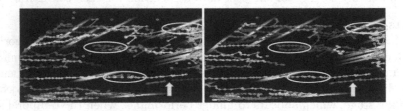

Fig. 4. Top: Initial ground plane trajectories at the start of MCMC processing of the Oxford Town Centre Dataset. Bottom: Final trajectories after 10000 iterations. Several places have been highlighted to illustrate improvements due to gap spanning and trajectory smoothing.

Figure 5 shows sample tracking results from each sequence. Consistency of estimated identity is indicated by bounding boxes of the same color on the same person over time. Videos suitable for qualitative assessment of the results across all frames are available in the online supplemental material.

5   Summary

Traditional tracking-by-detection methods must incorporate complex data association models to handle missed detections and false detections. Our approach, on the other hand, continually explores the set of multi-frame detections and uses a simple data association model for which an optimal solution can be computed efficiently. The burden of dealing with missed and false detections is now handled by the search over multi-frame detections, relying on the power of MCMC

Fig. 5. Sample output frames from the three test sequences. Top: Doohan sequence, Middle: APIDIS camera 6, Bottom: Oxford TownCentre. Color is used to indicate identity across frames.

sampling to produce a near-optimal set of detections. Unlike typical MCMC tracking, which must hypothesize both detections and their associations (and therefore propose complex multi-track moves such as split, merge or swap), our MCMC approach only proposes detections using simple local update moves of birth, death and diffusion while the corresponding associations are computed in a deterministic fashion. As we have shown, incorporating this deterministic aspect into the random search does not jeopardize the necessary conditions of MCMC to have a unique stationary distribution corresponding to our desired target distribution $\Psi(\mathcal{D})$. Additionally, our experiments show how re-estimating the set of multi-frame detections leads to significant improvements in tracking performance.

In future work, the approach in this paper could be generalized in several ways. Three specific ideas are: 1) use proposal moves that refer to the current trajectory estimates when hypothesizing new detections, for example to favor proposing detections that extend a partial track; 2) to use an appearance-based pedestrian detector confidence map in the image to propose pedestrian locations and evaluate their likelihood; and 3) to use a deterministic data association approach that is not strictly guaranteed to yield a global optimum, but that would allow use of more expressive objective functions that include terms of higher-order than the pairwise terms used in network flow / MDA.

References

1. Alahi, A., Jacques, L., Boursier, Y., Vandergheynst, P.: Sparsity driven people localization with a heterogeneous network of cameras. Journal of Mathematical Imaging and Vision 41(1-2), 39–58 (2011)
2. Andriyenko, A., Schindler, K., Roth, S.: Discrete-continuous optimization for multi-target tracking. In: CVPR (2012)
3. Ben Shitrit, H., Berclaz, J., Fleuret, G., Fua, P.: Multi-Commodity Network Flow for Tracking Multiple People. PAMI (2013)
4. Benfold, B., Reid, I.: Stable multi-target tracking in real-time surveillance video. In: CVPR (2011)
5. Berclaz, J., Turetken, E., Fleuret, F., Fua, P.: Multiple Object Tracking using K-Shortest Paths Optimization. PAMI 33(9), 1806–1819 (2011)
6. Bernardin, K., Stiefelhagen, R.: Evaluating multiple object tracking performance: The CLEAR MOT metrics. EURASIP Journal on Image and Video Processing, Special Issue on Video Tracking in Complex Scenes for Surveillance Applications 2008, article ID 246309 (May 2008)
7. Brau, E., Barnard, K., Palanivelu, R., Dunatunga, D., Tsukamoto, T., Lee, P.: A generative statistical model for tracking multiple smooth trajectories. In: CVPR, pp. 1137–1144 (2011)
8. Breitenstein, M., Reichlin, F., Leibe, B., Koller-Meier, E., Van Gool, L.: Online multiperson tracking-by-detection from a single, uncalibrated camera. PAMI 33(9), 1820–1833 (2011)
9. Brendel, W., Amer, M., Todorovic, S.: Multiobject tracking as maximum weight independent set. In: CVPR (2011)
10. Carr, P., Sheikh, Y., Matthews, I.: Monocular object detection using 3D geometric primitives. In: Fitzgibbon, A., Lazebnik, S., Perona, P., Sato, Y., Schmid, C. (eds.) ECCV 2012, Part I. LNCS, vol. 7572, pp. 864–878. Springer, Heidelberg (2012)
11. Collins, R.: Multitarget data association with higher-order motion models. In: CVPR (2012)
12. Fleuret, F., Berclaz, J., Lengagne, R., Fua, P.: Multi-Camera People Tracking with a Probabilistic Occupancy Map. PAMI 30(2), 267–282 (2008)
13. Ge, W., Collins, R.: Marked point processes for crowd counting. In: CVPR. pp. 2913–2920 (2009)
14. Ge, W., Collins, R.: Multi-target data association by tracklets with unsupervised parameter estimation. In: BMVC (2008)
15. Green, P.: Reversible jump markov chain monte carlo computation and bayesian model determination. Biometrika 82(4), 711–732 (1995)
16. Huang, C., Wu, B., Nevatia, R.: Robust object tracking by hierarchical association of detection responses. In: Forsyth, D., Torr, P., Zisserman, A. (eds.) ECCV 2008, Part II. LNCS, vol. 5303, pp. 788–801. Springer, Heidelberg (2008)
17. Khan, Z., Balch, T., Dellaert, F.: Mcmc data association and sparse factorization updating for real time multitarget tracking with merged and multiple measurements. PAMI 28(12), 1960–1972 (2006)
18. Kim, W., Lee, K.: Markov chain monte carlo combined with deterministic methods for markov random field optimization. In: CVPR (2009)
19. Leibe, B., Schindler, K., Gool, L.J.V.: Coupled detection and trajectory estimation for multi-object tracking. In: ICCV, pp. 1–8 (2007)
20. van Lieshout, M.: Depth map calculation for a variable number of moving objects using markov sequential object processes. PAMI 30(7), 1308–1312 (2008)

21. Milan, A., Roth, S., Schindler, K.: Continuous energy minimization for multitarget tracking. PAMI 36(1), 58–72 (2014)
22. Oh, S., Russell, S., Sastry, S.: Markov chain monte carlo data association for multi-target tracking. IEEE Transactions on Automatic Control 54(3), 481–497 (2009)
23. Pirsiavash, H., Ramanan, D., Fowlkes, C.C.: Globally-optimal greedy algorithms for tracking a variable number of objects. In: CVPR (2011)
24. Possegger, H., Sternig, S., Mauthner, T., Roth, P., Bischof, H.: Robust real-time tracking of multiple objects by volumetric mass densities. In: CVPR, pp. 2395–2402 (2013)
25. Shafique, K., Shah, M.: A noniterative greedy algorithm for multiframe point cor-respondence. PAMI 27(1), 51–65 (2005)
26. Wu, Z., Thangali, A., Sclaroff, S., Betke, M.: Coupling detection and data associ-ation for multiple object tracking. In: CVPR, pp. 1–8. Rhode Island (June 2012)
27. Roshan Zamir, A., Dehghan, A., Shah, M.: Gmcp-tracker: Global multi-object tracking using generalized minimum clique graphs. In: Fitzgibbon, A., Lazebnik, S., Perona, P., Sato, Y., Schmid, C. (eds.) ECCV 2012, Part II. LNCS, vol. 7573, pp. 343–356. Springer, Heidelberg (2012)
28. Zhang, L., Li, Y., Nevatia, R.: Global data association for multi-object tracking using network flows. In: CVPR (2008)
29. Zhao, T., Nevatia, R.: Bayesian human segmentation in crowded situations. In: CVPR (2003)

What Do I See? Modeling Human Visual Perception for Multi-person Tracking*

Xu Yan, Ioannis A. Kakadiaris, and Shishir K. Shah

Department of Computer Science, University of Houston
Houston, TX 77204-3010, USA
{xyan5,ioannisk}@uh.edu, sshah@central.uh.edu

Abstract. This paper presents a novel approach for multi-person tracking utilizing a model motivated by the human vision system. The model predicts human motion based on modeling of perceived information. An attention map is designed to mimic human reasoning that integrates both spatial and temporal information. The spatial component addresses human attention allocation to different areas in a scene and is represented using a retinal mapping based on the log-polar transformation while the temporal component denotes the human attention allocation to subjects with different motion velocity and is modeled as a static-dynamic attention map. With the static-dynamic attention map and retinal mapping, attention driven motion of the tracked target is estimated with a center-surround search mechanism. This perception based motion model is integrated into a data association tracking framework with appearance and motion features. The proposed algorithm tracks a large number of subjects in complex scenes and the evaluation on public datasets show promising improvements over state-of-the-art methods.

1 Introduction

Multi-person tracking is a fundamental problem for many computer vision tasks, such as video surveillance and activity recognition. The computer vision community has begun to explore social behavior modeling to improve accuracy of multi-target tracking systems in recent years. Various social behavior models [29,24,39,31] have been explored and incorporated into the multi-person tracking frameworks. Unlike the traditional motion model, the social behavior model, in essence, treats human motion as the result of both a person's intention and their interaction with environment rather than the outcome of a motion dynamics model alone. This is a critical aspect of tracking humans and enables incorporation of the basic understanding that human beings invariably will make motion decision based on their intent and understanding of the environment. In general, typical social behavior models are built on constraints over spatial proximity and

---

* This work was supported in part by the US Department of Justice, grant number 2009-MU-MU-K004. Any opinions, findings, conclusions or recommendations expressed in this paper are those of the authors and do not necessarily reflect the views of our sponsors.

D. Fleet et al. (Eds.): ECCV 2014, Part II, LNCS 8690, pp. 314–329, 2014.

(a)   (b)   (c)   (d)

Fig. 1. Examples of reconstructed virtual world. (a) The original surveillance image, (b) the virtual vision image, (c) the first-person view image from the person under the arrow, (d) the retinal mapping image. The bounding boxes in (a,b,c) with same color represent the same person.

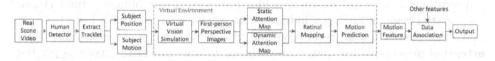

Fig. 2. System Framework. The components in red outline are implemented in virtual environment.

treat nearby subjects and objects with equal importance [38,2,18]. However, a person does not plan his/her movements based on a holistic understanding of the scene but reasons about it based on the local field of visual perception [17]. Therefore, in this paper, we propose building a perception based motion model from the first-person perspective. Intuitively, a person does not react to all subjects in his/her perspective with equal intensity. For example, a person will react strongly to a person moving faster in their direction as compared to someone moving slower. In other words, a person moving quickly towards one will take priority in one's perception and hence in their motion planning. We argue that people's attention has two kinds of variations: (1) spatial variations that are related to subjects that are near or far; and (2) temporal variations that are related to subjects that are moving fast or slow. To explore a more realistic motion model, we propose an attentive vision based tracking framework.

Benfold and Reid [6] utilized a person's head pose to locate areas of attention to guide surveillance systems. However, this information was not incorporated into a multi-person tracking framework. In our case, to visualize the scene from each person's point of view we utilize the *virtual vision simulation* [36] so that the scene can be rendered graphically and further used to simulate a first-person view assuming the camera to be located at the head height for each person in the scene. Figure 1(a) shows the real world, (b) shows the virtual scene, and (c) shows the first-person view image of person in the red bounding box in (a) and (b). Finally, Figure 1(d) shows the retinal mapping of the first-person view image of the specific person based on the log-polar transformation wherein the center of the first-person view image is assumed to be the focal point. Alternate approaches for simulating the scene can also be utilized [32].

We generate "attention maps" of the simulated first-person view image that guides the person's motion as shown in Figure 2. The static attention map is built based on human detection, which treats human subjects in the first-person view image as obstacles. In this paper, we assume that the human motion is dominated by the intent of obstacle avoidance. The dynamic attention map is derived from optical flow displacement of human subjects in a person's view. Human subjects further away or moving slowly will have a smaller optical flow displacements than those in closer proximity or moving fast. Further, the optical flow displacement from first-person view image, when mapped according to retinal mapping, implicitly incorporates the effect of motion direction in which humans subjects moving towards the person along the direction of the person's focal point will exhibit expansion and occupy more area than those moving away from the person. After combining static and dynamic attention maps, retinal mapping is overlaid on the combined map to mimic human retinal vision, i.e., spatial regions far from individual's visual center will have low attention and hence lower spatial resolution and vice-versa for closer regions. The final attention map combines spatial and temporal variations of the scene as per the person's visual priority. Our method identifies regions of high interest from subject's attention map that guides the estimation of subject's next movement and serves as a novel feature in a person tracking framework. The advantage of visual attention over direct use of motion information is that it provides a reasonable mechanism to estimate the motion probability while automatically weighting the proximal and peripheral information together. The key contributions of our work are as follows:

– *Perception based multi-person tracking.* We simulated the virtual vision and get the first-person view image. Such transformation facilitates intuitive analysis of human perception and reaction to subjects in the environment and induces a more realistic motion model. This also serves to enhance social behavior models by weighting relationship graphs.
– *Attentive vision model.* We propose an attentive vision model that approximates the spatial and temporal variance of human attention. The combined attention map enables motion path prediction of a person without explicit knowledge of other person's motion. Our model predicts human motion and is combined with data association for tracking.

We define human motion as a direct consequence of human attentive vision system. The problem is then transformed into a human attentive vision modeling problem (Sec. 3), which operates in a virtual simulation world that has the same physical world coordinates as the real world. We show how to integrate attention features into a tracking-by-detection framework (Sec. 4). Finally, we test our approach in real world challenging surveillance videos and evaluate the tracking performance in comparison to other tracking methods (Sec. 5).

2   Related Work

Multi-person Tracking. Tracking-by-detection has becomes increasingly popular for multi-person tracking due to the improvement of human detector. Progress on tracking-by-detection can be attributed to development in two areas, both of which bring the benefit to tracking performance. The first is the design of efficient data association methods. Brender *et al.* [10] used maximum weighted independent set to converge to a data association optimum. Andriyenko *et al.* [4] combined discrete with continuous optimization to solve both data association and trajectory estimation. Butt *et al.* [13] use Lagrangian relaxation to transfer the global data association to solvable min-cost flow problem. The second area is in the learning of discriminative features. In this category, multi-person tracking algorithms either exploit appearance variance feature [16,9] or model complex motion dynamics feature [33,26]. We contribute to build discriminative motion feature in this work.

Social behavior modeling has attracted more attention with its ability to quantify complex human interactions. Luber *et al.* [24] proposed to use repulsion effects to incorporate scene obstacles. Choi *et al.* [14] considered the group motion dynamics within a joint prediction model. Yan *et al.* [39] integrated the social attraction and repulsion effects into an interactive tracking framework. Qin *et al.* [31] and Bazzani *et al.* [5] exploited the social group effect associated with the tracking performance. Manocha *et al.* [8,23] leveraged reciprocal velocity obstacles model to take into account local interactions as well as physical and personal constraints. All the aforementioned works treat the social behavior from surveillance camera view angle instead of understanding social behavior from subject's own viewpoint. In this paper, we model the target motion behavior from the first person view and utilize it for multiple target tracking. To the best of our knowledge, no previous tracking method has leveraged first-person perspective.

Visual Attention Modeling. By mimicking the human vision system, computational visual attention modeling is investigated by psychologists, microbiologists, and computer scientists. A number of computational models of attention are proposed and can be categorized based on whether they are biological, purely computational, or hybrid [15]. All plausible biological methods are directly or indirectly inspired by cognitive concepts. In contrast, Ma *et al.* [25] proposed a method based on local contrast for generating saliency maps that is not based on any biological model. Achanta *et al.* [1] had incorporated both biological and computational parts in their method. Our work falls in the area of purely computational methods. Related work in crowd simulation [27,21] has leveraged human visual attention to model the motion of virtual agents in a synthesized environment.

3   Attentive Vision Modeling

Given a configuration $C^t = \{c_i^t\}$ of subjects ($i = 1 \ldots N$) at time t, each subject is modeled as $c_i^t = (p_i^t, s_i^t, a_i^t)$, where p_i^t denotes the world coordinate position, s_i^t its speed, and a_i^t its motion angle. Our method models the human perception of each subject i at the time step t based on the configuration C^t. For simplicity, we will explain one subject's attentive vision model in a scene with a fixed number of subjects. This can easily be generalized to an arbitrary number of subjects. Unlike previous approaches, we don't assume each person's prior knowledge about other subjects' position.

3.1   Virtual Vision Simulation

We assume a person's consistent moving direction in the next step $t+1$ is same as the person's current motion direction. Based on the calibration of the real scene (Figure 1(a)) and the output of human detection, we can get the position parameter p_i^t for each subject i. The motion parameters s^i and a^i estimation will be explained in section 4. Here we assume we have the parameters c_i^t for each subject. To simplify the configuration, we also set every person's height as 1.7 meter and the eye position is 1.6 meter from the ground, which is also set as the first-person view camera's position. Using the configuration C^t, we construct the virtual scene as shown in Figure 1(b) with virtual vision simulator [36]. In the simulator, we simulate human motion based on the start point, end point and the time we set to match the estimated speed. All movements are assumed to be piece-wise linear. In the virtual scene, the first-person view image is generated by putting the virtual camera at the virtual person's head location and directed towards the virtual person's moving direction in the simulated world. The focal length is fixed for each person. Here we assume the head pose is same as the subject motion direction. An example of a first-person view image is shown in Figure 1(c). The first-person view image shares the same world coordinate with virtual vision image and real world image. In the following sections, all computations of attentive vision are performed on first-person view images. The corresponding retinal mapping image is shown in Figure 1(d) further explained in the following section.

3.2   Attention Map

Visual saliency is one of the most popular computational model for visual attention [19]. Similar to saliency based attention model [28], we compute an attention map that leverages both static and dynamic components of attention. The attention map is built as shown in Figure 2 (red outline). The first step is to construct static and dynamic maps, then to overlap retinal mapping on the combined map.

Static Map. With virtual scene, all the pedestrian's motion are simulated with virtual agents that have the same velocity as the real world scene. The images of first-person perspective are collected from virtual vision simulator for frame $\{1, \ldots, i, \ldots, K\}$. Background subtraction is performed to detect the human subjects within the controlled foreground-background contrast in virtual scene [30]. The static map is built based on human detection results in frame 1. The output of human detection of frame 1 is denoted as $R^1 = \{r_1^1, \ldots, r_n^1\}$ where r_n^1 is represented by binary foreground mask. The static map of human attention is modeled as $S_s = r_1^1 \cup \ldots \cup r_n^1$.

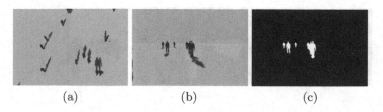

(a)   (b)   (c)

Fig. 3. The static map in first-person perspective view. (a) The over-head view image.(b) The first-person view image. (c) The static map is generated based on the human detection.

Dynamic Map. Human perception is sensitive to moving subjects and human attentive vision treats moving subjects with different velocities differently. The dynamic map is built to address the temporal variance component of attentive vision. Optical flow (O_x^i, O_y^i) is calculated for frame $\{2, \ldots, i, \ldots, K\}$, which implicitly models the relative motion between observer's and all the other subjects' motion [11]. With the virtual vision images, the human in $\{2, \ldots, i, \ldots, K\}$ frames is detected by background subtraction and the locations are denoted as $R^{2,\ldots,i,\ldots,K}$. We set $K = 25$ in this paper. The motion saliency in frame i is defined as

$$M^i(x,y) = \begin{cases} sqrt((O_x^i)^2 + (O_y^i)^2) & (x,y) \in R^i \\ 0 & \text{otherwise} \end{cases} \tag{1}$$

The final dynamic map combines all the motion saliency denoted as $S_d(x,y) = max\{M^2(x,y), \ldots, M^i(x,y), \ldots, M^K(x,y)\}$, which is determined by taking the maximum of motion intensity. A dynamic map example for one person is shown in Figure 4(a).

Static-Dynamic Map Combination. We hypothesize that the human perception drives attention to specific areas when the motion intensity in that region is above a certain threshold. Thus the combination of static and dynamic map is fulfilled in a motion-conditioned strategy. The combined attention map is computed as follows:

$$S(x,y) = \begin{cases} 1 & \text{if } S_d(x,y) \geq \epsilon \text{ or } S_s(x,y) = 1 \\ 0 & \text{otherwise} \end{cases} \tag{2}$$

where, ϵ denotes the threshold on motion intensity and is set to 0.1 in this paper. After combination, a binary mask is generated and is overlaid on the original image as shown in Figure 4(b) and 4(c). A crucial point to note here is that even though subjects receive higher perceptual attention, the regions they occupy may have lower probability as potential future target positions.

Retinal Mapping. Attentive vision refers to the reaction of people according to the visual stimuli in a dynamically changing environment, which is characterized by selective sensing in space and time as well as selective processing with respect to a specific task [34]. Selection in space involves the splitting of the visual field

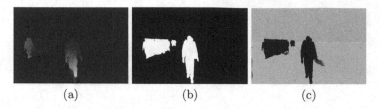

(a)   (b)   (c)

Fig. 4. (a) The dynamic map is generated based on virtual vision simulation. (b) The combined static-dynamic attention map. (c) The combined map mask is applied on first-person perspective image.

in a high resolution area, the fovea, and a space-variant resolution area, the periphery, which are denoted as retinal mapping. Log-polar transformation is the most common method to represent visual information with a space-variant resolution [37] and to achieve retinal mapping. The log-polar transformation conserves high resolution in the center of the image and the resolution gradually decreases away from center.

We denote (x, y) for the image coordinates and $(r_{(x,y)}, \theta_{(x,y)})$ for the corresponding polar coordinates and r_{max} denotes the maximum value of $r_{(x,y)}$. The polar mapping of image pixel (x, y) with origin (x_0, y_0) is defined as

$$r_{(x,y)} = \sqrt{(x-x_0)^2 + (y-y_0)^2}, \text{ and } \theta_{(x,y)} = tan^{-1}(\frac{y-y_0}{x-x_0}). \tag{3}$$

The foveal region is defined as a round disk with the radius r_0 and origin (x_0, y_0). The image in the foveal region retains uniform resolution while the non-foveal region exhibits decreasing resolution, which is also used to indicate the importance of observations . We apply the log-polar transformation on the non-foveal part of a first-person perspective image, which is defined as the ring-shaped area $r_{max} > r_{(x,y)} > r_0$. The unified retina mapping is defined as:

$$r'_{(x,y)} = \begin{cases} r_{(x,y)} & r_{(x,y)} < r_0 \\ log(r_{(x,y)}) & r_{max} > r_{(x,y)} > r_0 \end{cases} \tag{4}$$

and $\theta'(x, y) = \theta(x, y)$. With the transformed log-polar coordinates, the quantization is applied along θ' and r' axes that results in G and R elements, respectively. As shown in Figure 5, each pixel (x, y) undergoes a transform to the log-polar space and the log-polar space is quantized. The retinal mapping of combined static-dynamic attention map is computed based on the remapping of log-polar space that transforms the log-polar image back to the Cartesian space. The remapping follows the Eq. 3 and 4 utilizing the inverse mapping of θ' and r' to x' and y', respectively. Certain number of pixels will be allocated as the same intensity value due to the quantization in log-polar space. After doing so, we get the retinal mapping on combined attention map as shown in Figure 5(b). Another attention search map is generated for motion prediction as shown in Figure 5(c). For attention search map, we compute the mean of the mapped

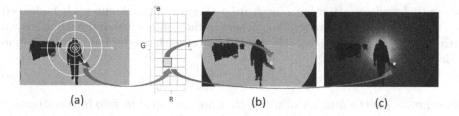

Fig. 5. The diagram of retinal mapping. (a)The first-person view image overlaid by static-dynamic map. (b) Retina mapping image. (c) Attention search map.

pixel locations and assign the intensity value from the log-polar space to the pixel position nearest to the computed mean position. The remaining pixels are assigned a value of zero. This allows us to generate a sparse map where the pixels that do not have a value of zero represent positions that can be probable locations for a target's next position.

3.3 Motion Prediction Based on Attentive Vision

This paper assumes that people follow their intuition, which means that people will find the most feasible and most attentive point as their destination. We divide this process into two step. The first step is to find the most attentive

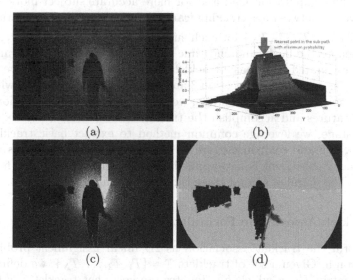

Fig. 6. (a) Center-surround search path. Red line is a sub-path, which is sparse here for visualization purpose. (b) The generated 3d probability map. The yellow point represents the nearest point in the sub path with maximum probability of being the destination point. X and Y are the original image coordinates and Z is the probability. (c) Potential destination point in first-perspective view image. (d) The calculated moving angle based on attentive vision.

sub-path based on attention search map (Figure 6(a)). A sub-path is defined as a line between two consecutive corners in the center-surround path as shown with red color in Figure 6(a). The probability of each sub-path in attention map is denoted as

$$P_{path} = \frac{m_{valid}}{m_{total}} \tag{5}$$

where, m_{valid} is the number of pixels that are not equal to zero in the attention map along the sub-path and m_{total} is the total number of pixels in the sub-path. Following the center-surround search path, the probability map of attentive vision is generated as shown in Figure 6(b). The sub-paths with maximum probability are selected as most attentive sub-path by exhaustive search.

For the second step, we calculate the corresponding world coordinate of each pixel in previous optimal sub-paths. With known observer's position, the point with the shortest distance to the observer is selected as potential destination from the optimal sub-path as shown in Figure 6(c). The predicted human motion direction π^{att} is calculated correspondingly based on the vector from the current position to found destination and is depicted in Figure 6(d). This is used to guide tracking later due to the shared world coordinate between the observer and the surveillance camera's view.

4   Tracking Framework

To reduce the computation load and for more accurate subject motion estimation, we leverage a two-stage tracking framework. In first stage, we extracts basic tracklets $\{T_1, \ldots, T_i, \ldots, T_N\}$ for each subject i in which $T_i = \{c_i^{t_i^b}, \ldots, c_i^{t_i^e}\}$ and t_i^b and t_i^e denote the begin and end time frame of T_i. The motion parameters s_i^t and a_i^t are estimated from basic tracklets. With these parameters, we simulate the virtual vision as shown in section 3 and get the motion prediction with attentive vision modeling. In second stage, we combine the predicted motion feature and other features and accomplish the tracklets association.

In first stage, we leverage common method to extract basic tracklet based on position, size and color histogram similarity in consecutive frames [31]. The color similarity constraint is also applied between current frame and first frame of tracklet. The detail of second stage is further explained in section 4.2 and 4.3.

4.1   Tracklet Association Formulation

We transform the tracklet association as 2D linear assignment problem on a bipartite graph. Given a set of tracklets $\mathbb{T} = \{T_1, T_2, \ldots, T_N\}$, we define a pairwise cost matrix H, in which h_{ij} denotes the cost that tracklet j is linked as first tracklet after tracklet i. The data association is formulated as

$$\arg\min_{\{i,j\}} \sum_{i=1}^{N} \sum_{j=1}^{N} h_{ij} x_{ij} \quad s.t. \begin{cases} \sum_{j=1}^{N} x_{i,j} = 1; \\ \sum_{i=1}^{N} x_{i,j} = 1; \\ x_{ij} \in \{0, 1\} \end{cases} \tag{6}$$

where $x_{ij} = 1$ iff tracklet j immediately follows tracklet i, otherwise, $x_{ij} = 0$. The cost is defined as the combination of five features including our attentive vision feature:

$$h_{ij} = \beta \cdot \Phi(T_i, T_j) \cdot Z(\Delta t) \tag{7}$$

where, $\beta = [\beta_1; \beta_2; \beta_3; \beta_4]$ is a vector of model parameters and set empirically in this paper, $\Phi(\cdot) = [\phi_1(\cdot), \phi_2(\cdot), \phi_3(\cdot), \phi_4(\cdot)]$ represents the association feature set, and $Z(\cdot)$ is the time gap component defined by an exponential model:

$$Z(\Delta t) = \begin{cases} \lambda^{\Delta t - 1} & 1 \leq \Delta t \leq \xi \\ \infty & \Delta t < 1 \text{ or } \Delta t > \xi \end{cases} \tag{8}$$

where ξ is the threshold of time gap and $\Delta t = t_j^b - t_i^e$.

4.2   Features Extraction

Given each tracklet pair (T_i, T_j), four features are calculated to get the association cost. The color feature ϕ_1 is build based on the 3D color histogram in the Red-Green-Intensity (RGI) space with 8 bins per channel. We perform a kernel density estimate for both the tracklets across their live frames. The similarity between two kernels $g(T_i)$ and $g(T_j)$ is measured by the Bhattacharyya coefficient B given by:

$$\phi_1 \propto \exp(-B[g(T_i), g(T_j)]). \tag{9}$$

The speed feature ϕ_2 is modeled by the Normal distribution: $\phi_2 \propto \mathcal{N}(\mu_j^s; \mu_i^s, \sigma_i^s)$ where, $\mu_j^s = mean(\sum_{t=t_j^b}^{t_j^e} s_j^t)$ is the average speed of T_j in its living period and μ_i^s, σ_i^s is the mean and variance of T_i's speed.

The angular likelihood is divided to two angular regions. The first one incorporates the attentive vision feature that assumes the next tracklet should appear at the predicted angle. It is modeled by the *von Mises* distribution [35], which is formulated as:

$$\phi_3 = \frac{e^{\kappa cos(\pi - \pi^{att})}}{2\pi I_0(\kappa)}, \tag{10}$$

where $I_0(.)$ is the modified Bessel function of order zero, and π denotes the motion angle between the spatial location of the middle point of tracklet i and the corresponding location of T_j. The π^{att} is our attentive vision model's predicted angle. κ corresponds to variance in a normal distribution and is set empirically. To get the informative attentive vision feature, the human motion direction history should be estimated accurately. Due to the uncertainty of detection output, we design a threshold strategy to estimate the human motion direction. When the basic tracklet is shorter than 10 frames, we compute the average optical flow to estimate the motion direction and we rule out the region overlapped by other tracklets. Otherwise, the motion direction is computed based on tracklet position information.

The second angular feature models smooth motion and penalizes motion change. This is described by the normal distribution; $\phi_4 \propto \mathcal{N}(\mu_j^a; \mu_i^a, \sigma_i^a)$, where

μ_j^a is the moving angle mean of T_j, μ_i^a and σ_i^a are the moving angle mean and variance of T_i.

4.3 Data Association

Given the cost matrix H, we solve the assignment problem through a strategy similar to the cut-while-linking strategy proposed in [31]. The cost matrix H is extended to H^{new} to solve the initialization and termination of tracks, which is defined as,

$$
H^{new} = \left[
\begin{array}{cccc|cccc}
h_{11} & h_{12} & \dots & h_{1N} & \tau & \infty & \dots & \infty \\
h_{21} & h_{22} & \dots & h_{2N} & \infty & \tau & \dots & \infty \\
\vdots & \vdots & \vdots & \vdots & \vdots & \vdots & \vdots & \vdots \\
h_{n1} & h_{n2} & \dots & h_{NN} & \infty & \infty & \dots & \tau \\
\infty & \infty & \dots & \infty & \infty & \infty & \dots & \infty \\
\infty & \infty & \dots & \infty & \infty & \infty & \dots & \infty \\
\vdots & \vdots & \vdots & \vdots & \vdots & \vdots & \vdots & \vdots \\
\infty & \infty & \dots & \infty & \infty & \infty & \dots & \infty
\end{array}
\right].
\tag{11}
$$

The thresholds τ decides when a trajectory ends and is fixed for each scene. When h_{ij} exceeds τ, the link between two tracklets is cut and the track will be linked to extended columns which indicates the track terminates. The initialization of tracks is solved along with determined termination. The extended version of data association formulation is defined as

$$
\arg\min_{\{i,j\}} \sum_{i=1}^{2N} \sum_{j=1}^{2N} h_{ij}^{new} x_{ij} \quad s.t. \begin{cases} \sum_{j=1}^{2N} x_{i,j} = 1; \\ \sum_{i=1}^{2N} x_{i,j} = 1; \\ x_{ij} \in \{0,1\} \end{cases}
\tag{12}
$$

The optimal association is solved by Munkres' assignment algorithm [12].

5   Experiments

We evaluate how attentive vision helps to improve multi-person tracking on two public datasets: TUD stadtmitte [3] and TownCentre [7]. We follow the popular evaluation metrics [22], which includes mostly tracked trajectories (MT), mostly lost trajectories (ML), fragments (Frag) and ID switches (IDS). In addition, we also report the false positive rate (FPR) of our results on each dataset. The TUD statmitte dataset has a short video, but with very low camera angle and frequent full occlusions among pedestrians. The TownCentre video is a high definition video with 1920×1280 resolution. This sequence is very crowded with frequent occlusion and interaction among pedestrians. The pedestrians appearing briefly at the image boundaries are excluded. We also collected a video in an outdoor uncontrolled environment. It is a high definition video with 1280×720 resolution and 1200 frames in total. This sequence is crowded with 40 trajectories in total. The activity inside is challenging for tracking algorithms since a large amount of interactions are observed among the people. Walking, skateboarding and biking activity also exists in the scene. We have manually annotated the video to identify the locations and provide unique IDs for all the people in the video.

5.1 Component-Wise Evaluation

To understand the benefit of the attentive vision feature proposed in this paper, we first present the component-wise evaluation. The baseline method turns off the attentive vision feature and re-tuning to the best performance while the default methods keep all the merits of the proposed method. Table 1 presents results of quantitative comparison. The default method out-performs the baseline method in most measures across all the datasets.

Table 1. Component-wise evaluation on each dataset. The best result is in bold.

Dataset	With attentive vision	MT	ML	Frag	IDS
TUD stadtmitte	No	60.0%	**0.0%**	3	2
TUD stadtmitte	Yes	**70.0%**	**0.0%**	2	1
TownCentre	No	81.3%	6.2%	**33**	45
TownCentre	Yes	**85.6%**	**4.8%**	43	19
OURS	No	47.5%	20.0%	22	21
OURS	Yes	**77.5%**	**10.0%**	13	18

5.2 Comparative Evaluation

To compare fairly with different tracking method, we use the same detector's output. For TUD stadtmitte, we use the same detection and groundtruth provided by [40] and show comparable performance. The quantitative results are show in Table 2. We can see that our result is comparable or better than state-of-the-art methods. Our result is better than *Energy Min* [3], *Disc-Continue* [4] and *PRIMPT* [20] as our attentive vision incorporated model gives more informed prediction. Our approach does not provide an obvious advantage over *Online CRF* [40] since this video has low camera angle and several very short tracklets, which makes it difficult to estimate the tracklet motion direction. In this case, the power of online learned appearance model in *Online CRF* gives more benefit than motion prediction. Some sample tracking results are shown in Figure 7(a). The FPR of our method is 3.2%.

For TownCentre dataset, we use the original detection and groundtruth provided by [7], which are used in [31], and we show improvement by incorporating the attentive vision features. The quantitative comparison is shown in Table 2. The results show that the attentive vision based tracking model outperforms *Basic affinity model* [31] and *SGB model* [31] in terms of MT, ML, and IDS. Fragment of trajectories under our model increased due to threshold setting in cut-while-linking strategy. Example qualitative result is shown in Figure 7(b,c,d). The FPR of our method is 7.6%.

We compare our method's performance with *SGB model*. We also replace the attentive vision model in our framework with *LTA model* [29] and keep all the other components fixed. The quantitative results are shown in Table 2, which show that attentive vision model outperforms *SGB model* and *LTA model* in terms of MT, ML and Frag. LTA does a little better in IDS than our model. The qualitative evaluation is shown in Figure 7(e). The FPR of our method is 5.9%.

326   X. Yan, I.A. Kakadiaris, and S.K. Shah

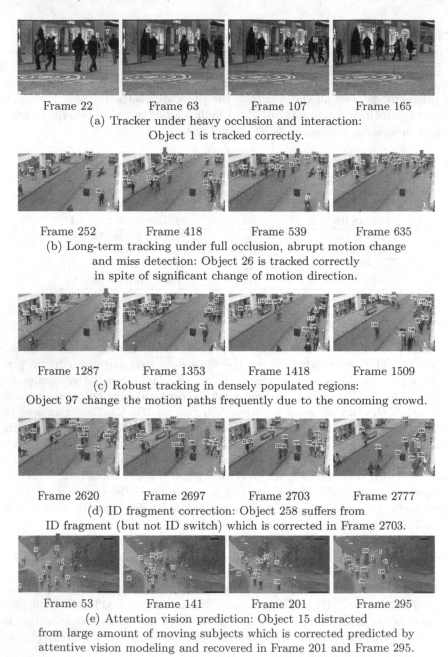

Frame 22   Frame 63   Frame 107   Frame 165
(a) Tracker under heavy occlusion and interaction:
Object 1 is tracked correctly.

Frame 252   Frame 418   Frame 539   Frame 635
(b) Long-term tracking under full occlusion, abrupt motion change
and miss detection: Object 26 is tracked correctly
in spite of significant change of motion direction.

Frame 1287   Frame 1353   Frame 1418   Frame 1509
(c) Robust tracking in densely populated regions:
Object 97 change the motion paths frequently due to the oncoming crowd.

Frame 2620   Frame 2697   Frame 2703   Frame 2777
(d) ID fragment correction: Object 258 suffers from
ID fragment (but not ID switch) which is corrected in Frame 2703.

Frame 53   Frame 141   Frame 201   Frame 295
(e) Attention vision prediction: Object 15 distracted
from large amount of moving subjects which is corrected predicted by
attentive vision modeling and recovered in Frame 201 and Frame 295.

Fig. 7. Tracking results of our approach on TUD statmitte, TownCentre and our campus datasets. For visualization purpose, certain false positive trajectories are not shown.

Table 2. Comparison of results on TUD statmitte, TownCentre and Our dataset. The best result is in bold. [31] (a) and [31] (b) represent the baseline method and proposed method in [31] respectively.

Dataset	Method	MT	ML	Frag	IDS
TUD stadtmitte	Andriyenko *et al.* [3]	60.0%	**0.0%**	4	7
TUD stadtmitte	Kuo *et al.* [20]	60.0%	10.0%	**0**	1
TUD stadtmitte	Andriyenko *et al.* [4]	60.0%	**0.0%**	1	4
TUD stadtmitte	Yang *et al.* [40]	**70.0%**	**0.0%**	1	**0**
TUD stadtmitte	Proposed method	**70.0%**	**0.0%**	2	1
TownCentre	Qin *et al.* [31] (a)	76.8%	7.7%	37	60
TownCentre	Qin *et al.* [31] (b)	83.2%	5.9%	**28**	39
TownCentre	Proposed method	**85.6%**	**4.8%**	43	**19**
OURS	Qin *et al.* [31]	45.0%	22.5%	24	22
OURS	Pellegrini *et al.* [29]	62.5%	15.0%	19	**16**
OURS	Proposed method	**77.5%**	**10.0%**	**13**	18

6   Conclusion

We have presented a novel tracking method using an attentive vision model where motion analysis is performed in the first-person view. The attentive vision is created from virtually reconstructed scene. A visual attention map is generated based on attentive vision mechanism, including both static and dynamic components. The most feasible path taken by the person is searched and decided from this constructed map. The predicted motion direction is integrated into data-association tracking with color and motion features. The association is solved by a greedy algorithm. As the experiments show, the proposed approach achieves promising improvements on different public datasets. Finally, the performance of the algorithm could be improved if we enhance the short tracklet motion estimation method and the virtual simulation details.

References

1. Achanta, R., Susstrunk, S.: Saliency detection for content-aware image resizing. In: Proc. ICIP, pp. 1005–1008 (2009)
2. Ali, S., Shah, M.: Floor fields for tracking in high density crowd scenes. In: Forsyth, D., Torr, P., Zisserman, A. (eds.) ECCV 2008, Part II. LNCS, vol. 5303, pp. 1–14. Springer, Heidelberg (2008)
3. Andriyenko, A., Schindler, K.: Multi-target tracking by continuous energy minimization. In: Proc. CVPR, pp. 1265–1272 (2011)
4. Andriyenko, A., Schindler, K., Roth, S.: Discrete-continuous optimization for multi-target tracking. In: Proc. CVPR, pp. 1926–1933 (2012)
5. Bazzani, L., Cristani, M., Murino, V.: Decentralized particle filter for joint individual-group tracking. In: Proc. CVPR, pp. 1886–1893 (2012)
6. Benfold, B., Reid, I.: Guiding visual surveillance by tracking human attention. In: Proc. BMVC, pp. 1–11 (2009)

7. Benfold, B., Reid, I.: Stable multi-target tracking in real-time surveillance video. In: Proc. CVPR, pp. 3547–3464 (2011)
8. Bera, A., Manocha, D.: Realtime multilevel crowd tracking using reciprocal velocity obstacles. CoRR abs/1402.2826 (2014)
9. Breitenstein, M.D., Reichlin, F., Leibe, B., Koller-Meier, E., Gool, L.V.: Robust tracking-by-detection using a detector confidence particle filter. In: Proc. ICCV, pp. 1515–1522 (2009)
10. Brendel, W., Amer, M., Todorovic, S.: Multiobject tracking as maximum weight independent set. In: Proc. CVPR, pp. 1273–1280 (2011)
11. Brox, T., Malik, J.: Large displacement optical flow: descriptor matching in variational motion estimation. IEEE T-PAMI 33(3), 500–513 (2011)
12. Burkard, R., Dell'Amico, M., Martello, S.: Assignment Problems. Society for Industrial and Applied Mathematics, Philadelphia (2009)
13. Butt, A.A., Collins, R.T.: Multi-target tracking by lagrangian relaxation to min-cost network flow. In: Proc. CVPR, pp. 1846–1853 (2013)
14. Choi, W., Savarese, S.: Multiple target tracking in world coordinate with single, minimally calibrated camera. In: Daniilidis, K., Maragos, P., Paragios, N. (eds.) ECCV 2010, Part IV. LNCS, vol. 6314, pp. 553–567. Springer, Heidelberg (2010)
15. Filipe, S., Alexandre, L.A.: From the human visual system to the computational models of visual attention: a survey. Artificial Intelligence Review 39(1), 1–47 (2013)
16. Grabner, H., Bischof, H.: On-line boosting and vision. In: Proc. CVPR, pp. 260–267 (2006)
17. Hari, R., Kujala, M.V.: Brain basis of human social interaction: From concepts ot brain imaging. Physiological Reviews 89(2), 453–479 (2009)
18. Kim, S., Guy, S.J., Liu, W., Lau, R.W.H., Lin, M.C., Manocha, D.: Predicting pedestrian trajectories using velocity-space reasoning. In: Proc. WAFR, pp. 609–623 (2012)
19. Koch, C., Ullman, S.: Shifts in slective visual attention: Towards the underlying neural circuitry. Human Neurbiology 4, 219–227 (1985)
20. Kuo, C., Nevatia, R.: How does person identity recognition help multi-person tracking? In: CVPR, pp. 1217–1224 (2011)
21. Lee, K.H., Choi, M.G., Hong, Q., Lee, J.: Group behavior from video: A data-driven approach to crowd simulation. In: Proc. SCA, pp. 109–118 (2007)
22. Li, Y., Huang, C., Nevatia, R.: Learning to associate: Hybridboosted multi-target tracker for crowded scene. In: Proc. CVPR, pp. 2953–2960 (2009)
23. Liu, W., Chan, A.B., Lau, R.W.H., Manocha, D.: Leveraging long-term predictions and online-learning in agent-based multiple person tracking. CoRR abs/1402.2016 (2014)
24. Luber, M., Stork, J., Tipaldi, G., Arras, K.: People tracking with human motion prediction from social forces. In: Proc. ICRA, pp. 464–469 (2010)
25. Ma, Y., Zhang, H.: Contrast-based image attention analysis by using fuzzy growing. In: Proc. International Conference on Multimedia, pp. 374–281 (2003)
26. Mei, X., Ling, H.: Robust visual tracking using l_1 minimization. In: Proc. ICCV, pp. 1436–1443 (2009)
27. Ondrej, J., Pettré, J., Olivier, A.H., Donikian, S.: A Synthetic-Vision Based Steering Approach for Crowd Simulation. In: Proc. SIGGRAPH, pp. 123:1–123:9 (2010)
28. Ouerhani, N.: Visual attention: from bio-inspired modeling to real-time implementation. Ph.D. thesis, Univeristy of Neuchâtel, Switzerland (2003)
29. Pellegrini, S., Ess, A.: K.Schindler, van Gool, L.: You'll never walk alone: modeling social behavior for multi-target tracking. In: Proc. ICCV, pp. 261–268 (2009)

30. Piccardi, M.: Background subtraction techniques: a review. In: Proc. IEEE conference on Systems, Man and Cybernetics, pp. 3099–3104 (2004)
31. Qin, Z., Shelton, C.R.: Improving multi-target tracking via social grouping. In: Proc. CVPR, pp. 1972–1978 (2012)
32. Qureshi, F., Terzopoulos, D.: Smart camera networks in virtual reality. In: Proc. International Conference on Distributed Smart Cameras, pp. 87–94 (2007)
33. Ross, D.A., Lim, J., Lin, R., Yang, M.: Incremental learning for robust visual tracking. IJCV 77(1), 125–141 (2008)
34. Schwartz, E.L., Greve, D.N., Bonmassar, G.: Space-variant active vision: Definition, overview and examples. Neural Networks 8(7), 1297–1308 (1995)
35. Song, B., Jeng, T.-Y., Staudt, E., Roy-Chowdhury, A.K.: A stochastic graph evolution framework for robust multi-target tracking. In: Daniilidis, K., Maragos, P., Paragios, N. (eds.) ECCV 2010, Part I. LNCS, vol. 6311, pp. 605–619. Springer, Heidelberg (2010)
36. Thiebaux, M., Marshall, A., Marsella, S., Kallman, M.: Smartbody: Behavior realization for embodied conversational agents. In: Proc. AAMAS, pp. 1151–1158 (2008)
37. Traver, V.J., Bernardino, A.: A review of log-polar imaging for visual perception in robotics. Robotics and Autonomous Systems 58(4), 378–398 (2010)
38. Treuille, A., Cooper, S., Popović, Z.: Continuum crowds. In: Proc. SIGGRAPH, pp. 1160–1168 (2006)
39. Yan, X., Kakadiaris, I., Shah, S.: Predicting social interactions for visual tracking. In: Proc. BMVC, pp. 102.1–102.11 (2011)
40. Yang, B., Nevatia, R.: An online learned CRF model for multi-target tracking. In: Proc. CVPR, pp. 2034–2041 (2012)

Consistent Re-identification in a Camera Network

Abir Das*, Anirban Chakraborty*, and Amit K. Roy-Chowdhury**

Dept. of Electrical Engineering, University of California, Riverside, CA 92521, USA

Abstract. Most existing person re-identification methods focus on finding similarities between persons between pairs of cameras (camera pairwise re-identification) without explicitly maintaining consistency of the results across the network. This may lead to infeasible associations when results from different camera pairs are combined. In this paper, we propose a network consistent re-identification (NCR) framework, which is formulated as an optimization problem that not only maintains consistency in re-identification results across the network, but also improves the camera pairwise re-identification performance between all the individual camera pairs. This can be solved as a binary integer programing problem, leading to a globally optimal solution. We also extend the proposed approach to the more general case where all persons may not be present in every camera. Using two benchmark datasets, we validate our approach and compare against state-of-the-art methods.

Keywords: Person re-identification, Network consistency.

1   Introduction

In many computer vision tasks it is often desirable to identify and monitor people as they move through a network of non-overlapping cameras. While many object tracking algorithms can achieve reasonable performance for a single camera, it is a more challenging problem for a network of cameras where issues such as changes of scale, illumination, viewing angle and pose start to arise. For non-overlapping cameras it is extremely challenging to associate the same persons at different cameras as no information is obtained from the "blind gaps" between them. This inter-camera person association problem is known as the person re-identification problem.

Person re-identification across non-overlapping fields-of-view (FOVs) is a well studied topic. Most widely used re-identification approaches focus on pairwise re-identification. Although the re-identification accuracy for each camera pair is high, it can be inconsistent if results from 3 or more cameras are considered. Matches of targets given independently by every pair of cameras might not conform to one another and in turn, can lead to inconsistent mappings. Thus, in

---

* The first two authors should be considered as joint first authors.
** Corresponding author.

D. Fleet et al. (Eds.): ECCV 2014, Part II, LNCS 8690, pp. 330–345, 2014.
© Springer International Publishing Switzerland 2014

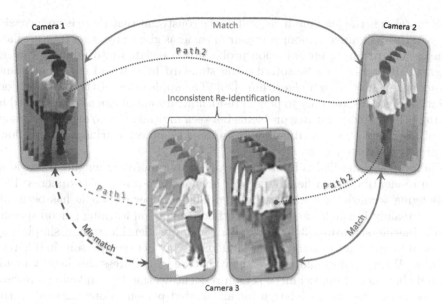

Fig. 1. Example of inconsistency in re-identification: Among the 3 possible re-identification results, 2 are correct. The match of the target in camera 1 to camera 3 can be found in two ways. The first one is the direct pairwise re-identification result between camera 1 and 3 (shown as 'Path 1'), and the second one is the indirect re-identification result in camera 3 given via the matched person in camera 2 (shown as 'Path 2'). The two outcomes do not match and thus the re-identification of the target across 3 cameras is not consistent.

person re-identification across a camera network, multiple paths of correspondences may exist between targets from any two cameras, but ultimately all these paths must point to the same correspondence maps for each target in each camera. An example scenario is shown in Fig. 1. Even though camera pairs 1-2 and 2-3 have correct re-identification of the target, the false match between the targets in camera pair 1-3 makes the overall re-identification across the triplet inconsistent. In this paper we propose a novel re-identification scheme across multiple cameras by incorporating the consistency requirement. We show that the consistency requirement not only makes the interpretation of re-identification more meaningful, but also makes the pairwise re-identification accuracy high. Since consistency across the camera network is the motivation as well as the building block of the proposed method, we term this as the 'Network Consistent Re-identification' (NCR) strategy.

To achieve a consistent and optimal re-identification, we pose the problem of re-identification as an optimization problem that minimizes the global cost of associating pairs of targets on the entire camera network constrained by a set of consistency criteria. The pairwise re-identification similarity scores obtained using any feasible approach are the input to the proposed method. Unlike assigning a match for which the similarity score is maximum among a set of probable candidates, our formulation picks the assignments for which the total similarity of all matches is the maximum, as well as the constraint that there is no inconsistency in the assignment among any pair of cameras given any other intermediate camera. The resulting optimization problem is translated into a binary integer program (IP) which can be solved using standard branch and cut, branch and bound or dynamic search algorithms [20]. The application of the proposed formulation is not limited only to person re-identification, but can also be applied in solving other correspondence problems between multiple nodes/instances arising out of the same object at different instants, *e.g.*, object tracking, optical flow, feature correspondences etc.

The proposed method is further generalized to a more challenging scenario in person re-identification when all persons are not present in all the cameras. This challenging scenario of dealing with a variable number of people has been addressed mainly in single cameras by methods relying on learning person specific discriminating signature [3,8]. For multi camera re-identification, a simple way has been to apply a threshold to the similarity score between persons in different cameras. With our formulation we show that we can address this largely unaddressed challenge of multicamera person re-identification by employing a reward for true negatives (no association for an isolated person in one camera) in the binary IP framework.

We compare the performance of our approach to state-of-the-art person re-identification methods using a publicly available benchmark dataset - WARD [16] having 3 cameras, and a new 4 camera dataset, RAiD (Reidentification Across indoor-outdoor Dataset) introduced by us. More details about the datasets are provided in sections 4.1 and 4.2.

2   Related Works and Our Contributions

In the last few years there has been increasing attention in the field of person re-identification across camera networks. The proposed approaches addressing the pairwise re-identification problem across non-overlapping cameras can be roughly divided into 3 categories, (i) discriminative signature based methods [2,3,15,16], (ii) metric learning based methods [1,4,23], and (iii) transformation learning based methods [11,18]. Multiple local features (color, shape and texture) are used in [3,15,16] to compute discriminative signatures for each person using multiple images. Similarity between person images is computed by measuring the distance between shape descriptors of color distributions projected in the log-chromaticity space [12] or by using an unsupervised salient feature learning framework in [24]. The authors in [9], propose a metric learning framework whereby a set of training data is used to learn an optimal non-Euclidean metric which minimizes the distance between features of pairs of true matches, while maximizing the same between pairs of wrong matches. Some of the recent works try to improve the re-identification performance by learning a relaxed Mahalanobis metric defined on pairs of true and wrong matches, by learning multiple metrics in a transfer learning set up [14] or by maintaining redundancy in colorspace using a local Fisher discriminant analysis based metric [17]. Works exploring transformation of features between cameras tried to learn a brightness transfer function (BTF) between appearance features [18], a subspace of the computed BTFs [11], linear color variations model [10], or a Cumulative BTF [19] between cameras. Some of these works [10,11] learned space-time probabilities of moving targets between cameras which may be unreliable if camera FoVs are significantly non-overlapping. As the above methods do not take consistency into account, applying them to a camera network does not give consistent re-identification. Since the proposed method is built upon the pairwise similarity scores, any of the above methods can be the building block to generate the camera pairwise similarity between the targets.

There have been a few correspondence methods proposed in recent years in other aspects of computer vision, *e.g.*, point correspondence in multiple frames and multi target tracking that are relevant to the proposed method. In one of the early works [21], finding point correspondences in monocular image sequences is formulated as finding a graph cover and solved using a greedy method. A suboptimal greedy solution strategy was used in [22] to track multiple targets by finding a maximum cover path of a graph of detections where multiple features like color, position, direction and size determined the edge weights. In [6], the authors linked detections in a tracking scenario across frames by solving a constrained flow optimization. The resulting convex formulation of finding k-shortest node-disjoint paths guaranteed the global optima. However, this method does not actively use appearance features into the data association process which might lead to ID switches among different pairs of cameras resulting in inconsistency. An extension of the work using sparse appearance preserving tracklets was proposed in [5]. With known flow direction, a flow formulation of re-identification will be consistent. But in a re-identification problem with no temporal or spatial layout information, the flow directions are not natural and thus re-identification performance may widely vary with different choices of temporal or spatial flow.

Contributions of the paper: To summarize, the contributions of the proposed approach to the problem of person re-identification are the followings. Network consistent person re-identification problem is formulated as an optimization problem which not only maintains consistency across camera pairwise re-identification results, but also improves the re-identification performance across different camera pairs. To the best of our knowledge, this is the first time that consistency in re-identification across a network of cameras is explored, and an optimization strategy with consistency information from additional cameras is used to improve the otherwise standard camera pairwise re-identification. Due to the formulation of the optimization problem as a binary IP, it is guaranteed to reach the global optima as opposed to the greedy approaches applied in some of the correspondence methods. The method is not tuned to any camera pairwise similarity score generation approach. Any existing re-identification strategy giving independent camera pairwise similarity scores can be incorporated into the framework. The proposed method is also extensible to situations where every person is not present in every camera.

3   Network Consistent Re-identification Framework

In this section we describe the proposed approach in details. The Network Consistent Re-identification (NCR) method starts with the camera pairwise similarity scores between the targets. Section 4 gives a brief description of the process in which the pairwise similarity scores for each person is generated. First we describe the notation and define the terminologies associated to this problem that would be used throughout the rest of the section before delving deeper into the problem formulation.

Let there be m cameras in a network. The number of possible camera pairs is $\binom{m}{2} = \frac{m(m-1)}{2}$. For simplicity we, first, assume, that the same n person are present in each of the cameras. In section 3.4 we will extend the formulation for a variable number of targets.

1. <u>Node:</u> The ith person in camera p is denoted as $\mathcal{P}_i^p$ and is called a 'node' in this framework.

2. <u>Similarity score matrix:</u> Let $\mathbf{C}^{(p,q)}$ denote the similarity score matrix between camera p and camera q. Then $(i,j)^{th}$ cell in $\mathbf{C}^{(p,q)}$ denotes the similarity score between the persons $\mathcal{P}_i^p$ and $\mathcal{P}_j^q$.

3. <u>Assignment matrix:</u> We need to know the association between the persons $\mathcal{P}_i^p$ and $\mathcal{P}_j^q, \forall i, j = \{1, \cdots n\}$ and $\forall p, q = \{1, \cdots m\}$. The associations between targets across cameras can be represented using 'assignment matrices', one for each camera pair. Each element $x_{i,j}^{p,q}$ of the assignment matrix $\mathbf{X}^{(p,q)}$ between the camera pair (p,q) is defined as follows:

$$x_{i,j}^{p,q} = \begin{cases} 1 & \text{if } \mathcal{P}_i^p \text{ and } \mathcal{P}_j^q \text{ are the same targets} \\ 0 & \text{otherwise} \end{cases} \tag{1}$$

As a result $\mathbf{X}^{(p,q)}$ is a permutation matrix, *i.e.*, only one element per row and per column is 1, all the others are 0. Mathematically, $\forall x_{i,j}^{p,q} \in \{0,1\}$

$$\sum_{j=1}^{n} x_{i,j}^{p,q} = 1 \; \forall i = 1 \text{ to } n \text{ and } \sum_{i=1}^{n} x_{i,j}^{p,q} = 1 \; \forall j = 1 \text{ to } n. \tag{2}$$

4. <u>Edge:</u> An 'edge' between two nodes $\mathcal{P}_i^p$, and $\mathcal{P}_j^q$ from two different cameras is a probable association between the ith person in camera p and the jth person in camera q. It should be noted that there will be no edge between the nodes of the same camera, *i.e.*, two targets from the same camera. There are two attributes connected to each edge. They are the similarity score $c_{i,j}^{p,q}$ and the association value $x_{i,j}^{p,q}$.

5. <u>Path:</u> A 'path' between two nodes $(\mathcal{P}_i^p, \mathcal{P}_j^q)$ is a set of edges that connect $\mathcal{P}_i^p$ and $\mathcal{P}_j^q$ without traveling through a camera twice. A path between $\mathcal{P}_i^p$ and $\mathcal{P}_j^q$ can be represented as the set of edges $e(\mathcal{P}_i^p, \mathcal{P}_j^q) = \{(\mathcal{P}_i^p, \mathcal{P}_a^r), (\mathcal{P}_a^r, \mathcal{P}_b^s), \cdots (\mathcal{P}_c^t, \mathcal{P}_j^q)\}$, where $\{\mathcal{P}_a^r, \mathcal{P}_b^s, \cdots \mathcal{P}_c^t\}$ are the set of intermediate nodes on the path between $\mathcal{P}_i^p$ and $\mathcal{P}_j^q$. The set of association values on all the edges between the nodes is denoted as $\mathcal{L}$, *i.e.*, $x_{i,j}^{p,q} \in \mathcal{L}, \forall i, j = [1, \cdots, n], \forall p, q = [1, \cdots, m]$

and $p < q$. Finally, the set of all paths between any two nodes $\mathcal{P}_i^p$ and $\mathcal{P}_j^q$ is represented as $\mathcal{E}(\mathcal{P}_i^p, \mathcal{P}_j^q)$ and any path $e^{(z)}(\mathcal{P}_i^p, \mathcal{P}_j^q) \in \mathcal{E}(\mathcal{P}_i^p, \mathcal{P}_j^q)$.

3.1 Global Similarity of Association

For the camera pair (p, q), the sum of the similarity scores of association is given by $\sum_{i,j=1}^{n} c_{i,j}^{p,q} x_{i,j}^{p,q}$. Summing over all possible camera pairs the global similarity score can be written as

$$\mathbf{C} = \sum_{\substack{p,q=1 \\ p<q}}^{m} \sum_{i,j=1}^{n} c_{i,j}^{p,q} x_{i,j}^{p,q} \tag{3}$$

3.2 Set of Constraints

The set of constraints are as follows.

1. Association constraint: A person from any camera p can have only one match from another camera q. This is mathematically expressed by the set of equations (2). This is true for all possible pairs of cameras which can be expressed as,

$$\sum_{j=1}^{n} x_{i,j}^{p,q} = 1 \ \forall i = 1 \text{ to } n \ \forall p, q = 1 \text{ to } m, \ p < q$$

$$\sum_{i=1}^{n} x_{i,j}^{p,q} = 1 \ \forall j = 1 \text{ to } n \ \forall p, q = 1 \text{ to } m, \ p < q \tag{4}$$

2. Loop constraint: This constraint comes from the consistency requirement. Given two nodes $\mathcal{P}_i^p$ and $\mathcal{P}_j^q$, it can be noted that for consistency, a logical 'AND' relationship between the association value $x_{i,j}^{p,q}$ and the set of association values $\{x_{i,a}^{p,r}, x_{a,b}^{r,s}, \cdots x_{c,j}^{t,q}\}$ of a possible path between the nodes has to be maintained. The association value between the two nodes $\mathcal{P}_i^p$ and $\mathcal{P}_j^q$ has to be 1 if the association values corresponding to all the edges of any possible path between these two nodes are 1. Keeping the binary nature of the association variables and the association constraint in mind the relationship can be compactly expressed as,

$$x_{i,j}^{p,q} \geq \left(\sum_{(\mathcal{P}_k^r, \mathcal{P}_l^s) \in e^{(z)}(\mathcal{P}_i^p, \mathcal{P}_j^q)} x_{k,l}^{r,s} \right) - |e^{(z)}(\mathcal{P}_i^p, \mathcal{P}_j^q)| + 1, \tag{5}$$

$\forall$ paths $e^{(z)}(\mathcal{P}_i^p, \mathcal{P}_j^q) \in \mathcal{E}(\mathcal{P}_i^p, \mathcal{P}_j^q)$, where $|e^{(z)}(\mathcal{P}_i^p, \mathcal{P}_j^q)|$ denotes the cardinality of the path $|e^{(z)}(\mathcal{P}_i^p, \mathcal{P}_j^q)|$, i.e., the number of edges in the path. The relationship holds true for all i and all j. For the case of a triplet of cameras the constraint in eqn. (5) simplifies to,

$$x_{i,j}^{p,q} \geq x_{i,k}^{p,r} + x_{k,j}^{r,q} - 2 + 1 = x_{i,k}^{p,r} + x_{k,j}^{r,q} - 1 \tag{6}$$

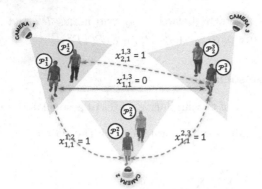

Fig. 2. An illustrative example showing that inconsistent re-identification is captured by the loop constraint given by eqn. (6) for a simple scenario involving 2 persons in 3 cameras.

An example involving 3 cameras and 2 persons is illustrated with the help of Fig. 2. Say, the raw similarity score between pairs of targets across cameras suggests associations between $(\mathcal{P}_1^1, \mathcal{P}_1^2)$, $(\mathcal{P}_1^2, \mathcal{P}_1^3)$ and $(\mathcal{P}_2^1, \mathcal{P}_1^3)$ independently. However, when these associations are combined together over the entire network, it leads to an infeasible scenario - $\mathcal{P}_1^1$ and $\mathcal{P}_2^1$ are the same person. This infeasibility is also correctly captured through the constraint in eqn. (6). $x_{1,1}^{1,3} = 0$ but $x_{1,1}^{1,2} + x_{1,1}^{2,3} - 1 = 1$, thus violating the constraint.

For a generic scenario involving a large number of cameras where similarity scores between every pair of cameras may not be available, the loop constraint equations (*i.e.*, eqn. (5)) have to hold for every possible triplet, quartet, quintet (and so on) of cameras. On the other hand, if the similarity scores between all persons for every possible pair of cameras are available, the loop constraints on quartets and higher order loops are not necessary. If loop constraint is satisfied for every triplet of cameras then it automatically ensures consistency for every possible combination of cameras taking 3 or more of them. So the loop constraint for the network of cameras become,

$$x_{i,j}^{p,q} \geq x_{i,k}^{p,r} + x_{k,j}^{r,q} - 1$$
$$\forall i, j = [1, \cdots n], \ \forall p, q, r = [1, \cdots m], \text{ and } p < r < q$$

(7)

3.3 Overall Optimization Problem

Thus, by combining the objective function in eqn. (3) with the constraints in eqn. (4) and eqn. (7) we pose the overall optimization problem as,

$$\underset{\substack{x_{i,j}^{p,q} \\ i,j=[1,\cdots,n] \\ p,q=[1,\cdots,m]}}{\operatorname{argmax}} \left(\sum_{\substack{p,q=1 \\ p<q}}^{m} \sum_{i,j=1}^{n} c_{i,j}^{p,q} x_{i,j}^{p,q} \right)$$

$$\text{subject to } \sum_{j=1}^{n} x_{i,j}^{p,q} = 1 \ \forall i = [1, \cdots, n] \ \forall p, q = [1, \cdots, m], \ p < q$$

$$\sum_{i=1}^{n} x_{i,j}^{p,q} = 1 \ \forall j = [1, \cdots, n] \ \forall p, q = [1, \cdots, m], \ p < q \tag{8}$$

$$x_{i,j}^{p,q} \geq x_{i,k}^{p,r} + x_{k,j}^{r,q} - 1$$

$$\forall i, j = [1, \cdots n], \ \forall p, q, r = [1, \cdots m], \text{ and } p < r < q$$

$$x_{i,j}^{p,q} \in \{0, 1\} \ \forall i, j = [1, \cdots, n], \ \forall p, q = 1 \text{ to } m, \ p < q$$

The above optimization problem for optimal and consistent re-identification is a binary integer program.

3.4 Network Consistent Re-identification for Variable Number of Targets

As explained in the previous sub-section, the NCR problem can be solved by solving the binary IP formulated in eqn. (8). However, there may be situations when every person does not go through every camera. In such cases, the values of assignment variables in every row or column of the assignment matrix can all be 0. In other words, a person from any camera p can have *at most* one match from another camera q. As a result, the association constraints now change from equalities to inequalities as follows:

$$\sum_{j=1}^{n_q} x_{i,j}^{p,q} \leq 1 \ \forall i = [1, \cdots, n_p] \ \forall p, q = [1, \cdots, m], \ p < q$$

$$\sum_{i=1}^{n_p} x_{i,j}^{p,q} \leq 1 \ \forall j = [1, \cdots, n_q] \ \forall p, q = 1 \text{ to } m, \ p < q, \tag{9}$$

where n_p snd n_q are the number of persons in camera p and q respectively. But with this generalization, it is easy to see that the objective function (ref. eqn. (8)) is no longer valid. Even though the provision of 'no match' is now available, the optimal solution will try to get as many association as possible across the network. This is due to the fact that the current objective function assigns reward to both true positive (TP) associations (correctly matching a person present in both cameras) and false positive (FP) associations (wrongly associating a match to a person who is present in only one camera). Thus the optimal solution may contain many false positive associations. This situation can be avoided by incorporating a modification in the objective function as follows:

$$\sum_{\substack{p,q=1 \\ p<q}}^{m} \sum_{i,j=1}^{n_p,n_q} (c_{i,j}^{p,q} - k) x_{i,j}^{p,q}, \tag{10}$$

where 'k' is any value in the range of the similarity scores. This modification leverages upon the idea that, typically, similarity scores for most of the TP matches in the data would be much larger than majority of the FP matches. In the new cost function, instead of rewarding all positive associations we give reward to most of the TPs, but impose penalties on the FPs. As the rewards for all TP matches are discounted by the same amount 'k' and as there is penalty for FP associations, the new cost function gives us optimal results for both 'match' and 'no-match' cases. The choice of the parameter 'k' depends on the similarity scores generated by the chosen method, and thus can vary from one pairwise similarity score generating methods to another. Ideally, the distributions of similarity scores of the TPs and FPs are non-overlapping and 'k' can be any real number from the region separating these two distributions. However, for practical scenarios where TP and FP scores overlap, an optimal 'k' can be learned from training data. A simple method to choose 'k' could be running NCR for different values of 'k' over the training data and choosing the one giving the maximum accuracy on the cross validation data. So, for this more generalized case, the NCR problem can be formulated as follows,

$$\underset{\substack{x_{i,j}^{p,q} \\ i=[1,\cdots,n_p] \\ j=[1,\cdots,n_q] \\ p,q=[1,\cdots,m]}}{\operatorname{argmax}} \left(\sum_{\substack{p,q=1 \\ p<q}}^{m} \sum_{i,j=1}^{n_p,n_q} (c_{i,j}^{p,q} - k)x_{i,j}^{p,q} \right)$$

$$\text{subject to } \sum_{j=1}^{n_q} x_{i,j}^{p,q} \leq 1 \ \forall i = [1,\cdots,n_p] \ \forall p,q = [1,\cdots,m], p<q \tag{11}$$

$$\sum_{i=1}^{n_p} x_{i,j}^{p,q} = 1 \ \forall j = [1,\cdots,n_q] \ \forall p,q = [1,\cdots,m], p<q$$

$$x_{i,j}^{p,q} \geq x_{i,k}^{p,r} + x_{k,j}^{r,q} - 1$$

$$\forall i = [1,\cdots,n_p], \ j = [1,\cdots,n_q], \ \forall p,q,r = [1,\cdots m], \text{ and } p<r<q$$

$$x_{i,j}^{p,q} \in \{0,1\} \ \forall i = [1,\cdots,n_p], \ j = [1,\cdots,n_q], \ \forall p,q = [1,\cdots,m], p<q$$

A rigorous proof showing that the problem in eqn. (8) is a special case of the more generalized problem described in this section can be found in the supplementary.[1]

4   Experiments

<u>Datasets and Performance Measures:</u> To validate our approach, we performed experiments on two benchmark datasets - WARD [16] and one new dataset RAiD introduced in this work. Though state-of-the-art methods for person re-identification e.g., [3,8,13] evaluate their performances using other datasets too (e.g., ETHZ, CAVIAR4REID, CUHK) these do not fit our purposes since these are either two camera datasets or several sequences of different 2 camera datasets.

---

[1] Supplementary materials are available at www.ee.ucr.edu/~amitrc/publications.php

WARD is a 3 camera dataset and RAiD is a 4 camera dataset. Results are shown in terms of recognition rate as Cumulative Matching Characteristic (CMC) curves and normalized Area Under Curve (nAUC) values (provided in the supplementary), as is the common practice in the literature. The CMC curve is a plot of the recognition percentage versus the ranking score and represents the expectation of finding the correct match inside top t matches. nAUC gives an overall score of how well a re-identification method performs irrespective of the dataset size. In the case where every person is not present in all cameras, we show the accuracy as total number of true positives (true matches) and true negatives (true non-matches) divided by the total number of unique people present. All the results used for comparison were either taken from the corresponding works or by running codes which are publicly available or obtained from the authors on datasets for which reported results could not be obtained. We did not re-implement other methods as it is very difficult to exactly emulate all the implementation details.

Pairwise Similarity Score Generation: The camera pairwise similarity score generation starts with extracting appearance features in the form of HSV color histogram from the images of the targets. Before computing these features, the foreground is segmented out to extract the silhouette. Three salient regions (head, torso and legs) are extracted from the silhouette as proposed in [3]. The head region S^H is discarded, since it often consists of a few and less informative pixels. We additionally divide both body and torso into two horizontal sub-regions based on the intuition that people can wear shorts or long pants, and short or long sleeves tops.

Given the extracted features, we generate the similarity scores by learning the way features get transformed between cameras in a similar approach as [11,18]. Instead of using feature correlation matrix or the feature histogram values directly, we capture the feature transformation by warping the feature space in a nonlinear fashion inspired by the principle of Dynamic Time Warping (DTW). The feature bin number axis is warped to reduce the mismatch between feature values of two feature histograms from two cameras. Considering two non-overlapping cameras, a pair of images of the same target is a feasible pair, while a pair of images between two different targets is an infeasible pair. Given the feasible and infeasible transformation functions from the training examples, a Random Forest (RF) [7] classifier is trained on these two sets. The camera pairwise similarity score between targets are obtained from the probability given by the trained classifier of a test transformation function as belonging to either the set of feasible or infeasible transformation functions. In addition to the feature transformation based method, similarity scores are also generated using the publicly available code of a recent work - ICT [2] where pairwise re-identification was posed as a classification problem in the feature space formed of concatenated features of persons viewed in two different cameras.

Experimental Setup: To be consistent with the evaluations carried out by state-of-the-art methods, images were normalized to 128×64. The H, S and V color histograms extracted from the body parts were quantized using 10 bins

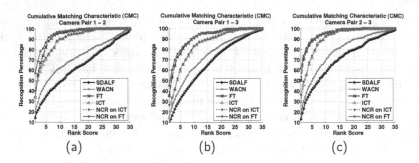

Fig. 3. CMC curves for the WARD dataset. Results and comparisons in (a), (b) and (c) are shown for the camera pairs 1-2, 1-3, and 2-3 respectively..

each. Image pairs of the same or different person(s) in different cameras were randomly picked to compute the feasible and infeasible transformation functions respectively. All the experiments are conducted using a multi-shot strategy where 10 images per person is taken for both training and testing The RF parameters such as the number of trees, the number of features to consider when looking for the best split, etc. were selected using 4-fold cross validation. For each test we ran 5 independent trials and report the average results.

4.1   WARD Dataset

The WARD dataset [16] has 4786 images of 70 different people acquired in a real surveillance scenario in three non-overlapping cameras. This dataset has a huge illumination variation apart from resolution and pose changes. The cameras here are denoted as camera $1, 2$ and 3. Fig. 3(a), (b) and (c) compare the performance for camera pairs $1 - 2, 1 - 3$, and $2 - 3$ respectively. The 70 people in this dataset are equally divided into training and test sets of 35 persons each. The proposed approach is compared with the methods SDALF [3], ICT [2] and WACN [16]. The legends 'NCR on FT' and 'NCR on ICT' imply that the NCR algorithm is applied on similarity scores generated by learning the feature transformation and by ICT respectively. For all 3 camera pairs the proposed method outperforms the rest. The difference is most clear in the rank 1 performance. For all the camera pairs 'NCR on FT' shows the best rank 1 performance of recognition percentages as high as 57.14, 45.15 and 61.71 for camera pairs 1-2, 1-3 and 2-3 respectively. The runner up in camera pair 1-2 is 'NCR on ICT' with rank 1 recognition percentage of 40. The runner up for the rest of the camera pairs is 'FT' with corresponding numbers for camera pairs 1-3 and 2-3 being 35.43 and 50.29 respectively Fig. 4 shows two example scenarios from this dataset where inconsistent re-identifications are corrected on application of NCR algorithm.

4.2   RAiD Dataset

Unlike the publicly available person re-identification datasets, Re-identification Across indoor-outdoor Dataset (RAiD) is collected so that a large number of

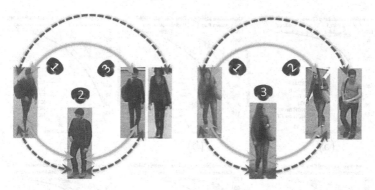

Fig. 4. Two examples of correction of inconsistent re-identification from WARD dataset. The red dashed lines denote re-identifications performed on 3 camera pairs independently by FT method. The green solid lines show the re-identification results on application of NCR on FT. The NCR algorithm exploits the consistency requirement and makes the resultant re-identification across 3 cameras correct.

people are seen in multiple cameras in a wide area camera network. This new dataset also has large illumination variation as this was collected using both indoor (camera 1 and 2) and outdoor cameras (camera 3 and 4). 43 subjects were asked to walk through these 4 cameras resulting in 6920 annotated images. 41 of the total 43 persons appear in all the cameras. We took these 41 persons to validate the proposed approach. The dataset is publicly available to download in http://www.ee.ucr.edu/~amitrc/datasets.php

The proposed approach is compared with the same methods as for the WARD dataset. 21 persons were used for training while the rest 20 were used in training. Figs. 5(a) - (f) compare the performance for camera pairs 1-2, 1-3, 1-4, 2-3, 2-4 and 3-4 respectively. We see that the proposed method performs better than all the rest for both the cases when there is not much appearance variation (for camera pair 1-2 where both cameras are indoor and for camera pair 3-4 where both cameras are outdoor) and when there is significant lighting variation (for the rest 4 camera pairs). Expectedly, for camera pairs 1-2 and 3-4 the performance of the proposed method is the best. For the indoor camera pair 1-2 the proposed method applied on similarity scores generated by feature transformation (NCR on FT) and on the similarity scores by ICT (NCR on ICT) achieve 86% and 89% rank 1 performance respectively. For the outdoor camera pair 3-4 the same two methods achieve 79% and 68% rank 1 performance respectively. For the rest of the cases where there is significant illumination variation the proposed method is superior to all the rest.

In all the camera pairs, the top two performances come from the NCR method applied on two different camera pairwise similarity score generating methods. It can further be seen that for camera pairs with large illumination variation (*i.e.* 1-3, 1-4, 2-3 and 2-4) the performance improvement is significantly large. For camera pair 1-3, the rank 1 performance shoots up to 67% and 60% on application of NCR algorithm to FT and ICT compared to their original rank 1 performance of 26% and 28% respectively. Clearly, imposing consistency improves

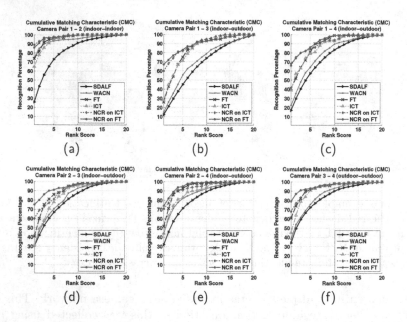

Fig. 5. CMC curves for RAiD dataset. In (a), (b), (c), (d), (e), (f) comparisons are shown for the camera pairs 1-2 (both indoor), 1-3 (indoor-outdoor), 1-4 (indoor-outdoor), 2-3 (indoor-outdoor), 2-4 (indoor-outdoor) and 3-4 (both outdoor) respectively.

the overall performance with the best absolute accuracy achieved for camera pairs consisiting of only indoor or only outdoor cameras. On the other hand, the relative improvement is significantly large in case of large illumination variation between the two cameras.

4.3 Re-identification with Variable Number of Persons

Next we evaluate the performance of the proposed method for the generalized setting when all the people may not be present in all cameras. For this purpose we chose two cameras (namely camera 3 and 4) and removed 8 (40% out of the test set containing 20 people) randomly chosen people keeping all the persons intact in cameras 1 and 2. For this experiment the accuracy of the proposed method is shown with similarity scores as obtained by learning the feature transformation between the camera pairs. The accuracy is calculated by taking both true positive and true negative matches into account and it is expressed as $\frac{(\text{\# true positive}+\text{\# true negative})}{\text{\# of unique people in the testset}}$.

Since the existing methods do not report re-identification results on variable number of persons nor is the code available which we can modify easily to incorporate such a scenario, we can not provide a comparison of performance here. However we show the performance of the proposed method for different values of 'k'. The value of 'k' is learnt using 2 random partitions of the training data in the same scenario (*i.e.*, removing 40% of the people from camera 3 and 4).

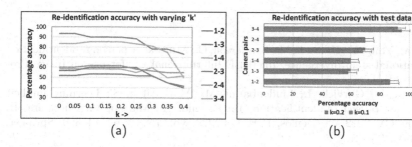

(a)   (b)

Fig. 6. performance of the NCR algorithm after removing 40% of the people from both camera 3 and 4. In (a) re-identification accuracy on the training data is shown for every camera pair by varying the parameter k after removing 40% of the training persons. (b) shows the re-identification accuracy on the test data for the chosen values of $k = 0.1$ and 0.2 when 40% of the test people were not present.

The average accuracy over these two random partitions for varying 'k' for all the 6 cameras are shown in Fig. 6(a). As shown, the accuracy remains more or less constant till $k = 0.25$. After that, the accuracy for camera pairs having the same people (namely camera pairs 1-2 and 3-4) falls rapidly, but for the rest of the cameras where the number of people are variable remains significantly constant. This is due to the fact that the reward for 'no match' increases with the value of 'k' and for camera pair 1-2 and 3-4 there is no 'no match' case. So, for these two camera pairs, the optimization problem (in eqn. (11)) reaches the global maxima at the cost of assigning 0 label to some of the true associations (for which the similarity scores are on the lower side). So, any value of 'k' in the range $(0 - 0.25)$ will be a reasonable choice. The accuracy of all the 6 cameras for $k = 0.1$ and 0.2 is shown in Fig. 6(b), where it can be seen that the performance is significantly high and does not vary much with different values of 'k.'

5   Conclusions

In this work we addressed the problem of person re-identification in a camera network by exploiting the requirement of consistency of re-identification results. A novel binary integer programing formulation of the problem is provided. The proposed method not only boosts camera pairwise re-identification performance but also can handle a largely unaddressed problem of matching variable number of persons across cameras. The future directions of our research will be not only to apply our approach to bigger networks with large numbers of cameras, and cope with wider space-time horizons but to apply also to other areas, (*e.g.*, social network analysis, medical imaging to name a few) where consistency is the key to robustness.

Acknowledgements. This work was partially supported by NSF grants IIS-1316934 and CNS-1330110. We acknowledge the authors of [16] for providing the code of WACN. We would also like to thank Andrew Yu, a current UCR undergraduate student, for helping in the annotation of the RAiD dataset.

References

1. Alavi, A., Yang, Y., Harandi, M., Sanderson, C.: Multi-shot person re-identification via relational stein divergence. In: IEEE International Conference on Image Processing (2013)
2. Avraham, T., Gurvich, I., Lindenbaum, M., Markovitch, S.: Learning implicit transfer for person re-identification. In: Fusiello, A., Murino, V., Cucchiara, R. (eds.) ECCV 2012 Ws/Demos, Part I. LNCS, vol. 7583, pp. 381–390. Springer, Heidelberg (2012)
3. Bazzani, L., Cristani, M., Murino, V.: Symmetry-driven accumulation of local features for human characterization and re-identification. Computer Vision and Image Understanding 117(2), 130–144 (2013)
4. Bellet, A., Habrard, A., Sebban, M.: A survey on metric learning for feature vectors and structured data. ArXiv e-prints (2013)
5. Ben Shitrit, H., Berclaz, J., Fleuret, F., Fua, P.: Tracking multiple people under global appearance constraints. In: IEEE International Conference on Computer Vision, pp. 137–144 (2011)
6. Berclaz, J., Fleuret, F., Turetken, E., Fua, P.: Multiple object tracking using k-shortest paths optimization. IEEE Transactions on Pattern Analysis and Machine Intelligence 33(9), 1806–1819 (2011)
7. Breiman, L.: Random forests. Machine Learning 45(1), 5–32 (2001)
8. Cheng, D.S., Cristani, M., Stoppa, M., Bazzani, L., Murino, V.: Custom pictorial structures for re-identification. In: British Machine Vision Conference (2011)
9. Dikmen, M., Akbas, E., Huang, T.S., Ahuja, N.: Pedestrian recognition with a learned metric. In: Kimmel, R., Klette, R., Sugimoto, A. (eds.) ACCV 2010, Part IV. LNCS, vol. 6495, pp. 501–512. Springer, Heidelberg (2011)
10. Gilbert, A., Bowden, R.: Tracking objects across cameras by incrementally learning inter-camera colour calibration and patterns of activity. In: Leonardis, A., Bischof, H., Pinz, A. (eds.) ECCV 2006. LNCS, vol. 3952, pp. 125–136. Springer, Heidelberg (2006)
11. Javed, O., Shafique, K., Rasheed, Z., Shah, M.: Modeling inter-camera space–time and appearance relationships for tracking across non-overlapping views. Computer Vision and Image Understanding 109(2), 146–162 (2008)
12. Kviatkovsky, I., Adam, A., Rivlin, E.: Color invariants for person re-identification. IEEE Transactions on Pattern Analysis and Machine Intelligence 35(7), 1622–1634 (2013)
13. Li, W., Wang, X.: Locally aligned feature transforms across views. In: IEEE International Conference on Computer Vision and Pattern Recognition (2013)
14. Li, W., Zhao, R., Wang, X.: Human reidentification with transferred metric learning. In: Lee, K.M., Matsushita, Y., Rehg, J.M., Hu, Z. (eds.) ACCV 2012, Part I. LNCS, vol. 7724, pp. 31–44. Springer, Heidelberg (2013)
15. Liu, C., Gong, S., Loy, C.C., Lin, X.: Person re-identification: What features are important? In: European Conference on Computer Vision, Workshops and Demonstrations, Florence, Italy, pp. 391–401. Springer, Heidelberg (2012)
16. Martinel, N., Micheloni, C.: Re-identify people in wide area camera network. In: International Conference on Computer Vision and Pattern Recognition Workshops, pp. 31–36. IEEE, Providence (2012)
17. Pedagadi, S., Orwell, J., Velastin, S.: Local fisher discriminant analysis for pedestrian re-identification. In: IEEE International Conference on Computer Vision and Pattern Recognition, pp. 3318–3325 (2013)

18. Porikli, F., Hill, M.: Inter-camera color calibration using cross-correlation model function. In: IEEE International Conference on Image Processing (ICIP), pp. 133–136 (2003)
19. Prosser, B., Gong, S., Xiang, T.: Multi-camera matching using bi-directional cumulative brightness transfer functions. In: British Machine Vision Conference (September 2008)
20. Schrijver, A.: Theory of linear and integer programming. John Wiley and Sons (1998)
21. Shafique, K., Shah, M.: A noniterative greedy algorithm for multiframe point correspondence. IEEE Transactions on Pattern Analysis and Machine Intelligence 27(1), 51–65 (2005)
22. Taj, M., Maggio, E., Cavallaro, A.: Multi-feature graph-based object tracking. In: Stiefelhagen, R., Garofolo, J.S. (eds.) CLEAR 2006. LNCS, vol. 4122, pp. 190–199. Springer, Heidelberg (2007)
23. Yang, L., Jin, R.: Distance metric learning: A comprehensive survey. Tech. rep., Michigan State University (2006)
24. Zhao, R., Ouyang, W., Wang, X.: Unsupervised salience learning for person re-identification. In: IEEE International Conference on Computer Vision and Pattern Recognition (2013)

Surface Normal Deconvolution: Photometric Stereo for Optically Thick Translucent Objects

Chika Inoshita[1], Yasuhiro Mukaigawa[2]
Yasuyuki Matsushita[3], and Yasushi Yagi[1]

[1] Osaka University, Japan
[2] Nara Institute of Science and Technology, Japan
[3] Microsoft Research Asia, China

Abstract. This paper presents a photometric stereo method that works for optically thick translucent objects exhibiting subsurface scattering. Our method is built upon the previous studies showing that subsurface scattering is approximated as convolution with a blurring kernel. We extend this observation and show that the original surface normal convolved with the scattering kernel corresponds to the blurred surface normal that can be obtained by a conventional photometric stereo technique. Based on this observation, we cast the photometric stereo problem for optically thick translucent objects as a deconvolution problem, and develop a method to recover accurate surface normals. Experimental results of both synthetic and real-world scenes show the effectiveness of the proposed method.

1 Introduction

Photometric stereo estimates the surface normals of a scene from multiple shading images taken under different lighting conditions [1]. While conventional methods are developed for simple Lambertian diffuse surfaces [2], recent generalizations can handle more complex reflections in real-world scenes [3, 4]. However, surface normal estimation of translucent materials is still a difficult task, where subsurface scattering is significant [5].

In a translucent object, incident light travels randomly and exits from various neighboring locations. This global light transport effect makes it hard to directly associate the shading observations with its surface geometry. As a result, shape-from-intensity techniques that only assume local illumination models naturally suffer from the unmodeled error of subsurface scattering. One of the directions to address this issue is to remove the subsurface scattering component from the observations, therefore conventional shape-from-intensity techniques can be used to the remaining direct lighting component. Recently, Nayar *et al.* [6] have demonstrated an approach to effectively remove subsurface scattering from the scene observations, with an expense of additional measurements under high-frequency illuminations. In general, removing the subsurface scattering component requires

D. Fleet et al. (Eds.): ECCV 2014, Part II, LNCS 8690, pp. 346–359, 2014.

an additional preprocessing stage, and a shape-from-intensity method that can directly account for subsurface scattering is wanted.

While exact modeling of subsurface scattering is still a difficult task that requires complicated models, prior studies in the field of computer graphics show that the image formation model of subsurface scattering can be well approximated as convolution of the scattering kernel and surface radiance on optically thick materials, which distribute light regardless of the incident directions [7]. We use this approximation to develop *surface normal deconvolution*, which recovers original surface normal from the *blurry* surface normal obtained by conventional photometric stereo on translucent objects. This idea is similar to Dong *et al.*'s method [8], which estimates surface normal by deconvolved input images to remove the subsurface scattering effect. While Dong *et al.* assume parametric subsurface scattering, *i.e.*, photon beam diffusion of optically homogeneous media, we represent subsurface scattering by non-parametric convolution kernels for either optically homogeneous or inhomogeneous media. The convolution kernels can be either calibrated or estimated, and various deconvolution techniques in the literature (such as image deblurring methods) can be used for the implementation to recover deblurred surface normal. We show estimation results by both our deconvolution formulation and existing deconvolution in experiments.

2   Related Works

Conventional photometric stereo methods recover surface normals at a pixel-level detail based on local illumination models. While the original work of Woodham [1] uses a simple Lambertian reflection model [2], more recent approaches make various generalizations by explicitly accounting for more flexible reflectance models [9, 10], or by robust estimation framework [3, 4]. These methods are shown effective; however, for translucent objects, global light interactions need to be accounted for to achieve accurate surface normal estimation. A seminal work of Nayar *et al.* [11] explicitly takes interreflections into account, which are global light transports among opaque surfaces. While the problem is similar, subsurface scattering remains as an un-addressed light transport effect in shape-from-intensity methods.

Recently, structured-light methods for measuring the shape of translucent surfaces are proposed. To reduce effect of subsurface scattering, combination of polarizers and phase shifting [12], multiplication of low-frequency and high-frequency projection pattern [13], and high frequency illumination with multiplexed light source [14] have been used. In addition, Gupta *et al.* [15] use several binary projection codes to decrease estimation errors caused by subsurface scattering and interreflections. These techniques are shown effective, with an expense of specialized hardware setups.

Modeling subsurface scattering has been more studied in computer graphics as bidirectional scattering surface reflection distribution function (BSSRDF). Although the general BSSRDFs can represent various translucent appearances, it is difficult to exactly model BSSRDFs because of its high-dimensionality. Hence,

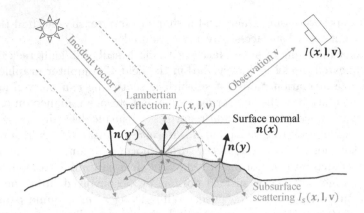

Fig. 1. Light interactions on a translucent surface. Incident light is partially reflected off the surface, while the rest of the light transmits and spreads inside the subsurface.

researchers previously approximate BSSRDFs as a low dimensional function with an assumption of homogeneous media [16], or isotropic scattering based on the diffusion theory [17–19]. In our work, we also approximate subsurface scattering by a simple model with an assumption of optically thick materials. In optically thick materials, incident light repeatedly scatters and loses its directionality, and as a result, the scattering strength becomes invariant to the illumination and observation directions. Based on this characteristics, subsurface scattering is approximated by a convolutional model in [7]. Our method is built upon this observation and extends it to develop a photometric stereo method for optically thick translucent objects.

3   Convolutional Image Formation Model

We begin with the image formation model for a translucent surface. When light illuminates a translucent surface, it is partially reflected, transmitted and also absorbed as depicted in Fig. 1. A portion of the transmitted light comes back to the surface via subsurface scattering; thus, the radiance $I(x, l, \mathbf{v})$ at a scene point x with incident vector l and observation vector $\mathbf{v}$ becomes the sum of the reflection $I_r(x, l, \mathbf{v})$ and subsurface scattering $I_s(x, l, \mathbf{v})$ components as

$$I(x, l, \mathbf{v}) = I_r(x, l, \mathbf{v}) + I_s(x, l, \mathbf{v}). \tag{1}$$

The subsurface scattering component $I_s(x, l, \mathbf{v})$ is modeled as [17]

$$I_s(x, l, \mathbf{v}) = \gamma(x) \, F(\mathbf{v}, \mathbf{n}(x), \eta) \int_{y \in A} R(x, y) F(l, \mathbf{n}(y), \eta) \mathbf{n}(y)^T l \, dy, \tag{2}$$

where $\gamma(x)$ is a scale factor for the subsurface scattering component, F represents Fresnel transmission, and $\mathbf{v}, \mathbf{n}, l \in \mathbb{R}^3$ are the obervation, surface normal, and incident vectors, respectively. η is a refractive index, $R(x, y)$ represents an extinction term for light from scene point x to its neighbor y such as dipole model [17], and A defines a neighboring area. Generally, the subsurface scattering component describes a nonlinear relation between the surface normals and observed intensity due to the Fresnel transmission term. To relax this complexity, we approximate the original model in a simpler form by assuming an optically thick material, as in [7]. On the surface of an optically thick material, subsurface scattering does not depend on the direction of the light, because the transmitted light scatters uncountable times and loses its directionality as same as diffusion approximation. Thus, subsurface scattering is invariant to the incident direction and outgoing direction, and the Fresnel terms F can be regarded as constants on optically thick materials. As a result the subsurface scattering component $I_s(x, \mathbf{l}, \mathbf{v})$ is simplified to

$$I_s(x, \mathbf{l}) = \gamma'(x) \int_{y \in A} R(x, y) \mathbf{n}(y)^T \mathbf{l} dy, \tag{3}$$

where $\gamma'(x)$ is a new scale factor of subsurface scattering that includes constant Fresnel transmission terms.

Assuming a Lambertian reflectance model for the reflection component $I_r(x, \mathbf{l}) = \rho(x) \mathbf{n}(x)^T \mathbf{l}$ with a diffuse albedo $\rho(x)$, the intensity observation $I(x, \mathbf{l}, \mathbf{v})$ can be written as

$$I(x, \mathbf{l}) = \left(\rho(x) \mathbf{n}(x) + \gamma'(x) \int_{y \in A} R(x, y) \mathbf{n}(y) dy \right)^T \mathbf{l}. \tag{4}$$

The first factor of Eq. (4) can be regarded as a simple convolution model as

$$I(x, \mathbf{l}) = \left(\int_{y \in A} h(x, y) \mathbf{n}(y) dy \right)^T \mathbf{l} = (h * \mathbf{n}(x))^T \mathbf{l}, \tag{5}$$

where $*$ is the convolution operation, the kernel h represents a scattering effect for the surface normals as

$$h(x, y) = \rho(x)\delta(x - y) + \gamma'(x) R(x, y). \tag{6}$$

A similar convolutional approximation of subsurface scattering is also discussed in the work of Munoz et al. [7] for the forward rendering of optically thick materials. This method is also inspired by the works of convolutional approximated subsurface scattering by d'Eon et al. [18] for the rendering of human skin and Donner et al. [16] for multi-layered materials. Unlike their method where the extinction term $R(x, y)$ is defined as a function parameterized only by the relative position of x and y, our method allows more flexibility for the extinction term $R(x, y)$ so that inhomogeneous translucent materials can also be handled.

4   Solution Method

Based on the convolutional image formation model, we develop a photometric stereo method for estimating the surface normals of an optically thick translucent surface. Our input is the same as traditional photometric stereo: A set of images is taken under varying lighting directions from a fixed view point. To simplify the discussion, we assume that the light directions are calibrated and the observations do not include shadows. In the rest of the paper, we work in the discretized pixel sites u and v that correspond to scene points x and y, respectively; thus Eq. (5) becomes

$$I(u, \mathbf{l}) = (h(u, v) * \mathbf{n}(u))^T \mathbf{l}. \tag{7}$$

The convolution equation Eq. (7) has a simple linear algebraic expression as

$$\mathbf{D} = \mathbf{HNL}, \tag{8}$$

where $\mathbf{D} \in \mathbb{R}^{m \times k}$ is an observation matrix, m and k are the numbers of pixels and light directions, respectively, $\mathbf{H} \in \mathbb{R}^{m \times m}$ is a scattering matrix, $\mathbf{N} \in \mathbb{R}^{m \times 3}$ is a surface normal matrix, and $\mathbf{L} \in \mathbb{R}^{3 \times k}$ is an incident light matrix, which is assumed to be known. This linear expression indeed has a similarity to the Lambertian photometric stereo [1], where the observation $\mathbf{D}$, scaled surface normal $\mathbf{N}_s$, and light matrix $\mathbf{L}$ has the following relationship:

$$\mathbf{D} = \mathbf{N}_s \mathbf{L}. \tag{9}$$

From Eqs. (8) and (9), we can see that the scaled surface normal $\mathbf{N}_s$ corresponds to $\mathbf{HN}$ as

$$\mathbf{N}_s = \mathbf{HN}. \tag{10}$$

Therefore, we could regard the scaled surface normal $\mathbf{N}_s$ as a *blurry* version of the original surface normal $\mathbf{N}$ that we wish to estimate. In the following we call $\mathbf{N}_s$ a smoothed surface normal.

Based on this observation, we estimate the surface normal $\mathbf{N}$ by taking the following two-step approach: (a) Obtain the smoothed surface normal $\mathbf{N}_s$ by Lambertian photometric stereo [1], (b) Estimate surface normal $\mathbf{N}$ in a deconvolution framework using the subsurface scattering matrix $\mathbf{H}$.

(a) Estimation of smoothed surface normal $\mathbf{N}_s$. We use a conventional Lambertian photometric stereo [1] for deriving the smoothed surface normal $\mathbf{N}_s$ as

$$\mathbf{N}_s = \mathbf{DL}^\dagger, \tag{11}$$

where † represents a Moore-Penrose pseudo inverse.

(b) Estimation of original surface normal **N**. Once the smoothed surface normal **N**$_s$ is obtained, we use Eq. (10) for deriving the original surface normal **N**. If the scattering matrix **H** is available and invertible, we can directly obtain the estimate of the original surface normal **N** in a linear least-squares fashion as **N** = **H**$^{-1}$**N**$_s$. Since the estimation result produced by such a simple deconvolution is often degraded by ringing artifacts due to the loss of high-frequency information in the original signal, we use a smoothness constraint to stabilize the estimation. We design the smoothness term s as a weighted second-order difference of $\mathbf{n}(u)$ among u's neighborhood locations t and v as

$$\mathbf{n}''(u) = w(t,u)\,(\mathbf{n}(t) - \mathbf{n}(u)) - w(u,v)\,(\mathbf{n}(u) - \mathbf{n}(v))\,. \tag{12}$$

The weight $w(u,v)$ controls the discontinuity of surface normals by taking the difference of intensity observations across varying lightings $\mathbf{l}_i$ as

$$w(u,v) = \exp\left(-\frac{1}{m}\sum_i^k (I(u,\mathbf{l}_i) - I(v,\mathbf{l}_i))^2\right). \tag{13}$$

The matrix expression of the smoothness **N**'' is given as

$$\mathbf{N}'' = \mathbf{W}\mathbf{N}, \tag{14}$$

where $\mathbf{W} \in \mathbb{R}^{a \times m}$ is a matrix of the second-order derivative filter, a is the number of triplets used for computing the second-order derivatives. In our case, we define the triplets along horizontal and vertical directions in the image coordinates. Finally, our estimation problem becomes a ridge regression problem as

$$\hat{\mathbf{N}} = \underset{\mathbf{N}}{\mathrm{argmin}}\,||\mathbf{H}\mathbf{N} - \mathbf{N_s}||_F^2 + \lambda||\mathbf{W}\mathbf{N}||_F^2, \tag{15}$$

where λ controls smoothness of the estimates. An explicit solution to this problem is given by setting its first-order derivative to be zero as

$$\mathbf{N} = \left(\mathbf{H}^T\mathbf{H} + \lambda\mathbf{W}^T\mathbf{W}\right)^{-1}\mathbf{H}^T\mathbf{N_s}. \tag{16}$$

In this manner, the estimates for the original surface normal **N** can be obtained in a closed-form.

The mathematical expression of the problem is equivalent to the image deblurring problem, where the original sharp image is recovered via deconvolution. The important difference is, however, that our problem deals with the deconvolution of surface normals. Therefore, conventional image priors that are developed for natural images may not be suitable. Other than this aspect, existing deconvolution techniques can be alternatively used for estimating the surface normal **N** from the smoothed surface normal **N**$_s$. The convolution kernel **H** is generally unknown but can be either calibrated (non-blind deconvolution) or estimated (blind deconvolution). While most of image deblurring techniques are limited to spatially-invariant point spread functions (PSFs), which corresponds to handling optically homogeneous materials in our case, the formulation of Eq. (16) can naturally handle optically inhomogeneous materials, corresponding to the case of spatially-varying PSFs.

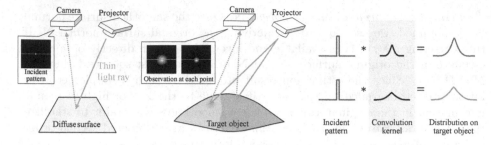

Fig. 2. Setting for measuring the convolution kernel. Projector casts a thin light ray to target object. We estimate the convolution kernel from the incident pattern and light distributions on the target object. In the case of inhomogeneous media, we capture light distributions at optically different regions.

4.1 Calibration of Convolution Kernel

As mentioned above, the surface normal deconvolution can be performed without knowing the convolution kernel by using blind deconvolution techniques; however, the knowledge of the convolution kernel is useful for stabilizing the estimation. Here we describe a simple procedure for measuring the convolution kernel. Fig. 2 shows our setting for measuring the convolution kernel. By illuminating a diffuse surface and the target translucent material individually by a thin ray emitted from a projector, we obtain the measurements of the incident light distribution and scattering response on the surface, respectively. The measured scattering response corresponds to the convolution between the incident light distribution and the convolution kernel. From this relationship, we calibrate the convolution kernel h. When target media is optically inhomogeneous, we need to calibrate convolution kernels at each optically different region.

5   Experiments

Now we evaluate our method using both synthetic and real-world data for the purposes of quantitative and qualitative evaluations.

5.1 Synthetic Data

Homogeneous Media. For the synthetic data, we use two types of scenes, scene A and B, as shown in Fig. 3. The image sizes of scene A and B are 150×113 and 160×160 pixels, respectively. For synthesizing the input images under varying lightings, we use Eq. (1) with the subsurface scattering model of Eq. (2). For the extinction term $R(x, y)$ in Eq. (2), we use the Dipole model [17] with the same parameters that are described in their paper. The camera model is orthographic and a pixel area corresponds to $(4/15)^2 [\text{mm}^2]$ in the metric system.

Figure 3 (b) shows the result of Lambertian photometric stereo based on Eq. (11) and its angular error in the pseudo color. Although the estimated surface normals are smoothed out due to subsurface scattering, especially around edges, the low-frequency signal of the overall surface normal directions are largely obtained.

To apply our surface normal deconvolution of Eq. (16), we use the extinction term $R(x, y)$ as the convolution kernel. The distance between scene points x and y is approximated to the distance between pixel sites u and v in the image coordinates. Figures 3 (c) and (d) show the result of our method with varying smoothness factors, $\lambda = 0.01$ and $\lambda = 0.1$, respectively. While the results with a small smoothness factor $\lambda = 0.01$ yield sharper reconstructions, they suffer from ringing artifacts around surface normal edges. Although the choice of the proper value for λ is scene-dependent and thus difficult as is the case with any regularization techniques, with a proper value of λ, our method significantly improves the reconstruction accuracy over the Lambertian photometric stereo that only considers the local illumination model, even though we also assume the same Lambertian model as the reflectance component. Table 1 summarizes the maximum and mean angular errors of the surface normal estimates using various material parameters. In general, we have observed that the smaller magnitude of subsurface scattering yields better accuracy, because stronger subsurface scattering cuts off the high-frequency signals more significantly. It shows that, by properly accounting for subsurface scattering, the accuracy improves by roughly 2 ~ 5 times in comparison with the baseline technique that only considers the local illumination model.

For optically homogeneous materials, we can also use conventional deconvolution methods in place of solving Eq. (16). Figures 4 and 5 show results of conventional non-blind deconvolution and blind deconvolution for scene B, respectively. For the non-blind deconvolution methods, we use the same convolution kernel with the one that is used for producing the result of Fig. 3. The results show consistent improvement over Lambertian photometric stereo, although these original methods are not particularly designed for deblurring surface normal fields. In addition, the results of blind deconvolution methods in Fig. 5, where the convolution kernel is not given but simultaneously estimated, also show improvement. While the blind deconvolution is a harder problem than non-blind deconvolution and the results are generally worse, when the knowledge of the convolution kernel is unavailable, it is a viable option for our method.

Inhomogeneous Media. Our solution method is naturally applicable to the case of inhomogeneous materials as long as the convolution kernel **H** in Eq. (16) is defined. To evaluate the performance of our method for inhomogeneous materials, we produce synthetic images that contain different optical thicknesses using masks that indicate the material regions as shown in Fig. 6 (a) and (b). Due to the difference of the magnitudes of subsurface scattering in the material regions, the surface normal estimates obtained by Lambertian photometric stereo, shown in Fig. 6 (d) and (e), exhibit varying smoothnesses; smoother in the gray mask region, and sharper in the white mask region.

By applying our method, the surface normal field is consistently improved regardless of the material regions as shown in the figure. This recovery shows higher accuracy than that of Fig. 3, because of the fact that this inhomogeneous example contains a region where scattering is less significant.

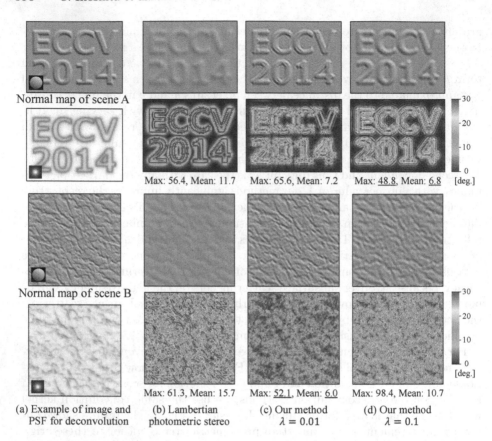

Max: 56.4, Mean: 11.7   Max: 65.6, Mean: 7.2   Max: 48.8, Mean: 6.8   [deg.]

Max: 61.3, Mean: 15.7   Max: 52.1, Mean: 6.0   Max: 98.4, Mean: 10.7

(a) Example of image and   (b) Lambertian   (c) Our method   (d) Our method
    PSF for deconvolution   photometric stereo $\lambda = 0.01$ $\lambda = 0.1$

Fig. 3. Result of synthetic scenes A and B. (a) shows an example of synthetic images using the Dipole model with the skim milk parameters in [17]. (b) is the surface normal and error maps of the Lambertian photometric stereo. More faithful surface normals are obtained with our method in (c) and (d) with the varying smoothness factor λ.

Table 1. Max and mean angular errors [deg.] of scene A and B with various materials. Parameters of each materials are described in [17].

Plot of kernels	Scene A						Scene B					
	Lambertian PS		Our method $\lambda = 0.01$		Our method $\lambda = 0.1$		Lambertian PS		Our method $\lambda = 0.01$		Our method $\lambda = 0.1$	
	max	mean	max	mean	max	mean	max	mean	max	mean	max	mean
1. Marble	41.5	7.7	40.1	3.0	30.5	2.6	56.2	11.9	29.1	1.9	36.2	5.6
2. Skim milk	56.4	11.7	65.6	7.2	48.8	6.8	61.3	15.7	52.1	6.0	98.4	10.7
3. Whole milk	37.7	6.6	30.7	2.5	25.4	1.9	52.4	10.7	22.1	1.5	28.5	4.4
4. Skin1	54.4	10.7	61.4	7.6	50.6	6.3	63.4	15.3	43.1	6.5	105.1	10.6
5. Skin2	50.3	9.8	59.5	5.1	44.1	4.7	61.5	14.3	47.9	4.2	86.2	8.7

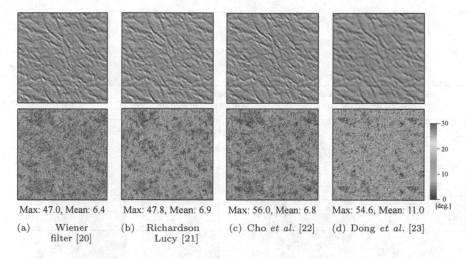

Max: 47.0, Mean: 6.4   Max: 47.8, Mean: 6.9   Max: 56.0, Mean: 6.8   Max: 54.6, Mean: 11.0

(a)   Wiener   (b)   Richardson   (c) Cho et al. [22]   (d) Dong et al. [23]
        filter [20]   Lucy [21]

Fig. 4. Surface normal estimates of scene B using non-blind deconvolution methods

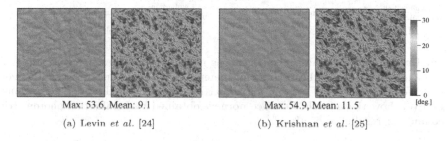

Max: 53.6, Mean: 9.1   Max: 54.9, Mean: 11.5

(a) Levin et al. [24]   (b) Krishnan et al. [25]

Fig. 5. Surface normal estimates of scene B using blind deconvolution methods

5.2   Real-World Data

We also tested our method using the real-world translucent objects. Figure 7 (a) shows our experiment setting. We used a Nikon D90 camera with a linear radiometric response function (RAW mode) and with a telescopic lens to approximate an orthographic projection. The target scenes are illuminated under directional lightings, and the light directions are calibrated using a dark specular sphere. In addition, to avoid specular reflections from the scene, we placed polarizers in front of both the light source and camera. We used three target objects: a soap as a homogeneous medium, angel and unicorn ornaments as inhomogeneous media as shown in Fig. 7 (b). Each scene is recorded under 12 different lighting directions. The image size of the soap, angel, and unicorn scenes are 232×164, 206×257, and 158×230 pixels, respectively. Prior to the measurement, the convolution kernels are measured using the procedure described in Sec. 4.1. For the inhomogeneous objects, we measured two distinct kernels which depend on different material regions, one for the white region and the other for the pink region. Examples of the recorded intensity images are shown in the left-most

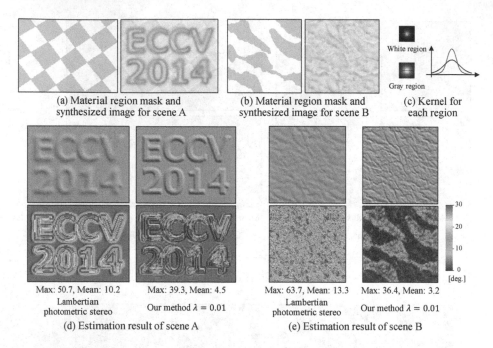

(a) Material region mask and synthesized image for scene A

(b) Material region mask and synthesized image for scene B

(c) Kernel for each region

White region

Gray region

| Max: 50.7, Mean: 10.2 | | Max: 63.7, Mean: 13.3 | Max: 36.4, Mean: 3.2 |

Max: 50.7, Mean: 10.2
Lambertian photometric stereo

Max: 39.3, Mean: 4.5
Our method $\lambda = 0.01$

Max: 63.7, Mean: 13.3
Lambertian photometric stereo

Max: 36.4, Mean: 3.2
Our method $\lambda = 0.01$

(d) Estimation result of scene A

(e) Estimation result of scene B

Fig. 6. Results with optically inhomogeneous media using scenes A and B. (a) and (b) show the masks that indicate different material regions and one of the synthesized images. We use two types of convolution kernels shown in (c) for these distinct regions. (d) and (e) show the smoothed surface normals obtained by Lambertian photometric stereo and our results, respectively.

column of Fig. 8. These images are not significantly blurry, but the details are smoothed out due to subsurface scattering.

The top row of Fig. 8 shows the result for the soap scene. While the surface normal recovered by Lambertian photometric stereo is significantly smoothed out, our method produces a much sharper estimate. The middle and bottom rows show the results of the angel and unicorn scenes, respectively. To assess the reconstruction accuracy, we created replicas of those by making molds with plaster. Assuming that the plaster reflectance is close to Lambertian, we obtained the reference surface normal by applying Lambertian photometric stereo to the replicas. The surface normal of plaster replicas exhibits details of the original shape, while the result of Lambertian photometric stereo is smoother. Our method makes the blurry surface normal much sharper and closer to the reference surface normal.

5.3 Discussion

Computation Time. Previous experiments show, in the case of optically homogeneous materials, we can apply various fast deconvolution methods for image deblurring to recover surface normal. However, in the case of inhomogeneous media, we have to solve Eq. (16) to deal with spatially variant convolution kernels.

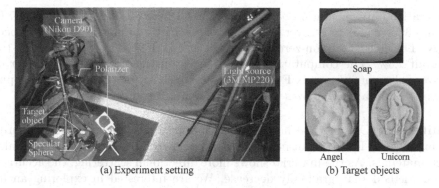

(a) Experiment setting   (b) Target objects

Fig. 7. Experiment setting and target objects. We use a projector as a light source. The camera is equipped with a telescopic lens. Polarizers are used to reduce the effects of specular reflection on the target object.

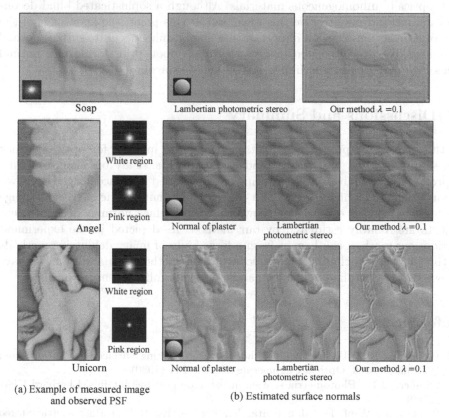

(a) Example of measured image and observed PSF

(b) Estimated surface normals

Fig. 8. Result of the real-world scenes. The soap scene in the top row is a homogeneous medium, while the middle and bottom rows (angel and unicorn scenes) are made of inhomogeneous media.

Our matlab implementation on Intel Core i7 CPU (3.5 GHz) takes about 17.6, 39, and 3.5 seconds to recover surface of soap, angel, and unicorn scenes, respectively. The density of non-zero elements of matrix $\mathbf{F}^T\mathbf{F} + \lambda\mathbf{W}^T\mathbf{W}$ in Eq. (16) is about 2.5%. The computation time depends on the size and the number of non-zero elements of matrix $\mathbf{F}^T\mathbf{F} + \lambda\mathbf{W}^T\mathbf{W}$, which are determined by the input image size and apparent sizes of PSFs in the image coordinates.

Limitations. Our method has a couple of limitations. First, we have ignored the influence of Fresnel transmissions, thus our method is restricted to optically thick materials. As the material shows more directional scattering, the accuracy of our method may gradually decrease. We are interested in exploring an iterative estimation framework to adaptively update the convolution kernels for incorporating the Fresnel transmission effects. The second limitation is that our method in practice relies on known convolution kernels, especially when dealing with optically inhomogeneous materials. Although a sophisticated blind deconvolution method may resolve this issue, but at this point, the knowledge of the convolution kernel plays an important role in obtaining accurate surface normal estimates. We are interested in investigating a good prior for surface normal fields that may potentially improve the blind deconvolution.

6 Discussions and Summary

In this paper, we proposed a photometric stereo method for optically thick translucent objects. We have extended the previous study on a convolutional approximation of subsurface scattering and developed a surface normal deconvolution technique, which consists of a conventional photometric stereo and image deconvolution. Our experiment shows that the surface normals of translucent objects are reliably estimated by our method. As depicted in the experiment section, our method can benefit from a large body of image deblurring methods in the literature including blind deconvolution methods. In addition, we have shown that our method is able to handle optically inhomogeneous media.

References

1. Woodham, R.J.: Photometric Method For Determining Surface Orientation From Multiple Images. Optical Engineering 19, 139–144 (1980)
2. Lambert, J.H.: Photometria sive de mensure de gratibus luminis. Eberhard Klett (1760)
3. Ikehata, S., Wipf, D., Matsushita, Y., Aizawa, K.: Robust Photometric Stereo using Sparse Regression. In: Proc. of IEEE Conference on Computer Vision and Pattern Recognition (CVPR) (2012)
4. Wu, L., Ganesh, A., Shi, B., Matsushita, Y., Wang, Y., Ma, Y.: Robust Photometric Stereo via Low-Rank Matrix Completion and Recovery. In: Kimmel, R., Klette, R., Sugimoto, A. (eds.) ACCV 2010, Part III. LNCS, vol. 6494, pp. 703–717. Springer, Heidelberg (2011)

5. Moore, K.D., Peers, P.: An empirical study on the effects of translucency on photometric stereo. The Visual Computer 29(6-8), 817–824 (2013)
6. Nayar, S.K., Krishnan, G., Grossberg, M.D., Raskar, R.: Fast separation of direct and global components of a scene using high frequency illumination. ACM Trans. on Graph. (ToG) 25(3), 935–944 (2006)
7. Munoz, A., Echevarria, J.I., Seron, F.J., Gutierrez, D.: Convolution-based simulation of homogeneous subsurface scattering. Computer Graphics Forum 30(8), 2279–2287 (2011)
8. Dong, B., Moore, K., Zhang, W., Peers, P.: Scattering Parameters and Surface Normals from Homogeneous Translucent Materials using Photometric Stereo. In: Proc. of IEEE Conference on Computer Vision and Pattern Recognition (CVPR) (2014)
9. Alldrin, N., Zickler, T., Kriegman, D.: Photometric stereo with non-parametric and spatially-varying reflectance. In: Proc. of IEEE Conference on Computer Vision and Pattern Recognition (CVPR) (2008)
10. Goldman, D.B., Curless, B., Hertzmann, A., Seitz, S.M.: Shape and spatially-varying BRDFs from photometric stereo. IEEE Trans. Pattern Analysis and Machine Intelligence (PAMI) 32, 1060–1071 (2010)
11. Nayar, S.K., Ikeuchi, K., Kanade, T.: Shape from interreflections. In: Proc. of International Conference on Computer Vision (ICCV) (1990)
12. Chen, T., Lensch, H.P.A., Fuchs, C., Seidel, H.P.: Polarization and Phase-shifting for 3D Scanning of Translucent Objects. In: Proc. of IEEE Conference on Computer Vision and Pattern Recognition (CVPR) (2007)
13. Chen, T., Seidel, H.P., Lensch, H.P.A.: Modulated phase-shifting for 3D scanning. In: Proc. of IEEE Conference on Computer Vision and Pattern Recognition (CVPR) (2008)
14. Gu, J., Kabayashi, T., Gupta, M., Nayar, S.K.: Multiplexed Illumination for Scene Recovery in the Presence of Global Illumination. In: Proc. of International Conference on Computer Vision (ICCV) (2011)
15. Gupta, M., Agrawal, A., Veeraraghavan, A., Narasimhan, S.G.: A Practical Approach to 3D Scanning in the Presence of Interreflections, Subsurface Scattering and Defocus. International Journal of Computer Vision (IJCV) 102, 33–55 (2012)
16. Donner, C., Lawrence, J., Ramamoorthi, R., Hachisuka, T., Jensen, H.W., Nayar, S.: An empirical BSSRDF model. ACM Trans. on Graph. (ToG) 28(3) (2009)
17. Jensen, H.W., Marschner, S.R., Levoy, M., Hanrahan, P.: A practical model for subsurface light transport. In: Proc. ACM SIGGRAPH, pp. 511–518 (2001)
18. d'Eon, E., Irving, G.: A quantized-diffusion model for rendering translucent materials. ACM Transactions on Graphics (TOG) 30 (2011)
19. Borshukov, G., Lewis, J.: Realistic human face rendering for "the matrix reloaded". In: Proc. ACM SIGGRAPH Sketches and Applications (2003)
20. Wiener, N.: Extrapolation, Interpolation, and Smoothing of Stationary Time Series:With Engineering Applications, 1st edn. MIT Press (1949)
21. Richardson, W.H.: Bayesian-based iterative method of image restoration. Journal of the Optical Soceity of America (JOSA) 62, 55–59 (1972)
22. Cho, S., Wang, J., Lee, S.: Handling outliers in non-blind image deconvolution. In: Proc. of International Conference on Computer Vision (ICCV) (2011)
23. Dong, W., Zhang, L., Shi, G.: Centralized sparse representation for image restoration. In: Proc. of International Conference on Computer Vision (ICCV) (2011)
24. Levin, A., Weiss, Y., Durand, F., Freeman, W.T.: Efficient marginal likelihood optimization in blind deconvolution. In: Proc. of IEEE Conference on Computer Vision and Pattern Recognition (CVPR) (2011)
25. Krishnan, D., Tay, T., Fergus, R.: Blind deconvolution using a normalized sparsity measure. In: Proc. of IEEE Conference on Computer Vision and Pattern Recognition (CVPR) (2011)

Intrinsic Video

Naejin Kong, Peter V. Gehler, and Michael J. Black

Max Planck Institute for Intelligent Systems, Tübingen, Germany
{naejin.kong,peter.gehler,black}@tuebingen.mpg.de

Abstract. Intrinsic images such as albedo and shading are valuable for later stages of visual processing. Previous methods for extracting albedo and shading use either single images or images together with depth data. Instead, we define *intrinsic video* estimation as the problem of extracting temporally coherent albedo and shading from video alone. Our approach exploits the assumption that albedo is constant over time while shading changes slowly. Optical flow aids in the accurate estimation of intrinsic video by providing temporal continuity as well as putative surface boundaries. Additionally, we find that the estimated albedo sequence can be used to improve optical flow accuracy in sequences with changing illumination. The approach makes only weak assumptions about the scene and we show that it substantially outperforms existing single-frame intrinsic image methods. We evaluate this quantitatively on synthetic sequences as well on challenging natural sequences with complex geometry, motion, and illumination.

Keywords: intrinsic images, video, temporal coherence, optical flow.

1 Introduction

Albedo and shading are fundamental view-centric features of the visual world that are closely related to physical properties of surfaces and light [5]. Many computer vision algorithms work directly with pixel values, which are a combination of albedo and shading. These same algorithms, whether image/video segmentation, flow estimation, object detection, or 3D shape reconstruction, may work significantly better if applied to more physical quantities. Consequently we seek to decompose images into their intrinsic albedo and shading components. This problem has been studied since the 1970's but previous work focuses on individual images. Here we extend these methods to video sequences and show that, by exploiting temporal constraints on albedo and shading, our method outperforms single-frame methods.

While today "intrinsic images" are typically taken to mean shading and albedo, the original meaning of Barrow and Tenenbaum [5] includes additional "images" related to object shape, such as surface normals, depth, and occluding contours. By using sequences of images, rather than static images, we extract a richer set of intrinsic images that include: albedo, shading, optical flow, occlusion regions, and motion boundaries. Our formulation provides an integrated framework for modeling video sequences in terms of such intrinsic images.

D. Fleet et al. (Eds.): ECCV 2014, Part II, LNCS 8690, pp. 360–375, 2014.

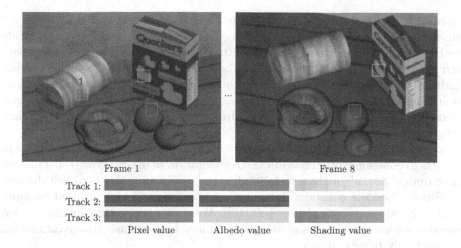

Fig. 1. Intrinsic Video. Top: two frames from a synthetic sequence with camera motion and illumination change. Bottom: pixel, albedo, and shading values for marked locations in 8 consecutive frames. Pixel values and shading change over time, while albedo is constant.

For a Lambertian surface, albedo and shading are mixed and encoded in observed pixel values according to

$$i_t(\mathbf{x}) = a_t(\mathbf{x}) \times s_t(\mathbf{x}), \tag{1}$$

where i is the known image, a and s are unknown albedo and shading variables, respectively, $\mathbf{x}$ is pixel location, and t is time. Since there are two unknowns and one observation, the recovery (factorization) of albedo and shading is ill-posed at a single pixel. To recover the intrinsic images from a single image, there have been several proposals for priors on albedo and shading that show promising results [4,12]. Previous work, however, has typically not considered videos of general scenes, non-rigid motions, and changing illumination. Our experiments with single-frame methods show that they do not produce temporally coherent results when applied independently to video frames.

If we know the optical flow of the scene, then we actually have additional constraints on the albedo and shading. If a surface is changing orientation with respect to the illumination, then the image values change, but the albedo does not. Thus, correspondence in time can provide additional constraints that make solving for the albedo well posed. We define *intrinsic video* as the factorization of video into sequences of albedo, shading, motion, occlusion, and motion boundaries.

Consider the synthetic image sequence in Fig. 1, containing camera motion and changing illumination. Given optical flow, the change in albedo and shading over time can be physically motivated. First, albedo is a unique value for each material that determines surface color, and its value is constant as long as the material stays unchanged. Second, shading is generated from physical interaction between surface geometry and incoming light. It is reasonable to assume that a camera, or objects in the scene, move or transform smoothly while the lighting condition changes only a little within a short time interval. Then, each scene point will exhibit constant albedo but smoothly (and slowly) varying shading over the video sequence. We use these insights to formulate new priors for intrinsic video estimation. Of course, these assumptions are sometimes violated (e.g., by cast shadows) and we address this below using a robust statistical formulation.

Note also that if pixel values change over time, they violate the assumption of brightness constancy often used in the computation of optical flow [15]. This can cause optical flow algorithms to fail unless they are made robust to such changes [7]. Since albedo is constant, however, we show that it can be used to more accurately estimate optical flow (cf. [10]). We thus suggest that intrinsic video provides a framework for combining optical flow and intrinsic image estimation in a mutually beneficial way.

Specifically, our intrinsic video method uses optical flow to establish a temporal constancy term for albedo and a temporal smoothness term for shading. Our spatial priors on albedo are similar to those suggested in [4]; these encourage the estimated albedo to be sparse and uniformly smooth. We develop a non-local spatial prior on shading that encourages spatial smoothness of the estimated shading based on a median of local and non-local pixel neighbors. Optical flow also provides us with information about the structure of the scene that we can use to improve intrinsic image estimation from video. In estimating shading, we use geometric information available in the flow, such as motion boundaries and occlusion, to enhance the quality of the estimated shading images. The full solution uses the Classic+NL flow algorithm [26] as a foundation and extends it for intrinsic video estimation.

We show results on synthetic and real sequences with complex motions and illumination change. Previous datasets for static intrinsic image evaluation are not appropriate so we develop a new synthetic dataset that we make publicly available. Both quantitatively on synthetic sequences, and qualitatively on real sequences, we substantially outperform single-frame methods on the estimation of albedo and shading.

2   Previous Work

A classic approach to constrain albedo and shading estimation from a single image is based on the Retinex theory [19], which says that albedo edges tend to be stronger than shading edges. Its usefulness was first proved in [16]. The performance of Retinex-based algorithms depends on correct labeling of albedo and shading edges. Learning-based approaches automatically determine this labeling [6,28], or directly predict shading edges [27]. Grosse et al. [13] conduct a quantitative analysis using their ground truth dataset and find that Retinex-based approaches perform well (in 2009). The dataset, however, contains static images of single segmented objects.

Recent Retinex-based algorithms add more constraints on albedo or shading. Bousseau et al. [8] require a small number of user-labeled albedo and shading pixels. In [25] and [24], non-local texture cues or a local continuity assumption on albedo are used, respectively. Gehler et al. [12] develop a probabilistic model and add a new global sparsity prior on albedo that models natural image statistics.

Intrinsic images are related to the physics of image formation. Barron and Malik [2,3] exploit the physics by explicitly modeling the shape and lighting that generate shading. Their shape priors, however, cannot model a whole scene involving multiple objects and surface discontinuities. This limits their scope to single objects, pre-segmented from the single image. Their extension in [4] jointly estimates several depths and lights given depth constraints and estimated depths (e.g. from a range scanner). In [11], shading estimation is constrained by relying on surface points reconstructed from given depth. Current depth sensors are still noisy, however, and for archival images and videos, no explicit depth information exists. Scene structure, however, is *implicit* in an RGB video sequence and we show that the optical flow already contains enough approximate geometric information to estimate albedo and shading in scenes with multiple objects. In particular, optical flow allows us to extract occlusion regions and putative surface boundaries. We exploit these in estimating piecewise-smooth shading.

Lee et al. [20] extract intrinsic images from an RGB-D video. Their temporal constraints are mainly built upon pixel correspondences obtained from 3D coordinates reconstructed with depth. Laffont et al. [17,18] used a collection of photographs that capture the same scene from different views under varying illumination. These methods also need pixel correspondences including their normals across the photographs, which are obtained by applying multi-view stereo; this assumes a rigid scene. Our approach uses optical flow instead, thus making no strong assumption about the scene structure. By not assuming a rigid scene, our intrinsic video method can deal with non-rigid and independently moving objects. In addition, optical flow is useful for imposing image-based temporal constraints, since it provides dense pixel correspondences at the image level. Weiss [29] and Hauagge et al. [14] estimate a single albedo image from a series of images of the same scene captured under significantly varying lighting conditions. These methods do not work if anything in the scene moves or if there is camera motion; each pixel in the image series should represent a single point and contain as much light variation as possible.

Like us, Ye et al. [30] extract coherent intrinsic images from an RGB video. They use optical flow to propagate an initial albedo decomposition of the first frame over the video sequence. In contrast, our model comes from physical properties of visible surfaces under motion and illumination variation. We optimize a full objective function containing both shading and albedo that integrates priors on each, including the spatial albedo priors from [4], new temporal priors on albedo and shading in Section 3.2, and new spatial shading priors that approximate object boundaries in Section 3.3. Using optical flow, the approach integrates information throughout all frames in the video and extracts additional intrinsic images related to occlusions and motion boundaries.

3   Formulation

Given a sequence of images, $\{I_t\}$, we extract the *intrinsic video* sequence, $\{A_t, S_t\}$, of albedo and shading images at each time instant t. Unless otherwise specified, and without loss of generality, all images are in the log domain. We recover the intrinsic video sequence by minimizing this objective function

$$\underset{\{A_t, S_t\}}{\text{argmin}} \, E(\{A_t, S_t\} \mid \{I_t\}, \{\mathbf{u}_t\}) =$$

$$\sum_t f_D(A_t, S_t | I_t) + f_{T_A}(A_{t+1}, A_t | \mathbf{u}_t) + f_{T_S}(S_{t+1}, S_t | \mathbf{u}_t) + f_A(A_t) + f_S(S_t), \quad (2)$$

where $\mathbf{u}_t$ is the optical flow between input images I_t and I_{t+1}. This flow is pre-computed from the input video using Classic+NL [26]. We assume that the estimated flow establishes reasonably accurate pixel correspondences robust to some illumination variation in the video.

The data term, $f_D(\cdot)$, enforces similarity between the input and reconstructed images (Section 3.1). The temporal coherence terms, $f_{T_A}(\cdot)$ and $f_{T_S}(\cdot)$, are pixel-wise temporal constraints on albedo and shading, respectively (Section 3.2); the formulation of these is one of our key novelties and goes beyond previous work. The spatial terms, $f_A(\cdot)$ and $f_S(\cdot)$, are priors, based on the statistics of albedo and shading, that constrain the solution (Section 3.3 and 3.4). Our spatial shading prior exploits optical flow in a novel way. Note that we assume the illuminant is white and thus shading is a grayscale image that has the same effect in each RGB channel. While the images are RGB, we often drop the index over RGB for clarity. Each term is described in detail below.

3.1   Image Similarity

The Lambertian equation (1), in the log domain, defines the data term. It measures similarity between each input log-image and the reconstructed log-image:

$$f_D(A_t, S_t) = \lambda_D \sum_{c \in \{R, G, B\}} \sum_{\mathbf{x}} \rho_D \Big(w_t^{\text{lum}}(\mathbf{x})(I_t(\mathbf{x}, c) - A_t(\mathbf{x}, c) - S_t(\mathbf{x})) \Big), \quad (3)$$

where $\mathbf{x}$ is pixel location, c is color channel, $w^{\text{lum}}(\mathbf{x}) = \text{lum}(i(\mathbf{x})) + \varepsilon$, and $\text{lum}(i)$ takes the luminance from the input intensity image i and $\varepsilon = 0.001$. This weight has been proven to be useful in [11] to prevent disproportionally strong contributions of dark pixels. The function $\rho_D(\cdot)$ penalizes differences between the observed and predicted log image. To deal with violations of our assumptions, we use a robust Charbonnier function $\rho_{\text{Charb}}(x) = \sqrt{x^2 + \epsilon^2}$ (a differentiable variant of the L1 penalty [9]; $\epsilon = 0.001$). The weight $\lambda_D = 10$ in all experiments.

3.2   Temporal Constraints

Inspired by Barrow and Tenenbaum [5], we formulate the intrinsic video problem to exploit physical properties of albedo and shading on the visible surfaces

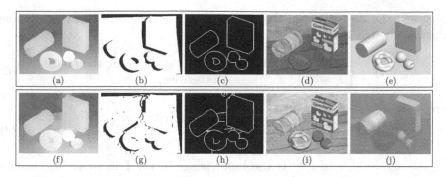

Fig. 2. Five types of intrinsic images. The occlusion map $w_{\mathbf{u}_t}^{\text{occ}}$ (Section 3.2) and the boundary map $w_{\mathbf{u}_t}^{\text{bnd}}$ (Section 3.3) are detected from optical flow. (a) Ground truth flow. (b) $w_{\mathbf{u}_t}^{\text{occ}}$ detected from (a). (c) $w_{\mathbf{u}_t}^{\text{bnd}}$ detected from (a). (d) Ground truth albedo. (e) Ground truth shading. (f) Estimated flow. (g) $w_{\mathbf{u}_t}^{\text{occ}}$ detected from (f). (h) $w_{\mathbf{u}_t}^{\text{bnd}}$ detected from (f). (i) Albedo estimated using (f)-(h). (j) Shading estimated using (f)-(h).

under motion and illumination variation. Specifically, we assume that albedo is typically constant over time while shading information changes slowly. Exploiting these assumptions requires that we know the correspondence of pixels over time. This is given by the optical flow, $\{\mathbf{u}_t\}$, over the sequence.

Temporal albedo constancy is defined as

$$f_{T_A}(A_t, A_{t+1}) = \lambda_{T_A} \sum_{c \in \{R,G,B\}} \sum_{\mathbf{x}} w_{\mathbf{u}_t}^{\text{occ}}(\mathbf{x}) \cdot \rho_{T_A}\Big(A_{t+1}(\mathbf{x} + \mathbf{u}_t(\mathbf{x}), c) - A_t(\mathbf{x}, c) \Big), (4)$$

where $A_{t+1}(\mathbf{x} + \mathbf{u}_t(\mathbf{x}))$ represents the albedo warped by the optical flow and where $w_{\mathbf{u}_t}^{\text{occ}}$ is a weight map computed from the optical flow that is 0 if the pixel is occluded and 1 otherwise. This weight map is a type of intrinsic image that disables temporal coherence of albedo at occlusion boundaries; see Fig. 2 (g).

The choice of penalty function, ρ_{T_A}, is critical. Although a pixel $A_t(\mathbf{x})$ and a warped pixel $A_{t+1}(\mathbf{x} + \mathbf{u}_t(\mathbf{x}))$ should have the same values theoretically, they are in practice similar but not strictly equal due to aliasing and finite image sampling. Also any errors in the optical flow could lead to errors in albedo because the pixels do not correspond to the same physical location in the scene. Consequently we adopt the smooth but robust Tukey function:

$$\rho_{T_A}(x) = \rho_{\text{Tukey}}(x) = \begin{cases} \frac{1}{3} & \text{if } x < -\alpha \text{ or } x > \alpha \\ \frac{x^2}{\alpha^2} - \frac{x^4}{\alpha^4} + \frac{x^6}{3\alpha^6} & \text{otherwise,} \end{cases} (5)$$

where $\alpha = 5$. This function is robust to various outliers caused by sampling, brightness variation, complex motion, occlusion and noise; it is also differentiable.

Optical flow is by nature undetermined in an image region occluded in the next image. The occlusion map $w_{\mathbf{u}_t}^{\text{occ}}$ is useful to prevent minor image artifacts where the flow is not defined. We detect occlusions by using the difference of input images and the divergence of the optical flow. We threshold this and exclude pixels moving outside the image boundaries:

$$w_{\mathbf{u}_t}^{occ}(\mathbf{x}) = \begin{cases} 1, & \text{if } o(\mathbf{x}) \geq 0.5 \text{ and } \mathbf{x} + \mathbf{u}(\mathbf{x}) \text{ stays inside the image} \\ 0, & \text{otherwise}, \end{cases} \qquad (6)$$

where

$$o(\mathbf{x}) = \exp\left(-\frac{(i_t^{\text{Lab}}(\mathbf{x}) - i_{t+1}^{\text{Lab}}(\mathbf{x}+\mathbf{u}))^2}{2\sigma_e^2} - \frac{d_{\mathbf{u}_t}^2(\mathbf{x})}{2\sigma_d^2} \right), \qquad (7)$$

$\sigma_d = 0.3$, $\sigma_e = 20$, and i^{Lab} is the input image in the Lab space. $d_{\mathbf{u}_t}$ is one-sided divergence computed from the flow $\mathbf{u}_t$. A similar detection heuristic is used in [23,26] for disabling the spatial regularization of optical flow and works well in our experiments.

Temporal shading similarity is defined as

$$f_{T_S}(S_t, S_{t+1}) = \lambda_{T_S} \sum_{\mathbf{x}} w_{\mathbf{u}_t}^{occ}(\mathbf{x}) \cdot \rho_{T_S}\left(S_{t+1}(\mathbf{x}+\mathbf{u}_t(\mathbf{x})) - S_t(\mathbf{x}) \right), \qquad (8)$$

where the same Tukey function is used as ρ_{T_S}. We also tried a quadratic function, but Tukey performed better. Here, we set λ_{T_S} much smaller than λ_{T_A} ($\lambda_{T_A} = 10$ and $\lambda_{T_S} = 1$) so that the shading term has less impact than the albedo term.

3.3 Spatial Shading Prior

Our spatial priors on shading encourage local and non-local smoothness of the estimated shading image. One of our key contributions is to exploit optical flow information in this spatial smoothness prior, resulting in a method that does not require object segmentation or depth data. A similar idea is used to define priors on optical flow in the Classic+NL method [26] and a slightly modified formulation works well for enforcing shading smoothness. Note that optical flow and shading information have some things in common. Both lack the high frequency structure of image texture. Flow and shading are both related to surfaces and change smoothly on smooth surfaces. They also are discontinuous at surface boundaries. These similarities may explain why a spatial smoothness model for flow works well for shading. Our shading term is

$$f_S(S_t) = \lambda_{S_s} \sum_{\mathbf{x}} \sum_{\mathbf{y} \in N_3(\mathbf{x})} \rho_S(S_t(\mathbf{x}) - S_t(\mathbf{y}))$$

$$+ \lambda_{S_m} \sum_{\mathbf{x}} w_{\mathbf{u}_t}^{bnd}(\mathbf{x}) \cdot \sum_{\mathbf{y} \in N_{nl}(\mathbf{x})} w_{\mathbf{u}_t}^{nl}(\mathbf{x}, \mathbf{y}) \left| S_t(\mathbf{x}) - S_t(\mathbf{y}) \right|, \qquad (9)$$

where ρ_S is the Charbonnier as above. The weight map $w_{\mathbf{u}_t}^{bnd}$ is another type of intrinsic image computed from optical flow as shown in Fig. 2 (h); the value is 1 if the pixel is near a motion boundary and 0 otherwise. For this we use a simple

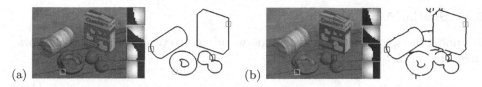

Fig. 3. Examples on the non-local weights defined in Eq. (10). (a) Weights computed from ground truth flow. (b) Weights computed from estimated flow. In each of (a) and (b), small boxes in the middle visualize 15×15 weights corresponding to the regions marked on the left image, and the right image shows motion boundaries detected from optical flow, visualized as $1 - w_{\mathbf{u}_t}^{\mathrm{bnd}}$. Note that the weight function stops spatial propagation around the motion boundaries.

Sobel filter applied to $\mathbf{u}_t$ and dilate the result to obtain the weight map $w_{\mathbf{u}_t}^{\mathrm{bnd}}$. N_3 means a 3×3 window around each pixel to encourage local smoothness, while N_{nl} is a non-local window of 15×15 pixels. Minimizing the non-local term, with the L1 penalty, corresponds to computing a weighted median in the region N_{nl} [21]. Note that we only take the weighted median near the motion boundaries by using $w_{\mathbf{u}_t}^{\mathrm{bnd}}$. While the non-local term improves results at boundaries, applying it everywhere in the image produces over smoothing away from boundaries.

The spatially-varying weight $w_{\mathbf{u}_t}^{\mathrm{nl}}$ encodes information about motion boundaries, which serves as a proxy for surface boundaries. It is defined as follows:

$$w_{\mathbf{u}_t}^{\mathrm{nl}}(\mathbf{x}, \mathbf{y}) = \exp\left(-\frac{|\mathbf{x} - \mathbf{y}|^2}{2\sigma_\partial^2}\right) \cdot \mathrm{surf}_{\mathbf{u}_t}(\mathbf{x}, \mathbf{y}), \tag{10}$$

where $\mathbf{x}$ is the center of a non-local (15×15) window, $\mathbf{y}$ is a pixel in the neighborhood of $\mathbf{x}$, and $\sigma_s = 7$. A binary function $\mathrm{surf}_{\mathbf{u}_t}$ depends on the flow field, $\mathbf{u}_t$, and helps the weight function stop spatial propagation around motion boundaries. It returns 1 at $\mathbf{y}$ if $\mathbf{y}$ and $\mathbf{x}$ stay within the same object region but 0 otherwise: we segment the non-local region into two pieces using the motion boundary inside, and assign 1's to the piece that includes $\mathbf{x}$ and 0's to the other. The boundary weights are illustrated in Fig. 3.

The two weights in Eq. (9) play an important role in preventing over smoothing at motion boundaries (and hence at object boundaries). Note that the weight function used for flow estimation in [26] uses occlusion and color boundaries. For shading, color boundaries are irrelevant and hence we use only motion boundaries. Note that there is no flow for the last frame in the sequence and there we use only the local term; this works well thanks to the information propagated from the previous frames. Other approaches could be used for smoothing with discontinuities; for example, bilateral filtering [22]. In contrast, our approach makes the intrinsic images for occlusions and boundaries explicit.

3.4 Spatial Albedo Prior

To model the spatial variation of albedo we adopt the two relevant spatial priors suggested in [2,4]:

$$f_A(A_t) = \tag{11}$$

$$\lambda_{A_s} \sum_{\mathbf{x}} \sum_{\mathbf{y} \in N_5(\mathbf{x})} \left[-\log \sum_{m=1}^{40} \alpha_m \cdot \mathcal{N}\left(\mathbf{A}_t(\mathbf{x}) - \mathbf{A}_t(\mathbf{y}); \ \mathbf{0}, \sigma_m \mathbf{\Sigma}\right) \right]$$

$$-\lambda_{A_p} \log \left[\frac{1}{N^2 \sqrt{4\pi \cdot \sigma_p^2}} \sum_{\mathbf{x}}^N \sum_{\mathbf{y}}^N \exp\left(-\frac{\|\mathbf{W}(\mathbf{A}_t(\mathbf{x}) - \mathbf{A}_t(\mathbf{y}))\|_2^2}{4\sigma_p^2} \right) \right], \tag{12}$$

where $\mathbf{A}_t(\mathbf{x})$ defines an RGB vector at pixel $\mathbf{x}$, α_m is a mixture constant for each multivariate Gaussian $\mathcal{N}(\cdot)$ whose covariance matrix $\mathbf{\Sigma}$ is scaled by σ_m, $\mathbf{W}$ is a whitening transform matrix to nullify dependency between color channels, σ_p is a standard deviation, N is the number of pixels. The first term shares the concept that underlies Retinex algorithms and encourages small spatial variation of the estimated albedo image based on a multivariate Gaussian scale mixture. The second term models global sparsity of albedo values as proposed in [12]. We use the distribution parameters for these priors learned in [4].

4 Optimization

Traditional approaches optimize for either albedo or shading by assuming that the Lambertian equation (1) is strictly satisfied. However, this assumption does not always hold in practice and thus the solution may be biased to either albedo or shading. Instead, we use the Lambertian equation as a soft constraint (Eq. (3) in Section 3.1) and solve for both variables concurrently. The concurrent optimization is challenging, but our temporal coherence terms effectively constrain the problem. To minimize our objective function, Eq. (2), we adopt a coarse to fine pyramid-based approach and incremental update scheme similar in spirit to the flow estimation method in [26]. Note that the objective function is defined over the entire sequence (not individual frames).

Our new spatial shading prior (Eq. (9) in Section 3.3) is difficult to directly optimize because of the non-local energy term. Instead, an auxiliary "coupling" variable $\tilde{S}_t$ is introduced to assist minimization of the non-local median energy:

$$f'_S(S_t, \tilde{S}_t) = \lambda_{S_s} g_l(S_t) + \lambda_{S_m} g_{nl}(\tilde{S}_t) + \lambda_{S_{cpl}} \sum_{\mathbf{x}} w_{\mathbf{u}_t}^{bnd}(\mathbf{x}) \left\| S_t(\mathbf{x}) - \tilde{S}_t(\mathbf{x}) \right\|^2, \tag{13}$$

where g_l and g_{nl} are the local and non-local terms in Eq. (9), respectively. The quadratic term above encourages the estimated S_t and $\tilde{S}_t$ to be the same. We found that $\lambda_{S_{cpl}} = 10$ works well in our shading estimation problem, with $\lambda_{S_s} = 2$ and $\lambda_{S_m} = 10000$. We alternate between minimizing S_t and $\tilde{S}_t$ as in [26]. More details are given in the supplementary material.

5   Experiments

We evaluate our intrinsic video estimation using three synthetic and three real sequences that illustrate different types of the motion and illumination variation. Due to limited space, we only show the first two frames of two sequences. Our supplementary material[1] includes data generation details and full results, in addition to the optical flow, occlusion and boundary intrinsic images, which are omitted here due to space. The computation time linearly increases with the number of frames (2.2h for 8 frames on average). We use 7 to 9 frame sequences here and, while shorter sequences can be used, we find that the quality improves with more frames because information propagates over all frames.

We compare our results with a baseline color-Retinex algorithm in [13] (CRET) and a more advanced Retinex-based method in [12] (GS). Note that both are *single-image* methods. Existing non-Retinex-based single-image methods only work with additional depth data [4,11] or segmentation of each object [2,3]. Our method deals with a general scene with multiple objects without depth information while making no assumption of rigidity. We obtained CRET results by using the color-Retinex term in the implementation of GS. Our intrinsic video method is denoted "IV". The optical flow used by our method is computed from the input video using Classic+NL [26] .

5.1   Synthetic Examples

Figures 4 and 5 show two synthetic examples with different types of motion and illumination variation. For each sequence we have ground truth values of albedo, shading, optical flow and occlusion. The CRET and GS methods are applied to each frame of the video independently.

As shown in (g)-(r) of the figures, both of CRET and GS put too much high-frequency albedo information into the shading image, and the albedo changes significantly from frame to frame. In contrast, our albedo image retains textural details and the shading is piecewise smooth, mostly obeying object boundaries. Our recovered albedo is consistent over time. One way to see this is by computing the optical flow using the recovered albedo sequences from each method; this is shown in (c)-(f) of the figures. We applied Classic+NL (using brightness instead of texture decomposition), to each reconstructed albedo sequence and the original images. This provides a measure of how temporally coherent the albedo is; an albedo sequence with better temporal coherence will produce flow images that look closer to the ground truth flow (u^{GT}).

Quantitative Analysis. In Fig. 6 (left), we measure the local mean squared error (LMSE) [13] of the reconstructed albedo and shading images; this is a standard error measure for evaluating intrinsic images. We calculate the LMSE at each frame and average this over all frames, and then average this over all three synthetic examples. We ran IV with both the computed optical flow as

---

[1] http://ps.is.tuebingen.mpg.de/project/Intrinsic_Video

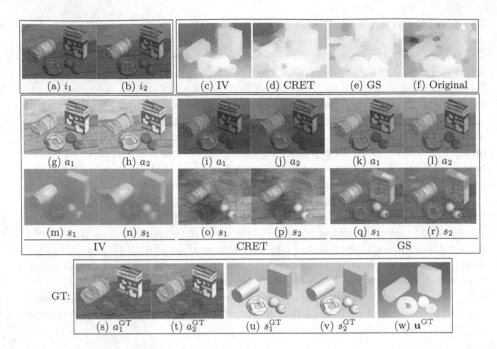

Fig. 4. Synthetic example in which a camera is freely moving and illumination varies significantly over time. (a),(b) Two frames from the sequence. (c)-(e) Flow from the albedo estimated from our method (IV), CRET and GS. (f) Flow from the original images. (g)-(l) Albedo from IV, CRET and GS. (m)-(r) Shading from IV, CRET and GS. (s)-(w) Ground truth albedo, shading and flow.

well as ground truth flow to evaluate the effect of flow errors on the solution. The results are shown in Fig. 6 (left).

Our reconstructed intrinsic images have smaller errors than the GS method: 13.3% with estimated flow and 14.5% with ground truth flow. Note that while ground truth flow improves results slightly, the estimate flow works well. We also disabled the temporal terms (IV w/o flow) to evaluate the importance of motion. In this case we do not use the temporal terms or the motion-based spatial smoothness weighting. More details are given in the supplemental material.

In Fig. 6 (right), we introduce a new temporal incoherence measure that assesses how consistent the reconstructed albedo is over time. Optical flow methods typically assume brightness constancy, which is violated if the illumination is inconsistent over time. Since violations of constancy increase errors in optical flow, the optical flow error provides a measure of how constant an albedo sequence is in time. We compute EPE (averaged end-point-error) [1] of the estimated flow (using estimated albedo sequences) compared with the ground truth flow and then average this over the three synthetic examples. Our albedo sequence is significantly more coherent (lower EPE) than the albedo estimated by previous methods. In addition, note that the flow computed from our albedo is more

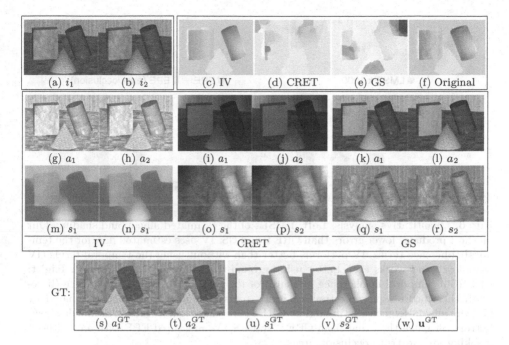

Fig. 5. Synthetic example in which all objects in the scene are moving while the camera translates. Illumination does not change much in this case. (a),(b) Two frames from the sequence. (c)-(e) Flow from the albedo estimated from our method (IV), CRET and GS. (f) Flow from the original images. (g)-(l) Albedo from IV, CRET and GS. (m)-(r) Shading from IV, CRET and GS. (s)-(w) Ground truth albedo, shading and flow.

accurate than the flow computed from the original images. The illumination changes in the original images violate brightness constancy. This result suggests that intrinsic video may be useful to improve optical flow estimation.

5.2   Real Examples

Figures 7 and 8 show two of our real examples. We captured real videos by serially taking photographs with a flashlight or static lighting. The real sequences involve different types of motion and illumination variation, corresponding to those in the synthetic examples. The results are consistent with those on synthetic sequences. As shown in (g)-(r) of the figures, our method significantly outperforms the previous methods. The shading from previous methods carries a lot of albedo information, but our shading sequence has few albedo details and well captures the overall shape of the scene with clean boundaries. The previous methods sometimes almost completely miss the shape of the scene in their shading images and the albedo is overall inconsistent between frames. While there is no ground true flow for this sequence, our reconstructed albedo produces less

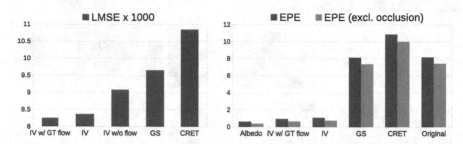

Fig. 6. Quantitative analysis. **Left**: LMSEs of the estimated albedo and shading. Our method produces lower errors than CRET and GS. IV uses estimated flow for the temporal coherence terms. IV performs better than without using the temporal terms (IV w/o flow), and works even better using ground truth flow (IV w/ GT flow). **Right**: EPE (our temporal incoherence measure) of the ground truth albedo sequence (baseline), the albedo sequence estimated by IV (ours), the albedo sequence estimated by GS, the albedo sequence estimated by CRET, and the original video. Our albedo shows better coherence than that from CRET and GS. We measured EPE with and without masking ground truth occlusion areas.

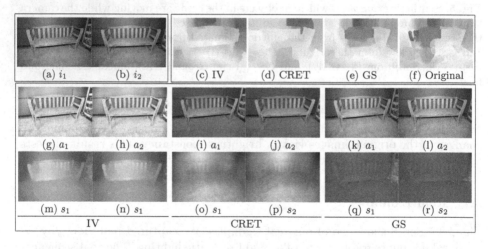

Fig. 7. Real example in which the input video captures a static outdoor scene with a freely moving camera. A flashlight on top of the camera was used to vary illumination over time fairly drastically. (a),(b) Two frames from the sequence. (c)-(e) Flow from the albedo estimated from our method (IV), CRET and GS. (f) Flow from the original images. (g)-(l) Albedo from IV, CRET and GS. (m)-(r) Shading from IV, CRET and GS.

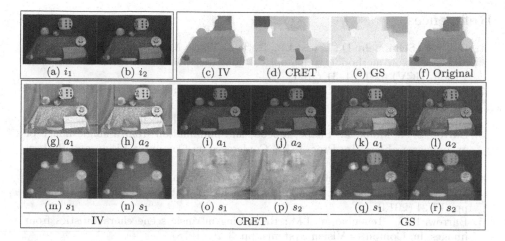

Fig. 8. Real example in which all objects continuously move but the background stays still. The camera and light sources are fixed. (a),(b) Two frames from the sequence. (c)-(e) Flow from the albedo estimated from our method (IV), CRET and GS. (f) Flow from the original images. (g)-(l) Albedo from IV, CRET and GS. (m)-(r) Shading from IV, CRET and GS.

noisy flow fields, suggesting that our albedo has better temporal coherence than the others as illustrated in (c)-(f) of the figures.

6 Conclusions and Future Work

We have introduced the idea of intrinsic video and an algorithm for extracting it automatically from video alone. Experiments with real and synthetic sequences demonstrate that our method generates accurate and temporally coherent albedo and shading, even from videos with non-rigid motion and illumination change. Key to our formulation is the assumption that albedo is mostly constant over time, while shading changes slowly. Optical flow provides the correspondence across time that we exploit to enforce novel temporal constraints on albedo and shading. Our experiments show that these temporal constraints significantly improve albedo and shading estimation. In addition to providing temporal continuity, optical flow gives us information about occlusion and putative surface boundaries; these intrinsic images are important for estimating accurate albedo and spatially coherent shading that is not blurred between objects. As a result of incorporating optical flow, our method works for general scenes, with multiple objects, without need of additional depth data or object segmentation.

According to our incoherence measure, intrinsic video may be useful for optical flow estimation because the resulting albedo sequences obey brightness constancy. Beyond our current work, we believe that integration of the intrinsic video and optical flow problems may produce better results for both. This work provides a new direction for research on both problems. As future work, we will explore the simultaneous estimation of both intrinsic video and optical flow.

References

1. Baker, S., Scharstein, D., Lewis, J.P., Roth, S., Black, M.J., Szeliski, R.: A database and evaluation methodology for optical flow. International Journal of Computer Vision (IJCV) 92(1), 1–31 (2011)
2. Barron, J.T., Malik, J.: Color constancy, intrinsic images, and shape estimation. In: Fitzgibbon, A., Lazebnik, S., Perona, P., Sato, Y., Schmid, C. (eds.) ECCV 2012, Part IV. LNCS, vol. 7575, pp. 57–70. Springer, Heidelberg (2012)
3. Barron, J.T., Malik, J.: Shape, albedo, and illumination from a single image of an unknown object. In: Proc. IEEE Conference on Computer Vision and Pattern Recognition (CVPR), pp. 334–341 (2012)
4. Barron, J.T., Malik, J.: Intrinsic scene properties from a single RGB-D image. In: Proc. IEEE Conference on Computer Vision and Pattern Recognition (CVPR), pp. 17–24 (2013)
5. Barrow, H.G., Tenenbaum, J.M.: Recovering intrinsic scene characteristics from images. In: Computer Vision Systems, pp. 3–26 (1978)
6. Bell, M., Freeman, W.T.: Learning local evidence for shading and reflectance. In: Proc. IEEE International Conference on Computer Vision (ICCV), pp. 670–677 (2001)
7. Black, M.J., Anandan, P.: The robust estimation of multiple motions: Parametric and piecewise-smooth flow fields. Computer Vision and Image Understanding 63(1), 75–104 (1996)
8. Bousseau, A., Paris, S., Durand, F.: User-assisted intrinsic images. ACM Trans. Graphics (TOG) – Proc. SIGGRAPH Asia 28(5), 130:1–130:10 (2009)
9. Bruhn, A., Weickert, J., Schnorr, C.: Lucas/kanade meets horn/schunck: Combining local and global optic flow methods. International Journal of Computer Vision (IJCV) 61, 211–231 (2005)
10. Butler, D.J., Wulff, J., Stanley, G.B., Black, M.J.: A naturalistic open source movie for optical flow evaluation. In: Fitzgibbon, A., Lazebnik, S., Perona, P., Sato, Y., Schmid, C. (eds.) ECCV 2012, Part VI. LNCS, vol. 7577, pp. 611–625. Springer, Heidelberg (2012)
11. Chen, Q., Koltun, V.: A simple model for intrinsic image decomposition with depth cues. In: Proc. IEEE International Conference on Computer Vision (ICCV), pp. 241–248 (2013)
12. Gehler, P., Rother, C., Kiefel, M., Zhang, L., Schölkopf, B.: Recovering intrinsic images with a global sparsity prior on reflectance. In: Shawe-Taylor, J., Zemel, R.S., Bartlett, P.L., Pereira, F.C.N., Weinberger, K.Q. (eds.) Advances in Neural Information Processing Systems (NIPS), pp. 765–773 (2011)
13. Grosse, R., Johnson, M.K., Adelson, E.H., Freeman, W.T.: Ground-truth dataset and baseline evaluations for intrinsic image algorithms. In: Proc. IEEE International Conference on Computer Vision (ICCV), pp. 2335–2342 (2009)
14. Hauagge, D., Wehrwein, S., Bala, K., Snavely, N.: Photometric ambient occlusion. In: Proc. IEEE Conference on Computer Vision and Pattern Recognition (CVPR), pp. 2515–2522 (2013)
15. Horn, B.K.P., Schunk, B.G.: Determining optical flow. Artificial Intelligence 17, 185–203 (1981)
16. Horn, B.K.P.: Determining lightness from an image. Computer Graphics and Image Processing 3(1), 277–299 (1974)
17. Laffont, P.Y., Bousseau, A., Drettakis, G.: Rich intrinsic image decomposition of outdoor scenes from multiple views. IEEE Transactions on Visualization and Computer Graphics 19(2), 210–224 (2013)

18. Laffont, P.Y., Bousseau, A., Paris, S., Durand, F., Drettakis, G.: Coherent intrinsic images from photo collections. ACM Transactions on Graphics (TOG) – Proc. SIGGRAPH Asia 31(6), 202:1–202:11 (2012)
19. Land, E.H., McCann, J.J.: Lightness and Retinex theory. Journal of the Optical Society of America 61(1), 1–11 (1971)
20. Lee, K.J., Zhao, Q., Tong, X., Gong, M., Izadi, S., Lee, S.U., Tan, P., Lin, S.: Estimation of intrinsic image sequences from image+depth video. In: Fitzgibbon, A., Lazebnik, S., Perona, P., Sato, Y., Schmid, C. (eds.) ECCV 2012, Part VI. LNCS, vol. 7577, pp. 327–340. Springer, Heidelberg (2012)
21. Li, Y., Osher, S.: A new median formula with applications to PDE based denoising. Communications in Mathematical Sciences 7(3), 741–753 (2009)
22. Paris, S., Kornprobst, P., Tumblin, J., Durand, F.: Bilateral filtering: Theory and applications. Foundations and Trends in Computer Graphics and Vision 4(1), 1–73 (2009)
23. Sand, P., Teller, S.: Particle video: Long-range motion estimation using point trajectories. International Journal of Computer Vision 80(1), 72–91 (2008)
24. Shen, J., Yang, X., Jia, Y., Li, X.: Intrinsic images using optimization. In: Proc. IEEE Conference on Computer Vision and Pattern Recognition (CVPR), pp. 3481–3487. IEEE (2011)
25. Shen, L., Tan, P., Lin, S.: Intrinsic image decomposition with non-local texture cues. In: Proc. IEEE Conference on Computer Vision and Pattern Recognition (CVPR), pp. 1–7 (2008)
26. Sun, D., Roth, S., Black, M.J.: A quantitative analysis of current practices in optical flow estimation and the principles behind them. International Journal of Computer Vision (IJCV) 106(2), 115–137 (2014)
27. Tappen, M.F., Adelson, E.H., Freeman, W.T.: Estimating intrinsic component images using non-linear regression. In: Proc. IEEE Conference on Computer Vision and Pattern Recognition (CVPR), pp. II: 1992–1999 (2006)
28. Tappen, M.F., Freeman, W.T., Adelson, E.H.: Recovering intrinsic images from a single image. IEEE Transactions on Pattern Analysis and Machine Intelligence 27(9), 1459–1472 (2005)
29. Weiss, Y.: Deriving intrinsic images from image sequences. In: Proc. IEEE International Conference on Computer Vision (ICCV), pp. II: 68–75 (2001)
30. Ye, G., Garces, E., Liu, Y., Dai, Q., Gutierrez, D.: Intrinsic video and applications. ACM Transactions on Graphics 33(4) (2014)

Robust and Accurate Non-parametric Estimation of Reflectance Using Basis Decomposition and Correction Functions

Tobias Nöll[1,2], Johannes Köhler[1,2], and Didier Stricker[1,2]

[1] German Research Center for Artificial Intelligence, Kaiserslautern, Germany
{Tobias.Noell,Johannes.Koehler,Didier.Stricker}@dfki.de
[2] University of Kaiserslautern, Germany

Abstract. A common approach to non-parametric BRDF estimation is the approximation of the sparsely measured input using basis decomposition. In this paper we greatly improve the fitting accuracy of such methods by iteratively applying a novel correction function to an initial estimate. We also introduce a basis to efficiently represent such a function. Based on this general concept we propose an iterative algorithm that is able to explicitly identify and treat outliers in the input data. Our method is invariant to different error metrics which alleviates the error-prone choice of an appropriate one for the given input. We evaluate our method based on a large set of experiments generated from 100 real-world BRDFs and 16 newly measured materials. The experiments show that our method outperforms other evaluated state-of-the-art basis decomposition methods by an order of magnitude in the perceptual sense for outlier ratios up to 40%.

Keywords: Non-parametric BRDF estimation, reflectance, basis decompostion, correction function, error metric, sparse data, outliers.

1 Introduction

How an object *appears* in reality is essentially determined by the complex interaction of its shape, its surface materials and the lighting environment it is currently observed in. Reproduction of this appearance is important in the context of various application domains such as advertisement, movie-production and cultural heritage preservation where realistic images of real objects need to be synthesized. This can be achieved by capturing and modeling the shape and surface material properties of the objects. In the last decades a considerable amount of progress has been made that allows to capture and model the 3D shape of an object precisely. This paper thus focuses on the robust and precise modeling of captured surface material properties only.

It is well known that the appearance properties for opaque materials are effectively described using the *Bidirectional Reflectance Distribution Function* (BRDF) [22]. For a specific material this function describes how much light from a specific *incident* direction is reflected to an *outgoing* direction. Various

D. Fleet et al. (Eds.): ECCV 2014, Part II, LNCS 8690, pp. 376–391, 2014.

types of BRDF measuring devices were proposed in the past – one device group for measuring isolated material probes (e.g. [18,19]), another group allowing a combined acquisition of geometry and reflectance of general objects (e.g. [12,14]). Regardless of the respective technical implementation all devices have in common that they can independently drive a light source and a sensor to different positions around the object of interest and thereby sample how the BRDF responds at these specific incident / outgoing directions. Densely sampling the BRDF is however intractable: As pointed out in [13], sampling at an angular resolution of 1 degree would already amount to a total number of 2×10^8 required measurements. Further, the BRDF is usually a complex function that can change drastically by several orders of magnitude for even small angular changes. This makes the extrapolation of a complete BRDF from a sparse set of measurements a complicated task that has not been completely solved yet. However, a *full* reconstruction that describes how the BRDF behaves under all configurations is essential for photo-realistic image generation.

In this paper we assume that we are provided with a sparse, irregularly sampled set of angular measurements. The task is to reconstruct the complete BRDF that accurately describes the sparsely measured behavior. This is particularly difficult for the following two properties of real measured data: First, even if the light and capturing directions were sampled in a regular way, the measurements themselves are usually irregular for curved objects, because the local coordinate system changes over the surface. Additionally, holes exist for areas that were occluded during acquisition. Second, measured reflectance data often contains outliers originating from imprecise calibration of the devices, imprecise reconstruction of the geometry, global illumination artifacts or self-shadowing. Our method is robust with respect to these practical considerations, achieves more accurate solutions than proposed state-of-the-art methods and to the best of our knowledge we are the first to explicitly consider and identify outliers during BRDF reconstruction (an overview of the problem is given in Figure 1).

1.1 Related Work

Parametric Model Fitting. Traditionally, parametric models – either empirical or based on a theoretical model – provide the BRDFs currently used in computer graphics. These range from ad-hoc models (e.g. Blinn-Phong [3], Lafortune [15], Ashikhmin [2], DSBRDF [23]) designed for efficiency, to physically derived descriptions either based on micro-facet theory (e.g. Ward [30], Cook-Torrance [4], Schlick [28]) or wave optics (e.g. He [11]). Independent of the derivation all parametric models are analytic functions that are well defined over the whole BRDF domain and only depend on a small set of meaningful parameters. Consequently, an obvious solution to the task would be to choose a parametric model and tune its parameters in a way that best fits the sparse set of actual measurements (in fact some models [15,30] were designed especially with this purpose in mind). The ability of analytic functions to describe measured reflectance behavior was examined in [21]. As it turns out, reducing a rich set of measurements to only a small set of parameters can introduce significant

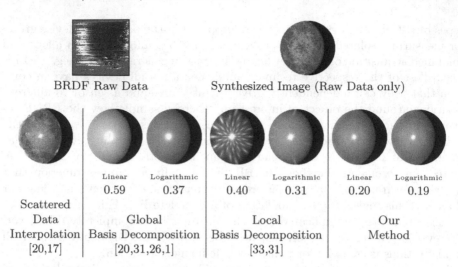

Fig. 1. Problem overview: First row (left) shows raw measured isotropic BRDF data (a 2D projection of the 3D BRDF table for visualization). Red corresponds to unmeasured areas. The right side of the first row shows a synthesized sphere based on the raw BRDF data. Note that for this specific camera / light configuration e.g. the specular lobe was never measured. A BRDF estimation algorithm tries to compute the full BRDF data based on the sparse raw input. The second row shows synthesized spheres using the estimates of different non-parametric algorithms (numerical values indicate the fitting error). The different state-of-the-art algorithms compute either physically implausible results (see scattered data interpolation and local basis decomposition) or non-accurate solutions (see global basis decomposition). Further, the estimate for the basis decomposition methods is highly dependent on the choice of an appropriate error metric for the current dataset (compare linear vs. logarithmic error metric) which can result in unpredictable solutions. Our method achieves accurate estimates that are additionally physically plausible. Additionally, our method is invariant with respect to different error metrics

errors: First, a specific reflectance model must be chosen *a priori*. However, each model was designed having a specific reflectance behavior in mind. In an extreme case there might not be *any* parameter configuration for the chosen model that describes the measured data well. Second, an error metric has to be chosen in order to mathematically define what the *best* parameter setting is. As pointed out in [9] this is non-trivial because choosing a parameter setting that minimizes a specific numerical error might not lead to a well fitting result in the perceptual sense. For BRDF fitting it is not yet clear which error metric is the most suitable to model human perception. Third, the models are usually highly nonlinear in their parameters which requires nonlinear optimization techniques for the parameter fitting. However, for these methods the quality of the fit is dependent on a good initial guess, and reaching a global minimum cannot be guaranteed. Because of these issues, research has shifted towards a non-parametric description of measured materials.

Non-parametric Description. The methods in this category allow for a potentially greater accuracy and generality for describing measured reflectance behavior. The most general, non-parametric description of a BRDF is a regularly sampled multidimensional *table* where the available scattered data points are resampled to. To fill the unmeasured entries, it was proposed in [20,17] to use the general purpose scattered data interpolation technique *Pull-Push* [10].

Most non-parametric techniques however describe the BRDF using basis decomposition. Hereby a BRDF ρ is approximated using a weighted linear combination of basis functions Ψ_i as

$$\rho(\boldsymbol{x}) \approx \sum_i \alpha_i \Psi_i(\boldsymbol{x}) \ . \tag{1}$$

The literature proposes a large set of suitable basis functions Ψ_i: Spherical harmonics [32,25], Zernike polynomials [13], spherical wavelets [29,16,20], radial basis functions [33,31], measured BRDFs [20,31,26,1] and rational functions [24]. The basis operates either *globally* (i.e. each Ψ_i is non-zero in large areas of the parameter domain) or *locally* (i.e. each Ψ_i is non-zero only in a small area of the parameter domain).

In this paper we address two problems that exist for all basis decomposition methods in general:

1. The choice of a local or global basis is until today a choice of accuracy versus robustness (as also examined in [31]): Choosing a local basis will allow for a better matching of the measured input since the weighting factors α_i can be chosen more independently. However, outliers in the input will then directly propagate to the final solution. Choosing a global basis behaves reversely: While it is in general more robust with respect to outliers, the weighting factors are less independent, thus the approximation accuracy is degraded.
2. Previous methods are not robust with respect to different error metrics (see Figure 1): The weighting factors a_i are chosen in a way that the linear combination fits best to the measured input data. Thus, an appropriate error metric to be minimized must be chosen *a priori*. This generates the same problems as in the parametric case: The estimated solution quality is highly dependent on this choice and a minimization in the numerical sense is not necessarily a minimization in the perceptual sense.

We propose a non-parametric method that addresses these problems as follows: It operates globally, thus is very robust with respect to outliers in the input. Our key idea is then to avoid the inevitably reduced accuracy of a global basis by iteratively applying different corrections to the initial solution. We therefore introduce the novel concept of BRDF correction functions and provide a novel global basis that can be used to model these functions effectively. In order to converge to the best solution during this iterative process we explicitly consider and identify outliers in the measured data. To the best of our knowledge this was not done by any previously proposed method. Additionally, our method is intrinsically robust with respect to different error metrics due to its iterative nature: A specific error metric only changes the iteration sequence but the overall estimate still converges to the same solution. We show in the evaluation section that our method has a higher robustness and accuracy than previous global and even local and tabular state-of-the-art methods.

1.2   Background

In its most general form a BRDF ρ can be represented as a 4-dimensional table $\rho(\theta_i, \phi_i, \theta_o, \phi_o)$ which is indexed by the spherical coordinates (θ, ϕ) of the incident and outgoing direction. This function then defines how much light from an incident direction i is reflected to an outgoing direction o.

It was shown that the *Rusinkiewicz re-parametrization* [27] is much more suitable for basis decomposition because features in common BRDFs are aligned with the transformed coordinate axes. The BRDF is therefore usually expressed as a function based on the half-vector h between incoming and outgoing light direction and a difference vector d (please refer to [19,20,27] for a more detailed explanation). This yields

$$\rho(\theta_h, \phi_h, \theta_d, \phi_d) . \tag{2}$$

Several constraints can be formulated regarding the estimated solution which can reduce the dimensionality (i.e. the complexity) of the BRDF function: Many methods [20,25,13,33,31,26,24] (and also our) estimate a solution in the space of *isotropic* materials and such materials can already be represented using a 3-dimensional function $\rho(\theta_h, \theta_d, \phi_d)$. All opaque materials without "grain" are in fact isotropic, hence this establishes a valid and meaningful complexity reduction.

2   Method

To robustly initialize our method we use a global basis: It was examined in [20,31,26,1] that novel BRDFs can be described using a basis of previously measured BRDFs. In [19] a publicly available database is introduced that contains 100 densely and precisely measured isotropic materials M_i that are used in [20,31,1] as basis functions.

Our initial estimate ϱ for a sparsely measured BRDF ρ can thus be written as a weighted linear combination

$$\varrho(\theta_h, \theta_d, \phi_d) = \sum_i \alpha_i M_i(\theta_h, \theta_d, \phi_d) \approx \rho(\theta_h, \theta_d, \phi_d) . \tag{3}$$

Our key idea is to formulate a BRDF correction function σ that represents the error of this initialization. There exist many different possibilities to do this, but we chose to represent σ by means of scaling factors, which yields

$$\sigma(\theta_h, \theta_d, \phi_d) = \frac{\rho(\theta_h, \theta_d, \phi_d)}{\varrho(\theta_h, \theta_d, \phi_d)} . \tag{4}$$

Using scaling factors is very reasonable because we will later only transform *similar* BRDFs, thus its values will be closely distributed around 1 for the whole parameter domain. Consequently, a correction function (as defined in Equation 4) is usually of drastically lower complexity than a BRDF which may change rapidly. If the correction function σ is known, the initial estimate is corrected by

$$\rho(\theta_h, \theta_d, \phi_d) = \sigma(\theta_h, \theta_d, \phi_d)\varrho(\theta_h, \theta_d, \phi_d) \ . \tag{5}$$

It is clear that finding the *true* correction function σ is as hard as finding the *true* BRDF ρ. However, it will turn out later that finding a good *approximation* can be performed robustly and more efficiently than in the BRDF case. When applying such an approximate correction function on ϱ we can improve our initial estimate and iterate this process until convergence.

Our approach to approximate σ is to perform another basis decomposition using a set of suitable basis functions C_i, which yields

$$\sigma(\theta_h, \theta_d, \phi_d) \approx \sum_i \beta_i C_i(\theta_h, \theta_d, \phi_d) \ . \tag{6}$$

Our intuition was – analogous to the BRDF approximation – that novel correction functions can be well described using a basis of previously generated correction functions C_i.

To generate a large set of correction functions we again used the material database provided in [19]: For each BRDF M_i from this database, we compute an approximation ϱ using the remaining 99 materials as a basis. We then compute the corresponding correction function σ using Equation 4 (with $\rho = M_i$). Note that σ is well defined over the whole isotropic BRDF parameter domain.

For each correction function C_i generated this way, we observed two important characteristics:

1. The values of each correction function are distributed within a narrow range.
2. Each correction function itself is a relatively smooth function.

These characteristics are in sharp contrast to measured BRDF data whose minimal and maximal values often differ by several orders of magnitude and usually show a disproportionately steep increase close to the specular lobe. This justifies our concept of using BRDF corrections since it indicates that the *space of all correction functions* is a less complex space than the *space of all materials*.

To verify that C_i indeed defines an expressive basis we evaluated how well each correction function itself is described using the remaining 99 correction functions as a basis. Even though the functions are of very different appearance they are in general very well represented within this basis (see Figure 2) with an average deviation to the original scaling function of only 0.076 units. This indicates that the space of *all* correction functions is well described through our generated basis. In the supplementary material we additionally analyze how the size of the generated basis affects the fitting accuracy of the final solution.

2.1   Algorithm

Based on the previous considerations we outline the following algorithm that exploits the concept of correction functions to provide a robust and accurate BRDF estimate for a sparse set of material measurements:

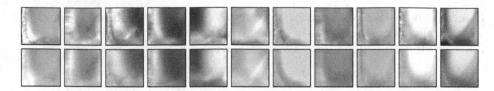

Fig. 2. Our novel BRDF corrections basis (11 out of 100); 1st row: Color coded 2D slices (x-Axis $\hat{=}$ θ_h, y-Axis $\hat{=}$ θ_d, $\phi_d = 90°$) of our generated 3D BRDF correction functions C_i for densely measured materials. 2nd row: Approximations of the upper correction functions using the remaining 99 correction functions as basis. Each of these functions is well approximated even though they have very different appearance

1. We compute a *dense* initial material estimate for the sparse input using M_i as basis functions.
2. We compute a correction factor for each value of this estimate where an input measurement is available. During this process outliers are identified and assigned with a low weight.
3. For this weighted sparse set of correction factors we can approximate the underlying *dense* correction function using our generated C_i as basis functions.
4. We improve our initial estimate by applying this correction function.
5. We iterate this procedure until convergence (go to step 2).

2.2 Basis Decomposition

In this subsection we demonstrate how we perform the basis decomposition used for the initialization and for each iteration step of our algorithm.

We assume that we are initially provided with a sparse set of n measurements $(\theta_{hi}, \theta_{di}, \phi_{di}, \rho_i, w_i)$, i.e. a function was measured at $\rho(\theta_{hi}, \theta_{di}, \phi_{di}) = \rho_i$ with a confidence of w_i (w_i could e.g. be provided by the measurement device or set to 1 if unknown). Given an error metric ε we compute the *best* representation of this function by a dense basis $\Psi = \{\Psi_1, \dots \Psi_m\}$ as

$$\begin{pmatrix} \varepsilon(\rho_1) \\ \vdots \\ \varepsilon(\rho_n) \end{pmatrix} \approx \begin{bmatrix} \varepsilon(\Psi_1(\theta_{h1}, \theta_{d1}, \phi_{d1})) & \dots & \varepsilon(\Psi_m(\theta_{h1}, \theta_{d1}, \phi_{d1})) \\ \vdots & & \vdots \\ \varepsilon(\Psi_1(\theta_{hn}, \theta_{dn}, \phi_{dn})) & \dots & \varepsilon(\Psi_m(\theta_{hn}, \theta_{dn}, \phi_{dn})) \end{bmatrix} \begin{pmatrix} \alpha_1 \\ \vdots \\ \alpha_m \end{pmatrix}, \quad (7)$$

abbreviated as $b \approx Ax$.

We can write the squared error of this basis decomposition as

$$d^T d = (Ax - b)^T (Ax - b) = (x^T A^T - b^T)(Ax - b)$$
$$= x^T A^T Ax - 2b^T Ax + b^T b. \quad (8)$$

To include the given confidence weighting we define $W = \text{diag}(w_1, \dots, w_n)$ and extend Equation 8 as

$$d^T d = x^T A^T W Ax - 2b^T W Ax + b^T W b. \quad (9)$$

We want to minimize the squared error, thus we can drop the constant term $b^T W b$ and define $Q = A^T W A$ and $c^T = b^T W A$. This leads to the canonical form of a *quadratic programming* (QP) problem, which is

$$\text{minimize}_{x} \quad J(x) = \frac{1}{2}\mathbf{x}^T Q \mathbf{x} + c^T \mathbf{x} ,$$
$$\text{subject to} \quad D\mathbf{x} \leq \mathbf{d} \text{ (inequality constraint) and} \tag{10}$$
$$E\mathbf{x} = \mathbf{e} \text{ (equality constraint)} .$$

We can solve this efficiently, e.g. using an online active set strategy [7] implemented in [6]. We set $D = -I$ and $d, E, e = 0$ to constrain $x \geq 0$ for a basis decomposition with only positive factors. The final solution is then given as

$$\rho(\theta_h, \theta_d, \phi_d) \approx \varepsilon^{-1}(\sum_{i=1}^{m} \alpha_i \varepsilon(\Psi_i(\theta_h, \theta_d, \phi_d))) . \tag{11}$$

2.3 BRDF Correction

If we are provided with a dense BRDF estimate ϱ for a sparse set of n measurements $(\theta_{hi}, \theta_{di}, \phi_{di}, \rho_i, w_i)$ we may generate a sparse set of correction factors $(\theta_{hi}, \theta_{di}, \phi_{di}, \sigma_i, v_i)$ by setting

$$\sigma_i = \frac{\rho_i}{\varrho(\theta_{hi}, \theta_{di}, \phi_{di})} . \tag{12}$$

Using our novel basis functions C_i, the underlying *dense* correction function σ may be generated from this sparse set. We can then use σ to correct the current BRDF estimate (Equation 5).

However, very relevant in this context are outliers in the measured BRDF values ρ_i. These will result in wrong scaling factors that will affect the quality of σ. In the worst case the generated correction function could even degrade the current estimate. As a result our method would diverge. It is thus extremely important to identify and treat all outliers accordingly. An intrinsic feature of our algorithm is that at each iteration step ϱ is already a robust, non-parametric approximation of the sparsely measured BRDF ρ. By comparing each measured input value with its corresponding estimate $\varrho_i = \varrho(\theta_{hi}, \theta_{di}, \phi_{di})$ we can thus robustly estimate outliers even in the non-parametric case and assign a low weight v_i to them before estimating the dense correction function. We set

$$v_i = w_i e^{-\gamma \frac{|\rho_i - \varrho_i|}{\varrho_i}} , \tag{13}$$

i.e. we assign an exponentially lower weight to the correction factor the more ϱ_i and ρ_i differ. γ is the only parameter of our algorithm and needs to be chosen appropriately depending on the dynamic range of the input values and the estimated outlier ratio.

Note that there might be more elaborate heuristics for detecting outliers. However, we found this simple one to work quite robustly. During any of the experiments performed for the evaluation we never experienced our method diverging (though we cannot guarantee this formally).

384   T. Nöll, J. Köhler, and D. Stricker

2.4 Implementation

Before our algorithm can be applied, we need to compute the new basis C_i once. This can be done as explained in Section 2. We used a logarithmic error metric $\varepsilon(x) = \ln(1 + x)$ and $W = I$ for the basis decomposition (Subsection 2.2). The *same* basis C_i is used for all iterations of our algorithm.

When provided with a sparse set of measurements $(\theta_{hi}, \theta_{di}, \phi_{di}, \rho_i, w_i)$ our algorithm performs the following steps (individually per RGB color channel) to estimate the complete BRDF ρ:

1. Initialize a dense BRDF ϱ for the sparse input using basis decomposition with

$$\Psi = \{M_1, \ldots, M_{100}\} \text{ and } \varepsilon(x) = \ln(1 + x) . \tag{14}$$

2. Generate a sparse set of correction factors $(\theta_{hi}, \theta_{di}, \phi_{di}, \sigma_i, v_i)$ with:

$$\sigma_i = \frac{\rho_i}{\varrho(\theta_{hi}, \theta_{di}, \phi_{di})} \text{ and } v_i = w_i e^{-\gamma \frac{|\rho_i - \varrho_i|}{\varrho_i}} \ (\varrho_i = \varrho(\theta_{hi}, \theta_{di}, \phi_{di})) . \tag{15}$$

3. Using these correction factors, estimate a dense BRDF correction function σ using basis decomposition with

$$\Psi = \{C_1, \ldots, C_{100}\} \text{ and } \varepsilon(x) = x . \tag{16}$$

4. Correct the current BRDF estimate ϱ using

$$\varrho(\theta_h, \theta_d, \phi_d) := \sigma(\theta_h, \theta_d, \phi_d)\varrho(\theta_h, \theta_d, \phi_d) . \tag{17}$$

5. Stop if the maximum iteration count has been reached or σ is 1 *almost everywhere*, otherwise go to 2.

3 Evaluation

We first demonstrate how our method is executed based on an example. We assume a sparse and irregular sampling of an isotropic BRDF to be given as input which was obtained by capturing a specular red material under different viewing and lighting directions. Our task is to extrapolate this sparse input to a consistent tabular dense BRDF representation suitable for image synthesis. We assume that only 10% of the discretized BRDF domain has been sampled at random positions. However, due to inevitable inaccuracies in the geometry reconstruction as well as in the sensor and light calibration, the data set exhibits a significant amount of outliers: In 40% of the cases a BRDF measurement value does not belong to the provided calibrated pair of incident and outgoing direction but to a random value of the BRDF.

The high ratio of outliers makes this dataset extremely challenging for existing non-parametric methods. In Figure 3 we show the solutions provided by different types of non-parametric state-of-the-art methods:

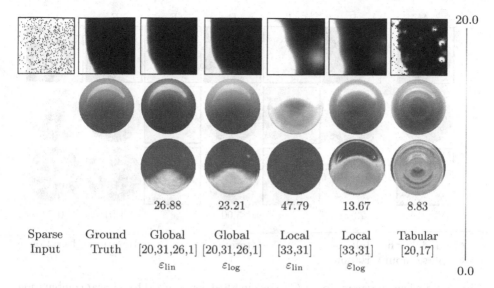

		Global	Global	Local	Local	Tabular
		26.88	23.21	47.79	13.67	8.83
Sparse	Ground	Global	Global	Local	Local	Tabular
Input	Truth	[20,31,26,1]	[20,31,26,1]	[33,31]	[33,31]	[20,17]
		ε_{lin}	ε_{log}	ε_{lin}	ε_{log}	

Fig. 3. Evaluation of different BRDF estimation techniques: The top row shows a 2D slice of the underlying 3D BRDF data (x-Axis $\hat{=} \theta_h$, y-Axis $\hat{=} \theta_d$, $\phi_d = 90°$), while the center row shows a rendered sphere of this material in a natural environment. The bottom as well as the numerical values indicate the image difference in the CIELAB [5] space of the current sphere with respect to the ground truth (from blue (0.0), over green to red (20.0 and higher)). All evaluated method types (global, local, tabular) could not provide a satisfactory solution. Moreover, the solution quality also depends highly on the chosen error metric (e.g. linear $\varepsilon_{\text{lin}}(x) = x$, logarithmic $\varepsilon_{\text{log}}(x) = \ln(1+x)$)

– *Global basis decomposition*: Using a linear combination of measured materials (as proposed in [20,31,26,1]) performs most physically meaningful with respect to the outliers. The reason for this is that each basis function is *globally* defined over the whole BRDF domain, thus physically non-meaningful outliers cannot be part of the solution. However, the outliers do affect the global solution quality, leading to a bad overall fit for in example.

– *Local basis decomposition*: In this class of methods the solution is provided by a basis decomposition where each basis function only has a *local* support on the BRDF domain (such as radial basis functions as proposed in [33,31]). These methods have a larger flexibility and allow for a potentially better fitting. However, outliers directly contribute to each basis function making the overall fitting less robust and less physically plausible.

– *Tabular representation*: This representation provides the largest flexibility because each measured value is *directly* represented. The missing values are completed using scattered data interpolation techniques (such as *Pull-Push* [10] as propsed in [20,17]). However, because the outliers are also interpolated over the BRDF domain this results in a physically implausible solution in this example.

All these evaluated method types cannot provide a satisfactory solution for our examplary dataset. Also the final solution quality is highly dependent on the chosen error metric. The various steps that our algorithm executes for this

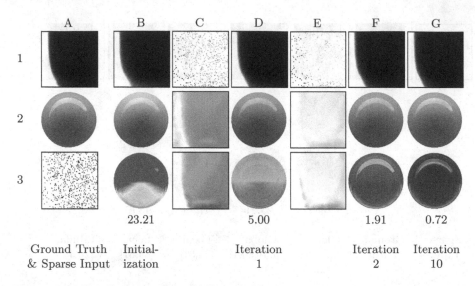

Fig. 4. Based on the sparse input (A3) our method is initialized by a linear combination of measured BRDFs (B1), the error of this initialization is shown in B2-3. Using this initialization we compute a sparse set of correction factors (C1) for which we estimate a dense correction function (C2). Note the similarity to the ground truth correction function (C3) even in the significant presence of outliers. Column D shows the corrected initial estimate, the error is already drastically reduced (D2-3) (error scale as in Figure 3). Columns E-F correspond to C-D for the second iteration. The last column shows the estimated solution after 10 iterations with almost no perceptual difference

example are illustrated and explained in Figure 4. Already after a single iteration we can achieve a solution that is significantly better than those of all other evaluated methods. After a few more iterations our estimate is perceptually almost indistinguishable from the original BRDF.

3.1 Benchmark

To give a representative evaluation how our algorithm performs when compared to other state-of-the art methods we performed a large number of experiments and compared the results. The material database in [19] provides 100 densely measured materials which served as a ground truth for our experiments. From each material we generated several sparse input sets with different characteristics. These differed in the data ratio (i.e. the number of randomly chosen samples from the ground truth BRDF table) and the outlier ratio (i.e. the probability for each sample to have consistent information). We assigned to each outlier a randomly chosen reflectance from the ground truth BRDF table (which is actually a more difficult problem than assigning completely random outlier values).

Similar to the previously given example we evaluated representative methods from each solution type in the literature: For global basis decomposition we chose a linear combination (LC) of measured materials (as proposed in [20,31,26,1])

Table 1. Mean CIELAB [5] error of all evaluated methods under varying outlier and data ratio. To give a visual impression of these numerical values the table cells are colored using the same colors as for the error visualizations in Figure 3 and 4

Our	Data ratio					LC	Data ratio				
Our	1.0	0.7	0.5	0.3	0.1	**LC**	1.0	0.7	0.5	0.3	0.1
0.00	0.28	0.29	0.29	0.29	0.31	0.00	4.88	4.89	4.91	4.96	5.05
0.20	0.36	0.37	0.44	0.44	0.49	0.20	6.32	6.58	6.76	7.57	7.59
0.40	0.73	0.72	0.75	0.78	0.92	0.40	7.97	8.22	7.93	8.32	9.03
0.60	2.06	2.10	2.05	2.23	2.31	0.60	9.64	9.74	9.46	9.59	9.53
0.80	4.86	4.89	4.83	4.81	4.83	0.80	11.33	11.16	11.05	11.05	10.61

RBF	Data ratio					PP	Data ratio				
RBF	1.0	0.7	0.5	0.3	0.1	**PP**	1.0	0.7	0.5	0.3	0.1
0.00	4.11	4.11	4.13	4.15	4.17	0.00	0.00	0.05	0.20	0.46	2.14
0.20	6.85	6.78	6.96	7.12	7.74	0.20	17.32	15.59	17.28	14.00	12.30
0.40	9.74	9.98	9.79	10.41	11.04	0.40	26.12	26.38	24.80	24.35	22.90
0.60	12.49	12.63	12.49	12.56	13.45	0.60	33.32	34.90	32.71	32.13	28.22
0.80	15.18	15.32	15.28	15.16	15.92	0.80	39.86	41.70	40.75	38.94	34.09

with a logarithmic error metric. For local basis decomposition we chose radial basis functions (RBF) as proposed in [33,31] with a logarithmic error metric. We distributed 758 RBF centers for each color channel as proposed in [31] on a radially re-parametrized BRDF domain which is more suitable for RBF interpolation [33]. For a tabular representation we used the *Pull-Push* (PP) method [10] as proposed in [20,17] for the scattered data interpolation. Finally, we initialized our method with the LC solution and performed 10 iterations. In the outlier free case we set the parameter $\gamma = 0$, otherwise to 3 (for an outlier ratio of 0.2) or to 6 (for larger outlier ratios). For LC and our algorithm we removed the current material from the underlying database before the methods were executed. All steps of our algorithm (including the estimation of the correction basis) were therefore executed without any remaining traces of the current material.

As demonstrated in [8], surface reflectance properties are clearer and better comparable when objects are viewed under real-world illuminations. For each estimated solution we thus synthesized a sphere of this material under a natural illumination given by a HDR environment map (*Grace Cathedral*, courtesy of Paul Debevec, see supplementary material). We compared each rendered sphere with the ground truth sphere in the perceptually uniform CIELAB [5] space.

The mean CIELAB [5] error values for all experiments are given in Table 1. The evaluation confirms the observations sketched in the previously given example: Compared to the local RBF method the global LC method is more robust if the sparse input contains many outliers. However, the local RBF method has an overall larger flexibility and thereby allows to better approximate the data (for small outlier ratios). The tabular PP method performs well in the outlier free case, however its quality decreases drastically even for very small outlier ratios, since outliers are also interpolated within the table.

The experiments indicate that our method performs significantly better than all other evaluated method types: In the outlier free case the proposed method

Table 2. Mean CIELAB [5] error for different error metric. In contrast to LC or RBF our method performs robust for different choices of error metrics.

Our			LC			RBF		
ε_{lin}	$\varepsilon_{\text{root}}$	ε_{log}	ε_{lin}	$\varepsilon_{\text{root}}$	ε_{log}	ε_{lin}	$\varepsilon_{\text{root}}$	ε_{log}
0.44	0.31	0.28	13.39	5.05	4.88	24.14	3.32	4.11

has a precision comparable to the tabular PP method. As less input data is available we can even outperform this purely tabular representation. We expect this is because our method implicitly uses physically meaningful BRDF domain knowledge by its underlying measured material and correction database. If compared to the LC and RBF method our approach has a significantly lower error value in all experiments (an order of magnitude lower perceptual error for outlier ratios up to 40%). Additionally, our method is almost invariant to increasing sparsity and behaves robust for increased outlier ratios.

We also evaluated how the individual methods based on basis decomposition performed for different error metrics. The choice of the error metric can have a significant impact on the estimation quality. As also pointed out in [21] it is difficult in practice to make a single choice that consistently performs well for all materials. To quantify which effect this choice can have, we compared the results of all methods using different error metrics. For this we chose the following three metrics that were proposed by researchers before: linear $\varepsilon_{\text{lin}}(x) = x$, square root $\varepsilon_{\text{root}}(x) = \sqrt{x}$ and logarithmic $\varepsilon_{\text{log}}(x) = \ln(1 + x)$. These metrics were then used for LC, RBF and in the initialization stage of our algorithm. We only considered the case of full data and zero outlier ratio (which allows a more consistent comparison without any randomness in the generated input). The results of this experiment are shown in Table 2. It can be seen that our algorithm performs robust with respect to different error metrics, whereas the outcome of the other basis decomposition methods is highly dependent on this choice. This indicates that *any* meaningful metric can be used along with our algorithm which alleviates the choice of an appropriate one. This choice then only affects the iteration sequence but the overall method converges to the same solution.

Fig. 5. Exemplary fitting result for 1 of the 16 newly measured materials. Left: Raw measured isotropic BRDF data (a 2D projection of the 3D BRDF table for visualization). Red corresponds to unmeasured areas. Right: Synthesized spheres using the computed estimates under point light illumination (numerical values indicate the fitting error). In contrast to our method the different state-of-the-art algorithms compute either physically implausible results (PP, RBF) or non-accurate solutions (LC)

Regarding the runtime our algorithm operates highly efficient, requiring only a few seconds per iteration on our hardware (3 GHz CPU, 24 GB RAM).

We additionally evaluated our method based on 16 newly measured materials (see Figure 5). This is important because real measured material samples can show different characteristics than our synthetically generated experiments. We found that our method allows to represent the measured data significantly better (in the numerical sense and in terms of physical plausibility). Summarized, for these newly measured materials our algorithm achieves a lower mean perceptual error (error of 0.19) compared to LC (error of 0.50) and RBF (error of 0.38). Please see the supplementary material for a detailed report.

4   Conclusion

We introduced a novel, non-parametric method that can be used for accurate and robust reflectance data fitting. It is based on the novel concept of BRDF correction functions that are iteratively applied to improve an initial BRDF estimate. Moreover, we introduced a new basis that allows to efficiently represent these correction functions. During execution the resulting algorithm explicitly identifies and excludes outliers in the input data. This is challenging (in particular for *non-parametric* methods) and was not handled by any previously proposed method that we are aware of.

We evaluated and compared our method using a large number of experiments and showed that it performs very robust with respect to sparse and outlier afflicted input – in contrast to other evaluated methods. We further showed that our method is invariant to different error metrics. This alleviates the choice of an appropriate error metric for a given input which was challenging until now.

The main limitation of our method is its current exclusive applicability to isotropic materials. The only reason for this is that there is currently no large enough database of measured anisotropic materials available. We have successfully tested our method in the isotropic (3D) case and we see no particular conceptual limitation why it should not be adaptable for the general anisotropic (4D) case once such data is available. It may be possible to synthesize such a database by using a variety of physically based anisotropic BRDF models with varying parameters. However, we have not verified this yet and it is subject to future work.

Acknowledgment. Our work has been partially funded by the project DENSITY (01IW12001) and the Google Research Award received by Didier Stricker, University of Kaiserslautern.

References

1. Ali, M.A., Sato, I., Okabe, T., Sato, Y.: Toward efficient acquisition of bRDFs with fewer samples. In: Lee, K.M., Matsushita, Y., Rehg, J.M., Hu, Z. (eds.) ACCV 2012, Part IV. LNCS, vol. 7727, pp. 54–67. Springer, Heidelberg (2013), http://dx.doi.org/10.1007/978-3-642-37447-0_5

2. Ashikhmin, M., Shirley, P.: An anisotropic phong brdf model. J. Graph. Tools 5(2), 25–32 (2000), http://dx.doi.org/10.1080/10867651.2000.10487522

3. Blinn, J.F.: Models of light reflection for computer synthesized pictures. In: Proceedings of the 4th Annual Conference on Computer Graphics and Interactive Techniques, SIGGRAPH 1977, pp. 192–198. ACM, New York (1977), http://doi.acm.org/10.1145/563858.563893

4. Cook, R.L., Torrance, K.E.: A reflectance model for computer graphics. ACM Trans. Graph. 1(1), 7–24 (1982), http://doi.acm.org/10.1145/357290.357293

5. Fairchild, M.D.: Color appearance models. John Wiley & Sons (2013)

6. Ferreau, H.J.: qpOASES Library for Online Active Set Strategy, http://set.kuleuven.be/optec/Software/qpOASES-OPTEC/ (accessed: February 13, 2014)

7. Ferreau, H.J., Bock, H.G., Diehl, M.: An online active set strategy to overcome the limitations of explicit mpc. International Journal of Robust and Nonlinear Control 18(8), 816–830 (2008), http://dx.doi.org/10.1002/rnc.1251

8. Fleming, R.W., Dror, R.O., Adelson, E.H.: Real-world illumination and the perception of surface reflectance properties. Journal of Vision 3(5), 3 (2003)

9. Fores, A., Ferwerda, J., Gu, J.: Toward a perceptually based metric for brdf modeling. In: Twentieth Color and Imaging Conference, Los Angeles, California, USA, pp. 142–148 (November 2012)

10. Gortler, S.J., Grzeszczuk, R., Szeliski, R., Cohen, M.F.: The lumigraph. In: Proceedings of the 23rd Annual Conference on Computer Graphics and Interactive Techniques, SIGGRAPH 1996, pp. 43–54. ACM, New York (1996), http://doi.acm.org/10.1145/237170.237200

11. He, X.D., Torrance, K.E., Sillion, F.X., Greenberg, D.P.: A comprehensive physical model for light reflection. In: Proceedings of the 18th Annual Conference on Computer Graphics and Interactive Techniques, SIGGRAPH 1991, pp. 175–186. ACM, New York (1991), http://doi.acm.org/10.1145/122718.122738

12. Holroyd, M., Lawrence, J., Zickler, T.: A coaxial optical scanner for synchronous acquisition of 3d geometry and surface reflectance. ACM Trans. Graph. 29, 99:1–99:12 (2010)

13. Koenderink, J.J., Doorn, A.J.V.: Phenomenological description of bidirectional surface reflection. JOSA A 15, 2903–2912 (1998)

14. Köhler, J., Nöll, T., Reis, G., Stricker, D.: A full-spherical device for simultaneous geometry and reflectance acquisition. In: 2013 IEEE Workshop on Applications of Computer Vision (WACV), pp. 355–362 (2013)

15. Lafortune, E.P., Foo, S.C., Torrance, K.E., Greenberg, D.P.: Non-linear approximation of reflectance functions. In: SIGGRAPH, pp. 117–126 (1997), http://dblp.uni-trier.de/db/conf/siggraph/siggraph1997.html#LafortuneFTG97

16. Lalonde, P., Fournier, A.: A wavelet representation of reflectance functions. IEEE Transactions on Visualization and Computer Graphics 3(4), 329–336 (1997), http://dx.doi.org/10.1109/2945.646236

17. Lawrence, J., Ben-Artzi, A., DeCoro, C., Matusik, W., Pfister, H., Ramamoorthi, R., Rusinkiewicz, S.: Inverse shade trees for non-parametric material representation and editing. In: ACM SIGGRAPH 2006 Papers, SIGGRAPH 2006, pp. 735–745. ACM, New York (2006), http://doi.acm.org/10.1145/1179352.1141949

18. Marschner, S.R., Westin, S.H., Lafortune, E.P.F., Torrance, K.E.: Image-based bidirectional reflectance distribution function measurement. Applied Optics 39, 2592–2600 (2000)

19. Matusik, W., Pfister, H., Brand, M., McMillan, L.: A data-driven reflectance model. In: ACM SIGGRAPH 2003 Papers, SIGGRAPH 2003, pp. 759–769. ACM, New York (2003), http://doi.acm.org/10.1145/1201775.882343
20. Matusik, W., Pfister, H., Brand, M., McMillan, L.: Efficient isotropic brdf measurement. In: Proceedings of the 14th Eurographics Workshop on Rendering, EGRW 2003, pp. 241–247. Eurographics Association, Aire-la-Ville (2003), http://dl.acm.org/citation.cfm?id=882404.882439
21. Ngan, A., Durand, F., Matusik, W.: Experimental analysis of brdf models. In: Proceedings of the Sixteenth Eurographics Conference on Rendering Techniques, EGSR 2005, pp. 117–126. Eurographics Association, Aire-la-Ville (2005), http://dx.doi.org/10.2312/EGWR/EGSR05/117-126
22. Nicodemus, F.E.: Directional reflectance and emissivity of an opaque surface. Appl. Opt. 4(7), 767–775 (1965), http://ao.osa.org/abstract.cfm?URI=ao-4-7-767
23. Nishino, K.: Directional statistics brdf model. In: 2009 IEEE 12th International Conference on Computer Vision, pp. 476–483 (September 2009)
24. Pacanowski, R., Salazar-Celis, O., Schlick, C., Granier, X., Pierre, P., Annie, C.: Rational BRDF. IEEE Transactions on Visualization and Computer Graphics 18(11), 1824–1835 (2012), http://hal.inria.fr/hal-00678885
25. Ramamoorthi, R., Hanrahan, P.: A signal-processing framework for inverse rendering. In: Proceedings of the 28th Annual Conference on Computer Graphics and Interactive Techniques, SIGGRAPH 2001, pp. 117–128. ACM, New York (2001), http://doi.acm.org/10.1145/383259.383271
26. Ren, P., Wang, J., Snyder, J., Tong, X., Guo, B.: Pocket reflectometry. In: ACM SIGGRAPH 2011 Papers, SIGGRAPH 2011, pp. 45:1–45:10. ACM, New York (2011), http://doi.acm.org/10.1145/1964921.1964940
27. Rusinkiewicz, S.: A new change of variables for efficient brdf representation. In: Rendering Techniques, pp. 11–22 (1998)
28. Schlick, C.: An inexpensive brdf model for physically-based rendering. Comput. Graph. Forum 13(3), 233–246 (1994)
29. Schröder, P., Sweldens, W.: Spherical wavelets: Efficiently representing functions on the sphere. In: Proceedings of the 22Nd Annual Conference on Computer Graphics and Interactive Techniques, SIGGRAPH 1995, pp. 161–172. ACM, New York (1995), http://doi.acm.org/10.1145/218380.218439
30. Ward, G.J.: Measuring and modeling anisotropic reflection. In: Proceedings of the 19th Annual Conference on Computer Graphics and Interactive Techniques, SIGGRAPH 1992, pp. 265–272. ACM, New York (1992), http://doi.acm.org/10.1145/133994.134078
31. Weistroffer, R.P., Walcott, K.R., Humphreys, G., Lawrence, J.: Efficient basis decomposition for scattered reflectance data. In: Proceedings of the 18th Eurographics Conference on Rendering Techniques, EGSR 2007, pp. 207–218. Eurographics Association, Aire-la-Ville (2007), http://dx.doi.org/10.2312/EGWR/EGSR07/207-218
32. Westin, S.H., Arvo, J.R., Torrance, K.E.: Predicting reflectance functions from complex surfaces. In: Proceedings of the 19th Annual Conference on Computer Graphics and Interactive Techniques, SIGGRAPH 1992, pp. 255–264. ACM, New York (1992), http://doi.acm.org/10.1145/133994.134075
33. Zickler, T., Enrique, S., Ramamoorthi, R., Belhumeur, P.: Reflectance sharing: Image-based rendering from a sparse set of images. In: Proceedings of the Sixteenth Eurographics Conference on Rendering Techniques, EGSR 2005, pp. 253–264. Eurographics Association, Aire-la-Ville (2005), http://dx.doi.org/10.2312/EGWR/EGSR05/253-264

Intrinsic Textures for Relightable Free-Viewpoint Video*

James Imber[1], Jean-Yves Guillemaut[2], and Adrian Hilton[2]

[1] Imagination Technologies Ltd., Kings Langley, Hertfordshire, UK
james.imber@imgtec.com
[2] Centre for Vision, Speech and Signal Processing,
University of Surrey, Guildford, Surrey, UK
{j.guillemaut,a.hilton}@surrey.ac.uk

Abstract. This paper presents an approach to estimate the intrinsic texture properties (albedo, shading, normal) of scenes from multiple view acquisition under unknown illumination conditions. We introduce the concept of *intrinsic textures*, which are pixel-resolution surface textures representing the intrinsic appearance parameters of a scene. Unlike previous video relighting methods, the approach does not assume regions of uniform albedo, which makes it applicable to richly textured scenes. We show that intrinsic image methods can be used to refine an initial, low-frequency shading estimate based on a global lighting reconstruction from an original texture and coarse scene geometry in order to resolve the inherent global ambiguity in shading. The method is applied to relighting of free-viewpoint rendering from multiple view video capture. This demonstrates relighting with reproduction of fine surface detail. Quantitative evaluation on synthetic models with textured appearance shows accurate estimation of intrinsic surface reflectance properties.

Keywords: Free-Viewpoint Video Rendering, Image-Based Rendering, Relighting, Intrinsic Images.

1 Introduction

Free-viewpoint video rendering (FVVR) gives the user the freedom to choose the viewpoint from which to view a captured scene [1–3]. FVVR has been applied successfully in sports TV production [4, 5] and video conferencing [6] among other applications. In FVVR, video from several cameras is used to reconstruct scene geometry using Multiple-View Stereo (MVS), and appearance is reproduced by projectively texturing the scene with the original images [7].

Recently, FVVR research has shifted from straightforward reproduction of the original scene to extending FVVR functionality [8, 9] with the goal of adapting it to other applications. In particular, the ability to relight an actor's performance

---

* Electronic supplementary material -Supplementary material is available in the online version of this chapter at http://dx.doi.org/10.1007/978-3-319-10605-2_26. Videos can also be accessed at http://www.springerimages.com/videos/978-3-319-10604-5.

D. Fleet et al. (Eds.): ECCV 2014, Part II, LNCS 8690, pp. 392–407, 2014.
© Springer International Publishing Switzerland 2014

for seamless compositing into arbitrary real-world and computer-generated surroundings is highly desirable, and is termed Relightable Free-Viewpoint Video Rendering (RFVVR).

Convincing RFVVR requires estimation of the parameters of a bidirectional reflectance distribution function (BRDF) for each point on the surface of a mesh from the appearance. The final appearance of a scene is a function of multiple parameters, including albedo, surface normals and specularity, as well as scene lighting, making the estimation of these parameters ambiguous. In this paper we address the problem of extracting intrinsic textures under arbitrary uncontrolled lighting, which is poorly constrained and requires that scene lighting be inferred together with the scene appearance.

The problem of fitting parameters (usually albedo and shading) to each pixel of an image, for which scene geometry is not available, has been studied extensively as intrinsic image extraction. This paper combines principles from intrinsic image extraction with prior knowledge of the scene to resolve the global ambiguity between shading and albedo. RFVVR and intrinsic image extraction approach the same problem from two angles - the former is a top-down approach, with knowledge of scene structure at its disposal, whereas the latter is a bottom-up approach, which relies on local image structure to decompose into albedo and shading images. In short, the coarse geometry available in RFVVR can be leveraged to resolve the global ambiguity present in intrinsic image reconstruction methods.

The proposed method improves on previous RFVVR methods, which make heavy use of the fact that albedo in a scene is likely to be piecewise constant. The piecewise constant albedo assumption breaks down in the presence of multi-albedo regions (such as wood or patterned fabric), and any subsequent surface refinement or normal map extraction will be invalid for such regions. For this reason, we propose a two-stage coarse-to-fine optimisation approach for albedo and shading. We use a segmentation-based coarse albedo estimate to estimate the lighting for the scene, after which the segmentation is discarded and we resort to a surface-based bilateral filter technique to estimate per-pixel albedo for complex materials. Finally, a highly-detailed surface normal map is extracted using the refined albedo, shading and irradiance estimates.

2   Related Work

Our approach to relighting draws from recent contributions in RFVVR and intrinsic image extraction. The availability of underlying geometry, and multiple viewpoints of the same scene, can be used as a powerful aid to the extraction of intrinsic images, which in the context of RFVVR are referred to as *intrinsic textures* as they are intrinsic appearance properties over the surface manifold.

2.1   Free Viewpoint Video Rendering

A scene model is reconstructed using MVS, which is projectively textured from the camera viewpoints [10]. To reproduce view-dependent aspects of appearance, such as specularity, camera views are blended together at run-time depending on viewpoint [11]. In the case of near-Lambertian scenes with accurate stereo reconstruction and camera calibration, a single texture per frame can be produced without sacrificing quality, as has been done for the results presented in this paper.

2.2   Intrinsic Image Extraction

The problem of estimating albedo and lighting from an image, without knowledge of geometry, has been extensively studied in computer vision as the problem of intrinsic image extraction [12–15]. The interaction of physical objects with light is governed by its intrinsic colours (albedo), specular properties, transmission properties and surface normals. Any image of a physical scene can be decomposed into intrinsic images corresponding to each material property.

No knowledge of global scene shape is available in these image-based techniques, and they invariably require additional constraints (or assumptions) to be introduced for good global solutions to be found. For example, Bousseau et al. [16] has a user interact with the system to guide the process, whereas Barron and Malik [17] use a set of shape and albedo priors based on general localised properties of natural images.

2.3   Material Properties from Multi-View Video

RFVVR requires the estimation of shape and reflectance properties comprising the scene [18, 19]. Once the underlying geometry and surface reflectance properties are known, arbitrary lighting conditions can be introduced in what is then a conventional computer graphics rendering pipeline. This can be expressed as estimating the parameters of a BRDF. Commonly-used BRDFs include the Lambertian (diffuse reflection only) and Phong (a physically inaccurate, but simple) reflection models. Throughout this paper, the Lambertian reflectance model is used.

In this work, we combine prior shape estimates from MVS with intrinsic image texture estimation to resolve the inherent global ambiguity. This replaces the assumption of piecewise constant albedo [12] which has often been used in RFVVR to constrain reflectance estimation. This assumption commonly fails in natural scenes with textured surface appearance such as patterned fabric.

Active Lighting. Controlling capture and lighting conditions allows highly accurate models of albedo and lighting behaviour to be estimated, since it reduces the number of unknown parameters. These systems are termed *active illumination* or *light stage* [18, 20]. This requires dedicated equipment, calibrated light sources and calibrated cameras. Active lighting is less practical for dynamic scenes, since it greatly increases the complexity of capture techniques. Einarsson et al. [21] demonstrate high-quality image-based relightable free-viewpoint video using a complex active capture system with time-multiplexed lighting. High-speed synchronised illumination and cameras, and post-registration of the images are required for reconstruction of reflectance properties and shape.

Fixed Calibrated Lighting. Passive techniques, which have a fixed lighting arrangement for the duration of capture, are better suited to the problem of dynamic scene relighting. Lensch et al. [22] introduce a robust method for the extraction of time-varying BRDF given a coarse geometric model of a real-world object. They propose extraction of surface normals as well as albedo in fitting the BRDF to give the illusion of high-frequency geometry. Ahmed et al. [19] use a similar technique for relighting of free-viewpoint video. They use calibrated point sources to iteratively refine surface normals and albedos given coarse scene geometry. A regularisation term is imposed on the surface normal to discourage poor fits to the reference data. To help resolve ambiguity, a clustering method based on the piecewise-constant albedo assumption is used.

Uncalibrated Lighting. More recently, the radiance from irradiance problem for Lambertian scenes is solved using spherical harmonics (SH) up to the second order [23]. Wu et al. [24] perform mesh refinement against the original images as opposed to normal extraction. Assuming a Lambertian reflectance model, the authors construct segment-based albedo and radiance estimates for each frame of the sequence. Local occlusion is used to resolve the radiance-from-irradiance problem to high SH orders.

This approach is extended to non-Lambertian cases in the work of Li et al. [9]. After solving the Lambertian radiance-from-irradiance problem, specular regions are used to localise light sources. The Phong model is fitted to the appearance. The techniques of both Wu et al. and Li et al. are for application to dynamic scenes, and temporal priors based on results from other frames form an important part of their methods.

Our proposed intrinsic texture approach performs a full-resolution fit of albedo and surface normal to the original texture. By contrast, Wu et al. and Li et al. optimise over the surface based on piecewise-constant albedo, which gives lower resolution due to the inherent smoothing of the regularisation. Our method accurately estimates the irradiance map for isolated frames, meaning that temporal priors from multi-frame sequences are not required.

3 Overview

We want to find albedo and surface normal textures for a coarse MVS scene reconstruction which give plausible results when rendered under arbitrary lighting conditions. No prior knowledge of lighting is assumed; the scenes were captured under unknown lighting conditions. To solve this problem, we propose first estimating the global scene irradiance, then using this to initialise localised refinement of albedo and shading, before finally fitting surface normals. An overview of the pipeline is given in Figure 1.

To estimate scene lighting, we start by coarsely segmenting the mesh surface into regions of similar albedo, making use of the observation that albedo is often piecewise constant. Unlike previous methods, this initial segmentation does not have to be accurate, and we make no attempt to refine it. Using this preliminary albedo estimate, we estimate the scene illumination which matches the shading

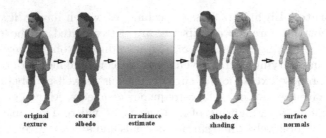

original   coarse   irradiance   albedo &   surface
texture   albedo   estimate   shading   normals

Fig. 1. Overview of the intrinsic texture extraction pipeline

distribution over the surface of the mesh. This provides a starting point for the albedo and shading texture extraction step, during which per-pixel albedo and shading textures are estimated. Finally, using the shading texture, surface normals are fitted to the lighting function. The normal map and albedo map can be used in conjunction to allow relighting of the FVV frame.

In using a coarse albedo estimate to determine the low-frequency global lighting, we do not lose any generality when applied to scenes with complex textures. The irradiance function is only recovered up to second order SH, meaning that any high-frequency variations in albedo within each segment will not corrupt the lighting estimate. Once the lighting has been estimated, the coarse albedo is discarded. This approach is in contrast to the current state-of-the-art method of first refining geometry based on a coarse albedo estimate, and then refining the BRDF parameters [9, 24]. It is thus capable of achieving full image-resolution albedo and surface normal maps for accurate surface detail.

4   Albedo and Shading Textures

The projectively textured, coarse MVS geometry is used to estimate the low-frequency irradiance. This irradiance accounts for the large, attached shadows at the scale of the MVS geometry, and is used to remove them from the original texture (section 4.1). To recover the missing high-frequency shading, an intrinsic image method is applied to the texture (section 4.2).

4.1   Low-Frequency Lighting Estimation

The global scene irradiance is reconstructed assuming Lambertian reflectance and infinitely displaced lighting. Ramamoorthi and Hanrahan [23] show that any irradiance map can be represented efficiently using spherical harmonics (SH) up to the second order, which requires only nine coefficients. This makes SH convenient for approximating the irradiance from a noisy set of samples.

The Lambertian reflectance model relates irradiance L to the radiance R by equation 1. The scene appearance I is related to the irradiance by $I(\boldsymbol{x}) = A(\boldsymbol{x})L(\boldsymbol{x})$. $V(\theta, \phi, \boldsymbol{x})$ is a visibility mask which can only take the values 0 and 1.

$$L(\boldsymbol{n}(\boldsymbol{x}), \boldsymbol{x}) = \int_{\Omega} \max\left(\boldsymbol{u}(\theta, \phi)^{\mathsf{T}} \boldsymbol{n}(\boldsymbol{x}), 0\right) R(\theta, \phi)\, V(\theta, \phi, \boldsymbol{x})\, \mathrm{d}\Omega \qquad (1)$$

Fig. 2. Local irradiance estimates (left and centre) for two materials (polar projection). On the right, the intersection between the two irradiance estimates, Q_{ij}. Also shown are the positions of the materials on the mesh surface, highlighted in cyan.

$u(\theta, \phi)$ is the unit vector in the direction of the spherical polar co-ordinates (θ, ϕ), and $n(x)$ is the normal at surface position x. The integral is over the sphere Ω with incremental surface area $d\Omega = \sin(\theta)d\theta d\phi$. Under the assumption of a convex scene, the dependence on surface position x in equation 1 disappears, and this can be considered as a convolution of the radiance function with a large low-pass filter, termed the clamped-cosine kernel (equation 2).

$$L(n) = \int_{\Omega} \max\left(u(\theta, \phi)^{\mathsf{T}} n \,,\, 0\right) R(\theta, \phi)\, d\Omega \qquad (2)$$

Due to this low-pass filtering, only spherical harmonics up to the second order can be reliably extracted in the case of convex objects [23]. Wu et al. extract the radiance function to higher orders by using the additional information provided by local self-occlusions in non-convex objects. For our purposes a low-order SH reconstruction of the irradiance suffices, since we rely on our intrinsic texture technique to extract high-frequency albedo, shading and surface normals. The lighting estimate is only used to globally balance the intrinsic albedo and shading textures in our case.

The texture is first segmented by albedo, using the segmentation of Felzenszwalb et al. [25] adapted to work in the tangent space of the mesh. This gives a set of materials, M. The material boundaries of this initial, coarse segmentation do not need to be pixel-accurate, since it is only used to recover the irradiance function. For each material u in M, an initial estimate of average albedo A'_u is given as the average colour of all texels (texture "pixels") comprising that material:

$$A'_u = \frac{1}{|u|} \sum_{x \in u} I(x) \quad \forall u \in M \qquad (3)$$

In the case of monochrome lighting, this initial estimate of albedo is a scaled version of the final albedo, A_u, so that $k_u A_u = A'_u$. The problem of finding the correct ratios of material albedos A_u to each other is now a problem of determining the multipliers k_u.

The per-material coarse shading estimate is given by:

$$S_u(\boldsymbol{x}) = \frac{I(\boldsymbol{x})}{A'_u(\boldsymbol{x})} \tag{4}$$

Making use of the fact that the low-frequency shading can be considered as samples of the irradiance function, $S_u(\boldsymbol{x})$ can be projected along the coarse surface normal $\boldsymbol{n}_c(\boldsymbol{x})$ provided by the MVS scene reconstruction to give an estimate L'_u of the irradiance function at that point.

$$L(\boldsymbol{n}_c(\boldsymbol{x})) \approx k_u L'_u(\boldsymbol{n}_c(\boldsymbol{x})) = k_u S_u(\boldsymbol{x}) \tag{5}$$

The sum of squared error in the overlap between the local irradiance estimates L'_u needs to be minimised by appropriate choices of k_u. For two materials $i, j \in M$, let $Q_{i,j}$ be the binary support function giving the overlap between L'_i and L'_j (Figure 2). The sum of squared error is given by:

$$E = \sum_i \sum_{j>i} \left[\int_\Omega (k_i L'_i(\theta, \phi) - k_j L'_j(\theta, \phi)) Q_{i,j}(\theta, \phi) \mathrm{d}\Omega \right]^2 \tag{6}$$

$$E = \sum_i \sum_{j>i} [k_i b_{ij} - k_j b_{ji}]^2 \tag{7}$$

$$\text{where} \quad b_{ij} = \int_\Omega L'_i(\theta, \phi) Q_{i,j}(\theta, \phi) \, \mathrm{d}\Omega \tag{8}$$

A greedy algorithm with a least-squares update step for each k_u is now used to minimise E. All k_u are initialised to 1. Since we are only interested in the ratios of the multipliers, the first multiplier, k_1, remains unchanged throughout, otherwise only the trivial solution $k_u = 0 \ \forall u \in M$ would be found. $Q_{i,j}(\theta, \phi)$ does not take into account local occlusion of the lighting.

Let k_c represent the multiplier currently being optimised. Letting $d_j = k_j b_{ji}$, the update step is given by:

$$k_c \leftarrow \operatorname*{argmin}_{k_c} ||k_c \boldsymbol{b}_c - \boldsymbol{d}||^2 = \frac{\boldsymbol{b}_c^\mathsf{T} \boldsymbol{d}}{\boldsymbol{b}_c^\mathsf{T} \boldsymbol{b}_c} \tag{9}$$

In this way, we can iterate over all the multipliers except for k_1, scaling the albedos to optimise the material overlaps, until convergence. This gives a refined estimate of the actual albedos A_u up to a global scale factor. These albedos may now be combined into a single coarse albedo estimate, A_c. The global irradiance estimate L is then found as the best fit of the SH basis up to the second order to L' (equation 10).

$$L'(\boldsymbol{n}_c(\boldsymbol{x})) = \frac{I(\boldsymbol{x})}{A_c(\boldsymbol{x})} \tag{10}$$

To test the effectiveness of this greedy approach, the order in which the materials were optimised was randomised. This was found to have no significant

Fig. 3. Example intrinsic image decompositions (albedo and shading) using the proposed modified bilateral filter

impact on the resulting $A_c(\boldsymbol{x})$. In the case of coloured irradiance, which is common in studio capture, the above can be done for each of the red, green and blue channels independently. It should be noted that this method only works on smooth meshes, since it relies on overlaps between per-material lighting estimates. In particular, it gives good results for human actors, but it would degrade for man-made objects with orthogonal faces.

4.2 Intrinsic Texture Extraction Filter

Our intrinsic texture extraction method builds upon the image-based method of Shen et al. [26] to incorporate global lighting information and operate over the surface of a mesh. To achieve this, a fast, bilateral filter based intrinsic image decomposition method is introduced. The use of an adaptive FIR filter for intrinsic image extraction, rather than explicitly minimising an energy functional, simplifies the method and is efficient in application to textures.

The contribution of Shen et al. [26] is an energy functional, which when minimised splits an image I into its constituent albedo A and shading S images, such that $I(\boldsymbol{x}) = A(\boldsymbol{x})S(\boldsymbol{x})$ (equation 11). It is show that this functional can be well approximated using a modified bilateral filter to remove local shading contributions from the original image.

$$E(A, S) = \sum_{\boldsymbol{x} \in P} \left(A(\boldsymbol{x}) - \sum_{\boldsymbol{y} \in N(\boldsymbol{x})} w(\boldsymbol{x}, \boldsymbol{y}) A(\boldsymbol{y}) \right)^2 + \sum_{\boldsymbol{x} \in P} (I(\boldsymbol{x})/S(\boldsymbol{x}) - A(\boldsymbol{x}))^2 \quad (11)$$

$$w(\boldsymbol{x}, \boldsymbol{y}) = \exp\left(-\frac{[\cos^{-1}(\hat{I}(\boldsymbol{x})^{\mathsf{T}} \hat{I}(\boldsymbol{y}))]^2}{\sigma_{i1}^2} \right) \exp\left(-\frac{[\mathrm{luma}(I(\boldsymbol{x})) - \mathrm{luma}(I(\boldsymbol{y}))]^2}{\sigma_{i2}^2} \right)$$
$$(12)$$

$$\mathrm{luma} = 0.299 \times \mathrm{Red} + 0.587 \times \mathrm{Green} + 0.114 \times \mathrm{Blue} \quad (13)$$

In equation 11, $N(\boldsymbol{x})$ is the neighbourhood of pixel $\boldsymbol{x}$, and P is the set of pixel positions. Equation 11 is made up of two parts. The first part imposes a metric for similarity in albedo between pixels which flattens out regions of similar albedo when minimised. The second part satisfies the condition that the observed image matches the estimated shading and albedo: $I(\boldsymbol{x}) = A(\boldsymbol{x})S(\boldsymbol{x})$. $S(\boldsymbol{x})$ is not dependent on the neighbourhood of pixels except through A, so a similar result can be achieved by minimising the following:

$$\operatorname*{argmin}_{A} E(A) = \sum_{\boldsymbol{x} \in P} \left(A(\boldsymbol{x}) - \sum_{\boldsymbol{y} \in N(\boldsymbol{x})} w(\boldsymbol{x}, \boldsymbol{y}) A(\boldsymbol{y}) \right)^2 \qquad (14)$$

Where $S = I/A$. This is equivalent to flattening out regions which are similar according to the metric defined in equation 12. This can be performed efficiently using a modified bilateral filter [27]:

$$A(\boldsymbol{x}) = \frac{1}{u} \int_{\boldsymbol{\mu}} I(\boldsymbol{\mu}) \exp\left(-\frac{\|\boldsymbol{x} - \boldsymbol{\mu}\|_2^2}{\sigma_w^2} \right) \exp\left(-\frac{[\cos^{-1}(\hat{I}(\boldsymbol{x})^\mathsf{T} \hat{I}(\boldsymbol{\mu}))]^2}{\sigma_{i1}^2} \right)$$
$$\times \exp\left(-\frac{[\operatorname{luma}(I(\boldsymbol{x})) - \operatorname{luma}(I(\boldsymbol{\mu}))]^2}{\sigma_{i2}^2} \right) d\boldsymbol{\mu} \qquad (15)$$

In addition to the usual bilateral filter term which gauges similarity between pixels by luma, the chromaticity similarity term from equation 12 is also present. Some examples of image decompositions using this method are given in figure 3. The variances σ_{i1}^2 and σ_{i2}^2 adapt to the local region, as described in Shen et al.'s paper. u is a normalisation term to ensure the filter weights sum to unity.

The method of Shen et al. is based upon a local similarity metric, so it requires additional high-level constraints in order to achieve a good global solution. The same is true of the bilateral filtering based method described here. In the original paper, these constraints are provided by a user via a stroke-based interaction method, whereas we use the irradiance estimate from the MVS shape reconstruction to provide automatic global albedo balancing.

The quality of the results depends on the choice of kernel size in equation 15. Large kernels will have high variances σ_{i1}^2 and σ_{i2}^2, which will cause bleeding between regions which have similar albedo. In addition, it will take a long time to convolve large kernels with the image. Conversely, small kernels will not pick up large shading gradients, even with a large number of iterations. Throughout this paper, a 15x15 kernel was used.

Iteratively applying the kernel in equation 15 can reduce the computational cost and bleeding effects of using large kernels whilst still allowing some global shading effects to be extracted. The shading image is formed as $S = I/A$ after every iteration. The colour component of A should be preserved between iterations, which is equivalent to enforcing $\hat{A} = \hat{I}$ whilst preserving the RGB "length" of each pixel of A. We found only a single iteration to be necessary for the intrinsic texture results presented here.

This filter is adapted to work in the tangent space of the mesh by filtering directly on the texture in texture space. Where sample points fall off the edge

Fig. 4. Processing of original texture (a) to produce shading (e) and albedo (f) textures. Coarse albedos (b) are rebalanced (c) to allow a global shading estimate (d), which initialises the fine shading/albedo extraction method (equation 16). (g) shows part of the original texture in texture space.

of the triangle containing the centre of the filter, the sample point is offset to the triangle containing the required texel. To prevent distortion from mapping the surface onto the UV plane, the UV chart is split into individual triangles (Figure 4g). This preserves the shape and relative size of each triangle between the mesh and texture space. Figure 4 shows the result of albedo refinement on a texture. It was found that increasing the luma variance σ_{i2}^2 gives better results in the case of texture filtering.

To account for the global scene lighting, the original image is first divided by the irradiance estimate sampled using the coarse surface normals $\boldsymbol{n}_c(\boldsymbol{x})$:

$$W(\boldsymbol{x}) = \frac{I(\boldsymbol{x})}{L(\boldsymbol{n}_c(\boldsymbol{x}))} \tag{16}$$

The filter is then applied to W to obtain the albedo estimate A. The shading texture S is formed from I and A.

5   Refined Surface Normal Estimation

Since both a global lighting estimate and a surface shading estimate are available, it is possible to fit surface normals to the data. This is done by minimising an error function defined against the shading texture, S, at each point on the surface of the mesh $\boldsymbol{x}$:

$$E(\boldsymbol{n}(\boldsymbol{x})) = \left\| S(\boldsymbol{x}) - L(\boldsymbol{n}) \right\|_1 + \Lambda(\boldsymbol{n}, \boldsymbol{n}_c) \tag{17}$$

$$\boldsymbol{n}_{opt}(\boldsymbol{x}) = \underset{\boldsymbol{n}}{\operatorname{argmin}} E(\boldsymbol{n}(\boldsymbol{x})) \tag{18}$$

The L1 norm was chosen for its robustness in the presence of noise. When fitting surface normals, the MVS reconstruction gives a good indication of likely normal fits. Large deviations of the fitted normals $\boldsymbol{n}$ from the coarse normals $\boldsymbol{n}_c$ are unlikely, and are therefore penalised using a regularisation term Λ. To minimise this function, an exhaustive search of all possible fits in the direction of the gradient of the irradiance function is performed.

Table 1. Quantitative evaluation on synthetic datasets

Model	Shading Acc.	Colour Angle	Irradiance MSE	Time Taken
Smooth Sphere	0.911	3.162°	0.0059	102s
Rough Sphere	0.858	6.145°	0.0030	118s
Bunny	0.928	2.495°	0.0032	149s
Dragon	0.935	3.406°	0.0012	179s
Average	0.908	3.802°	0.0033	137s

The regularisation term Λ is a function of the angle between the two vectors, defined as:

$$\Lambda(n, n_c) = \begin{cases} \lambda \left(\cos^{-1}(n^\intercal n_c)\right)^2 & n^\intercal n_c > 0 \\ \infty & \text{otherwise} \end{cases} \tag{19}$$

Where λ is determined experimentally. A value of 0.025 was used for all examples in this paper.

Since there is no inter-pixel dependency in equation 17, it is a good target for parallelisation. In our implementation, all surface normals are fitted in parallel on a GPU using a GLSL fragment shader. In all, the normal fitting stage takes of the order of 0.5 seconds to complete with a low-performance (Nvidia GeForce GT 240) graphics card, for a 1024x1024 texel texture.

6   Results

Ground-truth albedo and shading information is not available for multi-view sequences of actors. For this reason, a synthetic dataset consisting of multi-view renders of textured meshes, for which ground truth is available, is used to quantitatively evaluate the intrinsic texture method. Relit frames from public multiple view reconstruction datasets are also qualitatively evaluated to assess the performance for the target relightable FVVR application.

6.1   Quantitative Evaluation

A synthetic dataset was generated consisting of four models for evaluating the quality of the albedo and shading intrinsic images (Figure 5). The *bunny* and *dragon* models come from the Stanford 3D Scanning Repository. Each of these models was textured with a complex image, making albedo and lighting extraction comparatively difficult. A ray-tracer was used instead of a rasteriser to achieve more realistic lighting, including inter-reflections and ambient occlusions. A set of eight renders from virtual cameras arranged around the objects were combined into a single texture, in the same way as images from physical cameras are combined in the case of studio data. For each of the meshes, a low-polygon mesh (less than 6500 vertices in all cases) was used to generate the texture and provide coarse normals for irradiance and shading extraction. Ground truth

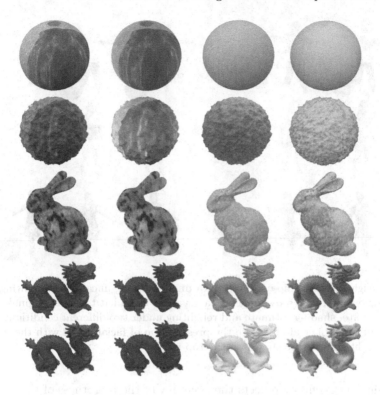

Fig. 5. Decomposition of synthetic textures and meshes into intrinsic textures. From left to right: original texture, albedo texture, shading texture and surface normals. The final row shows the result of omitting the local albedo/shading refinement stage.

shading and albedo was used for quantitative evaluation, with results given in Table 1. Our average runtime of 137 seconds per frame compares to 10 minutes reported by Wu et al. [24] and 7-8 minutes by Li et al. [9].

Two metrics were used to measure the accuracy of the separation between albedo and shading: shading accuracy and average colour angle, both measured in normalised RGB space (all axes in the range 0 to 1). Shading accuracy is given on a scale of 0 to 1 (equation 20).

$$\text{shading acc.} = 1 - \frac{1}{\sqrt{3}|P|} \sum_{x \in P} ||A(x) - A_G(x)||_2 \qquad (20)$$

Here, P is the set of all texel positions, and $A_G(x)$ is the ground-truth albedo.

Fig. 6. Relighting of studio-captured data under general, uncalibrated lighting conditions using our method (see supplementary video). From left to right: original texture, albedo estimate, shading estimate and relighting under two different conditions. On far right, result from Li et al. [9]. Note the preservation of facial detail with the proposed method. Light spheres are shown on the top row.

The shading accuracy reflects the accuracy of the brightness of the albedo as well as R:G:B ratio. The colour angle is a measure of the accuracy of the R:G:B ratio only (equation 21).

$$\text{avg. RGB angle} = \frac{1}{|P|} \sum_{x \in P} \cos^{-1}\left(\hat{A}(x)^{\mathsf{T}} \hat{A_G}(x)\right) \tag{21}$$

A colour angle of zero indicates that the R:G:B ratios in the albedo estimate perfectly match those in the ground truth.

6.2   Qualitative Evaluation

The method was validated on three studio capture datasets and rendered under various lighting conditions. The first two sequences [8] were recorded with 8 cameras at a resolution of 1920x1080, whereas the last sequence [24] was recorded with 11 cameras at 1296x972. In all renders a high level of detail is achieved, and challenging textures are faithfully reconstructed, as shown in Figure 6. In particular, the faces of the actors are reproduced accurately, which is vital for perceived realism. By using normal fitting rather than geometry refinement (Figure 7), we achieve a higher resolution in our relighting results than in current state-of-the-art methods [9, 24]. The supplementary video gives results for the full sequences.

The main shortcomings of this approach are misclassification of high-frequency dark albedos as shading, and noise in the extracted normal maps. The former is

Fig. 7. Surface normals before and after refinement

most obvious as the representation of the edges of the dancer's t-shirt logo, and some facial features, in the shading texture. The noise in the relit images results because each texel in the extracted normal map is fitted independently of the others, so no neighbour-based smoothing takes place.

7 Conclusions and Future Work

This paper introduces a new method for reconstruction of accurate high resolution albedo and surface normal textures from approximate multiple view scene reconstruction with unknown illumination. The approach enables estimation of albedo, shading and surface normals at the resolution of the original texture. Unlike previous approaches, this approach does not assume regions of near-constant albedo, but also works with rich, multi-albedo textures. A novel bilateral filter approach is proposed for efficient shading refinement.

The proposed intrinsic texture estimation method is based on the observation that RFVVR and intrinsic image estimation are complementary approaches to appearance property estimation. It is shown that a global, low-frequency lighting estimate obtained from an original texture and coarse scene geometry can be used to initialise a local, high-frequency refinement step.

Intrinsic textures are applied to relighting of free-viewpoint rendering from multiple view video capture. This demonstrates relighting with reproduction of detailed surface appearance. Quantitative evaluation on synthetic models with non-uniform surface appearance shows accurate estimation of per-pixel albedo and normals.

A number of refinements to this method are possible. Improved global lighting estimation by solving the radiance-from-irradiance problem taking into account occlusions would give a more accurate global lighting estimate. Extension to non-Lambertian surfaces would improve the generality of the approach. Finally, additional temporal and spatial priors may further improve the quality of the intrinsic textures.

Acknowledgements. The authors would like to thank Imagination Technologies Limited for funding this research. We would also like to thank Chenglei Wu and Christian Theobalt for kindly providing access to their datasets.

References

1. Zitnick, C., Kang, S., Uyttendaele, M.: High-quality video view interpolation using a layered representation. ACM Transactions on Graphics 1(212), 600–608 (2004)
2. Matusik, W., Buehler, C., Raskar, R., Gortler, S.J., McMillan, L.: Image-based visual hulls. In: Proceedings of the 27th Annual Conference on Computer Graphics and Interactive Techniques, pp. 369–374 (2000)
3. Vedula, S., Baker, S., Kanade, T.: Image-based spatio-temporal modeling and view interpolation of dynamic events. ACM Transactions on Graphics 24(2), 240–261 (2005)
4. Kanade, T., Rander, P., Narayanan, P.: Virtualized reality: constructing virtual worlds from real scenes. IEEE Multimedia 4(1), 34–47 (1997)
5. Guillemaut, J.Y., Hilton, A.: Joint Multi-Layer Segmentation and Reconstruction for Free-Viewpoint Video Applications. International Journal of Computer Vision 93(1), 73–100 (2010)
6. Pan, C.H., Huang, S.C., Chang, Y.L., Lian, C.J., Chen, L.G.: Real-time free viewpoint rendering system for face-to-face video conference. In: Proceedings of IEEE International Conference on Consumer Electronics, pp. 1–2 (2008)
7. Debevec, P., Taylor, C., Malik, J.: Modeling and rendering architecture from photographs: A hybrid geometry-and image-based approach. In: Proceedings of the 23rd Annual conference on Computer Graphics and Interactive Techniques, pp. 1–10 (1996)
8. Starck, J., Hilton, A.: Surface capture for performance-based animation. IEEE Computer Graphics and Applications 27(3), 21–31 (2007)
9. Li, G., Wu, C., Stoll, C., Liu, Y., Varanasi, K., Dai, Q., Theobalt, C.: Capturing Relightable Human Performances under General Uncontrolled Illumination. Computer Graphics Forum 32(2), 275–284 (2013)
10. Debevec, P., Taylor, C., Malik, J.: Image-based modeling and rendering of architecture with interactive photogrammetry and view-dependent texture mapping. In: Proceedings of the 1998 IEEE International Symposium on Circuits and Systems, pp. 14–17 (1998)
11. Starck, J., Kilner, J., Hilton, A.: A Free-Viewpoint Video Renderer. Journal of Graphics, GPU, and Game Tools 14(3), 57–72 (2009)
12. Land, E.H., McCann, J.J.: Lightness and retinex theory. Journal of the Optical Society of America 61(1), 1–11 (1971)
13. Barrow, H., Tenenbaum, J.: Recovering intrinsic scene characteristics from images. Computer Vision Systems, 3–26 (1978)
14. Tappen, M.F., Freeman, W.T., Adelson, E.H.: Recovering intrinsic images from a single image. IEEE Transactions on Pattern Analysis and Machine Intelligence 27(9), 1459–1472 (2005)
15. Shen, L., Yeo, C.: Intrinsic images decomposition using a local and global sparse representation of reflectance. In: 2011 IEEE Conference on Computer Vision and Pattern Recognition (CVPR) (2011)
16. Bousseau, A., Paris, S., Durand, F.: User-assisted intrinsic images. ACM Transactions on Graphics 28(5), 1 (2009)
17. Barron, J., Malik, J.: Shape, albedo, and illumination from a single image of an unknown object. In: 2012 IEEE Conference on Computer Vision and Pattern Recognition (CVPR), pp. 334–341 (2012)
18. Debevec, P., Hawkins, T., Tchou, C.: Acquiring the reflectance field of a human face. In: Proceedings of the 27th Annual Conference on Computer Graphics and Interactive Techniques, pp. 145–156 (2000)

19. Ahmed, N., Theobalt, C., Seidel, H.-P.: Spatio-temporal Reflectance Sharing for Relightable 3D Video. In: Gagalowicz, A., Philips, W. (eds.) MIRAGE 2007. LNCS, vol. 4418, pp. 47–58. Springer, Heidelberg (2007)
20. Matusik, W., Pfister, H., Ngan, A., Beardsley, P., Ziegler, R., McMillan, L.: Image-based 3D photography using opacity hulls. In: Proceedings of the 29th Annual Conference on Computer Graphics and Interactive Techniques, p. 427 (2002)
21. Einarsson, P., Chabert, C., Jones, A., Ma, W.C., Lamond, B., Hawkins, T., Bolas, M., Sylwan, S., Debevec, P.: Relighting human locomotion with flowed reflectance fields. ACM Transactions on Graphics 2006 Sketches (2006)
22. Lensch, H.P.A., Kautz, J., Goesele, M., Heidrich, W., Seidel, H.P.: Image-based reconstruction of spatial appearance and geometric detail. ACM Transactions on Graphics 22(2), 234–257 (2003)
23. Ramamoorthi, R., Hanrahan, P.: On the relationship between radiance and irradiance: determining the illumination from images of a convex Lambertian object. Journal of the Optical Society of America A 18(10), 2448 (2001)
24. Wu, C., Varanasi, K., Liu, Y., Seidel, H.P., Theobalt, C.: Shading-based dynamic shape refinement from multi-view video under general illumination. In: 2011 International Conference on Computer Vision, pp. 1108–1115 (November 2011)
25. Felzenszwalb, P.F., Huttenlocher, D.P.: Efficient graph-based image segmentation. International Journal of Computer Vision 59(2), 167–181 (2004)
26. Shen, J., Yang, X., Jia, Y., Li, X.: Intrinsic images using optimization. In: 2011 IEEE Conference on Computer Vision and Pattern Recognition (CVPR) (2011)
27. Durand, F., Dorsey, J.: Fast bilateral filtering for the display of high-dynamic-range images. ACM Transactions on Graphics (TOG) (2002)

Reasoning about Object Affordances
in a Knowledge Base Representation

Yuke Zhu, Alireza Fathi, and Li Fei-Fei

Computer Science Department, Stanford University, USA
{yukez,alireza,feifeili}@cs.stanford.edu

Abstract. Reasoning about objects and their affordances is a fundamental problem for visual intelligence. Most of the previous work casts this problem as a classification task where separate classifiers are trained to label objects, recognize attributes, or assign affordances. In this work, we consider the problem of object affordance reasoning using a knowledge base representation. Diverse information of objects are first harvested from images and other meta-data sources. We then learn a knowledge base (KB) using a Markov Logic Network (MLN). Given the learned KB, we show that a diverse set of visual inference tasks can be done in this unified framework without training separate classifiers, including zero-shot affordance prediction and object recognition given human poses.

1 Introduction

Visual reasoning is one ultimate goal of visual intelligence. Take an apple in Fig. 1 for example. Given a picture of an apple, humans can recognize the object name, its shape, color, texture, infer its taste, and think about how to eat it. Much of our field's effort in visual reasoning is focused on assigning a class label to some part of an image. Indeed casting the reasoning problem as a classification problem is intuitive. Most of the powerful machine learning tools are based on optimizing a classification objective. But this classifier-based paradigm also has limitations. Compared to the rich reasoning that can go through a person's mind upon seeing an apple, a typical object classifier is doing a "shallow" reasoning.

In this paper, we focus on the task of predicting the affordances of objects, and illustrate how a new representation of the visual and semantic information can go beyond this "shallow" reasoning and allow for more flexible and deeper visual reasoning. Gibson in his seminal paper [16] in 1979 refers to affordance as "properties of an object [...] that determine what actions a human can perform on them." Inspired by this, and a number of recent studies in computer vision [17,21,18,37], we define the full description of affordance as a combination of three things: (1) an affordance label (e.g. edible), (2) a human pose representation of the action (e.g. in skeleton form) and (3) a relative position of the object with respect to the human pose (e.g. next to).

A Naïve Approach. One way to make a rich prediction of affordance is to train a battery of different classifiers, each focusing on one aspect (color, shape,

D. Fleet et al. (Eds.): ECCV 2014, Part II, LNCS 8690, pp. 408–424, 2014.

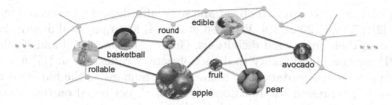

Fig. 1. An example knowledge structure for visual reasoning. Relevant nodes are interconnected in the knowledge graph. Different types of edges (indicated by color) depict a diverse range of relations between nodes, which relate different concepts, such as objects, their attributes and affordances, to each other.

texture, etc.) of the object. However, assuming we can do this for an exhaustive list of attributes of an apple, the reverse question remains — namely, inferring the type of fruit given an image of a person eating a piece of fruit or an image of a red, round piece of fruit.

Knowledge-Based Approach. Another way to consider the problem of visual reasoning is through a knowledge structure, such as the one illustrated in Fig. 1. Apple, in a knowledge graph, is a node (or entity) connected to other nodes, some depicting its visual attributes such as shape, color, texture, and other nodes depicting its affordance, such as edible. Each node connecting apple is further connected to other relevant nodes. In Fig. 1, the edible node is connected with pear, and the round node is connected to basketball, etc.

This representation is well known in the database and NLP communities, often called *knowledge base* (KB) or *knowledge graph*. Compared to classifiers that tackle one specific task, using a knowledge-based representation can enable querying a much larger array of questions. In one unified system, once the building and training the KB is complete, we are able to perform tasks such as zero-shot inference of object affordances, estimation of action pose given a visual object, prediction of an object given a likely action, etc. When using the aforementioned naïve approach, we would have trained separate classifiers for each of these tasks, each requiring a different set of training data and labels.

This paper presents a principled way of building a knowledge base (KB) of objects, their attributes, and affordances by extracting information from images as well as online textual sources such as Amazon and eBay. We use a Markov Logic Network (MLN) model [28] to represent the KB. We emphasize that once the KB of objects and their properties are trained, we can perform a number of different inference tasks in a unified framework without any further training. We demonstrate the effectiveness of this representation by testing on a number of sub-tasks related to zero-shot object affordance inference as well as object prediction given human poses. Our system outperforms classifiers trained for each individual sub-task.

2 Previous Work

Object Affordances. While the majority of visual recognition work focus on learning visual appearance based classifiers of objects [12,11,23], there is a growing interest in recognizing object and scene affordances (some call "function-alities") [21,17,15,37,20,22,19]. Winston et al. [34] learn physical descriptions of objects from their functional definitions. Gupta and Davis [18] and Kjellström et al. [21] use the functionality to detect objects. Grabner et al. [17] and Jiang et al. [20] represent affordances by hallucinating humans as the hidden context. Yao et al. [37] represent the functionality of an object based on the majority's human poses during interactions with it. None of the work, however, can predict affordance in novel objects. Furthermore, most of these work predict affordance as a single label whereas we can simultaneously predict affordance label, human pose and relative object location in a unified framework.

Zero-Shot Learning of Objects and Attributes. The classic approach to recognizing unseen objects is based on the visual similarity of the novel object with previously seen examples (e.g. [14,2]). More recently, Lampert et al. [25] introduced a method that recognizes unseen objects by transferring attributes from previously observed classes. Parikh and Grauman [27] extend this work by replacing binary attributes with relative attributes. Rohrbach et al. [29] compare three methods for knowledge transfer: object similarity, attributes, and object hierarchy. Furthermore, they mine attributes from the web to improve the performance of their method. In contrast to these methods, (a) we can predict affordances of unseen objects and infer much richer information beyond visual similarities, and (b) we use a knowledge based approach for reasoning and answering various types of queries, both through images and text.

Knowledge Base Representation. There is a growing trend towards building large-scale knowledge bases with statistical learning methods. NELL [5] learns probabilistic horn clauses by extracting and analyzing information from web text. NEIL [6] is a framework to automatically extract common sense relationships from web images. The *Jeopardy!*-winning DeepQA project [13] proposes a proba-bilistic evidence-based question-answering architecture involving more than 100 different techniques. Similar to this work, StatSnowball [38] and Elementary [26] use Markov Logic Networks [28] as the underlying knowledge representation and perform statistical inference for knowledge base construction. Tran and Davis [33] use Markov Logic Network to model events that contain complex interac-tions of people and vehicles. In contrast to these models, our knowledge base incorporates a wide range of heterogeneous information, allowing us to answer a diverse set of visual and textual queries.

3   Knowledge Base Construction and Representation

We first present our method for constructing a KB that relates objects, their attributes, and their affordances comprised of the three aforementioned compo-nents (affordance labels, human poses and human-object relative locations). To illustrate our idea, we use 40 objects and their properties for constructing the KB. However, our method is scalable to an arbitrary number of objects.

3.1   Overview of the Knowledge Base

A knowledge base (KB) refers to a repository of entities and rules that can be used for problem solving. One can also think of the KB as a graph (similar to Fig. 1), where the nodes denote the entities and the edges, denoting the general rules, characterize their relations.

Entities. The entities in our KB consist of object attributes and affordances. We use three types of attributes to describe an object:

1. **Visual attributes** – correspond to knowledge acquired from visual perception. Inspired by recent work on attribute learning [9,25,27], we define a set of visual attributes as a mid-level description of visual appearance.
2. **Physical attributes** – constitute a form of knowledge from the physical world. Each physical attribute is a measurable quantity that describes one aspect of the object. We select two relevant properties, weight and size, to describe the objects.
3. **Categorical attributes** – reflect a semantic understanding (generalization) of the object. Object categories form a hierarchy consisting of several levels of abstraction [8]. Knowledge of categorical attributes (e.g. a *dog* is an *animal*) often facilitates the ability of affordance reasoning.

These attributes serve as an intermediate representation of objects. This representation allows us to transfer knowledge across objects, and thus to predict the affordances of an object even if it has never seen before, which are represented by three types of entities:

1. **Affordance labels** – a verb or a verb phrase (e.g. *ride* and *sit on*).
2. **Human poses** – an articulated skeleton of human poses.
3. **Huamn-object relative locations** – the spatial relations between the human and the object during a human-object interaction.

General Rules. The general rules describe the relations between the entities. One can think of them as the edges in the knowledge graph. We model three types of relations between these entities:

1. **Attribute-Attribute Relations.** Strong correlations exist between attributes. We model these correlations with *attribute-attribute* relations. Positive weights indicate a positive correlation between two attributes; conversely, negative weights indicate that these attributes are not likely to co-occur.
2. **Attribute-Affordance Relations.** We observe that the affordances of an object are largely dependent upon its attributes (e.g. laptops and umbrellas are *lift-able* because they are not *heavy*). We model these dependency relationships by a set of *attribute-affordance* relations.

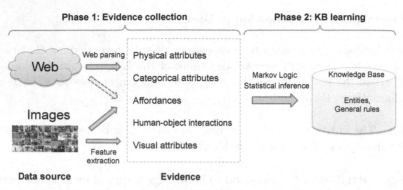

Fig. 2. A system overview of knowledge base learning. This process consists of two phases (Section 3.2). First we collect the evidence from diverse data sources, including images and online text. Then we learn the KB using Markov Logic Network.

3. **Human-Object-Interaction (HOI) Relations.** Humans are likely to interact with different objects in different ways. Furthermore, an object's attributes affect the way that a human interacts with it (e.g. the weight of an object changes the way it is grasped). Therefore, human poses and human-object spatial relations are jointly determined by the object attributes and the affordance. We define four sets of HOI relations to model the correlations (*attribute-pose*, *affordance-pose*, *attribute-location* and *affordance-location*).

3.2   Learning the Knowledge Base

Now that we have defined the entities and rules of the KB, we are ready to learn it from source data. There are two phases in learning the KB. First we collect evidence from diverse sources containing images and online textual sources. Then we employ Markov Logic Network (MLN) [28] for knowledge representation. Fig. 2 is a system overview of the key steps in the learning process. We now elaborate each of these steps below.

Phase 1: Collecting Evidence for KB Construction. A KB is populated by evidence, a set of facts and assertions about the entities. As Fig. 1 and Fig. 2 illustrate, we would like our KB to incorporate a wide range of heterogeneous information, including object attributes, affordances, human poses, etc.

Data source — We choose 40 objects offered by Stanford 40 Actions dataset [36] to seed the KB. For each object, we sample 100 images from the ImageNet dataset [7]. We select 14 affordances from human actions in Stanford 40 Actions. Fig. 3 shows 10 out of the 40 objects and the 14 different affordance labels. On average, each object has 4.25 out of the 14 affordances. Note that, the first four affordances are low-level physical interactions, which are a major interest in the robotics community; while, the rest are daily actions that often involve more complex human-object interaction and demand a higher-level understanding.

Evidence — Given the 40 objects, we are now ready to collect a set of evidence for the KB from the images as well as a number of online sources, such

bicycle
dog
guitar
horse
laptop
pen
shopping cart
small boat
teapot
violin
grasp
lift
throw
push
fix
ride
play
watch
sit on
feed
row
pour from
write with
type on
bicycle
pen
dog
shopping cart
guitar
small boat
horse
teapot
laptop
violin

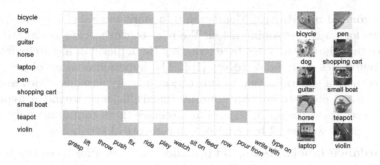

Fig. 3. Object images and affordance labels. We illustrate 10 objects in our KB and their affordance labels. The x-axis lists the 14 affordances and the y-axis provides the names of the 10 objects with sample images on the right. The presence of an affordance is indicated by blue color.

as Freebase [3], WordNet [10] and online shopping sites. For constructing a good KB, we would like the evidence to be diverse, accurate and consistent.

1. **Visual attributes.** Following [9], we choose 33 pre-trained visual attribute classifiers[1] to describe the shape, material and parts of the objects.
2. **Physical attributes.** We extract the real-world weights and real-world sizes of the objects from the *animal synopsis* fields on Freebase [3] and *product details* data from Amazon[2] and eBay[3]. To accommodate the noise in web data, we take the medians of the top K retrieved results as the true values. We quantize the weights into four bins (<1kg, 1–10kg, 10–100kg and >100kg) and the sizes into three bins (<10in, 10–100in and >100in). Fig. 4 shows a list of objects ranked by their weights and the four bins for quantization.

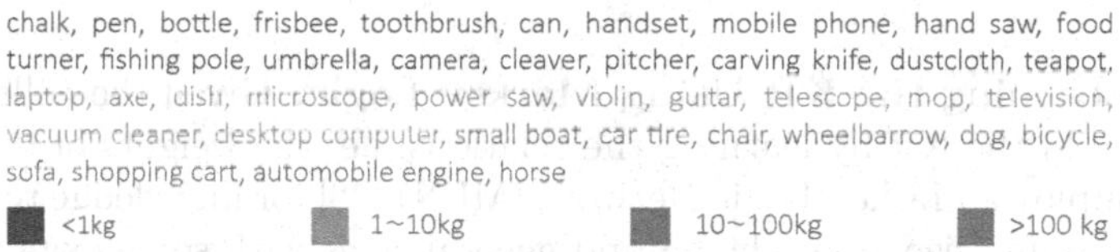

chalk, pen, bottle, frisbee, toothbrush, can, handset, mobile phone, hand saw, food turner, fishing pole, umbrella, camera, cleaver, pitcher, carving knife, dustcloth, teapot, laptop, axe, dish, microscope, power saw, violin, guitar, telescope, mop, television, vacuum cleaner, desktop computer, small boat, car tire, chair, wheelbarrow, dog, bicycle, sofa, shopping cart, automobile engine, horse
<1kg
1~10kg
10~100kg
>100 kg

Fig. 4. (Best viewed in color) Objects ranked by their physical weights. The weights are automatically collected from web sources. The quantization bins are indicated by the font colors. These estimates roughly reflect real-world weights of objects. Some objects (e.g. toothbrush and dustcloth) get larger estimates than expected since they are usually sold in batch on the shopping sites we use as data sources.

---

[1] **Visual attributes:** boxy 2D, boxy 3D, clear, cloth, feather, furn. arm, furn. back, furn. leg, furn. seat, furry, glass, handlebars, head, horiz. cyl., label, leather, metal, pedal, plastic, pot, rein, round, saddle, screen, shiny, skin, tail, text, vegetation, vert. cyl., wheel, wood, wool

[2] `http://www.amazon.com/`

[3] `http://www.ebay.com/`

3. **Categorical attributes.** Membership to more general classes can be informative for object reasoning [24,8]. We refer to this as categorical attributes. We obtain these attributes by extracting the hypernym hierarchy from lexical ontologies such as WordNet [10]. The hypernyms of an object can be regarded as a generalization of this object (e.g. hypernyms of *dog* are *mammal, animal*, etc.). To improve computational efficiency, we merge hypernyms that cover the same set of objects and remove those containing only one object. Finally, we use 22 hypernyms[4] as categorical attributes.

4. **Affordance labels.** As Fig. 3 illustrates, multiple affordance labels are assigned to each object in the KB. For this paper, we provide a manual labeling of the affordances to the 40 objects used for training. But one alternative approach would be to obtain a few canonical affordances is to extract the most frequent verbs associated with a noun phrase in large corpus like Google N-gram (the dashed arrow in Fig. 2).

5. **Human poses.** Human poses can be extracted from human action images in Stanford 40 Actions. Many approaches [35,1,37] have been proposed for this task, yet the state-of-the-art methods fail to perform robustly on images with large variations. To ensure the robustness of our KB in the training phase, we annotate the human poses of the images manually. We compute a pose descriptor based on the tilt angles of body parts (see Fig. 5(a)). The body part descriptors are discretized by k-means. The number of cluster centroids is determined by the Elbow Method. In practice, we choose 3 clusters for torsos, 8 for lower bodies and 8 for upper bodies.

6. **Human-object relative locations.** We extract human-object spatial relations based on the relative locations and sizes of their bounding boxes from human action images. The spatial relations are quantized into five bins: *above, on-top, below, next-to* and *in-hand* (see Fig. 5(b)).

Phase 2: Learning the KB Using Markov Logic. Given the collected evidence, we build the KB by learning the relations, i.e. the weights of the general rules. We employ a Markov Logic Network (MLN) [28] for knowledge representation. Fig. 6 summarizes the schema and general rules with some examples. The idea of MLN is to unify Markov Random Fields (MRF) and first-order logic. Markov Logic is a widely used language in statistical relational learning, which specifies an MRF by a weighted first-order logic knowledge base. Learning and inference in MLN resemble the standard algorithms for MRF, where a ground MRF is first instantiated by the weighted logic formulae. The formulae representing the entities and general rules define the structure of the KB. MLN can be considered as a log-linear model with one node per ground atom and one feature

---

[4] **Categorical attributes:** animal, instrumentality, implement, device, container, tool, equipment, vehicle, machine, wheeled vehicle, vessel, electronic equipment, edge tool, handcart, seat, musical instrument, cooking utensil, computer, scientific instrument, knife, telephone, writing implement

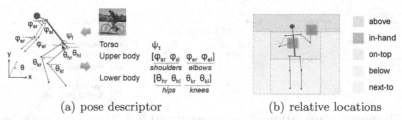

(a) pose descriptor   (b) relative locations

Fig. 5. Pose descriptors and human-object relative locations. (a) Human pose is represented by the tilt angles of body parts. The upper bodies are described by the angles of left and right shoulders and elbows, and the lower bodies by the angles of hips and knees. (b) Relative object locations are represented as quantized bins based on the centers and sizes of their bounding boxes. We use a total of five spatial bins to describe the human-object spatial relations.

Schema	General Rules	Examples
hasAffordance(*object, affordance*)	Attribute-attribute relations	isA(x, Vehicle) ⇒ isA(x, Animal)
isA(*object, category*)		
hasVisualAttribute(*object, attribute*)	Attribute-affordance relations	hasVisualAttribute(x, Furry) ⇒ hasAffordance(x, Feed)
hasWeight(*object, weight*)		hasWeight(x, W4) ⇒ hasAffordance(x, SitOn)
hasSize(*object, size*)		
locate(*object, location*)	Human-object-interaction relations	hasAffordance(x, Ride) ∧ locate(x, Below)
torso(*object, torso_id*)		isA(x, Animal) ∧ locate(x, Below)
upperBody(*object, ubody_id*)		hasAffordance(x, Push) ∧ torso(x, T1)
lowerBody(*object, lbody_id*)		isA(x, Vehicle) ∧ upperBody(x, U3)

Fig. 6. Knowledge base schema and general rules. The arguments in the schema specify the types of the variables. $W2$, $T1$ and $U3$ correspond to the quantized object weight (1–10kg), the first cluster for the torso and the third cluster for the upper body.

per ground formula. The joint distribution over possible worlds x is given by

$$P(X = x) = \frac{1}{Z} \exp \left(\sum_{i=1}^{n} w_i f_i(x_{\{i\}}) \right) \tag{1}$$

where Z is the partition function, F is the set of first-order formulae in MLN and n is the number of formulae in F, $x_{\{i\}}$ is a state of ground atoms appearing in the formula F_i and the feature function $f_i(x_{\{i\}}) = 1$ if $F_i(x_{\{i\}})$ is true and 0 otherwise. The weights w indicate the likelihood of the formulae being true. We learn the optimal weights w^* by maximizing the pseudo-likelihood given the evidence collected in Section 3.2 using the L-BFGS algorithm [28].

3.3   Visualizing the Knowledge Base

Fig. 7 visualizes a part of the constructed knowledge base. In this graph, each node (entity) corresponds to an atomic formula in MLN, and each edge (general rule) corresponds to a first-order logic formula that composes two atomic formulae with logic connectives and quantifiers. The weights of the edges are learned in Markov Logic (Section 3.2), where positive weights indicate that two entities are likely to co-occur (e.g. *furry* and *feed*), and negative weights indicate the entities are negatively correlated (e.g. *fix* and *animal*).

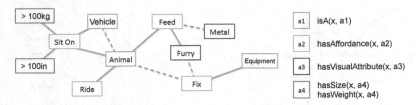

Fig. 7. Graphical illustration of the constructed KB. The nodes denote the entities (atomic formulae in MLN) illustrated on the right. The edges denote the *attribute-attribute* and *attribute-affordance* relations. The green solid edges indicate positive weights and the red dashed edges indicate negative weights.

0.8232 hasVisualAttribute(x, Saddle) ⇒ hasAffordance(x, SitOn)	-1.0682 hasVisualAttribute(x, Metal) ⇒ hasAffordance(x, Feed)
0.7467 hasVisualAttribute(x, Pedal) ⇒ hasAffordance(x, Lift)	-1.0433 hasVisualAttribute(x, Shiny) ⇒ hasAffordance(x, Feed)
0.7155 hasVisualAttribute(x, Screen) ⇒ hasAffordance(x, Fix)	-1.0115 hasVisualAttribute(x, Boxy_3D) ⇒ hasAffordance(x, Feed)
0.7012 hasVisualAttribute(x, Head) ⇒ hasAffordance(x, Feed)	-0.8317 hasVisualAttribute(x, Wheel) ⇒ hasAffordance(x, Feed)
0.6540 hasVisualAttribute(x, Furry) ⇒ hasAffordance(x, Feed)	-0.7987 hasVisualAttribute(x, Text) ⇒ hasAffordance(x, Feed)

(a) Top positive attributes (Visual) | (b) Top negative attributes (Visual)

5.4734 isA(x, Animal) ⇒ hasAffordance(x, Feed)	-3.8636 isA(x, Animal) ⇒ hasAffordance(x, Fix)
3.3196 isA(x, Vehicle) ⇒ hasAffordance(x, Ride)	-2.2209 isA(x, Seat) ⇒ hasAffordance(x, Push)
3.2436 isA(x, Vehicle) ⇒ hasAffordance(x, Row)	-1.8066 isA(x, Vehicle) ⇒ hasAffordance(x, Lift)
2.7976 isA(x, Container) ⇒ hasAffordance(x, PourFrom)	-1.7254 isA(x, Instrumentality) ⇒ hasAffordance(x, Feed)
2.6208 isA(x, Animal) ⇒ hasAffordance(x, SitOn)	-1.3258 isA(x, Instrumentality) ⇒ hasAffordance(x, Fix)

(c) Top positive rules | (d) Top negative rules

Fig. 8. Top weighted attribute-affordance relations. The relations between categorical attributes and affordances have the largest weights, indicating their importance in determining object affordances. For comparison, we also provide the top weighted relations between visual attributes and affordances. The weighted rules can be well interpreted. For instance, the first rule in Fig. 8(b) denotes that "objects that look metal are less likely to be feed-able".

To ensure the quality of the KB, we further examine the weights of general rules learned by MLN statistical inference. Large positive/negative weights indicate a high confidence of the rule being true/false [28]. Fig. 8 lists the top positive and negative weighted attribute-affordance relations. In contrast to visual attributes, categorical attributes serve as a more discriminative semantic-level abstraction, and therefore have larger weights.

4   Affordance Reasoning with KB

Now that we have learned a KB containing rich information about objects, their attributes and affordances, we show in this section a number of experiments to illustrate the effectiveness of this knowledge representation. We emphasize on the word *reasoning*. One of the most important advantages of using a KB representation is to allow for different types of visual and textual queries in a unified framework, as opposed to training separate classifiers for each task. Section 4.1 and Section 4.2 show experimental results for a number of visual tasks. Section 4.3 further explores some important properties of the KB.

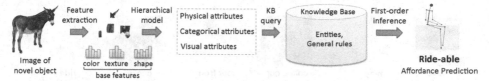

Fig. 9. The inference procedure of zero-shot affordance prediction. Given an image of a novel object, our model estimates the object attributes via a hierarchical model. These attributes serve as evidence for KB queries. We then employ first-order probabilistic inference to predict the affordances and to estimate human poses and human-object relative locations.

4.1   Zero-Shot Affordance Prediction

Given an unseen object, it is often useful to predict its affordances for both humans and robots. We remind readers that by *affordance*, we mean a combination of three pieces of information: an affordance label, the human pose and human-object relative location. We first briefly discuss the inference procedure, the testing data, and then show a number of experimental results.

Inference. Using the constructed KB, we propose a hierarchical model to perform affordance prediction. Given an image of a novel object, our model employs the visual information as cues to object attributes. The model first estimates visual attributes of the object, and infers its physical and categorical attributes. These attributes are taken as evidence to query the affordances and most likely human poses and object relative locations. We use lifted belief propagation for inference [31]. Fig. 9 illustrates an overview of the inference procedure.

Given an image I, we first extract the base features suggested in [9] and predict visual attributes. We then train a L1-regularized logistic regression classifier for each categorical attribute with both base features and visual attributes. Once we obtain the scores of visual and categorical attributes, we map the scores into a binary vector, where the nonzero entries indicate the presence of these attributes.

We predict the physical attributes by learning a ranking function. Based on the physical attributes of the training objects (see Fig. 4), we construct a set $\mathcal{P}_k$ of pairwise preferences where $(i, j) \in \mathcal{P}_k$ indicates i has a larger value than j of the k-th physical attribute. Our goal is to learn a ranking function $R_k(I) = w_k^T \phi(I)$ that attempts to satisfy $R_k(I_i) > R_k(I_j) \; \forall (i, j) \in \mathcal{P}_k$, where w_k is a model parameter and $\phi(I)$ is the base features. We train the model parameters using the ranking SVM formulation in [27]. Given a novel object, we estimate its physical attributes by comparing its ranking scores to the average scores of training objects.

Testing Data. Based on the 40 objects in the KB, we select a different set of 22 semantically similar objects[5] (close synsets in WordNet hierarchy) for testing.

---

[5] **Testing objects:** banjo, bench, bowl, broom, camel, cat, coffee cup, donkey, flagon, hammer, hand truck, kayak, monitor, motorcycle, pencil, rhinoceros, serving cart, sickle, spoon, stool, typewriter, walkie-talkie.

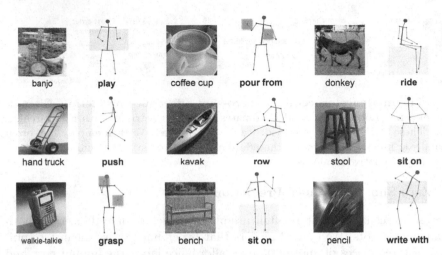

Fig. 10. Results of affordance prediction. We visualize the predicted affordances for a few testing objects. The relative locations are indicated by the color boxes defined in Fig. 5. The first seven examples are correct predictions; while the last two examples fail to match the ground-truth poses/locations.

For each object, we randomly sample 50 images from ImageNet [7]. These images of novel objects are taken as the inputs for affordance prediction.

Result 1: Predicting Affordance Labels. Some results are shown in Fig. 10. Our model can correctly predict the affordances of a novel object given object images from various viewpoints. Besides assigning affordance labels, the model simultaneously estimates the human poses and object relative locations.

For quantitative evaluation, we use the mean *area under the ROC curve* (mAUC) over all the affordances to evaluate the performance of our model (Table 1). We compare our method with two attribute-based classifiers based on previous work [9,25]. From the hierarchical model, we extract the base features and estimate the object attributes. Following [9] and [25], we train linear classifiers with L1-regularized logistic regression and SVMs with a multi-channel χ^2-kernel on four types of features: base features (BF), visual attributes (VA) and categorical & physical attributes (CP) and combined attributes (VA+CP).

Table 1. Performance of Zero-shot Affordance Prediction (measured in mAUC)

Method	L1-LR [9]	χ^2-SVM [25]	Ours
base features (BF)	0.7858	-	-
visual attributes (VA)	0.7525	0.7533	0.7432
categorical & physical (CP)	0.7919	0.7924	0.8234
combined (VA+CP)	0.8006	0.7985	**0.8409**

Our results in Table 1 indicate a combination of features achieve the best performance for the classifiers. In comparison, the knowledge-based model achieves the best performance with a 4% improvement over the best classification-based method. We attribute the better performance of the knowledge-based model to the complex general rules. Such relations can be readily represented in Markov Logic; however, classifiers fail to take the correlations into account.

Result 2: Estimating Human Poses. We now evaluate how our model predicts the poses of its canonical affordance. Each pose can be represented as a triple index $\mathcal{T}$ of the cluster centroids of the torso, lower body and upper body. We compute a Hamming distance between the index and its nearest neighbor in the ground-truth poses:

$$hamming(\mathcal{T}) = \min_{\mathcal{T}' \in P_o \cup \hat{P}_o} \sum_{i=1..3} \mathbb{1}(\mathcal{T}_i = \mathcal{T}_i') \qquad (2)$$

where P_o and its horizontal mirroring $\hat{P}_o$ are the set of ground-truth poses of the canonical affordance of the object, $\mathcal{T}_i$ is an index of the cluster centroid, and $\mathbb{1}(\cdot)$ is an indicator function. This distance metric ranges from 0 to 3, and a smaller value implies a better estimation of the poses.

Table 2. Performance of Estimating Human Poses (in Hamming distance)

Method	nearest neighbor	attributes	affordances	attributes+affordances
Distance	0.928	1.027	0.630	**0.527**

We compare our method with a nearest neighbor baseline, where we assign the canonical affordance and a corresponding human pose of its nearest neighbor to a testing object. The nearest neighbors are defined upon the Euclidean distance between the VA+CP attributes. We report the mean Hamming distance over all the testing samples in Table 2. To see how attributes and affordances affect the performance, we compare it with two methods, where we provide only the attributes and the affordances as evidence respectively. The best performance is achieved by combining affordances and attributes together. However, using affordances alone significantly outperforms its attribute counterpart. This may be due to the limited number of objects in the KB that have a certain affordance; thus in many cases, it is sufficient to predict the poses given the affordance.

4.2 Prediction from Human-Object Interactions

A reverse direction towards affordance prediction is to recognize the action and hypothesize the object in human-object interactions. When actions are seen at a distance and objects appear small, it is hard to observe object's visual attributes. In such cases, human poses and human-object spatial relations provide complementary information. We demonstrate the effectiveness of our KB in predicting the actions and the objects from human-object interactions.

Inference. From human action images, we extract the quantized human poses as evidence and query the affordance labels as well as object attributes. The affordance label with the highest likelihood is taken as the predicted action. We perform Maximum *a posteriori* (MAP) inference on MLN to estimate the most

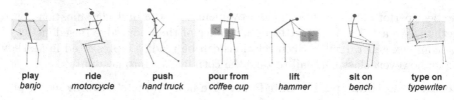

play   ride   push   pour from   lift   sit on   type on
banjo   motorcycle hand truck   coffee cup   hammer   bench   typewriter

Fig. 11. Prediction results from human-object interactions. We provide some examples of correct predictions of the actions and the objects. The last two examples illustrate two similar poses. Both are predicted as *sit on bench* using only the poses. The relative locations in the full model disambiguate those two poses.

likely 0/1 state of each object attribute. The predicted attributes can be used to retrieve the nearest neighbor among all the testing objects in Euclidean distance. We further evaluate how human-object spatial relations affect the performance. The relative locations between humans and objects are extracted from human action images as described in Fig. 5. We add the quantized locations in the evidence and perform the same queries.

Testing Data. We collect five human action images for each of the 22 testing objects from Stanford 40 Actions [36] and Google Image Search. We focus on one canonical affordance (e.g. *riding* for *motorcycle*) for each object.

Results. Fig. 11 provides some prediction results. Our model utilizes the information of the poses and relative locations to predict the actions and the objects.

We use prediction accuracy to quantitatively measure whether the model is able to correctly predict the action and the object in Table 3. One can see that human poses provide useful information about the actions. However, poses alone are sometimes insufficient to characterize an action. Human-object spatial relations disambiguate similar poses and therefore boost the performance. Besides, our model works better in predicting the affordance labels than the objects. In cases where humans interact with objects in similar ways, it is hard to tell apart objects but easier to identify the actions.

Table 3. Predicting Actions and Objects from Human-Object Interactions

Method	Action	Object
human poses	50.4%	46.2%
poses + locations	81.2%	64.5%

4.3   Why KB - Empirical Results

Partial Observation. Humans are proficient in inferring information given a few clues. For instance, people can easily identify a gray, heavy animal with a long trunk as an elephant. The ability of reasoning from partial observation is derived from the knowledge that connects the dots of various concepts together. In this section, we demonstrate the robustness of our model against partial observation.

To evaluate the robustness of our model, we test the performance of our model in affordance prediction given a randomly selected portion of evidence. For comparison, we evaluate the performance of the classification-based method. During testing, a portion of attribute feature dimensions are randomly selected and zeroed out. Fig. 12 depicts how the performance (mAUC) varies as a larger portion of attributes become unobserved.

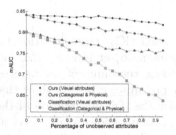

Fig. 12. Performance variations against partial observation. The x-axis denotes the percentage of unobserved evidence. The y-axis denotes the performance (mAUC). The top two curves correspond to our method. The bottom two are the classification-based method. In comparison, the knowledge base representation is more robust against partial observation.

We observe that performance drops significantly as information of categorical and physical attributes get removed; while, both models are relatively robust against the removal of visual attributes. In general, the performance of classification-based model drops more rapidly than the knowledge-based approach. This result provides evidence for KB's ability to utilize its rich structure for inference against partial observations, while there is no such mechanism built in traditional classifiers.

Diverse Question Answering. Compared to the classifiers, a KB representation can enable querying and inferencing of a much larger array of questions. Given a set of weighted MLN formulae, a user may write arbitrary queries in

Question	Evidence	Query	Top Answers
What do animals look like?	isA(N1, **Animal**)	hasVisualAttribute(N1, x)	hasVisualAttribute(N1, **Leather**) hasVisualAttribute(N1, **Head**) hasVisualAttribute(N1, **Tail**) hasVisualAttribute(N1, **Furry**)
I saw something shiny and metallic. What is it?	hasVisualAttribute(N1, **Shiny**) hasVisualAttribute(N1, **Metal**)	isA(N1, x)	isA(N1, **Instrumentality**) isA(N1, **Device**) isA(N1, **Container**) isA(N1, **Computer**)
Here is a vehicle and it's quite heavy. What can I do with it?	isA(N1, **Vehicle**) hasWeight(N1, W4) **(> 100 kg)**	hasAffordance(N1, x)	hasAffordance(N1, **Ride**) hasAffordance(N1, **Row**) hasAffordance(N1, **SitOn**) hasAffordance(N1, **Fix**)
Tell me how heavy and large a wooden musical instrument is.	isA(N1, **Musical_instrument**) hasVisualAttribute(N1, **Wood**)	hasWeight(N1, x) hasSize(N1, x)	hasSize(N1, D2) **(10-100 in)** hasWeight(N1, W2) **(1-10 kg)**

Fig. 13. Examples of question answering. We convert each question into the form of evidence and queries, where $N1$ is used for grounding. Predicates with the highest probabilities computed from MLN inference are presented in the last column as answers to the queries.

terms of the entities and rules. To answer these queries, MLN infers the probability or the most likely state of each query from the evidence. In Fig. 13, we provide examples to show the power of the KB in diverse question answering. Note that in a unified framework, we are able to query with both textual (e.g. *isA*) and visual (e.g. *hasVisualAttribute*) questions. Furthermore, the answers returned by the KB can also be textual (e.g. *hasSize*) or visual (e.g. *hasVisualAttribute*).

5   Conclusion

In this paper, we presented a knowledge-based (KB) representation to reason about objects, and their affordances in human-object interactions, motivated by a need to conduct deeper and more diverse reasoning of the heterogeneous data in the form of images and text. Our preliminary results show that a KB representation is a powerful tool to organize the rich information of the visual world, and to allow us to query different types of questions related to objects and their affordances, compared to a number of traditional classification schemes. A natural future direction is to extend the KB into a much larger scale for richer inferences. In this work, we choose to express our data structure and inference in a Markov Logic Network (MLN). A number of recent advances in database and machine learning [30,32,4] also point ways to different inference algorithms.

Acknowledgement. This work is partially supported by an NSF CAREER grant (IIS-0845230), an ONR MURI grant, the DARPA VIRAT program and the DARPA Mind's Eye program. We would like to thank Kevin Tang, Andrej Karpathy, Justin Johnson and anonymous reviewers for useful comments.

References

1. Andriluka, M., Roth, S., Schiele, B.: Pictorial structures revisited: People detection and articulated pose estimation. In: CVPR (2009)
2. Bart, E., Ullman, S.: Single-example learning of novel classes using representation by similarity. In: BMVC (2005)
3. Bollacker, K., Evans, C., Paritosh, P., Sturge, T., Taylor, J.: Freebase: A collaboratively created graph database for structuring human knowledge. In: ACM SIGMOD International Conference on Management of Data (2008)
4. Bordes, A., Weston, J., Collobert, R., Bengio, Y.: Learning structured embeddings of knowledge bases. In: AAAI Conference on Artificial Intelligence (2011)
5. Carlson, A., Betteridge, J., Kisiel, B., Settles, B., Hruschka Jr., E.R., Mitchell, T.M.: Toward an architecture for never-ending language learning. In: AAAI Conference on Artificial Intelligence (2010)
6. Chen, X., Shrivastava, A., Gupta, A.: Neil: Extracting visual knowledge from web data. In: IEEE International Conference on Computer Vision (2013)
7. Deng, J., Dong, W., Socher, R., Li, L.-J., Li, K., Fei-Fei, L.: Imagenet: A large-scale hierarchical image database. In: IEEE International Conference on Computer Vision (2009)

8. Deng, J., Krause, J., Berg, A.C., Fei-Fei, L.: Hedging your bets: Optimizing accuracy-specificity trade-offs in large scale visual recognition. In: Computer Vision and Pattern Recognition (2012)
9. Farhadi, A., Endres, I., Hoiem, D., Forsyth, D.: Describing objects by their attributes. In: Computer Vision and Pattern Recognition (2009)
10. Fellbaum, C.: Wordnet: An electronic lexical database. Bradford Books (1998)
11. Felzenszwalb, P., McAllester, D., Ramaman, D.: A discriminatively trained, multiscale, deformable part model. In: CVPR (2008)
12. Fergus, R., Fei-Fei, L., Perona, P., Zisserman, A.: Learning object categories from google's image search. In: ICCV (2005)
13. Ferrucci, D., Brown, E., Chu-Carroll, J., Fan, J., Gondek, D., Kalyanpur, A.A., Lally, A., Murdock, J.W., Nyberg, E., Prager, J., Schlaefer, N., Welty, C.: Building watson: An overview of the deepqa project. AI Magazine (2010)
14. Fink, M.: Object classification from a single example utilizing class relevance pseudo-metrics. In: NIPS (2004)
15. Fouhey, D.F., Delaitre, V., Gupta, A., Efros, A.A., Laptev, I., Sivic, J.: People watching: human actions as a cue for single view geometry. In: Fitzgibbon, A., Lazebnik, S., Perona, P., Sato, Y., Schmid, C. (eds.) ECCV 2012, Part V. LNCS, vol. 7576, pp. 732–745. Springer, Heidelberg (2012)
16. Gibson, J.J.: The Ecological Approach to Visual Perception. Houghton Mifflin, Boston (1979)
17. Grabner, H., Gall, J., Gool, L.V.: What makes a chair a chair? In: CVPR (2011)
18. Gupta, A., Kembhavi, A., Davis, L.S.: Observing human-object interactions: using spatial and functional compatibility for recognition. PAMI (2009)
19. Gupta, A., Satkin, S., Efros, A., Hebert, M.: From 3d scene geometry to human workspace. In: CVPR (2011)
20. Jiang, Y., Koppula, H.S., Saxena, A.: Hallucinated humans as the hidden context for labeling 3d scenes. In: CVPR (2013)
21. Kjellstrom, H., Romero, J., Kragic, D.: Visual object action recognition: inferring object affordances from human demonstration. In: CVIU (2010)
22. Koppula, H.S., Saxena, A.: Anticipating human activities using object affordances for reactive robotic response. In: Robotics: Science and Systems (RSS) (2013)
23. Krizhevsky, A., Sutskever, I., Hinton, G.E.: Imagenet classification with deep convolutional neural networks. In: NIPS (2012)
24. Kuettel, D., Guillaumin, M., Ferrari, V.: Segmentation propagation in imagenet. In: European Conference on Computer Vision (2012)
25. Lampert, C.H., Nickisch, H., Harmeling, S.: Learning to detect unseen object classes by between-class attribute transfer. In: CVPR (2009)
26. Niu, F., Zhang, C., Ré, C., Shavlik, J.: Elementary: Large-scale knowledge-base construction via machine learning and statistical inference. In: International Journal on Semantic Web and Information Systems - Special Issue on Web-Scale Knowledge Extraction (2012)
27. Parikh, D., Grauman, K.: Relative attributes. In: International Conference on Computer Vision (2011)
28. Richardson, M., Domingos, P.: Markov logic networks. Machine Learning 62(1-2), 107–136 (2006)
29. Rohrbach, M., Stark, M., Schiele, B.: Evaluating knowledge transfer and zero-shot learning in a large-scale setting. In: CVPR (2011)
30. Singh, A.P., Gordon, G.J.: Relational learning via collective matrix factorization. In: ACM SIGKDD International Conference on Knowledge Discovery and Data Mining (2008)

31. Singla, P., Domingos, P.: Lifted first-order belief propagation. In: AAAI Conference on Artificial Intelligence (2008)
32. Socher, R., Chen, D., Manning, C.D., Ng, A.Y.: Reasoning with neural tensor networks for knowledge base completion. In: Conference on Neural Information Processing Systems (2013)
33. Tran, S.D., Davis, L.S.: Event modeling and recognition using markov logic networks. In: Forsyth, D., Torr, P., Zisserman, A. (eds.) ECCV 2008, Part II. LNCS, vol. 5303, pp. 610–623. Springer, Heidelberg (2008)
34. Winston, P.H., Binford, T.O., Katz, B., Lowry, M.: Learning physical descriptions from functional definitions, examples, and precedents. In: AI Memos (1982)
35. Yang, Y., Ramanan, D.: Articulated pose estimation with flexible mixtures of parts. In: CVPR (2011)
36. Yao, B., Jiang, X., Khosla, A., Lin, A.L., Guibas, L., Fei-Fei, L.: Human action recognition by learning bases of action attributes and parts. In: IEEE International Conference on Computer Vision (2011)
37. Yao, B., Ma, J., Fei-Fei, L.: Discovering object functionality. In: ICCV (2013)
38. Zhu, J., Nie, Z., Liu, X., Zhang, B., Wen, J.-R.: Statsnowball: a statistical approach to extracting entity relationships. In: International World Wide Web Conference (2009)

Binary Codes Embedding
for Fast Image Tagging with Incomplete Labels

Qifan Wang*, Bin Shen*, Shumiao Wang, Liang Li, and Luo Si

Department of Computer Science
Purdue University
West Lafayette, IN 47907-2107, USA
{wang868,bshen,wang845,li900,lsi}@purdue.edu

Abstract. Tags have been popularly utilized for better annotating, organizing and searching for desirable images. Image tagging is the problem of automatically assigning tags to images. One major challenge for image tagging is that the existing/training labels associated with image examples might be incomplete and noisy. Valuable prior work has focused on improving the accuracy of the assigned tags, but very limited work tackles the efficiency issue in image tagging, which is a critical problem in many large scale real world applications. This paper proposes a novel Binary Codes Embedding approach for Fast Image Tagging (BCE-FIT) with incomplete labels. In particular, we construct compact binary codes for both image examples and tags such that the observed tags are consistent with the constructed binary codes. We then formulate the problem of learning binary codes as a discrete optimization problem. An efficient iterative method is developed to solve the relaxation problem, followed by a novel binarization method based on orthogonal transformation to obtain the binary codes from the relaxed solution. Experimental results on two large scale datasets demonstrate that the proposed approach can achieve similar accuracy with state-of-the-art methods while using much less time, which is important for large scale applications.

Keywords: Image Tagging, Binary Codes, Hashing.

1 Introduction

The purpose of image tagging, assigning tags or keywords to images, is to benefit people for managing, organizing and searching desired images from various resources. For example, Flickr has more than 2 billion images with millions of newly uploaded photos per day. Users can better categorize or search desired images based on the tags associated with them. Due to the rapid growth of the Internet, a huge amount of images have been generated and users can only manually tag a very small portion of the images. Therefore, it is a challenging task to automatically assigning accurate tags to images for large scale data.

---

* The two authors contributed equally to this work.

D. Fleet et al. (Eds.): ECCV 2014, Part II, LNCS 8690, pp. 425–439, 2014.

Numerous research have been conducted on improving the accuracy of image tagging, such as automatic image annotation techniques [28,31] and multi-label learning [3,10]. Although these methods generate promising results of effectively assigning tags to image examples, they usually require a large set of training images with clean and complete tags/labels. But for many Web image applications, the annotated tags are incomplete and noisy, making it difficult to directly apply these methods for image tagging. Several tag completion [2,14,30] methods have been recently proposed to deal with incomplete and noisy tags, which achieve better results in terms of tag predicting accuracy by modeling global tag consistency. However, most existing methods only focus on the effectiveness without paying much attention to efficiency. In real world applications, the data size grows explosively and there are often a large number of possible tags and thus it is a practical and important research problem to design efficient methods for large scale image tagging.

This paper proposes a novel Binary Codes Embedding approach for Fast Image Tagging (BCE-FIT) by designing compact binary codes for both image examples and tags. In particular, each image example is represented by a C-bit binary code and each tag is also represented using a C-bit binary code. Our key ideas of constructing the binary codes are that *(1) if a tag is associated to an image, then the Hamming distance between their corresponding binary codes should be small; (2) two similar images should have similar codes; (3) the codes of two semantically similar tags should also be similar.* We then formulate the problem of learning binary codes as a discrete optimization problem by simultaneously ensuring the observed tags to be consistent with the constructed binary codes and preserving the similarities between image examples and tags. An iterative optimization method together with a novel binarization method is proposed to obtain the optimal binary codes. In tag predicting process, we calculate the Hamming distances between the code of a query image and the codes of all possible tags, and choose those tags within small Hamming distance to the query image. The Hamming distances between the binary codes of images and tags can be efficiently calculated using the bitwise XOR operation. In this way, assigning tags to images can be efficiently conducted.

We summarize the contributions in this work as follows: (1) To our best knowledge, we propose the first research work to learn compact binary codes for both images and tags in order to efficiently assigning tags to image examples. (2) We propose a learning framework to obtain the optimal binary codes and develop an efficient coordinate descent method as the optimization procedure. (3) We prove the orthogonal invariant property of the optimal relaxed solution and learn an orthogonal matrix to further improve the code performance.

2   Related Work

2.1   Image Tagging

Image tagging can be viewed as a multi-label learning problem where each image is associated with multiple tags. Numerous work have been proposed on multi-label learning for automatic image annotation and classification by exploiting the dependence among tags [1,3,10,28]. Desai et al. [6] propose a discriminative structured prediction model for multi-label object recognition. Hariharan et al. [10] introduce a max-margin framework for large scale multi-label classification. In [3], Chen et al. propose an efficient multi-label classification method using hypergraph regularization. Bao et al. [1] formulate a scalable multi-label propagation framework for image annotation. Liu et al. [17] propose a constrained nonnegative matrix factorization method for multi-label learning.

Besides the multi-label learning methods, several machine learning approaches have been proposed for image tagging, including tag propagation [9,19], distance metric learning [12] and tag recommendation [23]. Li et al. [12] propose a neighbor voting algorithm for social tagging which accurately and efficiently learns tag relevance by accumulating votes from visual neighbors. A tag propagation (TagProp) method has been proposed in [9] which propagates tag information from the labeled examples to the unlabeled examples via a weighted nearest neighbor graph. Makadia et al. [19] propose a widely-used annotation baseline denoted as JEC, which is a straightforward but sophisticated greedy algorithm propagating labels from nearest visual neighbors to the target image. Zhou et al. [32] develop a hybrid probabilistic model for unified collaborative and content based image tagging.

Image tag completion [2,14,24,30] methods have been recently proposed for image tagging task by recovering the missing entries in the tag matrix. Cabral et al. [2] propose two convex algorithms for matrix completion based on a rank minimization criterion. Wu et al. [30] introduce a direct tag matrix completion algorithm by ensuring the completed tag matrix to be consistent with both the observed tags and the visual similarity. Lin et al. [14] propose a image-specific and tag-specific linear sparse reconstruction model for automatic image tag completion. Although existing image tagging methods generate promising results, very limited prior research addresses the efficiency problem, which is a practical and critical issue in many large scale real world applications.

2.2 Learning Binary Codes

Extensive research on learning binary codes for fast similarity search [5,8,25,26] have been proposed in recent years. Locality Sensitive Hashing (LSH) [5] method utilizes random linear projections to map data examples from a high-dimensional Euclidean space to a low-dimensional one. The work in [21] uses stacked Restricted Boltzman Machine (RBM) to generate compact binary hashing codes for fast similarity search of documents. The PCA Hashing (PCAH) [13] method projects each example to the top principal components of the training set, and then binarizes the coefficients by setting a bit to 1 when its value is larger than the median value seen for the training set, and -1 otherwise.

Recently, Spectral Hashing (SH) [29] is proposed to learn compact binary codes that preserve the similarity between data examples by balancing the binary codes. The work in [15] proposes a graph-based hashing method to automatically discover the neighborhood structure inherent in the data to learn appropriate compact codes. A Canonical Correlation Analysis with Iterative Quantization (CCA-ITQ) method has been proposed in [7,8] which treats the image features and tags as two different views. The hashing function is then learned by extracting a common space from these two views. More recently, a bit selection method [16] has been proposed to select the most informative hashing bits from a pool of candidate bits generated from different hashing methods.

Existing hashing methods focus on constructing binary codes on images for fast similarity search and can not be directly applied for fast assigning tags to images. The reason is that image tagging requires to design compact binary codes for both image examples and tags. Therefore, different from prior work, we propose a binary codes embedding approach for fast image tagging which learns binary codes for both image examples and tags simultaneously.

3   Binary Codes Embedding for Fast Image Tagging

3.1   Problem Setting and Overview

We first introduce the problem of BCE-FIT. Assume there are total n training images in the dataset, denoted as: $x_i, i \in \{1, 2, \ldots, n\}$, where x_i is the d-dimensional feature of the i-th image. There are total m possible tags denoted as: $t_j, j \in \{1, 2, \ldots, m\}$. Denote the observed tag matrix as: $T \in \{0, 1\}^{n \times m}$, where a label $T_{ij} = 1$ means the j-th tag is assigned to the i-th image, and $T_{ij} = 0$ means a missing tag or the i-th image is not associated with the j-th tag. Note that the i-th row of T is the tag vector associated with image x_i. In our approach, the training tags could be noisy and incomplete, which is the case in real world applications. The main purpose of BCE-FIT is to obtain optimal binary codes $y_i \in \{-1, 1\}^{C \times 1}, i \in \{1, 2, \ldots, n\}$ for the training images and $z_j \in \{-1, 1\}^{C \times 1}, j \in \{1, 2, \ldots, m\}$ for all possible tags, where C is the code length. We also want to learn a hashing function $f : R^d \rightarrow \{-1, 1\}^C$, which maps each image x_i to its binary code y_i (i.e., $y_i = f(x_i)$).

The proposed BCE-FIT approach is a general learning framework and we first describe the problem formulation of how to construct the objective function. Then we represent the optimization method to obtain the optimal binary codes and the hashing function. Fig.1 shows an example of the proposed approach.

3.2   Problem Formulation

The goal of image tagging is to automatically assign tags to both training images and query images. Three main ingredients of constructing the compact binary codes are: (1) if a tag t_j is assigned to an image x_i, then their corresponding binary codes z_j and y_i should be similar; (2) visually similar images x_i and x_j should have similar codes y_i and y_j; and (3) semantically similar tags, e.g. 'human' vs. 'people', t_i and t_j should also have similar codes z_i and z_j. The similarity between two binary codes can be measured based on their normalized Hamming distance as follows:

$$s(y_i, z_j) = 1 - \frac{1}{C} dist_{Ham}(y_i, z_j) = \frac{1}{2} + \frac{y_i^T z_j}{2C} \tag{1}$$

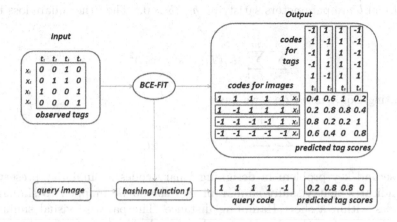

Fig. 1. An example of the proposed BCE-FIT. In this example, there are 4 training images ($n = 4$) with 4 possible tags ($m = 4$). 5 bits are used to represent the binary codes ($C = 5$). The predicted tag score is the similarity between the binary code of an image and a tag, which is calculated based on the normalized Hamming distance in Eqn.1. For the query image in this example, we will assign tags t_2 and t_3 to the query image since the corresponding tag scores are relatively high (0.8).

where $dist_{Ham}$ is the Hamming distance between two binary codes, which is just the number of bits that they differ. It can be seen from Eqn.1 that the smaller the Hamming distance is, the more similar their binary codes become. Note that the similarity between two binary codes is a real value between 0 and 1.

The first key problem in designing binary codes is to ensure the consistency between the observed tags and the constructed binary codes. Specifically, we propose to minimize the squared loss of the observed tags and the similarity estimated from the binary codes, which is a commonly used loss function in many machine learning applications.

$$\sum_{i=1}^{n} \sum_{j=1}^{m} (T_{ij} - s(y_i, z_j))^2 \tag{2}$$

As discussed before, $T_{ij} = 0$ can be interpreted in two ways that tag T_{ij} is missing or the i-th image is not related to the j-th tag, which indicates that $T_{ij} = 1$ contains more useful information than a tag with value 0. Therefore, an importance matrix $I \in R^{n \times m}$ is introduced to denote the confidence of how we trust tag information in tag matrix T. We set I_{ij} to a higher value when $T_{ij} = 1$ than $T_{ij} = 0$ as follows:

$$I_{ij} = \begin{cases} a, & if \ T_{ij} = 1 \\ b, & if \ T_{ij} = 0 \end{cases} \tag{3}$$

where a and b are parameters satisfying $a > b > 0$.[1] Then the square loss term becomes:

$$\sum_{i=1}^{n}\sum_{j=1}^{m} I_{ij}(T_{ij} - s(y_i, z_j))^2 \tag{4}$$

Substituting Eqn.1 into Eqn.4 we have:

$$\sum_{i=1}^{n}\sum_{j=1}^{m} I_{ij}(T_{ij} - \frac{1}{2} - \frac{y_i^T z_j}{2C})^2 \tag{5}$$

The second key problem in designing binary codes is similarity preserving, which indicates that visually similar images should be mapped to similar binary codes within a short Hamming distance. The pairwise visual similarity, S_{ij}, between two images x_i and x_j can be pre-calculated as:

$$S_{ij} = e^{-\frac{\|x_i - x_j\|^2}{\sigma^2}} \tag{6}$$

where σ^2 is the bandwidth parameter. Note that we use the Gaussian function/kernel to calculate the similarity in this work due to its popularity in many hashing methods [29,27], but other similarity criteria may also be used, such as cosine similarity or inner product similarity. To measure the similarity between images represented by the binary codes, one natural way is to minimize the follow quantity:

$$\sum_{i,j=1}^{n} (s(y_i, y_j) - S_{ij})^2 \tag{7}$$

The third criteria in designing binary codes is to ensure that semantically similar tags have similar codes. For example, we wish that the binary hashing codes for tags 'car' and 'automobile' be as close as possible since these two tags represent similar semantic meaning. In the extreme case, if two tags t_i and t_j appear in exactly the same set of images, i.e. the column i and j of tag matrix are identical, their binary codes should also be identical. However, since the tag information might be incomplete, we only assume that semantically similar tags tend to appear in the same image. Therefore, in order to measure the semantical similarity between two tags t_i and t_j, we use the number of images that are commonly shared by both tags, which can be calculated as: $\frac{T_i^T T_j}{m}$. Here T_i is the i-th column of tag matrix T. Dividing m is to normalize this quantity from 0 to 1. Then the similarity preservation between tags represented by the binary codes can be measured as:

$$\sum_{i,j=1}^{m} (s(z_i, z_j) - \frac{T_i^T T_j}{m})^2 \tag{8}$$

---

[1] In our experiments, we set the importance parameters a=1 and b=0.01 consistently throughout all experiments.

The entire objective function of the proposed BCE-FIT approach consists of three components: the square loss of tag consistency term in Eqn.4 and two similarity preservation term given in Eqn.7 and 8 as follows:

$$\min_{y,z} \quad \sum_{i=1}^{n}\sum_{j=1}^{m} I_{ij}(T_{ij} - s(y_i, z_j))^2$$

$$+\alpha \sum_{i,j=1}^{n} (s(y_i, y_j) - S_{ij})^2 + \beta \sum_{i,j=1}^{m} (s(z_i, z_j) - \frac{T_i^T T_j}{m})^2 \qquad (9)$$

$$s.t. \quad y_i, z_j \in \{-1, 1\}^{C\times 1}, \quad \sum_{i=1}^{n} y_i = 0 \quad \sum_{j=1}^{m} z_j = 0$$

where α and β are trade-off parameters. The constraints $\sum_{i=1}^{n} y_i = 0$ and $\sum_{j=1}^{m} z_j = 0$ are the bit balance constraints, which are equivalent to maximizing the entropy of each bit of the binary codes to ensure each bit carrying as much information as possible.

3.3 Optimization Algorithm

Relaxation. Directly minimizing the objective function in Eqn.9 is intractable since it is a constrained discrete optimization problem which is NP-hard to solve [29]. Therefore, we propose to relax the balance constraints into soft penalty terms and then relaxing the space of solution to $[-1, 1]^{C\times 1}$. Then the relaxed objective function becomes:

$$\min_{\tilde{y},\tilde{z}} \quad \sum_{i=1}^{n}\sum_{j=1}^{m} I_{ij}(T_{ij} - \frac{1}{2} - \frac{\tilde{y}_i^T \tilde{z}_j}{2C})^2$$

$$+\alpha \sum_{i,j=1}^{n} (\frac{1}{2} + \frac{\tilde{y}_i^T \tilde{y}_j}{2C} - S_{ij})^2 + \beta \sum_{i,j=1}^{m} (\frac{1}{2} + \frac{\tilde{z}_i^T \tilde{z}_j}{2C} - \frac{T_i^T T_j}{m})^2 \qquad (10)$$

$$+\gamma (\| \sum_{i=1}^{n} \tilde{y}_i \|^2 + \| \sum_{j=1}^{m} \tilde{z}_j \|^2)$$

$$s.t. \quad \tilde{y}_i, \tilde{z}_j \in [-1, 1]^{C\times 1}$$

where γ is a trade-off parameter. $\| \sum_{i=1}^{n} \tilde{y}_i \|^2$ and $\| \sum_{j=1}^{m} \tilde{z}_j \|^2$ are soft penalty terms converted from the bit balance constraints. However, even after the relaxation, the objective function is still non-convex with respect to $\tilde{y}$ and $\tilde{z}$ jointly, which makes it difficult to optimize. Fortunately, this relaxed problem is differentiable with respect to either one of the two sets of parameters when the other one is fixed, and therefore we propose to solve the problem by coordinate descent method. In particular, we alternatively update $\tilde{y}$ and $\tilde{z}$ while fixing the other set of parameters by doing the following two steps until convergence.

Step 1: Fix $\tilde{y}$, Optimize $\tilde{z}$. By taking the partial derivative of Eqn.10 with respect to $\tilde{z}_j$, we can obtain the gradient and LBFGS method is then applied for solving this optimization problem to obtain optimal $\tilde{z}$.

Step 2: Fix $\tilde{z}$, Optimize $\tilde{y}$. Similar to step 1, we use LBFGS method to solve for the optimal $\tilde{y}$ using the gradient of Eqn.10 with respect to $\tilde{y}_i$.

Due to the space limitation, we will provide the two gradients in supplemental material. We alternate the process of updating $\tilde{y}$ and $\tilde{z}$ for several iterations to find a locally optimal solution. In practice, we have found that a reasonable small number of iterations can achieve good performance.

Binarization. After obtaining the optimal real value solution $\tilde{y}$ and $\tilde{z}$ for the relax problem, we need to binarize them to obtain binary hashing codes y and z. A direct binarization method is to obtain binary codes y and z that are closest to $\tilde{y}$ and $\tilde{z}$. In particular, we seek to minimize the quantization error between the binary codes and the relaxed solution as follow:

$$\min_{y,z} \sum_i \|y_i - \tilde{y}_i\|^2 + \sum_j \|z_j - \tilde{z}_j\|^2 \tag{11}$$
$$s.t. \quad y_i, z_j \in \{-1, 1\}^{C \times 1}$$

which leads to the close form solution:

$$y_i = sgn(\tilde{y}_i), \quad z_j = sgn(\tilde{z}_j) \tag{12}$$

where $sgn()$ is the signum function of a real value vector.

In this work, we propose a novel binarization method that improves the quantization error through an orthogonal transformation by making use of the structure of the relaxed solution. We first prove the following theorem.

Theorem 1. *Assume Q is a $C \times C$ orthogonal matrix, i.e., $Q^T Q = I$. If $\tilde{y}$ and $\tilde{z}$ are an optimal solution to the relaxed problem Eqn.10, then $Q\tilde{y}$ and $Q\tilde{z}$ are also an optimal solution.*

Proof. By substituting $Q\tilde{y}$ and $Q\tilde{z}$ into Eqn.10, we have $\sum_{i,j} I_{ij}(T_{ij} - \frac{1}{2} - \frac{(Q\tilde{y}_i)^T Q\tilde{z}_j}{2C})^2 = \sum_{i,j} I_{ij}(T_{ij} - \frac{1}{2} - \frac{\tilde{y}_i^T \tilde{z}_j}{2C})^2$. Similarly, the value of the second and third terms will also not change. $\|\sum_i Q\tilde{y}_i\|^2 = \|Q \sum_i \tilde{y}_i\|^2 = \|\sum_i \tilde{y}_i\|^2$ and $\|\sum_j Q\tilde{z}_j\|^2 = \|Q \sum_j \tilde{z}_j\|^2 = \|\sum_j \tilde{z}_j\|^2$. We also have that $Q\tilde{y}, Q\tilde{z} \in [-1, 1]^{C \times 1}$. Thus, the value of the objective function in Eqn.10 does not change by the orthogonal transformation.

Based on the above observation, we propose to binarize $\tilde{y}$ and $\tilde{z}$ by minimizing the quantization error between the binary hashing codes and the orthogonal transformation of the relaxed solution as follow:

$$\min_{y,z,Q} \sum_i \|y_i - Q\tilde{y}_i\|^2 + \sum_j \|z_j - Q\tilde{z}_j\|^2 \tag{13}$$
$$s.t. \quad y_i, z_j \in \{-1, 1\}^{C \times 1}, \quad Q^T Q = I$$

Note that the direct binarization method can be achieved by simply setting $Q = I$. The intuitive idea behind this method is that the orthogonal transformation not only preserves the optimality of the relaxed solution but also provides us more flexibility to achieve more effective hashing codes with low quantization error. Similar ideas have also been investigated in other applications such as [8] for applying orthogonal transformation for only images in similarity search. However, our new research not only applies orthogonal transformation for images but also for tags. The above optimization problem can be solved by minimizing Eqn.13 with respect to y, z and Q alternatively.

Fix Q, update y and z. The close form solution can be expressed as:

$$y_i = sgn(Q\tilde{y}_i), \; z_j = sgn(Q\tilde{z}_j) \tag{14}$$

Fix y and z, update Q. The objective function becomes:

$$\min_{Q^T Q = I} \sum_i \|y_i - Q\tilde{y}_i\|^2 + \sum_j \|z_j - Q\tilde{z}_j\|^2 \tag{15}$$

Let $Y = [y_1, y_2, \ldots, y_n]$ and $Z = [z_1, z_2, \ldots, z_m]$. Then the above objective function can be rewritten to:

$$
\begin{aligned}
\min_{Q^T Q = I} \;& \|Y - Q\tilde{Y}\|_F^2 + \|Z - Q\tilde{Z}\|_F^2 \\
= \;& \|Y\|_F^2 + \|\tilde{Y}\|_F^2 + \|Z\|_F^2 + \|\tilde{Z}\|_F^2 \\
& - trace((Y\tilde{Y}^T + Z\tilde{Z}^T)Q^T)
\end{aligned}
\tag{16}
$$

which is equivalent to:

$$\max_{Q^T Q = I} trace((Y\tilde{Y}^T + Z\tilde{Z}^T)Q^T) \tag{17}$$

here $trace()$ is the matrix trace function and $\|\|_F$ is the matrix *Frobenius* norm. In this case, the objective function is essentially a variant of classic Orthogonal Procrustes problem [22], which can be solved efficiently by singular value decomposition using the following theorem (we refer to [22] for the detailed proof).

Theorem 2. *Let $U\Lambda V^T$ be the singular value decomposition of $Y\tilde{Y}^T + Z\tilde{Z}^T$. Then $Q = UV^T$ minimizes the objective function in Eqn.15.*

We then perform the above two steps alternatively to obtain the optimal binary codes y and z. After obtaining the binary codes, we can assign tags to images by calculating the predicted tag score using Eqn.1 (see figure 1).

In order to deal with the out-of-example problem in image tagging, where we need to generate binary codes for query images. A linear hashing function is used to map the image examples into binary codes as:

$$y_i = f(x_i) = sgn(Hx_i) \tag{18}$$

Algorithm 1. Binary Codes Embedding for Fast Image Tagging (BCE-FIT)

Input: Images X, Observed tag matrix T
Output: Hashing codes y and z, Hashing function H
 1: Initialize $\tilde{y}$ and Q
 2: **repeat**
 3:     Update $\tilde{z}$ in **Step 1**.
 4:     Update $\tilde{y}$ in **Step 2**.
 5: **until** the solution converges
 6: **repeat**
 7:     Update y and z using Eqn.14
 8:     Update $Q = UV^T$ according to Theorem 2.
 9: **until** the solution converges
10: Obtain hashing function H using Eqn.18.

---

where H is a $C \times d$ parameter matrix representing the hashing function. Then the optimal hashing function can be directly obtained by minimizing $\sum_i (\tilde{y}_i - Hx_i)^2 + \lambda\|H\|_F^2$, where λ is a weight parameter for the regularization term to avoid overfitting and $X = [x_1, x_2, \ldots, x_n]$ is the data feature matrix. The full learning algorithm is described in Algorithm 1.

3.4 Analysis

The optimization algorithm of (BCE-FIT) consists of two main loops. In the first loop, we iteratively optimize over $\tilde{z}$ and $\tilde{y}$ to obtain the optimal relaxed solution, where the time complexities for updating $\tilde{z}$ and $\tilde{y}$ are bounded by $O(nC^2 + nmC)$ and $O(nmC + nC)$ respectively. The second loop iteratively optimizes the binary hashing codes and the orthogonal transformation matrix, where the time complexities for updating y, z and Q are bounded by $O(nC^2 + mC^2 + C^3)$. Thus, the total time complexity of the learning algorithm is bounded by $O(nmC + nC + nC^2 + mC^2 + C^3)$, which scales linearly with n given $n \gg m > C$. For each query, the time for obtaining its binary code is constant $O(Cd)$.

4   Experiments

4.1   Datasets and Implementation

We conduct our experiments on two large scale datasets, *Flickr1m* [11] and *NUS-WIDE* [4]. *Flickr1m* is collected from Flicker images for image annotation and retrieval tasks. This benchmark contains 1 million image examples associated with more than $7k$ unique tags. A subset of $250k$ image examples with the most common $2k$ tags is used in our experiment by filtering out those images with less than 10 tags. 512-dimensional GIST descriptors [20] are used as image features. We randomly choose $240k$ image examples as training set and $10k$ for testing. *NUS-WIDE* [4] is created by NUS lab, which contains $270k$ images associated with $5k$ unique tags. We use the most common $2k$ tags in our experiment. We

Table 1. Performance of different algorithms with varying number of training tags on both datasets with 32 hashing bits

Flickr1m	AP@10					AP@20				
training tags	2	4	6	8	10	2	4	6	8	10
BCE-FIT	65.4	**68.9**	71.1	73.4	77.4	65.2	66.3	**70.4**	71.6	74.5
LSR[14]	**66.3**	68.6	**71.7**	**76.2**	**79.5**	**65.4**	**66.9**	69.3	**72.1**	**75.3**
TMC[30]	62.9	64.1	66.8	71.7	73.4	57.2	61.8	62.7	66.4	70.1
LM3L[10]	60.4	65.8	68.3	71.6	74.7	58.5	62.0	65.8	68.7	70.8
CCA-ITQ[7,8]	55.2	57.5	59.7	61.1	64.6	53.3	55.2	56.3	57.8	60.2
SH[29]	53.7	55.3	57.5	58.4	60.7	52.4	53.8	55.1	55.6	57.5
NUS-WIDE	AP@10					AP@20				
training tags	2	4	6	8	10	2	4	6	8	10
BCE-FIT	51.1	56.2	63.4	71.7	74.5	48.4	54.2	**61.8**	**70.2**	75.1
LSR[14]	**51.7**	**56.5**	**66.4**	**72.5**	**76.7**	**49.2**	**54.6**	59.4	67.5	**76.4**
TMC[30]	48.3	53.1	61.4	72.0	73.6	46.6	51.7	58.4	62.9	67.7
LM3L[10]	47.6	53.4	59.1	70.6	74.0	47.2	52.0	58.1	60.5	64.8
CCA-ITQ[7,8]	46.8	51.5	57.7	61.4	65.2	44.3	47.1	50.6	55.8	59.0
SH[29]	43.2	47.0	52.9	56.8	58.3	40.7	43.8	47.2	51.5	56.1

also filter out those images with less than 10 tags, resulting in a subset of $110k$ image examples. 500-dimensional visual features are extracted using a bag-of-visual-word model with local SIFT descriptor [18]. We randomly partition this dataset into two parts, $10k$ for testing and around $100k$ for training.

We implement our method using Matlab on a PC with Intel Duo Core i5-2400 CPU 3.1GHz and 8GB RAM. The parameters α, β and γ are tuned by cross validation on the training set and we will discuss how they will affect the performance of our approach later in detail. We repeat each experiment 10 times and report the result based on the average over the 10 runs. Each run adopts a random separation of the dataset.

4.2   Results and Discussion

The proposed BCE-FIT approach is compared with five state-of-the-art methods, including three non-hashing methods TMC [30], LM3L [10] and LSR [14], and two hashing methods CCA-ITQ [7,8] and SH [29]. For LM3L, we use linear kernels in this method to obtain fair comparison. For CCA-ITQ, the tags are treated as a different view and a common space is then learned between tags and images to form the hashing codes. For SH, the observed labels are viewed as the similarities between images and tags and a bipartite graph is constructed between nodes representing images and tags. Then, spectral hashing is applied to obtain binary codes for images and tags based on this graph. Four sets of experiments are conducted on both datasets to evaluate the effectiveness and efficiency of the proposed BCE-FIT for image tagging.

Table 2. Training time and testing time (sec) for different methods on both datasets. The length of hashing code is fix to 32 for all hashing methods.

method	Flickr1m		NUS-WIDE	
	training	testing	training	testing
BCE-FIT	232	1.23	86.45	0.38
LSR[14]	337	24.31	108	7.39
TMC[30]	837	5.36	528	2.57
LM3L[10]	489	23.52	154	7.86
CCA-ITQ[7,8]	254	1.23	91.83	0.37
SH[29]	198	1.22	79.44	0.38

In the first set of experiments, we evaluate the performance of different algorithms by varying the number of training tags. In particular, we vary the number of training tags for each image from $\{2, 4, 6, 8, 10\}$. We then rank the tags based on their relevance scores (Eqn.1) and return the top K ranked tags. We use the average precision (AP@K) of top 10 and 20 ranked tags as the evaluation metric. Table 1 summarizes the results for different methods. Note that for all hashing methods in this set of experiments, we fix the length of hashing codes to be 32. It is not surprising to see that the performance of all methods improve with the increasing number of training tags. From these comparison results, we can also see that BCE-FIT achieves similar or comparable accuracy results to the non-hashing methods and substantially outperforms the other hashing methods. Our hypothesis is that both CCA-ITQ and SH only focus on encoding the consistency of the binary codes to the observed tags without preserving the visual similarities among the image examples and the semantical similarities among tags, which tend to over fit. On the other hand, the proposed BCE-FIT constructs binary codes by simultaneously ensuring the learned codes to be consistent with observed tags and preserving the similarity between images and

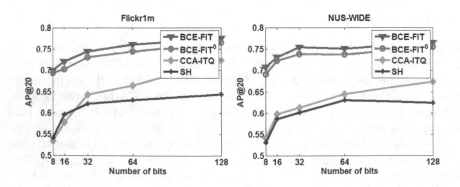

Fig. 2. Results of image tagging by varying number of hashing bits on two datasets

tags, which indicates that BCE-FIT generates more effective codes and predicts tags accurately. We also evaluate the precision and recall behavior of different methods. Due to the space limitation, we will include the precision and recall results in supplemental material.

In the second set of experiments, we evaluate the efficiency of different methods on both datasets. The training time and tag prediction time are reported in Table 2. We also fix the hashing bits to be 32 for all hashing methods. From the reported results, it is clear that image tagging process of hashing methods is 20 to 25 times faster than multi-label learning method LM3L, tag sparse reconstruction method LSR and tag matrix completion method TMC. The reason is that hashing methods use binary codes to calculate the tag relevance scores, which only involves efficient bit-wise operations XOR, while these non-hashing methods need to deal with real value vectors to compute the tag scores. We also observe that the training time of our method is comparable with other hashing methods and is much faster than TMC since the learning algorithm of TMC is quite involved with multiple terms.

In the third set of experiments, we evaluate the effectiveness of all hashing methods on both datasets by varying the number of hashing bits. We fix the number of training tags to be 10 in our experiments. We also compare our BCE-FIT with direct binarization method from Eqn.12 and call this $BCE-FIT^0$. The comparison results are reported in Fig.2. It is clear that the proposed BCE-FIT substantially outperforms other hashing methods on all different number of hashing bits. We can also observe that the binarization method with orthogonal transformation is consistently better than directly binarizing method. This is because BCE-FIT generates more effective hashing codes with lower quantization error than $BCE-FIT^0$ through orthogonal transformation, which preserves the optimality of the relaxed solution.

The fourth set of experiments study the performance of BCE-FIT with respect to the parameters α, β and γ. To prove the robustness of the proposed method, we conduct parameter sensitivity experiments on both datasets. In each experiment, we tune only one parameter from $\{0.5, 1, 2, 4, 8, 16, 32, 128\}$, while

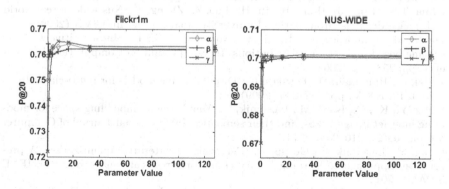

Fig. 3. Parameter Sensitivity for α, β and γ. Results of average precision with 32 hashing bits.

fixing the other two to the optimal values obtained from the first set of experiments. We report the results on *Flickr1m* and *NUS-WIDE* in Fig.3. It is clear from these experimental results that the performance of BCE-FIT is relatively stable with respect to α, β and γ.

5   Conclusion

This paper proposes a novel Binary Codes Embedding approach for Fast Image Tagging (BCE-FIT) by designing compact binary hashing codes for both images and tags. We formulate the problem of learning binary hashing codes as a discrete optimization problem by simultaneously ensuring the observed tags to be consistent with the constructed hashing codes and preserving the similarities between images and tags. An efficient coordinate descent method is developed as the optimization procedure. Extensive experiments on two large scale datasets demonstrate that the proposed approach can achieve comparable performance with state-of-the-art methods while using much less time. There are several possible directions to explore in the future research. For example, we plan to apply some sequential learning approach to accelerate the training speed of our method.

Acknowledgments. This work is partially supported by NSF research grants IIS-0746830, DRL-0822296, CNS-1012208, IIS-1017837, CNS-1314688 and a research grant from Office of Naval Research (ONR-11627465). This work is also partially supported by the Center for Science of Information (CSoI), an NSF Science and Technology Center, under grant agreement CCF-0939370.

References

1. Bao, B.K., Ni, B., Mu, Y., Yan, S.: Efficient region-aware large graph construction towards scalable multi-label propagation. Pattern Recognition 44(3), 598–606 (2011)
2. Cabral, R.S., la Torre, F.D., Costeira, J.P., Bernardino, A.: Matrix completion for multi-label image classification. In: NIPS, pp. 190–198 (2011)
3. Chen, G., Zhang, J., Wang, F., Zhang, C., Gao, Y.: Efficient multi-label classification with hypergraph regularization. In: CVPR, pp. 1658–1665 (2009)
4. Chua, T.S., Tang, J., Hong, R., Li, H., Luo, Z., Zheng, Y.: Nus-wide: a real-world web image database from national university of singapore. In: CIVR (2009)
5. Datar, M., Immorlica, N., Indyk, P., Mirrokni, V.S.: Locality-sensitive hashing scheme based on p-stable distributions. In: Symposium on Computational Geometry, pp. 253–262 (2004)
6. Desai, C., Ramanan, D., Fowlkes, C.: Discriminative models for multi-class object layout. In: ICCV, pp. 229–236 (2009)
7. Gong, Y., Ke, Q., Isard, M., Lazebnik, S.: A multi-view embedding space for modeling internet images, tags, and their semantics. International Journal of Computer Vision 106(2), 210–233 (2014)
8. Gong, Y., Lazebnik, S., Gordo, A., Perronnin, F.: Iterative quantization: A procrustean approach to learning binary codes for large-scale image retrieval. IEEE TPAMI (2012)
9. Guillaumin, M., Mensink, T., Verbeek, J.J., Schmid, C.: Tagprop: Discriminative metric learning in nearest neighbor models for image auto-annotation. In: ICCV, pp. 309–316 (2009)

10. Hariharan, B., Zelnik-Manor, L., Vishwanathan, S.V.N., Varma, M.: Large scale max-margin multi-label classification with priors. In: ICML, pp. 423–430 (2010)
11. Huiskes, M.J., Thomee, B., Lew, M.S.: New trends and ideas in visual concept detection: the mir flickr retrieval evaluation initiative. In: Multimedia Information Retrieval, pp. 527–536 (2010)
12. Li, X., Snoek, C.G.M., Worring, M.: Learning social tag relevance by neighbor voting. IEEE Transactions on Multimedia 11(7), 1310–1322 (2009)
13. Lin, R.S., Ross, D.A., Yagnik, J.: Spec hashing: Similarity preserving algorithm for entropy-based coding. In: CVPR, pp. 848–854 (2010)
14. Lin, Z., Ding, G., Hu, M., Wang, J., Ye, X.: Image tag completion via image-specific and tag-specific linear sparse reconstructions. In: CVPR, pp. 1618–1625 (2013)
15. Liu, W., Wang, J., Kumar, S., Chang, S.F.: Hashing with graphs. In: ICML, pp. 1–8 (2011)
16. Liu, X., He, J., Lang, B., Chang, S.F.: Hash bit selection: A unified solution for selection problems in hashing. In: CVPR, pp. 1570–1577 (2013)
17. Liu, Y., Jin, R., Yang, L.: Semi-supervised multi-label learning by constrained non-negative matrix factorization. In: AAAI, pp. 421–426 (2006)
18. Lowe, D.G.: Distinctive image features from scale-invariant keypoints. IJCV 60(2), 91–110 (2004)
19. Makadia, A., Pavlovic, V., Kumar, S.: A new baseline for image annotation. In: Forsyth, D., Torr, P., Zisserman, A. (eds.) ECCV 2008, Part III. LNCS, vol. 5304, pp. 316–329. Springer, Heidelberg (2008)
20. Oliva, A., Torralba, A.: Modeling the shape of the scene: A holistic representation of the spatial envelope. IJCV 42(3), 145–175 (2001)
21. Salakhutdinov, R., Hinton, G.E.: Semantic hashing. Int. J. Approx. Reasoning 50(7), 969–978 (2009)
22. Schonemann, P.: A generalized solution of the orthogonal procrustes problem. Psychometrika 31(1), 1–10 (1966)
23. Toderici, G., Aradhye, H., Pasca, M., Sbaiz, L., Yagnik, J.: Finding meaning on youtube: Tag recommendation and category discovery. In: CVPR, pp. 3447–3454 (2010)
24. Wang, Q., Ruan, L., Zhang, Z., Si, L.: Learning compact hashing codes for efficient tag completion and prediction. In: CIKM, pp. 1789–1794 (2013)
25. Wang, Q., Si, L., Zhang, D.: Learning to hash with partial tags: Exploring correlation between tags and hashing bits for large scale image retrieval. In: Fleet, D., Pajdla, T., Schiele, B., Tuytelaars, T. (eds.) ECCV 2014, Part I. LNCS, vol. 8691, pp. 378–392. Springer, Heidelberg (2014)
26. Wang, Q., Si, L., Zhang, Z., Zhang, N.: Active hashing with joint data example and tag selection. In: SIGIR (2014)
27. Wang, Q., Zhang, D., Si, L.: Semantic hashing using tags and topic modeling. In: SIGIR, pp. 213–222 (2013)
28. Wang, S., Jiang, S., Huang, Q., Tian, Q.: Multi-feature metric learning with knowledge transfer among semantics and social tagging. In: CVPR, pp. 2240–2247 (2012)
29. Weiss, Y., Torralba, A., Fergus, R.: Spectral hashing. In: NIPS, pp. 1753–1760 (2008)
30. Wu, L., Jin, R., Jain, A.K.: Tag completion for image retrieval. IEEE Trans. Pattern Anal. Mach. Intell. 35(3), 716–727 (2013)
31. Zheng, J., Jiang, Z.: Tag taxonomy aware dictionary learning for region tagging. In: CVPR, pp. 369–376 (2013)
32. Zhou, N., Cheung, W.K., Qiu, G., Xue, X.: A hybrid probabilistic model for unified collaborative and content-based image tagging. IEEE Trans. Pattern Anal. Mach. Intell. 33(7), 1281–1294 (2011)

Recognizing Products: A Per-exemplar Multi-label Image Classification Approach

Marian George and Christian Floerkemeier

Department of Computer Science
ETH Zurich, Switzerland

Abstract. Large-scale instance-level image retrieval aims at retrieving specific instances of objects or scenes. Simultaneously retrieving multiple objects in a test image adds to the difficulty of the problem, especially if the objects are visually similar. This paper presents an efficient approach for per-exemplar multi-label image classification, which targets the recognition and localization of products in retail store images. We achieve runtime efficiency through the use of discriminative random forests, deformable dense pixel matching and genetic algorithm optimization. Cross-dataset recognition is performed, where our training images are taken in ideal conditions with only one single training image per product label, while the evaluation set is taken using a mobile phone in real-life scenarios in completely different conditions. In addition, we provide a large novel dataset and labeling tools for products image search, to motivate further research efforts on multi-label retail products image classification. The proposed approach achieves promising results in terms of both accuracy and runtime efficiency on 680 annotated images of our dataset, and 885 test images of GroZi-120 dataset. We make our dataset of 8350 different product images and the 680 test images from retail stores with complete annotations available to the wider community.

1 Introduction

Many image classification techniques try to recognize the object classes present in the image through training multiple binary classifiers or a multi-class classifier using a large number of training images. Improving the performance of such algorithms requires learning the model using as many images as possible that are drawn from the same distribution as the test images [29]. However, in many real-world applications, we face the challenge that the testing images are taken in completely different settings than the training images. For example, in the domain of assisting the visually impaired, or vision for mobile robots, images are very likely to suffer from blur, specularities, unusual viewing angles, a lot of background clutter and very different lighting conditions. Gathering and labeling images that try to mimic the natural environments for which the system is used, is a tedious and very time-consuming task.

Recently, image recognition in the retail products domain has become an interesting research topic due to the remarkable advancements in the capabilities

D. Fleet et al. (Eds.): ECCV 2014, Part II, LNCS 8690, pp. 440–455, 2014.

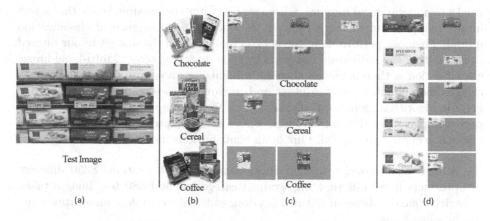

Fig. 1. System overview: (a) Given a test image, (b) we first filter the categories that the test image may belong to, (c) then we match the test image against all images in the filtered categories. (d) An energy function is then optimized given the top-ranked matches to obtain the final list, along with inferred locations, of recognized products.

of mobile phones and mobile vision systems [27,30]. A mobile vision algorithm to recognize products in an image has a wide range of potential applications, ranging from identifying individual products to provide review and price information, to the assisted navigation in supermarkets. Furthermore, mobile retail products recognition can assist the visually impaired in shopping, encouraging them to independently perform daily activities, which promotes their social wellness.

Building a system that parses an image featuring several retail products taken with a smart phone introduces several challenges. This includes the cross-dataset recognition challenges mentioned earlier. Product images available through on-line shopping websites are taken in ideal studio-like conditions, which are very different from real life images taken with mobile phones in shops, as illustrated in figure 2. These challenges are aggravated when having only one image per product for training and thousands of products (labels) to match against. Due to the increasing number of new products every day, the system also needs to be scalable with no or minimal retraining whenever a new product is introduced. To be applicable in the visually impaired domain, the designed scheme cannot rely on any feedback from the user in improving the retrieved results. The system has to work in a completely autonomous manner. Recognizing grocery products, in particular, is challenging as there are multiple products that have very similar visual appearance except for minor features like the color of the package, or some text describing the product. Finally, runtime efficiency is crucial for mobile vision systems, which makes semantic segmentation or sliding window detection approaches computationally expensive for our problem.

To this end, we designed an efficient per-exemplar multi-label image classification technique (as shown in figure 1) which targets simultaneous recognition and localization of all the individual products in a retail store image. Our algorithm works in a hierarchical manner, where we first filter the possible labels that a test image may contain through ranking the output of a fine-grained classification model. Then, we perform fast dense pixel matching on the images in our filtered list, and rank the individual products by their matching score. Multi-label image classification is then achieved through minimizing an energy function that correlates the matching score, context and recognition localization results through genetic algorithm global optimization. Our proposed approach is evaluated in a per-exemplar cross-dataset settings, where we show promising results in terms of both accuracy and speed. Our main contributions include:

- A large-scale novel retail products dataset, which contains 8350 different products in 80 different fine-grained categories, and 680 test images taken with a smart phone in natural environments with complete annotations and labeling tools.
- A fast technique to simultaneously recognize and localize all retail products in a test image, which scales to thousands of different labels.
- Automatically infer the total number and approximate locations of objects present in a test image in a single optimization round, unlike other more expensive object detection techniques.
- Experimental evaluation of our proposed system with an analysis of its different components, showing promising results.

2   Related Work

General-purpose object detection and recognition techniques [10,11,24] have been extensively used in image classification and retrieval problems. Some approaches [4] use binary classifiers trained on bag-of-words features [4] or compressed Fisher Vectors [25] to obtain a binary decision whether an object class is present or absent in a given test image. Hamming embedding[14] provides binary signatures that refine the matching based on visual words. It has been very successful in instance-level image retrieval domain. Others [11,7] try to detect and localize object classes in the image through extracting dense features like HOG [5] features and apply sliding window detectors or deformable part-based models [11]. However, these techniques require a large number of labeled training examples, which makes them unsuitable for classes with sparse examples.

Other approaches explore fine-grained image classification [3,26] to capture discriminative image regions that distinguish between different classes. In [1], randomization and discrimination are combined in a computationally efficient scheme to achieve fine-grained classification in a large feature space.

Multi-label image classification [17,34,16] differs from multi-class recognition [28] in that a single image is classified using multiple labels. Multi-label classification usually incorporates modelling the correlation between the labels, which significantly boosts the semantic classification performance [16]. In [35], Genetic Algorithm optimization is utilized for filtering the selected features, which are then used for classification. Unlike us, they rely on multi-label training data.

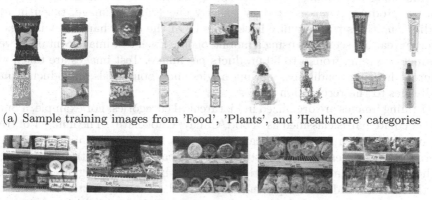

(a) Sample training images from 'Food', 'Plants', and 'Healthcare' categories

(b) Sample testing images from our collected dataset

Fig. 2. Sample images from our collected dataset

There have been relatively limited research attempts to recognize products in images [27,30,15,20,33]. In systems like [15,20], a product image search engine is built. However, these systems deal with recognizing only one product per image, with training images having similar conditions to query images. In [27], cross-dataset single product recognition is targeted through query object segmentation combined with iterative retrieval. They achieve good results in searching an image that contains only a single product. In our work, however, we target multi-products image parsing.

A related dataset to our proposed one is presented in [22], however the dataset size is much smaller than ours with only 120 grocery products in the training set. Each product category represents a single specific product (i.e. no hierarchies or classes of products). In [27], a sports product image dataset is collected. Both the training images and 67 query images contain a single product per image. Other existing object datasets include Caltech 101 [9], Caltech 256 [13], and VOC [8] datasets, which target more general-purpose object category recognition. Fine-grained object datasets include Oxford Flower [23], and Stanford Dogs [18] dataset. We run our experiments on our proposed dataset, as well as the one presented in [22].

In the following sections, we first present our proposed novel dataset in section 3. Then, we detail our approach in section 4. Experimental results and performance evaluation are discussed in section 5. Finally, conclusions and future work are summarized in section 6.

3 Grocery Products Dataset

We built a new supermarket products dataset, which can be used in multi-label, fine-grained cross-dataset object recognition. Our dataset consists of 8350 training images spanning 80 product categories, downloaded from the Web. Each grocery product is represented by exactly one training image, taken in ideal studio conditions with a white background. On the other hand, test images are taken in real-life scenarios using a mobile phone. Each test image contains several products, ranging from 6 to 30 products per image. Test images are taken with different lighting conditions, viewing angles and zoom levels, introducing many challenges to the recognition process.

Training images are organized in hierarchical categories. For example, a Snickers chocolate bar is classified as "Food/Candy/Chocolate". The number of training images in each fine-grained category ranges from 25 to 415 images, with an average of 112 different retail products in each category – one training image for each product. We added an additional label for background regions. The images for the background label represent shelves and price tags, extracted from test images. Examples of training images are shown in figure 2 (a).

Grocery products introduce many challenges to the object recognition problem. First, many products have similar appearance, with only minor differences in the color of the package, size of the package, or some text on the box. Also, non-planar products, like bottles or jars, lower the matching performance, considering that we only have one training image per product. Furthermore, evaluation images contain very little background regions, which makes it a rather challenging task to recognize every single product in the image. This is due to the fact that other regions in the image represent confusing background clutter relative to the specific region of each object.

One of the main goals of this work is to investigate cross-dataset multi-label image classification. Accordingly, our evaluation set is collected in completely different conditions from the training set. A total of 680 images are taken in different grocery stores covering the different classes in the training dataset. Testing images impose additional challenges, like specularities, different viewing angles, rotated or occluded products as shown in figure 2 (b).

We ran our experiments on 27 classes of the "Food" category products in addition to the background class, which represents shelves and price tags, with a total number of 3235 images. Deformable objects, like nuts bags, chips and bakery are included in the "Food" category of our datast. To evaluate the performance of our algorithm, we annotated 680 test images with all the products from the 27 training classes. The ground truth of each test image specifies bounding boxes with a corresponding single product label for each bounding box. A single bounding box covers a group of instances of the same product in a test image as shown in figure 3.

4   Exemplar-Based Multi-label Image Classification

In this section, we describe the design and implementation details of our algorithm. Figure 1 shows an overview of our system. Our proposed technique consists of three main steps. The first two steps filter the best matching products to a given test image through two successive ranking procedures. The third

Fig. 3. Sample test images with ground truth annotations from our proposed dataset

step simultaneously localizes and infers the total number of objects present in the test image through globally minimizing an energy function.

Although we are going to use specific algorithms for each step of our pipeline, any other algorithm that fits to a single step can be applied. For example, we used discriminative decision trees for multi-class ranking, but it would suffice to use SVM or k-NN for classification. Similarly, we can use any matching algorithm for the second step of our pipeline like SIFT flow or sparse features matching.

4.1   Multi-class Ranking

To reduce our search space from thousands of possible matches to tens up to a few hundreds of images, we train a classification model using the given training images, and then use a voting scheme, explained below, to retrieve the top-ranked object classes.

For training, we use the recently proposed discriminative random forests [1] technique. The training set contains a single image for each product with a total number of 3235 images in 27 classes. We extract dense SIFT feature descriptors [21] on each image with a spacing of four pixels, with five patch sizes: 8, 12, 16, 24 and 30. Visual vocabulary codebook of 256 code words is then constructed using k-means. Descriptors are assigned to code words using Locality-constrained Linear Coding (LLC) [31].

To retrieve the top ranked object classes for a given test image, we designed a voting algorithm, which first divides the test image into grids with different sizes. We, then, classify each grid region separately using the trained model. We gather votes for each class in the trained model by counting the number of grid segments belonging to that class. For each test image, we return the top k classes.

Our proposed class ranking technique handles two important challenges faced in cross-dataset object recognition, specifically in the products recognition domain. First, each object in the test image is surrounded by many other objects that have very similar features, which can easily confuse the classifier. By dividing the image into patches of different sizes, we limit such confusion. Second, by collecting the total number of votes for grids, we lower the impact of regions in the image suffering from difficult imaging conditions in affecting the final classification decision.

In the experiments section, we detail the parameters used for multi-ranking, and we show how the multi-label ranking performance is improved through gathering votes over grid patches rather than classifying the whole image once.

4.2   Fast Dense Pixel Matching

To achieve simultaneous recognition and localization of specific object instances in each test image, we apply fast dense pixel matching through deformable spatial pyramid matching [19]. No training is required to perform this step. Furthermore, it contributes to the scalability of our system, in such a way that adding new specific objects to the dataset does not require retraining the random forests step, as long as these objects fall under one of the pre-existing classes.

The goal is to rank the images in terms of appearance agreement while enforcing geometrical smoothness between neighboring pixels. The matching objective can be expressed formally by minimizing the energy function [19]:

$$E(t) = \sum_i D_i(t_i) + \alpha \sum_{i,j \in N} V_{ij}(t_i, t_j), \tag{1}$$

where D_i is a data term which measures the average distance between local descriptors within node i in the first image to those located within a region in the second image after shifting by t_i. V_{ij} is a smoothness term, α is a constant weight, and N denotes pairs of nodes linked by graph edges. The energy function is minimized using loopy belief propagation. Training images are scaled to 200x200 pixels, and test images are scaled to 600x450 pixels. We use the mean difference of dense color SIFT feature descriptors of patch size of 4 as our data term. In all the experiments, the value of α was fixed at 0.005 following [19].

A segmentation mask is obtained specifying the inferred location of every pixel in each matched image with respect to the current test image. The matching costs, along with the segmentation masks are used in the next step of our pipeline to produce the final multi-labeling results as explained in section 4.3.

4.3   A Genetic Algorithm-Based Multi-label Image Classification

Once we obtain a ranked list of matching correspondences, we then consider only the top N images, which will be in the range of very few tens of images, to obtain our final multi-labeling results. We formulate our problem in a genetic algorithm (GA) optimization model [12]. The quality of a given solution is determined using a fitness function, which is the objective function to be minimized using GA.

To define our multi-label image classification objective function, let q be our current test image. We want to find the $L \subset N$ images that minimize the following energy function:

$$E(L) = \alpha \sum_{l \in L} D_{lq}(l, q) + \beta U_{Lq}(L, q) + \gamma C_L, \tag{2}$$

where D_{lq} is the data term between image $l \in L$ and the current test image q, U_{Lq} is the uncoverage term, which measures the proportion of pixels not covered

(a)   (b)

Fig. 4. Sample (a) training and (b) testing images from Grozi-120 dataset

by any image l in L when the whole set is warped to q. Finally, our context term C_L models the prior knowledge about the co-occurrence of recognized products in the query image. α, β, and γ are weight parameters.

We chose our data term D_{lq} to measure the mean difference between the dense SIFT descriptors between the two images, as defined by [19]. We experimented with adding other features like normalized RGB color histogram. However, the performance was worse with global color, where most products are colorful, and the lighting conditions of test images are very different from training images.

The coverage term U_{Lq} penalizes results that do not cover a big proportion of the test image. If we define S_{lq} to be the set of non-overlapping pixels in q covered by l when warped to q, then U_{Lq} can be defined as:

$$U_{Lq}(L,q) = 1 - \frac{1}{z} \sum_{l \in L} |S_{lq}|, \tag{3}$$

where z is the total number of pixels in the test image q, and $|S_{lq}|$ is the cardinality of the set S_{lq}. This, again, helps in overcoming the challenge of having multiple database images with very similar visual appearance. Such images will all be ranked as top matches, but for only one object in the test image. Just taking the top ranked results, would then yield very poor coverage of the objects present in the test image.

The context term C_L models the prior probability that the labels which appear in the final retrieved set of images occur together. In other multi-label classification approaches, this knowledge is usually inferred from the training images. In our case, this knowledge cannot be obtained from the training images, as each image in our training set contains only a single product. We overcome this problem through utilizing the hierarchical structure of our solution. We model the prior distribution such that images (or labels) which fall under the same category are more likely to occur together than those which fall in different categories. The probability of co-occurrence is higher for more restrictive categories than for broader categories.

$$C_L = 1 - \sum_{l_i, l_j \in L} \tilde{P}(l_i, l_j), \tag{4}$$

where $\tilde{P}(l_i, l_j)$ is the prior distribution over the pairwise co-occurence of labels.

The overall energy function in Eq. 2 is globally minimized using constrained genetic algorithm (GA) [12]. We represent the population of possible solutions as a binary vector of length N, where each element represents the decision of inclusion for each image in the set. We used the "ga" method provided in the Matlab Global Optimization Toolbox. To constrain the type of children that the algorithm creates at each step to be binary, we implemented special creation, crossover, and mutation functions [6].

5   Experimental Results

Datasets: We evaluated the performance of our approach on two datasets:

1. 680 annotated test images from the proposed **"Grocery Products"** dataset, with a total number of 3235 products in 27 leaf node classes. Test images contain products of all subcategories in the "Food" category ranging from 6 to 30 product items per image. Regions in the test images which contain objects that do not belong to the database are given a null label.
2. 885 extracted test images from **GroZi-120** [22] dataset. There is a total of 676 training images representing 120 grocery products. Each product is represented by 2-14 training images with an average of 5.6 images. There are no classes of products (i.e. each class has only one specific product). The originally provided test images were unsuitable, since each image contains a single product item. No shelves images were provided. We, instead, extracted video frames from the provided 29 video files, each representing the whole frame as shown in figure 4. Each test image contains 4-15 grocery product items. Training images are downloaded from the web in ideal conditions, while test images are taken in grocery stores with different conditions.

Implementation Details: We trained 100 trees with a maximum depth of 10. We gathered votes for each test image over 57 patches of 5 different grid sizes. The motivation behind choosing these values is explained in section 5.4. The values of the parameters for the energy function (defined in Eq. 2): α, β and γ are optimized using coordinate descent as detailed in section 5.2.

Evaluation Metrics: We measure the performance of our proposed system using three metrics: mean average precision (mAP), mean average product recall (mAPR), and mean average multi-label classification accuracy (mAMCA) [2]. We chose non-standard measures because standard measures usually address the performance of single-instance retrieval. mAP is measured by computing the average precision over all test images for different values of the number of top matched images (n) that we consider in the matching step, and then the mean is taken over all values of n (ranging from 5 to 70). Averaging helps to capture the joint precision-recall performance. We count groups of specific products in a test image not individual product items (figure 3). We measure the mAPR by computing the average labeling performance (recall) of the retail product items present in an image, and then the mean is computed across all images. To

Table 1. Multi-label image classification performance for baseline labeling, different versions of our system, and state-of-the-art classification and retrieval techniques

Method	mAP(%)	mAMCA(%)	mAPR(%)
Baseline [19]	13.53	11.77	37.33
Full	23.49	21.19	43.13
without global optimization	16.93	15.07	43.36
with ground truth ranking	42.56	38.02	45.63
ground truth ranking without global optimization	30.7	27.8	68.5
FV(1024 dim)	8.62	6.41	20.73
FV(4096 dim)	11.26	9.95	22.14
FV(4096 dim) + RANSAC	12.3	10.1	24.5
HE(k=200000, h_t=22)	4.26	3.96	12.13

compute mAMCA over the test dataset D, suppose Y_x is the set of ground truth labels for test image x, and P_x is the set of prediction labels. We can define the multi-label score for image x as $score(P_x) = \frac{|Y_x \cap P_x|}{|Y_x \cup P_x|}$, and

$$accuracy_D = \frac{1}{|D|} \sum_{x \in D} score(P_x), \tag{5}$$

To analyze the performance of our multi-class ranking approach, we, also, use two measures: mean average recall (mAR) per-class and mean average accuracy (mAA) over the test images. We vary K, i.e. the number of predicted classes from 1 to the total number of classes, and measure the true positive and false positive rates accordingly.

In the next sections, we first perform quantitative and qualitative evaluation of our system (Sec. 5.1). We perform in-depth analysis of our GA optimization in Sec. 5.2. Results on the GroZi-120 dataset are reported in Sec. 5.3. Finally, multi-class ranking and runtime efficiency are discussed in Sec. 5.4 and Sec. 5.5.

5.1 Multi-label Image Classification Performance

To evaluate the performance of our proposed approach, we vary the number of predicted classes of the multi-class ranking (K) from 1 to the total number of classes and report the mAMCA and mAPR values on different variants of our system (see table 1): (1) full system (Full), (2) our system without performing global optimization (i.e. retreive all the n top-ranked images from the dense pixel matching results on the k top-ranked class categories), (3) our system if we have perfect ranking performance of the multi-class ranking step, and (4) ground truth ranking without performing global optimization. We compare the performance of our algorithm to state-of-the-art classification and instance-level image retrieval techniques, Fisher Vectors [25] (FV) and Hamming Embeddings [14] (HE). For FV, we use 1024 and 4096 dim. encodings without PCA. We, also, compare to FV (4096 dim) with Geometric Consistency Checks with RANSAC

Fig. 5. Examples of two multi-label classification results. Left column shows the test image, then the retrieved products, and finally their inferred locations in the test image.

re-ranking on the top 100 images. For HE, we use $k = 200,000$ visual words for building the bag-of-words histogram representation which was shown to yield good performance and we use a fixed Hamming threshold $h_t = 22$ following [14]. Finally, we compare to the baseline method of ranking all the images by just dense pixel matching score [19] and taking the top n matches.

Our full system achieves 23.49% mAP and 21.19% mAMCA over all the 680 test images, which outperforms the baseline method by over 9%. Our method also significantly performs better than other state-of-the-art approaches. FV and HE are efficient algorithms which achieve impressive precision on other benchmarks. However, for our case, the distribution of the training data from which the GMM model is built (for FV), or the BOF dictionary is built (for HE) is significantly different from the data distribution of the test set. In addition, these methods are better suited for general rather than fine-grained object recognition.

We also show the performance results if we run our dense pixel matching ranking and global optimization steps using the images of the ground truth classes (i.e., we assume that the multi-label ranking step gives a perfect ranking of predicted categories for each test image). This yields a substantial improvement in the mAP and mAMCA, which shows that our system's performance could be further improved by experimenting with different classification techniques. When evaluating the system, the parameters are optimized for maximizing the precision and accuracy of recognition. Accordingly, the recall performance is not much improved given the chosen values of the parameters. Showing the improvement of precision for the same achieved recall values gives an indication of how ground truth ranking can improve the performance of the system.

To verify the impact of our global optimization step, we report results when we pick the top n-ranked images from the matching step as our final multi-label classification result without any global optimization. We have two cases: (1) with random forests model ranking, and (2) with ground truth ranking. We notice that the mAMCA degrades by more than 6%, as more irrelevant images appear in the final result. In case of ground truth ranking, our system still performs better with global optimization.

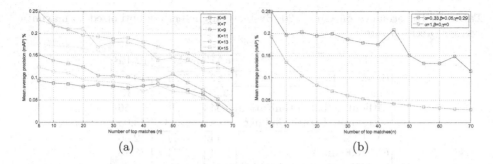

Fig. 6. (a) Mean average precision as a function of the total number of matches (n) for different values of the number of filtered classes (K). (b) Mean average precision as a function of the total number of top matches (n) when turning on (and off) the GA optimization. Our GA step significantly yields better performance.

In figure 5, we show sample results from running our full system on different test images to illustrate the effectiveness of our proposed technique. We show the original test image, the inferred labels, and their predicted locations in the test image. Failure cases are mainly due to significant visual resemblance between training images (like the cereal box in the figure), severe specularities, and blurry conditions of test images. We also fail to recognize wrong facing products, which can be addressed with additional training images.

Discussion: Although the absolute value of the results may seem unsatisfactory, we have to consider the challenging settings of our problem. Other fine-grained classification datasets like Caltech-UCSD Birds dataset [32] report a state-of-the-art performance of average accuracy of 19.2%, considering that there are 15 training images per category, and each image contains only one object instance. Whereas for our dataset, we have a single training image per category, and each test image contains an average of 20 objects per image.

5.2   GA Optimization

We analyze the performance of our GA optimization by investigating the mAP when choosing different parameter values for K, n, α, β and γ. We first study the effect of the number of filtered classes K, in the multi-ranking step, and the number of top matches n, in the dense pixel matching step, on the mAP performance of the system. Figure 6 (a) shows the mAP as a function of n for different values of $K = 5, 7, 9, 13, 15$. For each combination of n and K, we obtain the optimal values of α, β and γ which maximize the mAP using coordinate descent optimization. It is shown that increasing the number of classes K generally improves the mAP. However, as K keeps increasing, more noise is added to the filtered set which decreases the mAP. Best performance is obtained for $K = 13$ classes. As expected, mAP decreases as n increases, but at the same time the recall improves. In figure 6 (b), we plot the mAP as a function of n for

Table 2. Performance on Grozi-120. System parameters are optimized to maximize average precision rate.

Method	mAP	mAMCA	mAPR
Baseline [19]	7.62	6.24	16.59
Full	13.21	7.5	9.37
without global optimization	9.54	7.1	17.56
with ground truth ranking	N/A	43.03	43.03
FV(1024 dim)	4.44	5.49	12.50
FV(4096 dim)	7.34	5.74	15.16
FV(4096 dim) + RANSAC	8.13	6.65	15.2
HE(k=200000, h_t=22)	6.32	5.23	10.54

$K = 13$ when turning off the GA optimization, by setting $\alpha = 0$, $\beta = 0$ and $\gamma = 0$, and when turning on the GA optimization by fixing $\alpha = 0.33$, $\beta = 0.05$ and $\gamma = 0.29$ (obtained using coordinate descent). Our GA step significantly improves the mAP performance. Also, our curve is flatter which shows that our method is more tolerant to noise imposed by adding more images in the dense pixel matching step.

5.3   Performance on GroZi-120 Dataset

We ran our experiments on 885 extracted test images (see figure 4). We used the same metrics and compared to the same approaches as in Sec. 5.1. Our system significantly outperforms other methods and the baseline method as shown in table 2. Please note that mAP value for ground truth ranking variant of our system will always have a value of 100.0% because each product category represents a specific product in Grozi-120 dataset. For similar reasons, the ground truth ranking without global optimization setting cannot be applied to Grozi-120 dataset. Figure 7 shows sample results from running our algorithm on Grozi-120. We effectively recognize and infer the locations of the objects in a test image.

We note that our system achieves lower mAP values on the Grozi-120 dataset than on our proposed dataset. This is due to the fact that there are only 5.6 images per product (which represents a class) on average for training which greatly degrades the results of the discriminative random forests. This is verified in the significant improvement of the system performance when using ground truth ranking. Further more, a large proportion of the test images in the Grozi-120 dataset suffer from blurriness. Nevertheless, our system outperforms other approaches. Also, there is no available prior information. We adjusted the prior model to be the $l1$-norm of the total number of recognized products in the image.

5.4   Multi-class Ranking Analysis

To demonstrate the impact of our multi-class ranking scheme, we report the mAA and mAR values using (1) different number of segments (i.e. votes), as

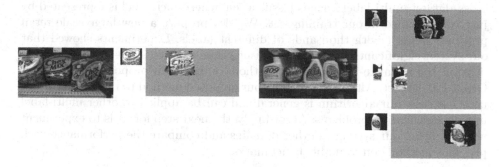

Fig. 7. Examples of two multi-label classification results on Grozi-120. Left column shows the test image, then the retrieved products, and finally their inferred locations.

Table 3. Multi-class ranking analysis. Baseline is the binary classification of images.

	Baseline	1 seg	5 seg	57 seg
mAA	25.56	63.55	62.52	**64.00**
mAR	22.4	57.22	53.32	**58.35**

opposed to (2) using the whole image (i.e. 1 segment) for ranking, and (3) performing binary classification of a test image (baseline). We have experimented with different, empirically chosen, segment sizes. Results in table 3 show that ranking classes through gathering classification votes consistently yields better performance. The impact of regions in the image that suffer from specularities or very wide variation in viewing angles is regularized by considering other patches that have better conditions.

5.5   Runtime Efficiency

Our system consists of 3 steps: (1) Multi-class ranking, (2) fast dense pixel matching, and (3) global optimization. We ran our experiments on a single 2.4G CPU with 4 GB of RAM without code optimization. Step (1) takes an average of 0.2 seconds per test image, not considering feature extraction time. Step (2) takes 0.35 seconds per each matching operation, and finally step (3) converges to an optimal solution in around 1.4 seconds when we consider the top 20 images for optimization. Accordingly, the total runtime of our algorithm is 1.95 seconds, where the time for dense pixel matching is parallelized for n top-ranked images. The most time consuming task is the LLC feature extraction.

6   Conclusions and Future Work

We presented a fast and scalable novel approach to recognize and localize all specific product instances in a retail store image with minimum training. We perform cross-dataset multi-label image classification, where each label is represented by just one instance in our training set. We also propose a new large-scale retail products dataset with thousands of different labels. Experiments showed that our system significantly yields better results than existing state-of-the-art classification and instance-level retrieval methods on both our proposed dataset, and Grozi-120 dataset. Although we apply our proposed method to the grocery products use case, our algorithm is general and can be applied to other multi-label image classification problems. Accordingly, the next step for us is to experiment with applying our system in other domains and compare the performance with previous methods on available benchmarks.

References

1. Bangpeng, Y., Aditya, K., Fei-Fei, L.: Combining randomization and discrimination for fine-grained image categorization. In: CVPR (2011)
2. Boutella, M.R., Luob, J., Shena, X., Brown, C.M.: Learning multi-label scene classification. Pattern Recognition 37(9), 1755–1771 (2004)
3. Branson, S., Wah, C., Schroff, F., Babenko, B., Welinder, P., Perona, P., Belongie, S.: Visual recognition with humans in the loop. In: Daniilidis, K., Maragos, P., Paragios, N. (eds.) ECCV 2010, Part IV. LNCS, vol. 6314, pp. 438–451. Springer, Heidelberg (2010)
4. Csurka, G., Dance, C., Bray, C., Fan, L.: Visual categorization with bags of keypoints. In: Workshop on Statistical Learning in Computer Vision (2004)
5. Dalal, N., Triggs, B.: Histograms of oriented gradients for human detection. In: CVPR (2005)
6. Deep, K., Singh, K.P., Kansal, M.L., Mohan, C.: A real coded genetic algorithm for solving integer and mixed integer optimization problems. Applied Mathematics and Computation 212(2), 505–518 (2009)
7. Duan, G., Huang, C., Ai, H., Lao, S.: Boosting associated pairing comparison features for pedestrian detection. In: ICCV Workshop on Visual Surveillance (2009)
8. Everingham, M., Gool, L.V., Williams, C., Winn, J., Zisserman, A.: The pascal visual object classes (voc) challenge. IJCV 88(2) (2010)
9. Fei-Fei, L., Fergus, R., Perona, P.: Learning generative visual models from few training examples: an incremental bayesian approach tested on 101 object categories. In: Workshop on Generative-Model Based Vision, CVPR (2004)
10. Fei-Fei, L., Fergus, R., Torralba, A.: Recognizing and learning object categories. In: ICCV Tutorial (2005)
11. Felzenszwalb, P.F., Girshick, R.B., McAllester, D., Ramanan, D.: Object detection with discriminatively trained part-based models. IEEE T. Pattern Anal. 32(9), 1627–1645 (2010)
12. Goldberg, D.E.: Genetic Algorithms in Search, Optimization and Machine Learning. Addison-Wesley (1989)
13. Griffin, G., Holub, A., Perona, P.: Caltech-256 object category dataset. Technical report, Caltech (2007)
14. Jegou, H., Douze, M., Schmid, C.: Hamming embedding and weak geometric consistency for large scale image search. In: Forsyth, D., Torr, P., Zisserman, A. (eds.) ECCV 2008, Part I. LNCS, vol. 5302, pp. 304–317. Springer, Heidelberg (2008)

15. Jing, Y., Baluja, S.: Pagerank for product image search. In: WWW (2008)
16. Jurie, Y.S.F.: Improving image classifcation using semantic attributes. IJCV 100(1), 59–77 (2012)
17. Kang, F., Jin, R., Sukthankar, R.: Correlated label propagation with application to multi-label learning. In: CVPR (2006)
18. Khosla, A., Jayadevaprakash, N., Yao, B., Fei-Fei, L.: Novel dataset for fine-grained image categorization. In: First Workshop on Fine-Grained Visual Categorization, CVPR (2011)
19. Kim, J., Liu, C., Sha, F., Grauman, K.: Deformable spatial pyramid matching for fast dense correspondences. In: CVPR (2013)
20. Lin, X., Gokturk, B., Sumengen, B., Vu, D.: Visual search engine for product images. In: Multimedia Content Access: Algorithms and Systems II (2008)
21. Lowe, D.G.: Distinctive image features from scale-invariant keypoints. IJCV 60(2), 91–110 (2004)
22. Merler, M., Galleguillos, C., Belongie, S.: Recognizing groceries in situ using in vitro training data. In: CVPR (2007)
23. Nilsback, M.E., Zisserman, A.: A visual vocabulary for ower classification. In: CVPR (2006)
24. Pandey, M., Lazebnik, S.: Scene recognition and weakly supervised object localization with deformable part-based models. In: ICCV (2011)
25. Perronnin, F., Liu, Y., Sanchez, J., Poirier, H.: Large-scale image retrieval with compressed fisher vectors. In: CVPR (2010)
26. Sharma, G., Jurie, F., Schmid, C.: Discriminative spatial saliency for image classification. In: CVPR (2012)
27. Shen, X., Lin, Z., Brandt, J., Wu, Y.: Mobile product image search by automatic query object extraction. In: Fitzgibbon, A., Lazebnik, S., Perona, P., Sato, Y., Schmid, C. (eds.) ECCV 2012, Part IV. LNCS, vol. 7575, pp 114–127. Springer, Heidelberg (2012)
28. Shotton, J., Winn, J., Rother, C., Criminisi, A.: Textonboost: Joint appearance, shape and context modeling for multi-class object recognition and segmentation. In: Leonardis, A., Bischof, H., Pinz, A. (eds.) ECCV 2006, Part I, LNCS, vol. 3951, pp. 1–15. Springer, Heidelberg (2006)
29. Torralba, A., Efros, A.: Unbiased look at dataset bias. In: CVPR (2011)
30. Tsai, S.S., Chen, D.M., Chandrasekhar, V., Takacs, G., Cheung, N.M., Vedantham, R., Grzeszczuk, R., Girod, B.: Mobile product recognition. In: ACM Multimedia (ACM MM) (2010)
31. Wang, J., Yang, J., Yu, K., Lv, F., Huang, T., Gong, Y.: Locality-constrained linear coding for image classification. In: CVPR (2010)
32. Welinder, P., Branson, S., Mita, T., Wah, C., Schroff, F., Belongie, S., Perona, P.: Caltech-ucsd birds 200. Technical report cns-tr-201, Caltech (2010)
33. Winlock, T., Christiansen, E., Belongie, S.: Toward real-time grocery detection for the visually impaired. In: CVAVI (2010)
34. Zha, Z., Hua, X., Mei, T., Wang, J., Qi, G., Wang, Z.: Joint multi-label multi-instance learning for image classification. In: CVPR (2008)
35. Zhang, M., Pena, J., Robles, V.: Feature selection for multi-label naive bayes classification. Information Sciences 179(19), 3218–3229 (2009)

Part-Pair Representation for Part Localization

Jiongxin Liu, Yinxiao Li, and Peter N. Belhumeur

Columbia University, USA
{liujx09,yli,belhumeur}@cs.columbia.edu

Abstract. In this paper, we propose a novel part-pair representation for part localization. In this representation, an object is treated as a collection of part pairs to model its shape and appearance. By changing the set of pairs to be used, we are able to impose either stronger or weaker geometric constraints on the part configuration. As for the appearance, we build pair detectors for each part pair, which model the appearance of an object at different levels of granularities. Our method of part localization exploits the part-pair representation, featuring the combination of non-parametric exemplars and parametric regression models. Non-parametric exemplars help generate reliable part hypotheses from very noisy pair detections. Then, the regression models are used to group the part hypotheses in a flexible way to predict the part locations. We evaluate our method extensively on the dataset CUB-200-2011 [32], where we achieve significant improvement over the state-of-the-art method on bird part localization. We also experiment with human pose estimation, where our method produces comparable results to existing works.

Keywords: part localization, part-pair representation, pose estimation.

1 Introduction

As a fundamental problem in computer vision, object part localization has been well studied in the last decade. Previous methods have been applied to different tasks, such as facial landmark detection [22,9,16,10,3,7], human pose estimation [26,19,34,24,25], and animal part localization [2,6,20,8]. In this paper, we use birds and humans as the test cases to design a unified framework for object detection and part localization, further improving the performance.

Existing works mainly focus on two directions: one is to build strong part detectors, and the second is to design expressive spatial models. To model the appearance of local parts that are variable and inherently ambiguous, mixture of components [34,36], and mid-level representations [24,25] are used. As for the spatial model, pictorial structure [18] and its variants have been proved to be very effective in different domains including human pose estimation. However, the pair-wise constraints in pictorial structure are sometimes not strong enough to combat detection noise, as shown in [20]. As a non-parametric spatial model, exemplar [3,35,20] has great success on the human face and birds. But as shown in Sec. 6.3, [20] does not work very well on the human pose, presumably due to

D. Fleet et al. (Eds.): ECCV 2014, Part II, LNCS 8690, pp. 456–471, 2014.

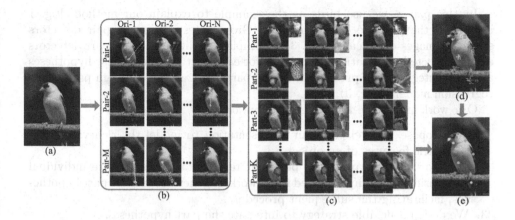

Fig. 1. Illustration of our method. (a) A testing image. (b) Pair detections for different pairs in different orientations. Each dashed line denotes a detected part pair. (c) Exemplar-conditioned part response maps. The exemplar is shown on the right side of the testing sample. (d) Candidate part detections. (e) Predicted part configuration. The brightness of colors indicates the confidence. Please see Fig. 6(a) for the color code

insufficient training exemplars and the limitations of the Consensus of Exemplars approach.

To better model the appearance and shape of an object, we propose part-pair representation where the object is represented as a set of part pairs. For the appearance, we build an ensemble of pair detectors, each of which targets a pair of parts. For the shape, we use the orientations and scales of the pairs to represent the global part configuration. The part-pair representation has two benefits. First, the ensemble of pair detectors cover overlapping regions on an object at different levels of granularities, thus capturing rich visual information. In spirit, pair detectors share some similarities with Poselet detectors [5]. But as pair detectors explicitly target pairs of parts, they are more suitable for our part-pair representation. Second, as the part-pair representation uses a complete graph to connect the parts, we have the luxury of adjusting the set of pairs to be considered when enforcing geometric constraints, making it either stronger (more rigid) or weaker (more flexible). Such flexibility is missing in the original exemplar-based models [3,20].

Using the part-pair representation, our method harnesses non-parametric exemplars and parametric models. As shown in [3,20], the exemplars help enforce relatively strong geometric constraints to suppress false part detections. But our instantiation of the idea is quite different, as we only expect to obtain an accurate estimation for a particular part, rather than for the global shape. After obtaining such part-centric hypotheses, the parametric regression models score pair-wise hypotheses to select the best ones to infer the global configuration. Such composition is flexible, as it only uses a subset of part predictions from each hypothesis that are likely to be correct.

In this paper, we use birds as the example to explain our method. Fig. 1 illustrates the pipeline of our method. Given a testing image, pair detectors scan the images over scales (Sec. 3). Exemplar-conditioned super part detectors are constructed, generating hypotheses for each part (Sec. 4). These hypotheses are then integrated to predict the global part configuration through parametric regression models (Sec. 5).

Our work makes the following contributions:

1. We propose a novel part-pair representation to model the rich visual and geometric features of an object.
2. We show how to apply the part-pair representation to localize individual parts using an exemplar-based framework. It generates reliable part hypotheses, facilitating the subsequent procedure.
3. We design a flexible strategy to integrate the part hypotheses.
4. Our method produces state-of-the-art results on bird part localization, as well as comparable results on human pose estimation.

2   Related Work

An important component in part localization is the appearance model, which has been studied in the context of object detection. Haar-like wavelets have been used in AdaBoost classifier [31] for human face detection. Subsequently, the paradigm of Linear SVMs trained on HOG features proved very popular [11,5,17]. A sufficiently fast non-linear detector which combines soft cascade with integral channel features is studied in [15,14,13]. Higher-level features have also shown promising results on object detection [27]. Recently, deep neural network has been applied to pedestrian detection and general object detection [23,30]. In our work, we follow [14,13] to build pair detectors that capture the appearance of geometrically rectified pair of parts. Note that our pair detectors differ from "pairs" of detectors in [28] which capture the mutual position of two independently learned part detectors.

Various shape models have been proposed in facial landmark detection. Statistical shape models [22,9,21] use multivariate Gaussian distribution to model the shape and appearance of a face. To better capture the shape and appearance variations, Constrained Local Models [3,1,35] constrain the global shape on top of local part detections, while tree-structured models jointly optimize the appearance and spatial terms to infer the part locations [18,16,36]. Shape regression [7] also works well on the human face, which is attributed to the strong correlation between low level features like pixel values and the shape increment.

As for human pose estimation, the tree-structured model has gained favor due to its generalization ability and efficiency. More importantly, the tree structure fits the kinematic skeleton of the human body, enabling effective modeling of the spatial relations. Starting from the work of [18], variants of the method have been developed [26,19,34,29,24,25]. To learn the model with large-scale datasets, a fast structured SVM solver is introduced in [6]. Recently, Poselet detectors are incorporated to capture additional mid-level information [33,24,25]. [33] designs a complex hierarchical model by organizing the Poselets in a coarse-to-fine hierarchy. [24,25] extends the pictorial structure by using Poselet dependent unary and pairwise terms. Our pair detectors share some similarities with the original Poselet detectors [5], but as pair detectors explicitly target pairs of parts rather than a random set of multiple parts, they can be easily manipulated to predict the part locations under the part-pair representation.

However, the tree-structured model does not work very well in the case where the parts to be estimated do not follow a kinematic tree, and the object resides in a cluttered scene with unknown position and size, as shown in [20]. The reason is that the first-order spatial constraints from tree-structured models are not strong enough to combat noisy detections. [20] manages to impose stronger and more precise constraints through exemplar-based models. But the rigidity of the models and the requirement of sufficiently large number of training samples limit its efficacy in human pose estimation, which will be shown in Sec. 6.3.

To combine the merits of tree-structured models and exemplars, we propose a novel part-pair representation. Under such representation, we employ exemplars to generate high quality hypotheses for each part. Then we design parametric models that exploit part-pair scores to combine these hypotheses in an optimal way. Our method demonstrates good performance on two challenging datasets [32,19].

3   Part-Pair Representation

Unlike part-based models that treat an object as a collection of parts, the part-pair representation breaks down the object into part pairs, forming a complete graph connecting the parts. Under such representation, the shape and appearance modeling focuses on the pairs (*i.e.*, the edges of the graph).

3.1   Shape Modeling

Assuming an object X has n parts with x^i denoting the location of part i, then part-pair representation treats X as a set of $n(n-1)/2$ part pairs $\{(x^i, x^j)|i, j \in [1, n], i \neq j\}$. For each pair (i, j) of X, we record its center location c^{ij}, orientation θ^{ij}, and length l^{ij}. Ideally, as any set of $n - 1$ pairs that span all the parts uniquely define the global part configuration, the other pairs seem to be redundant. In practice, such redundancy allow us to adjust the strength of the enforced geometric constraints by changing the set of pairs to be considered, which will be addressed in Sec. 4 and Sec. 5.

3.2   Appearance Modeling

We build pair detectors to model the appearance of each pair (pair detectors can be seen as specialized Poselet detectors [5], aiming at localizing two parts simultaneously). These detectors cover different regions on an object at different levels of granularities, with possibly significant overlap. For this reason, we have a rich representation of the object appearance.

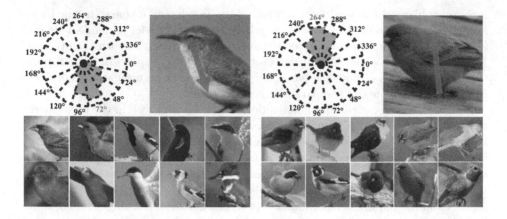

Fig. 2. Training samples after normalization. The left figure is for the pair (Left Eye, Belly), and the right figure corresponds to (Left Leg, Back). In each figure, sample frequencies over 15 orientations are visualized as blue sectors in the pie chart. The red arrow superimposed over the sample image of each figure indicates the pair orientation

Mixtures of Pair Detectors. To deal with rotation variations of the pairs, we discretize the rotation space in 15 different bins, corresponding to a span of 24 degrees. We then build one detector for each pair and each orientation[1]. For efficiency, we measure the sample frequencies in each orientation bin, and ignore the bins with frequencies smaller than 1%. So we have 776 rather than 1,575 detectors altogether for the bird dataset [32] where the number of parts is 15.

Inspired by POOF [4], we normalize the samples for each pair detector by rotating and rescaling the images, so that they are aligned at the two corresponding parts. Please see Fig. 2 for some aligned examples. For rotation, the rotation angle is determined based on the center of the target orientation bin. For rescaling, we rescale the samples of different pairs to different reference sizes, as they contain different granularities of information. For example, (Eye, Forehead) pair is typically much smaller than (Eye, Tail) pair in an image, resizing the (Eye, Tail) samples to a very small size may lose useful information.

To automate the process of deciding the reference sizes, we first estimate the average length $\bar{l}$ for each pair from the training data. After that, we know the minimum and maximum average lengths $\bar{l}_{min}$ and $\bar{l}_{max}$ among all the pairs. Assuming that the normalized length lies in the range $[\hat{l}_{min}, \hat{l}_{max}]$, we use a linear function $f(l)$ to map the range $[l_{min}, l_{max}]$ to $[\hat{l}_{min}, \hat{l}_{max}]$. Therefore, the reference size for pair (i, j) is $f(\bar{l}^{ij})$. We empirically set $\hat{l}_{min} = 24$ and $\hat{l}_{max} = 52$ to ensure reasonable image quality and avoid up-sampling the images too much.

---

[1] In our work, we use a single non-linear detector to handle pose & appearance variations within the same orientation bin. Alternatively, one can build multiple linear detectors (*e.g.*, Linear SVM + HOG) to explicitly decompose the visual complexity.

Training and Testing. After normalization, we use the toolbox [12] to extract the first-order integral channel features within an outer bounding box (*i.e.*, feature window) that contain both parts inside. Note that the feature window is placed at the center of the corresponding pair. We randomly generate up to $2,000$ rectangles to compute the features, and follow [13] to build a soft cascade detector with constant rejection thresholds. The details are as follows.

We build a cascade with $T = mT_0$ weak classifiers, and each weak classifier is a depth-two decision tree. $m = 30$ is the number of rounds of bootstrapping. After each round, we mine up to 400 hard negatives, and increase the number of weak classifiers by $T_0 = 50$ to build an AdaBoost classifier. Instead of performing a rejection test at every weak classifier, we check it after every T_0 weak classifiers (to accumulate enough observations). Assuming the score of a sample s at the kT_0-th weak classifier is $H_k(s) = \sum_{j \leq kT_0} \alpha_j h_j(s)$ where $\alpha_j > 0$ and $h_j(s)$ is the output of the j-th weak classifier, then the threshold is set as $\tau_k = b \sum_{j \leq kT_0} \alpha_j$ ($b = 0.45$ in our experiment).

At the testing stage, we build an image pyramid with 6 scales per octave, and apply the pair detectors in a sliding-window paradigm (with stride 4 pixels). To facilitate the following procedures, we normalize the scores so that an early rejected sample will not be penalized too much. To do this, we use $\bar{H}_k(s) = \frac{H_k(s)}{\sum_{j \leq kT_0} \alpha_j}$, and the normalized score $\bar{H}_k(s)$ is within the range $[0, 1]$ (early rejected samples will have scores below 0.45). Note that we do not apply Non-Maximum Suppression to the detection results; instead, we cache them as response maps at each scale.

4   Super Part Detector

Our method of part localization follows a bottom-up paradigm, and an important step is to generate reliable estimations for each part. In detection and localization tasks, the output from a single detector is usually very noisy. Therefore, additional contextual information such as the output from other related detectors is needed. Part-pair representation allows us to exploit such context, featuring the use of exemplar-based models. The motivation is that there are multiple pair detectors sharing the same part, and exemplars guide which pair detectors should be used (a way of imposing geometric constraint). In [3,20], the basic element of an exemplar is the part, and exemplars are used to dictate plausible global configuration of parts. In building super part detector, however, the basic element of an exemplar is the part pair, and exemplars provide an example of relevant pairs to a particular part (please see Fig. 3(a)).

4.1   Part Response Maps

Given the detection output from the pair detectors (in the form of pair response maps), our goal is to generate the response map for each part. The idea is similar to Hough Voting: a part pair activation votes for the positions of its two related parts. However, to gather the votes for a particular part i, exemplars are used

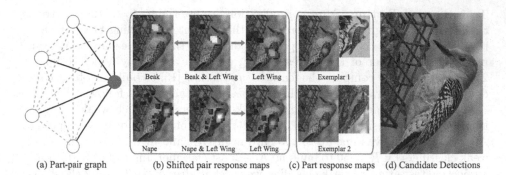

(a) Part-pair graph   (b) Shifted pair response maps   (c) Part response maps   (d) Candidate Detections

Fig. 3. (a) shows the part-pair representation as a complete graph for an object with 6 parts. To build the super part detector for a part (solid circle), only the pairs sharing the part are considered (solid lines). (b) illustrates the shifting of pair response maps. (c) shows the response maps for Left Wing conditioned on two exemplars. (d) shows the candidate detections for Left Wing.

to specify which pairs, orientations, and scales should be used. Assuming X_k is an exemplar being scaled to a particular size, we can obtain the response map for part i conditioned on X_k as follows.

Let $R^{ij}(x)$ denote the response maps for pair (i, j) where x is the pixel location in the testing image, then the exemplar X_k specifies the particular response map to use (at certain scale and orientation), which is denoted as $R_k^{ij}(x)$. To vote for part i based on the detections of pair (i, j), we can simply shift $R_k^{ij}(x)$ to obtain the corresponding map for part i, as illustrated in Fig. 3(b):

$$r_k^{ij}(x) = R_k^{ij}(x + o), \quad o = c_k^{ij} - x_k^i, \tag{1}$$

where o is the shifting offset, computed from $c_k^{i,j}$ – the center location of pair (i, j), and x_k^i – the location of part i. In our implementation, we quantize the offset o based on the discretization of pair rotations after normalizing the scales (please refer to Sec. 3.2). During testing, we pre-shift and cache the response maps using the quantized offset o. Therefore, given an exemplar X_k, we can easily retrieve its corresponding map $r_k^{ij}(x)$.

As exemplar X_k tells all the visible pairs (*i.e.*, both parts of a pair should be visible) sharing part i, the part response map for part i is then estimated as

$$R_k^i(x) = \frac{1}{N_k^i} \sum_j r_k^{ij}(x), \tag{2}$$

where N_k^i is the number of visible pairs containing part i. Assuming there is a detector that directly generates such response map, then we name it as *Super Part Detector*, which is conditioned on a particular exemplar. Fig. 3(c) shows two such maps from two exemplars.

4.2   Part Hypotheses

In this section, we will describe how to generate part hypotheses from the super part detectors. As described in Sec. 4.1, different exemplars give us different super part detectors for part i. However, only the detectors from exemplars that match the testing sample at the part are meaningful. By "match at the part", we mean that the exemplar has similar configuration of parts in the neighborhood of the target part; by "meaningful", we mean that the detector has reasonably high score at the correct part location rather than the background. Therefore, we simultaneously find the good exemplars and possible part locations.

A reasonable indicator about the goodness of an exemplar is the peak value of its corresponding part response map. So, for part i, score of X_k is

$$S_k^i = \max_x R_k^i(x). \tag{3}$$

To search for good exemplars, a naive way is to go through all the training exemplars, rescale them to each possible scale, evaluate their scores with Eq. 3 and keep the top-scoring ones. This process can be made faster using a heuristic strategy: we compute the upper bound of S_k^i with much lower cost, and obtain an initial set of promising exemplars. Then we use Eq. 3 to recompute their scores. The upper bound is computed as $\hat{S}_k^i = \frac{1}{N_k^i} \sum_j \max_x r_k^{ij}(x)$, where the addend can be reused to evaluate different exemplars. In our experiment, we keep the best 100 exemplars for part i, and extract up to five local maximas from each corresponding part response map. The locations and scores of these maximas form the candidate part detections as in Fig. 3(d).

We have a by-product from the above procedure. As the candidate part detections indicate where to place the exemplar in the image, we also obtain the predictions for the other parts. For instance, given X_k and a candidate detection of part i at x_0, the location of part j is $x_0 - x_k^i + x_k^j$ with confidence value $r_k^{ij}(x_0)$.

4.3   Discussion

The super part detector demonstrates one way of using part-pair representation, where a subset of up to $n-1$ pairs are used to impose the geometric constraints (please see Fig. 3(a)). Because multiple pair detections are accumulated, the super part detector is tolerable to the noise from certain pairs. Because of the discretization in the spatial domain, rotation space, and scale space, the super part detector is also tolerable to the displacement between the exemplar's parts and the testing sample's parts, especially for the distant parts with respect to the target part. For these reasons, the strength of geometric constraint from exemplars is weaker than that in [3,20]. In other words, exemplars that do not match the testing sample globally can still be useful in localizing a particular part.

5   Predicting Part Configuration

Recall that in Sec. 4.2, we obtain a set of hypotheses for each part. Each hypothesis consists of the candidate part detection, as well as the corresponding exemplar. Then we need to use the hypotheses to predict the global part configuration. We have two approaches, one is rigid and the other if more flexible.

5.1   Rigid Method

The idea is similar to [20]: assuming we place the exemplar X_k at a position in the testing image, then we evaluate the overall score of the exemplar as $S_k = \frac{1}{N_k} \sum_{i,j} R_k^{ij}(c_k^{ij})$, where N_k is the number of visible pairs.

To predict the global configuration, we evaluate the overall scores for all the candidate exemplars (*i.e.*, the exemplars placed in the testing image at the corresponding candidate part locations). Once we obtain the best $N = 30$ exemplars, we follow [20] to predict the visibilities and locations of all the parts using Consensus of Exemplars (CoE). As can be seen here, the method is very rigid, expecting the exemplars to match the testing sample globally; also, the strength of geometric constraints is very strong, as all the pairs in the part-pair representation are used. Therefore, it may fail if good matches to the testing sample do not exist in the training data, which is likely to happen when we do not have a large set of representative training samples.

5.2   Flexible Integration

One limitation of the rigid method is that all the parts from a single exemplar are taken into consideration at the consensus stage, some of which are purely distractors. The simple non-linear consensus operation is likely to fail if such noise is above a certain level. In our flexible method, we attempt to filter out the noise in a more effective way.

To do this, we construct a number of groups of part hypotheses, with at most one hypothesis corresponding to a particular part in each group. We evaluate these groups, and use the best one to predict the global part configuration. As the top-scoring hypotheses already have very high accuracy as shown in Tab. 1, we only keep a few of them (15 in our experiment) for each part.

Grouping Hypotheses. Following the discussion in Sec. 4.3, we first define the UR (uncertainty region) for each part inherited from an exemplar in a part hypothesis. Assuming we have a hypothesis for part i, then the uncertainty region for part j is a circle with radius equal to a fraction (20% in our experiment) of the distance between part i and j. Given this definition, we claim that two part hypotheses agree on a particular part if its two corresponding URs are close enough to each other (based on the center distance divided by the larger radius). To control the strength of geometric constraint, we require that two hypotheses to be paired should agree on at least N parts including themselves, where N can be tuned. Fig. 4 shows two part hypotheses and the parts they agree on.

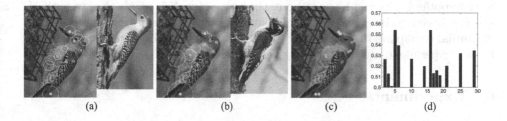

(a)   (b)   (c)   (d)

Fig. 4. (a) shows a Back hypothesis, which predicts the locations of all the parts in the form of uncertainty regions marked by white circles. The corresponding exemplar is shown on the right. (b) shows a Crown hypothesis. (c) shows eight parts on which the two hypotheses in (a) and (b) agree. (d) shows the features of this pair of hypotheses

To make the problem tractable, we group the hypotheses in a pair-wise manner. To evaluate the goodness of two paired hypotheses for parts i and j, we design a feature vector with $2 \times n$ entries where n is the total number of object parts. The first n entries correspond to the scores of part pairs in the hypothesis of part i, with the k-th value to be the pair score of (i, k). The second n entries are formed in the same way. We zero out the entries for the parts the two hypotheses do not agree on. One example of such feature is shown in Fig. 4(d). Using a held-out validation set, we train a logistic regression model that map the features to the percentage of correctly predicted parts: if two hypotheses agree on m parts, and the ground-truth locations for those parts are close enough to the mean predictions, then the percentage is $\frac{m}{n}$. As the features carry semantic meaning, we build different regression models for different pairs of parts.

The pair-wise grouping procedure is as follows. Initially, each part hypothesis forms a group. Starting from the initial group, we sequentially add another hypothesis that can be paired with an existing hypothesis in the group. We keep track of the parts the newly paired hypotheses agree on (by marking them as detected), and subsequent pairing should have new parts detected. The procedure terminates when there is no more hypothesis to add. In the end, we obtain a number of groups. The score of each group is computed as $S = \frac{1}{M}\sum_p \alpha_p s(p)$, where p is the paired hypotheses, $s(p)$ is the output of the regression model, M is the total number of detected parts and α_p is the percentage of newly detected parts from the parts the paired hypotheses agree on.

Predicting the Part Locations. Given the highest-scoring group, we directly use the candidate part detections from the hypotheses as the final results; for each of the other detected parts, we use the mean prediction from the corresponding paired hypotheses; for each of the undetected parts, if there are hypotheses in this group having a related part pair with scores above 0.5, then we use the predicted location with the highest pair score; Otherwise, the part is marked as invisible. If there does not exist group with more than one hypothesis (which is unlikely to happen), we use the part predictions from the exemplar in the best part hypothesis. As can be seen here, the parameter N controls the strength of geometric constraints. Smaller N indicates weaker constraints as it allows more dissimilar exemplars to contribute by only using their promising part predictions. In our experiment, we find $N = 5$ gives the best result.

6 Experiments

We evaluate our part localization method on the bird dataset CUB-200-2011 [32] and the human pose dataset LSP (Leeds Sports Poses) [19]. For all the experiments, we use the train/test split provided by the dataset. We withhold 15% of the training data as the validation set.

To evaluate the localization performance, we mainly use the PCP measure (Percentage of Correct Parts). For bird part localization, a correct part estimation should be within 1.5 standard deviation of an MTurk workers click from the ground truth part location. For human pose estimation, correct part should have end points within 50% of the part length from the ground truth end points.

6.1 Performance of Super Part Detector

To have an idea about the importance of the super part detector in our method, we evaluate its performance in localizing a particular part, and compare it with that of regular part detector and our pair detector. In the experiment, we do not try to reach an optimal solution for all the parts jointly. Instead, we predict the location of a single part, assuming it's visible.

For the regular part detector, we use the pose detectors designed by [20], where there are 200 detectors for each part. At the testing stage, the best five activations across all the pose detectors are outputted. As for the pair detector, recall that the activation of a pair detector casts a vote for its related parts. As such, to localize a part, we run all the relevant pair detectors (up to $14 \times 15 = 210$ detectors), and collect the highest-scoring predictions. For the super part detector, we use the best five candidate part detections obtained in Sec. 4.2. Note that we do not use Non-Maximum Suppression for all the detectors, and the activations are just local maximas in the response maps.

The PCPs for each part as well as the total PCP are listed in Tab. 1. We also report the top-5 accuracy, where at least one of the best five predictions is correct. From the comparison between pair detectors and pose detectors, we can see that using the different features and classifiers from [20] does not give us much better raw detectors. However, after building the super part detector from the pair detectors, we achieve significant improvement. This is reasonable as the super part detectors are context-aware. What we want to emphasize is that by imposing geometric constraints at an early stage, we have high quality part hypotheses which make it promising to design effective integration method.

Table 1. Comparison of different detectors in localizing individual parts. The super part detectors produce very reliable part activations. From left to right, the parts are: Back, Beak, Belly, Breast, Crown, Forehead, Eye, Leg, Wing, Nape, Tail, and Throat.

PCP	Ba	Bk	Be	Br	Cr	Fh	Ey	Le	Wi	Na	Ta	Th	Total
Part	23.4	23.8	31.1	28.1	35.0	28.8	11.5	17.3	18.3	29.4	10.0	34.7	23.9
Pair	27.2	28.4	39.7	31.8	21.4	28.4	5.3	14.5	13.2	38.6	17.9	44.7	25.1
SupP	**62.2**	**57.3**	**66.4**	**61.4**	**74.2**	**65.6**	**40.1**	**40.9**	**53.5**	**66.9**	**34.9**	**71.5**	**57.1**
Part-top5	49.1	47.2	56.2	55.7	62.3	51.1	23.9	37.9	43.9	53.5	26.6	59.1	46.7
Pair-top5	50.1	54.0	66.1	57.0	44.5	49.4	15.2	29.6	31.8	64.7	37.0	68.7	46.1
SupP-top5	**76.9**	**75.8**	**79.8**	**77.1**	**86.3**	**81.7**	**66.0**	**56.1**	**66.9**	**81.4**	**48.3**	**83.8**	**72.5**

Table 2. Comparison of part localization results on CUB-200-2011 [32]. Our method outperforms state-of-the-art techniques on all the parts.

PCP	Ba	Bk	Be	Br	Cr	Fh	Ey	Le	Wi	Na	Ta	Th	Total
DPM [6]	34.6	26.0	42.0	37.0	47.9	28.7	48.2	-	55.0	41.8	22.4	42.4	40.7
CoE [20]	62.1	49.0	69.0	67.0	72.9	58.5	55.7	40.7	71.6	70.8	40.2	70.8	59.7
Ours-rigid	59.7	59.0	69.5	67.3	**77.1**	**72.2**	67.9	39.9	69.7	75.2	34.7	76.7	63.1
Ours-flex	**64.5**	**61.2**	**71.7**	**70.5**	76.8	72.0	**70.0**	**45.0**	**74.4**	**79.3**	**46.2**	**80.0**	**66.7**

6.2   Predicting the Part Configuration

We evaluate our rigid and flexible methods (*i.e.*, Ours-rigid and Ours-flex) on predicting the global part configuration, including the visibilities. We compare with DPM implemented by [6] and exemplar-based method [20].

Tab. 2 shows the comparisons. DPM [6] has much lower accuracy possibly for two reasons: there is very large intra-class variability to be captured by few DPM components (14 detectors per part); the first-order spatial constraints in DPM are not strong enough to combat the detection noise. Although Ours-rigid does not outperform CoE [20] by a large margin, the improvement is still remarkable. First, we do not use subcategory labels; Second, the pair detectors does not have better performance than pose detectors as shown in Tab. 1. We attribute such improvement to the aggregation of a much richer set of appearance models that largely suppresses the false detections from individual detectors. Ours-flex further improves the overall PCP over Ours-rigid by about 3.6%. It clearly shows the benefit of adding some flexibility to the estimation of global configuration on top of the part hypotheses. Fig. 5 shows similar comparisons. As exemplars usually sacrifice Tail to match other parts, the improvement of Ours-flex over Ours-rigid on Tail is very large.

Fig. 6(a) shows some qualitative results. We can see that Ours-rigid fails to accurately localize the parts with large deformation. Because the constraints in the rigid method strongly restrict the prediction of part configuration, the estimations from Ours-rigid respect the exemplars much more than the particular

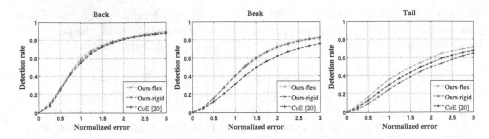

Fig. 5. Detection rates of Back, Beak, and Tail given varying degrees of localization precision. 1.5 is the threshold for a correct detection

Table 3. Comparison of part localization results on LSP dataset [19]. Our flexible method generates comparable results to the state-of-the-art works.

PCP	Torso	Upper leg	Lower leg	Upper arm	Forearm	Head	Total
Strong-PS [25]	**88.7**	**78.8**	**73.4**	**61.5**	**44.9**	**85.6**	**69.2**
Poselet-PS [24]	87.5	75.7	68.0	54.2	33.9	78.1	62.9
CoE [20]	83.4	69.0	61.7	47.5	28.1	79.3	57.5
Ours-rigid	84.2	69.3	61.5	48.7	28.5	79.9	58.0
Ours-flex	87.6	76.4	69.7	55.4	37.6	82.0	64.8

testing image, which is problematic when the exemplars do not match the testing sample well. Our flexible method mitigates this issue by allowing more flexible composition of part hypotheses.

Similar to [20], we conduct the experiment of species classification using the localized parts from our method. On the 200-species dataset, the mAP (mean average precision) is 48.32%; on the 14-species subset, the mAP is 65.18%.

6.3   Human Pose Estimation

We also apply our method to human pose estimation using LSP dataset [19]. Similar to [25], we use observer-centric (OC) annotations. The pair detectors are trained in the same way as those for bird dataset, and altogether we have 796 pair detectors. We also implement [20] with only pose consistency on this dataset.

The quantitative results are listed in Tab. 3. [20] and Ours-rigid do not work well on human pose estimation. Compared with the bird dataset, the number of training samples is much smaller in LSP, and human body is generally more articulated. These factors make the Consensus of Exemplar framework less effective in this experiment. Also note that the rigid method has only marginal improvement over [20]. One possible reason is that the images in the LSP dataset have already been rescaled and cropped (unlike [32]), making the effect of better suppressing false detections not prominent.

Tab. 3 also shows that Ours-flex method significantly improves over Ours-rigid. It also outperforms one state-of-the-art technique [24]. Compared with the

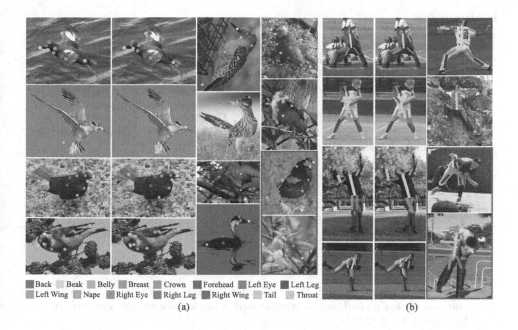

| Back | Beak | Belly | Breast | Crown | Forehead | Left Eye | Left Leg |
| Left Wing | Nape | Right Eye | Right Leg | Right Wing | Tail | Throat |

(a)   (b)

Fig. 6. (a) Qualitative results on CUB-200-2011 [32]. The color codes of the bird parts are at the bottom. (b) Qualitative results on LSP [19]. In both subfigures, the first two columns compare Ours-rigid (left) with Ours-flex (right), the other columns show more examples from Ours-flex. Failures are denoted with red frames.

well-constructed method [25], which employs many strong appearance models (some are tailored to human body), our method produces comparable results. The experiment demonstrates that our part-pair representation can be applied to the categories with large articulated deformation.

Some qualitative results are shown in Fig. 6(b). Similar to the comparison in Fig. 6(a), Ours-flex achieves more accurate localization by balancing the shape prior from exemplars and the detector activations in the testing image.

7   Conclusions

In this paper, we propose a part-pair representation to model an object, and study its application to part localization. Such representation enables us to capture rich visual information of the object, and impose adjustable geometric constraints on the part configuration. By combining part-pair representation with exemplars, we construct very powerful super part detectors, generating reliable part hypotheses. We also show that adding flexibility to the integration of part hypotheses largely improve the performance. Our method produces state-of-the-art results on bird part localization and promising results on human pose estimation.

References

1. Amberg, B., Vetters, T.: Optimal landmark detection using shape models and branch and bound. In: Proc. ICCV (2011)
2. Azizpour, H., Laptev, I.: Object detection using strongly-supervised deformable part models. In: Fitzgibbon, A., Lazebnik, S., Perona, P., Sato, Y., Schmid, C. (eds.) ECCV 2012, Part I. LNCS, vol. 7572, pp. 836–849. Springer, Heidelberg (2012)
3. Belhumeur, P.N., Jacobs, D.W., Kriegman, D.J., Kumar, N.: Localizing parts of faces using a consensus of exemplars. In: Proc. CVPR (2011)
4. Berg, T., Belhumeur, P.N.: POOF: Part-based one-vs-one features for fine-grained categorization, face verification, and attribute estimation. In: Proc. CVPR (2013)
5. Bourdev, L., Maji, S., Brox, T., Malik, J.: Detecting people using mutually consistent poselet activations. In: Daniilidis, K., Maragos, P., Paragios, N. (eds.) ECCV 2010, Part VI. LNCS, vol. 6316, pp. 168–181. Springer, Heidelberg (2010)
6. Branson, S., Beijbom, O., Belongie, S.: Efficient large-scale structured learning. In: Proc. CVPR (2013)
7. Cao, X., Wei, Y., Wen, F., Sun, J.: Face alignment by explicit shape regression. In: Proc. CVPR (2012)
8. Chen, X., Mottaghi, R., Liu, X., Fidler, S., Urtasun, R., Yuille, A.: Detect what you can: Detecting and representing objects using holistic models and body parts. In: Proc. CVPR (2014)
9. Cootes, T., Edwards, G., Taylor, C.: Active appearance models. IEEE TPAMI (2001)
10. Cristinacce, D., Cootes, T.: Feature detection and tracking with constrained local models. In: Proc. BMVC (2006)
11. Dalal, N., Triggs, B.: Histograms of oriented gradients for human detection. In: Proc. CVPR (2005)
12. Dollár, P.: Piotr's Image and Video Matlab Toolbox (PMT), http://vision.ucsd.edu/~pdollar/toolbox/doc/index.html
13. Dollár, P., Appel, R., Kienzle, W.: Crosstalk cascades for frame-rate pedestrian detection. In: Fitzgibbon, A., Lazebnik, S., Perona, P., Sato, Y., Schmid, C. (eds.) ECCV 2012, Part II. LNCS, vol. 7573, pp. 645–659. Springer, Heidelberg (2012)
14. Dollár, P., Belongie, S., Perona, P.: The fastest pedestrian detector in the west. In: Proc. BMVC (2010)
15. Dollár, P., Tu, Z., Perona, P., Belongie, S.: Integral channel features. In: Proc. BMVC (2009)
16. Everingham, M., Sivic, J., Zisserman, A.: "Hello! my name is... buffy" automatic naming of characters in tv video. In: Proc. BMVC (2006)
17. Felzenszwalb, P.F., Girshick, R.B., McAllester, D., Ramanan, D.: Object detection with discriminatively trained part based models. In: IEEE TPAMI (2010)
18. Felzenszwalb, P.F., Huttenlocher, D.P.: Pictorial structures for object recognition. IJCV 61(1), 55–79 (2005)
19. Johnson, S., Everingham, M.: Clustered pose and nonlinear appearance models for human pose estimation. In: Proc. BMVC (2010)
20. Liu, J., Belhumeur, P.N.: Bird part localization using exemplar-based models with enforced pose and subcategory consistency. In: Proc. ICCV (2013)
21. Matthews, I., Baker, S.: Active appearance models revisited. In: IJCV (2004)
22. Milborrow, S., Nicolls, F.: Locating facial features with an extended active shape model. In: Forsyth, D., Torr, P., Zisserman, A. (eds.) ECCV 2008, Part IV. LNCS, vol. 5305, pp. 504–513. Springer, Heidelberg (2008)

23. Ouyang, W., Wang, X.: Joint deep learning for pedestrian detection. In: Proc. ICCV (2013)
24. Pishchulin, L., Andriluka, M., Gehler, P., Schiele, B.: Poselet conditioned pictorial structures. In: Proc. CVPR (2013)
25. Pishchulin, L., Andriluka, M., Gehler, P., Schiele, B.: Strong appearance and expressive spatial models for human pose estimation. In: Proc. ICCV (2013)
26. Ramanan, D.: Learning to parse images of articulated bodies. In: Proc. NIPS (2006)
27. Ren, X., Ramanan, D.: Histograms of sparse codes for object detection. In: Proc. CVPR (2013)
28. Singh, S., Gupta, A., Efros, A.A.: Unsupervised discovery of mid-level discriminative patches. In: Fitzgibbon, A., Lazebnik, S., Perona, P., Sato, Y., Schmid, C. (eds.) ECCV 2012, Part II. LNCS, vol. 7573, pp. 73–86. Springer, Heidelberg (2012)
29. Sun, M., Savarese, S.: Articulated part-based model for joint object detection and pose estimation. In: Proc. ICCV (2011)
30. Szegedy, C., Toshev, A., Erhan, D.: Deep neural networks for object detection. In: Proc. NIPS (2013)
31. Viola, P., Jones, M.: Robust real-time object detection. IJCV 57(2), 137–154 (2001)
32. Wah, C., Branson, S., Welinder, P., Perona, P., Belongie, S.: The caltech-ucsd birds-200-2011 dataset. Computation & Neural Systems Technical Report, CNS-TR-2011-001 (2011)
33. Wang, Y., Tran, D., Liao, Z.: Learning hierarchical poselets for human parsing. In: Proc. CVPR (2011)
34. Yang, Y., Ramanan, D.: Articulated pose estimation with flexible mixtures-of-parts. In: Proc. CVPR (2011)
35. Zhou, F., Brandt, J., Lin, Z.: Exemplar-based graph matching for robust facial landmark localization. In: Proc. ICCV (2013)
36. Zhu, X., Ramanan, D.: Face detection, pose estimation, and landmark localization in the wild. In: Proc. CVPR (2012)

Weakly Supervised Learning of Objects, Attributes and Their Associations

Zhiyuan Shi, Yongxin Yang, Timothy M. Hospedales, and Tao Xiang

Queen Mary, University of London, London E1 4NS, UK
{z.shi,yongxin.yang,t.hospedales,t.xiang}@qmul.ac.uk

Abstract. When humans describe images they tend to use combinations of nouns and adjectives, corresponding to objects and their associated attributes respectively. To generate such a description automatically, one needs to model objects, attributes and their associations. Conventional methods require strong annotation of object and attribute locations, making them less scalable. In this paper, we model object-attribute associations from weakly labelled images, such as those widely available on media sharing sites (e.g. Flickr), where only image-level labels (either object or attributes) are given, without their locations and associations. This is achieved by introducing a novel weakly supervised non-parametric Bayesian model. Once learned, given a new image, our model can describe the image, including objects, attributes and their associations, as well as their locations and segmentation. Extensive experiments on benchmark datasets demonstrate that our weakly supervised model performs at par with strongly supervised models on tasks such as image description and retrieval based on object-attribute associations.

Keywords: Weakly supervised learning, object attribute associations.

1 Introduction

Vision research is moving beyond simple classification, annotation and detection to encompass generating more structured and semantic descriptions of images. When humans describe images they use combinations of nouns and adjectives, corresponding to objects and their associated attributes respectively. For example, an image can be described as containing "a person in red clothes and a shiny car". In order to imitate this ability, a computer vision system needs to learn models about objects, attributes, and their associations. Object-attribute associations is important for avoiding the mistakes such as "a shiny person and a red car". Learning object-attribute association also provides new query capabilities, e.g., "find images with a furry brown horse and a red shiny car".

There has been extensive work on detecting and segmenting objects [33, 6, 31] and describing specified objects and images in terms of semantic attributes [9, 36, 3, 32]. However, these tasks have previously been treated separately; jointly learning about and inferring object-attribute association in images with potentially multiple objects is much less studied. The few existing studies on

D. Fleet et al. (Eds.): ECCV 2014, Part II, LNCS 8690, pp. 472–487, 2014.

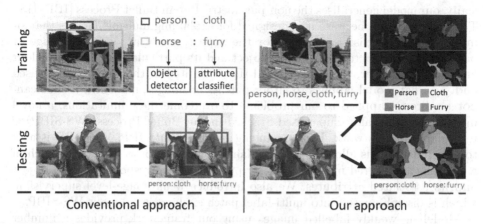

Fig. 1. Comparing our weakly supervised approach to object-attribute association learning to the conventional strongly supervised approach

modelling object-attribute association [17, 38, 20, 37, 36, 35] use fully annotated data [38, 20, 37] and/or are separately trained [17, 35]. In the conventional pipeline (Fig. 1) images are strongly labelled with object bounding boxes and associated attributes, from which object detectors and attribute classifiers are trained.Given a new image, the learned object detectors are first applied to find object locations, where the attribute classifiers are then applied to produce the object descriptions. However, there is a critical limitation of the existing approach: it requires strongly labelled objects and attributes. Considering there are over 30,000 object classes distinguishable to humans [18], even more attributes to describe them, and an infinite number of combinations, it is not scalable.

In this paper we propose to learn objects, attributes, and their associations from weakly labelled data. That is, images with object and attribute labels but not their associations nor their locations (see Fig. 1). Such weakly labelled images are abundant on media sharing websites such as Flickr. Therefore lack of training data would never be a problem. However, learning strong semantics, i.e. explicit object-attribute association from weakly labelled images is extremely challenging due to the label ambiguity: a real-world image with the tags "dog, white, coat, furry" could contain a furry dog and a white coat or a furry coat and a white dog. Furthermore, the tags/labels typically only describe the foreground/objects. There could be a white building in the background which is ignored by the annotator, and a computer vision model must infer that this is not what the tag 'white' refers to. Conventional methods cannot be applied without object locations and explicit object-attribute association being labelled.

To address the challenges of learning strong semantics from weak annotation, we develop a unified probabilistic generative model capable of jointly learning objects, attributes and their associations, as well as their location and segmentation. Our model is also able to learn from realistic images where there are multiple objects of variable sizes per image such as PASCAL VOC. More specifically, our model generalises the non-parametric Indian Buffet Process (IBP) [13]. The IBP is chosen because it is designed for explaining multiple factors that simultaneously co-exist to account for the appearance of a particular image or patch, e.g., such factors can be an object and its particular texture and colour attributes. However, the conventional IBP is limited in that it is unsupervised and, as a flat model, applies to either patches or images, not both; it thus cannot be directly applied to our problem. To overcome these limitations, a novel model termed Weakly Supervised Stacked Indian Buffet Process (WS-SIBP) is formulated in this work. By introducing hierarchy into IBP, WS-SIBP is able to group data, thus allowing it to explain images as groups of patches, each of which has an inferred multi-label description vector corresponding to an object and its associated attributes. We also introduce weak image-level supervision, which is disambiguated into multi-label patch explanations by our WS-SIBP.

Modelling weakly labelled images using our framework provides a number of benefits: (i) By jointly learning multiple objects, attributes and background clutter in a single framework, ambiguity in each is explained away by knowledge of the other. (ii) The infinite number of factors provided by the non-parametric Bayesian framework allows structured background clutter of unbounded complexity to be explained away. (iii) A sparse binary latent representation of each patch allows an unlimited number of attributes to co-exist on one object. The aims and capabilities of our approach are illustrated schematically in Fig. 1, where weak annotation in the form of a mixture of objects and attributes is transformed into object and attribute associations with locations.

2   Related Work

Learning Objects and Attributes. A central task in computer vision is understanding image content. Such an understanding has been shown in the form of an image description in terms of nouns (object detection or region segmentation), and more recently adjectives (visual attributes) [9, 27]. Attributes have been used to describe objects [9, 34], people [3], clothing [4], scenes [36], faces [32], and video events [12]. However, most previous studies have learned and inferred object and attribute models separately, e.g., by independently training binary classifiers, and require strong annotations/labels indicating object/attribute locations and/or associations if the image is not dominated by a single object.

Learning Object-Attribute Associations. A few recent studies have learned object-attribute association explicitly [35, 16, 17, 36–38, 20]. Different from our approach, [35, 37, 38, 20] only trains and tests on unambiguous data, i.e. images containing a single dominant object, assumes object-attribute association is known at training; and moreover allocates exactly one attribute per object. [17] tests on more challenging PASCAL VOC data with multiple objects and attributes coexisting. However, their model is pre-trained on object and attribute detectors learned on strongly annotated images with object bounding boxes provided. [36] also does object segmentation and object-attribute prediction. But their model is learned from strongly labelled images in that object-attribute association are given during training; and importantly prediction is restricted to object-attribute pairs seen during training. In summary none of the existing work learns object-attribute association from weakly labelled data as we do here.

Multi-attribute Query. Some existing work aims to perform attribute-based query [26, 15, 30, 32]. In particular, Recent studies have considered how to calibrate [30] and fuse [26] multiple attribute scores in a single query. We go beyond these studies in supporting conjunction of object+multi-attribute query. Moreover, existing methods either require bounding boxes or assume simple data with single dominant objects, and do not reason jointly about multiple attribute-object association. This means they would be intrinsically challenged in reasoning about (multi)-attribute-object queries on challenging data with multiple objects and multiple attributes in each image (e.g., querying furry brown horse, in a dataset with black horses and furry dogs in the same image). In other words, they cannot be directly extended to solve query by object-attribute association.

Probabilistic Models for Image Understanding. Discriminative kernel methods underpin many high performance recognition and annotation studies [9, 27, 3, 36, 28, 17, 5, 21, 6]. However the flexibility of generative probabilistic models has seen them successfully applied to a variety of tasks, especially learning structured scene representations, and weakly-supervised learning [12, 33, 31, 19]. These studies often generalise probabilistic topic models (PTM) [2]. However PTMs are limited for explaining objects and attributes in that latent topics are competitive - the fundamental assumption is that an object is a horse *or* brown *or* furry. They intrinsically do not account for the reality that it is *all* at once.

We therefore generalise instead the Indian Buffet Process (IBP) [7, 13]. The IBP is a latent feature model that can independently activate each latent factor, explaining imagery as a weighted sum of active factor appearances. However, conventional IBP is (i) fully unsupervised, and (ii) only handles flat data. Thus, it could explain patches or images, but not images composed of patches, thereby limiting usefulness for multiple object-attribute association within images. We therefore formulate a novel Weakly Supervised Stacked Indian Buffet Process (WS-SIBP) to model grouped data (images composed of patches), such that each patch has an infinite latent feature vector. This allows us to exploit image-level weak supervision, but disambiguate it to determine the best explanation in terms of which patches correspond to un-annotated background; which patch corresponds to which annotated object; and which objects have which attributes.

Weakly Supervised Learning. Weakly supervised learning (WSL) has attracted increasing attention as the volume of data which we are interested in learning from grows much faster than available annotation. Existing studies have generally focused on WSL of objects alone [31, 19, 6], with limited work on WSL of attributes [36, 12]. Some studies have treated this as a discriminative multi-instance learning (MIL) problem [22, 6], while others leveraged PTMs [31, 19]. Weakly supervised localisation is a particularly challenging variant where images are annotated with objects, but absent bounding boxes means their location is unknown. This has been solved by sampling bounding boxes for MIL treatment [6], or more 'softly' by PTMs [31]. In this paper we uniquely consider WSL of both objects, attributes, their associations and their locations simultaneously.

Our Contributions. In this paper we make three key contributions: (i) We for the first time jointly learn all object, attribute and background appearances, object-attribute association, and their locations from realistic weakly labelled images; (ii) We formulate a novel weakly supervised non-parametric Bayesian model by generalising the Indian Buffet Process; (iii) From this weakly labelled data, we demonstrate various image description and query tasks, including challenging tasks relying on predicting strong object-attribute association. Extensive experiments on benchmark datasets demonstrate that in each case our model is comparable to the strongly supervised alternatives and significantly outperforms a number of weakly supervised baselines.

3   Weakly Supervised Stacked Indian Buffet Process

We propose a non-parametric Bayesian model that learns to describe images composed of super-pixels/patches from weak object and attribute annotation. Each patch is associated with an infinite latent factor vector indicating if it corresponds to (an unlimited variety of) unannotated background clutter, or an object of interest, and what set of attributes are possessed by the object. Given a set of images with weak labels and segmented into super-pixels/patches, we need to learn: (i) which are the unique patches shared by all images with a particular label, (ii) which patches correspond to unannotated background, and (iii) what is the appearance of each object, attribute and background type. Moreover, since multiple labels (attribute and object) can apply to a single patch, we need to disambiguate which aspects of the appearance of the patch are due to each of the (unknown) associated object and attribute labels. To address all these learning tasks we build on the IBP [7] and introduce a weakly-supervised stacked Indian Buffet process (WS-SIBP) to model data represented as bags (images) of instances (patches) with bag-level labels (image annotations). This is analogous to the notion of documents in topic models [2].

3.1   Model Formulation

First, we associate each object category and each attribute to a latent factor. If there are K_o object categories and K_a attributes, then the first $K_{oa} = K_o + K_a$ latent factors correspond to these. An unbounded number of further factors are available to explain away background clutter in the data. At training time, we assume a binary label vector $L^{(i)}$ for objects and attributes is provided for each image i. So $L_k^{(i)} = 1$ if attribute/object k is present, and zero otherwise. Also $L_k^{(i)} = 1$ for all $k > K_{oa}$. That is, without any labels, we assume all background types can be present. With these assumptions, the generative process (illustrated in Fig. 2) for image i represented as bags of patches $\mathbf{X}^{(i)} = \{\mathbf{X}_{j\cdot}^{(i)}\}$ is as follows:

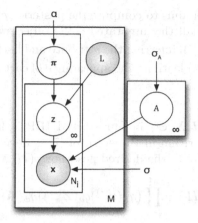

Fig. 2. The graphical model for WS-SIBP. Shaded nodes are observed.

For each latent factor $k \in 1 \ldots \infty$:

1. Draw an appearance distribution mean $\mathbf{A}_{k\cdot} \sim \mathcal{N}(0, \sigma_A^2 \mathbf{I})$.

For each image $i \in 1 \ldots M$:

1. Draw a sequence of i.i.d. random variables $v_1^{(i)}, v_2^{(i)} \cdots \sim \mathrm{Beta}(\alpha, 1)$,
2. Construct an image prior $\pi_k^{(i)} = \prod_{t=1}^{k} v_t^{(i)}$,
3. Input weak annotation $L_k^{(i)} \in \{0, 1\}$,
4. For each super-pixel patch $j \in 1 \ldots N_i$:
   (a) Sample state of each latent factor k: $z_{jk}^{(i)} \sim \mathrm{Bern}(\pi_k^{(i)} L_k^{(i)})$,
   (b) Sample patch appearance: $\mathbf{X}_{j\cdot}^{(i)} \sim \mathcal{N}(\mathbf{Z}_{j\cdot}^{(i)} \mathbf{A}, \sigma^2 \mathbf{I})$.

where $\mathcal{N}$, Bern and Beta respectively correspond to Normal, Bernoulli and Beta distributions with the specified parameters; and the notation $\mathbf{X}_{j\cdot}$ means the vector of row j in matrix $\mathbf{X}$. The Beta-Bernoulli and Normal-Normal conjugacy are chosen because they allow more efficient inference. α is the prior expected sparsity of annotations and σ^2 is the prior variance in appearance for each factor. Denote hidden variables by $\mathbf{H} = \{\boldsymbol{\pi}^{(1)}, \ldots, \boldsymbol{\pi}^{(M)}, \mathbf{Z}^{(1)}, \ldots, \mathbf{Z}^{(M)}, \mathbf{A}\}$, images by $\mathbf{X} = \{\mathbf{X}^{(1)}, \ldots, \mathbf{X}^{(M)}\}$, and parameters by $\boldsymbol{\Theta} = \{\alpha, \sigma_A, \sigma, \mathbf{L}\}$. Then the joint probability of the variables and data given the parameters is:

$$p(\mathbf{H}, \mathbf{X} | \boldsymbol{\Theta}) = \prod_{i=1}^{M} \left(\prod_{k=1}^{\infty} \left(p(\pi_k^{(i)} | \alpha) \prod_{j=1}^{N_i} p(z_{jk}^{(i)} | \pi_k^{(i)}, L_k^{(i)}) \right) \right.$$
$$\left. \cdot \prod_{j=1}^{N_i} p(\mathbf{X}_{j\cdot}^{(i)} | \mathbf{Z}_{j\cdot}^{(i)}, \mathbf{A}, \sigma) \right) \prod_{k=1}^{\infty} p(\mathbf{A}_{k\cdot} | \sigma_A^2). \tag{1}$$

Learning in our model aims to compute the posterior $p(H|X, \Theta)$ for: disambiguating and localising all the annotated ($L^{(i)}$) objects and attributes among the patches (inferring $Z_{j.}^{(i)}$), inferring the attribute and background prior for each image (inferring $\pi^{(i)}$), and learning the appearance of each factor (inferring A_k.).

3.2 Model Learning

Exact inference for $p(H|X, \Theta)$ in our stacked IBP is intractable, so an approximate inference algorithm in the spirit of [7] is developed. The mean field variational approximation to the desired posterior $p(H|X, \Theta)$ is:

$$q(H) = \prod_{i=1}^{M} \left(q_\tau(v^{(i)}) q_\nu(Z^{(i)}) \right) q_\phi(A) \tag{2}$$

where $q_\tau(v_k^{(i)}) = \text{Beta}(v_k^{(i)}; \tau_{k1}^{(i)} \tau_{k2}^{(i)})$, $q_\nu(z_{jk}^{(i)}) = \text{Bernoulli}(z_{jk}^{(i)}; \nu_{jk}^{(i)})$, $q_\phi(A_k.) = \mathcal{N}(A_k.; \phi_k, \Phi_k)$ and the infinite stick-breaking process for latent factors is truncated at K_{max}, so $\pi_k = 0$ for $k > K_{max}$. A variational message passing (VMP) strategy [7] can be used to minimise the KL divergence of Eq. (2) to the true posterior. Updates are obtained by deriving integrals of the form $\ln q(\mathbf{h}) = \mathbb{E}_{\mathbf{H} \backslash \mathbf{h}} [\ln p(\mathbf{H}, \mathbf{X})] + C$ for each group of hidden variables $\mathbf{h}$. These result in the series of iterative updates given in Algorithm 1, where $\varphi(\cdot)$ is the digamma function; and $q_{ms}^{(i)}$ and $\mathbb{E}_v[\log(1 - \prod_{t=1}^{k} v_t^{(i)})]$ are given in [7]. In practice, the truncation approximation means that our WS-SIBP runs with a finite number of factors K_{max} where truncation factor K_{max} can be freely set so long as it is bigger than the number of factors needed by both annotations and background clutter (K_{bg}), i.e., $K_{max} \gg K_o + K_a + K_{bg}$. Despite the combinatorial nature of the object-attribute association and localisation problem, our model is of complexity $\mathcal{O}(MNDK_{max})$ for M images with N patches, D feature dimension and K_{max} truncation factor.

3.3 Inference for Test Data

At testing time, the appearance of each factor k, now modelled by sufficient statistics $\mathcal{N}(A_k.; \phi_k, \Phi_k)$, is assumed to be known (learned from the training data), while annotations for each test image $L_k^{(i)}$ will need to be inferred. Thus Algorithm 1 still applies, but without the appearance update terms and with $L_k^{(i)} = 1 \ \forall k$, to reflect the fact that all the learned object, attribute, and background types could be present without any prior knowledge.

3.4 Applications of the Model

Given the learned model applied to testing data, we can perform the following tasks:

Free Annotation: This is to describe an image using a list of nouns and adjectives corresponding to objects and their associated attributes, as well as

Algorithm 1. Variational Inference for WS-SIBP

---

while *not converge* **do**

    for $k = 1$ **to** K_{max} **do**

$$\phi_k = (\tfrac{1}{\sigma^2} \sum_{i=1}^{M} \sum_{j=1}^{N_i} \nu_{jk}^{(i)} (\boldsymbol{X}_{j\cdot}^{(i)} - \sum_{l:l\neq k} \nu_{jl}^{(i)} \phi_l))(\tfrac{1}{\sigma_A^2} + \tfrac{1}{\sigma^2} \sum_{i=1}^{M} \sum_{j=1}^{N_i} \nu_{jk}^{(i)})^{-1}$$

$$\boldsymbol{\Phi}_k = \left(\tfrac{1}{\sigma_A^2} + \tfrac{1}{\sigma^2} \sum_{i=1}^{M} \sum_{j=1}^{N_i} \nu_{jk}^{(i)}\right)^{-1} \boldsymbol{I}$$

    end

    for $i = 1$ **to** M **do**

        for $k = 1$ **to** K_{max} **do**

$$\tau_{k1}^{(i)} = \alpha + \sum_{m=k}^{K_{max}} \sum_{j=1}^{N_i} \nu_{jm}^{(i)} + \sum_{m=k+1}^{K_{max}} (N_i - \sum_{j=1}^{N_i} \nu_{jm}^{(i)})(\sum_{s=k+1}^{m} q_{ms}^{(i)})$$

$$\tau_{k2}^{(i)} = 1 + \sum_{m=k}^{K_{max}} (N_i - \sum_{j=1}^{N_i} \nu_{jm}^{(i)}) q_{mk}^{(i)}$$

        for $j = 1$ **to** N_i **do**

$$\eta = \sum_{t=1}^{k} (\varphi(\tau_{t1}^{(i)}) - \varphi(\tau_{t2}^{(i)})) - \mathbb{E}_v[\log(1 - \prod_{t=1}^{k} v_t^{(i)})]$$
$$- \tfrac{1}{2\sigma^2} (\text{tr}(\boldsymbol{\Phi}_k) + \phi_k \phi_k^T - 2\phi_k(\boldsymbol{X}_{j\cdot}^{(i)} - \sum_{l:l\neq k} \nu_{jl}^{(i)} \phi_l)^T)$$

$$\nu_{jk}^{(i)} = \frac{L_k^{(i)}}{1+e^{-\eta}}$$

        end

    end

    end

end

---

locating them. To infer what objects are present in image i, the first K_o latent factors of the inferred $\boldsymbol{\pi}^{(i)}$ are thresholded or ranked to obtain a list of objects. This is followed by locating them via searching for the patches j^* maximising $\boldsymbol{Z}_{jk}^{(i)}$, then thresholding or ranking the K_a attribute latent factors in $\boldsymbol{Z}_{j^*k}^{(i)}$ to describe them.

Annotation given Object Names: This is a more constrained variant of the free annotation task above. Given a named (but not located) object k, its associated attributes can be estimated by first finding the location as $j^* = \arg\max_j \boldsymbol{Z}_{jk}^{(i)}$, then the associated attributes by $\boldsymbol{Z}_{j^*k}^{(i)}$ for $K_o < k \leq K_o + K_a$.

Object+Attribute Query: Images can be queried for a specified object-attribute conjunction $< k_o, k_a >$ by searching for $i^*, j^* = \arg\max_j \boldsymbol{Z}_{jk_o}^{(i)} \cdot \boldsymbol{Z}_{jk_a}^{(i)}$.

4 Experiments

Datasets: Various object and attribute datasets are available such as aPascal, ImageNet, SUN [24] and AwA [18]. We use aPascal because it has multiple objects per image; and ImageNet due to sharing attributes widely across categories.

480 Z. Shi et al.

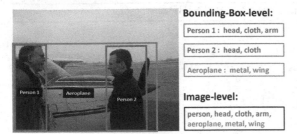

Bounding-Box-level:

Person 1 : head, cloth, arm

Person 2 : head, cloth

Aeroplane : metal, wing

Image-level:

person, head, cloth, arm,
aeroplane, metal, wing

Fig. 3. Strong bounding-box-level annotation and weak image-level annotations for aPascal are used for learning strongly supervised models and weakly supervised models respectively

Fig. 4. 43 subordinate classes of dog are converted into a single entry-level class 'dog'

aPascal: This dataset [9] is an attribute labelled version of PASCAL VOC 2008. There are 4340 images of 20 object categories. Each object is annotated with a list of 64 attributes that describe them by shape (e.g., isBoxy), parts (e.g., hasHead) and material (e.g., isFurry). In the original aPascal, attributes are strongly labelled for 12695 object bounding boxes, i.e. the object-attribute association are given. To test our weakly supervised approach, we merge the object-level category annotations and attribute annotations into a single annotation vector of length 84 for the entire image. This image-level annotation is much weaker than the original bounding-box-level annotation, as shown in Fig. 3. In all experiments, we use the same train/test splits provided by [9].

ImageNet Attribute: This dataset [27] contains 9600 images from 384 ImageNet synsets/categories. We ignore the provided bounding box annotation. Attributes for each bounding box are labelled as 1 (presence), -1 (absence) or 0 (ambiguous). We use the same 20 of 25 attributes as [27] and consider 1 and 0 as positive examples. Many of the 384 categories are subordinate categories, e.g. dog breeds. However, distinguishing fine-grained subordinate categories is beyond the scope of this study. We are interested in finding a 'black-dog' or 'white-car', rather than 'black-mutt' or 'white-ford-focus'. We thus convert the 384 ImageNet categories to 172 entry-level categories using [23] (see Fig. 4). We evenly split each class to create the training and testing sets.

Features: We first convert each image i to N_i super-pixels/patches by a recent segmentation algorithm [1]. We set the segmentation threshold to 0.1 to obtain a single over-segmentation from the hierarchical segmentation for each image. Each segmented patch is represented using two types of normalised histogram features: SIFT and Color. (1) SIFT: we extract regular grid (every 5 pixels) colorSIFT [29] at four scales. A 256 component GMM model is constructed on the collection of ColourSIFTs from all images. We compute Fisher Vector + PCA for all regular points in each patch following [14]. The resulting reduced descriptor is 512-D for every segmented region. (2) Colour: We convert the image to quantised LAB space $8\times8\times8$. A 512-D color histogram is then computed for each patch. The final 1024-D feature vector concatenates SIFT and Colour features together.

Compared Methods: We compare our WS-IBP to one strongly supervised model and three weakly supervised alternatives:

Strongly Supervised Model: A strongly supervised model uses bounding-box-level annotation. Two variants are considered for the two datasets respectively.

DPM+s-SVM: for aPascal, both object detector and attribute classifier are trained from fully supervised data (i.e. Bounding-Box-level annotation in Fig. 3). Specifically, we use the 20 pre-trained DPM detectors from [10] and 64 attribute classifiers from [9]. **GT+s-SVM:** for ImageNet attributes, there is not enough data to learn 172 strong DPM detectors as in aPascal. So we use the ground truth bounding box instead assuming we have perfect object detectors, giving a significant advantage to this strongly supervised model. We train attribute classifiers using our feature and liblinear SVM [8]. These strongly supervised models are similar in spirit to the models used in [17, 36, 35] and can provide a performance upper bound for the weakly supervised models compared.

w-SVM [9, 27]: In this weakly-supervised baseline, both object detectors and attribute classifiers are trained on the weak image-level labels as for our model (see Fig. 3). For aPascal, we train object and attribute classifiers using the feature extraction and model training codes (which is also based on [8]) provided by the authors of [9]. For ImageNet, our features are used, without segmentation.

MIML [41]: This is the multi-instance multi-label (MIML) learning method in [41]. In a way, our model can also be considered as a MIML method with each image a bag and each patch an instance. The MIML model provides a mechanism to use the same super-pixel/patch based representation for images as our model, thus providing the object/attribute localisation capability as our model does.

w-LDA: Weakly-supervised Latent Dirichlet Allocation (LDA) approaches [25, 31] have been used for object localisation. We implement a generalisation of LDA [2, 31] that accepts continuous feature vectors (instead of bag-of-words). Like MIML this method can also accept patch based representation, but w-LDA is more related to our WS-SIBP than MIML since it is also a generative model.

4.1   Image Annotation with Object-Attribute Association

An image description can be automatically generated by predicting objects and their associated attributes. Evaluating the performance of a multi-faceted framework covering annotation, association and localisation is non-trivial. To comprehensively cover all aspects of performance of our method and competitors, we perform three annotation tasks with different amount of constraints on test images: (1) *free annotation*, where no constraint is given to a test image, (2) *annotation given object names*, where named but not located objects are known

Table 1. Free annotation performance evaluated on t attributes per object

aPascal	w-SVM	MIML	w-LDA	WS-SIBP	DPM+s-SVM
AP@2	24.8	28.7	30.7	38.6	40.6
AP@5	21.2	22.4	24.0	28.9	30.3
AP@8	20.3	21.0	21.5	24.1	23.8
ImageNet	w-SVM	MIML	w-LDA	WS-SIBP	GT+s-SVM
AP@2	46.3	46.6	48.4	58.5	65.9
AP@3	41.1	43.2	43.1	51.8	60.7
AP@4	37.5	38.3	38.4	47.4	53.2

	w-SVM		MIML		w-LDA		WS-SIBP		DPM+s-SVM	
	bicycle	motorbike	person	bicycle	taillight	bicycle	person	motorbike	person	motorbike
	metal	metal	skin	headlight	taillight	wheel	cloth	wheel	cloth	engine
	row wind	row wind	cloth	window	label	rein	clear	shiny	skin	metal
	shiny	shiny	shiny	wheel	engine	beak	arm	pedal	hair	label
	text	text	leather	arm	shiny	metal	skin	exhaust	head	shiny
	wool	wool	foot/shoe	screen	glass	sail	head	round	leg	taillight
	cat	sheep	cat	dog	person	cat	person	cat	person	dog
	furry	furry	furry	mouth	cloth	nose	skin	furry	cloth	beak
	cloth	cloth	horn	furry	wood	furry	cloth	ear	torso	hand
	snout	snout	ear	torso	mast	arm	vegetation	beak	skin	arm
	leg	leg	occluded	taillight	torso	jet engine	torso	leg	clear	furry
	head	head	leg	shiny	arm	foot	arm	leather	head	skin
	car	person	person	train	car	cow	horse	car	car	horse
	window	window	hand	metal	wheel	furn.leg	furry	3d boxy	metal	furry
	glass	glass	screen	vert cyl	metal	head	leg	window	3d boxy	torso
	pedal	pedal	cloth	wing	propeller	furry	head	wheel	plastic	leaf
	3d boxy	3d boxy	arm	door	label	cloth	torso	handlebars	engine	saddle
	metal	metal	flower	leg	door	wool	rein	row wind	side mirror	feather

Fig. 5. Qualitative results on free annotation. False positives are shown in red. If the object prediction is wrong, the corresponding attribute box is shaded.

for each test image, and (3) *annotation given locations*, where objects locations are given in the form of bounding boxes, where the attributes can be predicted. **Free Annotation:** For WS-SIBP, w-LDA and MIML the procedure in Sec. 3.4 is used to detect objects and then describe them using the top t attributes. For the strongly supervised model on aPascal (DPM+s-SVM), we use DPM object detectors to find the most confident objects and their bounding boxes in each test image. Then we use the 64 attribute classifiers to predict top t attributes in each bounding box. In contrast, w-SVM trains attributes and objects independently, and cannot associate objects and attributes. We thus use it to predict only one attribute vector per image regardless of which object label it predicts.

Since there are variable number of objects per image in aPascal, quantitatively evaluating free annotation is not straightforward. Therefore, we evaluate only the most confident object and its associated top t attributes in each image, although more could be described. For ImageNet, there is only one object per image. We follow [11, 39] in evaluating annotation accuracy by average precision (AP), given varying numbers (t) of predicted attributes per object. Note that if the predicted object is wrong, all associated attributes are considered wrong.

Table 1 compares the free annotation performance of the five models. We have the following observations: (1) Our WS-SIBP, despite learned with the

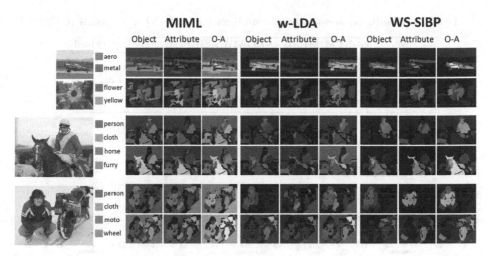

Fig. 6. Illustrating the inferred patch-annotation. Object and attributes are coloured, and multi-label annotation blends colours. The bottom two groups each have two rows corresponding to the two most confident objects detected.

weak image-level annotation, yields comparable performance to the strongly supervised model. The gap is particularly small for the more challenging aPascal dataset, whist for ImageNet, the gap is bigger as the strongly supervised GT | s-SVM has an unfair advantage by using the ground truth bounding boxes during testing. (2) WS-SIBP consistently outperforms the three weakly supervised alternatives. The margin is particularly large for $t = 2$ attributes per object, which is closest to the true number of attributes per object. For bigger t, all models must generate some irrelevant attributes thus narrowing the gaps. (3) As expected, the w-SVM model obtains the weakest results, suggesting that the ability to locate objects is important for modelling object-attribute association. (4) Compared to the two generative models, MIML has worse performance because a generative model is more capable of utilising weak labels [31]. (5) Between the two generative models, the advantage of our WS-SIBP over w-LDA is clear; due to the ability of IBP to explain each patch with multiple non-competing factors. (Training two independent w-LDA models for objects and attributes respectively is not a solution: the problem would re-occur for multiple competing attributes.)

Fig. 5 shows qualitative results on aPascal via the two most confident objects and their associated attributes. This is challenging data – even the strongly supervised DPM+s-SVM makes mistakes for both attribute and object prediction. Compared to the weakly supervised models, WS-SIBP has more accurate prediction – it jointly and non-competitively models objects and their attributes so object detection benefits from attribute detection and vice versa. Other weakly supervised models are also more likely to mismatch attributes with objects, e.g. MIML detects a shiny person rather than the correct shiny motorbike.

Table 2. Results on annotation given object names (GN) or locations (GL)

		w-SVM	MIML	w-LDA	WS-SIBP	strongly supervised
GN	aPascal	–	32.1	35.5	38.9	41.8
	ImageNet	32.4	33.5	39.6	51.5	56.8
GL	aPascal	33.2	35.1	35.8	43.8	42.1
	ImageNet	37.7	39.1	46.8	53.7	56.8

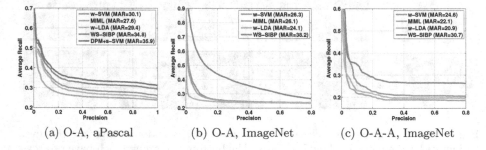

(a) O-A, aPascal   (b) O-A, ImageNet   (c) O-A-A, ImageNet

Fig. 7. Object-attribute query results as precision-average recall curve

To gain some insight into what has been learned by our model and why it is better than the weakly supervised alternatives, Fig. 6 visualises the attribute and object factors learned by WS-SIBP model and by the two baselines that also use patches as input. It is evident that without explicit background modelling, MIML suffers greatly by trying to explain the background patches using the weak labels. In contrast, both w-LDA and WS-SIBP have good segmentation of foreground objects, showing that both the learned foreground and background topics are meaningful. However, for w-LDA, since object and attributes topics compete for the same patch, each patch is dominated by either an object or attribute topic. In contrast, the object factors and attribute factors co-exist happily in WS-SIBP as they should do, e.g. most person patches have the clothing attribute as well.

Annotation Given Object Names (GN): In this experiment, we assume that object labels are given and we aim to describe each object by attributes, corresponding to tasks such as: "Describe the car in this image". For the strongly supervised model on aPascal, we use the object's DPM detector to find the most confident bounding box. Then we predict attributes for that box. Here, annotation accuracy is the same as attribute accuracy, so the performance of different models is evaluated following [40] by mean average precision (mAP) under the precision-recall curve. Note that for aPascal, w-SVM reports the same list of attributes for all co-existing objects, without being able to localise and distinguish them. Its result is thus not meaningful and is excluded. The same set of conclusions can be drawn from Table 2 as in the free annotation task: our WS-SIBP at par with the supervised models and outperforming the weakly supervised ones.

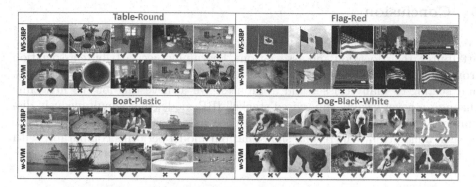

Fig. 8. Object-attribute query: qualitative comparison

Given Object Location (GL): If we further know the bounding box of an object in a test image, we can simply predict attributes inside each bounding box. This becomes the conventional attribute prediction task [9, 27] for describing an object. Table 2 shows the results, where similar observations can be made as in the other two tasks above. Note that in this case the strongly supervised model is the method used in [9]. The mAP obtained using our weakly supervised model is even higher than the strongly supervised model (though our area-under-ROC-curve value of 81.5 is slightly lower than the 83.4 figure reported in [9]).

4.2 Object-Attribute Query

In this task object-attribute association is used for image retrieval. Following work on multi-attribute queries [26], we use mean average recall over all precisions (MAR) as the evaluation metric. Note that unlike [26] which requires each queried *combination* to have enough (100) training examples to train conjunction classifiers, our method can query novel never-previously-seen combinations. Three experiments are conducted. We generate 300 random object-attribute combinations for aPascal and ImageNet respectively and 300 object-attribute-attribute queries for ImageNet. For the strongly supervised model, we normalise and multiply object detector with attribute classifier scores. No object detector is trained for ImageNet so no result is reported there. For w-SVM, we use [30] to calibrate the SVM scores for objects and attributes as in [26]. For the three WS models, the procedure in Sec. 3.4 is used to compute the retrieval ranking.

Quantitative results are shown in Fig. 7 and some qualitative examples in Fig. 8. Our WS-SIBP has a very similar MAR values to the strongly supervised DPM+s-SVM, while outperforming all the other models. w-SVM calibration [30] helps it outperform MIML and w-LDA. However, the lack of object-attribute association and background modelling still causes problems for w-SVM. This is illustrated in the 'dog-black-white' example shown in Fig. 8 where a white background caused an image with a black dog retrieved at rank 2 by w-SVM.

5   Conclusion

We have presented an effective model for weakly-supervised learning of objects, attributes, their location and associations. Learning object-attribute association from weak supervision is non-trivial but critical for learning from 'natural' data, and scaling to many classes and attributes. We achieve this for the first time through a novel weakly-supervised stacked IBP model that simultaneously disambiguates patch-annotation correspondence, as well as learning the appearance of each annotation. Our results show that our model performs comparably with a strongly supervised alternative that is significantly more costly to supervise.

References

1. Arbelaez, P., Maire, M., Fowlkes, C., Malik, J.: Contour detection and hierarchical image segmentation. TPAMI (2011)
2. Blei, D.M., Ng, A.Y., Jordan, M.I.: Latent dirichlet allocation. JMLR (2003)
3. Bourdev, L., Maji, S., Malik, J.: Describing people: A poselet-based approach to attribute classification. In: ICCV (2011)
4. Chen, H., Gallagher, A., Girod, B.: Describing clothing by semantic attributes. In: Fitzgibbon, A., Lazebnik, S., Perona, P., Sato, Y., Schmid, C. (eds.) ECCV 2012, Part III. LNCS, vol. 7574, pp. 609–623. Springer, Heidelberg (2012)
5. Chen, X., Shrivastava, A., Gupta, A.: Neil: Extracting visual knowledge from web data. In: ICCV (2013)
6. Deselaers, T., Alexe, B., Ferrari, V.: Weakly supervised localization and learning with generic knowledge. IJCV 100 (2012)
7. Doshi-Velez, F., Miller, K.T., Gael, J.V., Teh, Y.W.: Variational inference for the indian buffet process. Tech. rep., University of Cambridge (2009)
8. Fan, R.E., Chang, K.W., Hsieh, C.J., Wang, X.R., Lin, C.J.: LIBLINEAR: A library for large linear classification. JMLR (2008)
9. Farhadi, A., Endres, I., Hoiem, D., Forsyth, D.: Describing objects by their attributes. In: CVPR (2009)
10. Felzenszwalb, P.F., Girshick, R.B., McAllester, D., Ramanan, D.: Object detection with discriminatively trained part based models. TPAMI (2010)
11. Feng, Z., Jin, R., Jain, A.: Large-scale image annotation by efficient and robust kernel metric learning. In: ICCV (2013)
12. Fu, Y., Hospedales, T.M., Xiang, T., Gong, S.: Attribute learning for understanding unstructured social activity. In: Fitzgibbon, A., Lazebnik, S., Perona, P., Sato, Y., Schmid, C. (eds.) ECCV 2012, Part IV. LNCS, vol. 7575, pp. 530–543. Springer, Heidelberg (2012)
13. Griffiths, T.L., Ghahramani, Z.: The indian buffet process: An introduction and review. JMLR (2011)
14. Jégou, H., Perronnin, F., Douze, M., Sánchez, J., Pérez, P., Schmid, C.: Aggregating local image descriptors into compact codes. TPAMI (2011)
15. Kovashka, A., Grauman, K.: Attribute adaptation for personalized image search. In: ICCV (2013)
16. Kovashka, A., Vijayanarasimhan, S., Grauman, K.: Actively selecting annotations among objects and attributes. In: ICCV (2011)
17. Kulkarni, G., Premraj, V., Dhar, S., Li, S., Choi, Y., Berg, A., Berg, T.: Baby talk: Understanding and generating simple image descriptions. In: CVPR (2011)

18. Lampert, C.H., Nickisch, H., Harmeling, S.: Attribute-based classification for zero-shot visual object categorization. IEEE TPAMI (2013)
19. Li, L.J., Socher, R., Fei-Fei, L.: Towards total scene understanding:classification, annotation and segmentation in an automatic framework. In: CVPR (2009)
20. Mahajan, D., Sellamanickam, S., Nair, V.: A joint learning framework for attribute models and object descriptions. In: ICCV (2011)
21. Marchesotti, L., Perronnin, F.: Learning beautiful (and ugly) attributes. In: BMVC (2013)
22. Nguyen, N.: A new svm approach to multi-instance multi-label learning. In: ICDM (2010)
23. Ordonez, V., Deng, J., Choi, Y., Berg, A.C., Berg, T.L.: From large scale image categorization to entry-level categories. In: ICCV (2013)
24. Patterson, G., Hays, J.: Sun attribute database: Discovering, annotating, and recognizing scene attributes. In: CVPR (2012)
25. Rasiwasia, N., Vasconcelos, N.: Latent dirichlet allocation models for image classification. TPAMI (2013)
26. Rastegari, M., Diba, A., Parikh, D., Farhadi, A.: Multi-attribute queries: To merge or not to merge? In: CVPR (2013)
27. Russakovsky, O., Fei-Fei, L.: Attribute learning in large-scale datasets. In: Kutulakos, K.N. (ed.) ECCV 2010 Workshops, Part I. LNCS, vol. 6553, pp. 1 14. Springer, Heidelberg (2012)
28. Sadeghi, M., Farhadi, A.: Recognition using visual phrases. In: CVPR (2011)
29. van de Sande, K.E.A., Gevers, T., Snoek, C.G.M.: Evaluating color descriptors for object and scene recognition. TPAMI (2010)
30. Scheirer, W., Kumar, N., Belhumeur, P.N., Boult, T.E.: Multi-attribute spaces: Calibration for attribute fusion and similarity search. In: CVPR (2012)
31. Shi, Z., Hospedales, T.M., Xiang, T.: Bayesian joint topic modelling for weakly supervised object localisation. In: ICCV (2013)
32. Siddiquie, B., Feris, R., Davis, L.: Image ranking and retrieval based on multi-attribute queries. In: CVPR (2011)
33. Socher, R., Fei-Fei, L.: Connecting modalities: Semi-supervised segmentation and annotation of images using unaligned text corpora. In: CVPR (2010)
34. Turakhia, N., Parikh, D.: Attribute dominance: What pops out? In: ICCV (2013)
35. Wang, G., Forsyth, D.: Joint learning of visual attributes, object classes and visual saliency. In: ICCV (2009)
36. Wang, S., Joo, J., Wang, Y., Zhu, S.C.: Weakly supervised learning for attribute localization in outdoor scenes. In: CVPR (2013)
37. Wang, X., Ji, Q.: A unified probabilistic approach modeling relationships between attributes and objects. In: ICCV (2013)
38. Wang, Y., Mori, G.: A discriminative latent model of object classes and attributes. In: Daniilidis, K., Maragos, P., Paragios, N. (eds.) ECCV 2010, Part V. LNCS, vol. 6315, pp. 155–168. Springer, Heidelberg (2010)
39. Wu, L., Jin, R., Jain, A.K.: Tag completion for image retrieval. TPAMI (2013)
40. Zhang, N., Farrell, R., Iandola, F., Darrell, T.: Deformable part descriptors for fine-grained recognition and attribute prediction. In: ICCV (2013)
41. Zhou, Z.H., Zhang, M.L., Huang, S.J., Li, Y.F.: Multi-instance multi-label learning. Artificial Intelligence (2012)

Interestingness Prediction
by Robust Learning to Rank[*]

Yanwei Fu[1], Timothy M. Hospedales[1], Tao Xiang[1,**], Shaogang Gong[1],
and Yuan Yao[2,**]

[1] School of EECS, Queen Mary University of London, UK
[2] School of Mathematical Sciences, Peking University, China
{y.fu,t.hospedales,t.xiang,s.gong}@qmul.ac.uk, yuany@math.pku.edu.cn

Abstract. The problem of predicting image or video interestingness
from their low-level feature representations has received increasing interest. As a highly subjective visual attribute, annotating the interestingness value of training data for learning a prediction model is challenging.
To make the annotation less subjective and more reliable, recent studies
employ crowdsourcing tools to collect pairwise comparisons – relying on
majority voting to prune the annotation outliers/errors. In this paper,
we propose a more principled way to identify annotation outliers by formulating the interestingness prediction task as a unified robust learning
to rank problem, tackling both the outlier detection and interestingness
prediction tasks jointly. Extensive experiments on both image and video
interestingness benchmark datasets demonstrate that our new approach
significantly outperforms state-of-the-art alternatives.

1 Introduction

The problem of automatically predicting if people would find an image or video
interesting has started to receive increasing attention [7,16,21]. Interestingness
prediction has a number of real-world applications. In particular, since the number of images and videos uploaded to the Internet is growing explosively, people
are increasingly relying on image/video search engines or recommendation tools
to select which ones to view. Given a query, ranking the retrieved data with
relevancy to the query based on the predicted interestingness would improve the
user satisfaction. Similarly user stickiness can be increased if a media-sharing
website such as YouTube can recommend videos that are both relevant and interesting. Other applications such as web advertising and video summarisation
can also benefit.

Learning a computational model of how humans perceive interestingness is
however extremely challenging due to the following two reasons. First, what

---

[*] The research of Yuan Yao was supported in part by National Basic Research Program
of China (973 Program 2012CB825501), NSFC grant 61071157, and a joint NSFC-
Royal Society grant 61211130360, IE110976 with Tao Xiang.
[**] Corresponding authors.

D. Fleet et al. (Eds.): ECCV 2014, Part II, LNCS 8690, pp. 488–503, 2014.

defines interestingness and what cues contribute to the human perception of interestingness are still under investigation in psychophysics [39], cognitive sciences [4] and recently computer vision [7,16,21]. Therefore current research in computer vision on interestingness is primarily focused on designing relevant feature representations. Second, in order to predict interestingness from low-level features, training data with labelled interestingness values are required. This is problematic because as a highly subjective visual attribute, directly annotating an interestingness value for a data point is unreliable, e.g. on a scale of 1 to 10, 10 being the most interesting, different people will have very different ideas on what a scale 5 means for an image, especially without any common reference point.

In order to obtain more reliable interestingness annotation and thus learn better prediction models, recent studies [16,21] propose to model interestingness from human pairwise comparison data collected using crowdsourcing tools such as Amazon Mechanic Turk (AMT). The annotation task is to select between a pair of images or videos which one is more interesting. This is considered to be a much easier task, resulting in more reliable annotations. However, this brings about two new problems: (1) *sparsity* – the number of pairwise comparisons required is much bigger than for directly annotated interestingness values (there are $n^2 - n$ pairs give n data points); even with crowdsourcing tools, the annotation will be sparse, i.e. not all pairs are compared and each pair is only compared few times. (2) *Outliers* – it is well known that crowdsourced data are noisy [6,43,30]. Existing approaches [16,21] solve the outlier problem by majority voting which requires multiple comparisons for each pair of data points; but its effectiveness is severely limited by the sparsity of the data.

In this paper we propose a novel approach for predicting interestingness from sparse and noisy pairwise comparison data. Different from existing approaches which first remove outliers by majority voting, followed by regression [16] or learning to rank [21], we formulate a unified robust learning to rank framework to jointly solve both the outlier detection and interestingness prediction problems. Critically, instead of detecting outliers locally and independently at each pair by majority voting, our outlier detection method operates globally integrating all local pairwise comparisons together to minimise a cost that corresponds to global inconsistency of ranking order. This enables us to identify outliers that receive majority votes yet cause large global ranking inconsistency and thus should be removed. Furthermore, as a global method, only one comparison per pair is required, therefore significantly reducing the data sparsity problem compared to the conventional majority voting approach. Extensive experiments on benchmark image and video interestingness datasets demonstrate that our method significantly outperforms the state-of-the-art alternatives. In addition, since interestingness is a special case of relative attributes, we also validate our method on predicting more general image relative attributes for image classification tasks.

2   Related Work

Predicting Image and Video Interestingness. Early efforts on image interestingness prediction focus on different aspects than interestingness as such, including image quality [22], memorability [19], and aesthetics [7]. These properties are related to interestingness but different. For instance, it is found that memorability can have a low correlation with interestingness - people often remember things that they find uninteresting [16]. The work of Gygli et al [16] is the first systematic study of image interestingness. It shows that three cues contribute the most to interestingness: aesthetics, unusualness/novelty and general preferences, the last of which refers to the fact that people in general find certain types of scenes more interesting than others, for example outdoor-natural vs. indoor-manmade. Different features are then designed to represent these cues as input to a prediction model. In comparison, video interestingness has received much less attention, perhaps because it is even harder to understand its meaning and contributing cues. [28] focuses on key frames so essentially treats it as an image interestingness problem, whilst [21] is the first work that proposes benchmark video interestingness datasets and evaluates different features for video interestingness prediction. In a broader sense of attributes [26,11,12,27,13] interestingness can be considered as one type of relative attributes [35], although those attributes, such as how smiling a person is, are much less subjective.

Computational Models of Interestingness. Most earlier work casts the aesthetics or interestingness prediction problem as a regression problem [22,7,19,28]. However, as discussed before, obtaining an absolute value of interestingness for each data point is too subjective and affected too much by unknown personal preference/social background to be reliable. Therefore the most recent two studies on image [16] and video [21] interestingness all collect pairwise comparison data by crowdsourcing. Both use majority voting to remove outliers first. After that the prediction models differ – [16] converts pairwise comparisons into an absolute interestingness values and use a regression model, whilst [21] employs rankSVM [3] to learn a ranking function, with the estimated ranking score of an unseen video used as the interestingness prediction. We compare with both approaches in our experiments and demonstrate that our unified robust learning to rank approach is superior as we can remove better outliers – even if they correspond to comparisons receiving majority votes – thanks to its global formulation.

Learning from Noisy Crowdsourced Data. Beyond interesting prediction, many large-scale computer vision problems rely on human intelligence tasks (HIT) using crowdsourcing services, e.g. AMT (Amazon Mechanical Turk) to collect annotations. Many studies [23,40,36,30] highlight the necessity of validating the random or malicious labels/workers and give some filtering heuristics for data collection. However, existing approaches to annotation noise are primarily based on majority voting which requires a costly volume of redundant annotations. Moreover, as a local (per-pair) inconsistency filtering method, it has no effect on global inconsistency and even risks introducing additional inconsistency due to the well-known Condorcet's paradox [15].

Robust Learning to Rank. Statistical ranking has been widely studied in statistics [20,10] and computer science [44,45]. By aggregating pairwise local rankings into a global ranking, methods such as Huber-LASSO [46,18] have the potential to be robust against local ranking noise [5,31]. However, statistical ranking only concerns the ranking of the observed/training data, but not learning to predict unseen data by learning ranking functions. To learn such ranking functions for applications such as interestingness prediction, a feature representation of the data points must be used as model input in addition to the local ranking orders. This is addressed in learning to rank which is widely studied in machine learning [1,29,41,2]. However, existing learning to rank work does not explicitly model and remove outliers for robust learning: a critical issue for learning from crowdsourced data in practice. In this work, for the first time, we study the problem of robust learning to rank given extremely noisy and sparse crowdsourced pairwise labels. We show both theoretically and experimentally that by solving both the outlier detection and ranking estimation problems jointly, we achieve better outlier detection than existing statistical ranking methods and better ranking prediction than existing learning to rank method such as rankSVM without outlier detection.

Our Contributions. are threefold: (1) We propose a novel robust learning to rank method for interestingness prediction from noisy and sparse pairwise comparison data. (2) For the first time, the problems of detecting outliers and estimating ranking score are solved jointly in our unified framework. (3) We demonstrate both theoretically and experimentally that our method is superior to existing majority voting based methods as well as statistical ranking based methods.

3 A Unified Robust Learning to Rank (URLR) Framework

3.1 Problem Statement

We aim to learn an interestingness prediction model from a set of sparse and noisy pairwise comparisons, each comparison corresponding to a local ranking between a pair of images or videos. Suppose our training set has I data points/instances represented by a low-level feature matrix $\Phi = \left[\phi_i^T\right]_{i=1}^{I} \in R^{I \times d}$, where ϕ_i is a d-dimensional column feature vector for representing instance i. The annotations or data labels are represented as an annotation matrix Y. In particular, assume each pair of instances on average receive K votes by annotators. We will have $Y_{ij}^k = 1$ if the k-th vote indicates that instance i is more interesting than instance j, and $Y_{ji}^k = 1$ otherwise. The annotation matrix is then constructed as $Y_{ij} = \sum_k Y_{ij}^k$. These pairwise comparisons can be naturally represented by a directed graph $G = (V, E)$ with node set $V = \{i\}_{i=1}^{I}$ and edge set $E = \{i \rightarrow j | Y_{ij} > 0\}$. That is, an edge $i \rightarrow j$ exists if $Y_{ij} > 0$.

Given the training data Φ and Y, there are two tasks: (1) removing the outliers in Y and (2) estimating an interestingness prediction function. In this work a linear function is considered due to its low computational complexity, that is, given the low-level feature ϕ_x of a test instance x we use a linear function $f(x) = \beta^T \phi_x$ to predict its interestingness, where β is the coefficient weight vector of the low-level feature ϕ_x. All formulations can be easily updated to use a non-linear function.

Note that the annotation matrix Y is not symmetric – in an ideal case, one hopes that the votes received on each pair are unanimous, e.g. $Y_{ij} > 0$ and $Y_{ji} = 0$; but often there are disagreements, i.e. both $Y_{ij} > 0$ and $Y_{ji} > 0$. Assuming both cannot be true simultaneously, one of them will be an outlier. In this case, one is the majority and the other minority which will be pruned by the majority voting method. This is why majority voting is a local outlier detection method and requires as many votes per pair as possible to be effective (the wisdom of a crowd).

3.2   Framework Formulation

We propose to prune outliers globally. To this end, we introduce an unknown variable γ_{ij} for each element of Y which indicates whether Y_{ij} is an outlier. We thus aim to estimate both γ_{ij} for outlier detection and β for interestingness prediction in a unified framework. Specifically, for each edge $i \to j \in E$, Y_{ij} is modelled as,

$$Y_{ij} = \beta^T \phi_i - \beta^T \phi_j + \gamma_{ij} \tag{1}$$

where $\gamma_{ij} \in R$ is a variable that indicates annotation outliers. For an edge $i \to j$, if Y_{ij} is not an outlier, we expect $\beta^T \phi_i - \beta^T \phi_j$ should be approximately equal to Y_{ij}, therefore we have $\gamma_{ij} = 0$. On the contrary, when the prediction of $\beta^T \phi_i - \beta^T \phi_j$ differs greatly from Y_{ij}, we can explain Y_{ij} as an outlier and compensate for the discrepancy between the prediction and the annotation with a nonzero value of γ_{ij}. The only prior knowledge we have on γ_{ij} is that it is a sparse variable, i.e. in most cases $\gamma_{ij} = 0$.

For the whole training set, Eq (1) is written in its matrix form

$$Y = C\Phi\beta + \Gamma \tag{2}$$

where $Y = [Y_{ij}]$, $\Gamma = [\gamma_{ij}]$, and C is the incident matrix of the directed graph G, where $C_{ie} = -1/1$ if the edge e leaves/enters vertex i.

In order to estimate the $I^2 + d$ unknown parameters (I^2 for Γ and d for β), we aim to minimise the discrepancy between the annotation Y and our prediction $C\Phi\beta + \Gamma$, as well as keeping the outlier estimation Γ sparse. To that end, we put a l_2-loss on the discrepancy and a l_1- penalty on the outlier variables as a regularisation measure. This gives us the following cost function:

$$\min_{\beta,\Gamma} \frac{1}{2} \|Y - C\Phi\beta - \Gamma\|_2^2 + \lambda\|\Gamma\|_1 \tag{3}$$

$$:= \sum_{i \to j \in E} \left[\frac{1}{2}(Y_{ij} - \gamma_{ij} - \beta^T \phi_i + \beta^T \phi_j)^2 + \lambda|\gamma_{ij}| \right] \tag{4}$$

where λ is a free parameter corresponding to the weight for the regularisation term. With this cost function, our Unified Robust Learning to Rank (URLR) framework identifies outliers globally by integrating all local pairwise comparison together.

Figure 1(a) illustrates why our URLR framework is advantageous over the local majority voting method for outlier detection. Assume there are five images $A - E$ with five pairs compared three time each, and the correct ranking order of these 5 images in terms of interestingness is $A < B < C < D < E$. Figure 1(a) shows that among the five compared pairs, majority voting can successfully identify four outlier cases: $A > B$, $B > C$, $C > D$, and $D > E$, but not the fifth one $E < A$. However when considered globally, it is clear that $E < A$ is an outlier because if we have $A < B < C < D < E$, we can deduce $A < E$. Our formulation can detect this tricky outlier. More specifically, if the estimated β makes $\beta^T \phi_A - \beta^T \phi_E > 0$, it has a small local inconsistency cost for that minority vote edge $A \rightarrow E$. However, such β value will be 'propagated' to other images by using the voting edges $B \rightarrow A$, $C \rightarrow B$, $D \rightarrow C$, and $E \rightarrow D$, which are accumulated into much bigger global inconsistency with the annotation. This makes our model detect $E \rightarrow A$ as an outlier, contrary to the majority voting decision. In particular, the majority voting will introduce a loop comparison $A < B < C < D < E < A$ which is the well-known Condorcet's paradox [15]. We further give two more extreme cases in Fig. 1(b) and (c). Due to such Condorcet's paradox, in Fig. 1(b) the estimated β from majority voting is even worse than that from all annotation pairs which at least save the right annotation $A \rightarrow E$. Furthermore, Fig. 1(c) shows that when each pair only receives votes along one direction, majority voting will cease to work altogether, but our URLR can still detect outliers by examining the global cost.

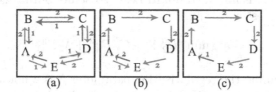

$$\begin{array}{ccc} \text{(a)} & \text{(b)} & \text{(c)} \end{array}$$

Fig. 1. Better outlier detection can be achieved using our URLR framework than majority voting. Green arrows indicate correct annotations, while red arrows are outliers.

3.3   Problem Decomposition

To solve Eq (3), we rewrite the cost function as,

$$L(\beta, \Gamma) = \frac{1}{2}\|Y - X\beta - \Gamma\|_2^2 + \lambda\|\Gamma\|_1. \tag{5}$$

where $X = C\Phi$. With $\frac{\partial L}{\partial \beta} = 0$, we have

$$\hat{\beta} = (X^T X)^\dagger X^T (Y - \Gamma). \tag{6}$$

The Moore-Penrose pseudo-inverse of $X^T X$ is equivalent to the limit of ridge regression solution: $(X^T X)^\dagger = \lim_{\mu \to 0}((X^T X)^T \cdot (X^T X) + \mu \mathbf{1})^{-1}(X^T X)^T$, where $\mathbf{1}$ is the eye matrix. To avoid numerical instability in many practical applications, we can replace the pseudo-inverse with ridge regression by setting $\mu > 0$. The standard solvers for Eq (6) will require $O(I^3)$ computational complexity. To reduce the complexity, the Krylov iterative and algebraic multi-grid methods [17] can be used.

Now plugging the solution of $\hat{\beta}$ back into Eq (5) and defining the hat matrix $H = H(X) = X(X^T X)^{-1}X^T$, we have

$$\hat{\Gamma} = \arg\min_{\Gamma} \|Y - \Gamma - H(Y - \Gamma)\|_2^2 + \lambda \| \Gamma \|_1 \tag{7}$$

The first term in Eq (7) is L_2- loss of the residuals of the observations $Y - \Gamma$ without the outliers Γ which is: $r = Y - \Gamma - H(Y - \Gamma) = (I - H)(Y - \Gamma)$. Interestingly, Eq (7) does not rely on the estimation of $\hat{\beta}$. We therefore can now decompose the optimisation problem (5) into two intervening sub-problems: outlier detection in (7) and estimation of β using (6).

3.4   Outlier Detection by Regularisation Path

For outlier detection, we can further simplify Eq (7) by Singular Value Decomposition (SVD),

$$X = U\Sigma A^T \tag{8}$$

where $U = [U_1, U_2]$ with U_1 an orthogonal basis of the column space of X and A is the conjugate transpose of U. Therefore, due to the orthogonality $U^T U = I$ and $U_2 X = 0$, Eq (7) is now a standard Least Absolute Shrinkage and Selection Operator (LASSO) estimator [9],

$$\hat{\Gamma} = \arg\min_{\Gamma} \|U_2^T Y - U_2^T \Gamma\|_2^2 + \lambda\|\Gamma\|_1 \tag{9}$$

Nevertheless, tuning the regularisation parameter λ is a notoriously difficult problem. Especially in our URLR framework, the λ value directly decides the ratio of outliers detected and the ratio is unknown. A number of methods for determining λ exist, but none is suitable for our formulation: (1) some heuristics rules like $\lambda = 2.5\hat{\sigma}$ [1] are popular in existing robust ranking models such as the M-estimator [18]. However setting a constant λ value independent of dataset is far from optimal because the ratio of outliers may vary for different crowdsourcing experiments. (2) Cross validation is also not applicable here because each edge $i \to j$ is associated with a γ_{ij} variable and any held-out edge $i \to j$ also corresponds to an unknown variable γ_{ij}. As a result, cross validation can only optimise part of the sparse variables while leaving those for the held-out validation set undetermined. (3) The other alternatives e.g. Akaike information criterion (AIC) and Bayesian information criterion (BIC) employ the relative

---

[1] $\hat{\sigma}$ is a Gaussian variance and is manually set by human prior knowledge.

quality and likelihood functions of the statistical models as the criterion for parameter selections. These statistical criteria however have no direct connection to the outliers pruned. Ideally λ should be a data-dependent parameter which selects a cut-off value and corresponds to the pruning rate p as the portion of the outliers among all comparisons.

This inspires us to sequentially consider all available solutions for all sparse variables along the Regularisation Path (RP) by gradually decreasing the value of the regularisation parameter λ from ∞ to 0. Specifically, based on the piecewise-linearity property of LASSO [9], RP can be efficiently computed by Least Angle Regression (LARS [8]). When $\lambda = \infty$, the regularisation parameter will strongly penalise outlier detection: if any annotation is taken as an outlier, it will greatly increase the value of the object function in Eq (9). When λ is changed from ∞ to 0, LASSO[2] will first select the variable subset accounting for the highest variances to the observations $U_2^T Y$ in Eq (9). These high variances should be assigned higher priority to represent the nonzero elements[3] of Γ of Eq (2), because Γ compensates the discrepancy between annotation and prediction. Based on this idea, we can order the edge set E by the λ values according to which nonzero γ_{ij} appears first when λ is decreased from ∞ to 0. In other words, if an edge γ_{ij} becomes nonzero at a larger λ_{ij} value, it has a higher probability to be an outlier. Following this order, we identify the top $p\%$ edge set Λ_p as the annotation outliers. And its complementary set $\Lambda_{1-p} = E \setminus \Lambda_p$ are the inliers. Therefore, the outcome of estimating Γ using Eq (9) is a binary outlier indication matrix $F_\Gamma = [F_{\gamma_{ij}}]$:

$$F_{\gamma_{ij}} = \begin{cases} 1 & i \to j \subset \Lambda_{1-p} \\ 0 & i \to j \in \Lambda_p \end{cases}$$

where each element $F_{\gamma_{ij}}$ indicates whether the corresponding edge $i \to j$ is an outlier or not. With this matrix, β can be solved by

$$\beta = (X^T X)^\dagger X^T (Y \odot F_\Gamma) \qquad (10)$$

where $\odot$ is the Hardmard product and $F_\Gamma = [F_{\gamma_{ij}}]$. The pseudo-code of learning our URLR model is shown in Alg. 1. Note that it is very efficient to solve the entire regularisation path by LARS: "roughly the same computational cost as a single least square fit" (P438[33]).

3.5   Theretoial Advantage over Huber-LASSO

Our URLR framework is related to a widely used statistical ranking method – Huber-LASSO [46,14]. Huber-LASSO addresses estimating the robust ranking

---

[2] For a thorough discussion from a statistical perspective, please read [9,10,8,38].
[3] This is related with LASSO for covariate selection in a graph. Please read [32] for more details.

Algorithm 1. Learning a unified robust learning to rank model

---

Input: A training dataset Φ with pairwise annotation Y and an outlier pruning rate $p\%$.

Output: Detection of outliers F_Γ and prediction model parameter β.

1. Perform SVD on X using Eq (8);
2. Solve Eq (9) using Regularisation Path;
3. Take the top $p\%$ pairs as outliers and estimate the outlier indicator matrix F_Γ;
4. Compute β using Eq (10).

---

of the training data rather than learning to predict the ranking of test data; therefore only the annotation part of the training data Y is required, instead of both Y and Φ in URLR. Specifically, given the annotation Y of the training data, Huber-LASSO estimates the global ranking order θ by

$$\hat{\theta} = \min_\theta \quad \frac{1}{2}\|Y - C\theta - \Gamma\|_2^2 + \lambda \parallel \Gamma \parallel_1 \tag{11}$$

$$:= \sum_{(i,j)\in E} \left[\frac{1}{2}(Y_{ij} - \gamma_{ij} - \theta_i + \theta_j)^2 + \lambda|\gamma_{ij}| \right]$$

where θ_i is the ranking score for instance i. Eq (11) is studied in [46,14] and is proved to be equivalent to the robust regression problem with Huber's loss function [18]. This is why it is called Huber-LASSO[4].

Our URLR model can be seen as an extension of Huber-LASSO for the ability to predict interestingness. It introduces the prediction model parameter β estimated as $\hat{\beta} = \hat{\theta}\Phi$. But this is not the most critical difference – one could still use Huber-LASSO to remove outliers and then use the same Eq (10) to estimate β. The more important difference is that URLR can better identify outliers, especially for sparse graphs. More specifically, to solve Eq (11), a similar formulation as Eq (9) can be used, solved by the same regularisation path method as in URLR. However, instead of SVD decomposing X in Eq (8), for Huber-LASSO, the matrix C is decomposed. This means the solution space of Eq (11) is $\dim(\Gamma) = |E| - I + 1$ where $|E|$ is the number of pairs compared and I is the number of graph nodes, i.e. training images or videos. Given a sparse dataset, this space is very small. In contrast, URLR enlarges $\dim(\Gamma)$ by including the subspace of original node space orthogonal to the feature space (Eq (9)). This means the solution space of Eq (9) is $\dim(\Gamma) \approx |E| - d$. When the feature dimension d is smaller than the number of images/videos I, the dimension of the solution space of Γ for URLR is higher than that of Huber-LASSO, leading to better outlier detection capability. Typically, we have $d < I$ in a large dataset; however if not, it can be made so by reducing the feature dimension.

---

[4] Note that broadly speaking, our method is still a special case of Huber-LASSO.

4   Experiments

Datasets. We conduct experiments on two image and video interestingness datasets and two relative image attribute datasets[5]. These datasets are summarised in Table 1. The image interestingness dataset was first introduced in [19] for studying memorability. It was later re-annotated as an image interestingness dataset by [16]. It consists of 2222 images, each represented as a 932 dimensional feature vector as in [16]. 16000 pairwise comparisons were collected by [16] using AMT and are used as annotation.

The video interestingness dataset is the YouTube interestingness dataset introduced in [21], which contains 14 different categories, each of which has 30 YouTube videos. $10 \sim 15$ annotators were asked to give complete interesting comparisons for all the videos in each category. So the original annotation is noisy but not sparse. We use bag-of-words of Scale Invariant Feature Transform (SIFT) and Mel-Frequency Cepstral Coefficient (MFCC) as the feature representation which are shown to be effective in [21] for predicting video interestingness.

We also carry out experiments on two relative attributes datasets –PubFig [25] and Scene [34] to test our URLR model's ability to predict other more general relative visual attributes. PubFig and Scene considered 11 ('smiling', 'round face', etc.) and 6 ('openness', 'natural' etc.) relative attributes respectively. Pairwise attribute annotation was collected by AMT [24]. Each pair was annotated by 5 crowdsourced workers. Gist and colour histograms features are used for PubFig, and Gist alone for Scene. Each image also belongs to a class (celebrity or scene type). These two datasets were designed for classification, with attribute scores as the representation, so the classification accuracy is determined by the attribute prediction accuracy.

Table 1. Dataset summary. We use the original features to learn the ranking model in Eq (10) and reduce the feature dimension (values in brackets) using KPCA to improve outlier detection in Eq (9) by enlarging the solution space (see Sec. 3.5).

Dataset	No. of pairs	No. img/video	Feature Dim.	No. class
Image Int.[19]	16000	2222	932(150)	1
Video Int. [21]	60000	420	1000(60)	14
PubFig [25,24]	2616	772	557(100)	8
Scene [34,24]	1378	2688	512(100)	8

Evaluation Metrics. For the image and video interestingness dataset, Kendall tau rank distance is employed to measure the rank correlation between the predicted ranking order and the ground truth ranking of unseen test data provided by [16] and [21] respectively[6]. Higher Kendall tau rank distance means lower

---

[5] All code and features are downloadable from Yanwei's website:
http://www.eecs.qmul.ac.uk/~yf300/ranking/

[6] Recent statistical theories [37,20] show that the dense human annotations collected in [16] and [21] can give a reasonable approximation of ground truth for interestingness.

quality of the ranking order predicted. For the scene and pubfig image dataset, the relative attributes are very sparsely collected and their prediction performance can only be evaluated indirectly by image classification accuracy with the predicted relative attributes as image representation.

Competitors. We compare our method (URLR) with four competitors. (1) Jiang *et al.* [21]: this method uses majority voting for outlier pruning and rankSVM for learning to rank. (2) Gygli *et al.* [16]: this method also first removes outliers by majority voting. After that, the fraction of selections by the pairwise comparisons for each data point is used as an absolute interestingness score and a regression model is then learned for prediction. (3) *Huber-LASSO*: this is a statistical ranking method that performs outlier detection as described in Sec. 3.5, followed by estimating β using Eq (10). (4) *Raw*: This is our URLR model without outlier detection, that is, all annotations are used to estimate β.

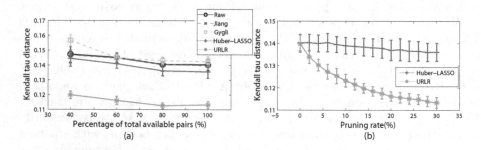

Fig. 2. Image interestingness prediction performance. Lower is better.

4.1   Image Interestingness Prediction

Experimental Settings. For this experiment, we randomly select 1000 images for training and the remaining 1222 are used for testing. All the experiments are repeated 10 times to reduce variance. The pruning rate p is set to 20%. We also vary the number of annotated pairs used to test how well each compared method copes with increasing annotation sparsity.

Comparative Results. The results are shown in Fig. 2 (a). It shows clearly that our URLR significantly outperforms the four alternatives for a wide range of annotation density. This validates the effectiveness of our method. In particular, the improvement over Jiang *et al.* [21] and Gygli *et al.* [16] demonstrates the superior outlier detection ability of URLR. URLR is superior to Huber-LASSO because the joint outlier detection and ranking estimation framework of URLR enables the enlargement of the solution space of Eq (9), resulting in better outlier detection performance. The performance of Gygli *et al.* [16] is the worst among all methods compared, particularly so given sparser annotation. This is not surprising – in order to get an reliable absolute interestingness value, dozens or even hundreds of comparisons per image are required, a condition not met by this dataset. The estimated value becomes less reliable given sparser annotations, explaining the worse relative performance. The performance of Huber-LASSO is also better than Jiang *et al.* [21] and Gygli *et al.* suggesting even a weaker global outlier detection approach is better then the majority voting based local one. Interestingly even the baseline method Raw gives a comparable result to Jiang *et al.* [21] and Gygli *et al.* [16] which suggests that just using all annotations without discrimination in a global cost function Eq (5) is as effective as majority voting.

Fig. 2 (b) evaluates how the performances of URLR and Huber-LASSO are affected by the pruning rate p. It can be seen that the performance of URLR is improving with an increasing pruning rate. This means that our URLR can keep on detecting true positive outliers. The gap between URLR and Huber-LASSO gets bigger when more comparisons are pruned showing Huber-LASSO stops detecting outliers much earlier on.

4.2 Video Interestingness Prediction

Experimental Settings. Because comparing videos across different categories is not very meaningful, we follow the same settings as in [21] and only compare the interestingness of videos within the same category. Specifically, we use 20 videos and their paired comparison for training and the remaining 10 videos for testing. The experiments are repeated for 10 rounds and the averaged results are reported. We use rankSVM with χ^2 kernel which is approximated by additive kernel of explicit feature mapping [42]. Kendall tau rank distance is used, and we find that the same results are obtained if the prediction accuracy used in [21] is used instead. The pruning rate is again set to 20%.

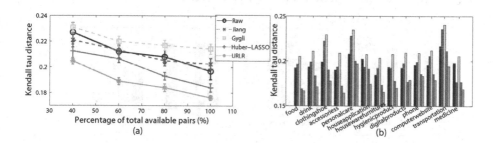

Fig. 3. Video interestingness prediction results

Comparative Results. The results of video interestingness prediction are shown in Fig 3. Fig. 3(a) compares different methods given varying amounts of annotations, and Fig. 3(b) shows the per category performance. The results show that all the observations we had for the image interestingness prediction experiment still hold here, and across all categories. However in general the gaps between our URLR and the alternatives are smaller as this dataset is densely annotated. In particular the performance of Huber-LASSO is much closer to our URLR now. This is because, as explained in Sec. 3.5, the advantage of URLR over Huber-LASSO is stronger when $|E|$ is close to I. Given a dense pairwise annotation $|E|$ is much greater than I and the effect of enlarging the solution space diminishes.

4.3   Relative Attributes Prediction for Image Classification

Experimental Settings. We evaluate image classification with relative attributes as representation on the PubFig and Scene datasets under two settings: multi-class classification where samples from all classes are available for training and zero-shot transfer learning where one class is held out during training (a different class is used in each trial with the result averaged). Our experiment setting is similar to that in [35], except that image-level, rather than class-level pairwise comparisons are used. Two variations of the setting are used:

- *Orig:* The original setting with the pairwise annotations is used as they are.
- *Orig+synth*: By visual inspection, there are limited annotation outliers in these datasets, perhaps because the relative attributes are less subjective compared to interestingness. To simulate more challenging situations, we randomly add 150 random comparison for each attribute, many of which would correspond to outliers. This will lead to around 20% extra outliers.

The pruning rate is set to 7% for original dataset (*Orig*) and 27% for dataset with additional outliers inserted for all attributes of both datasets (*Orig+synth*).

Comparative Results. Without the ground truth of relative attribute values, different models are evaluated indirectly via image classification accuracy in Fig. 4. Note that the method of Gygli *et al.* [16] is not compared here as the

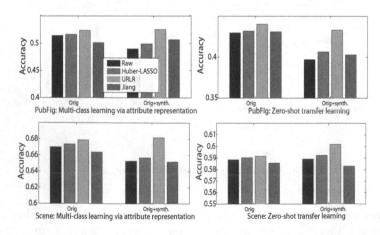

Fig. 4. Relative attribute performance evaluated indirectly as image classification rate (chance = 0.125)

annotation is too sparse for it to learn a meaningful model. The following observations can be made: (1) Our URLR always outperforms *Huber-LASSO*, *maj-voting* (Jiang) and *Raw* for all experiment settings. The improvement is more significant when the data contain more errors (*Orig+synth*). (2) The performance of other methods is in general consistent to what we observed in the image and video interestingness experiments: Huber-LASSO is better than majority voting (Jiang *et al.* [21]) and Raw often gives better results than majority voting too. (3) It is noted that for PubFig, Jiang *et al.* [21] is better than Raw given more outliers, but it is not the case for Scene. This is probably because the annotators are more familiar with the celebrity faces in PubFig hence their attributes than those in Scene. Consequently there should be more subjective/intentional errors for Scene, causing majority voting to choose wrong local ranking orders (e.g. not many people are sure how to compare the relative values of the 'diagonal plane' attribute for two images). These majority voting + outlier cases can only be rectified by using a global approach such as our URLR, even the Huber-LASSO method to a certain extent.

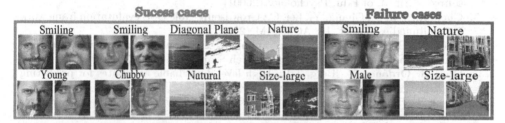

Fig. 5. Qualitative results on image relative attribute prediction

Qualitative Results. Figure 5 gives some examples of the pruned pairs for both datasets using URLR. In the success cases, the left images were (incorrectly) annotated to have more of the attribute than the right ones. However, they are either wrong or too ambiguous to give consistent answers, and as such are detrimental to learning to rank. A number of failure cases (false positive pairs identified by URLR) are also shown. Some of them are caused by unique view point (e.g. Hugh Laurie's mouth is not visible, so it is hard to tell who smiles more; the building and the street scene are too zoomed in compared to most other samples); others are caused by the weak feature representation, e.g. in the 'male' attribute example, the colour and Gist features are not discriminative enough for judging which of the two men has more 'male' attribute.

5   Conclusions

We have proposed a novel unified robust learning to rank (URLR) framework for predicting image and video interestingness. The key advantage of our method over the existing majority voting based approaches is that we can detect outliers globally by minimising a global ranking inconsistency cost. The joint outlier detection and ranking estimation formulation also provides our model with an advantage over the conventional statistical ranking methods such as Huber-LASSO for outlier detection. The effectiveness of our model in comparison with state-of-the-art alternatives has been validated using image and video interestingness datasets. Further, it is generally applicable to other relative attribute prediction tasks as demonstrated by our relative attribute based image classification experiments.

References

1. Cao, Z., Qin, T., Liu, T.Y., Tsai, M.F., Li, H.: Learning to rank: From pairwise approach to listwise approach. In: ICML (2007)
2. Carvalho, V.R., Elsas, J.L., Cohen, W.W., Carbonell, J.G.: A meta-learning approach for robust rank learning. In: SIGIR 2008 LR4IR - Workshop on Learning to Rank for Information Retrieval (2008)
3. Chapelle, O., Keerthi, S.S.: Efficient algorithms for ranking with svms. Inf. Retr. (2010)
4. Chen, A.: adn R. Pangrazi, P.D.: An examination of situational interest adn its sources. Brit. J. of Edu. Psychology (20001)
5. Chen, K., Wu, C., Chang, Y., Lei, C.: Crowdsourceable QoE evalutation framework for multimedia content. In: ACM MM (2009)
6. Chen, X., Bennett, P.N.: Pairwise ranking aggregation in a crowdsourced setting. In: ACM International Conference on Web Search and Data Mining (2013)
7. Dhar, S., Ordonez, V., Berg, T.L.: High level describable attributes for predicting aesthetics and interestingness. In: CVPR (2011)
8. Efron, B., Hastie, T., Johnstone, I., Tibshirani, R.: Least angle regression. Annals of Statistics (2004)
9. Fan, J., Li, R.: Variable selection via nonconcave penalized likelihood and its oracle properties. JASA (2001)
10. Fan, J., Tang, R., Shi, X.: Partial consistency with sparse incidental parameters. arXiv:1210.6950 (2012)
11. Fu, Y., Hospedales, T.M., Xiang, T., Gong, S.: Attribute learning for understanding unstructured social activity. In: Fitzgibbon, A., Lazebnik, S., Perona, P., Sato, Y., Schmid, C. (eds.) ECCV 2012, Part IV. LNCS, vol. 7575, pp. 530–543. Springer, Heidelberg (2012)
12. Fu, Y., Hospedales, T.M., Xiang, T., Fu, Z., Gong, S.: Transductive multi-view embedding for zero-shot recognition and annotation. In: Fleet, D., Pajdla, T., Schiele, B., Tuytelaars, T. (eds.) ECCV 2014, Part II. LNCS, vol. 8690, pp. 584–599. Springer, Heidelberg (2014)
13. Fu, Y., Hospedales, T.M., Xiang, T., Gong, S.: Learning multi-modal latent attributes. TPAMI (2013)
14. Gannaz, I.: Robust estimation and wavelet thresholding in partial linear models. Stat. Comput. 17, 293–310 (2007)
15. Gehrlein, W.V.: Condorcet's paradox. Theory and Decision (1983)
16. Gygli, M., Grabner, H., Riemenschneider, H., Nater, F., Gool, L.V.: The interestingness of images. In: ICCV (2013)
17. Hirani, A.N., Kalyanaraman, K., Watts, S.: Least squares ranking on graphs. arXiv:1011.1716 (2010)
18. Huber, P.J.: Robust Statistics. Wiley, New York (1981)
19. Isola, P., Xiao, J., Torralba, A., Oliva, A.: What makes an image memorable? In: CVPR (2011)

20. Jiang, X., Lim, L.H., Yao, Y., Ye, Y.: Statistical ranking and combinatorial hodge theory. Math. Program. (2011)
21. Jiang, Y.G., YanranWang, F.R., Xue, X., Zheng, Y., Yang, H.: Understanding and predicting interestingness of videos. In: AAAI (2013)
22. Ke, Y., Tang, X., Jing, F.: The design of high-level features for photo quality assessment. In: CVPR (2006)
23. Kittur, A., Chi, E.H., Suh., B.: Crowdsourcing user studies with mechanical turk. In: ACM CHI (2008)
24. Kovashka, A., Parikh, D., Grauman, K.: Whittlesearch: Image search with relative attribute feedback. In: CVPR (2012)
25. Kumar, N., Berg, A.C., Belhumeur, P.N., Nayar, S.K.: Attribute and simile classifiers for face verification. In: ICCV (2009)
26. Lampert, C.H., Nickisch, H., Harmeling, S.: Learning to detect unseen object classes by between-class attribute transfer. In: CVPR (2009)
27. Lampert, C.H., Nickisch, H., Harmeling, S.: Attribute-based classification for zero-shot visual object categorization. IEEE TPAMI (2013)
28. Liu, F., Niu, Y., Gleicher, M.: Using web photos for measuring video frame interestingness. In: IJCAI (2009)
29. Liu, Y., Gao, B., Liu, T.Y., Zhang, Y., Ma, Z., He, S., Li, H.: Browserank: letting web users vote for page importance. In: ACM SIGIR (2008)
30. Long, C., Hua, G., Kapoor, A.: Active visual recognition with expertise estimation in crowdsourcing. In: ICCV (2013)
31. Maire, M., Yu, S.X., Perona, P.: Object detection and segmentation from joint embedding of parts and pixels. In: ICCV (2011)
32. Meinshausen, N., Bühlmann, P.: High-dimensional graphs and variable selection with the lasso. Ann. Statist. (2006)
33. Murphy, K.P.: Machine learning: a probabilistic perspective. The MIT Press (2012)
34. Oliva, A., Torralba., A.: Modeling the shape of the scene: Aholistic representation of the spatial envelope. IJCV 42 (2001)
35. Parikh, D., Grauman, K.: Relative attributes. In: ICCV (2011)
36. Patterson, G., Hays, J.: Sun attribute database: Discovering, annotating, and recognizing scene attributes. In: Proc. CVPR (2012)
37. Rajkumar, A., Agarwal, S.: A statistical convergence perspective of algorithms for rank aggregation from pairwise data. In: Proceedings of the 31st International Conference on Machine Learning (2014)
38. She, Y., Owen, A.B.: Outlier detection using nonconvex penalized regression. Journal of American Statistical Association (2011)
39. Silvia, P.: Interest - the curious emotion. In: CDPS (2008)
40. Sorokin, A., Forsyth, D.: Utility data annotation with amazon mechanical turk. In: CVPR Workshops (2008)
41. Sun, Z., Qin, T., Tao, Q., Wang, J.: Robust sparse rank learning for non-smooth ranking measures. In: ACM SIGIR (2009)
42. Vedaldi, A., Zisserman, A.: Efficient additive kernels via explicit feature maps. In: IEEE TPAMI (2011)
43. Wu, O., Hu, W., Gao, J.: Learning to rank under multiple annotators. In: IJCAI (2011)
44. Xu, Q., Huang, Q., Jiang, T., Yan, B., Lin, W., Yao, Y.: Hodgerank on random graphs for subjective video quality assessment. IEEE TMM (2012)
45. Xu, Q., Huang, Q., Yao, Y.: Online crowdsourcing subjective image quality assessment. In: ACM MM (2012)
46. Xu, Q., Xiong, J., Huang, Q., Yao, Y.: Robust evaluation for quality of experience in crowdsourcing. In: ACM MM (2013)

Pairwise Probabilistic Voting:
Fast Place Recognition without RANSAC

Edward Johns and Guang-Zhong Yang

Imperial College London, UK

Abstract. Place recognition currently suffers from a lack of scalability
due to the need for strong geometric constraints, which as of yet are typically limited to RANSAC implementations. In this paper, we present
a method to successfully achieve state-of-the-art performance, in both
recognition accuracy and speed, without the need for RANSAC. We propose to discretise each feature pair in an image, in both appearance and
2D geometry, to create a triplet of words: one each for the appearance
of the two features, and one for the pairwise geometry. This triplet is
then passed through an inverted index to find examples of such pairwise
configurations in the database. Finally, a global geometry constraint is
enforced by considering the maximum-clique in an adjacency graph of
pairwise correspondences. The discrete nature of the problem allows for
tractable probabilistic scores to be assigned to each correspondence, and
the least informative feature pairs can be eliminated from the database
for memory and time efficiency. We demonstrate the performance of our
method on several large-scale datasets, and show improvements over several baselines.

Keywords: Place Recognition, Location Recognition, Instance Recognition, Image Retrieval, Bag Of Words, Inverted Index.

1 Introduction

This paper addresses place recognition [6][16][8][26], whereby the identity is
sought of a particular place or scene depicted in a query image. This is closely
related to the recognition or retrieval of object instances [13][1] and qualitative localisation [7][17][2]. In a typical place recognition framework, a Bag Of
Words (BOW) filtering stage yields a subset of candidate images [14], upon
which strong 3D constraints are imposed on local features based on a RAN-
dom SAmple Consensus (RANSAC) scheme [15]. Whilst such constraints offer
powerful verification of global geometric consistency, they are expensive to compute due to the need for generating multiple transformation hypotheses in the
RANSAC algorithm, and large-scale real-time recognition tasks are often forced
to forego 3D geometry entirely [2][7]. Although the use of an inverted index in
the BOW stage allows for very fast pre-filtering and has been studied extensively
in recognition and retrieval methods [5][1], geometric verification is typically re-
served as a separate stage altogether [14], or weakly represented in the BOW
vector [4], but typically is not incorporated directly in the inverted index.

D. Fleet et al. (Eds.): ECCV 2014, Part II, LNCS 8690, pp. 504–519, 2014.
© Springer International Publishing Switzerland 2014

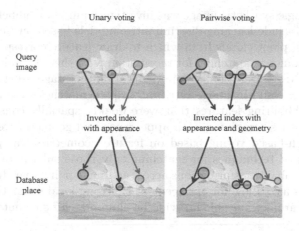

Fig. 1. A comparison of our proposed pairwise voting method with the standard single feature voting method, both using an inverted index

In this paper, we consider an alternative approach to geometric matching by building a generative model for each place, and embedding the learned 2D pairwise geometry directly in the inverted index to allow for much faster querying, which we denote *Pairwise Probabilistic Voting* (PPV). First, local features are tracked across training images for each place using wide baseline matching. Then, the relative geometry of pairs of features is discretised into a dictionary of *geometric words*, and the informative elements of an image are taken as the two visual words and one geometric word that defines each feature pair, which we denote a *word triplet*. Given a query image, rather than searching for candidate places that contain a particular visual word as with standard BOW, the search is for places that contain a particular pairwise configuration satisfying all three words in the triplet, as illustrated in Figure 1. By learning a probabilistic model of local geometry for each pair of features across training images for a particular place, votes for each place are weighted with a score reflecting the likelihood that the pairwise correspondence is a true positive. Finally, by ensuring that all votes for a candidate place agree globally with each other in pairwise geometry, an approximate constraint on global geometry can be applied without the need for an expensive RANSAC step.

1.1 Related Work

Instance recognition typically extends the image retrieval framework [14] to a recognition framework [26], by exploiting structure in the database [3] and learning models of places or objects over a training set of training images. Standard image retrieval approaches based on ranking database images form a simple solution [13], and in [16] a query was matched to each of a small subset of exemplar images for each place. Tracking local features across several training images to learn the expected behaviour of features was proposed in [6], and superimposing them onto a single synthetic image was investigated in [8]. Competing ideologies to recognition include learning discriminative models based on the BOW vector [9] and building point clouds from which to draw feature correspondences [17].

Although geometric matching for recognition with these techniques still relies on a costly RANSAC iteration, attempts to enrich this stage using 2D geometries have proven successful in image retrieval. In [22], matches were made between groups of neighbouring features that were weakly spatially consistent, and in [25][24] dictionaries combining both appearance and geometry were learned. In [20], fast Hough-based voting based on feature geometries was proposed, and [19][18] developed techniques for matching only those subsets of features with agreement on global transformations across an image pair. Near-duplicate image search methods also allow for enforcement of strong local geometric constraints [23], but these are not suitable for wide baseline matching or outdoor scenes.

2   A Geometric Dictionary

Concurrently with a standard visual dictionary [14], we propose to discretise pairwise geometry to enable geometric data to be sent through an inverted index alongside the appearance data. As with the visual dictionary Π of visual words $\pi \in \Pi$, we define a *geometric dictionary* Φ of *geometric words* $\phi \in \Phi$. Each geometric word represents a unique range in pairwise 2D image space.

The geometric dictionary is composed over 4-dimensional space, with each geometric word defined by 4 pairwise geometries. For a feature pair constituting features u and v, the pairwise geometries are as follows: scale-invariant distance δ_{uv}, scale ratio σ_{uv}, rotation-invariant orientation difference θ_{uv} and rotation-invariant angle ψ_{uv}. Scale-invariance and rotation-invariance are important in ensuring that the generative model of each place is not limited by the scales and rotations reflected in the training dataset. The distance between features, d_{uv}, is made scale-invariant by dividing by the scale of u, and the relative angle is made rotation-invariant by subtracting the orientation of u. The scale ratio and orientation difference are naturally invariant to in-plane transformation. This discretisation of geometry is similar to that of [25] except for we define the discretisation a priori rather than during querying, and is comparable to [24] but we limit to pairwise geometries to allow for inverted indexing with reasonable memory requirements.

Using the notation in Figure 2, the pairwise geometries are then calculated as follows:

$$\delta_{uv} = \frac{d_{uv}}{\sigma_u}, \qquad \sigma_{uv} = \frac{\sigma_v}{\sigma_u}, \qquad (1)$$
$$\theta_{uv} = \theta_v - \theta_u, \qquad \psi_{uv} = \psi_{uv} - \theta_u$$

Each of these four pairwise geometries is independently discretised by defining boundaries for each of the four geometries, with n divisions per geometry. However, rather than defining each boundary as a linear function of n, we instead use the expected distribution of each geometry from a training set of feature pairs,

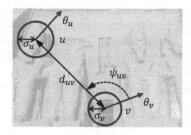

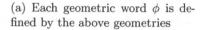

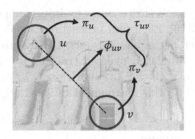

(a) Each geometric word ϕ is defined by the above geometries

(b) Each word triplet τ is defined by two visual words π_u, π_v and one geometric word ϕ_{uv}

Fig. 2. Notation for pairwise geometries

and compute the kth percentile from that distribution. This is because whilst the orientation and angle differences can be assumed to be distributed uniformly in the range $0 - 360°$, there is no such trend in the distribution of pairwise scale ratios and distances. By considering the observed distribution over a set of feature pairs from real data, this ensures that for a geometric dictionary with a fixed number of divisions per geometry, each division has an equal likelihood of assignment given a new pair of features, tending towards a uniform global distribution. We learned these distributions by randomly sampling one million pairs of features observed in images from the database.

Finally, the geometric word ϕ_{uv} for the feature pair is the discrete portion of 4-dimensional geometry defined by the quantised values of δ_{uv}, σ_{uv}, θ_{uv} and ψ_{uv}. This geometric word is then combined with the visual words π_u and π_v of the two features, to form a word triplet τ_{uv}. For our experiments, we used 30 divisions for each of the four geometries, yielding a geometric dictionary of size $810K$.

3   Pairwise Probabilistic Voting

The key idea behind our proposed method is to create a generative model for each place in the database, by learning distributions of word triplets over the place's training images, and then finding matches between pairs of query features and pairs of database landmarks. These matches then vote for the respective place, with the vote weighted probabilistically.

3.1   Learning a Distribution of Triplets

Let us define a *landmark* as a real-world point in the environment, that is observed in an image as a feature. Every database place $s \in S$ is represented by a set of such landmarks $\mathcal{X}_s$, with each built from a single feature track across

the place's entire set of training images using wide baseline matching, similar to
[6][8][16]. Each pair of features u and v, forming two tracks, is assigned one word
triplet per image in which the features co-occur, and thus a set of word triplets
is accumulated over all training images. The two tracks form two landmarks x
and y, with the landmark pair z_{xy} assigned the distribution of triplets $p(\tau|z_{xy})$
based on this learned set of word triplets from the feature tracks.

3.2   Voting

For the remainder of the paper, we drop the subscripts in z and let it represent
any particular landmark pair. During recognition, each feature pair w in the
query image is assigned a single word triplet τ_w. These query word triplets are
then sent through an inverted index to find landmark pairs in the database that
have also been assigned to this particular word triplet. The leaf node in the index
tree assigns a weighted vote μ_z to landmark pair z, and the overall score for a
place s is then the normalised summation of votes across all its landmark pairs:

$$f(s) = \frac{\sum\limits_{z \in \mathcal{Z}_s} \hat{\mu}_z}{\eta} \tag{2}$$

Here, $\mathcal{Z}_s$ is the set of landmarks in place s, and η is a normalisation term,
defined as the average number of landmark pairs observed in s's training images.
$\hat{\mu}_z$ is defined as the maximum value of μ_z achieved by all query feature pairs, to
account for cases when more than one feature pair matches a landmark pair.

The weighted vote μ_z is a probabilistic score representing how likely it is that
observed triplet τ_w is a true observation of landmark pair z. From the learned dis-
tribution $p(\tau|z)$, we can readily draw the value of $p(\tau_w|z)$. Furthermore, we can
also draw the values of $p(\tau_w|z^*)$ for any landmark pair z^* in the entire database.
Therefore, for a given triplet τ_w, the vote for landmark pair z is evaluated as:

$$\mu_z = p(z|\tau_w) = \frac{p(\tau_w|z)p(z)}{\sum\limits_{z^*} p(\tau_w|z^*)p(z^*)} \tag{3}$$

The value of $p(\tau_w|z)p(z)$ is proportional to the number of times τ_w is observed
for landmark pair z across all training images. Therefore, μ_z is simply the number
of times that τ_w is observed when z is present, divided by the number of times
that τ_w is observed when any landmark pair is present. This weight is calculated
in advance and stored at the leaf node in the index, such that voting for a place
involves simply traversing the index with a query triplet and adding weighted
votes to any database places, should a landmark pair for that place have an entry
at that leaf node. Figure 3 illustrates a set of landmark pairs and their associated
weights. Higher weights are assigned to pairs which are both frequently observed
at a place and discriminative with respect to all other landmark pairs in the
database.

Fig. 3. Vote weights μ_z for landmark pairs for an example place. The blue circle represents landmark x, with all other circles representing landmark y, and hence a landmark pair z_{xy}.

3.3   Index Structure

Our goal in designing an appropriate index is to link every word triplet to a leaf node, with each leaf node pointing to a set of weighted votes, and each one associated with a database place. The fastest inverted index is one which contains one pointer for every possible word triplet, where each pointer represents the leaf node. However, given a visual dictionary containing $100K$ words and a geometric dictionary containing $800K$ words,, this would require an index with at least $100K \times 100K \times 800K \approx 10^{16}$ pointers, which is impractical.

We therefore propose to divide the inverted index into two layers, each with a different structure. The first layer is a standard inverted index, and represents the combination of the two visual words in a word triplet, requiring $100K \times 100K = 10^{10}$ pointers (10 GB RAM). Then, the second layer is no longer an inverted index structure, but simply a list of geometric words for each visual word combination from the first layer. This list represents all geometric words from the entire database that have been assigned to by this visual word combination, and the list is structured as a binary search tree for efficient searching. In this way, whilst the first layer contains an entry for every possible combination of visual word pairs, the second layer only contains those geometric words which have actually been observed together with the particular visual word pair, reducing the memory requirements by several orders of magnitude.

Figure 4 illustrates this structure. In this example, suppose we have a query triplet consisting of visual words π_2 and π_3, and geometric word ϕ_4. Following the path of π_2 for the first landmark and then π_3 for the second, we see the list of two geometric words: ϕ_1 and ϕ_4. Then, taking ϕ_4, we see that there are two votes, targetting two different landmark pairs in the database that are represented by this particular word triplet, and we then add these weighted votes to scores for the respective places.

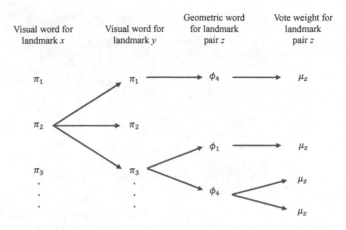

Fig. 4. The index structure, with an example distribution of wods. The arrows represent potential paths through the index in pursuit of the weighted votes.

4   Smoothing the Distributions

The discrete nature of the generative place models makes it tractable to learn a deep probabilistic model of landmark pairs, as a joint distribution across both appearance and geometry. Rather than treat the visual and geometric words assigned to a pair as independent, we propose to compute a full joint distribution across all three words in a triplet. In this way, effects on one word are modelled in the knock-on effect on another word. For example, if a particular illumination condition causes the visual word of one landmark to change, then we model the corresponding effect of this illumination condition on the visual word of the other landmark in the pair. Similarly, if the viewpoint on the place changes such that the pair's geometric word is affected, then the effect on the visual words due to the apparent change in scene appearance can be modelled. This involves updating the distribution $p(\tau|z)$ for each landmark pair by smoothing the explicit observations of word triplets from the feature tracks in the training images.

For an observed visual word $\pi \in \Pi$, let us define a set of a_π *alternative visual words*, $\bar{\pi} \in \Pi$, where an alternative word represents a possible assignment on a subsequent observation of the same landmark. This is similar to the soft assignment strategies in the BOW framework [13][11]. Each alternative visual word is designated a likelihood $p(\bar{\pi}_x|\pi_x)$ following Gaussian weighting proportional to the word centroid distance, with standard deviation σ_π, as in [13]. Similarly, for each geometric word $\phi \in \Phi$, a set of a_ϕ *alternative geometric words* $\bar{\phi} \in \Phi$ are defined as the α_ϕ nearest geometric words to ϕ, with their likelihoods $p(\bar{\phi}|\phi)$ again weighted by a Gaussian, with standard deviation σ_ϕ. We chose the values for a_π and a_ϕ by observing sets of landmark pairs, and determining the limit when the set of alternative words assigned to the pair accounted for future observations in 99% of the cases. The values of σ_π and σ_ϕ were fixed such that the furthest away alternative word had a value of $p(\bar{\pi}|\pi)$ or $p(\bar{\phi}|\phi)$ at 1% of that of the original word, i.e. when $\bar{\pi} \equiv \pi$ or $\bar{\phi} \equiv \phi$).

We now consider the probability that an observation of landmark pair z is assigned to a particular word triplet τ. Let us factorise the distribution as follows:

$$
\begin{aligned}
p(\tau|z) &= p(\pi_x, \pi_y, \phi_{xy}|z) \\
&= p(\pi_x|z)p(\pi_y|\pi_x, z)p(\phi_{xy}|\pi_x, \pi_y, z)
\end{aligned}
\tag{4}
$$

As such, we model y's visual word to be dependent on x's visual word, and the geometric word as dependent on both these visual words. We now introduce the smoothing effects of the alternative words, by considering that new word triplets should be included in the distribution, if each word in the triplet is in fact an alternative word for the respective original word. The probability of observing this new triplet is then calculated by taking the factorisation in Equation 4, and replacing each term with the probability of assignment to the alternative word. This is evaluated as:

$$
p(\tau|z) = p(\pi_x, \pi_y, \phi_{xy}|z)
$$

$$
= \overbrace{\sum_{\bar{\pi}_x} p(\bar{\pi}_x|\tau)p(\bar{\pi}_x|\pi_x)}^{\text{contribution from alternative visual words for landmark } x}
$$

$$
\times \overbrace{\sum_{\bar{\pi}_y} p(\bar{\pi}_y|\bar{\pi}_x)p(\bar{\pi}_y|\pi_y)}^{\text{contribution from alternative visual words for landmark } y}
\tag{5}
$$

$$
\times \overbrace{\sum_{\bar{\phi}_{xy}} p(\bar{\phi}_{xy}|\bar{\pi}_x, \bar{\pi}_y)p(\bar{\phi}_{xy}|\phi_{xy})}^{\text{contribution from alternative geometric words for landmark pair } z}
$$

where the probabilities in the bottom three rows are based on the maximum-likelihood distributions as before.

5   Geometric Cliques for Global Consistency

Whilst the pairwise geometry embedded in the inverted index offers strong constraints on local configurations, as of yet there is no enforcement of global geometric consistency. Thus, a set of feature pairs voting for one place may be independently representative of a landmark pair, but when considering the global relationships between all pairs, the overall configuration may be incompatible.

5.1   Defining a Compatibility Matrix

The proposed solution, which we denote the method of *Geometric Cliques* (GC), is based on finding a maximum clique in an adjacency matrix, whose elements indicate the *compatibility* of each pairwise match. Let us define a set of n pairwise matches $m \in M$ between an image and a place, generated by passing query feature pairs through the inverted index. Then, for each place, we construct an $n \times n$ binary *compatibility matrix* B, where element B_{ij} stores the compatibility of pairwise matches m_i and m_j, and is set to either 0 or 1. If m_i represents a match between feature pair $w_{u^i v^i}$ and landmark pair $z_{x^i y^i}$, the value of B_{ij} is 1 if, and only if, there also exist pairwise matches between every feature pair $w_{u^i u^j}$, $w_{u^i v^j}$, $w_{v^i u^j}$, $w_{v^i v^j}$ and every landmark pair $z_{x^i x^j}$, $z_{x^i y^j}$, $z_{y^i x^j}$, $z_{y^i y^j}$. In other words, all pairwise combinations of features and landmarks in m_i and m_j must have found a match through the inverted index for m_{ij} to be set to 1. If any pair of these features has not found a match to any pair of these landmarks, then m_i and m_j are not fully compatible and B_{ij} is set to 0. In the case that a pair of landmarks never co-occur in the place's training images, then the respective element of B is always set to 1, i.e. a value of 0 indicates that we have explicitly observed an inconsistent pairwise match that needs to be eliminated.

For example, in Figure 5a, the left image can be considered the query features, and the right image the database landmarks. Taking the red and blue pairs, all four features in the left image have a geometrically-similar configuration to the associated landmarks in the right image. Therefore, the respective element in B is set to 1 (see the first matrix in Fig 5b). However, taking the red and orange pairs, the configuration is not similar across all four features (only across the two features highlighted by the same colour), and hence the respective element in B is set to 0.

5.2   Searching for the Maximum Clique

The task now becomes to find a set of pairwise matches that are all compatible with each other, i.e. finding the maximum clique of B. Several solutions to this exist, including fast branch-and-bound methods [12], or approximate solutions using a fast search for a near-optimal maximum clique, followed by gradient descent to avoid local minima [21]. However, these methods are generalised and deal with a wide range of matrix structures, whereas we now propose our own fast approximate solution that exploits the unique nature of B.

There is a very low probability that both query features in a false positive pairwise match are also compatible with other pairwise matches. Thus, any false positive matches in B will have a very sparse row in the matrix, typically with very few elements set to 1. However, true positive pairwise matches will have a much larger number of compatible pairs, and hence the corresponding row will have a significant number of 1's. As such, we can very quickly eliminate false positives by detecting those rows with few 1's. The proposed algorithm exploits this by scoring each pairwise match by the number of consistent pairs, i.e. the number of elements in the respective row of B assigned to 1, and recursively removing the pair with the lowest score. After each iteration, the scores for each remaining pair are updated. The algorithm then converges when the entire matrix is devoid of any 0's.

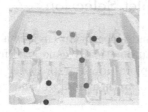

(a) Each colour represents one pairwise match found through the inverted index, and the resulting adjacency matrix is shown in (b)

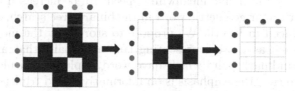

(b) The adjacency matrix iteratively eliminates the pairwise match with the lowest score, until a maximum clique is found

Fig. 5. Illustration of the Geometric Cliques algorithm to eliminate pairwise matches that, although may be locally consistent, are not globally consistent with other pairwise matches

See Figure 5b for an example of the evolution of B towards a maximum clique. Here, the green pairwise match is in fact a false positive, even though it may appear consistent with some of the other pairwise matches; in this example, the red pair. Our method is able to deal with this case because we require every pair to be consistent with every other pair in the final matrix.

Once the maximum clique has been established, the score for the respective place is determined in Equation 2 by considering only those pairs in the maximum clique. Given that false positive candidates exhibit zero or very few 1's in their respective row and hence are easy to eliminate, this method reproduced the same maximum clique as the methods of [12] and [21] over all experiments presented in Section 7, but with an average speed up factor of 13.7 compared with the fastest of these two.

During recognition of a query image, database places are ranked in order of their current scores, before elimination of these false positive matches as discussed. First, the place with the highest score is processed with geometric cliques, with its score updated, then the place with the second highest score, and so on. The algorithm stops when the score of the next place is lower than the maximum updated score for places which have been through the geometric cliques stage, because it is only possible for the score to reduce. Hence, only a small fraction of database places need to go through this stage, offering significant speed-up compared to RANSAC-based re-ranking strategies.

6   Boosting Efficiency by Triplet Selection

A key requirement of modern retrieval and recognition engines is scalability to web-scale tasks, whereby databases are automatically generated from vast user-generated databases [26][3]. We now explore how our proposed system scales appropriately to such demand, in terms of both memory efficiency and computational efficiency.

In order to both reduce the memory footprint and increase the recognition speed, albeit at a small cost to recognition accuracy, only a subset of all word triplets are stored in the index, with the rest discarded. Memory requirements will naturally be reduced, and meanwhile, speed will be increased when attempting to find a particular geometric word in the binary tree search, as each binary tree will be reduced in length. We propose to store only the most informative word triplets, such as those representing landmark pairs that are very stable in a place, or landmark pairs which have word triplets particularly unique to their place. Note that the emphasis is on informative word triplets, not informative landmark pairs; the triplets associated with each landmark pair will differ in their own discriminative power due to the number of other landmark pairs represented by each triplet.

To determine the level of information which each word triplet conveys, we consider the conditional entropy of the place identity, given that the knowledge of the triplet's presence or absence in a query image is available. Let us define $\mathbf{S}$ as the state of the place depicted in the query, which can take on all values $s \in S$, and the binary variable $\mathbf{T}$ as the state of word triplet τ, where $\mathbf{T} = 1$ indicates that the triplet is observed in a query. Word triplets are then ranked in order of the conditional entropy:

$$H(\mathbf{S}|\mathbf{T}) = \sum_{\mathbf{S}\in S} \sum_{\mathbf{T}=0,1} p(\mathbf{S},\mathbf{T}) \log \frac{p(\mathbf{T})}{p(\mathbf{S},\mathbf{T})}$$

$$= \sum_{\mathbf{S}\in S} \sum_{\mathbf{T}=0,1} p(\mathbf{T}|\mathbf{S}) \log \frac{p(\mathbf{T})}{p(\mathbf{T}|\mathbf{S})}$$

(6)

where the second row comes from $p(\mathbf{S},\mathbf{T}) = p(\mathbf{T}|\mathbf{S})p(\mathbf{S})$, where the terms $p(\mathbf{S})$ then cancel due to an equal prior probability across all places.

To calculate $p(\mathbf{T} = 1|\mathbf{S} = s)$, the probability of observing word triplet τ given place s, we consider the proportion of s's training images that contain a landmark pair with this triplet, based on the landmark's distribution of word triplets. The value of $p(\mathbf{T} = 0|\mathbf{S} = s)$ is then $1 - p(\mathbf{T} = 1|\mathbf{S} = s)$, and the value of $p(\mathbf{T})$ is the summation of $p(\mathbf{T}|\mathbf{S})$ over all places. In order to choose an optimal set of word triplets for a specified memory constraint, triplets are added to the inverted index in order of their conditional entropy, such that those which offer most information when observed, are added first. This is evaluated in Section 7 for a given memory allowance. Note that the empty index, before any triplets are added, is a constant for any scale of database.

7   Experiments

7.1   Experimental Procedure

We evaluated our method on three datasets: the *Oxford* [14] and *Paris* [13] Buildings, and our own new dataset *World* Buildings. The Oxford and Paris Buildings datasets consist of 17 and 12 places respectively, and the World Buildings dataset consists of 300 places acquire from Flickr.com using search terms such as "Sydney Opera House" and "Houses of Parliament", each with 1000 training images and 10 test images. It was decided to use this new dataset due to the large number of individual places compared to standard image retrieval datasets such as the Oxford and Paris Buildings, together with the large number of training images as is required for our method. SIFT features [10] were matched using fast geometric matching [14] to generate feature tracks, whilst discarding tracks between image pairs yielding less than 15 inlier feature matches. For each dataset, a further 1M random distractor images were added from Flickr, with each image acting as its own place, such that each feature is designated a landmark, and with the probabilistic model for PPV computed across the single image. A dictionary of 100k visual words was trained using approximate k-means [14].

Our PPV method was compared against implementations of two modelling techniques, each with three geometric querying methods, for a total of 6 competitors. The modelling techniques include the Iconic Images (IC) method [16], returning the image with the most inliers across a set of iconic images for each place, and the Scene Maps (SM) method [8], with each place represented by a single map of superimposed features and returning the scene map with the most inliers. The querying techniques include the Visual Phrases (VP) of [25] where small groups of geometrically-consistent features are voted for, and the spatially-constrained similarity measure (SCSM) of [18] where entire object transformations are voted for, both using an inverted index. Furthermore, a standard technique was implemented using RANSAC geometric verification on the top 50 places returned from a BOW stage (BOW + RANSAC) [14], using the recently-updated LO-RANSAC method [15]. For each implementation, both the Average Precision (AP) and the Recall at 100% precision (R@1) were recorded, with the latter being a useful measure for the applicability to robotics due to the need for very high precision in localisation.

For a fair comparison of scalability, each modelling technique was allocated the same memory to store the necessary data (excluding constant memory requirements such as the BOW and word triplet index structures, which are not affected by scale). For II, iconic images were added in order of their distance to the centroid of the place's training images until the memory limit was reached, with all these iconic images then stored in the database. Similarly, for SM, the superimposed features were added in order of the number of features in the respective feature track. For our PPV method, word triplets were added in order of their conditional entropy as in Section 6. Feature attributes (location, scale and orientation) were quantised to 2 bytes each for SM and II.

7.2   Results

Accuracy and Timing. Table 1 presents the average precision, recognition rate and query time (excluding feature extraction and quantisation) for all implementations of competing methods, each given an allocation of 16MB (excluding the distractor images). Furthermore, we show the incremental improvements on our PPV method as two key components are introduced: the smoothed parameter learning stage (as opposed to maximum-likelihood estimation), and the geometric cliques stage (as opposed to a purely local voting scheme). This new method outperforms all other competitors that forego a RANSAC stage, and offers similar if not greater recognition performance even when RANSAC is included in the competitors (but not in our method). Intuitively, our geometric cliques stage for global geometric verification is very powerful and offers similar constraints to a full RANSAC procedure. Furthermore, our method is significantly faster than all competitors on all datasets, and in particular, adding the GC stage incurs little timing penalty compared to the addition of a RANSAC stage for the competitors. Note that performance is generally higher on the Oxford and Paris datasets despite the smaller set of training images for each place due to the availability of bounding boxes, whereas the World Buildings dataset requires unsupervised feature tracking across the entire image.

Memory. Figure 6 demonstrates that as further triplets are accumulated in the index, the recognition accuracy improves because a larger number of votes are possible for the correct place, and so this score becomes less corrupted by competing places. In fact, average precision begins to flatten out at around 8MB, corresponding to less than half of the maximum memory requirement (16MB), showing that half of the word triplets offer little information and are typically drawn from unstable landmark pairs, or those landmark pairs with poorly discriminating visual word and geometric word combinations. As a further

Table 1. Summary of recognition results for all implementations. AP = Average Precision, R@1 = Recall at 100% precision. (Time in ms, 3.2GHz Intel Core i7).

Method	Oxford			Paris			World		
	AP	R@1	Time	AP	R@1	Time	AP	R@1	Time
II + VP	0.673	0.695	1211	0.704	0.732	1128	0.601	0.645	1379
SM + VP	0.700	0.739	1445	0.731	0.785	1379	0.622	0.656	862
II + SCSM	0.688	0.741	844	0.718	0.772	786	0.612	0.655	894
SM + SCSM	0.700	0.728	521	0.724	0.758	498	0.631	0.684	567
II + BOW + RANSAC	0.741	0.770	1511	0.777	0.802	1456	0.687	0.731	1872
SM + BOW + RANSAC	0.757	0.798	1236	0.778	0.822	1231	0.698	0.748	1560
PPV	0.702	0.731	144	0.741	0.761	137	0.635	0.655	168
PPV + Smoothing	0.737	0.768	166	0.758	0.792	156	0.653	0.686	195
PPV + GC	0.761	0.788	150	0.785	0.812	134	0.676	0.710	174
PPV + Smoothing + GC	0.769	0.803	175	0.790	0.830	165	0.685	0.723	202

consequence of reducing the number of stored triplets, the computational time decreases as a much smaller set of triplets must be searched across. The difference between an allocation of 16MB and 8MB was a decrease in computational time from 168ms to 137ms. The competing methods naturally increase in performance as greater memory is allocated, but the scalability of our method is comparable due to the allocation of memory based on an entropy measure, rather than the naive heuristics available for the competitors.

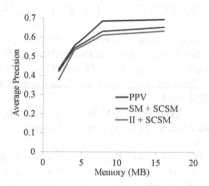

Fig. 6. The effect of the allocated memory on the average precision of recognition

8 Conclusions

In this paper a new framework for fast place recognition has been presented, called Pairwise Probabilistic Voting. It has been shown that it is possible to combine the merits of geometric constraints and inverted-index approaches, by voting for scenes through simple, local pairwise relationships. Geometry can be embedded in the inverted index by discretising image space over a number of geometry types, which also enables a strong generative model to be built, with joint distributions over pairwise appearance and geometry. We have also shown how global geometric constraints can be applied again by simply considering pairwise geometries, offering similar recognition performance to RANSAC approaches at a fraction of the required time. Our PPV method is also able to scale well with modest memory requirements due to its ability to remove most pairwise relationships from the index based on an entropy measure.

References

1. Arandjelovic, R., Zisserman, A.: Three things everyone should know to improve object retrieval. In: Proceedings of the IEEE Conference on Computer Vision and Pattern Recognition, pp. 2911–2918 (2012)
2. Cummins, M., Newman, P.: FAB-MAP: Probabilistic localization and mapping in the space of appearance. International Journal of Robotics Research 27, 647–661 (2008)

3. Heath, K., Gelfand, N., Ovsjanikov, M., Aanjaneya, M., Guibas, L.J.: Image-webs: Computing and exploiting connectivity in image collections. In: Proceedings of the IEEE International Conference on Computer Vision and Pattern Recognition, pp. 3432–3439 (2010)
4. Jegou, H., Douze, M., Schmid, C.: Hamming embedding and weak geometric consistency for large scale image search. In: Forsyth, D., Torr, P., Zisserman, A. (eds.) ECCV 2008, Part I. LNCS, vol. 5302, pp. 304–317. Springer, Heidelberg (2008)
5. Jégou, H., Chum, O.: Negative evidences and co-occurrences in image retrieval: The benefit of PCA and whitening. In: Fitzgibbon, A., Lazebnik, S., Perona, P., Sato, Y., Schmid, C. (eds.) ECCV 2012, Part II. LNCS, vol. 7573, pp. 774–787. Springer, Heidelberg (2012)
6. Johns, E., Yang, G.Z.: From images to scenes: Compressing an image cluster into a single scene model for place recognition. In: Proceedings of the IEEE International Conference on Comptuer Vision, pp. 874–881 (2011)
7. Johns, E., Yang, G.Z.: Generative methods for long-term place recognition in dynamic scenes. pp. 297–314 (2014)
8. Kalantidis, Y., Tolias, G., Avrithis, Y., Phinikettos, M., Spyrou, E., Mylonas, P., Kollias, S.: VIRaL: Visual image retrieval and localization. Multimedia Tools and Applications 51, 555–591 (2011)
9. Li, Y., Crandall, D.J., Huttenlocher, D.P.: Landmark classification in large-scale image collections. In: Proceedings of the IEEE International Conference on Computer Vision, pp. 1957–1964 (2009)
10. Lowe, D.G.: Distinctive image features from scale-invariant keypoints. International Journal on Computer Vision 60, 91–111 (2004)
11. Mikulík, A., Perdoch, M., Chum, O., Matas, J.: Learning a fine vocabulary. In: Daniilidis, K., Maragos, P., Paragios, N. (eds.) ECCV 2010, Part III. LNCS, vol. 6313, pp. 1–14. Springer, Heidelberg (2010)
12. Östergård, P.R.: A fast algorithm for the maximum clique problem. Discrete Appl. Math. 120, 197–201 (2002)
13. Philbin, J., Chum, O., Isard, M.: J. Sivic, A.Z.: Lost in quantization: Improving particular object retrieval in large scale image databases. In: Proceedings of the IEEE Conference on Computer Vision and Pattern Recognition, pp. 1–8 (2008)
14. Philbin, J., Chum, O., Isard, M., Sivic, J., Zisserman, A.: Object retrieval with large vocabularies and fast spatial matching. In: Proceedings of the IEEE Conference on Computer Vision and Pattern Recognition, pp. 1–8 (2007)
15. Raguram, R., Chum, O., Pollejeys, M., Matas, J., Frahm, J.M.: Usac: A universal framework for random sample consensus. Pattern Analysis and Machine Intelligence 35, 2022–2038 (2013)
16. Raguram, R., Wu, C., Frahm, J.M., Lazebnik, S.: Modeling and recognition of landmark image collections using iconic scene graphs. International Journal of Computer Vision 95, 213–231 (2011)
17. Sattler, T., Leibe, B., Kobbelt, L.: Fast image-based localization using direct 2D-to-3D matching. In: Proceedings of the IEEE International Conference on Computer Vision, pp. 667–674 (2011)
18. Shen, X., Lin, Z., Brandt, J., Wu, Y.: Spatially-constrained similarity measure for large-scale object retrieval. Pattern Analysis and Machine Intelligence 36, 1229–1241 (2014)
19. Tolias, G., Kalantidis, Y., Avrithis, Y., Kollias, S.: Towards large-scale geometry indexing by feature selection. Computer Vision and Image Understanding 120(3), 31–45 (2014)

20. Tolias, G., Avrithis, Y.: Speeded-up, relaxed spatial matching. In: Proceedings of the IEEE International Conference on Computer Vision, pp. 1653–1660 (2011)
21. Wang, R., Tang, Z., Cao, Q.: An efficient approximation algorithm for finding a maximum clique using hopfield network learning. Neural Computing 15(7), 1605–1619 (2003)
22. Wang, X., Yang, M., Cour, T., Zhu, S., Yu, K., Han, T.X.: Contextual weighting for vocabulary tree based image retrieval. In: Proceedings of the IEEE International Conference on Computer Vision, pp. 209–216 (2011)
23. Wu, Z., Ke, Q., Isard, M., Sun, J.: Bundling features for large scale partial-duplicate web image search. In: Proceedings of the IEEE International Conference on Computer Vision and Pattern Recognition, pp. 25–32 (2010)
24. Yuan, U., Wu, Y., Yang, M.: Discovery of collocation patterns: from visual words to visual phrases. In: Proceedings of the IEEE International Conference on Computer Vision and Pattern Recognition, pp. 1–8 (2007)
25. Zhang, Y., Jia, Z., Chen, T.: Image retrieval with geometry-preserving visual phrases. In: Proceedings of the IEEE International Conference on Computer Vision, pp. 809–816 (2011)
26. Zheng, Y., Zhao, M., Song, Y., Adam, H., Buddemeier, U., Bissacco, A., Brucher, F., Chua, T.S., Neven, H.: Tour the world: Building a web-scale landmark recognition engine. In: Proceedings of the IEEE Conference on Computer Vision and Pattern Recognition, pp. 1085–1092 (2009)

Robust Instance Recognition in Presence of Occlusion and Clutter

Ujwal Bonde, Vijay Badrinarayanan, and Roberto Cipolla

University of Cambridge, UK

Abstract. We present a robust learning based instance recognition framework from single view point clouds. Our framework is able to handle real-world instance recognition challenges, i.e, clutter, similar looking distractors and occlusion. Recent algorithms have separately tried to address the problem of clutter [9] and occlusion [16] but fail when these challenges are combined. In comparison we handle all challenges within a single framework. Our framework uses a soft label Random Forest [5] to learn discriminative shape features of an object and use them to classify both its location and pose. We propose a novel iterative training scheme for forests which maximizes the margin between classes to improve recognition accuracy, as compared to a conventional training procedure. The learnt forest outperforms template matching, DPM [7] in presence of similar looking distractors. Using occlusion information, computed from the depth data, the forest learns to emphasize the shape features from the visible regions thus making it robust to occlusion. We benchmark our system with the state-of-the-art recognition systems [9,7] in challenging scenes drawn from the largest publicly available dataset. To complement the lack of occlusion tests in this dataset, we introduce our *Desk3D* dataset and demonstrate that our algorithm outperforms other methods in all settings.

1 Introduction

A key limitation of supervised learning for object recognition is the need for large amounts of labelled training data so as to make it applicable to real world systems. One possible solution to address this limitation is to generate synthetic training data which closely resembles real world scenarios [21]. Object instance recognition is one such potential application where realistic training data can be easily synthesized using 3D object scans (using a Kinect sensor or dense reconstruction [17]) or which are available in large repositories such as the Google 3D warehouse [8]. Instance recognition in the presence of clutter and occlusion has several important applications, particularly in robotics and augmented reality. Recent methods [9,10,16,6] have begun to exploit the availability of cheap depth sensors to achieve success in instance recognition. Unlike earlier methods that relied on clean laser scanned data [14], these devices have encouraged research into the use of cheap depth data for real-time applications. However, these sensors are relatively noisy and contain missing depth values, thus making it difficult

D. Fleet et al. (Eds.): ECCV 2014, Part II, LNCS 8690, pp. 520–535, 2014.

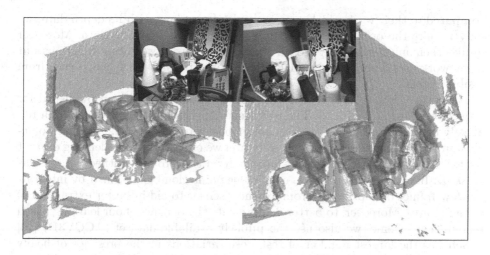

Fig. 1. Sample results of our instance recognition method which uses only point clouds as input. Meshed scenes from our *Desk3D* dataset with results of detection and pose classification on five object instances. Note meshed scenes are shown only for better visualization. Best viewed in color. See supplementary for videos.

to extract reliable object shape information. Recent development in 3D reconstruction [17] has made reliable shape information available in real time. In this work, we explore its use as an input for instance recognition (Fig. 1). However, to avoid being overly dependent on any particular reconstruction algorithm or sensor we use point clouds as input for recognition.

Object shape, unlike color, is invariant to changes in illumination or texture. The availability of cheap and real-time 3D data encourages the use of shape as a cue for recognition, particularly when color and texture cues are unreliable. An important example is in robotics, where the objects of interest can be textureless and often greased or discoloured. However, results from the state-of-the-art algorithm (LineMod) indicate that color is the dominant cue [9] and it outperforms depth cues in the majority of instances that were tested. In LineMod, surface normals were sampled densely over each 2.5D object template and these were used as depth cues for template matching. We believe this approach has not fully utilized the potential of depth data, especially the information present in the internal and external edges (contours) of the object. Moreover, a lack of discriminative selection of shape features in their approach degrades performance under presence of clutter and similar looking distractors. In contrast, given a 3D point-cloud model of an object, we encode its 3D shape using a discriminative set of edgelet/normal features learnt using a soft-label Random forest (slRF) [5].

Popular approaches to occlusion based recognition mainly rely on a parts-based strategy where the object is divided into smaller parts which vote for the presence of an object [14]. However as demonstrated in Sec. 4 most current depth based recognition systems suffer when the size of the object decreases. For this reason we explore the use of depth based occlusion cues similar to [16]. However compared to their work which uses multiple views along with its depth data, we only require the occlusion cues from a single view point cloud data. Moreover unlike their multi-staged approach that uses heuristic weighting functions our framework uses a single-stage slRF which learns to emphasize shape cues from visible region.

In recent years, several real-world RGB-D datasets have been published for object recognition [15,16,22]. The test scenes in these datasets either have a relatively clean background with not enough pose variations [16,22] or have no occlusion [15]. In the absence of such a dataset we create a new challenging dataset containing clutter as well as occlusion. We term this ground-truthed database as *Desk3D*. In the Desk3D dataset, each scene point-cloud is obtained by integrating few frames of depth data from a Kinect sensor to aid in better extraction of edge features. Moreover, to better demonstrate the benefits of our learning based recognition scheme, we also use the publicly available dataset (ACCV3D) [10] which has the largest number of test pose variations in the presence of heavy clutter with no occlusion. We benchmark our algorithm by extensive evaluation on Desk3D as well as on ACCV3D and show that our learning based method clearly outperforms the state-of-the-art recognition algorithms.

To summarize, our contributions are as follows:

1. We jointly address multiple instance recognition challenges of occlusion, clutter and similar looking distractors within a single learning based framework.
2. We introduce the challenging Desk3D dataset containing multiple clutter and occlusion scenarios to benchmark instance recognition methods.

2 Literature Review

A large portion of existing literature in instance recognition is dedicated to building descriptors to improve recognition [23,2]. In this work we use simple edge/normal orientation features and focus on achieving robust recognition in presence of clutter, similar looking distractors and occlusion. However these simple features can be replaced by more complex features that exist in literature.

Hinterstoisser *et al.* [9] use simple orientations features densely sampled to build robustness which they call the Dominant Orientation Templates (DOT). Using thousands of such templates for different viewpoints along with multi-modal signals (RGB+Depth) they achieve robustness to random clutter. Rios-Cabrera *et al.* [20] extend this work by discriminatively learning both the sampled features as well as the templates. Using a boosted classifier they are able to perform real time recognition on 10-15 objects. However as they still rely on 2D template matching its not clear how this work could be extended to handle occlusions as seen in the real world. In contrast our random forest framework exploits the depth ordering in single view for robustness to occlusion.

There has been a recent surge of interest in occlusion reasoning for object recognition [11,27,25]. These methods have primarily focused on jointly determining the occlusion and object location in single view RGB images. In this work, we are primarily interested in improving the robustness in presence of

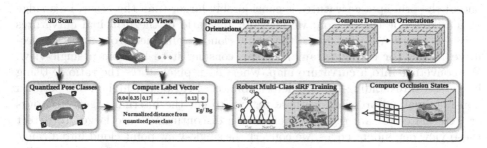

Fig. 2. Our training pipeline. Given a 3D object scan (point cloud) we simulate several thousand 2.5D object views, extract features for each view at various voxel offsets and assign them *soft labels* using the *quantized pose classes*. These features and soft labels are used to train a multi-class soft label Random Forest (slRF) [5] in a novel iterative manner to jointly classify location and pose of an object.

occlusion by utilizing the information obtained from single view point clouds. Our work is similar to [16] wherein they use multi-view RGB and depth images to compute occlusion information. Using multiple stages of reasoning along with a DPM [7] they achieve robustness to occlusion. In contrast we use a single-stage slRF which learns to emphasize shape cues from visible regions.

Deformable parts model have been successfully used for object category recognition [7]. Recently this has also been extended to object instance recognition in RGB [26]. However DPM's natural ability to exploit the similarity that exist within a category makes it unsuitable for detection in presence of similar looking distractors. On the other hand our slRF learns the most discriminative features for a given instance and hence is better able to deal with similar objects.

3   Learning Approach

An overview of our learning system is shown in Fig. 2. The input is a point cloud which is obtained from raw depth frames using Kinect or by integrating a few frames (typically 5-10 using Kinect Fusion [19]). The advantage of the latter approach is that it reduces noise and missing data from the sensor with minimal blurring of details. This makes it a stable input to estimate edges on the resulting point clouds. An advantage of working with point clouds is that the physical dimension of the scene does not change with the distance it is captured from. This eliminates the need to search over different object sizes for recognition. We first perform edgelet detection on point clouds as described below.

3.1   Edgelet Detection

Using the multi-scale method of Bonde *et al.* [3] we calculate the two principal curvatures λ_1, λ_2 for every point on the point cloud. We only consider the magnitude of the principal curvatures. In a point cloud, edges are regions where one of the principal curvatures is considerably larger than the other, i.e a ridge or a valley. For this reason, we consider the ratio of the principal curvatures $r = \frac{\lambda_1}{\lambda_2}$, where $\lambda_1 \geq \lambda_2$. Since the point cloud is obtained from a few consecutive frames (or a single frame) we can consider it to be from a single-view. We convert it into a curvature map, where each pixel stores the ratio r. Using hysteresis thresholding [18] we detect connected regions of high r. We perform non-maximal suppression on these regions to get the internal edges. Contours or external edges are regions where depth discontinuities are large. To detect these view dependent edges, we convert the single-view point cloud into a range image. Again, using hysteresis thresholding we detect regions of high depth discontinuities to obtain the external edges. These regions/edges are back projected onto the point cloud to get all the edgelet points (see Fig. 4). Finally, using local RANSAC line fitting we detect the orientation for each edgelet point. The orientations are quantized into 8 bins similar to [9] (to avoid ambiguity, we only consider camera facing orientations).

3.2   Encoding Occlusion Aware Features

We use a full 360 degree scan of the object for training. This scan is used to simulate different 2.5D views of the object. In each simulated view, edgelets are detected as described in Sec. 3.1. These edgelet points are quantized into a fixed voxel grid of size $w \times h \times d$ (typical values are $6 - 8$).

The dominant orientation of a voxel (v) is obtained by histogramming the orientation of all edgelet points within it and choosing the bin with maximum value. However, voxels containing corners or high curvature edges can have multiple dominant orientations. Therefore, at each voxel we also select all orientations whose histogram value is greater than one third the maximum value as dominant orientations. To achieve robustness to noise, we only consider those orientations whose histogram value is greater than a threshold (typically $10 - 30$). The feature vector for each voxel v is thus a vector x^v with eight elements and an element value is equal to 1 if the corresponding orientation is dominant.

Given the point cloud for the jth view we simulate an occluder in front of the object. Inspired by [11] we use a box world model for the occluder which are rectangular screens placed in front of the objects. The dimension of the screen have a truncated Gaussian distribution centered on $1/3^{rd}$ the dimensions of the simulated point cloud. As most natural occluders are resting on ground we simulate the occluder to start from the ground plane and not hanging in mid-air. Given the resulting point cloud we remove the occluded points from the simulated object. Using ray tracing (Fig 2) we assign an occlusion state $O^v = 1$ (or 0) for each of the visible voxels (or occluded) in the $w \times h \times d$ voxel grid. Finally for all the occluded voxels we modify their feature vector $x^v = \begin{bmatrix} -1 \end{bmatrix}$ where, $\begin{bmatrix} -1 \end{bmatrix}$ is an eight element vector with all elements -1. The resulting feature vector encodes the three possible states: -1 for occluded voxel, 0 for visible but no dominant orientation and 1 for visible and dominant orientation. Finally, we concatenated the vectors for all voxel in the jth view to get a feature vector x_j of dimension $w \times h \times d \times 8$.

3.3 Robust Training of Soft Label Random Forest

Soft Labelling: In order to assign labels for the simulated views, we first uniformly quantize the object viewpoints into 16 pose classes (2 along pitch, 2 along roll and 4 along yaw). As a simulated pose could be between two *quantized pose classes* it is assigned a *soft-label* with respect to each pose class. This helps to better explain simulated poses that are not close to any single pose class (see Sec. 3.5). Soft labels for each simulated pose are assigned based on the deviation of its *canonical rotational matrix* to the identity matrix [12]. For example, if R_j^i represents the canonical rotation matrix to take the jth simulated view to the ith quantized pose, then its distance is given by: $d_j^i = \|I - R_j^i\|_F$, where I is a 3×3 identity matrix and $\|.\|_F$ is the Frobenius norm. The soft labels are then given by:

$$l_j^i = \exp(-d_j^{i^2}), i \in \{1, ..., 16\}. \tag{1}$$

The final label vector for a simulated pose is normalized as $\sum_{i=1:16} l_j^i = 1$. We also add an additional label (16+1) to indicate foreground (fg) or background (bg) class. This is set to 0 for the simulated views (fg) and 1 for the bg examples (all the other 16 elements in the label vector are set to 0 in this case). We generate about 27000 such simulated views w/o occlusion and a similar number with occlusion spanning all the views of the object. For robustness, we augment the fg training set with a shifted version (2 voxels along all axes) of the simulated views. To improve localization, we augment the bg training set with a large shifted version (8 voxels) of the simulated views.

Given the complete training data $X = \{x_j, l_j\}$ a *conventional* 16+1 multi-class slRF is trained using the whole data. Similar to a multi-class RF, slRF computes a histogram of class membership at each node by element wise addition of the soft labels across all training examples falling into it. The split functions (features) query for occluded/presence or absence of a dominant orientation within a voxel. An information entropy measure [5] is used to evaluate the split function. We refer the reader to [5] for a detailed description of conventional slRF training. Each leaf node (Lf) in the trained slRF stores the foreground probability (p_{fg}) as the ratio of positive (fg) to negative (bg) samples as well as the pose class probabilities for fg samples $\left(p_{ps}^i = \frac{\sum_{j \in Lf} l_j^i}{\sum_{j \in Lf} \sum_{i \in [1,16]} l_j^i}\right)$. Note here that all the simulated views are considered as positive or fg samples irrespective of their pose. This is because the label assignment (Eq. 1) distributes the fg probability over all 16 pose classes. During testing fg and pose class probabilities are summed over 100 trees to get p_{fg}, p_{bg} for the forest.

Occlusion Queries: Given the tertiary nature of our feature vector $x_j \in \{-1, 0, 1\}$ two types of split questions exist. One which queries (> -1) for visible versus occluded voxel while the other queries (> 0) for a dominant orientation in a visible voxel. During the training of our slRF, split questions in the topmost nodes $(\approx 5 - 10)$ are restricted to only the second type of query. This is in accordance with the intuition that the decision for the presence of an object can be made from the features (dominant orientations) present in the visible regions

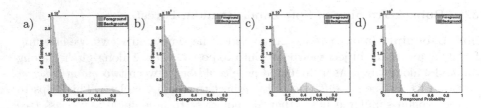

Fig. 3. (a) Foreground (fg) probability of training samples after *conventional training* of the slRF. No clear margin exists between the two classes. (b,c,d) show the fg probability over increasing number of iterations using our *robust iterative training* scheme (Alg. 1). A clear margin is visible between the class samples as the iterations progress.

and not based on the visibility/occlusion of a voxels. We remove this restriction for the bottom layers which allows the slRF to branch out based on the visibility of voxels and emphasize questions from visible regions.

Maximizing the Margin between Classes: Fig. 3(a) shows the p_{fg} predicted by the conventional slRF on the training data X for a sample class. We can observe that a subset of the two classes overlap and there does not exist a clear margin between the fg and bg samples. For robust recognition, we would ideally like to have a clear margin that would allow us to deal with sensor noise and also define a detection threshold. To this end, we propose an *novel iterative training* scheme which automatically mines these difficult examples lying in the overlapping parts and uses these to increase the margin between the two classes. We start by randomly selecting a subset of the training data $X_s \subset X$ such that $|X_s| \ll |X|$. We then train a multi-class slRF with this subset $|X_s|$ and calculate the leaf node distributions using the entire training corpus X. From the computed p_{fg} we then select *borderline positives* (fg examples with low p_{fg}) and *borderline negatives* (bg examples with high p_{fg}) and augment $|X_s|$ with these examples. However, for the classifier to learn to distinguish between borderline positive and similar or *confusing negative* examples, and vice versa, we also need to add these confusing examples to the training set. To mine the confusing negative examples we search for those negative examples that share the maximal number of leaf nodes with the borderline positive examples (and vice versa). Further, since our goal is to jointly predict both the location and pose, we follow a similar strategy for pose. After each iteration, we rank the accuracy of pose classification for each foreground sample as: $d_L^j = (l_j^c - \hat{l}_j^c)/l_j^c$, where $c = \arg\max_i l_j^i$ and $\hat{l}_j$ is the predicted class label vector. We then augment the training set with positive example having the largest d_L. Figs. 3 (b,c,d) show the fg probability margin increasing between fg and bg samples over iterations. Unlike most bootstrapping approaches, we start with a small training set for computational efficiency and low memory consumption. In our work, $|X_s| \approx |X|/20$. After each iteration we add a total of $|X|/20$ examples. We continue the process until the fg probability of all positive samples is greater than the fg probability of all negative samples. Usually this take 5-10 iterations. Our method shares some similarity to the work of [24], but they do not mine the

Algorithm 1. Proposed iterative training scheme for slRF.

Input: Training set $X = \{x_j, l_j\}$
Output: Learnt slRF classifier
1. Randomly select a subset: $X_s \subset X$ such that $|X_s| = |X|/20$.
2. Train slRF with X_s and compute p_{fg} for all X (see Sec. 3.3).
3. Augment X_s with borderline positive (low p_{fg}) and borderline negative (high p_{fg}).
4. Locate and augment X_s with confusing negative/ positive samples (see Sec. 3.3).
5. Compute pose class prediction accuracies d_L for all positive samples (see Sec. 3.3) and augment X_s with positive examples having high d_L.
6. Repeat steps 2 to 5 till p_{fg} for all positive data is greater than p_{fg} for all negative data.

---

confusing/similar examples which is crucial to establish the margin. We emphasize that this difference is crucial to achieve robustness Fig. 6(c) shows the performance improvement by mining these confusing examples. Alg. 1 summarizes the steps of our training scheme.

3.4   Addressing Challenges of Clutter and Occlusion.

Robustness to Clutter: In Sec. 3.3 we described the our iterative algorithm which increases the margin between similar looking examples. This increases the robustness of our framework allowing it reliably recognize difficult poses even in the presence of clutter (Fig. 6).

Dealing with Similar Looking Distractors. We set up an example case to understand how the slRF learns to discriminate between an object of interest and a similar looking distractor(s). We chose two car instances, a Mini and a Ferrari toy model (see Fig. 4). We select a quantized pose class and visualize the features (queries) learnt by their respective slRF by picking out all the training examples whose label vectors give this pose the maximum probability. We then pass these examples through the corresponding slRF. We select and plot the top few features that were repeatedly used as a node split feature (or queries) by the respective slRF (see Fig. 4). Each bold arrow in the figure represents an edgelet orientation query (feature). A pair or triplet of arrows correspond to multiple queries within a voxel. Note that different colors are used to represent the orientation queries and the encircled edgelets of the same color are those which responded positively to them. For the Mini, the queries capture the edgelets forming a corner of its windshield. For the Ferrari, the windshield and roof are smooth and hence no edgelets are detected at the windshield. On the other hand, the Ferrari's curved roof is a distinct feature which is captured by its slRF. These queries fail to find enough response on the Mini. Note that the slRF learns to query shape cues apart from simple corners.

Occlusion Training: To understand how the slRF uses the occlusion information we test two sample scenarios for the toy mini each having the same pose. For the first scenario, we generate examples wherein the front portion of the mini is occluded, while for the second scenario we occlude the middle portion. We then select the most frequently asked questions for both scenarios and only

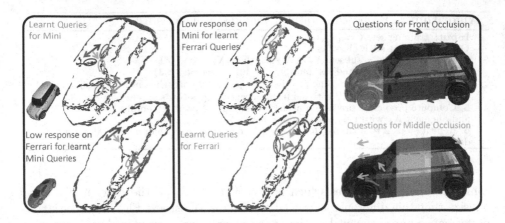

Fig. 4. Edgelet maps and some learnt features (queries) for a quantized pose class of the Ferrari and Mini. **Left** pane shows that when the learnt dominant orientation queries for the Mini (windshield) are projected onto the Ferrari they fail to find sufficient response. Similarly, **Middle** pane shows the learnt queries for the Ferrari (curved roof) fail to find sufficient response on the Mini. Note that the queries correspond to more than just corners and often capture intuitive shape features on the objects (see Sec. 3.4). **Right** pane shows the difference in the learnt dominant orientations when front/middle portion of Mini are occluded. Based on the occlusion information the slRF learns to emphasize questions from visible regions.

plot those questions that do not overlap in both scenarios. Fig. 4 (right top) shows the frequently asked questions for front occlusion which are absent in the second scenario. We observe that these questions shift to the middle/back (visible) portion of the mini. We also observe questions on the top portion of the front car. This is because of our assumption on the occluder model (Gaussian prior with the occluders resting on ground) which assigns a greater probability of the top portion been visible. Fig. 4 (right bottom) show the frequently asked questions for middle occlusion that are missing in the first scenario. A similar behavior is observed. This indicates that the slRF is using the occlusion questions to emphasize the visible portions and queries these regions to better deal with occlusion. Note that as compared to [16] who use a heuristic weighting our method automatically learns this from the occlusion queries.

3.5   Testing

We test our system on our Desk3D dataset as well as the publicly available ACCV3D dataset. For the Desk3D dataset, during testing, point clouds are obtained from the integration of a few Kinect frames (5) over a fixed region ($1.25m \times 1.25m \times 1.25m$). For the ACCV3D dataset, point clouds are obtained from individual depth frames to allow a fair comparison to other methods. This is followed by edgelet detection on the point cloud. The resulting edgelet points

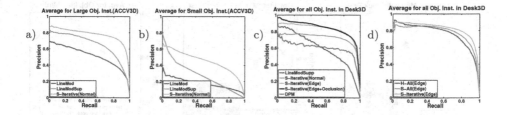

Fig. 5. Precision-Recall (PR) curves for joint pose+location. (a) and (b) PR curves for the ACCV3D dataset comparing LineMod with supervised removal of confusing templates (LineModSup) and w/o supervision, and our robust slRF (S-Iterative(Normals)). For fairness, we used surface normal features in our method as in LineMod. We clearly outperform LineMod and LineModSup on large objects. For small objects all methods do equally bad due to poor sensor resolution. (c) PR curves on non-occluded samples of Desk3D dataset for LineModSup, S-Iterative(Normals/Edge/Edge+Occlusion) and DPM. S-Iterative(Edge/Edge+Occlusion) outperform all other methods as they use both internal edge and contour cues for discrimination. DPM with HOG on depth images cannot not capture these details and performs poorly. (d) PR curves on Desk3D comparing hard (H-All(Edge)), soft label RF (S-All(Edge)) using conventional training. The use of soft-labels provides clear benefit over hard/scalar labels at high recall rates where several test examples which are not close to the quantized pose classes occur. Our robustly trained slRF (S-Iterative(Edge)) is more accurate as it learns a margin between classes.

---

are voxelized into a $128 \times 128 \times 128$ grid. We then compute shape features and occlusion states for these voxels as in the training stage. A *sliding cuboid* search is performed on the voxel grid. For each voxel location, the slRF is used to compute the fg class and pose probabilities. We pick the voxel with the maximum p_{fg} as the detected location and choose the pose class with the maximum p_{ps}. Note that we do not consider voxels close to the boundary of the grid. Also, we only consider voxel locations which have a sufficient number of edgelets within them.

4   Experiments and Results

We benchmark our system using the publicly available ACCV3D dataset [9] containing the largest number of test pose variation per object instance. Unlike other existing datasets [15,4,22] this dataset has high clutter and pose variations, thus closely approximating real world conditions. ACCV3D contains instances of 15 objects, each having over 1100 test frames (also see supplementary videos). For more extensive comparisons, we also tested on our *Desk3D* dataset. Desk3D contains multiple desktop test scenarios, where each test frame is obtained by integrating a few (5) frames from the Kinect sensor (see Fig. 4). In total there are over 850 test scenes containing six objects. The dataset also contains 450 test scenes with no objects to test the accuracy of the system.

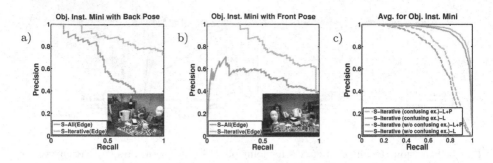

Fig. 6. Precision-Recall curves (joint pose+location) for the Mini on (a) near-back poses; (b) near-front poses in Desk3D . (c) PR curves (both location and joint pose+location) comparing the performance by mining confusing examples(see Sec. 3.3). Our iteratively trained slRF maximizes the margin between fg and bg (Sec. 3.3) and thus shows a large improvement on difficult poses compared to conventional training.

Scenario 1: Here we place two similar looking objects (Mini and Ferrari) along with similar looking distractors to confuse the recognition systems (see supplementary video). There are three test scenes wherein the objects are placed in different locations and poses. Each test scene/frame is recorded by smoothly moving the Kinect sensor over the scene. 110 test frames are automatically ground truthed using a known pattern on the desk (see Fig. 1).

Scenario 2: Here we test the performance of the algorithms in low clutter. We have five objects (Face, Kettle, Mini, Phone and Statue) of different 3D shape. We place the objects in clutter and record 60 − 90 frames for each object.

Scenario 3: Here we test the performance of the recognition algorithms in significant clutter. We capture six test scenes with the same five objects. Each test scene has 400 − 500 frames containing multiple objects with different backgrounds/clutter and poses.

Scenario 4: This scenario tests the performance of the recognition algorithms in occlusion and clutter. Current instance recognition datasets do not contain this challenge. We capture five test scenes similar to earlier scenario containing multiple objects with different backgrounds/clutter and poses.

For the background (bg) class, we record three scenes without any of the objects. The first two bg scenes contain 100 test frames each and are used as bg data to train the slRF. The third scene with 489 test frames are used to determine the accuracy of the learnt classifier. We quantify the performance of our proposed learning based system with the state-of-the-art template matching method of LineMod [9] using the two datasets. We use the open source implementation of their code [1].

For a fair comparison, we use only the depth modality based recognition set up of their system. As LineMod treats RGB/Depth separately and combines their

Table 1. Comparison of our robust sIRF with the state-of-the-art LineMod method on the ACCV3D dataset. We report both location only (L) and joint location and pose classification (L+P) results for both large and small objects. We outperform LineMod clearly with large objects and even with small objects, on an average, we perform better. Moreover, our overall pose classification is superior to that of LineMod. We see a large improvement on objects which have mainly smooth surfaces (can, holepunch, lamp, phone). For objects with high 3D detail (benchvise, driller, iron) all methods fare the same. Both systems are poor for very small objects (ape, cat, duck) as sensor resolution is low. Also, unlike LineMod, we currently do not adapt the size of voxels.

Object Instance	LineMod [9]		LineMod [9] (Supervision)		Our Work	
	L	L + P	L	L + P	L	L + P
BenchVise	82.88	74.57	83.79	75.23	**87.98**	86.50
Camera	67.94	57.70	**77.19**	68.94	58.20	53.37
Can	67.98	56.44	83.70	69.57	**94.73**	86.42
Driller	92.85	69.11	**94.70**	81.82	91.16	87.63
Iron	53.99	44.01	83.51	75.43	**84.98**	70.75
Lamp	89.81	75.39	92.91	80.93	**99.59**	98.04
Phone	53.02	48.27	77.72	70.47	**88.09**	87.69
Bowl	75.43	14.92	98.11	19.22	**98.54**	30.66
Box	**96.49**	55.31	63.37	27.69	95.21	63.53
Avg.(Large)	75.60	55.08	84.00	63.26	**88.62**	73.64
Ape	**28.32**	17.96	22.98	07.36	25.32	19.90
Duck	**50.80**	37.72	30.94	19.46	50.00	39.70
Cat	60.81	49.19	**63.10**	53.69	50.55	44.27
Cup	30.48	18.55	72.98	27.90	**73.55**	42.82
Glue	14.67	07.70	21.48	10.25	**62.70**	42.54
Holepunch	28.21	22.31	36.54	31.20	**73.00**	70.01
Avg.(Small)	33.88	23.91	41.34	24.98	**55.85**	43.10
Avg.(All)	59.58	43.28	66.93	47.94	**75.58**	61.43

individual matching score at the last stage of the detection pipeline, removing the RGB modality does not affect the training or testing of their depth alone system. As in our method, we train their system using the simulated views generated for each object. These simulated views are projected at different depths to learn scale-invariance for LineMod. Finally, their online training is used to learn the object templates. Except for the face category and small objects, each object instance contained more than 3000 templates after training. We observed that some of these learnt templates were often confused with the background. For this reason, we add a *supervised stage* wherein we test their detector on the two background test scenes with 100 frames. We remove templates that give a positive detection with high score (80) more than 200 times, i.e on an average once per frame. This significantly improved their recognition performance.

We also benchmark with DPM [7] which is widely considered as the state-of-the-art for category recognition. We use DPM with HOG feature on the depth images as a baseline. For training we use the simulated views similar to those used for training our work and LineMod. We observe that DPM with HOG on depth images does a poor job in describing instances and hence does poorly. These results were in in accordance with earlier observations [13]. For this reason we only compare DPM on the Desk3D dataset.   During testing, we consider localization to be correct if the predicted center is within a fixed radius ($\frac{max(w,d,h)}{3}$) of the ground truth position. We consider pose classification to be correct if the

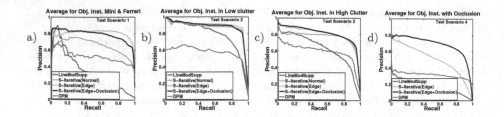

Fig. 7. PR curves for pose+location. (a) PR curves for test scenario 1 in Desk3D. Our discriminatively trained robust sIRF (both S-Iterative(Normals/Edge/Edge+Occlusion)) clearly outperforms DPM and LineMod even with supervision (removal of confusing templates - LineModSup). (b) Even in low clutter scenario DPM with HOG features on depth images does poorly. All other methods perform reasonable well (c) In high clutter, our method clearly shows significant gain at high recall rates. LineMod's dense feature sampling performs poorly on smooth objects.

predicted pose class (largest pose probability) or template is either the closest or second closest quantized pose to the ground truth.

Analysis: Fig. 5(a) and (b) shows the average PR curves for large and small objects in ACCV3D and Table 1 shows the accuracies of the methods. Approximately, large (small) objects have their axis-aligned bounding box volume greater (lesser) than $1000cm^3$. For a fair comparison, we used surface normal features as in LineMod. Overall we outperform LineMod (both with and w/o supervision) and a marked improvement is seen on pose classification. We have significant gains in performance on predominantly smooth objects (can, holepunch, lamp, phone) where dense feature sampling (LineMod) is confused by clutter. Both methods compare fairly on objects with more detail such as benchvise, driller, iron. Due to poor sensor resolution both methods perform poorly on small objects (ape, cat, duck).

Fig. 5(c) shows the average PR curves for Desk3D where our method outperforms LineMod even with supervision. Edgelets based sIRF does better than surface normals based sIRF as most objects in Desk3D (except Face, Kettle) have internal details which are better represented by edgelets. From Table 2 we can observe that iterative training with edgelet features performed best. A clear improvement is seen for similar looking (Ferrari, Mini) where our approach learns their fine discriminative features (Fig. 7(a)). From Fig. 7(b) we can see that except DPM all the methods perform well under low clutter, but as the clutter is increased (Fig. 7(c)) we clearly outperform LineMod, DPM. As in ACCV3D, for predominantly smooth objects (Kettle, Phone) LineMod's dense feature sampling performs poorly. For objects (Statue) which have high 3D detail the performance of all the methods are similar. For symmetrical objects (Face) pose classification suffers for all methods. From Table 3 and Fig. 7(d) we see that our occlusion based sIRF outperforms all method. This is because it learns to emphasize questions from visible regions.

Table 2. Comparison of our learning based system (for non-occluded scenes) under various training settings and features with the state-of-the-art instance recognition system (LineMod [9], DPM [7]) on the Desk3D dataset. We report location(L), joint location and pose classification (L+P) accuracies. H-All, S-All is conventional training with hard/soft labels respectively. S-Iterative is robust iterative training using soft labels. S-Iterative(Occlusion) uses the occlusion queries (see Sec. 3). Our system outperforms LineMod on 5/6 and DPM on all object instances. On an average, we outperform LineMod and DPM both with and w/o supervised removal of confusing templates (see Sec. 3.5). A marked improvement is seen in the discrimination between similar looking object instances (Ferrari, Mini).

Object Instance	LineMod [9]		LineMod [9] (Supervision)		DPM [7] (D-HoG)		H-All (Edges)		S-All (Edges)		S-Iterative (Edges)		S-Iterative (Occlusion)	
	L	L+P	L	L+P	L	L+P	L	L+P	L	L+P	L	L+P	L	L+P
Face	88.66	45.57	**91.55**	66.60	73.40	44.74	75.46	48.04	84.12	49.90	87.01	52.99	74.02	44.33
Kettle	76.19	38.80	83.95	60.49	65.32	53.34	81.31	71.96	82.19	73.02	87.83	78.48	**89.77**	79.19
Ferrari	24.37	12.61	75.63	47.90	52.14	32.41	95.80	73.95	98.32	74.79	**98.32**	77.31	96.64	65.55
Mini	26.22	12.27	68.76	55.09	53.26	30.64	81.31	70.15	84.80	73.22	87.03	76.71	**87.87**	79.78
Phone	53.55	43.85	89.77	79.03	57.43	64.32	96.71	90.81	**97.05**	91.68	96.53	90.99	96.71	91.16
Statue	90.15	83.27	91.64	84.76	74.50	70.29	89.78	84.20	89.22	85.50	91.45	86.25	**91.75**	86.80
Average	59.86	39.39	83.95	65.64	64.34	49.29	86.73	73.19	89.29	74.68	**91.36**	77.12	89.46	74.47

Table 3. Comparison of our learning based system with the state-of-the-art instance recognition system on occluded scenes in the Desk3D dataset. Our occlusion handling scheme is robust to occlusion and outperforms all methods by over 10%.

Object Instance	LineMod [9] (Supervision)		DPM [7] (D-HoG)		S-Iterative (Edges)		S-Iterative (Occlusion)	
	L	L+P	L	L+P	L	L+P	L	L+P
Face	73.21	26.29	44.00	08.86	88.79	45.11	**89.71**	40.00
Kettle	12.83	8.38	47.82	35.32	74.10	54.82	**83.25**	67.54
Mini	37.42	16.67	40.50	20.39	53.35	46.65	**69.18**	58.49
Phone	20.13	12.46	37.19	23.21	80.26	69.58	**86.26**	73.48
Statue	06.67	02.05	32.97	30.31	53.61	45.00	**81.03**	71.03
Average	30.15	13.17	40.50	23.72	70.70	52.62	**81.89**	62.11

In Fig. 5(d) we compare our slRF with conventional RF trained with hard/scalar labels. These scalar labels were assigned based on the pose class having the largest l^i (see Eq. 1). For pose classification, the conventional RF performs better at low recall rates as it does better than the slRF for test poses which are close to the quantized pose classes. However, for test poses which are further from the quantized pose classes, slRF fares better giving a higher precision at large recall rates. Fig. 5(d) also shows that our iteratively learnt slRF outperforms a conventional slRF. This is because our iterative strategy directs the slRF to concentrate harder on the difficult examples. To illustrate this, in Fig. 6(a) and (b) we show PR curves on two test scenes where the Mini is seen in near-back/front pose. Fig. 6(c) illustrates the advantage of mining confusing examples as proposed in Sec. 3.3 for the class Mini. Similar performance was seen on other classes as well.

5 Conclusion

We presented a learning based approach for depth based object instance recognition from single view point clouds. Our goal was to robustly estimate both the location and pose of an object instance in scenes with clutter, simialr looking distractors and occlusion. We employ a multi-class soft-label Random Forest to perform joint classification of location and pose. We proposed a novel iterative margin-maximizing training scheme to boost the performance of the forest on classification of difficult poses in cluttered scenes. By exploiting the depth ordering in single view point cloud data our method performs robustly even in the presence of large occlusions. We evaluated the performance of our algorithm on the largest publicly available dataset ACCV3D and our complementary Desk3D dataset focused on occlusion testing. We showed that our method outperforms the state-of-the-art LineMod and DPM algorithms on these challenging datasets. In future the performance of our unoptimized code (1.5 sec/object/frame) could be made real-time using GPUs.

Acknowledgements. This research is supported by the Boeing Company.

References

1. http://campar.in.tum.de/Main/StefanHinterstoisser
2. Aldoma, A., Tombari, F., Di Stefano, L., Vincze, M.: A Global Hypotheses Verification Method for 3D Object Recognition. In: Fitzgibbon, A., Lazebnik, S., Perona, P., Sato, Y., Schmid, C. (eds.) ECCV 2012, Part III. LNCS, vol. 7574, pp. 511–524. Springer, Heidelberg (2012)
3. Bonde, U., Badrinarayanan, V., Cipolla, R.: Multi Scale Shape Index for 3D Object Recognition. In: SSVM (2013)
4. Browatzki, B., Fischer, J., Graf, B., Bülthoff, H.H., Wallraven, C.: Going into depth: Evaluating 2D and 3D cues for object classification on a new, large-scale object dataset. In: ICCV Workshops on Consumer Depth Cameras (2011)
5. Criminisi, A., Shotton, J.: Decision Forests for Computer Vision and Medical Image Analysis. Springer (2013)
6. Drost, B., Ulrich, M., Navab, N., Ilic, S.: Model globally, match locally: Efficient and robust 3D object recognition. In: CVPR (2010)
7. Felzenszwalb, P.F., Girshick, R.B., McAllester, D., Ramanan, D.: Object detection with discriminatively trained part-based models. TPAMI 32, 1627–1645 (2010)
8. Google-3D-Warehouse, http://sketchup.google.com/3dwarehouse/
9. Hinterstoisser, S., Holzer, S., Cagniart, C., Ilic, S., Konolige, K., Navab, N., Lepetit, V.: Multimodal templates for real-time detection of texture-less objects in heavily cluttered scenes. In: ICCV (2011)
10. Hinterstoisser, S., Lepetit, V., Ilic, S., Holzer, S., Bradski, G., Konolige, K., Navab, N.: Model Based Training, Detection and Pose Estimation of Texture-Less 3D Objects in Heavily Cluttered Scenes. In: ACCV (2013)
11. Hsiao, E., Hebert, M.: Occlusion reasoning for object detection under arbitrary viewpoint. In: CVPR (2012)

12. Huynh, D.Q.: Metrics for 3D Rotations: Comparison and Analysis. JMIV 35, 155–164 (2009)
13. Janoch, A., Karayev, S., Jia, Y., Barron, J.T., Fritz, M., Saenko, K., Darrell, T.: A category-level 3d object dataset: Putting the kinect to work. In: Consumer Depth Cameras for Computer Vision (2013)
14. Knopp, J., Prasad, M., Willems, G., Timofte, R., Van Gool, L.: Hough Transform and 3D SURF for Robust Three Dimensional Classification. In: Daniilidis, K., Maragos, P., Paragios, N. (eds.) ECCV 2010, Part VI. LNCS, vol. 6316, pp. 589–602. Springer, Heidelberg (2010)
15. Lai, K., Bo, L., Ren, X., Fox, D.: A large-scale hierarchical multi-view RGB-D object dataset. In: ICRA (2011)
16. Meger, D., Wojek, C., Little, J.J., Schiele, B.: Explicit Occlusion Reasoning for 3D Object Detection. In: BMVC (2011)
17. Newcombe, R.A., Izadi, S., Hilliges, O., Molyneaux, D., Kim, D., Davison, A.J., Kohli, P., Shotton, J., Hodges, S., Fitzgibbon, A.W.: KinectFusion: Real-time dense surface mapping and tracking. In: ISMAR (2011)
18. Pauly, M., Keiser, R., Gross, M.H.: Multi-scale Feature Extraction on Point-sampled Surfaces. Comput. Graph. Forum 22, 281–290 (2003)
19. Point-Cloud-Library, http://pointclouds.org/
20. Rios-Cabrera, R., Tuytelaars, T.: Discriminatively Trained Templates for 3D Object Detection: A Real Time Scalable Approach. In: ICCV (2013)
21. Shotton, J., Sharp, T., Kipman, A., Fitzgibbon, A., Finocchio, M., Blake, A., Cook, M., Moore, R.: Real-time Human Pose Recognition in Parts from Single Depth Images (2011)
22. Tang, J., Miller, S., Singh, A., Abbeel, P.: A textured object recognition pipeline for color and depth image data. In: ICRA (2012)
23. Tombari, F., Salti, S., Di Stefano, L.: Unique signatures of histograms for local surface description. In: Daniilidis, K., Maragos, P., Paragios, N. (eds.) ECCV 2010, Part III. LNCS, vol. 6313, pp. 356–369. Springer, Heidelberg (2010)
24. Villamizar, M., Andrade-Cetto, J., Sanfeliu, A., Moreno-Noguer, F.: Bootstrapping Boosted Random Ferns for discriminative and efficient object classification. Pattern Recognition 45, 3141–3153 (2012)
25. Wang, T., He, X., Barnes, N.: Learning structured hough voting for joint object detection and occlusion reasoning. In: CVPR (2013)
26. Zhu, M., Derpanis, K.G., Yang, Y., Brahmbhatt, S., Zhang, M., Phillips, C., Lecce, M., Daniilidis, K.: Single Image 3D Object Detection and Pose Estimation for Grasping. In: ICRA (2014)
27. Zia, M., Stark, M., Schindler, K.: Explicit Occlusion Modeling for 3D Object Class Representations. In: CVPR (2013)

Learning 6D Object Pose Estimation
Using 3D Object Coordinates

Eric Brachmann[1], Alexander Krull[1], Frank Michel[1], Stefan Gumhold[1],
Jamie Shotton[2], and Carsten Rother[1]

[1] TU Dresden, Dresden, Germany
[2] Microsoft Research, Cambridge, UK

Abstract. This work addresses the problem of estimating the 6D Pose
of specific objects from a single RGB-D image. We present a flexible approach that can deal with generic objects, both textured and texture-less.
The key new concept is a learned, intermediate representation in form of
a dense 3D object coordinate labelling paired with a dense class labelling.
We are able to show that for a common dataset with texture-less objects,
where template-based techniques are suitable and state of the art, our
approach is slightly superior in terms of accuracy. We also demonstrate
the benefits of our approach, compared to template-based techniques, in
terms of robustness with respect to varying lighting conditions. Towards
this end, we contribute a new ground truth dataset with 10k images of
20 objects captured each under three different lighting conditions. We
demonstrate that our approach scales well with the number of objects
and has capabilities to run fast.

1 Introduction

The tasks of object instance detection and pose estimation are well-studied problems in computer vision. In this work we consider a specific scenario where the
input is a single RGB-D image. Given the extra depth channel it becomes feasible to extract the full 6D pose (3D rotation and 3D translation) of rigid object
instances present in the scene. The ultimate goal is to design a system that
is fast, scalable, robust and highly accurate and works well for generic objects
(both textured and texture-less) present in challenging real-world settings, such
as cluttered environments and with variable lighting conditions.

For many years the main focus in the field of detection and 2D/6D pose
estimation of rigid objects has been limited to objects with sufficient amount
of texture. Based on the pioneering work of [11,15], practical, robust solutions
have been designed which scale to large number of object instances [18,20]. For
textured objects the key to success, for most systems, is the use of a sparse
representation of local features, either hand crafted, e.g. SIFT features, or trained
from data. These systems run typically a two-stage pipeline: a) putative sparse
feature matching, b) geometric verification of the matched features.

Recently, people have started to consider the task of object instance detection
for texture-less or texture-poor rigid objects, e.g. [7,8,21]. For this particular challenge it has been shown that template-based techniques are superior. The main

D. Fleet et al. (Eds.): ECCV 2014, Part II, LNCS 8690, pp. 536–551, 2014.
© Springer International Publishing Switzerland 2014

Fig. 1. Overview of our system. Top left: RGB-D Test image (upper-half depth image and lower-half RGB image). The estimated 6D pose of the query object (camera) is illustrated with a blue bounding box, and the respective ground truth with a green bounding box. Top right: Visualization of the algorithms search for the optimal pose, where the inlet is a zoom of the centre area. The algorithm optimizes our energy in a RANSAC-like fashion over a large, continuous 6D pose space. The 6D poses, projected to the image plane, which are visited by the algorithm are color coded: *red poses* are disregarded in a very fast geometry check; *blue poses* are evaluated using our energy function during intermediate, fast sampling; *green poses* are subject to the most expensive energy refinement step. Bottom, from left to right: (a) Probability map for the query object, (b) predicted 3D object coordinates from a single tree mapped to the RGB cube, (c) corresponding ground truth 3D object coordinates, (d) overlay of the *3D model in blue* onto the test image (rendered according to the estimated pose)

focus of these works has been to show that template-based techniques can be made very fast, by using specific encodings [8] or additionally a cascaded framework [21]. The typical problems of template-based techniques, such as not being robust to clutter and occlusions as well as changing lighting conditions, have been partly overcome by carefully hand-crafted templates and additional discriminative learning. Nevertheless, template-based techniques have in our view two fundamental shortcomings. Firstly, they match the complete template to a target image, i.e. encode the object in a particular pose with one "global" feature. In contrast to this, sparse feature-based representations for textured objects are "local" and hence such systems are more robust with respect to occlusions. Secondly, it is an open challenge to make template-based techniques work for articulated or deformable object instances, as well as object classes, due to the growing number of required templates.

Our approach is motivated by recent work in the field of articulated human pose estimation from a pre-segmented RGB-D image [28]. The basic idea in [28] is not to predict directly the 60-DOF human pose from an image, but to first regress an intermediate so-called object coordinate representation. This means that each pixel in the image votes for a continuous coordinate on a canonical body in a canonical pose, termed the Vitruvian Manifold. The voting is done by a random forest and uses a trained assemble of simple, local feature tests. In the next step a "geometric validation" is performed, by which an energy function is defined that compares these correspondences with a parametric body model. Finally, the pose parameters are found by energy minimization. Hence, in spirit, this is akin to the two-stage pipeline of traditional, sparse feature-based techniques but now with densely learned features. Subsequent work in [24] applied a similar idea to 6D camera pose estimation, showing that a regression forest can accurately predict image-to-world correspondences that are then used to drive a camera pose estimaten. They showed results that were considerably more accurate than a sparse feature-based baseline.

Our system is based on these ideas presented in [28,24] and applies them to the task of estimating the 6D pose of specific objects. An overview of our system is presented in Fig. 1. However, we cannot apply [28,24] directly since we additionally need an object segmentation mask. Note that the method in [28] can rely on a pre-segmented human shape, and [24] does not require segmentation. To achieve this we jointly predict a dense 3D object coordinate labelling and a dense class labelling. Another major difference to [24] is a clever sampling scheme to avoid unnecessary generation of false hypotheses in the RANSAC-based optimization.

To summarize, the **main contribution** of our work is a new approach that has the benefits of local feature-based object detection techniques and still achieves results that are even slightly superior, in terms of accuracy, to template-based techniques for texture-less object detection. This gives us many conceptual and practical advantages. Firstly, one does not have to train a separate system for textured and texture-less objects. Secondly, one can use the same system for rigid and non-rigid objects, such as laptops, scissors, and objects in different states, e.g. a pot with and without lid. Thirdly, by using local features we gain robustness with respect to occlusions. Fourthly, by applying a rigorous feature learning framework we are robust to changes in lighting conditions. Fig. 2 shows the benefits of our system. The main technical contribution of our work is the use of a new representation in form of a joint dense 3D object coordinate and object class labelling. An additional minor contribution is a new dataset of 10k images of 20 objects captured each under three different lighting conditions and labelled with accurate 6D pose, which will be made publicly available.

2 Related Work

There is a vast literature in the area of pose estimation and object detection, including instance and category recognition, rigid and articulated objects, and

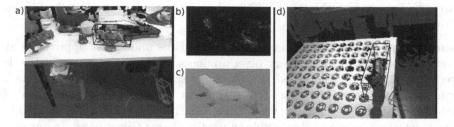

Fig. 2. Our method is able to find the correct pose, where a template-based method fails. (a) Test image showing a situation with strong occlusion. The pose estimate by our approach is shown in blue. The pose estimated by our reimplementation of the method by Hinterstoisser et al. from [8] is shown in red. (b) The coordinate predictions for a from one tree mapped to the RGB-cube and multiplied with $p_{c,i}$. (c) Ground truth object coordinates for a mapped to the RGB-cube. (d) Test image showing extreme light conditions, different from the training set. Estimated poses are displayed as in a.

coarse (quantized) and accurate (6D) poses. In the brief review below, we focus on techniques that specifically address the detection of instances of rigid objects in cluttered scenes and simultaneously infer their 6D pose. Some of the work was already mentioned above.

Template-Based Approaches. Perhaps the most traditional approach to object detection is to use templates, e.g. [11,26,7,8]. This means a rigid template is scanned across the image, and a distance measure is computed to find the best match. As the state of the art in template-based approaches, [8] uses synthetic renderings of a 3D object model to generate a large number of templates covering the full view hemisphere. They employ an edge-based distance metric which works well for textureless objects, and refine their pose estimates using ICP to achieve an accurate 6D pose. Such template-based approaches can work accurately and quickly in practice. The limitations of template-based approaches were discussed above.

Sparse Feature-Based Approaches. A popular alternative to templates are sparse feature-based approaches. These extract points of interest (often scale-invariant) from the image, describe these with local descriptors (often affine and illumination invariant), and match to a database. For example, Lowe [15] used SIFT descriptors and clustered images from similar viewpoints into a single model. Another great example of a recent, fast and scalable system is [16]. Sparse techniques have been shown to scale well to matching across vast vocabularies [18,20]. More recently a trend has been to *learn* interest points [22,10], descriptors [30], and matching [14,19,1]. Despite their popularity, a major limitation of sparse approaches for real applications is that they require sufficiently textured objects. Our approach instead can be applied densely at every image pixel regardless of texture, and can learn what are the most appropriate image features to exploit. Note that there is also large literature on contour and shape matching, which can deal with texture-less objects, e.g. [29], which is, however, conceptually different to our work.

Dense Approaches. An alternative to templates and sparse approaches are dense approaches. In these, every pixel produces some prediction about the desired output. In the generalized Hough voting scheme, all pixels cast a vote in some quantized prediction space (e.g. 2D object center and scale), and the cell with the most votes is taken as the winner. In [27,5], Hough voting was used for object detection, and was shown able to predict coarse object poses. In our work we borrow an idea from Gall et al. [5] to jointly train an objective over both Hough votes and object segmentations. However, in contrast to [5] we found a simple joint distribution over the outputs (in our case 3D object coordinates and object class labeling) to perform better than the variants suggested in [5]. Drost et al. [4] also take a voting approach, and use oriented point pair features to reduce the search space. To obtain a full 6D pose, one could imagine a variant of [5] that has every pixel vote directly for a *global* quantized 6D pose. However, the high dimensionality of the search space (and thus the necessary high degree of quantization) is likely to result in a poor estimate of the pose. In our approach, each pixel instead makes a 3D continuous prediction about only its *local* correspondence to a 3D model. This massively reduces the search space, and, for learning a discriminative prediction, allows a much reduced training set since each point on the surface of the object does not need to be seen from every possible angle. We show how these 3D object correspondences can efficiently drive a subsequent model fitting stage to achieve a highly accurate 6D object pose.

Finally, there are approaches for object class detection that use a similar idea as our 3D object coordinate representation. One of the first systems is the 3D LayoutCRF [9] which considers the task of predicting a dense part-labelling, covering the 3D rigid object, using a decision forest, though they did not attempt to fit a 3D model to those labels. After that the Vitruvian Manifold [28] was introduced for human pose estimation, and recently the scene coordinate regression forests was introduced for camera re-localization in RGB-D images [24]. Both works were discussed in detail above.

3   Method

We first describe our decision forest that jointly predicts both 3D object coordinates and object instance probabilities. Then we will discuss our energy function which is based on forest output. Finally, we will address our RANSAC based optimization scheme.

3.1   Random Forest

We use a single decision forest to classify pixels from an RGB-D image. A decision forest is a set $\mathcal{T}$ of decision trees T^j. Pixels of an image are classified by each tree T^j and end up in one of the tree's leafs l^j. Our forest is trained in a way that allows us to gain information about which object $c \in C$ the pixel i might belong to, as well as what might be its position on this object. We will denote a pixel's position on the object by $\mathbf{y}_i$ and refer to it as the pixel's *object coordinate*. Each leaf l^j stores a distribution over possible object affiliations $p(c|l^j)$, as well as a set of object coordinates $\mathbf{y}_c(l^j)$ for each possible object affiliation c. The term $\mathbf{y}_c(l^j)$ will be referred to as *coordinate prediction*. In the following we only discuss the interesting design decisions which are specific to our problem and refer the reader to the supplementary material for a detailed description.

Design and Training of the Forest. We build the decision trees using a standard randomized training procedure [2]. We quantized the continuous distributions $p(\mathbf{y}|c)$ into $5 \times 5 \times 5 = 125$ discrete bins. We use an additional bin for a background class. The quantization allows us to use the standard information gain classification objective during training, which has the ability to cope better with the often heavily multi-model distributions $p(\mathbf{y}|c)$ than a regression objective [6]. As a node split objective that deals with both our discrete distributions, $p(c|l^j)$ and $p(\mathbf{y}|c, l^j)$, we use the information gain over the joint distribution. This has potentially $125|C| + 1$ labels, for $|C|$ object instances and background, though many bins are empty and the histograms can be stored sparsely for speed. We found the suggestion in [5] to mix two separate information gain criteria to be inferior on our data.

An important question is the choice of features evaluated in the tree splits. We looked at a large number of features, including normal, color, etc. We found that the very simple and fast to compute features from [24] performed well, and that adding extra feature types did not appear to give a boost in accuracy (but did slow things down). The intuitive explanation is that the learned combination of simple features in the tree is able to create complex features that are specialized for the task defined by the training data and splitting objective. The features in [24] consider depth or color differences from pixels in the vicinity of pixel i and capture local patterns of context. The features are depth-adapted to make them largely depth invariant [23]. Each object is segmented for training. If a feature test reaches outside the object mask, we have to model some kind of background to calculate feature responses. In our experiments we will use uniform noise or a simulated plane the object sits on. We found this to work well and to generalize well to new unseen images. Putting objects on a plane allows the forest to learn contextual information.

For training, we use randomly sampled pixels from the segmented object images and a set of RGB-D background images. After training the tree structure based on quantized object coordinates, we push training pixels from all objects through the tree and record all the continuous locations $\mathbf{y}$ for each object c at each leaf. We then run mean-shift with a Gaussian kernel and bandwidth 2.5cm. We use the top mode as prediction $\mathbf{y}_c(l^j)$ and store it at the leaf. We furthermore store at each leaf the percentage of pixels coming from each object c to approximate the distribution of object affiliations $p(c|l^j)$ at the leaf. We also store the percentage of pixels from the background set that arrived at l^j, and refer to it as $p(bg|l^j)$.

Using the Forest. Once training is complete we push all pixels in an RGB-D image through every tree of the forest, thus associating each pixel i with a distribution $p(c|l_i^j)$ and one prediction $\mathbf{y}_c(l_i^j)$ for each tree j and each object c. Here l_i^j is the leaf outcome of pixel i in tree j. The leaf outcome of all trees for a pixel i is summarized in the vector $\mathbf{l}_i = (l_i^1, \ldots, l_i^j, \ldots, l_i^{|\mathcal{T}|})$. The leaf outcome of the image is summarized in $L = (\mathbf{l}_1, \ldots, \mathbf{l}_n)$. After the pixels have been classified we calculate for the object c we are interested in and for each pixel i in the image a number $p_{c,i}$ by combining the $p(c|l_i^j)$ stored at the leafs l_i^j. The number $p_{c,i}$ can be seen as the approximate probability $p(c|\mathbf{l}_i)$, that a pixel i belongs to object c given it ended up in all its leaf nodes $\mathbf{l}_i = (l_i^1, \ldots, l_i^j, \ldots, l_i^{|\mathcal{T}|})$. We will thus refer to the number $p_{c,i}$ as object probability. We calculate the object probability as

$$p_{c,i} = \frac{\prod_{j=1}^{|\mathcal{T}|} p(c|l_i^j)}{\prod_{j=1}^{|\mathcal{T}|} p(bg|l_i^j) + \sum_{\hat{c} \in C} \prod_{j=1}^{|\mathcal{T}|} p(\hat{c}|l_i^j)}. \tag{1}$$

A detailed deduction for Eq. 1 can be found in the supplementary material.

3.2 Energy Function

Our goal is to estimate the 6 DOF pose H_c for an object c. The pose H_c is defined as the rigid body transformation (3D rotation and 3D translation) that maps a point from object space into camera space. We formulate the pose estimation as an energy optimization problem. To calculate the energy we compare synthetic images rendered using H_c with the observed depth values $D = (d_1, \ldots, d_n)$ and the results of the forest $L = (\mathbf{l}_1, \ldots, \mathbf{l}_n)$. Our energy function is based on three components:

$$\hat{E}_c(H_c) = \lambda^{\text{depth}} E_c^{\text{depth}}(H_c) + \lambda^{\text{coord}} E_c^{\text{coord}}(H_c) + \lambda^{\text{obj}} E_c^{\text{obj}}(H_c). \tag{2}$$

While the component $E_c^{\text{depth}}(H)$ punishes deviations between the observed and ideal rendered depth images, the components $E_c^{\text{coord}}(H)$ and $E_c^{\text{obj}}(H)$ punish deviations from the predictions of the forest. Fig. 3 visualizes the benefits of each component. The parameters λ^{depth}, λ^{coord} and λ^{obj} reflect the reliability of the different observations. We will now describe the components in detail.

The Depth Component. This component is defined as

$$E_c^{\text{depth}}(H_c) = \frac{\sum_{i \in M_c^D(H_c)} f(d_i, d_i^*(H_c))}{|M_c^D(H_c)|}, \tag{3}$$

where $M_c^D(H_c)$ is the set of pixels belonging to object c. It is derived from the pose H_c by rendering the object into the image. Pixels with no depth observation d_i are excluded. The term $d_i^*(H_c)$ is the depth at pixel i of our recorded 3D model for object c rendered with pose H_c. In order to handle inaccuracies in the 3D model we use a robust error function: $f(d_i, d_i^*(H)) = \min(||\mathbf{x}(d_i) - \mathbf{x}(d_i^*(H))||, \tau_d)/\tau_d$, where $\mathbf{x}(d_i)$ denotes the 3D coordinates in the

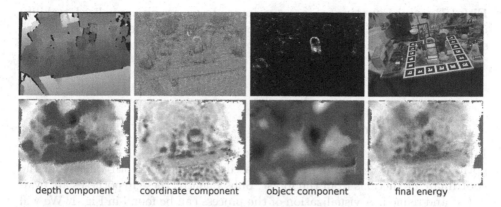

depth component   coordinate component   object component   final energy

Fig. 3. Benefits of the different energy components. While different energy components display strong local minima, their combination usually shows the strongest minimum at the correct pose. The energies were calculated for different poses and projected into image space using minimum projection. White stands for high energy dark blue for low energy. Each component is displayed below data it is related to. Left to right: depth component of test image together with $E_c^{\text{depth}}(H_c)$, predicted object coordinates from one of the trees with $E_c^{\text{coord}}(H_c)$, object probabilities with $E_c^{\text{object}}(H_c)$, the RGB components of test image is displayed with the final energy $E_c(H_c)$. The *estimated pose (blue)* and *ground truth pose (green)* are shown as bounding box.

camera system derived from the depth d_i. The denominator in the definition normalizes the depth component to make it independent of the object's distance to the camera.

The Object Component. This component punishes pixels inside the ideal segmentation M_c^D which are, according to the forest, unlikely to belong to the object. It is defined as

$$E_c^{\text{obj}}(H_c) = \frac{\sum_{i \in M_c^D(H_c)} \sum_{j=1}^{|\mathcal{T}|} - \log p(c|l_i^j)}{|M_c^D(H_c)|}. \tag{4}$$

The Coordinate Component. This component punishes deviations between the object coordinates $\mathbf{y}_c(l_i^j)$ predicted by the forest and ideal object coordinates $\mathbf{y}_{i,c}(H_c)$ derived from a rendered image. The component is defined as

$$E_c^{\text{coord}}(H_c) = \frac{\sum_{i \in M_c^L(H_c)} \sum_{j=1}^{|\mathcal{T}|} g(\mathbf{y}_c(l_i^j), \mathbf{y}_{i,c}(H_c))}{|M_c^L(H_c)|}. \tag{5}$$

where $M_c^L(H_c)$ is the set of pixels belonging to the object c excluding pixels with no depth observation d_i and pixels where $p_{c,i} < \tau_{pc}$. The latter is necessary because we find that pixels with small $p_{c,i}$ do not provide reliable coordinate predictions $\mathbf{y}_c(l_i^j)$. The term $\mathbf{y}_{i,c}(H_c)$ denotes the coordinates in object space at pixel i of our 3D model for object c rendered with pose H_c. We again use a robust error function $g(\mathbf{y}_c(l_i^j), \mathbf{y}_{i,c}(H_c)) = \min\left(||\mathbf{y}_c(l_i^j) - \mathbf{y}_{i,c}(H_c)||^2, \tau_y\right)/\tau_y$.

Final Energy Function. Since our energy terms are all normalized, stability can be an issue whenever the number of pixels to be considered becomes very small. To address the problem we use the following stable formulation:

$$E_c(H_c) = \begin{cases} \hat{E}_c(H_c), & \text{if } |M_c^L(H_c)| > 100 \\ \infty, & \text{otherwise} \end{cases} \tag{6}$$

3.3   Optimization

In order to find the solution to the task in Eq. 6 we use a RANSAC-based algorithm. It samples pose hypotheses based on observed depth values and the coordinate predictions from the forest. Subsequently, these hypotheses are evaluated and refined. A visualization of the process can be found in Fig. 1. We will now describe the procedure in detail.

Sampling of a Pose Hypothesis. We first draw a single pixel i_1 from the image using a weight proportional to the previously calculated $p_{c,i}$ each pixel i. We draw two more pixels i_2 and i_3 from a square window around i_1 using the same method. The width of the window is calculated from the diameter of the object and the observed depth value d_{i_1} of the pixel $w = f\delta_c/d_i$ where $f = 575.816$ pixels is the focal length. Sampling is done efficiently using an integral image of $p_{c,i}$. We randomly choose a tree index j_1, j_2 and j_3 for each pixel. Finally, we use the Kabsch algorithm to calculate the pose hypothesis H_c from the 3D-3D-correspondences $(\mathbf{x}(i_1), \mathbf{y}_c(l_{i_1}^{j_1}))$, $(\mathbf{x}(i_2), \mathbf{y}_c(l_{i_2}^{j_2}))$ and $(\mathbf{x}(i_3), \mathbf{y}_c(l_{i_3}^{j_3}))$.

We map each of the three predicted positions $\mathbf{y}_c(l_{i_\bullet}^{j_\bullet})$ into camera space using H_c and calculate a transformation error $e_{i_\bullet, j_\bullet}(H_c) = ||\mathbf{x}(i_\bullet) - H_c\mathbf{y}_c(l_{i_\bullet}^{j_\bullet})||$, which is simply the Euclidean distance to their counterpart. We accept a pose hypothesis H_c only if none of the three distances is larger than 5% of the object's diameter δ_c. The process is repeated until a fixed number of 210 hypotheses are accepted. All accepted hypotheses are evaluated according to Eq. 6.

Refinement. We refine the top 25 accepted hypotheses. To refine a pose H_c we iterate over the set of pixels $M_c^D(H_c)$ supposedly belonging to the object c as done for energy calculation. For every pixel $i \in M_c^D(H_c)$ we calculate the error $e_{i,j}(H_c)$ for all trees j. Let $\hat{j}$ be the tree with the smallest error $e_{i,\hat{j}}(H_c) \leq e_{i,j}(H_c)|\forall j \in \{1, \ldots, |\mathcal{T}|\}$ for pixel i. Every pixel i where $e_{i,\hat{j}}(H_c) < 20$mm is considered an inlier. We store the correspondence $(\mathbf{x}(i_1), \mathbf{y}_c(l_i^{\hat{j}}))$ for all inlier pixels and use them to reestimate the pose with the Kabsch algorithm. The process is repeated until the energy of the pose according Eq. 6 no longer decreases, the number of inlier pixels drops below 3, or a total of 100 iterations is reached.

The Final Estimate. The pose hypothesis with the lowest energy after refinement is chosen as final estimate. The estimates in Figs. 1 to 3 as well as our quantitative results in the experiments section were obtained using the exact algorithm described above. Our formulation of the task as energy optimization problem, however, allows for the use of any general optimization algorithm to further increase the precision of the estimate.

4   Experiments

Several object instance detection datasets have been published in the past [21,3], many of which deal with 2D poses only. Lai et al. [13] published a large RGB-D dataset of 300 objects that provides ground truth poses in the form of approximate rotation angles. Unfortunately, such annotations are to coarse for the accurate pose estimation task we try to solve. We evaluated our approach on the recently introduced Hinterstoisser et al. [8] dataset and our own dataset. The Hinterstoisser dataset provides synthetic training and real test data. Our dataset provides real training and real test data with realistic noise patterns and challenging lighting conditions. On both datasets we compare to the template-based method of [8]. We also tested the scalability of our method and comment on running times. In the supplementary material we provide additional experimental results for an occlusion dataset, for a detection task, and regarding the contribution of our individual energy terms. We train our decision forest with the following parameters. At each node we sample 500 color features and depth features. In each iteration we choose 1000 random pixels per training image, collect them in the current leafs and stop splitting if less than 50 pixels arrive. The tree depth is not restricted. A complete set of parameters can be found in the supplement.

Dataset of Hinterstoisser et al. Hinterstoisser et al. [8] provide colored 3D models of 13 texture-less objects[1] for training, and 1000+ test images of each object on a cluttered desk together with ground truth poses. The test images cover the upper view hemisphere at different scales and a range of $\pm 45°$ in-plane rotation. The goal is to evaluate the accuracy in pose estimation for one object per image. It is known which object is present. We follow exactly the test protocol of [8] by measuring accuracy as the fraction of test images where the pose of the object was estimated correctly. The tight pose tolerance is defined in the supplementary material. In [8] the authors achieve a strong baseline of 96.6% correctly estimated poses, on average. We reimplemented their method and were able to reproduce these numbers. Their pipeline starts with an efficient template matching schema, followed by two outlier removal steps and iterative closest point adjustment. The two outlier removal steps are crucial to achieve the reported results. In essence they comprise of two thresholds on the color and depth difference, respectively, between the current estimate and the test image. Unfortunately the correct values differ strongly among objects and have to be set by hand for each object[2]. We also compare to [21] who optimize the Hinterstoisser templates in a discriminative fashion to boost performance and speed. They also rely on the same two outlier removal checks but learn the object dependent thresholds discriminatively.

To produce training data for our method we rendered all 13 object models with the same viewpoint sampling as in [8], but skipped scale variations because

---

[1] We had to omit 2 objects since proper 3D models were missing.

[2] We verified this in private communication with the authors. These values are not given in the article.

of our depth-invariant features. Since our features may reach outside the object segmentation during training we need a background model to compute sensible feature responses. For our color features we use randomly sampled colors from a set of background images. The background set consists of approx. 1500 RGB-D images of cluttered office scenes recorded by ourselfs. For our depth features we use an infinite synthetic ground-plane as background model. In the test scenes all objects stand on a table but embedded in dense clutter. Hence, we regard the synthetic plane as an acceptable prior. Additionally, we also show results for a background model of uniform depth noise, and uniform RGB noise. The decision forest is trained for all 13 objects and a background class, simultaneously. For the background class we sample RGB-D patches from our office background set. To account for variance in appearance between purely synthetic training images and real test images we add Gaussian noise to the response of the color feature[25]. After optimizing our energy, we deploy no outlier removal steps, in contrast to [8,21].

Table 1. Results on the Hinterstoisser et al. dataset with synthetic training data, real training data and different background models (plane, noise). We see that our approach is consistently superior to [8,21].

	Synth. Training				Real Training	
	Linemod[8]	DTT-3D[21]	Our(plane)	Our(noise)	Our(plane)	Our(noise)
Avg.	96.6%	97.2%	98.3%	92.6%	98.1%	97.4%
Med.	97.1%	97.5%	98.9%	92.1%	99.6%	98.8%
Max.	99.9%	99.8%	100.0%	99.7%	100.0%	100%
Min.	91.8%	94.2%	95.8%	84.4%	91.1%	89.2%

Table 1 summarizes the results. We score an average of 98.3% with the synthetic plane background model. Hence we improve on both systems of [8] and [21]. See Fig. 4 for qualitative results. Using uniform noise as background model, we still report excellent results with 92.6% correctly estimated poses on average.

To verify that our approach is not restricted to synthetic training data, we performed an experiment where we trained with real images for each object. Since the dataset includes only one scene per object, we had to split each sequence into training and test. We sampled training images with at least 15° angular distance, to have an approximately regular coverage of the upper hemisphere similar to the Hinterstoisser et al. setup. The maximum distance of training images is ≈ 25° making this test slightly harder than in the synthetic setup. All other images are test images. To remove the background in the training images we do an intersection test with the 3D object bounding box. We substitute the background pixels with the two background model variants already discussed above. We do not add noise to the feature responses. In this experiment, we observe excellent accuracy which is stable even with the simple noise background model (compare right two columns in Table 1).

Fig. 4. Examples for pose estimation with our system (blue bounding box) versus the ground truth pose (green bounding box). The left test image shows an object from the Hinterstoisser et al. dataset[8], the right test image shows an object from our dataset. Next to each test image are the predicted object coordinates $\mathbf{y}$ from one tree of the forest. The inlay figures show the ground truth object coordinates (left) and the best object coordinates (right), where "best" is the best prediction of all trees with respect to ground truth (for illustration only).

Our Dataset. We recorded 20 textured and texture-less objects under three different lighting conditions: bright artificial light (*bright*), darker natural light (*dark*), and directional spot light (*spot*). For each light setting we recorded each object on a marker board in a motion that covers its upper view hemisphere. The distance to the object varied during the recording but the in-plane rotation was kept fixed. We added in-plane rotation artificially afterwards in the range of $\pm 45°$. We used KinectFusion [17,12] to record the external camera parameters for each frame. This serves as pose ground truth and is used to generate the object coordinates per pixel for training the decision forest. Recordings of the same object but different lighting conditions were registered using the marker board. Images that were used for training were segmented with the 3D object bounding box. An overview over the dataset and details about the recording procedure can be found in the supplement. We sampled training images with at least 15° angular distance. The maximal angular distance of training images is $\approx 25°$. We did not place our objects on a synthetic plane, because they were already recorded on a planar board. Depth features reaching outside the object mask during training will just use the depth in the original training image. For color features we sampled randomly from another set of office backgrounds that do not contain our objects.

To evaluate how well our approach generalizes with respect to varying lighting conditions, we trained our decision forest with the *bright* and *dark* training sets. Again we added Gaussian noise to the response of the color feature for robustness. In a first run we tested with images of the *bright* set that were not used for training. Here, the forest did not need to generalize to new lighting conditions but only to unseen views, which it does with excellent accuracy (avg. 95%, see Table 2). As before we measured performance as the percentage of correctly estimated poses of one object per test image which is always present. In a second run we tested with the complete *spot* set to demonstrate the capability of generalization to a difficult new lighting condition. We report an average rate of correctly estimated poses of 88.2%.

To demonstrate that the template based approach of Linemod[8] does not generalize as well with respect to lighting change we used our re-implementation to extract templates for one object based on the training set described above. Note, that the training set contains each view only with one scale. This can be problematic for Linemod if the test-data shows scale variation not covered by the training data. Hence, we render each training image from 2 larger and 3 smaller distances in 10cm steps. This gives us 6 different scales for each training image similar to the setup in [8]. As in [8] we tuned the outlier removal parameters by hand. However, we found that we had to disable these tests completely to get any detections under new lighting conditions. In a validation run we extracted templates from the *bright* training set and tested on the *bright* test set. Following the procedure of [8], we can estimate correct poses in 80.1% of the images. We account the difference to the performance on the Hinterstoisser dataset[8] to the fact that the object is textured and that our images are noisy. If we test with the same templates on the *spot* set, performance drops to 57.1%. Since our tree has seen both *bright* and *dark* in training we apply the following testing procedure to Linemod for a fair comparison. We also extract templates from the *dark* training set and apply it to the *spot* test set, observing 55.3%. For the final score, we consider an image solved by Linemod if one of the template sets, *dark* or *bright*, lead to the correct pose. Then we observe accuracy of 70.2%. So even under testing conditions in favor of Linemod performance drops by 10%. On the same object, we report accuracy of 96.9% on the *bright* test set (included in training lighting), and 91.8% on the *spot* test set (not seen in training).

Table 2. Accuracy on our dataset when testing with different lighting conditions. *Bright* lighting appeared in the training set, whereas *spot* lighting did not. We report average and median accuracy for our 20 objects. We also compare to Linemod [8] on one object. Details are given in the text.

	All		Toy(Battle Cat)			
Test Condition	Avg.	Med.	Our	[8](*dark*)	[8](*bright*)	[8](combined)
bright	95.6%	97.7%	96.9%	-	80.1%	-
spot	88.2%	93.0%	91.8%	55.3%	57.1%	70.2%

Scalability. We show the potential of our method with respect to scalability in two different ways: scalability in the object count, and scalability in the space of poses. The first concerns the number of objects the system is able to identify, while the latter concerns the range of poses it can recognize. We start with a forest that was trained for 5 objects, and a set of training images sampled form *dark* and *bright* lighting conditions, with an angular distance of min. 45°. We add ±45° in-plane rotation to each training image. During test, we consider images of the *spot* set which are at maximum 10° apart from the closest training image. This results in the same test difficulty as in the previous experiments. Performance is measured for one object (Stuffed Cat). We modify this setup in two ways. Firstly, we increased the object count to 30 by combining our dataset with real images of the Hinterstoisser dataset. We sampled the Hinterstoisser sets to have approximately the same amount of training images for our objects and the additional Hinterstoisser objects. Secondly, we increased the number of in-plane rotated training images 4-fold to the full ±180°. The results are shown in Fig. 5.

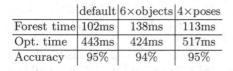 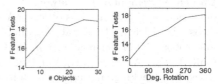

	default	6×objects	4×poses
Forest time	102ms	138ms	113ms
Opt. time	443ms	424ms	517ms
Accuracy	95%	94%	95%

Fig. 5. Left: Running time of our system with increasing object count and pose range. Accuracy stays stable. Right: Illustration of the sub-linear growth of the decision forest.

As the number of objects and the range of poses increase, the evaluation time of the tree does increase slightly, but considerably less than 6× resp. 4×. The runtime of the energy optimization is effected slightly due to variation in the forest prediction, and the accuracy of the system stays stable. Below the table in Fig. 5 we plot the sub-linear growth in the average number of feature tests per pixel with increasing object number and range of poses. Our proposed pipeline is linear in the number of objects but we demonstrate that with the forest the first essential step of our discriminatively trained method behaves sub-linearly in the number of objects.

Running Times. The complete running time of our pose estimation approach is the sum of forest prediction time and energy optimization time. Forest predictions are generated once per frame and the results are reused for every object in that frame. Our CPU implementation of the random forests takes 160ms avg. per frame on the dataset of [8]. Based on these predictions, energy optimization is done per object. We implemented energy evaluation on the GPU and report 398ms avg. per object on the dataset of [8] with the parameter settings suggested above. However, we found that a set of reduced parameters results in a large speed up while maintaining accuracy. We reduced the number of hypotheses from 210 to 42, the number of refinement steps from 100 to 20 and refined only the best 3 hypotheses. This still achieves 96.4% avg. accuracy on the dataset of [8] while reducing the average energy optimization time to 61ms.

Acknowledgements. This work has partially been supported by the European Social Fund and the Federal State of Saxony within project VICCI (#100098171). We thank Holger Heidrich for his reimplementation of Linemod. We also thank Stephan Ihrke, Daniel Schemala, Patrick Sprung and Sören König for their help preparing the different datasets und their contributions to our implementation.

References

1. Bo, L., Ren, X., Fox, D.: Unsupervised feature learning for RGB-D based object recognition. In: ISER (2012)
2. Criminisi, A., Shotton, J.: Decision Forests for Computer Vision and Medical Image Analysis. Springer (2013)
3. Damen, D., Bunnun, P., Calway, A., Mayol-Cuevas, W.: Real-time learning and detection of 3D texture-less objects: A scalable approach. In: BMVC (2012)
4. Drost, B., Ulrich, M., Navab, N., Ilic, S.: Model globally, match locally: Efficient and robust 3D object recognition. In: CVPR (2010)
5. Gall, J., Yao, A., Razavi, N., Van Gool, L., Lempitsky, V.: Hough Forests for object detection, tracking, and action recognition. IEEE Trans. on PAMI 33(11) (2011)
6. Girshick, R., Shotton, J., Kohli, P., Criminisi, A., Fitzgibbon, A.: Efficient regression of general-activity human poses from depth images. In: ICCV (2011)
7. Hinterstoisser, S., Cagniart, C., Ilic, S., Sturm, P., Navab, N., Fua, P., Lepetit, V.: Gradient response maps for real-time detection of texture-less objects. IEEE Trans. on PAMI (2012)
8. Hinterstoisser, S., Lepetit, V., Ilic, S., Holzer, S., Bradski, G., Konolige, K., Navab, N.: Model based training, detection and pose estimation of texture-less 3D objects in heavily cluttered scenes. In: Lee, K.M., Matsushita, Y., Rehg, J.M., Hu, Z. (eds.) ACCV 2012, Part I. LNCS, vol. 7724, pp. 548–562. Springer, Heidelberg (2013)
9. Hoiem, D., Rother, C., Winn, J.: 3D LayoutCRF for multi-view object class recognition and segmentation. In: CVPR (2007)
10. Holzer, S., Shotton, J., Kohli, P.: Learning to efficiently detect repeatable interest points in depth data. In: Fitzgibbon, A., Lazebnik, S., Perona, P., Sato, Y., Schmid, C. (eds.) ECCV 2012, Part I. LNCS, vol. 7572, pp. 200–213. Springer, Heidelberg (2012)
11. Huttenlocher, D., Klanderman, G., Rucklidge, W.: Comparing images using the hausdorff distance. IEEE Trans. on PAMI (1993)
12. Izadi, S., Kim, D., Hilliges, O., Molyneaux, D., Newcombe, R., Kohli, P., Shotton, J., Hodges, S., Freeman, D., Davison, A., Fitzgibbon, A.: KinectFusion: real-time 3D reconstruction and interaction using a moving depth camera. In: UIST (2011)
13. Lai, K., Bo, L., Ren, X., Fox, D.: A large-scale hierarchical multi-view rgb-d object dataset. In: ICRA. IEEE (2011)
14. Lepetit, V., Fua, P.: Keypoint recognition using randomized trees. IEEE Trans. on PAMI 28(9) (2006)
15. Lowe, D.G.: Local feature view clustering for 3d object recognition. In: CVPR (2001)
16. Martinez, M., Collet, A., Srinivasa, S.S.: Moped: A scalable and low latency object recognition and pose estimation system. In: ICRA (2010)
17. Newcombe, R., Izadi, S., Hilliges, O., Molyneaux, D., Kim, D., Davison, A., Kohli, P., Shotton, J., Hodges, S., Fitzgibbon, A.: KinectFusion: Real-time dense surface mapping and tracking. In: ISMAR (2011)
18. Nistér, D., Stewénius, H.: Scalable recognition with a vocabulary tree. In: CVPR (2006)
19. Ozuysal, M., Calonder, M., Lepetit, V., Fua, P.: Fast keypoint recognition using random ferns. IEEE Trans. on PAMI (2010)
20. Philbin, J., Chum, O., Isard, M., Sivic, J., Zisserman, A.: Object retrieval with large vocabularies and fast spatial matching. In: CVPR (2007)

21. Rios-Cabrera, R., Tuytelaars, T.: Discriminatively trained templates for 3D object detection: A real time scalable approach. In: ICCV (2013)
22. Rosten, E., Porter, R., Drummond, T.: FASTER and better: A machine learning approach to corner detection. IEEE Trans. on PAMI 32 (2010)
23. Shotton, J., Fitzgibbon, A., Cook, M., Sharp, T., Finocchio, M., Moore, R., Kipman, A., Blake, A.: Real-time human pose recognition in parts from a single depth image. In: CVPR (2011)
24. Shotton, J., Glocker, B., Zach, C., Izadi, S., Criminisi, A., Fitzgibbon, A.: Scene coordinate regression forests for camera relocalization in rgb-d images. In: CVPR (2013)
25. Shotton, J., Girshick, R.B., Fitzgibbon, A.W., Sharp, T., Cook, M., Finocchio, M., Moore, R., Kohli, P., Criminisi, A., Kipman, A., Blake, A.: Efficient human pose estimation from single depth images. IEEE Trans. on PAMI 35(12) (2013)
26. Steger, C.: Similarity measures for occlusion, clutter, and illumination invariant object recognition. In: DAGM-S (2001)
27. Sun, M., Bradski, G., Xu, B.-X., Savarese, S.: Depth-encoded hough voting for joint object detection and shape recovery. In: Daniilidis, K., Maragos, P., Paragios, N. (eds.) ECCV 2010, Part V. LNCS, vol. 6315, pp. 658–671. Springer, Heidelberg (2010)
28. Taylor, J., Shotton, J., Sharp, T., Fitzgibbon, A.: The Vitruvian Manifold: Inferring dense correspondences for one-shot human pose estimation. In: CVPR (2012)
29. Ferrari, V., Jurie, F., Schmid, C.: From images to shape models for object detection. In: IJCV (2009)
30. Winder, S., Hua, G., Brown, M.: Picking the best DAISY. In: CVPR (2009)

Growing Regression Forests by Classification: Applications to Object Pose Estimation

Kota Hara and Rama Chellappa

Center for Automation Research, University of Maryland, College Park, USA

Abstract. In this work, we propose a novel node splitting method for regression trees and incorporate it into the regression forest framework. Unlike traditional binary splitting, where the splitting rule is selected from a predefined set of binary splitting rules via trial-and-error, the proposed node splitting method first finds clusters of the training data which at least locally minimize the empirical loss without considering the input space. Then splitting rules which preserve the found clusters as much as possible are determined by casting the problem into a classification problem. Consequently, our new node splitting method enjoys more freedom in choosing the splitting rules, resulting in more efficient tree structures. In addition to the Euclidean target space, we present a variant which can naturally deal with a circular target space by the proper use of circular statistics. We apply the regression forest employing our node splitting to head pose estimation (Euclidean target space) and car direction estimation (circular target space) and demonstrate that the proposed method significantly outperforms state-of-the-art methods (38.5% and 22.5% error reduction respectively).

Keywords: Pose Estimation, Direction Estimation, Regression Tree, Random Forest.

1 Introduction

Regression has been successfully applied to various computer vision tasks such as head pose estimation [17,13], object direction estimation [13,30], human body pose estimation [2,28,18] and facial point localization [10,5], which require continuous outputs. In regression, a mapping from an input space to a target space is learned from the training data. The learned mapping function is used to predict the target values for new data. In computer vision, the input space is typically the high-dimensional image feature space and the target space is a low-dimensional space which represents some high level concepts present in the given image. Due to the complex input-target relationship, non-linear regression methods are usually employed for computer vision tasks.

Among several non-linear regression methods, regression forests [3] have been shown to be effective for various computer vision problems [28,9,10,8]. The regression forest is an ensemble learning method which combines several regression trees [4] into a strong regressor. The regression trees define recursive partitioning

D. Fleet et al. (Eds.): ECCV 2014, Part II, LNCS 8690, pp. 552–567, 2014.

of the input space and each leaf node contains a model for the predictor. In the training stage, the trees are grown in order to reduce the empirical loss over the training data. In the regression forest, each regression tree is independently trained using a random subset of training data and prediction is done by finding the average/mode of outputs from all the trees.

As a node splitting algorithm, binary splitting is commonly employed for regression trees, however, it has limitations regarding how it partitions the input space. The biggest limitation of the standard binary splitting is that a splitting rule at each node is selected by trial-and-error from a predefined set of splitting rules. To maintain the search space manageable, typically simple thresholding operations on a single dimension of the input is chosen. Due to these limitations, the resulting trees are not necessarily efficient in reducing the empirical loss.

To overcome the above drawbacks of the standard binary splitting scheme, we propose a novel node splitting method and incorporate it into the regression forest framework. In our node splitting method, clusters of the training data which at least locally minimize the empirical loss are first found without being restricted to a predefined set of splitting rules. Then splitting rules which preserve the found clusters as much as possible are determined by casting the problem into a classification problem. As a by-product, our procedure allows each node in the tree to have more than two child nodes, adding one more level of flexibility to the model. We also propose a way to adaptively determine the number of child nodes at each splitting. Unlike the standard binary splitting method, our splitting procedure enjoys more freedom in choosing the partitioning rules, resulting in more efficient regression tree structures. In addition to the method for the Euclidean target space, we present an extension which can naturally deal with a circular target space by the proper use of circular statistics.

We refer to regression forests (RF) employing our node splitting algorithm as KRF (K-clusters Regression Forest) and those employing the adaptive determination of the number of child nodes as AKRF. We test KRF and AKRF on Pointing'04 dataset for head pose estimation (Euclidean target space) and EPFL Multi-view Car Dataset for car direction estimation (circular target space) and observe that the proposed methods outperform state-of-the-art with 38.5% error reduction on Pointing'04 and 22.5% error reduction on EPFL Multi-view Car Dataset. Also KRF and AKRF significantly outperform other general regression methods including regression forests with the standard binary splitting.

2   Related Work

A number of inherently regression problems such as head pose estimation and body orientation estimation have been addressed by classification methods by assigning a different pseudo-class label to each of roughly discretized target value (e.g., [33,20,23,1,24]). Increasing the number of pseudo-classes allows more precise prediction, however, the classification problem becomes more difficult. This becomes more problematic as the dimensionality of target space increases. In general, discretization is conducted experimentally to balance the desired classification accuracy and precision.

[32,29] apply k-means clustering to the target space to automatically discretize the target space and assign pseudo-classes. They then solve the classification problem by rule induction algorithms for classification. Though somewhat more sophisticated, these approaches still suffer from problems due to discretization. The difference of our method from approaches discussed above is that in these approaches, pseudo-classes are fixed once determined either by human or cluster-ing algorithms while in our approach, pseudo-classes are *adaptively* redetermined at each node splitting of regression tree training.

Similarly to our method, [11] converts node splitting tasks into local classi-fication tasks by applying EM algorithm to the joint input-output space. Since clustering is applied to the joint space, their method is not suitable for tasks with high dimensional input space. In fact there experiments are limited to tasks with upto 20 dimensional input space, where their method performs poorly compared to baseline methods.

The work most similar to our method was proposed by Chou [7] who applied k-means like algorithm to the target space to find a locally optimal set of partitions for regression tree learning. However, this method is limited to the case where the input is a categorical variable. Although we limit ourselves to continuous inputs, our formulation is more general and can be applied to any type of inputs by choosing appropriate classification methods.

Regression has been widely applied for head pose estimation tasks. [17] used kernel partial least squares regression to learn a mapping from HOG features to head poses. Fenzi [13] learned a set of local feature generative model using RBF networks and estimated poses using MAP inference.

A few works considered direction estimation tasks where the direction ranges from 0° and 360°. [19] modified regression forests so that the binary splitting minimizes a cost function specifically designed for direction estimation tasks. [30] applied supervised manifold learning and used RBF networks to learn a mapping from a point on the learnt manifold to the target space.

3   Methods

We denote a set of training data by $\{\mathbf{x}_i, \mathbf{t}_i\}_{i=1}^{N}$, where $\mathbf{x} \in \mathbb{R}^p$ is an input vector and $\mathbf{t} \in \mathbb{R}^q$ is a target vector. The goal of regression is to learn a function $F^*(\mathbf{x})$ such that the expected value of a certain loss function $\Psi(\mathbf{t}, F(\mathbf{x}))$ is minimized:

$$F^*(\mathbf{x}) = \underset{F(\mathbf{x})}{\operatorname{argmin}} \operatorname{E}[\Psi(\mathbf{t}, F(\mathbf{x})]. \tag{1}$$

By approximating the above expected loss by an empirical loss and using the squared loss function, Eq.1 is reformulated as minimizing the sum of squared errors (SSE):

$$F^*(\mathbf{x}) = \underset{F(\mathbf{x})}{\operatorname{argmin}} \sum_{i=1}^{N} ||\mathbf{t}_i - F(\mathbf{x}_i)||_2^2. \tag{2}$$

However, other loss functions can also be used. In this paper we employ a spe-cialized loss function for a circular target space (Sec.3.5).

In the following subsections, we first explain an abstracted regression tree algorithm, followed by the presentation of a standard binary splitting method normally employed for regression tree training. We then describe the details of our splitting method. An algorithm to adaptively determine the number of child nodes is presented, followed by a modification of our method for the circular target space, which is necessary for direction estimation tasks. Lastly, the regression forest framework for combining regression trees is presented.

3.1 Abstracted Regression Tree Model

Regression trees are grown by recursively partitioning the input space into a set of disjoint partitions, starting from a root node which corresponds to the entire input space. At each node splitting stage, a set of splitting rules and prediction models for each partition are determined so as to minimize the certain loss (error). A typical choice for a prediction model is a constant model which is determined as a mean target value of training samples in the partition. However, higher order models such as linear regression can also be used. Throughout this work, we employ the constant model. After each partitioning, corresponding child nodes are created and each training sample is forwarded to one of the child nodes. Each child node is further split if the number of the training samples belonging to that node is larger than a predefined number.

The essential component of regression tree training is an algorithm for splitting the nodes. Due to the recursive nature of training stage, it suffices to discuss the splitting of the root node where all the training data are available. Subsequent splitting is done with a subset of the training data belonging to each node in exactly the same manner.

Formally, we denote a set of K disjoint partitions of the input space by $\mathcal{R} = \{r_1, r_2, \ldots, r_K\}$, a set of constant estimates associated with each partition by $\mathcal{A} = \{\mathbf{a}_1, \ldots, \mathbf{a}_K\}$ and the K clusters of the training data by $\mathbf{S} = \{S_1, S_2, \cdots, S_K\}$ where

$$S_k = \{i : \mathbf{x}_i \in r_k\}. \tag{3}$$

In the squared loss case, a constant estimate, $\mathbf{a}_k$, for the k-th partition is computed as the mean target vector of the training samples that fall into r_k:

$$\mathbf{a}_k = \frac{1}{|S_k|} \sum_{i \in S_k} \mathbf{t}_i. \tag{4}$$

The sum of squared errors (SSE) associated with each child node is computed as:

$$\text{SSE}_k = \sum_{i \in S_k} \|\mathbf{t}_i - \mathbf{a}_k\|_2^2, \tag{5}$$

where SSE_k is the SSE for the k-th child node. Then the sum of squared errors on the entire training data is computed as:

$$\text{SSE} = \sum_{k=1}^{K} \text{SSE}_k = \sum_{k=1}^{K} \sum_{i \in S_k} \|\mathbf{t}_i - \mathbf{a}_k\|_2^2. \tag{6}$$

The aim of training is to find a set of splitting rules defining the input partitions which minimizes the SSE.

Assuming there is no further splitting, the regression tree is formally represented as

$$H(\mathbf{x}; \mathcal{A}, \mathcal{R}) = \sum_{k=1}^{K} \mathbf{a}_k \mathbb{1}(\mathbf{x} \in r_k), \tag{7}$$

where $\mathbb{1}$ is an indicator function. The regression tree outputs one of the elements of $\mathcal{A}$ depending on to which of the $\mathcal{R} = \{r_1, \ldots, r_K\}$, the new data $\mathbf{x}$ belongs. As mentioned earlier, the child nodes are further split as long as the number of the training samples belonging to the node is larger than a predefined number.

3.2   Standard Binary Node Splitting

In standard binary regression trees [4], K is fixed at two. Each splitting rule is defined as a pair of the index of the input dimension and a threshold. Thus, each binary splitting rule corresponds to a hyperplane that is perpendicular to one of the axes. Among a predefined set of such splitting rules, the one which minimizes the overall SSE (Eq.6) is selected by trial-and-error.

The major drawback of the above splitting procedure is that the splitting rules are determined by exhaustively searching the best splitting rule among the predefined set of candidate rules. Essentially, this is the reason why only simple binary splitting rules defined as thresholding on a single dimension are considered in the training stage. Since the candidate rules are severely limited, the selected rules are not necessarily the best among all possible ways to partition the input space.

3.3   Proposed Node Splitting

In order to overcome the drawbacks of the standard binary splitting procedure, we propose a new splitting procedure which does not rely on trial-and-error. A graphical illustration of the algorithm is given in Fig.1. At each node splitting stage, we first find ideal clusters $\mathbf{T} = \{T_1, T_2, \cdots, T_K\}$ of the training data associated with the node, those at least locally minimize the following objective function:

$$\min_{\mathbf{T}} \sum_{k=1}^{K} \sum_{i \in T_k} ||\mathbf{t}_i - \mathbf{a}_k||_2^2 \tag{8}$$

where $T_k = \{i : ||\mathbf{t}_i - \mathbf{a}_k||_2 \leq ||\mathbf{t}_i - \mathbf{a}_j||_2, \forall 1 \leq j \leq K\}$ and $\mathbf{a}_k = \frac{1}{|T_k|} \sum_{i \in T_k} \mathbf{t}_i$. This minimization can be done by applying the k-means clustering algorithm in the target space with K as the number of clusters. Note the similarity between the objective functions in Eq.8 and Eq.6. The difference is that in Eq.6, clusters in $\mathbf{S}$ are indirectly determined by the splitting rules defined in the input space while clusters in $\mathbf{T}$ are directly determined by the k-means algorithm without taking into account the input space.

After finding $\mathbf{T}$, we find partitions $\mathcal{R} = \{r_1, \ldots, r_K\}$ of the input space which preserves $\mathbf{T}$ as much as possible. This task is equivalent to a K-class classification problem which aims at determining a cluster ID of each training data based on $\mathbf{x}$. Although any classification method can be used, in this work, we employ L2-regularized L2-loss linear SVM with a one-versus-rest approach. Formally, we solve the following optimization for each cluster using LIBLINEAR [12]:

$$\min_{\mathbf{w}_k} ||\mathbf{w}_k||_2 + C \sum_{i=1}^{N} (\max(0, 1 - l_i^k \mathbf{w}_k^T \mathbf{x}_i))^2, \tag{9}$$

where $\mathbf{w}_k$ is the weight vector for the k-th cluster, $l_i^k = 1$ if $i \in T_k$ and -1 otherwise and $C > 0$ is a penalty parameter. We set $C = 1$ throughout the paper. Each training sample is forwarded to one of the K child nodes by

$$k^* = \underset{k \in \{1, \cdots, K\}}{\operatorname{argmax}} \mathbf{w}_k^T \mathbf{x}. \tag{10}$$

At the last stage of the node splitting procedure, we compute $\mathbf{S}$ (Eq.3) and $\mathcal{A}$ (Eq.4) based on the constructed splitting rules (Eq.10).

Unlike standard binary splitting, our splitting rules are not limited to hyperplanes that are perpendicular to one of the axes and the clusters are found without being restricted to a set of predefined splitting rules in the input space. Furthermore, our splitting strategy allows each node to have more than two child nodes by employing $K > 2$, adding one more level of flexibility to the model. Note that larger K generally results in smaller value for Eq.8, however, since the following classification problem becomes more difficult, the larger K does not necessarily lead to better performance.

3.4   Adaptive Determination of K

Since K is a parameter, we need to determine the value for K by time consuming cross-validation step. In order to avoid the cross-validation step while achieving comparative performance, we propose a method to adaptively determine K at each node based on the sample distribution.

In this work we employ Bayesian Information Criterion (BIC) [21,27] as a measure to choose K. BIC was also used in [25] but with a different formulation. The BIC is designed to balance the model complexity and likelihood. As a result, when a target distribution is complex, a larger number of K is selected and when the target distribution is simple, a smaller value of K is selected. This is in contrast to the non-adaptive method where a fixed number of K is used regardless of the complexity of the distributions.

As k-means clustering itself does not assume any underling probability distribution, we assume that the data are generated from a mixture of isotropic weighted Gaussians with a shared variance. The unbiased estimate for the shared variance is computed as

$$\hat{\sigma}^2 = \frac{1}{N-K} \sum_{k=1}^{K} \sum_{i \in T_k} ||\mathbf{t}_i - \mathbf{a}_k||_2^2. \tag{11}$$

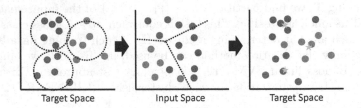

Target Space   Input Space   Target Space

Fig. 1. An illustration of the proposed splitting method ($K = 3$). A set of clusters of the training data are found in the target space by k-means (left). The input partitions preserving the found clusters as much as possible are determined by SVM (middle). If no more splitting is needed, a mean is computed as a constant estimate for each set of colored samples. The yellow stars represent the means. Note that the color of some points change due to misclassification. (right) If further splitting is needed, clusterling is applied to each set of colored samples separately in the target space.

We compute a point probability density for a data point **t** belonging to the k-th cluster as follows:

$$p(\mathbf{t}) = \frac{|T_k|}{N} \frac{1}{\sqrt{2\pi\hat{\sigma}^2}^q} \exp(-\frac{||\mathbf{t} - \mathbf{a}_k||_2^2}{2\hat{\sigma}^2}). \tag{12}$$

Then after simple calculations, the log-likelihood of the data is obtained as

$$\ln \mathcal{L}(\{\mathbf{t}_i\}_{i=1}^N) = \ln \mathbf{\Pi}_{i=1}^N p(\mathbf{t}_i) = \sum_{k=1}^K \sum_{i \in T_k} \ln p(\mathbf{t}_i) =$$

$$-\frac{qN}{2}\ln(2\pi\hat{\sigma}^2) - \frac{N-K}{2} + \sum_{k=1}^K |T_k|\ln|T_k| - N\ln N \tag{13}$$

Finally, the BIC for a particular value of K is computed as

$$\text{BIC}_K = -2\ln \mathcal{L}(\{\mathbf{t}_i\}_{i=1}^N) + (K-1+qK+1)\ln N. \tag{14}$$

At each node splitting stage, we run the k-means algorithm for each value of K in a manually specified range and select K with the smallest BIC. Throughout this work, we select K from $\{2, 3, \ldots, 40\}$.

3.5   Modification for a Circular Target Space

1D direction estimation of the object such as cars and pedestrians is unique in that the target variable is periodic, namely, $0°$ and $360°$ represent the same direction angle. Thus, the target space can be naturally represented as a unit circle, which is a 1D Riemannian manifold in R^2. To deal with a such target space, special treatments are needed since the Euclidean distance is inappropriate. For instance, the distance between $10°$ and $350°$ should be shorter than that between $10°$ and $50°$ on this manifold.

In our method, such direction estimation problems are naturally addressed by modifying the k-means algorithm and the computation of BIC. The remaining steps are kept unchanged. The k-means clustering method consists of computing cluster centroids and hard assignment of the training samples to the closest centroid. Finding the closest centroid on a circle is trivially done by using the length of the shorter arc as a distance. Due to the periodic nature of the variable, the arithmetic mean is not appropriate for computing the centroids. A typical way to compute the mean of angles is to first convert each angle to a 2D point on a unit circle. The arithmetic mean is then computed on a 2D plane and converted back to the angular value. More specifically, given a set of direction angles $t, \ldots, t_N$, the mean direction a is computed by

$$a = \text{atan2}(\frac{1}{N} \sum_{i=1}^{N} \sin t_i, \frac{1}{N} \sum_{i=1}^{N} \cos t_i). \tag{15}$$

It is known [15] that a minimizes the sum of a certain distance defined on a circle,

$$a = \underset{s}{\text{argmin}} \sum_{i=1}^{N} d(t_i, s) \tag{16}$$

where $d(q, s) = 1 - \cos(q - s) \in [0, 2]$. Thus, the k-means clustering using the above definition of means finds clusters $\mathbf{T} = \{T_1, T_2, \cdots, T_K\}$ of the training data that at least locally minimize the following objective function,

$$\underset{\mathbf{T}}{\min} \sum_{k=1}^{K} \sum_{i \in T_k} (1 - \cos(t_i - a_k)) \tag{17}$$

where $T_k = \{i : 1 - \cos(t_i - a_k) \leq 1 - \cos(t_i - a_j), \forall 1 \leq j \leq K\}$.

Using the above k-means algorithm in our node splitting essentially means that we employ distance $d(q, s)$ as a loss function in Eq.1. Although squared shorter arc length might be more appropriate for the direction estimation task, there is no constant time algorithm to find a mean which minimizes it. Also as will be explained shortly, the above definition of the mean coincides with the maximum likelihood estimate of the mean of a certain probability distribution defined on a circle.

As in the Euclidean target case, we can also adaptively determine the value for K at each node using BIC. As a density function, the Gaussian distribution is not appropriate. A suitable choice is the von Mises distribution, which is a periodic continuous probability distribution defined on a circle,

$$p(t|a, \kappa) = \frac{1}{2\pi I_0(\kappa)} \exp(\kappa \cdot \cos(t - a)) \tag{18}$$

where a, κ are analogous to the mean and variance of the Gaussian distribution and I_λ is the modified Bessel function of order λ. It is known [14] that the maximum likelihood estimate of a is computed by Eq.15 and that of κ satisfies

$$\frac{I_1(\kappa)}{I_0(\kappa)} = \sqrt{(\frac{1}{N}\sum_{i=1}^{N}\sin t_i)^2 + (\frac{1}{N}\sum_{i=1}^{N}\cos t_i)^2} = \frac{1}{N}\sum_{i=1}^{N}\cos(t_i - a). \qquad (19)$$

Note that, from the second term, the above quantity is the Euclidean norm of the mean vector obtained by converting each angle to a 2D point on a unit circle.

Similar to the derivation for the Euclidean case, we assume that the data are generated from a mixture of weighted von Mises distributions with a shared κ. The mean a_k of k-th von Mises distribution is same as the mean of the k-th cluster obtained by the k-means clustering. The shared value for κ is obtained by solving the following equation

$$\frac{I_1(\kappa)}{I_0(\kappa)} = \frac{1}{N}\sum_{k=1}^{K}\sum_{i\in T_k}\cos(t_i - a_k). \qquad (20)$$

Since there is no closed form solution for the above equation, we use the following approximation proposed in [22],

$$\kappa \approx \frac{1}{2(1 - \frac{I_1(\kappa)}{I_0(\kappa)})}. \qquad (21)$$

Then, a point probability density for a data point t belonging to the k-th cluster is computed as:

$$p(t|a_k, \kappa) = \frac{|T_k|}{N}\frac{\exp(\kappa \cdot \cos(t - a_k))}{2\pi I_0(\kappa)}. \qquad (22)$$

After simple calculations, the log-likelihood of the data is obtained as

$$\ln \mathcal{L}(\{t_i\}_{i=1}^{N}) = \ln \Pi_{i=1}^{N}p(t_i) = \sum_{k=1}^{K}\sum_{i\in T_k}\ln p(t_i) =$$

$$-N\ln(2\pi I_0(\kappa)) + \kappa\sum_{k=1}^{K}\sum_{i\in T_k}\cos(t_i - a_k) + \sum_{k=1}^{K}|T_k|\ln|T_k| - N\ln N. \qquad (23)$$

Finally, the BIC for a particular value of K is computed as

$$\text{BIC}_K = -2\ln\mathcal{L}(\{t_i\}_{i=1}^{N}) + 2K\ln N. \qquad (24)$$

where the last term is obtained by putting $q = 1$ into the last term of Eq.14.

3.6   Regression Forest

We use the regression forest [3] as the final regression model. The regression forest is an ensemble learning method for regression which first constructs multiple regression trees from random subsets of training data. Testing is done by computing the mean of the outputs from each regression tree. We denote the ratio of random samples as $\beta \in (0, 1.0]$. For the Euclidean target case, arithmetic mean is used to obtain the final estimate and for the circular target case, the mean defined in Eq.15 is used.

For the regression forest with standard binary regression trees, an additional randomness is typically injected. In finding the best splitting function at each node, only a randomly selected subset of the feature dimensions is considered. We denote the ratio of randomly chosen feature dimensions as $\gamma \in (0, 1.0]$. For the regression forest with our regression trees, we always consider all feature dimensions. However, another form of randomness is naturally injected by randomly selecting the data points as the initial cluster centroids in the k-means algorithm.

4   Experiments

4.1   Head Pose Estimation

We test the effectiveness of KRF and AKRF for the Euclidean target space on the head pose estimation task. We adopt Pointing'04 dataset [16]. The dataset contains head images of 15 subjects and for each subject there are two series of 93 images with different poses represented by pitch and yaw.

The dataset comes with manually specified bounding boxes indicating the head regions. Based on the bounding boxes, we crop and resize the image patches to 64×64 pixels image patches and compute multiscale HOG from each image patch with cell size 8, 16, 32 and 2×2 cell blocks. The orientation histogram for each cell is computed with signed gradients for 9 orientation bins. The resulting HOG feature is 2124 dimensional.

First, we compare the KRF and AKRF with other general regression methods using the same image features. We choose standard binary regression forest (BRF) [3], kernel PLS [26] and ϵ-SVR with RBF kernels [31], all of which have been widely used for various computer vision tasks. The first series of images from all subjects are used as training set and the second series of images are used for testing. The performance is measured by Mean Absolute Error in degree. For KRF, AKRF and BRF, we terminate node splitting once the number of training data associated with each leaf node is less than 5. The number of trees combined is set to 20. K for KRF, β for KRF, AKRF and BRF and γ for BRF are all determined by 5-fold cross-validation on the training set. For kernel PLS, we use the implementation provided by the author of [26] and for ϵ-SVR, we use LIBSVM package [6]. All the parameters for kernel PLS and ϵ-SVR are also determined by 5-fold cross-validation. As can been seen in Table

1, both KRF and AKRF work significantly better than other regression methods. Also our methods are computationally efficient (Table 1). KRF and AKRF take only 7.7 msec and 8.7 msec, respectively, to process one image including feature computation with a single thread.

Table 1. MAE in degree of different regression methods on the Pointing'04 dataset (even train/test split). Time to process one image including HOG computation is also shown.

Methods	yaw	pitch	average	testing time (msec)
KRF	5.32	3.52	4.42	7.7
AKRF	5.49	4.18	4.83	8.7
BRF [3]	7.77	8.01	7.89	4.5
Kernel PLS [26]	7.35	7.02	7.18	86.2
ε-SVR [31]	7.34	7.02	7.18	189.2

Table 2 compares KRF and AKRF with prior art. Since the previous works report the 5-fold cross-validation estimate on the whole dataset, we also follow the same protocol. KRF and AKRF advance state-of-the-art with 38.5% and 29.7% reduction in the average MAE, respectively.

Table 2. Head pose estimation results on the Pointing'04 dataset (5-fold cross-validation)

	yaw	pitch	average
KRF	5.29	2.51	3.90
AKRF	5.50	3.41	4.46
Fenzi [13]	5.94	6.73	6.34
Haj [17] Kernel PLS	6.56	6.61	6.59
Haj [17] PLS	11.29	10.52	10.91

Fig.2 shows the effect of K of KRF on the average MAE along with the average MAE of AKRF. In this experiment, the cross-validation process successfully selects K with the best performance. AKRF works better than KRF with the second best K. The overall training time is much faster with AKRF since the cross-validation step for determining the value of K is not necessary. To train a single regression tree with $\beta = 1$, AKRF takes only 6.8 sec while KRF takes 331.4 sec for the cross-validation and 4.4 sec for training a final model. As a reference, BRF takes 1.7 sec to train a single tree with $\beta = 1$ and $\gamma = 0.4$. Finally, some estimation results by AKRF on the second sequence of person 13 are shown in Fig.3.

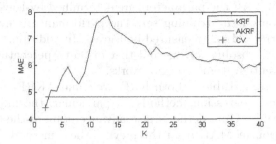

Fig. 2. Pointing'04: The effect of K of KRF on the average MAE. "CV" indicates the value of KRF selected by cross-validation.

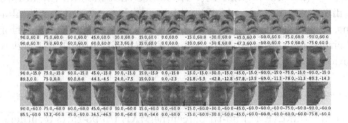

Fig. 3. Some estimation results of the second sequence of person 13. The top numbers are the ground truth yaw and pitch and the bottom numbers are the estimated yaw and pitch.

4.2 Car Direction Estimation

We test KRF and AKRF for circular target space (denoted as KRF-circle and AKRF-circle respectively) on the EPFL Multi-view Car Dataset [24]. The dataset contains 20 sequences of images of cars with various directions. Each sequence contains images of only one instance of car. In total, there are 2299 images in the dataset. Each image comes with a bounding box specifying the location of the car and ground truth for the direction of the car. The direction ranges from $0°$ to $360°$. As input features, multiscale HOG features with the same parameters as in the previous experiment are extracted from 64×64 pixels image patches obtained by resizing the given bounding boxes.

The algorithm is evaluated by using the first 10 sequences for training and the remaining 10 sequences for testing. In Table 3, we compare the KRF-circle and AKRF-circle with previous work. We also include the performance of BRF, Kernel PLS and ϵ-SVR with RBF kernels using the same HOG features. For BRF, we extend it to directly minimize the same loss function ($d(q, s) = 1 - \cos(q - s)$) as with KRF-circle and AKRF-circle (denoted by BRF-circle). For Kernel PLS and ϵ-SVR, we first map direction angles to 2d points on a unit circle and train regressors using the mapped points as target values. In testing phase, a 2d point coordinate (x, y) is first estimated and then mapped back to the angle by atan2(y, x). All the parameters are determined by leave-one-sequence-out cross-validation on the training set. The performance is evaluated by the Mean Absolute Error (MAE) measured in degrees. In addition, the MAE of 90-th percentile of the absolute errors and that of 95-th percentile are reported, following the convention from the prior works.

As can be seen from Table 3, both KRF-circle and AKRF-circle work much better than existing regression methods. In particular, the improvement over BRF-circle is notable. Our methods also advance state-of-the-art with 22.5% and 20.7% reduction in MAE from the previous best method, respectively. In Fig.4, we show the MAE of AKRF-circle computed on each sequence in the testing set. The performance varies significantly among different sequences (car models). Fig.5 shows some representative results from the *worst* three sequences in the testing set (seq 16, 20 and 15). We notice that most of the failure cases are due to the flipping errors ($\approx 180°$) which mostly occur at particular intervals of directions. Fig.6 shows the effect of K of KRF-circle. The performance of the AKRF-circle is comparable to that of KRF-circle with K selected by the cross-validation.

Table 3. Car direction estimation results on the EPFL Multi-view Car Dataset

Method	MAE (°) 90-th percentile	MAE (°) 95-th percentile	MAE (°)
KRF-circle	8.32	16.76	24.80
AKRF-circle	7.73	16.18	24.24
BRF-circle	23.97	30.95	38.13
Kernel PLS	16.86	21.20	27.65
ϵ-SVR	17.38	22.70	29.41
Fenzi et al. [13]	14.51	22.83	31.27
Torki et al. [30]	19.4	26.7	33.98
Ozuysal et al. [24]	-	-	46.48

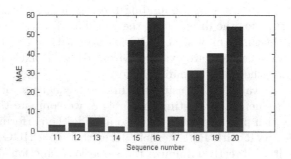

Fig. 4. MAE of AKRF computed on each sequence in the testing set

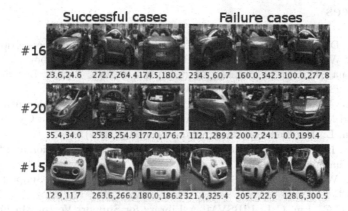

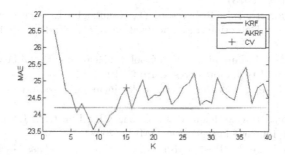

Fig. 5. Representative results from the *worst* three sequences in the testing set. The numbers under each image are the ground truth direction (left) and the estimated direction (right). Most of the failure cases are due to the flipping error.

Fig. 6. EPFL Multi-view Car: The effect of K of KRF on MAE. "CV" indicates the value of KRF selected by cross-validation.

5   Conclusion

In this paper, we proposed a novel node splitting algorithm for regression tree training. Unlike previous works, our method does not rely on a trial-and-error process to find the best splitting rules from a predefined set of rules, providing more flexibility to the model. Combined with the regression forest framework, our methods work significantly better than state-of-the-art methods on head pose estimation and car direction estimation tasks.

Acknowledgements. This research was supported by a MURI grant from the US Office of Naval Research under N00014-10-1-0934.

References

1. Baltieri, D., Vezzani, R., Cucchiara, R.: People Orientation Recognition by Mixtures of Wrapped Distributions on Random Trees. In: Fitzgibbon, A., Lazebnik, S., Perona, P., Sato, Y., Schmid, C. (eds.) ECCV 2012, Part V. LNCS, vol. 7576, pp. 270–283. Springer, Heidelberg (2012)
2. Bissacco, A., Yang, M.H., Soatto, S.: Fast Human Pose Estimation using Appearance and Motion via Multi-dimensional Boosting Regression. In: CVPR (2007)
3. Breiman, L.: Random Forests. Machine Learning (2001)
4. Breiman, L., Friedman, J., Stone, C.J., Olshen, R.A.: Classification and Regression Trees. Chapman and Hall/CRC (1984)
5. Cao, X., Wei, Y., Wen, F., Sun, J.: Face alignment by Explicit Shape Regression. In: CVPR (2012)
6. Chang, C.C., Lin, C.J.: LIBSVM: A Library for Support Vector Machines. ACM Transactions on Intelligent Systems and Technology (2011)
7. Chou, P.A.: Optimal Partitioning for Classification and Regression Trees. PAMI (1991)
8. Criminisi, A., Shotton, J.: Decision Forests for Computer Vision and Medical Image Analysis. Springer (2013)
9. Criminisi, A., Shotton, J., Robertson, D., Konukoglu, E.: Regression Forests for Efficient Anatomy Detection and Localization in CT Studies. Medical Computer Vision (2010)
10. Dantone, M., Gall, J., Fanelli, G., Van Gool, L.: Real-time Facial Feature Detection using Conditional Regression Forests. In: CVPR (2012)
11. Dobra, A., Gehrke, J.: Secret: A scalable linear regression tree algorithm. In: SIGKDD (2002)
12. Fan, R.E., Chang, K.W., Hsieh, C.J., Wang, X.R., Lin, C.J.: LIBLINEAR: A Library for Large Linear Classification. JMLR (2008)
13. Fenzi, M., Leal-Taixé, L., Rosenhahn, B., Ostermann, J.: Class Generative Models based on Feature Regression for Pose Estimation of Object Categories. In: CVPR (2013)
14. Fisher, N.I.: Statistical Analysis of Circular Data. Cambridge University Press (1996)
15. Gaile, G.L., Burt, J.E.: Directional Statistics (Concepts and techniques in modern geography). Geo Abstracts Ltd. (1980)
16. Gourier, N., Hall, D., Crowley, J.L.: Estimating Face Orientation from Robust Detection of Salient Facial Structures. In: ICPRW (2004)
17. Haj, M.A., Gonzàlez, J., Davis, L.S.: On partial least squares in head pose estimation: How to simultaneously deal with misalignment. In: CVPR (2012)
18. Hara, K., Chellappa, R.: Computationally Efficient Regression on a Dependency Graph for Human Pose Estimation. In: CVPR (2013)
19. Herdtweck, C., Curio, C.: Monocular Car Viewpoint Estimation with Circular Regression Forests. In: Intelligent Vehicles Symposium (2013)
20. Huang, C., Ding, X., Fang, C.: Head Pose Estimation Based on Random Forests for Multiclass Classification. In: ICPR (2010)
21. Kashyap, R.L.: A Bayesian Comparison of Different Classes of Dynamic Models Using Empirical Data. IEEE Trans. on Automatic Control (1977)
22. Mardia, K.V., Jupp, P.: Directional Statistics, 2nd edn. John Wiley and Sons Ltd. (2000)

23. Orozco, J., Gong, S., Xiang, T.: Head Pose Classification in Crowded Scenes. In: BMVC (2009)
24. Ozuysal, M., Lepetit, V., Fua, P.: Pose Estimation for Category Specific Multiview Object Localization. In: CVPR (2009)
25. Pelleg, D., Moore, A.: X-means: Extending K-means with Efficient Estimation of the Number of Clusters. In: ICML (2000)
26. Rosipal, R., Trejo, L.J.: Kernel Partial Least Squares Regression in Reproducing Kernel Hilbert Space. JMLR (2001)
27. Schwarz, G.: Estimating the Dimension of a Model. The Annals of Statistics (1978)
28. Sun, M., Kohli, P., Shotton, J.: Conditional Regression Forests for Human Pose Estimation. In: CVPR (2012)
29. Torgo, L., Gama, J.: Regression by classification. In: Brazilian Symposium on Artificial Intelligence (1996)
30. Torki, M., Elgammal, A.: Regression from local features for viewpoint and pose estimation. In: ICCV (2011)
31. Vapnik, V.: Statistical Learning Theory. Wiley (1998)
32. Weiss, S.M., Indurkhya, N.: Rule-based Machine Learning Methods for Functional Prediction. Journal of Artificial Intelligence Research (1995)
33. Yan, Y., Ricci, E., Subramanian, R., Lanz, O., Sebe, N.: No matter where you are: Flexible graph-guided multi-task learning for multi-view head pose classification under target motion. ICCV (2013)

Stacked Deformable Part Model with Shape Regression for Object Part Localization

Junjie Yan, Zhen Lei, Yang Yang, and Stan Z. Li*

Center for Biometrics and Security Research & National Laboratory
of Pattern Recognition, Institute of Automation, Chinese Academy of Sciences, China
{jjyan,zlei,yang.yang,szli}@nlpr.ia.ac.cn

Abstract. This paper explores the localization of pre-defined semantic object parts, which is much more challenging than traditional object detection and very important for applications such as face recognition, HCI and fine-grained object recognition. To address this problem, we make two critical improvements over the widely used deformable part model (DPM). The first is that we use appearance based shape regression to globally estimate the anchor location of each part and then locally refine each part according to the estimated anchor location under the constraint of DPM. The DPM with shape regression (SR-DPM) is more flexible than the traditional DPM by relaxing the fixed anchor location of each part. It enjoys the efficient dynamic programming inference as traditional DPM and can be discriminatively trained via a coordinate descent procedure. The second is that we propose to stack multiple SR-DPMs, where each layer uses the output of previous SR-DPM as the input to progressively refine the result. It provides an analogy to deep neural network while benefiting from hand-crafted feature and model. The proposed methods are applied to human pose estimation, face alignment and general object part localization tasks and achieve state-of-the-art performance.

1 Introduction

This paper focuses on localizing object parts from monocular image. For human and face category, this problem is often named as "human pose esti mation" or "face alignment". Accurate part localization serves as the basis of many high level applications. For example, a recent work [9] shows that directly extracting features around reliable face parts (landmarks) achieves leading face recognition performance. As surveyed in [28], human part localization can help with action recognition and human computer interaction. For general object, reliable part localization contributes to fine-grained object recognition, as proved in [46,6]. However, this problem is very challenging due to the variations in subject level (e.g., a human can take many different poses and dresses), category level (e.g., adult and baby) and image level (e.g., illumination and cluttered background).

---

* Corresponding author.

D. Fleet et al. (Eds.): ECCV 2014, Part II, LNCS 8690, pp. 568–583, 2014.
© Springer International Publishing Switzerland 2014

Human pose estimation and face alignment have been extensively explored for decades and achieved much progress. The critical issue is how to model the versatile spatial deformation and plausible appearance variation. The seminal work [21] exploits the pictorial structure (PS) from [23], which uses Gaussian distribution to capture the deformation of each part and constrain the relative position of interrelated parts via a tree structure. PS is improved by strong appearance representation (e.g., [17,25,29,30]), discriminative classifier (e.g., [25,44]) and powerful structure (e.g., [41,39,42,36,38,40]), and finally it becomes the leading method in localizing human parts on challenging benchmarks. DPM [20], as one of the representative works in this category, uses structural SVM training and HOG feature in pictorial structure for object detection, and it is lately extended by [44] for human pose estimation.

PS [21] and its widely used extension DPM [20,44] , however, cannot capture the global information and have limited flexibility, due to the deformation constraint by the fixed anchor location. To break the limitation of DPM, we propose a novel approach by incorporating shape regression into DPM, namely SR-DPM. Specifically, the shape regression estimates part locations using the appearance information globally. We set the regressed shape as the anchor locations in DPM and allow the deformations of parts around them to satisfy the local appearance consistency. Compared to traditional DPM, SR-DPM is of high degree of freedom to model global and local variations sufficiently. Due to the fact that shape regression and DPM can benefit from each other, we build an objective function to jointly learn them. It is a non-convex optimization problem, and we design a coordinate descent procedure to solve it.

In addition, we show that stacking SR-DPMs could further improve the performance. The complex shape variations are often beyond the representation capacity of single DPM or SR-DPM. To fully explore the data, we propose the stacked SR-DPM (S-SR-DPM), where each SR-DPM uses the output of previous SR-DPMs as the input and progressively refines the result. Note that the SR-DPMs in different layers use different parameters. The S-SR-DPM provides a natural analogy to deep convolutional neural network (DCNN) in increasing representation capacity [5]. Compared with the end-to-end learning in DCNN, the S-SR-DPM takes advantage of well designed hand-crafted pipelines and can achieve good performance with much fewer training data.

Previous works usually only consider part localization of a special category (e.g., human and face). In this paper we show wide applications of our method on human, face and general object. For human pose estimation, we conduct experiments on challenging LSP [25]. For face alignment, we use the LFPW [4] as the testbed. It terms of general object, we use the annotations [3] of animals from Pascal VOC [19]. We compare our method with different state-of-the-art methods on these three tasks and achieve the leading performance.

The rest of the paper is organized as follows. Section 2 reviews the related work. The proposed SR-DPM and its stacked form are described in section 3 and section 4. We show experiments in section 5 and finally conclude the paper in section 6.

2   Related Work

Many works on human pose estimation are based on pictorial structure in either generative or discriminative manner. The pictorial structure [21] uses Gaussian model to capture the deformation of each part and links parts by tree structure. Inference in pictorial structure is very efficient due to the dynamic programming and distance transform [21]. The pictorial structure is lately exploited in deformable part model (DPM) [20] with HOG feature and latent-SVM learning, and it achieves great success in Pascal VOC object detection. [44] extends DPM for articulated human pose estimation by adding part subtype and using part annotations in learning. [3] proves the advantage of fully supervised learning of parts over latent learning in [20] for general objects. [40] shows that automatically learning the tree is better than hand-crafted physical connections. [29] uses Poselets [7] to capture mid-level cues to latently capture high-order dependencies for pictorial structure. Many recent works improve PS in more part levels, more global models and more part models [39,42,36,38,26,33,15,31]. A very recent work [30] combines different appearance cues under the pictorial structure framework and achieves the current leading performance.

Although being similar to human pose estimation problem, face alignment field often uses very different methods, mainly due to the stronger spatial constraint of human face than human body. The most popular models include active shape model (ASM [11]), active appearance model (AAM [10]) and their extensions. Different from the Gaussian deformation of each local part in PS, ASM/AAM captures the shape deformation globally with PCA constraint. The global PCA constraint, however, has been indicated to be very sensitive and is lately extended to be constrained local model (CLM [12,34,4,2]) by a shape constraint on appearance of local parts. [47] exploits the DPM developed in [44] for joint face detection and alignment. [45] further improves the work with optimized mixtures and a two-step cascaded deformable shape model. In very recent, face alignment is taken as a regression problem [8,14,43,37], which directly learns the mapping the appearance to shape and achieves the leading performance on face alignment benchmarks and challenges (e.g., 300-W [32]). These methods, however, are sensitive to initialization, which makes them unsuitable for more difficult human and object part localization.

We stack multiple SR-DPMs, which is related to a very recent work [35]. In [35], multiple fisher vector coding layers are stacked to get a similar performance of deep neural network for image classification task. In [16], boosting is used to estimate the shape with pose-index feature, where the features are re-computed at the latest estimation of landmark localization. In [43], linear regression are stacked for face alignment.

Compared with previous works, the main contributions of this work are summarized as follows:

- We propose SR-DPM to incorporate DPM with shape regression and show how to jointly learn them. The SR-DPM is much more flexible than DPM in handling real world object deformation.

- We stack multiple SR-DPMs to increase the representation capacity, where each layer progressively refines the part locations. As shown empirically in experiments, the stacked SR-DPM is critical for better performance.
- To our best knowledge, it is the first work to simultaneously achieve state-of-the-art performance on human pose estimation, face alignment and general object part localization.

3   Deformable Part Model with Shape Regression

The DPM is composed of the root filter β_0 and some parts. Each part has a appearance filter β_i and deformation term d_i. Given an object part configuration specified by $S = [x_1, y_1, \cdots, x_N, y_N]^T$ and object location (x_0, y_0), the DPM favors some special part configurations by:

$$s(S, I) = \beta_0^T \phi_a(x_0, y_0, I) + \sum_{i=1}^{N} (\beta_i^T \phi_a(x_i, y_i, I) - d_i^T \phi_d(x_i, y_i, a_{x_i}, a_{y_i})), \quad (1)$$

where $\phi_a(x_i, y_i, I)$ is the HOG feature of the i-th part, and $\phi_d(x_i, y_i, a_{x_i}, a_{y_i})$ is the separable quadratic function to represent the deformation. $\phi_d(x_i, y_i, a_{x_i}, a_{y_i})$ is defined based on the relative location between the (x_i, y_i) and its anchor location (a_{x_i}, a_{y_i}), which is fixed after the specification of (x_0, y_0). It is straightforward to add mixture parts [44] or mixture components [20], but we leave them out to simplify the notation.

For each sliding window in localization, only the root location (x_0, y_0) is known in advance and each part location is inferred by maximizing the part appearance score minus the deformation cost associated with displacement to anchor location. Since parts are directly attached to the root, their locations are inferred independently given the fixed root by:

$$\max_{x_i, y_i} (\beta_i^T \phi_a(x_i, y_i, I) - d_i^T \phi_d(x_i, y_i, a_{x_i}, a_{y_i})), \quad (2)$$

where (x_i, y_i) traverses all possible locations of the part. The procedure can be efficiently solved by distance transform as used in [21,44].

Our improvement comes from the anchor location of each part. In DPM, the anchor location of each part is defined according to relative position of either the root [20] or its parent part [44]. It limits the flexibility since that each part can only have a small deformation around its fixed anchor location. Additionally, the star-structure used cannot capture global information, such as the high order spatial dependencies of left-arm, right-arm, left-leg and right-leg.

In this paper, we propose to use regression to estimate the anchor locations directly from the image appearance to capture the global information and increase the flexibility. After that we allow each part to have deformation based on these adaptive anchor part locations under the constraint of DPM. Let us use $\widehat{A} = [\widehat{a_{x_1}}, \widehat{a_{y_1}}, \cdots, \widehat{a_{x_N}}, \widehat{a_{y_N}}]^T$ to specify the estimated anchor part locations. Suppose the initial shape is A^0 and ground-truth shape is A^*, we always want that each (x_i, y_i) to have relationship with all the parts initialized by S_0 (which is the mean shape) to capture the global information. The function can be very complex, and in this paper we use a simple linear function to approximate it:

$$\widehat{A} = f(A^0, I) = A^0 + W^T \Phi(A^0, I), \tag{3}$$

where $\Phi(A^0, I)$ is the local appearance feature extracted around all parts. In this paper, we define it as the HOG feature [13] from the implementation in [20]. We concatenate feature vectors of all parts specified by A^0 to be a long vector, which has Nn_d values and n_d is the length of HOG vector for a part. The dimension of corresponding regression matrix W is $Nn_d \times 2N$. In Eq. 3, each new part location is estimated based on all the initial part locations, thus Eq. 3 encodes global information which previously cannot be captured in pictorial structure based models. No parametric shape prior, such as global shape PCA in ASM and local part Gaussian deformation in pictorial structure, is assumed in Eq. 3. It has advantage especially for real world objects, whose spatial deformation can be very complex and simple parametric prior cannot describe it well.

The above shape regression, however, is not enough for object part localization. The reason is that it cannot measure the confidence of the estimated part locations, which is very important for sliding window based scanning. Additionally, the global shape regression matrix not explicitly consider the appearance consistency of regressed part location. To this end, we further use the deformable part model to incorporate shape regression, by replacing the fixed anchor location with the shape regression output $\widehat{A}$:

$$s(S, I) = \beta_0^T \phi_a(x_0, y_0, I) + \sum_{i=1}^{N} (\beta_i^T \phi_a(x_i, y_i, I) - d_i^T \phi_d(x_i, y_i, \widehat{a_{x_i}}, \widehat{a_{y_i}})) \tag{4}$$

$$where \quad \widehat{A} = [\widehat{a_{x_1}}, \widehat{a_{y_1}}, \cdots, \widehat{a_{x_N}}, \widehat{a_{y_N}}]^T = A^0 + W^T \Phi(A^0, I).$$

For each sliding window in localization, we find the S to maximize the confidence score defined above, and take it the the estimated shape configuration of the sliding window. The deformable part model with shape regression (SR-DPM) provides the flexibility to capture large variations, but it also brings challenges, since the regression matrix W and the deformable part model parameter β are all unknown. In the following part, we present the objective function for joint learning and show the optimization method.

3.1   Model Learning

The objective function for model learning is motivated by the original DPM used in object detection, which is defined as:

$$\arg\min_{\beta, S_m} \frac{1}{2} \|\beta\|^2 + C \sum_{m=1}^{M} max(0, 1 - y_m \cdot s(S_m, I_m)), \tag{5}$$

where the first term is used for regularization and the second term is the hinge loss to punish error in detection. M is the number of training samples, and S_m

is the part configuration of the m-th image I_m. $y_m = 1$ for positive and -1 for negative. In this function, only the root location of S_m is annotated, and each part location is inferred according to Eq. 2. The loss function favors the score of positive sample above 1 and score negative sample below -1. It is a standard latent SVM problem and has many off-the-shelf solvers, such as the one used in [20]. One problem in solving is that the negative number is of combinatorial explosion, and we often use a negative sample mining step to gradually add negative samples.

In our SR-DPM for object part location, we also want to ensure that the estimated part configuration specified by S_m matches the ground truth part configuration specified by S_m^*. In this way, the objective function is extended to be:

$$\arg\min_{\beta,W,S_m} \frac{1}{2}\|\beta\|^2 + C_1 \sum_{m=1}^{M} max(0, 1 - y_m \cdot s(S_m, I_m)) + C_2\|W\|^2 + C_3 \sum_{m-1}^{M_p} \|S_m - S_m^*\|^2,$$

$$(6)$$

where C_1, C_2 and C_3 are used to control the relative weights of different terms. $\|W\|^2$ is used to regularize the regression matrix W. The last term $\sum_{m-1}^{M_p} \|S_m - S_m^*\|^2$ is used to measure the consistency of estimated shape S_m and ground truth shape S_m^*. In this function, the S_m is estimated according to the shape regression model parameterized by W and DPM parameterized by β in Eq. 4. Since only the shapes of positive samples are of interest, the shape loss is measured only on positive samples. The above object function provides a way to jointly learn the deformable part model and shape regression, which can benefit from each other. However, it also results in a highly non-convex problem, due to the inference procedure of S_m. We use a coordinate descent procedure to optimize them:

- When the W and S_m are fixed, the function only has the first two terms and becomes a SVM problem to learn the discriminative parameter β, and we use the solver from [44].
- When β is fixed, the optimal W is hard to solve directly since that the HOG transform is non-derivative. Instead, we find an approximation of W by relaxing the last term. We extensively search to find the part configuration $\widetilde{A_m}$, which can converge to a shape closest to ground truth shape S_m^* with regard to the DPM parameterized by β. Once we have $\widetilde{A_m}$, the regression matrix W just needs to ensure that the regressed shape is consistent with $\widetilde{A_m}$, so that we can approximately minimizing the term $\sum_{m=1}^{M_p} \|S_m - S_m^*\|^2$ by $\sum_{m=1}^{M_p} \|A_m^0 + W^T\Phi_a(A_m^0) - \widetilde{A_m}\|^2$. We concatenate shape vector $\widetilde{A_m} - A_m^0$ for $m \in [1, M_p]$ to be a matrix $\mathcal{A}$ and appearance feature vector $\phi(A_m^0, I_m)$ to be a matrix Φ_a, where $\mathcal{A} \in R^{2N \times M_p}$ and $\Phi_a \in R^{Nn_d \times M_p}$. Let I be an identity matrix in $R^{Nn_d \times Nn_d}$, the optimal W in Eq. 6 is approximated by:

$$W = \arg\min_{W_t} C_2\|W\|^2 + C_3 \sum_{m=1}^{M_p} \|A_m^0 + W^T\Phi_a(A_m^0) - \widetilde{A_m}\|^2 \qquad (7)$$

$$= (\Phi_a\Phi_a^T + \frac{C2}{C_3}I)^{-1}\Phi_a\mathcal{A}^T. \qquad (8)$$

– When W and β are fixed, we can use the standard inference procedure defined in Eq. 4 to find the optimal S_m.

Implementation Details. In our experience, the above procedure usually converges in 3 loop. To start the loop in learning, we need an initialization of W and S_m. The W is got by replacing the $\widetilde{S_m}$ in Eq. 7 with S_m^*, and the S_m is initialized by ground truth S_m^*. In the DPM training step, we always use the parameter got in last iteration as the "warm start", which leads to the fast convergence. We divide training samples into different views. For samples in each view, we align training shapes using similarity transform to remove the offset and normalize them into the same scale. After that, we estimate a multi-variate Gaussian distribution of the shape. For each sliding window in testing, we estimate the scale and translation of mean distribution, and then use it as the initialization A^0.

4   Stacked Deformable Part Model with Shape Regression

In this part, we further improve the part localization performance by stacking the proposed SR-DPM. The intuition comes from recent successes of deep convolutional neural networks (DCNN) in image classification [27] and object detection [24]. These works prove the representation capacity advantage of deep model for real world objects. However, to our best knowledge, no work has shown the advantage of DCNN for general object part localization, partially due to the conflict between the large variations and limited training data.

To balance the representation capacity of deep model and limited training data, we use hand-crafted feature and model for each layer and stack them to form a deep model. Compared with pure data-driven end-to-end learning, our method has much fewer parameters and benefits from reliable priors such as HOG feature and pictorial structure, while still keeps the advantage of rich representation capacity.

The SR-DPM can be taken as a map g, where the input is an image plus a shape and the output is a new shape on this image. Since the oracle map g^* is very complex, there exists an inconsistency between g and g^*. Suppose the training set is $\mathfrak{A}$, then the error on the training set is:

$$\sum_{A_i \in \mathfrak{A}} \|g^*(A_i^0, I_i) - g(A_i^0, I_i)\|^2, \tag{9}$$

where A_i^0 is the initial shape of i-th training sample. To further reduce the training error, we use a series of functions $\mathcal{G} = \{g_1, \cdots, g_K\}$, where K is number of functions. We want to approximate g^* by minimizing:

$$\sum_{A_i \in \mathfrak{A}} \|g^*(A_i^0, I_i) - g_T \circ g_{T-1} \circ \cdots \circ g_1(A_i^0, I_i)\|^2, \tag{10}$$

where each g_i is a SR-DPM, and it uses the output of g_{i-1} as the input. Since in each layer, the function g_i is nonlinear, the whole function is highly non-linear and has strong representation capacity to approximate the complex map from image to part locations. We name this model as the stacked SR-DPM (S-SR-DPM).

SR-DPMs in the S-SR-DPM are learned sequentially. The initial shape A_0 and image are taken as the input to train the first function g_1 specified by a SR-DPM on the training set, by the coordinate descent learning described in the above section. For the following g_i, we greedily optimize it by:

$$g_i = \arg\min_g \sum_{A_i \in \mathfrak{A}} \|g^*(A_i^0, I_i) - g(g_{i-1} \circ \cdots \circ g_1(A_i^0, I_i))\|^2. \qquad (11)$$

The map number keeps increasing until the training error does not decrease any more (typically in experiments, a 4 layer S-SR-DPM is enough). In our current implementation, we only use this layer-wise training procedure because of the limited computation resource, despite that the global training is possible. We find that just layer-wise training can significantly improve the performance.

The inference procedure of the S-SR-DPM can be divided into inference of each single layer SR-DPM, which has a global shape regression step and deformable part model step. The procedure is different from traditional iterative optimization in that in each iteration we use different model parameters. Given an image, sliding window based scanning is used, where a non-maximal suppression (NMS) is adopted to eliminate overlapping shape configurations and finally preserve the one with the highest confidence score. We show qualitative examples of S-SR-DPM inference on face alignment in Fig. 1.

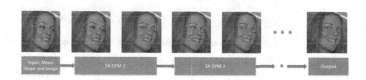

Fig. 1. Examples of S-SR-DPM inference on face alignment (best viewed in color)

5   Experiments

We conduct experiments on human pose estimation, face alignment and general object part localization task. We emphasize that our method achieves competitive performance on the three tasks, compared with different state-of-the-art methods.

5.1   Human Pose Estimation

For human pose estimation, we use the "Leeds Sport Poses" (LSP[1]) [25] to validate different settings and compare with the state-of-the-art methods. LSP is

---

[1] The dataset is available at http://www.comp.leeds.ac.uk/mat4saj/lsp.html

one of the most challenging datasets for human pose estimation, which includes 1000 sports humans for training and 1000 sports humans for testing. The performance is measured by Percentage of Correctly localized Parts (PCP) [22] on 10 object parts defined according to the 14 joints. 6 subtypes are used for each part. For all the experiments on LSP, we use the observer-centric annotations as suggested in [18].

Diagnostic Experiments. We report the mean PCP of 10 parts in different settings in Fig. 2. For the DPM, we use the code from [44] which is carefully tuned for human pose estimation. For our methods, we test the SR-DPM with independent shape regression and DPM learning, the SR-DPM with joint shape regression and DPM learning, and the S-SR-DPM whose depth is set to be among 2, 3 and 4. All these methods are trained on the training set of LSP and use the same 32 dimensional HOG feature from [20]. It can be found that adding shape regression improves a 1.2% margin over the original DPM. When the deformable part model and shape regression are jointly trained, we get a 1.9% further improvement. More improvements come from stacking multiple SR-DPMs to a deeper model. The 2-layer S-SR-DPM gets a 0.8% gain and 3-layer S-SR-DPM gets a 1.2% gain. In our final implementation, we use the 4-layer S-SR-DPM. It improves the final PCP performance by 4.5% over DPM and 1.4% over SR-DPM, which proves the advantage of our S-SR-DPM in capturing large variations for human pose estimation.

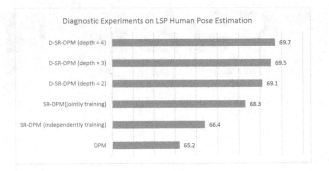

Fig. 2. Mean PCP of different settings on LSP

Comparison with State-of-the-Art Methods. We report the PCP of our methods and the state-the-art methods from recent works in Tab. 1. The "upper leg", "lower leg", "upper arm" and "fore arm" averages the left and right. The performance of our method is better than [1,44,29,18] and on par with a recent result from [30]. Note that [30] fuses multiple appearance cues such as specialized detector and mid-level Poselet, while our method only uses low-level HOG for appearance. Our method is better than [30] in localizing parts with large deformation, such as fore arm and upper arm, which proves the advantage of our method in representation capacity. [30] provides powerful appearance cues and achieves better performance for torso and head. [30] has advantage in appearance modeling and SR-DPM is better in deformation representation, thus they can be combined for further improvement.

Table 1. Comparisons on PCP results for human pose estimation on LSP

	torso	upper leg	lower leg	upper arm	fore arm	head	mean
Andriluka et al., [1]	80.9	67.1	60.7	46.5	26.4	74.9	55.7
Yang&Ramanan [44]	83.3	72.5	65.6	64.4	41.7	80.4	65.2
Pishchulin et al., [29]	87.5	75.7	68.0	54.2	33.9	78.1	62.9
Pishchulin et al., [30]	88.7	78.8	73.4	61.5	44.9	85.6	69.2
Eichner&Ferrari [18]	86.2	74.3	69.3	56.5	37.4	80.1	64.3
SR-DPM	85.4	75.2	68.8	67.6	45.3	83.6	68.3
S-SR-DPM	85.8	76.8	70.6	69.3	46.9	84.0	69.7

5.2 Face Alignment

For face alignment, we use the Labeled Face Parts in the Wild (LFPW[2]) from [4] as the testbed. It contains 29 face landmarks of real world faces with large appearance variations caused by expression, pose and illumination. Because some URLs are not available, we only get 811 of the 1132 training images and 224 of the 300 test images in this experiment. We only use a single component for face and a single subtype for each landmark. The Cumulative Error Distribution (CED) curve and mean error are used to report the performance. For the CED curve, we normalize the error by the inter-ocular distance to remove the influence of face scale.

The experimental comparisons are reported in Fig. 3. We first compare different settings of our method. The DPM performance is generated by a face-oriented DPM extension from [47]. By adding the shape regression, the normalized mean error has a 18.2% relative decrease. The joint learning of shape regression and DPM decreases the relative error by 14.5% over the independent learning. The stacked model is very effective for face alignment, and it has a 26.8% relative improvement over the single layer SR-DPM, and 48.8% relative improvement over the DPM.

We also compare our method with the state-of-the-art methods by CED curves. It can be found that our SR-DPM is already better than the strong method from [4]. The S-SR-DPM is better than the SDM [43] when the normalized error is below 0.061. Our method has a 0.0298 normalized mean error, while the SDM is 0.0347. The previous best result is [8], which reports a 0.0343 mean error and is sightly worse than our method. It is worth noting that the compared methods all needs reliable face bounding box for initialization, while our method can automatically find the bounding box by sliding window based scanning.

---

[2] http://homes.cs.washington.edu/$\sim$neeraj/projects/face-parts/

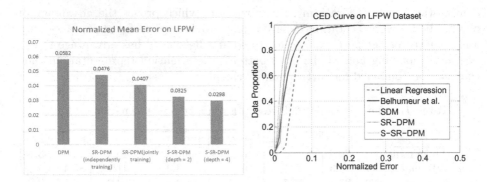

Fig. 3. Comparisons on LFPW face alignment dataset

5.3   Object Detection and Part Localization

Part localization for general object such as animal is more difficult than human and face, which is partially reflected by the detection performance on Pascal VOC. We use the images from Pascal VOC 2007 [19] and the annotation of parts from [3] [3], which includes "bird", "cat", "cow", "dog", "horse" and "sheep". Since the animals tend to be more flexible than human and face, we use the more sophisticated clustering techniques introduced in [3], where relative position, scale, aspect ratio and visibility of parts and the object are used as the feature for clustering, and finally 4 components are used for each category. We refer to [3] for the details. For our S-SR-DPM, the layer number is set to be 4, which is the same as the S-SR-DPM for human pose estimation and face alignment. The object detection is evaluated first and then the part localization.

Table 2. Average Precision of different methods for animal detection in VOC 2007

	Bird	Cat	Cow	Dog	Horse	Sheep	mAP
DPM Ver4 [20]	10.0	19.3	25.2	11.1	56.8	17.8	23.4
DPM Ver5 [20]	10.2	23.0	24.1	12.7	58.1	21.1	24.9
SS-DPM [3]	12.7	26.3	34.6	19.1	62.9	23.6	29.9
Proposed SR-DPM	14.9	27.5	35.7	21.9	64.4	25.5	31.7
Proposed S-SR-DPM	16.7	28.7	36.9	23.5	66.1	27.1	33.2

For object detection, we report the average precision (AP, defined in [19]) of each category on Pascal VOC 2007. The DPM release4[4], DPM release5 [5] and strongly supervised DPM (SS-DPM) [3] are used for comparison, as reported in Tab. 2. The part location information is important for large deformation, as

---

[3] www.csc.kth.se/cvap/DPM/part_sup.html

[4] http://cs.brown.edu/$\sim$pff/latent-release4/

[5] http://www.cs.berkeley.edu/$\sim$rbg/latent/

reflected by the large performance gain over DPM by strong supervised DPM and our methods. The SS-DPM and our proposed SR-DPM and S-SR-DPM use exactly the same training images and annotations. The SR-DPM improves SS-DPM by 1.8% AP and the S-SR-DPM further improves it by 1.5%. We note that the performance gain is more significant for categories with large deformations, such as bird and cat, which are the most difficult categories for current DPM based detection methods.

Table 3. Part Localization performance evaluated on PASCAL VOC 2007 animals. We report performance PCP of SS-DPM [3], the proposed SR-DPM and S-SR-DPM.

	Method	Bird	Cat	Cow	Dog	Horse	Sheep	mean per part
head	SS-DPM[3]	25.4	60.0	36.3	40.5	65.7	29.4	42.9
	SR-DPM	28.2	64.3	37.6	42.4	66.8	32.1	45.2
	S-SR-DPM	29.1	64.8	40.4	44.6	68.5	33.1	46.8
frontal legs	SS-DPM[3]	-	8.9	25.9	23.1	37.3	17.6	22.6
	SR-DPM	-	12.4	29.3	27.3	38.4	19.6	25.4
	S-SR-DPM	-	13.7	31.4	28.1	41.2	21.6	27.2
fore legs	SS-DPM[3]	12.1	-	37.1	-	39.3	10.9	24.9
	SR-DPM	14.4	-	39.1	-	42.7	12.5	27.2
	S-SR-DPM	17.9	-	41.2	-	44.5	14.6	29.3
torso/back	SS-DPM[3]	-	17.2	58.2	6.7	57.7	57.1	39.4
	SR-DPM	-	20.7	63.1	10.6	59.7	60.3	42.9
	S-SR-DPM	-	21.3	63.4	11.4	61.2	61.1	43.7
tail	SS-DPM[3]	6.1	1.7	-	0.9	32.0	2.4	8.6
	SR-DPM	10.2	4.2	-	5.9	35.0	5.7	12.2
	S-SR-DPM	11.1	6.7	-	5.4	36.1	5.3	12.9
mean per category	SS-DPM[3]	14.5	22.0	39.4	17.8	46.4	23.5	-
	SR-DPM	17.0	25.4	42.3	21.6	48.5	26.0	-
	S-SR-DPM	19.0	26.6	44.1	22.1	50.3	27.1	-

For part localization, we again use the PCP criterion [22], and compare our method with [3], which is the only available result on this setting. We report the PCP of each part in each category and mean PCP of strongly supervised DPM (SS-DPM), SR-DPM and S-SR-DPM in Tab. 3. By incorporating shape regression into deformation part model, while using exactly the same training data and parameter setting with SS-DPM, the proposed SR-DPM achieves a mean per part PCP improvement from 2.3% to 4.6% and a mean per category PCP improvement from 2.1% to 3.8%. When stacked model is used, S-SR-DPM further improves the mean per part/category PCP from 0.7%/0.5% to 1.8%/2.0%. Similar to the observations on object detection, our method has noticeably improvements for categories with large deformations such as bird, cat and dog. We show some qualitative results in Fig. 4.

Fig. 4. Qualitative results of S-SR-DPM for human pose estimation, face alignment and object part localization(best viewed in color)

6 Conclusion

In this paper, we propose two critical improvements over deformable part model to localize object parts from a single image. The first is that we extend DPM to SR-DPM, which exploits the shape regression to capture global information and provides flexible anchor locations. After that, we use the deformable part model to refine the result according to the anchor locations and measure the confidence score. We show how to learn the shape regression and DPM jointly by a coordinate descent procedure. The second improvement is that we prove stacked SR-DPM (S-SR-DPM) increases the representation capacity and leads to better localization performance. We show the advantages of SR-DPM and S-SR-DPM for human pose estimation, face alignment and object part localization, which are usually taken as three different problems.

Acknowledgement. This work was supported by the Chinese National Natural Science Foundation Projects #61105023, #61103156, #61105037, #61203267, #61375037, National Science and Technology Support Program Project #2013BAK02B01, Chinese Academy of Sciences Project No. KGZD-EW-102-2, and AuthenMetric R&D Funds.

References

1. Andriluka, M., Roth, S., Schiele, B.: Pictorial structures revisited: People detection and articulated pose estimation. In: CVPR. IEEE (2009)
2. Asthana, A., Zafeiriou, S., Cheng, S., Pantic, M.: Robust discriminative response map fitting with constrained local models. In: CVPR. IEEE (2013)
3. Azizpour, H., Laptev, I.: Object detection using strongly-supervised deformable part models. In: Fitzgibbon, A., Lazebnik, S., Perona, P., Sato, Y., Schmid, C. (eds.) ECCV 2012, Part I. LNCS, vol. 7572, pp. 836–849. Springer, Heidelberg (2012)
4. Belhumeur, P.N., Jacobs, D.W., Kriegman, D.J., Kumar, N.: Localizing parts of faces using a consensus of exemplars. In: CVPR. IEEE (2011)
5. Bengio, Y.: Learning deep architectures for ai. Foundations and trends® in Machine Learning (2009)
6. Berg, T., Belhumeur, P.N.: Poof: Part-based one-vs.-one features for fine-grained categorization, face verification, and attribute estimation. In: CVPR. IEEE (2013)
7. Bourdev, L., Maji, S., Brox, T., Malik, J.: Detecting people using mutually consistent poselet activations. In: Daniilidis, K., Maragos, P., Paragios, N. (eds.) ECCV 2010, Part VI. LNCS, vol. 6316, pp. 168–181. Springer, Heidelberg (2010)
8. Cao, X., Wei, Y., Wen, F., Sun, J.: Face alignment by explicit shape regression. In: CVPR. IEEE (2012)
9. Chen, D., Cao, X., Wen, F., Sun, J.: Blessing of dimensionality: High-dimensional feature and its efficient compression for face verification. In: CVPR. IEEE (2013)
10. Cootes, T.F., Edwards, G.J., Taylor, C.J.: Active appearance models. PAMI (2001)
11. Cootes, T.F., Taylor, C.J., Cooper, D.H., Graham, J.: Active shape models-their training and application. CVIU (1995)

12. Cristinacce, D., Cootes, T.: Automatic feature localisation with constrained local models. Pattern Recognition (2008)
13. Dalal, N., Triggs, B.: Histograms of oriented gradients for human detection. In: CVPR. IEEE (2005)
14. Dantone, M., Gall, J., Fanelli, G., Van Gool, L.: Real-time facial feature detection using conditional regression forests. In: CVPR. IEEE (2012)
15. Desai, C., Ramanan, D.: Detecting actions, poses, and objects with relational phraselets. In: Fitzgibbon, A., Lazebnik, S., Perona, P., Sato, Y., Schmid, C. (eds.) ECCV 2012, Part IV. LNCS, vol. 7575, pp. 158–172. Springer, Heidelberg (2012)
16. Dollár, P., Welinder, P., Perona, P.: Cascaded pose regression. In: CVPR. IEEE (2010)
17. Eichner, M., Ferrari, V.: Better appearance models for pictorial structures (2009)
18. Eichner, M., Ferrari, V.: Appearance sharing for collective human pose estimation. In: Lee, K.M., Matsushita, Y., Rehg, J.M., Hu, Z. (eds.) ACCV 2012, Part I. LNCS, vol. 7724, pp. 138–151. Springer, Heidelberg (2013)
19. Everingham, M., Van Gool, L., Williams, C.K.I., Winn, J., Zisserman, A.: The pascal visual object classes (voc) challenge. IJCV pp. 303–338 (2010)
20. Felzenszwalb, P.F., Girshick, R.B., McAllester, D., Ramanan, D.: Object detection with discriminatively trained part-based models. PAMI (2010)
21. Felzenszwalb, P.F., Huttenlocher, D.P.: Pictorial structures for object recognition. IJCV (2005)
22. Ferrari, V., Marin-Jimenez, M., Zisserman, A.: Progressive search space reduction for human pose estimation. In: CVPR. IEEE (2008)
23. Fischler, M.A., Elschlager, R.A.: The representation and matching of pictorial structures. IEEE Transactions on Computers (1973)
24. Girshick, R., Donahue, J., Darrell, T., Malik, J.: Rich feature hierarchies for accurate object detection and semantic segmentation. arXiv preprint (2013)
25. Johnson, S., Everingham, M.: Clustered pose and nonlinear appearance models for human pose estimation. In: BMVC (2010)
26. Johnson, S., Everingham, M.: Learning effective human pose estimation from inaccurate annotation. In: CVPR. IEEE (2011)
27. Krizhevsky, A., Sutskever, I., Hinton, G.E.: Imagenet classification with deep convolutional neural networks. In: NIPS (2012)
28. Moeslund, T.B., Hilton, A., Krüger, V., Sigal, L.: Visual Analysis of Humans. Springer (2011)
29. Pishchulin, L., Andriluka, M., Gehler, P., Schiele, B.: Poselet conditioned pictorial structures. In: CVPR. IEEE (2013)
30. Pishchulin, L., Andriluka, M., Gehler, P., Schiele, B.: Pstrong appearance and expressive spatial models for human pose estimation. In: ICCV. IEEE (2013)
31. Sadeghi, M.A., Farhadi, A.: Recognition using visual phrases. In: CVPR. IEEE (2011)
32. Sagonas, C., Tzimiropoulos, G., Zafeiriou, S., Pantic, M.: 300 faces in-the-wild challenge: The first facial landmark localization challenge (2013)
33. Sapp, B., Taskar, B.: Modec: Multimodal decomposable models for human pose estimation. In: CVPR. IEEE (2013)
34. Saragih, J.M., Lucey, S., Cohn, J.F.: Deformable model fitting by regularized landmark mean-shift. IJCV (2011)
35. Simonyan, K., Vedaldi, A., Zisserman, A.: Deep fisher networks for large-scale image classification. In: NIPS (2013)
36. Sun, M., Savarese, S.: Articulated part-based model for joint object detection and pose estimation. In: ICCV. IEEE (2011)

37. Sun, Y., Wang, X., Tang, X.: Deep convolutional network cascade for facial point detection. In: CVPR. IEEE (2013)
38. Tian, Y., Zitnick, C.L., Narasimhan, S.G.: Exploring the spatial hierarchy of mixture models for human pose estimation. In: Fitzgibbon, A., Lazebnik, S., Perona, P., Sato, Y., Schmid, C. (eds.) ECCV 2012, Part V. LNCS, vol. 7576, pp. 256–269. Springer, Heidelberg (2012)
39. Tran, D., Forsyth, D.: Improved human parsing with a full relational model. In: Daniilidis, K., Maragos, P., Paragios, N. (eds.) ECCV 2010, Part IV. LNCS, vol. 6314, pp. 227–240. Springer, Heidelberg (2010)
40. Wang, F., Li, Y.: Beyond physical connections: Tree models in human pose estimation. In: CVPR. IEEE (2013)
41. Wang, Y., Mori, G.: Multiple tree models for occlusion and spatial constraints in human pose estimation. In: Forsyth, D., Torr, P., Zisserman, A. (eds.) ECCV 2008, Part III. LNCS, vol. 5304, pp. 710–724. Springer, Heidelberg (2008)
42. Wang, Y., Tran, D., Liao, Z.: Learning hierarchical poselets for human parsing. In: CVPR. IEEE (2011)
43. Xiong, X., De la Torre, F.: Supervised descent method and its applications to face alignment. In: CVPR. IEEE (2013)
44. Yang, Y., Ramanan, D.: Articulated pose estimation with flexible mixtures-of-parts. In: CVPR. IEEE (2011)
45. Yu, X., Huang, J., Zhang, S., Yan, W., Metaxas, D.N.: Pose-free facial landmark fitting via optimized part mixtures and cascaded deformable shape model. In: ICCV (2013)
46. Zhang, N., Farrell, R., Iandola, F., Darrell, T.: Deformable part descriptors for fine-grained recognition and attribute prediction. In: ICCV (2013)
47. Zhu, X., Ramanan, D.: Face detection, pose estimation, and landmark localization in the wild. In: CVPR. IEEE (2012)

Transductive Multi-view Embedding
for Zero-Shot Recognition and Annotation

Yanwei Fu, Timothy M. Hospedales, Tao Xiang, Zhenyong Fu,
and Shaogang Gong

School of EECS, Queen Mary University of London, UK
{y.fu,t.hospedales,t.xiang,z.fu,s.gong}@qmul.ac.uk

Abstract. Most existing zero-shot learning approaches exploit transfer
learning via an intermediate-level semantic representation such as visual
attributes or semantic word vectors. Such a semantic representation is
shared between an annotated auxiliary dataset and a target dataset with
no annotation. A projection from a low-level feature space to the semantic space is learned from the auxiliary dataset and is applied without
adaptation to the target dataset. In this paper we identify an inherent limitation with this approach. That is, due to having disjoint and
potentially unrelated classes, the projection functions learned from the
auxiliary dataset/domain are biased when applied directly to the target
dataset/domain. We call this problem the *projection domain shift* problem and propose a novel framework, *transductive multi-view embedding*,
to solve it. It is 'transductive' in that unlabelled target data points are
explored for projection adaptation, and 'multi-view' in that both low-
level feature (view) and multiple semantic representations (views) are
embedded to rectify the projection shift. We demonstrate through extensive experiments that our framework (1) rectifies the projection shift
between the auxiliary and target domains, (2) exploits the complementarity of multiple semantic representations, (3) achieves state-of-the-art
recognition results on image and video benchmark datasets, and (4) enables novel cross-view annotation tasks.

1 Introduction

Humans can distinguish 30,000 basic object classes [3] and many more subordinate ones (e.g. breeds of dogs). To recognise such high number of classes, humans
have the ability to "learning to learn" and transfer knowledge from known classes
to unknown ones. Inspired by this ability and to minimise the necessary labelled
training examples for conventional supervised classifiers, researchers build the
recognition models that are capable of classifying novel classes with no training example, i.e. zero-shot learning. The key underpinning idea is to exploit
transfer learning via an intermediate-level semantic representation. Specifically,
two datasets with disjoint classes are considered: a labelled known auxiliary set
where a semantic representation is given for each data point, and a target dataset
to be classified with no labelled instance and semantic representation. Such a

D. Fleet et al. (Eds.): ECCV 2014, Part II, LNCS 8690, pp. 584–599, 2014.

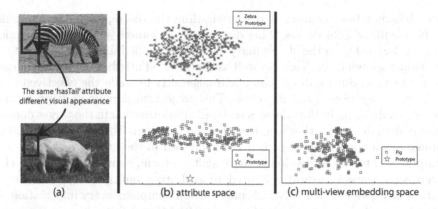

Fig. 1. An example of the projection domain shift problem. Zero-shot prototypes are shown as red stars and image low-level feature projections shown in blue. See text for details.

semantic representation is assumed to be shared between the auxiliary and target datasets. More specifically, apart from class label, each auxiliary data point is labelled by a semantic representation such as visual attributes [18,6,21,11], semantic word vectors [23,7,34] or others [28]. A projection function mapping low-level features to the semantic space is learned from the auxiliary dataset by either classification or regression models. Such a projection is then applied directly to map each unlabelled target class instance into the same semantic representation space. Within this semantic space, a zero-shot classifier is pre-defined by "extra-knowledge" to recognise all unseen instances. In particular, a single 'prototype' of each target class is specified in the semantic space. Depending on the semantic space, this prototype can be an attribute annotation vector [18] or a word vector inferred from the target class name [7].

An inherent problem exists in this zero-shot learning approach: Since the two datasets have different and potentially unrelated classes, the underlying semantic prototypes of classes also differ, as do the 'ideal' projection functions between the low-level feature space and the semantic spaces. Therefore, using the projection functions learned from the auxiliary dataset/domain without any adaptation to the target dataset/domain causes an unknown shift/bias. We call it the *projection domain shift* problem. This problem is illustrated in Fig. 1, which shows two object classes from the Animals with Attributes (AwA) dataset [20]: Zebra is one of the 40 auxiliary classes whilst Pig is one of 10 target classes. Both of them share the same 'hasTail' attribute, but the visual appearance of their tails differs greatly (Fig. 1(a)). Similarly, many other attributes of Pig are visually very different from those in the 40 auxiliary classes. Fig. 1(b) plots (in 2D using t-SNE [22]) a 85D attribute space representation of the image feature projections and class prototypes (85D binary attribute vectors) to illustrate the existence of the projection domain shift problem: a great discrepancy between the Pig prototype position in the semantic attribute space and the projections of its class member instances is observed, while the discrepancy does not exist for the auxiliary Zebra class. This discrepancy is caused when the projection functions learned from the 40 auxiliary classes are applied directly to project the Pig instances – what 'hasTail' (as well as the other 84 attributes) visually means is different now. Such a discrepancy will inherently degrade the effectiveness of zero-shot recognition of the Pig class. This projection domain shift problem is uniquely challenging in that there is no labelled information in the target domain to guide domain adaptation in mitigating the problem. To our knowledge, this problem has neither been identified nor addressed in the literature.

In addition to the projection domain shift problem, conventional approaches to zero-shot learning are also limited in exploiting multiple intermediate semantic spaces/views, each of which may contain complementary information. In particular, while both visual attributes [18,6,21,11] and linguistic semantic representations such as word vectors [23,7,34] have been independently exploited successfully, it remains unattempted and not straightforward to exploit synergistically multiple semantic 'views'. This is because they are of very different dimensions and types and each suffers from different domain shift effects discussed above. This exploitation has to be transductive for zero-shot learning as only unlabelled data are available for the target classes and the auxiliary data cannot be used directly due to the projection domain shift problem.

In this paper, we propose a transductive multi-view embedding framework to solve both the problems of projection domain shift and synergistic exploitation of multiple semantic views. Specifically, in the first step, each instance of an unlabelled target class is represented by multiple views: its low-level feature view and its (biased) projections in multiple semantic spaces (visual attribute space and word space in this work). To rectify the projection domain shift between auxiliary and target datasets, we introduce a multi-view semantic space alignment process to correlate different semantic views and the low-level feature view by projecting them onto a latent embedding space learned using multi-view Canonical Correlation Analysis (CCA) [13]. The objective of this new embedding space is to transductively (using the unlabelled target data) align each semantic view with each other, and with the low-level feature view to rectify the projection domain shift and exploit their complementarity. This can be seen as an unalignment process and its effects are illustrated by Fig. 1(c), where after alignment, the target Pig class prototype is much closer to its member points in this embedding space, making zero-shot recognition more accurate.

In the second step of our framework, we introduce a novel transductive multi-view Bayesian label propagation (TMV-BLP) algorithm for recognition. This allows us to exploit the manifold of unlabelled test data to compensate for the impoverished supervision available in zero-shot learning, as well as N-shot learning scenario where few target classes instances are available. In particular, a graph is constructed from the projection of each view in the embedding space, plus any available zero-shot prototypes. Zero-shot learning is then performed by semi-supervised label propagation from the prototypes to the target data points within and across the graphs. Overall our framework has the following advantages: (1) TMV-BLP can accommodate multiple semantic representations and exploit their complementarity to better rectify the projection domain shift problem and improve recognition. (2) Recognition generalises seamlessly whether none (zero-shot), few (N-shot), ample (fully supervised) examples of the target classes become available. Uniquely it can also synergistically exploit zero + N-shot (i.e., both prototypes and examples) learning. (3) It enables a number of novel cross-view annotation tasks including *zero-shot class description* and *zero attribute learning*. Extensive experiments on benchmark object and video activity datasets demonstrate that our method outperforms state-of-the-art alternatives on both zero-shot and N-shot recognition tasks.

2   Related Work

Semantic Spaces for Zero-Shot Learning. Learning visual attributes has been topical in the past 5 years. Attribute-centric models have been explored for images [18,6,12,31] and to a lesser extent videos [8,11,21]. Most existing studies [18,17,25,26,30,37,1] assume that an exhaustive ontology of attributes has been manually specified at either the class or instance level. However, annotating attributes scales poorly as ontologies tend to be domain specific. This is despite efforts exploring augmented data-driven/latent attributes at the expense of name-ability [6,21,11]. To overcome this problem, semantic representations that do not rely on an explicit attribute ontology have been proposed [29,28], notably *word vectors*. A word space is extracted from linguistic knowledge bases e.g. WordNet or Wikipedia by natural language processing models e.g. [5,23]. Instead of manually defining an attribute prototype, a novel target class' textual name can be projected into this space and then used as the prototype for zero-shot learning [7,34]. Importantly, regardless of the semantic space used, existing methods focus on either designing better semantic spaces or how to best learn the projections. The former are orthogonal to our work – any semantic spaces can be used in our framework and better ones would benefit our model. For the latter, no existing work has identified or addressed the projection domain shift problem.

Learning Multi-View Embedding Spaces. Relating the low-level feature view and semantic views of data has been exploited in visual recognition and cross modal retrieval. Most existing work [33,13,16,36,10,9] focuses on modelling images/videos with associated text (e.g. tags on Flickr/YouTube). Multi-view CCA is often exploited to provide unsupervised fusion of different modalities. However, there are two fundamental differences between previous multi-view embedding work and ours: (1) our embedding space is transductive, that is, learned from unlabelled target data from which all semantic views are estimated by projection rather than being the original views; These projected views thus have the projection domain shift problem that the previous work does not have. (2) The objectives are different: we aim to rectify the projection domain shift via the embedding in order to perform better recognition and annotation while they target primarily cross-modality retrieval.

Multi-View Label Propagation. In most previous zero-shot learning studies (e.g., direct attribute prediction (DAP) [20]), only semantic space prototypes are used for classification. Since the available knowledge (single zero-shot prototype per target class) is very limited, there has been recent interests in additionally exploiting the unlabelled target data by transductive learning [27]. However, apart from suffering from the projection domain shift problem, [27] has limited ability to exploit multiple semantic representations/views. In contrast, after alignment in the embedding space, our framework synergistically integrates the multiple graphs of low-level feature and semantic representations of each instance by transductive multi-view Bayesian label propagation (TMV-BLP). Moreover, TMV-BLP generalises beyond zero-shot to N-shot learning if labelled instances are available for the target classes. Classification on multiple graphs (C-MG) is well-studied in semi-supervised learning. Most solutions are based on the seminal work of Zhou *et al* [38] which generalises spectral clustering from a single graph to multiple graphs by defining a mixture of random walks on multiple graphs. However crucially, the influence/trustworthiness of each graph is given by a weight that has to be pre-defined and its value has a great effect on the performance of C-MG [38]. In this work, we extend the C-MG algorithm in [38] by introducing a Bayesian prior weight for each graph, which can be measured automatically from data. Our experiments show that our TMV-BLP algorithm is superior to [38] and [27].

Our Contributions. are as follows: (1) To our knowledge, this is the first attempt to investigate and provide a solution to the projection domain shift problem in zero-shot learning. (2) We propose a transductive multi-view embedding space that not only rectifies the projection shift, but also exploits the complementarity of multiple semantic representations of visual data. (3) A novel transductive multi-view Bayesian label propagation algorithm is developed to improve both zero-shot and N-shot learning tasks in the embedding space. (4) The learned embedding space enables a number of novel cross-view annotation tasks.

3   Learning a Transductive Multi-View Embedding Space

Problem Setup. We have c_S source/auxiliary classes with n_S instances $S = \{X_S, Y_S^i, \mathbf{z}_S\}$ and c_T target classes $T = \{X_T, Y_T^i, \mathbf{z}_T\}$ with n_T instances. X indicates the $t-$dimensional low-level feature of all instances; so $X_S \subseteq R^{n_s \times t}$ and $X_T \subseteq R^{n_T \times t}$. $\mathbf{z}_S$ and $\mathbf{z}_T$ are the training and test class label vectors. We assume the auxiliary and target classes are disjoint: $\mathbf{z}_S \cap \mathbf{z}_T = \varnothing$. We have I different types of intermediate semantic representations; Y_S^i and Y_T^i represent the $i-th$ type of m_i dimensional semantic representation for the auxiliary and target datasets respectively; so $Y_S^i \subseteq R^{n_S \times m_i}$ and $Y_T^i \subseteq R^{n_T \times m_i}$. Note that for the auxiliary dataset, Y_S^i is given as each data point is labelled. But for the target dataset, Y_T^i is missing, and its prediction $\hat{Y}_T^i$ from X_T is used instead. As we will see later, this is obtained using a projection function learned from the auxiliary dataset. Each target class c has a pre-defined class-level semantic prototype $\mathbf{y}_c^i$ in each semantic view i. In this paper, we consider two types of intermediate semantic representation (i.e. $I = 2$) – attributes and word vectors, which represent two distinct and complementary sources of information.

We use $\mathcal{X}$, $\mathcal{A}$ and $\mathcal{V}$ to denote the low-level feature, attribute and word vector spaces respectively. The attribute space $\mathcal{A}$ is typically manually defined using a standard ontology. For the word vector space $\mathcal{V}$, we employ the state-of-the-art skip-gram neural network model [23,24] on all English Wikipedia articles[1] which has higher accuracy and lower computational cost than alternatives such as [5]. Using this learned model, we can project the textual name of any class into the $\mathcal{V}$ space to get its word vector representation. It is a 'free' semantic representation in the sense that the generating process does not need any human annotations. We next address how to project low-level features into these spaces.

Learning the Projections of Semantic Spaces. Mapping images and videos into a semantic space i requires a projection function $f^i : \mathcal{X} \rightarrow \mathcal{Y}^i$. This is typically realised by classifiers [18] or regressors [34]. In this paper, using the auxiliary set S, we train support vector classifiers $f^{\mathcal{A}}(\cdot)$ and support vector regressors $f^{\mathcal{V}}(\cdot)$ for each dimension of the attribute and word vectors respectively. Then the target class instances X_T have the semantic projections: $\hat{Y}_T^{\mathcal{A}} = f^{\mathcal{A}}(X_T)$ and $\hat{Y}_T^{\mathcal{V}} = f^{\mathcal{V}}(X_T)$. However, these predicted intermediate semantics have the projection domain shift problem illustrated in Fig. 1. To solve this, we learn a transductive multi-view semantic embedding space to align the semantic projections with the low-level features of target data.

Learning Transductive Multi-View Semantic Embedding. To learn an embedding space capable of rectifying the domain shift, we employ multi-view Canonical Correlation Analysis (CCA) for E views, each denoted as $\boldsymbol{\Phi}^i$. Specifically, in this work we project three views of each target class instance $f^{\mathcal{A}}(X_T)$, $f^{\mathcal{V}}(X_T)$ and X_T (i.e. $E = I + 1 = 3$) into a shared embedding space and the three projection functions W^i are learned by

$$
\begin{aligned}
\min \quad & \sum_{i,j=1}^{E} \quad Trace(W^i \Sigma_{ij} W^j) \\
= \quad & \sum_{i,j=1}^{E} \quad \| \boldsymbol{\Phi}^i W^i - \boldsymbol{\Phi}^j W^j \|_F^2 \\
\text{s.t.} \quad & \left[W^i\right]^T \Sigma_{ii} W^i = I \quad \left[\mathbf{w}_k^i\right]^T \Sigma_{ij} \mathbf{w}_l^j = 0 \\
& i \neq j, k \neq l \quad i,j = 1, \cdots, E \quad k,l = 1, \cdots, n_T
\end{aligned}
\tag{1}
$$

where W^i is the projection matrix which maps the view $\boldsymbol{\Phi}^i$ (a n_T row matrix) into the embedding space and $\mathbf{w}_k^i$ is the kth column of W^i. Σ_{ij} is the covariance matrix between $\boldsymbol{\Phi}^i$ and $\boldsymbol{\Phi}^j$. The dimensionality of the embedding space is the sum of that of $\boldsymbol{\Phi}^i$ – there is obviously feature redundancy. Since the importance

---

[1] Only articles are used without any user talk/discussion. To 13 Feb. 2014, it includes 2.9 billion words and 4.33 million vocabulary (single and bi/tri-gram words). It is downloadable from Yanwei's website.

of each dimension is reflected by its corresponding eigenvalue [14,13,4], we use the eigenvalues to weight the dimensions and define a *weighted embedding space* Γ:

$$\boldsymbol{\Psi}^i = \boldsymbol{\Phi}^i W^i \left[D^i\right]^\lambda = \boldsymbol{\Phi}^i W^i \tilde{D}^i, \tag{2}$$

where D^i is a diagonal matrix with its diagonal elements set to the eigenvalues of each dimension in the embedding space, λ is a power weight of D^i and empirically set to 4 [13], and $\boldsymbol{\Psi}^i$ is the final representation of data from view i in Γ. In this work, three views are considered; for notational convenience, we index $i \in \{\mathcal{X}, \mathcal{V}, \mathcal{A}\}$. The same formulation can be used if more than three views are available.

Similarity in the Embedding Space. The choice of similarity metric is important for the high-dimensional embedding spaces Γ [13]. In particular, extensive evidences in text analysis and information retrieval have shown that high-dimensional embedding vectors are naturally directional and using cosine similarity provides significant robustness against noise [2,13,14]. Therefore for the subsequent recognition and annotation tasks, we compute cosine similarity in Γ by l_2 normalisation: normalising any vector $\psi_k^i \in \boldsymbol{\Psi}^i$ to unit length (i.e. $\| \psi_k^i \|_2 = 1$). Thus cosine similarity is given by the inner product of any two vectors in Γ. Finally, equipped with a weighted and normalised embedding space Γ, any two vectors can be directly compared no matter whether the original view is $\mathcal{X}$, $\mathcal{A}$ or $\mathcal{V}$.

4   Recognition by Multi-view Bayesian Label Propagation

We now introduce a unified framework for exploiting unlabelled target data transductively to improve zero-shot recognition as well as N-shot learning if sparse examples are available. We assume a target class c has a prototype $\mathbf{y}_c^i$ (either a manual binary attribute vector, or the class name representation in the word space as a word vector) in each semantic view for zero-shot, and/or a few labelled instances for N-shot classification. To exploit the learned embedding Γ for recognition, we project three views of each target class instance $f^{\mathcal{A}}(X_T)$, $f^{\mathcal{V}}(X_T)$ and X_T as well as the target class prototypes into this space. The prototypes $\mathbf{y}_c^i$ for views $i \in \{\mathcal{A}, \mathcal{V}\}$ are projected as $\psi_c^i = \mathbf{y}_c^i W^i \tilde{D}^i$. So we have $\psi_c^{\mathcal{A}}$ and $\psi_c^{\mathcal{V}}$ for the attribute and word vector prototypes of each target class c in Γ. In the absence of a prototype for the (non-semantic) low-level feature view $\mathcal{X}$, we synthesise it as $\psi_c^{\mathcal{X}} = (\psi_c^{\mathcal{A}} + \psi_c^{\mathcal{V}})/2$.

Most if not all of the target class instances are unlabelled. To exploit the unlabelled data transductively for classification, we consider graph-based semi-supervised learning in Γ. However, since our embedding space contains multiple projections of the target data, it is hard to define a single graph that exploits the manifold structure of each view. We therefore consider the graphs defined by the projection of each view in a multi-view label propagation algorithm (TMV-BLP). Thanks to the shared embedding space Γ, these heterogeneous graphs become comparable and can be connected by a Bayesian prior weight estimated from data. TMV-BLP provides multi-view label propagation by unifying the multi-graph into a single graph via a random walk within and across the graphs. The initial label information from the prototypes (zero-shot) and/or the few labelled target data points (N-shot learning) is then propagated to the unlabelled data.

Multi-view Bayesian Graph Construction. In Γ we aim to build a graph $\mathcal{G}$ relating labelled and unlabelled data and prototypes. Each view projection defines a node, and the distance between any pair of nodes is:

$$\omega(\psi_k^i, \psi_l^j) = \exp(\frac{< \psi_k^i, \psi_l^j >^2}{\delta}) \tag{3}$$

where $< \psi_k^i, \psi_l^j >^2$ is the square of inner product between the $i-th$ and $j-th$ projections of nodes k and l with a free parameter[2] δ. However, exhaustively connecting all projections of all data is computationally expensive. To balance efficiency and reflecting the topological manifold structure of the graphs, we simplify Eq (3) by two strategies: (1) We construct a k-nearest-neighbour graph $\mathcal{G}^i$ within each projection i, i.e., $i = j$ and $k \neq l$ in Eq (3) with $K = 30$ nearest neighbours[3]. (2) To connect heterogeneous graphs $\mathcal{G}^i$ and $\mathcal{G}^j$ ($i \neq j$), we only compute the similarity across projections at the same data point ($k = l$ but $i \neq j$ in Eq (3)).

To propagate label information from labelled nodes to other target instances, a classic strategy is random walks [38]. We define a random walk process within and across graphs. A natural random walk within $\mathcal{G}^i$ for two nodes k and l has the following transition probability,

$$p(k \to l|\mathcal{G}^i) = \frac{\omega(\psi_k^i, \psi_l^i)}{\sum_m \omega(\psi_k^i, \psi_m^i)}, \tag{4}$$

and the stationary probability for node k,

$$\pi(k|\mathcal{G}^i) = \frac{\sum_l \omega(\psi_k^i, \psi_l^i)}{\sum_k \sum_l \omega(\psi_k^i, \psi_l^i)}. \tag{5}$$

To connect the graphs across views $i \neq j$, we need to model the overall graph probability. Let $p(\mathcal{G}^i)$ denote the prior probability of graph $\mathcal{G}^i$ in the random walk. This prior reflects how informative $\mathcal{G}^i$ is. Then the posterior probability to choose graph $\mathcal{G}^i$ at projection/node ψ_k^i will be:

$$p(\mathcal{G}^i|k) = \frac{\pi(k|\mathcal{G}^i)p(\mathcal{G}^i)}{\sum_i \pi(k|\mathcal{G}^i)p(\mathcal{G}^i)}. \tag{6}$$

---

[2] Most previous work [27,38] needs to do cross validation for δ. Inspired by [19], a rule of thumb for setting δ is $\delta \approx \underset{k,l=1,\cdots,n}{\text{median}} < \psi_k^i, \psi_l^j >^2$ to balance roughly the same number of similar as dissimilar example pairs. This makes the edge weight invariant to the value scale of the heterogeneous graph.

[3] It can be varied from $10 \sim 50$ with little effects in our experiments.

For any pair of nodes k and l, the transition probability across multiple graphs can be computed by Bayesian model averaging,

$$p(k \rightarrow l) = \sum_i p(k \rightarrow l|\mathcal{G}^i) \cdot p(\mathcal{G}^i|k). \qquad (7)$$

In addition, the stationary probability across multiple graphs is computed as:

$$\pi(k) = \sum_i \pi(k|\mathcal{G}^i) \cdot p(\mathcal{G}^i). \qquad (8)$$

Finally, the prior probability of each graph $p(\mathcal{G}^i)$ is computed as

$$p(\mathcal{G}^i) = \frac{\sum_k \sum_{j \in \{\mathcal{X},\mathcal{V},\mathcal{A}\}, j \neq i} \omega(\psi_k^i, \psi_k^j)}{\sum_k \sum_{r \in \{\mathcal{X},\mathcal{V},\mathcal{A}\}} \sum_{u \in \{\mathcal{X},\mathcal{V},\mathcal{A}\}, r \neq u} \omega(\psi_k^r, \psi_k^u)} \qquad (9)$$

The intuition is that this is the relative consensus of each graph to all the others. A graph that is on average similar/in consensus with the others gets a stronger prior compared to an outlying graph which is not in consensus with others.

Label Propagation. Given the graph and random walk process defined above, we can derive the semi-supervised label propagation. Let P denote the transition probability matrix defined by Eq (7) and Π the diagonal matrix with the elements $\pi(k)$ computed by Eq (8). The Laplacian matrix $\mathcal{L}$ combines information of different views and is defined as: $\mathcal{L} = \Pi - \frac{\Pi P + P^T \Pi}{2}$. The label matrix Z for labelled N-shot data or zero-shot prototypes is defined as:

$$Z(q_k, c) = \begin{cases} 1 & q_k \in class\, c \\ -1 & q_k \notin class\, c \\ 0 & unknown \end{cases} \qquad (10)$$

Given the label matrix Z and Laplacian $\mathcal{L}$, label propagation on multiple graphs has the closed-form solution: $\hat{Z} = \eta(\eta \Pi + \mathcal{L})^{-1} \Pi Z$ where η is a regularisation parameter[4]. Note that in our framework, both labelled target class instances and prototypes are modelled as graph nodes. Thus the difference between zero-shot and N-shot learning lies only on the initial labelled instances: Zero-shot learning has the prototypes as labelled nodes; N-shot has instances as labelled nodes; and a new condition exploiting both prototypes and N-shot together is possible. This unified recognition framework thus applies when either or both of prototypes and labelled instances are available.

5   Annotation and Beyond

Our multi-view embedding space Γ bridges the semantic gap between low-level features $\mathcal{X}$ and semantic representations $\mathcal{A}$ and $\mathcal{V}$. Leveraging this cross-view

---

[4] It can be varied from $1 - 10$ with little effects in our experiments

mapping, annotation [15,36,13] can be improved and applied in novel ways. We consider three annotation tasks here.

Instance Level Annotation via Attribute Classification. Given a new instance u, we can describe/annotate it by predicting its attributes. The conventional solution is directly applying $\hat{\mathbf{y}}_u^{\mathcal{A}} = f^{\mathcal{A}}(\mathbf{x}_u)$ for test data. However as we have shown this suffers from projection domain shift problem. With the learned embedding Γ, we can now infer attributes for each target class instance $\hat{\mathbf{y}}_u^{\mathcal{A}} = \mathbf{x}_u W^{\mathcal{X}} \tilde{D}^{\mathcal{X}} \left[W^{\mathcal{A}} \tilde{D}^{\mathcal{A}} \right]^{-1}$.

Zero-Shot Class Description. From a broader pattern recognition perspective, one might be interested to ask what are the attributes of an unknown class, based solely on the name of the class. This *zero-shot class description* task could be useful, for example, to hypothesise the zero-shot attribute prototype of a class instead of defining it by experts [18] or ontology [11]. Our transductive embedding space enables this task by connecting semantic word space (i.e. naming) and discriminative attribute space (i.e. describing). Therefore, given the prototype $\mathbf{y}_c^{\mathcal{V}}$ from the name of a novel target class c, we compute $\hat{\mathbf{y}}_c^{\mathcal{A}} = \mathbf{y}_c^{\mathcal{V}} W^{\mathcal{V}} \tilde{D}^{\mathcal{V}} \left[W^{\mathcal{A}} \tilde{D}^{\mathcal{A}} \right]^{-1}$ to generate their class-level attribute description.

Zero Attribute Learning. This task is the inverse of the previous task: *inferring the name of a class given a set of attributes*. It is useful, for example, to validate or assess a proposed zero-shot attribute prototype, or to provide an automated semantic-property based index into a dictionary or database. To our knowledge, this is the first attempt for evaluating the quality of a class attribute prototype because no previous work has directly and systematically linked linguistic knowledge space with visual attribute space. Specifically given an attribute prototype $\mathbf{y}_c^{\mathcal{A}}$, we can use $\hat{\mathbf{y}}_c^{\mathcal{V}} = \hat{\mathbf{y}}_c^{\mathcal{A}} W^{\mathcal{A}} \tilde{D}^{\mathcal{A}} \left[W^{\mathcal{V}} \tilde{D}^{\mathcal{V}} \right]^{-1}$ to name the corresponding class and do retrieval on dictionary words in $\mathcal{V}$ using $\hat{\mathbf{y}}_c^{\mathcal{V}}$.

6 Experiments

Datasets and Settings. We evaluate our framework on two widely used image/video attribute datasets: Animal with Attribute (AwA) and Unstructured Social Activity Attribute (USAA). AwA [18] provides 50 classes of animals (30475 images) and 85 associated class-level attributes (such as furry, and has-Claws). It provides a defined source/target split for zero-shot learning with 10 classes and 6180 images held out. USAA is a video dataset [8,11] with 69 instance-level attributes for 8 classes of complex social group activity videos from YouTube. Each class has around 100 training and testing videos respectively. USAA provides instance-level attributes since there are significant intra-class variabilities. We use the thresholded mean of instances from each class to define a binary attribute prototype as in [11]. We use the same transfer learning setting in [11]: 4 classes as source and 4 classes as target data. We used exactly

Table 1. Comparison with the state-of-the-art on zero-shot learning on AwA and USAA. Mo, Ma, O and D represent the highest results in the mined object class-attribute associations, mined attributes, objectness as attributes and direct similarity methods used in [29] respectively. Note *: our implementation.

Approach	AwA	USAA
TMV-BLP	**47.1**	**47.8**
DAP	40.5([18]) / 41.4([20]) / 38.4*	33.2([11]) / 35.2*
IAP	27.8([18]) / 42.2([20])	–
M2LATM [11]	41.3	41.9
ALE/HLE/AHLE [1]	37.4/39.0/43.5	–
Mo/Ma/O/D [29]	27.0 / 23.6 / 33.0 / 35.7	–
PST [27]	42.7	36.2*
[35]	43.4	–

the same RGB colour histograms, SIFT, rgSIFT, PHOG, SURF and local self-similarity histograms in [18] for AwA, and SIFT, MFCC and STIP as low-level features for USAA as in [8]. We report absolute classification accuracy on USAA and mean accuracy for AwA for direct comparison to published results. The word vector space is trained by the skip model [23] with 100 dimensions[5].

6.1   Evaluating Zero-Shot Learning

Comparisons with State-of-the-Art. Our method (TMV-BLP) is compared against the state-of-the-art models for zero-shot learning in Table 1. For fair comparison, human effort exploited by all compared methods is limited to attribute annotation as in [20,8]. This excludes methods such as [37] which require additional human interventions. Note that our semantic vectors are 'zero' cost for human annotations, because they are generated by projecting classes' textual name into the $\mathcal{V}$ space. Apart from our method, the AHLE method in [1] also use two semantic spaces: attribute and WordNet hierarchy. Different from our embedding framework, AHLE simply concatenates the two spaces. Our TMV-BLP outperforms all the other methods by a noticeable margin on both datasets, showing the effectiveness of our approach.

Effectiveness of Transductive Multi-view Embedding. We validate the contribution of our transductive multi-view embedding space by splitting up and comparing the results of different combinations in Fig. 2 (a): $\mathcal{V}$ vs. $\Gamma(\mathcal{X}+\mathcal{V})$, $\mathcal{A}$ vs. $\Gamma(\mathcal{X}+\mathcal{A})$ and $[\mathcal{V},\mathcal{A}]$ vs. $\Gamma(\mathcal{X}+\mathcal{V}+\mathcal{A})$ (see the caption of Fig. 2(a) for definitions). We use DAP for $\mathcal{A}$ and nearest neighbour for $\mathcal{V}$ and $[\mathcal{V},\mathcal{A}]$, because the prototypes of $\mathcal{V}$ are not binary vectors so DAP cannot be applied. We use TMV-BLP for $\Gamma(\mathcal{X}+\mathcal{V})$ and $\Gamma(\mathcal{X}+\mathcal{A})$. We highlight the following observations: (1) After transductive embedding, $\Gamma(\mathcal{X}+\mathcal{V}+\mathcal{A})$, $\Gamma(\mathcal{X}+\mathcal{V})$ and $\Gamma(\mathcal{X}+\mathcal{A})$ outperform $[\mathcal{V},\mathcal{A}]$, $\mathcal{V}$ and $\mathcal{A}$ respectively. This means that the transductive embedding

---

[5] All codes/features are downloadable from Yanwei's website:
   http://www.eecs.qmul.ac.uk/~yf300/embedding/.

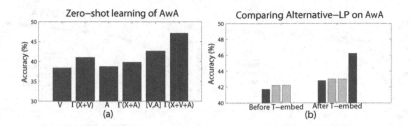

Fig. 2. (a)Effectiveness of transductive multi-view embedding for zero-shot learning on AwA and USAA. $[\mathcal{V}, \mathcal{A}]$ indicates the concatenation of semantic word and attribute space vectors. $\Gamma(\mathcal{X}+\mathcal{V})$ and $\Gamma(\mathcal{X}+\mathcal{A})$ mean using low-level+semantic word spaces and low-level+attribute spaces respectively to learn the embedding. $\Gamma(\mathcal{X}+\mathcal{V}+\mathcal{A})$ indicates using all 3 views to learn the embedding.(b) Comparing alternative label propagation methods. Note: T-embed means Transductive embedding spaces.

is helpful whichever semantic space is used; and validates the effectiveness of the embedding space in rectifying the projection domain shift by aligning the semantic views with low-level features. (2) The results of $[\mathcal{V}, \mathcal{A}]$ are higher than those of $\mathcal{A}$ and $\mathcal{V}$ individually, showing that the two semantic views are indeed complementary. However, our TMV-BLP on all views $\Gamma(\mathcal{X} + \mathcal{V} + \mathcal{A})$ further improves individual embeddings $\Gamma(\mathcal{X} + \mathcal{V})$ and $\Gamma(\mathcal{X} + \mathcal{A})$.

Comparison with Alternative Label Propagation Methods. We also compare two alternative label propagation methods: C-MG [38] and PST [27]. We use equal weights for each graph for C-MG and the same parameters from [27] for PST. We compare all methods before and after the embedding, as shown in Fig. 2(b). The performance of [27] depends on good quality initial labels while our TMV-BLP uses the trivial initial labels in Eq (10). We conclude that: (1) TMV-BLP in our embedding space outperforms both alternatives. (2) The embedding also improves C-MG and PST, due to alleviated projection domain shift via aligning the semantic projections and low-level features. This result shows that both the proposed embedding space and the Bayesian label propagation algorithm contributes to the superior performance of our method.

6.2 Evaluating N-Shot Learning

We next consider N-shot learning on AwA and USAA varying the number of training target class instances. This is challenging when there are few training examples per target class. We also consider the situation [27] where both a few training examples *and* a zero-shot prototype may be available (denoted with suffix +), and contrast it to conventional N-shot learning (denoted with suffix −). Note that our TMV-BLP can be used in both conditions but the PST method [27] mainly applies to the + condition[6]. All experiments use the same training instances and are repeated for 10 rounds to reduce variance. Evaluation is done

---

[6] PST- corresponds to the standard label propagation (see Fig 3(b) in [27]).

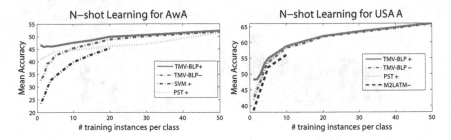

Fig. 3. N-shot learning comparison. PST+ is the method in [27] which uses prototypes for the initial label matrix. SVM+ and M2LATM- are the SVM and M2LATM methods used in [20] and [11] respectively. For fair comparison, we modify the SVM- used in [20] into SVM+.

on the remaining available images from the test split after removing the N instances. From the results shown in Fig. 3, we have the following observations and conclusions: (1) TMV-BLP+ always achieves the best performance, particularly given few training examples. This shows the effectiveness of our framework by combining complementary semantic and low-level feature information. We note that with 50 labelled instances per target class (fully supervised), using SVM with RBF kernel in the embedded space Γ obtains the same results as our TMV-BLP+, because the transductive kernel matrix (inverse of the Laplacian matrix $\mathcal{L}$) essentially models the same information as the SVM kernel matrix [32]. (2) As clearly shown in the AwA results, PST+ outperforms TMV-BLP- with less than 10 instances per class because PST+ exploits the prototypes. This suggests that a single good prototype is more informative than a few labelled instances in N-shot learning. This also explains when only few training labels are observed why the N-shot learning results of TMV-BLP+ are worse than its zero-shot learning results. (3) Nevertheless, TMV-BLP- still surpasses PST+ with more training instances because TMV-BLP combines the different views of the training instances, and the strong effect of the prototype is outweighed as more labelled instances become available.

6.3   Evaluating Annotation

Instance Annotation by Attributes. To quantify the annotation performance, we predict attributes/annotations for each target class instance for USAA. We employ two standard measures: mean average precision (mAP) and F-measure (FM) between the estimated and true annotation list. Using our three-view embedding space, our method (FM:0.341, mAP: 0.355) outperforms significantly the baseline of directly estimating $\mathbf{y}_u^{\mathcal{A}} = f^{\mathcal{A}}(\mathbf{x}_u)$ (FM:0.299, mAP: 0.267).

Novel Annotation Tasks Beyond Visual Recognition. We next illustrate two novel annotation tasks. In the *Zero-Shot Description* task, we explicitly infer the member attributes, given only the textual name of a novel class. Table 2 illustrates this for AwA by showing that the top/bottom 5 attributes associated

Table 2. Ranking attributes of AwA unseen testing classes. Bold font illustrates true positives; italic illustrates true negatives

AwA	raccoon	giant panda	humpback+whale	rat
top-5	**furry, quadrupedal, tail, nest spot, tree**	**vegetation, furry,** hops, grazer, **quadrupedal**.	nest spot, **slow, tail,** quadrupedal, weak	**tail,** nest spot, weak, **quadrupedal,** grazer
bot-5	*smart, bipedal, swims, tough skin, hairless*	*swims, ocean, hairless,* new world	*claws, hands,* big, new world, *bipedal*	*tusks,* small, new world, *bipedal*

with each class are meaningful (in ideal cases, all top 5 should be true positives and all bottom 5 true negatives). In the *Zero-Attribute Learning* task we attempt the reverse, inferring class names given a list of attributes. Table 3(a) shows the query attributes used for USAA (note that class name is shown for brevity, but it is the attributes of the classes that are queried) and the top-4 ranked list of classes returned. We emphasise the average rank of the true class is an impressive 2.13 (out of 4.33M vocabulary with chance-level 2.3×10^{-7}), compared with the average rank of 110.24 by directly querying word space [23] by using the textual descriptions of attributes. Table 3(b) shows an example of "incremental" query of using ontology definition of birthday party [11]. We firstly query by the *wrapped presents* attribute only, followed by adding *small balloon* and all the other attributes (*birthday songs* and *birthday caps*). The changing list of top ranked retrieved words intuitively reflects the expectation of the combinatorial meaning of the attributes.

Table 3. (a) Querying by attributes of classes. g,m and w_c indicate graduation party, music_performance and wedding_ceremony respectively. (b) An incrementally constructed query for birthday party. Bold indicates true positive words retrieved.

(a)	Query via embedding space	Query attribute words in word space
g	**party, graduation,** audience, caucus	cheering, proudly, dressed, wearing
m	**music, performance,** musical, heavy metal	sing, singer, sang, dancing
w_c	**w_c,** wedding, glosses, stag	nun, christening, bridegroom, **w_c**

(b) Attribute Query	Top Ranked Words
wrapped presents	music; performance; solo_performances;performing
+small balloon	wedding; wedding_reception; birthday_celebration; birthday
+All attitutes	**birthday_party;** prom; wedding reception

7   Conclusions and Future Work

We identified the challenge of projection domain shift in zero-shot learning and presented a new framework TMV-BLP to solve it by rectifying the biased projections in an embedding space. TMV-BLP synergistically exploits multiple intermediate semantic representations, as well as the manifold structure of unlabelled

598 Y. Fu et al.

test data to improve recognition in a unified way for both zero and N-shot learning tasks. So we achieve state-of-the-art performance on the challenging AwA and USAA datasets. Finally, we demonstrate that our framework enables novel tasks of relating textual class names and their semantic attributes.

References

1. Akata, Z., Perronnin, F., Harchaoui, Z., Schmid, C.: Label-embedding for attribute-based classification. In: CVPR (2013)
2. Banerjee, A., Dhillon, I.S., Ghosh, J., Sra, S.: Clustering on the unit hypersphere using von mises-fisher distributions. JMLR (2005)
3. Biederman, I.: Recognition by components - a theory of human image understanding. Psychological Review (1987)
4. Blitzer, J., Foster, D.P., Kakade, S.M.: Zero-shot domain adaptation: A multi-view approach (2009)
5. Brown, P.F., Pietra, V.J.: V.deSouza, P., C.Lai, J., L.Mercer, R.: Class-based n-gram models of natural language. Journal Computational Linguistics (1992)
6. Farhadi, A., Endres, I., Hoiem, D., Forsyth, D.: Describing objects by their attributes. In: CVPR (2009)
7. Frome, A., Corrado, G.S., Shlens, J., Bengio, S., Dean, J., Ranzato, M., Mikolov, T.: Devise: A deep visual-semantic embedding model andrea. In: NIPS (2013)
8. Fu, Y., Hospedales, T.M., Xiang, T., Gong, S.: Attribute learning for understanding unstructured social activity. In: Fitzgibbon, A., Lazebnik, S., Perona, P., Sato, Y., Schmid, C. (eds.) ECCV 2012, Part IV. LNCS, vol. 7575, pp. 530–543. Springer, Heidelberg (2012)
9. Fu, Y.: Multi-view metric learning for multi-view video summarization (2014), http://arxiv.org/abs/1405.6434
10. Fu, Y., Guo, Y., Zhu, Y., Liu, F., Song, C., Zhou, Z.H.: Multi-view video summarization. IEEE TMM 12(7), 717–729 (2010)
11. Fu, Y., Hospedales, T.M., Xiang, T., Gong, S.: Learning multi-modal latent attributes. TPAMI (2013)
12. Fu, Y., Hospedales, T.M., Xiang, T., Gongy, S., Yao, Y.: Interestingness prediction by robust learning to rank. In: Fleet, D., Pajdla, T., Schiele, B., Tuytelaars, T. (eds.) ECCV 2014, Part II. LNCS, vol. 8690, pp. 488–503. Springer, Heidelberg (2014)
13. Gong, Y., Ke, Q., Isard, M., Lazebnik, S.: A multi-view embedding space for modeling internet images, tags, and their semantics. IJCV (2013)
14. Hardoon, D.R., Szedmak, S., Shawe-Taylor, J.: Canonical correlation analysis; an overview with application to learning methods. In: Neural Computation (2004)
15. Hospedales, T., Gong, S., Xiang, T.: Learning tags from unsegmented videos of multiple human actions. In: ICDM (2011)
16. Hwang, S.J., Grauman, K.: Learning the relative importance of objects from tagged images for retrieval and cross-modal search. IJCV (2011)
17. Hwang, S.J., Sha, F., Grauman, K.: Sharing features between objects and their attributes. In: CVPR (2011)
18. Lampert, C.H., Nickisch, H., Harmeling, S.: Learning to detect unseen object classes by between-class attribute transfer. In: CVPR (2009)
19. Lampert, C.H.: Kernel methods in computer vision. Foundations and Trends in Computer Graphics and Vision (2009)

20. Lampert, C.H., Nickisch, H., Harmeling, S.: Attribute-based classification for zero-shot visual object categorization. IEEE TPAMI (2013)
21. Liu, J., Kuipers, B., Savarese, S.: Recognizing human actions by attributes. In: CVPR (2011)
22. van der Maaten, L., Hinton, G.: Visualizing high-dimensional data using t-sne. JMLR (2008)
23. Mikolov, T., Chen, K., Corrado, G., Dean, J.: Efficient estimation of word representation in vector space. In: Proceedings of Workshop at ICLR (2013)
24. Mikolov, T., Sutskever, I., Chen, K., Corrado, G., Dean, J.: Distributed representations of words and phrases and their compositionality. In: Proceedings of NIPS (2013)
25. Palatucci, M., Hinton, G., Pomerleau, D., Mitchell, T.M.: Zero-shot learning with semantic output codes. In: NIPS (2009)
26. Parikh, D., Grauman, K.: Relative attributes. In: ICCV (2011)
27. Rohrbach, M., Ebert, S., Schiele, B.: Transfer learning in a transductive setting. In: NIPS (2013)
28. Rohrbach, M., Stark, M., Schiele, B.: Evaluating knowledge transfer and zero-shot learning in a large-scale setting. In: CVPR (2012)
29. Rohrbach, M., Stark, M., Szarvas, G., Gurevych, I., Schiele, B.: What helps where—and why semantic relatedness for knowledge transfer. In: CVPR (2010)
30. Scheirer, W.J., Kumar, N., Belhumeur, P.N., Boult, T.E.: Multi-attribute spaces: Calibration for attribute fusion and similarity search. In: CVPR (2012)
31. Shi, Z., Yang, Y., Hospedales, T.M., Xiang, T.: Weakly supervised learning of objects, attributes and their associations. In: Fleet, D., Pajdla, T., Schiele, B., Tuytelaars, T. (eds.) ECCV 2014, Part II. LNCS, vol. 8690, pp. 472–487. Springer, Heidelberg (2014)
32. Smola, A.J., Kondor, R.: Kernels and regularization on graphs. In: Schölkopf, B., Warmuth, M.K. (eds.) COLT/Kernel 2003. LNCS (LNAI), vol. 2777, pp. 144–158. Springer, Heidelberg (2003)
33. Socher, R., Fei-Fei, L.: Connecting modalities: Semi-supervised segmentation and annotation of images using unaligned text corpora. In: CVPR (2010)
34. Socher, R., Ganjoo, M., Sridhar, H., Bastani, O., Manning, C.D., Ng, A.Y.: Zero-shot learning through cross-modal transfer. In: NIPS (2013)
35. Wang, X., Ji, Q.: A unified probabilistic approach modeling relationships between attributes and objects. In: ICCV (2013)
36. Wang, Y., Gong, S.: Translating topics to words for image annotation. In: ACM CIKM (2007)
37. Yu, F.X., Cao, L., Feris, R.S., Smith, J.R., Chang, S.F.: Designing category-level attributes for discriminative visual recognition. In: CVPR (2013)
38. Zhou, D., Burges, C.J.C.: Spectral clustering and transductive learning with multiple views. In: ICML 2007 (2007)

Self-explanatory Sparse Representation
for Image Classification

Bao-Di Liu[1,*], Yu-Xiong Wang[2,*], Bin Shen[3,**], Yu-Jin Zhang[4],
and Martial Hebert[2]

[1] Col. of Information and Control Engineering, China University of Petroleum,
Qingdao 266580, China
`thu.liubaodi@gmail.com`
[2] Robotics Institute, Carnegie Mellon University, Pittsburgh, PA 15213, USA
`yuxiongw@cs.cmu.edu, hebert@ri.cmu.edu`
[3] Dept. of Computer Science, Purdue University, West Lafayette, IN 47907, USA
`bshen@purdue.edu`
[4] Dept. of Electronic Engineering, Tsinghua University, Beijing 100084, China
`zhang-yj@mail.tsinghua.edu.cn`

Abstract. Traditional sparse representation algorithms usually operate
in a single Euclidean space. This paper leverages a self-explanatory reformulation of sparse representation, i.e., linking the learned dictionary
atoms with the original feature spaces explicitly, to extend simultaneous
dictionary learning and sparse coding into reproducing kernel Hilbert
spaces (RKHS). The resulting single-view self-explanatory sparse representation (SSSR) is applicable to an arbitrary kernel space and has
the nice property that the derivatives with respect to parameters of the
coding are independent of the chosen kernel. With SSSR, multiple-view
self-explanatory sparse representation (MSSR) is proposed to capture
and combine various salient regions and structures from different kernel
spaces. This is equivalent to learning a nonlinear structured dictionary,
whose complexity is reduced by learning a set of smaller dictionary blocks
via SSSR. SSSR and MSSR are then incorporated into a spatial pyramid
matching framework and developed for image classification. Extensive experimental results on four benchmark datasets, including UIUC-Sports,
Scene 15, Caltech-101, and Caltech-256, demonstrate the effectiveness of
our proposed algorithm.

Keywords: Reproducing Kernel Hilbert Spaces, Sparse Representation,
Multiple View, Image Classification.

1 Introduction

After decades of effort, the power of sparse representation has been gradually
revealed in visual computation areas, such as image annotation [21,22], image

---

* Contributed equally to this paper.
** Corresponding author.

D. Fleet et al. (Eds.): ECCV 2014, Part II, LNCS 8690, pp. 600–616, 2014.

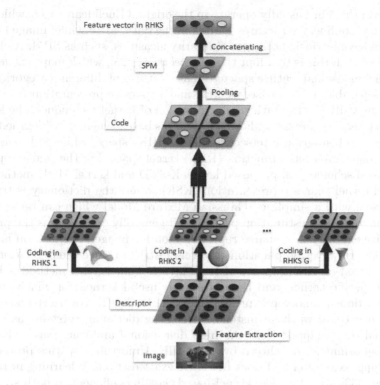

Fig. 1. Flowchart of the proposed SSSR & MSSR dictionary learning and coding process for image classification

inpainting [27,36], and have achieved impressive performance. Different from traditional decomposition frameworks like PCA, non-negative matrix factorization [28,29,37,39], and low-rank factorization [30,31,35], sparse representation [16] allows coding under over-complete bases (i.e., the number of bases is greater than the input data dimension), and thus generates sparse codes capable of representing the data more adaptively.

One example task is image classification [18,19,40], which aims to associate images with semantic labels automatically. The most common framework is the discriminative model [12,38,40]. There are five main steps: feature extraction, dictionary learning, image coding, image pooling, and SVM-based classification. Dictionary (also called vocabulary) learning is the key step here. One standard version of vocabulary learning is K-means clustering on image patches combined with hard- or soft-assignment vector quantization (VQ) [7]. Spatial pyramid matching (SPM) is typically incorporated in the pipeline to compensate the loss of spatial information [12]. In 2009, [40] introduced sparse representation algorithm for learning dictionary and coding images based on SPM, resulting in state-of-the-art performance in image classification.

Works of this kind usually operate in the original Euclidean space, which cannot capture nonlinear structures hidden in the data. Meanwhile, image descriptors often have intrinsic nonlinear similarity measures, such as SPM. A classical way to deal with this is to adopt the *"kernel trick"* [25], which maps the features into high dimensional feature space to make features of different categories more linearly separable. In this case, we may find a sparse representation for the features more easily [5,41]. With the introduction of kernel techniques, the learned dictionary becomes versatile. For the K-means based scheme, [38] learned a dictionary in the histogram intersection kernel (HIK) space, while [8] learned it in the Gaussian radial basis function (RBF) kernel space. For the sparse representation based scheme, [23] proposed kernel K-SVD and kernel MOD methods. [4] proposed kernel sparse representation (KSR), where the dictionary is trimmed to work well with a simplified Gaussian Mixture Model which can be viewed as a solution to density estimation problems. It generally outperforms the previous alternative extensions of sparse representation for image classification and face recognition. However, applications are very restricted since the derivation is exclusively based on the property of RBF kernel. That is, this method is limited to a few specific kernels and there are many useful kernels for which even the kernel functions cannot be expressed mathematically. To cover arbitrary kernel spaces, their other work [5] instead learned the dictionary first in the original space, and then mapped it to the high dimensional ambient space, whose improved performance was shown by using HIK. Unfortunately, this procedure is only an approximation and does not solve exact dictionary learning in the kernel space. [33] aims to make kernel-based classifiers efficient in both space and time. Sparse coding here is exploited to approximate the mapped features in the kernel space. There is no dictionary learning involved. They apply it to large image feature vectors, such as Fisher encoding, and the cost of non-linear SVM prediction is reduced by this approximation while maintaining the classification accuracy above an acceptable threshold. [3,20] point out that the data are self-explanatory. These approaches have many applications. However, treating the samples as a dictionary is almost impossible for the application of image classification based on bags of words, since we may easily have more than millions of local features to form the matrix. Thus, it is usually too expensive to calculate the sparse codes. [17] proposed a self-explanatory convex sparse representation for image classification. However, the additional convexity constraint is too restrictive to obtain better performance in practice.

Given that existing work either handles specific kernels or is implemented as an approximation, an issue arises naturally: we need a systematic scheme to generalize sparse representation into reproducing kernel Hilbert spaces (RKHS), which can directly learn dictionaries for arbitrary kernels. This leads to the first contribution of this paper, i.e., single-view self-explanatory sparse representation (SSSR). The key idea here is a new formulation as self-explanatory sparse representation inspired by the representer theorem of Schölkopf et al. [26], which enforces each dictionary atom in the RKHS to lie in the span of the features. Owing to the properties of this reformulation, the sparse representation can be tractably solved in arbitrary kernel spaces. The procedures do not require that the mathematical form of any kernel function be known, rather they work directly on the kernel matrices. It thus has the nice property that the derivatives with respect to parameters of the coding are independent of the used kernel. It also presents an explicit relationship between the basis vectors and the original image features, leading to enhanced interpretability.

On the other hand, a single kernel is generally not enough. Multiple kernel learning (MKL) and multiple view learning have thus been flourishing in computer vision [9]. Different kernels correspond to different implicit feature transformations, which result in different measures of similarity in the original feature space. MKL tries to integrate the power of different kernels by learning a weighted linear combination of them. A typical example is [42], which selects different input features and combines them by mapping them to a homogeneous Gaussian RBF kernel space.

Motivated by the success of the above SSSR for arbitrary kernels and multiple kernel learning [32], we propose multiple-view self-explanatory sparse representation (MSSR) to identify and combine various salient regions and structures from different kernel spaces. This is the second contribution of this paper. It is equivalent to learning a dictionary with non-linear structure, whose complexity is reduced by learning a set of smaller dictionary blocks via SSSR. Slightly different from the typical MKL scenario metioned above [42], here we exploit the nonlinear representation capability. That is, only a single source of the original image features is chosen while various kernel subspaces are merged. To effectively solve the corresponding sparse coding subproblem and dictionary learning subproblem, feature-sign search [13] and Lagrange multipliers are then generalized in the high dimensional space. As an application example, we incorporate SSSR and MSSR into the spatial pyramid matching framework and develop them for image classification. In fact, SSSR and MSSR could also be used in many other applications. The extensive experimental results demonstrate that the proposed SSSR and MSSR algorithms can learn more discriminative sparse codes than sparse coding, leading to improved performance in image classification. A flowchart of the proposed algorithm is illustrated in Figure 1.

The rest of the paper is organized as follows. Section 2 overviews sparse representation briefly, and introduces self-explanatory sparse representation reformulation naturally. SSSR and MSSR algorithms are proposed in Section 3. The solutions to the corresponding optimization problems are elaborated in Section 4. The overall algorithm is also summarized. Experimental results on several benchmark datasets are given in Section 5. Finally, discussions and conclusions are drawn in Section 6.

2   Self-explanatory Sparse Representation

We assume that the data vectors can be represented as linear combinations of only few active basis vectors that carry the majority of the energy of the data.

Formally, we solve the following problem:

$$\min_{\boldsymbol{B},\boldsymbol{S}} f(\boldsymbol{B},\boldsymbol{S}) = \|\boldsymbol{X} - \boldsymbol{B}\boldsymbol{S}\|_F^2 + 2\alpha\|\boldsymbol{S}\|_1$$

$$s.t. \ \|\boldsymbol{B}_{\bullet i}\|_2 \leq 1, \forall i = 1, 2, \ldots, K. \tag{1}$$

Here, $\boldsymbol{X} \in \mathbb{R}^{D \times N}$ represents the local descriptors extracted from images, where D is the dimension of $\boldsymbol{X}$, and N is the number of samples in $\boldsymbol{X}$. $\boldsymbol{B} \in \mathbb{R}^{D \times K}$ is the dictionary, where K is the size of the dictionary. $\boldsymbol{S} \in \mathbb{R}^{K \times N}$ is the corresponding sparse codes. $\|\cdot\|_F^2$ represents the Frobenius norm. $\boldsymbol{B}_{\bullet i}$ and $\boldsymbol{B}_{j\bullet}$ denote the i-th column and j-th row vectors of matrix $\boldsymbol{B}$, respectively. The regularization term is to control sparsity in $\boldsymbol{S}$, where α is a regularization parameter balancing the tradeoff between fitting goodness and sparseness.

However, there is no explicit relationship between the learned dictionary and the original features in the above formulation. Notice that K-means can be viewed as a special case of sparse representation with $\|\boldsymbol{S}_{\bullet i}\|_0 = 1, \|\boldsymbol{S}_{\bullet i}\|_1 = 1, \boldsymbol{S}_{\bullet i} \geq 0$, while its learned dictionary atoms are the centroids of the input data. Hence, for reasons of interpretability it may be useful to impose the constraint that each basis vector lies within the column space of the original features $\boldsymbol{X}$. By introducing the weight matrix $\boldsymbol{W} \in \mathbb{R}^{N \times K}$ and substituting the bases $\boldsymbol{B}$ in (1) with $\boldsymbol{X}\boldsymbol{W}$, we get a new formulation as self-explanatory sparse representation:

$$\min_{\boldsymbol{W},\boldsymbol{S}} f(\boldsymbol{W},\boldsymbol{S}) = \|\boldsymbol{X} - \boldsymbol{X}\boldsymbol{W}\boldsymbol{S}\|_F^2 + 2\alpha\|\boldsymbol{S}\|_1$$

$$s.t. \ \|\boldsymbol{X}\boldsymbol{W}_{\bullet k}\|_2 \leq 1, \forall k = 1, 2, \ldots, K. \tag{2}$$

Typically $K \ll N$, and the trivial solution $\boldsymbol{W} = \boldsymbol{I}$ is thus naturally ruled out. Actually, these two formulations can be unified from the perspective of the representer theorem of Schölkopf et al. [26]. When applied to the linear kernel, the solution to Eqn. 1, when minimizing over $\boldsymbol{B}$, is going to be of the form $\boldsymbol{B} = \boldsymbol{X}\boldsymbol{W}$. Hence, Eqn. 2 can be intuitively viewed as the "dual" reformulation of Eqn. 1, the "primal" form of the sparse representation problem, and gives the same solution. This is better understood if one draws an analogy with linear SVM training: one can formulate the training problem as an optimization over 1) either directly the weights of a linear classifier vector of the same dimension as the input signal 2) or the support vectors weights, that is a vector of dimension equal to the size of the training set that is used to linearly combine the training inputs. In the context of the problem here, the linear classifier is analogous to the dictionary $\boldsymbol{B}$, and the support vector weights are analogous to the weights $\boldsymbol{W}$.

Replacing the bases with linear combinations of image features has several advantages. The atoms now capture a notion of centroids similar to K-means, which explicitly expresses what happens during dictionary learning, leading to enhanced interpretability. Correspondingly, the code $\boldsymbol{S}$ can be interpreted as the posterior cluster probabilities and the weight $\boldsymbol{W}$ can be considered as the contributions of each data point when learning bases. Sparse representation and K-means can be thus unified in the same framework. Moreover, by confining the search space of potential bases, it might limit overfitting. The weight $\boldsymbol{W}$ makes the scenario more flexible, and different constraints like non-negativity can be incorporated into it so as to adapt to various tasks, while they might be difficult to directly impose on B. An obvious cost of the reformulation is the increased computational complexity, because $D \ll N$ generally for over-complete representation. However, we will soon discover in the next section that it actually facilitates our solution with executable steps in the nonlinear kernel spaces.

3   Single- and Multiple-View Self-explanatory Sparse Representation

3.1   Single View Formulation

Besides the interpretability, another important property for self-explanatory sparse representation is that it is easy to kernelize due to the separation of original data. Suppose that there exists a feature mapping function $\phi : \mathbb{R}^D \to \mathbb{R}^t$. It maps the original feature space to the high dimensional kernel space: $X = [X_{\bullet 1}, X_{\bullet 2}, \cdots, X_{\bullet N}] \to \phi(X) = [\phi(X_{\bullet 1}), \phi(X_{\bullet 2}), \cdots, \phi(X_{\bullet N})]$. Then, the objective function of (2) can be generalized to reproducing kernel Hilbert spaces as

$$\min_{W,S} f(W, S) = \|\phi(X) - \phi(X)WS\|_H^2 + 2\alpha \|S\|_1$$
$$\text{s.t. } \|\phi(X)W_{\bullet k}\|_H \leq 1, \forall k = 1, 2, \ldots, K, \tag{3}$$

which is single-view self-explanatory sparse representation (SSSR).

Now, the Frobenius norm has been replaced by the inner-product norm of that Hilbert space, such that $\|\phi(X)\|_H^2 = \kappa(X, X)$, with kernel function $\kappa(X_{\bullet i}, X_{\bullet j}) = \phi(X_{\bullet i})^T \phi(X_{\bullet j})$. The dictionary becomes a set of K arbitrary functions in that Hilbert space. Using the "kernel trick", we get

$$\|\phi(X) - \phi(X)WS\|_H^2 + 2\alpha\|S\|_1$$
$$= trace\{\kappa(X, X)\} - 2trace\{\kappa(X, X)WS\} \tag{4}$$
$$+ trace\{S^T W^T \kappa(X, X)WS\} + 2\alpha\|S\|_1.$$

On the other hand, if directly kernelizing the primal form (1), we get

$$\min_{B,S} f(B, S) = \|\phi(X) - \phi(B)S\|_H^2 + 2\alpha\|S\|_1. \tag{5}$$

Still, according to the representer theorem [26], the solution $\phi(B)$ to problem (5) has the form $\phi(B) = \phi(X)W$. This is already explicitly encoded in the formulation (3). That is, Eqns. 5, 3 are intuitively akin to the primal and dual forms of sparse representation in the Hilbert spaces.

There are also some benefits which make the dual form (3) preferable. Exactly optimizing to the standard formulation (5) is quite difficult. In the new high dimensional space, t, the dimension of $\phi(X) \gg$ the number of samples N, perhaps even infinite. By leveraging the "kernel trick", this can only be partially tackled.

Since $\boldsymbol{B}$ is involved in $\kappa(\boldsymbol{B}, \boldsymbol{B})$, the optimal solution to $\boldsymbol{B}$ is always related to the partial derivative of $\kappa(\boldsymbol{B}, \boldsymbol{B})$ with respect to $\boldsymbol{B}$, which is relatively easy only for some specific kernels [4]. For others, only an approximation strategy is feasible, where the dictionary in the kernel space is transformed from the one learned in the original space [5]. There is no guarantee that the transformation of the optimal dictionary in the original space will remain optimal in the kernel space. However, using the equivalent formulation (3), we can now search an optimal dictionary directly in the kernel space through optimizing $\boldsymbol{W}$ instead of $\boldsymbol{B}$. Since (4) only depends on the kernel function $\kappa(\boldsymbol{X}, \boldsymbol{X}) = \phi(\boldsymbol{X})^T \phi(\boldsymbol{X})$, which can be pre-computed before sparse representation, we can now handle arbitrary kernels with tractable computation.

3.2 Multiple View Joint Formulation

Using a single specific kernel may be a source of bias, and in allowing a learner to combine a set of kernels, a better solution can be found. Here, instead of choosing a single kernel function, a feasible alternative is to use a combination of kernels as in multiple kernel learning (MKL) methods.

Assume there are G candidate Hilbert spaces forming a set as $\mathcal{H} = \{H_1, ..., H_g, ..., H_G\}$, and the corresponding kernel functions $\left\{\kappa_g : \mathbb{R}^{D_g} \times \mathbb{R}^{D_g} \to \mathbb{R}\right\}_{g=1}^{G}$ with $\kappa_g(\boldsymbol{X}_{\bullet i}, \boldsymbol{X}_{\bullet j}) = \phi_g(\boldsymbol{X}_{\bullet i})^T \phi_g(\boldsymbol{X}_{\bullet j})$. Candidate spaces include the well-known linear kernel space, the polynomial kernel space, the Gaussian RBF kernel, and widely used ones in vision community such as the Hellinger kernel space and the histogram intersection kernel space. Given the original G feature representations $\boldsymbol{X}^g$ with dimension $D_g \times N$ (not necessarily different) of data instances and mapping them to these different Hilbert spaces, the general formulation for multiple kernel learning sparse representation is

$$\kappa_\eta \left(\boldsymbol{X}_{\bullet i}, \boldsymbol{X}_{\bullet j}\right) = f_\eta \left(\left\{\kappa_g \left(\boldsymbol{X}_{\bullet i}^g, \boldsymbol{X}_{\bullet j}^g\right)_{g=1}^{G}\right\}\right), \tag{6}$$

where $f_\eta : \mathbb{R}^G \to \mathbb{R}$ is a linear or nonlinear function combination function. The weight matrix $\boldsymbol{W}$ and $\boldsymbol{S}$ are also redefined in different spaces as $\boldsymbol{W} = \{\boldsymbol{W}^g\}_{g=1}^{G}$ and $\boldsymbol{S} = \{\boldsymbol{S}^g\}_{g=1}^{G}$.

For visual tasks, $\boldsymbol{S}$ is the most important part in that it serves as the newly mapped feature representation and the input of the final classifiers. Since different kernels correspond to different notions of similarity, $\{\boldsymbol{S}^g\}_{g=1}^{G}$ in different Hilbert spaces will capture various salient regions or structures, making the final representation more discriminative. Here, we fix the input features from a single source, and focus on its combination, and then generalize (3) to multiple-view self-explanatory sparse representation (MSSR):

$$\min_{\boldsymbol{W}, \boldsymbol{S}} f(\boldsymbol{W}, \boldsymbol{S}) = \sum_{H_g \in \mathcal{H}} \|\phi^g(\boldsymbol{X}) - \phi^g(\boldsymbol{X})\boldsymbol{W}^g \boldsymbol{S}^g\|_{H_g}^2 + 2\alpha \|\boldsymbol{S}^g\|_1$$

$$s.t. \|\phi^g(\boldsymbol{X})\boldsymbol{W}^g_{\bullet k}\|_{H_g} \leq 1, \forall k = 1, \ldots, K, g = 1, \ldots, G. \tag{7}$$

After obtaining $\{S^g\}$, we concatenate them to form the final representation as S. Another notable benefit is that since each set $\{W^g, S^g\}$ can be learned and inferred independently from each other, the computational cost is significantly reduced if a large weight matrix W is required. Generally speaking, for sparse representation a larger dictionary will lead to better performance while the computational consumption grows beyond linear increase. Moreover, since our dictionary blocks are built from different kernel spaces, it will outperform the one coming from the same kernel space. In our experiments, we show that learning 4,096 bases in total by learning four sets of 1,024 bases separately, outperforms 4,096 bases obtained from the single kernel space both in speed and classification accuracy.

4   Optimization of the Objective Function

In this section, we focus on solving the optimization of the objective function proposed in the last section. This optimization problem is not jointly convex in both W^g and S^g, but is separately convex in either W^g or S^g with S^g or W^g fixed. So the objective function can be optimized by alternating minimization to two optimization subproblems as follows.

– With fixed W^g, the objective function of finding sparse codes S^g can be written as an ℓ_1- regularized least-squares ($\ell_1 - ls$) minimization subproblem:

$$f(S^g) = \|\phi^g(X) - \phi^g(X)W^g S^g\|_F^2 + 2\alpha\|S^g\|_1 \qquad (8)$$

– With fixed S^g, the objective function of learning weight W^g can be written as an ℓ_2- constrained least-squares ($\ell_2 - ls$) minimization subproblem:

$$f(W^g) = \|\phi^g(X) - \phi^g(X)W^g S^g\|_F^2$$
$$s.t. \|\phi^g(X)W^g_{\bullet k}\|_2^2 \le 1, \ \forall k = 1, 2, \cdots, K. \qquad (9)$$

4.1 $\ell_1 - ls$ Minimization Subproblem

Eqn. 8 can be simplified as

$$f(S^g) = trace\{\kappa^g(X, X)\} - 2\sum_{n=1}^{N} [\kappa^g(X, X)W^g]_{n\bullet} S^g_{\bullet n}$$
$$+ \sum_{n=1}^{N} S^{g^T}_{\bullet n}[W^{g^T}\kappa^g(X, X)W^g]S^g_{\bullet n} + 2\alpha\sum_{k=1}^{K}\sum_{n=1}^{N}|S^g_{kn}|. \qquad (10)$$

For each feature x in X, the objective function in Eqn. 10 can be rewritten as

$$f(s^g) = \kappa^g(x, x) + s^{g^T}U s^g - 2V s^g + 2\alpha\|s^g\|_1, \qquad (11)$$

where $U = W^{g^T}\kappa^g(X, X)W^g$, $V = \kappa^g(x, X)W^g$. Once the W^g and $\kappa^g(X, X)$ are fixed, we can easily extend the feature-sign search algorithm [13] to optimize the objective function.

Denoting $L(s^g) = \kappa^g(x, x) + s^{gT} U s^g - 2V s^g$, then

$$\frac{\partial L(s^g)}{\partial s^g} = 2U s^g - 2V^T, \tag{12}$$

$$\frac{\partial^2 L(s^g)}{\partial^2 s^g} = 2U. \tag{13}$$

The sparse coding algorithm can be represented as solving the problem: $\min_{s^g} L(s^g)$ $+2\alpha \|s^g\|_1$. The detailed algorithmic procedure uses Algorithm 1 in [5]. Note that the computational cost of SSSR or MSSR is the same as that of sparse coding in [13] except for the additional expenditure in calculating the different kernel matrix.

4.2 $\ell_2 - ls$ Minimization Subproblem

Ignoring the unrelated term, Eqn. 9 can be simplified as

$$f(W^g) = -2 \sum_{k=1}^{K} [S^g \kappa^g(X, X)]_{k\bullet} W^g_{\bullet k} + \sum_{k=1}^{K} W^{gT}_{\bullet k} [\kappa^g(X, X) W^g S^g S^{gT}]_{\bullet k} \tag{14}$$
$$s.t. \|\phi^g(X) W^g_{\bullet k}\|_2^2 \leq 1, \forall k = 1, 2, \cdots, K.$$

We optimize each column of W^g alternately. Specifically, ignoring the constant term $trace\{\kappa^g(X, X)\}$, the Lagrangian is

$$\mathcal{L}(W^g, \lambda_k) = \sum_{k=1}^{K} W^{gT}_{\bullet k} [\kappa^g(X, X) W^g S^g S^{gT}]_{\bullet k} - 2 \sum_{k=1}^{K} [S^g \kappa^g(X, X)]_{k\bullet} W^g_{\bullet k} \tag{15}$$
$$+ \lambda_k (1 - [W^{gT} \kappa^g(X, X) W^g]_{kk}).$$

The partial derivative with respect to $W^g_{\bullet k}$ is

$$\frac{\partial \mathcal{L}(W^g, \lambda_k)}{\partial W^g_{\bullet k}} = 0. \tag{16}$$

Hence, the solution to $W^g_{\bullet k}$ is obtained as

$$W^g_{\bullet k} = \frac{S^{gT}_{k\bullet} - [\widetilde{W^g}^k F]_{\bullet k}}{F_{kk} - \lambda_k}, \tag{17}$$

where $F = S^g S^{gT}$, $\widetilde{W^g}^k = \begin{cases} W^g_{\bullet p}, & p \neq k \\ 0, & p = k \end{cases}$. Now, substituting $W^g_{\bullet k}$ into the Lagrangian and only keeping the term including $W^g_{\bullet k}$, we then have

$$\mathcal{L}(W^g, \lambda_k) = \lambda_k + \frac{(S^T_{k\bullet} - [\widetilde{W^g}^k F]_{\bullet k})^T \kappa^g(X,X)(S^g_{k\bullet}{}^T - [\widetilde{W^g}^k F]_{\bullet k})}{\lambda_k - F_{kk}}. \tag{18}$$

Thus, λ_k can be obtained. Substituting λ_k into $W^g_{\bullet k}$,

$$W^g_{\bullet k} = \frac{S^g_{k\bullet}{}^T - [\widetilde{W^g}^k F]_{\bullet k}}{\pm\sqrt{(S^g_{k\bullet}{}^T - [\widetilde{W^g}^k F]_{\bullet k})^T \kappa^g(X,X)(S^g_{k\bullet}{}^T - [\widetilde{W^g}^k F]_{\bullet k})}}. \tag{19}$$

From Eqn. 19, two solutions are obtained with $\pm$ signs. The sign of $W^g_{\bullet k}$ is not essential since it can be easily absorbed by converting between $S^g_{k\bullet}$ and $-S^g_{k\bullet}$.

Algorithm 1 Algorithm for SSSR or MSSR

Require: Data matrix $\boldsymbol{X} \in \mathbb{R}^{D \times N}$, α and K
1: Compute the kernels $\kappa(\boldsymbol{X}, \boldsymbol{X})$ on $\boldsymbol{X}$.
2: $\boldsymbol{W} \leftarrow rand(N,K) - 0.5$, $\boldsymbol{S} \leftarrow zeros(K,N) - 0.5$
3: Compute $\boldsymbol{F} = \boldsymbol{S}\boldsymbol{S}^T$, $\boldsymbol{G} = \boldsymbol{F} \odot (1 - \boldsymbol{I})$
4: **for** $k = 1; k \leq K; k{+}{+}$ **do**
5:     $\delta = \boldsymbol{W}_{\bullet k}^T \kappa(\boldsymbol{X}, \boldsymbol{X}) \boldsymbol{W}_{\bullet k}$
6:     $\boldsymbol{W}_{\bullet k} = \boldsymbol{W}_{\bullet k}/\sqrt{\delta}$
7: **end for**
8: $iter = 0$
9: **while** $(f(iter) - f(iter + 1))/f(iter) > 1e - 5$ **do**
10:     $iter \leftarrow iter + 1$
11:     **Update** $\boldsymbol{S}$:
12:     Sparse coding: compute using feature-sign search algorithm
13:     **Update** $\boldsymbol{W}$:
14:     Compute $\boldsymbol{F} = \boldsymbol{S}\boldsymbol{S}^T$, $\boldsymbol{G} = \boldsymbol{F} \odot (1 - \boldsymbol{I})$
15:     **for** $k = 1; k \leq K; k{+}{+}$ **do**
16:         $\boldsymbol{W}_{\bullet k} = \boldsymbol{S}_{k \bullet}^T - \boldsymbol{W}\boldsymbol{G}_{\bullet k}$
17:         $\delta = \boldsymbol{W}_{\bullet k}^T \kappa(\boldsymbol{X}, \boldsymbol{X}) \boldsymbol{W}_{\bullet k}$
18:         $\boldsymbol{W}_{\bullet k} = \boldsymbol{W}_{\bullet k}/\sqrt{\delta}$
19:     **end for**
20:     **Update the objective function:**
21:         $f = trace\{\kappa(\boldsymbol{X}, \boldsymbol{X})\} - 2trace\{\boldsymbol{A}\boldsymbol{S}^T\} + trace\{\boldsymbol{F}\boldsymbol{E}\} + 2\alpha\|\boldsymbol{S}\|_1$
22: **end while**
23: **return** $\boldsymbol{W}$, and $\boldsymbol{S}$

4.3 Overall Algorithm

Our algorithm for SSSR or MSSR is shown in Algorithm 1. Here, $1 \in \mathbb{R}^{K \times K}$ is a square matrix with all elements 1, $\boldsymbol{I} \in \mathbb{R}^{K \times K}$ is the identity matrix, and $\odot$ indicates the Hadamard product. By iterating $\boldsymbol{S}$ and $\boldsymbol{W}$ alternately, the sparse codes are obtained, and the bases are learned.

5 Experimental Results

In this section, we present our experimental results for SSSR and MSSR compared with several baselines and previous published techniques on four benchmark datasets, such as UIUC-Sports dataset [15], Scene 15 dataset [12], Caltech-101 dataset [14], and Caltech-256 dataset [10].

5.1 Experimental Settings

For each dataset, the data are randomly split into training set and testing set based on published protocols. The experimental process is repeated 8 times, and the mean and standard deviation of the classification accuracy are record. Each image is resized with maximum side 300 pixels firstly, except 400 pixels for UIUC-Sports dataset due to the high resolution of original images. As for the image features, two types of densely sampled SIFT features are used to demonstrate the effectiveness of SSSR and MSSR. One feature is extracted with patch size 16×16 and step size 8 pixels, which we call single scale SIFT. The other one is extracted under three scales 16×16, 24×24, and 32×32, and the step size 8 pixels, which

Table 1. Performance comparisons on UIUC-Sports dataset and Scene 15 dataset (%).

Methods	UIUC-Sports	Scene 15
Single scale SIFT		
ScSPM(1024) [40,6]	82.74 ± 1.46	80.28 ± 0.93
EMK [1]	74.56 ± 1.32	NA
KSR [4]	84.92 ± 0.78	83.68 ± 0.61
SCSR(1024) [17]	87.97 ± 1.11	81.51 ± 0.32
DLSM(1024) [18]	86.82 ± 1.04	83.40 ± 0.44
DLMM(1024) [18]	86.93 ± 0.99	83.67 ± 0.49
Ours(SSSR)		
Hellinger+1024+linearSVM	88.49 ± 1.25	82.25 ± 0.31
HIK+1024+linearSVM	88.41 ± 1.11	84.42 ± 0.33
POLY+1024+linearSVM	88.26 ± 1.12	83.59 ± 0.26
linear+1024+linearSVM	88.07 ± 1.33	83.84 ± 0.40
Ours(MSSR)		
4096+linearSVM	89.77 ± 1.12	85.18 ± 0.26
4096+polySVM	89.79 ± 0.96	**85.36 ± 0.29**
Multiple scale SIFT		
KSRSPM-HIK(4096)[5]	86.85 ± 0.45	NA
Ours(SSSR)		
Hellinger+4096+linearSVM	88.36 ± 0.82	84.89 ± 0.37
HIK+4096+linearSVM	88.54 ± 1.09	84.18 ± 0.47
POLY+4096+linearSVM	88.93 ± 0.81	84.09 ± 0.35
linear+4096+linearSVM	88.83 ± 0.81	83.67 ± 0.46
Ours(MSSR)		
16384+linearSVM	**89.95 ± 0.64**	84.89 ± 0.38
16384+polySVM	89.61 ± 0.70	84.93 ± 0.45

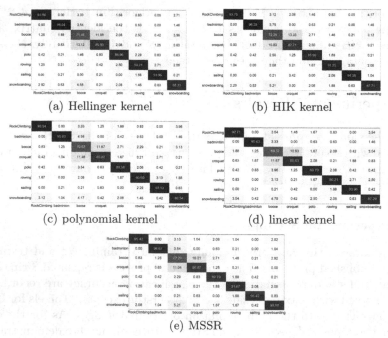

(a) Hellinger kernel   (b) HIK kernel

(c) polynomial kernel   (d) linear kernel

(e) MSSR

Fig. 2. Confusion matrix on UIUC-Sports dataset (%) with single scale SIFT features

Table 2. Performance comparisons on Caltech-101 dataset (%)

Methods	5train	10train	15train	20train	25train	30train
Single scale SIFT						
ScSPM(1024) [40]	NA	NA	67.0 ± 0.45	NA	NA	73.2 ± 0.54
DLSM(1024) [18]	NA	NA	66.88 ± 0.53	NA	NA	74.39 ± 0.82
DLMM(1024) [18]	NA	NA	67.54 ± 0.41	NA	NA	74.87 ± 0.67
Ours(SSSR)						
Hellinger+1024+linearSVM	47.42 ± 0.61	60.64 ± 0.48	65.65 ± 0.30	68.83 ± 0.50	71.35 ± 0.58	73.04 ± 1.27
HIK+1024+linearSVM	47.66 ± 0.41	60.44 ± 0.44	65.91 ± 0.54	69.05 ± 0.39	71.59 ± 0.73	73.43 ± 0.65
POLY+1024+linearSVM	48.10 ± 0.35	60.67 ± 0.37	65.91 ± 0.68	69.43 ± 0.21	71.77 ± 0.63	73.80 ± 0.64
linear+1024+linearSVM	48.27 ± 0.47	61.04 ± 0.59	66.26 ± 0.57	69.31 ± 0.65	71.72 ± 0.71	73.47 ± 0.42
Ours(MSSR)						
4096+linearSVM	49.52 ± 0.47	62.50 ± 0.23	67.97 ± 0.53	71.21 ± 0.38	73.68 ± 0.74	76.04 ± 0.67
4096+polySVM	49.34 ± 0.45	62.48 ± 0.26	67.79 ± 0.48	71.39 ± 0.36	73.63 ± 0.70	76.06 ± 0.83
Multiple scale SIFT						
LLC(4096) [34]	51.15	59.77	65.43	67.74	70.16	73.44
SC(AxMin@n)(4k) [11][1]	NA	NA	**74.6 ± 0.4**	NA	NA	**81.3 ± 0.6**
Ours(SSSR)						
Hellinger+4096+linearSVM	51.43 ± 0.82	64.60 ± 0.47	70.09 ± 0.27	73.70 ± 0.50	75.60 ± 0.51	77.43 ± 1.13
HIK+4096+linearSVM	51.81 ± 0.75	64.83 ± 0.56	69.93 ± 0.43	73.40 ± 0.57	75.25 ± 0.47	77.16 ± 1.01
POLY+4096+linearSVM	52.22 ± 1.02	65.39 ± 0.44	70.26 ± 0.50	73.79 ± 0.57	75.72 ± 0.48	77.31 ± 0.90
linear+4096+linearSVM	52.76 ± 0.81	65.67 ± 0.54	70.62 ± 0.60	74.18 ± 0.55	75.90 ± 0.60	77.51 ± 0.88
Ours(MSSR)						
16384+linearSVM	**53.36 ± 0.71**	**66.20 ± 0.56**	71.58 ± 0.43	**75.23 ± 0.68**	**76.89 ± 0.60**	78.74 ± 0.81
16384+polySVM	53.10 ± 0.70	66.10 ± 0.45	71.41 ± 0.38	75.08 ± 0.61	76.82 ± 0.52	78.59 ± 0.95

we call multiple scales SIFT. 128 dimensional SIFT descriptors are obtained and normalized to 1 with ℓ_2-norm. For learning the dictionaries, 30,000~50,000 samples are used. For single scale SIFT, the dictionary size is 1,024 for each kernel space. For multiple scales SIFT, the dictionary size is 4,096. The spatial pyramid matching kernel is with 1, 4, and 16 segments. We use a max pooling strategy [40]. An image is represented by the concatenation of each segment and normalized to 1 with ℓ_2-norm.

We use four different kernels: the Hellinger kernel $\left(\kappa(\boldsymbol{x}, \boldsymbol{y}) = \sum_{d=1}^{D} \sqrt{\mathbf{x}_d \mathbf{y}_d}\right)$, histogram intersection kernel $\left(\kappa(\boldsymbol{x}, \boldsymbol{y}) = \sum_{d=1}^{D} \min\{\mathbf{x}_d, \mathbf{y}_d\}\right)$, polynomial kernel $\left(\kappa(\boldsymbol{x}, \boldsymbol{y}) = (1 + \boldsymbol{x}^T \boldsymbol{y})^p\right)$, and linear kernel $\left(\kappa(\boldsymbol{x}, \boldsymbol{y}) = \boldsymbol{x}^T \boldsymbol{y}\right)$. Here, we set $p = 2$. Now only one parameter α needs tuning in the objective functions of SSSR and MSSR. The choice of α is obtained by cross-validation (CV). The CV results indicated that the optimal performance is achieved when maintaining approximate 10 non-0 elements, which agrees with the empirical conclusion in [40]. The parameter α is 0.15 for linear kernel, 0.3 for polynomial kernel, 0.4 for histogram intersection kernel, and 0.5 for hellinger kernel. Linear or Polynomial kernel SVM classifier is used with one-vs-all multi-class, and the LIBSVM [2] package is used.

---

[1] In [11], the image features are extracted with $16, 24, 32, 40$ patch size and $4, 6, 8, 10$ step size, respectively. Besides, the experimental setting in [11] is "approximate pooling (AxMin@n) with 4 levels of SPM".

612   B.-D. Liu et al.

Table 3. Performance comparisons on Caltech-256 dataset (%)

Methods	15train	30train	45train	60train
Single scale SIFT				
ScSPM(1024) [40]	27.73 ± 0.51	34.02 ± 0.35	37.46 ± 0.55	40.14 ± 0.91
LLC(1024) [34,6]	27.74 ± 0.32	32.07 ± 0.24	35.09 ± 0.44	37.79 ± 0.42
KSR(1024) [4]	29.77 ± 0.14	35.67 ± 0.10	38.61 ± 0.19	40.30 ± 0.22
SCSR(1024) [17]	29.23 ± 0.38	35.51 ± 0.32	38.68 ± 0.29	41.05 ± 0.42
DLSM(1024) [18]	29.31 ± 0.58	35.12 ± 0.34	37.62 ± 0.57	39.96 ± 0.62
DLMM(1024) [18]	30.35 ± 0.42	36.22 ± 0.33	38.97 ± 0.56	41.09 ± 0.44
Ours(SSSR)				
Hellinger+1024+linearSVM	32.74 ± 0.35	39.68 ± 0.33	43.18 ± 0.41	45.33 ± 0.34
HIK+1024+linearSVM	32.38 ± 0.47	39.13 ± 0.48	42.40 ± 0.34	44.86 ± 0.32
POLY+1024+linearSVM	31.58 ± 0.22	38.32 ± 0.32	41.74 ± 0.47	44.24 ± 0.43
linear+1024+linearSVM	31.52 ± 0.31	38.19 ± 0.33	41.39 ± 0.49	43.95 ± 0.63
Ours(MSSR)				
4096+linearSVM	34.06 ± 0.36	41.14 ± 0.43	44.72 ± 0.42	47.26 ± 0.43
4096+polySVM	35.38 ± 0.31	42.92 ± 0.46	46.88 ± 0.52	49.70 ± 0.43
Multiple scale SIFT				
LLC(4096) [34]	34.36	41.19	45.31	47.68
KSRSPM-HIK(4096)[5]	33.61 ± 0.34	40.63 ± 0.22	44.41 ± 0.12	47.03 ± 0.35
IFK [24][2]	34.7 ± 0.2	40.8 ± 0.1	45.0 ± 0.2	47.9 ± 0.4
Ours(SSSR)				
Hellinger+4096+linearSVM	37.11 ± 0.50	44.73 ± 0.37	48.65 ± 0.43	51.24 ± 0.60
HIK+4096+linearSVM	35.95 ± 0.36	43.45 ± 0.29	47.27 ± 0.33	49.96 ± 0.56
POLY+4096+linearSVM	35.54 ± 0.33	42.94 ± 0.40	46.70 ± 0.41	49.42 ± 0.62
linear+4096+linearSVM	35.66 ± 0.43	43.10 ± 0.28	46.98 ± 0.38	49.52 ± 0.60
Ours(MSSR)				
16384+linearSVM	37.12 ± 0.41	44.95 ± 0.38	48.89 ± 0.37	51.47 ± 0.72
16384+polySVM	**37.76 ± 0.25**	**45.70 ± 0.47**	**49.83 ± 0.18**	**52.81 ± 0.53**

5.2 UIUC-Sports Dataset

For the UIUC-Sports dataset [15], there are 8 classes with 1,579 images in total. We follow the common setup: 70 images per class are randomly selected as the training data, and 60 images per class for testing. Figure 2 shows the confusion matrices with single scale SIFT features. Table 1 shows the performance of different methods. Our proposed MSSR algorithm outperforms the traditional sparse representation based image classification [40] by 7.05% with single scale SIFT features.

5.3 Scene 15 Dataset

For the Scene 15 dataset [12], there are 15 classes with 4,485 images in total. We use an identical experimental setup as [12]: 100 images per class are randomly selected as the training data, and the rest for testing. Table 1 lists the comparisons of our SSSR and MSSR methods with previous work. Our proposed MSSR algorithm outperforms the traditional sparse representation based image classification [40] by 5.08% with single scale SIFT features.

---

[2] In [24], 5 scales are used for extracting the image features, and the total length of the vector to represent each image is 30k.

5.4   Caltech-101 Dataset

The Caltech-101 dataset [14] contains 102 classes, one of which is the background. After removing the background class, the remaining 101 classes with 8,677 images in total are used for classification, with each class varying from 31 to 800 images. We follow the standard experiment setup for this dataset: 5, 10, 15, 20, 25, and 30 images per category are selected as the training set, and the rest for testing (the maximum is 50 images per category for testing). Table 2 shows performances of different methods. The best results reported in [11] are 74.6% and 81.3% with 15 and 30 images per class as the training set. With single scale SIFT features, our proposed MSSR algorithm outperforms the traditional sparse representation based image classification [40] by 0.97% and 2.86% for 15 and 30 training images per class, respectively.

5.5   Caltech-256 Dataset

The Caltech-256 dataset [10] contains 257 classes, one of which is the background. After removing the background class, the remaining 256 classes with a total of 29,780 images are used for classification. We follow the standard experimental setup for this dataset: 15, 30, 45, and 60 training images per category, and 25 testing images per category. Table 3 shows the performance of different methods. With single scale SIFT features, our proposed MSSR algorithm outperforms the traditional sparse representation based image classification [40] by 7.65%, 8.9%, 9.42% and 9.56% for 15, 30, 45 and 60 training images per class, respectively.

6   Conclusions

In this paper, motivated by the fact that sparse representation, kernel representation, and multiple kernel learning are powerful tools in discovering hidden structure of complex data, we proposed novel single- and multiple-view self-explanatory sparse representation (SSSR and MSSR) schemes. By leveraging a self-explanatory reformulation of sparse representation, where the bases lie in the span of the image features, the new formula is readily generalized into reproducing kernel Hilbert spaces for arbitrary kernels with computational tractability and conceptual interpretability. SSSR is capable of identifying both nonlinear structural information and sparse active components. The multiple-view joint representation not only captures various structure information of the image features under different kernels, but also reduces the complexity of dictionary learning. This leads to enhanced visual representation power as has been demonstrated by extensive experiments on image classification tasks.

Acknowledgment. This work was supported by the National Natural Science Foundation of P.R. China (No. 61271407, No. 61301242, No. 61171118), Shandong Provincial Natural Science Foundation, China (No. ZR2011FQ016), and the Fundamental Research Funds for the Central Universities (No. R1405012A).

References

1. Bo, L., Sminchisescu, C.: Efficient match kernel between sets of features for visual recognition. In: Proceedings of Advances in Neural Information Processing Systems, vol. 2, pp. 135–143. The MIT Press (2009)
2. Chang, C.C., Lin, C.J.: LIBSVM: A library for support vector machines. ACM Transactions on Intelligent Systems and Technology 2(3), 27:1–27:27 (2011)
3. Elhamifar, E., Vidal, R.: Sparse subspace clustering: Algorithm, theory, and applications. IEEE Transactions on Pattern Analysis and Machine Intelligence 35(11), 2765–2781 (2013)
4. Gao, S., Tsang, I.W.-H., Chia, L.-T.: Kernel sparse representation for image classification and face recognition. In: Daniilidis, K., Maragos, P., Paragios, N. (eds.) ECCV 2010, Part IV. LNCS, vol. 6314, pp. 1–14. Springer, Heidelberg (2010)
5. Gao, S., Tsang, I.W.H., Chia, L.T.: Sparse representation with kernels. IEEE Transactions on Image Processing 22(2), 423–434 (2013)
6. Gao, S., Tsang, I.H., Chia, L.T.: Laplacian sparse coding, hypergraph laplacian sparse coding, and applications. IEEE Transactions on Pattern Analysis and Machine Intelligence 35(1), 92–104 (2013)
7. van Gemert, J.C., Veenman, C.J., Smeulders, A.W., Geusebroek, J.M.: Visual word ambiguity. IEEE Transactions on Pattern Analysis and Machine Intelligence 32(7), 1271–1283 (2010)
8. van Gemert, J.C., Veenman, C.J., Smeulders, A.W., Geusebroek, J.M.: Visual word ambiguity. IEEE Transactions on Pattern Analysis and Machine Intelligence 32(7), 1271–1283 (2010)
9. Gönen, M., Alpaydın, E.: Multiple kernel learning algorithms. Journal of Machine Learning Research 12, 2211–2268 (2011)
10. Griffin, G., Holub, A., Perona, P.: Caltech-256 object category dataset. Technical Report 7694, California Institute of Technology (2007)
11. Koniusz, P., Yan, F., Mikolajczyk, K.: Comparison of mid-level feature coding approaches and pooling strategies in visual concept detection. Computer Vision and Image Understanding 117(5), 479–492 (2013)
12. Lazebnik, S., Schmid, C., Ponce, J.: Beyond bags of features: Spatial pyramid matching for recognizing natural scene categories. In: Proceedings of the 19th CVPR, vol. 2, pp. 2169–2178. IEEE (2006)
13. Lee, H., Battle, A., Raina, R., Ng, A.: Efficient sparse coding algorithms. In: Proceedings of Advances in Neural Information Processing Systems, pp. 801–808. MIT Press (2006)
14. Li, F.F., Fergus, R., Perona, P.: Learning generative visual models from few training examples: An incremental bayesian approach tested on 101 object categories. In: Workshop of the 17th CVPR, vol. 12, p. 178. IEEE (2004)
15. Li, L.J., Li, F.F.: What, where and who? classifying events by scene and object recognition. In: Proceedings of the 11th ICCV, pp. 1–8. IEEE (2007)
16. Liu, B.D., Wang, Y.X., Bin, S., Zhang, Y.J., Wang, Y.J.: Blockwise coordinate descent schemes for sparse representation. In: Proceedings of the 39th ICASSP, pp. 5304–5308. IEEE (2014)
17. Liu, B.D., Wang, Y.X., Shen, B., Zhang, Y.J., Wang, Y.J., Liu, W.F.: Self-explanatory convex sparse representation for image classification. In: Proceedings of Systems, Man, and Cybernetics (SMC). pp. 2120–2125. IEEE (2013)
18. Liu, B.D., Wang, Y.X., Zhang, Y.J., Shen, B.: Learning dictionary on manifolds for image classification. Pattern Recognition 46(7), 1879–1890 (2013)

19. Liu, B.D., Wang, Y.X., Zhang, Y.J., Zheng, Y.: Discriminant sparse coding for image classification. In: Proceedings of the 37th ICASSP, pp. 2193–2196. IEEE (2012)
20. Liu, G., Lin, Z., Yan, S., Sun, J., Yu, Y., Ma, Y.: Robust recovery of subspace structures by low-rank representation. IEEE Transactions on Pattern Analysis and Machine Intelligence 35(1), 171–184 (2013)
21. Liu, W., Tao, D.: Multiview hessian regularization for image annotation. IEEE Transactions on Image Processing 22(7), 2676–2687 (2013)
22. Liu, W., Tao, D., Cheng, J., Tang, Y.: Multiview hessian discriminative sparse coding for image annotation. Computer Vision and Image Understanding 118, 50–60 (2014)
23. Nguyen, H.V., Patel, V.M., Nasrabadi, N.M., Chellappa, R.: Kernel dictionary learning. In: Proceedings of the 37th ICASSP, pp. 2021–2024. IEEE (2012)
24. Perronnin, F., Sánchez, J., Mensink, T.: Improving the fisher kernel for large-scale image classification. In: Daniilidis, K., Maragos, P., Paragios, N. (eds.) ECCV 2010, Part IV. LNCS, vol. 6314, pp. 143–156. Springer, Heidelberg (2010)
25. Schölkopf, B., Smola, A., Müller, K.: Kernel principal component analysis. In: Gerstner, W., Hasler, M., Germond, A., Nicoud, J.-D. (eds.) ICANN 1997. LNCS, vol. 1327, pp. 583–588. Springer, Heidelberg (1997)
26. Schölkopf, B., Herbrich, R., Smola, A.J.: A generalized representer theorem. In: Helmbold, D.P., Williamson, B. (eds.) COLT 2001 and EuroCOLT 2001. LNCS (LNAI), vol. 2111, pp. 416–426. Springer, Heidelberg (2001)
27. Shen, B., Hu, W., Zhang, Y., Zhang, Y.J.: Image inpainting via sparse representation. In: Proceedings of the 34th ICASSP, pp. 697–700. IEEE (2009)
28. Shen, B., Si, L.: Non-negative matrix factorization clustering on multiple manifolds. In: Proceedings of the 24th AAAI, pp. 575–580. IEEE (2010)
29. Shen, B., Si, L., Ji, R., Liu, B.: Robust nonnegative matrix factorization via l_1 norm regularization. arXiv preprint arXiv:1204.2311 (2012)
30. Tan, H., Cheng, B., Feng, J., Feng, G., Wang, W., Zhang, Y.J.: Low-n-rank tensor recovery based on multi-linear augmented lagrange multiplier method. Neurocomputing 119, 144–152 (2013)
31. Tan, H., Cheng, B., Wang, W., Zhang, Y.J., Ran, B.: Tensor completion via a multi-linear low-n-rank factorization model. Neurocomputing 133, 161–169 (2014)
32. Thiagarajan, J., Ramamurthy, K., Spanias, A.: Multiple kernel sparse representations for supervised and unsupervised learning. IEEE Transactions on Image Processing 23(7), 2905–2915 (2014)
33. Vedaldi, A., Zisserman, A.: Sparse kernel approximations for efficient classification and detection. In: Proceedings of the 25th CVPR, pp. 2320–2327. IEEE (2012)
34. Wang, J., Yang, J., Yu, K., Lv, F., Huang, T., Gong, Y.: Locality-constrained linear coding for image classification. In: Proceedings of the 23rd CVPR, pp. 3360–3367. IEEE (2010)
35. Wang, Y.X., Gui, L.Y., Zhang, Y.J.: Neighborhood preserving non-negative tensor factorization for image representation. In: Proceedings of the 37th ICASSP, pp. 3389–3392. IEEE (2012)
36. Wang, Y.X., Zhang, Y.J.: Image inpainting via weighted sparse non-negative matrix factorization. In: Proceedings of the 18th ICIP, pp. 3409–3412. IEEE (2011)
37. Wang, Y.X., Zhang, Y.J.: Nonnegative matrix factorization: a comprehensive review. IEEE Transactions on Knowledge and Data Engineering 25(6), 1336–1353 (2013)

38. Wu, J., Rehg, J.M.: Beyond the euclidean distance: Creating effective visual code-books using the histogram intersection kernel. In: Proceedings of the 12th ICCV, pp. 630–637. IEEE (2009)
39. Wu, Y., Shen, B., Ling, H.: Visual tracking via online non-negative matrix factor-ization. IEEE Transactions on Circuits and Systems for Video Technology 24(3), 374–383 (2014)
40. Yang, J., Yu, K., Gong, Y., Huang, T.: Linear spatial pyramid matching us-ing sparse coding for image classification. In: Proceedings of the 22nd CVPR, pp. 1794–1801. IEEE (2009)
41. Yang, M., Zhang, L., Shiu, S.K., Zhang, D.: Robust kernel representation with sta-tistical local features for face recognition. IEEE Transactions on Neural Networks and Learning Systems 24(6), 900–912 (2013)
42. Yuan, X.T., Yan, S.: Visual classification with multi-task joint sparse representa-tion. In: Proceedings of the 23th CVPR, pp. 3493–3500. IEEE (2010)

Efficient k-Support Matrix Pursuit

Hanjiang Lai[1,3], Yan Pan[2,*], Canyi Lu[1], Yong Tang[4], and Shuicheng Yan[1]

[1] Department of Electrical and Computer Engineering, National University of Singapore
[2] School of Software, Sun Yat-sen University, China
[3] School of Information Science and Technology, Sun Yat-sen University, China
[4] School of Computer Science, South China Normal University, China
{laihanj,canyilu}@gmail.com, panyan5@mail.sysu.edu.cn,
ytang@scnu.edu.cn, eleyans@nus.edu.sg

Abstract. In this paper, we study the k-support norm regularized matrix pursuit problem, which is regarded as the core formulation for several popular computer vision tasks. The k-support matrix norm, a convex relaxation of the matrix sparsity combined with the ℓ_2-norm penalty, generalizes the recently proposed k-support vector norm. The contributions of this work are two-fold. First, the proposed k-support matrix norm does not suffer from the disadvantages of existing matrix norms towards sparsity and/or low-rankness: 1) too sparse/dense, and/or 2) column independent. Second, we present an efficient procedure for k-support norm optimization, in which the computation of the key *proximity operator* is substantially accelerated by binary search. Extensive experiments on subspace segmentation, semi-supervised classification and sparse coding well demonstrate the superiority of the new regularizer over existing matrix-norm regularizers, and also the orders-of-magnitude speedup compared with the existing optimization procedure for the k-support norm.

Keywords: k-support norm, subspace segmentation, semi-supervised classification, sparse coding.

1 Introduction

We consider the following matrix pursuit problem:

$$\min_{W} \lambda \Omega(W) + \frac{1}{2}||A - BW||_F^2, \tag{1}$$

where $\lambda > 0$ is a non-negative trade-off parameter, $||\cdot||_F$ is the Frobenius norm of a matrix and $\Omega(W)$ is the regularization term. A, B are two given matrices with compatible dimensions.

(1) is a typical problem formulation for many computer vision tasks. For example, with $A = B = X$ and X being a set of column samples, (1) becomes the formulation of subspace segmentation [11,3] which seeks to learn an affinity matrix W satisfying $X \approx XW$: $\min_{W} \lambda \Omega(W) + \frac{1}{2}||X - XW||_F^2$. With $A = X$ being a set of column samples (e.g., SIFT features [12]) and $B = D$ being an over-complete dictionary, (1) becomes

---

* Corresponding author.

D. Fleet et al. (Eds.): ECCV 2014, Part II, LNCS 8690, pp. 617–631, 2014.

Table 1. The characteristics of the five matrix norms. Here w_i is the ith column of the matrix W and $\mathrm{Diag}(w_i)$ is the diagonal matrix whose diagonal elements are w_i.

	ℓ_1-norm	Frobenius	Nuclear	Trace Lasso	k-Support
Form	$\|W\|_1$	$\|W\|_F$	$\|W\|_*$	$\sum_i \|B\mathrm{Diag}(w_i)\|_*$	$\|W\|_k^{sp}$
Sparsity	Sparse	Dense	Dense	Balanced	Balanced
Column Dependency	Independent	Independent	Dependent	Independent	Dependent
Efficiency	Efficient	Efficient	Slow	Slow	Slow $\rightarrow$ Efficient

the formulation of sparse coding for image classification [20,21]: $\min_W \lambda\Omega(W) + \frac{1}{2}\|X - DW\|_F^2$.

In this paper, we focus on designing the regularization term $\Omega(W)$. In the past few years, there has been considerable research work on matrix regularization. The representative regularization norms include ℓ_1-norm [3], nuclear norm [11], Frobenius norm [13] and trace lasso [5]. In addition to the four representative norms, the k-support norm [1] has recently been proposed, which is the tightest convex relaxation of sparsity combined with ℓ_2-norm penalty. Table 1 lists the characteristics of these norms.

Regularization with the ℓ_1-norm [3,20] is a commonly-used technique to pursue sparse models for variable or feature selection, which makes the models more interpretable. However, it tends to over-shrink large coefficients, which often degrades the model accuracies. Besides, in the context of matrix pursuit, regularization with the ℓ_1 norm usually seeks a sparse representation of each row/column of the target matrix individually, regardless of the possible correlation between these rows/columns. For example, in multi-task learning or sparse coding problems, different rows/columns of the target matrix may be related in some sense, and it is advantageous to simultaneously pursue these rows/columns [21].

Regularization with the Frobenius norm has a grouping effect [13] and can reveal the correlated information. More importantly, it has the closed form solution, which makes it very efficient. However, it fails to encourage the sparsity and is also column independent as the ℓ_1-norm.

Regularization with the nuclear norm is used to approximate the rank of a matrix. For example, Low Rank Representation (LRR) [11] jointly optimizes the affinity matrix under a global low rank constraint which makes it better capture the global structure of the data. However, it often results in dense solutions as the Frobenius norm. Also solving the nuclear norm minimization problem requires Singular Value Decomposition (SVD) operation, which limits its scalability on large datasets.

Regularization with the trace lasso [5] is a data correlation dependent method which can adaptively balance the ℓ_1-norm and the Frobenius norm. For instance, Correlation Adaptive Subspace Segmentation (CASS) [14] uses the trace lasso to exhibit both sparsity and grouping effect, which makes it effective for subspace clustering. However, it also requires SVD for optimization as LRR and is column independent as ℓ_1 and Frobenius norms.

It can be seen that these four norms all suffer from one or two of the following disadvantages: 1) too dense/sparse solution, 2) column independency. To overcome these disadvantages, in this paper, we consider the matrix pursuit problem regularized with the k-support norm [1], i.e. $\Omega(W) = (||W||_k^{sp})^2$, where we denote $||W||_k^{sp}$ as the k-support norm of the matrix W. Specifically, assuming $W \in \mathbb{R}^{d \times n}$, and $w = \text{vec}(W)$ represents the vector constructed by concatenating the columns of W, $||W||_k^{sp}$ is defined as:

$$||W||_k^{sp} = \Big(\sum_{i=1}^{k-r-1} (|w|_i^{\downarrow})^2 + \frac{1}{r+1} \Big(\sum_{i=k-r}^{nd} |w|_i^{\downarrow} \Big)^2 \Big)^{\frac{1}{2}}, \tag{2}$$

where $|w|_i^{\downarrow}$ denotes the ith largest element in $|w|$ and $|w|_0^{\downarrow}$ is assumed to be $+\infty$. $r \in \{0, 1, ..., k-1\}$ satisfies $|w|_{k-r-1}^{\downarrow} > \frac{1}{r+1}(\sum_{i=k-r}^{nd} |w|_i^{\downarrow}) \geq |w|_{k-r}^{\downarrow}$. The k-support norm has two terms: ℓ_2-norm penalty for the large components, and ℓ_1-norm penalty for the small components. $k(1 \leq k \leq nd)$ is a tunable parameter of the cardinality to achieve a balance between the ℓ_2-norm (when $k = nd$) and the ℓ_1-norm (when $k = 1$). The k-support matrix norm provides an appropriate trade-off between model sparsity (by ℓ_1-norm) and algorithmic stability[1] (by Frobenius norm) [19], which yields more stable solutions than the ℓ_1-norm. Moreover, in (1), the k-support matrix norm facilitates simultaneously learning all the columns of the target matrix, and thus transferring knowledge from one column to another to improve generalization performance.

The k-support norm regularization problem can be solved by the Accelerated Proximal Gradient (APG) method [2] or Alternating Direction Method [10] (ADM), which both require computing the *proximity operator* of the k-support norm. The time complexity of the method in [1] is $O(nd(k + log(nd)))$ when the k-support norm is applied on a $d \times n$ matrix. This time complexity is impractically high when n, d and k are large. To tackle this issue, we propose a novel efficient procedure, which reduces the time complexity to $O((nd + k) \log(nd))$. Since k is usually set to be much larger than n in practice, such time reduction (with a factor of k) can substantially accelerate the optimization procedure with the k-support norm.

The main contributions of this paper can be summarized as follows:

1) We propose the k-support matrix regularizer, which can well balance the sparsity and density of the solution, and is column dependent. We apply the proposed regularizer to several popular computer vision problems. The experiment results show that the k-support matrix regularizer outperforms the state-of-the-art popular norms/regularizers.

2) We propose an efficient procedure to solve the *proximity operator* of the k-support norm, which is $100 \sim 1000$ times faster than the method in [1] for moderate or large matrix pursuit problems.

2 k-Support Matrix Pursuit and Optimization

2.1 Problem Definition and Optimization Overview

In this paper, we particularly address the matrix pursuit problem with the k-support norm:

$$\min \frac{\lambda}{2}(||W||_k^{sp})^2 + \frac{1}{2}||A - BW||_F^2. \tag{3}$$

---

[1] Algorithmic stability means that given two similar datasets, the outputs of the algorithm change very little [15].

The k-support norm is a convex relaxation to seek a sparse, low ℓ_2-norm linear predictor [1], as shown in the following convex hull:

$$C_k = \text{conv}\{w \in \mathbb{R}^{nd} \mid ||w||_0 \leq k, ||w||_2 \leq 1\},$$

where $w = vec(W)$. It consists of two parts: one is the ℓ_0-norm constraint and the other is the ℓ_2-norm constraint. The k-support norm is defined as the norm whose unit ball equals C_k. An equivalent but more intuitive definition is in Eq. (2).

The main advantage of the k-support norm is that it provides the flexibility of tuning the cardinality k in W (i.e., the number of non-zero elements in W). This parameter, which is often selected by cross validation, can be regarded as an upper bound estimation of the number of non-zero elements in the optimal W. The k-support regularized matrix pursuit with a fine-tuned k has the potential to obtain more predictive [1] and more stable [19] solutions. Another advantage of the k-support norm is that it is column dependent, which makes it effective for selecting the informative variables cross all columns.

The optimization problem (3) can be solved by first-order proximal gradient algorithms, such as the Accelerated Proximal Gradient (APG) method as in [2]. As shown in Algorithm 1, the problem (3) is solved based on the APG scheme.

Algorithm 1. Accelerated Proximal Gradient method

Input: A, B, λ, k, T and L.
Initialize: $W_0 = P_1 = 0, \alpha_1 = 1, M = B^T B, N = B^T A$.
For $t = 1, \cdots, T$
  Let $G_t = MP_t - N$ (**gradient**)
  $W_t = arg \min_W \frac{\lambda}{2}(||W||_k^{sp})^2 + \langle W - P_t, G_t \rangle + \frac{L}{2}||W - P_t||_F^2$ (***proximity operator***)
  $\alpha_{t+1} = \frac{1+\sqrt{1+4\alpha_t^2}}{2}$
  $P_{t+1} = W_t + \left(\frac{\alpha_t - 1}{\alpha_{t+1}}\right)(W_t - W_{t-1})$
End For
output: W_T.

In Algorithm 1, the *proximity operator* is a computationally expensive step in each iteration:

$$\min_W \frac{\beta}{2}||W - V||_F^2 + \frac{1}{2}(||W||_k^{sp})^2, \tag{4}$$

where $V = P_t - G_t/L$ and $\beta = L/\lambda$. It is equivalent to the following problem:

$$\min_w \frac{\beta}{2}||w - v||_F^2 + \frac{1}{2}(||w||_k^{sp})^2, \tag{5}$$

where $w = vec(W) \in \mathbb{R}^{nd}$, and $v = vec(V) \in \mathbb{R}^{nd}$. Argyriou *et al.* [1] proposed an algorithm to solve (5) with time complexity $O(nd(k + \log(nd)))$. Since the parameter k is regarded as an upper bound estimation of the number of non-zero elements in W, k is usually set to be much larger than n (e.g., $k = O(nd)$). Hence, the computation of the *proximity operator* generally dominates the whole algorithm, and its complexity

$O(nd(k + \log(nd))) \approx O(ndk)$ is impractically high for matrix pursuit problems with large n, d and k.

To accelerate Algorithm 1, in the next subsection, we propose a much more efficient procedure to solve the *proximity operator* problem, where the time complexity is reduced to $O((nd + k) \log(nd))$.

2.2 Binary Search Procedure to Solve the Proximity Operator

In this subsection, we present an efficient procedure to solve (5) based on binary search [8]. For ease of description, some notations are defined. We define z as the vector obtained by sorting the absolute values of the elements in v in a descending order, i.e., $z = |v|^{\downarrow}$. We also define s_i as z_i's corresponding index in v: $|v_{s_i}| = z_i$. The sign function is defined as: $\text{sign}(x) = 1$ if and only if $x \geq 0$, and otherwise $\text{sign}(x) = -1$.

According to the work [1], the solution w of the optimization problem (5) can be obtained by:

$$w_{s_i} = \text{sign}(v_{s_i})q_i, \tag{6}$$

where q_i is defined by:

$$q_i = \begin{cases} \frac{\beta}{\beta+1}z_i & \text{if } i = 1, ..., k - r - 1; \\ z_i - \frac{\sum_{i=k-r}^{l} z_i}{l-k+r+1+\beta(r+1)} & \text{if } i = k - r, ..., l; \\ 0 & \text{if } i = l + 1, ..., nd. \end{cases} \tag{7}$$

In (7), the integers r and l must satisfy

$$\begin{cases} \frac{1}{\beta+1}z_{k-r-1} > \frac{\sum_{i=k-r}^{l} z_i}{\beta(r+1)+l-k+r+1} \geq \frac{1}{\beta+1}z_{k-r}; \\ z_l > \frac{\sum_{i=k-r}^{l} z_i}{\beta(r+1)+l-k+r+1} \geq z_{l+1}. \end{cases} \tag{8}$$

To obtain every w_i (and corresponding q_i), two integers r and l must be efficiently found for (7) which satisfy the constraints in (8), which is very challenging. For example, in Algorithm 1 in the work [1], the time complexity $O(ndk)$ is needed to find the integer pair r, l for all q_i, $i = 1, 2, ..., nd$. Since k is usually set to be much larger than n, this complexity is unaffordable in large matrix pursuit problems.

To tackle this issue, we propose a new method to find the integer pair r, l for all q_i based on binary search. The proposed procedure to solve (5) is shown in Algorithm 2, in which we define $T_{r,l} = \sum_{i=k-r}^{l} z_i$. In each iteration, given r, we search for an l that satisfies the second condition in (8), by a binary search procedure (see Algorithm 3). If the obtained l also satisfies the first condition in (8), we jump out of the loop and calculate the final w with the obtained l and r. Otherwise we increase r by one and continue the loop.

To efficiently obtain l that satisfies the second condition in (8), we propose to use a binary search scheme as shown in Algorithm 3. In Algorithm 3, we search for l in the range from $k - r$ to nd.

If z_{low} is zero, which implies that z_j, $j = low, ..., high$, are all zeros, we obtain $l = low = k - r$. Otherwise, we use a trick like the binary search scheme [8] to reduce the search range by half in each iteration. Specifically, with the assumption that the obtained l satisfies the second condition in (8), we consider two cases:

Algorithm 2. Procedure to solve the *proximity operator*

Input: $v \in R^{nd}$, β, k.

Initialize: $z = |v|^{\downarrow}$, $z_0 = +\infty$, $z_{nd+1} = -\infty$.

For r = k-1,...,0

    Obtain l by **BinarySearch**(z,k-r,nd) (**see Algorithm 3**);

    If $\frac{1}{\beta+1} z_{k-r-1} > \frac{T_{r,l}}{l-k+r+1+\beta(r+1)} \geq \frac{1}{\beta+1} z_{k-r}$

      break;

    End If

End For

For $i = 1, 2, ..., nd$, calculate q_i by (7);

For $i = 1, 2, ..., nd$, calculate w_i by (6);

Output: w.

- **Case 1.** If we also have $z_{mid} > \frac{T_{r,mid}}{mid-k+r+1+\beta(r+1)}$ for a certain index mid, then we can prove that $mid \leq l$ (see Lemma 1). Hence, we only need to search for l in the range $[mid, high]$, by ignoring the search in $[low, mid-1]$.
- **Case 2.** If we also have $z_{mid} \leq \frac{T_{r,mid}}{mid-k+r+1+\beta(r+1)}$, then we can prove that $l \leq mid - 1$ (see Lemma 1). Hence, we only need to search for l in the range $[low, mid - 1]$, by ignoring the search in $[mid, high]$.

By using these facts, we follow the binary search scheme to design a loop to find l. In each iteration, we set mid to be $\lceil \frac{low+high}{2} \rceil$ (Line 7 in Algorithm 3) where $\lceil x \rceil$ represents the smallest integer which is larger than x. Then we reduce the search range of l by either Case 1 (Line 9 in Algorithm 3) or Case 2 (Line 11 in Algorithm 3).

Algorithm 3. Binary search procedure to find l

---

1. **Input**: $z, low, high$,
2. **Output**: l.
3. If $z_{low} = 0$
4.   return $l = low$.
5. End If
6. While $low < high - 1$
7. $mid = \lceil \frac{low+high}{2} \rceil$.
8.   If $z_{mid} > \frac{T_{r,mid}}{mid-k+r+1+\beta(r+1)}$
9. $low = mid$.
10.   Else
11. $high = mid - 1$.
12.   End If
13. End While
14. return $l = low$.

Justification. We give the following two lemmas to prove the correctness of Algorithm 3. The detailed proof of these lemmas can be found in the supplementary material.

Lemma 1 provides the foundation to design a binary search for l in Algorithm 3 so that we can efficiently reduce the search range.

Lemma 1. *Suppose that l satisfies $z_l > \frac{T_{r,l}}{l-k+r+1+\beta(r+1)} \geq z_{l+1}$. Let low, high, mid be variables generated by Algorithm 3. Then*

(1) If $z_{mid} > \frac{T_{r,mid}}{mid-k+r+1+\beta(r+1)}$ then $mid \leq l$;

(2) If $z_{mid} \leq \frac{T_{r,mid}}{mid-k+r+1+\beta(r+1)}$ then $l \leq mid - 1$.

A natural question arises in Algorithm 3: whether there always is an l satisfying the second condition in (8) in the range $[k - r, d]$? The answer is "yes" by the following lemma.

Lemma 2. *For any $r \in [0, k - 1]$, if $z_{k-r} > 0$, there exists an l such that $z_l > \frac{T_{r,l}}{l-k+r+1+\beta(r+1)} \geq z_{l+1}$ and $l \in [k - r, nd]$. If $z_{k-r} = 0$, we can obtain $l = k - r$.*

3 Applications of k-Support Matrix Pursuit

The matrix pursuit problem is the core for various vision applications. In this section, we apply the k-support regularizer to the following popular vision related problems: subspace clustering, semi-supervised learning and sparse coding, and show how these tasks benefit from the k-support regularizer.

3.1 Subspace Segmentation and Semi-supervised Learning

Subspace segmentation aims to partition a set of data points into multiple (linear or affine) subspaces. It is a widely-used technique in various visual tasks, such as face clustering [11] and motion segmentation [3].

Semi-supervised learning has received considerable attention in computer vision literature. In this work, we consider the graph based semi-supervised learning (SSL) [22], where the label information can be propagated to the unlabeled data through a certain affinity matrix.

A core step in both subspace segmentation and graph based semi-supervised learning is to learn a good affinity matrix to represent the structure of the data points. Here, we describe how to apply the k-support graph for these two tasks.

Let $X = [x_1, x_2, \cdots, x_n] \in \mathbb{R}^{m \times n}$ be a matrix whose columns are n data samples of m-dimension. Suppose that these samples are drawn from different subspaces, and each sample can be expressed as a linear combination of all the data points X: $x_i = Xw_i$, where w_i characterizes how other samples contribute to the reconstruction of x_i. Since x_i should be associated with only a few samples drawn from the same subspace, W should be sparse but not too sparse. Thus we use the k-support norm to infer such an affinity matrix: $\min_W \frac{1}{2}(\|W\|_k^{sp})^2$, s.t. $X = XW$. For the case with noises, we consider the following problem instead:

$$\min_W \frac{\lambda}{2}(\|W\|_k^{sp})^2 + \frac{1}{2}\|X - XW\|_F^2, \tag{9}$$

where $\lambda > 0$ is a parameter for controlling the tradeoff between the model complexity and the reconstruction error.

The detailed steps of the two learning tasks based on the inferred k-support norm are as follows. First, a good affinity matrix W is learned, that is, solving the problem (9), after which we symmetrize it by $W = (|W| + |W^T|)/2$. Then, for subspace clustering, the spectral clustering algorithm [17] is used on the matrix W to segment data, while for semi-supervised learning, the Markov random walks algorithm [16] is adopted to propagate label information to the unlabeled data through the matrix W.

3.2 Collaborative Sparse Coding

Let X be a set of m-dimensional local descriptors extracted from an image, i.e., $X = [x_1, x_2, \cdots, x_n] \in \mathbb{R}^{m \times n}$. The dictionary $D \in \mathbb{R}^{m \times d}$ contains d bases. Sparse coding is a task which seeks a sparse linear combination of the bases from an over-complete dictionary D, to recover the input signal x with low reconstruction errors.

Two representative works are locally linear codes (LLC) [18] and the ℓ_1-norm regularized sparse coding (ScSPM) [20]. LLC chooses the k nearest bases of the input x_i within the dictionary D by Euclidean distance: $\min_W \sum_{i=1}^{n} ||x_i - Dw_i||_2^2 + \lambda(||h_i \odot w_i||)^2, s.t.\ 1^T w_i = 1, \forall i$, where $\odot$ denotes the element-wise multiplication, and h_i is the locality adaptor, i.e., the similarity between each basis vector and the input descriptor. ScSPM minimizes the following optimization problem: $\min_W \sum_{i=1}^{n} ||x_i - Dw_i||_2^2 + \lambda ||w_i||_1$.

Suppose each image is partitioned into M sub-regions, and the jth sub-region X_j includes n_j local descriptors: $X_j = [x_{j_1}, \ldots, x_{j_{n_j}}]$. If M is large, the local descriptors within the same sub-region would be similar or have high correlations to some extent, and the sparse codes of these local descriptors would have correlated patterns. Hence, from the viewpoint of multi-task learning, it is natural to jointly learn the sparse codes for the local descriptors within the same sub-region. However, both ScSPM and LLC solve the sparse coding problem of each local descriptor individually, regardless of the possible correlations of descriptors in the same sub-region. To address this problem, we propose collaborative sparse coding using the k-support matrix norm:

$$\min_W \sum_{j=1}^{M} \frac{1}{2} ||X_j - DW_j||_2^2 + \frac{\lambda}{2} (||W_j||_k^{sp})^2, \tag{10}$$

where W_j is the sparse code matrix of the descriptors in the jth sub-region. Note that all the elements in W_j are sorted in a descending order, with ℓ_2-norm penalty being applied to the large elements and ℓ_1-norm penalty being applied to the small elements. Hence, $||W_j||_k^{sp}$ can be regarded as a global regularizer on the jth sub-region, where the informative variables in W_j are assigned with large values and the irrelevant variables are assigned with small values. Moreover, Xu et al. [19] showed that sparsity and algorithmic stability are two desired properties for designing a leaning algorithm. Xu et al. [19] proved that ℓ_1-regularized regression is sparse but not stable, while ℓ_2-regularized regression has strong stability. Hence, for some similar local descriptors (e.g., they are from the same sub-region), ScSPM would output different codes although they have high correlations. Intuitively, it is benefitial to consider these correlated descriptors together and collaborative sparse coding is desirable. The k-support matrix norm makes a trade-off between model sparsity (by ℓ_1-norm) and model stability (by Frobenius norm), and also is column dependent. Hence, it is a natural choice for collaborative sparse coding.

4 Experiments

In this section, we evaluate the effectiveness of the proposed k-support matrix regularization on three applications: 1) subspace segmentation, 2) semi-supervised classification and 3) sparse coding for image classification. Also we evaluate in detail the running time of our solver for the k-support norm by comparing it with the previous method shown in [1].

4.1 Experiments on Subspace Segmentation

We apply the proposed algorithm to solve the k-support matrix regularized subspace segmentation problem (9). The performance is compared with the following baselines: Sparse Subspace Clustering (SSC) [3], Low-Rank Representation (LRR) [11], Least Squares Regression (LSR) [13], Non-Negative Low-Rank and Sparse graph (NNLRS) [22] and Correlation Adaptive Subspace Segmentation (CASS) [14]. Our proposed method is referred to as KMP for **K**-support norm regularized **M**atrix **P**ursuit. The results of SSC, LRR, LSR and CASS are cited from [14]. The results of NNLRS and KMP are obtained by our careful implementations. For fair comparison, we follow the experimental settings as [14], where the parameters are tuned to the best for each method.

After constructing the affinity matrix, the normalized cuts method [17] is used to segment the data into different subspaces. The clustering result is evaluated by the accuracy/error, where the accuracy is calculated by the best matching rate of the predicted label and the ground truth, while the error rate is calculated by $1 -$ accuracy.

The experiments are conducted on Extended Yale B [4] for face clustering, and on Hopkins 155 [2] for motion segmentation.

The Extended Yale B dataset consists of 16,128 images of 28 human subjects with 9 poses and 64 illumination conditions. Following the settings in [14], we conduct two experiments on Extended Yale B. In the first experiment, we use the images in the first 5 classes, and then project the images onto 30 dimensions by principal component analysis (PCA). In the second experiment, we use the samples in the first 10 classes, and the images are projected onto 60 dimensions by PCA. Each class contains 64 images and each image is resized into 32×32 pixels. Table 2 shows the segmentation accuracy of each method.

The Hopkins 155 motion database contains 156 video sequences and each sequence has two or three motions (each motion corresponds to a subspace). Since each sequence is a sole data set, there are 156 subspace segmentation problems in total. We project the data onto 12 dimensions by PCA as in [14]. Table 3 shows the maximum, mean and standard deviation of the error rates of the 156 sequences.

The comparison results on Extended Yale B database and Hopkins 155 motion database indicate that KMP performs better than all the baselines. For example, in the first 5 classes, KMP achieves 94.69% accuracy, which indicates an improvement of 14.38% over SSC and 2.50% over LSR. The experimental results can empirically

---

[2] http://www.vision.jhu.edu/data/hopkins155/

Table 2. The accuracies of different algorithms on the Extended Yale B database (%). Note that the results of SSC, LRR, LSR and CASS are directly cited from [14].

	SSC [14]	LRR [14]	LSR [14]	NNLRS	CASS [14]	KMP
5	80.31	86.56	92.19	89.69	94.03	**94.69**
10	52.19	65.00	73.59	79.37	81.88	**82.25**

Table 3. The error rates of different algorithms on the Hopkins 155 database (%). Note that the results of SSC, LRR, LSR and CASS are directly cited from [14].

	SSC [14]	LRR [14]	LSR [14]	NNLRS	CASS [14]	KMP
Max	39.53	36.36	36.36	33.09	**32.85**	39.58
Mean	4.02	3.23	2.50	3.27	2.42	**1.99**
STD	10.04	6.06	5.62	6.82	5.84	**4.93**

justify that balancing the ℓ_1-norm and the Frobenius norm can help significantly improve the accuracy. On Hopkins 155 motion database, the mean error of KMP is 1.99%, compared with 2.42% of the second best algorithm CASS. KMP is column dependent, which may be the underlying reason for KMP to outperform CASS.

4.2   Experiments on Semi-supervised Classification

For semi-supervised classification, we compare the performances of the algorithms on two datasets: Extended Yale B and USPS [6]. USPS [3] is a handwritten digit dataset which has ten classes (the digits range from 0 to 9).

Following the settings in [14], on Extended Yale B, we use the images in the first 10 classes. On USPS, we randomly select 100 images from each class for our experiments. Each image in USPS is resized into 16×16 pixels. In all experiments, we randomly select 4, 8, 16, 32 images from each class as labeled samples, respectively, and the rest images are used as unlabeled samples. After obtaining the matrix W, we select the Markov random walks algorithm [16] for semi-supervised learning. For fair comparison with previous work, the parameters of all methods are tuned to achieve the best performance. We run each experiment for 20 times and report the averaged accuracies.

Fig. 1 shows the comparison results, from which two observations can be made. First, the k-support matrix norm can well balance the ℓ_1-norm and the Frobenius norm. SSC (ℓ_1-norm) achieves a good performance on USPS dataset, but performs poorly on Extended Yale B. LSR (Frobenius norm) performs well on Extended Yale B, but yields a poor performance on USPS. Compared with them, the k-support matrix norm performs well on both datasets. Second, the KMP performs better than CASS. The reason may be that the k-support matrix norm can capture the cross column information while CASS cannot.

---

[3] http://www.cad.zju.edu.cn/home/dengcai/Data/MLData.html

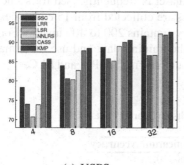 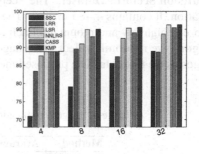

(a) USPS   (b) Extended Yale B

Fig. 1. The accuracies of semi-supervised classification based on different affinity matrices (%). Note that the results of SSC, LRR, LSR and CASS are directly cited from [14] on Extended Yale B database, and obtained by directly running their open source codes on USPS database.

4.3 Experiments on Collaborative Sparse Codings

The proposed algorithm is also applied to the sparse coding problem (10) for image classification, and compared with two state-of-the-art sparse coding methods: ScSPM [20] and LLC [18]. The performances are evaluated on two datasets: UIUC-Sport [9] and Scene15 [7].

On each dataset, we obtain a dictionary containing 1,024 bases using the k-means clustering. The results of ScSPM and LLC are obtained by directly using the online source codes[4]. In our image classification system, we use the open source code of ScSPM [20] to implement SIFT extraction, spatial pyramid matching and max pooling. For our collaborative sparse coding, we partition each image into a set of 20×20 non-overlap sub-regions. Then the proposed k-support matrix pursuit algorithm is performed on each sub-region to obtain the sparse codes, respectively.

Results on UIUC-Sport Dataset. The UIUC-Sport dataset contains images collected from 8 classes of different sports such as badminton, rock climbing and sailing. There are 1,579 images in total and the number of images in each category ranges from 137 to 250. For each category, we randomly select 70 images as training data, and another 60 images as test data. As shown in Table 4, the k-support regularized sparse coding method shows superior performance over ScSPM and LLC.

Table 4. Image classification results on UIUC-Sport dataset(%)

Method	Average Classification Accuracy
ScSPM [20]	82.74 ± 1.46
LLC [18]	84.58 ± 1.19
KMP	$\mathbf{85.55 \pm 1.23}$

---

[4] www.ifp.illinois.edu/~jyang29

Results on Scene15 Dataset. The Scene15 dataset is frequently used for scene classification. It contains 4,485 images. The images are collected from 15 categories such as forest, highway and mountain. Each category contains 200 to 400 images. For each category, we randomly select 100 images as the training data and use the remaining images as the test data. The proposed method outperforms ScSPM and LLC.

Table 5. Image classification results on Scene15 dataset(%)

Method	Average Classification Accuracy
ScSPM [20]	80.28 ± 0.93
LLC [18]	81.57 ± 0.50
KMP	**83.04 ± 0.43**

From the two results, we can observe that it is advantageous to jointly learn the sparse codes within the same sub-region. KMP also considers the sparsity and stability of the algorithm, while ScSPM (with ℓ_1 norm) is not stable [19], which may be the underlying reason for the better performance of KMP than ScSPM.

4.4 Experiments on Algorithmic Complexity

In this subsection, we evaluate the running time of our solver by comparing it with the previous method shown in [1]. We use the open source code of the k-support norm [5] to make a fair comparison. Since it uses the linear search algorithm, we call it "LS-KMP". Our method is referred to as "BS-KMP", which means using binary search for the k-support norm.

We report the running time of LS-KMP and BS-KMP on all the above databases. Note that both algorithms use the same implementation except for the computation of the *proximity operator*. The running time shown in Table 6 is the cost to compute the affinity or sparse code matrix. For Scene15 and UIUC datasets, we only report the average running time of the first 10 images. We can see that the proposed procedure performs 2 or 3 orders of magnitude faster than the LS-KMP on the first three datasets. On Scene15 and UIUC datasets, BS-KMP only has 10 times faster than the LS-KMP. This is because the value of k is set to be a small integer in these two datasets, e.g., $k = 10$.

Table 6. Running time comparison between LS-KMP and BS-KMP on five real datasets (in sec)

	YaleB	Hopkins	USPS	Scene15	UIUC
LS-KMP	3530	66174	30707	31.14	33.16
BS-KMP	**5.25**	**400.55**	**191.05**	**3.31**	**3.01**

---

[5] http://cvc.centrale-ponts.fr/personnel/andreas/

We conduct simulated experiments to observe the effects of the parameters on the running time of the *proximity operator* with different values of β and k:

$$\min_{w} \frac{\beta}{2}||w - v||^2 + \frac{1}{2}(||w||_k^{sp})^2. \tag{11}$$

We generate a vector $v \in \mathbb{R}^{10000}$, which is randomly sampled from the norm distribution $N(0, 1)$. For each setting, the running time is averaged over 10 different v.

Parameter k. Table 7 shows how the running time varies with the different values of the predefined parameter k. The parameter k is chosen from the set $\{1000, 2000, \cdots, 9000\}$. We fix $\beta = 10$ in these experiments.

Table 7. Running time comparison under different k on synthetic data (in sec)

k	1000	2000	3000	4000	5000	6000	7000	8000	9000
LS-KMP	6.1842	12.4235	16.3917	18.0764	17.8485	16.1820	13.3029	9.5786	5.0788
BS-KMP	0.0020	0.0024	0.0032	0.0083	0.0159	0.0252	0.0371	0.0497	0.0627

It can be seen that the proposed method runs significantly faster than the LS-KMP, especially when k is set near half value of the dimension, e.g., $k = [4000, 5000, 6000]$. Table 7 shows that BS-KMP is $81 \sim 5177$ times faster than the LS-KMP on simulated data.

Parameter β. Table 8 shows how the running time varies with the different values of β. The parameter β is chosen from the set $\{0.01, 0.1, 1, 10, 100\}$. We fix $k = 5000$ in these experiments. As shown in Table 8, the running time of LS-KMP sharply changes

Table 8. Running time comparison under different β on synthetic data (in sec)

β	0.01	0.1	1	10	100
LS-KMP	0.0737	0.7016	5.6410	17.8485	22.4130
BS-KMP	0.0401	0.0374	0.0293	0.0159	0.0124

with different β, while BS-KMP is more stable.

5 Conclusions and Future Work

In this paper, we proposed to use the k-support matrix norm to address the matrix pursuit problem, which is valuable for a wide range of applications including subspace segmentation, semi-supervised classification and sparse coding. The k-support matrix norm is advantageous and provides a flexible trade-off between model sparsity and prediction accuracy. To tackle the time-consuming *proximity operator* problem of the k-support norm, we also developed an efficient binary search procedure, which can substantially reduce the running time. Extensive experiments showed the superior effectiveness of the k-support matrix norm over the state-of-the-art baseline norms.

In future work, we plan to study the effects of using the k-support matrix norm for the construction error term, and intend to investigate the relationship between the k-support loss function and the outlier/Gaussian noise of the data.

Acknowledgements. This work was funded in part by National Science Foundation of China (grant No. 61370021, 61003045, 61100080), Natural Science Foundation of Guangdong Province, China (grant No. S2013010011905). The corresponding author is Yan Pan.

References

1. Argyriou, A., Foygel, R., Srebro, N.: Sparse prediction with the k-support norm. In: Advances in Neural Information Processing Systems, pp. 1466–1474 (2012)
2. Beck, A., Teboulle, M.: A fast iterative shrinkage-thresholding algorithm for linear inverse problems. SIAM Journal on Imaging Sciences 2(1), 183–202 (2009)
3. Elhamifar, E., Vidal, R.: Sparse subspace clustering. In: IEEE Conference on Computer Vision and Pattern Recognition, pp. 2790–2797 (2009)
4. Georghiades, A.S., Belhumeur, P.N., Kriegman, D.J.: From few to many: Illumination cone models for face recognition under variable lighting and pose. IEEE Transactions on Pattern Analysis and Machine Intelligence 23(6), 643–660 (2001)
5. Grave, E., Obozinski, G., Bach, F.: et al.: Trace lasso: a trace norm regularization for correlated designs. Advances in Neural Information Processing Systems 2, 5 (2011)
6. Hull, J.J.: A database for handwritten text recognition research. IEEE Transactions on Pattern Analysis and Machine Intelligence 16(5), 550–554 (1994)
7. Lazebnik, S., Schmid, C., Ponce, J.: Beyond bags of features: Spatial pyramid matching for recognizing natural scene categories. In: IEEE Computer Society Conference on Computer Vision and Pattern Recognition, vol. 2, pp. 2169–2178 (2006)
8. Lewis, G.N., Boynton, N.J., Burton, F.W.: Expected complexity of fast search with uniformly distributed data. Information Processing Letters 13(1), 4–7 (1981)
9. Li, L.J., Fei-Fei, L.: What, where and who? classifying events by scene and object recognition. In: IEEE International Conference on Computer Vision, pp. 1–8 (2007)
10. Lin, Z., Liu, R., Su, Z.: Linearized alternating direction method with adaptive penalty for low-rank representation. In: Advances in Neural Information Processing Systems, pp. 612–620 (2011)
11. Liu, G., Lin, Z., Yu, Y.: Robust subspace segmentation by low-rank representation. In: International Conference on Machine Learning, pp. 663–670 (2010)
12. Lowe, D.G.: Object recognition from local scale-invariant features. In: IEEE International Conference on Computer Vision, vol. 2, pp. 1150–1157 (1999)
13. Jia, K., Chan, T.-H., Ma, Y.: Robust and efficient subspace segmentation via least squares regression. In: Fitzgibbon, A., Lazebnik, S., Perona, P., Sato, Y., Schmid, C. (eds.) ECCV 2012, Part IV. LNCS, vol. 7575, pp. 331–344. Springer, Heidelberg (2012)
14. Lu, C., Feng, J., Lin, Z., Yan, S.: Correlation adaptive subspace segmentation by trace lasso. In: IEEE International Conference on Computer Vision (2013)
15. Shalev-Shwartz, S., Shamir, O., Sridharan, K., Srebro, N.: Learnability and stability in the general learning setting. In: Annual Conference of Learning Theory (2009)

16. Szummer, M., Jaakkola, T.: Partially labeled classification with markov random walks. In: Advances in Neural Information Processing Systems, pp. 945–952 (2001)
17. Von Luxburg, U.: A tutorial on spectral clustering. Statistics and Computing 17(4), 395–416 (2007)
18. Wang, J., Yang, J., Yu, K., Lv, F., Huang, T., Gong, Y.: Locality-constrained linear coding for image classification. In: IEEE Conference on Computer Vision and Pattern Recognition, pp. 3360–3367 (2010)
19. Xu, H., Caramanis, C., Mannor, S.: Sparse algorithms are not stable: A no-free-lunch theorem. IEEE Transactions on Pattern Analysis and Machine Intelligence 34(1), 187–193 (2012)
20. Yang, J., Yu, K., Gong, Y., Huang, T.: Linear spatial pyramid matching using sparse coding for image classification. In: IEEE Conference on Computer Vision and Pattern Recognition, pp. 1794–1801 (2009)
21. Yuan, X.T., Liu, X., Yan, S.: Visual classification with multitask joint sparse representation. IEEE Transactions on Image Processing 21(10), 4349–4360 (2012)
22. Zhuang, L., Gao, H., Lin, Z., Ma, Y., Zhang, X., Yu, N.: Non-negative low rank and sparse graph for semi-supervised learning. In: IEEE Conference on Computer Vision and Pattern Recognition, pp. 2328–2335 (2012)

Geodesic Regression on the Grassmannian

Yi Hong[1], Roland Kwitt[2], Nikhil Singh[1], Brad Davis[3], Nuno Vasconcelos[4], and Marc Niethammer[1,5]

[1] Department of Computer Science, UNC Chapel Hill, NC, USA
[2] Department of Computer Science, University of Salzburg, Austria
[3] Kitware Inc., Carrboro, NC, USA
[4] Statistical and Visual Computing Lab, UCSD, CA, USA
[5] Biomedical Research Imaging Center, UNC Chapel Hill, NC, USA

Abstract. This paper considers the problem of regressing data points on the Grassmann manifold over a scalar-valued variable. The Grassmannian has recently gained considerable attention in the vision community with applications in domain adaptation, face recognition, shape analysis, or the classification of linear dynamical systems. Motivated by the success of these approaches, we introduce a principled formulation for regression tasks on that manifold. We propose an *intrinsic* geodesic regression model generalizing classical linear least-squares regression. Since geodesics are parametrized by a starting point and a velocity vector, the model enables the synthesis of new observations on the manifold. To exemplify our approach, we demonstrate its applicability on three vision problems where data objects can be represented as points on the Grassmannian: the prediction of traffic speed and crowd counts from dynamical system models of surveillance videos and the modeling of aging trends in human brain structures using an affine-invariant shape representation.

Keywords: Geodesic regression, Grassmann manifold, Traffic speed prediction, Crowd counting, Shape regression.

1 Introduction

Data objects in many computer vision problems admit a subspace representation. Examples include feature sets obtained after dimensionality reduction via PCA, or observability matrix representations of linear dynamical systems. Assuming equal dimensionality, such subspace representations allow to interpret the data as points on the Grassmann manifold $\mathcal{G}(p, n)$, *i.e.*, the manifold of p-dimensional linear subspaces of $\mathbb{R}^n$. The seminal work of [10] and the introduction of efficient processing algorithms to manipulate points on the Grassmannian [12] has led to a variety of principled approaches to solve different vision and learning problems. These include domain adaptation [13,29], gesture recognition [19], face recognition under illumination changes [20], or the classification of visual dynamic processes [27]. Other works have explored subspace estimation via conjugate gradient decent [21], mean shift clustering [6], and the definition

D. Fleet et al. (Eds.): ECCV 2014, Part II, LNCS 8690, pp. 632–646, 2014.
© Springer International Publishing Switzerland 2014

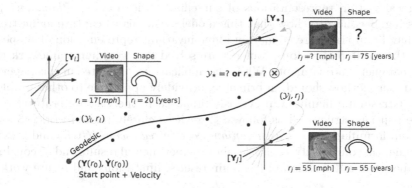

Fig. 1. Illustration of Grassmannian geodesic regression and inference. At the point marked $\otimes$, the inference objective for (i) traffic videos is to predict the independent variable r_* (here: speed), whereas for (ii) corpus callosum shapes we seek the manifold-valued $\mathcal{Y}_*$ for a value of the independent variable (here: age). For illustration, elements on the Grassmannian are visualized as lines through the origin, *i.e.*, $\mathcal{Y}_i \in \mathcal{G}(1,2)$.

of suitable kernel functions [14,18] that can be used with a variety of machine learning techniques.

While many vision applications primarily focus on performing classification or recognition tasks on the Grassmannian, the problem of regression has gained little attention (see §2). Yet, this statistical methodology has the potential to address many problems in a principled way. For instance, it enables predictions of an associated scalar-valued variable while, at the same time, respecting the geometry of the underlying space. Further, in scenarios such as shape regression, we are specifically interested in summarizing continuous trajectories that capture variations in the manifold-valued variable as a function of the scalar-valued independent variable. Fig. 1 illustrates these two inference objectives. While predictions about the scalar-valued variable could, in principle, be formulated within existing frameworks such as Gaussian process regression, *e.g.*, by using Grassmann kernels [14,18], it is not clear how to or if it is possible to address the second inference objective in such a formulation.

Contribution. We propose a formulation that directly fits a geodesic to a collection of data points. This is beneficial for several reasons. First, it is a *simple* and natural extension of linear regression to the Grassmannian; second, it provides a compact representation of the complete geodesic path; third, since the geodesic is parametrized by a starting point and a velocity, we can freely move along it and synthesize additional observations; fourth, it opens up the possibility of statistical analysis on Grassmannian geodesics; finally, this concept easily extends to more complex models, such as piecewise regression. The approach is extremely versatile which we demonstrate on three vision problems where data objects admit a representation on the Grassmannian. First, we show that the geodesic regression model can predict traffic speed and crowd counts from dynamical system representations of surveillance video clips *without* any pre-processing. Second, we show that this model allows us to capture aging trends of human brain structures under an affine-invariant representation of shape [3]. These three different vision problems are solved in a common framework with minor parameter adjustments. While the applications presented in this paper are limited, our method should, in principle, be widely applicable to other problems on the Grassmann manifold, previously proposed in the vision literature.

The paper is structured as follows: §2 reviews closely related work; §3 introduces our formulation of *Grassmannian geodesic regression (GGR)* and presents two numerical solution strategies. §4 shows experimental results and §5 concludes the paper with a discussion of the main results, limitations and future work.

2   Related Work

While differential geometric concepts, such as geodesics and intrinsic higher-order curves, have been well studied [23,5], their use for regression has only recently gained interest. A variety of methods extending concepts of regression in Euclidean spaces to *nonflat* manifolds have been proposed. Rentmeesters [24], Fletcher [11] and Hinkle *et al.* [15] address the problem of geodesic fitting on Riemannian manifolds, mostly focusing on symmetric spaces. Niethammer *et al.* [22] generalized linear regression to the manifold of diffeomorphisms to model image time-series data, followed by works extending this concept [16,25,26].

In principle, we can distinguish between two groups of approaches: first, *geodesic shooting* based strategies which address the problem using adjoint methods from an optimal-control point of view [22,16,25,26]; the second group comprises strategies which are based on optimization techniques that leverage *Jacobi fields* to compute the required gradients [11,24]. Unlike Jacobi field approaches, solutions using adjoint methods do not require computation of the curvature explicitly and easily extend to higher-order models, *e.g.*, polynomials [15], splines [26], or piecewise regression models. Our approach is a representative of the first category which ensures extensibility to more advanced models.

In the context of computer-vision problems, Lui [19] recently adapted the known Euclidean least-squares solution to the Grassmann manifold. While this strategy works remarkably well for the presented gesture recognition tasks, the formulation does not guarantee to minimize the sum-of-squared geodesic distances within the manifold. Since, in the regression literature, this is the natural extension of least-squares to Riemannian manifolds, the geometric and variational interpretation of [19] remains unclear. In contrast, we address the problem from an energy-minimization point of view which allows us to guarantee, by design, consistency with the geometry of the manifold.

To the best of our knowledge, the closest works to ours are [2] and [24]. Batzies *et al.* [2] discusses only a theoretical characterization of the geodesic fitting problem on the Grassmannian, but does not provide a numerical strategy for estimation. In contrast, we derive alternative optimality conditions using principles from optimal-control. These optimality conditions not only form the basis for our shooting approach, but also naturally lead to a convenient iterative algorithm. By construction, the obtained solution is guaranteed to be a geodesic. As discussed above, Rentmeesters [24] follows the Jacobi field approach. While both optimization methods have the same computational complexity for the gradient, *i.e.*, $O(np^2)$ on the Grassmannian $\mathcal{G}(p, n)$, it is non-trivial to generalize [24] to higher-order or piecewise models. Our approach, on the other hand, offers an alternative, simple solution that is (i) extensible and (ii) easy to implement.

3 Grassmannian Geodesic Regression (GGR)

To develop the framework for GGR, we first briefly review the Riemannian structure of the Grassmannian. For a more detailed treatment of this topic we refer the reader to [10,4,1]. We then discuss exact geodesic matching for two points and inexact geodesic matching for multiple points in §3.1 and present two strategies to solve these problems in §3.2 and §3.3.

Riemannian Structure of the Grassmann Manifold. The *Grassmann* manifold $\mathcal{G}(p, n)$ is defined as the set of p-dimensional linear subspaces of $\mathbb{R}^n$, typically represented by an orthonormal matrix $\mathbf{Y} \in \mathbb{R}^{n \times p}$, such that the column vectors span $\mathcal{Y}$, *i.e.*, $\mathcal{Y} = \mathrm{span}(\mathbf{Y})$. The Grassmannian can equivalently be defined as a quotient space within the special orthogonal group $SO(n)$ as $\mathcal{G}(p, n) := SO(n)/(SO(n-p) \times SO(p))$. The *canonical metric* $g_{\mathcal{Y}} : T_{\mathcal{Y}}\mathcal{G}(p, n) \times T_{\mathcal{Y}}\mathcal{G}(p, n) \to \mathbb{R}$ on $\mathcal{G}(p, n)$ is given by

$$g_{\mathcal{Y}}(\mathbf{\Delta}_{\mathcal{Y}}, \mathbf{\Delta}_{\mathcal{Y}}) = \mathrm{tr}\ \mathbf{\Delta}_{\mathcal{Y}}^{\top}\mathbf{\Delta}_{\mathcal{Y}} = \mathbf{C}^{\top}(\mathbf{I}_n - \mathbf{Y}\mathbf{Y}^T)\mathbf{C}\ , \tag{1}$$

where $\mathbf{I}_n$ denotes the $n \times n$ identity matrix, $T_{\mathcal{Y}}\mathcal{G}(p, n)$ is the tangent space at $\mathcal{Y}$, $\mathbf{C} \in \mathbb{R}^{n \times p}$ arbitrary and $\mathbf{Y}$ is a *representer* for $\mathcal{Y}$. Under this choice of metric, the arc-length of the geodesic connecting two subspaces $\mathcal{Y}, \mathcal{Z} \in \mathcal{G}(p, n)$ is related to the *canonical angles* $\phi_1, \ldots \phi_p \in [0, \pi/2]$ between $\mathcal{Y}$ and $\mathcal{Z}$ as $d^2(\mathcal{Y}, \mathcal{Z}) = ||\phi||_2^2$. In what follows, we slightly change notation and use $d^2(\mathbf{Y}, \mathbf{Z})$, with $\mathcal{Y} = \mathrm{span}(\mathbf{Y})$ and $\mathcal{Z} = \mathrm{span}(\mathbf{Z})$. In fact, the (squared) geodesic distance can be computed from the SVD decomposition $\mathbf{U}(\cos \mathbf{\Sigma})\mathbf{V}^{\top} = \mathbf{Y}^{\top}\mathbf{Z}$ as $d^2(\mathbf{Y}, \mathbf{Z}) = ||\cos^{-1}(\mathrm{diag}\ \mathbf{\Sigma})||^2$ (cf. [12]), where $\mathbf{\Sigma}$ is a diagonal matrix with principal angles ϕ_i.

Finally, consider a curve $\gamma : [0, 1] \to \mathcal{G}(p, n), r \mapsto \gamma(r)$ with $\gamma(0) = \mathcal{Y}_0$ and $\gamma(1) = \mathcal{Y}_1$, where $\mathcal{Y}_0$ represented by $\mathbf{Y}_0$ and $\mathcal{Y}_1$ represented by $\mathbf{Y}_1$. The *geodesic equation* for such a curve on $\mathcal{G}(p, n)$ is given (in terms of representers) by

$$\ddot{\mathbf{Y}}(r) + \mathbf{Y}(r)[\dot{\mathbf{Y}}(r)^{\top}\dot{\mathbf{Y}}(r)] = \mathbf{0}, \text{ with } \dot{\mathbf{Y}}(r) \doteq \frac{d}{dr}\mathbf{Y}(r)\ . \tag{2}$$

Eq. (2) also defines the Riemannian exponential map on the Grassmannian as an ODE for convenient numerical computations. Integrating the geodesic equation, starting with initial conditions, "shoots" the geodesic forward in time.

3.1 Exact/Inexact Geodesic Matching

Exact Matching between Two Points. To generalize linear regression in Euclidean space to geodesic regression on the Grassmannian, we replace the *line* equation by the geodesic equation (2), *i.e.*, the Euler-Lagrange equation of

$$E(\mathbf{Y}(r)) = \int_{r_0}^{r_1} \text{tr } \dot{\mathbf{Y}}(r)^\top \dot{\mathbf{Y}}(r) \, dr, \text{ such that } \mathbf{Y}(r_0) = \mathbf{Y}_0, \ \mathbf{Y}(r_1) = \mathbf{Y}_1 \quad (3)$$

and $\dot{\mathbf{Y}}(r) = (\mathbf{I}_n - \mathbf{Y}(r)\mathbf{Y}(r)^\top)\mathbf{C}$. To generalize residuals, we need the derivative of the squared geodesic distance of points to the regression geodesic with respect to its base point, *i.e.*, $\nabla_{\mathbf{Y}_0} d^2(\mathbf{Y}_0, \mathbf{Y}_1)$. Since the squared distance can be formulated as $d^2(\mathbf{Y}_0, \mathbf{Y}_1) = \min_{\mathbf{Y}(r)} E(\mathbf{Y}(r))$ for $r_0 = 0$ and $r_1 = 1$, we can derive $\nabla_{\mathbf{Y}_0} d^2(\mathbf{Y}_0, \mathbf{Y}_1)$, at optimality, as $\nabla_{\mathbf{Y}_0} d^2(\mathbf{Y}_0, \mathbf{Y}_1) = -2\dot{\mathbf{Y}}(0)$ (see supplementary material for details). The geodesic connecting the subspaces spanned by $\mathbf{Y}_0, \mathbf{Y}_1$, and its initial condition $\dot{\mathbf{Y}}(0)$ can be efficiently computed following [12], resulting in an efficient computation of $\nabla_{\mathbf{Y}_0} d^2(\mathbf{Y}_0, \mathbf{Y}_1)$ which will be used to solve the regression problem with multiple points. Since the geodesic can connect two points *exactly*, we refer to the case of two points as the *exact* matching problem.

Inexact Matching for Multiple Points. In order to fit a geodesic, given by an initial point $\mathbf{Y}(r_0)$ and an initial velocity $\dot{\mathbf{Y}}(r_0)$, to a collection of points $\{\mathbf{Y}_i\}_{i=0}^{N-1}$ at N measurement instances $\{r_i\}_{i=0}^{N-1}$, exact matching is relaxed to *inexact* matching through the minimization of the energy

$$E(\mathbf{Y}(r_0), \dot{\mathbf{Y}}(r_0)) = \alpha \int_{r_0}^{r_{N-1}} \text{tr } \dot{\mathbf{Y}}(r)^\top \dot{\mathbf{Y}}(r) \, dr + \frac{1}{\sigma^2} \sum_{i=0}^{N-1} d^2(\mathbf{Y}(r_i), \mathbf{Y}_i), \quad (4)$$

fulfilling the constraints for initial conditions $\mathbf{Y}(r_0)^\top \mathbf{Y}(r_0) = \mathbf{I}_p, \mathbf{Y}(r_0)^\top \dot{\mathbf{Y}}(r_0) = \mathbf{0}$, and the geodesic equation of (2); $\alpha \geq 0$ and $\sigma > 0$. The search for the curve $\mathbf{Y}(r)$ that minimizes this energy is denoted as *inexact* matching. As in the Euclidean case, $\mathbf{Y}(r_0)$ and $\dot{\mathbf{Y}}(r_0)$ can be interpreted as the initial *intercept* and *slope* that parametrize the geodesic. The first term in (4) is a norm-penalty on the slope of the geodesic, whereas α and σ are balancing constants. In practice, α is typically set to 0, unless we have specific prior knowledge about the slope, similar to a slope-regularized least-squares fit.

3.2   Approximate Solution by Pairwise Searching

One possibility to finding a geodesic that best approximates all data points $\{\mathbf{Y}_i\}$ is to adopt an extension of the well-known random sample consensus (RANSAC) procedure. This consists of picking pairs of points $\{\mathbf{Y}_a, \mathbf{Y}_b\}$; assuming $r_a < r_b$, we can compute the corresponding initial velocity $\dot{\mathbf{Y}}(r_a)$ (using the procedures of [12]) and then integrate the geodesic equation (2) forward and backward to span the full measurement interval of all data points $\{\mathbf{Y}_i\}$. As for a geodesic, $\dot{\mathbf{Y}}(r)^\top \dot{\mathbf{Y}}(r) = const.$, we can measure the regression energy in (4), given the geodesic specified by $\{\mathbf{Y}_a, \mathbf{Y}_b\}$, to evaluate model fit. By either randomly sampling a sufficient number of pairs of data points, or (for small datasets) exhaustively sampling all possible pairs, we obtain the approximate solution as the geodesic of the data point pair with the smallest energy. This solution, denoted as *GGR (pairwise searching)*, can be used directly, or to initialize the iterative numerical solution described in §3.3. Note that by dividing points into inliers and outliers, given distance thresholds, this defines a RANSAC-like estimation methodology on the Grassmannian.

3.3 Optimal Solution by Geodesic Shooting

To solve the energy minimization problem in (4), we discuss the shooting solution for the special case $N = 2$ first; the general solution then follows accordingly. Specializing (4) to $N = 2$ and $\mathbf{Y}(r_0) = \mathbf{Y}_0$, the geodesic determined by two representers, $\mathbf{Y}_0$ and $\mathbf{Y}_1$, can be obtained by minimizing the shooting energy

$$E(\mathbf{Y}(r_0), \dot{\mathbf{Y}}(r_0)) = \alpha \operatorname{tr} \dot{\mathbf{Y}}(r_0)^\top \dot{\mathbf{Y}}(r_0) + \frac{1}{\sigma^2} d^2(\mathbf{Y}(r_1), \mathbf{Y}_1) \qquad (5)$$

subject to constraints for initial conditions and the geodesic equation. To simplify computations, we replace the second order geodesic constraint by a system of first order. That is, we introduce auxiliary variables $\mathbf{X}_1(r) = \mathbf{Y}(r)$ and $\mathbf{X}_2(r) = \dot{\mathbf{Y}}(r)$ to rewrite the shooting energy of (5) and its constraints. By adding the constraints through Lagrangian multipliers, computing the associated variation, collecting terms and integration by parts, we obtain the optimality conditions with boundary conditions and constraints as shown in the forward and backward steps of Algorithm 1. Since the geodesic is determined by the unknown initial conditions, we need the gradients with respect to the sought-for initial conditions $\nabla_{\mathbf{X}_1(r_0)} E$ and $\nabla_{\mathbf{X}_2(r_0)} E$, which are also given in Algorithm 1[1].

The extension to the full GGR formulation is conceptionally straightforward. The goal is now to fit a best-approximating geodesic, *cf.* (4), to N data points $\{\mathbf{Y}_i\}_{i=0}^{N-1}$. Unlike the case for $N = 2$, instead of a fixed initial condition and one inexact final matching condition, we have (i) both initial $\mathbf{Y}(r_0)$ and $\dot{\mathbf{Y}}(r_0)$ free and (ii) multiple inexact matching terms. This creates jump conditions for the Lagrangian multiplier $\lambda_1(r)$ at each measurement instant when integrating backward in time. Algorithm 1 performs this computation.

4 Experiments

In the experiments, we demonstrate the versatility of our approach on three vision problems with data objects represented on the Grassmannian. First, on traffic speed prediction and crowd counting based on linear dynamical system models of surveillance video clips and second, on modeling the aging trend that is visible in the 2D shape of the human *corpus callosum*.

Dynamical Systems as Points on the Grassmannian. We demonstrate GGR in the context of modeling video clips by linear dynamical systems (LDS), commonly referred to as *dynamic texture* models [9] in the computer vision literature. For videos, represented by a collection of vectorized frames $\mathbf{y}_1, \ldots, \mathbf{y}_\tau$ with

---

[1] More details about the derivation are included in the supplementary material.

Algorithm 1. Grassmannian geodesic regression (GGR)

Data: $\{(r_i, \mathbf{Y}_i)\}_{i=0}^{N-1}$, $\alpha \geq 0$ and $\sigma > 0$

Result: $\mathbf{Y}(r_0)$, $\dot{\mathbf{Y}}(r_0)$

Set initial $\mathbf{Y}(r_0)$ and $\dot{\mathbf{Y}}(r_0)$, *e.g.*, using pairwise searching of §3.2.

while *not converged* **do**

Solve $\begin{cases} \dot{\mathbf{X}}_1 = \mathbf{X}_2, \ \mathbf{X}_1(r_0) = \mathbf{Y}(r_0), \\ \dot{\mathbf{X}}_2 = -\mathbf{X}_1(\mathbf{X}_2^\top \mathbf{X}_2), \ \mathbf{X}_2(r_0) = \dot{\mathbf{Y}}(r_0) \end{cases}$ forward for $r \in [r_0, r_{N-1}]$.

Solve $\begin{cases} \dot{\lambda}_1 = \lambda_2 \mathbf{X}_2^\top \mathbf{X}_2, \ \lambda_1(r_{N-1}+) = \mathbf{0}, \\ \dot{\lambda}_2 = -\lambda_1 + \mathbf{X}_2(\lambda_2^\top \mathbf{X}_1 + \mathbf{X}_1^\top \lambda_2), \ \lambda_2(r_{N-1}) = \mathbf{0} \end{cases}$ backward with

jump conditions

$$\lambda_1(r_i-) = \lambda_1(r_i+) - \frac{1}{\sigma^2} \nabla_{\mathbf{X}_1(r_i)} d^2(\mathbf{X}_1(r_i), \mathbf{Y}_i)$$

and $\nabla_{\mathbf{X}_1(r_i)} d^2(\mathbf{X}_1(r_i), \mathbf{Y}_i)$ computed as in §3.1. For multiple measurements at a given r_i, the jump conditions for each measurement are added up. Compute gradient with respect to initial conditions:

$$\nabla_{\mathbf{X}_1(r_0)} E = -(\mathbf{I}_n - \mathbf{X}_1(r_0)\mathbf{X}_1(r_0)^\top)\lambda_1(r_0-) + \mathbf{X}_2(r_0)\lambda_2(r_0)^\top \mathbf{X}_1(r_0),$$

$$\nabla_{\mathbf{X}_2(r_0)} E = 2\alpha \mathbf{X}_2(r_0) - (\mathbf{I}_n - \mathbf{X}_1(r_0)\mathbf{X}_1(r_0)^\top)\lambda_2(r_0).$$

Use a line search with these gradients to update $\mathbf{Y}(r_0)$ and $\dot{\mathbf{Y}}(r_0)$ as described in Algorithm 2 in Appendix A.

end

$\mathbf{y}_i \in \mathbb{R}^n$, the standard dynamic texture model has the form: $\mathbf{x}_{k+1} = \mathbf{A}\mathbf{x}_k + \mathbf{w}_k$, $\mathbf{w}_k \sim \mathcal{N}(\mathbf{0}, \mathbf{W})$; $\mathbf{y}_k = \mathbf{C}\mathbf{x}_k + \mathbf{v}_k$, $\mathbf{v}_k \sim \mathcal{N}(\mathbf{0}, \mathbf{R})$, with $\mathbf{x}_k \in \mathbb{R}^p$, $\mathbf{A} \in \mathbb{R}^{p \times p}$ and $\mathbf{C} \in \mathbb{R}^{n \times p}$. When relying on the prevalent (approximate) estimation approach of [9], the matrix $\mathbf{C}$ is, by design, of (full) rank p (*i.e.*, the number of states) and by construction we obtain an *observable* system, where the *observability* matrix $\mathbf{O} = [\mathbf{C} \ (\mathbf{CA}) \ (\mathbf{CA}^2) \ \cdots \ (\mathbf{CA}^{p-1})]^\top \in \mathbb{R}^{np \times p}$ also has full rank. System identification is not unique in the sense that systems $(\mathbf{A}, \mathbf{C})$ and $(\mathbf{TAT}^{-1}, \mathbf{CT}^{-1})$ with $\mathbf{T} \in \mathcal{GL}(p)^2$ have the same transfer function. Hence, the realization subspace spanned by $\mathbf{O}$ is a point on the Grassmannian $\mathcal{G}(p, n)$ and the observability matrix is a representer of this subspace. In our experiments, we identify an LDS model for a video clip by its $np \times p$ orthonormalized observability matrix.

Shapes as Points on the Grassmannian. We also apply GGR in the context of landmark-based shape analysis. A *shape matrix* is constructed based on its m landmarks, $\mathbf{L} = \{(x_1, y_1, ...); (x_2, y_2, ...); ...; (x_m, y_m, ...)\}$. Using SVD on the shape matrix, *i.e.*, $\mathbf{L} = \mathbf{U}\mathbf{\Sigma}\mathbf{V}^\top$, we obtain an affine-invariant shape representation from the left-singular vectors $\mathbf{U}$ [3]. This establishes a mapping from the shape matrix to a point on the Grassmannian (with $\mathbf{U}$ as the representative).

---

^{2} $\mathcal{GL}(p)$ is the general linear group of $p \times p$ invertible matrices.

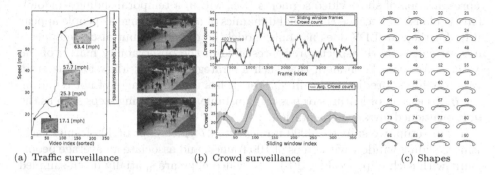

(a) Traffic surveillance   (b) Crowd surveillance   (c) Shapes

Fig. 2. Illustration of the datasets: (a) surveillance videos of highway traffic [7] for speed regression; (b) surveillance videos of a sidewalk [8] for regressing *average* crowd count and (c) corpus callosum shapes [11] for shape regression

4.1   Datasets

Synthetic Sine/Cosine Signals. To first demonstrate GGR on a toy-example, we embed 25 synthetic 2D sine/cosine signals, sampled at 630 points in $[0, 10\pi]$, in $\mathbb{R}^{24}$; the signal frequencies are uniformly sampled in $(0, 10)$. The 2D signals $\mathbf{s} \in \mathbb{R}^{2 \times 630}$ are then linearly projected via $\bar{\mathbf{s}} = \mathbf{Us}$, where $\mathbf{W} \sim \mathcal{N}(\mathbf{0}, \mathbf{I}_{24})$ and $\mathbf{W} = \mathbf{U\Sigma V}^\top$. Finally, white Gaussian noise with $\sigma = 0.1$ is added to $\bar{\mathbf{s}}$. Given a collection of training signals, our objective is to predict the signal frequency based on the LDS models of the 24-dimensional data.

UCSD Traffic Dataset [7]. This dataset was introduced in the context of clustering traffic flow patterns with LDS models. It contains a collection of short traffic video clips, acquired by a surveillance system monitoring highway traffic. There are 253 videos in total and each video is roughly matched to the speed measurements from a highway-mounted speed sensor. We use the pre-processed video clips introduced in [7] which were converted to grayscale and spatially normalized to 48 × 48 pixels with zero mean and unit variance. Our rationale for using an LDS representation for speed prediction is the fact that clustering and categorization experiments in [7] showed compelling evidence that dynamics are indicative of the traffic class. We argue that the notion of speed of an object (*e.g.*, a car) could be considered a property that humans infer from its visual dynamics.

UCSD Pedestrian Dataset [8]. We use the Peds1 subset of the UCSD pedestrian dataset which contains 4000 frames with a ground-truth people count (both directions and total) associated with each frame. Similar to [8] we ask the question whether we can infer the number of people in a scene (or clip) without actually detecting the people. While this has been done by resorting to crowd/motion segmentation and Gaussian process regression on low-level features extracted from these segments, we go one step further and try to avoid any preprocessing at all. In fact, our objective is to infer an *average* people count from an LDS representation of short video segments (*i.e.*, within a temporal sliding window). This is plausible because the visual dynamics of a scene change as people appear in it. Further, an LDS does not only model the dynamics, but also the appearance of videos; both aspects are represented in the observability matrix of the system. We remark, though, that such a strategy does not allow for fine-grain frame-by-frame predictions as in [8]. Yet, it has the advantages of not requiring any pre-selection of features or possibly unstable preprocessing steps such as the aforementioned crowd segmentation.

In our setup, we split the 4000 frames into 37 video clips of 400 frames each, using a sliding window with steps of 100 frames, and associate an average people count with each clip, see Fig. 2(b). The video clips are spatially down-sampled to a resolution of 60×40 pixel (original: 238×158) to keep the observability matrices at a reasonable size. Since the overlap between the clips potentially biases the experiments, we introduce a weighted variant of system identification (see Appendix B) with weights based on a Gaussian function centered at the middle of the sliding window and a standard deviation of 100. While this ensures stable system identification, by still using 400 frames, it reduces the impact of the overlapping frames on the parameter estimates. With this strategy, the average crowd count is localized to a smaller region.

Corpus Callosum Shapes [11]. To demonstrate GGR for modeling shape changes, we use a collection of 32 *corpus callosum* shapes with ages varying from 19 to 90 years, shown in Fig. 2(c). Each shape is represented by 64 2D boundary landmarks, and is projected to a point on the Grassmannian using the left-singular vectors obtained from the SVD decomposition of the 64×2 shape matrix.

4.2   Results

We compare the performance of (i) *GGR (pairwise searching)* (*i.e.*, the approximate solution), (ii) *Full GGR*, and (iii) *Full piecewise GGR*. For (iii), the regression space is subdivided into regression intervals and a full regression solution is computed for each interval independently. Given a (test) measurement, a regressor is estimated for all intervals. We search over each interval and find the closest point on the geodesic with the smallest distance. The value of the regressor at this optimal point is then regarded as the predicted value for the measurement. For full GGR, we set $\alpha = 0$ because no prior information is known about the measurements, and $\sigma^2 = 1$. Two segments were used in *Full piecewise GGR* and the breakpoint (separating the regression intervals) varied with the dataset, but was roughly chosen to separate the data into two equal-sized groups or two classes. While this is certainly an ad–hoc choice and could be fully data-driven, our choice of two segments is only to demonstrate the easy extensibility of our method to a piecewise regression formulation. To compare the three GGR variants, we report the *mean absolute error (MAE)*, computed over all folds in a cross validation (CV) setup with a dataset-dependent number of folds.

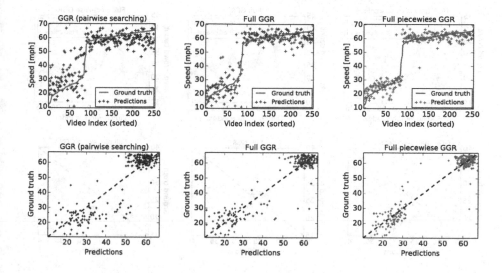

Fig. 3. Visualization of traffic speed predictions via 5-fold cross validation. The top row shows the predictions vs. the videos sorted by *speed*; the bottom row shows the correlation with the ground-truth.

Signal Frequency Prediction (Toy Data). For this experiment, the number of LDS states is set to $p = 2$ which is, in theory, sufficient to capture sine/cosine signals. We divide the 25 signals into 5 groups for 5-fold CV. For *Full piecewise GGR*, we regress on the signals with frequencies in the two intervals $(0,5)$ and $[5,10)$. The testing MAE ranges from 0.49e-15±0.32e-15 for both *GGR (pairwise searching)* and *Full GGR* to 0.58e-15±0.28e-15 for *Full piecewise GGR*, *cf.* Table 1. On this toy data, this shows that all our regression formulation(s) can essentially capture the data perfectly.

Traffic Speed Prediction. For each video clip, we estimate LDS models with $p = 10$ states. The breakpoint of *Full piecewise GGR* is set at 50 [mph], which roughly divides the videos into two categories, *i.e.*, fast and slow. Results are reported for 5-fold CV. A visualization of the predictions is shown in Fig. 3 with the predictions versus the sorted speed measurements, as well as the correlation with the ground-truth. As we can see from the MAEs in Table 1, the results gradually improve as we switch from *GGR (pairwise searching)* to *Full GGR* and *Full piecewise GGR*, with a top MAE of 3.35 ± 0.38 [mph] for testing.

Crowd Counting. For each of the 37 video clips we extract from the Peds1 dataset, we estimate LDS models with $p = 10$ states using weighted system identification as described in Appendix B. For *Full piecewise GGR*, the breakpoint is set to a count of 23 people; this choice separates the 37 videos into two groups of roughly equal size. Results are reported for 4-fold CV. From the results shown in Fig. 4, we see that both *Full GGR* and *Full piecewise GGR* provide visually close predictions to the ground-truth. From Table 1, we further see that

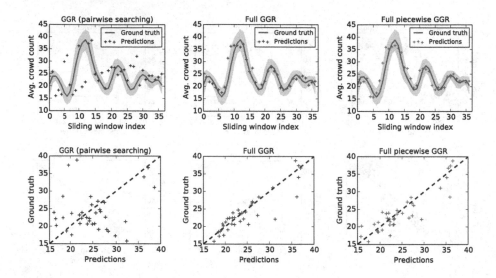

Fig. 4. Visualization of crowd counting results via 4-fold cross validation. The top row shows the crowd count predictions as a function of the sliding window index, overlaid on the ground-truth counts; the bottom row shows the predictions versus the ground-truth. The gray bands indicate the weighted standard deviation ($\pm 1\sigma$) of the number of people in the sliding window.

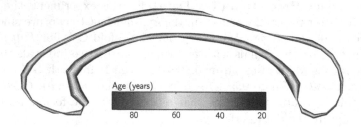

Fig. 5. Corpus callosum shapes along *Full GGR* geodesic; colored by age in years

these two GGR variants have significantly better performance than the pairwise searching strategy. In fact, *Full GGR* achieves the top prediction by improving from 5.14 ± 0.64 to 1.65 ± 0.79. Although, *Full piecewise GGR* has lowest training error among the three variants, its testing error is higher than for *Full GGR*, indicating an overfit to the data.

Corpus Callosum Aging. We generate corpus callosum shapes along the geodesic fit by *Full GGR*, as shown in Fig. 5. The shapes are recovered from the points along the geodesic on the Grassmann manifold through scaling by the mean singular values of the SVD results. As we can see, the shape shrinks from blue to red, corresponding to 19 and 90 years of age; this demonstrates the thinning trend of the corpus callosum with age and is consistent with [11].

Table 1. Mean absolute errors (MAE, computed via cross validation) ±1 standard deviation on both training and testing data. Either *Full GGR* or *Full piecewise GGR* give the best results. *Full piecewise GGR* leads to overfitting for the crowd counting case, hence *Full GGR* is preferable in this case.

	GGR (pairwise searching)		Full GGR		Full piecewise GGR	
	Train	Test	Train	Test	Train	Test
Signal freq. (x 10⁻¹⁵)	0.50 ± 0.09	0.49 ± 0.32	0.50 ± 0.09	0.49 ± 0.32	0.52 ± 0.06	0.58 ± 0.28
Traffic speed	6.46 ± 0.55	6.20 ± 0.77	2.98 ± 0.20	4.59 ± 0.43	**1.65 ± 0.13**	**3.35 ± 0.38**
Crowd counting	4.27 ± 0.33	5.14 ± 0.64	0.81 ± 0.21	**1.65 ± 0.79**	**0.63 ± 0.08**	2.05 ± 0.88

It is critical to note that since the Grassmann manifold has non-negative sectional curvature, conjugate points do exist. This implies that there can be multiple geodesics that connect any two points, resulting in a potentially non-unique solution for the regression problem. However, Wong [28] proves that geodesics are unique as long as subspace angles ϕ_i are less than $\pi/2$. We evaluated all subspace angles in our experiments against this criteria and found *no* violation which ensures that all estimated geodesics were unique. While the issue of conjugate points exists with any manifold of non-negative curvature, this criteria can certainly serve as a sanity check for any solution to the regression problem.

5   Discussion

In this paper, we developed a general theory for Grassmannian geodesic regression. This allowed us to compute regression geodesics that explain the variation in the data on the Grassmannian. We demonstrated the utility of our method for modeling a dependent Grassmannian-valued variable in the form of observability matrices from LDS and affine-invariant shape data, with respect to a scalar-valued independent variable. We also showed that our formulation naturally extends to piecewise regression models.

The experimental results on the traffic speed data show that the dynamics captured by the LDS models correlate with traffic speed, leading to predictions with an MAE error of 3.35 ± 0.38 [mph]. This is an encouraging result, especially since the dataset has an unbalanced design and requires no higher-level preprocessing (*e.g.*, tracking). For crowd counting, an MAE of 1.65 ± 0.79 does not beat the frame-by-frame counting results in [8] (1.31 for frame counting on **Peds1**, and 0.59 for our measure of *average* counting). However, in our case, information is captured by the LDS model directly from the raw image data, whereas frame-by-frame counting typically requires a collection of suitable features and thus involves more preprocessing. Additionally, our approach is not directly comparable to [8], since regressing an average people count is influenced by the variation of the counts within the LDS estimation window.

In our shape regression experiment, we show that the resulting estimated geodesic effectively summarizes the trajectory of changes in the corpus callosum for a population. In fact, the corpus callosum exhibits a clear thinning with progressing age. Since the estimated geodesic summarizes the complete nonlinear variability of aging related biological changes, and is compactly represented by its initial conditions, this modeling opens the possibility of nonlinear statistics on changes in (anatomical) shapes.

Some open questions need to be addressed in future work. For example, piecewise GGR has the advantage of greater flexibility but inherently depends upon the *optimal* number of segments. While the breakpoints could, in principle, be chosen in a data-driven way, the increased flexibility makes the model susceptible to overfitting issues (especially with unbalanced data). Furthermore, since we fit the segments independently, this results in discontinuous piecewise geodesic curves. Thanks to the adjoint method it is, however, possible to derive a *continuous-piecewise* GGR variant by constraining the geodesics to match at the segment boundaries (see supplementary material for details).

Another interesting avenue to pursue in future work would be to leverage the concept of *time-warping* in which the time-axis is bent according to some parametric function. This increases flexibility and could be beneficial in vision applications where we have specific prior knowledge about the data, *e.g.*, traffic speed measurements exhibiting saturation in the upper and lower ranges. The general strategy to incorporate time-warping into the regression formulation is developed in [17] and exemplified on the Grassmannian, using the numerical machinery developed in this work.

A   Line Search on the Grassmannian

Performing a line search is not as straightforward as in Euclidean space since we need to assure that the constraints for $\mathbf{Y}(r_0)$ and $\dot{\mathbf{Y}}(r_0)$ are fulfilled for any given step. In particular, changing $\mathbf{Y}(r_0)$ will change the associated tangent vector $\dot{\mathbf{Y}}(r_0)$. Once, we have updated $\mathbf{Y}(r_0)$ to $\mathbf{Y}^u(r_0)$ by moving along the geodesic defined by $\mathbf{Y}(r_0)$ and the gradient of the energy with respect to this initial point, *i.e.*, $\nabla_{\mathbf{X}_1(r_0)} E$, we can transport the tangent $\dot{\mathbf{Y}}(r_0)$ to $\mathbf{Y}^u(r_0)$ using the closed form solution for *parallel transport* of [10]. In particular,

$$\dot{\mathbf{Y}}^u(r_0) = [\mathbf{Y}(r_0)\mathbf{V}\ \mathbf{U}] \begin{pmatrix} -\sin t\boldsymbol{\Sigma} \\ \cos t\boldsymbol{\Sigma} \end{pmatrix} \mathbf{U}^\top + (\mathbf{I}_n - \mathbf{U}\mathbf{U}^\top)\dot{\mathbf{Y}}(r_0) \tag{6}$$

where $\mathbf{H} = \mathbf{U}\boldsymbol{\Sigma}\mathbf{V}^\top$ is the compact SVD of the tangent vector at $\mathbf{Y}(r_0)$ along the geodesic connecting $\mathbf{Y}(r_0)$ and $\mathbf{Y}^u(r_0)$. Algorithm 2 lists the line search procedure in full technical detail.

Algorithm 2. Grassmannian equivalent of $x^{k+1} = x^k - \Delta t g$, where Δt is the timestep and g is the gradient.

Data: $\mathbf{Y}(r_0)$, $\dot{\mathbf{Y}}(r_0)$, $\nabla_{\mathbf{Y}(r_0)}E$, $\nabla_{\dot{\mathbf{Y}}(r_0)}E$, Δt
Result: Updated $\mathbf{Y}^u(r_0)$ and $\dot{\mathbf{Y}}^u(r_0)$
Compute $\dot{\overline{\mathbf{Y}}}^u(r_0) = \dot{\mathbf{Y}}(r_0) - \Delta t \nabla_{\mathbf{x}_2(r_0)}E$
Compute $\mathbf{Y}^u(r_0)$ by flowing for Δt along geodesic with initial condition
$(\mathbf{Y}(r_0), -\nabla_{\mathbf{x}_1(r_0)}E)$ (using algorithm in [10])
Transport $\dot{\overline{\mathbf{Y}}}^u(r_0)$ along the geodesic connecting $\mathbf{Y}(r_0)$ to $\mathbf{Y}^u(r_0)$, using (6),
resulting in $\dot{\overline{\mathbf{Y}}}^u_T(r_0)$
Project updated initial velocity onto the tangent space (for consistency):
$\dot{\mathbf{Y}}^u(r_0) \leftarrow (\mathbf{I}_n - \mathbf{Y}^u(r_0)\mathbf{Y}^u(r_0)^\top)\dot{\overline{\mathbf{Y}}}^u_T(r_0)$.

B   Temporally Localized System Identification

To support a non-uniform weighting of samples during system identification, we propose a *temporally* localized variant of [9]. This is beneficial in situations where we need a considerable number of frames for stable system identification, yet not all samples should contribute equally to the LDS parameter estimates. Specifically, given the measurement matrix $\mathbf{M} = [\mathbf{y}_1, \cdots, \mathbf{y}_\tau]$ and a set of weights $\mathbf{w} = [w_1, \cdots, w_\tau]$, such that $\sum_i w_i = \tau$, we perform a weighted SVD of $\mathbf{M}$, *i.e.*,

$$\mathbf{U}\boldsymbol{\Sigma}\mathbf{V}^\top = \mathbf{M}\mathrm{diag}(\sqrt{\mathbf{w}}) \ . \tag{7}$$

Then, as in [9], $\mathbf{C} = \mathbf{U}$ and $\mathbf{X} = \boldsymbol{\Sigma}\mathbf{V}^\top$. Once the state matrix $\mathbf{X}$ has been determined, $\mathbf{A}$ can be computed as $\mathbf{A} = \mathbf{X}_2^\tau \mathbf{W}^{\frac{1}{2}}(\mathbf{X}_1^{\tau-1}\mathbf{W}^{\frac{1}{2}})^\dagger$, where † denotes the pseudoinverse, $\mathbf{X}_2^\tau = [\mathbf{x}_2, \cdots, \mathbf{x}_\tau]$, $\mathbf{X}_1^{\tau-1} = [\mathbf{x}_1, \cdots, \mathbf{x}_{\tau-1}]$ and $\mathbf{W}^{\frac{1}{2}}$ is a diagonal matrix with $W_{ii}^{\frac{1}{2}} = [\frac{1}{2}(w_i + w_{i+1})]^{1/2}$.

Acknowledgements. This work was supported by NSF grants EECS-1148870, EECS-0925875 and IIS-1208522.

References

1. Absil, P.A., Mahony, R., Sepulchre, R.: Optimization Algorithms on Matrix Manifolds. Princeton University Press (2008)
2. Batzies, E., Machado, L., Silva Leite, F.: The geometric mean and the geodesic fitting problem on the Grassmann manifold,
   http://www.mat.uc.pt/preprints/ps/p1322.pdf (unpublished manuscript)
3. Begelfor, E., Werman, W.: Affine invariance revisited. In: CVPR (2006)
4. Boothby, W.: An Introduction to Differentiable Manifolds and Riemannian Geometry. Academic Press (1986)
5. Camarinha, M., Leite, F.S., Crouch, P.: Splines of class C^k on non-Euclidean spaces. IMA J. Math. Control Info. 12(4), 399–410 (1995)
6. Çetingül, H., Vidal, R.: Intrinsic mean shift for clustering on Stiefel and Grassmann manifolds. In: CVPR (2009)

7. Chan, A., Vasconcelos, N.: Classification and retrieval of traffic video using auto-regressive stochastic processes. In: Intelligent Vehicles (2005)
8. Chan, A., Vasconcelos, N.: Counting people with low-level features and Bayesian regression. Trans. Image Process. 12(4), 2160–2177 (2012)
9. Doretto, G., Chiuso, A., Wu, Y., Soatto, S.: Dynamic textures. Int. J. Comput. Vision 51(2), 91–109 (2003)
10. Edelman, A., Arias, T., Smith, S.T.: The geometry of algorithms with orthogonality constraints. SIAM J. Matrix Anal. Appl. 20(2), 303–353 (1998)
11. Fletcher, T.P.: Geodesic regression and the theory of least squares on Riemannian manifolds. Int. J. Comput. Vision 105(2), 171–185 (2012)
12. Gallivan, K., Srivastava, A., Xiuwen, L., Dooren, P.V.: Efficient algorithms for inferences on Grassmann manifolds. In: Statistical Signal Processing Workshop, pp. 315–318 (2003)
13. Gopalan, R., Li, R., Chellappa, R.: Domain adaption for object recognition: An unsupervised approach. In: ICCV (2011)
14. Hamm, J., Lee, D.: Grassmann discriminant analysis: A unifying view on subspace learning. In: ICML (2008)
15. Hinkle, J., Fletcher, P.T., Joshi, S.: Intrinsic polynomials for regression on Riemannian manifolds. J. Math. Imaging Vis., 1–21 (2014)
16. Hong, Y., Joshi, S., Sanchez, M., Styner, M., Niethammer, M.: Metamorphic geodesic regression. In: Ayache, N., Delingette, H., Golland, P., Mori, K. (eds.) MICCAI 2012, Part III. LNCS, vol. 7512, pp. 197–205. Springer, Heidelberg (2012)
17. Hong, Y., Singh, N., Kwitt, R., Niethammer, M.: Time-warped geodesic regression. In: Hata, N., Barillot, C., Hornegger, J., Howe, R. (eds.) MICCAI 2014, Part II. LNCS, vol. 8674, pp. 105–112. Springer, Heidelberg (2014)
18. Jayasumana, S., Hartley, R., Salzmann, M., Li, H., Harandi, M.: Optimizing over radial kernels on compact manifolds. In: CVPR (2014)
19. Lui, Y.: Human gesture recognition on product manifolds. JMLR 13, 3297–3321 (2012)
20. Lui, Y., Beveridge, J., Kirby, M.: Canonical Stiefel quotient and its application to generic face recognition in illumination spaces. In: BTAS (2009)
21. Mittal, S., Meer, P.: Conjugate gradient descent on Grassmann manifolds for robust subspace estimation. Image Vision Comput. 30, 417–427 (2012)
22. Niethammer, M., Huang, Y., Vialard, F.-X.: Geodesic regression for image time-series. In: Fichtinger, G., Martel, A., Peters, T. (eds.) MICCAI 2011, Part II. LNCS, vol. 6892, pp. 655–662. Springer, Heidelberg (2011)
23. Noakes, L., Heinzinger, G., Paden, B.: Cubic splines on curved spaces. IMA J. Math. Control Info. 6(4), 465–473 (1989)
24. Rentmeesters, Q.: A gradient method for geodesic data fitting on some symmetric Riemannian manifolds. In: CDC-ECC (2011)
25. Singh, N., Hinkle, J., Joshi, S., Fletcher, P.: A vector momenta formulation of diffeomorphisms for improved geodesic regression and atlas construction. In: ISBI (2013)
26. Singh, N., Niethammer, M.: Splines for diffeomorphic image regression. In: Hata, N., Barillot, C., Hornegger, J., Howe, R. (eds.) MICCAI 2014, Part II. LNCS, vol. 8674, pp. 121–129. Springer, Heidelberg (2014)
27. Turuga, P., Veeraraghavan, A., Srivastrava, A., Chellappa, R.: Statistical computations on Grassmann and Stiefel manifolds for image and video-based recognition. IEEE Trans. Pattern Anal. Mach. Intell. 33(11), 2273–2285 (2011)
28. Wong, Y.C.: Differential geometry of Grassmann manifolds. Proc. Natl. Acad. Sci. USA 57(3), 589–594 (1967)
29. Zheng, J., Liu, M.Y., Chellappa, R., Phillips, P.: A Grassmann manifold-based domain adaption approach. In: ICML (2012)

Model Selection by Linear Programming

Joseph Wang, Tolga Bolukbasi, Kirill Trapeznikov, and Venkatesh Saligrama

Boston University, USA

Abstract. Budget constraints arise in many computer vision problems. Computational costs limit many automated recognition systems while crowdsourced systems are hindered by monetary costs. We leverage wide variability in image complexity and learn adaptive model selection policies. Our learnt policy maximizes performance under average budget constraints by selecting "cheap" models for low complexity instances and utilizing descriptive models only for complex ones. During training, we assume access to a set of models that utilize features of different costs and types. We consider a binary tree architecture where each leaf corresponds to a different model. Internal decision nodes adaptively guide model-selection process along paths on a tree. The learning problem can be posed as an empirical risk minimization over training data with a non-convex objective function. Using hinge loss surrogates we show that adaptive model selection reduces to a linear program thus realizing substantial computational efficiencies and guaranteed convergence properties.

Keywords: test-time budget, adaptive model selection, cost-sensitive learning.

1 Introduction

Image recognition often relies on expensive intermediate visual processing tasks that can hinder test-time applicability. In automated systems, low-level representations (e.g., histograms of oriented gradients) typically incur a high computation cost and impact test time tractability. In crowdsourced systems, humans are paid to identify intermediate visual cues/attributes and can be prohibitively expensive for test-time.

On the other hand, we can leverage the fact that images exhibit wide diversity in complexity. Indeed, recognition for many typical instances can be performed to desired accuracy with relatively cheap models that utilize computationally inexpensive features or only a few expensive attributes. This key insight motivates our model selection policies that adapts to problem difficulty. We learn decision rules from training data, which when presented with a new example selects the most informative and cost-effective model for that example.

We describe our work in the context of handwriting recognition and scene categorization. In handwriting recognition the objective is to predict a word given a sequence of letter images. While a more complex model, that uses several feature types or processing at multiple resolutions yields better predictive

D. Fleet et al. (Eds.): ECCV 2014, Part II, LNCS 8690, pp. 647–662, 2014.

performance, the system suffers from the prohibitively slow computation time
[24]. Scene recognition– another scenario where budget constraints arise–is a
difficult task due to the large number of classes and interclass similarity [15].
Low-level features are often insufficient for acceptable performance; and high-
level attributes crowdsourced by Amazon Mechanical Turk (AMT) are often
used in predictive models incurring monetary costs. Due to the wide diversity
of images, high-cost attributes/features are often unnecessary for many images
to meet acceptable performance. Indeed "cheap" models can often be used for
typical cases. The goal of this paper is to learn policies that adaptively utilizes
cost-effective models while ensuring desired performance. If we represent an input data instance as $\mathbf{x}$, its unknown response as y and our adaptive selection
system as $\mathbf{g}(\mathbf{x})$ then the high level objective is to minimize the average prediction
error subject to an average budget B.

$$\min_{\mathbf{g}} \ \mathbf{E}\left[\, \mathrm{error}(\mathbf{g}(\mathbf{x}), y) \,\right] \quad s.t. \ \ \mathbf{E}\left[\, \mathrm{cost}(\mathbf{g}(\mathbf{x})) \,\right] \leq B$$

Several researchers have explored similar problems ([8,10,11,24]) which we will
describe later.

The novel contribution that differentiates our work is a convex formulation
for learning an adaptive model selector. We assume we are given a collection of
precomputed models. Each model operates on features with different costs. Our
decision system is described by a binary tree (see Fig.1). Each leaf corresponds to
a particular model. Due to this structure, models can share features/attributes.
The internal decision nodes route examples along the paths in a tree culminating
in a model that is cost-effective while meeting desired accuracy levels.

Learning decision functions at each node of such a tree can be posed as an
empirical risk minimization(ERM) problem that balances acquisition cost and
misclassification error. We express ERM as an extremal(maxima) point of sums
of indicator functions. This key transformation enables us to introduce convex
surrogates for the indicator functions and, in turn, results in a convex objective.
Without our transformation, direct substitution of surrogates in the original
empirical risk results in a non-convex multi-linear formulation which is known
to be NP-complete [14].

Next, by choosing a hinge loss for upper-bounding surrogate, we reduce the
objective to a linear program (LP): a very well studied problem with strong
convergence guarantees and efficient optimization algorithms. However, other
convex surrogates are also possible and our formulation carries all the advantage
of convex programming such as repeatability, global convergence and computation efficiency. In contrast, alternating non-convex optimization approaches
[18,2,21] applied to similar problems do not have such guarantees.

1.1   Related Work

Our work is broadly related to detection cascades (see [20,27,5] and references
therein) and the more recent work on classifier cascades [18]. Detection cascades

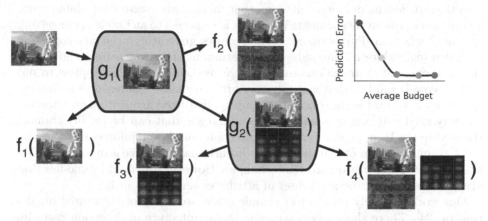

Fig. 1. An illustration of our model selection tree. We have access to four models: $f_1, \ldots f_4$. The models use a different combination of three representations: rgb, hog, and gist. The system has two internal decisions nodes. $g_1(rgb)$ uses the raw pixel values to either select a low cost model $f_1(rgb)$, medium cost model $f_2(rgb, hog)$ or delay the decision. The last decision node, $g_2(rgb, gist)$, acquired the gist feature selects between predicting with available information, $f_3(rgb, gist)$, or processing hog and predicting with the most expensive model, $f_4(rgb, gist, hog)$. The performance of an adaptive model selection can be represented by an budget vs error curve in the upper right corner. The colors correspond to different operating points as we vary the trade off between cost and error. The overall goal is to operate close the performance of the most complex model (red) with much lower budgets. The green point will an example of a desired system.

have been used for highly skewed problems for object detection and realize efficiency by using simpler models to reject examples as negative without needing to evaluate the more complex models farther along the cascade. Classifier cascades generalize this to multi-class scenarios with a series of increasingly informative models that adapt to problem difficulty. More recently, these ideas have also been generalized to cost-sensitive tree classifiers for web page ranking [26]. Our work differs from these contributions in several ways. First, our architecture is flexible and account for tree structures unlike cascades. Second, our approach can deal with a wider variety of prediction tasks including structured learning and sequence prediction with combinatorial output spaces in contrast to [20,27,5,18,26]. Finally, unlike much of this existing work that involve nonconvex objectives and resort to alternative minimization schemes we formulate a globally convex objective with guaranteed convergence properties. We generalize the work on convex classifier cascades in [23] to more flexible architectures and broader range of prediction problems. Also, related convex optimization techniques were used by [22] in local learning problems.

Our work can be placed within the broader context of MDP approaches as well. MDP methods unlike ours do not assume fixed architectures. [10,9] apply an imitation learning (IL) algorithm introduced by [16] to the problem of feature selection. IL learns decision functions that mimics an *oracle* on training data. Many issues arise in this context. We do not have access to an oracle in our setting of model selection. Furthermore, IL [9] requires generating arbitrary collection of states (candidate feature subsets) from training data to ensure a sufficiently rich collection of state-actions to mimic. Nevertheless this idea applied to our setting entails models that can take any arbitrary subset of features as inputs, which is not tractable. In contrast by employing a fixed acquisition architecture we only need a relatively small number of models that can be readily trained. Related to the IL approach is another direction based on reinforcement learning [12,4,7]. In lieu of an oracle the authors linearly parameterize a reward function and estimate it with standard RL techniques. However, the need for models that are customized to arbitrary subset of attributes remains as in IL.

Our work is closely related to dynamic model selection for structured prediction of [24]. There the authors combine the architecture of detection cascades with decision structure of RL. The authors define a value for selecting a more complex model to make predictions, and approximate the selection policy as a linear combination of meta-features computed on previous model outputs. The goal is to improve inference accuracy while satisfying a budget on a batch of test data. Our approach is more general. Instead of being limited to cascades, we have the ability to construct a binary tree architecture. Also, instead of a single policy that controls model selection at every step, we learn a separate decision function for every internal node of the tree. These advantages produce a more cost-effective model selection policy as we demonstrate in our experiments.

2   Empirical Risk Problem

In a typical learning problem, a data instance, $\mathbf{x} \in \mathcal{X}$ has a corresponding response $y \in \mathcal{Y}$. The goal is to learn a model $f(\mathbf{x}) \in \mathcal{Y}$ that correctly predicts the response variable y. For notational purposes we let $\mathcal{D}$ denote the unknown joint distribution for $(\mathbf{x}, y)$.

For example, in scene categorization, the objective is to predict a scene category, y, in an image $\mathbf{x}$. Here, the response space $\mathcal{Y}$ consists of L possible classes, $\{1, \ldots, L\}$. In structured prediction, the input, $\mathbf{x}$, is a sequence of handwritten letter images. The goal is predict the written word. Here, $\mathcal{Y}$ is a combinatorial output space consisting of all admissible letter sequences.

Each instance $\mathbf{x}$ is composed of M different vector-valued feature/attribute components. The mth feature component has an associated cost c_m. We assume we have access to K prediction models: $f_1(\mathbf{x}), \ldots, f_K(\mathbf{x})$ that are a priori given and fixed. The input to each model, $f_k(\cdot)$, is a sub-collection, S_k, of the M attributes or features. Each model has an associated cost of prediction: $\sum_{m \in S_k} c_m$. In addition, each model's prediction performance is evaluated with a loss function given the ground truth response variable: $\mathcal{L}(f(\mathbf{x}), y) \in \mathbb{R}^+$. For instance, in classification, the loss is simply a 0/1 error, $\mathcal{L}(f(\mathbf{x}), y) = \mathbb{1}_{[f(\mathbf{x}) \neq y]}$.

Our goal is to learn a decision system that dynamically selects one of these models for every instance $\mathbf{x}$. We represent our system as a binary tree. The binary tree is composed of K leafs and $K-1$ internal nodes. At each internal node, $j = 1, \ldots, K-1$, is a binary decision function, $\text{sign}[g_j(\mathbf{x})] \in \{+1, -1\}$. This function determines which action should be taken for a given example. The binary decisions, $g_j(\mathbf{x})$'s, represent actions from the following set: stop and predict with the model that uses the current set of features or choose which feature to request next. Each leaf node, $k = 1, \ldots, K$, corresponds to a terminal decision of predicting with the model $f_k(\mathbf{x})$ based on the available information. For notational simplicity, we denote applying a decision node and a leaf model as $g_j(\mathbf{x})$ and $f_k(\mathbf{x})$ respectively. Note the functions implicitly operate only on the feature sets that have been acquired along the associated path to each node.

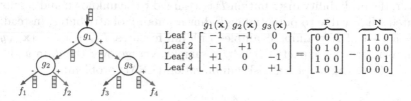

Fig. 3. An example decision system of depth two: node $g_1(x_1)$ selects either to acquire feature 2 for a cost c_2 or 3 for a cost c_3. Node $g_2(x_1, x_2)$ selects either to stop and predict with features $\{1, 2\}$ or to acquire 3 for c_3 and then terminate. Node $g_3(x_1, x_3)$ selects to predict with $\{1, 3\}$ or with $\{1, 2, 3\}$.

The objective is to learn the internal decision functions, $y_j(\mathbf{x})$'s. We define the system risk:

$$R(\mathbf{g}, \mathbf{x}, y) = \sum_{k=1}^{K} R_k(f_k, \mathbf{x}, y) G_k(\mathbf{g}, \mathbf{x}) \qquad (1)$$

Here, $\mathbf{g} = \{g_1, \ldots g_{K-1}\}$ is the set of decision functions. $R_k(f_k, \mathbf{x}, y)$ is the risk of making a decision at a leaf k. It consists of two terms: loss of the model at the leaf and the cost of features corresponding to the sub-collection of attributes, S_k, acquired along the path from the root node to the leaf; and α is a parameter that controls trade-off between acquisition cost and model performance.

$$R_k(f_k, \mathbf{x}, y) = \mathcal{L}(f_k(\mathbf{x}), y) + \alpha \sum_{m \in S_k} c_m \qquad (2)$$

$G_k(\mathbf{g}, \mathbf{x}) \in \{0, 1\}$ is a binary state variable indicating whether or not an instance $\mathbf{x}$ is terminated at the kth leaf. As illustrated in Fig. 3 we compactly encode the path from the root to every leaf in terms of internal decisions, $g_j(\mathbf{x})$'s, by two auxiliary binary matrices: $\mathbf{P}, \mathbf{N} \in \{0, 1\}^{K \times K-1}$. If $\mathbf{P}_{k,j} = 1$ then, on the path to leaf k, a decision node j must be positive: $g_j > 0$. If $\mathbf{N}_{k,j} = 1$ then on the path to leaf k, a decision at node j must be negative: $g_j \leq 0$. A kth row in $\mathbf{P}$ and $\mathbf{N}$ jointly encode a path from the root node to a leaf k. The sign pattern for each path is obtained by $\mathbf{P} - \mathbf{N}$. Using this path matrix, the state variable can be defined:

$$G_k(\mathbf{g}, \mathbf{x}) = \prod_{j=1}^{K-1} [\mathbb{1}_{g_j(\mathbf{x})>0}]^{\mathbf{P}_{k,j}} [\mathbb{1}_{g_j(\mathbf{x})\leq0}]^{\mathbf{N}_{k,j}} \tag{3}$$

Our goal is to learn decision functions $g_1, \ldots, g_{K-1}$ that minimize the expected system risk:

$$\min_{\mathbf{g}} \mathbb{E}_{\mathcal{D}} [R(\mathbf{g}, \mathbf{x}, y)] \tag{4}$$

However, the probability distribution $\mathcal{D}$ is assumed to be unknown and cannot be estimated reliably due to potential high-dimensionality of attributes. Instead, we are given a set of N training examples with full features, $(\mathbf{x}_1, y_1), \ldots, (\mathbf{x}_N, y_N)$. We approximate the expected risk by a sample average over the data and construct the following empirical risk minimization (ERM) problem:

$$\min_{\mathbf{g}} \sum_{i=1}^{N} R(\mathbf{g}, \mathbf{x}_i, y_i) = \sum_{i=1}^{N} \sum_{k=1}^{K} \overbrace{R_k(f_k, \mathbf{x}_i, y_i)}^{\text{risk of leaf } k} \underbrace{\prod_{j=1}^{K-1} [\mathbb{1}_{g_j(\mathbf{x}_i)>0}]^{\mathbf{P}_{k,j}} [\mathbb{1}_{g_j(\mathbf{x}_i)\leq0}]^{\mathbf{N}_{k,j}}}_{G_k(\cdot) = \text{state of } \mathbf{x}_i \text{ in a tree}}$$

$$\tag{5}$$

Note that by the definition of risk in (1), the ERM problem can be viewed as a minimization over a function of indicators with respect to decisions: $g_1, \ldots, g_{K-1}$.

3   Model Selection by Linear Programming

A popular approach to solving ERM problems is to substitute indicators with convex upper-bounding surrogates, $\phi(z) \geq \mathbb{1}_{[z]}$ and then to minimize the resulting surrogate risk. However, this strategy leads to a non-convex, multi-linear optimization problem in our setting. Previous attempts to solve problems of this form have focused on computationally costly alternating minimization approaches [18,2,21] with no guarantees on optimality. A key point of this paper is that rather than attempting to solve this non-convex surrogate problem, we instead reformulate the indicator empirical risk in (5) as a maximization over sums of indicators before introducing convex surrogate. Our approach yields a globally convex upper-bounding surrogate of the empirical loss function.

3.1   Convex Risk Objective

In reformulating the risk, it is useful to define the "savings" for an example. The *savings*, π_k^i, for an example i, represents the difference between the worst case outcome, R_{max} and the risk $R_k(f_k, \mathbf{x}_i, y_i)$ for terminating at the kth leaf.

Intuitively R_{max} is the cost of incorrectly predicting with the most expensive model (the model that uses all the features): $R_{max} = \max_{y'} \mathcal{L}(y, y') + \alpha \sum_m c_m$.

$$\pi_k^i = R_{max} - R_k(f_k, \mathbf{x}_i, y_i) \tag{6}$$

Note that the savings do not depend on the decisions, $g_j's$, that we are interested in learning.

For a binary tree, $\mathcal{T}$, composed of $K - 1$ internal nodes and K leaves, it turns out that the risk in (5) can be rewritten as a maxima of K terms. Each term is a weighted linear combination of indicators, and each weight corresponds to the *savings lost* if the decision inside the indicator argument is true. Before stating the result, we define the weights for the linear combination in each term of the max. For an internal node j, we denote C_j^n as the set of leaf nodes in a subtree corresponding to a negative decision $g_j(\mathbf{x}) \leq 0$. And C_j^p is the set of leaf nodes in a subtree corresponding to a positive decision. For instance in Fig. 1, $C_1^p = \{Leaf\ 3, Leaf\ 4\}$.

For a compact representation, recall that the kth rows in matrices $\mathbf{P}$ and $\mathbf{N}$ define a path to leaf k in terms of $g_1, \ldots, g_{K-1}$, and a non-zero $\mathbf{P}_{k,j}$ or $\mathbf{N}_{k,j}$ indicates if $g_j \lessgtr 0$ is on the path to leaf k. So for each $\mathbf{x}_i$ and each leaf k, we introduce two positive weight row vectors of length $K - 1$:

$$\mathbf{w}_{n,k}^i = \mathbf{N}_{k,1} \sum_{l \in C_1^p} \pi_l^i, ..., \mathbf{N}_{k,K-1} \sum_{l \in C_{K-1}^p} \pi_l^i, \quad \mathbf{w}_{p,k}^i = \mathbf{P}_{k,1} \sum_{l \in C_1^n} \pi_l^i, ..., \mathbf{P}_{k,K-1} \sum_{l \in C_{K-1}^n} \pi_l^i \tag{7}$$

Using these weight definitions, the empirical risk in (5) can be rewritten as:

Lemma 31. *The empirical risk of tree $\mathcal{T}$ is:*

$$R(\mathbf{g}, \mathbf{x}_i, y_i) = R_{max} - \sum_{k=1}^{K} \pi_k^i + \max_{k \in \{1,...,K\}} \mathbf{w}_{p,k}^i \begin{bmatrix} \mathbb{1}_{g_1(\mathbf{x}_i)>0} \\ \vdots \\ \mathbb{1}_{g_{K-1}(\mathbf{x}_i)>0} \end{bmatrix} + \mathbf{w}_{n,k}^i \begin{bmatrix} \mathbb{1}_{g_1(\mathbf{x}_i)\leq 0} \\ \vdots \\ \mathbb{1}_{g_{K-1}(\mathbf{x}_i)\leq 0} \end{bmatrix} \tag{8}$$

The proof of this lemma is included in the Supplementary Material

The jth component of $\mathbf{w}_{n,k}^i$ multiplies $\mathbb{1}_{[y_j(\mathbf{x}_i)\leq 0]}$ in the term corresponding to the kth leaf. For instance in our four leaf example in Fig. 1, the weight multiplying $\mathbb{1}_{[g_1(\mathbf{x}_i)\leq 0]}$ is the sum of these savings for leaves 3 and 4 (i.e. savings lost if $g_1 \leq 0$). $(\mathbf{w}_{n,1}^i)_1 = \pi_3^i + \pi_4^i$. Therefore, sets C_j^p, C_j^n define which π_k^i's contribute to a weight for a decision term. If $\mathbf{P}_{k,j}$ or $\mathbf{N}_{k,j}$ is zero then decision $g_j \lessgtr 0$ is not on the path to leaf k and the weight is zero.

Intuitively, the empirical risk in (8) represents a scan over the paths to each leaf ($k = 1, \ldots, K$), and each term in the maximization encodes a path to one of the K leaves. The active term in the maximization corresponds to the leaf to which an observation is assigned by the decision functions $g_1, \ldots, g_{K-1}$. Additionally, the weights on the indicators represent the *savings lost* if the argument of the indicator is active. In our example, if the decision function $g_1(\mathbf{x}_i)$ is negative, leaves 3 and 4 cannot be reached by $\mathbf{x}_i$, and therefore π_3^i and π_4^i, the savings associated with leaves 3 and 4, cannot be realized and are lost.

An important observation is that each term in the max in (8) is a linear combination of indicators instead of a product as in (5). This transformation enables us to upper-bound each indicator function with a convex surrogate, $\phi(z)$: $\phi[g_j(\mathbf{x})] \geq \mathbb{1}_{[g_j(\mathbf{x})>0]}$, $\phi[-g_j(\mathbf{x})] \geq \mathbb{1}_{[g_j(\mathbf{x})\leq 0]}$. And the result is a novel convex upper-bound on the empirical risk in (8). We denote this risk as $R_\phi(\mathbf{g})$. And the optimization problem over a set of training examples, $\{\mathbf{x}_i, y_i\}_{i=1}^N$ and a family of decision functions $\mathcal{G}$:

$$\max_{\mathbf{g}\in\mathcal{G}} \sum_{i=1}^{N} R_\phi\left(\mathbf{g}, \mathbf{x}_i, y_i\right) \tag{9}$$

3.2   Linear Programming

There are many valid choices for the surrogate $\phi(z)$. However, if a hinge loss is used as an upper bound and $\mathcal{G}$ is a family of linear functions of the data then the optimization problem in (9) becomes a linear program (LP).

Proposition 32. *For* $\phi(z) = \max(1 - z, 0)$ *and linear decision functions* $g_1, \ldots, g_{K-1}$, *the minimization in* (9) *is equivalent to the following linear program:*

$$\min_{\substack{g_1,\ldots,g_{K-1},\gamma^1,\ldots,\gamma^N \\ \alpha_1^1,\ldots,\alpha_{K-1}^N,\beta_1^1,\ldots,\beta_{K-1}^N}} \sum_{i=1}^{N} \gamma^i \text{ subject to:} \tag{10}$$

$$\gamma^i \geq \mathbf{w}_{p,k}^i \begin{bmatrix} \alpha_1^i \\ \vdots \\ \alpha_{K-1}^i \end{bmatrix} + \mathbf{w}_{n,k}^i \begin{bmatrix} \beta_1^i \\ \vdots \\ \beta_{K-1}^i \end{bmatrix}, i \in [N], \ k \in [K]$$

$$1 + g_j(\mathbf{x}_i) \leq \alpha_j^i, \quad 1 - g_j(\mathbf{x}_i) \leq \beta_j^i, \quad \alpha_j^i \geq 0, \ \beta_j^i \geq 0,$$

$$j \in [K-1], i \in [N]$$

We introduce the variable γ^i for each example $\mathbf{x}_i$ to convert from a maximization over leaves to a set of linear constraints. Similarly, the maximization within each hinge loss is converted to a set of linear constraints. The variables α_j^i upper-bound the indicator $\mathbb{1}_{g_j(x_i)>0}$ and the variables β_j^i upper-bound the indicator $\mathbb{1}_{g_j(x_i)\leq 0}$. Additionally, the constant terms in the risk are removed for notational simplicity, as these do not effect the solution to the linear program. For details please refer to Suppl. materials.

Complexity: Linear programming is a relatively well-studied problem, with efficient algorithms previously developed. Specifically, for K leaves, N training points, and a maximum feature dimension of D, we have $O(KD+KN)$ variables and $O(KN)$ constraints. The state of the art primal-dual methods for LP are fast in practice, with an expected number of iterations $O(\sqrt{n}\log n)$, where n is the number of variables [1].

Kernelization: Our formulation can handle more complex decision functions $\mathbf{g}(\mathbf{x})$ by kernelization. The observations x_i are replaced in the LP by $\psi(\mathbf{x}_i)$ for some expanded basis function $\psi(\cdot)$. For expanded basis functions, a natural solution is to add ℓ_2 regularization on the decision functions, converting the LP to a quadratic program. Addition of ℓ_2 regularization removes non-unique solutions, with solution of the regularized problem equal to the minimum norm solution of the unregularized problem (for a sufficiently small regularization parameter value). Furthermore, the ℓ_2 regularization allows for the problem to be kernelized, as the optimization can be expressed with respect to expanded basis inner products of the form $\psi(\mathbf{x}_i)^T \psi(\mathbf{x}_j)$ in the dual problem. While this is possible, yielding a quadratic optimization problem in place of the proposed LP, empirical evidence indicates that on real-world data the family of linear and low-order polynomial decision functions is sufficiently rich and therefore we do not explore kernelization in the experimental section.

Algorithm 1. Model Selection by LP

INPUT: $f_1(\mathbf{x}), f_2(\mathbf{x}), \ldots, f_K(\mathbf{x})$ {Models}; $S_1, S_2, \ldots, S_K$ {Features used by each model}; $\mathbf{P}, \mathbf{N}$ {Tree structure}; $(\mathbf{x}_1, y_1), (\mathbf{x}_2, y_2), \ldots, (\mathbf{x}_N, y_N)$ {Training Data}; α {Trade-off parameters}
for $(i, k) = \{1, \ldots, N\} \times \{1, \ldots, K\}$ do
    Compute savings in (6): $\pi_k^i \leftarrow R_{max} - R_k(f_k, \mathbf{x}_i, y_i)$
    Compute weight vectors in (7): $\mathbf{w}_{n,k}^i, \mathbf{w}_{p,k}^i$
end for
Solve linear program in (10): $[g_1(\mathbf{x}), g_2(\mathbf{x}), \ldots, g_{K-1}(\mathbf{x})] \leftarrow LPsolver(\{\mathbf{w}_{n,k}^i, \mathbf{w}_{p,k}^i\})$
OUTPUT: Model Selection Tree: $\mathbf{g}(\mathbf{x})$

---

4   Experiments

We demonstrate our LP model selection approach in Algorithm 1 on two important prediction tasks in computer vision. First, we apply our method to the problem of structured prediction. We use the handwriting dataset for word prediction and compare our method to the RL based model selection ([24]). Here, the cost is computation time for processing HOG transforms of different scales. For the second experiment, we apply our method to the SUN scene categorization [15] dataset. Here instead of using image processing features, we use human generated descriptor as inputs to a classifier. In this set-up, the cost of feature acquisition is the monetary value paid to Amazon Mechanical Turk workers.

Performance Metric: Our goal is to train a set of decision functions for a fixed tree that minimizes prediction loss subject to an average budget constraint. We examine average acquisition cost vs. average prediction loss to compare performance of the proposed LP approach. We sweep over values of the tradeoff parameter α in order to learn systems of varying average budget, resulting in a series of learned trees of differing prediction rates and average budgets. Increasing the value of α biases the system to learn decisions with low average acquisition cost with an increased system error, while decreasing the value α yields systems with smaller error at the expense of an increase in cost. Although a system may not be learned that exactly matches a desired budget, any point in the convex hull of budget/error points learned is achievable by weighted randomization over learned systems. As a result, we take the lower convex hull of points in the space of average error vs. average cost to learn a decision system for any average budget. Note that in the experimental results, a convex hull over the training points is taken, with the corresponding policies applied to unseen test data, and therefore the resulting curve is not necessarily a convex hull. In all experiments, we first divide the data into 10 training/test folds. Within each fold, we further divide the training data of each fold into 10 sub-folds. In these sub-folds, we use all but one subfold to train the models, and apply this learned predictor to estimate the losses for the unused subfold. These sub-folds are used to more accurately represent the prediction ability of the models for learning our adaptive system.

Leaf Models: Each individual leaf model, $f_1, \ldots, f_K$, operates on a subset of the features acquired on the path to that leaf. We assume f_k's are pre-computed prior to learning the decision system. The goal of our paper is to demonstrate the advantage of an adaptive selection system therefore we do not seek to learn the most accurate models. We simply illustrate the gain in relative performance: same level of accuracy as the most complex model achieved with lower budgets.

4.1   Model Selection in Structured Learning

Structured Learning Problem: In structured learning, the goal is to learn a model from a set of training samples that maps inputs $x \in \mathcal{X}$ to the outputs $y \in \mathcal{Y}$. In a typical structured prediction setup [19], the response space $\mathcal{Y}$ is not simply a discrete label but instead a more complex structured output. In particular, we focus on the problem of predicting words from handwritten characters, where the output space, $\mathcal{Y}$, is a string of letters of varying length. The goal is to learn a scoring function, $\Psi_w(\mathbf{x}, y)$, over training data such that the prediction model, $f(\mathbf{x}) = \arg\max_{y \in \mathcal{Y}} \Psi_w(\mathbf{x}, y)$ matches the given training structure.

We use a function $\Psi_w(\mathbf{x}, y) = \mathbf{w} \cdot \mathbf{h}[\mathbf{x}, y]$ which is linear in the score features $\mathbf{h} : \mathcal{X} \times \mathcal{Y} \to \mathbb{R}^p$. In general, there are exponentially many outputs and solving this inference is computationally infeasible. However, $\mathbf{h}$ is usually constructed to decompose over subsets of y that enables this problem to be solved efficiently. In our experiment, we adopted a first-order linear conditional random field model which is commonly used in optical character recognition (OCR) tasks [24,13]. In this model, the score features decompose into sum of unary and pairwise terms. Given an input character image sequence of $\mathbf{x} = \{x(1), \ldots, x(l)\}$, the score of output sequence can be written as, $\Psi_w(\mathbf{x}, y) = \sum_{j=1}^{\ell} \mathbf{h}[x(j), y(j)] \cdot \mathbf{w} + \sum_{j=2}^{\ell} \mathbf{h}[\mathbf{x}, y(j-1), y(j)] \cdot \mathbf{w}$, where $y(1), \ldots, y(\ell)$ are labels for individual characters in the word y. Given the weight vector $\mathbf{w}$, we use max-sum algorithm [3] to solve the inference problem. To learn the weight vector

w, we solve maximum conditional likelihood using stochastic gradient descent. We used the implementation in [13] for this purpose.

Dataset and Simulation Details: We used the OCR data set from [17]. This data set has 6,877 handwritten words where each word is represented as sequence of 16x8 binary letter images. There are 55 unique words, 26 unique characters and 55,152 letters.

Following [17], we use three sets of features: raw images, histogram of gradients (hog1) [6] computed in 3x3 bins and a finer HoG computed on 2x2 bins (hog2). We train three CRF models: $f_{rgb}, f_{rgb,hog1}, f_{rgb,hog2}$. Note that once hog2 is computed, hog1 does not add additional information. The computational cost of processing the raw images is assumed to be negligible, while the computational cost of the 2x2 and 3x3 HOG features are assumed to be equal and proportional to the length of the word.

The goal is to learn a system to minimize character recognition error subject to an average computational cost constraint per letter. We train two architectures: a two stage cascade and a three decision node binary tree as illustrated in Fig. 4a. Note the tree allows greater flexibility by allowing us to acquire hog2 directly from rgb while a cascade has to acquire hog1 before processing hog2.

Following the framework presented in [24], the decision functions in our LP tree also act on meta features as opposed to the raw features. These meta features reflect the fit of the structured predictor $f_{(.)}$ to the training set population. The meta-features used are the difference in the score for the top two sequence predictions, the average of the min/max and mean entropies of the marginal distributions as predicted at each position in the word by the predictor at that stage. Additional meta-features count the number of times a 3-gram 4-gram and 5-gram are predicted but never occur in the training set.

Dynamic Model Selection Baseline: We compare our approach to dynamic structured model selection method (DMS) in [24]. There the authors employ a cascade architecture with models arranged sequentially in the order of increasing cost, and learn a policy that controls whether an example should be predicted using the current model or rejected to the next more expensive model. For their DMS architecture, we use the same cascade as for our approach.

The authors define the value of delaying a decision as a decrease in the loss when a sample is moved from stage i to $i + 1$. This value function is modeled as a linear combination of the meta-features. The policy then sends the instance that suffer the maximum predicted loss reduction to the next stage until a predetermined budget limit is hit. The value of skipping a stage is defined as: $V(f_i, x, y) = L(f_{i-1}(x), y) - L(f_i(x), y)$. The policy parameter β is found by ridge regression, $\arg\min_\beta \lambda||\beta||_2^2 + \sum_{i=2}^{3} \sum_{j=1}^{n} (V(f_i, x_j, y_j) - \beta^T \phi(x_j, f_{1:i-1}))^2$, where ϕ denotes the meta-features for given sample and stage predictors. The test time value is then defined as $J(\tau_1, ..., \tau_n, \eta) = \sum_{j=1}^{n} \sum_{i=2}^{\tau_j} \beta^T \phi(x^j, f_{1:i-1})$, where τ_j denotes how many features are computed for example j. During test time, the total value is greedily maximized until the budget constraint B prevents any other features from being computed.

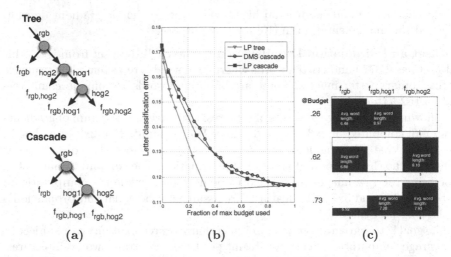

Fig. 4. (a) shows two system structures used in the OCR experiment: a two stage cascade and a three node tree. In (b), we display the budget vs error plot for three methods: cascade and tree architecture of our LP model selection system and a DMS cascade system. While performance of LP and DMS are on par in the cascade structure, LP Tree has a significant advantage over DMS. LP tree achieves same accuracy with a significant speedup and lower computation cost($\geq$70% savings). Panel (c) displays the distribution of examples that end up at 3 different stages/models in the LP cascade at three budget operating points. For the tree, this is not illustrative since the best accuracy is achieved at .33 budget point.

Fig. 5. Here, we examine the histogram at .62 budget from Fig. 4c. We provide examples of three different words being classified at the cheapest/simplest model (f_{rgb}) and at the complex/expensive model ($f_{rgb,hog2}$). As expected, more obscure and rotated words require the complex model.

Discussion: We report average error for different values of average budget (see Fig. 4b). For simplicity, we normalize the units to the fraction of the maximum budget allowed. For example, if the system operates at budget 1 then every example is routed to the most expensive model $f_{rgb,hog2}$ (the best accuracy). For budget 0, every example remains with the cheapest model, f_{rgb}. An adaptive system with a budget between 0 and 1, utilized the cheap model for some examples and the expensive model for others resulting in a lower budget but accuracy equivalent to the expensive model.

The experiments clearly highlight the advantages of our approach. Our LP cascade performance matches the accuracy for all budget values of a DMS cascade. However, when we introduce a more flexible tree architecture instead of a cascade, the performance dramatically improves. Our LP tree exhibits significant computational-savings($\geq 70\%$) and speedup to achieve similar accuracy as a DMS cascade. In a cascade, an example cannot go directly to the most complex model, $f_{rgb,hog2}$ while in a tree this decision is possible and results in higher cost efficiency. In addition, our approach learns a separate decision for every internal node in the tree allowing for more complex selection functions. In contrast in DMS, the same policy function is used at every stage of the cascade limiting the discriminative power of the decision system. Note that DMS does not generalize to trees in an obvious way since it is in essence an early stopping policy.

In addition to the error vs budget performance, we explore the distribution of examples that are being routed to the three models in our LP cascade architecture. We examine systems corresponding to budgets: .26,.62 and .73. As expected at a budget of .26, model utilization is evenly distributed between the cheapest, f_{rgb} and the medium complexity model, $f_{rgb,hog1}$. At the other end of the spectrum, at a higher budget of .73, most examples are being routed to the most expensive/complex model, $f_{rgb,hog2}$. However, in the middle of the spectrum at the .62 budget system, for half of the examples, f_{rgb} is being utilized and the rest are routed to the last model $f_{rgb,hog2}$. This however may not be that surprising. Since the performance of hog1 and hog2 are similar, the system decides to use the more expensive feature. We do not explore the distributions for the LP Tree since the best performance is already achieved at a .33 budget.

We also report the average word length that each model sees. As expected longer (presumably harder to classify) end up at a later more complex model. We next look at the actual images being classified at the cheapest (simplest) model (f_{rgb}) and at the most expensive, $f_{rgb,hog2}$ levels. We look at different instances of the same word. Fig. 5 illustrates more obscure instances of the same word are routed to the last stage (the most complex/expensive model).

4.2   Scene Recognition

Next, we apply our system to another challenging task in computer vision: scene recognition. The problem can be posed as multi-class classification problem, where $\mathbf{x}$ is an image of a scene, and y is one of L scene categories. We focus on the popular scene dataset SUN [25].

The difficulty in this problem is due to several factors. First, the number of classes, L, is very large, $L > 700$, and the number of examples per class is small, 20. Partly due to this data limitation and the difficulty of the task itself, automatic visual recognition features such as HoG or GIST do not achieve suitably high accuracy rates. In an attempt to improve performance, authors in [15] proposed exploring human annotated attributes. Amazon Mechanical Turk workers were asked to vote whether images fit certain descriptions such as: camping, cluttered space, fire. For each attribute, an average of three votes is reported, with a total of 102 attributes. The attributes are then grouped into three sets: (1), functions (camping, hiking, biking...), (2), materials (trees, clouds, grass,...), and (3) surface/spatial properties (dirty, glossy, rusty,open area, warm,...).

To simplify our experiment, we use the second level of the class hierarchy, which groups the scenes into more general categories, and then we discard the indoor categories, resulting in only 10 classes. From this data, we randomly construct an even training/test split, resulting in around 400 training and 400 test points per class.

We then train 3 models: $f_1, f_{1,2}, f_{1,2,3}$, with the subscripts indicating which attribute groups are used to construct the model. Since attributes are acquired by paying AMT workers, the goal is to make accurate predictions while using the smallest number of total attributes. Additionally, due to the nature of the system, dynamic model selection must be performed in a streaming test data setting as opposed to collecting data for all test examples before acting.

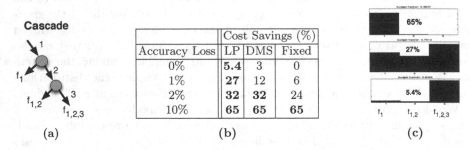

Cascade

Accuracy Loss	Cost Savings (%)		
	LP	DMS	Fixed
0%	**5.4**	3	0
1%	**27**	12	6
2%	**32**	**32**	24
10%	**65**	**65**	**65**

(a)   (b)   (c)

Fig. 6. SUN Scene Categorization Results. (a) shows cascade structure used in the experiment. In (b), we report cost savings for four accuracy levels. Loss is the difference between the accuracy of the most complex model and the dynamic model at different budget points. Cost savings is the percent saved from the most expensive model. In (c), we display example distribution among stages.

Fig. 7. Sample images from the railroad category sent to different models

We compare the performance of our system to a DMS cascade and non-adaptive fixed-length systems. Note that the DMS cascade cannot be applied to individual test examples, as the system ceases to dynamically select the models. To accommodate for this shortcoming, we randomly partition the test data into subsets of 10 examples, with performance of the learned DMS cascades averaged over all subsets. In contrast, the system learned using the proposed LP operates on single examples allowing for streaming/parallel application as opposed to a batch/centralized strategy.

Table 6b compares change in classification accuracy vs. cost reduction for the three approaches. For all 4 changes in classification accuracy, the proposed LP approach matches or exceeds the performance of the fixed-length systems or the adaptive DMS system. In particular, the proposed LP approach produces an adaptive system that reduces the budget by 27% while reducing accuracy by only 1%. In comparison, the DMS cascade is only able to reduce the budget by 12% when maintaining a classification performance within 1% of the full system.

References

1. Anstreicher, K.M., Ji, J., Potra, F.A., Ye, Y.: Probabilistic analysis of an infeasible-interior-point algorithm for linear programming. Math. Oper. Res. 24(1), 176–192 (1999)
2. Bennett, K.P., Mangasarian, O.L.: Bilinear separation of two sets in n-space. Computational Optimization and Applications 2 (1993)
3. Bishop, C.M., et al.: Pattern recognition and machine learning, vol. 1. Springer, New York (2006)
4. Busa-Fekete, R., Benbouzid, D., Kégl, B.: Fast classification using sparse decision dags. In: 29th International Conference on Machine Learning (ICML) (2012)
5. Chen, M., Xu, Z., Weinberger, K.Q., Chapelle, O., Kedem, D.: Classifier cascade: Tradeoff between accuracy and feature evaluation cost. In: International Conference on Artificial Intelligence and Statistics (AISTATS), pp. 235–242 (2012)
6. Dalal, N., Triggs, B.: Histograms of oriented gradients for human detection. In: IEEE Computer Society Conference on Computer Vision and Pattern Recognition, CVPR 2005, vol. 1, pp. 886–893. IEEE (2005)
7. Dulac-Arnold, G., Denoyer, L., Preux, P., Gallinari, P.: Datum-wise classification: a sequential approach to sparsity. In: Gunopulos, D., Hofmann, T., Malerba, D., Vazirgiannis, M. (eds.) ECML PKDD 2011, Part I. LNCS, vol. 6911, pp. 375–390. Springer, Heidelberg (2011)
8. Gao, T., Koller, D.: Active classification based on value of classifier. In: NIPS, vol. 24, pp. 1062–1070 (2011)
9. He, H., Daume III, H., Eisner, J.: Imitation learning by coaching. In: Advances In Neural Information Processing Systems (NIPS), pp. 3158–3166 (2012)
10. Jiang, J., Teichert, A.R., Daumé III, H., Eisner, J.: Learned prioritization for trading off accuracy and speed. In: NIPS, pp. 1340–1348 (2012)
11. Karayev, S., Baumgartner, T., Fritz, M., Darrell, T.: Timely object recognition. In: NIPS, pp. 899–907 (2012)
12. Karayev, S., Fritz, M., Darrell, T.: Dynamic feature selection for classification on a budget. In: International Conference on Machine Learning (ICML): Workshop on Prediction with Sequential Models (2013)

13. Maaten, L., Welling, M., Saul, L.K.: Hidden-unit conditional random fields. In: International Conference on Artificial Intelligence and Statistics, pp. 479–488 (2011)
14. Megiddo, N.: On the complexity of polyhedral separability. Discrete & Computational Geometry 3(1) (1988)
15. Patterson, G., Hays, J.: Sun attribute database: Discovering, annotating, and recognizing scene attributes. In: Proceeding of the 25th Conference on Computer Vision and Pattern Recognition (CVPR) (2012)
16. Ross, S., Bagnell, D.: Efficient reductions for imitation learning. In: International Conference on Artificial Intelligence and Statistics (AISTATS), pp. 661–668 (2010)
17. Taskar, B., Guestrin, C., Koller, D.: Max-margin markov networks. In: NIPS (2003)
18. Trapeznikov, K., Saligrama, V.: Supervised sequential classification under budget constraints. In: International Conference on Artificial Intelligence and Statistics (AISTATS) (2013)
19. Tsochantaridis, I., Joachims, T., Hofmann, T., Altun, Y., Singer, Y.: Large margin methods for structured and interdependent output variables. Journal of Machine Learning Research 6(9) (2005)
20. Viola, P., Jones, M.: Robust Real-time Object Detection. International Journal of Computer Vision 4, 34–47 (2001)
21. Wang, J., Saligrama, V.: Local supervised learning through space partitioning. Advances in Neural Information Processing Systems 25 (2012)
22. Wang, J., Saligrama, V.: Locally-Linear Learning Machines (L3M). In: Asian Conference on Machine Learning, pp. 451–466 (2013)
23. Wang, J., Trapeznikov, K., Saligrama, V.: An LP for Sequential Learning Under Budgets. In: Proceedings of the Seventeenth International Conference on Artificial Intelligence and Statistics, pp. 987–995 (2014)
24. Weiss, D., Sapp, B., Taskar, B.: Dynamic structured model selection. In: ICCV (2013)
25. Xiao, J., Hays, J., Ehinger, K.A., Oliva, A., Torralba, A.: Sun database: Large-scale scene recognition from abbey to zoo. In: 2010 IEEE Conference on Computer Vision and Pattern Recognition (CVPR), pp. 3485–3492. IEEE (2010)
26. Xu, Z., Kusner, M., Chen, M., Weinberger, K.Q.: Cost-sensitive tree of classifiers. In: Proceedings of the 30th International Conference on Machine Learning (ICML 2013), pp. 133–141 (2013)
27. Zhang, C., Zhang, Z.: A Survey of Recent Advances in Face Detection. Tech. rep., Microsoft Research (2010)

Perceptually Inspired Layout-Aware Losses for Image Segmentation

Anton Osokin[1] and Pushmeet Kohli[2]

[1] Moscow State University, Moscow, Russia
[2] Microsoft Research, Cambridge, UK

Abstract. Interactive image segmentation is an important computer vision problem that has numerous real world applications. Models for image segmentation are generally trained to minimize the Hamming error in pixel labeling. The Hamming loss does not ensure that the topology/structure of the object being segmented is preserved and therefore is not a strong indicator of the quality of the segmentation as perceived by users. However, it is still ubiquitously used for training models because it decomposes over pixels and thus enables efficient learning. In this paper, we propose the use of a novel family of higher-order loss functions that encourage segmentations whose layout is similar to the ground-truth segmentation. Unlike the Hamming loss, these loss functions do not decompose over pixels and therefore cannot be directly used for loss augmented inference. We show how our loss functions can be transformed to allow efficient learning and demonstrate the effectiveness of our method on a challenging segmentation dataset and validate the results using a user study. Our experimental results reveal that training with our layout-aware loss functions results in better segmentations that are preferred by users over segmentations obtained using conventional loss functions.

Keywords: structured prediction, image segmentation, loss-based learning, max-margin learning, perceptual error metrics.

1 Introduction

Interactive image segmentation is an important problem in Computer Vision that involves separating an object (foreground 'fg') of interest, specified by some user provided seeds, from the rest of the image (background 'bg'). Like many other problems in Computer Vision, and Machine learning in general, fg-bg segmentation can be formulated in terms of learning a prediction function $f : \mathcal{X} \to \mathcal{Y}$ that maps a set of inputs $x \in \mathcal{X}$ (e.g. images or features) to some desired outputs $y \in \mathcal{Y}$ (eg. locations or pixel-wise segmentations of one or more objects in the image). The prediction function for image segmentation is typically assumed to take the form of a minimization of a low order (typically pairwise) energy function. Such prediction functions have become very popular in computer vision because certain classes of pairwise energies can be efficiently minimized (either exactly or approximately) using Min-cut/Max-flow algorithms [14].

D. Fleet et al. (Eds.): ECCV 2014, Part II, LNCS 8690, pp. 663–678, 2014.

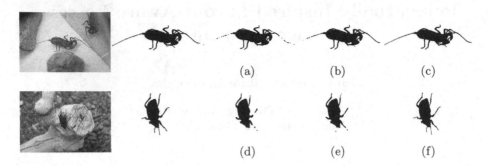

(a)   (b)   (c)

(d)   (e)   (f)

Fig. 1. *The left column shows* 2 images from "twigs and legs" dataset [10]. *The second left column* shows the zoomed ground-truth labelings. *The other columns* correspond to different distortions of the ground truth: *(a)* and *(d)* – morphological opening of the ground truth; *(b)* and *(e)* – averaging over 5x5 window; *(c)* and *(f)* – thinning of "fat" parts of the ground truth. Table 1 shows 4 different loss functions computed for these segmentations

Table 1. Different losses computed for segmentations (a)-(f) in figure 1 (the lower the loss is the better the segmentation is w.r.t. it)

Loss	1a	1b	1c	1d	1e	1f
Hamming	**0.19**	0.20	0.24	0.11	**0.10**	0.12
Jaccard	**3.91**	4.18	4.95	5.14	**4.91**	5.83
Area	0.20	**0.05**	0.21	0.11	**0.06**	0.12
Skeleton	3.72	0.71	**0.45**	2.90	1.53	**0.59**

Most discriminative methods for learning prediction functions such as Max-Margin Markov Networks (M^{3}N) [23], and Structured Support Vector Machines (SSVMs) [24] are based on the principle of Empirical Risk Minimization (ERM). This technique has gained wide-spread acceptance in Computer Vision by producing impressive results for many vision problems including image segmentation [18,21] and object detection [3,6]. ERM requires choosing the prediction function that makes the best predictions under some metric or *loss function*. More formally, given a family of prediction functions $f_\mathbf{w} : \mathcal{X} \to \mathcal{Y}$ parameterized by $\mathbf{w}$ and a training set of examples of input/output pairs $\mathcal{D} = \{(\mathbf{x}_n, \mathbf{y}_n); n \in \{1, ..., N\}, \mathbf{x}_n \in \mathcal{X}, \mathbf{y}_n \in \mathcal{Y}\}$, the learning algorithm tries to find the optimal weight vector $\mathbf{w}^*$ that minimizes the total task-dependent loss as:

$$\mathbf{w}^* = \arg\min_\mathbf{w} L(\mathbf{w}) = \arg\min_\mathbf{w} \frac{1}{N} \sum_{n=1}^{N} \Delta(\mathbf{y}_n, f_\mathbf{w}(\mathbf{x}_n)) \tag{1}$$

where loss function $\Delta(\mathbf{y}_n, \hat{\mathbf{y}}_n)$ denotes the cost of predicting output $\hat{\mathbf{y}}_n$ when the correct prediction is $\mathbf{y}_n$. The Hamming distance (number of mislabelled pixels) between the prediction and the ground truth is widely used as the loss for training models for image segmentation. One of the reasons for this choice is the fact that Hamming distance decomposes over pixel variables and thus results in a tractable learning problem (see sec. 2). Although the choice of the Hamming loss allows efficient learning, it also poses a problem. The Hamming loss is not a strong indicator of the quality of the segmentation results as perceived by users. This point is illustrated in figure 1 and table 1.

A number of loss functions have been proposed in the literature as a replacement for the Hamming loss. Lempitsky et al. [16] balance costs for false positives and false negatives in order to compensate for differences in prior probabilities. The PASCAL VOC segmentation challenge [5] uses Jaccard distance (the intersection/union metric). Pletscher and Kohli [18] use a loss that encourages segmentations to be of the correct size (area loss). All the above-mentioned losses can be computed using the confusion matrix of the mislabeled pixels. These loss functions consider how many errors were made but ignore *where* these errors were made, i.e. they do not care if the topology/structure of the object being segmented is preserved.

In this paper, we address the problem of computing layout preserving segmentations. We propose a skeleton-based loss function that allows to learn a low order model using higher order loss functions that penalize segmentations that differ from the ground truth in terms of the layout. This approach can be combined for further improvement with recently proposed high-order models (e.g. [17,1]) or densely-connected pairwise models [15]. Our work generalizes the loss functions used in [18] to a much larger family of layout-aware losses that still allow efficient training. We propose two layout-aware loss functions: the Row-Column loss and the Skeleton loss. Both losses take into account the spatial relationships between image pixels. Figure 1 and table 1 show examples of segmentations that are ranked differently using Hamming, Jaccard, Area, and Skeleton losses. It can be observed that only the skeleton loss selects the segmentation with the preserved structure as the best.

We evaluate the proposed loss functions together with several other baseline losses on a challenging interactive image segmentation dataset. We perform a user study to quantify the difference between the human notion of similarity of image segmentations and the similarities defined by our loss functions. Experimental results reveal that the skeleton loss leads to better segmentation results that are considered better by users.

2 Loss-Based Training

In this section we introduce our notation and review the loss-based max-margin approach [24,23]. For a given input $\mathbf{x} \in \mathcal{X}$ we consider a model that predicts output $\mathbf{y} \in \mathcal{Y}^1$ by maximizing a linearly parameterized score function:

$$f_{\mathbf{w}}(\mathbf{x}) = \arg\max_{\mathbf{y} \in \mathcal{Y}} \langle \mathbf{w}, \varphi(\mathbf{x}, \mathbf{y}) \rangle \qquad (2)$$

---

[1] Formally the set of possible labelings $\mathcal{Y}$ itself depends on the object $\mathbf{x}$, e.g. the number of variables in each $\mathbf{y}$ depends on the resolution on image $\mathbf{x}$. In this paper we omit the dependency of $\mathcal{Y}$ on $\mathbf{x}$ to lighten the notation.

where $\mathbf{w}$ is a vector of the model parameters and $\varphi(\mathbf{x}, \mathbf{y})$ is a mapping of a joint input/output space to a space of so-called generalized features. Generalized features are usually predefined and depend on the nature of the task.

In computer vision, problems are very often formulated using graphical models which represent the factorized form of a score function. We consider a pairwise model with structure specified by graph $\mathcal{G} = (\mathcal{V}, \mathcal{E})$, where $\mathcal{V}$ is a set of nodes (each node $i \in \mathcal{V}$ corresponds to a variable y_i in output space $\mathcal{Y}$) and $\mathcal{E}$ is a set of edges that correspond to direct dependencies between the variables. Each variable y_i can take values from set $\mathcal{K} = \{0, 1\}$. The score function (negative energy) of the model takes the following form:

$$\langle \mathbf{w}, \varphi(\mathbf{x}, \mathbf{y}) \rangle = \sum_{i \in \mathcal{V}} \psi_i(y_i, \mathbf{x}, \mathbf{w}^u) + \sum_{(ij) \in \mathcal{E}} \psi_{ij}(y_i, y_j, \mathbf{x}, \mathbf{w}^p) \qquad (3)$$

where ψ_i and ψ_{ij} are linear function w.r.t. model parameters $\mathbf{w}$. For convenience the set of model parameters is separated into unary ($\mathbf{w}^u$) and pairwise ($\mathbf{w}^p$) parameters. It is well known that if the score function is supermodular w.r.t. variables $\mathbf{y}$ than it can be maximized efficiently over labelings $\mathbf{y}$ using min-cut/max-flow algorithms [14].

Having defined the form of the predictor function we formulate the problem of learning the model parameters $\mathbf{w}$ given the set of input/output pairs

$$\{(\mathbf{x}^1, \mathbf{y}^1), \ldots, (\mathbf{x}^N, \mathbf{y}^N)\}.$$

The margin-rescaled version of the max-margin approach (also referred to as structured SVM, SVM-struct) formulates a convex upper bound on the regularized empirical risk in the following way:

$$\frac{\lambda}{2} \|\mathbf{w}\|^2 + \frac{1}{N} \sum_{n=1}^{N} \left(\max_{\mathbf{y} \in \mathcal{Y}} \left(\langle \mathbf{w}, \varphi(\mathbf{x}^n, \mathbf{y}) \rangle + \Delta(\mathbf{y}, \mathbf{y}^n) \right) - \langle \mathbf{w}, \varphi(\mathbf{x}^n, \mathbf{y}^n) \rangle \right). \qquad (4)$$

Here $\Delta(\mathbf{y}, \mathbf{y}^n)$ is a loss function, specifying the penalty for prediction $\mathbf{y}$ in place of ground-truth labeling $\mathbf{y}^n$.

The traditional approach to minimize (4) is to formulate it as a quadratic program (QP) with exponentially many constraints,

$$\min_{\mathbf{w}\xi} \quad \frac{\lambda}{2} \|\mathbf{w}\|^2 + \sum_{n=1}^{N} \xi^n \qquad (5)$$

$$\text{s.t.} \quad \langle \mathbf{w}, \varphi(\mathbf{x}^n, \mathbf{y}) \rangle + \Delta(\mathbf{y}, \mathbf{y}^n) - \langle \mathbf{w}, \varphi(\mathbf{x}^n, \mathbf{y}^n) \rangle \leq \xi^n,$$

$$\forall n = 1, \ldots, N, \quad \forall \mathbf{y} \in \mathcal{Y}, \qquad (6)$$

and to solve it via a cutting plane algorithm [24]. Algorithm 1 states the simplest version of this approach.

3   Choosing the Loss Function

The choice of loss function $\Delta(\mathbf{y}, \mathbf{y}^n)$ is a crucial component of the max-margin formulation (4). The only requirement that algorithm 1 imposes on the loss

---

Algorithm 1. Cutting plane algorithm to solve SSVM problem (5)-(6) [24]

Input: $\{(\mathbf{x}^1, \mathbf{y}^1), \ldots, (\mathbf{x}^N, \mathbf{y}^N)\}$, λ, ε.
Output: $\mathbf{w}^*$ – the solution of 5-6;
 1: $S^n = \emptyset$, $\forall n = 1, \ldots, N$;
 2: **repeat**
 3:   **for** $n = 1, \ldots, N$ **do**
 4:     $H(\mathbf{y}) := \Delta(\mathbf{y}, \mathbf{y}^n) + \langle \mathbf{w}, \varphi(\mathbf{x}^n, \mathbf{y}) - \varphi(\mathbf{x}^n, \mathbf{y}^n) \rangle$;
 5:     $\hat{\mathbf{y}} = \arg\max_{\mathbf{y} \in \mathcal{Y}} H(\mathbf{y})$;   // find the most violated constraint
 6:     $\xi^n = \max\{0, \max_{\mathbf{y} \in S^n} H(\mathbf{y})\}$;   // compute the current slack
 7:     **if** $H(\hat{\mathbf{y}}) > \xi^n + \varepsilon$ **then**
 8:       $S^n := S^n \cup \{\hat{\mathbf{y}}\}$;
 9:       $\mathbf{w} \leftarrow$ optimize (5) with constraints defined by $\bigcup_n S^n$
10: **until** no S^n has changed during iteration

---

function is that it should allow the solution of the loss-augmented MAP inference problem in step 5:

$$\max_{\mathbf{y} \in \mathcal{Y}} \Big(\langle \mathbf{w}, \varphi(\mathbf{x}^n, \mathbf{y}) \rangle + \Delta(\mathbf{y}, \mathbf{y}^n) \Big). \tag{7}$$

In this section we review the loss functions typically used to evaluate segmentation quality and describe new layout-aware losses.

3.1 Decomposable Loss Functions

From a computational stand-point, the simplest loss functions are the ones that can be represented as the sum of the unary potentials w.r.t. labeling $\mathbf{y}$. In this case, the loss-augmented inference problem (7) is as hard as the vanilla MAP-inference problem (2). Arguably the simplest and most often used decomposable loss function is the Hamming distance to the ground-truth labeling:

$$\Delta_{\mathrm{H}}(\mathbf{y}, \mathbf{y}^n) = \frac{1}{|\mathcal{V}|} \sum_{i \in \mathcal{V}} [y_i \neq y_i^n]. \tag{8}$$

Here $[\cdot]$ is the Iverson bracket notation: $[A]$ equals 1 if a logical expression A is true and 0 otherwise.

A more flexible version of Hamming loss can be obtained by associating weights to all terms in (8) as follows:

$$\sum_{i \in \mathcal{V}} \sum_{k \in \mathcal{K}} c_{ik} [y_i = k][y_i^n \neq k]. \tag{9}$$

In this formulation weights c_{ik} can be conditioned on the ground-truth labeling $\mathbf{y}^n$ without making optimization w.r.t. $\mathbf{y}$ harder. This manipulation allows us to construct the more general weighted Hamming loss (wH) function.

The weighted Hamming loss follows the intuition that the pixels at the boundary of the object are harder to segment correctly [12] and thus are more valuable: $c_{ik} = 1 + A \exp\left(-d_i(\mathbf{y}^n)/B\right)$, where $d_i(\mathbf{y}^n)$ is the distance between pixel i and the closest point on the foreground-background boundary in the labeling $\mathbf{y}^n$, and A, B are distance parameters. In our experiments we use $A = 10$ and $B = 7$.

3.2 High-Order Loss Functions

The Hamming loss (and even its weighted variant) do not represent the "perceptual quality" of the segmentation well. This has led researchers to adopt other metrics for evaluating results. For instance, the PASCAL VOC segmentation challenge [5] uses the Jaccard distance (also known as "the intersection/union metric") between the sets of pixels belonging to the object according to the predicted and the ground-truth segmentations. This metric is defined as follows:

$$\Delta_J(\mathbf{y}, \mathbf{y}^n) = 1 - \frac{TP}{TP + FP + FN} = 1 - \frac{\sum_{i \in \mathcal{V}} y_i y_i^n}{\sum_{i \in \mathcal{V}} y_i y_i^n + y_i(1 - y_i^n) + (1 - y_i)y_i^n} \tag{10}$$

where TP, FP, FN denote the number of True Positives, False Positives, and False Negatives, correspondingly. Jaccard loss (10) is not decomposable which makes the loss-augmented MAP-inference (7) problem different from MAP inference. Tarlow and Zemel [22] proposed a message passing scheme that can approximately solve the loss-augmented MAP-inference problem with the Jaccard loss function.

3.3 Supermodular Loss Functions

Pletscher and Kohli [18] make the observation that certain high-order loss functions $\Delta(\mathbf{y}, \mathbf{y}^n)$ are supermodular and can thus be maximized in polynomial time. They used a supermodular higher-order loss function that penalized segmentations that differed in terms of the area of the foreground segment:

$$\Delta_A(\mathbf{y}, \mathbf{y}^n) = \frac{1}{|\mathcal{V}|} \left| \sum_{i \in \mathcal{V}} y_i - \sum_{i \in \mathcal{V}} y_i^n \right|. \tag{11}$$

They showed that the loss-augmented MAP-inference problem can be solved by solving an equivalent st-mincut/maxflow problem.

3.4 Layout Dependent Losses

High-order losses (11), (10) and the decomposable Hamming loss (8) view the segmentation as a sequence of pixels and are unaware of the spatial layout of the pixels. Weighted Hamming loss (9) is in some sense smarter and tries to introduce the notion that for "good" segmentation not all pixels are equally important: the closer the pixel is to the ground-truth boundary the more important it is. We believe that for human perception, layout and topology of the segmentation are very important criteria for the segmentation to be "good". In this section we present two new higher-order loss functions that take the spatial layout of pixels into account.

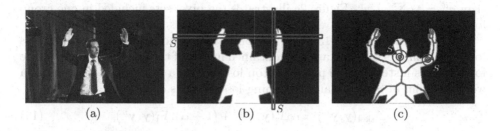

(a)   (b)   (c)

Fig. 2. The initial image – *(a)*; pixel sets that form groups for the row-column loss – *(b)*, and skeleton loss – *(c)*

Row-Column loss. One way to characterize a segmentation is through its silhouette: an orthogonal projection of the 2-D set of pixels in a certain direction. The silhouette-based loss requires that for each line in a certain direction the number of pixels that belong to the object should be as close to the number of pixels of the ground-truth segmentation as possible. Formally, this loss can be expressed as follows:

$$\Delta_{RC}(\mathbf{y}, \mathbf{y}^n) = \sum_{d \in \mathcal{D}} \sum_{S \in \mathcal{S}_d} \left| \sum_{i \in S} y_i - \sum_{i \in S} y_i^n \right|. \tag{12}$$

Here $\mathcal{S}_d$ is a set of all lines in direction d that intersect the image domain and $\mathcal{D}$ is a set of directions considered. In our experiments we restrict ourselves to 2 directions: horizontal and vertical. Figure 2b illustrates the pixel sets included in one group for the row-column loss for the case where $\mathcal{D} = \{\text{Horizontal, Vertical}\}$.

Skeleton loss. A skeleton of the object segment is an important morphological characteristic for human perception. The notion of skeleton is well-known in the image processing and mathematical morphology communities (see e.g. [8] for a review).

Our skeleton-based loss function is motivated from the intuition that pixels around the skeleton of the ground-truth segmentation are very important and should be segmented correctly. We achieve this by using the following loss function:

$$\Delta_s(\mathbf{y}, \mathbf{y}^n) = \sum_{d \in \mathcal{D}} \sum_{S \in \mathcal{S}_d} a_S^d \left| \sum_{i \in S} y_i - \sum_{i \in S} y_i^n \right| \tag{13}$$

where $\mathcal{D}$ is a set of all points on the skeleton, $\mathcal{S}_d$ is a set of all pixel sets associated with pixel d of the skeleton, a_S^d are the weighting coefficients.

For each pixel on the skeleton, we define the following three sets: a circle centered at the pixel with a radius 25% larger than the distance to the boundary, and circles with the radius equal to 50% and 25% of the radius of the first circle. To make the number of sets smaller, we sub-sample the points on the skeleton such that the loss only considers 25% of the points. We set the weighting coefficients in such a way that all the sets have equal impact regardless of their size: $a_S^d = 1/\sum_{i\in S} y_i^n$. Figure 2c illustrates the pixel sets included in one group for the skeleton loss.

As defined in equation 13, the skeleton loss does not penalize segmentations for mislabeling pixels that are not contained in any of the circles. To compensate for this bias instead of the pure skeleton loss we use a composite loss which is a weighted sum of Skeleton and Hamming losses and is defined as:

$$\Delta_{\mathrm{skel}}(\mathbf{y},\mathbf{y}^n) = \alpha\Delta_{\mathrm{s}}(\mathbf{y},\mathbf{y}^n) + (1-\alpha)\Delta_{\mathrm{H}}(\mathbf{y},\mathbf{y}^n) \tag{14}$$

where α is a mixing coefficient. In our experiments we use $\alpha = 0.5$ and normalize both losses in such a way that the maximum possible loss equals 1.

4   Inference with High-Order Losses

We now describe how the loss-augmented inference problem can be solved for the layout-aware loss functions. Both skeleton (14) and row-column (12) losses can be written down in the following form:

$$\Delta(\mathbf{y},\hat{\mathbf{y}}) = \sum_{S\in\mathcal{S}} a_S \left|\sum_{i\in S} y_i - b_S\right| \tag{15}$$

where set $\mathcal{S}$ is a set of subsets of nodes: $\mathcal{S} \subset 2^{\mathcal{V}}$, $a_S \geq 0$, b_S are the coefficients. Note that this form is very general. In fact, decomposable losses like the Hamming loss as well as higher-order losses such as the area loss (11) can be viewed as special cases of this general form. It is also easy to see that this general form is supermodular and thus can be maximized in polynomial time. However, the worst case complexity of supermodular maximization is still quite high which prevents their application to large scale maximization problems such as the ones encountered in this paper.

Instead, we follow the approach used in [12,18,11] to transform the problem to the pairwise one:

$$\left|\sum_{i\in S} y_i - b_S\right| = \max_{z_S\in\{0,1\}} \left(z_S \left(\sum_{i\in S} y_i - b_S\right) + (1-z_S)\left(b_S - \sum_{i\in S} y_i\right)\right)$$

$$= \max_{z_S\in\{0,1\}} \left((1-2z_S)\left(b_S - \sum_{i\in S} y_i\right)\right). \tag{16}$$

The function in the r.h.s. is supermodular and pairwise w.r.t. variables z_S and y_i. Such functions can be maximized efficiently using standard max-flow/min-cut algorithms [14].

5   Image Segmentation Model

In this section we provide the details of the pairwise random field model (3) for image segmentation that was trained using the different loss functions. Following the approach of [18], we have one variable in $\mathcal{V}$ for each pixel of the image. We define the set of edges $\mathcal{E}$ using the 8-connected pixel grid. For each node and edge in the model we compute a set of unary and pairwise features respectively. Afterwards, we combine corresponding unary features of each pixel to form a vector of unary generalized features (which is later multiplied by unary weights $\mathbf{w}^U$). The pairwise features define the Potts pairwise potentials combined into the two groups for each pairwise feature: diagonal and horizontal/vertical edges.

Unary potentials. For every node in the model we compute the following 51 unary features: 3 RGB channels, the likelihood from 5-component Gaussian mixture models fitted to the predefined foreground and background seeds in RGB and CIELUV spaces independently, 3 CIELUV color channels, 40 distance transform features, and 1 constant bias feature. Every feature $f_k(i)$ is used to define a unary potential:

$$\psi_i(y_i, \mathbf{x}, \mathbf{w}^u) = \sum_k \left(w_k^u f_k(i)[y_i = \text{'}fg\text{'}] - w_k^u f_k(i)[y_i = \text{'}bg\text{'}] \right). \qquad (17)$$

All the features are normalized in such a way that the maximum value equals 1, and the minimum value – 0. We use the approach from [9] to learn the GMM-based appearance models from pixels that belong to user-specified "seed" regions.

To construct the distance transform features we use generalized distance transforms to background and foreground seeds. Following [9] we define the distance from a pixel to the seed region as the minimum length of a discrete path that leads form the pixel to the region, where the length of each path is defined as follows:

$$L(\Gamma) = \sum_{i=0}^{n-1} \sqrt{(1 - \gamma)d(\Gamma^i, \Gamma^{i+1})^2 + \gamma\|\Delta I(\Gamma^i, \Gamma^{i+1})\|^2}. \qquad (18)$$

Here $\Gamma = \{\Gamma^i\}_{i=0}^n$ is a discrete path connecting point Γ_0 and Γ_n. All neighboring elements of the path are connected in 8-connectivity sense and $d(\cdot, \cdot)$ is the Euclidian distance between them. $\Delta I(\cdot, \cdot)$ is a vector in color space equal to the color difference of the corresponding points; γ is a weight factor between Euclidian and color differences. We construct features using distance transforms to both foreground and background seeds with the following parameters: $\gamma = 0$ (Euclidian distance); I – CIELUV color channels, $\gamma = 1$; I – RGB color channels, $\gamma = 1$; I – appearance model response channel, $\gamma = 1$. Two feature responses for an example image are shown in figure 3e and 3f. In addition we threshold each of the distances at 5 levels uniformly distributed between the minimum and the maximum values. In total we get 40 distance transform features.

Pairwise potentials. We use one constant pairwise feature and 5 contrast dependent features. All the pairwise features define Potts pairwise potentials with separate weights for diagonal and horizontal/vertical edges (12 pairwise generalized

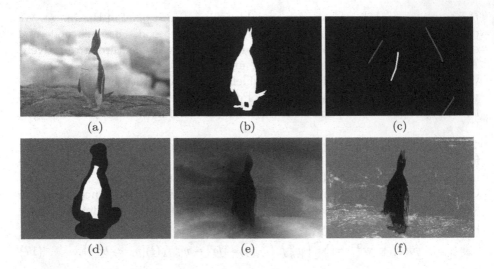

Fig. 3. *(a)* – the initial image from the dataset; *(b)* – the ground truth; *(c)* – the initial seed provided by [9]; *(d)* – the extended seeds that we use in out experiments; geodesic distance from the foreground seeds in the *(e)* RGB channels; *(f)* appearance model response channel

features in total). Formally, the pairwise potentials of the image segmentation model are defined as follows:

$$\psi_{ij}(y_i, y_j, \mathbf{x}, \mathbf{w}^p) = \sum_k \exp\left(-c_k \beta \|I_i - I_j\|^2\right)[y_i \neq y_j] \tag{19}$$

where I_i is the color of the i-th pixel in the RGB color space, β is the inverse average difference between the neighboring pixels on the current image (as suggested in [19]), c_k is a weighting coefficient that we varied to get different features; we used the following values of c_k: 0, 0.1, 0.3, 1, 3, 10.

6   Experiments

In this section we present the details of our experimental evaluation including the dataset, the implementation details and the results.

Dataset. We perform our experiments on a subset of the dataset provided by [9], which is an extended version of the GrabCut dataset [2]. The dataset contains 151 images, their ground-truth segmentations, and user-defined object/background seeds. Prior to all experiments we've chosen 60 images which seemed to be hard for the model and on which different losses seemed to show different properties: objects with thin and long structure, mixed color statistics, etc. Figure 3 shows an image from the data set (a), the corresponding ground truth (b), and the predefined seeds (c). To avoid model mis-specification we've enlarged the user defined seeds, making them more similar to tight trimaps [13] (see fig. 3d). To do this we apply the following morphological operations. We dilate the user defined seeds by 50% of the maximum distance to segment boundary, intersect the obtained region with 10 pixel eroded segment, union the result with 20 pixel eroded segment.

Implementation details. We implemented algorithm 1 in Matlab. In all our experiments, finding the most violated constraints (step 5) was the computational bottleneck. We used the interior-point method provided by MATLAB Optimization Toolbox to solve the QP (step 9) and called the QP-solver after adding each individual constraint. To solve the min-cut/max-flow problem we used the C++ code connected to Matlab via the MEX interface. Following [18] we use the IBFS algorithm [7][2] instead of the popular Boykov-Kolmogorov [4] algorithm. The latter is slower for denser graph structures. For the majority of image processing operations mentioned in section 5 we use the software provided by [9][3] and [18].[4] All the losses in our experiments are normalized to $[0, 1]$ segment. Although the worst possible configuration w.r.t. the skeleton and the row-column losses can be non-trivial we can always obtain it by solving the loss-augmented inference (7) with weights $\mathbf{w}$ fixed to 0.

Experimental evaluation. We split our dataset half and half 8 times into train and test sets. We train the segmentation algorithm (2) on each training set with Hamming loss (8), weighted Hamming loss (9), area loss (11), row-column loss (12), and skeleton loss (14). For each loss we select a value of regularization parameter λ using the cross-validation over the generated 8 sets.

For each combination of train and test losses we report the test-loss value averaged over all generated train/test datasets and images within one dataset (table 2). As a baseline we add the GrabCut method [2] implemented in the OpenCV library. Note that the best performance with respect to a certain loss is achieved not necessarily with training with the same loss. Figure 4 shows some qualitative results of images achieved via training with different losses.

User study. To evaluate the quality of the proposed loss functions, we conducted a user study. The user study consisted of 2 stages. In the first stage, a participant not associated with the project was shown all segmentations and asked to select images in the test set (selected randomly prior to the study) where the difference in the segmentation results was most significant. The person was not told about the objective of the research. The resulting 15 images were used for the second stage of the user study.

In the second stage of the user study each of the 18 participants for each image selected in the first stage was shown a page containing the following images: the original image, the ground-truth segmentation, and the results obtained from

---

[2] http://www.cs.tau.ac.il/~sagihed/ibfs/
[3] http://www.robots.ox.ac.uk/~vgg/software/iseg/
[4] https://github.com/ppletscher/hol

Table 2. Values of different losses on Train and Test sets when the model is trained using different losses at the Training stage

Training Stage	Hamming		HammingW		Area		Row-Column		Skeleton	
	Train	Test	Train	Test	Train	Test	Train	Test	Train	Test
Hamming	7.62	9.56	10.56	12.86	6.26	8.31	10.06	12.81	20.65	23.32
HammingW	7.75	9.99	10.54	13.17	6.91	9.60	10.41	13.67	21.47	24.35
Area	7.43	**9.32**	10.57	12.86	**3.54**	**7.07**	9.22	**12.12**	17.63	19.57
Row-Column	7.22	9.40	**10.27**	**12.82**	4.39	7.24	**9.07**	12.30	17.79	20.37
Skeleton	**7.09**	9.61	10.36	13.33	4.65	7.43	9.11	12.58	**13.30**	**15.20**
GrabCut	13.14	13.14	15.97	15.97	12.08	12.08	18.17	18.17	28.04	28.04

Table 3. Results of the user study. For each training loss (Hamming, Area, Row-Column, and Skeleton) we report (a) the percentage of times users gave the particular loss the best rank (these numbers do not sum up to one because participants were allowed to assign equal ranks to multiple segmentation results); (b) the mean ranks given by participants (the lower, the better)

	Hamming	Area	Row-Col.	Skeleton
Best vote	20%	17%	12%	**64%**
Mean rank	2.62	2.66	2.76	**1.96**

the models trained with 4 different loss functions (Hamming, area, row-column, and skeleton) in a randomized order (see fig. 5 for an example). To avoid framing biases, no annotations were provided with the segmentations. We asked the participants to rank the 4 segmentation results according to the "similarity" to the ground-truth segmentation and to also specify the magnitude of the differences – on a scale of 1 to 3 (1 being most significant).

The summary of the user-study results is presented in table 3. For each loss function we report the percentage of times the prediction from the model trained using the loss was marked as the best segmentation (among significant results) and the average rank. We also applied the nonparametric Friedman's test together with the Tukey-Kramer multiple comparison procedure [20]. The analysis showed that the skeleton loss performed best[5] and the other losses did not have significant differences. Figure 6 shows the correlations between the quality of segmentation results as perceived by users and as measured by the weighted combination of loss functions.

---

[5] 95% confidence intervals for the difference between the ranks of Hamming/Area/Row-Column loss and Skeleton loss are $[0.39, 0.92]$, $[0.43, 0.96]$, $[0.53, 1.06]$, correspondingly.

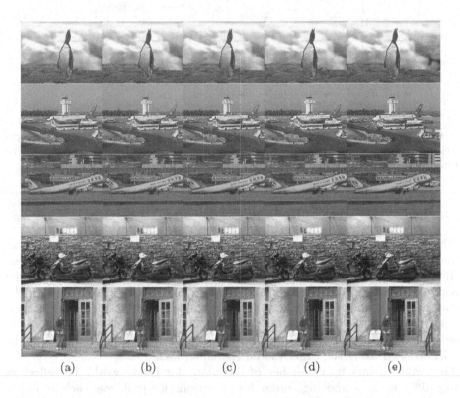

(a)   (b)   (c)   (d)   (e)

Fig. 4. Results of the prediction function trained by SSVM with *(a)* Hamming loss; *(b)* weighted Hamming loss; *(c)* area loss; *(d)* row-column loss; *(e)* skeleton loss.

Fig. 5. A sample slide of the conducted user study. The slide contains the initial image, the ground truth, 4 segmentations produced by maximizing the score function trained using different losses (Hamming, area, row-column, and skeleton). The order of segmentations is random.

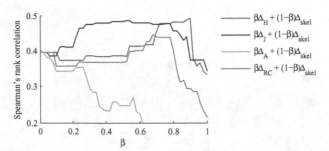

Fig. 6. The analysis of the user study results. We show Spearman's rank correlation coefficient between the weighted combination of the Skeleton and the Hamming/Jaccard/Area/Row-Column losses and rankings produced by the users.

7   Discussion and Conclusions

In this paper we have proposed the use of higher-order layout-aware loss functions for learning conventional pairwise random field models for the problem of interactive image segmentation. We have shown that models trained using layout-aware loss functions produce segmentations that are consistent with the layout of the ground truth while still allowing efficient MAP inference. Further, the segmentation results produced by these models are considered perceptually closer to the ground truth by human judges compared to the results from the models trained using the conventional Hamming loss.

Our work throws up a number of directions for future work. The effect of using different low- and high-order loss functions for problems such as image denoising, optical flow, image compression are all important topics that could be investigated. A characterization of higher-order loss functions that allow efficient learning is another important direction.

In our experiments we have observed that the best results on the test set according to a certain loss are not necessarily achieved when training with the convex upper bound (4) of the same loss. This effect might be the consequence of the fact that such convex uppers bounds are not tight and the correlation between the bound and the target empirical risk (1) near the minimum of (4) is not high enough. Investigation of these effects is another important direction for future work.

Acknowledgments. This work was supported by Microsoft – Moscow State University Joint Research Center (RPD# 1053945) and Russian Foundation for Basic Research (project 12-01-33085).

References

1. Alexe, B., Deselaers, T., Ferrari, V.: What is an object? In: IEEE Conference on Computer Vision and Pattern Recognition, CVPR (2010)
2. Blake, A., Rother, C., Brown, M., Perez, P., Torr, P.: Interactive image segmentation using an adaptive GMMRF model. In: Pajdla, T., Matas, J(G.) (eds.) ECCV 2004. LNCS, vol. 3021, pp. 428–441. Springer, Heidelberg (2004)
3. Blaschko, M.B., Lampert, C.H.: Learning to localize objects with structured output regression. In: Forsyth, D., Torr, P., Zisserman, A. (eds.) ECCV 2008, Part I. LNCS, vol. 5302, pp. 2–15. Springer, Heidelberg (2008)
4. Boykov, Y., Kolmogorov, V.: An experimental comparison of Min-Cut/Max-Flow algorithms for energy minimization in vision. IEEE Transactions on Pattern Analysis and Machine Intelligence (PAMI) 26(9), 1124–1137 (2004)
5. Everingham, M., Van Gool, L., Williams, C.K.I., Winn, J., Zisserman, A.: The PASCAL visual object classes (VOC) challenge. IJCV 88(2), 303–338 (2010)
6. Felzenszwalb, P.F., Girshick, R.B., McAllester, D.A., Ramanan, D.: Object detection with discriminatively trained part-based models. IEEE Transactions on Pattern Analysis and Machine Intelligence (PAMI) 32(9), 1627–1645 (2010)
7. Goldberg, A.V., Hed, S., Kaplan, H., Tarjan, R.E., Werneck, R.F.: Maximum flows by incremental breadth-first search. In: European Symposium on Algorithms (ESA), pp. 457–468 (2011)
8. Gonzalez, R., Woods, R.: Digital image processing. Prentice Hall (2002)
9. Gulshan, V., Rother, C., Criminisi, A., Blake, A., Zisserman, A.: Geodesic star convexity for interactive image segmentation. In: IEEE Conference on Computer Vision and Pattern Recognition, CVPR (2010)
10. Jegelka, S., Bilmes, J.: Submodularity beyond submodular energies: Coupling edges in graph cuts. In: IEEE Conference on Computer Vision and Pattern Recognition, CVPR (2011)
11. Kohli, P., Kumar, M.P.: Energy minimization for linear envelope MRFs. In: IEEE Conference on Computer Vision and Pattern Recognition, CVPR (2010)
12. Kohli, P., Ladický, L., Torr, P.: Robust higher order potentials for enforcing label consistency. International Journal of Computer Vision (IJCV) 82(3), 302–324 (2009)
13. Kohli, P., Nickish, H., Rother, C., Rhemann, C.: User-centric learning and evaluation of interactive segmentation systems. International Journal of Computer Vision (IJCV) 100(3), 261–274 (2012)
14. Kolmogorov, V., Zabih, R.: What energy functions can be minimized via graph cuts? IEEE Transactions on Pattern Analysis and Machine Intelligence (PAMI) 26(2), 147–159 (2004)
15. Krahenbuhl, P., Koltun, V.: Efficient inference in fully connected CRFs with gaussian edge potentials. In: Advances in Neural Information Processing Systems, NIPS (2011)
16. Lempitsky, V., Vedaldi, A., Zisserman, A.: A Pylon model for semantic segmentation. In: Advances in Neural Information Processing Systems, NIPS (2011)
17. Nowozin, S., Lampert, C.H.: Global interactions in random field models: A potential function ensuring connectedness. SIAM Journal on Imaging Sciences (SIIMS) 3(4) (2010)
18. Pletscher, P., Kohli, P.: Learning low-order models for enforcing high-order statistics. In: International Conference on Artificial Intelligence and Statistics, AISTATS (2012)

19. Shotton, J., Winn, J., Rother, C., Criminisi, A.: Textonboost for image understanding: Multi-class object recognition and segmentation by jointly modeling texture, layout, and context. International Journal of Computer Vision 81(1), 2–23 (2009)
20. Sprent, P., Smeeton, N.: Applied Nonparametric Statistical Methods. Chapman & Hall/CRC (2001)
21. Szummer, M., Kohli, P., Hoiem, D.: Learning CRFs using graph cuts. In: Forsyth, D., Torr, P., Zisserman, A. (eds.) ECCV 2008, Part II. LNCS, vol. 5303, pp. 582–595. Springer, Heidelberg (2008)
22. Tarlow, D., Zemel, R.: Structured output learning with high order loss functions. In: International Conference on Artificial Intelligence and Statistics, AISTATS (2012)
23. Taskar, B., Guestrin, C., Koller, D.: Max-Margin Markov networks. In: Advances in Neural Information Processing Systems, NIPS (2003)
24. Tsochantaridis, I., Joachims, T., Hofmann, T., Altun, Y.: Large margin methods for structured and interdependent output variables. Journal of Machine Learning Research (JMLR) 6(9), 1453–1484 (2005)

Large Margin Local Metric Learning

Julien Bohné[1,2], Yiming Ying[3], Stéphane Gentric[2], and Massimiliano Pontil[1]

[1] University College London, Department of Computer Science, London, UK
m.pontil@cs.ucl.ac.uk
[2] Safran Morpho, Issy-les-Moulineaux, France
{julien.bohne,stephane.gentric}@morpho.com
[3] University of Exceter, Department of Computer Science, Exceter, UK
y.ying@exeter.ac.uk

Abstract. Linear metric learning is a widely used methodology to learn a dissimilarity function from a set of similar/dissimilar example pairs. Using a single metric may be a too restrictive assumption when handling heterogeneous datasets. Recently, local metric learning methods have been introduced to overcome this limitation. However, they are subjects to constraints preventing their usage in many applications. For example, they require knowledge of the class label of the training points. In this paper, we present a novel local metric learning method, which overcomes some limitations of previous approaches. The method first computes a Gaussian Mixture Model from a low dimensional embedding of training data. Then it estimates a set of local metrics by solving a convex optimization problem; finally, a dissimilarity function is obtained by aggregating the local metrics. Our experiments show that the proposed method achieves state-of-the-art results on four datasets.

Keywords: Dissimilarity learning, local metric learning, face recognition, nearest neighbor classification.

1 Introduction

An effective dissimilarity function is of great importance for many pattern recognition applications such as face verification, speech recognition or text categorization. As it might be hard to design such a function by hand for each task, especially when the input dimensionality is large, learning dissimilarity functions from labeled data has received a growing interest over the last years, see, for example, [4,7,24] and references therein.

A well studied class of dissimilarity functions is a linear metric of the form $(x_i - x_j)^\top M (x_i - x_j)$ where x_i and x_j are two data points which we wish to compare and M is a positive semidefinite matrix (PSD). This approach has been shown to be quite effective on various tasks but it suffers a strong limitation: it makes use of a single linear metric to compare data over all the input space which is inappropriate to handle heterogeneous data. This observation is the root of the development of local metric learning methods which adapt the dissimilarity function to the local specificities of the data. For illustrative purpose let us

D. Fleet et al. (Eds.): ECCV 2014, Part II, LNCS 8690, pp. 679–694, 2014.

consider two examples. It is well known that in digit classification some digits are easily mistaken for another such as "1" and "7" or "3" and "8", it seems therefore reasonable to reduce the number of misclassification to focus on different features to discriminate digits in the "1-7" region and in the "3-8" one. Our second example is face verification: should we put the emphasis on the very same features to compare two pictures of Caucasian males and two pictures of Asian females? Our answer is "no" and our experiments show that local metric learning improves the performance for these two applications.

Dissimilarity function can be employed in nearest neighbor classifiers or to take decisions based on the thresholding of the dissimilarity. Those two situations are different as the former depends only on the ranking of the nearest neighbors whereas the latter is concerned about the absolute meaning of the dissimilarity. In this work we propose a flexible local metric learning method called Large Margin Local Metric Learning (LMLML) which can be employed in both settings and can handle an arbitrary large number of classes. Its training procedure does not need one to know the class labels but only a set of pairs labeled "similar" (both points belong to the same class) or "dissimilar" (the two points belong to different classes). Our method computes a set of local metrics which are combined into an adaptive dissimilarity function with the help of a soft partitioning of the training data. The optimization of the local metrics is formulated as a convex problem which favors a large margin solution. The problem also involves a novel regularization term encouraging matrices which are close to a simple baseline solution. Our experiments show that LMLML outperforms or matches state-of-the-art results on various datasets.

After describing the related work in the next section we present LMLML and explain how to train the model in Section 3 and demonstrate its effectiveness on various datasets in Section 4. Finally, in Section 5 we summarize our findings.

2   Related Work

Global metric learning methods such as ITML [4], LDML [7] or LMNN [24] are precursors of this work. They formulate metric learning as the optimization of an objective function which decreases when the distances of similar pairs is made small while increasing those of dissimilar pairs. Some of these methods also include a regularization term which aims at limiting the risk of over-fitting.

Local metric learning has recently been investigated from several angles. It has sometimes been linked to semi-supervised clustering such as in [1] where labeled data are used to find local transformations of the data points in order to improve a clustering process. This kind of method cannot compute dissimilarity measures between pairs of never seen points which is the goal of our work.

Metric learning is often used in nearest neighbor schemes (NN) to perform multi-class classification. Several local metric learning algorithms have been developed to improve NN classifiers. Weinberger and Saul proposed an extension of LMNN to local metric (MM-LMNN [23]), in which a specific metric is associated to each class and all the metrics are jointly learned to optimize a classification criterion. LMNN has also been extended to a multi-tasks setting [5] where multiple metrics are jointly learned [17]. Our work can be considered to be a generalization of these methods as it uses a weighted combination metrics instead of activating a single metric for each comparison (see Section 3.2).

KISSME [11] has also been extended to local metric in [12] where one KISSME metric is learned separately for each class. These class-specific metrics are averaged with a global one to limit the risk of over-fitting due to the fact that each metric might be learned using only a limited number of training samples. GLML [15] proposes to use local metric to limit the performance bias due to finite sampling using the class conditional probability distribution.

All the previously presented methods suffer from the same drawback, namely they need enough training samples per class to estimate the metrics and therefore cannot easily be employed when the number of classes is very large. To overcome this problem [22] introduces a local metric learning method based on finite number of linear metrics named PLML. The number of metrics is different from the number of classes and hence the method can scale to a larger number of classes. However this method is specifically designed for NN classification as it can only compute the dissimilarity of pairs for which at least one point is in the training set. This strongly limits the range of tasks PLML can deal with and for example prevent its use for face verification.

As we shall see in the next sections, our approach overcomes the limitations mentioned above and, as we demonstrate by a set of experiments, obtains better results than previous local metric learning methods.

3   Large Margin Local Metric Learning

This section describes the proposed method. We start by presenting our data preprocessing and then detail LMLML's model and each step of its optimization.

3.1   Data Preprocessing

A preprocessing is applied to the data before training the model. This step serves two purposes: first it reduces the dimensionality to speed up the computation for both training and testing, and second it reduces the noise thereby improving the overall performance of the algorithm.

Like most of the metric learning methods we first center the dataset and reduce the dimensionality to a n-dimensional space by PCA; n is often chosen so that 95% of the energy is preserved. Let $\mathcal{D} = \{(i,j)\}$ denote the index set of training pairs and let y_{ij} be a label which is equal to 1 if (x_i, x_j) is a similar pair and -1 otherwise. We compute the within-class scatter matrix defined by

$$S = U \left(\sum_{(i,j) \in \mathcal{D} | y_{ij}=1} (x_i - x_j)(x_i - x_j)^\top \right) U^\top \tag{1}$$

where U is the matrix formed by the n leading eigenvectors of the covariance matrix of the data, and then multiply the data by $S^{-1/2}$ to make the classes, on average, isotropic. This transformation is known under different names such as *mapping in the intra-personal subspace* in face recognition [3] or *Within-Class Covariance Normalization (WCCN)* in the speaker recognition community [8]. The transformed data points are now $x' = S^{-1/2}U(x - m)$ where m is the mean of the data. Like in [3], we finally rescale each feature vector so that it has a unit L2-norm. To simplify the notation, whenever we mention a feature vector x in the reminder of the document, it in fact refers to the n-dimensional preprocessed vector $x'/\|x'\|_2$.

3.2 Model

The square distance associated with a pair of data points (x_i, x_j) using the matrix $M \in \mathcal{S}_+^n$ (the set of $n \times n$ PSD matrices) is defined by

$$d^2(x_i, x_j, M) = (x_i - x_j)^\top M (x_i - x_j). \tag{2}$$

In LMLML the metric is adapted to each pair so the matrix M is replaced by a matrix-valued function $\mathcal{M} : \mathbb{R}^n \times \mathbb{R}^n \mapsto \mathcal{S}_+^n$. It is defined, for every $x_i, x_j \in \mathbb{R}^n$, as a convex combination a $K + 1$ matrices

$$\mathcal{M}(x_i, x_j) = \sum_{k=0}^{K} w_k(x_i, x_j) M_k \tag{3}$$

where $w_k(x_i, x_j)$ are nonnegative weights which we define below. The smoothness of the function $\mathcal{M}$ is a very desirable property because it guarantees the dissimilarity function to be local and also because abrupt changes would make the thresholding of the dissimilarity more difficult to handle. In order to ensure this property, we use weights w_k which vary smoothly across the input space. As we want the dissimilarity function to be *local* it makes sense to use a soft partitioning of the input space to compute the weights $w_k(x_i, x_j)$ and we propose to rely on a Gaussian Mixture Model (GMM) with K components as follow:

$$w_k(x_i, x_j) = \begin{cases} \beta & \text{if } k = 0 \\ P(k|Vx_i) + P(k|Vx_j) & \text{otherwise} \end{cases} \tag{4}$$

where $V \in \mathbb{R}^{r \times n}$ is a dimensionality reduction matrix to be described in Section 3.3, β is a positive constant and $P(k|Vx)$ is the posterior probability that the point Vx has been generated by the Gaussian k. Notice that $\forall x_i, x_j \in \mathbb{R}^n$, $\sum_{k=0}^{K} w_k(x_i, x_j) = 2 + \beta$. The GMM has to be computed on a low dimensional space, typically less than 50, to ensure the smoothness of w_k because $P(k|Vx)$ tends not to be smooth otherwise. We illustrate this in Section 4.3. The GMM is trained using the standard Maximum Likelihood EM algorithm. Even if this procedure is totally unsupervised, the soft partitioning depends on the labels as V is learned in a supervised manner.

Thanks to the weights $w_k(x_i, x_j)$, each local metric has a strong influence only within a specific region, M_k has a large weight in $\mathcal{M}(x_i, x_j)$ if x_i or x_j is strongly associated with Gaussian k and even more so if both are. In the face verification example mentioned in the introduction, the soft partitioning tends to roughly regroup faces by gender and ethnicity (see Section 4.4). Thus $\mathcal{M}(x_i, x_j)$ emphasizes those features which are most discriminative to compare people with similar gender/ethnicity than x_i and/or x_j.

The metric M_0 is associated with a constant weight and is therefore a global metric, it handles the part of the dissimilarity function which is common to the whole input space. The metrics M_k with $1 \leq k \leq K$ deal with the local adaptations of the dissimilarity function over the regions defined by the Gaussians of the GMM. Our model is a generalization of global metric and purely local metric as the parameter β allows to balance the influence of the global metric M_0 and the local metrics M_k in the matrix $\mathcal{M}(x_i, x_j)$. The larger K is, the more the model will be able to handle subtle local adaptations but the more it might overfit. Among values obtaining comparable performance during cross-validation, the smallest should be preferred because speed and memory occupancy for training and testing grow linearly with K. The impact of K on the performance is studied in Section 4.3. If $K = 0$ or $\beta \to \infty$ our model is equivalent to a global linear metric.

One could think that it is not necessary to add the M_0 metric in our model because the very same dissimilarity function can be written without M_0 by integrating it into the others M_k. However the actual formulation allows one to use all the training points to learn the part of the dissimilarity function which is common to the whole space and this leads to better generalization performance.

We summarize here the 4 steps of LMLML's training:

1. Data preprocessing (Section 3.1),
2. Optimization of V which maps the data into a low dimensional embedding (Section 3.3),
3. Training of the GMM and computation of the weights $w_k(x_i, x_j)$ using (4),
4. Optimization of the PSD matrices $M_0, \ldots, M_k$ (Section 3.4).

3.3   Low Dimensional Embedding

The weights $w_k(x_i, x_j)$ are based on the soft partitioning of the space derived from the GMM. Training the GMM on a discriminative low dimensional embedding is one of the key points of our method for two reasons. First, the low dimensionality favors the smoothness of weight functions. Second, for local metric to be effective it is needed that points which are hard to discriminate using a global metric have similar weights so that the local metrics focus on the locally discriminative information. To fulfill these two requirements the computation of the embedding is inspired by low rank global metric learning methods [20]. Let $V \in \mathbb{R}^{r \times n}$ denote the transformation matrix embedding the data into the low dimensional feature space of size r. We define the following loss function based on the hinge loss:

$$\ell_\gamma(y, z) = \max\left(0, 1 - \frac{y}{\gamma}(1 - z)\right) \tag{5}$$

where $y \in \{-1, 1\}$ is a label, z a dissimilarity value and γ the margin width parameter. We propose to find the transformation V by minimizing the objective function

$$J(V, \alpha) = \frac{1}{|\mathcal{D}|} \sum_{(i,j) \in \mathcal{D}} \ell_\gamma \left(y_{ij}, d^2(x_i, x_j, V^\top V) \right) + \lambda \|V^\top V - \alpha I\|_F \qquad (6)$$

with respect to V and α, d^2 is the distance function defined by (2), $|\cdot|$ is the cardinality operator and λ is a parameter tuning the strength of the regularization. Thanks to the preprocessing step described in Section 3.1 the Euclidean distance is already a reasonable metric so, to limit over-fitting, the regularizer favors solutions close to the identity up to a scale factor parameter α. The scale factor being unknown, the optimization is also performed with respect to α.

The parameter γ is typically between 0.5 and 1: only the more difficult pairs impact the objective function when γ is small but a larger proportion of them does if γ is large. Its optimal value depends on how helpful easy pairs are to improve the performance on the part of the ROC curve we care about. It also depends on the size of the training set: larger values of γ are better with small training sets because when few pairs are available it is better not to discard too many of them even if they are not the most helpful ones. Both λ and γ have to be selected by cross-validation but can be set by looking only at the performance of low dimensional transformation alone. Objective functions similar to (6) have already been proposed in the literature [20,13], they mainly differ by the choice of the regularizer.

This optimization problem is not convex so there is no guarantee to find the global minimum but in practice we observed that the initialization of the optimization does not impact much the final performance. We use a stochastic mini-batch gradient descent to minimize $J(V, \alpha)$. At each iteration, it uses the gradient of $J_{\mathcal{D}'}(V, \alpha)$ which is the approximation of the objective function using only a randomly selected subset of size t of the training set $\mathcal{D}' \subset \mathcal{D}$. Its computation is straightforward and gives

$$\frac{\partial J_{\mathcal{D}'}(V, \alpha)}{\partial \alpha} = \frac{\alpha t - \|V\|_F^2}{\|V^\top V - \alpha I\|_F}, \qquad (7)$$

$$\frac{\partial J_{\mathcal{D}'}(V, \alpha)}{\partial V} = \frac{1}{|\mathcal{D}'|} \sum_{(i,j) \in \mathcal{D}'} \frac{\partial \ell_\gamma \left(y_{ij}, d^2(x_i, x_j, V^\top V) \right)}{\partial V} + \lambda \frac{\partial \|V^\top V - \alpha I\|_F}{\partial V} \qquad (8)$$

with

$$\frac{\partial \ell_\gamma \left(y_{ij}, d^2(x_i, x_j, V^\top V) \right)}{\partial V} = \begin{cases} 0 \text{ if } y_{ij}(1 - d^2(x_i, x_j, V^\top V)) < \gamma \\ \frac{2 y_{ij} V (x_i - x_j)(x_i - x_j)^\top}{\gamma} \text{ otherwise} \end{cases}, \qquad (9)$$

$$\frac{\partial \|V^\top V - \alpha I\|_F}{\partial V} = \frac{2V(V^\top V - \alpha I)}{\|V^\top V - \alpha I\|_F}. \qquad (10)$$

3.4   Local Metrics Optimization

LMLML training is a two steps procedure: we first learn the low dimensional transformation and the GMM allowing to compute the weights $w_k(x_i, x_j)$ as previously described, and then we optimize over the PSD matrices M_k considering the weights fixed. In this section, we explain how to achieve the latter step.

We define an objective function similar to (6) but adapted to local metrics:

$$H(\mathbf{M}, \boldsymbol{\alpha}) = \frac{1}{|\mathcal{D}|} \sum_{(i,j) \in \mathcal{D}} \ell_\gamma \left(y_{ij}, d^2(x_i, x_j, \mathcal{M}(x_i, x_j))\right) + \lambda' \sum_{k=0}^{K} \|M_k - \alpha_k I\|_F \quad (11)$$

where $\mathbf{M} = \{M_0, \ldots, M_K\}$, $\boldsymbol{\alpha} = \{\alpha_0, \ldots, \alpha_K\}$ is a vector of scale factors and λ' tunes the intensity of the regularization; λ' is usually very close to λ of (6) but can be tuned by cross-validation to optimize the performance of LMLML. We seek to minimize $H(\mathbf{M}, \boldsymbol{\alpha})$ with respect to $\mathbf{M}$ and $\boldsymbol{\alpha}$ under the constraint that $\forall k \in \{0, \ldots, K\}$, $M_k \in \mathcal{S}_+^n$.

When replacing $\mathcal{M}(x_i, x_j)$ by its definition (3) in the expression of the squared distance (2), we notice that $d^2(x_i, x_j, \mathcal{M}(x_i, x_j))$ is linear with respect to each of the matrices M_k so ℓ_γ is convex. Each term of the regularizer can be written as $\| [\text{vec}(M_k)^\top, \alpha] A \|_2$ with the appropriate matrix $A \in \mathbb{R}^{(n^2+1) \times n^2}$. The composition of a convex function with a linear mapping is convex (see [2], 3.2.2) therefore $H(\mathbf{M}, \boldsymbol{\alpha})$ is jointly convex.

The optimization of a constrained problem can be slow but we can transform it into an unconstrained problem. We make the change of variable $M_k = L_k^\top L_k$ where $L_k \in \mathbb{R}^{n \times n}$, define the objective function H' such that $H'(\mathbf{L}, \boldsymbol{\alpha}) = H(\mathbf{M}, \boldsymbol{\alpha})$ where $\mathbf{L} = \{L_0, \ldots, L_K\}$ and optimize H'. This new problem is no longer convex but as it has been shown in [13], if we consider two functions f and h such that $f(L) = h(L^\top L)$ then every minimum of f corresponds to a minimum of h. The proof can easily be extended to the multi metric case and therefore, as H is convex, we can optimize the unconstrained problem H' without risking to be stuck in a non optimal local minimum. Notice that this reasoning does not apply to the minimization of (6) because the matrix V is rectangular whereas the L_k are square. Using a rectangular matrix is equivalent to adding a rank constraint on the metric and therefore makes the initial optimization problem non convex.

The optimization is also performed using a stochastic mini-batch gradient descent. Let $H'_{\mathcal{D}'}(\mathbf{L}, \boldsymbol{\alpha})$ be the approximation of the objective function using only a subset of size t of the training set $\mathcal{D}' \subset \mathcal{D}$, its gradient is

$$\frac{\partial H'_{\mathcal{D}'}(\mathbf{L}, \boldsymbol{\alpha})}{\partial \alpha_k} = \frac{\alpha_k t - \|L_k\|_F^2}{\|L_k^\top L_k - \alpha_k I\|_F}, \quad (12)$$

$$\frac{\partial H'_{\mathcal{D}'}(\mathbf{L}, \boldsymbol{\alpha})}{\partial L_k} = \frac{1}{|\mathcal{D}'|} \sum_{(i,j) \in \mathcal{D}'} \frac{\ell_\gamma \left(y_{ij}, d^2(x_i, x_j, \mathcal{M}(x_i, x_j))\right)}{\partial L_k} + \lambda' \frac{\partial \|L_k^\top L_k - \alpha_k I\|_F}{\partial L_k}$$

$$(13)$$

with

$$\frac{\ell_\gamma\left(y_{ij}, d^2(x_i, x_j, \mathcal{M}(x_i, x_j))\right)}{\partial L_k} = \begin{cases} 0 \text{ if } y_{ij}(1 - d^2(x_i, x_j, \mathcal{M}(x_i, x_j))) < \gamma \\ \\ \frac{2y_{ij}w_k(x_i, x_j)L_k(x_i - x_j)(x_i - x_j)^\top}{\gamma} \text{ otherwise} \end{cases} \tag{14}$$

$$\frac{\partial \|L_k^\top L_k - \alpha_k I\|_F}{\partial L_k} = \frac{2L_k(L_k^\top L_k - \alpha_k I)}{\|L_k^\top L_k - \alpha_k I\|_F}. \tag{15}$$

Note that in LMLML, the L_k are jointly optimized: all the metrics impact the value of $\mathcal{M}(x_i, x_j)$ and therefore the gradient of each L_k.

3.5   Parameters Setting

The regularization strength λ' and the number of local metrics K are the two key parameters of LMLML. They have to be set by cross-validation for each dataset, the others parameters don't need to be fine tuned. The dimensionality after PCA n is common to most metric learning algorithm and is usually chosen so that 95% of the energy is preserved. Parameter γ is not very sensitive, it takes value in $[0.5, 1]$ and should be close to 0.5 on big datasets and closer to 1 on smaller ones. Among the additional parameters added specifically to deal with the local metrics, namely K, r and β, only K needs to be tuned, we have set $r = 30$ and $\beta = 1.5$ in all our experiments.

4   Experiments

The set of experiments presented in this section demonstrates the performance of LMLML on various datasets and provides some insights into the method.

4.1   Datasets and Setup

MNIST. Handwritten digits classification has been widely used to assess the performance of dissimilarity functions for classification. The MNIST[1] dataset is composed of 70000 images of size 28×28, 60000 for training and 10000 for testing. We used the same setup as in [22] to compare the performance with other dissimilarity measures. The PCA is computed directly on the pixel values and 164 dimensions are kept after the PCA to retain 95% of the energy. The classification is performed using a simple nearest neighbor classifier.

FRGC. Face verification is a very popular application of dissimilarity function learning. The task consists in determining whether two images depict the same person, usually by thresholding a dissimilarity measure. The identities used for testing are not included in the training set. FRGC Experiment 1 [18] is a face

---

[1] http://yann.lecun.com/exdb/mnist/

dataset of more than 15000 images of more than 500 people. The pose of the subject and the illumination have been controlled during the acquisition so compared to datasets like Labeled Faces in the Wild presented hereafter this dataset is fairly easy. However, on this type of dataset, the interest is focused on the verification rate at low false positive rates (1% and below). This is a realistic setting for many security applications of face recognition (like smartphone unlocking or passport check at the border) where a false accept is a security breach and therefore must be very rare. After aligning the images using the eyes locations, we computed UoCTTI HOG descriptors [6] extracted using the *VLFeat* library [21] to obtain 6076-dimensional feature vectors. We retained 700 dimensions after the PCA and trained all the dissimilarity functions we compare on these vectors.

LFW. Label Faces in the Wild (LFW) [9] is another face verification dataset. It is composed of 13233 images of 5749 people taken from *Yahoo! News* in wide range of acquisition conditions (pose, illumination, expression, age, *etc.*) therefore considered to be challenging. We have followed the same feature extraction procedure as [3]: the "aligned" image are first cropped to 150 × 80 to remove most of the background, then descriptors composed of histograms of Local Binary Patterns [16] are extracted and their dimensionality is reduced to 300 by PCA. The within-class whitening is also activated on LFW. As discussed in Section 4.2 the choice of the training pairs has a great impact on the overall performance of dissimilarity function methods. To get rid of this bias we report the performance on LFW in the Image Restricted setting where only a limited number of labeled training pairs are provided but not the identity information associated with each image making impossible the use of all possible pairs. We followed the recommended 10-folds cross-validated experiment for evaluation [9] and selected the parameters and the threshold using a 9-folds cross-validation scheme for each training.

Reuters. Finally we demonstrate the performance of LMLML on the text categorization dataset Reuters-21578 R52[2]. It consists of 9100 text documents which appeared on the Reuters newswire in 1987, 6532 in the training test and 2568 in the testing set. Each text belongs to one of the 52 topics and every topic has at least one text in the training set and one in the testing set. The classes are very unbalanced as some topics have more than 1000 text documents whereas others have just a few. Each text is described as a histogram of word occurrence spanning 5180 terms. A very large number of dimensions should be kept after the PCA to preserve 95% of the energy but to speed up the experiments we kept only the first 100 dimensions retaining only 62% of the energy.

---

[2] http://www.cad.zju.edu.cn/home/dengcai/Data/TextData.html

4.2   Choosing Training Pairs from Class Labels

Many dissimilarity function learning methods consist in optimizing an objective function depending on pairs of feature vectors, see for example [4,7,22,3,13]. The number of possible pairs grows quadratically with the number of training points therefore it is often impracticable to use all of them because the training would require a prohibiting amount of time. The choice of the training pairs has a huge impact on the performance of the method. On some datasets like LFW in the Image Restricted setting the pairs are provided with the dataset but most of the time the pairs have to be created from the class labels, in this section we give some guidelines about how to choose the training pairs.

When the dissimilarity function is employed for nearest neighbor classification like on the MNIST and Reuters datasets, the training pairs should consist of neighboring points because nearest neighbor classifiers base their decision only from such points. We propose to proceed as follow: for each data point x, create q similar pairs, formed by x and each of its q closest neighbors of the same class, and q dissimilar pairs, formed by x and each of its q closest neighbors of a different class. This results in $2q$ training pairs per data point. For both MNIST and Reuters we used $q = 5$.

Dissimilarity measures are also often thresholded to take a decision such as in face verification application. The choice of the threshold leads to a specific trade-off between false positive error and verification rates and this choice depends on the target application. On a dataset like FRGC the number of possible similar pairs is limited and all of them can be used during training but a selection must be made for the dissimilar ones. As people are mainly interested in performance at low false positive rates on such datasets, the training set should include a large number of dissimilar pairs. To speed up the training, we propose a simple hard dissimilar pairs mining scheme. We first randomly pick a number of dissimilar pairs equal to the number of similar pairs and train our model with this set. Then we compute the dissimilarity for a large number of dissimilar pairs and select the 5 or 10% hardest pairs to learn the metrics again. This step could be repeated many times but in practice we observed little improvement after the first iteration.

4.3   Results on MNIST

We argued in Section 3.2 that the dimensionality of the data needs to be reduced before computing the GMM in order to ensure the smoothness of the posterior probability $P(k|x)$ with respect to x and therefore of the weights w_k and the function $\mathcal{M}$. We performed an experiment on MNIST to support our claim. We computed low dimensional embeddings of several dimensionalities using the procedure described in Section 3.3 and for each performed the following operations:

1. Estimation of the GMM parameters (for this experiment we have arbitrary chosen $K = 5$),

2. Computation of the posterior probability distribution $P(\cdot|x)$ for every x in the training set,
3. Computation of the Bhattacharyya distance

$$d_B\left(P(\cdot|x_i), P(\cdot|x_j)\right) = -\log\sum_k \sqrt{P(k|x_i)P(k|x_j)} \qquad (16)$$

between the distribution associated with each x and those of its 3 nearest neighbors.

Figure 1a shows the 75th and 90th percentiles of the computed Bhattacharyya distance function of the dimensionality of the embedding. We can see that larger embedding dimensionality leads to larger Bhattacharyya distance between nearby points which means less smooth weights w_k and therefore justify our choice of a low dimensional embedding. When $r = 30$, the largest weight accounts for less than 80% of the total for 18% of MNIST samples.

We also studied on this dataset the impact of the parameter K, the number of local metrics used in LMLML. As the training of the GMM only finds a local minimum we performed the training 10 times for each value of K and report the mean and standard deviation of the classification rate on Figure 1b. We see that the local metrics significantly outperform the global one ($K = 0$) even if only 2 metrics are used. The classification rate increases for K up to 17 and stays stable afterwards. The speed and memory occupancy for training and testing grows linearly with K so smaller values should be favored. We also notice that LMLML's overall performance has little sensitivity to the local minima proneness of the GMM as the average standard deviation is only 0.015%.

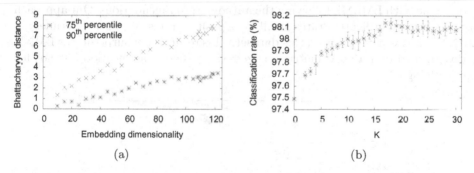

Fig. 1. (a) Percentiles of Bhattacharyya distance between neighbors function of the embedding dimensionality. (b) Impact of K on LMLML's performance.

On the MNIST dataset we compare LMLML with 6 others methods designed for nearest neighbor classification using the same features: 2 global metric learning algorithms LMNN [24] and BoostMetric [19], 3 local metric learning methods MM-LMNN [23], GLML [15] and PLML [22] and a multi-class SVM with one-against-all strategy (the best kernel has been chosen by inner cross-validation). The performance of the other methods have been taken from [22]. Table 1 reports the results. It is worth noticing that the idea of local metric learning needs to be carefully handled to be effective, MM-LMNN and GLML obtain worse results than the global metric learning methods. A possible explanation is that they learn one metric per class and fail to share the information among the classes. LMLML ($K = 19$ set by cross-validation) has an accuracy of 98.10% and outperforms all the other methods including non linear SVM.

Table 1. Classification Rates on MNIST

Local Metric Learning & SVM		Global Metric Learning	
Method	Class. Rate	Method	Class. Rate
LMLML $K = 19$	98.10%	LMLML $K = 0$	97.49%
SVM [22]	97.62%	LMNN [24]	97.30%
PLML [22]	97.30%	BoostMetric [19]	96.03%
MM-LMNN [23]	93.24%		
GLML [15]	84.00%		

4.4   Results on FRGC

To perform face verification a method needs to be able to compute a dissimilarity with pairs of never seen points so we cannot compare LMLML to the local metric learning methods presented in Section 2. Figure 2 shows the ROC curves of LMLML, KISSME [11], ITML [4] and LDML [7]. We used the code available on their respective author's website and cross-validated their parameters in the same way we did with LMLML following the authors' recommendations. Our approach obtains better verification rates at all false positive rates. We also experimented LMNN but it works poorly on this dataset. This result is not surprising as LMNN is designed to find a good metric for nearest neighbor classification but not for thresholding.

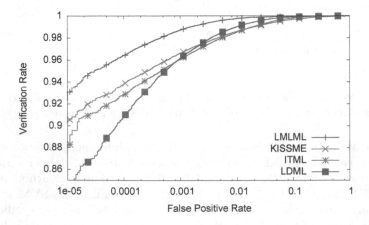

Fig. 2. ROC curves on FRGC

In order to gain more insights into the good performance achieved by our method we observed the distribution of the faces among the different Gaussians of the GMM. Each line of Figure 3 shows faces for which the posterior probability is greater than 0.7 for a specific Gaussian. Thanks to the use of our discriminative low dimensional embedding, the GMM capture interesting properties of the faces: the first group is mostly populated of Asian people (both males and females), the second of Caucasian females, the third and fourth of Caucasian males and the last one of Asian females. This grouping is totally unsupervised as no gender or ethnicity information has been given to the algorithm and allows LMLML to adapt the dissimilarity function to the specificities of these groups and contribute to its good performance on FRGC.

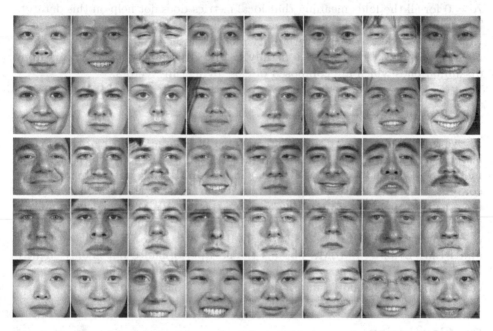

Fig. 3. Samples of faces belonging to the different Gaussians of the GMM, each line is constituted of faces for which $P(k|Vx) > 0.7$ for a specific Gaussian

4.5   Results on LFW

The best methods on LFW rely on fine tuning of the feature extraction: combination of several image descriptors, detection of numerous feature points, use of multiple alignments of the images. To fairly evaluate our approach we followed the feature extraction procedure described in [3,14] and compare our results to those given in these papers in Table 2. CSML's accuracy is copied from [14] and all the others come from [3].

LMLML obtains the 2nd best performance with 0.8613 just behind Sub-SML which got 0.8673. However, the parameter selection process consistently chooses

Table 2. Accuracy on LFW

Method	Accuracy	Method	Accuracy
LMLML	0.8613 ± 0.0053	ITML [4]	0.7998 ± 0.0039
Sub-SML [3]	0.8673 ± 0.0053	Sub-ITML [3]	0.8398 ± 0.0048
CSML [14]	0.8557 ± 0.0052	LDML [7]	0.8065 ± 0.0047
KISSME [11]	0.8337 ± 0.0054	Sub-LDML [3]	0.8227 ± 0.0058
DML-eig [25]	0.8228 ± 0.0041	SILD [10]	0.8007 ± 0.0135

$K = 0$ for all the folds meaning that local metrics does not help on this dataset. The main explanation for this observation might be that the major challenge of LFW is the wide intra-class variability and this issue is not addressed by local metric learning as local metrics mainly help to discriminate similar pairs from dissimilar ones which are composed of close by feature vectors.

4.6   Results on Reuters

As we noted before this dataset is composed of a large number of classes and is very unbalanced. This makes local metric learning methods which learn one metric per class such as MM-LMNN [23] or GLML [15] not well suited. We compared LMLML with one global metric learning method: LMNN, and one local learning metric method: PLML. We used the code downloaded from their respective author's website and cross-validated their parameters. The results are the following: LMLML $K = 3$: 89.03%, LMLML $K = 0$: 88.75%, LMNN: 88.87% and PLML 87.39%. LMLML obtains the best performance but is only slightly better than LMNN. Once again these results show that handling local metric can be tricky as the global metric learning LMNN outperforms PLML.

5   Conclusion

In this paper, we have introduced a new local metric learning algorithm. The data are embedded into a discriminative low dimensional space to compute a soft partitioning which allows to define a smooth locally adapting dissimilarity function. Our method overcomes the limitations of previous local metric learning methods, it is as flexible as global metric learning methods and can therefore be applied to wide variety of scenarios. The good performance of LMLML has been demonstrated on four different datasets including the popular and challenging LFW. In the future, LMLML could be extended to a more generic multi metrics method by performing the soft partitioning with respect to other criteria such as image quality. Furthermore, an interesting direction for future research is to integrate the soft partitioning and the learning of the local metrics into a single optimization problem.

References

1. Bilenko, M., Basu, S., Mooney, R.J.: Integrating constraints and metric learning in semi-supervised clustering. In: ICML, pp. 11–18 (2004)
2. Boyd, S., Vandenberghe, L.: Convex Optimization. Cambridge University Press, New York (2004)
3. Cao, Q., Ying, Y., Li, P.: Similarity metric learning for face recognition. In: ICCV (2013)
4. Davis, J.V., Kulis, B., Jain, P., Sra, S., Dhillon, I.S.: Information-theoretic metric learning. In: ICML, pp. 209–216 (2007)
5. Evgeniou, T., Pontil, M.: Regularized multi-task learning. In: SIGKDD, pp. 109–117 (2004)
6. Felzenszwalb, P.F., Girshick, R.B., McAllester, D., Ramanan, D.: Object detection with discriminatively trained part-based models. PAMI 32(9), 1627–1645 (2010)
7. Guillaumin, M., Verbeek, J., Schmid, C.: Is that you? metric learning approaches for face identification. In: ICCV, pp. 498–505 (2009)
8. Hatch, A.O., Kajarekar, S., Stolcke, A.: Within-class covariance normalization for svm-based speaker recognition. In: ICSLP, pp. 1471–1474 (2006)
9. Huang, G.B., Ramesh, M., Berg, T., Learned-Miller, E.: Labeled faces in the wild: A database for studying face recognition in unconstrained environments. Tech. Rep. 07-49, University of Massachusetts, Amherst (2007)
10. Kan, M., Shan, S., Xu, D., Chen, X.: Side-information based linear discriminant analysis for face recognition. In: BMVC, pp. 1–12 (2011)
11. Köstinger, M., Hirzer, M., Wohlhart, P., Roth, P.M., Bischof, H.: Large scale metric learning from equivalence constraints. In: CVPR, pp. 2288–2295 (2012)
12. Köstinger, M., Roth, P.M., Bischof, H.: Synergy-based learning of facial identity. In: Pinz, A., Pock, T., Bischof, H., Leberl, F. (eds.) DAGM and OAGM 2012. LNCS, vol. 7476, pp. 195–204. Springer, Heidelberg (2012)
13. Maurer, A.: Learning similarity with operator-valued large-margin classifiers. JMLR 9, 1049–1082 (2008)
14. Nguyen, H.V., Bai, L.: Cosine similarity metric learning for face verification. In: Kimmel, R., Klette, R., Sugimoto, A. (eds.) ACCV 2010, Part II. LNCS, vol. 6493, pp. 709–720. Springer, Heidelberg (2011)
15. Noh, Y.K., Zhang, B.T., Lee, D.D.: Generative local metric learning for nearest neighbor classification. In: NIPS, pp. 1822–1830 (2010)
16. Ojala, T., Pietikäinen, M., Mäenpää, T.: Multiresolution gray-scale and rotation invariant texture classification with local binary patterns. PAMI 24(7), 971–987 (2002)
17. Parameswaran, S., Weinberger, K.Q.: Large margin multi-task metric learning. In: NIPS, pp. 1867–1875 (2010)
18. Phillips, P.J., Flynn, P.J., Scruggs, T., Bowyer, K.W., Chang, J., Hoffman, K., Marques, J., Min, J., Worek, W.: Overview of the face recognition grand challenge. In: CVPR, pp. 947–954 (2005)
19. Shen, C., Kim, J., Wang, L., van den Hengel, A.: Positive semidefinite metric learning with boosting. In: NIPS, pp. 1651–1659 (2009)
20. Simonyan, K., Parkhi, O.M., Vedaldi, A., Zisserman, A.: Fisher vector faces in the wild. In: BMVC (2013)

21. Vedaldi, A., Fulkerson, B.: VLFeat: An open and portable library of computer vision algorithms (2008), http://www.vlfeat.org/
22. Wang, J., Kalousis, A., Woznica, A.: Parametric local metric learning for nearest neighbor classification. In: NIPS, pp. 1610–1618 (2012)
23. Weinberger, K., Saul, L.: Fast solvers and efficient implementations for distance metric learning. In: ICML, pp. 1160–1167 (2008)
24. Weinberger, K., Saul, L.: Distance metric learning for large margin nearest neighbor classification. JMLR 10, 207–244 (2009)
25. Ying, Y., Li, P.: Distance metric learning with eigenvalue optimization. JMLR 13, 1–26 (2012)

Movement Pattern Histogram for Action Recognition and Retrieval

Arridhana Ciptadi[1], Matthew S. Goodwin[2], and James M. Rehg[1]

[1] College of Computing, Georgia Institute of Technology, USA
{arridhana,rehg}@gatech.edu
[2] Department of Health Sciences, Northeastern University, USA
m.goodwin@neu.edu

Abstract. We present a novel action representation based on encoding the global temporal movement of an action. We represent an action as a set of movement pattern histograms that encode the global temporal dynamics of an action. Our key observation is that temporal dynamics of an action are robust to variations in appearance and viewpoint changes, making it useful for action recognition and retrieval. We pose the problem of computing similarity between action representations as a maximum matching problem in a bipartite graph. We demonstrate the effectiveness of our method for cross-view action recognition on the IXMAS dataset. We also show how our representation complements existing bag-of-features representations on the UCF50 dataset. Finally we show the power of our representation for action retrieval on a new real-world dataset containing repetitive motor movements emitted by children with autism in an unconstrained classroom setting.

1 Introduction

The recognition and retrieval of actions in videos is challenging due to the need to handle many sources of variations: viewpoint, size and appearance of actors, scene lighting and video quality, etc. In this paper we introduce a novel action representation based on motion dynamics that is robust to such variations.

Currently, state-of-the-art performance in action classification is achieved by extracting dense local features (HOG, HOF, MBH) and grouping them in a bag-of-features (BOF) framework [26]. The basic BOF representation ignores information about the spatial and temporal arrangement of the local features by pooling them over the entire video volume. More recently, it has been shown that considering the spatial and temporal arrangements (dynamics) of an action (eg. extracting separate BOF model for each subvolume of a video [14,26] or modelling the spatio-temporal arrangements of the interest points [29]) adds more discriminative power to the representation.

Our approach is based on the observation that the dynamics of an action provide a powerful cue for discrimination. In Johansson's moving light display experiment, it was shown that humans perceive actions by abstracting a coherent structure from the spatio-temporal pattern of local movements [9]. While humans respond to both spatial and temporal information, the spatial configuration of movements that comprise an action is strongly affected by changes in viewpoint. This suggests that representing the temporal

D. Fleet et al. (Eds.): ECCV 2014, Part II, LNCS 8690, pp. 695–710, 2014.

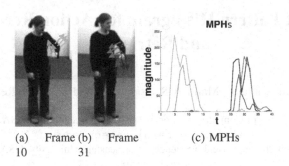

(a)   Frame (b)   Frame   (c) MPHs
10   31

Fig. 1. Movement Pattern Histogram for *checkwatch* action. (a)-(b): Arrows indicate optical flow direction and are color coded according to the flow words (flows are subsampled for presentation). (c): MPH set for *checkwatch*. (Best viewed in color).

structure of an action could be valuable for reducing the effect of viewpoint. Motivated by this observation, we define human actions as a composition of temporal patterns of movements.

Our key hypothesis is that the temporal dynamics of an action are similar across views. For example, the timing pattern of acceleration and deceleration of the limbs is largely preserved under viewpoint changes. In our representation, an action is decomposed into movement primitives (corresponding roughly to body parts). We encode the fine-grained temporal dynamics of each movement primitive using a representation that we call the *movement pattern histogram* (MPH). We describe an action as a collection of MPHs (see Fig. 1).

An advantage of video-level pooling methods such as BOF is that computing similarity between representations can be done reliably using $L2$ or χ^2 distance function. In part this is because these representations discard the temporal structure of an action, obviating the need for temporal alignment as a part of the matching process. In contrast, computing similarity between two sets of MPH requires alignment and we describe an novel method to do so using a simultaneous alignment and bipartite matching formulation. Such formulation allows for matching across viewpoints and we present an efficient algorithm to solve it.

Our MPH representation can be used in two ways: 1) as a stand-alone action representation for action recognition/retrieval across multiple viewpoints; and 2) to complement existing BOF representations for action recognition. We demonstrate that our approach outperforms standard representations for cross-view recognition tasks in the IXMAS dataset [27]. We also show that our representation complements existing representations for the classification task in the UCF50 dataset [21]. Finally, we show that our representation yields state-of-the-art results for the task of action retrieval in the novel Stereotypy dataset that we introduce (stereotypies are repetitive body movement patterns frequently associated with autism and are often the target of behavioral therapy). In summary, this paper makes three contributions:

– We introduce the *movement pattern histogram*, a novel representation of actions as a multi-channel temporal distribution of movement primitives.

– We present a novel optimization approach to matching movement pattern histograms across videos based on maximum bipartite graph matching.
– We introduce the Stereotypy dataset, a new annotated video corpus obtained by recording children with autism in a classroom setting[1]. We will make this dataset publicly available.

2   Related Work

There is a vast literature on action/activity representation (a recent survey can be found in [20]). A classic representation of action in videos is based on space-time templates [6,11]. While this approach captures the fine-grained detail of an action, it is challenging to achieve robustness to variations. A popular framework used by many authors is the bag-of-features model, with varying local features: interest points [14,5], tracks of points [18,10,26] or frame based descriptors [25]. Many of these methods use descriptors such as HOG/HOF [14,5,26], MBH [26], MIP [13] or shape-flow [25] that are not robust to variations in viewpoint and thus may not support accurate matching of actions across views. Moreover, the BOF framework typically only have a very coarse model of action dynamics (eg. by dividing a video into several subvolumes). *In contrast, our representation captures the fine-grained dynamics of an action while being robust to variations in viewpoint.*

Recently, interesting work has been done to address the challenge of viewpoint variation in action recognition. Liu et.al. [17] tackle the viewpoint problem through transfer learning by building a mapping between codebooks from different viewpoints. However, their framework requires knowledge of the camera viewpoint associated with each action (in testing and training). In a similar spirit, [16,30] learn a series of linear transformations of the feature vector extracted from a video to make it invariant to viewpoint changes. However, a linear transformation is not guaranteed to accurately model view-invariant mapping. Also, performance of their method drops significantly in the absence of multi-view observations of actions in training examples. In addition, [17,16,30] use the shape-flow descriptor that requires extraction of a bounding box and silhouette of an action, which can be challenging in real-world videos. Note that these methods assume a discrete number of pre-defined camera positions, which limits applicability of the methods since the need to collect examples across viewpoints can be burdensome.

Junejo et.al. [10] propose the self similarity matrix (SSM) which exhibits invariance to viewpoint changes. They compute SSM by either point tracking or pairwise frame similarity. However, point tracking is not always accurate and computing pairwise frame similarity means the feature will not be robust to slowly changing background. Another representation robust to changes in viewpoints is the hankelet ([15]). Hankelet is a hankel matrix representation of a tracklet that is invariant to affine transformations. Results in [10] and [15] show that SSM and hankelet are susceptible to large viewpoint changes.

---

[1] Note that the Stereotypy dataset was collected under an IRB-approved protocol, following best-practices for research with vulnerable subject populations. Consent to publish has been obtained for all images and results.

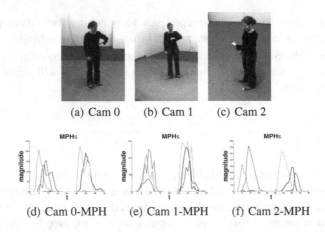

(a) Cam 0   (b) Cam 1   (c) Cam 2

(d) Cam 0-MPH   (e) Cam 1-MPH   (f) Cam 2-MPH

Fig. 2. (a)-(c): Three different views of the checkwatch action. (d)-(f): MPH representations of checkwatch for each view. Note the structural similarity of the MPH curves despite huge changes in viewpoint.

3   Action Representation

In this section we describe our action representation, the *movement pattern histogram* (MPH). MPH encodes the global temporal pattern of an action without requiring explicit tracking of features over time. In Sec. 4 we present an iterative method for matching two sets of MPHs.

3.1   The Movement Pattern Histogram

To illustrate our approach, consider the action of a person checking a watch seen from frontal view (Fig. 1). This action can be characterized by the upward movement of the hand and upper arm during the early part of the action (to bring the watch to a readable distance) and the downward movement of the same body parts at the end of the action. We can imagine encoding these body part movements with a cluster of flow vectors, where each cluster explains some portion of the total flow across the video. We denote these clusters as *flow words*. In the check-watch example, the upward hand movement might be mapped to a single flow word. That word would be present in the first half of the frames and absent in the other half (when the hand moves downward).

Given a set of extracted flow words, our goal is to represent an action by encoding the pattern of temporal occurrence of the flow words. In the example of Fig.1, the green and cyan words occur early in the action (when the hand and upper arm are raised) while the blue and magenta words occur later in the action. We construct an MPH for each flow word which encodes its dynamics.

We now describe the process of constructing the MPH representation. We assume that the video is captured using a static camera (we relax this assumption in Section 3.2). First we compute dense optical flow over the video clip. Then, we use EM to cluster together the flow vectors from all frames based only on the flow direction (we only consider flow vectors whose magnitudes are above a certain threshold). Each flow cluster defines a single flow word. In Figure 1(a)-1(b) we can see the flows color-coded according to the five flow words. We then generate an MPH for each of the flow clusters by binning the flow vectors. Each bin t in the MPH h_c corresponds to frame number t, and contains the sum of flow magnitudes for all pixel flows f that corresponds to cluster c in that frame. Let m_c denote the set of flow vectors that map to cluster c:

$$h_c(t) = \sum_{f(t) \in m_c} \| f(t) \| \tag{1}$$

In Fig. 1(c) we can see that the green MPH corresponding to upward hand movement is active at the beginning of the action and the blue MPH that corresponds to downward hand movement is active at the end. Note that MPH is quite different from other flow-based models such as the histograms of oriented optical flow (HOOF) [4]. HOOF models the distribution of optical flow direction in each frame, making it a viewpoint-dependent representation, while MPH models the temporal distribution of the *magnitudes* of the different flow clusters.

MPH differs in two ways from the standard histogram representations of visual words which are used in action recognition. First, each MPH corresponds to a single flow word and describes the variation in its magnitude over time. In contrast, BOF uses a single fixed histogram describing the co-occurrence of all visual words. Second, the MPH provides a very fine-grained temporal description (one bin per frame) but a very coarse spatial description (all occurrences of a word in a frame are binned together), in order to gain robustness to viewpoint variations.

Figure 2 illustrates the robustness of the MPH representation to viewpoint variation. We can see that the shapes of the MPH sets are quite similar in spite of substantial changes in viewpoint.

Figure 3 shows MPHs for different actions. The MPH representation achieves a certain invariance property under viewpoint changes because it marginalizes out information about appearance, spatial configuration, and flow direction of an action. While spatial configuration and appearance can be important for discriminating certain actions (eg. high punch vs low punch), Fig. 3 demonstrates that the temporal nature of an action can also be very discriminative. Note how MPH captures the dynamics of the different actions: wave (Fig. 3(c)) consists of hand moving left and right and this periodicity is reflected in the MPH. Even in cases where the mechanics of two actions are similar (checkwatch and scratchhead both involve upward and downward movement of the hand), the dynamics of the actions make the MPH sets distinct (Fig. 3(d) vs 3(f)).

3.2 Compensating for Camera Motion

Sometimes action in the real-world is captured using a moving camera. This can cause problems for our representations if we assume that all flows in the video are relevant to the action. To minimize the effect of camera motion we can apply a video stabilization technique such as [7] before computing dense optical flow. However, since we only need to remove the background motion between two consecutive frames (i.e. we don't need to produce smooth camera trajectory for the whole video), we can apply a simpler solution. We estimate the background motion by computing homography between frames from the optical flow motion vectors (this is similar to [8] but instead of assuming affine motion between frames we use homography). Using the dense optical flow computed,

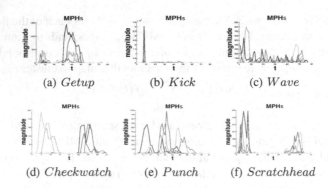

(a) *Getup*   (b) *Kick*   (c) *Wave*

(d) *Checkwatch*   (e) *Punch*   (f) *Scratchhead*

Fig. 3. MPHs of different actions

we select a subset of flow vectors located in textured regions (using criteria in [23]) and perform homography estimation with RANSAC. From the estimated homography, we compute the camera-induced background motion for every pixel in that frame and then subtract the background motion from the computed flow vectors. We do this background motion estimation for every frame in the video and use the corrected flow vectors to compute MPH. Figure 4 shows the result of our motion compensation.

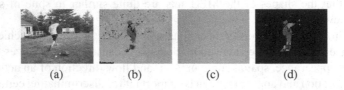

(a)   (b)   (c)   (d)

Fig. 4. Motion compensation results from UCF50: b) Original flow, c) Estimated background motion, d) Motion compensated flow. Flows are color coded following the Middlebury convention.

4   Computing Similarity

Given our new MPH representation, how can we compute similarity between two videos – *target* and *source*? Accurate similarity measure is important for action recognition and retrieval. Our assumption is that if the two videos correspond to the same action, we can find matching in which the MPH pairs are highly correlated. Let $h_i^t \in \mathbb{R}^{l_t}$ and $h_j^s \in \mathbb{R}^{l_s}$ be the movement pattern histogram for primitives (clusters) i and j in the *target* and *source* videos, respectively (l_s and l_t are the number of frames of the videos). Note that since each video is clustered independently, there is no a priori relationship between MPHs from separate videos. Let $T = \{h_1^t, h_2^t, ...h_K^t\}$ and $S = \{h_1^s, h_2^s, ...h_K^s\}$, where K is the total number of flow words in the target and source video. We can construct an undirected bipartite graph $G = (V, E)$ where every single element of T is connected to every single element of S, the vertex set $V = T \cup S$, and $e_{ij} \in E$ is the edge between h_i^t and h_j^s. The weight of edge e_{ij} is the similarity measure between two signals h_i^t and h_j^s.

We use the Pearson correlation coefficient (PCC) to compute e_{ij} due to its invariance to scaling: $e_{ij} = PCC(h_i^t, h_j^s) = \frac{cov(h_i^t, h_j^s)}{\sigma_{h_i^t}\sigma_{h_j^s}}$

The similarity between the target and source video is the maximum weighted bipartite matching score of graph G.

Simultaneous Alignment and Matching

Since an action can be performed at different speeds, the two sets of histograms S and T might not be temporally aligned. This negatively impacts our correlation measure. In order to overcome this problem, we propose a simultaneous alignment and matching method where we iteratively perform alignment and matching of S and T.

Let $\boldsymbol{H_s} = [h_1^s, h_2^s, ...h_K^s]$ and $\boldsymbol{H_t} = [h_1^t, h_2^t, ...h_K^t]$ be the matrices that we construct from S and T. Without loss of generality, let us assume that we normalize the MPH in S and T so that they all have zero mean and unit standard deviation. Also, we zero-pad each vectors h_j^s and h_i^t such that $l_s = l_t = l$. Under this condition, finding the maximum weighted bipartite matching of graph G is equivalent to computing a $K \times K$ binary matrix M that minimizes $C_m = \|\boldsymbol{H_s}M - \boldsymbol{H_t}\|_F^2$, where $\Sigma_i M(i,j) = 1, \Sigma_j M(i,j) = 1$.

To align $\boldsymbol{H_s}$ and $\boldsymbol{H_t}$, we can use dynamic time warping (applying DTW or its variants eg. [31] on a time series data is a common approach for doing activity alignment) to compute binary matrices $(\boldsymbol{D_s}, \boldsymbol{D_t})$ that minimize $C_{dtw} = \|\boldsymbol{D_s}\boldsymbol{H_s} - \boldsymbol{D_t}\boldsymbol{H_t}\|_F^2$, where $\Sigma_j \boldsymbol{D_s}(i,j) = 1$ and $\Sigma_j \boldsymbol{D_t}(i,j) = 1$. Note that DTW optimization infers $\boldsymbol{D_s}$ and $\boldsymbol{D_t}$ using dynamic programming such that the temporal ordering of the rows in $\boldsymbol{H_s}$ and $\boldsymbol{H_t}$ is preserved. The DTW solution $(\boldsymbol{D_s}, \boldsymbol{D_t})$ are binary matrices of size $l' \times l$ where l' is the length of the alignment path between $\boldsymbol{H_s}$ and $\boldsymbol{H_t}$. Putting the previous two steps together, we get the final cost function that we want to minimize:

$$C_{mdtw} = \|\boldsymbol{D_s}\boldsymbol{H_s}M - \boldsymbol{D_t}\boldsymbol{H_t}\|_F^2$$
$$\text{where } \Sigma_i M_{ij} = 1, \ \Sigma_j M_{ij} = 1$$
$$\Sigma_j \boldsymbol{D_s}(i,j) = 1 \tag{2}$$
$$\Sigma_j \boldsymbol{D_t}(i,j) = 1$$

Optimizing C_{mdtw} is a non-convex optimization problem with respect to the matching matrix M and alignment matrices $\boldsymbol{D_s}$ and $\boldsymbol{D_t}$. We can perform iterative optimization by alternating between computing $(\boldsymbol{D_s}, \boldsymbol{D_t})$ and M:

1. Set M as $K \times K$ identity matrix
2. Fix M and minimize $C_{dtw} = \|\boldsymbol{D_s}\boldsymbol{H_s^m} - \boldsymbol{D_t}\boldsymbol{H_t}\|_F^2$, where $\boldsymbol{H_s^m} = \boldsymbol{H_s}M$, to optimize for $(\boldsymbol{D_s}, \boldsymbol{D_t})$
3. Fix $(\boldsymbol{D_s}, \boldsymbol{D_t})$ and minimize $C_m = \|\boldsymbol{H_s^{dtw}}M - \boldsymbol{H_t^{dtw}}\|_F^2$, where $\boldsymbol{H_s^{dtw}} = \boldsymbol{D_s}\boldsymbol{H_s}$ and $\boldsymbol{H_t^{dtw}} = \boldsymbol{D_t}\boldsymbol{H_t}$, to optimize for M
4. Iterate 2-3 until convergence

Both step 2 and 3 monotonically decrease/non-increase C_{mdtw}. Since C_{mdtw} has a lower bound of 0 this optimization will converge. DTW can be solved in $O(l^2)$ and minimizing C_m using Hungarian algorithm takes $O(K^3)$. Hence the complexity of this algorithm is $O(l^2) + O(K^3)$ and since l and K are typically small this is efficient to compute (l is typically between 60-150 depending on how long the action is. K depends on the number of peaks of the flow distribution, typically between 4-6). Empirically we observe that this optimization converges after 2-3 iterations.

To optimize for M, the task is to find the set of edges $e_{ij} \in E$ that defines a perfect matching in G such that the sum of the edges in the matching is maximum. We solve this using the Hungarian algorithm to compute a set of λ for the following problem:

$$\max_{\lambda} \sum_{(i,j)\in E} \lambda_{ij} e_{ij}$$
$$\text{s.t.} \sum_{j\in N(i)} \lambda_{ij} = 1 \; \forall i \in source \tag{3}$$
$$\sum_{i\in N(j)} \lambda_{ij} = 1 \; \forall j \in target$$
$$\lambda_{ij} \in \{0,1\}$$

where e_{ij} is the correlation between the i-th column of H_s and j-th column of H_t, and $N(i)$ is the set of vertices that are adjacent to vertex i.

After obtaining the λ for maximum matching, we define the similarity score between two videos as the maximum weighted bipartite matching score of graph G:

$$score = \sum_{(i,j)\in E} \lambda_{ij} e_{ij} \tag{4}$$

Figure 5 illustrates an example of the matching result. Note that while the two actions are captured from widely different viewpoints, our matching algorithm is able to establish the correspondence between flow clusters by exploiting the temporal property of MPH. For instance, the matched MPH pair 1 (Fig. 5(c)) corresponds to flow words that belong to the hand while it is moving up at the beginning of the action (Fig. 5(a)-5(b)) and the matched pair 3 (Fig. 5(f)) corresponds to flow words of the hand while it is moving down at the end of the action (Fig. 5(d)-5(e)). This intuitive interpretation of the matching result is possible since our flow words map to well-defined spatial regions in the video. We believe this interpretability is a highly desirable property for real-world applications.

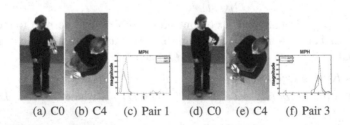

(a) C0   (b) C4   (c) Pair 1   (d) C0   (e) C4   (f) Pair 3

Fig. 5. Matching of cam 0 and cam 4 for checkwatch. Note how the matched MPH pair correspond to the same body part movements ((a)-(b): Hand moving up, (d)-(e): Hand moving down).

5   Experimental Results

To evaluate the performance of our method we performed experiments on the IXMAS dataset [27], UCF50 dataset [21] and a new real-world Stereotypy dataset that consists of a collection of videos ranging from 10 to 20 minutes each (with total length of 2 hours). We consider three tasks. First, to show robustness of our representation to variations in viewpoint, we perform cross-view action recognition experiments on the IXMAS dataset. Second, to show how our feature complements BOF representation, we perform action recognition on the UCF50 dataset. Finally, we demonstrate the power of our approach on a real-world problem by doing action retrieval on the Stereotypy dataset.

For the action retrieval task, we compare retrieval results against several BOF representations: cuboid [5], self-similarity matrix (SSM) [10], shapeflow [25], dense trajectories [26], and cuboid+shapeflow (used in [17,16,30]). Note that BOF representation has been previously used for action retrieval (eg. [3]).

To compute MPH we used GPU-based dense optical flow [28]. To select the K for MPH we examined the number of peaks in the distribution of flow directions in sample videos. We chose $K = 5$ (5 MPH per video) for all experiments. The details for competing methods are in the supplemental material.

5.1 Results on IXMAS Dataset

The IXMAS dataset contains videos of 11 types of actions captured from 5 viewpoints. There are 30 examples per action performed by several actors. We perform the standard cross-view classification task on the IXMAS dataset and compare it against methods described in [10,16,15,30]. It is important to note that in this particular experiment we are not assuming any view-correspondence in the training data. For this experiment we use 1NN classifier and a 6-fold cross validation procedure (identical cross-validation procedure as in [16,15,30]).

Table 1. Classification results by using a single view for training on IXMAS. Each row is a training view, and column a test view.

	c0	c1	c2	c3	c4	Avg.
	Ours, [16], [15], [10]	Ours, [16], [15], [10]	Ours, [16], [15], [10]	Ours, [16], [15], [10]	Ours, [16], [15], [10]	Ours, [16], [15], [10]
c0		80.3, 63.6, **83.7**, 75.2	63.6, 60.6, 59.2, **69.7**	68.5, 61.2, 57.4, **71.8**	**56.4**, 52.6, 33.6, 49.4	**67.2**, 59.5, 58.5, 66.5
c1	80.0, 61.0, **84.3**, 78.5		62.1, 62.1, 61.6, **67.9**	59.7, 65.1, 62.8, **71.5**	47.9, **54.2**, 27.0, 48.0	62.4, 60.6, 58.9, **66.5**
c2	63.6, 63.2, 62.5, **70.0**	62.1, 62.4, 65.2, **73.0**		79.7, 71.7, 72.0, 68.5	75.5, 58.2, 60.1, 55.2	**70.2**, 63.9, 64.9, 66.7
c3	67.0, 64.2, 57.1, **73.6**	65.8, 71.0, 61.5, **72.4**	**83.6**, 64.3, 71.0, 67.3		46.4, **56.6**, 31.2, 45.9	**65.7**, 64.0, 55.2, 64.8
c4	**54.5**, 50.0, 39.6, 44.5	49.4, **59.7**, 32.8, 41.5	**72.1**, 60.7, 68.1, 55.2	50.0, **61.1**, 37.4, 37.9		56.5, **57.9**, 44.5, 44.8
Avg.	66.3, 59.6, 60.9, **66.7**	64.4, 64.2, 60.8, **65.5**	**70.4**, 61.9, 65.0, 65.0	64.5, **64.8**, 57.4, 62.4	**56.5**, 55.4, 38.0, 49.6	**64.4**, 61.2, 56.4, 61.9

We focus on two recognition tasks: 1) classifying videos captured from the *test* view using training data captured from the *train* view, and 2) classifying videos captured from the *test* view using training data from all of the other views. We compare against results in [16,15,30] using the non-correspondence mode, since in many applications the need to have multi-view correspondence in training data can be burdensome.

The results for the first recognition task (classifying videos from the test view using training from the train view) can be seen in Table 5.1. For this task, our method improves the average recognition accuracy by 2.5% compared to the next best approach (see the highlighted cell in Table 5.1). Hankelet ([15]) is only robust to affine transformation and thus achieves low accuracy when classifying videos trained from very different viewpoints (eg. c0 vs c4).

The results for classifying videos from the test view by using training from all of the other views can be seen in Table 2. Note that even though the result of [10] is achieved by including videos from all the views (including the test view) for training, our approach still yields the best result. *Our method can use the additional training views more effectively due to its ability to generalize across viewpoints.*

Table 2. Cross-view recognition accuracy on IXMAS (trained on videos captured from all views except the *test* view). Note how our representation gives a significantly more accurate result.

Method	Test View					
	c0	c1	c2	c3	c4	Avg.
Ours	**83.9**	**81.8**	**87.6**	**83.0**	**73.6**	**82.0**
[30] (test view used for transfer learning)	66.4	73.5	71.0	75.4	66.4	70.5
[16] (test view used for transfer learning)	62.0	65.5	64.5	69.5	57.9	63.9
[10] (trained on all cameras)	77.0	78.8	80.0	73.9	63.6	74.6

5.2   Results on UCF50 Dataset

The UCF50 dataset contains 6618 videos of 50 types of actions. For this experiment we use the leave-one-group-out (LoGo) cross validation as suggested in [21].

Many videos in UCF50 were captured using low-res handheld cameras with various motion artifacts due to camera shake and rolling shutter. Clearly, the fine-grained motion features that our method exploits are difficult to extract in this case. However we still believe that it is valuable to characterize the limitations of our approach by analyzing the UCF50. Another important characteristic of this dataset is that the scene context gives a significant amount of information about the type of action in the video. For example, many of the actions are performed using a specific set of instruments (eg. barbell in bench press) and representing those cues can help immensely for classification. This suggests the need to combine our representation (which only models the dynamics of an action) with a complementary appearance-based representation.

We combine our representation with Fisher Vector (FV) encoding [19] (which can be seen as an extension to BOF) of the dense trajectory descriptor described in [26]. To convert our pairwise action similarity measure to a feature vector we use a method similar to ActionBank [22]. In ActionBank, the videos in the training set function as the bases of a high-dimensional action-space. For example, if we have N videos in the training set, the feature vector for video v is a vector of length N where the value of $N(i)$ is our similarity measure between video v and the i-th video in the training set. The full feature vector for each video is then simply a concatenation of the FV representation of dense trajectory and our ActionBank-like representation. For this experiment we use 1-vs-all linear SVM (with $C = 0.1$) for training and classification.

Classification results on this dataset can be seen in Table 3. The accuracy improvement obtained by adding our representation suggests that MPH encodes information that is complementary to HOG, HOF and MBH.

Comparing results of MPH + FV of dense trajectory against only FV of dense trajectory, the most significant improvement in accuracy comes from the class PizzaTossing (an improvement of 10.5% from 65.8% to 76.3%). A large part of this improvement comes from a better discrimination between PizzaTossing and Nunchucks classes. Many of the videos of these these two classes share a significant similarity in appearance: a person performing an action in a small room captured from close to frontal view. Thus, MPH (which models the dynamics of the action) increases discrimination between these two classes. Another notable improvement comes from the class RockClimbing (an improvement of 6.9% from 85.4% to 92.3%). About half of the improvement for this class comes from a better discrimination against RopeClimbing. While the actual movement of climbing a rope vs climbing a wall with a rope is different, the context of these two classes are very similar since wall and rope tend to be the prominent features in the video. Thus, MPH provides a powerful cue to help discriminate between these two classes. On the other hand, MPH can also increase confusion between classes. We observe the biggest drop in accuracy in the class HorseRace (a decrease of 3.1% from 98.4% to 95.3%) partly due to increased confusion with Biking. This is likely due to the fact that from a distance, the movement dynamics of HorseRace and Biking look similar: people moving on a trajectory with their body moving slightly up-and-down with a particular frequency. Human action is a complex concept defined by the interplay of a number of elements: movements, human pose, instruments used, and surrounding background context. A better approach to modelling any of these elements is a step towards a better action representation.

Table 3. Classification results on UCF50

Method	Accuracy (LoGo)
Ours (MPH) + FV of [26]	90.5
Dense trajectories [26] w/ FV encoding	88.9
MBH + scene context[21]	76.9
GIST3D + STIP [24]	73.7
MIP [13]	72.7

5.3 Results on Stereotypy Dataset

We also address the problem of *action retrieval*: Given a single example video clip containing an action of interest, the task is to retrieve all matching instances of that action from an unstructured video collection. The strength of our bottom-up matching approach is that it can compute a similarity measure between activities without learning. It can therefore be used in situations where the space of possible activities is very large and difficult to define a priori and when it is difficult to find an extensive amount of training examples across different views.

In the domain of behavioral psychology, there is currently great interest in studying the effectiveness of behavioral therapy for children with autism [2]. These children frequently exhibit repetitive motor movements, known as *stereotypies*. In comparison to more traditional functional activities, stereotypies are often unique expressions of

Fig. 6. The Stereotypy dataset. Region of interest is indicated by the bounding box.

individual behavior and highly person-dependent, making it challenging to construct a general model of such behaviors [1]. At the same time, it would be very useful to be able to retrieve all instances of a particular stereotypy exhibited by a child across multiple therapy sessions given only a single example. We conducted an experiment to evaluate the effectiveness of our algorithm in this context.

We collaborated with experimental and educational psychologists on analyzing videos obtatined of children with autism who engage in stereotypies in a classroom setting. The dataset consists of videos captured from various viewing locations. Representative frames are shown in Figure 6 (note the variations in viewpoints and appearance of the videos). We are interested in three types of stereotypies exhibited by the children: jumping up from chair (S1), jumping on the floor (S2), and paddling movement of the hands (S3). A psychologist with autism expertise and familiarity of the children provided ground truth labels for the stereotypies. The dataset contains 54 instances of S1 behavior, 12 instances of S2 behavior and 51 instances of S3 behavior. For each video in the dataset we manually identified a bounding box of the region of interest, which defines the input for the retrieval task.

We used sliding window to split the videos into a series of 60-frame clips where the window slides 15 frames at a time. We extracted 12410 clips from all of the videos in the dataset.

Action Retrieval Task: We identified all clips containing stereotypies, and used eac of those clips as the *target* input for retrieval. Given a *target* clip, we computed the similarity of the clip against the rest of the clips in the dataset. The similarity score for our algorithm is described in Section 4. For BOF, we found that $L2$ distance between the normalized feature vectors yielded the best results. We then ranked the videos according to the similarity score and measured performance by using precision-recall (PR) curve, a common metric for retrieval. We counted a clip as a hit if it overlapped with at least 50% of the groundtruth annotation.

The PR curves for retrieving stereotypies can be seen in Figure 7(a). Note that our method performed significantly better than various BOF representations. This is likely because a therapist sometimes came to interact with a child during the course of the video (Fig. 8(b)) and the child often moved, changing his relative angle to the camera. These variations will affect any appearance-based representation. The accuracy of dense trajectories drops significantly after around 50% recall. While dense trajectories representation is good at capturing the discriminative aspect of the behavior, it is very viewpoint dependent and thus can only retrieve instances of the behavior captured from the same viewpoint (the videos in the dataset are captured either from overhead view or side view). Note that shapeflow and SSM perform especially poorly in this setting due to the therapist sometimes appearing in the background. Shapeflow relies on successful extraction of silhouette of the foreground actor (we use [12] for computing silhouette), which is challenging in videos. SSM uses pairwise frame similarity, thus a slowly changing background (eg. due to the therapist moving) has a huge effect on the representation.

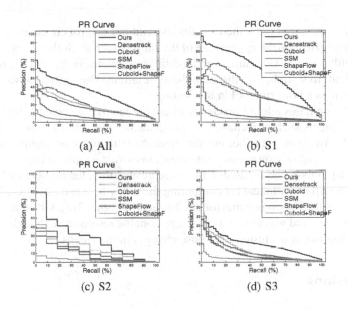

(a) All   (b) S1

(c) S2   (d) S3

Fig. 7. Precision-recall for curves for all behaviors

To better illustrate our retrieval results, we performed the retrieval task using a single example of S1 that can be seen in Figure 8(a). In this particular example, we were able to retrieve a clip containing another S1 behavior ranked 1 in the retrieval results. Note that since our representation is agnostic to camera viewpoint, the retrieved results can contain clips captured from viewpoints that are different from the input (Fig. 8(b)). Behavior S1 has very distinct dynamics and as a result our approach performed very well, often able to retrieve the top 3 results with 100% accuracy. The PR curves for the S1 behavior can be seen in Figure 7(b).

Another visual example of our retrieval results can be seen in Figure 8(c)-8(d). Note how our method is able to retrieve the same behavior under massive variations in appearance (different room, clothing, viewpoint, lighting condition and scaling). Indeed

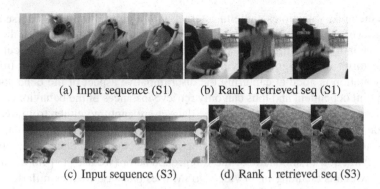

(a) Input sequence (S1)   (b) Rank 1 retrieved seq (S1)

(c) Input sequence (S3)   (d) Rank 1 retrieved seq (S3)

Fig. 8. Retrieval results for behavior S1 (a-b) and S3 (c-d)

in real-world videos, it is often the case that we can not control elements of the scene that have a large effect on the appearance of the subject such as clothing worn, subject's orientation with respect to the camera and lighting conditions. In the absence of training data it is difficult to learn how to discount these variations. Our motion-based matching approach provides a powerful tool in this setting.

Behavior S3 contains a lot of instances where the hands are occluded by the child's own torso or objects such as a chair. Due to occlusion, there will be some MPHs that are observable from one view, but not the other. Note that this occlusion problem affects all methods that rely on seeing movements to extract a representation (such as all of the interest-points-based methods). In our representation, the number of MPHs not occluded often will be sufficient for computing similarity between activities. The quantitative result for the paddling behavior can be seen in Figure 7(d). Given the difficulty of the task, our method was able to produce reasonable results even though there were a significant number of occlusions and pose changes in the videos.

6 Conclusions

We present a novel action representation that encodes the fine-grained dynamics of an action and is robust to variations in appearance. Our simultaneous matching and alignment formulation explicitly handles variations in the dynamics of an activity and allows matching of features extracted from different viewpoints. Our representation naturally complements existing BOF representations and performs well on traditional action recognition datasets as well as on a new real-world stereoypy dataset.

Acknowledgment. The authors would like to thank the Center for Discovery for assistance with collection and annotation of the Stereotypy dataset. This research was supported in part by NSF Awards 0960618 and 1029679 and NIH grant P50 DC013027.

References

1. Albinali, F., Goodwin, M.S., Intille, S.S.: Recognizing stereotypical motor movements in the laboratory and classroom: A case study with children on the aautism spectrum. In: UbiComp (2009)
2. American Psychiatric Association: Diagnostic and Statistical Manual of Mental Disorders DSM-IV-TR, 4th edn. Text Revision. American Psychiatric Pub. (2000)
3. Cao, L., Ji, R., Gao, Y., Liu, W., Tian, Q.: Mining spatiotemporal video patterns towards robust action retrieval. Neurocomputing (2012)
4. Chaudhry, R., Ravichandran, A., Hager, G., Vidal, R.: Histograms of oriented optical flow and binet-cauchy kernels on nonlinear dynamical systems for the recognition of human actions. In: CVPR (2009)
5. Dollar, P., Rabaud, V., Cottrell, G., Belongie, S.: Behavior Recognition via Sparse Spatio-Temporal Features. ICCV-VS PETS (2005)
6. Gorelick, L., Blank, M., Shechtman, E., Irani, M., Basri, R.: Actions as Space-Time Shapes. PAMI (2007)
7. Grundmann, M., Kwatra, V., Essa, I.: Auto-directed video stabilization with robust l1 optimal camera paths. In: CVPR (2011)
8. Jain, M., Jégou, H., Bouthemy, P., et al.: Better exploiting motion for better action recognition. In: CVPR (2013)
9. Johansson, G.: Visual Perception of Biological Motion and a Model for Its Analysis. Attention, Perception, & Psychophysics 14(2), 201–211 (1973)
10. Junejo, I., Dexter, E., Laptev, I., Pérez, P.: View-Independent Action Recognition from Temporal Self-Similarities. PAMI (2010)
11. Ke, Y., Sukthankar, R., Hebert, M.: Volumetric features for video event detection. IJCV (2010)
12. Kim, K., Chalidabhongse, T.H., Harwood, D., Davis, L.: Real-time foreground–background segmentation using codebook model. Real-time imaging 11(3), 172–185 (2005)
13. Kliper-Gross, O., Gurovich, Y., Hassner, T., Wolf, L.: Motion interchange patterns for action recognition in unconstrained videos. In: Fitzgibbon, A., Lazebnik, S., Perona, P., Sato, Y., Schmid, C. (eds.) ECCV 2012, Part VI. LNCS, vol. 7577, pp. 256–269. Springer, Heidelberg (2012)
14. Laptev, I., Marszalek, M., Schmid, C., Rozenfeld, B.: Learning Realistic Human Actions from Movies. In: CVPR (2008)
15. Li, B., Camps, O.I., Sznaier, M.: Cross-view activity recognition using hankelets. In: CVPR (2012)
16. Li, R., Zickler, T.: Discriminative Virtual Views for Cross-View Action Recognition. In: CVPR (2012)
17. Liu, J., Shah, M., Kuipers, B., Savarese, S.: Cross-View Action Recognition via View Knowledge Transfer. In: CVPR (2011)
18. Messing, R., Pal, C., Kautz, H.: Activity Recognition Using the Velocity Histories of Tracked Keypoints. In: ICCV (2009)
19. Perronnin, F., Sánchez, J., Mensink, T.: Improving the fisher kernel for large-scale image classification. In: Daniilidis, K., Maragos, P., Paragios, N. (eds.) ECCV 2010, Part IV. LNCS, vol. 6314, pp. 143–156. Springer, Heidelberg (2010)
20. Poppe, R.: A survey on vision-based human action recognition. Image and Vision Computing 28(6), 976–990 (2010)
21. Reddy, K.K., Shah, M.: Recognizing 50 human action categories of web videos. Machine Vision and Applications (2012)

22. Sadanand, S., Corso, J.J.: Action bank: A high-level representation of activity in video. In: CVPR (2012)
23. Shi, J., Tomasi, C.: Good features to track. In: CVPR (1994)
24. Solmaz, B., Assari, S.M., Shah, M.: Classifying web videos using a global video descriptor. Machine Vision and Applications (2012)
25. Tran, D., Sorokin, A.: Human Activity Recognition with Metric Learning. In: Forsyth, D., Torr, P., Zisserman, A. (eds.) ECCV 2008, Part I. LNCS, vol. 5302, pp. 548–561. Springer, Heidelberg (2008)
26. Wang, H., Kläser, A., Schmid, C., Liu, C.L.: Dense trajectories and motion boundary descriptors for action recognition. In: IJCV (2013)
27. Weinland, D., Boyer, E., Ronfard, R.: Action Recognition from Arbitrary Views using 3D Exemplars. IJCV (2007)
28. Werlberger, M., Trobin, W., Pock, T., Wedel, A., Cremers, D., Bischof, H.: Anisotropic Huber-L1 optical flow. BMVC (2009)
29. Yuan, C., Li, X., Hu, W., Ling, H., Maybank, S.: 3d r transform on spatio-temporal interest points for action recognition. In: CVPR (2013)
30. Zhang, Z., Wang, C., Xiao, B., Zhou, W., Liu, S., Shi, C.: Cross-view action recognition via a continuous virtual path. In: CVPR (2013)
31. Zhou, F., de la Torre, F.: Canonical Time Warping for Alignment of Human Behavior. NIPS (2009)

Pose Filter Based Hidden-CRF Models for Activity Detection

Prithviraj Banerjee and Ram Nevatia

University of Southern California, Los Angeles, USA

Abstract. Detecting activities which involve a sequence of complex pose and motion changes in unsegmented videos is a challenging task, and common approaches use sequential graphical models to infer the human pose-state in every frame. We propose an alternative model based on detecting the key-poses in a video, where only the temporal positions of a few key-poses are inferred. We also introduce a novel pose summarization algorithm to automatically discover the key-poses of an activity. We learn a detection filter for each key-pose, which along with a bag-of-words root filter are combined in an HCRF model, whose parameters are learned using the latent-SVM optimization. We evaluate the performance of our model for detection on unsegmented videos on four human action datasets, which include challenging crowded scenes with dynamic backgrounds, inter-person occlusions, multi-human interactions and hard-to-detect daily use objects.

Keywords: Activity detection, Key-poses, CRFs, Latent-SVM.

1 Introduction

There has been considerable research in classifying segmented videos, however there has been comparatively less progress on the more challenging task of activity detection, where multiple instances of an activity are simultaneously localized and classified in un-segmented videos. Detection is an important task, as in real world applications like surveillance, the activities of interest occur only for a part of the video. We propose a novel activity detection algorithm based on automatically discovering the key-poses in the activity, and learning a key-pose filter based Hidden Conditional Random Field (HCRF) model. We focus on activities primarily defined by a sequence of complex pose and motion changes, which can involve interactions with objects or other humans in the scene.

Activity recognition algorithms can be broadly categorized based on their structure modeling capabilities. A common class of approaches [9,26] train classifiers on video-wide statistics of local features, and ignore the local temporal dynamics of the activity. To classify unsegmented videos, they typically use an inefficient sliding window approach [30], which can be sensitive to window size. A complementary approach [11,12] learns a sequential motion model, and performs classification based on state assignments inferred from every frame in the video; to keep the inference tractable, these further require a Markovian assumption

D. Fleet et al. (Eds.): ECCV 2014, Part II, LNCS 8690, pp. 711–726, 2014.

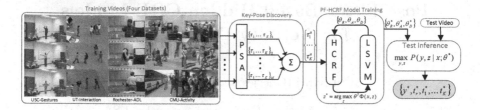

Fig. 1. Flow diagram of our proposed algorithm

between adjacent frames, and fail to capture long range dynamics in the activity, making them sensitive to variations in activity styles and action-durations.

We argue that for activity *detection*, it is sufficient to determine the *presence or absence* of certain key states in an observation sequence, and whether certain temporal relationships between the state detections are satisfied. Recognizing actions using a subset of the frames has been explored previously [3,15,20,21], however these do not address the problem of automatically discovering the important states/sub-sequences of an activity, and either perform exhaustive search over all possible sub-sequences [20], rely on hand annotations [3,21], or use a manually defined list of relevant poses [15], requiring separate annotated pose data for each pose-detector. There exist methods for automatic discovery of key-states [11,31], however [11] relies on hard to obtain mocap data, and [31] ignores temporal structure.

We propose a novel graphical model for activity detection, where the random variables to be inferred are the temporal locations of the key-poses. Key-poses represent the important human pose configurations in an activity, and are a natural choice for defining a key-state in our model. Our algorithm automatically discovers the relevant key-pose definitions in an activity, and learns a set of key-pose detection filters, and pools their detection responses, while satisfying the temporal relationships between them.

Our contributions are multi-fold: (1) The relevant key-poses are discovered automatically, (2) the key-pose detection filters are learned jointly in a discriminative HCRF framework, and do not require manually annotated pose-specific training data, (3) the temporal locations of the key-pose detections correspond to the active segments in the video stream, enabling activity detection in unsegmented videos, and (4) the key-poses correspond to a natural semantic interpretation. We show results on 4 datasets, which include challenging crowded scenes with dynamic backgrounds and inter-person occlusions, multi-person interactions, and actions involving hard-to-detect daily use objects.

2 Related Work

We briefly survey classification methods using subsequence based models, and methods for activity detection.

[**Subsequence Models**] The discriminative advantage of short snippets of video for activity classification has been recognized before [21]. There exist approaches that identify the single most important subsegment of a video [21], while others represent the video as a sequence of manually annotated atomic actions [3], or a set of discriminative spatio-temporal patches [5], while ignoring their temporal ordering and distribution. [14,24] extended the deformable part object detector [2] to the temporal domain for activity classification, and decompose the video into discriminative sub volumes based on their correlations to a global feature distribution. The sub-volumes need not correspond to any semantic interpretation, and classify pre-segmented videos only. [15,25] propose a closely related model for learning discriminative key-pose sequences, with focus on interactions between a pair of humans. These models ensure only ordering constraints, but ignore the uncertainty in temporal placement of the poses and do not detect multiple instances of the activity in a video. [15] also manually defines a list of relevant poselets, where each poselet detector requires separate annotated training data, placing a practical limit on the range of poses it can model.

[**Activity Detection**] Structure models like in [11,13] perform automatic video segmentation by learning densely linked finite state machines, which combine all the activities in a single model. They do not scale well with the number of activities (inference is quadratic in the number of states), and require extensive manual annotations. Spatio-temporal volumetric feature based algorithms [6,29] rely on global statistics to detect action events, with no semantic reasoning of the underlying activity. [6] further requires enumeration of all possible sub volumes, and resorts to sub-sampling for tractable learning. There exist techniques [17,22] based on maximizing the volumetric correlation of 3D templates to localize single primitive actions, however it is unclear how multiple templates for complex activities can be combined.

3   Model Overview

We define a human activity as a sequence of key-poses. Pose inference is a difficult problem in itself; instead, we compute features that are related to pose but do not make the pose information, such as joint positions, explicit. We introduce a novel Pose Summarization Algorithm (PSA) to discover the key-poses in an activity during training, along with their expected temporal positions. Key-pose detection filters are discriminatively learned from the observed HoG-HoF features at the discovered key-pose locations. We also define a probabilistic temporal position distribution for each key-pose, to model its detection uncertainty.

The pose features in a video are quantized to a vocabulary of pose-codewords. The global distribution of the poses present in the sequence is learned using a *root filter*, which is a function of the histogram of pose-codewords. The multiple key-pose filters, root filters and their corresponding temporal relationships are jointly modeled in a probabilistic framework, resulting in an HCRF model. The parameters of this model are learned in a discriminative max margin framework using a latent support vector machine. Figure 1 shows the flow diagram of our proposed algorithm. Final classification and detection is performed by inferring the class labels, and temporal positions from the HCRF model.

While there exist methods [6,17,22,29] which perform detection in both space and time dimensions, we argue that spatial detection of the human is better solved by dedicated pedestrian trackers. We use trajectory results $x = \{x_t\}$ from a standard tracking algorithm [4] as input to our activity detection framework, where x_t is the human detection box in the tth frame. HoG/HoF [2] features $f(x_t) \in \mathcal{R}^D$ are computed from the detection box x_t centered around the human, and hence the features capture the human pose configuration at time t.

4   Key-Pose Discovery

Automatic decomposition of an activity in a video segment into its constituent key-poses is defined as the Key Pose Discovery problem. This is a prerequisite for learning a key-pose detector, as we need to first discover what are the important key-poses in an activity, and determine their expected temporal position in an activity sequence, before learning how to detect them. Algorithms for automatic key pose discovery rely on variants of change detection in the pose dynamics [11], however they require accurate human limb estimates from motion capture data, which are difficult to obtain. Another approach is to perform hierarchical clustering of the pose features [31], followed by vector quantization to learn a vocabulary of pose based codewords. However these codewords do not take into account the temporal structure present in the pose sequence of an activity.

Inspired by existing techniques for video summarization [10], we solve the key pose discovery problem using *pose sequence summarization*. Given N poses in an activity sequence, our task is to select the $K < N$ subset of poses, which best summarize the complete pose sequence w.r.t. a cost function defined on the pose space.

4.1   Pose Summarization Algorithm (PSA)

Let $f(x_t) \in \mathcal{R}^D$ define a D dimensional feature vector describing the human pose present in the window x_t. Let $\tau_1 \cdots \tau_K$ define the temporal location of the K key poses in an activity segment. By definition, each key pose $f(x_{\tau_k})$ best summarizes the poses present in the pose sequence $\{f(x_{b_k}) \cdots f(x_{b_{k+1}})\}$ present between frames b_k and b_{k+1}. Hence, for a given temporal range $[b_k, b_{k+1})$, the optimal key-pose location τ_k is computed as $\tau_k = \arg\min_{\hat{\tau}} C(\hat{\tau}, b_k, b_{k+1})$, where function $C(\hat{\tau}, b_k, b_{k+1}) = \sum_{t=b_k}^{b_{k+1}-1} \|f(x_t) - f(x_{\hat{\tau}})\|_2^2$ is the Pose Summarization Error. The total cost incurred in summarizing the entire pose sequence using just K key-poses is given by the error function $E(K, \{\tau_k\}, \{b_k\}) = \sum_{k=1}^{K} C(\tau_k, b_k, b_{k+1})$.

The optimal assignments of key-poses $\{\tau_k\}$, and their respective temporal boundaries $\{b_k\}$ are determined by minimizing $E(\cdot)$. A dynamic programming algorithm for video summarization was proposed in [10], which is easily adapted for our purpose. The key insight is that given the temporal boundaries $\{b_k\}$, the corresponding key-pose locations $\{\tau_k\}$ can be determined in $O(T^2)$ time for a video segment of length T. This suggests an algorithm which recursively determines the optimal temporal boundary locations. The dynamic program has

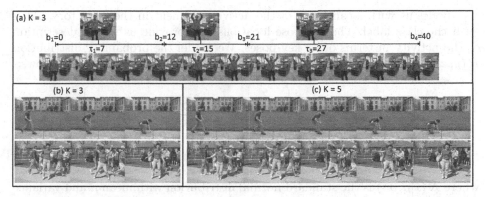

Fig. 2. (a) PSA discovers the key-poses for K=3 in a video segment. (b-d) Sample results for K={3, 5}. (Detection boxes x_t are omitted for clarity).

a computational complexity of $O\left(KT^3\right)$, and hence is efficient for reasonably sized video segments with $T < 200$ frames.

We present results of the key-pose discovery on a sample video in Fig. 2, and observe that the discovered key-poses match closely to an intuitive definition of key-poses by humans. Note that with increasing K, adjacent key poses are more similar in appearance, and harder to distinguish from each other. The optimum value of K varies depending on the activity. The expected temporal location of the kth key-pose in an activity segment is given by the temporal *anchor position* $\tau_k^a = N^{-1}\sum_n^N \tau_k^{(n)}$ computed over N videos. This is analogous to the anchor position of parts in object detection frameworks [2].

5   Pose Filter based HCRF Model (PF-HCRF)

We define temporal distributions to model the location of the key-poses relative to their anchor positions, and define an HCRF model to learn a set of discriminative key-pose detection filters by searching in the neighborhood of their corresponding anchor positions. Running inference on the HCRF model solves the detection and classification tasks simultaneously. HCRFs have been used before for part-based object and action classification [27]. We define the individual key-pose filters as the 'parts' in our HCRF model, resulting in a Pose Filter Hidden Conditional Random Field (PF-HCRF) model. Let y be a binary class variable signifying the presence/absence of an activity class. Our objective is to learn a distribution $P(y|\boldsymbol{x})$ to infer the class label y, given the trajectory $\boldsymbol{x}$:

$$y^* = \arg\max_{y\in\{+,-\}} P\left(y|\boldsymbol{x}\right) \propto \arg\max_{y,\boldsymbol{z}} P\left(y|\boldsymbol{z},\boldsymbol{x}\right) P\left(\boldsymbol{z}|\boldsymbol{x}\right) \qquad (1)$$

where $\boldsymbol{z} = \{t_r, t_1, t_2 \cdots t_K\}$ are the latent variables in our model. t_r determines the starting position of the action segment in the trajectory, while the variables $\{t_k\}$ determine the temporal location of the key poses constituting the activity. Figure 3(a) shows the factor graph representation of the PF-HCRF. Solving eqn.

1 provides us with localization of the activity segment in the trajectory, along with the class label. The key-pose locations also provide us with a description of the activity in terms of its key-poses. We model the probability distribution $P(y, z|x)$ using root $\theta_R^T \Phi_R$ and key-pose appearance $\theta_A^T \Phi_A$ filters, as follows:

$$P(y_{+1}|z, x) \propto exp\left\{\theta_R^T \Phi_R(x, t_r) + \sum_{k \in \mathcal{K}} \theta_{A_k}^T \Phi_A(x, t_k)\right\}$$

$$P(z|x) \propto P(t_r|x) \prod_{k \in \mathcal{K}} P(t_k|x) \propto \mathcal{C} \prod_{k \in \mathcal{K}} \mathcal{N}\left(t_k|\tau_k^a + \delta_k, \sigma_k^2\right)$$

where $\mathcal{N}(x|\mu, \sigma^2)$ is the standard normal distribution with mean μ and variance σ^2. The filters $\{\theta_R, \theta_A\}$ are a single dimensional template specifying the weights of the features $\{\Phi_R, \Phi_A\}$ appearing in a segment of the trajectory. Their dot product is the filter score when applied to the segment.

5.1   Root Filter

The root filter $\theta_R^T \Phi_R$ captures the global distribution of poses present in a given activity segment. First, a vocabulary of codewords $\mathcal{W}$ is learned over the pose features $f(x_i)$ extracted from all the videos in the training set. Then, each trajectory window x_i is assigned to the closest pose-codeword $w \in \mathcal{W}$, the mapping being defined by a function $g(x_t) : \mathcal{R}^D \to \mathcal{W}$. An activity segment is said to start from time t_r and has a length of L frames. The root filter computes the histogram of pose-code words (Fig. 3 c,d) present in the temporal window $[t_r, t_r + L]$, and is defined as:

$$\theta_R^T \Phi_R(x, t_r) = \sum_{w \in \mathcal{W}} \eta_w \sum_{t=t_r}^{t_r+L} \mathbf{1}_{g(x_t)=w} \tag{2}$$

where $\mathbf{1}_{g(x_t)=w}$ returns 1 if $g(x_t)=w$ is true, otherwise returns 0. Parameter L is the temporal bandwidth of the root filter, and is set to the average length of an activity segment determined from training examples.

5.2   Key-Pose Appearance Filter

Filter $\theta_{A_k}^T \Phi_A$ models the appearance of the kth key-pose. Accurate key-pose detection requires the HoG-HoF descriptors to be computed from detections centered at the human figure. Misaligned detections (Fig. 4(c)) capture only the partial human image, and produce noisy HoG-HoF features, which in turn leads to inaccurate key-pose detections. We incorporate a scale-alignment search around the trajectory detection box $x_{t_k} = [c, w, h]$, where c is the center of the detection box and (w, h) are its width and height:

$$\theta_{A_k}^T \Phi_A(x, t_k) = \max_{s \in \mathcal{S}, p \in \mathcal{P}} \gamma_k^T f\left(x_{t_k} = [c + p, sw, sh]\right) \tag{3}$$

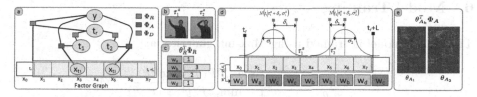

Fig. 3. Panel (a) shows the factor graph representation of the PF-HCRF model for $K = 2$ key-poses. Panel (b) shows the two key-poses identified by the pose summarization algorithm, with their corresponding anchor times: τ_1^a, τ_2^a. Panel (d) shows the feature descriptors x_t, and their corresponding codewords assignments $w_t \in W$ below. The root filter $\boldsymbol{\theta}_R^T \boldsymbol{\Phi}_R$ is shown in cyan, being applied between frames t_r and $t_r + L$ where it models the pose-codeword frequencies, as shown in panel (c). Sample results of key-pose filters $\boldsymbol{\theta}_{A_k}^T \boldsymbol{\Phi}_A$ learned by the LSVM are shown in panel (e). Their temporal location is modeled with a normal distribution about their corresponding anchor location τ_k^a, shown in panel (d).

where S is the scale pyramid and P is the alignment search grid. We learn a conditional model, and hence the weight vector $\boldsymbol{\gamma}_k$ corresponds to the discriminative ability of the appearance of the kth key-pose to classify the overall activity segment. Figure 3(e) show examples of appearance models learned for detecting key-poses. The weight magnitudes show a clear visual correlation with the discriminative key-pose present in the video.

5.3 Temporal Location Distribution

The latent variables $\boldsymbol{z} = \{t_r, t_1, t_2 \cdots t_K\}$ define the temporal location of the activity segment, and its constituent key-pose locations. As we do not have prior knowledge of the global temporal location of the activity segment, we set its distribution to a constant : $P(t_r|\boldsymbol{x}) \propto C$.

The temporal distribution of the key-poses $P(t_k|\boldsymbol{x})$ is modeled using a standard normal distribution $\mathcal{N}(\cdot)$ with mean $\tau_k^a + \delta_k$ and variance σ_k^2:

$$\log P(t_k|\boldsymbol{x}) \propto \boldsymbol{\theta}_{D_k}^T \boldsymbol{\Phi}_D (t_k, t_r) \propto \log \mathcal{N} \left(t_k | \tau_k^a + \delta_k, \sigma_k^2 \right) \qquad (4)$$

where parameter τ_k^a is the temporal anchor position (section 4.1) of the kth key-pose, and remains unchanged during model training. The optimal key-pose locations τ_k in each video (determined by the pose summarization algorithm) need not be centered within their corresponding temporal boundaries $[b_k, b_{k+1})$ (see Fig. 2). Parameter δ_k accounts for this offset, and measures the linear shift in the key-pose location from its anchor position τ_k^a, while parameter σ_k^2 measures the uncertainty in the temporal location. Figure 3(d) shows the parameterization of the normal distribution. Both δ_k and σ_k are learned during model training, however it is more convenient to learn the equivalent log-probability parameters $a_k = 1/\sigma_k^2$ and $c_k = 2\delta_k a_k$.

6   Model Training

The HCRF model is trained using Max-margin criteria:

$$\theta^* = \arg\max_{\theta} \Lambda : \forall_i \frac{\max_{z^i} P(y^i, z^i | x^i; \theta)}{1 - \min_{z^i} P(y^i, z^i | x^i; \theta)} > \Lambda \tag{5}$$

where Λ is the margin between the positive and negative examples. It has been argued [27] that the max-margin criteria is better suited for the classification task compared to the traditional Max Likelihood criteria. Solving equation 5 is equivalent to optimizing a Latent Support Vector Machine [28] in the log-probability domain. Transforming the probability distributions to the log domain results in the following energy function:

$$E(x, z) = \log P(y = +1, z | x) = \theta^T \Phi(x, z) \tag{6}$$
$$= \theta_R^T \Phi_R(x, t_r) + \sum_{k \in \mathcal{K}} \left\{ \theta_{D_k}^T \Phi_D(t_k, t_r) + \theta_{A_k}^T \Phi_A(x, t_k) \right\}$$

6.1   Latent Support Vector Machine

A Latent Support Vector Machine (LSVM) incorporates latent variable inference in the SVM optimization algorithm. Yu et al [28] proposed a Concave-Convex Procedure (CCCP) for efficiently solving the LSVM optimization:

$$\min_{\theta} \left[\frac{1}{2} \|\theta\|_2^2 + C \sum_{i=1}^{n} \max_{\hat{y}, \hat{z}} \left[\theta^T \Psi(x_i, \hat{y}, \hat{z}) + \Delta_L(y_i, \hat{y}, \hat{z}) \right] \right]$$
$$- \left[C \sum_{i=1}^{n} \max_{\tilde{z}} \theta^T \Psi(x_i, y_i, \tilde{z}) \right] \tag{7}$$

where Δ_L is the loss function, and Ψ is the class augmented feature function. The optimization is solved using CCCP, which minimizes $f(\theta) - g(\theta)$ where both f and g are convex. To map our activity model into the LSVM formulation while satisfying the convexity requirements of f and g, the feature function Ψ is defined as: $\Psi(x_i, y_i, \hat{z}) = \Phi(x, z)$ for positive examples, and equal to 0 for negative examples. The CCCP algorithm requires solving two sub-problems iteratively: (1) Latent Variable Completion , and (2) Loss-Augmented Inference. Latent variable completion is equivalent to MAP inference on the HCRF model, defined as:

$$\max_{\tilde{z}} \theta^T \Phi(x, \tilde{z}) = \theta_R^T \Phi_R + \sum_{\substack{k \in \mathcal{K} \\ t_r = 0}} \max_{t_k} \left\{ \theta_{D_k}^T \Phi_D + \theta_{A_k}^T \Phi_A \right\} \tag{8}$$

where t_r is set to zero as training videos are pre-segmented. Maximization over t_k can be solved in $O(N)$ time (N is length of a trajectory) using distance transform

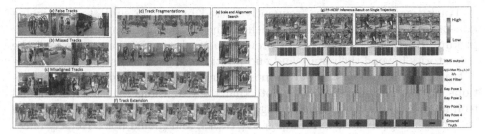

Fig. 4. (a-d) Noisy and erroneous tracks (e) Scale-Alignment search (f) Track extension (g) Heat maps represent the output scores of the key-pose filters, root filters and the inferred detection confidence $A(t)$, along with ground truth and predicted detection segments. Refer the text for more details. (Figure is best viewed in color and magnified)

algorithms [2]. The Loss Augmented Inference problem with zero-one loss for a binary decision problem is solved as follows:

$$\max_{\hat{y},\hat{z}} \left[\boldsymbol{\theta}^T \Psi\left(\boldsymbol{x}_i, \hat{y}, \hat{\boldsymbol{z}}\right) + \Delta(y_i, \hat{y}, \hat{\boldsymbol{z}}) \right] = \begin{cases} \max\left\{1, \max_{\hat{z}} \boldsymbol{\theta}^T \boldsymbol{\Phi}(\boldsymbol{x}, \hat{z})\right\} & \text{if } y_i = +1 \\ \max\left\{0, 1 + \max_{\hat{z}} \boldsymbol{\theta}^T \boldsymbol{\Phi}(\boldsymbol{x}, \hat{z})\right\} & \text{if } y_i = -1 \end{cases}$$

[Weight Initialization] LSVM optimization is non-convex, and careful initialization of the weights has been suggested in previous work [2,14]. We train standard SVMs separately on the root filter and the appearance filter features, and initialize $\boldsymbol{\theta}_R$ and $\boldsymbol{\theta}_A$ respectively to the learned weights. c_k is initialized using the mean displacement of the key-pose locations τ_k (obtained from Pose Summarization Algorithm) from the anchor position τ_k^a. Parameter a_k is initialized using the pose-boundary locations (b_k, b_{k+1}), as it represents the variance in the key pose location.

7   Model Inference for Multiple Detections

Detecting and tracking humans in cluttered and crowded environments is a challenging problem. We use a standard appearance based pedestrian tracker [4], trained independently of the datasets used here. Figure 4(a-d) shows some representative results highlighting the challenges. Common inaccuracies include false positive tracks, missed tracks, misaligned tracks, and track fragmentations. The PF-HCRF detector is less sensitive to false positive trajectories, and treats it as a valid human track where ideally no human activity will be detected. However, missed tracks are impossible to recover from; hence we prefer tracking algorithms with higher recall at the expense of precision. Misaligned tracks cause noisy key-pose detections, and hence we perform scale-alignment search (eqn. 3) around the detection box. Figure 4(e) shows the scale-alignment search about a candidate detection (blue ellipse), with the optimal box shown in red. In our experiments, we use a single octave scale pyramid $\mathcal{S}$ with 5 levels centered at the original scale, and a 3×3 alignment search grid $\mathcal{P}$ with 10 pixel step width.

Track fragmentations are frequently caused by human subjects undergoing non-pedestrian pose transitions, which commonly occur during actions such as pickup. To counter the effects of premature track termination, we extend the trajectories beyond their start and end positions. Figure 4(f) shows an example of track fragmentation, and our proposed track extension (shaded-dashed detections in blue and magenta). We note that the extensions may not correspond to human subjects in the video (magenta colored extensions in figure), in which case they are equivalent to false positive tracks, and should not adversely affect our performance.

Detection and classification on a test video is performed by inferring the optimal class labels and root filter location: $\{y^*, t_r^*\} = \max_{y,z} P(y, z|x; \theta^*)$. The optimal root filter location t_r^* is the detected position of the activity segment. For pre-segmented videos, t_r is fixed to zero, and only the optimal class label y^* is inferred. In an activity detection task, multiple instances of the same activity class can exist in a single video. The optimum t_r^* will return only a single detection result. To incorporate multiple detections, we infer the time series $A(t) = \max_{z/t_r} P(y = +1, t_r = t|x; \theta^*)$, representing the detection confidence at each time t. Following object detection algorithms, we apply a Non-Maxima Suppression (NMS) filter to $A(t)$, and declare the resulting maximas as our predicted activity detections.

Figure 4(g) shows an example of the multiple detection inference procedure for the two-handed wave action, where the outputs of the separate key-pose filters, root filters, and the inferred time series $A(t)$ are shown. The ground truth row shows the activity segments for two-handed wave action with positive labels (red), negative labels (green) for other actions and segments with no activity (cyan). The NMS output is given by pink bars, with the inferred key-pose locations marked in yellow, along with the key-pose frames shown above. The sequence of detected key-poses are consistent across segments and describe the activity. The video sequence contains action segments with partial occlusions, where some of the key-poses are not visible. We observe that the individual key-pose and root filter detection confidences are not sufficient for detecting the activity segments, whereas the combined inference result $A(t)$ provides a clear segmentation of the video, hence validating our algorithm. The NMS algorithm also detects a false positive due to the local maxima occurring in that segment; choosing an appropriate confidence-threshold for the detected maximas will remove the weakly scored false positives. We set the threshold to the confidence value corresponding to the maximum F1 score of each detector.

8   Results

We evaluate our algorithm on 4 datasets: UT-Interaction[18], USC-Gestures[13], CMU-Action[7] and Rochester-ADL[12]. The model is trained using a pose-codeword vocabulary size of 500, and by selecting an appropriate number of key-poses $K \in \{3, 4, 5\}$ based on action complexity. PF-HCRF model inference runs at 0.05 fps on a standard PC, and at 2 fps without scale-alignment search.

(a) UT-Interaction	50%-Video	Full-Video	(c) Rochester ADL		
PF-HCRF	83.33%	97.50%			
Raptis [15]	73.30%	93.30%	**Method**	**Accuracy**	**Features**
Ryoo [19]	70.00%	85.00%			
Cuboid+SVM [18]	31.70%	85.00%	PF-HCRF	88.67%	HoG+HoF
BP+SVM [19]	65.00%	83.30%	Wang [26]	85.00%	HoG+HoF
Vahdat [25]	-	93.30%			
Zhang [30]	-	95.00%	Wang [26]	96.00%	HoG+HoF+ContextFtrs
Kong [8]	-	88.30%	Messing [12]	67.00%	Key Point Tracks (KPT)
(b) USC-Gestures	Tr:Ts = 1:7	Tr:Ts = 3:5			
PF-HCRF (Classf.)	98.00%	99.67%	Messing [12]	89.00%	KPT+Color+FaceDets
Root-Filter	58.81%	85.57%			
Singh [23]	92.00%	-	Laptev [9]	59.00%	HoG+HoF
Natarajan [13]	79.00%	90.18%	Raptis [16]	82.67%	KPT+HoG+HoF
PF-HCRF (Det. MAP)	0.68	0.79			
Root-Filter (Det. MAP)	0.26	0.49	Satkin [20]	80.00%	HoF

Fig. 5. (a) UT-Interaction: Classification accuracy for observing the initial 50% of the video, and the full video. Result tables for (b) USC-Gestures and (c) Rochester-ADL.

8.1 UT-Interaction [18]

The UT-Interaction Set-1 dataset was released as a part of the contest on Semantic Description of Human Activities (SDHA) [18]. It contains 6 types of human-human interactions: hand-shake, hug, kick, point, punch and push. The dataset is challenging as many actions consist of similar human poses, like "outstretched-hand" occurs in point, punch, push and shake actions. There are 10 video sequences shot in a parking-lot, with 2-5 people performing the interactive actions in random order.

[**Classification**] SDHA contest [18] recommends using a 10-fold leave-one-out evaluation methodology. PF-HCRF achieves an average classification score of 97.50%, and outperforms all existing approaches (Figure 5a). We also evaluate our model on the streaming task (or activity prediction task), where only the initial θ fraction of the video is observable. This measures the algorithm's performance at classifying videos of incomplete activity executions. Figure 6a plots the classification accuracy for different values of observation ratio θ. The PF-HCRF model out-performs other methods, which can be attributed to its learning a small set of discriminative key-poses, where detecting even the first few key-poses helps in classifying the action. Moreover, the model returns the most likely position of key-poses in the unobserved section of the video, and hence is capable of "gap-filling". [15] also uses a key-frame based algorithm, however it is unable to perform gap-filling, as they only learn the temporal order of the key-frames, whereas PF-HCRF employs a probabilistic model for the key-pose locations, which is learned in a discriminative manner.

[**Detection**] SDHA contest [18] recommends evaluating the detection performance on the 10 videos using precision-recall curves for the 6 actions, and we present the same in Figure 6b. None of the contest participants report detection PR curves [18], making us the first ones to do so. [15] report detection results while assuming that each video contains one and only one instance of each action

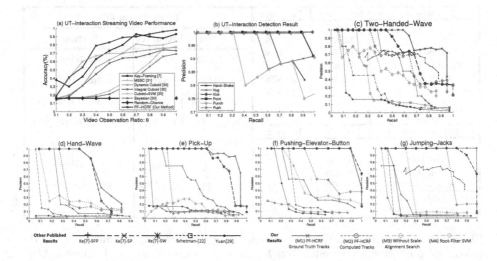

Fig. 6. UT-Interaction:(a) Streaming video performance and (b) Precision-Recall curves for activity detection. (c-g) Precision-Recall curves on CMU-Action.

type, and report an accuracy rate of 86.70% averaged over all actions, where the predicted action has a 50% temporal overlap with the groundtruth. Using the same metric, PF-HCRF model achieves an average detection accuracy of 90.00%.

8.2 USC-Gestures [13]

The dataset consists of 8 video sequences of 8 different actors, each performing 5-6 instances of 12 actions, resulting in 493 action segments. The actions correspond to hand gestures like attention, left-turn, right-turn, flap, close-distance, mount etc. The dataset has a relatively clean background with stationary humans, however it is still challenging due to relatively small pose differences between actions, causing pose-ordering to become a key discriminative factor in recognizing actions.

[**Classification**] Following [13,23], we evaluate the classification performance using two different train-test ratios: 1:8, and 3:5, averaged over all folds. The PF-HCRF algorithm outperforms previous results (Figure 5b) in all split ratios. Furthermore, [13,23] require manual construction of activity models using 2.5D joint locations for manually identified key-poses; the models also contain pre-defined motion styles and durations. PF-HCRF avoids cumbersome manual annotation of motion styles, while also automatically identifying the key-poses.

[**Detection**] The dataset has 8 videos (~12000 frames per video) containing continuous executions of 493 action segments. The action segments consist only ~10% of total video frames, and are interspersed with gesture actions other than the 12 gestures used for classification, making it a challenging dataset for activity detection. For baseline comparison, we implemented a Root-filter classifier (Sec.5.1), where a standard SVM is trained using the histogram of pose-codewords. Figure 5b shows the Mean Average Precision score averaged over 12 actions for the detection task. The root-filter does not capture temporal dynamics, and fails to differentiate between gestures with similar key-poses, but different temporal ordering, which explains their lower performance compared to PF-HCRF.

8.3 CMU-Action [7]

This dataset contain events representing real world activities such as picking up object from the ground, waving for a bus, pushing an elevator button, jumping jacks and two handed waves. The dataset consists of ~20 minutes of video containing 110 events of interest, with three to six actors performing multiple instances of the actions. The videos were shot using hand held cameras in a cluttered/crowded environment, with moving people and cars composing a dynamic background. The dataset is challenging due to its poor resolution (160×120), frequent occlusions, high variability in how subjects perform the actions, and also significant spatial and temporal scale differences in the actions.

We evaluate our performance using a 1:2 train:test split. Fig. 6 shows the Precision-Recall curves for the 5 action classes, and for four different method variations. First, PF-HCRF model is applied to manually annotated ground truth tracks (M1). Next it is applied to tracks computed from a pedestrian tracker [4] (M2), and then reapplied without "scale-alignment search and track extensions"(M3). Lastly, the Root-filter based SVM classifier is applied to the computed tracks (M4). We compare our performance to previously published results [7,22,29] on this dataset. Ke et al [7] show results using a flow consistency based correlation model of [22], and three variants of their super-pixel part-based method. Note, that these methods use only a single activity instance for training. Yuan et al [29] combine the two-handed-wave and jumping jack actions, and show results only on this single combined action.

Results on ground truth tracks (M1) provides an upper-bound on our performance in terms of reliance on tracks, and we achieve the best results using PF-HCRF across all actions. With computed tracks (M2), PF-HCRF still outperform other existing techniques across all actions, showing our model's tolerance to noisy tracks. Without "scale-alignment search and track extensions" (M3), the performance on hand-wave and pickup activities is poorer, which we attribute to misaligned and fragmented tracks caused by non-pedestrian poses, however, we still have good results for the other three activities. Lastly the results with the Root-filter classifier (M4) are significantly lower, which validates that our performance improvement is over and above simply using tracking results.

8.4 Rochester ADL [12]

The Activities of Daily Living (ADL) dataset contains 150 videos performed by 5 actors in a kitchen environment, and consists of 10 complex daily-living activities, involving interaction and manipulation of hard to detect objects: answering

Fig. 7. Key-pose sequences inferred by PF-HCRF gives a semantic description of activity with high consistency

phone, dialing phone, looking up phone directory, writing on whiteboard, drinking water, eating snacks, peeling banana, eating banana, chopping banana and eating using silverware. As we do not have access to an upper-body tracker, the PF-HCRF is applied to the entire frame instead of tracks. Figure 5c summarizes our results on the dataset. PF-HCRF achieves an accuracy rate of 88.67% using only HoG-HoF features. The choice of features is important for this dataset, as special features can be designed to capture elements of the kitchen scene and the various objects, like yellow-banana, white-board, phone-near-face etc. Messing et al [12] augment their model with color and face-detection based features, improving their accuracy from 67% to 89%. Similarly, [26] augments their HoG-HoF descriptors with contextual-interaction based features, causing their accuracy to improve from 85% to 96%; we expect that the PF-HCRF model will also benefit from using simmilar contextual features. Furthermore, PF-HCRF localizes the key-poses of the complex activities, and we observe high consistency in the key-pose appearance across actors (Fig.7), and they seem to correspond to a natural semantic interpretation. Such decompositions are not obtainable using [12,26].

9   Conclusion

We proposed a key-pose filter based HCRF model for detecting multiple instances of activity in unsegmented videos, and generate semantic descriptions. We presented a novel pose summarization algorithm to automatically identify the key poses of an activity sequence. Our model training does not require manual annotation of key-poses, and uses video segment level class labels only.

Acknowledgments. We thank Dr. Remi Trichet and Dr. SungChun Lee for their valuable help and advice. This research was supported, in part, by the Office of Naval Research under grant #N00014-13-1-0493.

References

1. Cao, Y., Barrett, D.: Recognizing Human Activities from Partially Observed Videos. In: CVPR (2013)
2. Felzenszwalb, P., McAllester, D.: A discriminatively trained, multiscale, deformable part model. In: CVPR (2008)
3. Gaidon, A.: Actom sequence models for efficient action detection. In: CVPR (2011)
4. Huang, C., Wu, B., Nevatia, R.: Robust object tracking by hierarchical association of detection responses. In: Forsyth, D., Torr, P., Zisserman, A. (eds.) ECCV 2008, Part II. LNCS, vol. 5303, pp. 788–801. Springer, Heidelberg (2008)
5. Jain, A., Gupta, A., Rodriguez, M., Davis, L.: Representing Videos using Mid-level Discriminative Patches. In: CVPR (2013)
6. Ke, Y., Sukthankar, R., Hebert, M.: Efficient visual event detection using volumetric features. In: ICCV (2005)
7. Ke, Y., Sukthankar, R., Hebert, M.: Volumetric Features for Video Event Detection. IJCV (2010)
8. Kong, Y., Jia, Y., Fu, Y.: Learning Human Interaction by Interactive Phrases. In: Fitzgibbon, A., Lazebnik, S., Perona, P., Sato, Y., Schmid, C. (eds.) ECCV 2012, Part I. LNCS, vol. 7572, pp. 300–313. Springer, Heidelberg (2012)
9. Laptev, I., Marszalek, M., Schmid, C., Rozenfeld, B.: Learning realistic human actions from movies. In: CVPR (2008)
10. Liu, T., Kender, J.R.: Computational approaches to temporal sampling of video sequences. MCCA (2007)
11. Lv, F., Nevatia, R.: Single view human action recognition using key pose matching & viterbi path searching. In: CVPR (2007)
12. Messing, R., Pal, C., Kautz, H.: Activity recognition using the velocity histories of tracked keypoints. In: ICCV (2009)
13. Natarajan, P., Singh, V., Nevatia, R.: Learning 3D Action Models from a few 2D videos. In: CVPR (2010)
14. Niebles, J.C., Chen, C.-W., Fei-Fei, L.: Modeling Temporal Structure of Decomposable Motion Segments for Activity Classification. In: Daniilidis, K., Maragos, P., Paragios, N. (eds.) ECCV 2010, Part II. LNCS, vol. 6312, pp. 392–405. Springer, Heidelberg (2010)
15. Raptis, M., Sigal, L.: Poselet Key-framing: A Model for Human Activity Recognition. In: CVPR (2013)
16. Raptis, M., Soatto, S.: Tracklet Descriptors for Action Modeling and Video Analysis. In: Daniilidis, K., Maragos, P., Paragios, N. (eds.) ECCV 2010, Part I. LNCS, vol. 6311, pp. 577–590. Springer, Heidelberg (2010)
17. Rodriguez, M., Ahmed, J., Shah, M.: Action Mach A spatio-temporal maximum average correlation height filter for action recognition. In: CVPR (2008)
18. Ryoo, M.S., Chen, C.-C., Aggarwal, J.K., Roy-Chowdhury, A.: An overview of contest on semantic description of human activities (SDHA) 2010. In: Ünay, D., Çataltepe, Z., Aksoy, S. (eds.) ICPR 2010. LNCS, vol. 6388, pp. 270–285. Springer, Heidelberg (2010)
19. Ryoo, M.: Human activity prediction: Early recognition of ongoing activities from streaming videos. In: ICCV. IEEE (2011)
20. Satkin, S., Hebert, M.: Modeling the Temporal Extent of Actions. In: Daniilidis, K., Maragos, P., Paragios, N. (eds.) ECCV 2010, Part I. LNCS, vol. 6311, pp. 536–548. Springer, Heidelberg (2010)

21. Schindler, K., Van Gool, L.: Action Snippets: How many frames does human action recognition require? In: CVPR (2008)
22. Shechtman, E., Irani, M.: Space-time behavior-based correlation-Or-how to tell if two underlying motion fields are similar without computing them? PAMI (2007)
23. Singh, V., Nevatia, R.: Action recognition in cluttered dynamic scenes using Pose-Specific Part Models. In: ICCV (2011)
24. Tian, Y., Sukthankar, R., Shah, M.: Spatiotemporal Deformable Part Models for Action Detection. In: CVPR (2013)
25. Vahdat, A., Gao, B., Ranjbar, M., Greg Mori: A discriminative key pose sequence model for recognizing human interactions. In: Workshop on Visual Surveillance (2011)
26. Wang, J., Chen, Z., Wu, Y.: Action Recognition with Multiscale Spatio-Temporal Contexts. In: CVPR (2011)
27. Wang, Y., Mori, G.: Hidden Part Models for Human Action Recognition: Probabilistic vs. Max-Margin. PAMI (2010)
28. Yu, C.N.J., Joachims, T.: Learning structural SVMs with latent variables. In: ICML (2009)
29. Yuan, J., Liu, Z., Wu, Y.: Discriminative Subvolume Search for Efficient Action Detection. In: CVPR (2009)
30. Zhang, Y., Liu, X., Chang, M.-C., Ge, W., Chen, T.: Spatio-Temporal Phrases for Activity Recognition. In: Fitzgibbon, A., Lazebnik, S., Perona, P., Sato, Y., Schmid, C. (eds.) ECCV 2012, Part III. LNCS, vol. 7574, pp. 707–721. Springer, Heidelberg (2012)
31. Zhuang, Y., Rui, Y.: Adaptive key frame extraction using unsupervised clustering. In: ICIP (1998)

Action Recognition Using Super Sparse Coding Vector with Spatio-temporal Awareness

Xiaodong Yang and YingLi Tian

Department of Electrical Engineering
City College, City University of New York, USA

Abstract. This paper presents a novel framework for human action recognition based on sparse coding. We introduce an effective coding scheme to aggregate low-level descriptors into the super descriptor vector (SDV). In order to incorporate the spatio-temporal information, we propose a novel approach of super location vector (SLV) to model the space-time locations of local interest points in a much more compact way compared to the spatio-temporal pyramid representations. SDV and SLV are in the end combined as the super sparse coding vector (SSCV) which jointly models the motion, appearance, and location cues. This representation is computationally efficient and yields superior performance while using linear classifiers. In the extensive experiments, our approach significantly outperforms the state-of-the-art results on the two public benchmark datasets, i.e., HMDB51 and YouTube.

1 Introduction

Action recognition has been widely applied to a number of real-world applications, e.g., surveillance event detection, human-computer interaction, content-based video search, etc. It is of great challenge to recognize actions in unconstrained videos due to the large intra-class variations caused by factors such as viewpoint, occlusion, motion style, performance duration, and cluttered background. Most of recent action recognition approaches rely on the bag-of-visual-words (BOV) representation which consists in computing and aggregating statistics from local space-time features [15] [26] [27]. In this framework, a video representation can be obtained by extracting low-level features, coding them over a visual dictionary, and pooling the codes in some well-chosen support regions. A significant progress has been made in the development of local space-time features [26] [27]. After low-level feature extraction, the approaches similar to those used for object recognition are generally employed.

In the basic BOV framework, a visual dictionary is learned by K-means and used to quantize low-level features through hard-assignment [15]. A number of coding variants have been proposed and reported to achieve the state-of-the-art results in image and video recognition, e.g., local soft assignment [19], sparse coding [30], and locality-constrained linear coding [28]. These approaches reduce information loss by relaxing the restrictive cardinality constraint in coding

D. Fleet et al. (Eds.): ECCV 2014, Part II, LNCS 8690, pp. 727–741, 2014.

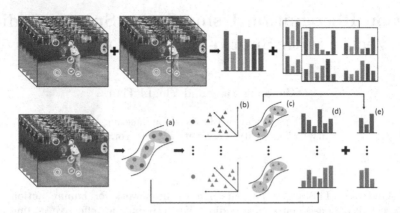

Fig. 1. Frameworks of STP (up) and SSCV (bottom). STP represents a video by concatenating BOVs from the entire sequence and spatio-temporal cells. SSCV jointly models the motion, appearance, and location information. (a) A visual dictionary of local descriptors is learned by sparse coding. (b) 3D space-time locations are associated to each visual word in (a) according to the assignments of descriptors. (c) A visual dictionary of locations is learned by sparse coding for each set in (b). SSCV is obtained by the combination of (d) SDV and (e) SLV.

descriptors. Accordingly, the average pooling can be replaced by the max pooling [30]. Recently, several coding schemes have emerged to encode descriptors with respect to the visual words that they are assigned to, e.g., Fisher vector [23], super vector coding [31], and vector of locally aggregated descriptors [10]. These methods usually retain high order statistics and have noticeably better performances [25].

The basic BOV aggregates the assignments over an entire video to generate the final representation. It obviously incurs a loss of information by discarding all the spatio-temporal locations of local space-time features. An extension to the completely orderless BOV for action recognition is the spatio-temporal pyramid (STP) [15] [26], inspired by the spatial pyramid matching (SPM) [16] for image classification. In this approach, a video sequence is repeatedly and evenly subdivided into a set of spatial and temporal cells where descriptor-level statistics are pooled. It can be used to roughly capture the spatial layout and temporal order of an action sequence. However, the concatenation of BOV histograms over many subvolumes of a video dramatically increases feature dimensions, which largely increase the learning and storage costs.

In this paper, we propose a novel action recognition framework on low-level feature coding and spatio-temporal information modeling, as illustrated in Fig. 1. We first employ a sparse coding approach [20] to compute the visual dictionary and coefficients of local descriptors. Each descriptor is coded by recording the difference of the local descriptor to all visual words. The coefficient-weighted difference vectors are then aggregated for each visual word through the whole video. These vectors of all visual words are in the end concatenated as the representation of super descriptor vector (SDV), which is used to characterize the motion and appearance cues. We further model the spatio-temporal information by computing the super location vector (SLV) of the space-time coordinates of local descriptors assigned to each visual word. We combine SDV and SLV as the super sparse coding vector (SSCV) which jointly models the motion, appearance, and spaio-temporal information.

The main contributions of this paper are summarized as follows. First, we provide an effective coding scheme to aggregate low-level features into a discriminative representation, which relies on a smaller visual dictionary. Second, we propose a novel approach to incorporate the spaio-temporal information in a much more compact representation, which correlates and models the motion, appearance, location cues in a unified way. Third, we perform a systematic evaluation of the state-of-the-art coding and pooling methods in the context of action recognition.

The remainder of this paper is organized as follows. Section 2 introduces the related work of feature aggregation and spatio-temporal information modeling. Section 3 describes the detailed procedures to compute SDV, SLV, and SSCV. A variety of experimental results and discussions are presented in Section 4. Finally, Section 5 summarizes the remarks of this paper.

2   Notations and Related Work

In this section, we introduce the notations used throughout this paper and summarize the related work on aggregating local descriptors and modeling spatial (temporal) information. We represent a video sequence $\mathcal{V}$ by a set of low-level descriptors $\mathcal{X} = \{x_1, \ldots, x_n\}$ in $\mathbb{R}^{m \times n}$ and associated locations $\mathcal{L} = \{l_1, \ldots, l_n\}$ in $\mathbb{R}^{3 \times n}$. C indicates the space-time cells defined in a spatio-temporal pyramid with C_j denoting the jth cell. $\mathbf{D} = \{\mathbf{d}_1, \ldots, \mathbf{d}_K\}$ is a visual dictionary with K visual words $\mathbf{d}_k \in \mathbb{R}^m$.

2.1   Feature Aggregation

Let $\mathcal{F}$ and $\mathcal{G}$ denote the coding and pooling operators, respectively. The final representation of $\mathcal{V}$ is the vector z obtained by sequentially coding, pooling, and concatenating over all space-time cells:

$$\alpha_i = \mathcal{F}(x_i), \quad i = 1, \ldots, n, \tag{1}$$

$$h_j = \mathcal{G}\left(\{\alpha_i\}_{i \in C_j}\right), \quad j = 1, \ldots, |C|, \tag{2}$$

$$z^T = \left[h_1^T \ldots h_{|C|}^T\right]. \tag{3}$$

In the basic BOV framework, hard assignment $\mathcal{F}$ minimizes the distance of x_i to $\mathbf{D}$ that is usually learned by K-means. $\mathcal{G}$ performs the averaging over each pooling cell C_j:

$$\alpha_i \in \{0,1\}^K, \alpha_{i,j} = 1 \text{ iff } j = \arg\min_k \|x_i - \mathbf{d}_k\|_2^2, \tag{4}$$

$$h_j = \frac{1}{|C_j|} \sum_{i \in C_j} \alpha_i. \tag{5}$$

In order to enhance the probability density estimation, soft assignment was introduced in [5]. It codes a descriptor x_i by multiple visual words in $\mathbf{D}$ using a kernel function (e.g., the Gaussian function) of the distance between x_i and $\mathbf{d}_k$. Liu et al. proposed local soft assignment in [19] to further improve the membership estimation to visual words. By taking account of the underlying manifold structure of local descriptors, $\mathcal{F}$ in local soft assignment only employs the $\mathcal{K}$ nearest visual words $N_{\mathcal{K}}(x_i)$ to code a descriptor x_i and sets its distances of the remaining visual words to infinity:

$$\alpha_{i,k} = \frac{\exp\left(-\beta \hat{d}(x_i, \mathbf{d}_k)\right)}{\sum_{j=1}^{K} \exp\left(-\beta \hat{d}(x_i, \mathbf{d}_j)\right)}, \tag{6}$$

$$\hat{d}(x_i, \mathbf{d}_k) = \begin{cases} \|x_i - \mathbf{d}_k\|^2 & \text{if } \mathbf{d}_k \in N_{\mathcal{K}}(x_i), \\ \infty & \text{otherwise}, \end{cases} \tag{7}$$

where β is a smoothing factor to control the softness of assignment. As for $\mathcal{G}$ in local soft assignment, it was observed that max pooling in the following equation outperformed average pooling:

$$h_{j,k} = \max_{i \in C_j} \alpha_{i,k}, \text{ for } k = 1, \dots, K. \tag{8}$$

Parsimony has been widely employed as a guiding principle to compute sparse representation with respect to an overcomplete visual dictionary. Sparse coding [20] approximates x_i by using a linear combination of a limited number of visual words. It is well known that the ℓ_1 penalty yields a sparse solution. So the sparse coding problem can be solved by:

$$\min_{\mathbf{D}, \alpha} \frac{1}{n} \sum_{i=1}^{n} \left(\frac{1}{2} \|x_i - \mathbf{D}\alpha_i\|_2^2 + \lambda \|\alpha_i\|_1 \right), \tag{9}$$

$$\text{subject to } \mathbf{d}_k^T \mathbf{d}_k \leq 1, \forall k = 1, \dots, K,$$

where λ is the sparsity-inducing regularizer to control the number of non-zero coefficients in α_i. It is customary to combine sparse coding with max pooling as shown in Eq. (8).

Fisher vector [23] extends the BOV representation by recording the deviation of x_i with respect to the parameters of a generative model, e.g., the Gaussian mixture model (GMM) characterized by $\{\pi_k, \mu_k, \sigma_k, k = 1, \dots, K\}$. π_k, μ_k, and σ_k are the prior mode probability, mean vector, and covariance matrix (diagonal), respectively. Let γ_i^k be the soft assignment of x_i to the kth Gaussian component. We obtain the Fisher vector of $\mathcal{X}$ by concatenating the gradient vectors from K Gaussian components:

$$\rho_k = \frac{1}{n\sqrt{\pi_k}} \sum_{i=1}^{n} \gamma_i^k \left(\frac{\boldsymbol{x}_i - \boldsymbol{\mu}_k}{\boldsymbol{\sigma}_k} \right), \quad \boldsymbol{\tau}_k = \frac{1}{n\sqrt{2\pi_k}} \sum_{i=1}^{n} \gamma_i^k \left[\frac{(\boldsymbol{x}_i - \boldsymbol{\mu}_k)^2}{\boldsymbol{\sigma}_k^2} - 1 \right], \quad (10)$$

where ρ_k and $\boldsymbol{\tau}_k$ are m-dimensional gradients with respect to $\boldsymbol{\mu}_k$ and $\boldsymbol{\sigma}_k$ of the kth Gaussian component. The relative displacements of descriptors to the mean and variance in Eq. (10) retain more information lost in the traditional coding process. The superiority of Fisher vector was recently identified in both image classification [25] and action recognition [29].

2.2 Spatial and Temporal Information

The orderless representation of a video completely ignores the spatial and temporal information, which could convey discriminative cues for action recognition. We outline the relevant representative work that attempts to account for the spatial and temporal locations of low-level features.

The dominant approach to incorporate spatial and temporal information is the spatio-temporal pyramid (STP), as illustrated in Fig. 1. Inspired by the spatial pyramid matching (SPM) [16], Laptev et al. [15] proposed to partition a video to a set of space-time cells in a coarse-to-fine manner. Each cell is represented independently and the cell-level histograms h_j are finally concatenated into the video-level histogram z as in Eq. (2-3). This representation has been proven to be effective when the action categories exhibit characteristic spatial layout and temporal order.

In image classification, the feature augmentation based methods were proposed in [21] [24] to append a weighted location l_i to the corresponding descriptor $\boldsymbol{x}_i$. As opposed to SPM, this approach does not increase the feature dimensionality thus makes the learning more efficient. Krapac et al. [12] introduced the spatial Fisher vector to encode the spatial layout of local image features. The location model can be learned by computing per visual word the mean and variance of spatial coordinates of the assigned local image patches. While these representations are more compact, the evaluation results only showed marginal improvement over SPM in terms of classification accuracy.

3   Super Sparse Coding Vector

We describe the detailed procedures of computing SSCV in this section. We propose a novel feature coding scheme based on sparse coding to aggregate descriptors and locations into discriminative representations. The space-time locations are included as part of the coding step, instead of only coding motion and appearance cues and leaving the spatio-temporal coherence to be represented in the pooling stage. This enables SSCV to jointly characterize the motion, appearance, and location information.

3.1 Modeling Space-Time Features

We represent each local feature as the descriptor-location tuple $f_i = (x_i, l_i)$. By employing a generative model (e.g., GMM) over descriptors and locations, we model f_i as:

$$p(f_i) = \sum_{k=1}^{K} p(w = k)p(x_i|w = k)p(l_i|w = k), \qquad (11)$$

where $p(w = k)$ denotes the prior mode probability of the kth Gaussian component in the descriptor mixture model, and w is the assignment index. We assume the prior mode probabilities are equal, i.e., $p(w = k) = 1/K, \forall k$. The kth Gaussian of descriptors is defined by:

$$p(x_i|w = k) = \mathcal{N}(x_i; \mu_k, \sigma_k), \qquad (12)$$

where μ_k and σ_k are the mean and covariance (diagonal) of the kth Gaussian. As illustrated in Fig. 1, we jointly model the spatio-temporal information by associating the locations of descriptors to the corresponding visual descriptor word, i.e., the Gaussian of descriptors in this context. We define the spatio-temporal model by using a GMM distribution over the locations associated with the kth visual word:

$$p(l_i|w = k) = \sum_{g=1}^{G} \pi_{k_g} \mathcal{N}\left(l_i; \mu_{k_g}, \sigma_{k_g}\right), \qquad (13)$$

where π_{k_g}, μ_{k_g}, and σ_{k_g} are the prior mode probability, mean, and covariance (diagonal) of the gth Gaussian of locations in the kth visual descriptor word. We again assume the prior mode probabilities are equal, i.e., $\pi_{k_g} = 1/G, \forall g$.

3.2 Computing Super Descriptor Vector (SDV)

We utilize sparse coding to learn a visual dictionary and code descriptors. We aggregate the coefficient-weighted differences between local descriptors and visual words into a vector, rather than directly pooling the coefficients.

The generation process of x_i is modeled by the probability density function in Eq. (12). The gradient of the log-likelihood of this function with respect to its parameters describes the contribution of the parameters to the generation process [8]. Here we focus on the gradient with respect to the mean:

$$\frac{\partial \ln p(x_i|w = k)}{\partial \mu_k} = \rho_i^k \sigma_k^{-1}(x_i - \mu_k), \qquad (14)$$

where ρ_i^k denotes the posterior $p(w = k|x_i)$. If making the three approximations:

1. the posterior is estimated by the sparse coding coefficient, i.e., $\rho_i^k = \alpha_i^k$,
2. the mean is represented by the visual word in sparse coding, i.e., $\mu_k = d_k$,
3. the covariance is isotropic, i.e., $\sigma_k = \epsilon \mathbb{I}$ with $\epsilon > 0$,

we can simplify Eq. (14) to $\alpha_i^k \left(\boldsymbol{x}_i - \mathbf{d}_k\right)$, where α_i^k is the coefficient of the ith descriptor $\boldsymbol{x}_i$ to the kth visual word $\mathbf{d}_k$ in Eq. (9).

We choose sparse coding in the approximation because it is much cheaper to compute the means (dictionary) compared to the Expectation Maximization (EM) algorithm in training GMM. Especially, it was recently shown in [3] that a reasonably good dictionary can be created by some simple methods, e.g., random sampling in a training set. Moreover, our empirical evaluations show the approximations based on sparse coding improves the recognition accuracy. We then apply average pooling to aggregate the coefficient-weighted difference vectors for each visual word:

$$\boldsymbol{u}_k = \frac{1}{n} \sum_{i=1}^{n} \alpha_i^k \left(\boldsymbol{x}_i - \mathbf{d}_k\right). \tag{15}$$

The final vector representation U of SDV is the concatenation of $\boldsymbol{u}_k$ from K visual words and is therefore with the dimensionality of mK:

$$U = \left[\boldsymbol{u}_1^T \dots \boldsymbol{u}_K^T\right]^T. \tag{16}$$

SDV has several remarkable properties: (1) the relative displacements of descriptors to visual words retain more information lost in the traditional coding process; (2) we can compute SDV upon a much smaller dictionary which reduces the computational cost; (3) it performs quite well with simple linear classifiers which are efficient in terms of both training and testing.

3.3   Computing Super Location Vector (SLV)

The descriptors quantized to the same visual word exhibit characteristic spatio-temporal layout. In order to capture this correlation between motion, appearance, and location, we associate space-time locations to the visual descriptor words that corresponding descriptors are assigned to. We also employ sparse coding to learn a visual location dictionary to code the location set associated with each visual descriptor word, as illustrated in Fig. 1(c). The coefficient-weighted differences between locations and visual location words are aggregated as the spatio-temporal representation.

In order to describe the contribution of the parameters to the generation process of l_i, we take the gradient of the log-likelihood of Eq. (13) with respect to the mean:

$$\frac{\partial \ln p \left(l_i | w = k\right)}{\partial \boldsymbol{\mu}_{k_g}} = \rho_i^{k_g} \boldsymbol{\sigma}_{k_g}^{-1} \left(l_i - \boldsymbol{\mu}_{k_g}\right), \tag{17}$$

where $\rho_i^{k_g}$ denotes posterior $p \left(t = g | l_i, w = k\right)$ and t is the assignment index. We can interpret $\rho_i^{k_g}$ as a spatio-temporal soft assignment of a descriptor location l_i associated with the kth visual descriptor word to the gth Gaussian component in the location mixture model.

Algorithm 1. Computation of SSCV

Input: a video sequence $\mathcal{V}$
a visual descriptor dictionary $\mathbf{D}^x = \{\mathbf{d}_k\}$
a visual location dictionary $\mathbf{D}^l = \{\mathbf{d}_{k_g}\}$
Output: SSCV $\mathbf{Z}$

1 compute spatio-temporal features $\mathcal{X} = \{\boldsymbol{x}_i\}$ and $\mathcal{L} = \{\boldsymbol{l}_i\}$ from $\mathcal{V}$
2 compute coefficients $\{\alpha_i^k\}$ of $\mathcal{X}$ on $\{\mathbf{d}_k\}_{k=1}^K$ by sparse coding
3 **for** visual descriptor word $k = 1$ **to** K **do**
4     $\boldsymbol{u}_k :=$ average pooling $\alpha_i^k (\boldsymbol{x}_i - \mathbf{d}_k)$, $\boldsymbol{x}_i \in \mathcal{X}$
5   associate locations to the kth visual descriptor word: $\mathcal{L}_k = \{\boldsymbol{l}_i | \alpha_i^k > 0\}$
6   compute coefficients $\left\{\alpha_i^{k_g}\right\}$ of $\mathcal{L}_k$ on $\{\mathbf{d}_{k_g}\}_{g=1}^G$ by sparse coding
7   **for** visual location word $g = 1$ **to** G **do**
8         $\boldsymbol{v}_{k_g} :=$ average pooling $\alpha_i^{k_g} (\boldsymbol{l}_i - \mathbf{d}_{k_g})$, $\boldsymbol{l}_i \in \mathcal{L}_k$
9   **end**
10     $\boldsymbol{Z}_k := [\boldsymbol{u}_k^T, \boldsymbol{v}_{k_1}^T \dots \boldsymbol{v}_{k_G}^T]^T$
11 **end**
12 $\boldsymbol{Z} := [\boldsymbol{Z}_1^T \dots \boldsymbol{Z}_K^T]^T$
13 signed square rooting and ℓ_2 normalization

If we enforce the approximations (1-3) in Section 3.2, Eq. (17) can be simplified to $\alpha_i^{k_g} (\boldsymbol{l}_i - \mathbf{d}_{k_g})$, where $\alpha_i^{k_g}$ is the sparse coding coefficient of the ith location $\boldsymbol{l}_i$ to the gth visual location word $\mathbf{d}_{k_g}$ associated with the kth visual descriptor word $\mathbf{d}_k$. As illustrated in Fig. 1(b), let $\mathcal{L}_k$ denote the set of locations that are associated to the kth visual descriptor word according to the positive assignments of their descriptors, i.e., $\mathcal{L}_k = \{\boldsymbol{l}_i | \alpha_i^k > 0\}$. We then employ the average pooling to aggregate the coefficient-weighted difference vectors for each visual location word:

$$\boldsymbol{v}_{k_g} = \frac{1}{|\mathcal{L}_k|} \sum_{\boldsymbol{l}_i \in \mathcal{L}_k} \alpha_i^{k_g} (\boldsymbol{l}_i - \mathbf{d}_{k_g}). \tag{18}$$

The concatenation of $\boldsymbol{v}_{k_g}$ from G visual location words associated with K visual descriptor words forms the final representation $\boldsymbol{V}$ of SLV with a dimensionality of $3GK$:

$$\boldsymbol{V} = [\boldsymbol{v}_{1_1}^T \dots \boldsymbol{v}_{1_G}^T \dots \boldsymbol{v}_{K_1}^T \dots \boldsymbol{v}_{K_G}^T]^T. \tag{19}$$

SLV shares the same remarkable properties as SDV. Moreover, SLV can be computed on much smaller visual descriptor dictionary (e.g., $K = 100$) and visual location dictionary (e.g., $G = 5$). If we combine SDV and SLV, the resulting vector is of $(m + 3G)K$ dimensions, where the descriptor dimensionality m (e.g., 162 in STIP [14]) is normally much larger than $3G$. So another major benefit is that, as opposed to STP, SLV only slightly increases feature dimensions thus making the learning and predicting more efficient.

We adopt the two normalization schemes introduced in [23] on SDV and SLV, i.e., signed square rooting and ℓ_2 normalization. As illustrated in Fig. 1, each visual word in (a) is in the end characterized by two parts, i.e., $\boldsymbol{u}_k$ in (d) and $[\boldsymbol{v}_{k_1} \dots \boldsymbol{v}_{k_G}]$ in (e). They are used to model the motion (appearance) and location cues, respectively. We summarize the outline of computing SSCV of an action sequence in Algorithm 1.

4 Experiments and Discussions

In this section, we extensively evaluate the proposed method on the two public benchmark datasets: HMDB51 [13] and YouTube [18]. In all experiments, we employ LIBLINEAR [4] as the linear SVM solver. Experimental results show that our algorithm significantly outperforms the state-of-the-art methods. Our source code for computing SSCV is available online.[1]

4.1 Experimental Setup

Datasets. The HMDB51 dataset [13] is collected from a wide range of sources from digitized movies to online videos. It contains 51 action categories and 6766 video sequences in total. This dataset includes the original videos and the stabilized version. Our evaluations are based on the original ones. We follow the same experimental setting as [13] using three training/testing splits. There are 70 videos for training and 30 videos for testing in each class. The average accuracy over the three splits is reported as the performance measurement. The YouTube dataset [18] contains 11 action classes collected under large variations in scale, viewpoint, illumination, camera motion, and cluttered background. This dataset contains 1168 video sequences in total. We follow the evaluation protocol as in [18] by using the leave-one-out cross validation for a pre-defined set of 25 groups. We report the average accuracy over all classes as the performance measurement.

Low-Level Feature Extraction. We evaluate our approach on five low-level visual contents using appearance and motion features. STIP is used to detect sparse interest points and compute HOG/HOF as the descriptor [14]. Motivated by the success of dense sampling in image classification and action recognition, we also employ the dense trajectories [26] to densely sample and track interest points from several spatial scales. Each tracked interest point generates four descriptors: HOG, HOF, trajectory (TRA), and motion boundary histogram (MBH). HOG focuses on static appearance cues, whereas HOF captures local motion information. TRA characterizes the geometric shape of a trajectory. MBH computes gradient orientation histograms from horizontal and vertical spatial derivatives of optical flow. It has been proven effective to represent motion information and suppress camera motion. So for each action sequence, we compute five features: STIP (162), HOG (96), HOF (108), TRA (30), and MBH (192), where the number in parentheses denotes the descriptor dimensionality.

---

[1] http://yangxd.org/code

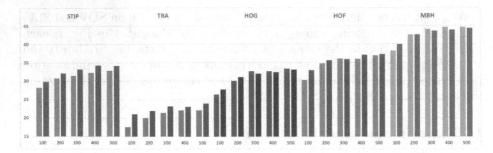

Fig. 2. Recognition accuracy (%) of FV and SDV using different descriptors with a variety of visual dictionary size K on the HMDB51 dataset. The bars in light color and deep color denote the results of FV and SDV, respectively. This figure is better viewed on screen.

4.2   Evaluation of Feature Aggregation Schemes

In this section, we compare and analyze the performance of a variety of feature aggregation schemes. We focus on the HMDB51 dataset for a detailed evaluation of the coding and pooling parameters. Note: the spatio-temporal information is discarded in the experiments of this section.

The baseline aggregation method is the hard assignment (Hard) paired with average pooling in Eq. (4-5). The local soft assignment (LocalSoft) and max pooling in Eq. (6-8) are employed with $K = 10$ nearest neighbors and $\beta = 1$. We also adopt the sparse coding (SC) with max pooling in Eq. (8-9) and set the regularizer $\lambda = 1.2/\sqrt{m}$ as suggested in [20]. As a successful feature aggregation scheme, Fisher vector (FV) in Eq. (10) is compared as well. Before computing FV, we follow the preprocess in [23] [25] to apply PCA to project the descriptors to half dimensions. This step is mainly used to decorrelate the data and make it better fit the diagonal covariance matrix assumption in GMM.

SDV is compared to other feature aggregation schemes in Table 1. We set the visual dictionary size $K = 4000$ for Hard, LocalSoft, SC, and $K = 500$ for FV and SDV. As shown in this table, LocalSoft consistently outperforms Hard due to the enhanced membership estimation of descriptors to visual words. While still inferior to our method, SC largely improves the accuracy over Hard and

Table 1. Recognition accuracy (%) of different aggregation schemes using a variety of descriptors on the HMDB51 dataset

	Hard	LocalSoft	SC	FV	SDV
STIP	19.2	24.5	28.6	32.8	**34.2**
TRA	17.3	18.7	21.9	22.1	**23.9**
HOG	21.0	25.3	31.5	**33.3**	33.1
HOF	22.0	25.8	34.5	36.9	**37.3**
MBH	31.1	32.6	36.1	**44.6**	44.3

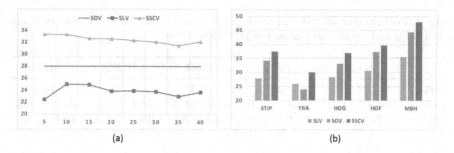

Fig. 3. Evaluations of SLV on the HMDB51 dataset. (a) Performance (%) of SLV and SSCV using STIP for a variety of visual location dictionary size G. (b) Performance (%) of SLV, SDV, and SSCV for a variety of features.

LocalSoft by introducing the sparsity in coding descriptors. SDV outperforms FV in STIP, TRA, and HOF, and yields comparable results to FV in HOG and MBH. We further conduct a detailed evaluation of FV and SDV as shown in Fig. 2. SDV systematically outperforms FV in STIP and TRA, irrespective of the visual dictionary size. For HOG, HOF, and MBH, SDV achieves higher recognition accuracy than FV in a relatively small size. SDV and FV tend to have comparable results as the visual dictionary size enlarges. In addition to the superior recognition accuracy, SDV is computationally more efficient. This is because more information is stored per visual word, which enables SDV to perform quite well by using a much more compact visual dictionary. We use $K = 500$ to compute SDV in the following experiments if not specified.

4.3 Evaluation of Spatio-temporal Models

Here we evaluate different approaches on modeling the spatio-temporal information and report results for the HMDB51 dataset.

STIP is first used to investigate the impact of the size of visual location dictionary on SLV. As shown in Fig. 3(a), the results of SLV ranges from 22.4% to 25.0% as G increases from 5 to 40. The performance of SDV is plotted as a reference. When SDV and SLV are combined to SSCV, it is not very sensitive to the size and achieves the best result using only 5 visual location words. In the following experiments, we use $G = 5$ to compute SLV. Fig. 3(b) demonstrates the results of SLV, SDV, and SSCV for a variety of features. SSCV consistently and significantly outperforms SDV for all features. This shows SLV is effective to model and provide the complementary spatio-temporal information to the motion and appearance cues in SDV. It is interesting to observe that SLV based on the pure space-time information even outperforms SDV in the feature TRA.

SSCV is then compared to the widely used spatio-temporal pyramid (STP) on modeling the space-time information. We use in our experiments four different spatio-temporal grids. For the spatial domain we employ a 1×1 whole spatial block and a 2×2 spatial grid. For the temporal domain we apply the

Table 2. Performance (%) of STP and SSCV on modeling the spatio-temporal information for a variety of features on the HMDB51 dataset

	STIP	TRA	HOG	HOF	MBH
SDV	34.2	23.9	33.1	37.3	44.3
STP	35.4 (+1.2)	28.8 (+4.9)	34.4 (+1.3)	38.1 (+0.8)	46.9 (+2.6)
SSCV	**37.4** (+3.2)	**29.9** (+6.0)	**36.9** (+3.8)	**39.7** (+2.4)	**48.0** (+3.7)

entire sequence and two temporal segments. The combination of these subdivisions in both spatial and temporal domains generate 15 space-time cells in total. We compute a separate SDV from each cell and concatenate them as the final representation of STP. As shown in Table 2, both STP and SSCV improve the results because of the spatio-temporal cues complemented to SDV. However, for all features SSCV achieves more significant improvement than STP, while with much more compact representation. In our experimental setting, the dimensions of STP and SSCV are $15mK$ and $(m + 15)K$, where m is the descriptor dimensionality. So in comparison to STP, our approach can also considerably reduce the computation and memory costs in both training and testing.

Table 3. Comparison of SSCV and the state-of-the-art method for each individual feature on the HMDB51 and YouTube datasets

	HMDB51 (%)					YouTube (%)				
	STIP	TRA	HOG	HOF	MBH	STIP	TRA	HOG	HOF	MBH
WKSL'13 [26]	-	28.0	27.9	31.5	43.2	69.2	67.5	72.6	70.0	80.6
SSCV	37.4	**29.9**	**36.9**	**39.7**	**48.0**	**77.4**	**70.9**	**80.4**	**77.0**	**83.2**

4.4   Comparison to State-of-the-Art Results

In this section, we compare our results to the state-of-the-arts on the two benchmark datasets: HMDB51 and YouTube. SSCV is first compared to the results in [26] for each individual feature as demonstrated in Table 3. SSCV significantly outperforms the approach in [26], though both methods are based upon the same features. This is mainly because SDV is more representative than BOV to capture the motion and appearance information, and SLV is more effective than STP to model the spatio-temporal cues. Moreover, SSCV employs the linear SVM which is more efficient than the non-linear SVM with χ^2 kernel used in [26]. We combine all the features and compare with the most recent results in the literature as displayed in Table 4. We can observe that SSCV significantly outperforms the state-of-the-art results on the two datasets.

Table 4. Comparison of SSCV to the state-of-the-art results as reported in the cited publications

HMDB51		%	YouTube		%
GGHW'12	[6]	29.2	ICS'10	[7]	75.2
WWQ'12	[29]	31.8	LZYN'11	[17]	75.8
JDXLN'12	[11]	40.7	BSJS'11	[1]	76.5
WKSL'13	[26]	48.3	BT'10	[2]	77.8
PQPQ'13	[22]	49.2	WKSL'13	[26]	85.4
JJB'13	[9]	52.1	PQPQ'13	[22]	86.6
SSCV		**53.9**	SSCV		**88.0**

5 Conclusion

In this paper, we have presented a novel framework for action recognition. An effective coding scheme SDV is proposed to capture motion and appearance cues by sparse coding low-level descriptors and average pooling coefficient-weighted difference vectors between descriptors and visual words. A novel approach SLV is introduced to incorporate the spatio-temporal cues in a compact and discriminative manner. The combination of SDV and SLV constitutes the final representation of SSCV which jointly models the motion, appearance, and location information in a unified way. Our approach is extensively evaluated on two public benchmark datasets and compared to a number of most recent results. Experimental results demonstrate that our approach significantly outperforms the state-of-the-art methods.

Acknowledgement. This work was supported in part by NSF Grant EFRI-1137172, IIS-1400802, and FHWA Grant DTFH61-12-H-00002.

References

1. Bhattacharya, S., Sukthankar, R., Jin, R., Shah, M.: A Probabilistic Representation for Efficient Large-Scale Visual Recognition Tasks. In: CVPR (2011)
2. Brendel, W., Todorovic, S.: Activities as Time Series of Human Postures. In: Daniilidis, K., Maragos, P., Paragios, N. (eds.) ECCV 2010, Part II. LNCS, vol. 6312, pp. 721–734. Springer, Heidelberg (2010)
3. Coates, A., Ng, A.: The Importance of Encoding versus Training with Sparse Coding and Vector Quantization. In: ICML (2011)
4. Fan, R., Chang, K., Hsieh, C., Wang, X., Lin, C.: LIBLINEAR: A Library for Large Linear Classification. JMLR (2008)
5. Gemert, J., Veenman, C., Smeulders, A., Geusebroek, J.: Visual Word Ambiguity. PAMI (2009)
6. Kliper-Gross, O., Gurovich, Y., Hassner, T., Wolf, L.: Motion Interchange Patterns for Action Recognition in Unconstrained Videos. In: Fitzgibbon, A., Lazebnik, S., Perona, P., Sato, Y., Schmid, C. (eds.) ECCV 2012, Part VI. LNCS, vol. 7577, pp. 256–269. Springer, Heidelberg (2012)

7. Ikizler-Cinbis, N., Sclaroff, S.: Object, Scene and Actions: Combining Multiple Features for Human Action Recognition. In: Daniilidis, K., Maragos, P., Paragios, N. (eds.) ECCV 2010, Part I. LNCS, vol. 6311, pp. 494–507. Springer, Heidelberg (2010)
8. Jaakkola, T., Haussler, D.: Exploiting Generative Models in Discriminative Classifiers. In: NIPS (1998)
9. Jain, M., Jegou, H., Bouthemy, P.: Better Exploiting Motion for Better Action Recognition. In: CVPR (2013)
10. Jegou, H., Douze, M., Schmid, C., Perez, P.: Aggregating Local Descriptors into a Compact Image Representation. In: CVPR (2010)
11. Jiang, Y.-G., Dai, Q., Xue, X., Liu, W., Ngo, C.-W.: Trajectory-Based Modeling of Human Actions with Motion Reference Points. In: Fitzgibbon, A., Lazebnik, S., Perona, P., Sato, Y., Schmid, C. (eds.) ECCV 2012, Part V. LNCS, vol. 7576, pp. 425–438. Springer, Heidelberg (2012)
12. Krapac, J., Verbeek, J., Jurie, F.: Modeling Spatial Layout with Fisher Vector for Image Categorization. In: ICCV (2011)
13. Kuehne, H., Jhuang, H., Garrote, E., Poggio, T., Serre, T.: HMDB: A Large Video Database for Human Motion Recognition. In: CVPR (2011)
14. Laptev, I.: On Space-Time Interest Points. IJCV (2005)
15. Laptev, I., Marszalek, M., Schmid, C., Rozenfeld, B.: Learning Realistic Human Actions from Movies. In: CVPR (2008)
16. Lazebnik, S., Schmid, C., Ponce, J.: Beyond Bags of Features: Spatial Pyramid Matching for Recognizing Natural Scene Categories. In: CVPR (2006)
17. Le, Q., Zou, W., Yeung, S., Ng, A.: Learning Hierarchical Invariant Spatio-Temporal Features for Action Recognition with Independent Subspace Analysis. In: CVPR (2011)
18. Liu, J., Luo, J., Shah, M.: Recognizing Realistic Actions from Videos in the Wild. In: CVPR (2009)
19. Liu, L., Wang, L., Liu, X.: In Defense of Soft-Assignment Coding. In: ICCV (2011)
20. Mairal, J., Bach, F., Ponce, J., Sapiro, G.: Online Dictionary Learning for Sparse Coding. In: ICML (2009)
21. McCann, S., Lowe, D.G.: Spatially Local Coding for Object Recognition. In: Lee, K.M., Matsushita, Y., Rehg, J.M., Hu, Z. (eds.) ACCV 2012, Part I. LNCS, vol. 7724, pp. 204–217. Springer, Heidelberg (2013)
22. Peng, X., Qiao, Y., Peng, Q., Qi, X.: Exploring Motion Boundary based Sampling and Spatio-Temporal Context Descriptors for Action Recognition. In: BMVC (2013)
23. Perronnin, F., Sánchez, J., Mensink, T.: Improving the Fisher Kernel for Large-Scale Image Classification. In: Daniilidis, K., Maragos, P., Paragios, N. (eds.) ECCV 2010, Part IV. LNCS, vol. 6314, pp. 143–156. Springer, Heidelberg (2010)
24. Sanchez, J., Perronnin, F., Campos, T.: Modeling the Spatial Layout of Images Beyond Spatial Pyramids. PRL (2012)
25. Sanchez, J., Perronnin, F., Mensink, T., Verbeek, J.: Image Classification with the Fisher Vector: Theory and Practice. IJCV (2013)
26. Wang, H., Klaser, A., Schmid, C., Liu, C.: Dense Trajectories and Motion Boundary Descriptors for Action Recognition. IJCV (2013)
27. Wang, H., Ullah, M., Klaser, A., Laptev, I., Schmid, C.: Evaluation of Local Spatio-Temporal Features for Action Recognition. In: BMVC (2009)
28. Wang, J., Yang, J., Yu, K., Lv, F., Huang, T., Gong, Y.: Locality-Constrained Linear Coding for Image Classification. In: CVPR (2010)

29. Wang, X., Wang, L., Qiao, Y.: A Comparative Study of Encoding, Pooling and Normalization Methods for Action Recognition. In: Lee, K.M., Matsushita, Y., Rehg, J.M., Hu, Z. (eds.) ACCV 2012, Part III. LNCS, vol. 7726, pp. 572–585. Springer, Heidelberg (2013)
30. Yang, J., Yu, K., Gong, Y., Huang, T.: Linear Spatial Pyramid Matching Using Sparse Coding for Image Classification. In: CVPR (2009)
31. Zhou, X., Yu, K., Zhang, T., Huang, T.S.: Image Classification Using Super-Vector Coding of Local Image Descriptors. In: Daniilidis, K., Maragos, P., Paragios, N. (eds.) ECCV 2010, Part V. LNCS, vol. 6315, pp. 141–154. Springer, Heidelberg (2010)

HOPC: Histogram of Oriented Principal Components of 3D Pointclouds for Action Recognition

Hossein Rahmani, Arif Mahmood, Du Q. Huynh, and Ajmal Mian

Computer Science and Software Engineering, The University of Western Australia,
35 Stirling Highway, Crawley, WA 6009 Australia

Abstract. Existing techniques for 3D action recognition are sensitive to viewpoint variations because they extract features from depth images which change significantly with viewpoint. In contrast, we directly process the pointclouds and propose a new technique for action recognition which is more robust to noise, action speed and viewpoint variations. Our technique consists of a novel descriptor and keypoint detection algorithm. The proposed descriptor is extracted at a point by encoding the Histogram of Oriented Principal Components (HOPC) within an adaptive spatio-temporal support volume around that point. Based on this descriptor, we present a novel method to detect Spatio-Temporal Key-Points (STKPs) in 3D pointcloud sequences. Experimental results show that the proposed descriptor and STKP detector outperform state-of-the-art algorithms on three benchmark human activity datasets. We also introduce a new multiview public dataset and show the robustness of our proposed method to viewpoint variations.

Keywords: Spatio-temporal keypoints, multiview action dataset.

1 Introduction

Human action recognition has many applications in smart surveillance, human-computer interaction and sports. The Kinect and other depth cameras have become popular for this task because depth sequences do not suffer from the problems induced by variations in illumination and clothing texture. However, the presence of occlusion, sensor noise and most importantly viewpoint variations still make action recognition a challenging task.

Designing an efficient depth sequence representation is an important task in many computer vision problems. Most existing action recognition techniques (e.g., [4,21,38]) treat depth sequences the same way as color videos and use color-based action recognition methods. However, while these methods are suitable for color video sequences, simply extending them to depth sequences may not be optimal [19]. Information captured by depth cameras actually allows geometric features to be extracted to form rich descriptors. For instance, Tang et al. [27] used histograms of the normal vectors for object recognition in depth images. Given a depth image, they computed spatial derivatives, transformed them to the polar coordinates and used the 2D histograms as object descriptors. Recently, Oreifej and Liu [19] extended the same technique to the temporal dimension by adding time derivative. A downside of treating depth sequences this way is that the noise in the depth images is enhanced by the differential operations [31]. Histogramming, on the other hand, is analogous to integration and is more resilient to

D. Fleet et al. (Eds.): ECCV 2014, Part II, LNCS 8690, pp. 742–757, 2014.

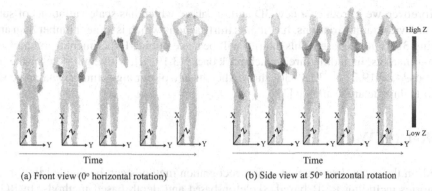

(a) Front view (0° horizontal rotation)   (b) Side view at 50° horizontal rotation

Fig. 1. Two sequences of 3D pointclouds of a subject performing the *holding head* action. Notice how the depth values (colours) have significantly changed with the change in viewpoint. Simple normalization cannot compensate for such depth variations. Existing depth based action recognition algorithms will not be accurate in such cases

the effect of noise. Furthermore, viewpoint variations are unavoidable in real scenarios. However, none of the existing 3D sensor based techniques is designed for cross-view action recognition where training is performed on sequences acquired from one view and testing is performed on sequences acquired from a significantly different view ($> 25°$).

We directly process the 3D pointcloud sequences (Fig. 1) and extract point descriptors which are robust to noise and viewpoint variations. We propose a novel descriptor, the *Histogram of Oriented Principal Components* (HOPC), to capture the local geometric characteristics around each point within a sequence of 3D pointclouds. To extract HOPC at a point p, PCA is performed on an adaptive spatio-temporal support volume around p (see Fig. 2) which gives us a 3×3 matrix of eigenvectors and the corresponding eigenvalues. Each eigenvector is projected onto m directions corresponding to the vertices of a *regular m-sided polyhedron* and scaled by its eigenvalue. HOPC is formed by concatenating the projected eigenvectors in decreasing order of their eigenvalues.

HOPC is used in a holistic and local setting. In the former approach, the sequence of 3D pointclouds is divided into spatio-temporal cells and HOPC descriptors of all points within a cell are accumulated and normalized to form a single cell descriptor. All cell descriptors are concatenated to form a holistic HOPC descriptor. In the latter approach, local HOPC are extracted at candidate spatio-temporal keypoints (STKP) and a HOPC quality factor is defined to rank the STKPs. Only high quality STKPs are retained. All points within the adaptive spatio-temporal support volume of each STKP are aligned along the eigenvectors of the spatial support around STKP. Thus the support volume is aligned with a local object centered coordinate basis and extracting HOPC, or any other feature, at the STKP will be view invariant. See Section 4.2 for details. Since humans may perform the same action at different speeds, to achieve speed invariance, we propose automatic temporal scale selection by minimizing the eigenratios over a varying temporal window size. The main contributions of this paper include:

- A HOPC descriptor for 3D pointclouds.
- A spatio-temporal key-point (STKP) detector and a view invariant descriptor.
- A technique for speed normalization of actions.

Moreover, we introduce a new 3D action dataset which has scale variations of subjects and viewpoint variations. It contains thirty actions which is larger number than any existing 3D action dataset. This dataset will be made public. Experimental comparison on four datasets, including three benchmark ones [13,19,32], with eight state-of-the-art methods [4,10,19,21,31,32,35,36] shows the efficacy of our algorithms. Data and code of our technique are available [1].

2   Related Work

Based on the input data, human action recognition methods can be divided into three categories including RGB based, skeleton-based and depth based methods. In RGB videos, in order to recognize actions across viewpoint changes, mostly view independent representations are proposed such as view invariant spatio-temporal features [2,20,22,23,25,33]. Some methods infer the 3D scene structure and use geometric transformations to achieve view invariance [5,9,15,26,39]. Another approach is to find a view independent latent space [7,8,12,14] in which features extracted from the actions captured at different view points are directly comparable. Our proposed approach also falls in this category. However, our approach is only for 3D pointclouds captured by depth sensors. To the best of our knowledge, we are the first to propose cross-view action recognition using 3D pointclouds. We propose to normalize the spatio-temporal support volume of each candidate keypoint in the 3D pointcloud such that the feature extracted from the normalized support volume becomes view independent.

In skeleton based methods, 3D joint positions are used for action recognition. Multicamera motion capture (MoCap) systems [3] have been used for human action recognition, but such special equipment is marker-based and expensive. Moreover, due to the different quality of the motion data, action recognition methods designed for MoCap are not suitable for 3D pointcloud sequences which is the focus of this paper [32].

On the other hand, some methods [36,31,37] use the human joint positions extracted by the OpenNI tracking framework (OpenNI) [24] as interest points. For example, Yang and Tian [37] proposed pairwise 3D joint position differences in each frame and temporal differences across frames to represent an action. Since 3D joints cannot capture all the discriminative information, the action recognition accuracy is compromised. Wang et al. [32] extended the previous approach by computing the histogram of occupancy pattern of a fixed region around each joint in a frame. In the temporal dimension, they used low frequency Fourier components as features and an SVM to find a discriminative set of joints. It is important to note that the estimated joint positions are not reliable and can fail when the human subject is not in an upright and frontal view position (e.g. lying on sofa) or when there is clutter around the subject.

Action recognition methods based on depth maps can be divided into holistic [19,21,13,38,29] and local approaches [32,35,11,31]. Holistic methods use global features such as silhouettes and space-time volume information. For example, Li et al. [13] sampled boundary pixels from 2D silhouettes as a bag of features. Yang et al. [38] added temporal derivative of 2D projections to get Depth Motion Maps (DMM). Vieira et al. [29] computed silhouettes in 3D by using the space-time occupancy patterns. Recently, Oreifej and Liu [19] extended histogram of oriented 3D normals [27] to 4D by adding time derivative. The gradient vector was normalized to unit magnitude and projected on a refined basis of 600-cell Polychrome to make histograms. The last component of normalized gradient vector was inverse of the gradient magnitude. As a result, information from very strong derivative locations, such as edges and silhouettes, may get suppressed [21]. The proposed HOPC descriptor is more informative than HON4D as it captures the spread of data in three principal directions. Thus, HOPC achieves more action recognition accuracy than exiting methods on three benchmark datasets.

Depth based local methods use local features where a set of interest points are extracted from the depth sequence and a feature descriptor is computed for each interest point. For example, Cheng et al. [4] used interest point detector proposed by Dollár et al. [11] and proposed a Comparative Coding Descriptor (CCD). Due to the presence of noise in depth sequences, simply extending color-based interest point detectors such as [6] and [11] may degrade the efficiency of these detectors [19].

Motion trajectory based action recognition methods[30,34] are also not reliable in depth sequences [19]. Therefore, recent depth based action recognition methods resorted to alternative ways to extract more reliable interest points. Wang et al. [31] proposed Haar features to be extracted from each random subvolume. Xia and Aggarwal in [35] proposed a filtering method to extract spatio-temporal interest points. Their approach fails when the action execution speed is faster than the flip of the signal caused by the sensor noise. Both techniques are sensitive to viewpoint variations.

In contrast to previous interest point detection methods, the proposed STKP detector is robust to variations in action execution speed, sensor viewpoint and the spatial scale of the actor. Since the proposed HOPC descriptor is not strictly based on the depth derivatives, it is more robust to noise. Moreover, our methods do not require skeleton data which may be noisy or unavailable especially in the case of side views.

3   Histogram of Oriented Principal Component (HOPC)

Let $Q = \{Q_1, Q_2, \cdots, Q_t, \cdots, Q_{n_f}\}$ represent a sequence of 3D pointclouds captured by a 3D sensor, where n_f denotes the number of frames (i.e. number of 3D pointclouds in the sequence) and Q_t is the 3D pointcloud at time t. We make a spatio-temporal accumulated 3D pointcloud by merging the sequence of individual pointclouds in the time interval $[t - \tau, t + \tau]$. Consider a point $\mathbf{p} = (x_t\ y_t\ z_t)^\top, 1 \le t \le n_f$ in Q_t. We define the spatio-temporal support of $\mathbf{p}$, $\Omega(\mathbf{p})$, as the 3D points which are in a sphere of radius r centered at $\mathbf{p}$ (Fig. 2). We propose a point descriptor based on the eigenvalue decomposition of the scatter matrix C of the points $\mathbf{q} \in \Omega(\mathbf{p})$:

$$C = \frac{1}{n_p} \sum_{\mathbf{q} \in \Omega(\mathbf{p})} (\mathbf{q} - \mu)(\mathbf{q} - \mu)^\top, \text{where } \mu = \frac{1}{n_p} \sum_{\mathbf{q} \in \Omega(\mathbf{p})} \mathbf{q}, \tag{1}$$

and $n_p = |\Omega(\mathbf{p})|$ denotes the number of points in the spatio-temporal support of $\mathbf{p}$. Performing PCA on the scatter matrix C gives us $CV = EV$, where E is a diagonal matrix of the eigenvalues $\lambda_1 \ge \lambda_2 \ge \lambda_3$, and V contains three orthogonal eigenvectors $[\mathbf{v}_1\ \mathbf{v}_2\ \mathbf{v}_3]$ arranged in the order of decreasing magnitude of their associated eigenvalues. We propose a new descriptor, the Histogram of Oriented Principal Components

(HOPC), by projecting each eigenvector onto m directions obtained from a *regular m-sided polyhedron*. We use $m = 20$ to make a *regular icosahedron* which is composed of 20 *regular pentagonal* facets and each facet corresponds to a histogram bin. Let $U \in \mathbb{R}^{3 \times m}$ be the matrix of the center positions $\mathbf{u}_1, \mathbf{u}_2, \cdots, \mathbf{u}_m$ of facets:

$$U = [\mathbf{u}_1, \mathbf{u}_2, \cdots, \mathbf{u}_i, \cdots, \mathbf{u}_m] \tag{2}$$

For a *regular icosahedron* with center at the origin, these normalized vectors are

$$\left(\frac{\pm 1}{L_u}, \frac{\pm 1}{L_u}, \frac{\pm 1}{L_u} \right), \left(0, \frac{\pm \varphi^{-1}}{L_u}, \frac{\pm \varphi}{L_u} \right), \left(\frac{\pm \varphi^{-1}}{L_u}, \frac{\pm \varphi}{L_u}, 0 \right), \left(\frac{\pm \varphi}{L_u}, 0, \frac{\pm \varphi^{-1}}{L_u} \right), \tag{3}$$

where $\varphi = (1 + \sqrt{5})/2$ is the golden ratio, and $L_u = \sqrt{\varphi^2 + 1/\varphi^2}$ is the length of vector $\mathbf{u}_i, 1 \leq i \leq m$. The eigenvectors are basically directions of maximum variance of the points in 3D space. Thus, they have a $180°$ ambiguity. To overcome this problem, we consider the distribution of vector directions and their magnitudes within the support volume of $\mathbf{p}$. We determine the sign of each eigenvector $\mathbf{v}_j$ from the sign of the inner products of $\mathbf{v}_j$ and all vectors within the support of $\mathbf{p}$:

$$\mathbf{v}_j = \mathbf{v}_j.sign \left(\sum_{\mathbf{q} \in \Omega(\mathbf{p})} sign(\mathbf{o}^\top \mathbf{v}_j)(\mathbf{o}^\top \mathbf{v}_j)^2 \right) \tag{4}$$

where $\mathbf{o} = \mathbf{q} - \mathbf{p}$ and the $sign$ function returns the sign of an input number. Note that the squared projection ensures the suppression of small projections, which could be due to noise. If the signs of eigenvectors $\mathbf{v}_1, \mathbf{v}_2$, and $\mathbf{v}_3$ disagree i.e. $\mathbf{v}_1 \times \mathbf{v}_2 \neq \mathbf{v}_3$, we switch the sign of the eigenvector whose $|\sum_{w=1}^{n_p} sign(\mathbf{o}_w^\top \mathbf{v}_j)(\mathbf{o}_w \mathbf{v}_j)^2|$ value is the smallest. We then project each eigenvector $\mathbf{v}_j$ onto U to give us:

$$\mathbf{b}_j = U^\top \mathbf{v}_j \in \mathbb{R}^m, \text{ for } 1 \leq j \leq 3. \tag{5}$$

In case $\mathbf{v}_j$ is perfectly aligned with $\mathbf{u}_i \in U$, it should vote into only i^{th} bin. However, all $\mathbf{u}_i$'s are not orthogonal, therefore $\mathbf{b}_j$ will have non-zero projection in other bins as well. To overcome this effect, we quantize the projection of $\mathbf{b}_j$. For this purpose, a threshold value ψ is computed by projecting any two *neighbouring* vectors $\mathbf{u}_k$ and $\mathbf{u}_l$,

$$\psi = \mathbf{u}_k{}^\top \mathbf{u}_l = \frac{\varphi + \varphi^{-1}}{L_u{}^2}, \quad \mathbf{u}_k, \mathbf{u}_l \in U. \tag{6}$$

Note that for any $\mathbf{u}_k \in U$, we can find a $\mathbf{u}_l \in U$ such that $\psi = (\varphi + \varphi^{-1})/L_u{}^2$. The quantized vector is given by

$$\hat{\mathbf{b}}_j(z) = \begin{cases} 0 & \text{if } \mathbf{b}_j(z) \leq \psi \\ \mathbf{b}_j(z) - \psi & \text{otherwise,} \end{cases}$$

where $1 \leq z \leq m$. We define $\mathbf{h}_j$ to be $\hat{\mathbf{b}}_j$ scaled by the corresponding eigenvalue λ_j,

$$\mathbf{h}_j = \frac{\lambda_j \cdot \hat{\mathbf{b}}_j}{||\hat{\mathbf{b}}_j||_2} \in \mathbb{R}^m, \text{ for } 1 \leq j \leq 3. \tag{7}$$

We concatenate the histograms of oriented principal components of all three eigenvectors in decreasing order of their eigenvalues to form a descriptor of point p:

$$h_p = [h_1^T \ h_2^T \ h_3^T]^T \in \mathbb{R}^{3m}. \tag{8}$$

The spatio-temporal HOPC descriptor at point p encodes information from both shape and motion in the support volume around it. Since the smallest principal component of the local surface is in fact the total least squares estimate of the surface normal [18], our descriptor, which inherently encodes the surface normal, is more robust to noise than gradient-based surface normal used in [27,19]. Using this descriptor, we propose two different action recognition algorithms in the following section.

4 Action Recognition

We propose a holistic and a local approach for human action recognition. Our holistic method is suitable for actions under occlusions, more inter-class similarities of local motions, and where the subjects do not change their spatial locations. On the other hand, our local method is more suitable for cross-view action recognition and in cases where the subjects change their spatial locations.

4.1 Action Recognition with Holistic HOPC

A sequence of 3D pointclouds is divided into $\gamma = n_x \times n_y \times n_t$ spatio-temporal cells along X, Y, and T dimensions. We use c_s, where $s = 1 \cdots \gamma$, to denote the sth cell. The spatio-temporal HOPC descriptor h_p in (8) is computed for each point p within the sequence. The cell descriptor h_{c_s} is computed by accumulating $h_{c_s} = \sum_{p \in c_s} h_p$ and then normalizing $h_{c_s} \leftarrow h_{c_s}/\|h_{c_s}\|_2$. The final descriptor h_v for the given sequence is a concatenation of h_{c_s} obtained from all the cells: $h_v = [h_{c_1}^T \ h_{c_2}^T \ ... \ h_{c_s}^T \ ... \ h_{c_\gamma}^T]^T$. We use h_v as the holistic HOPC descriptor and use SVM for classification.

Computing a Discriminative Cell Descriptor. The HOPC descriptor is highly correlated to the order of eigenvalues of the spatio-temporal support volume around p. Therefore, for each point a pruning approach is introduced to eliminate the ambiguous eigenvectors of each point. For this purpose, we define two eigenratios:

$$\delta_{12} = \frac{\lambda_1}{\lambda_2}, \delta_{23} = \frac{\lambda_2}{\lambda_3}. \tag{9}$$

For 3D symmetrical surfaces, the values of δ_{12} or δ_{23} will be equal to 1. The principal components of symmetrical surfaces are ambiguous. To get a discriminative h_p, the values of δ_{12} and δ_{23} must be greater than 1. However, to manage noise we choose a threshold value $\theta > 1 + \epsilon$, where ϵ is a margin and select only the discriminative eigenvectors as follows:

1. If $\delta_{12} > \theta$ and $\delta_{23} > \theta$: $h_p = [h_1^T \ h_2^T \ h_3^T]^T$.
2. If $\delta_{12} \leq \theta$ and $\delta_{23} > \theta$: $h_p = [0^T \ 0^T \ h_3^T]^T$.
3. If $\delta_{12} > \theta$ and $\delta_{23} \leq \theta$: $h_p = [h_1^T \ 0^T \ 0^T]^T$.
4. If $\delta_{12} \leq \theta$ and $\delta_{23} \leq \theta$: In this case, we discard p.

4.2   STKP: Spatio-Temporal Key-Point Detection

Consider a point $\mathbf{p} = (x_t \ y_t \ z_t)^\top$ within a sequence of 3D pointclouds. In addition to the spatio-temporal support volume around $\mathbf{p}$ defined in section 3, we further define a spatial only support volume around $\mathbf{p}$ as the 3D points of Q_t that fall inside a sphere of radius r centered at $\mathbf{p}$. Thus, we perform PCA on both the spatial and the spatio-temporal scatter matrices C' and C.

Let $\lambda'_1 \geq \lambda'_2 \geq \lambda'_3$ and $\lambda_1 \geq \lambda_2 \geq \lambda_3$ represent the eigenvalues of the spatial C' and spatio-temporal C scatter matrix, respectively. We define the following ratios:

$$\delta'_{12} = \frac{\lambda'_1}{\lambda'_2}, \ \delta'_{23} = \frac{\lambda'_2}{\lambda'_3}, \ \delta_{12} = \frac{\lambda_1}{\lambda_2}, \ \delta_{23} = \frac{\lambda_2}{\lambda_3}. \tag{10}$$

For a point to be identified as a potential keypoint, the condition $\{\delta_{12}, \delta_{23}, \delta'_{12}, \delta'_{23}\} > \theta$ must be satisfied. This process prunes ambiguous points and produces a subset of candidate keypoints. It reduces the computational burden of the subsequent steps. Let $\mathbf{h}'_{\mathbf{p}} \in \mathbb{R}^{3m}$ represent the spatial HOPC and $\mathbf{h}_{\mathbf{p}} \in \mathbb{R}^{3m}$ represent the spatio-temporal HOPC. A *quality* factor is computed at each candidate keypoint $\mathbf{p}$ as follows:

$$\eta_p = \frac{1}{2} \sum_{i=1}^{3m} \frac{(\mathbf{h}'_{\mathbf{p}}(i) - \mathbf{h}_{\mathbf{p}}(i))^2}{(\mathbf{h}'_{\mathbf{p}}(i) + \mathbf{h}_{\mathbf{p}}(i))}. \tag{11}$$

When $\mathbf{h}'_{\mathbf{p}} = \mathbf{h}_{\mathbf{p}}$, the *quality* factor has the minimum value of $\eta_p = 0$. It means that the candidate keypoint $\mathbf{p}$ has a stationary spatio-temporal support volume with no motion.

We define a locality as a sphere of radius r' (with $r' \ll r$) and a time interval $2\tau' + 1$ (with $\tau' \leq \tau$). We sort the candidate STKPs according to their quality values and starting from the highest quality keypoint, all STKPs within its locality are removed. The same process is repeated on the remaining STKPs. Fig. 2 shows the steps of our STKP detection algorithm. Fig. 3-a shows the extracted STKPs from three different views for a sequence of 3D pointclouds corresponding to the *holding head* action.

4.3   View-Invariant Key-Point Descriptor

Let $\mathbf{p} = (x_t \ y_t \ z_t)^\top$ represent an STKP. All points within the spatio-temporal support volume of $\mathbf{p}$ i.e., $\Omega(\mathbf{p})$, are aligned along the eigenvectors of its spatial scatter matrix, $B = PV'$, where $P \in \mathbb{R}^{n_p \times 3}$ is a matrix of points within $\Omega(\mathbf{p})$ and $V' = [\mathbf{v}'_1 \ \mathbf{v}'_2 \ \mathbf{v}'_3]$ denotes the 3×3 matrix of eigenvectors of the spatial scatter matrix C'. Recall that the signs of these eigenvectors have a 180° ambiguity. As mentioned earlier, we use the sign disambiguation method to overcome this problem. As a result, any feature (e.g. raw depth values or HOPC) extracted from the aligned spatio-temporal support volume around $\mathbf{p}$ will be view invariant.

In order to describe the points within the spatio-temporal support volume of keypoint $\mathbf{p}$, the spatio-temporal support of $\mathbf{p}$ is represented as a 3D hyper-surface in the 4D space (X, Y, Z) and T. We fit a 3D hyper-surface to the aligned points within the spatio-temporal support volume of $\mathbf{p}$. A uniform $m_x \times m_y \times m_t$ grid is used to sample the hyper-surface and its raw values are used as the descriptor of keypoint $\mathbf{p}$.

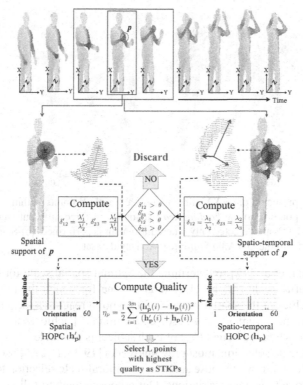

Fig. 2. STKP: Spatio-Temporal Key-Point detection algorithm

We use the bag-of-words approach to represent each 3D pointcloud sequence and build a codebook by clustering the keypoint descriptors using K-means. Codewords are defined by the cluster centers and descriptors are assigned to codewords using Euclidean distance. For classification, we use SVM with the histogram intersection kernel [16].

5   Adaptive Support Volume

So far we have used a fixed spatial (r) and temporal (τ) support volume to detect and describe each keypoint **p**. However, subjects can have different scales (in height and width) and perform actions with different speeds. Therefore, simply using a fixed spatial (r) and temporal (τ) support volume is not optimal. Large values of r and τ enable the proposed descriptors to encapsulate more information about shape and motion of a subject. However, this also increases sensitivity to occlusion and action speed.

A simple approach to finding the optimal spatial scale (r) for a STKP is based on the subject's height (h_s) e.g. $r = e \times h_s$, where e is a constant that is empirically chosen to make a trade-off between descriptiveness and occlusion. This approach is unreliable and may fail when a subject touches the background or is not in an upright position. Several automatic spatial scale detection methods [28] have been proposed for 3D object recognition. In this paper, we use the automatic spatial scale detection method

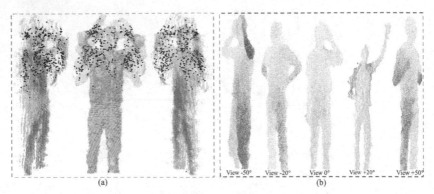

Fig. 3. (a)-STKPs projected onto XY dimensions on top of all points within a sequence of 3D pointclouds corresponding to the *holding head* action (from three different views). Note that a large number of STKPs are detected only where movement is performed. (b)-Sample pointclouds at different views from the UWA3D Multiview Activity dataset.

proposed by Mian et al. [17] to determine the optimal spatial scale for each keypoint. The optimal spatial scale (r_b) is selected as the one for which the ratio between the first two eigenvalues of the spatial support of a keypoint reaches a local maximum. Our results show that the automatic spatial scale selection [17] achieves the same accuracy as the fixed scale when the height (h_s) of each subject is available.

For temporal scale selection, most previous works [19,35,21,29,6] used a fixed number of frames. However, we propose automatic temporal scale selection to make our descriptor robust to action speed variations. Our proposed method follows the automatic spatial scale detection method by Mian et al. [17]. Let $Q = \{Q_1, Q_2, \cdots, Q_t, \cdots, Q_{n_f}\}$ represent a sequence of 3D pointclouds. For a point $\mathbf{p} = [x_t \ y_t \ z_t]^\top$, we start with points in $[Q_{t-\tau}, \cdots, Q_{t+\tau}]$ for $\tau = 1$ which are within its spatial scale r (note that we assume r as the optimal spatial scale for $\mathbf{p}$) and calculate the summation of ratio between the first two eigenvalues (λ_2/λ_1) and the last two eigenvalues (λ_3/λ_2) as:

$$A_{\mathbf{p}}^{\tau} = \frac{\lambda_2}{\lambda_1} + \frac{\lambda_3}{\lambda_2}, \tag{12}$$

where $\lambda_1 \geq \lambda_2 \geq \lambda_3$. This process continues for all $\tau = 1, \cdots, \Delta$ and the optimal temporal scale τ corresponding to the local minimum value of $A_{\mathbf{p}}$ found for point $\mathbf{p}$. A point which does not have a local minimum is not considered as a candidate keypoint.

6 Experiments

The proposed algorithms were evaluated on three benchmark datasets including MSRAction3D [13], MSRGesture3D [31], and ActionPairs3D [19]. We also developed a new "UWA3D Multiview Activity" dataset to evaluate the proposed cross-view action recognition algorithm. This dataset consists of 30 daily activities of ten subjects performed at different scales and viewpoints (Subsection 6.4). For our algorithms, we used $k = 1000, \theta = 1.12, m_x = m_y = 20$ and $m_t = 3$ in all experiments. To test the performance of our holistic approach, each sequence of 3D pointclouds was divided into $6 \times 5 \times 3$ spatio-temporal cells along X, Y, and T dimensions, respectively.

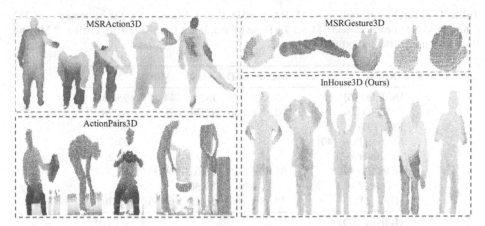

Fig. 4. Sample 3D pointclouds from the MSRAction3D, MSRGesture3D, ActionPairs3D, and UWA3D Multiview Activity datasets

The performance of the proposed algorithms was compared with seven state-of-the-art methods including Histogram of Oriented Gradient (HOG3D) [10], Random Occupancy Pattern (ROP) [31], Histogram of 3D joints(HOJ3D) [36], Actionlet Ensemble [32], Histogram of 4D Oriented Normals (HON4D) [19], Depth Spatio-Temporal Interest Points (DSTIP) [35], and Histograms of Depth Gradient (HDG) [21]. The accuracy is reported from the original papers or from the authors' implementations of DSTIP [35], HDG [21], HOG3D [10], and HON4D [19]. The implementation of HOJ3D [36] is not available, therefore we used our own implementation.

6.1 MSRAction3D Dataset

MSRAction3D dataset [13] consists of 20 actions each performed by 10 subjects 2-3 times (Fig. 4). The dataset is challenging due to high inter-action similarities. To test our holistic approach, we used five subjects for training and five for testing and repeated the experiments 252 folds exhaustively as proposed by [19]. To show the effectiveness of our automatic spatio-temporal scale selection, we used four different settings using fixed and varying values of r and τ. Table 1 compares our algorithms with existing state-of-the-art. Note that the proposed algorithm outperformed all techniques under all four settings. The maximum accuracy was achieved using constant r and adaptive τ. Adaptive r did not improve results since there is little scale variation in this dataset. Note that HOJ3D [36], Moving Pose [40] and Actionlet [32] use skeleton data which is not always available.

We also evaluated our local method with automatic spatial and temporal scale selection and achieved 90.90% accuracy (subjects {1,3,5,7,9} used for training and the rest for testing). This is higher than 89.30% of DSTIP [35] and 88.36% of HON4D [19]. Note that DSTIP [35] only reported the accuracy of the best fold and used additional steps such as mining discriminative features which can be applied to improve the accuracy of any descriptor. We did not include such steps in our method.

752   H. Rahmani et al.

Table 1. Accuracy comparison on MSRAction3D dataset. Mean ± STD is computed over 252 folds. Fold 5/5 means subjects {1,3,5,7,9} used for training and the rest for testing. [a] Moving Pose [40] used different setting.

Method	Mean±STD	Max	Min	5/5
HOJ3D [36]	63.55±5.23	75.91	44.05	75.80
HOG3D [10]	70.38±4.40	82.78	55.26	82.78
ROP [31]	-	-	-	86.50
Moving Pose [40]	-	-	-	91.70[a]
Actionlet [32]	-	-	-	88.20
HON4D [19]	81.88±4.45	90.61	69.31	88.36
DSTIP [35]	-	89.30	-	-
HDG [21]	77.68±4.97	86.13	60.55	83.70
Holistic HOPC				
constant r, constant τ	85.45±2.31	92.39	73.54	91.64
adaptive r, constant τ	84.78±2.89	91.64	72.41	90.90
constant r, adaptive τ	86.49±2.28	92.39	74.36	91.64
adaptive r, adaptive τ	85.01±2.44	92.39	72.94	91.27

6.2   MSRGesture3D Dataset

The MSRGesture3D dataset [31] contains 12 American sign language gestures performed 2-3 times by 10 subjects. For comparison with previous techniques, we use the leave-one-subject-out cross validation scheme proposed by [31]. Because of the absence of full body subjects (only hands are visible), we evaluate our methods in two settings only. Table 2 compares our method to existing state-of-the-art methods excluding HOJ3D [36] and Actionlet [32] since they require 3D joint positions which are not present in this dataset. Note that both variants of our method outperform all techniques by a significant margin achieving an average accuracy of 96.23% which is 3.5% higher than the nearest competitor HDG [21]. We also tested our local method with automatic spatial and temporal scale selection and obtained an accuracy of 93.61%.

6.3   ActionPairs3D Dataset

The ActionPairs3D dataset [19] consists of depth sequences of six pairs of actions (Fig. 4) performed by 10 subjects. This dataset is challenging as each action pair has similar motion and shape. We used half of the subjects for training and the rest for testing as recommended by [19] and repeated the experiments 252 folds. Table 3 compares the proposed holistic HOPC descriptor in two settings with existing state-of-the-art methods. Our algorithms outperformed all techniques with 2.23% improvement over the nearest competitor. Adaptive τ provides better improvement on this dataset compared to the previous two. We also evaluated our local method with automatic spatial and temporal scale selection and obtained 98.89% accuracy using subjects {6.7.8.9.10} for training and the rest for testing.

Table 2. Comparison with state-of-the-art methods on MSRGesture3D dataset

Method	Mean±STD	Max	Min
HOG3D [10]	85.23±12.12	100	50.00
ROP [31]	88.50	-	-
HON4D [19]	92.45±8.00	100	75
HDG [21]	92.76±8.80	100	77.78
Holistic HOPC			
adaptive r, constant τ	95.29±6.24	100	83.67
adaptive r, adaptive τ	96.23±5.29	100	88.33

Table 3. Accuracy comparisons on the ActionPairs3D dataset. Mean±STD arc computed over 252 folds. 5/5 means subjects {6,7,8,9,10} used for training and the rest for testing.

Method	Mean±STD	Max	Min	5/5
HOJ3D [36]	63.81±5.94	67.22	50.56	66.67
HOG3D [10]	85.76±4.66	85.56	65.00	82.78
Actionlet [32]	-	-	-	82.22
HON4D [19]	96.00±1.74	100	91.11	96.67
Holistic HOPC				
constant r, constant τ	97.15±2.21	100	88.89	97.22
constant r, adaptive τ	98.23±2.19	100	88.89	98.33

6.4 UWA3D Multiview Activity Dataset

We collected a new dataset using the Kinect to emphasize three factors: (1) Scale variations between subjects. (2) View-point variations. (3) All actions were performed in a continuous manner with no breaks or pauses. Thus, the start and end positions of body for the same actions are different. Our dataset consists of 30 activities performed by 10 human subjects of varying scales: *one hand waving, one hand Punching, sitting down, standing up, holding chest, holding head, holding back, walking, turning around, drinking, bending, running, kicking, jumping, moping floor, sneezing, sitting down(chair), squatting, two hand waving, two hand punching, vibrating, falling down, irregular walking, lying down, phone answering, jumping jack, picking up, putting down, dancing,* and *coughing* (Fig. 4). To capture depth videos from front view, each subject performed two or three random permutations of the 30 activities in a continuous manner. For cross-view action recognition, 5 subjects performed 15 activities from 4 different side views (see Fig. 3-b). We organized our dataset by segmenting the continuous sequences. The dataset is challenging due to self-occlusions and high similarity. For example, *drinking* and *phone answering* actions have very similar motion and only the hand location in these actions is slightly different. As another example, *lying down* and *falling down* actions have very similar motion, but the speed of action execution is different. Moreover, some actions such as: *holding back, holding head,* and *answering phone* have self-occlusions. The videos were captured at 30 frames per second at a spatial resolution of 640 × 480.

Table 4. Accuracy comparison on the UWA3D Activity dataset for same-view action recognition

Method	Mean±STD	Max	Min
HOJ3D [36]	48.59±5.77	58.70	28.93
HOG3D [10]	70.09±4.40	82.78	51.60
HON4D [19]	79.28±2.68	88.89	70.14
HDG [21]	75.54±3.64	85.07	61.90
Holistic HOPC			
constant r, constant τ	83.77±3.09	92.18	74.67
constant r, adaptive τ	84.93±2.75	93.11	74.67

We evaluate our proposed methods in the same-view, and cross-view action recognition settings. The holistic approach is used to classify actions captured from the same view and the local approach is used for cross-view action recognition where the training videos are captured from front view and the test videos from side views.

Same-View Action Recognition. We selected half of the subjects as training and the rest as testing and evaluated our holistic method in two settings: (1) constant r, constant τ, (2) constant r, adaptive τ. Table 4 compares our methods with existing state of the art. Both variants of our algorithm outperform all methods achieving a maximum of 84.93% accuracy. The adaptive τ provides minor improvement because there is no explicit action speed variation in the dataset. To further test the robustness of our temporal scale selection (adaptive τ) to action speed variations we use depth videos of actions performed by half of the subjects captured at 30 frames per second as training data and depth videos of actions performed by the remaining subjects captured at 15 frames per second as test data. The average accuracy of our method using automatic temporal scale selection was 84.64% which is higher than 81.92% accuracy achieved by our method using constant temporal scale and the 76.43% accuracy achieved by HON4D. Next, we swap the frame rates of the test and training data. The average accuracy of our method using automatic temporal scale selection was 84.70% which is higher than 81.01% accuracy achieved by our method using constant temporal scale. The accuracy of HON4D was 75.81% in this case.

Cross-View Action Recognition. In order to evaluate the STKP detector and HOPC descriptor for cross-view action recognition, we used front views of five subjects as training and side views of the remaining five subjects as test. Table 5 compares our method with existing state-of-the- art holistic and local methods for cross-view action recognition. Note that the performance of all other methods degrades when the subjects perform actions at different viewing angles. This is not surprising as existing methods assume that actions are observed from the same viewpoint i.e. frontal. For example, HON4D achieved 86.55% accuracy when the training and test samples were in the same view (frontal). The average accuracy of HON4D dropped to 48.89% when the training samples were captured from front view and the test samples were captured from four different side views. We also observed that the performance of existing methods did not degrade only for actions like *standing up, sitting down,* and *turning around*. This is due to the distinctness of these actions regardless of the viewpoint.

Table 5. Cross-view action recognition on the UWA3D Multiview Activity dataset. Depth sequences of five subjects at 0° are used for training and the remaining subjects at 0° and 4 different side-views are used for testing. Average accuracy is computed only for the cross-view scenario.

Method	View angle					
	0°	-25°	$+25^\circ$	-50°	$+50^\circ$	Average
Holistic Methods						
HON4D [19]	86.55	62.22	60.00	35.56	37.78	48.89
HDG [21]	79.13	60.00	64.44	33.33	35.56	48.33
Local Methods						
HOJ3D [36]	63.34	60.00	62.22	37.78	40.00	50.00
DSTIP+DCSF [35]	80.80	66.67	71.11	35.56	40.00	53.33
STKP+hyper-surface fitting	87.39	81.33	82.67	71.11	71.11	76.56
STKP+HOPC	**91.79**	**86.67**	**88.89**	**75.56**	**77.78**	**82.23**

We test two variants of our method. First, we apply our STKP detector on 3D point-cloud sequences and use the raw values of fitted hyper-surface as features. The average accuracy obtained over the four different side views ($\pm 25^\circ$ and $\pm 50^\circ$) was 76.56% in this case. Next, we use the STKP detector combined with the proposed HOPC descriptor. This combination achieved the best average accuracy i.e. 82.23%. Comparison with other methods and the accuracy of each method on different side views are shown in Table 5. These experiments demonstrate that our STKP detector in conjunction with HOPC descriptor significantly outperforms state-of-the-art methods for cross-view as well as same-view action recognition.

7 Conclusion

Performance of current 3D action recognition techniques degrades in the presence of viewpoint variations across the test and the training data. We proposed a novel technique for action recognition which is more robust to action speed and viewpoint variations. A new descriptor, Histogram of Oriented Principal Components (HOPC), and a keypoint detector are presented. The proposed descriptor and detector were evaluated for activity recognition on three benchmark datasets. We also introduced a new multiview public dataset and showed the robustness of our proposed method to viewpoint variations.

Acknowledgment. This research was supported by ARC Discovery Grant DP110102399.

References

1. UWA3D Multiview Activity dataset and Histogram of Oriented Principal Components Matlab code (2014), http://www.csse.uwa.edu.au/~ajmal/code.html
2. Blank, M., Gorelick, L., Shechtman, E., Irani, M., Basri, R.: Actions as space-time shapes. In: ICCV (2005)

3. Campbell, L., Bobick, A.: Recognition of human body motion using phase space constraints. In: ICCV (1995)
4. Cheng, Z., Qin, L., Ye, Y., Huang, Q., Tian, Q.: Human daily action analysis with multi-view and color-depth data. In: ECCVW (2012)
5. Darrell, T., Essa, I., Pentland, A.: Task-specific gesture analysis in real-time using interpolated views. PAMI (1996)
6. Dollár, P., Rabaud, V., Cottrell, G., Belongie, S.: Behavior recognition via sparse spatio-temporal features. In: ICCV (2005)
7. Farhadi, A., Tabrizi, M.K.: Learning to recognize activities from the wrong view point. In: Forsyth, D., Torr, P., Zisserman, A. (eds.) ECCV 2008, Part I. LNCS, vol. 5302, pp. 154–166. Springer, Heidelberg (2008)
8. Farhadi, A., Tabrizi, M.K., Endres, I., Forsyth, D.A.: A latent model of discriminative aspect. In: ICCV (2009)
9. Gavrila, D., Davis, L.: 3D model-based tracking of humans in action: a multi-view approach. In: CVPR (1996)
10. Klaeser, A., Marszalek, M., Schmid, C.: A spatio-temporal descriptor based on 3D-gradients. In: BMVC (2008)
11. Laptev, I.: On space-time interest point. IJCV (2005)
12. Li, R.: Discriminative virtual views for cross-view action recognition. In: CVPR (2012)
13. Li, W., Zhang, Z., Liu, Z.: Action recognition based on a bag of 3D points. In: CVPRW (2010)
14. Liu, J., Shah, M., Kuipersy, B., Savarese, S.: Cross-view action recognition via view knowledge transfer. In: CVPR (2011)
15. Lv, F., Nevatia, R.: Single view human action recognition using key pose matching and viterbi path searching. In: CVPR (2007)
16. Maji, S., Berg, A.C., Malik, J.: Classification using intersection kernel support vector machines is efficient. In: CVPR (2008)
17. Mian, A., Bennamoun, M., Owens, R.: On the repeatability and quality of keypoints for local feature-based 3D object retrieval from cluttered scenes. IJCV (2010)
18. Mitra, N.J., Nguyen, A.: Estimating surface normals in noisy point clouds data. In: SCG (2003)
19. Oreifej, O., Liu, Z.: HON4D: histogram of oriented 4D normals for activity recognition from depth sequences. In: CVPR (2013)
20. Parameswaran, V., Chellappa, R.: View invariance for human action recognition. IJCV (2006)
21. Rahmani, H., Mahmood, A., Huynh, D.Q., Mian, A.: Real time human action recognition using histograms of depth gradients and random decision forests. In: WACV (2014)
22. Rao, C., Yilmaz, A., Shah, M.: View-invariant representation and recognition of actions. IJCV (2002)
23. Seitz, S., Dyer, C.: View-invariant analysis of cyclic motion. IJCV (1997)
24. Shotton, J., Fitzgibbon, A., Cook, M., Sharp, T., Finocchio, M., Moore, R., Kipman, A., Blake, A.: Real-time human pose recognition in parts from single depth images. In: CVPR (2011)
25. Syeda-Mahmood, T., Vasilescu, A., Sethi, S.: Recognizing action events from multiple viewpoints. In: IEEE Workshop on Detection and Recognition of Events in Video (2001)
26. Syeda-Mahmood, T., Vasilescu, A., Sethi, S.: Action recognition from arbitrary views using 3D exemplars. In: ICCV (2007)
27. Tang, S., Wang, X., Lv, X., Han, T.X., Keller, J., He, Z., Skubic, M., Lao, S.: Histogram of oriented normal vectors for object recognition with a depth sensor. In: Lee, K.M., Matsushita, Y., Rehg, J.M., Hu, Z. (eds.) ACCV 2012, Part II. LNCS, vol. 7725, pp. 525–538. Springer, Heidelberg (2013)

28. Timbari, F., Stefano, L.D.: Performance evaluation of 3D keypoint detectors. IJCV (2013)
29. Vieira, A.W., Nascimento, E., Oliveira, G., Liu, Z., Campos, M.: STOP: space-time occupancy patterns for 3D action recognition from depth map sequences. In: CIARP (2012)
30. Wang, H., Klaser, A., Schmid, C., Liu, C.L.: Action recognition by dense trajectories. In: CVPR (2011)
31. Wang, J., Liu, Z., Chorowski, J., Chen, Z., Wu, Y.: Robust 3D action recognition with random occupancy patterns. In: Fitzgibbon, A., Lazebnik, S., Perona, P., Sato, Y., Schmid, C. (eds.) ECCV 2012, Part II. LNCS, vol. 7573, pp. 872–885. Springer, Heidelberg (2012)
32. Wang, J., Liu, Z., Wu, Y., Yuan, J.: Mining actionlet ensemble for action recognition with depth cameras. In: CVPR (2012)
33. Weinland, D., Ronfard, R., Boyer, E.: Free viewpoint action recognition using motion history volumes. In: CVIU (2006)
34. Wu, S., Oreifej, O., Shah, M.: Action recognition in videos acquired by a moving camera using motion decomposition of lagrangian particle trajectories. In: ICCV (2011)
35. Xia, L., Aggarwal, J.: Spatio-temporal depth cuboid similarity feature for activity recognition using depth camera. In: CVPR (2013)
36. Xia, L., Chen, C.C., Aggarwal, J.K.: View invariant human action recognition using histograms of 3D joints. In: CVPRW (2012)
37. Yang, X., Tian, Y.: EigenJoints-based action recognition using naive bayes nearest neighbor. In: CVPRW (2012)
38. Yang, X., Zhang, C., Tian, Y.: Recognizing actions using depth motion maps-based histograms of oriented gradients. In: ACM ICM (2012)
39. Yilmaz, A., Shah, M.: Action sketch: a novel action representation. In: CVPR (2005)
40. Zanfir, M., Leordeanu, M., Sminchisescu, C.: The moving pose: an efficient 3D kinematics descriptor for low-latency action recognition and detection. In: ICCV (2013)

Natural Action Recognition Using Invariant 3D Motion Encoding

Simon Hadfield, Karel Lebeda, and Richard Bowden

Centre for Vision, Speech and Signal Processing, University of Surrey, UK
{S.Hadfield,K.Lebeda,R.Bowden}@surrey.ac.uk

Abstract. We investigate the recognition of actions "in the wild" using 3D motion information. The lack of control over (and knowledge of) the camera configuration, exacerbates this already challenging task, by introducing systematic projective inconsistencies between 3D motion fields, hugely increasing intra-class variance. By introducing a robust, sequence based, stereo calibration technique, we reduce these inconsistencies from fully projective to a simple similarity transform. We then introduce motion encoding techniques which provide the necessary scale invariance, along with additional invariances to changes in camera viewpoint.

On the recent Hollywood 3D natural action recognition dataset, we show improvements of 40% over previous state-of-the-art techniques based on implicit motion encoding. We also demonstrate that our robust sequence calibration simplifies the task of recognising actions, leading to recognition rates 2.5 times those for the same technique without calibration. In addition, the sequence calibrations are made available.

Keywords: Action recognition, in the wild, 3D motion, scene flow, invariant encoding, stereo sequence calibration.

1 Introduction

In recent years, the field of action recognition has been exploring techniques for effectively exploiting the wealth of 3D video data which has recently become available. However, the area of natural or "in the wild" action recognition using 3D data offers it's own unique, and so far unaddressed, challenges. Attempting to make use of 3D data from disparate sources with unknown calibration, adds additional layers of variations into a field which is already typified by huge intra-class variance and limited training data. This is especially obvious in recent datasets such as Hollywood-3D [10] which contains a wide variety of 3D data, but provides no calibration information. This severely limits the amount of 3D information which can be extracted, forcing authors to resort on projected 2D motion fields [10] or implicit depth encodings [13]. In this paper we propose not only the use of true 3D motion fields (see Figures 1 and 2) as a descriptor for recognising action categories, but also techniques for reliably extracting robust, invariant and comparable descriptors from uncontrolled 3D data.

Motion information has long been one of the primary tools to distinguish actions. Interest points in natural videos are detected based on temporal gradients [15,33] and motion fields are directly encoded to describe videos [24,22,16]. This is perhaps unsurprising, as it can be argued that motions are what define an action. In recent years,

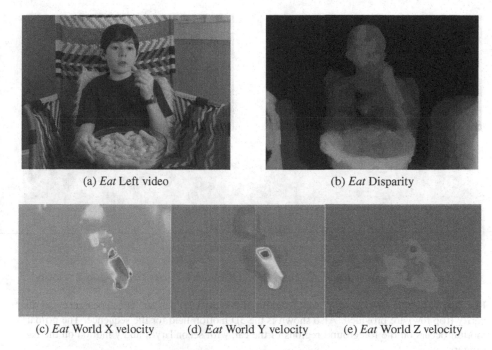

(a) *Eat* Left video   (b) *Eat* Disparity

(c) *Eat* World X velocity   (d) *Eat* World Y velocity   (e) *Eat* World Z velocity

Fig. 1. An example *Eat* action taken from the Hollywood 3D dataset. The appearance and disparity (top row) are provided. Also shown is a 3D motion field for the sequence. Note that motion is concentrated on the arm and head, which move towards each other.

3D structural data has seen increasing use in action recognition, however 3D motions remain conspicuously unexploited. This is primarily due to the difficulty in obtaining such data. Although the Kinect directly provides 3D structural information at every frame, the motion fields which warp from one structure to the next are unknown, and estimating them is still a topic of ongoing research [21,27,9,2].

In addition to the difficulty in extracting such data, there has recently been a rapid increase in the potential sources of 3D data. This includes consumer devices like the Kinect, 3D broadcast footage from television networks & film studios, and even upcoming mobile devices like Google's Project Tango. This variety of input domains further emphasises the need for invariant encoding, in order to fully exploit the diverse set of input data.

2   Related Work

In action recognition, it has long been standard practice to employ interest point detectors [15] to focus attention on salient regions of the scene during learning. This serves to suppress irrelevant background information and reduce the computational complexity of many algorithms [7,19,16]. The use of 3D data has removed the need for this step in much recent work recognising actions in constrained environments, due to the simplicity of segmenting the actor (for example by using the Kinect's user mask) [19,4,8]. This enables complex "volumetric" descriptions of the actors body over time [34,32,31,23].

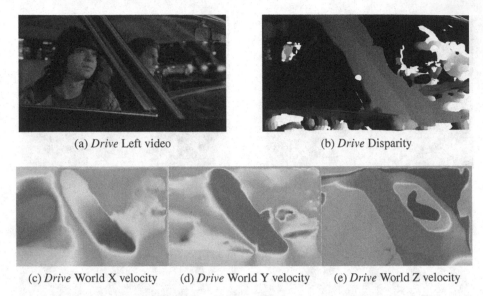

(a) *Drive* Left video   (b) *Drive* Disparity

(c) *Drive* World X velocity   (d) *Drive* World Y velocity   (e) *Drive* World Z velocity

Fig. 2. An example *Drive* action taken from the Hollywood 3D dataset. The appearance and disparity (top row) are provided. Also shown is the 3D motion field for the sequence. The primary motion occurs on the foreground regions of the car, with secondary x and y motion on the passengers.

However, for "in the wild" action recognition this is not the case as it generally remains impossible to segment the actor reliably, due to noisy 3D data, cluttered environments, and scenes containing multiple people. As such, it is still common to use interest point detectors as a kind of "soft user mask". In this paper, we use the depth-aware spatio-temporal corner detectors of [10] for this purpose.

Once salient parts of the sequence have been detected, various local feature descriptors are generally extracted from these regions. Local features which have proved effective in the past include gradient based appearance information [28,17], 2D motion information [22,5] and spatio-temporal extensions to SIFT and SURF descriptors [29,33]. For "in the wild" action recognition, the use of the Hollywood-3D dataset has prompted the investigation of local features based on 3D information. However, previous work has been limited by the lack of consistent calibration information. As such, authors have been forced to rely on the recognition system learning to generalise across variations arising from miscalibration [13,10]. It is here that one of the major contributions of this paper lies, overcoming this limitation and making it possible for a new and powerful type of local information to be extracted to encode actions, based on 3D motion fields.

The final stage of "in the wild" action recognition, is often for the collection of local features to be encoded into a single holistic description of the sequence, often via a Bag-of-Words approach with a codebook of exemplar features. This approach is analogous to the highly successful Bag-of-Words techniques for object recognition, but with an additional temporal dimension. The Bag-of-Words approach to sequence encoding is generally performed by accumulating occurrences spatially and temporally across the entire sequence. This provides invariance to a range of important deformations, such as spatial and temporal translation, stretching and reflection. This is invaluable for generalisation, but it also leads to much of the relational information being discarded, such as the spatial configuration and temporal ordering of features. Laptev *et al.* attempt to mitigate this by splitting the spatio-temporal volume into sub-blocks, creating a descriptor for each sub-block, and concatenating them to create the sequence descriptor [16]. Sapienza *et al.* follow a similar vein, encoding individual sub-sequences, however rather than concatenating to create a single descriptor, they employ Multiple Instance Learning (MIL) [26]. This accounts for some parts of the sequence being irrelevant, for example before and after the action. In this paper we propose a number of novel encoding schemes, incorporating invariances particularly suited to our 3D motion features, such as scale and viewpoint invariance.

The remainder of this paper is structured as follows. Section 3 describes the robust auto-calibration technique proposed for use with varied footage. We then explain how this calibration allows comparable 3D motion information to be extracted from varied sequences, and propose invariant encoding schemes in Section 4, allowing us to make the best use of the varied training sequences. Finally, in Section 5 the proposed techniques are evaluated on a recent dataset for 3D action recognition "in the wild" and compared against the existing state of the art results.

3   Stereo Sequence Auto-calibration

To extract comparable 3D motion information from multi-view sequences, we need some form of calibration between the views. This is particularly an issue for "in the wild" action recognition, where the camera models, and layout, change between sequences. Without accounting for these differences, extracted 3D information varies greatly from sequence to sequence. This introduces a huge amount of artificial variation to the action classes, making classification even more challenging. To mitigate this issue, we introduce an approach for stereo auto-calibration of video pairs.

The first step towards calibrating a pair of video sequences I^l and I^r, each of which consists of n frames ($I^l_{1...n}$ and $I^r_{1...n}$), is to detect a set of candidate correspondences. In this paper, sets (S^l and S^r) of SIFT [20] points $s = (x, y, \tau)$ are extracted, where,

$$S = \{s : \mathrm{SIFT}(I_\tau(x,y)) > \lambda_s\}. \tag{1}$$

based on the threshold λ_s. Each SIFT point s_i has an associated SIFT descriptor f_i. Correspondences between point detections are calculated subject to the condition that their descriptors are closer than a threshold λ_f, and that they occur at the same frame in both sequences,

$$C = \{(s^l_i, s^r_j) : |f^l_i - f^r_j| < \lambda_f \text{ and } \tau^l_i = \tau^r_j\}. \tag{2}$$

Given this set of cross sequence correspondences, the epipolar geometry of the scene is estimated using 7-point RANSAC with Local Optimisation [18]. The fundamental matrix is estimated by

$$F = \underset{F'}{\arg\min} \sum \epsilon_s\left(s^{l\top}_i, s^r_i | F'\right), \tag{3}$$

where ϵ_s is the Sampson error (linearised approximation to projection error). In this work ϵ_s also applies a truncated quadratic cost function (as in MSAC), which provides an approximation to the maximum likelihood estimate [30].

Given the estimated F we can also extract the set of inlier correspondences,

$$\hat{C} = \left\{ (s_i^l, s_i^r) : \left| s_i^{l\top} F s_i^r \right| < \lambda_r \right\}, \tag{4}$$

which obey the epipolar constraints estimated. For the experiments in this paper, the detection, matching and inlier thresholds (λ_s, λ_f and λ_r respectively) use the default values suggested by their respective authors.

3.1 Full 3D Sequence Calibration

Estimating the epipolar geometry between the sequences is only the first step to consistent 3D calibration. Next the focal length (and hence the Essential matrix E) must be estimated. This is feasible, subject to the assumption of square pixels, and that focal length is consistent between the two sequences (this assumption is reasonable, as stereo capture rigs generally utilise the same type of camera for both views). This can then be combined with constraints on the rank of F, and the trace of E, to construct a Polynomial Eigenvalue Problem (PEP) which may be efficiently solved [14]. As with the estimation of F, this is solved in a RANSAC framework, with the inliers to the epipolar geometry $\hat{C}$ used as input.

Unfortunately, in general 3D footage it is very common for cameras to be in a near-parallel configuration. This adversely affects the stability of the PEP, which (although deterministic) may become sensitive to changes in the input correspondences $\hat{C}$. In other words, for a given $\hat{C}$ a particular E is estimated consistently. However, adding or removing a small number of points from $\hat{C}$ can in some cases lead to significant differences in the estimated E. Luckily, the offline nature of the auto-calibration system, coupled with efficient PEP solvers, mean the process can be repeated a number of times. Each iteration finds a slightly different F and $\hat{C}$ which in turn leads to a different E.

Figure 3 shows the distribution of focal lengths estimated over 1000 repetitions, for two sequence pairs with different levels of zoom. The distribution of focal lengths arising due to the near-parallel camera configuration, follows the log-normal distribution which should be expected from a multiplicative entity such as the focal length. As such, we can achieve robustness to near-parallel cameras, by taking the mode of this distribution, for each sequence pair. In our experiments we use 100 calibration repetitions to model this distribution, which takes a few minutes in our single thread Matlab implementation.

Finally, given our robust estimate of E it is possible to estimate the projections matrices P^l and P^r for the cameras [12]. This leads to 4 possible solutions as shown in Figure 4. We select the solution that maximizes the number of corresponding point pairs $\hat{C}$ intersecting in front of the cameras,

$$P^l, P^r = \underset{P'^l, P'^r}{\arg\max} \sum_{(s_i^l, s_i^r) \in \hat{C}} \operatorname{sign}(d_l) + \operatorname{sign}(d_r), \tag{5}$$

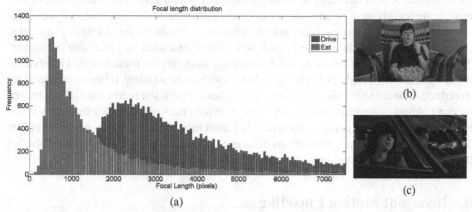

Fig. 3. Distribution of estimated focal lengths over 20000 repetitions, on the 2 different sequences pairs shown in B and C (wide-angle, close-up *Eat* shot, and extreme zoom *Drive* shot).

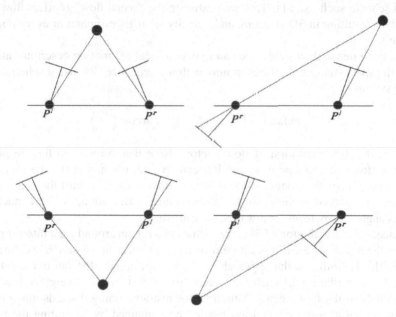

Fig. 4. The 4 possible solutions for stereo camera projection matrices, with a given E matrix. Note that only one solution leads to the 3D point being in front of both cameras [12].

where d_l and d_r are the distances along the rays defined by homogeneous points $\bar{s}_i^l$, $\bar{s}_i^r$ and $\mathcal{D}$ is the 3D position of the rays intersection,

$$d_l \bar{s}_i^l = P'^l \mathcal{D} \qquad \text{and} \qquad d_r \bar{s}_i^r = P'^r \mathcal{D}. \qquad (6)$$

The proposed approach to stereo sequence calibration has some limitations. Firstly, lens distortion is not included in the model. This is acceptable for a wide range of footage from Kinect devices and broadcast sources, which generally exhibit little distortion, however this may be an issue for upcoming 3D mobile devices. Secondly, in order to exploit correspondences over entire sequences, a consistent focal length is assumed (i.e. no zooming). In theory the technique could be extended by collecting correspondences within a sliding window, and estimating a time varying focal length. However, to obtain a sufficient number of correspondences within the window, it becomes necessary to reduce robustness by allowing weaker matches. Finally, the reconstructions achieved by our calibration technique, are only consistent with each other up to a similarity transform (reconstructions using a generic calibration are consistent up to a homography). The removal of projective distortions does greatly reduce the variability in the data, but the remaining scale ambiguity still must be addressed during encoding.

4   Invariant Motion Encoding

The estimated calibration can be used in conjunction with an efficient 3D motion estimation scheme such as [11]. This will estimate the "scene flow" (optical flows 3D counterpart) resulting in 3D structure and velocity (u, v, w) estimates at every point in the scene.

Given these dense flow fields, we can extract a local 3D motion descriptor around each of the spatio-temporal interest points within a sequence. We use a spherical coordinate system

$$\phi = \arctan\left(\frac{v}{u}\right) \quad \text{and} \quad \psi = \arctan\left(\frac{w}{v}\right), \tag{7}$$

to describe the 3D orientation of flow vectors. Note that ϕ refers to the "in plane" orientation (from the viewpoint of the left camera) i.e. when ϕ is $0°$, the motion is toward to the top of the image, when ϕ is $90°$ the motion is toward the right of the image, etc. In contrast ψ refers to the "out of plane" orientation, i.e. how much the motion is angled away from, or towards, the camera.

We encode the distribution of 3D orientations in a region around each interest point, capturing the nature of local motion field using a spherical histogram H as shown in Figure 5. This is similar to the approach used for shape context [3], but in the velocity domain. The contribution of each flow vector to the histogram is weighted based on the magnitude of the flow vector. Although this histogramming discards much of the spatial information, some general attributes are maintained by separating the region into several neighbouring blocks, and encoding each of them independently as $H_{1...n}$. These sub-region spherical histograms are then combined to form the overall descriptor H. It should be noted that placing histogram bins at regular angular intervals in this way leads to the bins covering unequal areas of the sphere's surface. An exaggerated version of this effect can be seen in Figure 5a, although in practice fewer bins are used and the difference is less pronounced. In the future regular or semi-regular sphere tessellations could be considered to remove this effect [25].

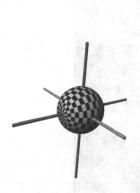

(a) Spherical orientation histogram   (b) An encoded motion field

Fig. 5. (a) The spherical orientation histogram. Different orientation bins are illustrated with alternating white and black squares. The ϕ orientation relates to rotation around the w axis (which points away from the camera). This leads to movement between the cells of one concentric rings in the histogram. The ψ orientation relates to rotation around the u axis, i.e. moving between concentric rings. (b) a scene divided into a 3 by 3 grid of subregions, with the motion of each subregion aggregated (for clarity aggregated motions are shown in 2D).

At this stage we introduce our first layer of invariance. By normalising the local descriptors, we are able to resolve the scale ambiguity which remained in our auto-calibration of Section 3. As mentioned previously, our motion fields are only consistent up to a similarity transform. However, the normalised spherical histograms,

$$\bar{H} = \frac{H}{|H|} \tag{8}$$

are consistent up to a 3D rotation, making these 3D motion descriptors much more comparable between camera configurations, and thus suitable for "in the wild" recognition. In addition to this, the normalised features provide invariance to the speed at which actions are performed, as only the shape and not the value of the motion field is encoded. This is again very import for "in the wild" recognition, with many different actors, each of whom have their own action style.

4.1 Rotational Invariance

Next we look at including viewpoint invariance in our 3D motion features (i.e. removing the final 3D rotation ambiguity, and making the descriptors completely consistent). This is one of the biggest challenges for "in the wild" action recognition. The the same action viewed from different angles looks completely different. However, as we are using the underlying 3D motion field, it is possible to modify our feature encoding to be invariant to such changes.

Fig. 6. $\bar{H}^r$ The subregions of the encoded motion field are re-arranged such that the region of maximum motion occurs first. This provides some degree of invariance to camera roll.

We firstly encode invariance to camera roll (i.e. rotation around the z axis) by cycling the order of the subregion histograms $H_{1...n}$ such that the the subregion containing the largest amount of motion occurs first. This re-arranged, roll-invariant, descriptor is referred to as $\bar{H}^r$ (see Figure 6).

We can follow a similar approach for the flow vectors within the subregion histograms, to make the direction of the motions as well as their positions, rotationally-invariant. If we find the strongest motion vector in H and label its 3D orientation as $\hat{\phi},\hat{\psi}$ then we can redefine our local orientations in relation to this flow vector,

$$\phi^p = \arctan\left(\frac{v}{u} - \hat{\phi}\right) \quad \text{and} \quad \psi^p = \arctan\left(\frac{w}{v} - \hat{\psi}\right). \tag{9}$$

The resulting descriptors $\bar{H}^p$ obtained when encoding ϕ^p, ψ^p makes the flow vectors robust to camera pitch (rotation around the x axis) in addition to roll, as shown in Figure 7.

However, due to the separation of ϕ and ψ our descriptors are still not resistant to camera pans (rotation around the y axis, which at 90 degrees causes ϕ orientation to become ψ orientation). In addition, normalising based on the maximum flow vector is sensitive to outliers in the flow field. As such, our final approach is to perform PCA on the local region of the motion field, extracting 3 new basis vectors u', v', w'. Computing orientation using these basis vectors,

$$\phi' = \arctan\left(\frac{v'}{u'}\right) \quad \text{and} \quad \psi' = \arctan\left(\frac{w'}{v'}\right), \tag{10}$$

leads to a descriptor $\bar{H}'$ which is invariant to all 3 types of camera viewpoint change, and also robust to outlier motions. See Figure 8 for an illustration.

Fig. 7. $\bar{H}^p$ The orientation $(\hat{\phi}, \hat{\psi})$ of the strongest motion vector in the scene, is used to normalise the orientation histograms, providing invariance to camera pitch and roll

4.2   Holistic Sequence Encoding

Whichever local descriptors are used, the final representation of the sequence is formed by a holistic Bag-of-words encoding. The sequence is described in terms of the frequency of occurrence for various exemplar descriptors (called the codebook). As in the case of the local descriptors, this space-time accumulation serves to provide invariance to spatio-temporal translations, scaling *etc.* but also implies a loss of relational information. To somewhat mitigate this, the sequence is divided into space-time blocks, each of which is encoded independently to provide the final description of the sequence.

5   Results

We evaluate our technique on the recently released Hollywood 3D dataset, which contains over an hour of "in the wild" action footage, taken from 3D broadcasts, covering 14 action categories. We compare our 3D motion features estimated using a single generic calibration, and estimated with sequence specific auto-calibration[1], against the current state of the art results on the dataset [13] which uses auto-encoders to implicitly model uncalibrated structural information. We also include results for a baseline method using 2D motion information from optical flow.

Performance is evaluated in terms of Average Precision [6] for each class. Classification is performed using an SVM with an RBF kernel, and encoding uses a Mahalonobis distance function and a codebook of 40000 elements, facilitating comparison with [10]. For the feature descriptors each subregion histogram uses 4×4 bins in the ϕ and ψ orientations, leading to a motion feature vector of 144 elements.

---

[1] Estimated calibrations are available at http://cvssp.org/Hollywood3D/

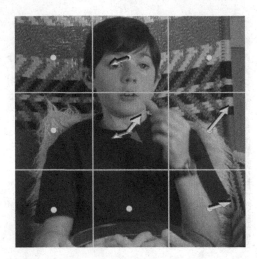

Fig. 8. $\bar{H}'$ A new set of 3D axes is chosen using PCA, relating to the dominant 3D motion orientations in the scene. This provides complete invariance to camera viewpoint change.

In Table 1 we can see that the raw 3D motion features ($\bar{H}$ -uncal), directly attainable from the dataset with a generic calibration, perform rather poorly, offering only a minor improvement over 2D motion based features (HOF[10]). The use of our proposed stereo sequence auto-calibration ($\bar{H}$) dramatically improves performance, more than doubling the average precision, by removing the projective distortion effects on the motion field. This helps to explain why 3D motion estimation techniques have not previously been exploited for "in the wild" action recognition, despite the fact that actions are generally defined by their 3D motions. The results also show that the unnormalised features (H), which are not scale invariant, perform uniformly worse than their normalised counterparts. It's worth noting, however, that Hollywood 3D doesn't contain the *Run/Jog/Walk* ambiguities of some datasets. Instead the wide range of viewpoints and zooms present in the data favour the more consistent $\bar{H}$ features.

The viewpoint invariant encoding schemes of Section 4.1 (upgrading the motion fields to fully consistent, rather than "up to a rotation") provide more modest improvements. Including roll invariance ($\bar{H}^r$) gives only a small performance increase, probably because broadcast footage such as that contained in the Hollywood-3D dataset contains few camera rolls. It may be expected that this scheme would prove more valuable in other scenarios such as on mobile devices. Attempting to include pitch invariance ($\bar{H}^p$) by normalising motion orientations actually reduces performance on many of the action classes. This is likely because normalising by the maximum motion makes the technique susceptible to outliers in the motion field. It is interesting to note however, that there is a marked improvement for a small number of actions such as *Run* and *Swim*. This may be because these actions experience greater variation in camera pitch (for example running shots being seen from above, and swimming shots from underwater). The final scheme ($\bar{H}'$), including full viewpoint invariance by estimating new motion orientation axes, provides the greatest performance, with more than 40 % improvement over the previously state of the art SAE-MD(av) [13] technique. It is interesting to note

Table 1. Per class Average Precision scores using various types of features encodings, including 2D motions [10], implicit depth and motion encoding [13], uncalibrated 3D motions, Unnormalised 3D motions, and calibrated motions encoding varying levels of invariance to camera viewpoint change

Action	HOF [10]	SAE-MD(av) [13]	$\bar{H}$-uncal	$\bar{H}$	H	$\bar{H}^r$	$\bar{H}^p$	$\bar{H}'$
NoAction	12.5	12.8	13.0	18.0	16.2	17.2	15.3	**21.2**
Run	18.0	50.4	21.5	44.3	41.1	40.8	55.9	**63.1**
Punch	2.9	38.0	10.9	48.7	45.6	51.6	52.1	**54.2**
Kick	3.6	7.9	8.1	18.2	18.2	**19.9**	18.1	**19.9**
Shoot	16.3	35.5	24.4	27.1	26.5	30.2	27.9	**31.0**
Eat	3.6	7.0	5.5	24.2	24.1	24.0	23.1	**24.2**
Drive	35.1	59.6	45.4	**62.3**	58.4	62.0	50.2	60.8
UsePhone	8.1	23.9	7.8	18.8	18.2	19.3	18.2	**22.3**
Kiss	6.7	16.4	7.0	24.2	24.1	24.0	26.3	**31.3**
Hug	2.6	7.0	3.5	21.8	21.0	22.2	23.8	**32.4**
StandUp	8.8	34.2	7.1	49.1	47.0	**51.8**	49.0	50.0
SitDown	4.3	7.0	4.8	16.3	14.1	17.9	16.9	**18.1**
Swim	6.4	29.5	14.0	28.8	27.1	30.0	**43.2**	43.0
Dance	2.8	36.3	3.7	45.3	41.8	44.2	**48.1**	44.9
Overall	9.4	26.1	12.6	31.9	30.2	32.5	33.4	**36.9**

that all of these encoding schemes actually *throw away* some of the information present within the original features. However, for the task of "in the wild" action recognition, camera viewpoint invariance outweighs this, by making it easier to generalise between sequences.

6 Conclusions

In this paper we have demonstrated that 3D motion is a powerful tool for recognising the actions being performed in a scene. However, in order for it to be truly exploited within the field of "in the wild" action recognition, appropriate sequence calibration techniques must be employed. To this end we introduce an approach for stereo sequence calibration which is robust to near parallel cameras setups, and we make available the estimated calibrations for the entirety of the Hollywood-3D dataset.

We have also shown that one of the biggest issues for "in the wild" recognition, is the intra-class variability. By using viewpoint invariant encoding schemes, we can significantly improve the value of our 3D motion features, particularly for actions which are commonly viewed from different angles.

In the future it would be useful to explore more advanced holistic encoding schemes for sequences, preserving the invariances encoded in our 3D motion features without discarding so much relational information. It would also be interesting to investigate online approaches to auto-calibration, allowing the calibration to change within sequences. This would prove valuable for sequences which include zooming cameras, and also in domains where the cameras are not rigidly attached together and may move independently (for example surveillance cameras and co-operating drones).

Acknowledgements. This work was supported by the EPSRC project "Learning to Recognise Dynamic Visual Content from Broadcast Footage" (EP/I011811/1).

References

1. BMVC, September 3-7 (2012)
2. Basha, T., Avidan, S., Hornung, A., Matusik, W.: Structure and motion from scene registration. In: 2012 IEEE Conference on Computer Vision and Pattern Recognition (CVPR), pp. 1426–1433 (June 2012)
3. Belongie, S., Malik, J., Puzicha, J.: Shape matching and object recognition using shape contexts. PAMI 24(4), 509–522 (2002)
4. Cheng, Z., Qin, L., Ye, Y., Huang, Q., Tian, Q.: Human daily action analysis with multi-view and color-depth data. In: Fusiello, A., Murino, V., Cucchiara, R. (eds.) ECCV 2012 Ws/Demos, Part II. LNCS, vol. 7584, pp. 52–61. Springer, Heidelberg (2012)
5. Dalal, N., Triggs, B., Schmid, C.: Human detection using oriented histograms of flow and appearance. In: Leonardis, A., Bischof, H., Pinz, A. (eds.) ECCV 2006. LNCS, vol. 3952, pp. 428–441. Springer, Heidelberg (2006)
6. Everingham, M., Van Gool, L., Williams, C.K.I., Winn, J., Zisserman, A.: The PASCAL visual object classes (VOC) challenge. International Journal of Computer Vision 88(2), 303–338 (2010)
7. Gilbert, A., Illingworth, J., Bowden, R.: Action recognition using mined hierarchical compound features. PAMI 33(5), 883 –897 (may 2011)
8. Gorelick, L., Blank, M., Shechtman, E., Irani, M., Basri, R.: Actions as space-time shapes. PAMI 29(12), 2247–2253 (2007)
9. Hadfield, S., Bowden, R.: Kinecting the dots: Particle based scene flow from depth sensors. In. In: Proceedings, International Conference on Computer Vision, Barcelona, Spain, November 6-13 (2011)
10. Hadfield, S., Bowden, R.: Hollywood 3d: Recognizing actions in 3d natural scenes. In: Proceedings of the Conference on Computer Vision and Pattern Recognition (CVPR), Oregon, USA, June 22-28 (2013)
11. Hadfield, S., Bowden, R.: Scene particles: Unregularized particle based scene flow estimation. IEEE Trans. on Pattern Analysis and Machine Intelligence 36(3), 564–576 (2014)
12. Hartley, R., Zisserman, A.: Multiple View Geometry in computer vision. Cambridge University press (2000)
13. Konda, K., Memisevic, R.: Learning to combine depth and motion. arXiv preprint arXiv:1312.3429 (2013)
14. Kukelova, Z., Bujnak, M., Pajdla, T.: Polynomial eigenvalue solutions to the 5-pt and 6-pt relative pose problems. In: BMVC, pp. 1–10 (2008)
15. Laptev, I., Lindeberg, T.: Space-time interest points. In: Proc. Ninth IEEE Int Computer Vision Conf, pp. 432–439 (2003)
16. Laptev, I., Marszalek, M., Schmid, C., Rozenfeld, B.: Learning realistic human actions from movies. In: Proc. IEEE Conf. Computer Vision and Pattern Recognition CVPR 2008, pp. 1–8 (2008)

17. Laptev, I., Perez, P.: Retrieving actions in movies. In: Proc. IEEE 11th Int. Conf. Computer Vision ICCV 2007. pp. 1–8 (2007)
18. Lebeda, K., Matas, J., Chum, O.: Fixing the locally optimized ransac. In: Bowden, et al. (eds.) [1], pp. 1013–1023
19. Li, W., Zhang, Z., Liu, Z.: Action recognition based on a bag of 3D points. In: 2010 IEEE Computer Society Conference on Computer Vision and Pattern Recognition Workshops (CVPRW), pp. 9–14. IEEE (2010)
20. Lowe, D.G.: Distinctive image features from scale-invariant keypoints. IJCV 60(2), 91–110 (2004)
21. Lukins, T., Fisher, R.: Colour constrained 4D flow. In: Proc. BMVC, Oxford, UK, September 6-8, pp. 340–348 (2005)
22. Messing, R., Pal, C., Kautz, H.: Activity recognition using the velocity histories of tracked keypoints. In: Proc. IEEE 12th Int. Computer Vision Conf, pp. 104–111 (2009)
23. Oreifej, O., Liu, Z.: Hon4d: Histogram of oriented 4d normals for activity recognition from depth sequences. In: 2013 IEEE Conference on Computer Vision and Pattern Recognition (CVPR), pp. 716–723. IEEE (2013)
24. Oshin, O., Gilbert, A., Bowden, R.: Capturing the relative distribution of features for action recognition. In: Proc. IEEE Int Automatic Face & Gesture Recognition and Workshops (FG 2011) Conf., pp. 111–116 (2011)
25. Saff, E.B., Kuijlaars, A.B.: Distributing many points on a sphere. The Mathematical Intelligencer 19(1), 5–11 (1997)
26. Sapienza, M., Cuzzolin, F., Torr, P.: Learning discriminative space-time actions from weakly labelled videos. In: Proc. BMVC [1]
27. Schuchert, T., Aach, T., Scharr, H.: Range flow in varying illumination: Algorithms and comparisons. PAMI, 1646–1658 (2009)
28. Schuldt, C., Laptev, I., Caputo, B.: Recognizing human actions: a local SVM approach. In: Proc. 17th Int. Conf. Pattern Recognition ICPR 2004, vol. 3, pp. 32–36 (2004)
29. Scovanner, P., Ali, S., Shah, M.: A 3-dimensional SIFT descriptor and its application to action recognition. In: Proceedings of the 15th International Conference on Multimedia, Multimedia 2007, pp. 357–360. ACM, New York (2007)
30. Torr, P., Zisserman, A.: Robust computation and parametrization of multiple view relations. In: Sixth International Conference on Computer Vision, pp. 727–732. IEEE (1998)
31. Vieira, A.W., Nascimento, E.R., Oliveira, G.L., Liu, Z., Campos, M.F.: Stop: Space-time occupancy patterns for 3d action recognition from depth map sequences. Progress in Pattern Recognition, Image Analysis, Computer Vision, and Applications, 252–259 (2012)
32. Wang, J., Liu, Z., Chorowski, J., Chen, Z., Wu, Y.: Robust 3D action recognition with random occupancy patterns. In: Fitzgibbon, A., Lazebnik, S., Perona, P., Sato, Y., Schmid, C. (eds.) ECCV 2012, Part II. LNCS, vol. 7573, pp. 872–885. Springer, Heidelberg (2012)
33. Willems, G., Tuytelaars, T., Van Gool, L.: An efficient dense and scale-invariant spatio-temporal interest point detector. In: Forsyth, D., Torr, P., Zisserman, A. (eds.) ECCV 2008, Part II. LNCS, vol. 5303, pp. 650–663. Springer, Heidelberg (2008)
34. Yang, X., Zhang, C., Tian, Y.: Recognizing actions using depth motion maps-based histograms of oriented gradients. In: Proceedings of the 20th ACM International Conference on Multimedia, pp. 1057–1060. ACM (2012)

Detecting Social Actions of Fruit Flies

Eyrun Eyjolfsdottir[1], Steve Branson[1], Xavier P. Burgos-Artizzu[1],
Eric D. Hoopfer[1], Jonathan Schor[1], David J. Anderson[1,2], and Pietro Perona[1]

[1] California Institute of Technology, Pasadena, California, USA
[2] Howard Hughes Medical Institute (HHMI)

Abstract. We describe a system that tracks pairs of fruit flies and automatically detects and classifies their actions. We compare experimentally the value of a frame-level feature representation with the more elaborate notion of 'bout features' that capture the structure within actions. Similarly, we compare a simple sliding window classifier architecture with a more sophisticated structured output architecture, and find that window based detectors outperform the much slower structured counterparts, and approach human performance. In addition we test our top performing detector on the CRIM13 mouse dataset, finding that it matches the performance of the best published method. Our Fly-vs-Fly dataset contains 22 hours of video showing pairs of fruit flies engaging in 10 social interactions in three different contexts; it is fully annotated by experts, and published with articulated pose trajectory features.

1 Introduction

Machine understanding of human behavior is potentially the most useful and transformative application of computer vision. It will allow machines to be better aware of their environment, enable rich and natural human-machine interaction, and it will unleash new applications in a number of industries including automotive, entertainment, surveillance and assisted living. Development of automated vision systems that can understand human behavior requires progress in object detection, pose estimation, tracking, action classification and detection, and activity analysis. Progress on the latter (actions and activities) is hampered by two difficulties. First, tracking and pose estimation is very difficult in humans due to variation in clothing, the amount of occlusion in natural environments and in social conditions, and the sheer complexity and number of human body motions. Second, it is difficult (both technically and legally) to film large numbers of humans acting spontaneously while they perform interesting activities. As a result, human action datasets are small and unrepresentative, especially when social behavior is concerned (see Table 1).

A good strategy for computer vision researchers to make progress on behavior analysis is to shift their attention to the simpler world of laboratory animals [1]. We collaborate with behavioral neurobiologists who are interested in measuring and analyzing behavior across genotypes, in order to understand the link between genes, brains and behavior. One of their most popular model organism is the

D. Fleet et al. (Eds.): ECCV 2014, Part II, LNCS 8690, pp. 772–787, 2014.

fruit fly, Drosophila melanogaster; it is easy to care for, has a fast life cycle, and exhibits a wide range of behaviors despite having merely 10^5 neurons. Through this collaboration we have put together a large annotated dataset of fruit flies interacting spontaneously in controlled environments. This dataset allows us to study natural actions and develop insight into how to represent, segment and classify them. If our effort is successful, we can both advance the state of the art in human action analysis and provide biologists with tools for automatic labeling of actions, enabling them to do experiments at a scale which would otherwise be extremely expensive or impossible.

In this paper we describe an end-to-end approach for detecting the actions of fruit flies from video. The main contributions of our study are:

1. We consider two different action detection architectures: sliding window detectors and structured output detectors. By comparing five variants of the two architectures on our dataset, we find that sliding window detectors outperform the structured output detectors, in spite of being orders of magnitude faster.

2. We describe *bout features* that extract statistical patterns from frame-level features over an interval of time, and emphasize the similarities of bouts within an action class. Our experiments show that actions cannot be well detected using frame-level features alone, and that bout features improve performance by 28%.

3. We discuss pitfalls of measures commonly used for benchmarking action detection in continuous video and demonstrate which measures are most suitable, suggesting a protocol for comparing the performance of different algorithms.

4. We introduce Caltech Fly-vs-Fly Interactions (Fly-vs-Fly for short), a dataset containing 22 hours of fruit flies interacting spontaneously and sporadically. It comes with complete labeling of 10 actions, annotated by neurobiologists, and a second layer of annotations that can be used as a reference point for action detection performance. Along with the videos and annotations we publish a number of time-varying trajectory features, computed from the tracked pose (position, orientation, wing angles, etc.) of the flies. The dataset is available at `www.vision.caltech.edu/Video_Datasets/Fly-vs-Fly`.

2 Related Work

Datasets – A large number of human action datasets have been published. KTH [2] and Weizmann [3] are early contributions that have been extensively used, but they are very small and consist of pre-segmented clips of acted actions. Hollywood 2 [4], Olympic Sports [5], HMDB51 [6], and UCF-101 [7], contain pre-segmented clips of natural actions, making them suitable for action classification, but not for detection and segmentation of actions, while UT-interactions [8] contains continuous social interactions that are acted. VIRAT [9] contains hours of continuous video of humans behaving naturally and intermittently, lending itself well to action detection research; however, the pose of the subjects cannot yet be robustly tracked and the human motion that can be explored is limited; furthermore, VIRAT does not contain social actions. HumanEva [10], HDM05 [11],

TUM Kitchen [12], CMU MMAC [13], and CAD-60/120 [14,15] are continuous and come with fully tracked skeletons which makes them useful for analyzing a range of human motions; however, these datasets are small, and their actions are acted. Table 1 compares details of the mentioned datasets.

The publicly available datasets of animal behavior video are Honeybee Dance [16], UCSD mice [17], Home-cage behaviors [18], and CRIM13 [1]. The latter two are suitable for action detection, containing long videos of spontaneous mouse actions, but both are parameterized with only the tracked centroid of the subject and spatial-temporal features. A large and well annotated dataset containing unsegmented, spontaneous, social actions, that includes tracking of articulated body motion has not yet been published. Our dataset aims to fill that place.

Table 1. Synoptic table of action datasets shown in chronological order, grouped by human vs. animal. Properties desired for detecting realistic social actions from articulated pose are highlighted in green.

Dataset	Year	#Citations	Duration	#Actions⁺	Natural	Social	Continuous	Articulated pose
KTH	2004	1634	3 hours*	6	x	x	x	x
Weizmann	2005	986	5 minutes*	10	x	x	x	x
HumanEva	2006	583	22 minutes	6	x	x	✓	✓
HDM05	2007	107	3 hours	70	x	x	✓	✓
TUM Kitchen	2009	98	1 hour*	13	x	x	✓	✓
CMU MMAC	2009	97	6 hours*	16**	x	x	✓	✓
Hollywood 2(1)	2009	436(1327)	20 hours	12	✓	✓	x	x
Olympic Sports	2010	196	2 hours*	16	✓	x	x	x
UT Interactions	2010	41	20 minutes	6	x	✓	✓	x
HMDB51	2011	137	2 hours	51	✓	✓	x	x
VIRAT	2011	91	29 hours	23	✓	x	✓	x
UCF-101(50,11)	2012	40(57,477)	27 hours	101	✓	✓	x	x
CAD-60/120	2011/13	175/34	2 hours*	22**	x	x	✓	✓
UCSD mice	2005	1458	2 hours	5	✓	x	x	x
Honeybee	2008	61	3 minutes	3	✓	x	✓	x
Home-cage	2010	60	13 hours	8	✓	x	✓	x
CRIM13	2012	15	37 hours	12	✓	✓	✓	x
Fly-vs-Fly	2014	-	22 hours	10	✓	✓	✓	✓

*estimated upper limit, **sub-activities (actions/verbs), ⁺excluding the null category

Action Detection – A common approach to action detection is frame-by-frame classification, where each frame is classified based on features extracted from the frame itself, or from a time window around it: Dankert et al. detected actions of fruit flies using manually set thresholds on frame-level features, along with nearest neighbor comparison [19]; Burgos et al. used boosting and auto-context on sliding windows for detecting actions between mice [1]; and Kabra et al. also use window based boosting for detecting actions of fruit flies in their interactive behavior annotation tool, JAABA [20]. More sophisticated approaches globally optimize over possible temporal segmentations, outputting structured sequences of actions: Jhuang et al. used an SVMHMM, described in [21], for detecting actions of single housed mice [18]; Hoai et al. used a multi-class SVM with structured inference for segmenting the dance of the honeybee [22]; and Shi et al. used a discriminative semi-Markov model for segmenting human actions [23].

We implemented three variants of the above approaches, specifically comparing a sliding window SVM detector against two structured output SVM detectors, expecting the latter to improve frame-wise consistency and better capture structured actions. For reference, we compare our results with the methods described in [20] and [1] and with the performance of trained novice annotators.

3   Fly-vs-Fly

In collaboration with biologists we have collected a new dataset, Fly-vs-Fly, which contains a total of 22 hours (1.5m frames recorded at 200Hz and 2.2m frames at 30Hz) of 47 pairs of fruit flies interacting. The videos are organized into three subsets, each of which was collected for a different study:

Boy meets boy is designed to study the sequence of actions between two male flies, whose behaviors range from courtship to aggression. The flies are placed in a 4x5 cm^2 chamber with a food patch in its center and walls coated with Fluon, constraining the flies to walking on the floor [24]. It contains six 20 minute videos recorded at 200Hz with 12 pix/mm (24 pixels covering the 2mm fly body length).

Aggression contains videos of two hyper aggressive males [25] and is used to quantify the effect of genetic manipulation on their behavior. The flies are placed in a circular 16mm diameter chamber with uniform food surface [26]. It consists of ten 30 minute videos recorded at 30Hz with 8 pix/mm.

Courtship videos contain a female and a male, which in some cases are wild type and in the rest are so-called hyper courters [25]. This set of videos was used to study how genetic manipulation affects male courtship behavior. It consists of 31 videos recorded with the same chamber and video settings as Aggression.

The filming setups for these experiments are shown in Supplementary Figure 2.

3.1   Annotations

The entire dataset was annotated by, or under the supervision of, biologists, with 10 action classes that have been identified for the study of fruit fly interactions [27,28,19]: *wing threat, charge, lunge, hold,* and *tussle* (aggressive), *wing extension, circle, copulation attempt,* and *copulation* (courtship), and *touch* (neutral). Each action is described and visualized in Supplementary Figure 1.

Annotating a video involves finding all time intervals that contain an action of interest, also referred to as action *bouts*, and requires recording the start frame, end frame, and class label of each detected bout. The dataset is annotated such that actions can overlap, for instance tussling usually includes lunging, wing threat sometimes includes a charge, and wing extension and circling tend to overlap. Each action class takes up less than 2% of the total frames in a video, apart from touch (7%) and copulation (57%), and some classes have substantial intraclass variation, both in terms of duration and appearance. Figure 1 summarizes the dataset.

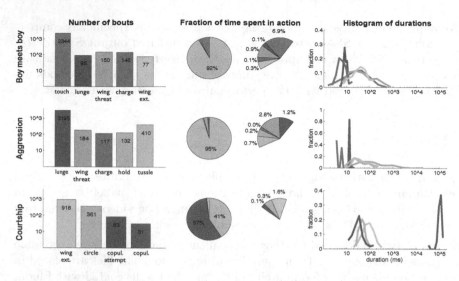

Fig. 1. Action statistics: *Left:* Number of bouts for each action. *Center:* Fraction of time a fly spends in each action, where the gray area represents the grab-bag category *other*. *Right:* Distribution of bout durations for each action class.

3.2   Feature Representation

For action classification, data representation is half the challenge. An ideal classifier is invariant of any intra-action variation, but to train such a classifier a complex model or large amounts of training data may be needed. Alternatively, this invariance can be encoded into the features. Following prior art [19,29,20] we have implemented a tool that tracks individual flies and segments them into body, wing, and leg pixels, which are parameterized further by fitting an oriented ellipse to the body component and line segments to the wing components.

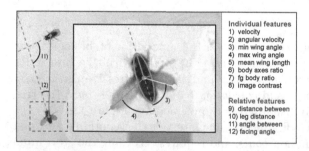

Fig. 2.   Illustration of features derived from the tracked fly skeletons, which are invariant of absolute position and orientation of the fly and relate the pose of the fly to that of the other fly.

From the tracking output we derive a set of features that are designed to be invariant of the absolute position and orientation of a fly, and relate its pose to that of the other fly. The features (illustrated in Figure 2) can be split into two categories: individual features which include the fly's *velocity, angular velocity, min and max wing angles, mean wing length, body axis ratio, foreground-body ratio,* and *image contrast* in a window around the fly; and relative features

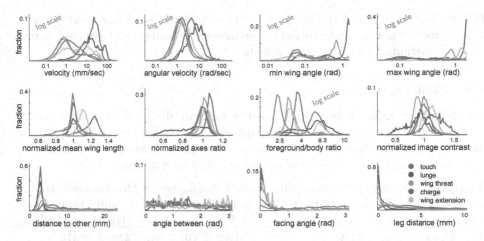

Fig. 3. Frame-wise feature distribution for the actions of the Boy meets boy sub-dataset, and the grab-bag action *other* shown in gray.

which relate one fly to the other with *distance between* their body centers, *leg distance* (shortest distance from its legs to the foreground of the other fly), *angle between*, and *facing angle*. Analysis of the feature distributions showed that the velocities, wing angles, and foreground-body ratio are better represented by their log values, becoming more normal distributed. Figure 3 shows the distribution of each feature, for all actions in the Boy meets boy sub-dataset, giving an idea of which features are important for which action. In addition, we take the first two time derivatives of each feature, resulting in a feature space of 36 *per-frame* features. The features are computed from the reference frame of each fly, yielding two asymmetrical feature vectors, and the actions we consider are always involve one fly 'performing' the action. Hence, an hour of video effectively results in 2 hours of labeled data.

Our software for tracking flies and annotating their actions is available, along with documentation, at `www.vision.caltech.edu/Tools/FlyTracker`.

4   Action Detection

In this paper we focus on detection by exhaustive classification, in particular we compare two different architectures: *Sliding window detection* which refers to classifying fixed size windows that move frame-by-frame over a video sequence, and *structured output detection* which refers to detection by optimizing over all possible segmentations of a sequence into actions. Both schemes involve a training algorithm that learns an action classifier from n labeled sequences, $\{(x_i, y_i)\}_{i \in \{1,\dots,n\}}$, and an inference algorithm that takes a new sequence x and predicts $y := \{y^j\} = \{(s^j, e^j, c^j)\}$, where y^j is the jth bout in the segmentation of x, s^j and e^j mark the start and end of the bout and c^j is its class label. We treat the problem of detecting different actions as disjoint detection problems, mainly because the data that we are interested in has many overlapping actions.

Before describing the detection architectures in detail we define *bout features* that aggregate per-frame features over an interval of frames, and are used in our implementation of both detection schemes.

4.1 Bout Features

We define a number of bout-level features that are designed to extract statistical patterns from an interval and emphasize the similarities of bouts within an action class, independent on bout duration. The following bout features, $\psi_k(x, t_{start}, t_{end})$, are functions of sequence x and interval $[t_{start} \; t_{end}]$:

Temporal region features capture statistics of frame-level features over subintervals, and emphasize patterns within an action composed of r subactions. They can be expressed as: $\{\text{op}(x(t_{start} + (i-1)\delta t : t_{start} + i\,\delta t - 1))\}_{i \in \{1,...,r\}}$, where $\delta t = (t_{end} - t_{start} + 1)/(r-1)$, $r \geq 1$, and op $\in \{\text{min, max, mean, std}\}$.

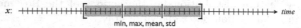

min, max, mean, std

Harmonic features are meant to capture harmonic actions and can be expressed as: $\sum_{i=1}^{r}(-1)^i \; \text{mean}(x(t_{start} + (i-1)\delta t : t_{start} + i\,\delta t - 1))$, where $\delta t = (t_{end} - t_{start} + 1)/(r-1)$ and $r \geq 1$.

Boundary features emphasize the change in features at the start and end of a bout, and help with locating boundaries. For a fixed δt, they can be expressed as: $\text{mean}(x(t_{start/end} : t_{start/end} + \delta t)) - \text{mean}(x(t_{start/end} - \delta t : t_{start/end}))$.

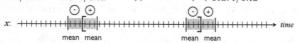

Bout change features capture the difference in features between the beginning and end of a bout, expressed as: $x(t_{end}) - x(t_{start})$.

Global difference features compare the mean of a bout to global statistics of data, expressed as: $\text{mean}(x(t_{start} : t_{end})) - \text{op}(x)$, where op $\in \{\text{min, max, mean}\}$.

Histogram features represent the normalized distribution of each feature within the bout, expressed as: $\text{hist}(x(t_{start} : t_{end}), \text{bins})$, where bins are extracted from the training data, such that an equal number of frames falls into each bin.

In our experiments we use three temporal region splits, $r \in \{1, 2, 3\}$, and set the number of histogram bins to be 2^3, resulting in a total of $K = 48$ bout functions. With K bout functions applied to each of the N per-frame features, the feature representation for a bout ends up being a $D = KN$ dimensional vector, ψ.

4.2 Sliding Window Framework

Our sliding window implementation has 4 main components: a *training* algorithm that learns a classifier from labeled sequences, a *classifier* module, an *inference* algorithm that predicts labels for unseen sequences, and a *post processing* module that promotes continuity in the prediction labels.

Training: The training algorithm converts each sequence of input labels, $\{y_i\} = \{(s^j, e^j, c^j)_i\}$, to indicator vectors, $\{z_i\}$, that specify whether a frame belongs to an action or not. It extracts normalized bout features over fixed sized windows surrounding each frame of all sequences, obtaining high dimensional data points whose labels are the same as those of the frames around which the windows were placed. With this data it trains a classifier using a bootstrapping scheme that overcomes memory limitations that may be associated with large data, and allows us to indirectly optimize with respect to performance measures that involve the number of predicted positives. At each iteration it learns a classifier from a subset of the data, using a learning algorithm suitable for the classifier type, applies it to all of the data and adds misclassified samples to the training set - repeating until the desired performance measure stops increasing.

Inference: The inference algorithm extracts bout features from a window around each frame in x, normalized with statistics from the training data, and classifies each window using the classifier obtained from the training step. The resulting sequence of scores is thresholded to obtain an action indicator vector, $\hat{z}$, whose connected components make up the predicted label sequence, $\hat{y}$, assigning each bout the label, start frame, and end frame of its component.

Post Processing: Classifying a sequence frame-by-frame often results in noisy labels, that is, within a bout of an action a few frames may be just below a threshold and therefore split the bout into multiple bouts. To account for this we fit an HMM to the scores to achieve smoother transitions: we convert scores to posterior probabilities, $P(x(t)|z(t) = 1) := 1/(1+\exp(-\text{score}(t)))$, $P(x(t)|z(t) = 0) := 1 - P((t)|z(t) = 1)$, compute prior probabilities, $P(z(1) = c)$, and transition matrix, $P(z(t + 1) = c_i|z(t) = c_j)$, from the training data, and run the Viterbi algorithm [30] to find the most probable frame-wise sequence of actions.

Classifier: The classifier module consists of a binary classifier and its associated learning algorithm. For comparison with our structured SVM implementation, we choose to use a linear SVM classifier, learnt using the LIBLINEAR implementation described in [31]. The classifier can be substituted by any other binary classifier, such as boosting, regression, neural net, or a generative model.

This approach can be converted to a frame-based detector, by simply substituting the bout features around a frame with its per-frame features.

4.3   Structured Output Framework

Structured output detectors differ from sliding windows in that they optimize over all possible segmentations of a sequence into action intervals, finding the best start and end frame of all bouts, allowing for varying sized intervals.

Structured SVM. We extend the structured SVM [32] to train a model that can be utilized for segmenting sequences into actions, by defining a *score* *function, $f(x, y)$*, which assigns high scores to good segmentations, and a *loss function, $\mathcal{L}(y, \hat{y})$*, which penalizes poor segmentations.

Training: The goal is to learn the weights w of a score function from a given training set, such that for each training example the score of the true segmentation y_i is higher than the score of any other segmentation y by at least $\mathcal{L}(y_i, y)$. If these constraints cannot be satisfied, a hinge loss is suffered. To learn these weights we use the primal structured SVM objective:

$$w^* \leftarrow \arg\min_w \|w\|^2 + C\frac{1}{n} \sum_{i=1}^{n} \left(\max_y \left[f(x_i, y) + \mathcal{L}(y_i, y) \right] - f(x_i, y_i) \right),$$

which we minimize using a cutting plane algorithm [32] that iteratively finds the most violated constraint: $\hat{y} = \arg\max_y \left[f(x_i, y) + \mathcal{L}(y_i, y) \right]$. Searching over all possible segmentations is intractable, but since our score- and loss functions are linear in the bouts of y, dynamic programming [33] can solve for the optimal y.

Score Function: We define a score function $f(x, y)$, which measures how well y segments x into actions and can be represented as the sum of a bout score, unary cost, transition cost, and duration cost, over all bouts in the segmentation:

$$f(x, y) = \sum_{(s^j, e^j, c^j) \in y} [w_{c^j} \cdot \psi(x, s^j, e^j) - \tau(c^j) - \lambda(c^{j-1}, (c^j)) - \gamma(c^j, s^j, e^j)].$$

Weights w_{c^j} are used to calculate the score for a bout of class c^j, $\tau(c^j)$ is the cost of detecting a bout of class c^j, $\lambda(c^{j-1}, c^j)$ is the cost of moving from action c^{j-1} to c^j, and $\gamma(c^j, s^j, e^j)$ is the cost of spending $e^j - s^j + 1$ frames in action c^j. These terms are inspired by a hidden semi Markov model, comparable to [23].

Loss function: The loss function penalizes discrepancies between ground truth segmentation y and a predicted segmentation $\hat{y}$, and should be constructed such that a small loss indicates satisfactory results. We define it as:

$$\mathcal{L}(y, \hat{y}) = \sum_{(s,e,c) \in y} \frac{\ell_{fn}^c}{e - s + 1} \left(\bigcap_{\hat{y}, \hat{c} \neq c} (s, e) \right) + \sum_{(\hat{s}, \hat{e}, \hat{c}) \in \hat{y}} \frac{\ell_{fp}^c}{\hat{e} - \hat{s} + 1} \left(\bigcap_{y, c \neq \hat{c}} (\hat{s}, \hat{e}) \right),$$

where $\bigcap_{\hat{y}, \hat{c} \neq c}(b, e)$ is the number of frames in $\hat{y}$ intersecting with $[b\ e]$ with different action class $\hat{c} \neq c$, ℓ_{fn}^c is the cost for missing a bout of class c, and $\ell_{fp}^{\hat{c}}$ is the cost for incorrectly detecting a bout of class $\hat{c}$. This loss function softly penalizes predictions where the start or end of the bout is slightly incorrect. On the other hand, since the loss is normalized by the bout duration, it effectively counts the number of incorrectly predicted bouts and, unlike a per-frame loss, long actions are not deemed to be more important than short ones.

Inference: Given a score function, $f(x, y)$, and an input x, the optimal segmentation can be found by solving $\hat{y} = \arg\max_y f(x, y)$. Again, similarly to the learning phase, searching over all possible segmentations is intractable but we can solve for y using dynamic programming.

Semi-structured SVM. This approach is a hybrid of the sliding window SVM and the structured SVM; its inference algorithm optimizes over possible segmentations of a sequence, using dynamic programming, but the classifiers are trained using a linear SVM on fixed bouts from the training set, similar to [22].

Training: We extract bout features from the positive bouts, $\{(s^{j_i}, e^{j_i})\}_i$, for each sequence x_i in the training set, and from randomly sampled negative bouts. We consider a bout as negative if its intersection with a positive bout is less than half of their union, so that large intervals containing positive bouts and small intervals that are parts of a positive bout are still considered as negatives. Inference involves considering all possible intervals of any duration as potential action bouts, however training on all such possible intervals would be intractable. Instead, we generate a limited number of randomly sampled negatives and use a bootstrapping training process that gradually adds useful negative samples. At each iteration we train a classifier on the current training data, run inference with the learnt classifier, and add falsely detected positives to the set of negative training samples - repeating until no new false positives are detected.

Inference: Here the goal is the same as in the structured SVM approach, to find the optimal segmentation of a new input sequence x, $\hat{y} = \arg\max_y f(x, y)$, but with a simpler score function: $f(x, y) = \sum_{(s^j, e^j, c^j) \in y} w_{c^j} \cdot \psi(x, s^j, e^j)$. Again, we solve this using dynamic programming. We speed up the inference by setting upper limits on the duration of an action, which we obtain from the training set.

5 Experiments and Analysis

5.1 Measures

The performance measure used to compare algorithms should favor desirable predictions; in the case of action detection for behavior analysis it is important that there are few false hits and misses compared to the number of true action instances, which becomes difficult the more sparsely actions occur in the data. We have generated a synthetic ground truth sequence with 5 sporadic action classes, and two different prediction sequences, to demonstrate the difference between three common measures: a *confusion matrix*, *ROC* curves, and *precision-recall* curves. This comparison shows that precision-recall most effectively emphasizes the large performance discrepancy between the two predictions (see Figure 4).

   Precision-recall curves, used for measuring detection performance for a single class, plot *precision* against *recall*, favoring minimum number of false positives and false negatives with respect to the number of positives. **ROC** curves are similar but instead of precision they plot the *false positive rate*, which places little emphasis on false positives when negatives take up vast majority of the frames. A **confusion matrix**, used in multi-class classification, is a square matrix whose entry (i, j) represents the fraction of ground truth instances of class i that are predicted as class j, and is commonly summarized by its diagonal mean. However, its diagonal effectively measures the recall of each class and fails to emphasize false positive instances which get absorbed into the grab-bag class *other*.

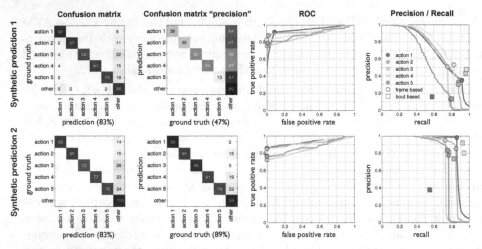

Fig. 4. Confusion matrices and ROC are unreliable diagnostics for assessing experimental results. Each row shows the result of a different synthetic experiment. The confusion matrices (first column) and the ROC (third column) suggest that both experiments yield the same result and hide the large difference in the number of false detections. This fact is revealed by the "precision" confusion matrix (second column) and by the precision-recall curve (fourth column). The last column also shows how bout-wise and frame-wise measurements can differ.

To account for this, one must also look at the 'dual' confusion matrix, where entry (i, j) represents the fraction of predicted instances of class i that belong to class j according to ground truth, in which case the diagonal effectively measures the precision of each class. We conclude that "precision" and "recall" confusion matrices are good measures for multi-class detection problems, where classes are mutually exclusive, but for experiments such as ours, where classes overlap and false positives are expensive, precision-recall curves are the best performance measurement tools.

For behavior analysis, correctly counting the number of action instances is equally important as correctly measuring the duration spent in an action, hence we must also measure the **bout-wise performance**. To do that we use an overlap criteria, that deems a ground truth bout (s_g, e_g, b) and predicted bout (s_p, e_p, b) to match only if, $\frac{min(e_g, e_p) - max(s_g, s_p)}{max(e_g, e_p) - min(s_g, s_p)} > threshold$. If multiple bouts fit that criteria, we match the one with the highest ratio. Figure 4 shows that there can be large discrepancies between frame-wise and bout-wise performance. This is the case when predicted bouts are more fragmented than ground truth bouts, or when bouts are consistently predicted to be shorter than, or offset from, the ground truth (see more detail in Supplementary Figure 3).

In order to rank different methods we combine precision and recall into a single value using the *F-score*, defined as $F_\beta = (1 + \beta^2) \cdot \frac{precision \cdot recall}{\beta^2 \cdot precision + recall}$, which for $\beta = 1$ represents the harmonic mean that favors balanced precision-recall combinations. To further combine bout-wise and frame-wise performance we define the *F*-score* as the harmonic mean of F1-frame and F1-bout.

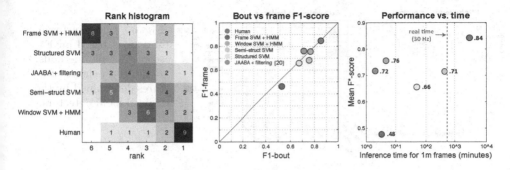

Fig. 5. Method comparison on the Fly-vs-Fly dataset. *Left*: Histogram of method ranks over all actions, based on their F*-score, ordered by mean rank. *Center*: Comparison of F1-scores of each method, averaged over all actions. *Right*: F*-score of each method as a function of inference time.

5.2 Method Comparison

Here we explore how a window based SVM compares to structured, and semi-structured SVMs, which we find very interesting as they all make use of linear classifiers and the same bout features, but differ in their training and inference procedures. In addition, we compare them with a frame based SVM to get a sense for how much bout features contribute to performance, and to JAABAs back-end [20], another window based detector, for comparison with methods currently deployed in action detection systems.

Each method's free parameters were optimized using a subset of the training data for validation, and we found that HMM post processing improved the mean F*-score of the window- and frame based SVMs by 11% and 3% respectively. For comparison with JAABA we trained detectors by substituting their boosting classifier implementation into the learning and inference modules of our window based framework. JAABA as presented in [20] does not include post processing, but here we apply a box filter suggested on their project website [34] for a fair bout-wise performance comparison, improving its mean F*-score by 6%.

To measure the performance of our action detectors, we computed bout- and frame-wise precision, recall and F1-scores, and the F*-score which can be used to rank the different methods. These measures, broken down for each behavior in Supplementary Figures 6-8, show considerable variation in method rank depending on the action. Here we summarize the results in a detector rank histogram (Figure 5), which shows the number of times each detector achieved each rank and orders methods according to their mean rank. For a finer resolution view of how the methods line up we show the mean F1-scores, averaged over all actions, and the mean F*-score as a function of time it takes to run the detector on 1 million frames. This view mostly preserves the rank observed in the rank histogram, but it also shows that most methods cluster around 70% performance, apart from humans at 84% and frame based SVM at 48%. In addition, it shows that the window based methods perform slightly better than the structured output counterparts, in spite of being orders of magnitude faster.

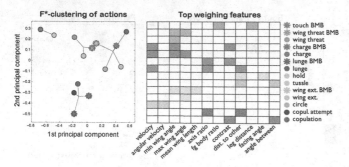

Fig. 6. *Left*: clustering of actions based on F*-score of all methods. *Right*: top weighted features determined by the trained SVM detectors.

These summary measures abstract away information about performance patterns between actions that may give insights into the different types of actions. To explore that, we cluster actions based on their F*-score for each method, by applying principal component analysis to the F*-matrix, and fitting k-means to the dimension-reduced matrix, splitting actions into 4 groups. Figure 6 shows that this clustering groups together lunge, charge, and copulation attempt, which all share the characteristic of being short and concise but poorly captured by the frame based detector, and, as one might expect, it groups actions (wing threat and wing extension) from different sub-datasets together. From the learnt detectors of the three different SVM approaches we found that the window based detector made most use of the bout statistics and histogram features, while structured ones used boundary dependent features to a similar extent, and that the top per-frame features used by all methods are those listed in Figure 6, showing that each feature is the highest contributing feature to at least one action.

5.3   Performance on CRIM13

Finally, to give a better idea of where these methods place within state of the art, we test the top ranked detector on the most recently published animal dataset, CRIM13, and compare our results with those presented in [1]. Actions in CRIM13 are non-overlapping, and the detection problem is treated as multiclass. To make a similar comparison we covert our binary action detectors to a single multi-class detector by fitting them to an HMM with 13 states. By shifting output scores of individual binary classifiers, before converting them to posterior probabilities, we can trade off the performance of different classes. We obtain the optimal shift-parameters by greedily maximizing w.r.t. the diagonal mean of the "recall" confusion matrix, to match the measure used in [1], and since we are interested in high precision-recall combination, we also optimize w.r.t. the mean F1-score of the "recall" and "precision" matrix diagonals. Figure 7 shows the confusion matrices produced for each of our optimization criteria, and Figure 8 shows our results compared with those presented in [1]. We ran our algorithm only on tracking features (TF) provided with the CRIM13 dataset, obtaining performance just above the top results reported in [1], which includes spatial-temporal features (STF), and 3.2% higher than their performance on tracking features alone. Optimizing w.r.t. F1-score results in approximately 6% F1-performance gain over the "recall" optimization.

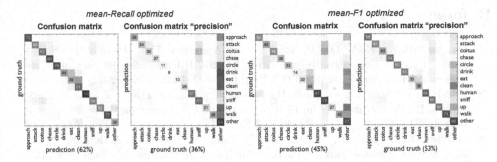

Fig. 7. Confusion matrices for Window SVM + HMM on the CRIM13 test dataset. *Left*: performance optimized w.r.t. the diagonal mean of confusion matrix. *Right*: performance optimized w.r.t. "recall" and "precision" confusion matrices.

Method	mean recall	mean F1
Boosting (TF) + Autocontext [1]	58.30%	-
Boosting (TF + STF) + Autocontext [1]	61.20%	-
Window SVM+HMM (recall shift)	**61.66%**	40.76%
Window SVM+HMM (F1 shift)	45.42%	47.22%

Fig. 8. Comparison of the window based SVM to the methods used in [1], showing performance on the CRIM13 test dataset.

6   Conclusions

We collected a large dataset of fruit fly videos that, with its natural and sporadic interactions and rich set of articulated pose features, fills a gap in existing datasets. We developed a framework for comparing action detection performance, showing that precision and recall are the best suited measures for evaluating detection algorithms, and that results should be reported both in terms of bout- and frame-wise performance. Using these measures, we showed that bout features highly improve performance upon frame-level features. We compared sliding window classifiers to the more sophisticated structured output detectors, and found that window based classifiers outperformed their structured counterparts, despite having much lower time complexity. This was surprising to us as the structured output methods allow for elastic sized windows which should better capture structure within bouts. A caveat is that the more complex actions in our dataset have low duration variation, therefore fixed sized window classifiers with good bout features may suffice. Our results also show (Supplementary Figures 6-8) that the structured output methods suffer from over-segmenting long bouts of actions that do not have much structure, which leads to a lower bout-wise performance. We believe this may be overcome by incorporating higher order Markov terms in the score function, and will explore that in future work. In our experiments, the top performing algorithm, a window based SVM + HMM, reached a 76% F*-score on Fly-vs-Fly, compared to 84% achieved by humans, and matches the performance of the best published method on CRIM13.

Acknowledgements. This work was supported by the ONR MURI Grant N00014-10-1-0933 and the Gordon and Betty Moore Foundation.

References

1. Burgos-Artizzu, X.P., Dollár, P., Lin, D., Anderson, D.J., Perona, P.: Social behavior recognition in continuous video. In: 2012 IEEE Conference on Computer Vision and Pattern Recognition (CVPR), pp. 1322–1329. IEEE (2012)
2. Schuldt, C., Laptev, I., Caputo, B.: Recognizing human actions: a local svm approach. In: Proceedings of the 17th International Conference on Pattern Recognition, ICPR 2004, vol. 3, pp. 32–36. IEEE (2004)
3. Gorelick, L., Blank, M., Shechtman, E., Irani, M., Basri, R.: Actions as space-time shapes. Transactions on Pattern Analysis and Machine Intelligence 29(12), 2247–2253 (2007)
4. Marszałek, M., Laptev, I., Schmid, C.: Actions in context. In: IEEE Conference on Computer Vision & Pattern Recognition (2009)
5. Niebles, J.C., Chen, C.W., Fei-Fei, L.: Modeling temporal structure of decomposable motion segments for activity classification. In: Daniilidis, K., Maragos, P., Paragios, N. (eds.) ECCV 2010, Part II. LNCS, vol. 6312, pp. 392–405. Springer, Heidelberg (2010)
6. Kuehne, H., Jhuang, H., Garrote, E., Poggio, T., Serre, T.: HMDB: a large video database for human motion recognition. In: Proceedings of the International Conference on Computer Vision (ICCV) (2011)
7. Soomro, K., Zamir, A.R., Shah, M.: Ucf101: A dataset of 101 human actions classes from videos in the wild. arXiv preprint arXiv:1212.0402 (2012)
8. Ryoo, M., Aggarwal, J.: Ut-interaction dataset, icpr contest on semantic description of human activities (sdha) (2010)
9. Oh, S., Hoogs, A., Perera, A., Cuntoor, N., Chen, C.C., Lee, J.T., Mukherjee, S., Aggarwal, J., Lee, H., Davis, L., et al.: A large-scale benchmark dataset for event recognition in surveillance video. In: 2011 IEEE Conference on Computer Vision and Pattern Recognition (CVPR), pp. 3153–3160. IEEE (2011)
10. Sigal, L., Black, M.J.: Humaneva: Synchronized video and motion capture dataset for evaluation of articulated human motion. Brown Univertsity TR 120 (2006)
11. Müller, M., Röder, T., Clausen, M., Eberhardt, B., Krüger, B., Weber, A.: Documentation mocap database hdm05 (2007)
12. Tenorth, M., Bandouch, J., Beetz, M.: The tum kitchen data set of everyday manipulation activities for motion tracking and action recognition. In: 2009 IEEE 12th International Conference on Computer Vision Workshops (ICCV Workshops), pp. 1089–1096. IEEE (2009)
13. De la Torre, F., Hodgins, J., Montano, J., Valcarcel, S., Forcada, R., Macey, J.: Guide to the carnegie mellon university multimodal activity (cmu-mmac) database. Tech. rep., Citeseer (2009)
14. Sung, J., Ponce, C., Selman, B., Saxena, A.: Unstructured human activity detection from rgbd images. In: 2012 IEEE International Conference on Robotics and Automation (ICRA), pp. 842–849. IEEE (2012)
15. Koppula, H.S., Gupta, R., Saxena, A.: Learning human activities and object affordances from rgb-d videos. arXiv preprint arXiv:1210.1207 (2012)
16. Oh, S.M., Rehg, J.M., Balch, T., Dellaert, F.: Learning and inferring motion patterns using parametric segmental switching linear dynamic systems. International Journal of Computer Vision 77(1-3), 103–124 (2008)
17. Dollár, P., Rabaud, V., Cottrell, G., Belongie, S.: Behavior recognition via sparse spatio-temporal features. In: VS-PETS (October 2005)

18. Jhuang, H., Garrote, E., Yu, X., Khilnani, V., Poggio, T., Steele, A.D., Serre, T.: Automated home-cage behavioural phenotyping of mice. Nature Communications 1, 68 (2010)
19. Dankert, H., Wang, L., Hoopfer, E.D., Anderson, D.J., Perona, P.: Automated monitoring and analysis of social behavior in drosophila. Nature Methods 6(4), 297–303 (2009)
20. Kabra, M., Robie, A.A., Rivera-Alba, M., Branson, S., Branson, K.: Jaaba: interactive machine learning for automatic annotation of animal behavior. Nature Methods (2012)
21. Altun, Y., Tsochantaridis, I., Hofmann, T., et al.: Hidden markov support vector machines. In: ICML, vol. 3, pp. 3–10 (2003)
22. Hoai, M., Lan, Z.Z., De la Torre, F.: Joint segmentation and classification of human actions in video. In: 2011 IEEE Conference on Computer Vision and Pattern Recognition (CVPR), pp. 3265–3272. IEEE (2011)
23. Shi, Q., Cheng, L., Wang, L., Smola, A.: Human action segmentation and recognition using discriminative semi-markov models. International Journal of Computer Vision 93(1), 22–32 (2011)
24. Hoyer, S.C., Eckart, A., Herrel, A., Zars, T., Fischer, S.A., Hardie, S.L., Heisenberg, M.: Octopamine in male aggression of drosophila. Current Biology 18(3), 159–167 (2008)
25. Hoopfer, E.D., Anderson, D.J.: Unpublished work
26. Asahina, K., Watanabe, K., Duistermars, B.J., Hoopfer, E., González, C.R., Eyjólfsdóttir, E.A., Perona, P., Anderson, D.J.: Tachykinin-expressing neurons control male-specific aggressive arousal in drosophila. Cell 156(1), 221–235 (2014)
27. Chen, S., Lee, A.Y., Bowens, N.M., Huber, R., Kravitz, E.A.: Fighting fruit flies: a model system for the study of aggression. Proceedings of the National Academy of Sciences 99(8), 5664–5668 (2002)
28. Hall, J.C.: The mating of a fly. Science 264(5166), 1702–1714 (1994)
29. Branson, K., Robie, A.A., Bender, J., Perona, P., Dickinson, M.H.: High-throughput ethomics in large groups of drosophila. Nature Methods 6(6), 451–457 (2009)
30. Viterbi, A.: Error bounds for convolutional codes and an asymptotically optimum decoding algorithm. IEEE Transactions on Information Theory 13(2), 260–269 (1967)
31. Fan, R.E., Chang, K.W., Hsieh, C.J., Wang, X.R., Lin, C.J.: Liblinear: A library for large linear classification. The Journal of Machine Learning Research 9, 1871–1874 (2008)
32. Tsochantaridis, I., Joachims, T., Hofmann, T., Altun, Y.: Large margin methods for structured and interdependent output variables. Journal of Machine Learning Research, 1453–1484 (2005)
33. Bellman, R.: Dynamic programming and lagrange multipliers. Proceedings of the National Academy of Sciences of the United States of America 42(10), 767 (1956)
34. http://jaaba.sourceforge.net

Progressive Mode-Seeking on Graphs
for Sparse Feature Matching

Chao Wang[1], Lei Wang[1], and Lingqiao Liu[2]

[1] School of Computer Science & Software Engineering
University of Wollongong, NSW, Australia
[2] School of Computer Science, University of Adelaide, Australia

Abstract. Sparse feature matching poses three challenges to graph-based methods: (1) the combinatorial nature makes the number of possible matches huge; (2) most possible matches might be outliers; (3) high computational complexity is often incurred. In this paper, to resolve these issues, we propose a simple, yet surprisingly effective approach to explore the huge matching space in order to significantly boost true matches while avoiding outliers. The key idea is to perform mode-seeking on graphs progressively based on our proposed guided graph density. We further design a density-aware sampling technique to considerably accelerate mode-seeking. Experimental study on various benchmark data sets demonstrates that our method is several orders faster than the state-of-the-art methods while achieving much higher precision and recall.

Keywords: Feature matching, Mode-seeking.

1 Introduction

Matching sparse features between two images is a longstanding research problem for a variety of applications in computer vision, such as motion estimation, object recognition, image retrieval and 3D reconstruction [8]. Since the matches have meaningful interrelations and structures, they are often used to construct an association graph in which graph nodes represent candidate matches while graph edges represent relationships between them. As a result, feature matching is modeled as a node selection problem in an association graph. Although there are many other feature matching algorithms, we restrict ourselves to the ones based on the association graph in this paper.

There have been a myriad of algorithms proposed to address this problem, ranging from classical methods like graph matching [8,2,10,16,22] and hypergraph matching [23,9,15], through various agglomerative clustering approaches [1,24], to recently popular mode-seeking methods [17,14,3,4]. While tremendous progress has been made, current methods are still far from being practical when dealing with many real-world images due to three challenges.

(1) The combinatorial nature makes the matching space of all the possible matches huge. Let n_1 and n_2 denote the numbers of sparse features of two images P and Q respectively, there are $n_1 \times n_2$ possible candidate matches. Generally,

D. Fleet et al. (Eds.): ECCV 2014, Part II, LNCS 8690, pp. 788–802, 2014.

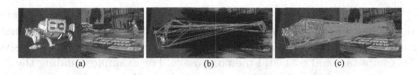

(a)   (b)   (c)

Fig. 1. (a) Input images P and Q. (b) Two types of feature detectors (MSER [19] and Harris-Affine [20]) extract 2539 SIFT features from image P and 3013 SIFT features from image Q. The 2539 matches produced by SIFT feature matching include only 64 true matches shown with green lines and 2475 false matches shown with black lines. (c) All the 281 true matches. Since there are 2539×3013 possible matches, the probability of true matches is much less than 1%.

we have $n_1, n_2 > 1000$ and $n_1 \times n_2 > 1000,000$. Building a full association graph G^F of millions of nodes is not tractable. To address this issue, most methods establish candidate matches by using discriminative features, such as SIFT [18], at a relatively low cost. However, those candidate matches usually include only a small portion of all the true matches, as shown in Fig.1.

(2) Most possible matches might be outliers. For many real-world image pairs, there are only several hundreds of true matches which account for less than 1% of the total candidate matches, as shown by Fig.1. To detect the inlier nodes from the full association graph is like looking for a needle in a haystack.

There have been a few attempts to handle the outliers. A popular method is to first solve an affine transform by using RANSAC, and then remove outliers with the affine. This naive scheme often fail when there exist significant outliers, non-rigid transforms or many-to-many object correspondences. Graph-matching methods [8,2,10,16,22] impose pair-wise constraints and the hyper-graph matching methods [23,9,15] impose high-order constraints (e.g., projective invariance) on graph nodes. The nodes that do not satisfy those constrains are considered as outliers. These methods work well for rigid transformations but perform poorly in the case of large non-rigid motions. Agglomerative clustering methods [1,24] cluster nodes with a bottom-up aggregation strategy and filter out outlier clusters with small sizes. Such methods are based on a set of heuristic rules and therefore global optimum often cannot be achieved. Recently, mode-seeking methods [17,14,3,4] have received a lot of attentions because they have appealing advantages over other techniques: the structure of the clusters may be rather arbitrary [4], the number of clusters does not need to be known in advance, and the convergence can be guaranteed. They assume that inlier nodes for true matches have larger graph density [17](or authority[4]) than outliers, and remove outliers by eliminating the clusters with small density (or authority). They work very well for the small graph constructed from the SIFT feature matching. When exploring the huge matching space which includes all possible matches, however, they might completely fail because the probability of true matches can be so small (e.g.,< 1%) that their assumptions do not hold anymore.

(3) High computational complexity is often incurred. A common starting point for constructing an association graph is the computation of the similarity matrix. Its time and space complexity is $O(N^2)$ with N denoting the number of graph

nodes ($N = n_1 \times n_2$ in the full graph). Therefore the computational costs in both time and memory are huge for large graphs. In addition to the similarity matrix construction, many other steps involved in existing methods are also expensive in terms of computational cost and memory usage. For examples, finding the principal eigenvectors of the similarity matrix in [16], high-order power iterations in [9], bottom-up building clusters in [1,24], shifting among the power set of a given graph in [17,14], and computing the PageRank matrix in [3] all take at least $O(N^2)$ time and memory. Then the usefulness of these techniques on large graphs is hampered by the high complexity. Several techniques have been developed to reduce the complexity of the classical mode-seeking method[7][13][21][12]. However, they are restricted to traditional data representation as points in a metric feature space, and it is very difficult to adapt them to graph representation. As far as we know, no work has been designed to speed up mode-seeking on graphs.

The above three challenges make detection of all the true matches in the huge matching space extremely difficult. To resolve these challenges, we propose a simple, yet surprisingly effective approach to explore the huge matching space in order to significantly boost true matches while avoiding outliers. The key idea is to perform mode-seeking on graphs progressively. Our method, called the progressive mode-seeking algorithm (PMA), starts from a small graph built by the matches obtained based on SIFT distances as in [1], and then explores a huge matching space in a progressive manner. The high performance of PMA comes from our proposed guided graph density (GGD). Totally different from the traditional graph density [17][3][4] which is calculated based on a single graph, our GGD of a node in one graph is calculated based on another reference graph. More specifically, the GGD of a node in a huge graph is calculated based on a small clean graph which mainly includes true matches. This leads the GGD values of outliers to nearly zero, and therefore makes mode-seeking much more robust to outliers even in a huge matching space. To reduce the complexity, we further design a density-aware sampling technique to considerably accelerate mode-seeking. The resultant method has a time complexity linear in the number of graph nodes.

Our PMA is inspired by the progressive graph matching (PGM) method [5] which performs graph matching progressively. PGM can greatly boost the number of true matches. However, it fails to handle many-to-many object correspondences due to its single cluster assumption, and tends to introduce many outliers because graph matching results are often noisy. Different from PGM, our PMA performs mode-seeking in a progressive manner. It excels in handling many-to-many object correspondences because each cluster of matches naturally corresponds to one object correspondence. Furthermore, it successfully avoids introducing many outliers by suppressing their graph density values.

PMA works well on a very wide variety of images. Experimental study on several benchmark data sets shows that it is several orders faster than the state-of-the-art mode-seeking methods on images with thousands of features, while producing much higher precision and recall.

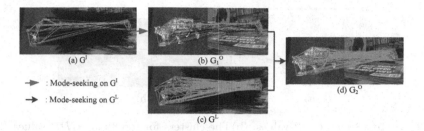

(a) G^I

→ : Mode-seeking on G^I

➡ : Mode-seeking on G^L

(b) G_1^O

(c) G^L

(d) G_2^O

Fig. 2. The framework of our PMA. It performs mode-seeking on G^I to produce G_1^O, and mode-seeking on G^L based on G_1^O to produce G_2^O. G^I is a small graph obtained by the matches obtained based on SIFT distances as in [1], and G^L is a much larger graph covering most true matches. (a) G^I contains 64 true matches and 2475 false matches. (b) G_1^O contains 38 true matches and 21 false matches. (c) G^L contains 252 true matches and 101308 false matches. (d) G_2^O contains 233 true matches and 48 false matches.

To summarize, this paper has three main contributions. Firstly, we propose a novel way to compute graph density which enables a progressive framework for robustly exploring the huge matching space. Secondly, we bring forward a density-aware sampling technique to significantly speed up mode-seeking on graphs. The third is that we design a novel mode-seeking method for clustering graph nodes in order to solve for sparse feature matching.

2   Algorithm

Following [2,4,16,18], an association graph is defined as $G = (V, E, W)$ which consists of nodes V, edges E and attributes W. $\omega(i, j) \in W$ is the attribute of edge $e(i, j) \in E$, characterizing similarity between node v_i and node v_j. In this paper, we use N, the number of nodes, to denote the size of graph G.

Fig.2 shows the progressive framework of our PMA. First, n_1 and n_2 salient features are extracted from two input images P and Q respectively with multiple types of detectors. N_I candidate matches are then established by the matches obtained based on SIFT distances as in [1], and are taken as the nodes of a small initial graph G^I. We also build a much larger graph G^L and ensure that it covers most of all the true matches. Here, G^L is much smaller than the full graph G^F. Different from other methods, we do not compute the full similarity matrix W. Instead, we only compute the similarity between each node in G^L and each node randomly sampled in G^L, as will be detailed later. Second, we perform mode-seeking on the small graph G^I similar to [17,14,3,4] in order to detect the inlier clusters G_1^O. We find out that this kind of method works well because SIFT distance at low cost can increase the probability of true matches greatly. Finally, we perform mode-seeking on the large graph G^L guided by G_1^O, producing graph G_2^O. A density-aware sampling technique is proposed to considerably accelerate the mode-seeking process. We can further run mode-seeking

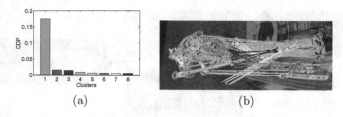

Fig. 3. (a) Top 8 max CDP values. (b)The clusters for top 8 max CDP values. The inlier clusters (denoted with green lines) have CDP values significantly larger than those of the outlier clusters.

on G^L iteratively guided by G_2^O to detect more true matches. In most cases, the first iteration brings significant performance improvement. For efficiency we use only two iterations which already produce satisfying results.

2.1   Mode-Seeking on G^I

Recent methods [3,17,4] define the graph density based on node characteristics such as the probability of visits by the random walker, and are therefore quite different from the classical kernel density estimate (KDE)[7] defined in a metric space. The high computational complexity hampers their usefulness for huge matching spaces. Differently, we define the graph density similar to KDE by representing the kernel on a joint domain. This frames a graph-based analogue to the classical KDE, and therefore makes the fast methods designed to accelerate KDE applicable to the graph density, as will be shown. Our graph density at node v_j is defined as

$$f(j) = \frac{1}{N_I} \sum_i^{N_I} K(i,j) \tag{1}$$

with $K(i,j) = g(d_S(i,j), h_S) g(d_G(i,j), h_G)$. $g(d,h)$ is a Gaussian function of d with h denoting the standard deviation. d_S is the Euclidean distance in spatial domain on the image. d_G is the node distance in graph domain and is set as the Symmetric Transfer Error (STE) used in [5,15,1,4]. h_S and h_G denote the kernel bandwidths which determine the resolution of the mode detection. Here we set $h_G = 20$ and $h_S = H/10$ with H^2 denoting the image size.

As pointed out by [7], a truncated Gaussian kernel always provides satisfactory performance, that is, only the nearest neighbors $v_i \in \Omega(j)$ are adopted to calculate the graph density. Let $\Omega(j) = \{v_i \in G^I | d_S(i,j) \leq \gamma h_S, d_G(i,j) \leq \gamma h_G\}$ with $\gamma = 2$, Eq.(1) becomes $f(j) = \frac{1}{n_j} \sum_{v_i \in \Omega(j)} K(i,j)$ with n_j denoting the size of $\Omega(j)$. To efficiently find $\Omega(j)$, we firstly use axis-aligned box windows [7] to obtain the nearest neighbors in the spatial domain, and then test each one in the graph domain.

Similar to the classical methods [7], our mode-seeking is achieved by shifting each node to the local mode in which the local maximum of graph density is attained. The node-shifting $NS(j)$ of v_j is formulated as

$$NS(j) = \arg \max_{v_i \in \Omega(j)} p(j,i)(f(i) - f(j)), \qquad (2)$$

where $p(j,i) = K(j,i)/\sum_{v_i \in \Omega(j)} K(j,i)$ denotes the probability of the transition from node v_j to node v_i. $NS(j)$ refers to the neighboring node of v_j with the highest expected graph density increment. Therefore node-shifting is the steepest ascent over the graph density within $\Omega(j)$. Similar to other mode-seeking methods [14,4,3], ours is guaranteed to converge, as proved below.

Theorem 1. A finite sequence of node-shifting from any node converges to a graph density mode.

Proof. Since $\Omega(j)$ of any node v_j includes itself, the graph density values of a sequence of shifts from v_j keep strictly increasing until the shifts attain a node whose node-shifting is itself. The final node, therefore, is the density mode $DM(j)$, and the length of the sequence is the graph size N_I at most.

Starting from any node, successive shifts progress toward its graph density mode. The shifting trajectory of nodes sharing a common density mode builds a tree, and leads to a natural cluster. For each node, we only need to compute its node-shifting once. This makes the next node-shifting for any node already exist. Then the cluster label of all nodes associated with each disjoint tree can be assigned in a single tree traversal.

As observed by [17,4], the nodes for true matches usually have larger graph density values than outliers for the graph built by the matches obtained based on SIFT distances[1]. So we can utilize this observation to detect outlier clusters in the small graph G^I. We define the cluster density of each cluster as the sum of the graph density values of its members, and its cluster density percentage (CDP) as the ratio between its cluster density and the sum of all the nodes' graph density values. According to the above observation, the outlier clusters usually have small cluster densities and therefore have small CDP. So CDP provides a reliable measure for detecting and eliminating outliers, as shown in Fig.3. We remove outlier clusters whose CDP is less than a small threshold $t = 0.03$. The final output is the inlier clusters of nodes which compose graph G_1^O with size N_1^O.

2.2 Mode-seeking on G^L

We build G^L by using top Z matches for each feature based on the SIFT feature distances. By testing the ETHZ toys dataset[11], we plot the percentage of all the true matches that G^L includes as a function of Z in Fig.4(a). It can be seen that over 90% true matches for each image pair are included in G^L when $Z = 40$. This suggests that we can perform the mode-seeking on G^L rather than on the full graph G^F to achieve great complexity reduction since the size of G^L is only Zn_1 as opposed to $n_1 \times n_2$ for G^F.

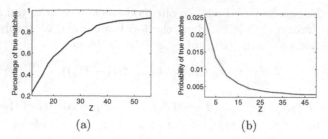

Fig. 4. (a) The percentage of all the true matches included by G^L as a function of Z. (b) The probability of true matches in G^L as a function of Z. $Z = 1$ in SIFT matching[18].

We also give the probability of the true matches in G^L as a function of Z in Fig.4(b). As can be seen, the probability attains the maximum when $Z = 1$. This indicates that SIFT distance ($Z = 1$) at low cost can greatly increase the probability of true matches. When Z become very large ($Z > 40$), the probability of true matches gradually reduces to a small value (0.0028) and keeps almost unchanged. This is because most matches are overlapped by each other for large Z. It further verifies that exploring the full graph G^F might be unnecessary.

For each node v_j in G^L, we define its **guided graph density (GGD)** as $f(j) = \frac{1}{n_j} \sum_{v_i \in \Omega(j,G^L,G_1^O)} K(i,j)$ with

$$\Omega(j, G^L, G_1^O) = \{v_i \in G_1^O | v_j \in G^L, d_S(i,j) \le \gamma h_S, d_G(i,j) \le \gamma h_G\} \quad (3)$$

Our GGD searches for Ω in another reference graph, i.e., $\Omega \subset G_1^O$. This is in sharp contrast with the traditional methods in which $\Omega \subset G^L$. As can be seen in Fig.2(b), G_1^O is mainly composed of inliers. Then the GGD values of most outliers in G^L become nearly zero because: (1) the d_S and d_G between outliers and inliers are often very large, and (2) the nodes of G_1^O might be far away from many outliers so that the nearest neighbor set Ω of many outliers are empty. Many mode-seeking methods fail when exploring huge matching space because their assumption that inlier clusters often have larger graph density than outliers does not hold when the probability of inliers is very low, say the case in G^L. Our GGD solves this problem nicely because it makes the assumption hold again by suppressing the graph density of outliers. Then we can perform mode-seeking based on GGD to detect and eliminate outliers, as done in Section 2.1. The output N_2^O nodes compose a G_2^O. Fig.5 shows the impact of GGD.

The mode-seeking on G^L is guaranteed to converge, and the proof is the same as that for Theorem 1. So our PMA is guaranteed to converge.

2.3   A Density-Aware Sampling Technique

To accelerate the classical mode-seeking method, D.Freedman et al.[12] approximate the whole feature space by using a greatly reduced number of points

(a)   (b)

Fig. 5. (a) Mode-seeking result on graph G^L with $\Omega \subset G^L$. None of the top 8 clusters is inlier cluster. Each color indicates on cluster of matches. (b) Mode-seeking result on graph G^L with GGD ($\Omega \subset G_1^O$). The inlier cluster is detected in a clean manner.

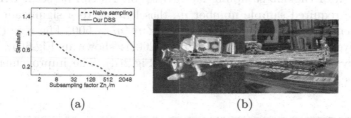

(a)   (b)

Fig. 6. Impact of our density-aware sampling (DAS) technique. (a)Two kinds of similarities as functions of sub-sampling factor Zn_1/m are shown. One similarity is between the result by original mode-seeking method (without sampling) and the result by the naive sampling method. The other similarity is between the result by original mode-seeking method (without sampling) and the result by our density-aware sampling (DAS) method. (b)The result by the naive sampling method with $m = 200$. Three outlier clusters are detected. The result by our DAS with $m = 200$ is given in Fig.2(d).

randomly sampled from the distribution defined by KDE. The speed-up is proportional to the sub-sampling factor. However, different from sampling metric feature space for KDE, directly sampling the graph density in Eq.(1) can not produce graph node samples. A naive sampling method to solve this issue is to randomly sample from the set of graph nodes. Since most graph nodes might be outliers, the number of samples need to be sufficiently large in order to cover the modes of inliers with a large probability. Then the complexity reduction will be limited. To solve this problem, we propose a simple approach called the density-aware sampling (DAS) technique which samples graph nodes according to the graph density in mode-seeking on G^I (or the GGD in mode-seeking on G^L). In DAS, the probability of accepting v_i is $f(i)/\sum_i f(i)$. As mentioned before, inliers often have larger graph density values (or GGD values) than outliers, so DAS tends to sample more inliers, thus solving the problem of the naive sampling method nicely.

We use DAS to sample m nodes of G (G can be G^I and G^L) to approximate G, obtaining graph G^{sample}. Then instead of computing modes directly on G, we perform mode-seeking on G^{sample} to obtain the density modes. We further map backwards from each node v_i in G to the closest sample s_{i*} by $s_{i*} = \arg\max_{s_i \in \Omega(i)} K(i, s_i)$ with $\Omega(i) \subset G^{sample}$. Finally, we set the graph density mode $DM(i)$ of v_i to $DM(s_{i*})$ in order to obtain the final clustering results.

We adopt DAS in the mode-seeking on both G^I and G^L. When performing it on G^L, we randomly sample $R = min(m, N_1^O)$ nodes from G_1^O which is the mode-seeking result on G^I to further reduce the complexity. The details are given in Algorithm 1.

To show the impact of our DAS, we measure the similarity between the result obtained by the original mode-seeking method and those obtained by two sampling techniques: the naive sampling method and our DAS. The similarity between any two graphs G^1 and G^2 is calculated by the normalized intersect $|G^1 \cap G^2|/|G^1 \cup G^2|$ with $|G|$ denoting the size of G. Fig.6(a) plots the similarity as a function of the sub-sampling factor Zn_1/m. As can be seen, DAS greatly reduces the required sample number m, thus leading to a significant speed-up Zn_1/m. Generally, we set $m = 200$ to get $Zn_1/m > 500$. The result obtained by the naive sampling method with $m = 200$ is shown in Fig.6(b), and that obtained by our DAS is given in previous Fig.2(d). The improvement by our DAS can be clearly seen.

Algorithm 1: mode-seeking on G^I (G^L)

Input G^I (G_1^O and G^L)

Output G_1^O (G_2^O)

1. Sampling: sample m nodes of G^I
(sample m nodes of G^L and R nodes of G_1^O)
2. Node-shifting: solve for the node-shifting for all the m matches with Eq.(2)
3. Tree traversal: assign each sample s_i to its density mode $DM(s_i)$ by a tree traversal along $NS(s_i)$
4. Map backwards: for each node v_i, find s_{i*} by $\arg\max_{s_i \in \Omega(i)} K(i, s_i)$, then let $DM(i) = DM(s_{i*})$
5. Remove outliers: compute CDP for each cluster, and remove outlier clusters with $CDP < t$

---

3   Analysis

Complexity. In mode-seeking on G^I, in order to cluster m samples, we need to search for the nearest neighbors $\Omega(j)$ for each node v_j. Assuming that the matches are uniformly distributed in image, the time complexity for finding $\Omega(j)$ is $O(mr)$ by using the axis-aligned box windows, with $r = (2\gamma h_S)^2/H^2$ denoting the area ratio of the region we explore to the whole image. Then computing the graph density for all the m nodes takes $O(m^2 r)$ time, and node-shifting also takes $O(m^2 r)$ time. Mapping backwards takes $O(N_I mr)$ time. Therefore the time complexity of mode-seeking on G^I reaches $O(2m^2 r + N_I mr) \approx O(N_I mr)$ since $N_I \gg m$. In mode-seeking on G^L, searching for $\Omega(j)$ on graph G_1^O takes $O(Rr)$ time, and clustering the m samples takes $O(2Rmr)$ time. Mapping backwards takes $O(Zn_1 mr)$ time. Then the time complexity is about $O(Zn_1 mr)$ since $Zn_1 \gg R$. So the total time complexity of our PMA is $O(N_I mr + Zn_1 mr) \approx O(Zn_1 mr)$ which is linear in the number of graph nodes Zn_1.

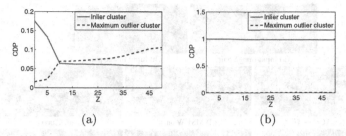

Fig. 7. The effect of our guided graph density (GGD) ($\Omega \subset G_1^O$) on eliminating outliers. (a) The result by mode-seeking with $\Omega \subset G^L$. With the increase of outliers, the max CDP for outlier clusters becomes much larger than the CDP for the inlier cluster. (b) The result by our mode-seeking with $\Omega \subset G_1^O$. The CDP for the inlier cluster is nearly independent of the number of outliers, and accounts for the majority of all the graph density values. No outlier cluster whose CDP is larger than t is detected.

Revisiting the literature on the subject, mode-seeking by using the methods [17,14,3,4] takes $O((Zn_1)^2)$ time on graph G^L. So the speed-up by our PMA is a factor of $(Zn_1)^2/(N_I mr + Zn_1 mr)$. In practical cases of interest, n_1 is about 2000, and N_1 is set to 2000. Then we have $(Zn_1)^2/(N_I mr + Zn_1 mr) \approx 2439$. So this is quite an impressive speed-up.

Effect of our GGD. Taking the image pair in Fig.1(a) as an example, we gradually increase the percentage of outliers by increasing Z. Fig.7 shows the results by mode-seeking with $\Omega \subset G^L$ and with our GGD ($\Omega \subset G_1^O$). With the increase of outliers, the max CDP for outliers becomes larger than the CDP for the inlier cluster. This is why many existing mode-seeking methods fail. By using GGD, no outlier cluster is detected at all because the GGD values of outliers become nearly zero. Then the CDP for the inlier cluster accounts for the majority of all the graph density values, and is almost independent of the number of outliers, as shown in Fig.7(b).

Limitations. Our method starts from mode-seeking on a small graph G^I built the matches obtained based on SIFT distances as in [1], and assumes that the nodes for true matches usually have larger graph density values than outliers in the small graph G^I. Although this assumption has been widely used [17,4], we did find that it does not hold for two extreme cases: large smooth regions such as white plates with little texture, and tiny-sized objects with few features extracted. To handle these cases will be our future work.

4   Experiments

We compare our PMA with three leading graph-based feature matching methods: the progressive graph matching (PGM) [5], the agglomerative correspondence clustering (ACC) [1] and the mode-seeking via random walk (RRWM) [4]. PGM improves the true matches progressively by exploring the full matching space

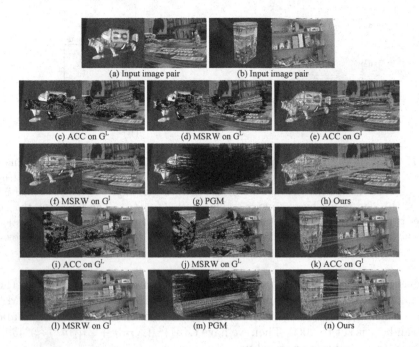

(a) Input image pair   (b) Input image pair

(c) ACC on G^L (d) MSRW on G^L (e) ACC on G^I

(f) MSRW on G^I (g) PGM   (h) Ours

(i) ACC on G^L (j) MSRW on G^L (k) ACC on G^I

(l) MSRW on G^I (m) PGM   (n) Ours

Fig. 8. Comparison on two image pairs of ETHZ toys dataset [11]. True matches are shown with green lines and outliers are shown with black lines.

based on an initial graph. We set G^I as its initial graph as done by our PMA. Both ACC and RRWM are only based on the similarity matrix of the association graph. We perform ACC and RRWM on graph G^L as done by PMA. We also run ACC and RRWM on graph G^I as their original work did for comparison. The algorithms of [17,3] were not compared in this paper because the source code provided by the authors on the internet produce 'out of memory' problem when handling our data sets.

We tested the above methods on three challenging benchmark data sets: ETHZ toys dataset [11], Co-recognition dataset [6] and Intra-class dataset [1]. ETHZ toys dataset includes 9 different rigid/non-rigid object pairs with significant transforms and clutters. Co-recognition dataset contains 6 image pairs with

Table 1. Precision/Recall (%) by four methods. ACC and RRWM denote their results on graph G^I. Since both ACC and RRWM fail to handle G^L, we do not show their results on G^L.

Data sets	ACC[1]	RRWM[4]	PGM[5]	Our PMA
ETHZ	63/15	66/23	11/66	**82/74**
Co-recognition	67/68	69/75	13/69	**88/79**
Intra-class	71/24	52/22	25/81	**72/83**

(a) Two input image pairs

(b) Results by ACC on G^I

(c) Results by MSRW on G^I

(d) Results by PGM

(e) Our results

Fig. 9. Comparison on two image pairs of Co-recognition dataset [6]

complex many-to-many object correspondences. Intra-class dataset consists of 30 image pairs of large intra-class variation. The ground truth feature matches are manually constructed for each image pair to enable quantitatively evaluation. Here, we use the MSER[19] and the Harris affine detectors [20] with SIFT descriptor [18]. Our testing environment is MS Windows 7 Professional with Intel Core i5-3550 CPU 3.3GHz, 16GB RAM.

Fig.8 shows the matching results for two examples of ETHZ toys dataset. A prominent phenomenon observed is that the results on graph G^L by both ACC and RRWM are totally cluttered by the background outliers, with precisions and recalls close to zero. Actually, this happens for each image pair in the data sets. In the following parts we will not show the results on graph G^L by ACC or RRWM. The results obtained by both ACC and RRWM on graph G^I are much better, with about 20% of all the true matches detected. PGM fails to handle these two examples due to the significant outliers. In comparison, our PMA successfully detects about 80% of all the true matches with much higher precisions, despite large object transforms and outliers.

Fig.9 demonstrates a comparison on two challenging image pairs in Co-recognition data set. These image pairs have three and four object correspondences respectively. Since PGM assumes that the true matches belong to a single cluster, it can not deal with many-to-many object correspondences. Therefore the results on these two examples are far from being satisfactory. ACC and RRWM accurately detect the three inlier clusters but also introduce many outliers. Our PMA solves this problem effectively by successfully distinguishing the inliers from outliers.

Fig.10 illustrates feature matching for two image pairs in Intra-class data set. To solve this, it is required to address appearance difference as well as intra-class variation. As can be seen, PGM cannot distinguish true matches from outliers. Both ACC and RRWM fail to recover most inlier matches. In contrast, the result by our PMA has much more inlier matches with less outliers.

Table 1 gives quantitative results on the three benchmark data sets. As mentioned before, since both ACC and RRWM fail to handle G^L and the precisions are nearly zero, we do not show their results. As can been seen, our PMA largely outperforms the other methods in both precision and recall.

Table 2. Average running time (in second) by four methods. ACC and RRWM denote their running time on graph G^L.

Data sets	ACC[1]	RRWM[4]	PGM[5]	Our PMA
ETHZ	245257	16462	23	6
Co-recognition	264379	19873	28	7
Intra-class	673	65	10	2

Table 2 gives the computational time. For ETHZ toys dataset [11] and Co-recognition dataset [6], our PMA is more than 1000 times faster than the leading mode-seeking method RRWM on graph G^L. We also test RRWM on the small graph G^I. The average time to process each image pair in the three data sets is 4, 6 and 2 seconds respectively. As shown in Table 2, our PMA has comparable performance. Compared with the ACC and PGM methods which are not mode-seeking methods, our PMA is also much faster. For Intra-class dataset [1], the feature numbers of most images are very small (in some cases, even less than fifty). Therefore the speed-up by our method is less significant than that on the other two data sets. However, more than 10 times speed-up over RRWM on G^L can still be observed.

The space complexity of our PMA is also linear in the number of graph nodes. By using 16GB RAM, our method can handle about 819×2000 nodes at most.

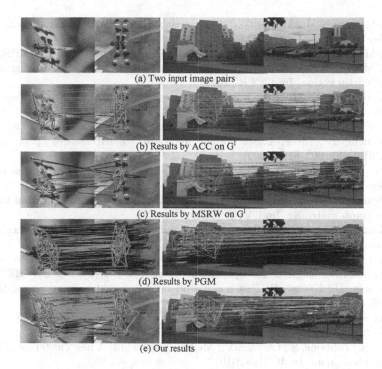

(a) Two input image pairs

(b) Results by ACC on G^I

(c) Results by MSRW on G^I

(d) Results by PGM

(e) Our results

Fig. 10. Comparison on two image pairs of Intra-class dataset [1]

5   Conclusion

Feature matching is a long-standing and important problem for many applications in computer vision. This paper tried to address it by focusing on a novel issue: efficiently exploring the huge matching space based on the graph-based method. The crucial component of our proposed algorithm is to compute the graph density for one graph based on a reference graph. This enables a progressive mode-seeking framework for robustly exploring the huge matching spaces. To reduce the complexity of mode-seeking, we utilize the property that inliers often have larger graph density values than outliers and propose a simple density-aware sampling scheme. Results on several standard data sets demonstrated that our method significantly outperforms state-of-the-art methods, in terms of precision, recall and run time.

References

1. Cho, M., Lee, J., Lee, K.M.: Feature correspondence and deformable object matching via agglomerative correspondence clustering. In: ICCV (2009)
2. Cho, M., Lee, J., Lee, K.M.: Reweighted random walks for graph matching. In: Daniilidis, K., Maragos, P., Paragios, N. (eds.) ECCV 2010, Part V. LNCS, vol. 6315, pp. 492–505. Springer, Heidelberg (2010)

3. Cho, M., Lee, K.M.: Authority-shift clustering: Hierarchical clustering by authority seeking on graphs. In: CVPR (2010)
4. Cho, M., Lee, K.M.: Mode-seeking on graphs via random walks. In: CVPR (2012)
5. Cho, M., Lee, K.M.: Progressive graph matching: Making a move of graphs via probabilistic voting. In: CVPR (2012)
6. Cho, M., Shin, Y.M., Lee, K.M.: Co-recognition of image pairs by data-driven monte carlo image exploration. In: Forsyth, D., Torr, P., Zisserman, A. (eds.) ECCV 2008, Part IV. LNCS, vol. 5305, pp. 144–157. Springer, Heidelberg (2008)
7. Comaniciu, D., Meer, P.: A robust approach toward feature space analysis. TPAMI 24(5), 603–619 (2002)
8. Conte, D., Foggia, P., Sansone, C., Vento, M.: Thirty years of graph matching in pattern recognition. IJPRAI, 265–298 (2004)
9. Duchenne, O., Bach, F., Kweon, I., Ponce, J.: A tensor-based algorithm for high-order graph matching. In: CVPR (2009)
10. Duchenne, O., Joulin, A., Ponce, J.: A graph-matching kernel for object categorization. In: ICCV (2011)
11. Ferrari, V., Tuytelaars, T., Gool, L.V.: Simultaneous object recognition and segmentation from single or multiple model views. IJCV 67(2), 159–188 (2006)
12. Freedman, D., Kisilev, P.: Fast mean shift by compact density representation. In: CVPR (2009)
13. Georgescu, B., Shimshoni, I., Meer, R.: Mean shift based clustering in high dimensions: A texture classification example. In: ICCV (2003)
14. Jouili, S., Tabbone, S., Lacroix, V.: Median graph shift: A new clustering algorithm for graph domain. In: ICPR (2010)
15. Lee, J., Cho, M., Lee, K.M.: Hyper-graph matching via reweighted random walks. In: CVPR (2011)
16. Leordeanu, M., Hebert, M.: A spectral technique for correspondence problems using pairwise constraints. In: ICCV (2005)
17. Liu, H., Latecki, L.J., Yan, S.: Fast detection of dense subgraph with iterative shrinking and expansion. TPAMI (2013)
18. Lowe, D.G.: Object recognition from local scale-invariant features. In: ICCV (1999)
19. Matas, J., Chum, O., Urban, M., Pajdla, T.: Robust wide baseline stereo from maximally stable extremal regions. In: BMVC (2002)
20. Mikolajczyk, K., Schmid, C.: Scale and affine invariant interest point detectors. In: IJCV (2004)
21. Paris, S., Durand, F.: A topological approach to hierarchical segmentation using mean shift. In: CVPR (2007)
22. Torresani, L., Kolmogorov, V., Rother, C.: Feature correspondence via graph matching: Models and global optimization. In: Forsyth, D., Torr, P., Zisserman, A. (eds.) ECCV 2008, Part II. LNCS, vol. 5303, pp. 596–609. Springer, Heidelberg (2008)
23. Zass, R., Shashua, A.: Probabilistic graph and hypergraph matching. In: CVPR (2008)
24. Zhang, W., Wang, X., Zhao, D., Tang, X.: Graph degree linkage: agglomerative clustering on a directed graph. In: Fitzgibbon, A., Lazebnik, S., Perona, P., Sato, Y., Schmid, C. (eds.) ECCV 2012, Part I. LNCS, vol. 7572, pp. 428–441. Springer, Heidelberg (2012)

Globally Optimal Inlier Set Maximization with Unknown Rotation and Focal Length

Jean-Charles Bazin[1], Yongduek Seo[2], Richard Hartley[3], and Marc Pollefeys[1]

[1] Department of Computer Science, ETH Zurich, Switzerland
[2] Department of Media Technology, Sogang University, South Korea
[3] Australian National University and NICTA, Canberra, Australia

Abstract. Identifying inliers and outliers among data is a fundamental problem for model estimation. This paper considers models composed of rotation and focal length, which typically occurs in the context of panoramic imaging. An efficient approach consists in computing the underlying model such that the number of inliers is maximized. The most popular tool for inlier set maximization must be RANSAC and its numerous variants. While they can provide interesting results, they are not guaranteed to return the globally optimal solution, i.e. the model leading to the highest number of inliers. We propose a novel globally optimal approach based on branch-and-bound. It computes the rotation and the focal length maximizing the number of inlier correspondences and considers the reprojection error in the image space. Our approach has been successfully applied on synthesized data and real images.

Keywords: Consensus set maximization, branch-and-bound, inlier detection, RANSAC.

1 Introduction

Distinguishing inliers and outliers among data is a fundamental problem and constitutes a necessary step for model estimation, notably in computer vision. An efficient approach to identify inliers and outliers consists in estimating the underlying model in such a way that the number of inliers is maximized. The most popular technique must be RANSAC [8] and has been applied for numerous computer vision tasks ranging from 3D reconstruction to object recognition. Despite its popularity and that interesting results can be obtained, RANSAC is not guaranteed to maximize the number of inliers in a globally optimal way. This paper is dedicated to rotational homography with unknown focal length, i.e. models composed of rotation and focal length, which typically occurs in the context of panoramic imaging [5]. We propose a globally optimal approach that computes the camera rotation and the focal length so that the maximum number of inlier correspondences between two images is guaranteed to be obtained.

Previous work investigated how to maximize the number of inliers. First, several variants of RANSAC have been proposed, for example MLESAC, LO-RANSAC and preemptive-RANSAC [22,17,19,7]. While they generally perform

D. Fleet et al. (Eds.): ECCV 2014, Part II, LNCS 8690, pp. 803–817, 2014.

better than the original RANSAC in terms of the number of identified inliers, they are not guaranteed to obtain the optimal result. In contrast to random sampling, Li [13] applied an optimal branch-and-bound technique in combination with convex and concave envelops [15]. However this approach is limited to distance definitions and constraints that are strictly linear with respect to the sought model. Kahl et al. [12] proposed an optimal method also based on branch-and-bound in combination with L_1-norm to partially reduce the sensitivity to outliers. A post-validation step was proposed by Olsson et al. [18]. While this approach is useful to verify the optimality of a potential solution, it does not provide a mechanism to explicitly compute the optimal solution. Bazin et al. [2] proposed an approach to maximize the number of inliers under a pure rotational model. In contrast to their work, (i) we do not assume that the focal length is known in advance, (ii) we compute the focal length, in addition to the rotation, (iii) instead of the angular error, we consider the meaningful Euclidian distance in the image space in pixels [10], which requires deriving the reprojection bounds in the image, and (iv) we introduce a rotation parametrization that permits to reduce the correlation between the focal length and the rotation parameters. Yang et al. [23] recently proposed a globally optimal Iterative Closest Point (ICP) algorithm for rigid registration (rotation + translation) of two 3D point sets and can be applied to maximize the number of inlier correspondences between these two sets. This method is dedicated to 3D point sets (e.g. registration error in 3D space) and thus cannot be straightforwardly generalized for unknown focal length and used for our application in the image space.

2 Formulation

Let us note $\mathbf{x}_i = (x_i, y_i)$ and $\mathbf{x}_i' = (x_i', y_i')$ the ith input pair of 2D feature points in correspondence (e.g. obtained by SIFT [14]), respectively in the first and second images, with $i = 1 \ldots N$ and where N is the number of matches. The two images are taken with a camera located at a fixed position and turning with any 3D rotation R. It is assumed that the camera is intrinsically calibrated (e.g. camera center is known), except for the focal length f which is unknown and same for the two images. In the following, all the measurements $(\mathbf{x}_i, \mathbf{x}_i')$ are centered, i.e. the camera center's coordinates (C_x, C_y) are subtracted to the points' coordinates in pre-processing, and thus the intrinsic calibration matrix is reduced to $\mathsf{K}_f = \mathrm{diag}(f, f, 1)$ [10]. In the absence of noise and outliers, any two measurements $(\mathbf{x}_i, \mathbf{x}_i')$ in correspondence verify:

$$\mathbf{x}_i' = \mathsf{T}\mathbf{x}_i = \mathsf{K}_f\, \mathsf{R}\, \mathsf{K}_f^{-1}\mathbf{x}_i \text{ and } d_{\mathsf{R},f}(\mathbf{x}_i, \mathbf{x}_i') = 0\, \forall i \tag{1}$$

where $d_{\mathsf{R},f}(\mathbf{x}, \mathbf{x}') = \|\mathsf{K}_f\, \mathsf{R}\mathsf{K}_f^{-1}\mathbf{x} - \mathbf{x}'\|_2$, that is the Euclidian distance in pixels between the measurement in the right image $\mathbf{x}'$ and the measurement of the left image $\mathbf{x}$ projected into the right image by the transformation T that depends on the camera rotation R and the focal length f. In the following, $d_{\mathsf{R},f}(\mathbf{x}, \mathbf{x}')$ is called the reprojection error.

Due to noise and outliers, these relations might not be verified for all the input matches. Following the "residual tolerance method" [8], we define a match $(\mathbf{x}_i, \mathbf{x}_i')$ as an inlier if the reprojection error is lower than a residual tolerance δ, i.e. $d_{\mathtt{R},f}(\mathbf{x}_i, \mathbf{x}_i') \leq \delta$. Otherwise the match is considered an outlier.

Let $\mathcal{S}$ represent the set of input matches: $\mathcal{S} = \{(\mathbf{x}_i, \mathbf{x}_i'), i = 1 \ldots N\}$. The set $\mathcal{S}$ is partitioned into an inlier-set $\mathcal{S}_I \subseteq \mathcal{S}$ containing the inlier matches and an outlier-set $\mathcal{S}_O \subseteq \mathcal{S}$ with $\mathcal{S}_O = \mathcal{S} - \mathcal{S}_I$. The cardinality of $\mathcal{S}_I$ corresponds to the number of inlier matches. Maximizing the number of inliers with unknown rotation and unknown focal length can now be formulated as:

$$\max_{\mathcal{S}_I, \mathtt{R}, f} \quad card(\mathcal{S}_I) \tag{2a}$$

$$\text{s.t.} \quad d_{\mathtt{R},f}(\mathbf{x}_i, \mathbf{x}_i') \leq \delta, \forall i \in \mathcal{S}_I \subseteq \mathcal{S} \tag{2b}$$

$$\mathtt{R} \in SO(3) \tag{2c}$$

Solving System 2 in a globally optimal way is a challenging task mainly due to the non-linearity, the non-convexity and the rotation constraint. System 2 can also be considered as a typical chicken-and-egg problem: if the inliers are known, then the underlying model (rotation and focal length) can be computed [6], and reciprocally, if the model is known, the inliers can be retrieved (simple check of the inlier constraint at Eq. (2b)). Unfortunately neither the inliers nor the model is known apriori. A method would be to test all the possible combinations of inliers/outliers. While the number of combinations is finite (2^N), it is generally untractable in practice. Another naive method would be to test all the possible models but the model search space has an infinite cardinality and thus is untractable. In practice, a popular method to solve System 2 is to apply RANSAC in combination with a 2-point algorithm [4], but as explained above, RANSAC is not guaranteed to return the globally optimal solution.

3 Proposed Approach

This section presents the proposed approach to solve System 2 in a globally optimal way. We start by introducing a particular parametrization of the transformation T, then study the projection bounds when the parameters of the transformation lie in a given range, and finally explain how to use these bounds in the framework of branch-and-bound.

3.1 Parametrization

Rotation can be parameterized in several ways such as Euler angles, quaternion and axis-angle. In our work, we propose to use a parametrization of the form

$$\mathtt{R} = \mathtt{R}_z(\theta) \, \mathtt{R}_r \, \mathtt{R}_z(\phi) \tag{3}$$

where $\mathtt{R}_z(\theta)$ is a rotation about the z-axis (optical axis) by an angle θ and R_r is a rotation about the y-axis to be explained presently.

One key advantage of this parametrization is the way it interacts with K_f in the definition (1) of T. One may easily verify that K_f commutes with a rotation R_z, i.e. $K_f R_z = R_z K_f$. This important observation provides a simple form for T:

$$\begin{aligned}
T &= K_f \, R \, K_f^{-1} = K_f \, R_z(\theta) R_r R_z(\phi) \, K_f^{-1} \\
&= R_z(\theta) \, K_f R_r K_f^{-1} R_z(\phi) \; .
\end{aligned} \tag{4}$$

We define R_r as the rotation about the y-axis with the property that $K_f R_r K_f^{-1}$ takes origin $(0,0,1)^\top$ to the point $(r,0,1)^\top$. The mapping $K_f R_r K_f^{-1}$ is of the form

$$K_f \, R_y(\alpha) K_f^{-1} = \begin{bmatrix} \cos(\alpha) & 0 & f\sin(\alpha) \\ 0 & 1 & 0 \\ -\sin(\alpha)/f & 0 & \cos(\alpha) \end{bmatrix} = \begin{bmatrix} 1 & 0 & f\tan(\alpha) \\ 0 & 1/\cos(\alpha) & 0 \\ -\tan(\alpha)/f & 0 & 1 \end{bmatrix} \tag{5}$$

up to (irrelevant) scale. In order to take $(0,0,1)^\top$ to $(r,0,1)^\top$, it follows that $\tan(\alpha) = r/f$, so $\cos(\alpha) = f/\sqrt{f^2 + r^2}$. For easier notation, let us consider the reciprocal focal length $g = 1/f$ instead of the focal length. After some mathematical manipulations, we finally obtain the mapping

$$U(g,r) = K_f \, R_r K_f^{-1} = \begin{bmatrix} 1 & 0 & r \\ 0 & \sqrt{1 + r^2 g^2} & 0 \\ -rg^2 & 0 & 1 \end{bmatrix} \; . \tag{6}$$

Finally, the complete transformation T gets simplified to:

$$T = R_z(\theta) \begin{bmatrix} 1 & 0 & r \\ 0 & \sqrt{1 + r^2 g^2} & 0 \\ -rg^2 & 0 & 1 \end{bmatrix} R_z(\phi) \; . \tag{7}$$

Interpretation. The two rotations $R_z(\phi)$ and $R_z(\theta)$ carry out rotations about the image origin. One may think of these as being rotations in the left and right hand images respectively. Thus, the way a point is transformed by T is as follows:

1. The point in the left image is rotated around the origin by an angle ϕ by $R_z(\phi)$.
2. Then it is mapped into the right image by $U(g,r)$ (see (6)), parameterized by g and r (i.e. f and α).
3. Finally, it is rotated around the origin of the right image by an angle θ by $R_z(\theta)$.

An interesting observation is that in order to test a correspondence between points x_i (in the left image) and x'_i (in the right image), one may do a pre-rotation of x_i by ϕ and x'_i by $-\theta$. In this operation, the circular inlier neighbourhoods (of radius δ) remain circular and the radius is unchanged.

All this is possible thanks to the rotation parametrization of (3) that permits R_z to commute with K_f, and in turn, to "separate" R_z and f. This reduces the correlation of f and the rotation parameters, which is desirable in the reduction of the error bound, and also simplifies the derivations of the bounds in pixel error (more details in the next sections).

Additional Properties. The mapping $\mathsf{U}(g,r)$ applied to a point $\mathbf{x} = (x,y,1)^\top$ provides a point $\mathbf{x}'$ given by

$$\mathbf{x} = (x,y,1) \to \mathbf{x}' = (x+r,\ y\sqrt{1+r^2g^2},\ 1-rxg^2)^\top . \tag{8}$$

After dehomogenizing, this becomes

$$(x,y) \to (x',y') = \left(\frac{x+r}{1-rxg^2},\ \frac{y\sqrt{1+r^2g^2}}{1-rxg^2} \right) . \tag{9}$$

An important note is that x' depends only on x, and not on y. In particular, this mapping takes a (vertical) line of the form $x = c$ to a new line $x' = (c + r)/(1 - rcg^2)$. This will be used for a quick-and-easy way of checking whether a match is a potential inlier given a certain transformation.

Another important property is the "trajectory" of the point $(x,y)^\top$ mapped into the right image as r varies. From (9), one can show that this trajectory is a hyperbola with the equation

$$(1 + g^2 x_0^2)\,(y')^2 - (g^2 y_0^2)\,(x')^2 = y_0^2 \tag{10}$$

where (x_0, y_0) represents the initial point when $r = 0$. The initial point (x_0, y_0) is the same as (x,y), but written with the subscript so as to indicate that this point is constant here and (x', y') are the variables.

3.2 Intervals of r and g

This section investigates where a point $\mathbf{x} - (x,y)$ is mapped to under a transformation $\mathsf{U}(g,r)$, when the parameters r and g lie in a range. Let us suppose that $r_{\min} \leq r \leq r_{\max}$ and $g_{\min} \leq g \leq g_{\max}$. With these intervals, the mapped point $\mathsf{U}(g,r)\mathbf{x}$ must lie inside some bounded region in the right image and in the following, we compute the bounds on its x and y coordinates.

Bounds on y. Based on the above observations and derivations, $\mathsf{U}(g,r)\mathbf{x}$ must lie between the two hyperbolas defined by (10) for $g = g_{\min}$ and $g = g_{\max}$. This gives a very convenient way to determine whether the mapping of $\mathbf{x}$ into the right image passes "close" to (i.e. up to δ) its putative corresponding point $\mathbf{x}'$ for any value of r. The hyperbolas are illustrated in Figure 1. This figure shows that for values of g close to zero (very large focal lengths), the point moves almost horizontally, whereas for larger values of g (shorter focal lengths) the trajectory becomes more curved.

Bounds on x. As shown previously, where a point $\mathbf{x} = (x,y)$ maps to does not depend on y, only on x (see (9)). As y varies in the point (x,y), the mapped point (x',y') varies along a vertical line as well. Thus, U maps vertical lines to vertical lines. Taking derivatives of the line $x' = (x+r)/(1-rxg^2)$ with respect to r and g gives

$$\frac{\partial x'}{\partial r} = \frac{1 + g^2 x^2}{(-1 + g^2 rx)^2} \quad \text{and} \quad \frac{\partial x'}{\partial g} = \frac{2grx(r+x)}{(-1 + g^2 rx)^2} . \tag{11}$$

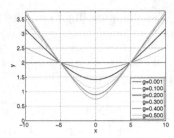

Fig. 1. Hyperbolic trajectories of a point transformed by $\mathsf{U}(g,r)$ with different values of g, given the initial point $(x_0, y_0) = (5,2)$ and for any values of r.

The derivative with respect to r is always positive. Therefore, the minimum value x_{min} of x' will be achieved at $r = r_{\min}$ and the maximum x_{max} at $r = r_{\max}$.

The sign of the derivative with respect to g corresponds to the sign of $2grx(r + x)$, which depends on the values of x and r (note that $g = 1/f \geq 0$ since focal length is always positive). Let us study the minimum of x'. As explained right above, it is achieved with $r = r_{min}$. Let note $s = \text{sign}(r_{min}x(r_{min} + x))$. Thus the sign of the derivative is the same as s: if $s \geq 0$ (rec. $s \leq 0$) then the derivative is positive (rec. negative), then the minimum of x' is obtained at $g = g_{min}$ (rec. $g = g_{max}$). Concretely, the minimum value of x' is achieved at one of the two parameter values $(r, g) = (r_{min}, g_{min})$ or (r_{min}, g_{max}) depending on the sign of $r_{min}x(r_{min} + x)$. A similar derivation can be followed for the maximum of x': the value at which x' takes its maximum value is at either $(r, g) = (r_{max}, g_{min})$ or (r_{max}, g_{max}) depending on the sign of $r_{max}x(r_{max} + x)$.

Summarizing this, the minimum and maximum of x' are achieved at two of the four corners of the rectangle defined by the range of the parameters r and g. Thus, we see that we can bound the range of the point $\mathbf{x}' = (x', y')$ to lie between two vertical lines $x' = x_{\min}$ and $x' = x_{\max}$ and to lie between the two hyperbolas corresponding to the values of $g_{\min}$ and $g_{\max}$. This gives a simple test to see whether the point $\mathbf{x}$ can transform to the target point $\mathbf{x}'$ within a suitable radius (i.e. up to δ). Concretely, the test can be conducted as follows:

1. In terms of the initial point $\mathbf{x} = (x_0, y_0)$ compute the bounds $x_{\min}$ and $x_{\max}$ and test if x' lies between them.
2. Test if $\mathbf{x}'$ lies between the two hyperbolas defined for $g_{\min}$ and $g_{\max}$ and with the initial point (x_0, y_0).

If either of these two tests fails, then it is sure that $\mathbf{x}'$ is not within range. Otherwise, $\mathbf{x}'$ *might* be within range: $(\mathbf{x}, \mathbf{x}')$ is a potential inlier match but this has to be confirmed with further investigations, as detailed in the next section.

3.3   Branch-and-Bound

To efficiently deal with bounds, we follow the branch and bound algorithm (noted BnB in the following). BnB is a general framework for global optimization [11] that recently gained popularity in the field of computer vision [21,24,9]. Given a search space of the model to estimate, BnB iteratively subdivides this search space into smaller subspaces, identifies and removes the subspaces that do not contain the optimal solution via a feasibility test and refines the remaining subspaces, i.e. the subspaces that can potentially contain the optimal solution.

Our search space is composed of the rotation space $SO(3)$ parameterized by the angles (θ, ϕ, α) (see Section 3.1) and the focal length range. We call "cube" a delimited part of that space. We now ask the question: how to estimate the lower and upper bounds of the number of inliers that can be obtained by any models in a given cube?

Lower bound. Let us start with the lower bound. The center of a given cube $\mathcal{C}$ corresponds to a specific point in the search space and thus corresponds to known rotation angles (θ, ϕ, α) and focal length f, which in turn provides R and K_f. Then we can simply count the number of matches $(\mathbf{x}_i, \mathbf{x}_i')$ verifying the inlier constraint (2b). One may note that this number does not necessarily correspond to the lowest number of inliers that could be obtained in the cube $\mathcal{C}$, but provides a practical lower bound of the maximum number of inliers that can be obtained in the cube $\mathcal{C}$.

Upper bound. Computing the upper bound is more challenging. We note $[\theta_l, \theta_u]$, $[\phi_l, \phi_u]$, $[\alpha_l, \alpha_u]$ and $[f_l, f_u]$ the definition ranges of these parameters in a given cube $\mathcal{C}$. The rotation of a point $\mathbf{x}_i$ (in the left image) by $R_z(\phi)$ with $\phi \in [\phi_l, \phi_u]$ defines a circular arc centered at the origin and of length $\phi_u - \phi_l$. The x and y bounds of this arc can be easily obtained analytically and we note them $([x_i], [y_i]) = ([x_{i,l}, x_{i,u}], [y_{i,l}, y_{i,u}])$ where l and u stand for lower and upper values. Similarly, let us note $([x_i'], [y_i']) = ([x_{i,l}', x_{i,u}'], [y_{i,l}', y_{i,u}'])$ the bounds of the point $\mathbf{x}_i'$ (in the right image) rotated by $R_z(\theta)$ with $\theta \in [\theta_l, \theta_u]$.

In Section 3.2, we investigated how the ranges of r and g (i.e. α and f) influence the mapping U and we derived the x and y bounds of the point $\mathbf{x}$ mapped by U. This approach can be easily generalized to an interval of point $([x_i], [y_i])$ instead of a given point $\mathbf{x}$. The "extended" x and y bounds of the interval $([x_i], [y_i])$ mapped by U can be computed in a similar way, analytically or by simple interval arithmetics [16]. This provides the interval of $\mathbf{x}_i$ mapped by U in the right image (obtained by the definition ranges of ϕ, α, f) and we compare this interval to the interval of $([x_i'], [y_i'])$ (obtained by the definition range of θ). If the intervals intersect (up to δ), then the match $(\mathbf{x}_i, \mathbf{x}_i')$ is a potential inlier under a model contained in $\mathcal{C}$. If they do not intersect, then it is definitively an outlier for the cube $\mathcal{C}$. We conduct this procedure for all the input matches and count the number of potential inliers, which in turn provides an upper bound of the number of inliers for $\mathcal{C}$.

Search strategy. We explained above how to compute the lower and upper bounds of the number of inliers for a given cube. We now discuss how to iteratively discard the non-feasible cubes and conduct the search strategy.

First of all, the search starts with a cube list $\mathcal{L}$ that is initialized with one cube covering the entire search space (see above). During the subdivision of a cube $\mathcal{C}_j$, each dimension of this cube is split into two intervals of equal length, which provides, in total, $2^4 = 16$ disjoint smaller cubes whose side length is half of the side length of the original cube $\mathcal{C}_j$. The cube $\mathcal{C}_j$ is removed from $\mathcal{L}$ and replaced by its subdivided cubes.

Let l^* be the highest lower bound obtained so far or the number of inliers computed beforehand by any existing methods. Let us note l_j and u_j the lower and upper bounds of the number of inliers of a cube $\mathcal{C}_j$. If $u_j < l^*$ then it is sure that the optimal model (i.e. the model leading to the highest number of inliers) is not contained in $\mathcal{C}_j$ because $\mathcal{C}_j$ does not contain any models that can lead to at least or more than l^* inliers. Thus the cube $\mathcal{C}_j$ is considered non-feasible and can be removed from the search space. On the contrary (i.e. if $u_j \geq l^*$) then the cube $\mathcal{C}_j$ is subdivided for further investigation. In case $l_j > l^*$ then l^* is updated by l_j. This procedure is applied iteratively for all the cubes contained in the cube list $\mathcal{L}$. We define the maximum upper bound u^* as the highest upper bound among the feasible cubes currently present in the list $\mathcal{L}$. Along the BnB iterations, the non-feasible cubes are discarded (the search space reduces), the size of the cubes decreases (by subdivision), the gap between the lower and upper bounds l_j and u_j computed for each cube $\mathcal{C}_j$ diminishes, and l^* and u^* converge. The search stops when the list $\mathcal{L}$ contains at least one cube $\mathcal{C}_j^*$ whose lower bound l_j equals the maximum upper bound u^* because it means that the model at the center of $\mathcal{C}_j^*$ (i.e. used to compute l_j) provides the maximum number of inliers u^*. Finally the BnB procedure simply returns the model $(\mathtt{R}^*, f^*)$ associated to the center of $\mathcal{C}_j^*$ and this model leads to the maximum number of inliers u^* that can be obtained inside the search space.

4   Results

This section presents some experimental results obtained for synthesized data and real images. Implementation details, additional algorithmic explanations and supplementary results are available on the authors' website. Our branch-and-bound approach has been implemented in C++ and ran on a computer equipped with an Intel Core i7 CPU 2.8GHz (a single core is used) and 12GB RAM. We run BnB on the whole rotation search space $SO(3)$ and a conservative realistic range for the focal length $[200, 4500]$, unless otherwise stated. Our approach takes between a few seconds and a few minutes depending mainly on the number of points and the search space size.

We compare our approach to the conventional RANSAC and the optimized LO-RANSAC [7], both being referred to as RANSACs. They both embed the state-of-the-art minimal solution approach of Brown et al. [4], that we refer to as the 2-point algorithm. We consider LO-RANSAC in addition to the conventional RANSAC, because it is known to perform very well in practice. Among the versions of LO-RANSAC, we apply the *inner RANSAC with iteration* because it has been shown that it provides the best results [7]. The number of RANSAC iterations is automatically computed with the true outlier ratio (if not available, e.g.

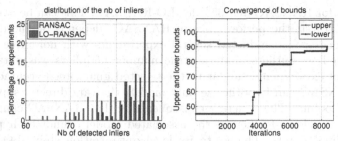

Fig. 2. Comparison between RANSACs and the proposed approach. Left: distribution of the number of inliers obtained by RANSAC and LO-RANSAC. Their best run leads to 88 and 89 inliers respectively. Right: convergence of the BnB bounds to 90 inliers.

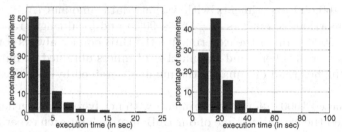

Fig. 3. Distribution of the execution time of our approach for $N = 30$ (left) and $N - 300$ data points (right) with 70% of outliers

for real data, set to 80%), a guaranteed accuracy of 99% and a minimal sampling of 2 points for the 2-point algorithm [10]. Since different runs of RANSACs might lead to different results (because of the random data sampling), we repeat each experiment over 1000 runs with the same input data and parameters. Finally, the algorithms are compared with respect to the number of inliers detected.

4.1   Synthesized Data

We randomly generate a set of $N = 300$ correspondences of 2D points between the left and right images. To reproduce realistic settings, we corrupt the x and y coordinates of the points by a Gaussian noise (std=0.5pixels) and create a percentage $p = 70\%$ of outliers with $\delta = 2$pixel. Figure 2 compares the number of inliers obtained by the proposed approach and RANSACs. Our BnB approach obtains 90 inliers, which corresponds to the number of synthesized inliers. On the contrary, RANSAC spans between 61 and 88 inliers and never obtains the number of synthesized inliers, that is 90. As expected, LO-RANSAC performs better than RANSAC: results span between 71 and 89 inliers. While it does not obtain the number of synthesized inliers neither, the distribution is clearly improved: RANSAC obtained more than 84 inliers in 26% of the 1000 runs, whereas it occurred in 72% of the runs for LO-RANSAC.

One might wonder why neither RANSAC nor LO-RANSAC managed to obtain the true number of inliers. This actually happened in about 80% of our experiments for RANSAC and 65% for LO-RANSAC. This can be explained by two reasons. First, the performance of RANSACs depends on the data noise: for completeness, we conducted several experiments with noise-free data, but still corrupted by outliers, and the true number of inliers was obtained in a percentage of experiments similar to the selected guaranteed accuracy of 99%. Second, RANSAC can hypothesize only models that are directly supported by the selected points. The concrete consequence is that RANSAC cannot return the optimal number of inliers if the associated model cannot be hypothesized by the minimal points. Thanks to its local optimization steps, LO-RANSAC performs better than RANSAC, but still relies on the data points support to hypothesize models, and therefore this limitation is removed only partially.

For a complete comparison of RANSACs and our BnB approach, we conducted more than 100,000 experiments with various data amounts ($N = 10 \sim 600$ points), proportions of outliers ($p = 0\% \sim 90\%$) and focal length ranges ([500 , 700] to [10 , 5000]). In *all* the experiments, the BnB bounds always converged to the true number of inliers, and the number of inliers obtained by our approach was always higher than or equal to the number obtained by RANSAC and LO-RANSAC.

We conducted 1000 different experiments with newly randomly generated data and measured the execution time of our BnB approach for each experiment. The distribution of the execution time for $N = 30$ and $N = 300$ data points (70% of outliers) is illustrated in Figure 3. As expected, the execution time increases with the number of points since there are more data to process, and the figure shows that the approach is scalable with the data amount. RANSACs definitely run faster than the BnB approach but we do not aim to compete with RANSACs in terms of speed: our key goal is to obtain the globally optimal solution.

4.2   Real Data

We now present results obtained by our approach on real images. We perform the intrinsic calibration of the camera by Bouguet's toolbox [3], and the camera center is then applied to the point measurements to center their coordinates. Putative correspondences between two images are obtained by extracting and matching SIFT features [14]. The number of RANSAC iterations is computed with a very conservative outlier ratio of 80% and we run RANSACs 1000 times for each experiment. In the case the focal length and its limits are totally unknown, we use a conservative focal length range [200 , 4500]. This focal length range covers most of the practical cases and can be enlarged if needed. Optionally, a rough focal length estimation and/or its limits can be obtained via EXIF tags like in [1,20] or known approximately from the camera device.

A first representative result with a small overlap is shown in Figure 4. The images are acquired with a Sony NEX-3 camera. A rough estimate of the focal length is available from the EXIF tag and we use a range of ±200 around this value (we will show results without any EXIF tag information in Figure 5). 163 putative correspondences are obtained by SIFT. The number of inliers obtained by RANSAC and LO-RANSAC span between 75 and 80, and between 77 and 80

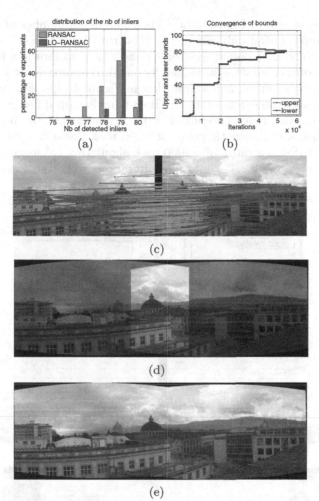

Fig. 4. (a) Distribution of the number of inliers obtained by RANSAC and LO-RANSAC. (b) Convergence of the BnB bounds to 80 inliers. (c) Inlier (green) and outlier (red) matches detected by our approach. (d) Highlighted overlap of the input images on the resulting panoramic view. (e) The final panoramic view.

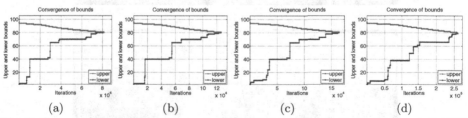

Fig. 5. Convergence of the BnB bounds to 80 inliers with a focal length range of ± 300 (a), ± 500 (b), ± 1000 (c) around a rough focal length estimation, and with a very conservative focal length range of $[200, 4500]$ (d).

respectively, as shown in Figure 4-(a). Their maximum number of inliers, that is 80, is obtained during only 9% of the 1000 runs by RANSAC, and 19% by LO-RANSAC. The BnB bounds converge to 80 inliers, as shown in Figure 4-(b). The inlier and outlier matches identified by our BnB approach are shown in Figure 4-(c), and the resulting panoramic view in Figure 4-(d,e). For completeness, Figure 5 illustrates the evolution of the BnB bounds with different focal length ranges for the image pair of Figure 4. First it shows that the bounds always converged. Also, a focal length range of ± 200 took about 5.4×10^4 iterations (see Figure 4-(b)) and a range of ± 1000 took about 16×10^4 iterations (see Figure 5-(c)), that is about 2.96 times more iterations while the search space is 5

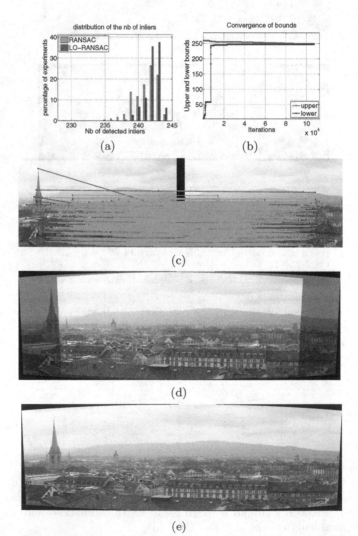

(a)

(b)

(c)

(d)

(e)

Fig. 6. Same legend as in Figure 4. The best run of RANSAC and LO-RANSAC leads to 244 inliers and our BnB bounds converge to 248 inliers.

times larger. This shows that the method is scalable with the focal length range. Figure 5-(d) shows the convergence of the BnB bounds with a very conservative focal length range, which shows that our method can be applied for practical cases when the focal length and its limits are totally unknown.

An additional representative result with a large overlap is shown in Figure 6. 275 putative correspondences are obtained by SIFT. The number of inliers obtained by RANSAC and LO-RANSAC span between 229 and 244, and between 238 and 244 respectively. Their maximum number of inliers, that is 244, is ob-

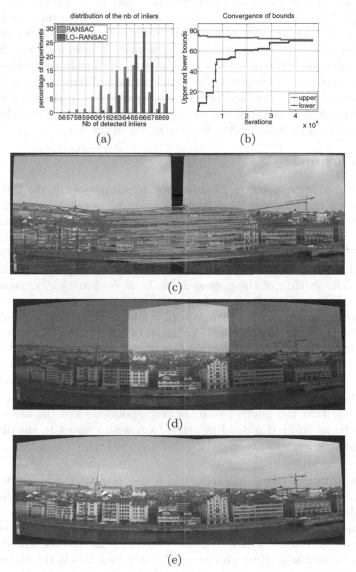

Fig. 7. Same legend as in Figure 4. The best run of RANSAC and LO-RANSAC leads to 69 inliers and our BnB bounds converge to 70 inliers.

tained during only 3%, by RANSAC, and 6%, by LO-RANSAC, of the 1000 runs. In contrast, our BnB bounds converge to 248 inliers, which is 4 additional inliers than the best result of RANSAC and LO-RANSAC among the 1000 runs. For this image pair, the lower bound increases very quickly to 243 inliers, and the gap between the lower and the upper bounds reduces slowly. This is because the reprojection errors of some correspondences were close to the inlier threshold and thus the size of the cubes (i.e. the uncertainty of the model) needs to be sufficiently small to be able to decide whether such correspondence is inlier or outlier, and this cube size is continuously reduced along the BnB iterations.

We also apply our approach on images acquired by a smartphone. Figure 7 shows a representative result with a conservative focal length range: the RANSAC distribution, the convergence of the BnB bounds, the inlier/outlier correspondences obtained by our approach and the resulting panoramic view. Some additional results for different scenes and cameras are available on the authors' website. Similarly to the experiments with synthesized data, the number of inliers obtained by our approach on *all* our experiments with real images was always higher than or equal to the number of inliers obtained by RANSAC and LO-RANSAC, which confirms the validity of our approach.

5   Conclusion

This paper faced the problem of inlier set maximization in the image space with unknown rotation and focal length. The most popular approach to solve this problem is RANSAC but it has several limitations especially the lack of optimality. We proposed a new approach based on branch-and-bound that maximizes the inlier set in a globally optimal way: it returns the rotation and the focal length leading to the highest number of inlier correspondences in the image space. The validity of the approach has been confirmed by experiments on synthesized data and real images.

An interesting direction for future work would be to estimate, in addition to the focal length, some extra intrinsic parameters, such as the camera center. We also plan to investigate the generalization of our approach of inlier set maximization in the image space beyond pure-rotation motion and for other models. Especially, in the context of fundamental matrix estimation, the goal would be to compute the rotation and translation of the camera, as well as the focal length, in such a way that the number of inlier correspondences in the image is maximized, up to an inlier threshold in pixels (e.g. with respect to the distance to the epipolar line).

Acknowledgments. This research, which has been partially carried out at BeingThere Centre, was supported by the Singapore National Research Foundation under its International Research Centre @ Singapore Funding Initiative and administered by the IDM Programme Office. The work was also supported by the Sogang University Research Grant of 201210029. NICTA is funded by the Australian Government through the ARC. Yongduek Seo is the corresponding author.

References

1. Agarwal, S., Snavely, N., Simon, I., Seitz, S.M., Szeliski, R.: Building Rome in a day. In: ICCV (2009)
2. Bazin, J.-C., Seo, Y., Pollefeys, M.: Globally optimal consensus set maximization through rotation search. In: Lee, K.M., Matsushita, Y., Rehg, J.M., Hu, Z. (eds.) ACCV 2012, Part II. LNCS, vol. 7725, pp. 539–551. Springer, Heidelberg (2013)
3. Bouguet, J.Y.: Camera calibration toolbox for Matlab
4. Brown, M., Hartley, R., Nister, D.: Minimal solutions for panoramic stitching. In: CVPR (2007)
5. Brown, M., Lowe, D.: Automatic panoramic image stitching using invariant features. IJCV (2007)
6. Choi, K., Lee, S., Seo, Y.: A branch-and-bound algorithm for globally optimal camera pose and focal length. Image and Vision Computing (2010)
7. Chum, O., Matas, J.: Optimal randomized RANSAC. TPAMI (2008)
8. Fischler, M.A., Bolles, R.C.: Random sample consensus: A paradigm for model fitting with applications to image analysis and automated cartography. Communications of the ACM (1981)
9. Hartley, R., Kahl, F.: Global optimization through rotation space search. IJCV (2009)
10. Hartley, R.I., Zisserman, A.: Multiple View Geometry in Computer Vision, 2nd edn. Cambridge University Press (2004)
11. Horst, R., Tuy, H.: Global optimization: deterministic approaches. Springer (2006)
12. Kahl, F., Agarwal, S., Chandraker, M., Kriegman, D., Belongie, S.: Practical global optimization for multiview geometry. IJCV (2008)
13. Li, H.: Consensus set maximization with guaranteed global optimality for robust geometry estimation. In: ICCV (2009)
14. Lowe, D.: Distinctive image features from scale-invariant keypoints. IJCV (2003)
15. McCormick, G.: Computability of global solutions to factorable nonconvex programs: part I - convex underestimating problems. Mathematical Programming (1976)
16. Moor, R.: Interval Analysis. Prentice-Hall (1966)
17. Nistér, D.: Preemptive RANSAC for live structure and motion estimation. In: ICCV (2003)
18. Olsson, C., Enqvist, O., Kahl, F.: A polynomial-time bound for matching and registration with outliers. In: CVPR (2008)
19. Raguram, R., Frahm, J.-M., Pollefeys, M.: A comparative analysis of RANSAC techniques leading to adaptive real-time random sample consensus. In: Forsyth, D., Torr, P., Zisserman, A. (eds.) ECCV 2008, Part II. LNCS, vol. 5303, pp. 500–513. Springer, Heidelberg (2008)
20. Snavely, N., Seitz, S.M., Szeliski, R.: Photo tourism: Exploring photo collections in 3D. In: SIGGRAPH (2006)
21. Sun, M., Telaprolu, M., Lee, H., Savarese, S.: An efficient branch-and-bound algorithm for optimal human pose estimation. In: CVPR (2012)
22. Torr, P., Zisserman, A.: MLESAC: A new robust estimator with application to estimating image geometry. Computer Vision and Image Understanding (2000)
23. Yang, J., Li, H., Jia, Y.: Go-ICP: solving 3D registration efficiently and globally optimally. In: ICCV (2013)
24. Yu, C., Seo, Y., Lee, S.W.: Global optimization for estimating a BRDF with multiple specular lobes. In: CVPR (2010)

Match Selection and Refinement for Highly Accurate Two-View Structure from Motion

Zhe Liu, Pascal Monasse, and Renaud Marlet

Université Paris-Est, LIGM (UMR 8049), ENPC, F-77455 Marne-la-Vallée, France

Abstract. We present an approach to enhance the accuracy of structure from motion (SfM) in the two-view case. We first answer the question: "fewer data with higher accuracy, or more data with less accuracy?" For this, we establish a relation between SfM errors and a function of the number of matches and their epipolar errors. Using an accuracy estimator of individual matches, we then propose a method to select a subset of matches that has a good quality vs. quantity compromise. We also propose a variant of least squares matching to refine match locations based on a focused grid and a multi-scale exploration. Experiments show that both selection and refinement contribute independently to a better accuracy. Their combination reduces errors by a factor of 1.1 to 2.0 for rotation, and 1.6 to 3.8 for translation.

1 Introduction

3D reconstructions from pictures are increasingly being used to model real scenes or objects. For some applications such as video games or virtual film sets, capturing the general shape and appearance is enough. The reconstruction method does not have to be particularly accurate. However, in industrial settings, where 3D models are used for measurement, accuracy is crucial. Moreover, even for less demanding tasks, accurate reconstruction reduces the quantity of required images, thus reducing the costs and increasing the applicability. Better estimates also lessen the impact of outliers.

In this paper, we propose a method to greatly enhance the accuracy of two-view structure from motion (SfM), i.e., the estimation of the camera poses (positions and orientations) and of the basic structure of the scene (3D point cloud). As 3D reconstruction methods strongly rely on the quality of the estimated calibration, this is a crucial initial step. In most cases, being wrong at calibration time cannot be recovered later.

Match Selection. Most SfM approaches are based on the detection and matching of interest points (features) in image pairs [11]. Given point matches between two images, we can estimate a fundamental matrix F relating them. If internal calibration parameters are known (calibration matrix K), this also provides an estimate of the camera motion (rotation R, translation t) and 3D position of matched points. As feature detection and matching is not perfect, two main things can go wrong in the SfM process: the matches can be either incorrect

D. Fleet et al. (Eds.): ECCV 2014, Part II, LNCS 8690, pp. 818–833, 2014.

or inaccurate. There is actually a grey area between these notions: incorrect matches reduce SfM accuracy, sometimes to the point of making it fail, while inaccurate matches are considered as good enough for calibrating, even though they also degrade SfM accuracy. Incorrect matches are generally dealt with using RANSAC [9] or one of its numerous variants [7,8,19,26]. It separates "good matches" (inliers) from "wrong matches" (outliers), trying to find the largest consensus on an estimated fundamental matrix, using a threshold (fixed or adaptive) to assess consistency. While this robust selection method can eliminate many outliers, a number of false positives can remain among the selected inliers because the rejection criterion is mostly based on the distance to epipolar lines, which provides a necessary but not sufficient condition (ambiguity along lines).

Compromises at two different levels impact SfM accuracy. First of all, statistically, the more matches to calculate the fundamental matrix, the more accurate the estimation. A first compromise thus concerns the RANSAC selection criterion: if it is too permissive, matches considered as inliers are more numerous but are also more likely to be contaminated by wrong matches, and accuracy drops; if the criterion is too strict, there are too few inliers to get a good accuracy. The second compromise concerns the accuracy heterogeneity of individual inliers: keeping only the most accurate inliers can naturally improve SfM accuracy; but it can also degrade it as the estimation is based on fewer points. The first compromise has indirectly been widely studied: people try to select as many good matches as possible, while excluding as many wrong matches as possible. But the second compromise, quality vs. quantity, has been poorly addressed. This paper presents an original method to find a good balance between the number of inliers to consider for SfM estimation and their expected accuracy.

Match Refinement. Another way to obtain a better SfM accuracy is to improve the accuracy of feature detection and matching.

Due to differences in imaging conditions, in particular changes of viewpoint or illumination, a salient point or region detected in one image is not detected in the other image at the exact same location. The most popular features are by design only invariant (at most) to affine transformation (e.g., Harris-affine [18], MSER [17], ASIFT [20]), or to small affine transformation (e.g., SIFT [16]). But they are not invariant under perspective transformation, which is enough to offset most detections. Methods to add some perspective invariance to existing feature detectors have been proposed, but they require full 3D information (depth map or mesh) [13,28], which is computationally expensive or requires more than just image data; others are suited to specific classes of scenes only, mostly urban environments, as they strongly rely on the presence of vanishing points and large planar surfaces [2,5]. Besides, they have been designed to improve the repeatability of feature detection and matching, which is generally measured using a threshold on the relative overlap of corresponding regions [18], not in terms of the closest distance between feature centers.

Traditionally, two detected feature points can nonetheless be considered as matching although their position in the images does not correspond exactly to the same 3D point in the observed scene. For a number of tasks, being close is enough. But for highly accurate calibration, it is not satisfactory. In fact, we do not care whether a specific 3D point is accurately identified in both images, such as the very tip of a corner. What we need is possibly arbitrary pairs of points in the images as long as they correspond to extremely close 3D points. In this sense, feature detection and matching is just a way for us to identify corresponding regions rather than corresponding points: their center generally corresponds only to close but different 3D points. Our match refinement only uses them as initial estimates to find a neighboring pair of points that is likely to correspond to closer 3D points because they have a better photometric consistency (assuming an unknown affine transformation).

Finely relating image regions can be addressed with optical flow methods [3]. But they are not well adapted here because they suppose small variations, both in viewpoint (very small baseline, quasi-affine transformation) and in illumination (controlled light scenes). Refining the position of image regions to overlap them better has been studied in the photogrammetry community. One of the most popular methods is adaptive least squares matching (LSM), that tries simultaneously to find radiometric and geometric corrections to best fit two images patches [10]. The most complex geometric correction generally considered in this framework is affine transformation, because projective transformations are assumed to be sufficiently approximated by an affinity. We present here an improvement of LSM based on a focused irregular grid and made robust with coarse-to-fine exploration. We show that it outperforms affine correction.

Our Contributions follow the structure of the paper: We establish an empirical statistical relationship between the inaccuracy of matches, their number, and various indicators of SfM inaccuracy (Section 2). We describe an original method that exploits this relationship to select matches that are likely to improve SfM accuracy (Section 3). We present a novel method to locally refine the position of matches to improve their accuracy (Section 4). We show on extensive experiments that both methods improve substantially the accuracy of structure from motion, and even more when combined (Section 5). Section 6 concludes.

2   Statistical Behavior of SfM Errors

2.1   Theoretical Results

We consider a pair of images I, I', obtained by cameras C, C' with 3×4 projection matrices P, P' and 3×3 calibration matrices K, K'. We also consider a set of matches M between I and I', i.e., pairs of points $m = (\mathbf{x}, \mathbf{x}')$ where $\mathbf{x}$ is the projection of a 3D point X on I, i.e., $\mathbf{x} = PX$ in homogeneous coordinates, and where $\mathbf{x}'$ is a point in I' considered as matching with $\mathbf{x}$, possibly with some inaccuracy. In the general case, a fundamental matrix F_M between I and I' can be estimated from matches M, and F_M may in turn be used with K, K' to estimate projection matrices P_M, P_M' on I, I'. The resulting reprojection error of $\mathbf{x}$ in I', i.e., the discrepancy in I' between the exact reprojection of X by P' and the estimated reprojection of X by P_M' is the distance $e_{2D}(M, m) = d(P'X, P_M'X)$.

In case images I and I' are related by homography H, and considering matching points $\mathbf{x}'$ as possibly inaccurate measurements of reprojected points $P'X = H\mathbf{x}$ in I', Hartley and Zisserman [11, §5.1.3, Eq.(5.5)] show that, if these measurements are subject to independent Gaussian noise with standard deviation $\sigma_{2D}(M)$, then the estimation error $e_{2D}(M)$ of reprojected points in I' by the estimated homography H_M, or equivalently via P'_M, is:

$$e_{2D}(M) = \mathbb{E}_{m \in M} [\, e_{2D}(M,m)^2 / |M| \,]^{1/2} = 2\,\sigma_{2D}(M)/\sqrt{|M|}. \tag{1}$$

Dividing the estimation error by 2 thus requires 4 times as many matches, or matches with location error divided by 2. This bound is optimal (assuming no other errors such as distortion), and achieved for the Maximum Likelihood Estimator (MLE). Finding a similar bound for the fundamental matrix is impractical because it is a non convex problem in very high dimension. We do not try to solve it, but we draw inspiration of the MLE bound in what follows.

Another reading of (1) is that if we can find a subset $M_{\text{sub}} \subset M$ such that matching points $\mathbf{x}'$ in M_{sub} are subject to independent Gaussian noise with standard deviation $\sigma_{2D}(M_{\text{sub}}) < \sigma_{2D}(M)$ compared to their expected location $H\mathbf{x}$, and if $\sigma_{2D}(M_{\text{sub}})/\sqrt{|M_{\text{sub}}|} < \sigma_{2D}(M)/\sqrt{|M|}$, then $e_{M_{\text{sub}}} < e_M$, and $H_{M_{\text{sub}}}$ is thus a better estimate of H than H_M. Now if we have a way to evaluate $\sigma_{2D}(M_{\text{sub}})$ for any M_{sub}, the optimal subset M^*_{sub} of matches for estimating H is:

$$M^*_{\text{sub}} = \underset{M_{\text{sub}} \subset M}{\arg\min}\ \sigma_{2D}(M_{\text{sub}})/\sqrt{|M_{\text{sub}}|}. \tag{2}$$

$H_{M^*_{\text{sub}}}$ minimizes reprojection errors w.r.t. ground truth H (not w.r.t. $H_{M^*_{\text{sub}}}$ that has a trivial solution with any 4 points).

To our knowledge, a similar result is not known for the fundamental matrix. The situation is more complex in this case as estimating F, with 7- or 8-point methods, relies on SVD and/or requires solving complex polynomial systems.

2.2   Empirical Results

As a theoretical result is difficult to obtain, we study empirically the influence of $|M|$ and $\sigma_{2D}(M)$ on SfM accuracy. Using a collection of images with accurate ground-truth calibration, presenting various feature distributions, we measure:

- F_M is the fundamental matrix estimated from M using ORSA (a RANSAC variant) and iterative re-weighted least squares (IRLS) [19].
- $e_F(M)$ is the root mean square error (RMSE) of the distance $e_F(M,m)$ of $\mathbf{x}'$ to the F_M-epipolar line of $\mathbf{x}$ in I', for $m = (\mathbf{x}, \mathbf{x}') \in M$.
- $e_R(M) = \angle R_{\text{gt}} R_M^{-1}$ is the angle between the ground-truth rotation R_{gt} and its estimate R_M based on M.
- $e_t(M) = \angle(t_{\text{gt}}, t_M)$ is the angle between the ground-truth translation direction t_{gt} and its estimate t_M.
- $e_{3D}(M, R, t)$ is the RMSE of the distance of the 3D point $\widehat{X}$ triangulated from $\mathbf{x}, \mathbf{x}'$ using a given rotation and translation R, t, to the ground-truth 3D point X, for $m = (\mathbf{x}, \mathbf{x}') \in M$. We also define $e_{3D}(M) = e_{3D}(M, R_M, t_M)$.

Realistic, Semi-synthetic Dataset. Estimating SfM errors requires a ground truth for both calibration and matched points. While accurate camera calibrations can be determined using LiDAR data [23], it is difficult to construct a significant number of accurate ground-truth point matches. For this, we resort to semi-synthetic ground-truth datasets: the images, the camera poses and the distribution of matching points are real, but the actual point locations are adjusted to make sure they are error-free.

Concretely, given a pair of images I, I' with known calibration P_{gt}, P'_{gt}, we detect and match SIFT feature points in each image. We use a descriptor distance ratio to next best match at most 0.8, which is the standard setting [16]. As these matches may still contain outliers, we first clean them using the K-VLD method of Liu and Marlet [15], that eliminates many false matches, including near the epipolar lines, and then using ORSA, an adaptive state-of-the-art variant of RANSAC by Moisan and Stival [19], known for its robustness in practical SfM systems [21]. It results in an almost outlier-free set of matches $\tilde{M}$. Treating them as inliers, for each match $\tilde{m} = (\tilde{\mathbf{x}}, \tilde{\mathbf{x}}') \in \tilde{M}$, we construct a 3D point X by triangulation using ground truth calibration P_{gt}, P'_{gt}, and reproject it onto images I, I' as new 2D points $(\mathbf{x}, \mathbf{x}') = m$. The resulting set of matches M_{gt} yields a perfect ground truth that is realistic in terms of feature distribution in images (location and number) and in space.

We then add noise by randomly moving in image I' the matched points $\mathbf{x}'$, using an isotropic Gaussian distribution with given standard deviation σ_{2D}. This asymmetric setting reproduces the theoretical hypothesis mentioned in Section 2.1. (Adding noise to points in both images experimentally leads to almost identical results, scaled by a constant.) To also conform to this hypothesis, the noise is independent of the characteristics of the features that originated the synthetic points, such as scale. Moreover, we add variation to the number of matches by randomly selecting only a given ratio r. This defines new sets $M = M(\sigma_{2D}, r)$.

In our experiments, we use Strecha et al.'s dataset [23]. It consists of 6 groups of 8 to 30 images with both internal and external accurate ground-truth calibration. We consider all pairs of consecutive images in all image groups, in which we detect and match SIFT features. The number of matches typically varies between 300 and 6000. For each image pair, we consider discrete ratios of matches $r = k^2/100$ with $k = 4, \ldots, 10$ (thus different point configurations), and discrete deviation $\sigma_{2D} = 0.2 + 0.3k$ with $k = 0, \ldots, 6$ (in pixels). For each combination of r and σ_{2D}, we sample 50 noisy variants of the data, estimate their SfM accuracy, and average the corresponding error measures by quadratic mean (RMS).

Analysis. Adding noise σ_{2D} and ratio r as $M = M(\sigma_{2D}, r)$ has a direct impact on epipolar error $e_F(M)$ and on rotation and translation errors e_R, e_t. It has an impact in turn on the error e_{3D} of estimated 3D points, which depends both on noisy matches M and estimated calibration R_M, t_M.

We observe that e_{3D}, e_R and e_t all are highly correlated to $N = |M|$ and σ_{2D}: although there are some variations, we notice experimentally that $\log e_{3D}, \log e_R$ and $\log e_t$ are more or less linear with respect to $\log N$ when σ_{2D} is fixed, with some slope α depending on the image pair, and more or less linear with $\log \sigma_{2D}$

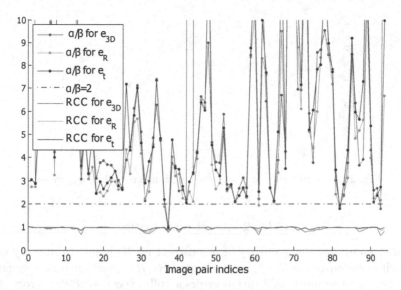

Fig. 1. Dotted curves: estimated α/β for different image pairs (the order is irrelevant). Plain curves: regression correlation coefficient between e_R, e_t, or e_{3D}, and $\sigma_{2D}^\alpha/N^\beta$.

when N is fixed (but not the configuration), with some slope $-\beta$ also depending on the image pair. It is confirmed by computing the regression correlation coefficient (RCC) of e_{3D}, e_R, e_t with $\sigma_{2D}^\alpha/N^\beta$, which is in general very close to 1, as can be seen in Figure 1 (bottom 3 curves, plotted on the same diagram).

Besides, we also found empirically that σ_{2D} is more or less proportional to e_F, not only to the exact epipolar error. We thus hypothesize the relation:

$$e_R, e_t, e_{3D} \propto \frac{\sigma_{2D}^\alpha}{N^\beta} \propto \frac{e_F^\alpha}{N^\beta} \tag{3}$$

With a fixed distribution of points, we should have $\alpha = 1$ for small errors. Still with a fixed configuration, but duplicating all matches, the covariance matrix of estimated parameters is halved; we should thus have $\beta = 0.5$. This is consistent with equation (1). However, it does not hold when point configuration varies. Experimentally, α and β can vary significantly depending on images pairs and match sampling. In our semi-synthetic dataset, β varies between 0.2 and 1.5. Yet, assuming relation (3), knowing α/β is sufficient to compare errors for a given image pair:

$$\frac{e_F^\alpha}{N^\beta} < \frac{e_F'^\alpha}{N'^\beta} \Leftrightarrow \frac{e_F^{\alpha/\beta}}{N} < \frac{e_F'^{\alpha/\beta}}{N'} \tag{4}$$

The situation where all matched points are treated as inliers and contribute to estimating F amounts to preferring the largest N (smallest $1/N$) independently of e_F, i.e., to $\alpha/\beta = 0$. On the contrary, the larger α/β, the more aggressively low-accuracy features should be discarded. As can be seen in Figure 1,

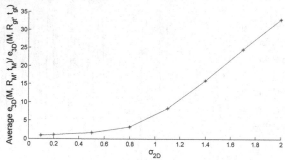

Fig. 2. Amplification of 3D reconstruction error when σ_{2D} grows

$$\alpha/\beta \geq 2 \quad \text{almost consistently.} \tag{5}$$

Figure 2 compares the accuracy of reconstructing 3D points from noisy image points with ground-truth R_{gt}, t_{gt} vs estimated R_M, t_M (average on image pairs). The bigger σ_{2D}, the more calibration errors amplify reconstruction errors.

3   Match Selection to Improve Accuracy

To improve accuracy, we estimate SfM using a selected subset of good matches.

Cleaning up Input Matches. Although we use IRLS for estimating F, the level of accuracy we target may be sensitive to outliers remaining after RANSAC. We thus try to eliminate outliers from the set of input matches. We have to do it without introducing the bias of an early approximate calibration estimation, which would be the case if we were to first filter the matches using RANSAC. For this reason, we first clean up the matches using the K-VLD method [15]. Based on semi-local geometric and photometric consistency, it eliminates many outliers without any calibration assumption. Running ORSA afterwards on the resulting set of matches M typically only removes on the order of 10% of matches with a found threshold of less than 2-pixel error for estimating F.

Comparing Subsets of Matches. The SfM errors we want to reduce are $e_R(M), e_t(M), e_{3D}(M)$. But what can be easily measured given a pair of images and a set of matches M is just $e_F(M)$. However, as indicated by Eq. (3) and (4), $e_R(M), e_t(M), e_{3D}(M)$ vary monotonically with $e_F(M)^{\alpha/\beta}/|M|$. The basic idea of match selection is to use only a subset of matches $M_{\text{sub}} \subset M$ as soon as:

$$\frac{e_F(M_{\text{sub}})^{\alpha/\beta}}{|M_{\text{sub}}|} < \frac{e_F(M)^{\alpha/\beta}}{|M|} \tag{6}$$

However, α/β is a priori unknown for an arbitrary image pair. Moreover, we want to improve SfM without taking the risk to degrade it. What we need is a sufficient condition that reducing the number of matches will probably improve accuracy but most certainly will not reduce it. For this, we look for a possible value $\gamma \geq 1$

such that, for any image pair, any set of matches M with corresponding α, β parameters, and any subset of matches $M_{\text{sub}} \subset M$,

$$\frac{e_F(M_{\text{sub}})^\gamma}{|M_{\text{sub}}|} < \frac{e_F(M)^\gamma}{|M|} \Rightarrow \frac{e_F(M_{\text{sub}})^{\alpha/\beta}}{|M_{\text{sub}}|} < \frac{e_F(M)^{\alpha/\beta}}{|M|} \tag{7}$$

We can then choose this optimal subset of matches M_{sub}^* for estimating F:

$$M_{\text{sub}}^* = \arg\min_{M_{\text{sub}} \subset M} \frac{e_F(M_{\text{sub}})^\gamma}{|M_{\text{sub}}|} \tag{8}$$

The fundamental $F_{M_{\text{sub}}^*}$ minimizes reprojection errors w.r.t. ground truth F_{gt}.

Noting that $(e_F(M_{\text{sub}})/e_F(M))^\gamma < |M_{\text{sub}}|/|M| < 1$ and hypothesizing (5), we can choose $\gamma = 2$ because then $(e_F(M_{\text{sub}})/e_F(M))^{\alpha/\beta} < e_F(M_{\text{sub}})/e_F(M))^\gamma$, ensuring condition (7). Parameter γ is chosen as a safe empirical lower bound, not an average value, which is more robust. Still, a general method to treat a specific class of images would be to run experiments as in Section 2.2 and pick a value $\gamma \leq \alpha/\beta$. Without loss of generally, we assume $\gamma = 2$ in the following.

Exploring Subsets of Matches. The difficulty to find M_{sub}^* is to explore $M_{\text{sub}} \subset M$, as there are too many such subsets ($2^{|M|}$). We propose to evaluate just a fraction of them, that has the most chances to lead to smaller ratios $e_F(M_{\text{sub}})^2/|M_{\text{sub}}|$. For this, we rank the matches in M and use this ordering to explore only subsets of top-rank matches. More precisely, we look for a ranking function $\phi: M \to \mathbb{R}$ to order the matches into a sequence $(m_i)_{1 \leq i \leq |M|}$ such that $i < j \Rightarrow \phi(m_i) < \phi(m_j)$, and consider $M_{\text{sub}}(N) = \{m_i \mid 1 \leq i \leq N\}$. If the ranking function ϕ is highly correlated to the reprojection errors $e_{\mathcal{D}}(M, m)$, and hence to the epipolar errors $e_F(M, m)$, then

$$\min_{M_{\text{sub}} \subset M} \frac{e_F(M_{\text{sub}})^2}{|M_{\text{sub}}|} = \min_{N \leq |M|} \frac{1}{N} \min_{\substack{M_{\text{sub}} \subset M \\ |M_{\text{sub}}| = N}} e_F(M_{\text{sub}})^2$$

$$\approx \min_{N \leq |M|} \frac{1}{N} e_F(M_{\text{sub}}(N))^2 \tag{9}$$

We may thus resort to:

$$N^* = \arg\min_{N \leq |M|} \frac{e_F(M_{\text{sub}}(N))^2}{N} \tag{10}$$

$$M^* = M_{\text{sub}}(N^*) \tag{11}$$

The number of subsets to explore is then reduced from $2^{|M|}$ to $|M|$, which is still a lot given that M generally contains a few thousands of matches. Note that $e_F(M_{\text{sub}}(N))^2/N$ is not necessarily convex. However, it is in practice "smooth" enough for a reduced exploration of $8 \leq N \leq |M|$ to make sense. In our various experiments, we found it robust and accurate enough to ensure a minimum of 40% of matches in $M_{\text{sub}}(N)$ and to explore fractions of M with a 5% step, i.e., to consider $N = r|M|$ with ratio $r = 0.4 + 0.05k$ and $k = 0, \ldots, 12$.

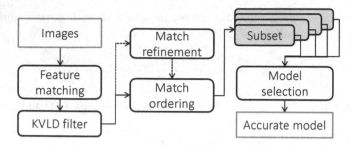

Fig. 3. A global view of our algorithm

Ranking Matches. The choice of a ranking function ϕ varies with the kind of feature. For SIFT, it seems natural to consider the distance between feature descriptors $d(desc(\mathbf{x}), desc(\mathbf{x}'))$ as an indicator of feature accuracy. Besides, Tang [25] showed that SIFT subsampling amplifies location error by the feature scale factor $scale(\mathbf{x})$. This leads us to define the following ranking function:

$$\phi(\mathbf{x}, \mathbf{x}') = \max(scale(\mathbf{x}), scale(\mathbf{x}'))\, d(desc(\mathbf{x}), desc(\mathbf{x}')) \qquad (12)$$

Large features thus tend to be ordered last, unless their descriptors match well. Still, although they have a poor accuracy, they are often useful for robustness, which could be a issue if too many of them are discarded. But our use of K-VLD [15] provides enough (if not better) robustness improvement to compensate.

On semi-synthetic data, made with first images from Mikolajczyk et al.'s dataset [18] and after applying an known homography, we found a correlation coefficient of 0.42 between ϕ and σ_{2D}, which proves the relevance of ϕ for ordering M. It outperforms other indicators, such as feature saliency that has a correlation score of 0.02. The Lowe score (ratio of descriptor distance to next best match) has an individual correlation of 0.2, but it does not improve the global correlation when combined with ϕ.

Note that the definition of ϕ relies only on detection scale and on the SIFT *descriptor*, not on the detector. It can thus be used, e.g., for all detectors of Mikolajczyk et al. [18], including SURF, Harris-Affine and MSER. Transposition to other descriptors is direct, but the correlation coefficient should be checked.

Algorithm. Our match selection algorithm is summarized on Figure 3. After feature detection and matching, matches M are cleaned up using K-VLD and ordered using the ranking function ϕ. Subsets M_{sub} of sorted matches are explored to minimize $e_F(M_{\mathrm{sub}})^\gamma/|M_{\mathrm{sub}}|$ and the subset with the lowest value if used to construct the estimated model.

Comparison to Related Methods. The PROSAC variant of RANSAC also constructs a series of match subsets and iterates first on better ones [7]. However, the target is not accuracy but fast convergence; robustness and precision are similar to RANSAC. Note that our method is not an alternative to RANSAC nor a fundamental matrix estimator, but a complement: a RANSAC variant as well as a fundamental matrix estimator are still needed to compute the calibration and the corresponding epipolar error e_F for the different M_{sub} subsets considered.

As a matter of fact, Section 5 shows that our method, combined with different variants of RANSAC, consistently provides much better results.

4   Least Square Focused Matching

We now present an extension of least squares matching (LSM) [10,22] to better adjust the location of matching features. LSM is based on the hypothesis that, *locally*, the region around the feature center is mostly planar, so that two matching regions are approximately related by homography, which in turn can be approximated by an affinity if the change of viewpoint is moderate. Besides, image intensity is also considered to possibly vary with an affine transformation.

Finding the affine parameters (both geometric and radiometric) that best map the two regions provides a good estimate of point displacement. This is a non-linear adjustment problem. It can be addressed by an iterative scheme based on a first-order Taylor expansion expressing optical flow constraints: differentiating the affine relation between the two regions, a small change in the affine parameters can be related to a small change in the dissimilarity measure of the regions, to be minimized. Yet, contrary to ordinary optical flow [3], LSM is not restricted to small light changes, small rotation angles and small baselines.

With LSFM, we propose two improvements. First, instead of using a regular sampling grid around the features, we use an irregular grid focused on the center of the region to match. Second, we combine it with an image scale traversal to make it more robust to local minima. (We also tried estimating a homography rather than just an affinity, but it did not produce substantial improvements.)

Note that feature detection covariance [4,12,24,29] is irrelevant here. What we do is, given a position p in I for which we know a roughly corresponding position p' in I', adjust p' so that the regions around p in I and p' in I' correlate better, under some geometric and photometric affinity to estimate. Feature points that match just happen to provide good initial correspondences for the refinement process. This is also widely different from refining the location of features detected as salient [16,18]. Moreover, refining given matches leads to a better accuracy than refining detections before matching.

Initialization. Given two matching features, we measure the dissimilarity η between the region with the lowest scale s and the region with the highest scale s' after enlarging by a factor of s'/s the sampling grid. We also rotate the grid according to the difference of orientation between the features. This initializes the affinity parameters in the iteration process.

Focused Grid. The image dissimilarity measure η in LSM is traditionally based on a regular sampling grid centered on interest points. This assumes a uniform transformation of the whole patches, which is true locally and slowly breaks down when moving away from the center. For this reason, we propose to use a grid focused on the patch center, i.e., denser in the center than in the border, which is additionally weighted by a Gaussian kernel to further concentrate on the center. Concretely, we use a grid whose lines are defined by a geometric progression:

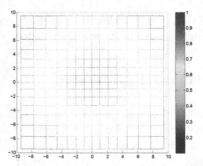

Fig. 4. Focused grid: denser and heavier center (colors represent the Gaussian weight)

its coordinates are $(u, v) = (sign(i)\frac{\rho^{|i|}-1}{\rho-1}, sign(j)\frac{\rho^{|j|}-1}{\rho-1})$ for $i, j \in \{-n, \dots, n\}$.
A standard Gaussian weight of $\frac{1}{2\pi\sigma^2} \exp(-\frac{u^2+v^2}{2\sigma^2})$ is used on grid nodes (u, v).
Figure 4 illustrates the shape of our grid, with color representing the Gaussian weight. In experiments, we use a spline interpretation of order 5 to get subpixel intensity in a focused grid with $n = 7$, $\sigma = 0.9\,n$ and $\rho = 1.1$: samples at the grid border are then almost twice as dense (in one direction) as at the center.

Scale Exploration. Additionally, rather than directly adjusting the feature positions at their original scale, we perform a coarse-to-fine refinement. We start adjusting point location at a higher scale and progressively refine the location by reducing the scale until we reach the original scale. (An optimal scale is not search as in [14]: the original scale is best for accuracy.) It improves robustness, preventing some refinements to be caught in local minima. For this, we create a pyramid of images similar to the one used in SIFT detection. After convergence of the geometric and photometric parameters at a given scale, we restart with the corresponding location and parameters at the scale below. As a high blur may also cause deviation from the optimal solution, we make sure there is an actual improvement: if the measure of dissimilarity computed with the estimated parameters at the current scale is less than the dissimilarity on the lower scale using just feature scale and orientation, the latter is kept as initial parameters for the refinement at the lower scale. In our experiments, we explore 5 octaves of scale, dividing each octave in 2, i.e., with a geometric progression of ratio $\sqrt{2}$.

Impact of the Feature Detector. SSD-based refinement is more accurate for regions with high gradients. SIFT does not necessarily detect points in such regions, but its robustness compensates. Besides it tends to find points within objects, where relative intensity is more stable, compared to corners that have strong but less stable gradients because they often correspond to occlusion edges.

Match Selection with Match Refinement. Match selection and match refinement are independent improvements that can be combined, match refinement coming first (see Fig. 3). However, match refinement changes the correlation between the match errors and the indicators of feature accuracy. When combined, the match ranking to create subset candidates (cf. Section 3) has to be changed.

Based on experiments with the same semi-synthetic data as in Section 3, we found that, after match refinement, the dissimilarity measure η using the focused grid has correlates with the actual feature localization error, with score of 0.27. Besides, intuitively, the scaling and shearing of the image, as defined by the affinity estimate A, also has an impact on the quality of matching. Given orthogonal vectors (u, v) in I, we consider the value $\max_{u,v} \frac{|u^T A^T A v|}{|Au||Av|}$, which is the cosine of the maximum crushing after transformation. It can be shown to be simply expressed as $\chi = \frac{|\lambda_1 - \lambda_2|}{\lambda_1 + \lambda_2}$, where $\lambda_1, \lambda_2 > 0$ are the eigenvalues of $A^T A$. It has a correlation score of 0.12 with the localization error. By a linear regression over the same semi-synthetic data, we empirically define $\phi(m) = 0.3\,\eta + 42.6\,\chi$, which has a correlation of 0.34 with the location error. Note that feature scales no longer correlate with the location error (correlation is only 0.01) and are thus discarded from the ranking function.

5   Experiments

To evaluate our method, we consider some RANSAC variants among those that are considered the most suited for accuracy (as opposed, e.g., to robustness or speed) [6,27]: RANSAC with iterative re-weighted least squares (IRLS) for final model estimation [27, method S1], RANSAC with M-estimator (MSAC), LO-RANSAC [8], MLESAC [26], and ORSA with IRLS [19]. IRLS tries to minimize the sum of squares of geometric error between points in the right image and the epipolar line of corresponding points in left image. For each of these variants, we compare 4 settings: RANSAC alone, RANSAC preceded by match selection (MS), RANSAC preceded by match refinement (MR) using LSFM, and RANSAC preceded both by match refinement and match selection (MR+MS). A uniform threshold of 3 pixels (distance to epipolar line) is used in the RANSAC variants for outlier rejection, apart from ORSA that chooses the threshold automatically. All the results we provide are averaged over 20 runs.

Only datasets with highly accurate ground-truth calibration can be used for validation. We experimented with the full dataset of Strecha et al. [23], a de facto standard in camera calibration: 6 groups of 8 to 30 images totaling 95 pairs of successive images. For each pair, SIFT feature points are detected and matched with the usual setting [16] (no tweaking as in Sect. 2.2), i.e., a descriptor distance ratio to next best match at most 0.8. We ran the same experiment with the DTU robot dataset [1]. However, as it is huge (about 0.5 To), we only considered 9 of the 60 groups of images, covering various themes (scenes 1, 2, 4, 9, 10, 12, 21, 28, 52), in the reduced format (fewer images, yielding 12 images pairs: 1-12, 12-24, 24-25, 25-26, 26-37, 37-49, 50-57, 57-64, 57-65, 57-94, 64-95, 64-119), with identical illumination condition (number 08 for all tests), but full-size images.

Match Selection and Refinement. Figure 5 shows the average rotation and translation errors e_R, e_t for each scene of each dataset. Table 1 shows the average results, illustrating both the separate and combined benefits of MS and MR. Gain factors attain 2.0 for rotation and 3.8 for translation. Note that most

Table 1. Average rotation and translation errors: RANSAC alone (raw), +match selection (MS), +match refinement (MR), +both (MR+MS), and gain raw/(MR+MS)

Dataset	Strecha et al. [23]					DTU robot [1]				
e_R (deg $\times 10^{-2}$)	raw	MS	MR	MR+MS	gain	raw	MS	MR	MR+MS	gain
RANSAC	16.4	9.52	10.3	8.87	1.9	26.5	22.3	21.5	21.3	1.2
MSAC	14.1	9.53	8.86	8.43	1.7	21.3	21.7	20.4	20.1	1.1
LO-RANSAC	16.4	9.54	10.3	8.97	1.8	26.8	22.2	21.5	21.3	1.3
MLESAC	15.8	7.81	9.50	7.76	2.0	21.8	22.6	20.8	20.2	1.1
ORSA	12.2	7.24	6.48	6.60	1.9	21.9	21.7	20.8	20.3	1.1
e_t (deg)	raw	MS	MR	MR+MS	gain	raw	MS	MR	MR+MS	gain
RANSAC	1.85	1.09	1.23	1.04	1.8	3.83	2.12	1.81	1.02	3.7
MSAC	1.59	1.08	1.03	0.96	1.6	1.27	1.03	0.93	0.70	1.8
LO-RANSAC	1.83	1.10	1.21	1.05	1.7	3.89	2.14	1.76	1.02	3.8
MLESAC	2.16	0.95	1.09	0.87	2.5	2.02	1.34	1.23	0.77	2.6
ORSA	1.38	0.81	0.68	0.74	1.9	1.22	0.88	0.66	0.66	1.8

parameters are learned on other, widely different images [18]; only the lower bound $\gamma = 2$ is defined from feature distribution in [23] and nothing else. Our excellent results on [1,23] suggests that these parameters make sense for a wide range of images.

Focused Matching. We compare our focused matching (LSFM, Section 4) with standard least square matching (LSM). Rather than considering planar

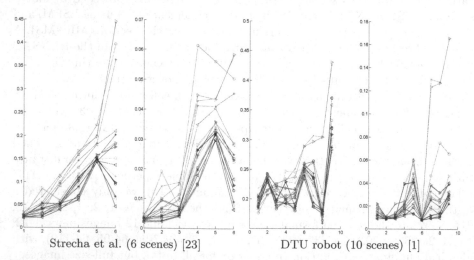

Strecha et al. (6 scenes) [23]   DTU robot (10 scenes) [1]

Fig. 5. Average results on the datasets. Left: rotation error e_R. Right: translation error e_t. Color red: raw RANSAC; blue: with match selection (MS); green: with match refinement using LSFM (MR); **black**: with both match selection and match refinement (MR+MS). Line symbol -▷-: RANSAC with IRLS; -*-: MSAC; -x-: LO-RANSAC; -o-: MLESAC; -◁-: ORSA. Scenes are reordered by increasing rotation error of RANSAC

Table 2. Match refinement evaluation using LSM, LSM with focused grid, LSM with focused grid and scale exploration (LSFM), gain as improvement of LSFM over LSM

e_R (deg $\times 10^{-2}$)	LSM	LSM + foc. grid	LSFM	gain
Strecha et al. [23]	7.55	6.73	6.48	1.17
DTU robot [1]	20.97	21.22	20.79	1.01
e_t (deg)	LSM	LSM + foc. grid	LSFM	gain
Strecha et al. [23]	0.84	0.72	0.68	1.25
DTU robot [1]	0.77	0.71	0.66	1.16

scenes and measuring reprojection errors, we directly measure e_R and e_t using the datasets and settings as above. Matches are then refined by the following methods: LSM, LSM with focused grid, and LSM with focused grid and scale exploration (LSFM). We estimate errors after calibrating with ORSA+IRLS, which has the best performance in the above tests (see Table 1). Table 2 shows that, apart from a poor reduction of rotation error in the DTU robot dataset, the LSFM factor gain is 1.16 to 1.25.

6   Conclusion

In this paper we have studied, in the two-view case, the "quality vs. quantity" balance of point matches for structure from motion — a poorly addressed issue in the literature. We have found a correlation between SfM errors and a function of the number of matches and their epipolar errors. Using this relation, we have presented a new method for selecting relevant subsets of points to improve SfM accuracy. We have also proposed an improvement of an existing method to refine match locations. Using extensive experiments involving real data with ground-truth calibration, we have shown that match selection and match refinement independently lead to a major reduction of SfM errors over the best methods targeted at accuracy. Combining both methods, the error is reduced by factors up to 2.0 for rotations and 3.8 for translations, which is an enormous improvement.

Our work is valuable for stereovision. Extending it to the multi-view case is not trivial because of track consistency. First, removing one match does not necessarily remove the associated points from the track and leads to a substantially different bundle adjustment problem. Second, the location of points in a track would need to be optimized simultaneously in all associated images. We actually want *track selection* (or *reduction*) as well as *track refinement*. Besides, a good term to minimize to assess the benefit of match reduction is likely to be linked to the total reprojection error with respect to all 3D points *after* bundle adjustment. A study similar to that of Section 2 thus has to be carried out.

Still, a lower bound of the possible improvement can be obtained by applying match selection (MS) on each image pair in an SfM pipeline, before actual processing by the system. A preliminary experiment on Strecha et al.'s dataset using OpenMVG [21], a competitor to Bundler, shows improvements up to 15% on the average camera location error, in particular on scenes with wider viewpoint changes and less images (HerzJesu-P8 vs -P25, Castle-P19 vs -P30). Conversely, it may be the case that bundle adjustment is doing a good job at averaging on long tracks, compensating for the inaccuracy of point location. Track selection and track refinement are thus likely to be more profitable on difficult scenes.

Finally, most of our results are constructed on empirical studies. We however believe the "quality vs. quantity" issue deserves a better theoretical treatment, including a study of the influence of the configuration of points in images.

Acknowledgements. This work was carried out in IMAGINE, a research project between ENPC and CSTB. It was partly supported by ANR project Stereo.

References

1. Aanæs, H., Dahl, A.L., Pedersen, K.S.: Interesting interest points. International Journal of Computer Vision 97(1), 18–35 (2012)
2. Baatz, G., Köser, K., Chen, D., Grzeszczuk, R., Pollefeys, M.: Leveraging 3D city models for rotation invariant place-of-interest recognition. IJCV 96(3), 315–334 (2012), http://dx.doi.org/10.1007/s11263-011-0458-7
3. Baker, S., Scharstein, D., Lewis, J., Roth, S., Black, M.J., Szeliski, R.: A database and evaluation methodology for optical flow. IJCV 92(1), 1–31 (2011)
4. Brooks, M.J., Chojnacki, W., Gawley, D., Van Den Hengel, A.: What value covariance information in estimating vision parameters? In: Proceedings of the 8th IEEE International Conference on Computer Vision (ICCV), vol. 1, pp. 302–308. IEEE (2001)
5. Cao, Y., McDonald, J.: Viewpoint invariant features from single images using 3D geometry. In: WACV (2009)
6. Choi, S., Kim, T., Yu, W.: Performance evaluation of RANSAC family. In: BMVC, pp. 1–12 (2009)
7. Chum, O., Matas, J.: Matching with PROSAC – progressive sample consensus. In: CVPR (2005)
8. Chum, O., Matas, J., Obdrzalek, S.: Enhancing RANSAC by generalized model optimization. In: ACCV (2004)
9. Fischler, M.A., Bolles, R.C.: Random sample consensus: a paradigm for model fitting with applications to image analysis and automated cartography. CACM 24(6) (1981)
10. Gruen, A.: Adaptive least squares correlation: a powerful image matching technique. S. Afr. J. of Photogrammetry, Remote Sensing and Cartography 14(3) (1985)
11. Hartley, R.I., Zisserman, A.: Multiple View Geometry in Computer Vision. Cambridge University Press (2004)
12. Kanazawa, Y., Kanatani, K.: Do we really have to consider covariance matrices for image features? In: Proceedings of the 8th IEEE International Conference on Computer Vision (ICCV), vol. 2, pp. 301–306. IEEE (2001)
13. Köser, K., Koch, R.: Perspectively invariant normal features. In: ICCV (2007)
14. Köser, K., Koch, R.: Exploiting uncertainty propagation in gradient-based image registration. In: BMVC (2008)
15. Liu, Z., Marlet, R.: Virtual line descriptor and semi-local graph matching method for reliable feature correspondence. In: BMVC (2012)
16. Lowe, D.: Distinctive image features from scale-invariant keypoints. IJCV 60(2), 91–110 (2004)

17. Matas, J., Chum, O., Urban, M., Pajdla, T.: Robust wide-baseline stereo from maximally stable extremal regions. Image and Vision Computing 22(10), 761–767 (2004)
18. Mikolajczyk, K., Schmid, C.: Scale & affine invariant interest point detectors. IJCV 60(1), 63–86 (2004)
19. Moisan, L., Stival, B.: A probabilistic criterion to detect rigid point matches between two images and estimate the fundamental matrix. IJCV 57(3), 201–218 (2004)
20. Morel, J.M., Yu, G.: ASIFT: A new framework for fully affine invariant image comparison. SIAM Journal on Imaging Sciences 2(2), 438–469 (2009)
21. Moulon, P., Monasse, P., Marlet, R.: Adaptive Structure from Motion with a contrario model estimation. In: Lee, K.M., Matsushita, Y., Rehg, J.M., Hu, Z. (eds.) ACCV 2012, Part IV. LNCS, vol. 7727, pp. 257–270. Springer, Heidelberg (2013)
22. Potůčková, M.: Image matching and its applications in photogrammetry. Ph.D. thesis, Aalborg Universitet (2004)
23. Strecha, C., von Hansen, W., Van Gool, L., Fua, P., Thoennessen, U.: On benchmarking camera calibration and multi-view stereo for high resolution imagery. In: CVPR (2008)
24. Sur, F., Noury, N., Berger, M.O.: Computing the uncertainty of the 8 point algorithm for fundamental matrix estimation. In: Proceedings of 19th British Machine Vision Conference (BMVC), pp. 96.1–96.10 (2008)
25. Tang, Z.: High precision in Camera calibration. Ph.D. thesis, ENS Cachan (2012)
26. Torr, P.H.S., Zisserman, A.: MLESAC: a new robust estimator with application to estimating image geometry. CVIU 78(1), 138–156 (2000)
27. Torr, P.H., Murray, D.W.: The development and comparison of robust methods for estimating the fundamental matrix. IJCV 24(3), 271–300 (1997)
28. Wu, C., Clipp, B., Li, X., Frahm, J.M., Pollefeys, M.: 3D model matching with viewpoint-invariant patches (VIP). In: CVPR (2008)
29. Zeisl, B., Georgel, P.F., Schweiger, F., Steinbach, E.G., Navab, N., Munich, G.: Estimation of location uncertainty for scale invariant features points. In: Proceedings of 20th British Machine Vision Conference (BMVC), pp. 1–12 (2009)

LSD-SLAM: Large-Scale Direct Monocular SLAM

Jakob Engel, Thomas Schöps, and Daniel Cremers

Technical University Munich, Germany

Abstract. We propose a direct (feature-less) monocular SLAM algorithm which, in contrast to current state-of-the-art regarding direct methods, allows to build large-scale, consistent maps of the environment. Along with highly accurate pose estimation based on direct image alignment, the 3D environment is reconstructed in real-time as pose-graph of keyframes with associated semi-dense depth maps. These are obtained by filtering over a large number of pixelwise small-baseline stereo comparisons. The explicitly scale-drift aware formulation allows the approach to operate on challenging sequences including large variations in scene scale. Major enablers are two key novelties: (1) a novel direct tracking method which operates on $\mathfrak{sim}(3)$, thereby explicitly detecting scale-drift, and (2) an elegant probabilistic solution to include the effect of noisy depth values into tracking. The resulting direct monocular SLAM system runs in real-time on a CPU.

1 Introduction

Real-time monocular Simultaneous Localization and Mapping (SLAM) and 3D reconstruction have become increasingly popular research topics. Two major reasons are (1) their use in robotics, in particular to navigate unmanned aerial vehicles (UAVs) [10,8,1], and (2) augmented and virtual reality applications slowly making their way into the mass-market.

One of the major benefits of *monocular* SLAM – and simultaneously one of the biggest challenges – comes with the inherent scale-ambiguity: The scale of the world cannot be observed and drifts over time, being one of the major error sources. The advantage is that this allows to seamlessly switch between differently scaled environments, such as a desk environment indoors and large-scale outdoor environments. Scaled sensors on the other hand, such as depth or stereo cameras, have a limited range at which they can provide reliable measurements and hence do not provide this flexibility.

1.1 Related Work

Feature-Based Methods. The fundamental idea behind feature-based approaches (both filtering-based [15,19] and keyframe-based [15]) is to split the overall problem – estimating geometric information from images – into two sequential steps: First, a set of feature observations is extracted from the image.

D. Fleet et al. (Eds.): ECCV 2014, Part II, LNCS 8690, pp. 834–849, 2014.
© Springer International Publishing Switzerland 2014

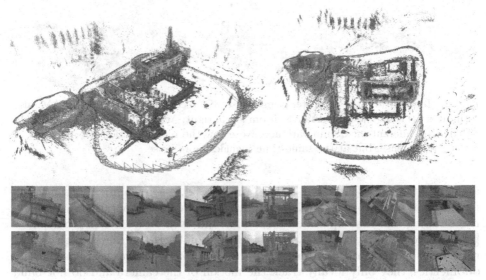

Fig. 1. Large-Scale Direct Monocular SLAM: LSD-SLAM generates a consistent global map, using direct image alignment and probabilistic, semi-dense depth maps instead of keypoints. Top: Accumulated pointclouds of all keyframes of a medium-sized trajectory (from a hand-held monocular camera), generated in real-time. Bottom: A selection of keyframes with color-coded semi-dense inverse depth map. See also the supplementary video.

Second, the camera position and scene geometry is computed as a function of these feature observations only.

While this decoupling simplifies the overall problem, it comes with an important limitation: *Only information that conforms to the feature type can be used.* In particular, when using keypoints, information contained in straight or curved edges – which especially in man-made environments make up a large part of the image – is discarded. Several approaches have been made in the past to remedy this by including edge-based [16,6] or even region-based [5] features. Yet, since the estimation of the high-dimensional feature space is tedious, they are rarely used in practice. To obtain dense reconstructions, the estimated camera poses can be used to subsequently reconstruct dense maps, using multiview stereo [2].

Direct Methods. Direct visual odometry (VO) methods circumvent this limitation by optimizing the geometry directly on the image intensities, which *enables using all information in the image*. In addition to higher accuracy and robustness in particular in environments with little keypoints, this provides substantially more information about the geometry of the environment, which can be very valuable for robotics or augmented reality applications.

While direct image alignment is well-established for RGB-D or stereo sensors [14,4], only recently monocular direct VO algorithms have been proposed: In [24,20,21], accurate and fully dense depth maps are computed using a variational formulation, which however is computationally demanding and requires

Fig. 2. In addition to accurate, semi-dense 3D reconstructions, LSD-SLAM also estimates the associated uncertainty. From left to right: Accumulated pointcloud thesholded with different maximum variance. Note how the reconstruction becomes significantly more dense, but at the same time includes more noise.

a state-of-the-art GPU to run in real-time. In [9], a semi-dense depth filtering formulation was proposed which significantly reduces computational complexity, allowing real-time operation on a CPU and even on a modern smartphone [22]. By combining direct tracking with keypoints, [10] achieves high frame-rates even on embedded platforms. All these approaches however are pure visual odometries, they only locally track the motion of the camera and do not build a consistent, global map of the environment including loop-closures.

Pose Graph Optimization. This is a well-known SLAM technique to build a consistent, global map: The world is represented as a number of keyframes connected by pose-pose constraints, which can be optimized using a generic graph optimization framework like g2o [18].

In [14], a pose graph based RGB-D SLAM method is proposed, which also incorporates geometric error to allow tracking through scenes with little texture. To account for scale-drift arising in monocular SLAM, [23] proposed a keypoint-based monocular SLAM system which represents camera poses as 3D similarity transforms instead of rigid body movements.

1.2   Contributions and Outline

We propose a **L**arge-**S**cale **D**irect monocular **SLAM** (LSD-SLAM) method, which not only locally tracks the motion of the camera, but allows to build consistent, large-scale maps of the environment (see Fig. 1 and 2). The method uses direct image alignment coupled with filtering-based estimation of semi-dense depth maps as originally proposed in [9]. The global map is represented as a pose graph consisting of keyframes as vertices with 3D similarity transforms as edges, elegantly incorporating changing scale of the environment and allowing to detect and correct accumulated drift. The method runs in real-time on a CPU, and as odometry even on a modern smartphone [22]. The main contributions of this paper are (1) a framework for large-scale, direct monocular SLAM, in particular a novel scale-aware image alignment algorithm to directly estimate the similarity transform $\xi \in \mathfrak{sim}(3)$ between two keyframes, and (2) probabilistically consistent incorporation of uncertainty of the estimated depth into tracking.

2   Preliminaries

In this chapter we give a condensed summary of the relevant mathematical concepts and notation. In particular, we summarize the representation of 3D poses as elements of Lie-Algebras (Sec. 2.1), derive direct image alignment as weighted least-squares minimization on Lie-manifolds (Sec. 2.2), and briefly introduce propagation of uncertainty (Sec. 2.3).

Notation. We denote matrices by bold, capital letters ($\mathbf{R}$) and vectors as bold, lower case letters ($\boldsymbol{\xi}$). The n'th row of a matrix is denoted by $[\cdot]_n$. Images $I \colon \Omega \to \mathbb{R}$, the per-pixel inverse depth map $D \colon \Omega \to \mathbb{R}^+$ and the inverse depth variance map $V \colon \Omega \to \mathbb{R}^+$ are written as functions, where $\Omega \subset \mathbb{R}^2$ is the set of *normalized* pixel coordinates, i.e., they include the intrinsic camera calibration. Throughout the paper we use d to denote the *inverse* of the depth z of a point, i.e., $d = z^{-1}$.

2.1   3D Rigid Body and Similarity Transformations

3D Rigid Body Transformations. A 3D rigid body transform $\mathbf{G} \in \mathrm{SE}(3)$ denotes rotation and translation in 3D, i.e. is defined by

$$\mathbf{G} = \begin{pmatrix} \mathbf{R} & \mathbf{t} \\ \mathbf{0} & 1 \end{pmatrix} \quad \text{with} \quad \mathbf{R} \in \mathrm{SO}(3) \text{ and } \mathbf{t} \in \mathbb{R}^3. \tag{1}$$

During optimization, a minimal representation for the camera pose is required, which is given by the corresponding element $\boldsymbol{\xi} \in \mathfrak{se}(3)$ of the associated Lie-algebra. Elements are mapped to $\mathrm{SE}(3)$ by the exponential map $\mathbf{G} = \exp_{\mathfrak{se}(3)}(\boldsymbol{\xi})$, its inverse being denoted by $\boldsymbol{\xi} = \log_{\mathrm{SE}(3)}(\mathbf{G})$. With a slight abuse of notation, we consistently use elements of $\mathfrak{se}(3)$ to represent poses, which we directly write as vector $\boldsymbol{\xi} \in \mathbb{R}^6$. The transformation moving a point from frame i to frame j is written as $\boldsymbol{\xi}_{ji}$. For convenience, we define the pose concatenation operator $\circ \colon \mathfrak{se}(3) \times \mathfrak{se}(3) \to \mathfrak{se}(3)$ as

$$\boldsymbol{\xi}_{ki} := \boldsymbol{\xi}_{kj} \circ \boldsymbol{\xi}_{ji} := \log_{\mathrm{SE}(3)} \left(\exp_{\mathfrak{se}(3)}(\boldsymbol{\xi}_{kj}) \cdot \exp_{\mathfrak{se}(3)}(\boldsymbol{\xi}_{ji}) \right). \tag{2}$$

Further, we define the 3D projective warp function ω, which projects an image point $\mathbf{p}$ and its inverse depth d into a by $\boldsymbol{\xi}$ transformed camera frame

$$\omega(\mathbf{p}, d, \boldsymbol{\xi}) := \begin{pmatrix} x'/z' \\ y'/z' \\ 1/z' \end{pmatrix} \quad \text{with} \quad \begin{pmatrix} x' \\ y' \\ z' \\ 1 \end{pmatrix} := \exp_{\mathfrak{se}(3)}(\boldsymbol{\xi}) \begin{pmatrix} \mathbf{p}_x/d \\ \mathbf{p}_y/d \\ 1/d \\ 1 \end{pmatrix}. \tag{3}$$

3D Similarity Transformations. A 3D similarity transform $\mathbf{S} \in \mathrm{Sim}(3)$ denotes rotation, scaling and translation, i.e. is defined by

$$\mathbf{S} = \begin{pmatrix} s\mathbf{R} & \mathbf{t} \\ \mathbf{0} & 1 \end{pmatrix} \quad \text{with} \quad \mathbf{R} \in \mathrm{SO}(3), \ \mathbf{t} \in \mathbb{R}^3 \text{ and } s \in \mathbb{R}^+. \tag{4}$$

As for rigid body transformations, a minimal representation is given by elements of the associated Lie-algebra $\boldsymbol{\xi} \in \mathfrak{sim}(3)$, which now have an additional degree of freedom, that is $\boldsymbol{\xi} \in \mathbb{R}^7$. The exponential and logarithmic map, pose concatenation and a projective warp function ω_s can be defined analogously to the $\mathfrak{se}(3)$ case, for further details see [23].

2.2   Weighted Gauss-Newton Optimization on Lie-Manifolds

Two images are aligned by Gauss-Newton minimization of the photometric error

$$E(\boldsymbol{\xi}) = \sum_i \underbrace{(I_{\text{ref}}(\mathbf{p}_i) - I(\omega(\mathbf{p}_i, D_{\text{ref}}(\mathbf{p}_i), \boldsymbol{\xi})))^2}_{=:r_i^2(\boldsymbol{\xi})}, \tag{5}$$

which gives the maximum-likelihood estimator for $\boldsymbol{\xi}$ assuming i.i.d. Gaussian residuals. We use a left-compositional formulation: Starting with an initial estimate $\boldsymbol{\xi}^{(0)}$, in each iteration a left-multiplied increment $\delta\boldsymbol{\xi}^{(n)}$ is computed by solving for the minimum of a Gauss-Newton second-order approximation of E:

$$\delta\boldsymbol{\xi}^{(n)} = -(\mathbf{J}^T\mathbf{J})^{-1}\mathbf{J}^T\mathbf{r}(\boldsymbol{\xi}^{(n)}) \quad \text{with} \quad \mathbf{J} = \left.\frac{\partial\mathbf{r}(\epsilon \circ \boldsymbol{\xi}^{(n)})}{\partial\epsilon}\right|_{\epsilon=0}, \tag{6}$$

where $\mathbf{J}$ is the derivative of the stacked residual vector $\mathbf{r} = (r_1, \ldots, r_n)^T$ with respect to a left-multiplied increment, and $\mathbf{J}^T\mathbf{J}$ the Gauss-Newton approximation of the Hessian of E. The new estimate is then obtained by multiplication with the computed update

$$\boldsymbol{\xi}^{(n+1)} = \delta\boldsymbol{\xi}^{(n)} \circ \boldsymbol{\xi}^{(n)}. \tag{7}$$

In order to be robust to outliers arising e.g. from occlusions or reflections, different weighting-schemes [14] have been proposed, resulting in an iteratively reweighted least-squares problem: In each iteration, a weight matrix $\mathbf{W} = \mathbf{W}(\boldsymbol{\xi}^{(n)})$ is computed which down-weights large residuals. The iteratively solved error function then becomes

$$E(\boldsymbol{\xi}) = \sum_i w_i(\boldsymbol{\xi})r_i^2(\boldsymbol{\xi}), \tag{8}$$

and the update is computed as

$$\delta\boldsymbol{\xi}^{(n)} = -(\mathbf{J}^T\mathbf{W}\mathbf{J})^{-1}\mathbf{J}^T\mathbf{W}r(\boldsymbol{\xi}^{(n)}). \tag{9}$$

Assuming the residuals to be independent, the inverse of the Hessian from the last iteration $(\mathbf{J}^T\mathbf{W}\mathbf{J})^{-1}$ is an estimate for the covariance $\boldsymbol{\Sigma_\xi}$ of a left-multiplied error onto the final result, that is

$$\boldsymbol{\xi}^{(n)} = \epsilon \circ \boldsymbol{\xi}_{\text{true}} \quad \text{with} \quad \epsilon \sim \mathcal{N}(\mathbf{0}, \boldsymbol{\Sigma_\xi}). \tag{10}$$

In practice, the residuals are highly correlated, such that $\boldsymbol{\Sigma_\xi}$ is only a lower bound - yet it contains valuable information about the correlation between noise

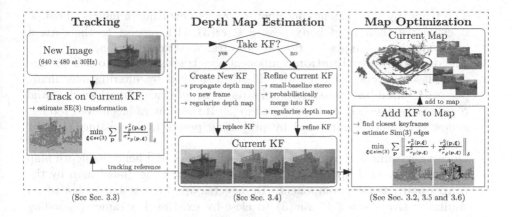

Fig. 3. Overview over the complete LSD-SLAM algorithm

on the different degrees of freedom. Note that we follow a **left-multiplication** convention, equivalent results can be obtained using a right-multiplication convention. However, the estimated covariance Σ_ξ depends on the multiplication order – when used in a pose graph optimization framework, this has to be taken into account. The left-multiplication convention used here is consistent with [23], while e.g. the default type-implementation in g2o [18] assumes right-multiplication.

2.3 Propagation of Uncertainty

Propagation of uncertainty is a statistical tool to derive the uncertainty of the output of a function $f(\mathbf{X})$, caused by uncertainty on its input $\mathbf{X}$. Assuming $\mathbf{X}$ to be Gaussian distributed with covariance $\Sigma_\mathbf{X}$, the covariance of $f(\mathbf{X})$ can be approximated (using the Jacobian $\mathbf{J}_f$ of f) by

$$\Sigma_f \approx \mathbf{J}_f \Sigma_\mathbf{X} \mathbf{J}_f^T. \tag{11}$$

3 Large-Scale Direct Monocular SLAM

We start by giving an overview of the complete algorithm in Sec. 3.1, and briefly introduce the representation for the global map in Sec. 3.2. The three main components of the algorithm are then described in Sec. 3.3 (tracking of new frames), Sec. 3.4 (depth map estimation), Sec. 3.5 (keyframe-to-keyframe tracking) and finally Sec. 3.6 (map optimization).

3.1 The Complete Method

The algorithm consists of three major components: **tracking, depth map estimation** and **map optimization** as visualized in Fig. 3:

- The **tracking** component continuously tracks new camera images. That is, it estimates their rigid body pose $\boldsymbol{\xi} \in \mathfrak{se}(3)$ with respect to the current keyframe, using the pose of the previous frame as initialization.
- The **depth map estimation** component uses tracked frames to either refine or replace the current keyframe. Depth is refined by filtering over many per-pixel, small-baseline stereo comparisons coupled with interleaved spatial regularization as originally proposed in [9]. If the camera has moved too far, a new keyframe is initialized by projecting points from existing, close-by keyframes into it.
- Once a keyframe is replaced as tracking reference – and hence its depth map will not be refined further – it is incorporated into the global map by the **map optimization** component. To detect loop closures and scale-drift, a similarity transform $\boldsymbol{\xi} \in \mathfrak{sim}(3)$ to close-by existing keyframes (including its direct predecessor) is estimated using scale-aware, direct $\mathfrak{sim}(3)$-image alignment.

Initialization. To bootstrap the LSD-SLAM system, it is sufficient to initialize a first keyframe with a *random* depth map and large variance. Given sufficient translational camera movement in the first seconds, the algorithm "locks" to a certain configuration, and after a couple of keyframe propagations converges to a correct depth configuration. Some examples are shown in the attached video. A more thorough evaluation of this ability to converge without dedicated initial bootstrapping is outside the scope of this paper, and remains for future work.

3.2   Map Representation

The map is represented as a pose graph of keyframes: Each keyframe $\mathcal{K}_i$ consists of a camera image $I_i \colon \Omega_i \to \mathbb{R}$, an inverse depth map $D_i \colon \Omega_{D_i} \to \mathbb{R}^+$, and the variance of the inverse depth $V_i \colon \Omega_{D_i} \to \mathbb{R}^+$. Note that the depth map and variance are only defined for a subset of pixels $\Omega_{D_i} \subset \Omega_i$, containing all image regions in the vicinity of sufficiently large intensity gradient, hence **semi-dense**. Edges $\mathcal{E}_{ji}$ between keyframes contain their relative alignment as similarity transform $\boldsymbol{\xi}_{ji} \in \mathfrak{sim}(3)$, as well as the corresponding covariance matrix $\boldsymbol{\Sigma}_{ji}$.

3.3   Tracking New Frames: Direct $\mathfrak{se}(3)$ Image Alignment

Starting from an existing keyframe $\mathcal{K}_i = (I_i, D_i, V_i)$, the relative 3D pose $\boldsymbol{\xi}_{ji} \in \mathfrak{se}(3)$ of a new image I_j is computed by minimizing the variance-normalized photometric error

$$E_p(\boldsymbol{\xi}_{ji}) = \sum_{\mathbf{p} \in \Omega_{D_i}} \left\| \frac{r_p^2(\mathbf{p}, \boldsymbol{\xi}_{ji})}{\sigma^2_{r_p(\mathbf{p}, \boldsymbol{\xi}_{ji})}} \right\|_\delta \tag{12}$$

$$\text{with} \quad r_p(\mathbf{p}, \boldsymbol{\xi}_{ji}) := I_i(\mathbf{p}) - I_j(\omega(\mathbf{p}, D_i(\mathbf{p}), \boldsymbol{\xi}_{ji})) \tag{13}$$

$$\sigma^2_{r_p(\mathbf{p}, \boldsymbol{\xi}_{ji})} := 2\sigma_I^2 + \left(\frac{\partial r_p(\mathbf{p}, \boldsymbol{\xi}_{ji})}{\partial D_i(\mathbf{p})} \right)^2 V_i(\mathbf{p}) \tag{14}$$

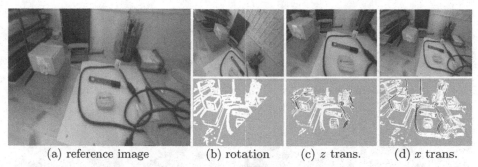

(a) reference image   (b) rotation   (c) z trans.   (d) x trans.

Fig. 4. Statistic normalization: (a) reference image. (b-d): tracked images and inverse variance $\sigma_{r_p}^{-2}$ of the residual. For pure rotation, depth noise has no effect on the residual noise and hence all normalization factors are the same. For z translation depth noise has no effect for pixels in the center of the image, while for x translation it only affects residuals with intensity-gradient in x direction.

where $\| \cdot \|_\delta$ is the Huber norm

$$\|r^2\|_\delta := \begin{cases} \frac{r^2}{2\delta} & \text{if } |r| \le \delta \\ |r| - \frac{\delta}{2} & \text{otherwise.} \end{cases} \tag{15}$$

applied to the *normalized* residual. The residual's variance $\sigma_{r_p(\mathbf{p},\boldsymbol{\xi}_{ji})}^2$ is computed using covariance propagation as described in Sec. 2.3, and utilizing the inverse depth variance V_i. Further, we assume Gaussian image intensity noise σ_I^2. Minimization is performed using iteratively re-weighted Gauss-Newton optimization as described in Sec. 2.2.

In contrast to previous direct methods, the proposed formulation explicitly takes into account varying noise on the depth estimates: This is of particular relevance as for direct, monocular SLAM, this noise differs significantly for different pixels, depending on how long they were visible – which is in contrast to approaches working on RGB-D data, for which the uncertainty on the inverse depth is approximately constant. Figure 4 shows how this weighting behaves for different types of motion. Note that no depth information for the new camera image is available – therefore, the scale of the new image is not defined, and the minimization is performed on $\mathfrak{se}(3)$.

3.4   Depth Map Estimation

Keyframe Selection. If the camera moves too far away from the existing map, a new keyframe is created from the most recent tracked image. We threshold a weighted combination of relative distance and angle to the current keyframe:

$$\text{dist}(\boldsymbol{\xi}_{ji}) := \boldsymbol{\xi}_{ji}^T \mathbf{W} \boldsymbol{\xi}_{ji} \tag{16}$$

where $\mathbf{W}$ is a diagonal matrix containing the weights. Note that, as described in the following section, each keyframe is scaled such that its mean inverse depth is one. This threshold is therefore relative to the current scale of the scene, and ensures sufficient possibilities for small-baseline stereo comparisons.

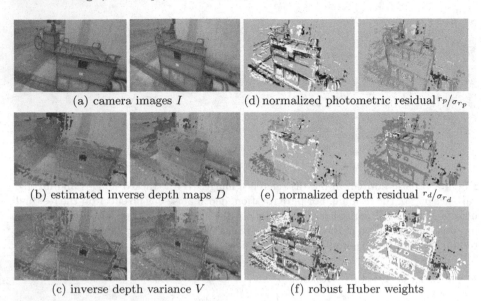

(a) camera images I (d) normalized photometric residual r_p/σ_{r_p}

(b) estimated inverse depth maps D (e) normalized depth residual r_d/σ_{r_d}

(c) inverse depth variance V (f) robust Huber weights

Fig. 5. Direct keyframe alignment on $\mathfrak{sim}(3)$: (a)-(c): two keyframes with associated depth and depth variance. (d)-(f): photometric residual, depth residual and Huber weights, before minimization (left), and after minimization (right).

Depth Map Creation. Once a new frame is chosen to become a keyframe, its depth map is initialized by projecting points from the previous keyframe into it, followed by one iteration of spatial regularization and outlier removal as proposed in [9]. Afterwards, the depth map is scaled to have a mean inverse depth of one - this scaling factor is directly incorporated into the $\mathfrak{sim}(3)$ camera pose. Finally, it replaces the previous keyframe and is used for tracking subsequent new frames.

Depth Map Refinement. Tracked frames that do not become a keyframe are used to refine the current keyframe: A high number of very efficient small-baseline stereo comparisons is performed for image regions where the expected stereo accuracy is sufficiently large, as described in [9]. The result is incorporated into the existing depth map, thereby refining it and potentially adding new pixels – this is done using the filtering approach proposed in [9].

3.5 Constraint Acquisition: Direct $\mathfrak{sim}(3)$ Image Alignment

Direct Image Alignment on $\mathfrak{sim}(3)$. Monocular SLAM is – in contrast to RGB-D or Stereo-SLAM – inherently scale-ambivalent, i.e., the absolute scale of the world is not observable. Over long trajectories this leads to scale-drift, which is one of the major sources of error [23]. Further, all distances are only defined up to scale, which causes threshold-based outlier rejection or parametrized robust kernels (e.g. Huber) to be ill-defined. We solve this by using the inherent correlation between scene depth and tracking accuracy: The depth map of each

Fig. 6. Two scenes with high scale variation. Camera frustums are displayed for each keyframe with their size corresponding to the keyframe's scale.

created keyframe is scaled such that the mean inverse depth is one. In return, edges between keyframes are estimated as elements of $\mathfrak{sim}(3)$, elegantly incorporating the scaling difference between keyframes, and, in particular for large loop-closures, allowing an explicit detection of accumulated scale-drift.

For this, we propose a novel method to perform *direct, scale-drift aware image alignment on* $\mathfrak{sim}(3)$, which is used to align two differently scaled keyframes. In addition to the photometric residual r_p, we incorporate a depth residual r_d which penalizes deviations in inverse depth between keyframes, allowing to directly estimate the scaled transformation between them. The total error function that is minimized becomes

$$E(\boldsymbol{\xi}_{ji}) := \sum_{\mathbf{p} \in \Omega_{D_i}} \left\| \frac{r_p^2(\mathbf{p}, \boldsymbol{\xi}_{ji})}{\sigma_{r_p(\mathbf{p}, \boldsymbol{\xi}_{ji})}^2} + \frac{r_d^2(\mathbf{p}, \boldsymbol{\xi}_{ji})}{\sigma_{r_d(\mathbf{p}, \boldsymbol{\xi}_{ji})}^2} \right\|_\delta, \tag{17}$$

where the photometric residual r_p^2 and $\sigma_{r_p}^2$ is defined as in (13) - (14). The depth residual and its variance is computed as

$$r_d(\mathbf{p}, \boldsymbol{\xi}_{ji}) := [\mathbf{p}']_3 - D_j([\mathbf{p}']_{1,2}) \tag{18}$$

$$\sigma_{r_d(\mathbf{p}, \boldsymbol{\xi}_{ji})}^2 := V_j([\mathbf{p}']_{1,2}) \left(\frac{\partial r_d(\mathbf{p}, \boldsymbol{\xi}_{ji})}{\partial D_j([\mathbf{p}']_{1,2})} \right)^2 + V_i(\mathbf{p}) \left(\frac{\partial r_d(\mathbf{p}, \boldsymbol{\xi}_{ji})}{\partial D_i(\mathbf{p})} \right)^2, \tag{19}$$

where $\mathbf{p}' := \omega_s(\mathbf{p}, D_i(\mathbf{p}), \boldsymbol{\xi}_{ji})$ denotes the transformed point. Note that the Huber norm is applied to the sum of the normalized photometric and depth residual – which accounts for the fact that if one is an outlier, the other typically is as well. Note that for tracking on $\mathfrak{sim}(3)$, the inclusion of the depth error is **required** as the photometric error alone does not constrain the scale. Minimization is performed analogously to direct image alignment on $\mathfrak{se}(3)$ using the iteratively re-weighted Gauss-Newton algorithm (Sec. 2.2). In practice, $\mathfrak{sim}(3)$ tracking is computationally only marginally more expensive than tracking on $\mathfrak{se}(3)$, as only little additional computations are needed[1].

Constraint Search. After a new keyframe $\mathcal{K}_i$ is added to the map, a number of possible loop closure keyframes $\mathcal{K}_{j_1}, ..., \mathcal{K}_{j_n}$ is collected: We use the closest

---

[1] We approximate the gradient of the depth map to be zero, which significantly speeds up the computation

ten keyframes, as well as a suitable candidate proposed by an appearance-based mapping algorithm [11] to detect large-scale loop closures. To avoid insertion of false or falsely tracked loop closures, we then perform a **reciprocal tracking check**: For each candidate $\mathcal{K}_{j_k}$ we independently track $\boldsymbol{\xi}_{j_k i}$ and $\boldsymbol{\xi}_{ij_k}$. Only if the two estimates are statistically similar, i.e., if

$$e(\boldsymbol{\xi}_{j_k i}, \boldsymbol{\xi}_{ij_k}) := (\boldsymbol{\xi}_{j_k i} \circ \boldsymbol{\xi}_{ij_k})^T \left(\boldsymbol{\Sigma}_{j_k i} + \mathrm{Adj}_{j_k i} \boldsymbol{\Sigma}_{ij_k} \mathrm{Adj}_{j_k i}^T \right)^{-1} (\boldsymbol{\xi}_{j_k i} \circ \boldsymbol{\xi}_{ij_k}) \quad (20)$$

is sufficiently small, they are added to the global map. For this, the adjoint $\mathrm{Adj}_{j_k i}$ is used to transform $\boldsymbol{\Sigma}_{ij_k}$ into the correct tangent space.

Convergence Radius for $\mathfrak{sim}(3)$ Tracking. An important limitation of direct image alignment lies in the inherent non-convexity of the problem, and hence the need for a sufficiently accurate initialization. While for the tracking of new camera frames a sufficiently good initialization is available (given by the pose of the previous frame), this is not the case when finding loop closure constraints, in particular for large loop closures.

One solution for this consists in using a very small number of keypoints to compute a better initialization: Using the depth values from the existing inverse depth maps, this requires aligning two sets of 3D points with known correspondences, which can be done efficiently in closed form using e.g. the method of Horn [13]. Still, we found that in practice the convergence radius is sufficiently large even for large-scale loop closures - in particular we found that the convergence radius can be substantially increased by the following measures:

- **Efficient Second Order Minimization (ESM)** [3]: While our results confirm previous work [17] in that ESM *does not significantly* increase the precision of dense image alignment, we observed that it *does* slightly increase the convergence radius.
- **Coarse-to-Fine Approach:** While a pyramid approach is commonly used for direct image alignment, we found that starting at a very low resolution of only 20×15 pixels – much smaller than usually done – already helps to increase the convergence radius.

An evaluation of the effect of these measures is given in Sec. 4.3.

3.6   Map Optimization

The map, consisting of a set of keyframes and tracked $\mathfrak{sim}(3)$-constraints, is continuously optimized in the background using pose graph optimization [18]. The error function that is minimized is – in accordance with the left-multiplication convention from Sec. 2.2 – defined by (W defining the world frame)

$$E(\boldsymbol{\xi}_{W1} \cdots \boldsymbol{\xi}_{Wn}) := \sum_{(\boldsymbol{\xi}_{ji}, \boldsymbol{\Sigma}_{ji}) \in \mathcal{E}} (\boldsymbol{\xi}_{ji} \circ \boldsymbol{\xi}_{Wi}^{-1} \circ \boldsymbol{\xi}_{Wj})^T \boldsymbol{\Sigma}_{ji}^{-1} (\boldsymbol{\xi}_{ji} \circ \boldsymbol{\xi}_{Wi}^{-1} \circ \boldsymbol{\xi}_{Wj}). \quad (21)$$

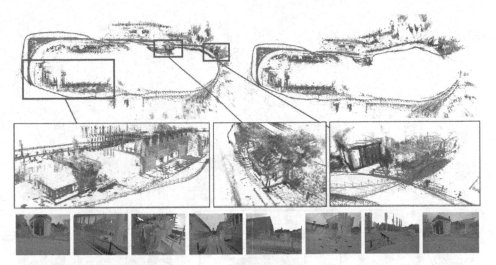

Fig. 7. Loop closure for a long and challenging outdoor trajectory (after the loop closure on the left, before on the right). Also shown are three selected close-ups of the generated pointcloud, and semi-dense depth maps for selected keyframes.

4   Results

We evaluate LSD-SLAM both quantitatively on publicly available datasets [25,12] as well as on challenging outdoor trajectories, recorded with a hand held monocular camera. Some of the evaluated trajectories are shown in full in the supplementary video.

4.1   Qualitative Results on Large Trajectories

We tested the algorithm on several long and challenging trajectories, which include many camera rotations, large scale changes and major loop closures. Figure 7 shows a roughly 500 m long trajectory which takes 6 minutes just before and after the large loop closure is found. Figure 8 shows a challenging trajectory with large variations in scene depth, which also includes a loop closure.

4.2   Quantitative Evaluation

We evaluate LSD-SLAM on the publicly available RGB-D dataset [25]. Note that for monocular SLAM this is a very challenging benchmark, as it contains fast rotational movement, strong motion blur and rolling shutter artifacts. We use the very first depth map to bootstrap the system and get the correct initial scale. Table 9 shows the resulting absolute trajectory error, and compares it to other approaches.

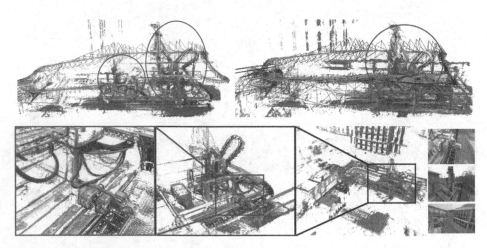

Fig. 8. Accumulated pointcloud of a trajectory with large scale variation, including views with an average inverse depth of less than 20 cm to more than 10 m. After the loop closure (top-right), the geometry is consistently aligned, while before (top-left) parts of the scene existed twice, at different scales. The bottom row shows different close-ups of the scene. The proposed scale-aware formulation allows to accurately estimate both fine details and large-scale geometry – this flexibility is one of the major benefits of a monocular approach.

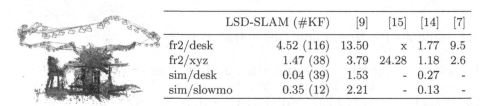

	LSD-SLAM (#KF)	[9]	[15]	[14]	[7]
fr2/desk	4.52 (116)	13.50	x	1.77	9.5
fr2/xyz	1.47 (38)	3.79	24.28	1.18	2.6
sim/desk	0.04 (39)	1.53	-	0.27	-
sim/slowmo	0.35 (12)	2.21	-	0.13	-

Fig. 9. Results on the TUM RGB-D benchmark [25], and two simulated sequences from [12], measured as absolute trajectory RMSE (cm). For LSD-SLAM, we also show the number of keyframes created. 'x' denotes tracking failure, '-' no available data. For comparison we show respective results from semi-dense mono-VO [9], keypoint-based mono-SLAM [15], direct RGB-D SLAM [14] and keypoint-based RGB-D SLAM [7]. Note that [14] and [7] use depth information from the sensor, while the others do not.

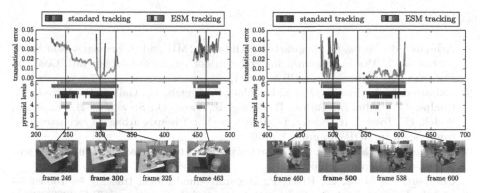

Fig. 10. Convergence radius and accuracy of sim(3) direct image alignment with and without ESM minimization (indicated by light / dark) for a different number of pyramid levels (color). All frames of the respective sequence are tracked on frame 300 (left) and frame 500 (right), using the identity as initialization. The bottom plots show for which frames tracking succeeds; the top plots show the final translational error. ESM and more pyramid levels clearly increase the convergence radius, however these measures have no notable effect on tracking precision: if tracking converges, it almost always converges to the same minimum.

4.3 Convergence Radius for sim(3) Tracking

We evaluate the convergence radius on two exemplary sequences, the result is shown in Fig. 10. Even though direct image alignment is non convex, we found that with the steps proposed in Sec. 3.5, surprisingly large camera movements can be tracked. It can also be observed that these measures only increase the convergence radius, and have no notable effect on tracking precision.

5   Conclusion

We have presented a novel direct (feature-less) monocular SLAM algorithm which we call LSD-SLAM, which runs in real-time on a CPU. In contrast to existing direct approaches – which are all pure odometries – it maintains and tracks on a global map of the environment, which contains a pose-graph of keyframes with associated probabilistic semi-dense depth maps. Major components of the proposed method are two key novelties: (1) a direct method to align two keyframes on sim(3), explicitly incorporating and detecting scale-drift and (2) a novel, probabilistic approach to incorporate noise on the estimated depth maps into tracking. Represented as point clouds, the map gives a semi-dense and highly accurate 3D reconstruction of the environment. We experimentally showed that the approach reliably tracks and maps even challenging hand-held trajectories with a length of over 500 m, in particular including large variations in scale within the same sequence (*average* inverse depth of less than 20 cm to more than 10 m) and large rotations – demonstrating its versatility, robustness and flexibility.

References

1. Achtelik, M., Weiss, S., Siegwart, R.: Onboard IMU and monocular vision based control for MAVs in unknown in- and outdoor environments. In: Intl. Conf. on Robotics and Automation (ICRA) (2011)
2. Akbarzadeh, A., Frahm, J.M., Mordohai, P., Engels, C., Gallup, D., Merrell, P., Phelps, M., Sinha, S., Talton, B., Wang, L., Yang, Q., Stewenius, H., Yang, R., Welch, G., Towles, H., Nistér, D., Pollefeys, M.: Towards urban 3d reconstruction from video. In: 3DPVT, pp. 1–8 (2006)
3. Benhimane, S., Malis, E.: Real-time image-based tracking of planes using efficient second-order minimization (2004)
4. Comport, A., Malis, E., Rives, P.: Accurate quadri-focal tracking for robust 3d visual odometry. In: Intl. Conf. on Robotics and Automation (ICRA) (2007)
5. Concha, A., Civera, J.: Using superpixels in monocular SLAM. In: Intl. Conf. on Robotics and Automation (ICRA) (2014)
6. Eade, E., Drummond, T.: Edge landmarks in monocular slam. In: British Machine Vision Conf. (2006)
7. Endres, F., Hess, J., Engelhard, N., Sturm, J., Cremers, D., Burgard, W.: An evaluation of the RGB-D slam system. In: Intl. Conf. on Robotics and Automation (ICRA) (2012)
8. Engel, J., Sturm, J., Cremers, D.: Camera-based navigation of a low-cost quadrocopter. In: Intl. Conf. on Intelligent Robot Systems (IROS) (2012)
9. Engel, J., Sturm, J., Cremers, D.: Semi-dense visual odometry for a monocular camera. In: Intl. Conf. on Computer Vision (ICCV) (2013)
10. Forster, C., Pizzoli, M., Scaramuzza, D.: SVO: Fast semi-direct monocular visual odometry. In: Intl. Conf. on Robotics and Automation (ICRA) (2014)
11. Glover, A., Maddern, W., Warren, M., Stephanie, R., Milford, M., Wyeth, G.: OpenFABMAP: an open source toolbox for appearance-based loop closure detection. In: Intl. Conf. on Robotics and Automation (ICRA), pp. 4730–4735 (2012)
12. Handa, A., Newcombe, R.A., Angeli, A., Davison, A.J.: Real-time camera tracking: When is high frame-rate best? In: Fitzgibbon, A., Lazebnik, S., Perona, P., Sato, Y., Schmid, C. (eds.) ECCV 2012, Part VII. LNCS, vol. 7578, pp. 222–235. Springer, Heidelberg (2012)
13. Horn, B.: Closed-form solution of absolute orientation using unit quaternions. Journal of the Optical Society of America (1987)
14. Kerl, C., Sturm, J., Cremers, D.: Dense visual SLAM for RGB-D cameras. In: Intl. Conf. on Intelligent Robot Systems (IROS) (2013)
15. Klein, G., Murray, D.: Parallel tracking and mapping for small AR workspaces. In: Intl. Symp. on Mixed and Augmented Reality (ISMAR) (2007)
16. Klein, G., Murray, D.: Improving the agility of keyframe-based SLAM. In: Forsyth, D., Torr, P., Zisserman, A. (eds.) ECCV 2008, Part II. LNCS, vol. 5303, pp. 802–815. Springer, Heidelberg (2008)
17. Klose, S., Heise, P., Knoll, A.: Efficient compositional approaches for real-time robust direct visual odometry from RGB-D data. In: Intl. Conf. on Intelligent Robot Systems (IROS) (2013)
18. Kümmerle, R., Grisetti, G., Strasdat, H., Konolige, K., Burgard, W.: g2o: A general framework for graph optimization. In: Intl. Conf. on Robotics and Automation (ICRA) (2011)
19. Li, M., Mourikis, A.: High-precision, consistent EKF-based visual-inertial odometry. International Journal of Robotics Research 32, 690–711 (2013)

20. Newcombe, R., Lovegrove, S., Davison, A.: DTAM: Dense tracking and mapping in real-time. In: Intl. Conf. on Computer Vision (ICCV) (2011)
21. Pizzoli, M., Forster, C., Scaramuzza, D.: REMODE: Probabilistic, monocular dense reconstruction in real time. In: Intl. Conf. on Robotics and Automation (ICRA) (2014)
22. Schöps, T., Engel, J., Cremers, D.: Semi-dense visual odometry for AR on a smartphone. In: Intl. Symp. on Mixed and Augmented Reality (ISMAR) (2014)
23. Strasdat, H., Montiel, J., Davison, A.: Scale drift-aware large scale monocular slam. In: Robotics: Science and Systems (RSS) (2010)
24. Stühmer, J., Gumhold, S., Cremers, D.: Real-time dense geometry from a handheld camera. In: Goesele, M., Roth, S., Kuijper, A., Schiele, B., Schindler, K. (eds.) Pattern Recognition. LNCS, vol. 6376, pp. 11–20. Springer, Heidelberg (2010)
25. Sturm, J., Engelhard, N., Endres, F., Burgard, W., Cremers, D.: A benchmark for the evaluation of RGB-D SLAM systems. In: Intl. Conf. on Intelligent Robot Systems (IROS) (2012)

Author Index

Printed in the United States
by Bookmasters

Printed in the United States
By Bookmasters